U.S. Department of State

CURRENT HOME OF THE DEPARTMENT OF STATE

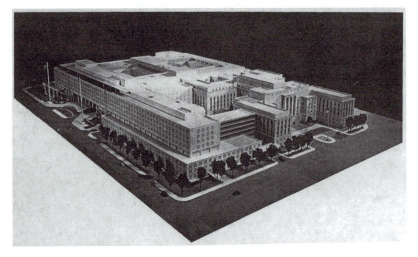

PREVIOUS HOMES OF THE DEPARTMENT OF STATE

First home, Philadelphia, 1781–1783

Washington, Pennsylvania Avenue near White House, 1820–1866

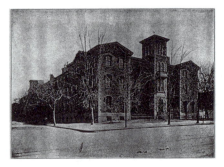

Washington, 14th and S. Streets, N.W., 1866–1875

Washington, State-War-Navy Building, Pennsylvania Ave. at 17th Street, N.W., 1875–1947

U.S. DEPARTMENT OF STATE

A Reference History

ELMER PLISCHKE

GREENWOOD PRESS
Westport, Connecticut • London

Library of Congress Cataloging-in-Publication Data

Plischke, Elmer, 1914–
    U.S. Department of State : a reference history / Elmer Plischke.
      p.   cm.
    Includes bibliographical references and index.
    ISBN 0–313–29126–8 (alk. paper)
    1. United States. Dept. of State—History. I. Title.
JZ1480.A4   1999
353.1'3'0973—dc21   98–53381

British Library Cataloguing in Publication Data is available.

Library of Congress Catalog Card Number: 98–53381
ISBN: 0–313–29126–8

First published in 1999

Greenwood Press, 88 Post Road West, Westport, CT 06881
An imprint of Greenwood Publishing Group, Inc.
www.greenwood.com

Printed in the United States of America

The paper used in this book complies with the
Permanent Paper Standard issued by the National
Information Standards Organization (Z39.48–1984).

10 9 8 7 6 5 4 3 2 1

To Audrey

For a lifetime of inspiration, dedication, and happy memories

Contents

Part II: 1801–1861

Part III: 1861–1945

Illustrations

TABLES

FIGURES

Preface

As with the Foreign Offices of other countries, the Department of State of the United States has inevitably been fashioned by slow and incremental growth and mutation. Those who direct and participate in it during each successive epoch are inclined to be influenced by pre-established practices, principles of law and policy, pragmatic institutions, administrative techniques, reservoirs of potential and experienced practitioners, and related factors. Issues and problems are often inherited from earlier times, others arise from changing circumstances, and some, after thoughtful scrutiny, may be deferred for later resolution. Occasionally there are those that are sublimated into nobler causes which generate determinations that both reflect the past and portend the future. Such developments have applied to the establishment and struggle to perfect the Department of State, the Foreign Service, American diplomatic and consular practice, and other features of the progression of American foreign relations.

A definitive history of the organization and functioning of the Department of State would require several volumes. This is a single-volume, comprehensive reference history covering more than two centuries, from the commencement of American diplomatic relations antedating the Constitution to the present. It is neither a traditional American diplomatic history nor an analysis of American foreign policy. Rather, constituting the primary American agency responsible for the conduct of foreign affairs, as the Department evolved to become one of the world's great foreign offices, this volume focusses on its origin, organization, reform, maturation, and functions, including its leadership, structure, machinery, principal officers, management, and staffing; its personnel system; its diplomatic and consular missions and representation abroad; its treaty making; its participation in international conferences and organizations; and its relations with other government agencies that possess foreign relations responsibilities.

In addition, it deals with more precise matters such as presidential and ministerial diplomacy; congressional legislation concerned with the Department, the Foreign Service, and diplomatic affairs; the establishment of the merit system for departmental, diplomatic, and consular personnel and the achievement of professionalism; diplomatic and consular titles and ranks; budgeting, salaries, and allowances; multiple diplomatic assignments of several kinds; domestic responsibilities of the Department; coordination of foreign relations agencies and functions abroad; many other factors and developments; and future challenges and issues.

The author acknowledges indebtedness to the earlier general histories of the State Department published by William H. Michael (1901), Gaillard Hunt (1914), and Graham H. Stuart (1949); the shorter studies and status reports of such authors as E. Wilder Spaulding and George Verne Blue (1936), William Gerber (1942 and 1955), and David F. Trask (1981); volumes on the Foreign Service and consular affairs produced Chester L. Jones (1906), Tracy H. Lay (1925), James Rives Childs (1948), and William Barnes and John Heath Morgan (1961); comprehensive analysis of the conduct of American foreign relations, such as those contributed by John W. Foster (1900 and 1906), John H. Mathews (1922 and 1938), James L. McCamy (1950), Graham H. Stuart (2d ed., 1952), and this author (3rd ed., 1967); various memoirs and biographies; diverse, more specialized analyses; and many U.S. government publications, especially those issued by the Office of the Historian of the Department of State and several Congressional Committees.

Special appreciation is extended to William Z. Slany, the Historian, and Paul Claussen, of the Office of the Historian of the Department of State, for their assistance, and to Kim Breighner, who provided word-processing service for this volume. However, the author assumes responsibility for its essence, structure, and analysis.

Glossary of Diplomatic Terms

Accession Process whereby a nonsignatory state becomes a party to a treaty or agreement that has already been concluded by other states, which is authenticated by an instrument of accession. Usually the treaty or agreement text specifies whether a nonsignatory state is entitled to accede and how to file the instrument of accession. Also see Adhesion.

Accord When used generically, means an agreement, convention, pact, or treaty. At times is used more precisely to denote such instruments other than treaties and conventions.

Ad referendum Principle applied to the negotiation of treaties and agreements, which recognizes that the final instruments are subject to subsequent approval by the governments of the signatories—in the case of the United States, by the President, and for a treaty, with the advice and consent of the Senate.

Adhesion Process whereby a state signifies its intention to abide by the stipulations of a treaty or agreement that has already been concluded by other states, which is authenticated by an instrument of adhesion. Some hold that such action does not signify that the state technically becomes a party to the treaty or agreement. Also referred to as adherence. Also see Accession.

Adjudication System of peaceful settlement of international disputes, in which parties submit their controversy to a court, which decides the case on the basis of principles of law and equity, the parties agreeing in advance to be bound by the court's decision. Also see Judicial Settlement and Arbitration.

Agréation Process of consultation of governments to arrive at an agreement respecting the appointment of a particular individual to serve as the diplomatic envoy of the sending government in the receiving country. Also see *Agrément*.

Agreement Generically used synonymously with accord, arrangement, joint declaration, or understanding but may be less formal than a treaty. In a narrower sense it constitutes a commitment between states that is comparable to a treaty. Also see Executive Agreement and Understanding.

Agrément   Agreement resulting from the process of *agréation.*

Aide-memoire   Written diplomatic communication in the form of a memorandom, which is concise, completely impersonal, and entirely factual and bears no signature. It also may be referred to simply as a *memoire* but generally is called a memorandum in contemporary U.S. practice.

Alliance   Commitment between two or more states to act together for general or specific purposes, often for mutual defense. Usually embodied in a formal treaty.

Alternat   Principle governing the signing of official copies of treaties and agreements, wherein signatories have their names and signatures appear first—or in the preferred position—in the copies they respectively keep, thus alternating positions in the copies signed.

Ambassador   Technically, the chief of a diplomatic mission of Embassy rank, accredited by a Chief of State to a foreign government or an international organization. Generally, the term also is used interchangeably with emissary or envoy.

Angary   International right of a belligerent nation in time of war to requisition, under certain conditions, or to destroy neutral property found within its territory or jurisdiction, subject to payment of full compensation.

Ante bellum   Means ''before the war'' (in the United States often used to denote before the Civil War).

Arbitration   System of peaceful settlement of disputes, in which the parties select an arbitral agent—a single individual, a commission, or a court—to decide the issue either by compromise or on the basis of principles of law and equity, as agreed to by the parties, and the parties acknowledge in advance that they will be bound by the award. Also see Adjudication and Conciliation.

Armistice   Formal agreement between belligerents in time of war to provide for a cessation of hostilities and disposition of military forces. Also see Cease-fire and Truce.

Asylum   Process of providing sanctuary or refuge for individuals to protect them from mistreatment or violence. Diplomatic and consular asylum, or exterritorial asylum, involves sanctuary in diplomatic and consular establishments, or the residence or property of foreign diplomats and consuls. Territorial asylum involves refuge within the territory of a foreign state.

Attaché   Generally, a member of the staff of an Ambassador or Minister, but, more specifically, the term either denotes certain types of functional specialists in overseas missions, such as agricultural, commercial, and military attachés, or simply applies to a category of career assignment distinguished from counselors, first and second secretaries, and the like.

Balance of power   Principle of international politics and diplomatic practice based on the notion that peace can be maintained by the proper distribution of economic, military, and political forces among nations so that no single nation or combination of nations can dominate or threaten others.

Belligerents   Applied to states and their military forces at war with another state, that, under international law, are subject to the laws of war.

Bilateral Applied to international treaties and agreements that have two signatories that contain reciprocal and complementary commitments, or it is applied to international conferences and meetings that are participated in by the representatives of two governments. Also see Multilateral.

Bipartite Applied to international treaties and agreements having two corresponding parts or commitments, one for each of the two signatories, or to negotiations or meetings and conferences participated in by representatives of two governments. Also see Multipartite.

Capitulation Act or instrument of surrender in time of hostilities, such as an armistice, surrender, or suspension of arms. Formerly, it also was used to denote the unequal treaties with countries of the Middle East and Asia that granted special privileges and extraterritorial rights to foreign governments.

Career Ambassador Highest ranked position in the career Foreign Service of the United States, to which officers rise through the ranks when appointed to duties comparable to those of ambassadors and ministers. This is a career rank, not an assignment title.

Career diplomat Member of the professional diplomatic career service of the United States, as distinguished from a diplomat appointed from outside the career.

Career Minister Second highest ranked position in the career Foreign Service of the United States, immediately under the rank of Career Ambassador.

Casus belli Event or set of circumstances that is a cause of war or is alleged to justify going to war.

Casus foederis Act or event provided for in a treaty of alliance that makes the alliance operative and renders it active.

Cease-fire Agreement for cessation of hostilities and military advances, and usually freezes the existing military situation. Also see Armistice and Truce.

Chancery The building where the head of a diplomatic mission and its members have their offices in the capital of the country to which they are accredited.

Chargé d'Affaires Technically, a chief of diplomatic mission accredited by the sending government to the Ministry of Foreign Affairs of the receiving country. Chargés rank below Ambassadors and Ministers. A **Chargé d'Affaires ad interim** serves as temporary or provisional diplomatic representative during the absence of the Ambassador or Minister or in the interim pending the appointment of a new Chief of Mission. A **Charge d'Affairés en titre** serves in this capacity on a permanent basis.

Chief of Mission The Ambassador, Minister, or chargé d'affaires, appointed by the President, with Senate approval, who heads a nation's diplomatic mission in a foreign capital.

Chief of Protocol Principal government official who manages and administers the rules of national and diplomatic ceremony and etiquette.

Chief of State Supreme agent or representative of a country in its diplomatic relations with other states, who may be an emperor, king, or president. In the parliamentary system, the Chief of State is distinguished from the Head of Government.

Collective security Principle of mutual commitment undertaken by a group of countries to guarantee the security of one another against foreign intervention or aggression. It usually is embodied as a basic element in the contemporary alliance and the international organization that has significant political and peacekeeping responsibilities.

Comity or international comity   Reciprocal courtesy and politeness, as distinguished from rules of international law, which governments accord to one another, including their diplomatic relations.

Commission   Official document certifying the designation of an appointee to the Foreign Service of the United States or to a diplomatic or consular assignment, which is signed by the President or some official designated by the President. Also denotes a diplomatic delegation sent on a special mission, usually to a conference to negotiate a treaty or agreement.

Communiqué   Official announcement or bulletin that reports the results of an international meeting, conference, or talks between high-level government officials.

Compromis d'arbitrage   Special understanding, often in the form of a treaty, to submit a particular dispute to international arbitration or adjudication, specifying the nature and organization of the arbitral agency or court, the issue to be decided, and, sometimes, the principles to be applied in deciding the award.

Compulsory jurisdiction   Principle that when one party to a dispute brings action, the dispute being under the jurisdiction of a court, the court may legally compel the other party to appear before it or forfeit the case. This commitment has been made voluntary under the International Court of Justice (see Optional clause).

Conciliation   System of peaceful settlement of disputes, in which the parties submit the dispute to a previously established agency or commission, which either simply files a report determining the facts at issue or, if so authorized by the parties, proceeds to make recommendations for the resolution of the controversy, based upon equity and mutual compromise. In either case, the parties are not bound in advance to accept the report or recommendation. Also see Arbitration.

Conclave   International conference that sometimes meets or negotiates in secret.

Concordat   Treaty or agreement signed by the Papacy with secular states, concerning the interests of the Roman Catholic Church and ecclesiastical matters.

Conference diplomacy   Multilateral diplomacy, as distinguished from traditional bilateral diplomacy and classical direct negotiation, usually involving some form of conferencing in ad hoc meetings, regularized conferences, or sessions of deliberative agencies of international organizations.

Congress   Type of international gathering. Formerly, it was distinguished from the international conference in that it was regarded as more important and dignified, generally for the purpose of negotiating a major peace settlement, and involved a greater number of states and the highest-level plenipotentiaries. Currently, the term is limited to the semipublic gathering or technical or administrative meetings concerned with nonpolitical matters, particularly in inter-American relations.

Consul   Member of the Foreign Service who heads a consulate and performs consular as distinct from diplomatic functions.

Consular agent   Consular officer who is subordinate to principal consular officers and who is usually appointed to a lesser consular post.

Consular convention   Treaty among governments providing for the establishment and governance of consular relations; not simply a custom or usage.

Consular post   Consular establishment, whether a consulate-general, consulate, vice consulate, or consular agency.

Consulate   Foreign mission, usually established in a major port or industrial or transportation center, that performs consular as distinct from diplomatic functions.

Contingency planning   Systematic advance planning of policy and action to be pursued if and when identified contingencies should occur.

Contingent fund   President's special or emergency fund, from which expenditures may be made for diplomatic purposes without rendering a full account of the details of its use.

Contraband   Merchandise that, though belonging to a neutral nation in time of war, may be seized by the forces of a belligerent power because such goods are deemed to be susceptible to use for hostile purposes by its enemy.

Convention   Generally used synonymously with the term "treaty". More specifically, it is restricted to multilateral treaties that concern cultural, commercial, and consular affairs or treatment of governmental, administrative, and legal matters, rather than political issues. In international affairs, it is not synonymous with an international conference or gathering.

Country team   Group of officers stationed in a given foreign country representing the Department of State and other agencies, who are amalgamated into a cooperative team to assist the Chief of Mission in an advisory capacity in coordinating U.S. policy, programs, and action in that country.

Coup d'état   Sudden, decisive blow or action in politics or diplomacy or a sudden, forceful overthrowing of a government.

Courier   Messenger who personally conveys diplomatic communications and pouches of documents from and to Washington and among U.S. diplomatic and consular establishments overseas.

Courtesy resignation   Formal, automatic resignation filed by every U.S. Ambassador and Minister when a new President takes office, which may be accepted or rejected in each case as the President decides.

Customary international law   Code of international practice accepted as legally binding by the prescriptive practice of states, which is not overtly or necessarily embodied in written legal commitments, such as treaties and agreements.

Dean of diplomatic corps   See Doyen.

Declaration   Simple statement of national policy concerning foreign affairs or an agreed statement of policy of two or more governments or of principles of international law as mutually understood. It may or may not be in the form of a formal treaty.

Deputy Chief of Mission (DCM)   The second in command and authority, under the Chief of Mission, in a foreign capital.

Detente   Denotes a relaxation of international tensions or conflict. Is not related to entente and therefore does not signify the opposite or absence of an understanding defined as an entente.

Diplomacy Practice involving the application of intelligence, tact, and judgment to the conduct of official relations between the governments of members of the family of nations. It is the science of management of foreign affairs and the art of representation and negotiation. It is not synonymous with substantive foreign policy goals and principles.

Diplomatic corps (or *Corps Diplomatique*) Generically used for the entire corps of diplomatic representatives of a government or for all of the diplomatic officers stationed in a given national capital. In a broader sense it also is applied to the diplomatic staff of a single state throughout the world. Also used to describe the combined foreign diplomatic staffs in a given capital.

Diplomatic list List, usually published periodically, of the names of persons who constitute the diplomatic missions accredited to the government of a state.

Diplomatic mission Establishment providing representation and negotiation as distinct from consular services. It may be a traditional Embassy or Legation, it may be accredited to an international conference or organization, or it may be ''special,'' concerned with some particular and temporary diplomatic assignment.

Diplomatic post Diplomatic establishment in a foreign capital, consisting of the Chief of Mission and all members of the mission.

Diplomatic pouch The mail container employed to transmit official diplomatic communications between the Department of State and American foreign missions and among such missions. It bears the official seal, is inviolable, is legally exempt from interference, and is conveyed by a diplomatic courier.

Diplomatist Applied generically to all officials who serve in diplomatic affairs.

Dispatch or despatch Generally represents the formal communication or report of a Chief of Mission to the Secretary of State (or Secretary of Foreign Affairs) and the latter's communication to the Chief of Mission stationed abroad.

Dollar diplomacy Term applied to U.S. policy and relations in the Caribbean area and Asia, involving emphasis on promoting and protecting the commercial and financial interests of U.S. nationals and the government abroad and of using financial strength and pressures to build diplomatic power and achieve foreign relations goals.

Doyen Ranking diplomat in a capital, who occupies this position by virtue of holding the highest diplomatic rank in the particular country for the longest period of time. On certain collective diplomatic matters, the *doyen* represents the interests of the entire diplomatic corps.

Embargo An order, decree, or regulation, issued by a government, prohibiting the departure of merchant ships from ports under its control or prohibiting them from carrying certain types of goods out of the country, which may be levied as a reprisal for an alleged injury committed by another government and as a means of securing redress.

Embassy Permanent, regular diplomatic establishment of the highest rank, accredited to a foreign government and headed by an Ambassador.

Emissary Diplomatic agent appointed to a representation or negotiating mission, regardless of diplomatic rank.

Entente Understanding between two or more states to establish a common course of action or a community of goals or interests concerning certain issues. It is not as formal as an alliance but stronger than peaceful or cordial relations.

Envoy Diplomatic agent appointed to a representation or negotiating mission. Technically, the term also is used for diplomatic agents of the second rank comparable to Ministers but inferior to Ambassadors.

Excellency Title of honor employed in addressing Ambassadors and Ministers in oral and written communications. Also used for some high-level officials, such as the Secretary of State.

Exchange of notes Denotes an agreement, mutually bilateral, between governments, often consummated by a diplomat with the Secretary of State or Foreign Minister. For the United States such an exchange usually constitutes an executive agreement, not a treaty.

Exchange of ratifications Formal act whereby signatories of a treaty or agreement provide one another with instruments that authenticate the mutual ratification of the treaty or agreement, thereby effectuating its implementation.

Executive agent or envoy (see Presidential agent, emissary, or envoy).

Executive agreement International understanding between governments that establish, alter, or terminate mutual rights and reciprocal obligations, without requiring the advice and consent of the Senate under the American constitutional treaty-making procedure.

Exequatur Official document granted to foreign consular officers by the government of the country in which they are to function, recognizing their official capacity and authorizing them to perform the functions appropriate to their offices.

Exterritoriality Legal principle recognizing that diplomats, together with their families and suite, staff, residence, and archives, lie outside the legal jurisdiction of the country to which they are assigned. Also see Extraterritoriality.

Extradition Practice of apprehending a fugitive criminal by the authorities of the country of refuge, for surrender to the authorities of the country in which the alleged crime was perpetrated, for trial and, if found guilty, for punishment under the latter's law. Usually, extradition does not apply to ''political'' crimes, and normally no obligation to extradite exists in the absence of specific treaty commitments.

Extraterritoriality Principle, based upon international custom or on treaties known as capitulations, under which foreign nationals are tried by diplomatic or consular courts operating in accordance with the laws of the country of the individual's nationality rather than by local courts under the law of the local jurisdiction. Also see Exterritoriality.

Final act Ultimate, comprehensive, and inclusive written end product of an international conference, reviewing its activities and embodying the texts of engagements concluded.

Foreign Service of the United States Career diplomatic and consular services of the United States, comprising the personnel to staff overseas diplomatic and consular missions and policy-making and other positions in the Department of State. It is distinguished from the regular Civil Service.

Foreign Service officer Career officer, selected on the basis of examination and appointed by the President with Senate approval, to perform diplomatic or consular duties for the United States.

Foreign Service Reserve officer Nonpermanent career officer who is appointed on a noncontinuing basis to fill immediate staffing needs, often to provide specialists in the Foreign Service who are not normally acquired through ordinary recruitment.

Foreign Service staff American personnel, other than Foreign Service and Reserve officers, who generally perform administrative, fiscal, managerial, and clerical services in U.S. missions abroad.

Full power Official document, signed by the President, authorizing a diplomatic agent to represent, negotiate, and sign a treaty or agreement for the United States. Full powers also may be incorporated into other official documents, such as a letter of credence or "letters patent." In the case of a negotiating conference, the full power is delivered to, or exchanged with, other conferees.

General act Formal document containing a summary of proceedings of an international meeting or conference, which posseses the character of a treaty by declaring that the annexed agreements, conventions, and treaties acquire the force of law and commitment as if they were textually embodied.

Good offices System of peaceful settlement of disputes, involving the voluntary inter-position of a third party, simply through suggestion or advice, to induce the disputing parties to join in attempting by direct negotiation or some other form of peaceful settle-ment to resolve their differences. Also see Mediation.

Handing diplomats their passports Expression figuratively employed to signify that a state finds an individual to be persona non grata and wishes that individual to depart. Does not imply the actual conferral of an exit passport or exit visa.

Head of Government Chief executive, that is, the actual, as distinct from the nominal, wielder of executive authority, who may be called Prime Minister, Premier, Chancellor, or President. In the presidential system of government, as in the United States, the offices of Chief of State and Head of Government are combined in a single official.

Hot line Special communications network established by the United States and the Soviet Union, providing the White House and the Kremlin with a direct and constantly available electronic facility.

Internuncio Diplomatic representative of the Papacy accredited to a government, of ministerial rank. Also see Nuncio.

Intervention Direct interference by one state in the foreign or domestic affairs of other states for the purpose of influencing or controlling them.

Inviolability Principle of exemption or guaranteed freedom from restraint, personal or legal injury, or interference of diplomats, their premises, their archives, and their com-munications.

Joint declaration An agreement concerning goals, policies, or actions jointly declared or proclaimed, usually in written form, by the representatives of two or more states. See Agreement.

Joint representation Arrangement whereby two or more states accredit the same per-son to represent them to another state. Differs from multiple or plural representation.

Judicial settlement System for the peaceful settlement of international disputes by an international tribunal, such as the International Court of Justice. Also see Adjudication.

As a method of peaceful settlement, it needs to be distinguished from arbitration, conciliation, mediation, and good offices.

Legation   Permanent, regular diplomatic establishment of the second highest rank, accredited to a foreign government and headed by a Minister.

Letter of credence   Official document, signed by the President, addressed and formally presented to the head of a receiving government or to an international organization, that identifies emissaries, indicates the object of their missions, and authorizes them to represent the government of the United States.

Letter of recall   Official document, signed by the President, addressed and formally presented to the head of a receiving country or an international organization, recalling particular envoys and terminating their participation in the mission on which they were engaged.

Letters patent   Official documents furnished a presidential or special agent in lieu of a letter of credence, often containing full powers. This expression also may be used for the documentation given consuls by their sending government, authenticating their appointments and authorizing them to perform their duties.

Mediation   System of peaceful settlement, in which a third party intervenes diplomatically, assuming the role of mediator, playing a leading and regular part in the conduct of negotiations, and serving as conciliator and neutral intermediary but not as arbiter or judge. Also see Good offices.

Memorandum   Usually a written instrument, on virtually any subject, often of a routine nature, sent by a diplomat to the Department of State (or Foreign Office) or to the diplomatic mission of another country.

Minister   Chief of a diplomatic mission of legation rank, accredited by a Chief of State to a foreign government. Ministers are of two grades—the Envoy Extraordinary and Minister Plenipotentiary, who ranks below the Ambassador, and the Minister Resident, who ranks below the Envoy Extraordinary and above the Chargé d'Affaires, but which rank was discontinued by the United States at the turn of the twentieth century.

Ministerial diplomacy   Diplomacy engaged in personally at the Secretary of State or Foreign Minister level.

Modus visendi   Provisional working arrangement pending the devisement of a more permanent undertaking for settling a dispute or resolving a problem. It may be formalized as a written agreement or informally embodied in written or oral exchanges or statements.

Most-favored-nation   Principle commonly applied in commercial, trade, and consular treaties that provides that contracting states reciprocally enjoy the commercial or consular advantages of the state that is accorded the greatest benefits, so that subsequent benefits granted to a third country by either of the parties are automatically extended to the other parties having most-favored-nation relations with the granting state.

Multilateral   Term applied to international treaties and agreements that have more than two signatories, containing reciprocal and complementary commitments, or applied to international conferences and meetings participated in by representatives of more than two governments. Also see Bilateral.

Multipartite   Term applied to international treaties and agreements having more than two signatories, with commitments involving more than two governments. Also see Multilateral.

Multiple representation   Arrangement whereby a diplomatic emissary is accredited to two or more states at the same time. Usually the envoy has a permanent residence in one of the capitals and periodically visits the other states. Or, as in early American diplomatic practice, the emissary remained in the capital of one country and negotiated with the envoys of other countries stationed in that capital. Differs from joint or plural representation.

Negotiation   Process of discussion and bargaining between the diplomatic emissaries of two or more states to agree to common goals and policies, settle international disputes, or conclude international treaties and agreements.

Neutralism   National policy position to refrain from involvement in a conflict between other states, often called noninvolvement, nonalignment, or noncommittal. Differs from neutrality and neutralization.

Neutrality   Voluntary status of a state that remains legally uninvolved and impartial toward belligerent states in time of war, which may be formally proclaimed by a declaration of neutrality, but accrues automatically under the laws of war. Differs from neutralism and neutralization.

Neutralization   Process whereby states agree, by means of an international treaty, to guarantee the integrity and independence of a given state, and the neutralized state binds itself not to take up arms against any of the other signatories unless it is attacked or invaded. Differs from neutralism and neutrality.

Non-self-executing treaty or agreement   Treaty or agreement that is not automatically enforceable on the basis of its own stipulations but requires implementing legislation or formal executive orders and regulations to render it executable.

Note diplomatique   Formal communication addressed by the Secretary of State to the Foreign Minister of another country, and vice versa.

Note verbale   Written diplomatic communication, which is impersonal, is drafted in the third person, and is unsigned.

Nuncio   Permanent or continuing diplomatic representative of the Papacy accredited to a government, of ambassadorial rank.

Open diplomacy   As applied to treaties and agreements, generally denotes that, when they are consummated, they are made public and formally published. However, agreement is not universal respecting the application of this principle to negotiations while they are under way.

Optional clause   Stipulation in Statute of the International Court of Justice that permits members, as a voluntary option, to accept ipso facto and without special agreement the compulsory adjudication of certain types of legal disputes. If one subscribing state brings suit against another, therefore, the court may compel the latter to appear or forfeit the case.

Overseas mission   General expression covering ordinary diplomatic and consular missions (such as embassies, legations, and consulates), regularized missions to international organizations, and temporary special diplomatic missions that take emissaries to foreign territory.

Pacific settlement Applies generically to the peaceful settlement of international disputes, which may take the form of adjudication, arbitration, mediation, conciliation, and good offices.

Pact Popular title for certain important treaties, usually creating significant commitments concerned with peacekeeping or collective security or with establishing an alliance.

Papal legate Diplomatic representative of the Papacy of the ambassadorial rank (see Nuncio).

Parliamentary diplomacy Diplomatic relations conducted in a multilateral forum—either the ad hoc or the regularized international conference or the agency of an international organization—with decision making handled by a formal voting process.

Passport Official document that authenticates the identity and nationality of a person for travel or sojourn abroad. They are of three types—diplomatic passports for diplomats and consuls, special passports for other government officials, and regular passports for private persons. Some countries also issue other types of passports for particular purposes.

Persona grata Diplomatic status signifying that a particular emissary is personally acceptable to the receiving government.

Persona non grata Diplomatic status signifying that particular diplomatic emissaries at the time of appointment are, or while serving in their appointments become, unacceptable to the receiving or host government.

Personal diplomacy Applied to the conduct of direct representation, meetings, and negotiations at the highest governmental levels, by Chiefs of State, Heads of Government, and Foreign Ministers. Also see Ministerial and Summit diplomacy.

Personal representative See Presidential agent.

Plural representation Arrangement whereby a state accredits more than one permanent diplomatic envoy to a foreign state or international organization, such as the United Nations. Differs from joint or multiple representation.

Precedence Order of relative ranking or priority of government leaders and diplomats for purposes of status, reception, seating, speaking, and otherwise participating in diplomatic affairs.

Presidential agent, emissary, or envoy Special diplomatic emissary, appointed and assigned by the President without Senate confirmation, to a special mission, usually of a temporary or nonpermanent nature. Such envoys represent the President and often are responsible directly to the Chief Executive. They may be appointed and/or function in secret and are then known as secret agents.

Privileges and immunities Encompasses more than a dozen different types of exemptions, based on principles of international law and comity, to guarantee inviolability to diplomatic and consular officers as well as to their facilities, to protect them and their work from a variety of local laws and regulations, including taxes, duties, and other matters, and to provide them with freedom of movement and communication.

Procès verbal Either simply an authenticated written record of the minutes of an international conference or of an exchange of treaty ratifications or an agreed written addition to the text of a treaty or agreement by way of explanation, elucidation, or interpretation.

Protocol   When used to denote a written instrument, this term is interchangeable with *proces verbal*. However, protocol also is used to denote proper international deportment, including such matters as formal procedures, etiquette, and precedence in ceremonies of state and diplomatic relations.

Rapporteur   Officer of an international meeting or committee who, as reporter, prepares a summary of deliberations in the form of an official record or report.

Ratification   Process whereby the provisions of a treaty are formally confirmed and approved by a state; it is an executive, not a legislative (Senate) act, and is signified by a document called an instrument of ratification, which is signed by the President.

Rebus sic stantibus   Legal principle that, literally meaning "things remaining the same," applies to treaty termination, inasmuch as, under certain limited conditions, the obligations of a treaty are deemed to terminate by virtue of a vital change in the circumstances or conditions under which the undertaking was concluded.

Reciprocity of ranks of diplomatic envoys   Principle of international comity that states exchange diplomatic envoys at the same diplomatic rank.

Recognition   Process whereby a state acknowledges or accepts a new state in the family of nations or a new government in an existing state. While essentially a national political action, it produces important international legal as well as political consequences.

Reservation (to treaty)   Formally stipulated condition respecting the text of a treaty that specifies such interpretations, limitations, or qualifications—but not actual text amendments—that a government makes a formal part of its ratification. Reservations may be initiated by the Senate or the President and are embodied in the ratification instrument.

Right of legation   Legal prerogative of members of the family of nations to engage in diplomacy, to send diplomatic agents to represent their interests in other states, and reciprocally to receive such emissaries.

Safe conduct   Authorization granting permission for a diplomatic envoy to pass unmolested into, out of, or through the territory of a belligerent state in time of war or of a country involved in revolution or civil disorder.

Secret agent   Presidential agent who is appointed and functions secretly (see Presidential agent).

Self-executing treaty or agreement   Treaty or agreement that is automatically enforceable on promulgation on the basis of its own stipulations, without requiring implementing legislation or regulations.

Shirtsleeve diplomacy   Direct, blunt, often brusque diplomatic conduct, avoiding delicate treatment, diplomatic finesse, and proper protocol—hence, a lack of customary proprieties. Thus, figuratively speaking, it implies that a diplomat removes his coat and, "businesslike," lays his cards on the table.

Sovereignty   Legal principle affording a state freedom from foreign control in the conduct of its domestic and foreign affairs.

Special diplomatic agent, envoy, or representative   See Presidential agent.

Special mission   Nontraditional mission, which is accredited to, and provides representation in, an international organization or to an international conference, to the government or leaders of a country with which the United States is not yet ready to engage in normal official relations, or for some other special purposes, such as the mission of a presidential special agent or emissary.

Sponsion   Pledge made by, or commitment or agreement entered into by, diplomatic agents who are not properly authorized or commissioned or who exceed their authority; it is voidable if not automatically null and void.

State visit   Technically, the formal visit by a Chief of State to a foreign country on the invitation of its government. This expression also is applied more generally to visits of others as well, such as Heads of Government and certain other leaders above the ministerial level.

Status quo   Existing situation or state of things; hence, an unchanged condition of affairs. Status quo ante bellum means the condition or state of affairs existing before war.

Statute   In international parlance, it is the title of a particular type of treaty or agreement, usually serving as the constitutive act of an international organization that specifies a system of regulations or to an international juridical agency, such as the International Court of Justice.

Summit diplomacy   Personal diplomacy engaged in by Chiefs of State and Heads of Government. Also see Personal diplomacy.

Treaty   International contract or understanding between states to establish, alter, or terminate mutual rights and reciprocal obligations. In U.S. constitutional practice, a treaty is subject to Senate advice and consent before it may be ratified and implemented by the President.

Truce   Agreement for the abatement or suspension of hostilities in time of military conflict, which often includes agreed conditions. Also see Armistice and Cease-fire.

Ultimatum   Written communication by one state to another containing demands or terms respecting an international dispute, the rejection of which may lead to rupture of diplomatic relations or to war.

Understanding   See Agreement.

Unilateral declaration   Formal announcement of a state, asserting its goals, policies, or courses of action, that is proclaimed or transmitted to other states for their information and guidance.

Visa   Endorsement or notation impressed on a passport, manifesting that it has been examined and found to be in order to permit the bearer to proceed to and into a foreign country. Visas are classified as diplomatic, official, and ordinary.

White paper   Report, often comprising a selected collection of documents, issued by a Foreign Office or the Department of State, to present a case or justify a policy or action.

Wristonization   Process of integrating the officer personnel of the Department of State and the Foreign Service. ''De-Wristonization'' refers to subsequent undoing of certain aspects of such amalgamation.

NOTE

For other lists of diplomatic and foreign relations terms, see Thomas A. Bailey, *A Diplomatic History of the American People*, 9th ed., 1974, pp. 957–61; Melquiades J.

Gamboa, *Elements of Diplomatic and Consular Practice: A Glossary*, 1966; Robert B. Harmon, *The Art and Practice of Diplomacy: A Selected and Annotated Guide*, 1971, pp. 160–74; and Elmer Plischke, *Conduct of American Diplomacy*, 3d ed., 1967, pp. 643–51. For foreign relations dictionaries, see Ferdinand De Cussy, *Dictionaire Ou Manuel-Lexique Du Diplomate Et Du Consul*, 1846; Jack C. Plano and Roy Olton, *The International Relations Dictionary*, 2d ed., 1979; and U.S. Department of State, *International Relations Dictionary*, 1978. For additional references to relevant materials, see Elmer Plischke, *U.S. Foreign Relations: A Guide to Information Sources*, 1980, pp. 12–14.

normal official relations, or for some other special purposes, such as the mission of a presidential special agent or emissary.

Sponsion Pledge made by, or commitment or agreement entered into by, diplomatic agents who are not properly authorized or commissioned or who exceed their authority; it is voidable if not automatically null and void.

State visit Technically, the formal visit by a Chief of State to a foreign country on the invitation of its government. This expression also is applied more generally to visits of others as well, such as Heads of Government and certain other leaders above the ministerial level.

Status quo Existing situation or state of things; hence, an unchanged condition of affairs. Status quo ante bellum means the condition or state of affairs existing before war.

Statute In international parlance, it is the title of a particular type of treaty or agreement, usually serving as the constitutive act of an international organization that specifies a system of regulations or to an international juridical agency, such as the International Court of Justice.

Summit diplomacy Personal diplomacy engaged in by Chiefs of State and Heads of Government. Also see Personal diplomacy.

Treaty International contract or understanding between states to establish, alter, or terminate mutual rights and reciprocal obligations. In U.S. constitutional practice, a treaty is subject to Senate advice and consent before it may be ratified and implemented by the President.

Truce Agreement for the abatement or suspension of hostilities in time of military conflict, which often includes agreed conditions. Also see Armistice and Cease-fire.

Ultimatum Written communication by one state to another containing demands or terms respecting an international dispute, the rejection of which may lead to rupture of diplomatic relations or to war.

Understanding See Agreement.

Unilateral declaration Formal announcement of a state, asserting its goals, policies, or courses of action, that is proclaimed or transmitted to other states for their information and guidance.

Visa Endorsement or notation impressed on a passport, manifesting that it has been examined and found to be in order to permit the bearer to proceed to and into a foreign country. Visas are classified as diplomatic, official, and ordinary.

White paper Report, often comprising a selected collection of documents, issued by a Foreign Office or the Department of State, to present a case or justify a policy or action.

Wristonization Process of integrating the officer personnel of the Department of State and the Foreign Service. "De-Wristonization" refers to subsequent undoing of certain aspects of such amalgamation.

NOTE

For other lists of diplomatic and foreign relations terms, see Thomas A. Bailey, *A Diplomatic History of the American People*, 9th ed., 1974, pp. 957–61; Melquiades J.

Gamboa, *Elements of Diplomatic and Consular Practice: A Glossary*, 1966; Robert B. Harmon, *The Art and Practice of Diplomacy: A Selected and Annotated Guide*, 1971, pp. 160–74; and Elmer Plischke, *Conduct of American Diplomacy*, 3d ed., 1967, pp. 643–51. For foreign relations dictionaries, see Ferdinand De Cussy, *Dictionaire Ou Manuel-Lexique Du Diplomate Et Du Consul*, 1846; Jack C. Plano and Roy Olton, *The International Relations Dictionary*, 2d ed., 1979; and U.S. Department of State, *International Relations Dictionary*, 1978. For additional references to relevant materials, see Elmer Plischke, *U.S. Foreign Relations: A Guide to Information Sources*, 1980, pp. 12–14.

Glossary of Symbols and Acronyms

DIPLOMATIC

Ad int	ad interim
AE/P	Ambassador Extraordinary and Plenipotentiary
Agt.	Diplomatic Agent
Asst Sec	Assistant Secretary of State
BEX	Board of Examiners (Foreign Service)
CA	Career Ambassador
CdA	Charge d'Affaires
CG	Consul General
CM	Career Minister
CDM	Chief of Diplomatic Mission
CN	Circular Note
Comm	Commission or Commissioner
Conf	International Conference
Conv	International Convention
Couns	Counselor of Embassy
DCM	Deputy Chief of Mission
Dep Sec	Deputy Secretary of State
Dep Under Sec	Deputy Under Secretary of State
Dip/Agt	Diplomatic Agent
Dir	Director
DPL	Diplomat

EA	Executive Agreement
EE/MP	Envoy Extraordinary and Minister Plenipotentiary
FAS	Foreign Agricultural Service
FCS	Foreign Commercial Service
FO	Foreign Office
FS	Foreign Service
FSI	Foreign Service Institute
FSN	Foreign Service National (recruited locally abroad)
FSO	Foreign Service Officer
FSR (DES)	Foreign Reserve (Domestic)
FSRO	Foreign Service Reserve Officer
FSRU	Foreign Service Reserve Officer (Unlisted)
FSSO	Foreign Service Staff Officer
MP	Minister Plenipotentiary
MR	Minister Resident
MR/CG	Minister Resident and Consul General
NC	Noncareer Appointee
PNG	Persona Non Grata
POLAD	Political Adviser
Rep	Representative (diplomatic)
Under Sec	Under Secretary of State
USLO	U.S. Liaison Office/Officer
USUN	U.S. Representative to the United Nations

NATIONAL

ACDA	Arms Control and Disarmament Agency
ACTION	Peace Corps
AEC	Atomic Energy Commission
AFSA	American Foreign Service Association
AID	Agency for International Development
BEW	Board of Economic Warfare
CAB	Civil Aeronautics Board
CCC	Commodity Credit Corporation
CEA	Council of Economic Advisers
CIA	Central Intelligence Agency
CM	Chief of Mission (diplomatic)

COMECON	Council for Mutual Economic Aid
CSC	Civil Service Commission
DCM	Deputy Chief of Mission
DEA	Drug Enforcement Administration
DIA	Defense Intelligence Agency
DOD	Department of Defense
EAS	Executive Agreement Series (U.S.), issued singly, superseded by TIAS in 1945
ECA	Economic Cooperation Administration
EO	Executive Order
EOP	Executive Office of the President
ERP	European Recovery Program (Marshall Plan)
EXIMBANK	Export-Import Bank
FAA	Federal Aviation Administration
FBI	Federal Bureau of Investigation
FBIS	Foreign Broadcast Information Service (of CIA)
FCC	Federal Communications Commission
FEA	Foreign Economic Administration
FOA	Foreign Operations Administration
FR	Federal Register
FRUS	*Foreign Relations of the United States*
FTC	Federal Trade Commission
GAO	General Accounting Office
GDP	Gross Domestic Product
GNP	Gross National Product
ICA	International Cooperation Administration (predecessor of AID)
IDA	International Development Association
IG	Interdepartmental Groups
INS	Immigration and Naturalization Service
IRG	Interdepartmental Regional Group
JCS	Joint Chiefs of Staff
MAAG	Military Assistance Advisory Group
MDAP	Mutual Defense Assistance Program
MFN	Most-Favored Nation Principle
MSA	Mutual Security Agency
MSP	Mutual Security Program
NASA	National Aeronautics and Space Administration

NIA	National Intelligence Authority
NSA	National Security Agency
NSC	National Security Council
OCB	Operations Coordinating Board
OEC	Office of Export Control
OMB	Office of Management and Budget
OPIC	Overseas Private Investment Corporation
OSS	Office of Strategic Services
OTA	Office of Technology Assessment
OWI	Office of War Information
OWM	Office of War Mobilization
P.L.	Public Laws
PRC	Policy Coordinating Committee
SANACC	State, Army, Navy, Air Coordinating Committee
SCC	Special Coordinating Committee
SIG	Senior Interdepartmental Group
STAT	U.S. Statutes at Large
SWNCC	State, War, Navy Coordinating Committee
TCA	Technical Cooperation Administration
TIAS	Treaties and Other International Acts Series (U.S.), issued singly since 1945
TS	Treaty Series (U.S.), issued singly, superseded by TIAS in 1945
USC	U.S. Code
USIA	U.S. Information Agency
USICA	U.S. International Communication Agency
USIS	U.S. Information Service
UST	U.S. Treaties and Other International Agreements (annual volumes since 1950)
USTR	U.S. Trade Representative
USTS	U.S. Treaty Series
USUN	U.S. Mission to United Nations
VOA	Voice of America

FOREIGN AND INTERNATIONAL

This is a selected list of organizations and other agencies, some of which temporary, are defunct, or have been superseded.

ABC Powers	Argentina, Brazil, and Chile
ADB	African Development Bank
ADB	Asian Development Bank
ADF	African Development Foundation
ANC	African National Congress
ANZUS	Australia, New Zealand, United States (Collective Security Agency)
ASEAN	Association of Southeast Asian Nations
BENELUX	Belgium, Netherlands, Luxembourg Customs Union
BIRPI	United International Bureau for the Protection of Intellectual Property
BIS	Bank of International Settlements
BNC	Binational Commission
CARICOM	Caribbean Community and Common Market
CCAC	Combined Civil Affairs Committee (United States and United Kingdom)
CCS	Combined Chiefs of Staff (United States and United Kingdom)
CEEC	Committee of European Economic Cooperation
CENTO	Central Treaty Organization (successor to METO)
CFM	Council of Foreign Ministers
CIAP	Inter-American Committee on the Alliance for Progress
CIEC	Conference on International Economic Cooperation
CITEJA	International Technical Committee of Aerial Legal Experts
COCOM	Coordinating Committee of NATO
COMECON	Council for Mutual Economic Assistance
CPRB	Combined Production and Resources Board
CRMB	Combined Raw Materials Board
CSCE	Conference/Council on Security and Cooperation in Europe
EAC	European Advisory Commission
EAEA	European Atomic Energy Agency
EBRD	European Bank for Reconstruction and Development
EC	European Community/ies
ECA	Economic Commission for Africa (UN)
ECAFE	Economic Commission for Asia and the Far East (UN)
ECE	Economic Commission for Europe (UN)
ECITO	European Central Inland Transport Organization
ECLA	European Commission for Latin America (UN)
ECO	European Coal Organization
ECSC	European Coal and Steel Community (Schuman Plan)

EDC	European Defense Community (Pleven Plan, defeated)
EDF	European Development Fund
EEA	European Environmental Agency
EEC	European Economic Community (Common Market)
EFTA	European Free Trade Association
EPC	European Political Community
EPU	European Payments Union
ESRO	European Space Research Organization
EU	European Union
EURATOM	European Atomic Energy Community
FAO	Food and Agriculture Organization
FEC	Far Eastern Commission
GATT	General Agreement on Tariffs and Trade
IA-ECOSOC	Inter-American Economic and Social Council
IACAC	Inter American Commercial Arbitration Commission
IACI	Inter-American Childrens Institute
IAEA	International Atomic Energy Agency
IADB	Inter-American Defense Board
IADB	Inter-American Development Bank
IAIAS	Inter-American Institute of Agricultural Sciences
IAII	Inter-American Indian Institute
IAR	International Authority for the Ruhr
IARA	Inter-Allied Reparation Agency
IASI	Inter-American Statistical Institute
IATA	International Air Transport Association
IB/IBRD	International Bank for Reconstruction and Development (World Bank)
ICAO	International Civil Aviation Organization
ICBM	Intercontinental Ballistic Missile
ICEM	Intergovernmental Committee for European Migration
ICES	International Council for the Exploration of the Seas
ICJ	International Court of Justice
ICM	Intergovernmental Committee for Migration
ICSU	International Council of Scientific Unions
IDA	International Development Association
IDB	Inter-American Defense Board
IDB	Inter-American Development Bank

IDCA	International Development Cooperation Agency
IEA	International Energy Agency
IEFC	International Emergency Food Council
IFAD	International Fund for Agricultural Development
IFC	International Finance Corporation
IGY	International Geophysical Year
ILC	International Law Commission (UN)
ILO	International Labor Orgainzation
IMCO	Intergovernmental Maritime Consultative Organization
IMF	International Monetary Fund
IMO	International Maritime Organization (formerly, IMCO)
IMO	International Meteorological Organization
INMARSAT	International Maritime Satellite Organization
INTELSTAT	International Telecommunications Satellite Organization
INTERPOL	International Criminal Police Commission
IOM	International Organization for Migration
IPPC	International Penal and Penitentiary Commission
IPU	Interparliamentary Union
IRO	International Refugee Organization
IRRI	International Rice Research Institute
ITC	International Trade Commission
ITO	International Trade Organization
ITU	International Telecommunication Union
IUOTO	International Union of Official Travel Organizations
IWC	International Whaling Commission
LAFTA	Latin American Free Trade Association
LASO	Latin American Solidarity Organization
LDC	Less Developed Country
LN	League of Nations
LNTS	League of Nations Treaty Series
LOS	Law of the Sea
MBFR	Mutual and Balanced Force Reduction
METO	Middle East Treaty Organization (succeeded by CENTO)
MFN	Most Favored Nation
MIGA	Multilateral Investment Guarantee Agency
MNF	Multinational Force
NAC	North Atlantic Council

NAM	Nonaligned Movement
NAMSO	NATO Maintenance Supply Organization
NAPMO	NATO Programme Management Organization
NATO	North Atlantic Treaty Organization
NGO	Nongovernmental Organization
NIEO	New International Economic Order
OAS	Organization of American States
OAU	Organization of African Unity
OCA	Organization of Central American States
OECD	Organization for Economic Cooperation and Development
OECS	Organization of Eastern Caribbean States
OEEC	Organization for European Economic Cooperation
OIR	Inter-American Radio Office
OPEC	Organization of Petroleum Exporting Countries
OPIC	Overseas Private Investment Corporation
OTC	Organization for Trade Cooperation
PAHO	Pan American Health Organization
PAIGH	Pan American Institute of Geography and History
PASO	Pan American Sanitary Organization
PAU	Pan American Union
PCA	Permanent Court of Arbitration (Hague Tribunal)
PCIJ	Permanent Court of International Justice
PLO	Palestine Liberation Organization
POW	Prisoner of War
SALT	Strategic Arms Limitation Talks/Treaty
SDI	Strategic Defense Initiative
SEATO	South East Asia Treaty Organization
SPC	South Pacific Commission
START	Strategic Arms Reduction Talks
STS	Space Transportation System
SUNFED	Special United Nations Fund for Economic Development
UN	United Nations
UN-AEC	United Nations Atomic Energy Commission
UN-CCA	United Nations Commission on Continental Armaments
UN-ECOSOC	United Nations Economic and Social Council
UN-GA	United Nations General Assembly
UN-SC	United Nations Security Council

UN-SYG	United Nations Secretary-General
UN-TC	United Nations Trusteeship Council
UNCDF	United Nations Capital Development Fund
UNCLOS	United Nations Conference on the Law of the Sea
UNCTAD	United Nations Trade and Development Board
UNDP	United Nations Development Program
UNDRO	United Nations Disaster Relief Office
UNEF	United Nations Emergency Force
UNEPTA	United Nations Expanded Program of Technical Assistance
UNESCO	United Nations Educational, Scientific and Cultural Organization
UNHCR	United Nations High Commissioner for Refugees
UNICEF	United Nations International Children's Emergency Fund
UNIDO	United Nations Industrial Development Organization
UNIDROIT	United Nations International Institute for the Unification of Private Law
UNITAR	United Nations Institute for Training and Research
UNREF	United Nations Refugee Fund
UNRRA	United Nations Relief and Rehabilitation Administration
UNSCOB	United Nations Committee on the Balkans
UNSCOP	United Nations Special Committee on Palestine
UNTS	United Nations Treaty Series
UNWCC	United Nations War Crimes Commission
UPU	Universal Postal Union
WEU	Western European Union
WFP	World Food Program
WHO	World Health Organization
WIPO	World Intellectual Property Organization
WMO	World Meteorological Organization
WTO	World Trade Organization

NOTE

For additional glossaries of abbreviations, symbols, and acronyms, see Melquiades J. Gamboa, *Elements of Diplomatic and Consular Practice: A Glossary* (Quezon City, Philippines: Central Law, 1966); Marian D. Irish and Elke Frank, *U.S. Foreign Policy: Context, Conduct, Content* (New York: Harcourt Brace Jonanovich, 1975); William Macomber, Jr., *The Angels' Game: A Handbook of Modern Diplomacy* (New York: Stein and Day, 1975); and Elmer Plischke, *Conduct of American Diplomacy* (New York: Van

Nostrand, 1967). Glossaries are also provided in various Department of State publications, such as the *Foreign Relations of the United States* series, the *Biographic Registers*, Macomber's *Diplomacy for the 70s* (Washington, D.C.: Government Printing Office, 1970), and others and also in the *U.S. Government Manual*.

PART I

TO 1801

1

Origins of American Diplomacy— Prelude

"What is past is prologue" reads the inscription emblazoned on the National Archives Building in Washington, D.C.—an expression coined by Shakespeare as used in *The Tempest*. Though widely acknowledged for their creation of the United States and its political system, the Founders of the American Government also determined the nature and use of foreign affairs techniques, such as diplomatic and consular representation, the issuing of official credentials and the handling of diplomatic ceremonies, international negotiations and bargaining, and the conclusion of treaties and agreements. This experience showcases the adoption and application—first by the newly independent States and then by the American Confederation—of the diplomatic and consular institutions and practices that provided the foundation on which the Government of the United States could function and build after the Constitution went into effect.

EARLY DEVELOPMENTS

Prior to 1789, development of the conduct of foreign relations may be segmented in three periods. The first—the extended colonial era—ran until 1774. The second, a short span of less than two years—marked by the movement toward union and the convening of the Continental Congress at Philadelphia in September 1774, the outbreak of the Revolutionary War the following year, and the signing of the Declaration of Independence in mid-1776—was the critical period in which the colonies asserted their independence and created a confederal union. The third period, from 1776 to 1789, involved the commencement of collegial foreign relations directed by the Continental Congress, the establishment of a Department of Foreign Affairs, the appointment of a Secretary for

Foreign Affairs, the commissioning of American diplomats and consuls, and the negotiation of America's first treaties with foreign powers.

Committees of Correspondence

During the first period, the extracontinental affairs of the colonies were managed by the British government. This applied to both the relations of individual colonies with one another and their collective interests. As a result, they neither dispatched nor received foreign diplomatic emissaries, nor did they create foreign offices, establish official communications with foreign governments, or sign treaties with them.

In time, however, they established intercolonial agencies and relationships that consisted of policies and programs of cooperation that were implemented by colonial committees of correspondence, joint or collective conferencing by means of congresses and conventions, and alliances and other agreements. The notion of creating such committees of correspondence to handle colonial interchange originated in the early 1760s and eventually included both local committees for intracolonial communication and colony committees for dealing with intercolonial exchanges and with the British government. In 1775 the Continental Congress also elected a Committee of Correspondence, which became the Department of Foreign Affairs, the precursor of the Department of State.

Intercolonial Conferencing

The colonies also chose delegates to represent them and their interests in a series of some fifteen negotiatory "congresses" and "conventions." These emissaries discussed issues, resolved differences, devised plans, and, in some cases, produced agreements and treaties.[1] Some conclaves were strictly ad hoc intercolonial meetings, involving small numbers of colonies and eventually all thirteen, which dealt with general political, economic, jurisdictional, and other cooperative issues. Others were convened to deal with security and relations with the Indians. The third group was devoted to promoting joint action and union among the American colonies. In 1643 four New England colonies held a conference in Boston to create the New England Confederation, to meet annually to act in common in their external relations with the Dutch, the French, and the Indians. In 1754, a convention held in Albany, New York, approved Benjamin Franklin's Plan of Union, creating an intercolonial confederal system of governance headed by a President-General appointed by the British Crown and a Grand Council of colonial delegates, which was rejected by both the British government and the colonies.

At the Stamp Act Congress in 1765, twenty-seven delegates from nine colonies adopted a "Declaration of Rights and Grievances," advised the colonies to appoint special agents or emissaries to solicit relief from the British government, and produced resolutions and petitions addressed to the British Crown concerning the rights and welfare of the colonies. Finally, shortly before the outbreak of the Revolutionary War, the Continental Congress began to convene annually.

Most of these early conclaves were multipartite, delegations varying from three or four to nine colonies and eventually to twelve at the time of the Continental Congress. Except for the New England Confederation and the Continental Congress, they were ad hoc, initiated by various officials for specific purposes. Many of them were promoted by colonial governors and legislative councils. Colonies were represented by their governors, council members, and others who were commonly designated as "commissioners." This initial experience introduced the colonies to the functions of devising policy, conferring and negotiating with one another and with the Indian nations, and choosing delegates to serve as emissaries to represent them. This acquainted the colonies with several basic elements of the diplomatic process in both inter- and extra-colonial political relations.

Colonial Agents and Representation

Prior to 1774 the colonies initiated the system of utilizing American agents abroad, initially in London, and the British government devised ways of communicating with them, which constituted the rudiments of mutual representation. They utilized commercial and political "agents" who were neither orthodox diplomats bearing the customary ranks of Ambassador or Minister nor consuls. They were elected or appointed and, for certain purposes, officially commissioned. Most functioned as ad hoc or temporary representatives, whereas some became resident envoys. They provided information to the Lords and Board of Trade and other British agencies, and they explained and defended colonial interests in such matters as commercial, financial, navigation, and tax matters, as well as in political organization, territorial and boundary issues, and relations with the Indians.

During the first half of the seventeenth century the British government made little attempt to formalize the management of the colonies through the American agents, who were usually sent to London for special missions. To 1774, as indicated in Table 1.1, a corps of at least sixty agents represented the American colonies in Great Britain. More than twenty, functioning largely as colony lobbyists, information brokers, advocates of colonial policy and legislation, and channels of communication, represented one or more colonies from the 1620s till 1754. Nearly forty agents were commissioned from 1755 to 1774, a few of whom overlapped the two periods. They presented colony petitions, transmitted documents, promoted trade, and sought to gain British acceptance of colonial legislation and other actions.

By the mid-eighteenth century they served as emissaries of both the colonies that appointed them and the larger community of the thirteen colonies. This combined role became even more imperative after the Continental Congress

Table 1.1
Colonial Foreign Agents, 1624–1774

Early Colony Agents, 1624–1754
(With colonies represented)

Sir Henry Ashurst
Sir William Berkeley (Va.)
William Byrd (Va.)
Leonard Calvert (Md.)
John Clarke (R.I.)
George Croghan (Pa.)
Joseph Dudley (Mass.)
Jeremiah Dummer (Conn., Mass., N.H.)
Thomas Hutchinson (Mass.)
Sir William Johnson (N.Y.)
Increase Mather (Mass.)

Ferdinand John Paris (Md., Pa.,
    East Jersey)
William Penn (Pa.)
Sir William Phipps (Mass.)
John Pountis (Va.)
Peyton Randolph (Va.)
Miles Standish (New Plymouth)
Nathaniel Weare (N.H.)
Roger Williams (R.I.)
Edward Winslow (Mass., Plymouth)
John Winthrop (Conn.)
Sir George Yeardley (Va.)

Colony Agents, 1755-1774 *

James Abercromby (N.C., Va.)
Sir David Barclay, Jr. (Del., Pa.)
Thomas Barker (N.C.)
William Bollan (Mass.)
Edmund Burke (N.Y.)
Robert Charles (N.Y., Pa.)
Dennis de Berdt, Jr. (N.J.)
Dennys de Berdt (Mass., Del.)
Alexander Elmsley (N.C.)
Benjamin Franklin (Ga., N.J., Mass., Pa.)
Charles Garth (Ga., Md., S.C.)
Jared Ingersoll (Conn.)
Richard Jackson (Conn., Mass., Pa.)
William Samuel Johnson (Conn.)
Peter Cuchet Jouvenal (N.C.)
Alexander Kellet (Ga.)
William Knox (East Fla., Ga.)
Arthur Lee (Mass.)
Thomas Life (Conn.)

William Little (Ga.)
Henry Eustace McCulloh (N.C.)
Henry Marchant (R.I.)
Benjamin Martyn (Ga.)
Jasper Mauduit (Mass.)
Israel Mauduit (Mass.)
Edward Montagu (N.H.)
Richard Partridge (Conn., Mass., N.J.,
    N.Y., Pa., R.I.)
Charles Pinckney (S.C.)
John Sargent (N.Y., Pa.)
Joseph Sherwood (N.J., R.I.)
Samuel Smith (N.C.)
John Thomlinson, Sr. (N.H.)
John Thomlinson, Jr. (N.H.)
Barlow Trecothick (N.H.)
John Wentworth (N.H.)
Paul Wentworth (N.H.)
Henry Wilmot (N.J., Pa.)
Sir James Wright (S.C.)

*Several of these began their careers as colony agents prior to 1755, such as Abercromby
(1748–), Bollan (1743–), Charles (1748–), Partridge (1715–), and John Thomlinson, Sr.
(1734–). A few of these agents were subsequently appointed as U.S. emissaries after the
Constitution went into effect. In addition to Benjamin Franklin, these included William Bollan,
Edmund Burke, Charles Garth, Arthur Lee, Thomas Life, Charles Pinckney, and Paul Wentworth.

convened in 1774 and the Declaration of Independence was signed. Surprisingly, only approximately one-fourth of the agents were born in the colonies.[2]

The length of service of individual agents differed considerably, varying from short, ad hoc assignments to ten to seventeen years or longer. Four who held long appointments—William Bollan (1755–62 and 1768–75), Benjamin Franklin (1757–62 and 1765–75), Thomas Life (1760–75), and Charles Garth (1762–75), each of whom served for fourteen or more years—are especially noteworthy because they later became Confederation agents employed by the Continental Congress.

Although three-fourths of these agents represented a single colony, more than a dozen held dual or multiple appointments. During the period from 1755 to 1774 at least eight served the interests of two colonies, and two represented three colonies. However, records were set by Franklin, who simultaneously was designated the agent of Georgia, New Jersey, and Massachusetts as well as Pennsylvania, and earlier, during a period of nearly half a century, Richard Partridge represented six of the northern colonies. In terms of longevity and multiple service, Partridge has been called a ''career agent.'' Similarly, in view of developments after the Confederation was established and Franklin was commissioned as Minister Plenipotentiary to France, the title ''first career American diplomat'' might well be applied to him. The largest number of agents served during the decade and a half from 1758 to 1775. The number of active agents doubled between 1758 and the mid-1760s, reaching a total of eighteen in 1765, but later the number declined to ten or fewer between 1772 and 1775.[3]

Treaty and Agreement Making

In the seventeenth and eighteenth centuries the colonies also became subject to a variety of treaties and agreements.[4] These were of three types. One category, negotiated by the British government, usually consisted of peace settlements following its wars with major European powers that among other matters, fixed territorial possession and other rights in America. The second category consisted of settlements negotiated with Indian tribes. Although, in some cases, British policy and negotiations were paramount, much of this negotiation was handled by colonial agents. These treaty actions included those that followed the wars of the European powers in North America, those that concluded North American or local wars between colonies and the Indians, and others. In addition, colonial leaders contributed to the planning of, and participation in, the negotiation of arrangements to establish union among the colonies—the third type of treaty making.

UNION AND INDEPENDENCE

From 1774 to 1776, the movement toward independence and union altered the status and relationships of the colonies not only with one another but also with Great Britain, other European powers, and the Indians. This short span of less than two years produced the transformation of the colonies into independent States, epitomized by three historic developments—the convening of the Continental Congress, the outbreak of the Revolutionary War, and the proclamation of the Declaration of Independence.

The launching of the Continental Congress, which met at Philadelphia on September 5, 1774,[5] issued a "Declaration of Resolves" on October 14, and, on October 24, its delegates signed an "Agreement on Association." This plan is unique in that it constituted a "legislative resolution" to create a mutual commitment for the nonimportation and nonconsumption of British goods, as well as nonexportation and nonshipping of American merchandise to Great Britain. Although these collective actions presaged the creation of a formal union, they did not treat such matters as independence, constitutional agencies of governance, or the conduct of external affairs with Great Britain, other foreign powers, or the Indians.

While ad hoc, without a unifying treaty or constitutive act, when the Congress adjourned on October 26, it recommended the convening of a second Congress, to meet at Philadelphia on May 10, 1775. During its second session, meeting in the midst of revolutionary ferment, Franklin proposed his "Plan for Perpetual Union" on July 21. It provided for agencies of government, authority of the Congress over war and peace, sending and receiving ambassadors, and entering into alliances. This plan was to be implemented by incorporation into a formal treaty to be ratified by colonial representatives at the next session of Congress.

In the meantime the Revolutionary War broke out at Lexington, Massachusetts, on April 19, 1775, and on July 4 of the following year the delegates of the Continental Congress signed the Declaration of Independence. American assertion of independence, reinforced by the surrender of General Cornwallis at Yorktown in 1781, marked the conversion of the colonies into independent and sovereign States. Although, under international law and practice, they were inchoate members of the society of nations, pending acceptance or formal recognition by foreign governments, the conduct of American interstate and foreign relations depended on further action.

Even before the Declaration of Independence was signed on June 12, 1776, the Continental Congress, seeking to legitimate collective action, appointed a committee to draft a document to serve as its constitutive act of confederation. This committee, consisting of a delegate from each of the thirteen States, produced the John Dickinson draft of the Articles of Confederation by July 12. Sixteen months later a revised draft was approved by Congress, which sent it to the States for approval, but it took more than three additional years before the Articles were ratified by all thirteen, and it went into effect at the beginning of March 1781.

These Articles amalgamated the thirteen States into a Confederation entitled "The United States of America," in which each of them, retaining its "sovereignty, freedom, and independence," joined in "a firm league of friendship" for "common defence" and "mutual and general welfare." State delegations were to meet annually in a Congress that, so far as foreign affairs were concerned, possessed sole and exclusive right and power to determine issues of peace and war, send and receive diplomats, enter into treaties and alliances, regulate land and naval forces, manage trade and relations with the Indians, and appoint civil officers to administer the general affairs of the Confederation, which, as it turned out, included relations with foreign nations. In form and content, the Articles of Confederation constituted a treaty among the constituent American States, rather than a simple legislative act or intercolonial compact.

FOREIGN RELATIONS OF THE AMERICAN CONFEDERATION, 1774–1789

Until the Constitution went into effect in 1789, the Continental Congress developed both agencies and processes for managing the foreign affairs of the Confederation and its constituent States. It exercised authority to formulate foreign policy determinations and to administer external relations with both the European powers and the Indians. The critical process of producing State constitutions was largely completed within four years after the Declaration of Independence, but these and later constitutions to 1789 evidenced little concern with foreign relations.[6] However, because the States regarded themselves as sovereign, the Congress decided that it needed to clarify its relations with them, particularly respecting the commitments embodied in the Treaty of Peace with Great Britain, signed in 1783.

In a lengthy report to the States in 1787, the Secretary for Foreign Affairs indicated that, by the Articles of Confederation, the States vested in Congress "a general though limited Sovereignty" for national purposes in the conduct of foreign affairs. Therefore, the States did not enjoy concurrent jurisdiction in this matter, and, when a treaty "is constitutionally made, ratified, and published," it is "binding on the whole nation and superadded to the laws of the land, without the intervention of State legislatures."

Management of Foreign Affairs

In administering relations with foreign governments, the Continental Congress dealt with four main areas of activity—the framing of external policy, the creation of agencies for administrative management, the sending and receiving of emissaries, and the consummation of treaties and agreements. During the fifteen years that the Continental Congress functioned, it assumed responsibility for the collective foreign affairs of the States in two respects. It established its own system and procedures of governance, and, in addition, it created subsidiary agencies to assist it in the administration of relations with foreign governments. From the outset Congress, representing the sovereignty of the people of the States (not the aggregate people of a united nation called the United States), commenced to exercise policy-making authority for dealing with both foreign powers and the Indian tribes that lay outside the territories of the thirteen States.[7]

To assist it, on November 29, 1775, Congress created a Committee of Correspondence, consisting of five members, to handle communications with the governments of Great Britain and other countries and with American agents abroad. This committee was the first formally constituted body charged with conducting American foreign correspondence. Its initial instructions, dated December 12, 1775, addressed to Arthur Lee in London and Charles F. W. Dumas, an American friend in The Hague, implored them to secretly provide the United States with critical information.[8] Two months later the Committee renamed itself the Committee of Secret Correspondence. In mid-April 1777 this was converted into the Committee for Foreign Affairs, headed by a Secretary for Foreign Affairs, who was instructed by, and reported to, Congress. Thomas Paine was elected the first Committee Secretary. Commentators generally regard this as marking the origin of the American Department of State.

The following year Congress became more aggressive in managing the conduct of American emissaries abroad. It established a three-member committee to prepare instructions for dealing with European Courts, ordered that the Foreign Affairs Committee provide it with "all letters and public papers" received "from the commissioners, agents, and other persons, who have transacted business for the United States in Europe" from the outset to date; committed the members of Congress to secrecy in dealing with such papers[9]; and resolved that the delegates would meet each evening to review the existing state of American foreign relations. In 1779 Congress appointed a committee, consisting of one member from each State, to review "the foreign affairs of the United States" and the activities of past and current Commissioners in Europe. Its report, filed on March 24, reviewed the appointments and actions of the first accredited emissaries. Another report was prepared by a special committee of Congress in 1782, presented on September 18, which detailed correspondence to and from American emissaries abroad.

To deputize the administration of foreign relations, early in 1781, less than two months before the ratification of the Articles of Confederation, Congress created a Department of Foreign Affairs, headed by a Secretary for Foreign Affairs, to supersede the Committee for Foreign Affairs.[10]. The Secretary was empowered to manage correspondence with American envoys abroad, as well as foreign representatives to the United States, to maintain foreign relations records, and to report to Congress and attend its sessions. On August 10 Congress elected Robert R. Livingston as the first Secretary.[11] He took office on October 20, and the following year he appointed Lewis Richard Morris and Pierre Etiene DuPonceau as Under Secretaries and also a Translator of French and a Clerk.

Early in May 1784 Congress elected John Jay to succeed Livingston, but, because Jay was then Minister Plenipotentiary in Europe, he did not assume the office until late in December. He remained Secretary not only until March 4,

1789, when the new Federal Government was launched, but also until Thomas Jefferson assumed the office on March 22, 1790.[12] During the hiatus of nearly a year and a half—June 1783 to December 1784–the President of Congress functioned as acting Secretary for Foreign Affairs. To provide continuing documentary service, however, in August 1783 Congress named Henry Remsen, Jr., to undertake this task, and in March the following year it elected him as Under Secretary. See Table 1.2, sections II and III.

Both Livingston and Jay found the office of Secretary to be frustrating, because its functions were not clearly defined and were severely circumscribed by Congress, so that the Secretary was regarded as little more than a congressional clerk. Early in 1782 Livingston sent a letter of protest to the President of Congress, which led to some reorganization of the Department, and on February 22 his title was changed to "Secretary to the United States of America, for the Department of Foreign Affairs." After his resignation, however, Congress returned to its custom of managing external relations through special committees to deal with both foreign policy and problems. Although Jay wrote to the President of Congress in January 1785 requesting special instructions to define the scope of his authority, existing conditions persisted throughout the Confederation years.

Beginning in 1783 and with the signing of the Peace Treaty with Great Britain, Congress became more active not only in prescribing objectives and devising foreign policy, but also in directing the activities of American diplomats and consuls abroad and foreign emissaries accredited to the United States, the designing of diplomatic credentials and ceremonies, and the negotiation of treaties and agreements.[13] It also provided a modest headquarters building for the Department of Foreign Affairs.[14] To comport with traditional international practice, on the same day that it signed the Declaration of Independence, Congress also launched a procedure to devise an official seal, to be applied in authenticating important Confederation documents. After six years a design for the Great Seal of the United States was approved, a die was cast, and thereafter it was applied by the Secretary of Congress to various types of Confederation documents, most of which were concerned with foreign affairs.[15]

Evidencing that the Secretary and Department of Foreign Affairs were adjuncts of the Congress, the Secretary submitted a good many reports to it for its information and guidance. Aside from those concerned with Indian and other treaty affairs, they dealt with both incoming and outgoing communications regarding relations with foreign governments (including the use of ciphers), the activities of American emissaries, assessment of their performance, the expenses entailed, a complete inventory of the organized files of the Department, and similar matters. On August 14, 1788, a comprehensive windup report was filed with Congress, which summarized the conduct, operation, and documents management of the Department.

An often overlooked, but major, aspect of the conduct of foreign relations at the time was the formidable difficulty encountered in maintaining expeditious

Table 1.2
Confederation Foreign Affairs Secretaries and Emissaries, 1774–1789

I. Early State Agents Inherited by Confederation *

	States Represented
William Bollan	Massachusetts
Edmund Burke	New York
Benjamin Franklin	Pennsylvania, Georgia, Massachusetts, and New Jersey
Charles Garth	South Carolina, Georgia, Maryland
Arthur Lee	Massachusetts
Thomas Life	Connecticut
Paul Wentworth	New Hampshire

II. Secretaries for Foreign Affairs

	Home State
Robert R. Livingston	New York
John Jay	New York

III. Under Secretaries for Foreign Affairs

Pierre Etiene DuPonceau
Lewis Richard Morris
Henry Remsen, Jr.

IV. Confederation Primary Diplomats

	Home State
John Adams	Massachusetts
Francis Dana	Massachusetts
Silas Deane	Connecticut
Charles F. W. Dumas	(Netherlands)
Benjamin Franklin	Pennsylvania
Ralph Izard	South Carolina
John Jay	New York

IV. Confederation Primary Diplomats (cont.)

	Home State
Thomas Jefferson	Virginia
Henry Laurens	South Carolina
Arthur Lee	Virginia
William Lee	Virginia

V. Additional Negotiators

Thomas Barclay	Pennsylvania
William Carmichael	Maryland
John Lamb	New York

VI. Confederation Consuls

Thomas Barclay	Massachusetts
William Palfrey	Pennsylvania

VII. Others—Ad Hoc Agents and Mission Secretaries

John Quincy Adams
Edward Bancroft
Uriah Forrest
William Temple Franklin
Josiah Harmar
Richard Harrison
Reuben Harvey
William Hodgder
David Humphreys
John Laurens
Richard Penn
John Marsden Pintard
William Shaw
William S. Smith
Samuel W. Stockton
Joseph Tascaud
Gaspar Vogt
Jonathan Williams, Jr.

*Beginning in 1774 these agents served the Continental Congress and have been called "secret agents."

Great Seal of the United States, Original Die of 1782. This seal was superseded by new versions in 1825, 1841, 1877, 1885, and 1904.

and effective communications between Congress and American representatives abroad. Often multiple copies of documents were transmitted by separate couriers. During the Revolutionary War these were accompanied with instructions to destroy them to avoid interception by the enemy. As a consequence, receipt of some of them overlapped, causing confusion abroad. At times there were long lapses between communications,[16] so that American diplomats were obliged to rely on their own initiative and discretion in their consultations and negotiations.

Among the many logistical and administrative problems of the Continental Congress during these fifteen years were the designation of a national "capital" and providing suitable headquarters facilities. The lack of a constant Confederation capital and its migratory condition prevented the establishment of a durable domicile for the Department of Foreign Affairs. When Livingston was elected Secretary in 1781, and Congress met at Philadelphia, the Department was housed in an unpretentious dwelling at 13 South Sixth Street. After he resigned, in June 1783, the Congress functioned without a Secretary for more than a year and a half (June 4, 1783, to December 1784), when it moved sequentially from Philadelphia to Princeton, Annapolis, and Trenton. In 1785 Congress convened in New York City, which remained its headquarters until 1789.

After the Constitution went into effect in 1789, the capital of the United States returned to Philadelphia, and Secretary Jay headed the Department of Foreign Affairs until Jefferson returned from Paris to take over the office in March 1790. Pending the move of the capital to Washington, D.C., ten years later, the Department was located first on Market Street, then on the corner of Arch and

Sixth Streets, then in North Alley, and finally at the northeast corner of Fifth and Chestnut Streets.

Diplomatic and Consular Representation

The need for diplomatic representation was apparent from the outset, even before the independence of the United States was assured, in order to establish its international status and to gain channels of communication and negotiation, recognition, and financial and other support from foreign countries. Historically, the diplomatic service of the United States traces its origin to the secret agents employed by the Continental Congress abroad in 1775 to sound out opinion in Europe regarding the conflict of the colonies with the British government.

Whereas most diplomatic histories of the United States recount the exploits of such early American diplomats as John Adams, Benjamin Franklin, John Jay, Thomas Jefferson, and Arthur Lee, little attention is devoted to the corps of some three dozen emissaries who served in Europe as Ministers Plenipotentiary, Commissioners, consular officers, other agents, secretaries to missions, and individual envoys. Nor do they elucidate the comprehensive way in which the Continental Congress received information and reports, framed the instructions and commissions issued to emissaries, provided them with letters of credence and foreign consular officers with exequaturs, formally received accredited foreign diplomats, prepared and transmitted drafts of treaties to guide American diplomats in their negotiations, considered complaints against them, ratified the treaties and agreements they signed, and either recalled them or acquiesced in their petitions to return to America.

According to the official *Journals of the Continental Congress*, initially, in 1774, the Continental Congress inherited and relied upon a number of colony agents stationed in London and converted them into its secret envoys. These included William Bollan, Edmund Burke, Benjamin Franklin, Charles Garth, Arthur Lee, Thomas Life, and Paul Wentworth.[17] See Table 1.2, section I. Of these, only Franklin and Lee remained in American service abroad and were later commissioned by Congress.

In addition, from 1774 to 1789 the American corps of principal diplomatic officers included many delegates to the Continental Congress. They were commissioned, and Congress provided them with diplomatic credentials and instructions. They were responsible to the Department of Foreign Affairs and the Congress, which could dismiss or recall them, and most were resident envoys. Their titles and ranks varied, and only John Adams, Franklin, Jay, and Jefferson were Ministers Plenipotentiary, the highest rank employed by the United States at the time.

After the Declaration of Independence was signed, in September 1776 Congress elected three of its members to serve as the first American diplomatic "Commissioners"—Silas Deane, Franklin, who had returned from London to America in 1775, and Jefferson—to represent the Confederation at the French

Court. When Jefferson declined the appointment, Arthur Lee, who had been serving as the colony agent of Massachusetts in London, was elected in October to take Jefferson's place in this triumvirate of official Confederation emissaries. These were the first formally commissioned American diplomats. Congress also elected a special committee to draft letters of credence for them.

The Committee of Correspondence's first diplomatic instructions to Deane in December 1775, prepared by Franklin, directed him to go abroad on America's initial, official mission to a foreign Court. He was instructed ''to transact such business, commercial and political, as the said Secret Committee had committed to its care, in behalf and by authority of the Congress of the thirteen United Colonies.'' The following March he was also charged with gaining support for the defense of the colonies and persuading the French government to support American independence. Deane arrived in Paris on July 6, 1776, only two days after the signing of the Declaration of Independence, and he was received ''unofficially.'' His letter of credence and instructions were signed by the Committee, whereas later such documents were normally signed by the President of the Continental Congress. Thus, Deane was the first American diplomat to serve abroad, he participated in negotiating and signing three treaties with France in 1778, and he was the first to be formally recalled.

During the following years, 1777–89, the Continental Congress appointed a corps of ten other primary diplomats, three additional negotiators, two consular officers, and eighteen ad hoc agents and mission secretaries. See Table 1.2, sections IV–VII. Late in 1776, following the Declaration of Independence, three American Commissioners were accredited to France—Franklin, Adams, and Arthur Lee. Franklin, the premier American emissary to Europe for a decade (1776–85), was stationed at Paris. He was the first American diplomat to be formally received abroad and the first to be designated Minister Plenipotentiary, and he negotiated and signed nine treaties and two executive agreements with the French Government and the representatives of other countries, including Great Britain (following the Revolutionary War) as well as Prussia and Sweden. Adams was initially assigned to Paris in 1776 and was later accredited as Minister Plenipotentiary to the Netherlands (1781–83) and as Minister Plenipotentiary to Great Britain (1785–88), and he participated in negotiating two treaties with the Netherlands, three with the British Government, and one with Prussia. Arthur Lee, also assigned to Paris in 1776, participated in the consummation of three early treaties with France in 1778 and was commissioned to negotiate with the Spanish Government.

At this time the Continental Congress also commissioned William Lee to the courts of Berlin and Vienna and Ralph Izard to the Grand Duchy of Tuscany. Subsequently, Francis Dana became the Secretary to Adams' mission to Great Britain and in 1780 was commissioned as Minister to Russia but was not officially received, and Jay was accredited as Minister Plenipotentiary to negotiate with Spain, and he joined Franklin's diplomatic team at Paris in 1779 and participated in signing the Peace Treaty with Great Britain in 1783. Jefferson was elected to assist Franklin in 1781, 1782, and 1783, but it was not until Franklin requested permission to return to the United States that in 1785 Jefferson was commissioned Minister Plenipotentiary at Paris to succeed him.

Exceptional were the cases of Charles Dumas and Henry Laurens. Dumas, although not an American citizen but a friend of American independence, was recruited secretly in 1780, served in the Netherlands to provide Congress with intelligence, and was made Chargé d'Affaires ad interim during Adams' absence while he served at London. He continued in this unique capacity without a formal commission until 1790.[18] Laurens was recruited in 1779 to seek a loan from the Netherlands, but as he sailed for Europe, he was captured by the British, charged with high treason, and held captive in the Tower of London. He was not released until 1782, in exchange for British Lieutenant General Cornwallis. He then joined the American diplomatic team at Paris to negotiate with the Netherlands and participated in negotiating and signing the Preliminary Articles of Peace with Great Britain.[19]

These early emissaries represented the American Confederation to most of the major European countries. In addition, even though he was not an official appointee, Richard Harrison, located at Cadiz, a Spanish seaport, began in 1780 to communicate economic intelligence to Congress through the Governor of South Carolina. William Carmichael was appointed in 1779 as Secretary to Minister Plenipotentiary Jay to Spain, and three years later he was commissioned Chargé d'Affaires when Jay left Spain, where Carmichael remained until 1795.[20] In 1784 David Humphreys was appointed Secretary to the American Commission in Europe to negotiate treaties of amity and commerce. Several others declined appointments as American diplomats during this period, including William Livingston and John Rutledge, both designated as Ministers Plenipotentiary to the Netherlands.

William Palfrey was commissioned as America's first consular officer, accredited to France in November 1780, but he was lost at sea en route to Europe. He was succeeded the following year by Thomas Barclay, a Pennsylvania merchant residing in France, and in 1783 he was commissioned as the first Consul General, with authority to recruit vice consuls and other agents at French ports, and in 1785 he was also made responsible for managing the public accounts of American diplomats in Europe. Three years later he concluded and signed a Peace and Friendship Treaty with Morocco.

Although diplomatic representation is normally regarded as a mutual endeavor, it was not unnatural for foreign governments to proceed cautiously in commissioning diplomats to the United States. During the Confederation period, only France and the Netherlands, after they had signed treaties with the Confederation, accredited ranking diplomatic emissaries to the United States. In August 1778 Congress received Conrad Alexandre Gerard de Reyneval, the first foreign Minister Plenipotentiary to be sent to this country by the French Government.[21] He was replaced the following year by Anne Cesar Chevalier de la Luzerne, who presented his credentials on November 4 and was officially received two weeks later, and he remained until 1784. He, in turn, was succeeded in February 1788 by Count de Moustier. The only other foreign diplomats accredited to the United States during this period were Peter John Van Berckel of the Netherlands, who was received as Minister Plenipotentiary late in October 1783, and Don Diego Gardoqui, received as Spanish Chargé d'Affaires in June 1785.

Supplementing these diplomatic appointments, the Continental Congress also launched a consular service. Because trade was so important to the colonies, early colony agents generally served commercial purposes, and the Confederation converted these agents into consular officers. After the Peace Treaty was signed with Great Britain in 1783, Congress augmented American consular relations. The consular service was not only expanded in Europe but also extended to the West Indies and even China. Similarly, European governments undertook to develop their consular representation in the United States.

In addition to sponsoring the negotiation of a consular convention with France, Congress undertook to organize and refine consular affairs. In 1783 it considered a proposal to empower American Ministers Plenipotentiary to also serve as Consuls General and to be personally invested "with consular powers," and it authorized them to control "all vice consuls or inferior commercial agents" within their areas of jurisdiction. It also specified that there should be as many vice consuls in foreign ports "as shall from time to time be found necessary" and that they "shall have free liberty" to engage in trade, a privilege denied to diplomats. To clarify the status of Consuls, in October 1785 the Secretary for Foreign Affairs declared that they are normally received by governments in accordance with existing treaties or in pursuance of general international custom observed by commercial countries. He also defined the duties and jurisdiction of consular officials and recommended that neither salaries nor fees should be paid to them for service in ports where they otherwise derived income from handling trade and shipping affairs.

In September and October 1785 the Secretary also filed two major reports with Congress that presented concrete plans for the organization and expansion of the American consular service. They provided for the appointment of Consuls General for specific consular districts in Europe and the Mediterranean countries and empowered them with authority to appoint as many consular officers for ports within their districts as they regarded necessary and to define the territorial jurisdiction of each; for the issuance by Congress of commissions to such consular officials; and for entitling Consuls General to suspend, for cause, any Consul within their districts. These plans recommended that Consuls also be appointed to serve the United States in Austria, the Canaries, Denmark, France, Germany, Great Britain, Ireland, Madeira, the Netherlands, Portugal, Russia, Spain, and certain ports in the Mediterranean.[22] The United States signed its first bilateral consular convention in November 1788 with France,[23] which became a precedent for later consular treaties with other countries.

Commentary on Foreign Representation

As a consequence, during the Confederation period the Continental Congress established practices for electing, appointing, commissioning, ranking, instructing, monitoring, and recalling American diplomats and other emissaries. It designed plans for the handling of diplomatic documents, for prescribing rules concerned with their confidentiality, and for reviewing the nature and status of the conduct of American foreign relations and emissaries. It also defined its authority to recall as well as to commission American diplomats, to restrict assignments to American citizens, and to prescribe their tenure. In 1785 it devised procedures for the reception of foreign diplomats accredited to the United States and instructed the Secretary for Foreign Affairs to draft an act "for securing the privileges and immunities of public ministers from foreign powers."[24]

The Secretary for Foreign Affairs was elected by, and responsible to, the Congress, functioned as its intermediary in communicating with envoys and agents abroad, and counseled the Congress on staffing, procedures, and policy. The American Ministers Plenipotentiary and Commissioners abroad were allowed a certain amount of latitude in their negotiations and, at times, were afforded discretion in handling their responsibilities. Their progress was hindered by serious impediments, ranging from the uncertainty and slowness of communications between North America and the European capitals, to the unwillingness of some governments to recognize and deal with a distant, weak confederation of sovereign States and the confusion and overlapping of appointments and assignments.

By the end of this era, however, despite the inherent constitutional and practical weaknesses of the Continental Congress, the American States had achieved their independence, which was recognized not only by Great Britain but also by France, Morocco, the Netherlands, Prussia, Spain, Sweden, and other countries. American diplomats succeeded in negotiating a series of treaties and agreements with six foreign powers. Half of them bore multiple signatures. Treaty ratification was regarded as a purely legislative function, handled by the Continental Congress.

Reviewing the nature and personnel of the American foreign relations corps during this period, several American emissaries were members of the Continental Congress when they were commissioned—initially, Deane and Franklin in 1775 and, subsequently, Adams (1777), Dana (1779), Jay (1779), Jefferson (1785), and Laurens (1779). A few, such as Adams and Franklin, remained elected delegates to Congress for a time while serving abroad, and a substantial number were later elected as delegates. At one time or another, therefore, all of them except William Lee and Dumas served as members of Congress. In addition, Jefferson had drafted, and he, Adams, and Franklin signed, the Declaration of Independence; Dana and Laurens signed the Articles of Confederation; and Franklin participated in the Convention at Philadelphia in 1787 and signed the Constitution.

Franklin, who represented the United States in France for nearly a decade, was lauded by diplomatic historian Samuel Flagg Bemis as one of the two persons "best known in the world at that time" and by Thomas A. Bailey as the ranking member of his "Hall of Fame for American Diplomats." He also has been called the "Father of the Foreign Service of the United States." Four of the leading emissaries were commissioned as Ministers Plenipotentiary—Franklin (France, Great Britain, and Sweden), Adams (Great Britain and the Netherlands), Jay (Spain and France), and Jefferson (France). Others who played a major role in early American diplomacy included Deane and Arthur Lee, whereas Dana, Izard, Jay, Laurens, and William Lee were less successful in their missions to Berlin, Russia, Spain, Tuscany, and Vienna. Barclay became the principal consular officer. Others served in lesser ad hoc or temporary assignments or as secretaries to the Paris mission and to individual diplomats. See Table 1.2, section VII for list of ad hoc agents and mission secretaries.

Prior to 1774 the American agents abroad came from, and represented, each of the colonies. Those who served as Secretary for Foreign Affairs, Commissioners, Ministers, and principal consular officers, beginning in 1775, were from six of these States (Connecticut, Massachusetts, New York, Pennsylvania, South Carolina, and Virginia), although Carmichael, Secretary to several missions and Chargé d'Affaires, came from Maryland.

Except, perhaps, for Franklin, it may be said that these early diplomatic officials were characterized as nonprofessionals, in the sense that they were not professionally trained and career-oriented for diplomatic service. Rather, they were selected because of the talents and ability they demonstrated as colonial leaders and the experience they acquired in earlier public service in America and, in some cases, also abroad, which equipped them for diplomacy. As a group their accomplishments under uncertain and difficult conditions both at home and in Europe were gratifying, if not remarkable, and laid a basis for, and provided a challenge to, their successors.

Treaty Making

The Continental Congress engaged actively in promoting the negotiation of treaties and agreements with European and Mediterranean powers and the Indians. Despite the fact that the colonies had little prior experience in this matter, except for intercolony agreements, and those with the British government and the Indians, the Confederation leaders rapidly devised treaty objectives and the essential elements of the process of agreement making.

The treaties and agreements consummated were of two general categories, those with foreign governments and those with Indian tribes. The former consisted of four types—the peace settlement with Great Britain, the alliance with France, treaties of amity and commerce with a number of countries, and a few others, some of which proved to be abortive, such as the attempt to join the Armed Neutrality, to produce comprehensive consular conventions, and to induce the Barbary states to terminate their piracy in the Mediterranean.

The confederal treaty-making process consisted of (1) policy making by the Continental Congress, which determined principles, made decisions, and instructed American emissaries; (2) advisory counsel and the handling of communications by the Secretary for Foreign Affairs; (3) negotiations by commissioned envoys; (4) signature; and (5) formal approval, promulgation, and ratification by Congress and the exchange of ratifications. In certain cases the President, as ceremonial head of the Congress, signed the documents to implement the treaty, but he did not play the central role in the process as it operates under the Constitution.

It may be noteworthy that, even before the Declaration of Independence was signed, Congress undertook to prepare a "Plan of Treaties," or what American historian Samuel Flagg Bemis has called the "Plan of 1776" or a "model treaty." This plan was proposed, articulated, and eventually presented on July 18, 1776, which Congress debated briefly and adopted in a revised version on September 17. The latter consisted of thirty detailed articles that promoted peace and friendship and stipulated arrangements concerning trade, duties and imposts, shipping and navigation, fisheries, the mutual exchange of consular officials, piracy and privateers, and the treatment of contraband in time of hostilities. It propounded a number of basic international principles, such as equality, reciprocity, most-favored-nation, and freedom of the seas, which became keystones of American commercial and navigation treaties.

This plan was sent to American representatives in France, accompanied by negotiation instructions, which included the specification that they were "to obtain as early as possible, a publick acknowledgment of the Independence of these States." This was accompanied on September 26 by the appointment of three Commissioners to the French Court to undertake this negotiation mission.

The primary objectives of this Treaty Plan were to obtain recognition of American independence and assistance from France, preferably by means of an alliance during the Revolutionary War, and to promote the mutual enhancement of commerce. After sixteen months of negotiations, on February 6, 1778, Confederation and French emissaries signed America's first formal treaties—a Treaty of Alliance to endure in perpetuity, "from the present time and forever," which proved to be the only formal international alliance joined by the United States prior to World War II, and a Treaty of Amity and Commerce, which became the precursor of later commercial treaties with a good many other governments.[25] At the same time the United States and France also signed a separate secret treaty providing for the right of accession of Spain to the two treaties with France. These treaties were signed by Deane, Franklin, and Arthur Lee. See Table 1.3 for a list of treaties and agreements.

The United States concluded five additional treaties with three countries during the years of the Revolutionary War, prior to the definitive Peace Treaty with Great Britain in 1783—two with France, two with the Netherlands, and one with Sweden. Those with France, called "Contracts," signed by Franklin in 1782 and 1783, dealt with financial aid for the Confederation. Two of them— with the Netherlands (1782), signed by Adams, and with Sweden (1783), signed by Franklin—were Treaties of Amity and Commerce modeled on that negotiated with France, and the fifth was a specialized treaty with the Netherlands that established commitments for the treatment of captured vessels in time of war (1782). A significant by-product of the Treaties of Amity and Commerce with the Netherlands and Sweden was that they also acknowledged the independence of the United States and its emergence into the community of nations.

Historically, the most important treaty consummated during this period was the Peace Treaty with Great Britain. In June 1781 Congress commissioned Adams, Franklin, Jefferson, and Henry Laurens to undertake negotiations in Paris for this peace settlement. Actually, it involved three separate instruments. The first, designated the Preliminary Articles of Peace, was signed on November 30, 1782, by a distinguished quadriumvirate of American diplomats—Adams, Franklin, Jay, and Laurens—and by Richard Oswald, who represented the British government. In keeping with instructions from Congress and the Secretary for Foreign Affairs, this treaty, consisting of nine articles, provided that Great Britain acknowledged the thirteen American States as "free Sovereign and independent States," that the British relinquished "all claims" to governmental and territorial rights in them, and that "there shall be a firm and perpetual Peace" between the signatories. It also defined American boundaries and dealt with fishing rights, the restitution of confiscated British properties, a guarantee against future American confiscations, and mutual freedom of navigation on the Mississippi River.

The second of these instruments, a Declaration on Cessation of Hostilities, signed by Adams and Franklin on January 20, 1783, was treated by the United States as an international agreement rather than a formal treaty, which went into effect when signed and therefore did not require the exchange of ratifications. Although General Cornwallis had surrendered at Yorktown on October 19, 1781, technically, the Revolutionary War did not end until this declaration was signed. It provided for the termination of hostilities between Great Britain and the United States but would become effective only on condition that Britain also concluded such declarations for the suspension of arms with France and Spain, which were signed that same day. This was the first cessation of hostilities, later known as an armistice or cease-fire, to be signed by American emissaries. It also was the first agreement, as distinguished from a formal treaty, signed by the United States.[26]

Some seven months later, after nearly two years of negotiations, the definitive Treaty of Peace, which has been called "the American birth certificate," was finally signed in Paris by Adams, Franklin, and Jay on September 3, 1783. It confirmed the end of the Revolutionary War and the independence of the United States. It reiterated the nine Preliminary Articles of Peace and added a tenth, which limited the time for the exchange of ratifications to six months. It was ratified and proclaimed by the United States the following January and became effective in May.[27]

Shortly after this peace settlement, Congress launched a new wave of treaty

Table 1.3
Treaties and Agreements—Confederation Period, 1774–1789

Country	Title	Where Signed	Treaty or Agreement[a]	Date Signed	Date Ratified[b]	Date in Effect	Signers for United States[c]	Citation Bevans[d]
France	Amity and Commerce	Paris	T	Feb. 6, 1778	May 4, 1778	July 17, 1778[1]	Deane, Franklin, Arthur Lee	7:763-76
France	Alliance	Paris	T	Feb. 6, 1778	May 4, 1778	July 17, 1778[2]	Deane, Franklin, Arthur Lee	7:777-80
France	Right of Accession of Spain to Treaties with France (1778)	Paris	T	Feb. 6, 1778	May 4, 1778	July 17, 1778[3]	Deane, Franklin, Arthur Lee	7:781-82
France	Contract for Financial Aid	Versailles	T	July 16, 1782	Jan. 22, 1783	Jan. 1, 1784[4]	Franklin	7:783-87
Netherlands	Amity and Commerce	The Hague	T	Oct. 8, 1782	Jan. 23, 1783	June 23, 1783[5]	Adams	10:6-18
Netherlands	Recaptured Vessels	The Hague	T	Oct. 8, 1782	Jan. 23, 1783	June 23, 1783[6]	Adams	10:19-21
Great Britain	Preliminary Articles of Peace	Paris	T	Nov. 30, 1782	Apr. 15, 1783	Aug. 13, 1783[7]	Adams, Franklin, Jay, Henry Laurens	12:1-5
Great Britain	Declaration on Cessation of Hostilities	Versailles	A	Jan. 20, 1783		Jan. 20, 1783[8]	Adams, Franklin	12:6-7
France	Contract for Financial Aid	Versailles	T	Feb. 25, 1783	Oct. 31, 1783	Jan. 1, 1784[9]	Franklin	7:788-91
Sweden	Amity and Commerce	Paris	T	Apr. 3, 1783	July 29, 1783	Feb. 6, 1784[10]	Franklin	11:710-22
Great Britain	Treaty of Peace	Paris	T	Sep. 3, 1783	Jan. 14, 1784	May 12, 1784[11]	Adams, Franklin, Jay	12:8-12
France	Amity and Commerce	Versailles	A	Aug. 27, Sep. 3 and 4, 1784		Sep. 9, 1784[12]	Franklin	7:792-93
Prussia	Amity and Commerce	Passy, Paris, and London	T	July 9 and 28, Aug. 5, 1785	May 17, 1786	Aug. 8, 1786[13]	Adams, Franklin, Jefferson	8:78-87
Morocco	Peace and Friendship	Morocco	T	June 23 and 28, July 6 and 15, 1786	July 18, 1787	July 18, 1787[14]	Barclay	9:1278-85
France	Consular Convention	Versailles	T	Nov. 14, 1788	Sep. 9, 1789	Jan. 6, 1790[15]	Jefferson	7:794-800

[a]Those labeled treaties (T) were ratified, whereas agreements (labeled A) were not and became effective at time of signature.

[b]During the days of the Confederation it was common for the Continental Congress to provide ratification of treaties. However, in the case of the Treaties of Amity and Commerce with Prussia and Morocco, they were ratified by the President of the Continental Congress. After the U.S. government was established under the Constitution in 1789, treaties have been ratified by the President of the United States.

[c]The signers of these treaties included John Adams, Thomas Barclay, Silas Deane, Benjamin Franklin, John Jay, Thomas Jefferson, Henry Laurens, and Arthur Lee.

[d]Citations are to Charles I. Bevans, *Treaties and Other International Agreements of the United States of America, 1776–1949*, 12 volumes, showing volume and page numbers.

[1]Declared abrogated by Act of Congress, July 7, 1798.

[2]Declared abrogated by Act of Congress, July 7, 1798.

[3]This was a secret treaty, which was declared abrogated by Act of Congress, July 7, 1798. In 1785–86 Secretary of Foreign Affairs Jay sought to negotiate a treaty of commerce and alliance with Spain, and no treaty was signed with Spain until 1795.

[4]Expired on execution of the contract.

[5]Forms of ships' passports and certificates were appended. Abrogated by the Netherlands government in 1795.

[6]Abrogated by the Netherlands government in 1795.

[7]Replaced by Treaty of Peace in 1783.

[8]This was America's first "agreement"; went into effect on signature.

[9]Expired on execution of the contract.

[10]Expired February 6, 1799; was renewed in part September 4, 1816 and July 4, 1827; and was terminated February 4, 1919.

[11]Several articles terminated upon fulfillment of terms, and Article 8 was annulled by the War of 1812.

[12]Consisted of an exchange of notes and was not a formal treaty; abrogated by Act of Congress July 7, 1798. A new Treaty of Amity and Commerce was signed with France September 30, 1800.

[13]Expired August 8, 1796; revived by treaty of July 1, 1799; and Article 12 was again revived by treaty of May 1, 1828. It was superseded by a new Treaty of Commerce and Navigation signed in 1839.

[14]Signed by Emperor of Morocco, June 23, 1786, and was delivered to the American agent in Morocco June 28, 1786, and additional articles were signed by Morocco, July 15, 1786; and it was signed by Thomas Barclay in 1786 and later approved and countersigned by Jefferson on January 1, 1787, and by Adams on January 25, 1787. It expired and was replaced by a New Treaty of Peace and Friendship, signed October 1, 1836.

[15]Although signed during the Confederation period, it was not ratified and did not go into effect until the government was established under the Constitution. This was America's first consular convention.

negotiation. Late in October 1783 and early April and May 1784, it considered ways to augment its Treaty Plan of 1776. Referred to as its "Treaty Plan of 1784," it stressed that in future negotiations American emissaries should seek to insist upon treatment of the United States "as one nation" and upon the international principles of "perfect" equality and reciprocity. It also specified that, so far as shipping and trade were concerned, signatories possessed the right to carry their own goods in their own ships and vessels and espoused the notion that they could carry the goods of other signatories, with duties based on the most-favored-nation principle; that the United States was to be permitted to engage in direct commerce with the territorial possessions of other signatories in North America; and that, in the event of war between the signatories, merchants of one of them would be allowed to remain in the other country for up to nine months to collect debts owed them and then depart freely. Finally, it was recommended that such new treaties would be valid for a limited period of ten years.

In December 1783 and the following year Congress sent a series of instructions and commissions to the American Ministers in France to negotiate such treaties with Denmark, Geneva, Genoa, Great Britain, Hamburg, Naples, the Ottoman Ports, Portugal, Prussia, Rome, Russia, Sardinia, Saxony, the two Sicilies, Spain, Tuscany, Venice, and Vienna, as well as Morocco and the regencies of Algiers, Tripoli, and Tunis. These embraced most of the countries and principalities of Europe and the Mediterranean area. Yet, by the time that the Constitution went into effect in 1789, such treaties were signed only with Prussia in 1785 and Morocco in 1786. To summarize, during the Confederation period, the United States became a party to fifteen treaties and agreements with five European powers and Morocco.

Evidencing how important international commerce was to the emerging United States and how anxious the government was to regularize the management of trade and navigation relations with other countries, eventually, after the Constitution went into effect, such treaties of amity and commerce—although their titles varied—were signed with many other governments. The precedent established by the Continental Congress continued for several decades and through the 1820s was applied to an aggregate of nearly thirty treaties with fourteen countries, mostly in Europe but also including the Mediterranean and the Western Hemisphere and even Hawaii.

It may be concluded that, during the Confederation period, the Continental Congress maintained as tight a rein on the treaty process as was feasible under existing circumstances. It commissioned specific envoys to negotiate particular treaties with individual foreign governments. It drafted model texts of certain treaties and sent them to American representatives abroad, it acted on their suggestions and recommendations and those of the Secretary for Foreign Affairs, and it approved, ratified, and promulgated the treaties that were signed, transmitted their texts to the American States, and, lacking a genuine executive to implement them, mandated State compliance. It also kept the records of negotiations and the official, signed copies in its archives. The Secretary for Foreign Affairs possessed little independent or even discretionary treaty authority. He filtered correspondence and reports from diplomats and consular officers and relayed instructions, commissions, and other documents to them as directed by Congress.

Frequently overlooked, during this flurry of treaty making, Congress also was faced with determining the role of the States respecting treaties and agreements with foreign nations. It resolved that State legislatures may not pass any acts for "interpreting, explaining or construing" a "national treaty" or for limiting, impeding, or counteracting the execution of any treaty that was constitutionally made, ratified, and published and therefore became "the law of the land" and was "binding and obligatory" on the States. Furthermore, it resolved that State enactments previously existing that were repugnant to the Treaty of Peace with Great Britain were to be automatically repealed.

The Confederation was also determined to promote and manage the collective negotiation of treaties with Indian nations. The process used paralleled, but differed from, that employed for negotiating with foreign powers. Whereas prior to 1774 this was handled by the colonies and the British, when the Continental Congress assembled, it gradually assumed responsibility for policy control and the administration of negotiations with the Indian tribes that lay outside the territory of the colonies and were therefore regarded as "foreign nations." However, it was not until the Articles of Confederation were ratified and became constitutionally binding and the Peace Treaty was signed with Great Britain that Congress exercised a leading role in promoting such treaties with the Indians.[28] In October 1783 it also resolved that no treaty entered into with Indian tribes by the States that provided for the purchase of Indian territory was to be valid until Commissioners appointed by the United States "completed" such treaties.

As one of the last major actions of the Congress respecting treaty negotiations with Indians, in August 1787, it contemplated a committee proposal that, instead of holding frequent negotiations with individual tribes, the strategy be changed to negotiate general treaties for related groups of Indian nations. Confederation Commissioners, elected and instructed by Congress and its committees, functioned largely as negotiators. In some cases they worked independently, and in others they cooperated with State agents.[29]

The numerous treaties concluded with the Indians dealt with a variety of issues. The principal goals of the Confederation were to prevent warfare between Indians and the settlers, to stabilize territorial jurisdiction, possession, and trade in the western frontier lands, and to restrain American settlers and their hunger for additional territory, especially north of the Ohio River. Substantively, these treaties encompassed such general subjects as peace and amity, the cession of lands to the United States, the securing of tribal land to the Indians, and commerce, as well as more specific matters, including boundaries, trading posts, hunting and fishing rights, the release of hostages, and even the extradition of criminals. So far as treaty procedure is concerned, Congress chose territorial

District Superintendents and negotiating agents, instructed them, approved the treaties, proclaimed and published them, and sent copies to the executives of the States concerned, sometimes with specific implementation instructions.

The Confederation dealt with more than forty Indian tribes, including the Six Iroquois Nations. A sampling of the many treaties signed with them in the mid- and late 1780s embraces a series of "organic treaties," concluded with most of the principal peripheral Indian nations. They acknowledged American Confederation suzereignty over its territory, which introduced a new relationship between the United States and the Indians. Difficulties continued with certain tribes because settlers pressed avidly westward, some local agents negotiated with individual tribal leaders for additional lands and other advantages, and at times the States regarded themselves as sovereign in dealing with the Indians. Moreover, "international neighbors," especially Great Britain and Spain, whose territorial interests in Canada, Florida, and elsewhere were threatened by American expansion, sought to undermine peace and cooperation between the Confederation and the Indians. Many of the problems and a great deal of treaty negotiation continued after the Constitution went into effect in 1789.[30]

During this early period the Confederation also sought to negotiate treaties respecting such issues as the depredations of the Barbary powers in the Mediterranean and piracy on the high seas. Although these matters involved marine and naval affairs, because they pertained to political and legal relations with other governments and nationals, they also became the concern of the Department of Foreign Affairs and necessitated the framing of foreign policy and engagement in negotiations with European and Mediterranean countries. The United States endeavored to gain cooperation and guarantees from European powers to cope with these problems; to negotiate bilateral treaties with the Barbary powers—Morocco, Algiers, Tripoli, and Tunis—respecting their plundering and brigandage in the Mediterranean; and, as authorized by the Articles of Confederation, to enact legislation to deal with piracy.[31]

In 1786 Thomas Barclay signed a Treaty of Peace and Friendship with Morocco, the only treaty concluded during the Confederation period with any Barbary power that dealt with corsair attacks in the Mediterranean. It survived for fifty years and, surprisingly, in its forty-ninth year, it was replaced by a new treaty that endured for another half century. However, after the Constitution went into effect, treaties were also signed with Algiers in 1795, Tripoli in 1796, and Tunis in 1797.

The Confederation also concerned itself with privateering—the longtime international practice of a nation at war to commission privately owned ships to arm themselves and engage in naval action, primarily against the commercial vessels of an enemy. By means of this technique the small naval power could seek to redress the imbalance of naval might with those countries that possessed substantial naval forces, and therefore it was advantageous to the United States for some decades. To cope with privateering, Congress passed a resolution to regularize American practice during the Revolutionary War and included the matter in its general Treaty Plan of 1776, incorporated stipulations concerning privateering in Articles 17 and 19 of the 1778 Treaty of Alliance with France as well as in the Treaties of Amity and Commerce with the Netherlands, Prussia, and Sweden signed in the 1780s, and issued an ordinance to govern American practice, including a warning ''to pay sacred regard'' to the rights of neutral powers and allies. Negotiations concerning privateering remained on the American agenda for more than another century.

CONCLUSION

During the early years of emergent American diplomacy, policies were initiated to deal with foreign relations, basic machinery was devised and refined, negotiations were undertaken, and treaties and agreements were concluded with both foreign governments and the Indian tribes. This experience provided the Framers of the Constitution and the Founders of the American government in 1789 with substantial precedents for establishing the Department of State, the management of the conduct of foreign affairs, the diplomatic and consular services, and forms of documentation essential to the development of American foreign relations practice.

This was achieved by the Confederation under difficult circumstances—waging the Revolutionary War while regulating relations with and among thirteen sovereign American States under a weak confederal system that lacked a genuine executive and promoting collective interests and welfare in dealing with foreign countries that needed to be induced to recognize U.S. independence, receive and deal with its emissaries, accredit envoys to the American Confederation, and rely on it to fulfill its international prescriptions and commitments.

To those who question or criticize these early actions and achievements it may be said that by 1789, the rudiments of the conduct of American foreign affairs had been laid. They embraced a policy-making process, an administrative Department of Foreign Affairs headed by a Secretary, methods of electing and appointing, commissioning, accrediting, instructing and recalling diplomats and consular officers, and a variety of diplomatic documentation, such as commissions, letters of credence, exequaturs, letters of recall, treaty drafts, ratification instruments, proclamations, and others, as well as a national seal to authenticate them.

Valuable experience was gained in defining collegial goals and interests, designing and implementing critical objectives, and testing strategies, tactics, and other courses of action to achieve them. Aside from acquiring international recognition of the independence of the American States at the time of their Revolution, these included negotiating an acceptable peace with Great Britain, fixing original territorial boundaries, engaging in mutual diplomatic and consular relations, promoting international commerce, and negotiating a series of treaties and agreements. In addition, a corps of individuals, many of whom were reputed statesmen and some of whom were later to hold important positions in the

American Government and diplomatic establishment, benefited from their experience during the Confederation years.

Critics emphasize the diplomatic problems and failures of the period, such as the overexpectations of Congress, its inability to conclude more consular conventions and treaties of amity and commerce, and the difficulty of getting the thirteen States to implement Confederation policy and commitments. However, when these are balanced by concrete achievements during the short span of only fifteen years—involving the transition from dependent colonies to weak, sparsely populated, independent States and then to an experimental federal republic—the progress made may be regarded as remarkable in laying the foundation for the control of external affairs and diplomacy when the Constitution went into effect in 1789 and the Federal Government was established.

NOTES

1. There were more than fifteen such conclaves between 1643 and the first session of the Continental Congress in 1774, at least seven of which involved Indian delegates. For a list and brief description of some ten international congresses and conventions attended by American colonies, see Richard Frothingham, *The Rise of the Republic of the United States* (Boston: Little, Brown, 1873), pp. 118–20, n. 1.

2. This category of "patriot agents" was represented particularly by Arthur Lee, William Samuel Johnson, William Bollan, Benjamin Franklin, and Henry Marchant, who were active during the decade prior to the signing of the Declaration of Independence. For additional comment on these agents, see Michael G. Kammen, *A Rope of Sand: The Colonial Agents . . .* , pp. 164–69. Among others, these agents of British nationality included such notables as Sir William Berkeley, William Bollan, Edmund Burke, Sir William Johnson, Roger Williams, Edward Winslow, John Winthrop, and William Penn, the founder of Pennsylvania. George Croghan and Sir William Johnson were born in Ireland, and Roger Williams in Wales.

3. For a comprehensive study of American colonial agents, see Kammen, *A Rope of Sand: The Colonial Agents . . .* Chapter 1 deals with "Decades of Development: The Agencies, 1624–1755," and Chapter 2 constitutes "A Profile of the Agency, 1756–1775." Kammen also discusses such matters as private agents, the political influence and collective cooperation among agents, their relations with their constituents and British administrators, their intercommunication with one another, colonial disillusionment with the agents, the petitioning process, and similar practices. A list of thirty-eight agents with their years of service is provided on pp. 20–21, and details of their service is summarized in his "Dramatis Personae, 1755–1775," pp. 323–26.

4. The term "treaty"—though normally denoting a written understanding negotiated by commissioned representatives of national governments that is formally signed and ratified—was used loosely in the literature on the colonies to encompass not only written treaties but also other agreements and even contracts and similar commitments, especially in intercolonial affairs and relations with Indian tribes. In the early period they were negotiated and officially accepted and approved, though not formally ratified. Some were personal, involving English proprietors and concluded with Indian chiefs or their representatives.

5. The title "congress"—a term denoting an international conference—was initiated by the Virginia House of Burgesses to consider and respond to the "Intollerable Acts" enacted by the British Parliament in 1774 in retaliation for the Boston Tea Party and other manifestations of colonial opposition to British rule. Twelve colonies were represented by roughly fifty delegates, chosen largely by colonial assemblies. Georgia and Canada, also invited, were not represented.

6. Beginning as early as January 1776 the States proceeded to devise their constitutions with surprising alacrity. The initial constitutions of New Hampshire, New Jersey, South Carolina, and Virginia antedated the Declaration of Independence, and in less than a year and a half six more States devised theirs (Delaware, Georgia, Maryland, New York, North Carolina, and Pennsylvania), whereas three States (Connecticut, Massachusetts, and Rhode Island) retained their charter governments. Of these early constitutions, four lasted for more than half a century—North Carolina (seventy-five years), New Jersey (sixty-eight), Maryland (sixty-five), and Virginia (fifty-four).

For the texts of these State constitutions, see Francis Newton Thorpe, *The Federal and State Constitutions, Colonial Charters, and Other Organic Laws of the States, Territories, and Colonies Now or Heretofore Forming the United States of America* (Washington, D.C.: Government Printing Office, 1909); also see William C. Morey, *The First State Constitutions* (Philadelphia: American Academy of Political and Social Science, no. 98, 1894); and for discussion on "The Writing of the State Constitutions," see Chapter 4 of Allan Nevins, *The American States during and after the Revolution, 1775–1789* (New York: Macmillan, 1924).

7. It needs to be noted that certain relations with the Indians, for purposes of management, were not regarded as "foreign affairs" and were, therefore, administered by agencies other than those concerned with Confederation foreign relations.

8. This message to Arthur Lee and Charles Dumas provided: "It would be agreeable to Congress to know the disposition of foreign powers towards us, and we hope that this object will engage your attention. We need not hint that great circumspection and impenatrable secrecy are necessary." Quoted in Spaulding and Blue, *The Department of State of the United States*, p. 4.

9. This resolution, passed on August 15, 1778, required that "members of this house keep secret from all but the members of this house, under like obligation of secrecy, such information as may be derived from an inspection of the papers of the Committee of Secret Correspondence." See *Journals of the Continental Congress*, vol. 11, pp. 793–94.

10. Although popularly this office has been called the "Secretary *of* Foreign Affairs," the *Journals* of the Continental Congress refer to it as the "Secretary *for* Foreign Affairs." Presumably, this reflected that the Secretary was elected and instructed by, and responsible to, Congress and that it was not an independent or discretionary administrative office. In this respect it differed substantially from its successor, the Secretary of State.

11. Livingston, a delegate to Congress from New York, 1775–76 and 1779–80, had served on several of its committees, including the one that drafted the Declaration of Independence, and later he was reelected to Congress, 1784–85 and served as Minister Plenipotentiary to France, 1801–4.

12. Before Jay was elected Minister Plenipotentiary to Spain in 1779, he had served in three sessions of the Continental Congress and as its President in 1778. He joined Franklin in Paris in 1782, where he participated in negotiating the Treaty of Peace with

Great Britain. Subsequently, he was appointed Chief Justice of the Supreme Court and was elected Governor of New York.

13. For example, Congress endeavored to mold diplomatic relations to accord with "the established policy of modern civilized nations"; passed a resolution to redefine the nature of the Department of Foreign Affairs, making the Secretary "the head of the Diplomatic corps of the United States of America," who was directed to present plans for conducting foreign political and commercial relations; dealt with protocol respecting the reception ceremonial for foreign emissaries to the United States; discussed the "secret manner" in which American Ministers negotiated with foreign governments; introduced the systematic establishment of consular relations with foreign nations; and devised the form of documentation for the ratification of treaties.

14. In those early days the "home" of the Department of Foreign Affairs was a modest facility. Soon after taking office as Secretary for Foreign Affairs, Livingston established his office in a small, brick, three-story house in Philadelphia, independent of the headquarters of the Continental Congress. He and his deputies occupied the second floor. After he resigned as Secretary and Jay was elected to succeed him, and the seat of the Confederation was located in New York City, the department moved to the Fraunces Tavern and later to two houses on Broadway.

15. On July 4, 1776, minutes after adopting the Declaration of Independence, Congress resolved that Franklin, Adams, and Jefferson constituted a committee "to bring in a device for a seal for the United States of America." The committee recruited the assistance of a gifted artist, Pierre Eugene Du Simitière, who prepared a variety of designs. In March 1780, after considering its report, Congress referred it to a second committee, consisting of James Lovell, John Morin Scott, and William Churchill Houston, which sought the assistance of Francis Hopkinson, a former member of Congress who had an interest in heraldry, and he produced new designs. The report of this committee, dated May 10, 1780, was debated and referred back to committee.

Although it did not yet have a Great Seal, in January 1782 Congress passed a resolution empowering the Secretary of Congress "to keep the public seal, and cause the same to be affixed to every act, ordinance or paper, which Congress shall direct."

On May 4, 1782, a third committee, composed of Arthur Middleton, Elias Boudinot, and John Rutledge, was directed to continue the task, and they recruited William Barton, who also had an interest in heraldry and who produced two sets of designs, the second of which was reported to Congress in only five days. The following month, on June 13, Congress placed the matter in the hands of its Secretary, Charles Thomson. With the reports of the three committees, their designs, and the continued assistance of Barton, Secretary Thomson produced a design of his own and presented his report to Congress on June 20, which finalized action on the Great Seal of the United States—known as "the Eagle and the Shield."

A die was cut, and it was first employed in September. Thereafter the seal was affixed to a variety of documents, including certain proclamations, commissions of civil and diplomatic officers, letters of credence and recall, other ceremonial letters to foreign heads of state, full powers to negotiate and sign treaties (including those with the Indian tribes), instruments of ratification, and sea letters or ships' passports.

For consideration by the Continental Congress, see *Journals*, 5:517–18; 17:423, 434; and 22:57, 338–40. For detailed commentary, with photographic and other depictions, see Patterson and Dougall, *The Eagle and the Shield: A History of the Great Seal of the*

United States, Chapters 2–7, with depiction of the 1782 Great Seal on pp. 124–25. This format was replaced by subsequent dies in 1841, 1871, 1877, 1885, and 1904.

No separate seal for the Department of Foreign Affairs was authorized by the Continental Congress. Such action was not taken until September 15, 1789, after the Constitution had gone into effect. The original seal of the Department of State was first used in 1790, and later dies were cast in 1834, 1880, 1911, 1917, and subsequently. See Patterson and Dougall, Chapter 18.

16. To illustrate, on occasion Congress received no communications for a period of eleven months from any of its emissaries in Europe. On the other hand, Franklin complained to Secretary Livingston that he had received no message from American authorities for "six full months" on so important a matter as the reception in the United States of the Preliminary Articles of Peace with Great Britain.

17. All of these agents were from the colonies except Burke, a prominent British statesman and a member of Parliament who was appointed by New York in 1775 as its agent in London; he sought conciliation and cooperation of the British government with the colonies and conferred independently with Franklin. Franklin went to England in 1757 and remained five years; in 1764 he sailed again to Great Britain and returned to America in 1775. He was a delegate to the second Continental Congress, and in 1776 he was elected to represent the United States in France. Arthur Lee, who had resided in London for some years, was later chosen to join Franklin and Silas Deane as emissary to Paris. Subsequently, in 1801 Charles Pinckney was also accredited as Envoy Extraordinary to Spain.

18. Dumas, a Swiss by birth, residing in The Hague, Netherlands, and a friend of Franklin, was charged by the Committee for Foreign Affairs to report on the disposition of foreign powers toward the United States. Records of the Continental Congress reveal that, despite the lack of an official appointment or commission, he was called an "agent" of the United States. He transmitted dozens of messages to America conveying intelligence and other information during the critical 1780s, and for a short time he served as American Chargé d'Affaires ad interim at The Hague.

19. When Laurens was captured, his diplomatic papers, appointing him as emissary to the Netherlands, though cast overboard, were retrieved by the British and were used against him during an examination before the Privy Council, which resulted in a charge of treason. He was approached with offers of a pardon and his liberty if he would serve the British government, but he declined. When released early in 1782, he proceeded to Paris.

20. Carmichael's status was somewhat confusing. On September 28, 1779, he was nominated to negotiate a treaty with Spain, but the following day Congress changed its mind and elected him Secretary to the American Minister (Jay) to negotiate such a treaty. In October, when Jay was elected Minister Plenipotentiary to Spain, Carmichael was confirmed as Secretary to Jay's mission.

21. Because Gerard was the first foreign emissary to be received by the United States and was accredited as either a Minister Plenipotentiary or merely as a "resident" envoy, Congress considered and decided how he was to be formally received. It opted for the rank of Minister Plenipotentiary, which, setting a precedent for such ranking and reception ceremonies, influenced subsequent actions.

During the Confederation period, ranking American envoys were also given the status of Ministers Plenipotentiary, and after the Constitution went into effect, this practice was continued, although some American emissaries were given the rank of Minister Resident, which, in diplomatic practice, ranks below the Minister Plenipotentiary.

22. These plans to organize the American consular service provided for appointing the American Minister in Madrid to serve as Consul General for Spain, the Canaries, and islands in the Mediterranean and assigning consuls to Bilboa, Cadiz, Malaga, Alicant, and Barcelona; appointing the American resident to Portugal to serve as Consul General for that kingdom and Madeira and for stationing consuls in Lisbon and Madeira; appointing the American Minister at The Hague to serve as Consul General for the Netherlands and assigning a consul in Amsterdam, to be responsible also for Denmark, Germany, Russia, and Sweden; appointing the American Minister in London to be Consul General for Great Britain and its adjacent islands, but until a treaty of commerce was concluded with Great Britain, it was sufficient to place American consuls in London and Bristol in Great Britain and in Dublin and Cork in Ireland; deferring the appointment of a consul to Sweden and relying on its consul in the United States; and deferring the appointment of consuls to Germany and the Mediterranean islands.

23. This Franco-American consular convention also dealt with such matters as displaying the national coat of arms, the use of official seals, the handling of ships' papers, accidents and losses at sea and shipwreck, and the treatment of personal estates of citizens who die within their jurisdiction. It embodied the principle of reciprocal or most-favored-nation treatment and was to run for a span of twelve years. Although negotiated and signed during the Confederation period, it was not ratified until September 1789 and entered into force on January 6, 1790. For the text of the proposed Franco–American consular convention, 1785, see *Journals of the Continental Congress*, vol. 29, pp. 500–515, and for the text of the commission and instructions to Jefferson, 1787, to negotiate it, see *Journals*, vol. 33, pp. 423–27. For the final text of the treaty, see *Treaties and Other International Agreements of the United States of America* (Washington, D.C.: Department of State, 1968–76) vol. 7, pp. 794–800.

24. For the texts of reception ceremonies for foreign emissaries to the United States, see *Journals of the Continental Congress*, vol. 24, pp. 390–92; vol. 25, pp. 750–52; vol. 28, pp. 402–3, 406–7, 466–67; and vol. 29, p. 515n. In 1783 Congress decided that American precedence would be: the President of Congress, members of Congress indiscriminately, the Secretary of Congress, the Secretary for Foreign Affairs, and other chief administrators; see *Journals*, vol. 24, p. 391. For commentary on privileges and immunities, see *Journals*, vol. 29, pp. 655.

25. The Franco–American Treaty of Amity and Commerce, also exaggerating its continuance in perpetuity, spoke of fixing "in an equitable and permanent manner the Rules which ought to be followed" between the signatories and indicated that the treaty "shall be perpetual." These two treaties, dealt with as a package, were ratified by the United States on May 4, 1778, and became effective on July 17. For the texts of these Franco–American treaties, see *Journals of the Continental Congress*, vol. 11, pp. 419–55. Although the United States also sought to conclude a consular convention with France, this was not consummated until ten years later and was not ratified until September 9, 1789, and entered into force on January 6, 1790, after the Constitution went into effect.

26. It is noteworthy that certain international instruments, including armistices and cease-fires, are normally regarded as agreements that enter into force when signed, without requiring legislative approval. This distinction between treaties and agreements, although not specified in the Constitution of the United States, was subsequently continued in American diplomatic practice and has increased in usage.

27. Illustrating the treaty ratification and implementation process of the Confederation, this final Peace Treaty, signed early in September 1783, was ratified and proclaimed by Congress on January 14 the following year and by D. Hartley for the British government on April 9; then ratifications were exchanged at Paris on May 12, at which time it formally went into effect for both countries. Copies of the treaty were sent to the American States with a covering note (dated August 2, 1784). See *Journals of the Continental Congress*, vol. 26, pp. 28–30; vol. 27, pp. 615–24, 719.

28. The Articles of Confederation specified, in Article 9, that the Continental Congress possessed ''the sole and exclusive right and power'' to regulate the trade and manage ''all affairs'' with the Indians that were not members of any States, provided that the legislative right of any State within its own jurisdictional limits was not infringed or violated. In Article 6 it also stipulated that no State could engage in any war without the consent of Congress unless the State was invaded by enemies or had information that threatened invasion by some Indian nation. Although the Articles were agreed to on November 15, 1777, and signed on July 9 the following year, they were not fully ratified and did not go into effect until March 1781. Technically, therefore, Congress did not possess this constitutional authority until the spring of 1781.

29. The title ''Commissioner'' denoted that these officials were elected or appointed and formally commissioned. They functioned in a representative capacity and participated in conferences with Indian representatives, but they differed from the diplomats who negotiated with European governments, who were accredited with the customary national and international credentials (including letters of credence and full powers). The State negotiators were commissioned by their State governments.

30. Thereafter, the executive branch of the Federal Government negotiated treaties with Indian tribes as well as with foreign governments. They became legally binding when approved by a new treaty process. The signed treaty, to be ratified by the President, required Senate approval by two-thirds vote.

Over the years more than 400 separate treaties were consummated with Indian tribes. For a descriptive tabulation of nearly seventy Indian treaties concluded between 1763 and 1796 (giving dates, places where the treaties were negotiated, the Indian tribes concerned, and documentation sources), see Dorothy V. Jones, *License for Empire: Colonialism by Treaty in Early America* (Chicago: University of Chicago Press, 1982), pp. 188–97. For a more comprehensive ''Chronology of Indian Treaties'' (giving the years and Indian tribes with which treaties were concluded), listing 372 treaties consummated between 1778 and 1883, see Rupert Costo and Jeanette Henry, *Indian Treaties: Two Centuries of Dishonor* (San Francisco: Indian Historian Press, 1977), pp. 208–18.

Although the subjects of these treaties varied widely, more than half of those negotiated after 1789 involved the exchange and cession of Indian lands and the prescription of boundaries. In 1871 Congress passed an act terminating the negotiation of ''treaties'' with Indians, but ''executive agreements''—which do not require Senate approval by two-thirds vote and may be approved by simple majority vote of both houses of Congress—could still be negotiated.

31. Privateering is distinguished from piracy in that it is officially authorized, whereas piracy does not possess official government sanction.

2

Federalist Period—
Creating the Department of
State and Diplomatic Corps,
1789–1801

When the Constitution of the United States went into effect in 1789, the conduct of foreign affairs was governed by both authorizations and prohibitions. The prescriptions for the Federal Government stipulated:

Article. I.

Section. 8. The Congress shall have Power . . . ;
To regulate Commerce with foreign Nations . . . ;
To . . . regulate the Value . . . of foreign Coin . . . ;
To define and punish Piracies and Felonies committed on the high Seas, and Offences against the Law of Nations;
To declare War, grant Letters of Marque and Reprisal, and make Rules concerning Captures on Land and Water;

* * *

Section. 9. . . .
No Title of Nobility shall be granted by the United States: And no Person holding any Office of Profit or Trust under them, shall, without the Consent of the Congress, accept of any present, Emolument, Office, or Title, of any kind whatever, from any King, Prince, or foreign State.

Article. II.

Section. 2. The President . . .
. . . shall have Power, by and with the Advice and Consent of the Senate, to make Treaties, provided two thirds of the Senators present concur; and he shall nominate, and by and with the Advice and Consent of the Senate, shall appoint Ambassadors, other public Ministers and Consuls, . . . and all other Officers of the United States, whose

Appointments are not herein otherwise provided for, and which may be established by Law; but the Congress may by Law vest the Appointment of such inferior Officers, as they think proper, in the President alone, . . . , or in the Heads of Departments.

The President shall have Power to fill up all Vacancies that may happen during the Recess of the Senate, by granting Commissions which shall expire at the End of their next Session.

Section. 3. . . . ; he shall receive Ambassadors and other public Ministers; . . . and shall Commission all the Officers of the United States.

Section. 4. The President, Vice President and all civil Officers of the United States, shall be removed from Office on Impeachment for, and Conviction of, Treason, Bribery, or other high Crimes and Misdemeanors.

Article. III.

Section. 2. The judicial Power shall extend to all Cases, in Law and Equity, arising under this Constitution, the Laws of the United States, and Treaties made, or which shall be made, under their Authority;—to all Cases affecting Ambassadors, other public Ministers and Consuls;—to all Cases of admiralty and maritime Jurisdiction; . . .

In all Cases affecting Ambassadors, other public Ministers and Consuls, . . . the Supreme Court shall have original Jurisdiction. In all the other Cases before mentioned, the Supreme Court shall have appellate Jurisdiction, both as to Law and Fact, with such Exceptions, and under such Regulations as the Congress shall make.

Section. 3. Treason against the United States, shall consist only in levying War against them, or in adhering to their Enemies, giving them Aid and Comfort. No Person shall be convicted of Treason unless on the Testimony of two Witnesses to the same overt Act, or on Confession in open Court.

Article. VI.

* * *

This Constitution, . . . and all Treaties made, or which shall be made, under the Authority of the United States, shall be the supreme Law of the Land; and the Judges in every State shall be bound thereby, any Thing in the Constitution or Laws of any State to the Contrary notwithstanding.

In addition, to regulate the relationship between the Federal Government and the States respecting foreign relations, the Constitution, in Article 1, section 10, provided:

No State shall enter into any Treaty, Alliance, or Confederation; grant Letters of Marque and Reprisal. . . .

No State shall, without the Consent of the Congress, lay any Imposts or Duties on Imports or Exports, except what may be absolutely necessary for executing its inspection Laws: and the net Produce of all Duties and Imposts, laid by any State on Imports or Exports, shall be for the Use of the Treasury of the United States, and all such Laws shall be subject to the Revision and Control of the Congress.

No State shall, without the Consent of Congress, lay any Duty of Tonnage, keep

Troops, or Ships of War in time of Peace, enter into any Agreement or Compact with another State, or with a foreign Power, or engage in War, unless actually invaded, or in such imminent Danger as will not admit of delay.

Subsequently, the Eleventh Amendment added:

Eleventh Amendment

The Judicial power of the United States shall not be construed to extend to any suit in law or equity, commenced or prosecuted against one of the United States by Citizens of another State, or by Citizens or Subjects of any Foreign State.

Although the powers and functions of the President and Congress were prescribed in the Constitution, there were no mandates for creating executive Departments, but they were taken for granted and later authorized by statute. Proposals for instituting a Department of Foreign Affairs, headed by a Secretary, were broached at the Constitutional Convention in 1787, but they were not incorporated into the Constitution. During the initial months of transition, it was natural that the new Federal Government continued to rely upon the agencies, processes, and personnel it inherited from the Confederation. In the interim, therefore, John Jay continued as Secretary for Foreign Affairs, assisted by Henry Remsen, Jr., his Chief Clerk, while Thomas Jefferson remained as Minister Plenipotentiary in France, and William Carmichael served as Chargé d'Affaires in Spain.

ESTABLISHMENT OF THE DEPARTMENT OF STATE

Act of July 1789

On May 19, 1789, the House of Representatives considered the creation of an executive Department of Foreign Affairs, as well as War and Treasury Departments. James Madison moved that

there shall be established an Executive Department, to be denominated the Department of Foreign Affairs, at the head of which there shall be an officer, to be called the Secretary to the Department of Foreign Affairs, who shall be appointed by the President, by and with the advice and consent of the Senate; and to be removable by the President.

After some debate by both houses of Congress, on July 27 it enacted the first constitutive foreign affairs statute, which provided:

That there shall be an Executive Department, to be denominated the Department of Foreign Affairs; and that there shall be a principal officer therein, to be called the Secretary for the Department of Foreign Affairs, who shall perform and execute such duties as shall, from time to time, be enjoined on or intrusted to him by the President of the

United States, agreeable to the Constitution, relative to correspondences, commissions, or instructions, to or with public ministers or consuls from the United States, or to negotiations with public ministers from foreign states or princes, or to memorials or other applications from foreign public ministers, or other foreigners, or to such other matters respecting foreign affairs as the President of the United States shall assign to the said Department: And furthermore, that the said principal officer shall conduct the business of the said Department in such manner as the President of the United States shall, from time to time, order or instruct.

. . . That there shall be in the said Department an inferior officer, to be appointed by the said principal officer, and to be employed therein as he shall deem proper, and to be called the chief clerk in the Department for Foreign Affairs; and who, whenever the said principal officer shall be removed from office by the President of the United States, or in any other case of vacancy, shall, during such vacancy, have the charge and custody of all records, books, and papers, appertaining to the said Department.

. . . That the said principal officer, and every other person to be appointed or employed in the said Department, shall, before he enters on the execution of his office or employment, take an oath or affirmation, well and faithfully to execute the trust committed to him.

. . . That the Secretary for the Department of Foreign Affairs, to be appointed in consequence of this act, shall, forthwith after his appointment, be entitled to have the custody and charge of all records, books, and papers, in the office of Secretary for the Department of Foreign Affairs, heretofore established by the United States in Congress assembled.[1]

Although this act retained the titles ''Department of Foreign Affairs'' and ''Secretary for the Department of Foreign Affairs,'' which had been employed by the Confederation, it created an entirely new foreign relations establishment. The Department was mandated by law, and the Secretary, to be appointed by the President with the approval of the Senate, was made responsible to the Chief Executive, not the Congress, as was the case during the Confederation period. In addition, the Secretary was entrusted with specific functions as an administrative agent to serve under the direction of the Chief Executive. From the onset it was manifest that the President was the primary foreign relations officer, and the Secretary was his principal deputy.

Act of September 1789

In order to handle various internal government functions, such as correlating communications and other relations with the States, maintaining the Great Seal of the United States, and servicing various records, which had previously been the responsibility of the Secretary of the Continental Congress and which normally are cared for by a separate department, on July 23, prior to enacting the organic act of the Department of Foreign Affairs, Congress debated whether to create a Home Department, headed by a Home Secretary, to handle such domestic functions. But this was rejected.[2]

Congress decided, rather, to ascribe these duties to the Department of Foreign

Great Seal of the United States, 1825. *Source*: Richard Patterson and Richardson
Dougall. Contemporary Great Seal of United States.

Affairs. It therefore passed another law, signed by the President on September
15, 1789, which renamed it the Department of State and changed the title of its
principal officer to Secretary of State. Among other matters, this act directed
the Secretary to have charge of printing, publishing, and distributing the bills
and resolutions of Congress and transmitting them to its members and the
States, to maintain custody of the Great Seal of the United States and imprint it on
commissions and other documents and produce a separate departmental seal,
and to preserve all books, records, and papers of the Continental Congress.

Although Congress passed legislation respecting the application of the Great
Seal, it did not legally mandate the documents requiring the President's signature. Thus, the presidential signing of documents became a matter of custom
and usage, introduced by President Washington and modified by subsequent
Presidents. However, when documents represent official executive action respecting legislation, executive orders and proclamations, formal communications
with Congress or either of its chambers, relations of the Federal Government
with the States and in some cases with foreign governments, it is customary that
they be signed personally by the President.

In addition to mandating that "the seal heretofore used by the United States
in Congress assembled shall be and hereby is declared to be the seal of the
United States" and making the Secretary of State responsible for its custody
and application, this law also authorized the Secretary to create a departmental
seal, subject to the approval of the President. From the outset, the Department
of State was empowered to authenticate not only its own documents, discussed
later, but also those that bear the Great Seal of the United States.

Concerned with amalgamating foreign and domestic functions, in March the
following year the House of Representatives considered whether the Secretary
of State should be instructed to report on the expediency of this action and
whether it would be necessary to appoint a separate departmental Chief Clerk

to handle internal duties, but this resolution was defeated. Nevertheless, Congress authorized the appointment of an additional Clerk in the Department of State.

Subsequently, as noted later, other domestic activities were added to the responsibilities of the Department. Consequently, the American executive system is unique in that, whereas other governments usually attribute foreign and domestic functions to separate ministries, and although many domestic tasks have been turned over to other American agencies as they were created, the Department of State has retained this singular title and still performs certain nonforeign relations functions.

The Department of State was the first executive Department established under the Constitution, in 1789, making the Secretary of State the senior Cabinet member and administrative officer of the United States. The Presidential Succession Acts of 1886 and 1947 also prescribed the sequence of succession to the presidency in the event of the death, removal, impeachment, resignation, or inability of both the President and Vice President.[3] Although no Secretary has actually risen to the presidency in this manner, the Secretary continues to enjoy this privileged position in the national government. In September 1789 Congress also passed an act for establishing the initial salary of the Secretary of State as well as a series of other officers, including the Chief Clerk and other clerks of the State Department. In this act the salary of the Secretary of State was fixed at $3,500.

Act of July 1790

To govern certain aspects of conducting relations with foreign nations, on July 1, 1790, Congress passed its first enactment to provide for the systematic funding of American diplomatic missions abroad. It specified:

That the President of the United States shall be, and hereby is, authorized to draw from the Treasury of the United States a sum not exceeding forty thousand dollars annually . . . , for the support of such persons as he shall commission to serve the United States in foreign parts, and for the expense incident to the business in which they may be employed: *Provided*, That . . . the President shall not allow to any Minister Plenipotentiary a greater sum than at the rate of nine thousand dollars per annum, as a compensation for all his personal services, and other expenses; nor a greater sum for the same than four thousand five hundred dollars per annum to a Chargé des Affaires; nor a greater sum for the same than one thousand three hundred and fifty dollars per annum to the secretary of any Minister Plenipotentiary.

By this act Congress set the important precedent of controlling annually the total funding of American diplomats and their secretaries, as well as the maximum compensation of individual diplomats. By implication, therefore, Congress assumed authority to prescribe the nature and size of the American diplomatic establishment. In addition, it fixed presidential accountability for such expenditures, delegated to the President the extent to which information concerning such funding be made public, and authorized the implementation of this prescription for the following two years.[4]

ORGANIZATION AND MANAGEMENT

Secretaries of State

Whereas during the Confederation period, the Continental Congress elected the Secretary for Foreign Affairs, who was responsible to the Congress, under the Constitution, Article 2, Section 2, the President was authorized to nominate and, with the consent of the Senate, to appoint all officers established by law, including the Secretary of State. This established the legal principle that the Secretary is the President's chief administrative officer for the conduct of foreign relations and is responsible to the President. During President Washington's administration, from the outset he also established the precedent of simultaneously sending multiple nominations of various officers to the Senate for confirmation, which later was also applied to diplomats and consuls.[5]

When the Constitution went into effect, John Jay, who had been Secretary for Foreign Affairs under the Confederation, continued informally in charge of external relations until President Washington appointed Thomas Jefferson, a fellow Virginian, as the first Secretary of State (1789–93). He was succeeded, in turn, by Edmund Randolph, also of Virginia (1794–95), and then by Timothy Pickering of Pennsylvania (1795–1800) and subsequently by John Marshall of Virginia (1800–1801), the only Secretary appointed by President John Adams. In addition to these four Secretaries, three Secretaries of State ad interim were appointed by the President to serve temporarily as acting officials pending the swearing in of successors. Naturally, these interim Secretaries did not require formal Senate confirmation. See Table 2.1.

In choosing his first Secretary, President Washington sought a proven statesman possessing not only ability and integrity but also experience. He selected Jefferson, who had been a member of the Continental Congress, drafted the Declaration of Independence, prepared the resolution to ratify the Peace Treaty with Great Britain, and succeeded Benjamin Franklin as Minister Plenipotentiary to France from March 1785 until September 1789, when he was commissioned Secretary of State.[6] During the four years of his Secretaryship, Jefferson participated in accrediting American emissaries to five European countries.[7]

The main diplomatic issues with which he was confronted were enhancing American international credibility, gaining additional foreign recognition, promoting international commerce, countering Barbary depredations, and establishing American neutrality when France went to war with Great Britain and Spain following the outbreak of the French Revolution. Jefferson, who was pro-French,

Table 2.1
Department of State Principal Officers, 1789–1801

Secretaries of State [1]	Residence	Date of Appointment	Entry on Duty	Termination of Appointment
Thomas Jefferson	Va.	Sep. 26, 1789	Mar. 22, 1790	Dec. 31, 1793
Edmund Randolph	Va.	Jan. 2, 1794	Jan. 2, 1794	Aug. 20, 1795
Timothy Pickering [2] (ad interim)	Pa.	Aug. 20, 1795		Dec. 9, 1795
Timothy Pickering	Pa.	Dec. 10, 1795	Dec. 10, 1795	May 12, 1800
Charles Lee [3] (ad interim)	Va.	May 13, 1800		June 5, 1800
John Marshall	Va.	May 13, 1800	June 6, 1800	Feb. 4, 1801
John Marshall [4] (ad interim)	Va.	Feb. 4, 1801		Mar. 4, 1801
Chief Clerks [5]				
Henry Remsen, Jr. [6]	N.Y.	July 27, 1789		Dec. 31, 1789
Roger Alden	Conn.	Jan. 1, 1790		July 25, 1790
Henry Remsen, Jr. [6]	N.Y.	Sep. , 1790		Mar. 31, 1792
George Taylor, Jr.	N.Y.	Apr. 1, 1792		Feb. 7, 1798
Jacob Wagner	Pa.	Feb. 8, 1798		Mar. 31, 1807

[1]There is no statutory specification of the title for an interim Secretary of State when the office is vacant.

[2]Pickering, Secretary of War, served as Secretary of State ad interim until a new Secretary of War was appointed, at which time he began serving as regular Secretary of State.

[3]Lee was then Attorney General, who also served as Secretary of State ad interim.

[4]Marshall continued to serve as Secretary of State ad interim for one month pending the appointment of his successor, James Madison, on March 5, 1801.

[5]The Chief Clerk was not a presidential appointee and therefore did not require Senate approval; individuals were appointed by the Secretary of State. The Chief Clerk was the ranking member of the Department of State under the Secretary.

[6]Remsen previously served as Under Secretary of Foreign Affairs during the Confederation period from March 2, 1784. Appointed Chief Clerk following the Congressional act of July 27, 1789, which created the Department of Foreign Affairs, he was reappointed in 1790 and served until the end of March 1792.

often was contested by Alexander Hamilton, the Secretary of the Treasury, who was pro-British.

The American desire for neutrality was complicated by the commitments of the Franco–American Alliance of 1778. At a Cabinet meeting summoned by the President, the matter was debated, and, because of Jefferson's reservation, when Washington issued America's first Proclamation of Neutrality in 1793, it avoided the term "neutrality" but enjoined Americans to maintain a friendly and impartial attitude toward both countries and to refrain from hostilities against any belligerent power. Muddling the issue was the question of recognizing the French revolutionary government, on which Jefferson propounded the de facto recognition doctrine, which continued as the policy of the United States for more than a century. He, therefore, recommended the reception of Edmond C. Genêt without qualifications as the French Minister to the United States.[8]

When Jefferson sought to resign as Secretary in July 1793, the President persuaded him to remain until the end of the year. In the meantime the Department of State had been invested with additional domestic responsibilities, including most functions that were not placed under the jurisdiction of other departments. These new duties included the issuing of commissions of appointment and letters of patent, implementing copyright laws and serving as depository of copyrighted books and other materials, printing the census and preserving census reports, and, strangely, even responsibility for the mint.

In the field of foreign affairs, although President Washington regarded himself as the primary decision maker on matters of executive policy and in some respects was viewed as his own Secretary of State, he sought Jefferson's advice, usually in writing. Jefferson required regular communications from diplomatic and consular officials abroad and issued carefully prepared instructions to them. When he left office, his diplomatic team consisted of American Ministers in France, Great Britain, and Portugal, William Carmichael as Chargé d'Affaires in Spain, and a corps of consular officers.

Washington picked Edmund Randolph, another Virginian, then serving as Attorney General, to succeed Jefferson.[9] He was appointed on January 2, 1794, and served for only a year and a half, until August 20, 1795. His tenure was marred by deteriorating relations with France and Great Britain, which, at war, attempted to use the American States against each other, by the actions of Genêt and his successor, Joseph Fauchet, and, surprisingly, by Washington's bypassing the diplomatic establishment when in 1794 he appointed John Jay, then Chief Justice of the Supreme Court, as Minister Extraordinary to Great Britain to negotiate a treaty of amity and commerce. Randolph opposed the Jay mission and later urged the President not to ratify the treaty. He was forced to resign peremptorily when it was alleged that he had engaged in an intrigue with the French Minister, even though Fauchet denied the allegations.

Washington found it difficult to recruit Randolph's successor. He offered the post successively to William Paterson of New Jersey, Thomas Johnson of Maryland, Charles Pinckney of South Carolina, Patrick Henry of Virginia, and Rufus King of Massachusetts, all of whom declined.[10] The President then asked Timothy Pickering of Pennsylvania, his Secretary of War, to serve in both posts. Pickering responded that he would serve in either office but preferred not to give up the Secretaryship of War until a replacement could be appointed. As a result, he functioned as Secretary of State ad interim from August 20, 1795, to December 9 and was then appointed Secretary of State, in which capacity he continued for nearly four and one-half years, until May 12, 1800. He supported American rights of neutrality, and, following the ratification of a commercial treaty with Great Britain, relations with France deteriorated.

John Adams was inaugurated as President in March 1797. Seeking to avert a rupture of diplomatic relations and possible war with France, he decided to send a special diplomatic mission to Paris, headed by an avowed friend of France. He thought of sending Jefferson, but he was then Vice President and was needed in the United States. Adams then decided to send Charles Cotesworth Pinckney, John Marshall, and Francis Dana. When Dana declined, the President substituted Elbridge Gerry of Massachusetts,[11] but the French Directorate refused to receive this trio of Envoys Extraordinary. When Adams contemplated a second special mission to France in 1799, he consulted his Cabinet members, but not Pickering, his Secretary of State, who opposed the venture and sought to prevent or forestall it. His rapport with the President declined during his three years of service under Adams, and he was finally dismissed.[12]

During Pickering's administration additional domestic functions were assigned to the Department of State. These included the preparation of an annual report to Congress on returns from collectors of customs at American ports, the filing of reports on the impressment of American seamen by foreign powers, and the issuing of letters of marque and reprisal, exequaturs to foreign consuls in the United States, and passports to Americans for travel abroad.

Adams next turned to John Marshall,[13] also of Virginia, and appointed him Secretary on May 13, 1800, but he did not assume his duties until June 6. In the meantime Charles Lee, the Attorney General, functioned as Secretary of State ad interim. As relations with France continued to erode, Adams sent another special mission to Paris to conclude a new Treaty of Friendship and Commerce. Headed by William Vans Murray, then American Minister in the Netherlands, the mission included Oliver Ellsworth, then Chief Justice, and William R. Davie,[14] the Governor of North Carolina. When the treaty was signed late in September, which acknowledged the right of American neutrality, Secretary Marshall recommended that it be ratified in order to avoid war, which some regarded as inevitable. Secretary Marshall was also confronted with declining relations with Great Britain, and he prepared comprehensive instructions to the American Minister in London respecting the fundamental international law principles governing neutrality and belligerency.

Marshall remained as Secretary for less than a year, until February 4, 1801, although he continued as Secretary of State ad interim until President Jefferson was inaugurated on March 4. When Chief Justice Oliver Ellsworth retired in December 1800, Adams appointed Marshall to that position.

Staffing the Department

During these early years the staff of the Department of State was very small. The original act of July 27, 1789, authorized the Secretary to appoint a Chief Clerk who, whenever the Secretary was removed by the President or in any other case of vacancy, would have "custody of all records, books, and papers" pertaining to the Department. The following year Congress empowered the Secretary to appoint an additional clerk. Henry Remsen, Jr., of New York, who had been the Confederation Under Secretary for Foreign Affairs from March 2, 1784, was appointed as the first Chief Clerk of the Department.[15] For a list of Chief Clerks see Table 2.1.

In January 1790 President Washington assigned custody of the Great Seal and various papers not concerned with foreign relations to Roger Alden of Connecticut, who had served previously as Deputy or Assistant Secretary to the Continental Congress and had custody of the Great Seal and responsibility for various Confederation documentation, and later Jefferson also appointed him to the rank of Chief Clerk.[16] This matter of the disposition and preservation of the Confederation seal and documents fortuitously instituted the practice of assigning domestic functions to the Department of State, which resulted in both the combining of foreign relations and home office functions within a single executive agency and the changing of its title to the Department of State. Remsen and Alden were assisted by a small group of clerks and a translator. When Alden resigned on July 25, 1790, the external and internal staffing functions of the Department were combined.

Later, on April 1, 1792, Secretary Jefferson appointed George Taylor, Jr., of New York as Chief Clerk, who remained until February 1798. Secretary Pickering superseded him with Jacob Wagner of Pennsylvania, who held this office for nine years, until March 1807.[17] Thus, three Chief Clerks—Remsen, Taylor, and Wagner—provided considerable departmental continuity for more than twenty years, spanning the period from the Confederation well into President Jefferson's second term.

Originally consisting of only three clerks and translators when Jefferson became Secretary, the staff of the Department expanded during the Pickering administration to eight or nine clerks and a few other employees. At the time the Secretary performed many clerical functions personally. By the end of the eighteenth century the total staff numbered only ten clerks, translators, and messengers to manage both foreign and domestic functions—not including diplomatic and consular officials stationed abroad.

Home of the Department

When the Federal Government was established, it had its capital in New York City during 1789 and part of 1790. For the following ten years it was located in Philadelphia, where the Department of State had its headquarters at Fifth and Chestnut Streets, although, because of a yellow fever epidemic, it moved temporarily to the State House in Trenton, New Jersey. In 1800 the Department moved twice, from Philadelphia to the building that housed the Treasury Department, located east of the White House in Washington, D.C., which was shared with other departments, and from there to a block of houses on Pennsylvania Avenue and Nineteenth Street.

Original Seal of the Department of State, 1790. Contemporary Seal of the Department of State.

Seal of the Department of State

In addition to the Great Seal of the United States, separate official seals have been devised for various executive officers, including the President, Vice President, Secretary of State, and heads of other Departments, as well as the Supreme Court. The seal of the Department of State dates back to 1790, which was authorized by Congress in September 1789 and was modified several times by 1934. This act of 1789 specified, in section 5, "That the said Secretary shall cause a seal of office to be made for the said department of such device as the President of the United States shall approve, and all copies of records and papers in the said office, authenticated under the said seal, shall be evidence equally as the original record or paper." The Department of State seal was originally used for validating certain general records and other papers. Eventually, it also came to be impressed on a variety of diplomatic and consular documents, certificates of assignment of consular officers, identification papers for diplomatic couriers, departmental orders and regulations, and other important instruments.[18]

DIPLOMATIC AND CONSULAR REPRESENTATION

Under the Constitution, U.S. foreign emissaries are executive officers, appointed by, and responsible to the President. The diplomatic and consular corps are administrative agencies, under the authority and direction of the President and Secretary of State. When he became President, Washington inherited only two commissioned Confederation diplomats in Europe. Thomas Jefferson remained as Minister Plenipotentiary in Paris for seven months until he was appointed Secretary of State and assumed his new duties in March 1790. The only other commissioned diplomat was William Carmichael, who had been appointed Chargé d'Affaires ad interim in Spain in February 1783. He was later accredited

on a permanent basis as Chargé d'Affaires en titre in April 1790, and he continued in this capacity until 1794. During this transition the new government
functioned for more than two years without any ranking envoys in the capitals
of Europe, except for Paris, to which the President appointed William Short on
April 20, 1790, to succeed Jefferson.

Diplomatic Corps

Between 1789 and March 1797, President Washington appointed nine new
diplomatic envoys to five countries, as indicated in Table 2.2. These included
John Quincy Adams, David Humphreys, Rufus King, James Monroe, Gouverneur Morris, William Vans Murray, Charles Cotesworth Pinckney, Thomas
Pinckney, and William Short,[19] several of whom served in more than one appointment.[20] Surprisingly, American emissaries were then accredited only to
France, Great Britain, the Netherlands, Portugal, and Spain.[21] This represented
a decline in direct representation to Austria, Prussia, Russia, Sweden, and Tuscany and reflected some hesitation in maximizing the diplomatic establishment
in Europe except for those countries with which the United States was then
directly involved. Three months after he became President, John Adams revived
diplomatic relations with Prussia. Reviewing the anatomy of the American diplomatic corps during the Federalist period, of the eighteen appointments made
(excluding Jefferson, who had been commissioned by the Confederation), Washington made fourteen, and Adams made four. For various reasons, four appointees did not serve.[22]

Apparently, Washington was somewhat diffident about expanding the American diplomatic corps abroad. During his first term, through 1792, he made only
five new appointments—two to France and one each to Portugal, Great Britain,
and the Netherlands—and he reappointed Carmichael to Spain. Further evidencing his trepidation, his first appointment, of William Short to France in
April 1790, was at the rank of Chargé d'Affaires, as was the reappointment of
Carmichael,[23] and two were commissioned as Ministers Resident, whereas Gouverneur Morris and Thomas Pinckney were accredited as his first Ministers Plenipotentiary. In his second term, 1793–97, he appointed eight envoys, of whom
five were Ministers Plenipotentiary (to France, Great Britain, Portugal, and
Spain), and three were Ministers Resident (to the Netherlands and Spain). During his presidency, 1797–1801, President Adams, who inherited a number of
these emissaries, made only four nominations, including two new Ministers
Plenipotentiary.[24]

Naturally, diplomats vary in the length of time they hold their assignments.
These ranged from those of William Short in the Netherlands (six months) and
Spain (fourteen months) to those of Humphreys in Portugal (more than six years)
and Rufus King in Great Britain (nearly seven years). After Adams succeeded
to the presidency, he made only two firm appointments, and in 1801, when
Thomas Jefferson became President, all American diplomats were recalled and

Table 2.2
American Diplomats, 1789–1801

Country	Name	Residence	Title	Appointment	Presentation of Credentials	Termination of Mission
France	Thomas Jefferson [1]	Va.	MP	Mar. 10, 1785	May 17, 1785	Left post, Sept. 20, 1789
	William Short	Va.	CdA	Apr. 20, 1790	June 14, 1790	Presented recall, May 15, 1792
	Gouverneur Morris	N.Y.	MP	Jan. 12, 1792	June 3, 1792	Recall requested by Govt. of France, Apr. 9, 1794 [2]
	James Monroe	Va.	MP	May 28, 1794	Aug. 15, 1794	Presented recall, Dec. 9, 1796
	Charles Cotesworth Pinckney [3]	S.C.	MP	Sep. 9, 1796		
	William Vans Murray [4]	Md.	MP			
Great Britain	James A. Bayard [5]	Del.	MP	Feb. 19, 1801		
	Thomas Pinckney	S.C.	MP	Jan. 12, 1792	Aug. 9, 1792	Presented recall, July 27, 1796
	Rufus King	N.Y.	MP	May 20, 1796	July 27, 1796	Presented recall, May 16, 1803
Netherlands	William Short	Va.	MR	Jan. 16, 1792	June 18, 1792	Left post, Dec. 19, 1792
	John Quincy Adams	Mass.	MR	May 30, 1794	Nov. 6, 1794	Presented recall, June 20, 1797
	William Vans Murray	Md.	MR	Mar. 2, 1797	June 20, 1797	Presented recall, Sept. 2, 1801
Portugal	David Humphreys	Conn.	MR	Feb. 21, 1791	May 13, 1791	Presented recall, July 25, 1797
	John Quincy Adams [6]	Mass.	MP	May 30, 1796		
Prussia	William L. Smith	S.C.	MP	July 10, 1797	Sept. 8, 1797	Presented recall, Sept. 9, 1801
	John Quincy Adams	Mass.	MP	June 1, 1797	Dec. 5, 1797	Presented recall, May 5, 1801
Spain	William Carmichael	Md.	CdA	Apr. 20, 1790	7	Presented recall, Sept. 5, 1794
	William Short	Va.	MR	May 28, 1794	Sept. 7, 1794	Left post, Nov. 1, 1795
	David Humphreys	Conn.	MP	May 20, 1796	Sept. 10, 1797	Presented recall, probably soon after Dec. 28, 1801

Symbols
MP   Minister Plenipotentiary
MR   Minister Resident, which ranks below Minister Plenipotentiary, but above a Chargé d'Affaires
CdA   Chargé d'Affaires

[1] Jefferson, commissioned Minister Plenipotentiary during the Confederation period, continued to serve the new federal government in Paris until he was appointed its first Secretary of State.

[2] Gouverneur Morris remained at his post until August, when James Monroe arrived and presented his credentials.

[3] Charles C. Pinckney proceeded to his post but was not received by the French Directory, and he left his post on February 5, 1797.

[4] Murray was not commissioned; his nomination was superseded by a new nomination with two others—Oliver Ellsworth and William R. Davie—to serve on a special joint commission to negotiate a new treaty with France.

[5] Bayard did not serve under this appointment.

[6] John Quincy Adams did not serve under this appointment; he was still Minister Resident in the Netherlands until June 1797 and then became the American Minister Plenipotentiary to Prussia later that year, where he was formally received on December 5.

[7] Carmichael, who had been appointed Chargé d'Affaires ad interim by the Confederation and was received on February 20, 1783, and was later appointed as Chargé d'Affaires en titre on April 20, 1790, by the new Federal government, but there appears to be no record of his presentation of his credentials in 1790.

replaced, except for Rufus King, who remained in Great Britain until May 1803. Thus, the practice of changing ranking diplomats as new Presidents were inaugurated was introduced as early as the beginning of the nineteenth century and is discussed later.

Other interesting features of these early diplomats are their origin and rank. All came from seven of the thirteen States—Connecticut, Delaware, Maryland, Massachusetts, New York, South Carolina, and Virginia. Two-thirds of the appointees hailed from South Carolina (three), New York (two), and Virginia (two). During the Confederation, only four envoys were given the diplomatic rank of Minister Plenipotentiary—John Adams, Benjamin Franklin, John Jay, and Thomas Jefferson. After Great Britain signed the Peace Treaty with the United States, and the Constitution came into effect, the American Government might have sought to elevate its diplomatic representation to the ambassadorial level. However, in part because it was officially and popularly believed that the very notion of an Ambassador smacked of aristocracy, which was vehemently rejected by the United States in the eighteenth century, the highest-ranking emissaries were designated as Ministers.

Except for two envoys accredited as Chargés d'Affaires, all diplomats appointed during the Federalist period were ranked as Ministers. Those accredited to France, Great Britain, and Prussia were all of the Minister Plenipotentiary rank, whereas those commissioned to the Netherlands and the initial ministerial appointees to Portugal and Spain were Ministers Resident, although subsequent envoys to these countries were also ranked as Ministers Plenipotentiary. This distinction probably reflected both American reservation concerning aristocratic ostentation and also, at least so far as France and Great Britain were concerned, an attitude of differentiating among foreign nations on the basis of their perceived importance to, and the foreign relations interests of, the United States.

Aside from four appointees who were not commissioned or failed to be received abroad, most formally "presented their recall" following normal tenures in their assignments, and three, according to the Department of State records, simply "left their posts," after serving from one and one-half to four years. Only one, Gouverneur Morris, Minister Plenipotentiary to France, was recalled at the request of its government.[25]

President Washington also introduced the unique practice of appointing special envoys to undertake exceptional, ad hoc diplomatic missions. As discussed later, he selected Gouverneur Morris, John Jay, and Thomas Pinckney for three separate, but important, assignments to Great Britain. Subsequently, President Adams experimented with the notion of commissioning two such special missions consisting of multiple envoys, assigned to France to negotiate a new treaty with the United States.

In an early appropriations act, July 1, 1790, Congress recognized the need for the position of secretaries employed by Ministers serving abroad. It also made the President accountable for expenditures for diplomats, including such secretaries, for whom the initial annual compensation was limited to $1,350 per person.

Consular Affairs

In the absence of congressional action, guided by both traditional international law and practice and the stipulations of the Franco–American Consular Convention concluded by the Confederation, Secretary Jefferson assumed initiative to govern and regularize certain consular functions. He directed consular officers to report regularly the names of American ships entering and clearing the ports to which they were assigned and to provide the Department of State with political and commercial information.

In 1790 President Washington appointed his first seventeen consular officers—twelve Consuls and five Vice Consuls. They were commissioned without salaries; they derived their remuneration from private trade and the fees that they collected for their services, a practice that continued for some decades. In 1791 Congress passed an act to implement the Franco–American Consular Convention, which had been concluded under the Confederation, signed in 1788, and ratified the following year and which went into effect in January 1790. It specified the rights, functions, and responsibilities of both French consular officers in the United States and American consular agents stationed abroad.

Early in April 1792 Congress enacted "the first organic law for consular affairs." It applied to all consular officials, prescribed regulations for the protection of American citizens and their interests abroad, fixed the fees to be collected for specified services rendered, required consuls to give bonds with sureties to guarantee faithful and effective service, and authorized additional functions that either inhered in traditional consular activities or flowed from existing and future treaties and conventions. Specifically, this law, enacted in part to implement the Franco–American Consular Convention, prescribed regulations for such matters as receiving and dealing with protests and declarations filed by Americans, taking custody of, and liquidating the estates of, Americans who died and possessed property within their consular jurisdictions, providing assistance to American ships and vessels stranded on the coasts of their consular districts, assisting at U.S. government expense (at the rate of twelve cents per diem) Americans who suffered shipwreck or illness, and monitoring action of ships' masters to return Americans to the United States when the vessels on which they served were sold abroad.[26]

American consular representation expanded more rapidly than diplomatic missions during the Federalist period. Because of the Barbary piracy problem in the Mediterranean, special attention was devoted to negotiating treaties to protect American vessels and their crews. This task was placed under the direction of David Humphreys, Minister to Portugal, who employed agents to deal with Algiers, Tripoli, and Tunis. By 1800 the number of American consular posts had increased to more than fifty.

Unauthorized Representation—The Logan Act, 1799

Finally, on January 30, 1799, Congress legislated to guarantee and control unilateral executive responsibility for official diplomatic communications with foreign governments and to prohibit unauthorized dealings with them. Dr. George Logan, a sincere, but meddling, Philadelphia pacifist, visited Paris on an unofficial diplomatic mission, hoping to avert the outbreak of war with France. Congress immediately passed what has come to be known as the Logan Act, holding such unofficial individuals like Logan to be criminally liable under penalty of fine and imprisonment, which still remains in effect. As subsequently amended, it provides:

Any citizen of the United States . . . who, without authority of the United States, directly or indirectly commences or carries on any correspondence or intercourse with any foreign government . . . with the intent to influence the measures or conduct of any foreign government . . . in relation to any disputes or controversies with the United States, or to defeat the measures of the United States, shall be fined not more than $5,000 or imprisoned not more than three years, or both.[27]

TREATY MAKING

Treaty Process

Under the Constitution, the law and procedure for treaty making were changed significantly. Previously, the Continental Congress played the central role—determining policy, preparing draft treaties, instructing negotiators, and approving and ratifying signed treaties, which, under the Articles of Confederation, had to be approved by at least nine of the States.

To recapitulate, the Constitution, Article 2, section 2 specifies that the President "shall have Power, by and with the Advice and Consent of the Senate, to make Treaties, provided two-thirds of the Senators present concur," and Article 6 specifies that "all Treaties made, or which shall be made, under the Authority of the United States, shall be the supreme law of the Land." In terms of both constitutional law and procedure, this produced a major innovation in the management of American treaty making, in which the President and the Department of State play the central role.

At the Constitutional Convention there were strong argument and, for a time, even some disposition in favor of ascribing the treaty-making power solely to the Senate. Toward the end of the Convention, however, the proposal was made to broaden legislative participation by associating the House of Representatives with the Senate in the process. Both plans were eventually defeated, and the President came to be viewed as the logical official to conduct foreign relations and therefore needed explicit authority in this matter. Nevertheless, the delegates were unwilling to grant the Chief Executive unlimited control, and a serious check on presidential action was readily provided in the Senate two-thirds approval requirement. During committee consideration of this formula at the Convention, a motion for Senate simple majority approval was proposed and defeated by only one vote. Although at times the two-thirds rule has caused difficulties in the treaty-making process, it has not prevented the United States from concluding thousands of treaties.

Of the six major steps in the American treaty process—negotiation, signature, Senate approval, ratification, exchange of ratifications, and proclamation or promulgation—Congress is directly involved in only one stage, Senate approval. All the rest became executive responsibilities, with the Secretary and Department of State playing the primary role for negotiation and signature, whereas the President is personally responsible for ratification and promulgation.[28]

These generalizations are subject to a number of important caveats. Thus, the President may determine the policy to be pursued in negotiations and may decide not to submit a signed treaty to the Senate for approval or may even decide not to ratify it after the Senate has given its approval, particularly if the Senate seeks to amend or interpret the treaty text. On the other hand, when a treaty requires implementing legislation, and particularly if appropriations are necessary to put it into effect, Congress becomes involved, and appropriations legislation must originate in the House of Representatives.

Congress may also legislate respecting certain other aspects of the treaty process. For example, in mid-1790 it required that "all treaties made, or which shall be made or promulgated under the authority of the United States . . . be published and annexed to their code of laws, by the Secretary of State." This set the early precedent in the conduct of American foreign relations that, when concluded, the texts of treaties be made public. The United States has subsequently not been a party to any formal secret treaty.[29]

Although the Continental Congress clearly supervised the negotiation of treaties with both foreign powers and the Indian tribes, this was modified under the Constitution. Not only was the procedure for negotiation and ratification changed, but administratively, while the Department of State has handled treaty making with foreign powers, negotiations and the conclusion of treaties and agreements with the Indians were turned over to the Department of War.

Treaty Record

Desiring to stay out of Europe's wars, to counter the closed trading system of the great maritime powers, and to promote and regularize relations with European and Mediterranean nations begun by the Confederation, action was taken to ratify the Franco–American Consular Convention signed in 1788 and to negotiate a series of nine new treaties during the Washington and Adams administrations. The first of these was not signed until November 1794, late in Washington's second administration. The remaining eight were concluded between September 1795 and September 1800. See Table 2.3.

Table 2.3
Treaties, 1789–1801

Country	Title	Where Signed	Date Signed	Date Ratified [a]	Date in Effect	Signers for United States	Citation Bevans [b]
France	Consular Convention	Versailles	Nov. 14, 1788	Sep. 9, 1789	Jan. 6, 1790 [1]	Thomas Jefferson	7:794-800
Great Britain	Amity, Commerce, and Navigation	London	Nov. 19, 1794	Aug. 14, 1795	Oct. 28, 1795 [2]	John Jay	12:13-33
Algiers	Peace and Amity	Algiers	Sep. 5, 1795	Mar. 7, 1796	Mar. 7, 1796 [3]	Joseph Donaldson	5:32-44
Spain	Friendship, Limits, and Navigation	San Lorenzo el Real	Oct. 27, 1795	Mar. 7, 1796	Apr. 25, 1796 [4]	Thomas Pinckney	11:516-25
Tripoli	Peace and Friendship	Tripoli and Algiers	Nov. 4, 1796 / Jan. 3, 1797	June 10, 1797	June 10, 1797 [5]	Joel Barlow	11:1070-80
Great Britain	Commerce	Philadelphia	May 4, 1796	May 9, 1796	Oct. 6, 1796 [6]	Timothy Pickering	12:34-35
Tunis	Amity, Commerce, and Navigation	Tunis	Aug. 28, 1797	Jan. 10, 1800	Jan. 10, 1800 [7]	William Eaton / James L. Cathcart	11:1088-95
Great Britain	Commerce	London	Mar. 17, 1798	June 7, 1798	June 9, 1798 [8]	Rufus King	12:36-37
Prussia	Amity and Commerce	Berlin	July 11, 1799	Feb. 19, 1800	June 22, 1800 [9]	John Quincy Adams	8:88-97
France	Friendship and Commerce	Paris	Sep. 30, 1800	Feb. 18, 1801	July 31, 1801 [10]	William Vans Murray / Oliver Ellsworth / W. B. Davie	7:801-811

[a] All of these were treaties, ratified by the President after receiving the consent of the Senate, as required by the Constitution.

[b] Citations are to Charles I. Bevans, *Treaties and Other International Agreements of the United States of America, 1776–1949*, 12 volumes, showing volume and page numbers.

[1] Signed during the Confederation period and was the first treaty ratified by President Washington. Also was the first U.S. Consular Convention.

[2] Popularly known as the "Jay Treaty." Specific articles were later supplemented, suspended, terminated, expired, or amended, 1796–1812.

[3] Only a Turkish text was signed in 1795. Superseded by treaty of June 30 and July 3, 1815.

[4] Popularly known as the "Pinckney Treaty." Several articles were later invalidated by the Treaty of Amity, Settlement, and Limits, February 22, 1819. It was terminated April 14, 1903, by treaty of July 3, 1902, and therefore remained in effect for more than a century.

[5] Superseded April 17, 1806, by treaty of June 4, 1805. Translated from Arabic into English by Joel Barlow.

[6] Constituted an article explanatory to the Treaty of Amity, Commerce, and Navigation of 1794 (Jay Treaty). Dealt with relations with Indians.

[7] Superseded May 7, 1904, by treaty of March 15, 1904, between the United States and France. Remained in effect for more than a century.

[8] Constituted an article explanatory to one of the articles of the Treaty of Amity, Commerce, and Navigation of 1794 (Jay Treaty). Dealt with boundary delineation. Terminated on the fulfillment of its terms.

[9] Superseded Treaty of Amity and Commerce, signed in 1785. Expired June 22, 1810, but several of its articles were revived by treaty of May 1, 1828.

[10] Superseded Treaty of Amity and Commerce of 1778 with its amendments. It expired July 31, 1809.

Most of them were titled and dealt with amity, peace, friendship, commerce, and navigation. In addition, they promoted consular relations, and the treaty with Spain also dealt with territorial jurisdiction in North America.[30] They were formal treaties, requiring Senate approval and presidential ratification and proclamation. The new treaties with France and Prussia superseded earlier engagements, whereas those with Great Britain and Spain—popularly known, respectively, as the Jay and Pinckney Treaties—were landmark ventures in U.S. diplomatic history.[31] New treaties were also concluded with the Barbary regencies of Algeria, Tripoli, and Tunis, which had been under negotiation since the 1780s.

During this Federalist period, as previously, the negotiation and signing of treaties were handled abroad, except for that concluded with Great Britain in 1796, which was signed at Philadelphia by Secretary of State Timothy Pickering. Six were signed by ranking American resident and special emissaries.[32] As had been the case during the Confederation years, when negotiations were conducted by consular officials, the Federal Government also used them to sign treaties with the Barbary regencies.[33]

As a result, by 1800 the United States had concluded twenty-four treaties and agreements and was signatory to treaties of amity and commerce with nine European and Mediterranean powers (Algiers, France, Great Britain, Morocco, the Netherlands, Prussia, Spain, Tripoli, and Tunis). All of these twenty-four treaties and agreements were bipartite. Twelve of them had been abrogated, fulfilled, or superseded, whereas the Peace Treaty with Great Britain (1783), the Treaty of Amity and Commerce with Morocco, and the Franco–American Consular Convention, together with the nine new treaties concluded by the Federal Government, were in effect when Thomas Jefferson became President. Surprisingly, two of them—the Pinckney Treaty with Spain (1795) and the treaty with Tunis (1797)—remained in force for more than a century. In addition, the Treaty of Amity and Commerce with Sweden (1783), which expired in 1799, was twice renewed and was not terminated until 1919 and therefore remained in effect for more than 135 years.

CONCLUSION—STATUS AT END OF FEDERALIST PERIOD

During the twelve years of the Federalist period, policy making and administration were experimental, and the Department of State developed slowly and modestly. Clearly, Congress was concerned less with controlling the details of the management of foreign relations, diplomatic and consular representation, and the conduct of the diplomatic process than was the Continental Congress. In addition to enacting legislation to create the foreign relations establishment, the Congress of the Federal Union was more concerned with the financing of the Department of State and the diplomatic and consular services, authorizing the staffing of the Department, legislating with respect to substantive foreign relations policy and programs, and providing Senate approval of diplomatic and consular appointees and treaties.[34]

It also became apparent that foreign policy was controlled and, in some cases, formulated by the President, that the presidency was the sole agency of official communications with foreign governments and their emissaries, and that the President had authority to commission American diplomats and consular officers. Similarly, it was manifest that the Secretaryship of State and its functions were subject to the laws enacted by Congress and the directives of the President. These precedents fixed the politicojuridical relationship of the Congress, the President, and the Secretary and Department of State for the future.

Not surprisingly, so far as substantive foreign policy making was concerned, Congress and the President played mutual, coordinating roles on many matters. In some cases foreign policies were proposed by the President. In others they were initiated in Congress and enacted into law. Sometimes Congress debated foreign relations issues in great detail, as it did when in 1797 and 1798 it considered action to deal with deteriorating relations with France and the abrogation of the Franco–American treaties of 1778.[35]

However, the most historic American foreign policy of that era was enunciated by President Washington in his Farewell Address in September 1796, in which he propounded the concept of noninvolvement in European political, as distinct from commercial and other, relations:

The great rule of conduct for us in regard to foreign nations is, in extending our commercial relations to have with them as little *political* connection as possible. So far as we have already formed engagements let them be fulfilled with perfect good faith. Here let us stop.

Europe has a set of primary interests which to us have none or a very remote relation. Hence she must be engaged in frequent controversies, the causes of which are essentially foreign to our concerns. . . .

Our detached and distant situation invites and enables us to pursue a different course. . . .

Why forego the advantages of so peculiar a situation? Why quit our own stand upon foreign ground? Why, by interweaving our destiny with that of any part of Europe, entangle our peace and prosperity in the toils of European ambition, rivalship, interest, humor, or caprice?

A few years later, in his first Inaugural Address on December 8, 1801, Thomas Jefferson synthesized this as a dictum of "peace, commerce and honest friendship with all nations, entangling alliances with none." He incorporated this into his "essential principles of Government" and "the brightest constellation" of American goals. This fundamental policy of political noninvolvement, epitomized as "no entangling alliances," which grew out of a long history of entanglement in Europe's wars and the difficulties that flowed from the commitments of the Franco–American Alliance of 1778, became the traditional policy that governed U.S. relations with Europe until World War II.

Some criticize that, beginning with Washington, some presidents have been inclined to serve "as their own Secretaries of State." If applied to policy formulation and decisions respecting the management of foreign relations in accordance with the law, this is scarcely subject to objection. Such criticism would seem credible only if applied to those cases in which the President ignores or bypasses the Secretary of State on matters of foreign affairs administration and the diplomatic process. Even in the matter of presidential commissioning of special agents and diplomatic missions, or undertaking diplomatic missions personally, which became common practice in the twentieth century, the Chief Executive functions within presidential rights and authority.

Presidents Washington and Adams appointed four Secretaries—Jefferson, Randolph, Pickering, and Marshall—and two of them and Charles Lee also served as Secretaries ad interim for short periods. Based on their prior experience, as a group the Secretaries were well qualified for public office. Their impressive combined prior experience included serving in Revolutionary War military service (Marshall, Pickering, and Randolph), election to the Continental Congress and drafting the Declaration of Independence (Jefferson), election as a delegate to the Constitutional Convention (Randolph), election to membership in Congress (Jefferson and Marshall), previous Cabinet membership (Pickering—Postmaster General and Secretary of War, Randolph—Attorney General), previous diplomatic experience (Jefferson as Minister Plenipotentiary and Marshall as Envoy Extraordinary), and service in State governments (Jefferson—Virginia legislature and Governor, Marshall—Virginia legislature, Pickering—New York judge; and Randolph—Virginia Attorney General and Governor).

The relations of Presidents Washington and Adams with their Secretaries of State naturally depended on their individual political dispositions, their character and interests, and the foreign issues and critical problems with which they were confronted. They set many precedents concerned with staffing, processes, and procedures for their successors. By the end of the eighteenth century the Office of Chief Clerk as the Secretary's principal deputy had become traditional, continuing for another half century, and the departmental staff was relatively modest.

The initial overseas diplomatic service was as unpretentious as the domestic facility. Secretary Jefferson drew a clear-cut distinction between the diplomatic corps, which was responsible for servicing political relations with foreign governments, and the consular officers, who dealt primarily with commercial matters. This also was reflected in the lack of interchange between diplomatic and consular officials and between those who served abroad and those in the Department of State. As a result, little attempt was made to develop a professional foreign relations establishment, and this continued for many years, which disaffected some aspects of the management of American foreign relations. In part, the size and expansion of the diplomatic corps were governed by congressionally mandated funding constraints, which may account for the restriction of American resident diplomatic representation to only six European countries.

The inner foreign relations teams of Presidents Washington and Adams were small and generally cohesive. They consisted principally of their Secretaries of State, other Cabinet members (insofar as they were concerned with aspects of external affairs on whom the President relied for counsel, such as Secretary of the Treasury Alexander Hamilton), the American diplomatic and consular representatives stationed abroad, the special envoys appointed to negotiate with foreign governments, and the departmental Chief Clerks and their staffs. In addition, Presidents Washington and Adams, and their Secretaries of State, maintained extensive official and personal correspondence with a good many foreign officials and friends of America.

Several developments introduced during these early years warrant special mention. Congressional action to ascribe domestic as well as foreign relations functions to the Secretary introduced a unique feature in departmental organization and management. The agency created to deal with foreign affairs was almost immediately converted into the Department of State and has since remained unchanged, even though most of its extensive domestic responsibilities were later turned over to other agencies as the American administrative mechanism expanded.[36]

The second development of major significance pertained to the manner in which President Washington fashioned executive-senatorial relations in implementing the treaty-making process. Had the Constitution simply specified that the President shall have authority to negotiate treaties and, with the approval of the Senate, shall be empowered to ratify them, instead of phrasing it as it did, the meaning would have been self-evident. Because the Constitution gave the President the power, by and with the advice and consent of the Senate, "to make" treaties, the question arose as to whether the Senate was to participate in negotiation as well as in approval for ratification. Was the Senate to advise and consent during the entire treaty-making process—was it to serve conjointly and cooperatively with the President, or were the two branches simply to function in sequential order?

At first Washington, with the concurrence of Secretary Jefferson, sought to obtain senatorial counsel during the early stages of negotiation. He therefore appeared personally before the Senate on August 22, 1789, to consider the matter of a treaty with the Indians. He posed a number of specific questions, on which he expected expeditious guidance, but the Senate decided to refer the matter to a committee, so that it could be considered without the presence of the Chief Executive.

Although Washington did not oppose delay for serious consideration, he failed to see justification for commitment to a congressional committee. When he returned a few days later, and the ensuing debate was tedious and interminable, he decided not to repeat this practice, allegedly declaring that "he would be damned if he ever went there again." Subsequently, he resorted to written communications instead of personal consultation for guidance purposes, but even this tactic proved to be so unfruitful that under subsequent Presidents, with a few exceptions, it, too, was abandoned.[37] Washington, therefore, established the precedent of presidential independence in treaty negotiation.

The third early innovation of historical consequence was presidential appointment of special diplomatic missions and presidential personal envoys, bypassing or supplementing regularly accredited emissaries, which was introduced into, and has continued to be employed as common practice in, the conduct of American foreign relations, which has come to be called summit diplomacy. It provided the President with diplomatic options to traditional foreign representation. The presidential personal representatives, also called executive agents or special envoys, usually have been ad hoc temporary agents commissioned to perform specific assignments.

Presidents Washington and Adams employed them for a variety of purposes. For example, in 1790, Washington instructed Gouverneur Morris, an experienced American statesman then in France on private business, to proceed to London to persuade the British government to enter into formal diplomatic relations and accredit a British Minister to the United States and to negotiate the settlement of disputes arising under the Peace Treaty of 1783.[38] In April 1794 Washington also appointed John Jay, then Chief Justice of the United States, as Envoy Extraordinary, who was provided with detailed instructions for negotiating the Treaty of Amity, Commerce, and Navigation with Great Britain, which was signed by him on November 19. Similarly, the following year Washington selected Thomas Pinckney, then U.S. Minister Plenipotentiary in Great Britain, to go to Spain as the President's Envoy Extraordinary and "sole Commissioner Plenipotentiary" to stimulate negotiations with the Spanish Government, and he finally concluded and signed the Treaty of Friendship, Limits, and Navigation on October 27 and then returned to his post in London.

President Adams also appointed a number of such presidential agents. He decided to send a multiple special mission to France in July 1797 to resolve differences with the French Government and to conclude a new treaty of amity and commerce. The mission consisted of Charles C. Pinckney, former Minister Plenipotentiary to France, whom the French Directory had refused to recognize; John Marshall, who was later to become Secretary of State and Chief Justice; and Elbridge Gerry, who had been a member of Congress and would later be elected Governor of Massachusetts. This mission failed, and two years later Adams contemplated a second such special mission to France, for which he had new instructions prepared, but this mission did not materialize. Finally, in March 1800 Adams created a new joint mission consisting of William Vans Murray, who had been commissioned by Washington and was then serving as Minister Resident to the Netherlands, assisted by Oliver Ellsworth and William R. Davie, to proceed to Paris. They concluded the new Franco–American Treaty of Friendship and Commerce, signed by them on September 30, whereupon Murray returned to his legation at The Hague.

Several aspects of these special missions are worthy of note. At the time, presidential appointments were normally made with the approval of the Senate;

yet, many later special envoys were sent on presidential diplomatic assignments without legislative confirmation. Some such early missions were undertaken by single individuals, whereas during the Adams administration they involved multiple accreditation. While several special envoys were temporarily taken from other diplomatic appointments, to which they returned on the completion of these missions, most were not then members of the executive service. Thus, the role of these presidential special emissaries was flexible and has proved to be a valuable diplomatic feature of American diplomacy.

As combined chief of state and head of government, Washington engaged in a number of aspects of summit diplomacy available to him at that time. He was the first "foreign-policy-maker-in-chief" of the United States. By virtue of his constitutional power to appoint American diplomatic representatives and receive foreign envoys, together with his responsibility for the negotiation of treaties, he possessed authority over diplomatic communications. Only seven months after the birth of the new Republic, he sent the first presidential message to a foreign leader when he wrote personally to the sultan of Morocco in December 1789, which he signed while he was at Mount Vernon, and the provisional capital was located approximately 150 miles away at Philadelphia.

Washington also signed personally a host of other documents. Aside from those concerned with domestic affairs, he signed letters of credence and full powers issued to accredited American diplomats to foreign governments, and he signed and issued a variety of presidential proclamations, some of which concerned foreign relations, such as the first Neutrality Proclamation in 1793 and those designed to implement treaties. In addition, he introduced the practice of appointing special presidential envoys to supplement regularly accredited resident diplomats abroad.

Thus, Washington introduced the practice of presidential diplomacy. This was historically important because, at a time when the stature of the United States and its government was uncertain, and the presidency lacked inherent prestige abroad, he lent his unique personal dignity, credibility, and eminence to the office and the nation in the conduct of foreign affairs. In *Presidential Greatness*, Thomas A. Bailey contends that Washington was "perhaps the only man in the history of the presidency bigger than the government itself." Moreover, by his use of the available techniques of summitry and the perspicacious manner in which he employed them, Washington warrants induction into the Summit Hall of Fame as its only pre–twentieth century dignitary.[39]

So far as the production and evolution of the variety of diplomatic documentation are concerned, during the Federalist period the President, Secretary, and Department of State instituted and formalized methods for the handling, format, and transmission of foreign relations credentials, such as nominations and appointments, diplomatic letters of credence and recall, full powers, instructions, and treaty negotiation directives and ratification instruments. They also devised processes for filing progress and other reports with Congress on American diplomatic and consular affairs. In addition, the President inaugurated the tradition of issuing foreign policy proclamations, and the Secretary and Department of State established a system of organizing, maintaining, and servicing their records and archives.

Building on the precedents set by the Continental Congress, on the traditions and practices of other countries, and more concretely on the interests and needs of the embryonic Federal Government, from the outset Congress, Presidents Washington and Adams, and their Secretaries of State dealt with the enactment of a series of fundamental and implementing laws, the creation of administrative machinery, and the formulation of policies, practices, and techniques for managing and conducting the foreign affairs of the United States. The essence of these determinations, agencies, instruments, and procedures, as later incrementally refined, for the conduct of relations with other nations not only provided the rudiments of the American system but also has endured for more than two centuries.

NOTES

1. On June 2, 1789, a House of Representatives committee presented the proposal to establish an executive "Department of Foreign Affairs," which was passed on June 24 and was also passed by the Senate on July 27. See *Annals of Congress*, 1st Cong. (1789–91), 2: 2187. For a detailed account of the House of Representatives debate on creating the Department and Secretary of Foreign Affairs, June 16–24, 1789, see *Annals of Congress*, 1st Cong. (1789–91), 1:473–613.

For an interesting analysis of the issue of using the title "United States" in the singular and plural in the Constitution and in diplomatic practice, determined by a circular of the Secretary of State for diplomatic relations in 1904, see Foster, *The Practice of Diplomacy*, pp. 83–90.

2. This proposal suggested that Home Department duties would embrace correspondence with the "several States," monitor "the execution of the laws of the Union," maintain and apply "the great seal," prepare commissions, affix the seal to commissions and other official documents, maintain "authentic copies of all public acts" and other documents and transmit them to the States, procure enactments of the States and report when they were "contrary to the laws of the United States," maintain "the archives of the late Congress" of the Confederation, "receive and record the census," maintain proposals for patents and keep records of those granted, and other functions as directed by the President. During the debate it was argued that a separate administrative Department was unnecessary, that other agencies could handle some of these functions, that it was doubtful that the funding of a separate Department was justifiable, and that the Secretary for Foreign Affairs "was not so much overcharged" with functions that this office might "attend to" most of these duties.

Examples of contemporary governments that have Home Affairs Ministries include Great Britain, India, Japan, the Netherlands, and South Africa. Most of them are headed by Ministers of Home Affairs, whereas in Great Britain it is titled Secretary of State for the Home Department. In other governments domestic functions are ascribed to other agencies.

3. The Presidential Succession Act of 1886 provided that the Secretary of State suc-

ceeded the President and Vice President, whereas the Act of 1947 changed the sequence by giving priority to the Speaker of the House of Representatives and the President of the Senate, followed by the Secretary of State and then the other Cabinet members in the order of their seniority.

4. Ten years later, in May 1800, in a general appropriations act, Congress reaffirmed these annual compensation amounts, both for individual diplomats and for the total annual salary funding of $40,000. Thus, these maximum compensation levels were maintained for more than a decade. But, in keeping with earlier practice, Congress also provided for additional specific amounts for the expenses of Commissioners and other agents to perform particular diplomatic tasks abroad totaling nearly $100,000, plus $56,000 for payment to the Regency of Algiers.

5. For example, in September 1789, in a single communication to the Senate, President Washington submitted the multiple nominations of nine officials, including Thomas Jefferson as Secretary of State, Edmund Randolph as Attorney General, and Samuel Osgood as Postmaster General, and the remainder as U.S. marshals, judges, and attorneys.

6. Jefferson, then the American Minister Plenipotentiary to France, was nominated by President Washington on September 25, 1789, and was appointed Secretary of State the following day. The President wrote him on October 13 offering him the position, to which Jefferson responded. He returned from Europe but did not take over the Secretaryship until March 22, 1790. In the meantime John Jay, who had been serving as Secretary for Foreign Affairs for the Confederation and continued until March 1790, was appointed the first Chief Justice of the United States.

7. These countries included France, Great Britain, the Netherlands, Portugal, and Spain.

8. President Washington requested the views of Secretaries Jefferson (State) and Hamilton (Treasury) on this matter. Jefferson maintained that the United States was bound by the Franco–American Alliance of 1778 and that Genêt should be received as the French Minister without reservation. When Genêt used neutral American territory to organize French attacks on British and Spanish colonies and commerce, established French prize courts on American soil, and appealed to Congress rather than to the President for an exequatur for a French Consul, Jefferson objected that this violated diplomatic protocol, and he pronounced that, so far as foreign relations are concerned, the President "is the only channel of communication between this country and foreign nations" and that official transactions with them is vested solely in the President. This fixed a firm precedent in American diplomatic practice. Also see n.25.

9. Previously, Randolph had been aide-de-camp to General Washington (1775–76), a member of the Continental Congress (1779–82), and Governor of Virginia (1786–88). He also headed its delegation to the Constitutional Convention, where he presented the Virginia Plan, but eventually he refused to sign the Constitution.

10. Paterson, a former delegate to the Constitutional Convention, was a Senator from New Jersey. Johnson, formerly Governor of Maryland and a member of the Continental Congress, was then Associate Justice on the Supreme Court. Charles Pinckney was formerly a member of the Continental Congress (1784–87), a delegate to the Constitutional Convention, Governor of South Carolina (1789–92, 1796–98, and later also 1806–8), and U.S. Senator (1798–1801). Henry, well-known American patriot and Revolutionary orator, was a former member of the Virginia House of Burgesses, delegate to the first Continental Congress, and Governor of Virginia (1776–79 and 1784–86). King, who previously served as a judge in the Massachusetts General Court and as a delegate to

the Constitutional Convention from that state, later moved to New York and was elected a member of the State Assembly and the U.S. Senate. Subsequently, he was appointed as Minister Plenipotentiary to Great Britain.

11. Charles C. Pinckney of South Carolina, who participated in several Revolutionary War battles, was a delegate to the Constitutional Convention and signed the Constitution and later was a candidate for both Vice President (1800) and President (1804 and 1808). Marshall of Virginia, who also served in the Revolutionary War to 1781, was a member of the Virginia Convention that ratified the Constitution, served in the Virginia Assembly (1782–91, 1795–97), was offered the post of Attorney General by President Washington, which he declined, and, when James Monroe returned from serving as Minister Plenipotentiary to France, was offered this appointment by the President in 1796. Gerry of Massachusetts was a member of the State legislature in 1772, was elected to the Continental Congress (1776–85), signed the Declaration of Independence, attended the Constitutional Convention but refused to sign the Constitution, and was a member of the House of Representatives (1789–93).

12. On May 10, 1780, President Adams wrote to Secretary Pickering, suggesting that he resign. When he refused, two days later the President discharged him. In his volume on *The Department of State*, Graham Stuart claims that, although Presidents relieved other Secretaries of their positions by various means, this was the only outright presidential dismissal of a Secretary of State.

13. Adams wished to appoint Marshall as Secretary of War, but he declined, and shortly thereafter Adams offered him the post of Secretary of State.

14. Ellsworth of Connecticut, former member of the Connecticut Assembly, delegate to the Continental Congress (1778–83) and the Constitutional Convention, and judge on the Connecticut Supreme Court (1785–89), served as a U.S. Senator (1789–96) and as Chief Justice of the United States (1796–1800). Ellsworth became ill while in France, and he resigned from both the Supreme Court and his diplomatic appointment, although he did sign the Franco–American Treaty of 1801. Davie of North Carolina had served in the Revolutionary War, as a delegate to the Constitutional Convention, and as Governor of North Carolina in 1799, when he was sent to France.

15. Remsen served the Confederation as Under Secretary until the end of 1789, was reappointed in September the following year, and remained Chief Clerk of the Department of State until the end of March 1792.

16. When the Confederation came to an end in July 1789, Charles Thomson, Secretary of the Continental Congress, presented the Great Seal and the collection of Confederation records to President Washington, with the recommendation that his Deputy Secretary of the Confederation, Roger Alden, be appointed by the new government to be responsible for them. Subsequently, on January 1, 1790, Washington appointed Alden to undertake these responsibilities, but he held this position for only seven months.

17. Taylor served several New York companies during the Revolutionary War, as a clerk for Lt. Col. Richard Varick. He was appointed a member of General Washington's staff in 1781 to handle his letters and papers. Two years later he moved to the office of the Confederation Secretary for Foreign Affairs. In 1790 he was employed by Secretary Jefferson as a clerk in the Department of State, and two years later he succeeded Remsen as Chief Clerk.

Wagner was already serving as a senior Clerk in the Department of State and therefore was familiar with the duties of the office of Chief Clerk, to which he was appointed on February 8, 1798, and in which he remained until he voluntarily retired in 1807.

18. To implement the act of September 1789, it appears that Jefferson, soon after he became Secretary of State, consulted with John Jay (formerly Secretary of Foreign Affairs but then Chief Justice), who had established a seal for the Supreme Court. The original Department of State seal resembles the Supreme Court seal of 1790, except for the departmental designation. Initially, it was variously called "the seal of office," "the privy seal," or simply "the office seal," but, since 1796, it has been known as "the seal of the Department of State."

At the outset it was used for authenticating copies made from records and papers in the possession of the Department of State and for certifying signatures, passports for citizens, and commissions issued to commercial agents and minor employees of the Department who received their appointments from the Secretary of State rather than the President. The original seal was used for more than forty years. Later dies were cast in 1834, 1880, 1911, 1917, and subsequently.

For a detailed account of the development and use of the Department of State seal with depictions of the versions of 1790, 1834, 1880, and 1934, see Patterson and Dougall, *The Eagle and the Shield*, Chapter 18 on "The Seal of the Department of State," pp. 470–509. Also see Hunt, *The Department of State of the United States*, pp. 74, 100.

19. They all served in one or more assignments, except for Charles C. Pinckney, who was not received by French authorities in 1796, so that he returned to the United States the following year.

20. Thus, John Quincy Adams was appointed Minister Resident to the Netherlands and was later commissioned Minister Plenipotentiary to Prussia, Humphreys served as Minister Resident in Portugal and was later appointed Minister Plenipotentiary to Spain, and William Short was accredited to three countries—France, the Netherlands, and Spain.

21. This may be explained, in part, by the fact that, except for Prussia, these were the countries that possessed territories in the Western Hemisphere and with which the United States traded and sought to promote cordial treaty relations.

22. Thus, Charles C. Pinckney, though appointed in 1796 and proceeding to his post in Paris, was not officially recognized by the French Government. Murray, intended to be his successor, was nominated but not commissioned, and he was then appointed a presidential special envoy to France. James A. Bayard, appointed as Murray's successor by President Adams in the twilight of his Administration, was not commissioned. He was superseded a few months later by Robert R. Livingston, who was appointed by President Jefferson early in his Administration. On the other hand, John Quincy Adams, American Minister Resident to the Netherlands, 1794–97, was appointed in May 1796 to serve in Portugal, but he remained at The Hague until June 1797 and then was immediately accredited to Prussia.

23. The reason for designating Short as Chargé d'Affaires in Paris was that Minister Plenipotentiary Jefferson was authorized to return to the United States on leave from his post in France, so that President Washington decided to accredit Short to temporarily "take charge of our affairs" at the French Court during Jefferson's absence. Among the reason for appointing Carmichael as Chargé d'Affairs was that he had previously held and continued in that rank.

24. John Quincy Adams was transferred from the Netherlands to Prussia (see n. 22). Murray, who was nominated for appointment to France in 1797, was not commissioned, and almost immediately he was accredited as Minister to the Netherlands. President Adams' two new Ministers were William L. Smith, who was commissioned to Portugal

to succeed Humphreys when he was sent to Spain, and James A. Bayard, a last-moment appointee, as Minister Plenipotentiary to France.

25. This recall of Gouverneur Morris from France in April 1794 was concurrent with the demand of the United States that Edmund C. Genêt, the French Minister to the United States, be recalled. During his service in the United States, 1793–94, Genêt sought to involve this country in the war that the new recolutionary French government was waging with its European neighbors, while the United States sought to maintain its neutrality, as formally proclaimed by the President on March 24, 1794.

As a result, President Washington requested that Genêt be recalled, and on April 9, 1794, the French government also requested that Morris be recalled from Paris. For President Washington's message to Congress, reporting on his action to have Genêt recalled, in which he asserted that the French Minister's "conduct has been unequivocally disapproved" and that his recall was to be "expedited without delay," see *Annals of Congress*, 3d Cong. (1793–95), 1:36. Also see n.8.

26. It is noteworthy that this act did not deal with such standard consular matters as regulations and fees for promoting and handling American trade, issuing and collecting the fees for providing shipping documents, including ship registrations and ships' passports, protecting Americans from arrest and mistreatment aboard ship or otherwise within their consular districts, and many other functions subsequently ascribed to consular officers. For the text of this act, approved April 14, 1792, see *Annals of Congress*, 2d Cong. (1791–93), pp. 1360–63. For an earlier version, considered by the Senate, November 20, 1791, see pp. 33–36.

27. For the text of the original Logan Act, see *Annals of Congress*, 5th Cong. (1797–1799) 3:3795, and 1 Stat. 613; for some recent revisions, see *U.S. Code* 1940, Title 18, sec. 5; 62 Stat. 744 (June 25, 1948), and for the current version, see Act of September 13, 1994 (108 Stat. 2147) and *U.S. Code*, Title 18, sec. 953.

28. For the texts of documentation to illustrate the treaty-making process, as presented by President Washington to the Senate in 1795 in the case of the Jay Treaty of Amity, Commerce, and Navigation with Great Britain, including copies of Washington's appointment, letter of credence, proclamation of full power, detailed instructions to Jay and dispatches from Secretary of State Edmund Randolph, see *Annals of Congress*, 4th Cong. (1795–1797), 1:2370–80. For an illustration of Senate detailed action in approving the Treaty of Friendship and Commerce with France, concluded in 1800, see *Annals of Congress*, 6th Cong. (1799–1801), pp. 768–78.

29. It should be noted that the same principle of openness does not apply to the negotiation process or to Senate approval proceedings and that, even though the texts of most executive agreements are also made public, some of them, especially military arrangements in time of war, naturally are not publicized.

30. Articles 2–4 of this treaty with Spain defined the southern and western boundary limits of the United States and provided for a joint survey and for mapping of its territorial jurisdiction.

31. For a comprehensive report of congressional debate on the historic Jay Treaty, illustrating presidential management and congressional oversight of the treaty process, see essay entitled "Treaty With Great Britain," April 1796, in *Annals of Congress*, 4th Cong., 1st Sess. (1795–97) 1:969–1291. For an earlier general discussion on the "Execution of Treaties" with Algiers, Great Britain, and Spain, also dated April 1796, see pp. 940–51, in which it was claimed that this was "one of the most important questions" to come before Congress "upon which the fate of the country depended."

32. Sequentially, these treaties with European governments included Thomas Jefferson, Minister Plenipotentiary, Consular Convention with France, signed in 1788; John Jay, Envoy Extraordinary, Treaty of Amity, Commerce, and Navigation with Great Britain, 1794; Thomas Pinckney, Envoy Extraordinary, Treaty of Friendship, Limits, and Navigation with Spain, 1795; Rufus King, Minister Plenipotentiary, Treaty of Commerce with Great Britain, 1798; John Quincy Adams, Minister Plenipotentiary, Treaty of Amity and Commerce with Prussia, 1799; and William Vans Murray, Minister Plenipotentiary, Treaty of Friendship and Commerce with France, 1800.

33. Thus, Joseph Donaldson, a consular officer in North Africa, signed the Treaty of Peace and Amity with Algiers in 1795; Joel Barlow, Consul General stationed in Algiers, translated and signed the Treaty of Peace and Friendship with Tripoli in 1796; and William Eaton, Consul at Tunis and James Leander Cathcart, Consul General at Tripoli, signed the treaty of Amity, Commerce, and Navigation with Tunis in 1797. The negotiation of these treaties was under the direction of David Humphries, Minister to Portugal, who employed Barlow and Donaldson, whereas Cathcart had been captured by the rulers of Algiers in 1785 and was commissioned as consular officer in July 1797, and Eaton was also commissioned that year.

34. For example, in addition to controlling the foreign relations establishment through appropriations legislation, Congress enacted laws that dealt with the form of oaths and affirmations, the home of the Department of State and, so far as substantive foreign relations were concerned, repayment of the U.S. foreign debt, retributive suspension of international intercourse, the establishment of a national shipping embargo, commerce and customs duties, peace and trade with external Indian tribes, nationality, naturalization of foreign immigrants, fisheries, the slave trade, privateering (prohibiting Americans from engaging in such acts ''against nations in amity'' with the United States), and navigation, shipping (including the registration of vessels), ships' passports, ports, and lighthouses.

35. See *Annals of Congress*, 4th Cong. (1795–1797), 2:2713–2777; 5th Cong. (1797–99), 2:2116–2128 and 3:3322–3559; and 6th Cong. (1799–1801), 1:1085–1207. Also see general debate on foreign affairs in *Annals of Congress*, 8th Cong. (1797–99), 1:848–945 and 1115–1215.

36. To summarize, during the Federalist period, in addition to providing custody of the records, books, and other papers of the Confederation that were turned over to the Federal Government and responsibility for printing and distributing the resolutions and laws passed by Congress together with the treaties concluded with foreign governments, the Department of State was saddled with a host of additional domestic responsibilities. To illustrate, in addition to maintaining files of official presidential communications and applications for appointment to federal office, transmitting all commissions of appointment (even those concerned with other Departments and agencies), and translating certain legislation and communications from foreign governments, these included issuing passports to Americans and exequaturs to foreign consuls in the United States, certifying letters patent, implementing copyright laws and preserving copyright papers, creating a depository of books produced in the United States, printing census returns, registering American ships and other vessels, issuing letters of marque and reprisal, producing copies of ships' passports to be handled by port agents, preparing annual reports on customs collections, administering the public mint, servicing correspondence of the Federal Government with the States, and even providing Congress with copies of the laws enacted by the government of the Northwest Territory.

Among the most unique assignments of the Secretary of State was the preparation of a plan to standardize weights and measures. By way of background, it should be noted that the Founders were concerned with this matter from the outset. The Articles of Confederation, Article IX, specified that the Congress possessed the "sole and exclusive right and power of regulating the alloy and value of coin" and of "fixing the standard of weights and measures throughout the United States." In 1789 this was reiterated in the Constitution, Article 1, Sec. 8, clause 5, which stipulates that Congress has the power to "coin money, regulate the value thereof, . . . and fix the standards of weights and measures."

In his first Annual Address to Congress, January 8, 1890, President Washington informed Congress: "Uniformity in the currency, weights, and measures of the United States is an object of great importance, and will, I am persuaded, be duly attended to." Congress delegated this task to Secretary of State Jefferson, who submitted a technical report six months later, on July 4. In it he proposed two alternative possibilities. The first was based on weights and measures then in use in the United States, with suggestions for achieving uniformity, and the second prescribed a decimal codification of weights and measures to conform with the decimal monetary system that had been established. The matter of standardizing weights and measures was reraised later, and again the preparation of a plan was assigned to the Secretary of State, John Quincy Adams, as noted in the next chapter.

For documentation, see *Messages and Papers of the Presidents*, 1:58 for President Washington's statement, and for Jefferson's preliminary plans, various drafts, the text of the final draft, and his transmittal communication, see *The Papers of Thomas Jefferson*, ed. Julian P. Boyd (Princeton: Princeton University Press, 1961), vol. 16, pp. 602–75, with the final report at pp. 650–74. Also see *Annals of Congress*, 1st Cong. (1789–1791), pp. 1094–95, 1738, 1782–83, 1826, which indicates that it was approved by the Senate.

In effect, therefore, the Department of State became the repository of all functions that were not made the responsibility of the Treasury, War, and Navy Departments and the Post Office. Secretary Jefferson viewed it as being burdened with all of the internal functions that were not ascribed to the Treasury Department.

37. As a result, the President has sought advice of the full Senate during the treaty negotiation process in less than twenty cases, half of which occurred during the incumbency of Washington prior to the negotiation of the Jay Treaty.

38. Subsequently, in 1792 Morris was appointed Minister Plenipotentiary to Paris.

39. For additional information on presidential summitry, see Plischke, *Summit Diplomacy: Personal Diplomacy of the President of the United States* and *Diplomat in Chief: The President at the Summit.*

PART II

1801–1861

3

Post-Federalist Period—
Germination and
Crystallization, 1801–1829

Grounded on developments of the Confederation and Federalist periods, in many respects during the years from 1801 to 1829 the United States reconfirmed, crystallized, and refined its fundamental and long-lived foreign relations policies and practices. These included (1) the maintenance of its independence and national security; (2) continental territorial expansion; (3) national self-determination and de facto recognition of new states and governments; (4) freedom of trade; (5) freedom of the seas; (6) isolation and noninvolvement in Europe's political affairs and wars; (7) nonintervention and neutrality in time of war; and (8) mutual negotiation on the basis of equality and reciprocity. Embracing these as goals and forging pragmatic objectives and substantive and procedural policies to implement them provided the government, especially the Department of State, with both challenges and opportunities.

During the early decades of the nineteenth century additional enduring policies were added, such as the termination of mercantilism of the major European maritime powers, the propagation of the rights of neutral countries in time of war, the acquisition of additional territory by purchase and cession, the peaceful settlement of international disputes by means of not only traditional negotiation but also arbitration, the participation in multilateral international cooperation both in treaty making and international conferencing, and, perhaps most historic, the proclamation of the Monroe Doctrine.

Two celebrated substantive policies—isolationism and neutrality, and the Monroe Doctrine (unique unilateral declarations)—warrant brief explanation. Isolationism, abstentionism, and neutrality in time of European wars were discussed in President Washington's Farewell Address in Chapter 2. The Monroe Doctrine, the second enduring policy pronouncement, was proclaimed by President James Monroe in a message to Congress, December 2, 1823. Addressing himself to the relations of the European imperial powers with the newly independent countries of Latin America, he declared:

We owe it, therefore, to candor and to the amicable relations existing between the United States and those powers to declare that we should consider any attempt on their part to extend their system to any portion of this hemisphere as dangerous to our peace and safety. With the existing colonies or dependencies of any European power we have not interfered and shall not interfere. But with the Governments who have declared their independence and maintained it, and whose independence we have, on great consideration and on just principles, acknowledged, we could not view any interposition for the purpose of oppressing them, or controlling in any other manner their destiny, by any European power in any other light than as the manifestation of an unfriendly disposition toward the United States. In the war between those new Governments and Spain we declared our neutrality at the time of their recognition, and to this we have adhered, and shall continue to adhere, provided no change shall occur which, in the judgment of the competent authorities of this Government, shall make a corresponding change on the part of the United States indispensable to their security.

These two fundamental policies permeated the political and diplomatic relations of the United States with Europe and Latin America into the twentieth century.

Between 1801 and 1830 the United States experienced many new developments and significant changes. It engaged in two wars—with Tripoli (1801–4) and Great Britain (1812–15)—which were concluded with formal peace treaties; augmented its own recognition as an independent member of the community of nations; reconfirmed and refined its isolation and nonintervention policies; stabilized future pretensions of European imperial expansion in the Western Hemisphere; purchased the Louisiana and Florida territories; settled boundary arrangements with Great Britain, Mexico, Russia, and Spain; and achieved disarmament of the Great Lakes.

In terms of the conduct of foreign relations, the United States extended its formal diplomatic representation to fifteen countries and the Hawaiian (or Sandwich) Islands and its consular relations not only to much of Europe but also to Latin America, the Caribbean, northern and southern Africa, and even the Pacific and the Orient. The Department of State concluded thirty-one new treaties and agreements, including its first multipartite arrangement, and nearly participated in its first multilateral international conference. It continued its central functions of participating in framing and implementing foreign substantive and procedural policy and procedures, maintaining the flow of correspondence with diplomatic envoys and consular officers abroad and with foreign diplomats and consuls stationed in the United States, and managing American treaty making. Meanwhile, its domestic functions proliferated, and two departmental proposals for administrative reform and functional reorganization were instituted in the 1820s.

ORGANIZATION AND MANAGEMENT

Four notable statesmen were elected as Presidents. Three of them—Thomas Jefferson, James Madison, and James Monroe—were elected for two terms,

Table 3.1
Department of State Principal Officers, 1801–1829

Secretaries of State

Secretaries of State	Appointed	Entry on Duty	Termination of Appointment
* John Marshall (Va.) (Chief Justice)	Feb. 4, 1801		Mar. 4, 1801
* Levi Lincoln (Mass.) (Attorney General)	Mar. 5, 1801		May 1, 1801
James Madison (Va.)	Mar. 5, 1801	May 2, 1801	Mar. 3, 1809
Robert Smith (Md.)	Mar. 6, 1809	Mar. 6, 1809	Apr. 1, 1811
James Monroe (Va.)[1]	Apr. 2, 1811	Apr. 6, 1811	Mar. 3, 1817
* John Graham (Va.) (Chief Clerk, Dept. of State)	Mar. 4, 1817		Mar. 9, 1817
* Richard Rush (Pa.) (Attorney General)	Mar. 10, 1817		Sept. 22, 1817
John Quincy Adams (Mass.)	Mar. 5, 1817	Sept. 22, 1817	Mar. 3, 1825
* Daniel Brent (Va.) (Chief Clerk, Dept. of State)	Mar. 4, 1825		Mar. 7, 1825
Henry Clay (Ky.)	Mar. 7, 1825	Mar. 7, 1825	Mar. 3, 1829

Chief Clerks

Jacob Wagner (Pa.)	Feb. 8, 1798[2]		Mar. 31, 1807
John Graham (Va.)	July 1, 1807		July 18, 1817
Daniel Brent (Va.)	Sept. 22, 1817		Aug. 22, 1833

*Indicates Secretary of State ad interim.
[1]Monroe was nominated when the Senate was not in session, was recommissioned after confirmation by the Senate, September 30, 1814, and was later reappointed and reconfirmed.
[2]Wagner was continued in this position from Secretary Timothy Pickering's administration.

whereas John Quincy Adams held office for only four years. All had served previously as Secretary of State, and, except for Madison, they had substantial prior diplomatic experience. They were, therefore, well qualified for managing the development of American foreign relations.

Secretaries of State

These Presidents appointed five Secretaries of State. As indicated in Table 3.1, sequentially, they were James Madison (Virginia), Robert Smith (Maryland), James Monroe (Virginia), John Quincy Adams (Massachusetts), and Henry Clay (Kentucky). Madison, Monroe, and Adams held the office for eight years, Monroe for nearly six years, and Smith for two years.

Although not previously an American diplomat, Madison, who was highly qualified by background, ability, and political experience, agreed to become

Secretary before Jefferson's election to the presidency. When Madison was elected President in 1809, he wanted to appoint Albert Gallatin, who had served as Secretary of the Treasury since 1801, but, because of some Senate opposition, the President left him in his Treasury post and chose Robert Smith (former Secretary of the Navy for eight years) to head the State Department. But after only two years, in April 1811, Madison dismissed him [1] and replaced him with Monroe, who had been Minister Plenipotentiary to both France and Great Britain.

Six years later, in 1817, when Monroe became President, he appointed John Quincy Adams, who had extensive experience serving diplomatically as private secretary to Francis Dana in St. Petersburg, Russia, as Secretary to the American mission, appointed to negotiate the Peace Treaty with Great Britain in the early 1780s, and as Minister to the Netherlands (1794–97), Prussia (1797–1801), Russia (1809–14), and Great Britain (1815–17). He also had participated in concluding ten other treaties with five European countries. Since few Secretaries had a more extensive and varied prior diplomatic experience, when appointed, he had virtually become a career diplomat. When he was later inaugurated as President in 1825, he appointed Henry Clay as his Secretary of State.[2] An able parliamentarian, Clay had little prior administrative experience, and held no diplomatic appointments. Like his predecessors, except for Smith, he continued in office until a new President was elected.

From 1789 to 1829, of the nine Secretaries of State, five were Virginians, and the remaining four came from Pennsylvania, Maryland, Massachusetts, and Kentucky. Prior to 1825, all of them came from the original thirteen States; Clay was the first to be appointed from one of the newly admitted States. The appointment of Monroe and his subsequent election as President ended the early "Virginia dynasty."[3]

As was customary, to provide for the administration of the Department of State during the hiatus between the inauguration of the President and the nomination and Senate confirmation of a new Secretary, the position was temporarily filled by ad interim Secretaries (see Table 3.1). After Jefferson became President, pending the appointment of Madison, he named John Marshall, the Chief Justice of the Supreme Court and former Secretary of State, to serve as interim Secretary for a month, followed by Levi Lincoln, newly appointed Attorney General, who served for nearly two months. Though commissioned on March 5, 1801, Madison was unable to assume his duties until May 2 because of the death of his father and the need to attend to private affairs.

Similarly, when President Monroe was inaugurated in 1817, he appointed two sequential Secretaries ad interim—John Graham, the Department Chief Clerk, and Richard Rush, the newly appointed Attorney General, who served from March 4 to September 22, 1817, pending the return of John Quincy Adams from his diplomatic post in London, where he did not present his recall until May. Before Clay took the oath of office as Secretary on March 7, 1825, for three days President Adams had Daniel Brent, Chief Clerk of the Department, function as interim Secretary.

These temporary appointments illustrated the practice of utilizing primarily Cabinet officers but also the Chief Justice and the departmental Chief Clerk pending the commissioning and entry on duty of the new Secretary of State. Some interim Secretaries served for only a few days, whereas others, such as Graham and Rush, together occupied the office for more than six months. Normally, interim Secretaries make little substantive foreign relations contributions. However, Rush negotiated and signed an important executive agreement with Great Britain in 1817.

Staffing the Department

Congress continued to control the size of the Department of State, primarily through legislation that restricted the size of its staff. Because the Chief Clerks and their assisting clerks were not political appointees, they remained in office for long tenures and therefore provided some administrative continuity. During the twenty-eight years from 1801 to 1829, only two new Chief Clerks were recruited, so that in the first four decades only six were appointed. President Madison inherited Jacob Wagner as Chief Clerk, who continued in this office for six more years until he voluntarily retired on March 31, 1807. He was succeeded by John Graham, who previously held the position of Secretary to the American Legation and then Chargé d'Affaires in Madrid, and he remained Chief Clerk for ten years from 1807 to 1817. Even more impressive, Daniel Brent, functioned as a clerk in the Department for a decade and was then promoted to the rank of Chief Clerk on September 22, 1817, and remained until August 22, 1833, thus serving in the Department for more than a quarter century. In addition, both Graham and Brent functioned as Secretaries of State ad interim. By the early nineteenth century the office of Chief Clerk had become a position of importance in managing the administration of foreign affairs. Structurally, so far as seniority was concerned, it was comparable to the twentieth-century offices of Under Secretaries and later Deputy Secretaries of State.

Not having created a Home Department or other agencies to which the domestic functions of the State Department could be transferred and in view of the congressional disposition to regard it as the residual repository of those functions that did not naturally accrue to the other Departments and the Postal System, the remaining option was to increase and systematize the staff of the Department of State. It numbered only ten in 1800, including the Secretary and the Chief Clerk. Congress continued its niggerdly attitude toward adding additional clerks. Despite the appeals of Secretaries Adams and Clay for more personnel,[4] by 1818 the authorized number of regular clerks had been increased from eight to merely ten, including a Superintendent for the Department's Patent Office, and by 1827 the number had risen only to thirteen.

Congress controlled the staffing and management of the Department primarily through appropriations legislation, which dealt with both the total departmental budget and specific compensation levels. Whereas originally in 1789 it fixed the annual salary of the Secretary at $3,500, by 1806 it was raised to $5,000 and by the 1820s to $6,000. During these four decades the compensation of the Chief Clerk rose from $800 to $2,000. Compensation of regular clerks was initially set at $500 for each of them, and by the 1820s it varied in amount, not to exceed $800 to $1,600 per individual, and messengers received $1,400. On total departmental budgets, in 1798 Congress fixed the limit at $9,162, which was increased in 1806 to $12,812 and in the mid-1820s to $24,500.[5] Appropriations for American diplomatic missions to foreign governments and special missions to negotiate treaties and participate in international conferences and agencies were embodied in separate legislation.

Home of the Department

As noted earlier, when in 1800 the National Government transferred the capital from Philadelphia to Washington, D.C., the Department moved its office twice. The following year it relocated to what was called the "War Office" on Seventeenth and G Streets and for the period 1814 to 1816 to a building at G Street near Eighteenth. In 1820 it returned to the Treasury Building near the White House on Pennsylvania Avenue, where it remained until 1866.

British forces invaded Washington during the War of 1812 and burned the Capitol, White House, and other public buildings, including the headquarters of the Department of State. Although the Department lost some of its library, Chief Clerk Graham salvaged many important records, including the originals of the Declaration of Independence, the Constitution, the papers of the Confederation, and other documents. He stored them in a gristmill several miles up the Potomac River and later moved them to Leesburg, Virginia, until after the war.

Functions and Responsibilities—Foreign and Domestic

The traditional foreign relations functions of the Department—including the implementation of policy, diplomatic and consular representation abroad, and negotiating treaties—remained unchanged in kind but increased in quantity. The major innovations were the commencement of participation in multipartite international conferencing and acceleration of treaty making.

More specifically, as summarized by Secretary Adams, the Department was responsible for correspondence with, and issuing instructions to, American diplomats and consular officers; communicating with foreign envoys in the United States; preparing, executing, and recording letters of credence, diplomatic commissions, and exequaturs; producing translations of treaties and other documents; handling papers concerned with pecuniary claims of Americans against foreign governments; maintaining foreign relations files, including treaty documents; monitoring consular responsibilities; and related activities. He noted that these functions increased in volume as the United States extended its diplomacy to more foreign countries and expanded its foreign interests, trade, and consular relations.

He also stressed the Department's burden of increasing domestic functions. By the 1820s Congress saddled the Secretary and Department of State with the preparation and distribution of copies of the acts and resolutions passed by Congress and other state papers to members of Congress, delegates of the American Territories, the President and Vice President and heads of the administrative Departments, the executives and legislatures of the States and Territories, and "each University and College in the United States." Other duties included preparing, printing, and distributing an alphabetical index to congressional legislation at the end of each session; caring for the books and papers of the Continental Congress and the Constitutional Convention of 1789; preparing all commissions; executing personal passports; preparing and recording Federal pardons and emissions of fines; operating the Patent Office; participating in the production and distribution of the decennial national census; subscribing for, and distributing to, members of Congress copies of Statistical Annals; providing custody and application of the Great Seal of the United States; and others. The incremental augmentation of these functions by Congress reconfirmed the practice of assigning to the Department of State all such responsibilities not entrusted to other departments and agencies.

Several aspects of this increase of domestic responsibility of the Department warrant special mention. In addition to service as the general custodian and transmission agency for the distribution of public documents, Secretary Adams' duties were extended to the planning, devisement, and actual production of the American census and to designing a system of weights and measures for the United States, a matter that had lain dormant since the days of Secretary Jefferson.

For producing the first American census of 1790, the count was ascertained by U.S. marshals, which was collated and sent to the President, who passed it on to Congress. The Department of State became involved increasingly in this process, beginning with the census of 1800, for which the Secretary was directed by Congress to devise instructions for taking the census. Ten years later the population census was taken under the direction of the Department of State, and a simultaneous census of manufactures was handled by the Treasury Department.

For the census of 1820, the Secretary of State was made fully responsible for its management and distribution. Secretary Adams personally devoted considerable attention to including additional details to provide a more comprehensive tabulation, which set the general pattern for the next three decades.[6] Thus, the Secretary of State was assigned the duties of what later became the Census Bureau in the Department of Commerce.

Emphasizing the unique assignment of domestic functions to the Secretary of State, three years earlier, in 1817, Congress directed Secretary Adams to develop a general system of weights and measures for the country. This matter had been introduced by President Washington and entrusted to Secretary Jefferson in 1790. At the time it was combined with the constitutional prescription for coining money. As early as 1786 the Continental Congress had mandated the establishment of a decimal system of coinage to replace the English pound and various coins that were circulating in the American States, and the Mint Act was adopted in 1792.[7]

The institution of standardized weights and measures was more complicated because they related to usage both within the United States and in other countries, involving an important, but difficult, problem of equivalencies that was under consideration by other countries and the subject of international negotiations for generations. Treatment of the matter in the United States during the 1820s parallelled that of 1790. In his last annual message to Congress, December 3, 1816, President Madison reiterated the proposal that a plan for national standardization be prepared:

Congress will call to mind, that no adequate provision has yet been made, for the uniformity of weights and measures, also contemplated by the Constitution. The great utility of a standard, fixed in its nature, and founded on the easy rule of decimal proportions, is sufficiently obvious. It led the Government, at an early stage, to preparatory steps for introducing it; and a completion of the work will be a just title to the public gratitude.

The following day the House of Representatives passed a series of fifteen resolutions and appointed special committees to implement each of them. Early in March 1817 the Senate passed a resolution to have the Secretary of State undertake the task of devising a system of weights and measures for the United States. Secretary Adams devoted nearly four years to study and prepare a scholarly, comprehensive report on the subject, which he filed with the House of Representatives on February 22, 1821, and which has been called an outstanding piece of research into an intricate subject that was long rated as the model of analysis on the matter.[8] No standardizing legislation was immediately passed by Congress, the National Government dealt with the problems of American practice and international standardization for more than a century and a half, and officially, the United States has subscribed to metric standards. Nevertheless, in everyday life the traditional or customary American units of weights and measures, though standardized, persist.[9]

A third major development pertained to the copyright, archival, and library functions of the Department of State. From the outset it maintained its own departmental, diplomatic, and consular records and papers, but it also had custody of the archives of the Continental Congress, the original collection of books of the Continental Congress, and the records of the Constitutional Convention. In addition, it maintained the documents that pertained to the administration of copyrights and patents and to such other matters as the issuing of executive commissions, personal passports, ships' passports, registers of American seamen, records of executive pardons, claims of Americans against foreign governments, and, naturally, its own library. It also was responsible for the preservation of books published and copyrighted in the United States.

A significant portion of developing a national library was assumed by the Library of Congress when it was established by laws enacted in 1800 and 1802.[10] However, the Department of State continued to maintain its own library. In 1820 Secretary Adams undertook to improve its organization and management. He found that much of it had been depleted—by removals, the British attack in 1814, fire, and general lack of systematic care. When the Department moved to its new facilities in January 1820, he reserved two rooms for the library and assigned its management to departmental clerk Thomas L. Thurston and, to amplify its holdings, incorporated important documents of the constituent American States.[11]

Departmental Reorganization

As the laws and their administrative implementation and the functions and responsibilities of the Department proliferated both in kind and in degree, the foreign and domestic burdens of the Secretary and his small staff of clerks mounted. It became necessary, therefore, to stabilize and improve departmental organization and administration. The government had three options—to assign particular duties to other existing or new agencies (as Congress did when it created the Library of Congress), to create a Home Department to handle the State Department's and other domestic responsibilities, or to increase the Department of State staff. Congress analyzed departmental settlement of financial accounts in relation to activities, which it required of all Executive Departments, and specifically reviewed the tasks in relation to the Department's costs.

In December 1816, responding to a congressional request, President Madison provided the Senate with a comprehensive report on the matter of ensuring "certainty in the accountability" and "annual settlement of accounts" by the administrative departments, in which he reraised the matter of creating a new independent agency to be called the "Home Department." His suggestion was that it be headed by a Secretary to execute presidential directives pertaining to territorial governments, national highways and canals, the general Post Office, Indian affairs, and patents. Apparently, he was more concerned with the disposition of these major executive responsibilities than with the host of domestic functions that burdened the Department of State, except for the time-consuming function of issuing patents, with which he personally had to wrestle when he was Secretary of State.

The Senate introduced a bill on January 6, 1817, to create a Home Department, headed by a Secretary, specifically to deal with correspondence and communications with the Governors of the States and territorial offices of the United States, trade and treaties with Indian nations, the Post Office, the District of Columbia, and patents. It also suggested that the Chief Clerk of the State Department be replaced by an Under Secretary to have charge of all departmental "records, books, and papers." But again this idea of establishing a separate Home Department was rejected.

When, in the early 1820s, Congress sought to restrain the increased cost of the Department, which had doubled in two decades, Secretary Adams responded that its domestic workload had increased its servicing correspondence from sixteen to twenty-four American States, that the handling of congressional documents and responding to requests from Congress for information had risen fivefold, and that the basic task of hand-copying documents was becoming an egregious burden. He concluded that the Department needed more, rather than fewer, clerks to fulfill its responsibilities.

Given the reluctant attitude of Congress and to systematize the operation of the Department and render it more efficient, Secretary Adams instituted its first administrative reorganization. He was motivated by the issuance of an executive order of 1818 that fixed the duties and compensation of departmental clerks and required that the Secretary's directives be implemented through the Chief Clerk. Daniel Brent, appointed to this office in 1817, was made responsible for superintending and monitoring all activities within the Department and for assisting the Secretary in preparing certain important classes of correspondence.

At the time, the departmental clerks included John B. Colvin, Richard Forrest, Josias W. King, Andrew McCormick, John H. Purviance, Dr. William Thornton, Thomas L. Thurston, Moses Young, a Mr. Bailey, and others. Adams assigned each of them specific duties. For example, under this reorganization Bailey handled consular correspondence, a record of domestic and foreign correspondence other than that pertaining to diplomatic affairs, and an account of departmental appropriations. Colvin prepared congressional acts for publication, executive pardons, and emissions of fines, and he performed other domestic duties. Forrest was made responsible for personal passports and exequaturs for foreign consuls in the United States. King had the task of preparing and registering commissions and letters of credence and was in charge of books and papers. McCormick and Young serviced the archives and files. Dr. Thornton continued in charge of patents. Clerks also were assigned such functions as translation, copying, recording in registers, and forwarding documents to diplomatic envoys, the President, and Congress.[12]

Reminiscent of earlier practice respecting the use of presidential special envoys to negotiate treaties, Secretary Adams also regularized the issuance of directions to resident diplomats abroad by providing each of them with two sets of instructions. The first type, general in nature, dealt with diplomatic procedure and deportment, relations with American consuls located within their foreign jurisdictions, duties pertaining to the issuance of American passports abroad, international proprieties governing the use of the *alternat* in signing treaties, and American rules pertaining to the acceptance of gifts from foreign governments and leaders. The second instruction was individualized and specified the goals, objectives, policies, and procedures for dealing with the government to which each emissary was accredited.

Less than a year after he became Secretary of State, in response to a House of Representatives select committee's circular message addressed to each of the four Executive Departments, requesting a report on the needs for staffing to fulfill departmental responsibilities, Secretary Clay petitioned the Ways and Means Committee of the House of Representatives for additional staff to handle the burgeoning work of the Department. The congressional overture raised two issues: whether the departmental service suffered "for want of suitable means and provision" for effective performance and "what evils are experienced in the despatch of official business" of the Department. In his report Clay emphasized both the quantity and incongruity of the Department's foreign and domestic functions, which, "without having the smallest connexion with each other," are "indiscriminately blended together." He also noted that within recent years the number of American diplomatic missions had doubled and consular agents had multiplied, and he reiterated that many functions were extraneous to those of the Department and ought to be committed to a Home Department.

Specifically, in his response of February 16, 1826, Clay reviewed fifteen types of departmental duties, grouped in two categories. The first, consisting of eight foreign relations functions, included:

1. Correspondence with fourteen American Ministers . . . in foreign countries, four Consuls to the Barbary Powers, charged also with Diplomatic Duties, two Agents of Claims in Paris, and London, and 110 Consuls abroad and including numerous translations; and likewise an extensive correspondence concerning claims of Citizens of United States on foreign Governments.

2. Correspondence, occasional treating and frequent official interviews on business with Foreign Ministers accredited by this Government, whose number varies from ten to fourteen; and also, correspondence with Foreign Consuls admitted in our Ports, whose Governments have no diplomatic representative.

3. The issuing and distributing to applicants personal passports, and the preparation and distribution of Sea-Letters and Mediterranean Passports.

4. A compilation from official returns of lists of Passengers arriving in the United States and of registered Seamen and of Commercial information.

5. The custody of the great seal and recording of all the Commissions to American Ministers and Consuls and of foreign Consuls residing in the United States and the making out and recording of their Exequaturs.

6. Examination and liquidation of accounts for foreign and other services under this Department, in order to handle their payment here or passage through the Offices of the Treasury and the application and disbursement of the fund for the relief and protection of distressed American Seamen.

7. Custody and care of the Books and Papers belonging to various Commissions, which are now dissolved, under different treaties . . . and making Extracts from some of those papers, on the application of Individuals.

8. Reports to Congress, and complying with calls for information, and other orders of the Senate and House of Representatives.

Some of the domestic functions of the Department, he added, embraced:

9. Correspondence with Governors of States and of Territories, with Federal Officers, Marshalls, and United States District Attornies.

10. The preservation of the rolls of Congress, the recording of the laws, the direction of the printing and distribution of them, and of Public Documents and the designation of and corresponding with, the printers of the laws.

11. Patent Office, and the reception and preservaton of books &c published in the United States, and giving necessary Certificates to procure the Copyrights.

12. Making out and recording all Commissions which do not pass through and belong particularly to the other Departments and compiling &c of the biennial Register of Officers &c, &c.

13. Issuing certificates under the official Seal of the Department for purposes of authentication of records, papers and documents and making out and recording of pardons, remissions of fines and penalties.

14. Care of the original manuscript Journal books, documents and papers belonging to the Congress of the Confederation, and of the Declaration of Independence, the Constitution of the United States and the Journal and Proceedings of the Convention.

15. The periodical superintendence of taking the Census and other matters of statistical information, connected with it, and making a Digest thereof.

Commenting on this matter, Clay observed that under the existing arrangement ''too many and too incompatible duties devolve upon the Department'' and that in no other Department was the Secretary personally saddled with so great a ''total quantity'' of functions. The obvious remedy, he concluded, was that the last seven of his items should be transferred to a Home Department and that, if this was not done, then Congress should increase the staff of the Department.[13] Although no immediate action was taken to relieve the Department of its domestic functions, in the course of time most of them were eventually ascribed to other agencies of the government.

DIPLOMATIC AND CONSULAR REPRESENTATION

As U.S. foreign relations and interests grew, the Department of State expanded American diplomatic and consular representation. By 1830 diplomats were accredited to fifteen European and Latin American countries. The consular service was more widespread, including not only Europe, Latin America, and the Mediterranean but also the Pacific and even the Orient and southern Africa. Whereas the United States continued its practice of not appointing Ambassadors and previously ranked its diplomats as Ministers Plenipotentiary, Ministers Resident, Chargés d'Affaires, and Commissioners, the new title Envoy Extraordinary and Minister Plenipotentiary was introduced. Most diplomats were resident emissaries, but Presidents and Secretaries of State continued to accredit special diplomatic missions and envoys for particular purposes, such as major treaty negotiations.

Diplomatic Corps

At the time of transition, President Jefferson and Secretary of State Madison inherited five Ministers, all appointed in 1796 and 1797, who continued in their assignments for a short time. These included Rufus King (Great Britain), William L. Smith (Portugal), and veterans John Quincy Adams (Prussia), David Humphries (Spain), and William Vans Murray (the Netherlands). During the first three decades of the nineteenth century, the Presidents made sixty-two new diplomatic appointments, of which twelve did not serve for various reasons.[14] These new commissions went to fifty-two persons, of whom ten received multiple appointments.[15] This practice denoted a tendency to introduce some continuity of ranking diplomatic personnel, which, in a few cases, approached the creation of an element of professionalism.[16] These emissaries, who came from sixteen American States and the District of Columbia,[17] were accredited to eight European countries, seven Latin American nations, and the Hawaiian Islands.[18] (see Table 3.2).

Due to the nomination of presidential candidates when the Senate was not in session; transition between presidential administrations; delay between executive nomination, Senate approval, and presentation of diplomatic credentials; Senate rejection of a few nominations; procrastination of foreign governments in scheduling reception by the receiving chief of state; and slowness of communications and travel in those days, sometimes months transpired between presidential nomination and commencement of the service of the diplomat abroad. This time lag ranged from two to three months to twelve to sixteen months and even to more than two years.[19] Similarly, the hiatus during which the United States was unrepresented in foreign capitals varied substantially, from immediate succession, as when Robert R. Livingston presented his recall to the French government on November 18, 1804, and his successor, John Armstrong, presented his credentials the same day, to three years in American relations with Great Britain during the War of 1812 and to nearly twelve years in American relations with Spain.[20]

Not surprisingly, the duration of service in individual appointments also fluctuated considerably, from a few months to more than ten years. Eight American envoys served for less than a year,[21] whereas seven held individual appointments for more than five years, and Henry Middleton was stationed in Russia for more than nine years.[22] Nearly half, however, held their assignments for two to six years.

Diplomatic service in specific posts was terminated for a variety of reasons. Aside from the outbreak of war with Great Britain, these included change in presidential administrations, the death of the emissary, the decision to transfer an envoy from one post to another, or, in exceptional cases, recall when the

Table 3.2
American Diplomats, 1801–1829

Country Name	Residence	Title	Appointment	Presentation of Credentials
Argentina				
Caesar R. Rodney	Del.	MP	Jan. 27, 1823	Dec. 27, 1823
John M. Forbes	Mass.	CdA	Mar. 9, 1825	Aug. 20, 1825
Brazil				
Condy Raguet	Pa.	CdA	Mar. 9, 1825	Oct. 29, 1825
William Tudor	Mass.	CdA	June 26, 1827	June 25, 1828
Chile				
Heman Allen	Vt.	MP	Jan. 27, 1823	Apr. 23, 1824
Samuel Larned	R.I.	CdA	Feb. 29, 1828	Nov. 9, 1828
Colombia				
Richard C. Anderson	Ky.	MP	Jan. 27, 1823	Dec. 16, 1823
Beaufort T. Watts	S.C.	CdA	Mar. 3, 1827	[1]
William H. Harrison	Ohio	EE/MP	May 24, 1828	Feb. 5-13, 1829
Thomas P. Moore	Ky.	EE/MP	Mar. 13, 1829	Sept. 26, 1829
Denmark				
Henry Wheaton	N.Y.	CdA	Mar. 3, 1827	Sept. 20, 1827
France				
Robert R. Livingston	N.Y.	MP	Oct. 2, 1801	Dec. 6, 1801
John Armstrong	N.Y.	MP	June 30, 1804	Nov. 18, 1804
Jonathan Russell	R.I.	CdA	Nov. 5, 1810	[2]
Joel Barlow	D.C.	MP	Feb. 27, 1811	Nov. 17, 1811
William H. Crawford	Ga.	MP	Apr. 9, 1813	Dec. 14, 1813
Albert Gallatin	Pa.	EE/MP	Feb. 28, 1815	July 16, 1816
James Brown	La.	EE/MP	Dec. 9, 1823	Apr. 13, 1824
Great Britain				
James Monroe	Va.	MP	Apr. 18, 1803	Aug. 17, 1803
William Pinkney	Md.	MP	Feb. 26, 1808	Apr. 27, 1808
Jonathan Russell	R.I.	CdA	July 27, 1811	Nov. 15, 1811
John Quincy Adams	Mass.	EE/MP	Feb. 28, 1815	June 8, 1815
Richard Rush	Pa.	EE/MP	Dec. 16, 1817	Feb. 12, 1818
Rufus King	N.Y.	EE/MP	May 5, 1825	Nov. 11, 1825
Albert Gallatin	Pa.	EE/MP	May 10, 1826	Sept. 1, 1826
James Barbour	Va.	EE/MP	May 23, 1828	Nov. 24, 1828
Guatemala[3]				
William Miller	N.C.	CdA	Mar. 7, 1825	Died en route
John Williams	Tenn.	CdA	Dec. 29, 1825	May 3, 1826
William B. Rochester	N.Y.	CdA	Mar. 3, 1827	Not present credentials
John Hamm	Ohio	CdA		Nomination withdrawn
Mexico				
Andrew Jackson	Tenn.	EE/MP	Jan. 27, 1823	Declined appointment
Ninian Edwards	Ill.	EE/MP	Mar. 4, 1824	Not proceed to post
Joel R. Poinsett	S.C.	EE/MP	Mar. 8, 1825	June 1, 1825
Netherlands				
William Eustis	Mass.	EE/MP	Dec. 19, 1814	July 20, 1815
Alexander H. Everett	Mass.	CdA	June 27, 1818	Jan. 4, 1819
Christopher Hughes	Md.	CdA	Mar. 9, 1825	July 10, 1826

Country Name	Residence	Title	Appointment	Presentation of Credentials
Peru				
John B. Prevost	N.Y.	CdA		Not commissioned
James Cooley	Ohio	CdA	May 2, 1826	May 21, 1827
Samuel Larned	R.I.	CdA	Dec. 29, 1828	Nov. 30, 1829 [4]
Emanuel J. West		CdA	Oct. 22, 1829	Died en route
Samuel Larned	R.I.	CdA	May 15, 1830	Not reaccredited [4]
Portugal				
Thomas Sumpter, Jr.	S.C.	MP	Mar. 7, 1809	June 7, 1810 [5]
John Graham		MP	Jan. 6, 1819	July 24, 1819 [5]
John James Appleton	Mass.	CdA		Not commissioned
Henry Dearborn, Sr.	Mass.	EE/MP	Mar. 9, 1822	Not known
Thomas L. L. Brent	Va.	CdA	Mar. 9, 1825	June 24, 1825
Russia				
William Short	Va.	MP	Sept. 8, 1808	Not proceed to post
John Quincy Adams	Mass.	MP	June 27, 1809 [6]	Nov. 5, 1809
James A. Bayard	Del.	EE/MP	Feb. 28, 1815	Not proceed to post
William Pinkney	Md.	EE/MP	Mar. 7, 1816	Jan. 13, 1817
George Washington Campbell	Tenn.	EE/MP	Apr. 16, 1818	Feb. 7, 1819
Henry Middleton	S.C.	EE/MP	Apr. 6, 1820	June 17, 1821
Spain				
Charles Pinckney	S.C.	MP	June 6, 1801	Jan.-Mar., 1802
James Bowdoin III	Mass.	MP	Nov. 22, 1804	Not proceed to post
George W. Erving	Mass.	MP	Aug. 10, 1814	Aug. 24, 1816
John Forsyth	Ga.	MP	Feb. 16, 1819	May 18, 1819
Hugh Nelson	Va.	MP	Jan. 15, 1823	Dec. 4, 1823
Alexander H. Everett	Mass.	EE/MP	Mar. 9, 1825	Sept. 4, 1825
Sweden				
Jonathan Russell	R.I.	MP	Jan. 18, 1814	Apr. 29, 1814
Christopher Hughes, Jr.	Md.	CdA	Jan. 21, 1819	Not known
William C. Somerville	Va.	CdA	Mar. 9, 1825	Not proceed to post
John James Appleton	Mass.	CdA	May 2, 1826	Oct. 28, 1826

Symbols: EE/MP (Envoy Extraordinary/Minister Plenipotentiary); MP (Minister Plenipotentiary); CdA (Chargé d'Affaires).

[1] Watts had been serving in Bogotá as Chargé d'Affaires ad interim since June 1826.

[2] Russell, commissioned in February 1811, was not issued a letter of credence but was then serving as Chargé d'Affaires ad interim in Paris.

[3] Technically, Miller was commissioned to the Central Republic of America, Williams to the Federation of the Center of America, and Rochester and Hamm to the Republic of Central America. Hawaii is not included: prior to 1853 the United States was represented by Commissioners to the Sandwich Islands, without the status of a diplomatic legation.

[4] Larned served as Chargé d'Affaires in Peru till 1829, and when West died en route to his assignment, Larned remained, was recommissioned in 1830, and served without interruption.

[5] Sumpter and Graham served at the Court of Portugal in Rio de Janeiro, 1810 to 1820, after it fled from Lisbon to Brazil, before U.S. representation to Argentina commenced.

[6] Adams was nominated March 6, 1809, which was rejected by the Senate; the nomination of June 26, 1809, was confirmed, and he was appointed the following day.

diplomat was declared to be persona non grata or when it was determined by the President or Secretary of State that representation in a given country was not needed. To summarize, official Department of State designation of the termination of diplomatic missions reveals that, in addition to the suspension of duties of Jonathan Russell in London in July 1812 following the declaration of war and five envoys who died at their posts and one whose recall was requested by the country to which he was accredited,[23] a dozen are listed as formally "presented recall" by the United States and a majority as "left posts," "had farewell audience," "was superseded," and similar general explanations.

This early experience evidences some of the special problems, developments, and techniques concerning transition from administration to administration and maintaining continuity of foreign representation. For example, although diplomats were not automatically replaced immediately when a new President was inaugurated, all of the Ministers inherited by President Jefferson in 1801 presented their recalls later that year, except for Rufus King, then Minister Plenipotentiary to Great Britain.[24] The United States seemed to have particular difficulty inaugurating dependable diplomatic relations with some of the new Latin American governments when they gained their independence, especially Guatemala, Mexico, and Peru.[25]

One of the strangest experiences involved continuity of diplomatic relations with Portugal. For a decade, from 1810 to 1820, U.S. representation to its government was handled not in Lisbon but in Rio de Janeiro, because the Portuguese royal family had fled to Argentina when Portugal was threatened by Napoleon's armies. Subsequently, beginning in 1823, the United States accredited its envoys Thomas Sumpter and John Graham to the Argentinian government.

As in the Federalist period, the lack of a systematic policy and method of staffing American diplomatic positions abroad and the lack of interchanging individuals between the Department of State in Washington and the diplomatic service—except for Robert R. Livingston, who served as Secretary for Foreign Affairs under the Continental Congress and later was appointed Minister Plenipotentiary to France; John Quincy Adams and James Monroe, who held diplomatic appointments and subsequently were appointed Secretary of State; and John Graham, who, following long service as Chief Clerk, was appointed Minister Plenipotentiary to Portugal—evidenced the continued nonprofessional nature of the American diplomatic corps. At the time, however, this was generally regarded as a virtue, rather than an impediment, in promoting the American democratic spirit and character.

Diplomatic Mission Secretaries

The early staffing of American diplomatic missions abroad was managed by Congress through the appropriations process. An act of July 1, 1790, which provided funding for diplomatic representation to foreign governments, authorized the appointment of Secretaries of Legation who were not exempt from

Senatorial confirmation. Presidents Washington and John Adams made no such appointments but permitted some American diplomats to engage private secretaries at government expense, who assumed the title and role of Secretaries of Legation.

Under Article 2, section 2, clause 2, of the Constitution, the President, with the advice and consent of the Senate, is empowered to appoint not only diplomats and consuls but also "all other Officers of the United States, whose Appointments are not herein otherwise provided for, and which shall be established by Law." Technically, Secretaries of Legation were appointable subject to Senate confirmation. When Jefferson became President, he nominated two such Secretaries and requested Senate approval, which initiated a precedent for future action, and Congress formally required this by an act passed on May 1, 1810.

Like others, such appointments were controlled by Congress through its budgetary legislation. Initially, it enacted lump-sum appropriations for foreign missions, including the use of Legation Secretaries, but in 1818 it introduced the method of specifying amounts for each foreign mission, and later, in 1831, it refined its appropriations procedure more narrowly by itemizing the funding of each diplomatic position. Thus, Congress maintained financial control over both existing and new members of all American foreign missions.

Change in Diplomatic Ranking and Titles

As indicated in Table 3.2, of American Diplomats, thirty-eight nominations were at the rank of Minister, of which nineteen were Ministers Plenipotentiary, and nineteen were designated as Envoys Extraordinary and Ministers Plenipotentiary. Some twenty-four were Chargés d'Affaires, and one, representing the United States in Hawaii (not included in the table), was simply designated as a Commissioner. During the early decades of the nineteenth century, significant changes were made in the ranking of American diplomats, including the raising of their status in some countries and virtually eliminating the appointment of Ministers Resident between the 1820s and the 1850s.

The rank of Envoys Extraordinary, a new title, was employed, beginning in 1814 and 1815,[26] largely for appointees to major European countries—France, Great Britain, Russia, and Spain—but also, temporarily, for accreditation to Colombia and Mexico.[27] On the other hand, prior to creating this new rank, Ministers Plenipotentiary were appointed to nine countries, especially France and Spain. The lesser rank of Chargé d'Affaires was ascribed for long periods to envoys appointed to Chile, Colombia, Denmark, Guatemala, Peru, and Sweden. For some countries, with which the United States subsequently initiated diplomatic relations, such as China (1844–58), Liberia (1863–66), and the Hawaiian Islands (1853–63), American envoys were designated as Commissioners, without the benefit of legation status.

When the United States commenced to employ this new rank of Envoy Extraordinary and Minister Plenipotentiary, it discontinued appointing Ministers

Resident and Ministers Plenipotentiary for half a century, until the mid-1850s,[28] except for Turkey.[29] It returned to using the Minister Resident rank in the 1880s and early 1890s[30] but continued to use the title Envoy Extraordinary and Minister Plenipotentiary for emissaries to major European powers and a few Latin American and other countries.[31]

Contemplating the reasons for this elevation to the rank of Envoy Extraordinary and Minister Plenipotentiary, it may be pointed out that following the War of 1812 and the Napoleonic War in Europe, the United States decided to raise the international status of its diplomatic emissaries, short of appointing Ambassadors. Second, a number of the appointees to this superior rank were acknowledged and, in some cases, distinguished statesmen who had previous diplomatic experience, such as John Quincy Adams, James A. Bayard, Albert Gallatin, Rufus King, William Pinkney, and Richard Rush.

Finally, perhaps most crucially, it is conceivable that when the United States acquired the Louisiana and Florida territories and became a continental power and following the promulgation of the Monroe Doctrine, its international status was enhanced. Paralleling this development, the signing of the historic Diplomatic Convention by Austria, France, Great Britain, Portugal, Prussia, Russia, Spain, Sweden, and the Papacy at the Congress of Vienna in 1815 systematized two important aspects of subsequent diplomacy. It both addressed the matter of the acceptability of individual diplomatic officers to receiving governments and prescribed their international ranking, precedence, and treatment.

On the matter of acceptability of envoys, the Convention required that, by the process of "*agreation*," the sending government obtain advance approval of its proposed emissary at a specified rank, which, in international parlance, is known as "*agrement*."[32] It appears, however, that the United States, not a signatory of the convention, which did not commit itself to this procedure until it began to appoint Ambassadors in 1893,[33] in order to observe the traditional proprieties of diplomatic representation, found it prudent, if not necessary, in dealing with foreign governments to act cooperatively on the matter of commissioning acceptable individuals at mutually agreeable ranks. Inasmuch as this is a reciprocal process in the management of diplomatic relations, therefore, diplomats above the rank of Chargés d'Affaires, who sometimes are interim appointees, were exchanged at the same rank, so that, in effect, foreign governments could influence the raising of diplomatic exchanges with the United States.

So far as stabilizing the titles, rank, and precedence of diplomats is concerned, the Vienna Convention, as amplified at the Congress of Aix-la-Chapelle in 1818, adopted a system of determining the status of diplomats in a national capital founded on titular rank and seniority of service rather than on the previous basis of the relative political preeminence of their countries and the importance of their sovereigns, the duration of their independent status, or their international power status.

According to the Vienna and Aix-la-Chapelle Conventions, diplomats were ranked in four categories, in the following sequence:

1. Ambassadors Extraordinary and Plenipotentiary, and Papal Legates or Nuncios.
2. Envoys Extraordinary and Ministers Plenipotentiary, and Papal Internuncios.
3. Ministers Resident (added at Aix-la-Chapelle).
4. Chargés d'Affaires and Chargés d'Affaires ad interim.

Within these categories precedence is simply based on individual seniority (or longevity) in a particular rank at a given capital. Ambassadors and Ministers are accredited to the receiving Chief of State, whereas Chargés d'Affaires are accredited to Foreign Ministers, or, in the United States, to the Secretary of State.[34]

Special Diplomatic Missions

Presidential special envoys were appointed for two types of missions, as preliminary agents prior to the establishment of formal diplomatic relations with certain countries and as representatives of the United States in the negotiation of a number of treaties. Prior to the recognition of the independence of the Latin American Republics, such special envoys were sent to obtain information on their independence movements and on the possibility of establishing trade with them. In 1810 President Madison commissioned Joel R. Poinsett to South America, who concluded a commercial arrangement with the revolutionary regime of Buenos Aires the following year. He also visited Chile, and other special agents were sent to Cuba, Mexico, and Venezuela. More formal missions, for information gathering and liaison purposes, were undertaken by Theodorick Bland, John Graham, John B. Prevost, and Caesar A. Rodney, three of whom were later accredited formally to Latin American countries.[35]

Such special emissaries also played a major role in initiating diplomatic relations with the revolutionary regimes of Latin America. By 1821 the United Provinces of La Plata (Argentina), Greater Colombia (Colombia and Venezuela), Chile, Mexico, and Central America achieved their independence from Spain, and the following year Brazil separated from Portugal. The United States was the first outside country to formally recognize these new Western Hemisphere nations,[36] and thereafter the special agents were superseded by regular diplomatic envoys, who were appointed to seven Latin American governments between 1823 and 1826.

As was the case during the Confederation and Federalist periods, Presidents also appointed special missions to negotiate treaties and for other purposes. To negotiate the Louisiana Purchase Treaty with France (1803), President Jefferson commissioned a delegation consisting of his Ministers to France and Great Britain. During the War of 1812, President Madison appointed an able team of five, who negotiated and signed the Peace Treaty in 1814. The following year another special commission, again consisting of Adams, Clay, and Gallatin, concluded a Commerce and Navigation Treaty with Great Britain, and three years later Richard Rush (Minister to London) and Gallatin (Minister to Paris) were recruited to conclude a Fisheries and Boundary Treaty, also with Great Britain. Two other treaties, signed with Algiers in 1815 and 1816, including a Peace Treaty ending the naval war with that Barbary power, were negotiated by special teams of two representatives, consisting of a consular official and a naval officer. Other treaties with European governments were negotiated by resident American diplomats, except for those concluded by the Secretary of State in Washington.

Introducing a new feature in American diplomatic practice, after several Latin American countries gained their independence, and President Monroe proclaimed his Doctrine, in 1825 the United States was invited by Simón Bolívar, the Latin American Liberator, to attend its first regional international conference, convened at Panama, to establish a Pan-American alliance and confederation. President Adams and Secretary Clay were anxious to commission delegates to represent U.S. interests. However, a substantial segment of the people and members of the Senate opposed involvement. The President, insisting on participation, persuaded the Senate to confirm his nomination of two Commissioners, and the House of Representatives voted to appropriate the necessary funds. This was the first U.S. attempt to attend such a multipartite congress, which proved to be the forerunner of the inter-American organization and other multipartite international agencies.[37]

Remarkable Foreign Relations Team

As a group this diplomatic corps of the early nineteenth century embraced a distinguished group of statesmen. Livingston had previously been Secretary for Foreign Affairs, and Adams, Rufus King, William Pinkney, and William Short had previous diplomatic experience. Five were later appointed to additional diplomatic assignments.[38] Three subsequently became Secretary of State—Monroe (1811), Adams (1817), and John Forsyth (1834), and several were later elected President—Madison (1809), Monroe (1817), Adams (1825), and William Henry Harrison (1841). Ten of these diplomats held other Cabinet posts, two as Secretary of the Treasury, six as Secretary of War, and several as Attorney General.[39] More than a dozen concluded and signed treaties for the United States.[40]

This constitutes a remarkable cumulative record of a corps of statesmen engaged in the cause of American diplomacy. History can scarcely forget the names and achievements of John Quincy Adams, Albert Gallatin, Robert R. Livingston, and James Monroe. Though amateurs at the outset, except for Adams, they emerged as gifted envoys. Of these, diplomatic historian Thomas A. Bailey acknowledges the good fortune of Livingston as being at the right place at the right time to purchase the Louisiana Territory, commends Adams as an able emissary and ranks him among the great Secretaries of State, and enshrines Galatin in his "nucleus of an American Diplomatic Hall of Fame." In his history of the Department of State, Graham Stuart concludes that Adams was The "Department's Greatest Secretary."

During the Federalist period, President Washington, three of the four Secretaries of State, and two of the ranking diplomats were from Virginia, of whom William Short was appointed to both France and the Netherlands. Similarly, during the first three decades of the nineteenth century, whereas the first three of four Presidents and two of five Secretaries came from Virginia, only six of some sixty diplomatic nominations were from that State. This marked the end of what some have called the "Virginia dynasty" in dominating the management and conduct of American foreign relations.

Consular Affairs

The consular service grew both quantitatively and geographically, but progress in the administration of its functions and operations was slow to develop. The organic law of 1792 was augmented by the acts of 1803, 1818, and 1823. These enlarged the responsibilities of consular officers, especially with respect to maintaining lists of ships' masters and crews; assisting in handling ships' papers, including sea letters and ships' passports; certifying invoices for goods exported from abroad to the United States that were subject to American duties, and stipulating the value of such goods; and providing protection and assistance to American seamen who were stranded or destitute abroad and facilitating their return to the United States. Consular officers also were rendered subject to penalties for issuing false certificates and personal passports.

The Department of State reports that the number of consular posts more than doubled from fifty-two in 1800 to some 140 by 1830. Most of these were in Europe, including the eight countries with which the United States had formal diplomatic relations, as well as with northern Germany and Italy. They also were commissioned to the Barbary powers after commercial treaties were concluded with them, to the newly independent Latin American countries, and to the Caribbean island possessions of France, Great Britain, the Netherlands, and Spain. A few also were located in the Pacific area, the Orient, and Africa.[41]

Most consular officers were Americans, some held their posts for extended periods, and a few consular establishments remained in a single family, as long as seventy years. Most individuals held a single post where they were also engaged in business, but others were given successive appointments.[42] Although the practice was uncommon, occasionally, they bridged from consular to diplomatic assignments as Chargés d'Affaires.[43] Like Joel Barlow, James L. Cathcart, Joseph Donaldson, and William Eaton, who had previously concluded treaties with Algiers, Tripoli, and Tunis, several consular officers of the early nineteenth century are also remembered for negotiating and signing treaties with the Barbary powers. These include William Shaler (Consul General at Algiers—

two treaties with Algiers) and Tobias Lear (also Consul General at Algiers—a Peace and Amity Treaty with Tripoli).

Assessing consular developments during these years, historians William Barnes and John Heath Morgan have written:

The pattern of the Consular Service that emerges in this early period is one of steady growth in geographic coverage, centering on Western Europe; predominantly American personnel; frequent cases of long tenure in a single post coupled with a few instances of service in more than one post; and occasional transfers of officers from the Consular to the Diplomatic Service. Consular duties formed an adjunct to the officers' business and commercial activities and were carried on with a minimum of guidance and supervision from the Department of State. Fee collections had not yet increased to the level where consular posts at important commercial centers became prizes to be eagerly sought after by partisans of the political party in power at home—a fact which helps to explain the relatively long tenure that consuls enjoyed in this period.[44]

TREATY MAKING

The essentials of American treaty making, founded during the Federalist period, remained largely unchanged. The President and Congress determined foreign policy, treaties and agreements were negotiated and signed under presidential authority, negotiating instructions were generally devised and transmitted by the Secretary of State, with the assistance of his departmental staff, to guide American negotiators, either resident emissaries or those on special missions. Most treaties and agreements were concluded abroad, but some were signed in Washington by the Secretary of State. Treaties were ratified by the President, with the advice and consent of the Senate. The major innovations were the conclusion of three executive agreements, one of which was America's first multipartite convention, and the signing of several treaties and agreements in the nation's capital.

Treaty Record

The Department of State continued to expand the American treaty relationship with foreign governments in both quantity and kind and in geographic distribution. During this period it concluded thirty-one treaties and agreements at an accelerating rate, with six signed in the 1880s, eight in the 1810s, and seventeen, or more than half, in the 1820s. All but three were formal treaties. The exceptions—executive agreements—included an exchange of diplomatic notes with Great Britain in 1817, called the Rush–Bagot Agreement, to mutually limit naval forces on the Great Lakes[45]; a short agreement with Hawaii called "Articles of Arrangement," concluded in 1826; and a multipartite declaration, called a "Presidential Agreement," signed in Algiers also in 1826. See Table 3.3 for a list of treaties and agreements.

Table 3.3
Treaties and Agreements, 1801–1829

Country	Title	T or A [a]	Where Signed	Date signed	Date Ratified	Date in Effect	Signers for United States	Citation Bevans [b]
				Bipartite				
Algiers	Peace Treaty	T	Algiers	June 30, 1815	Dec. 26, 1815	Dec. 26, 1815[1]	William Shaler Stephen Decatur	5:45-50
	Peace and Amity	T	Algiers	Dec. 22 and 23, 1816	Feb. 11, 1822	Feb. 11, 1822[2]	William Shaler I. Chauncey	5:51-57
Brazil	Peace, Friendship, Commerce, and Navigation	T	Rio de Janeiro	Dec. 12, 1828	Mar. 17, 1829	Mar. 18, 1829[3]	William Tudor	5:792-803
Central American Federation	Peace, Amity, Commerce, and Navigation	T	Washington	Dec. 5, 1825	Jan. 16, 1826	Aug. 2, 1826[4]	Henry Clay	6:503-14
Denmark	Friendship, Commerce, and Navigation	T	Washington	Apr. 12, 1826	May 6, 1826	Aug. 10, 1826[5]	Henry Clay	7:1-6
France	Cession of Louisiana	T	Paris	Apr. 30, 1803	Oct. 21, 1803	Oct. 21, 1803*	Robert R. Livingston James Monroe	7:812-15
	Cession of Louisiana (Financial Arrangement)	T	Paris	Apr. 30, 1803	Oct. 21, 1803	Oct. 21, 1803*	Robert R. Livingston James Monroe	7:816-17
	Claims	T	Paris	Apr. 30, 1803	Oct. 21, 1803	Oct. 21, 1803*	Robert R. Livingston James Monroe	7:818-21
	Navigation and Commerce	T	Washington	June 24, 1822	Feb. 12, 1823	Feb. 12, 1823	John Quincy Adams	7:822-25
Great Britain	Claims	T	London	Jan. 8, 1802	Apr. 27, 1802	July 15, 1802*	Rufus King	12:38-40
	Peace and Amity	T	Ghent	Dec. 24, 1814	Feb. 17, 1815	Feb. 17, 1815	John Quincy Adams James A. Bayard Henry Clay Albert Gallatin Jonathan Russell	12:41-48
	Commerce and Navigation	T	London	July 3, 1815	Dec. 21, 1815	July 3, 1815[6]	John Quincy Adams Henry Clay Albert Gallatin	12:49-53

Country	Title	T or A[a]	Where Signed	Date signed	Date Ratified	Date in Effect	Signers for United States	Citation Bevans[b]
Great Britain (cont.)	Naval Forces on Great Lakes	A	Washington	Apr. 28/29, 1817		Apr. 29, 1817[7]	Richard Rush	12:54-56
	Fisheries, Boundary, and Restoration of Slaves	T	London	Oct. 20, 1818	Jan. 28, 1819	Jan. 30, 1819[8]	Albert Gallatin Richard Rush	12:57-60
	Claims	T	St. Petersburg	July 12, 1822	Jan. 9, 1823	Jan. 10, 1823[9]	Henry Middleton	12:61-70
	Claims	T	London	Nov. 13, 1826	Dec. 27, 1826	Feb. 6, 1827*	Albert Gallatin	12:71-73
	Boundaries	T	London	Aug. 6, 1827	Feb. 21, 1828	Mar. 2, 1828[10]	Albert Gallatin	12:74-75
	Commerce and Navigation	T	London	Aug. 6, 1827	Jan. 12, 1828	Mar. 2, 1828[11]	Albert Gallatin	12:76-77
	Arbitration of Boundary	T	London	Sept. 29, 1827	Feb. 12, 1828	Mar. 2, 1828[12]	Albert Gallatin	12:78-81
Hanseatic Republic	Friendship, Commerce, and Navigation	T	Washington	Dec. 20, 1827	Jan. 8, 1828	June 2, 1828*	Henry Clay	8:41-45
	Friendship, Commerce, and Navigation	T	Washington	June 4, 1828	(Date not given)	Jan. 14, 1829*	Henry Clay	8:46-47
Hawaiian Islands	Commerce	A	Honolulu	Dec. 23, 1826		Dec. 23, 1826[13]	Thomas Ap Cotesby Jones	8:861-63
Mexico	Boundaries	T	Mexico City	Jan. 12, 1828	Apr. 5, 1832	Apr. 5, 1832*	Joel R. Poinsett	9:760-63
Prussia (Germany)	Commerce and Navigation	T	Washington	May 1, 1828	Mar. 12, 1829	Mar. 14, 1829[14]	Henry Clay	8:98-104
Russia	Navigation and Fisheries on Northwest Coast	T	St. Petersburg	Apr. 17, 1824	Jan. 7, 1825	Feb. 11, 1825*	Henry Middleton	11:1205-07
Spain	Settlement of Claims	T	Madrid	Aug. 11, 1802	Jan. 9, 1804	Dec. 21, 1818[15]	Charles Pinckney	11:526-27
	Amity, Settlement, and Limits	T	Washington	Feb. 22, 1819	Feb. 20, 1821	Feb. 22, 1821[16]	John Quincy Adams	11:528-36
Sweden and Norway	Friendship and Commerce	T	Stockholm	Sept. 24, 1816	May 27, 1818	Sept. 25, 1818*	Jonathan Russell	11:868-75
	Commerce and Navigation	T	Stockholm	Sept. 4, 1827	Jan. 17, 1828	Jan. 17, 1828[17]	John J. Appleton	11:876-83

Country	Title	T or A [a]	Where Signed	Date signed	Date Ratified	Date in Effect	Signers for United States	Citation Bevans [b]
Tripoli								
	Peace and Amity	T	Tripoli	June 4, 1805	Apr. 17, 1806	Apr. 17, 1806[18]	Tobias Lear	11:1081-87
	Multipartite							
	Cemetery in Algiers	A	Algiers	Mar. 21, 1826[19]			William Shaler	1:1-2

[a]Three of these were executive agreements; all the rest were formal treaties.

[b]Citations are to Charles I. Bevans, *Treaties and Other International Agreements of the United States of America, 1776–1949*, 12 volumes, showing volume and page numbers.

*Indicates that it expired, was terminated on the fulfillment of its terms, or became obsolete.

[1]Renewed and modified by Treaty of 1816.

[2]Became obsolete in 1830, when Algiers became a province of France.

[3]Operative from date signed, December 12, 1828; articles relating to commerce and navigation terminated December 12, 1841.

[4]Federation terminated in 1847.

[5]Supplemented with an exchange of notes, signed in Washington, April 25 and 26, 1826. Abrogated in April 1856, renewed in part the following year, supplemented in 1861, modified in 1946, and replaced in 1951, so that in effect, in part, it endured for a century and a quarter.

[6]Although effective on date of signature, it was not ratified and proclaimed by the President until five months later. Extended for ten years by Convention of 1818, and indefinitely by Convention of 1827.

[7]Popularly known as the Rush–Bagot Agreement. Although, as an executive agreement, it became effective on mutual signature, President Monroe sent it to the Senate, which approved it on April 16, 1818, and the President proclaimed it on April 28. Richard Rush was the first Secretary of State ad interim to sign a treaty for the United States.

[8]Article 3 was continued in force by the Convention of 1827.

[9]Under mediation of the Russian Emperor, provided for indemnification under Article 1 of Peace Treaty of Ghent. Superseded by Convention of 1826.

[10]Extended Article 3 of Convention of 1818; superseded by treaty of 1846.

[11]Extended Convention of 1815.

[12]Terminated in January 1831, when King of the Netherlands rendered arbitral award.

[13]Not approved by Senate. Superseded by Treaty of Commerce and Navigation with Hawaii in 1849.

[14]Not revived after World War I.

[15]Annulled by Treaty of 1819.

[16]Popularly known as the Transcontinental or the Adams–Onis Treaty. Terminated by treaty of 1902 and therefore was effective for some eight decades.

[17]Terminated by the United States for Sweden in 1919 and for Norway in 1932. Thus, survived for nearly a century.

[18]Terminated in 1912, so that it endured for more than a century.

[19]Called a "presidential agreement," which was also signed by Denmark, Great Britain, the Netherlands, Portugal, Sardinia, Spain, Sweden, Tuscany, and the Two Sicilies, to build a fence around an international cemetery, where Americans and Europeans were buried.

As in the past, most of these treaties and agreements were concluded with European countries, the largest number with Great Britain (ten) and France (four), together accounting for nearly half of them, but also with Prussia and Spain and with such other countries as Denmark, the Hanseatic Republic, Russia, and Sweden. After several Latin American countries gained their independence from Spain and Portugal, the United States also signed treaties with Brazil, the Central American Federation, and Mexico. The only other bipartite treaty partners were Algiers and Tripoli, in North Africa, and Hawaii, the first Pacific nation to engage in treaty relations with the United States.

Whereas previously, the American treaties were primarily concerned with amity, friendship, commerce, navigation, and consular affairs, during this period other matters were also introduced. Aside from new commercial treaties and two peace treaties (with Great Britain following the War of 1812 and with Algiers to conclude the naval war to rid the Mediterranean of the Barbary pirates, signed, respectively, in 1814 and 1815), these treaties and agreements dealt with such subjects as the cession of territory to the United States by France and Spain; boundaries with Great Britain and Mexico; claims settlements with France, Great Britain, and Spain; and more specialized matters. The latter included naval disarmament on the Great Lakes (with Great Britain), fishing rights (with Great Britain and Russia), the submission of international disputes to arbitration (primarily with Great Britain but also with Spain); and a multipartite agreement providing for the maintenance of an international cemetery in Algiers.

Evidencing both the rising international status of the United States and its initiation of treaty negotiations, eight of these treaties and one executive agreement were signed in Washington by Secretaries Adams (two) and Clay (five) and acting Secretary of State Richard Rush (one). Other bipartite treaties were signed in the capitals of other signatories,[46] except for the Peace Treaty with Great Britain concluded at Ghent in 1814 and the Anglo-American-mediated Claims Convention of 1822 signed at St. Petersburg, Russia. Most of these treaties and agreements were signed by American emissaries resident in these foreign capitals.[47]

Major Treaties

Aside from promoting interest in general matters of amity, commerce, and navigation, among the most important treaties and agreements were those that provided peace settlements to end warfare with Great Britain and Algiers, the acquisition of the Louisiana and Florida territories, the fixing of boundaries, and disarmament of the Great Lakes.

During the War of 1812, the Russian Chancellor asked American Minister Plenipotentiary Adams whether an overture for mediation would be viewed favorably by the United States, and the Russian Emperor tendered a formal offer. President Madison accepted it in March 1813 and nominated Albert Gallatin, his Secretary of the Treasury, and James A. Bayard, former Minister designate to France, to join Adams as a triune negotiating commission. But the British rejected the offer. Early in September the Emperor reissued his proposal for mediation, and again the British declined, preferring direct negotiations with American commissioners. President Madison then recommissioned the three American envoys[48] and added Henry Clay (Speaker of the House of Representatives) and Jonathan Russell (former Chargé d'Affaires in London when the war broke out and subsequently Minister Plenipotentiary to Sweden). Samuel Flagg Bemis regards this as one of the ablest negotiating commissions ever appointed by the United States, which, together with President Madison and Secretary of State Monroe, represented the leading American statesmen at the time.

The peace commissioners did not meet at Ghent (Belgium), a neutral site, until August 1814, and they concluded the Peace Treaty some four months later, which was ratified and went into effect in mid-February 1815. This treaty was important not only because it ended the war with one of the great powers but also because it reconfirmed American independence, acknowledged American territory on the basis of the status quo ante bellum, dealt with future territorial issues by providing for peaceful arbitral settlement, and marked the end of the first "European phase" of American diplomacy.

Despite the early treaties with Morocco (1786), Algiers (1795), Tripoli (1796), and Tunis (1797), relations with the Barbary Powers festered for years, during which the United States made customary payments of tribute and suffered the challenge of piracy and the confiscation of ships and goods and the seizure of American merchant seamen. This matter came to a head in the early nineteenth century, when, in 1802, President Jefferson launched a naval attack on Tripoli, without a declaration of war, to defend the commercial rights and interests of the United States in the Mediterranean. The Treaty of Peace and Amity concluded with Tripoli in 1805 failed to end the depredations, which continued for another decade.

However, following the War of 1812, during which the United States strengthened its naval power, which was augmented by the naval forces of several European maritime states, on March 3, 1815, Congress declared war on Algiers and forced it to conclude a Peace Treaty. It was signed in June by William Shaler, American Consul General in Algiers, and Stephen Decatur, the Commander of the American naval forces in the Mediterranean. This action, supported by British and Dutch bombardment of Algiers, mitigated the Barbary piracy problem.

Two historic treaties concluded with France in 1803 and Spain in 1819 provided for the cession of the Louisiana and Florida territories. These acquisitions constituted the initial post-Revolutionary additions to the continental domain of the United States and initiated the American practice of expanding its North American territory, which continued until the Gadsden Territory was purchased from Mexico in 1853, and Alaska was acquired from Russia in 1867.

The Louisiana Territory—a huge expanse between the Mississippi River and the Rocky Mountains—belonged to Spain in the 1790s and was ceded to France by the Treaty of San Ildefonso in 1800. The United States had long been concerned with its freedom of shipping on the Mississippi River and was anxious to gain control over transit at its mouth at New Orleans. Developments in Europe and the Caribbean induced Napoleon to offer to sell the entire territory to the United States. President Jefferson rapidly appointed Robert R. Livingston, then Minister Plenipotentiary to France, and James Monroe, who was serving as Minister Plenipotentiary to Great Britain, to negotiate the purchase treaty. It was signed on April 30, 1803, and ratified in October, and the physical transfer of sovereignty was formally celebrated on December 20. The cession arrangement involved two treaties, signed and ratified at the same time, one for the cession and the second for the method of payment by the United States.

Thus, the United States, largely as a windfall of European politics and war, acquired what has been called "the greatest real estate bargain in history," for $15 million (60 million francs), of which $3,750,000 was to be paid by the United States to satisfy American claims against the French government. The major consequences of this treaty were that it doubled U.S. territory, extended it westward to the Rocky Mountains, brought the mighty Mississippi River basin under American jurisdiction, presaged additional continental territory purchases, and facilitated the laying of the territorial foundation for developing into a mighty world power.

Following a series of revolts by immigrants from the United States and an insurrection in the Baton Rouge district of Florida in 1810, Congress passed a resolution in January the following year declaring that the United States "cannot . . . see any part of the said territory pass into the hands of any foreign power" (a prelude to enunciating the Monroe Doctrine) and authorizing President Madison to take custody of East Florida if it was likely to be occupied by any foreign nation. Negotiations were launched in 1817 by Secretary of State Adams and Don Luis de Onis, the Spanish Minister accredited to Washington. With the assistance of the good officers of the French Minister in Washington, a Treaty of Amity, Settlement, and Limits was signed on February 22, 1819, known as the Transcontinental or the Adams–Onis Treaty. It provided for the cession by Spain of all of its North American territory east of the Mississippi River, and the United States agreed to provide $5 million for the payment of claims by Americans against the Spanish government. It was ratified two years later. Adams regarded this as a major coup, and it concluded a territorial issue that had plagued the United States for three decades.

In the 1820s the United States also extended its territorial interests in northwest North America. The Russian Czar issued an imperial edict in 1821, assuming jurisdiction over the coast, including trading and fishing, as far south as 51 degrees north latitude, which included Alaska and the coastal area south to Vancouver Island. Britain joined the United States in protesting this pretension, and Secretary Adams informed the Russian government that "the American Continents are no longer subjects for any new European colonial establishments''—also heralding the Monroe Doctrine. By Article 3 of the Treaty of 1824 Russia and the United States mutually agreed not to establish ''any settlements'' beyond ''fifty-four degrees and forty minutes of north latitude,'' which left Alaska with its extensive panhandle within Russian control, but protected United States interests against Russia in the Oregon Territory.

Subsequently, in March 1825, President Adams appointed Joel R. Poinsett as the first Envoy Extraordinary and Minister Plenipotentiary to Mexico, where he served for more than four years. Secretary Clay instructed him to offer a flexible scale of payment for additional territory to move the U.S. boundary as far west as possible. But the treaty that was signed with Mexico on January 12, 1828, merely reconfirmed the boundary established by the Transcontinental Treaty concluded with Spain in 1819.

In addition to systematizing treaty relations regarding amity and commerce with a dozen countries, negotiating peace treaties, providing for territorial expansion, and fixing boundaries, the United States and Great Britain concluded an executive agreement to provide for naval disarmament on the Great Lakes. Beginning in the 1790s, such leaders as John Jay and Alexander Hamilton were anxious to disarm the lakes and land frontier between British and American territory. By an exchange of notes in 1817, popularly known as the Rush–Bagot Agreement, signed by Acting Secretary of State Richard Rush and Charles Bagot, the British Minister in Washington, such disarmament was achieved for the Great Lakes. It specified that neither government would maintain any naval vessels on these lakes and Lake Champlain, except for small revenue cutters. Although President Madison submitted it to the Senate, which gave its approval, it went into effect on signature and did not require formal ratification. Under its terms either government was entitled to nullify it on six months' notice, but it has endured and has served as a pilot for subsequent boundary disarmament arrangements.

Peaceful Settlement of Disputes

A major innovation in American treaty policy and implementation during these early years of the nineteenth century was the introduction of commitments to settle international disputes peacefully by means of arbitration. The Founders of the American Government adopted this principle in both the Articles of Confederation and the Constitution for disputes between or among the American States, which set a precedent for incorporating it into international treaty practice.[49]

Aside from traditional negotiation, the basic processes for resolving disputes peacefully are known as good offices, mediation, conciliation, arbitration, and adjudication. Usually, commitments to resort to these measures are embodied in bilateral and multilateral treaties, which specify the method, procedure, and consequences of conflict management.[50]

Most frequently, such peaceful settlement arrangements are utilized for resolving territorial, boundary, and claims disputes, and the agency relied on may be a single impartial individual, a small commission, or, in more recent times, a preestablished court.

The earliest use of peaceful settlement in American affairs occurred in 1650, when a territorial settlement between Connecticut and the Province of New York (under Dutch rule) was submitted to the Colony of Massachusetts for settlement.[51] Early in the 1780s a territorial dispute between Connecticut and Pennsylvania over the Susquehanna River Valley was resolved by a unanimous determination in favor of Pennsylvania.[52]

To resolve disputes with foreign countries, the United States has pursued two avenues of amicable settlement—by agreeing with other governments in advance to settle them by utilizing peaceful processes and by actually applying them to concrete cases. Negotiations and the appointment of Commissioners to settle international differences by mutual accommodation and arbitration became a major goal and function of the Department of State. Despite the fact that, from the outset, it played a significant role in supplementing direct negotiations with such peaceful settlement processes, little literary attention has been paid to this early development, except in some studies of international law. Procedurally, agreement for peaceful settlement is normally embodied in formal treaties, which usually are called conventions.

The modern era of arbitral or judicial settlement of international disputes, it is universally conceded, began with the signing of the Jay Treaty with Great Britain in 1794. Articles 5, 6, and 7 of this historic treaty provided for the creation of three separate commissions to deal with the boundary delineation of the St. Croix River, which had been made a part of the northeastern boundary of the United States by the Peace Treaty of 1783, the debts owed by the United States to compensate the British for private damages sustained during the Revolutionary War, and satisfaction of spoliation claims of Americans for depredations against their shipping. Even though these arrangements were required by treaty in 1794, they were not consummated until the early nineteenth century, when joint commissions were created to deal with these issues.[53]

Similarly, the Peace Treaty of Ghent, at the end of the War of 1812, provided for four boundary settlements with Great Britain. In implementing Article 4, the question of the ownership of certain islands in Passamaquoddy Bay and the Bay of Fundy was settled by a joint conciliation commission of two members, one from each country, without the involvement of a third, neutral party. The two governments also accepted the determination of another such commission, established under Article 6 of the treaty, to allocate the boundary along the middle of the Great Lakes. However, commissions for the remaining two boundary questions failed to agree, and they were deferred until the signing of the Webster–Ashburton Treaty in 1842.[54]

Four additional Anglo–American treaties, concerned with boundary, claims, and other matters, were concluded in the 1820s, two of which produced peaceful settlement. By the treaty of 1818, Article 5 of which dealt with the ''restitution of,'' or ''full compensation for,'' American slaves taken by the British, it was agreed that differences between the two governments were to be submitted ''to some friendly Sovereign of State.'' The Claims Conventions of 1822 and 1826, flowing from arbitrations under the Treaty of Ghent, transferred the issue of the amount of the indemnification of the United States to be arbitrated by the Emperor of Russia, who decided in favor of the United States without fixing the amount to be paid. Ultimately, by direct negotiation, the Claims Treaty of 1826, negotiated by Albert Gallatin and two British emissaries, fixed the amount of the indemnification at a lump sum of $1,200,000, payable by Great Britain in full payment of the American claims.[55]

The fourth treaty, signed in London on September 29, 1827, served as a *compromis d'arbitrage*, which was unique and constituted a convention for the settlement of the northeast boundary of the United States. Previously having failed to do so by a joint commission, this treaty provided for joint referral of the issue to ''some friendly Sovereign or friendly State,'' which was submitted to the King of the Netherlands, whose award was rejected.

The United States also resorted to arbitration to resolve boundary and claims disputes with Spain but used a different process. The Pinckney Treaty of 1795, Articles 2 and 3, prescribed that the southern boundary of the United States was to be determined by one Commissioner and one Surveyor from each government to produce an agreed demarcation, an explanatory plat, and a journal of proceedings. To deal with the settlement of American claims for damages resulting from losses of vessels and cargoes taken by the Spanish during the war between France and Spain, a commission was established, in Philadelphia, consisting of one Commissioner appointed by each government, who jointly selected a third, impartial umpire. They decided to indemnify Americans in the amount of more than $300,000. On August 11, 1802, the United States also signed a Claims Treaty with Spain, which provided for the same kind of arbitration, to be convened in Madrid. But it was not ratified and implemented until December 1818 and was superseded by the Transcontinental Treaty the following year.[56]

On the other hand, arbitration was bypassed in the Claims Convention of April 30, 1803, with France to provide for payment of claims owed Americans resulting from the capture and confiscation of American vessels and cargoes. It prescribed French indemnification of Americans without creating a claims conciliation or arbitration commission, but in Article 6 it authorized the United States to monitor the process by appointing three persons to examine French documents that dealt with such settlements.

The Boundary Treaty with Mexico, concluded January 12, 1828, which specified the demarcation between United States and Mexican territory, provided for no subsequent arbitration. However, as in the case of treaties with Great Britain, it created a joint team, consisting of a Commissioner and Surveyor from each country to jointly establish, mark, and record the fixing of the boundary.

Finally, despite all the conflict, negotiations, treaty stipulations, conciliation arrangements, and arbitrations over boundaries for more than three decades, when the United States purchased the Louisiana Territory—which the treaty of 1803 simply defined as the same that France had acquired from Spain three years earlier, without defining its boundary[57]—the United States and Great Britain agreed to a simple formula for its delineation in the Anglo–American Treaty of 1818. By bilateral negotiation this boundary was extended from the Lake of the Woods westward along the 49th parallel of north latitude to the crest of the "Stony (Rocky) Mountains," projecting this astronomical line of demarcation some 1,000 miles across North America. This was remarkable in several respects. It averted the problems that result from determining natural boundaries, it obviated the likelihood of subsequent conflict and the need for arbitration, it could be physically defined by careful surveying, and it later served as the basis of extension through the Oregon Territory to the Pacific. Half a century later, like the Great Lakes, it also was disarmed. Eventually, this enabled the United States to boast of its nearly 4,000 miles of undefended northern frontier, which Winston Churchill later described as "guarded only by neighborly respect and honorable obligations" serving as "an example to every country and a pattern for the future of the world."

In summary, after the Constitution went into effect, although treaty commitments for the peaceful settlement of international disputes had already been established in the Jay and Pinckney Treaties in the 1790s, during the first three decades of the nineteenth century the United States became a signatory to eleven more treaties that dealt with boundary, claims, and other issues that were regarded as amenable to conciliation and arbitration. These, together with the Jay and Pinckney Treaties, provided for at least a dozen peaceful settlement arrangements, all but one with Great Britain. Not all attempts at arbitration were successful, and most of those that failed were superseded by direct bilateral negotiations. The Department of State played the primary role in promoting the conclusion of the treaties that prescribed the amicable resolution of disputes and backing them up with conciliation negotiations when arbitration failed to produce a settlement. Based on this early experience, it promoted many subsequent peaceful settlement arrangements, eventuating in the creation of the Hague Tribunal, the International Court of Justice, and other agencies.

CONCLUSION

Major developments during this period may be grouped in two categories. At the time, the United States was engrossed with many foreign relations issues and practices, some of major historical significance, which the Department of State initiated or with which it otherwise became involved. Among the more important were the waging and consequences of two wars; superseding the commitment of the Alliance of 1778 with France; challenging the European mercantilist system and promoting freedom of trade; asserting the right of the freedom of the seas and the maritime rights of neutral governments in time of war; insisting on the rights of expatriation and naturalization; acquiring the Louisiana and Florida territories from France and Spain; and achieving a series of boundary and international claims settlements, not only by direct negotiation but also by international conciliation and arbitration.

On the other hand, so far as organization and administration of the Department of State were concerned, as might be expected, it expanded diplomatic relations and increased its diplomatic representation to several additional European countries and to Latin American countries following their revolutions and the achievement of their independence. To service trade and maritime interests, it concluded a series of new commercial treaties and more than doubled its consular force. It managed the negotiation of more than thirty new treaties and agreements, concerned substantially with commerce and navigation but also with peace settlements, the cession of extensive territory to the United States, boundary and claims settlements, fishing rights, and naval disarmament on the Great Lakes.

The Department did this with little fundamental change in structure or increase in its staff. Congress amplified departmental domestic responsibilities. Two plans for reorganization were produced, one providing for administrative realignment and stabilization under Secretary Adams, and the second, proposed by Secretary Clay, recommending the transferral of a portion of departmental internal functions to other Federal administrative agencies, which was not implemented by Congress.

In addition to the valuable service as both diplomatic officers and Secretaries of State of James Monroe and especially John Quincy Adams, many other developments during these three decades will be remembered. Of major significance were the promulgation of the Monroe Doctrine, identified with both the President and Secretary Adams, and the extensive Louisiana and Florida cession treaties, associated, respectively, with President Jefferson, Secretary of State Madison, and Ministers Plenipotentiary Robert R. Livingston and James Monroe, who signed the former in 1803, and President Monroe and Secretary Adams, who signed the Adams–Onis Treaty with Spain in 1819.

Other memorable developments include the appointment of the first Envoys Extraordinary and Ministers Plenipotentiary William Eustice in 1814 and John Quincy Adams and Albert Gallatin the following year; the initial signing of a series of treaties and agreements in Washington by the Secretary of State, beginning with the Rush–Bagot Agreement with Great Britain in 1817, which also was the first executive agreement and the first disarmament arrangement participated in by the United States; the signing of the first multipartite agreement; and the first appointment of diplomatic representatives to an international congress. Finally, Chief Clerk John Graham will be remembered for salvaging the Department of State's books and records from the flames of battle during the War of 1812, Secretary Adams for his meticulous report on weights and measures, and Joel R. Poinsett for importing the Poinsettia plant into the United States.

Though rare, on occasion the President continued the practice of corresponding personally with foreign Chiefs of State, bypassing the Department of State and diplomatic corps. In the early years of the nineteenth century, for example, President Jefferson communicated with the Bey of Tripoli (May 21, 1801), the Emperor of Morocco (December 20, 1803), the Dey of Algiers (March 27, 1804), and the Emperor of Russia (June 15, 1804). These were all concerned with Barbary depredations on U.S. commerce in the Mediterranean, although that with the Russian Czar also dealt with mutual commerce and consular affairs.

Relations of the President with the Secretary of State were both traditional and, in some respects, unique. The President continued as the principal foreign relations officer of the United States, who determined executive foreign policy, as illustrated by the proclamation of the Monroe Doctrine, and, for certain negotiations, he appointed special presidential missions and individual executive agents to both Europe and Latin America. One of the most exceptional features of this relationship between the President and the Secretary was that all four Presidents had the benefit of prior service as Secretary of State, and three of them also had diplomatic experience in Europe.

Turning to their personal relations, President Jefferson and Secretary Madison had been friends since 1776, worked together as Founders of the American Republic, and frequently corresponded and exchanged views on public and private matters, and Madison encouraged Jefferson to accept appointment as the first Secretary of State under President Washington. Although Jefferson has been regarded as ''an absolute President,'' he sought the counsel of Secretary Madison, whose influence was less apparent than that in earlier administrations, but they worked together with understanding of each other's views and merit, and they respected each other.

When President Madison selected Monroe as his Secretary in 1811, the latter sought assurance that he could influence foreign policy and that he would have actual direction of the nation's diplomacy. They usually agreed on American national objectives and interests and on the methods of achieving them, including the handling of the wars with Great Britain and Tripoli and the possibility of war with France.

After Monroe was elected President, he was blessed with the opportunity to appoint John Quincy Adams, a seasoned diplomat, as his Secretary of State. The President consulted freely with Adams, other Cabinet members, and the Chairman of the Senate Foreign Relations Committee. Adams was less inclined to compromise on important foreign affairs issues, and sometimes he differed with the President and other Cabinet members. But the President and Secretary agreed on nonintervention in Europe and Latin American independence and on the desirability of issuing a public declaration to draw a dividing line between the Old World and the Americas, and Adams worked closely with the President and influenced both the principles and language of the Monroe Doctrine.

In the contested presidential election of 1824, which was decided by the House of Representatives after the Electoral College failed to reach a decision, Henry Clay, an experienced and influential member of Congress, supported Adams and was appointed as his Secretary of State. Whereas Clay excelled and enjoyed his work in Congress, his service as Secretary probably was his least congenial public office, in part because he lacked prior diplomatic and administrative experience and because he had to deal not only with critical treaty negotiations but also with an unfriendly Congress. President Adams was inclined to impose his foreign policy views on his Secretary, and they differed in their dispositions and on a number of diplomatic nominations, but overall they maintained friendly relations in the cause of American foreign interests and diplomacy, and Clay generally enjoyed good relations with American diplomats abroad.

Thus, during this period involving wars, extensive territorial expansion, and stabilizing the status and role of the United States in foreign affairs, the country was fortunate to have a series of able statesmen at the helm in both the presidency and the Department of State. The major misfortune was the appointment of Robert Smith as Secretary in 1809.

NOTES

1. Madison was dissatisfied with Smith's manner of drafting important papers and the functioning of the diplomatic service in a number of key capitals. In addition, he was troubled by the factional differences between Smith and Secretary of the Treasury Gallatin in the Cabinet, which came to a head in March 1811. Gallatin tendered his resignation, declaring that either he or Secretary Smith needed to resign, but President Madison refused to accept Gallatin's resignation, solicited from James Monroe his willingness to become Secretary of State, informed Smith that he did not measure up to expectations, and offered him an alternative appointment as Minister to Russia, which Smith rejected.

2. In the presidential election of 1824, in which the candidates were John Quincy Adams, Andrew Jackson, William H. Crawford, and Henry Clay, Jackson received the largest popular vote, but none received a majority of the Electoral College vote. Adams was elected by the House of Representatives. Clay supported Adams in House of Representatives voting and was rewarded with this appointment as Secretary of State.

3. In addition, to this time two of the eight Chief Clerks were Virginians. After Monroe only two Secretaries of State to the time of World War II were from Virginia (Abel P. Upshur, 1843–44, and Edward R. Stettinius, Jr., 1944–45).

4. Early in 1821, when Congress sought to retrench the national administration, Secretary Adams argued that the Department of State needed more, rather than fewer, clerks and that they were inadequately compensated for their qualifications and responsibilities.

On January 14, 1826, Secretary Clay sent a message to the House of Representatives Ways and Mean Committee requesting additional staff for the Department. In it he stressed the increase in the number of American diplomatic missions to foreign governments and the burden of translating documents not only from French but also from other languages.

5. To indicate departmental differences for 1798, for example, whereas the Department of State had only a Secretary and a Chief Clerk as its top-level management staff, whose combined salaries totaled $4,300, the Treasury Department, in addition to the

Secretary, had more than five additional senior officials, including a Treasurer, Comptroller, Auditor, Register of the Treasury, and Commissioner of Revenue—whose combined authorized compensation amounted to more than $55,000.

By the mid-1820s the senior staff of the Treasury Department had been increased to the Secretary, two Comptrollers, the Treasurer, five Auditors, the Register of the Treasury, and several more specialized officers.

By the mid-1820s the combined salaries for the leaders of Department of State had risen to only $8,000 and remained at this level for the next twenty years.

6. The census act of March 14, 1820, spelled out some thirty categories of data to be surveyed and made the Secretary of State responsible for collating the information and having it printed and for providing Congress with 1,500 copies. See *Annals of Congress*, 16th Cong., 1st Sess. (1820), 2: 2559–64.

7. For earlier consideration of standardizing weights and measures, see Chapter 2, n.36.

8. In 1898 one of Adams' biographers called this venture one of those vast labors that involved more toil than all the negotiations required to conclude the Adams–Onis Treaty with Spain and that Adams described as "a fearful and oppressive task." Having been under study for more than half a century by the ablest Europeans, Adams' report constituted a "solid and magnificent monument of research and reflection which has not yet been superseded by later treatises." See John T. Morse, Jr., *John Quincy Adams* (Boston: Houghton Mifflin, 1898), American Statesmen Series, vol. 15, pp. 126–27.

For background, see *Annuals of Congress*, 14th Cong., 2d Sess. (1816–1817), pp. 14, 197, 202, 234; and 16th Cong., 2d Sess. (1820–21), pp. 375 and 1216.

9. The history of the standardization of weights and measures after Adams' report of 1821, among others, includes a congressional resolution of 1830 for the Secretary of the Treasury to determine various standards employed by American Customs Houses and legislation in 1836 and 1838 that required the Secretary of the Treasury to supply each American State with sets of standards and balances, so that by 1850 Secretary Adams' recommendations concerning domestic standardization had been implemented.

On the matter of international standardization, utilizing the metric system, the United States participated in the Diplomatic Conference on the Meter in 1875 and adhered to the Convention it adopted, international metric standards were produced in the late 1880s and early 1890s, and in 1960 these measurements were titled "International System of Units." In 1975 the United States adopted a Metric Conversion Act but provided no mandatory requirements for implementation, and a Metric Board was established to coordinate voluntary conversion to the metric system.

At the international level, the United States not only attended the initial conference held in Paris in 1875 and signed the original Convention as well as an amending Convention negotiated at Sevres in 1921 but also has been a member of the International Bureau of Weights and Measures since 1878.

10. An Act of Congress, January 26, 1802, provided that the libraries of the Senate and House of Representatives were to be combined and housed in the Capitol and that a Librarian of Congress be appointed to have charge of the library. It also authorized appropriations for the purchase of books and maps and for a per diem compensation for the services of the Librarian.

The Library of Congress was destroyed in the burning of the Capitol in 1814 during the War of 1812. It was replaced in 1815, when Congress purchased the private library of Thomas Jefferson. In 1851 its collection was reduced by fire to 20,000 volumes, but since then it has increased its holdings through congressional purchases, deposits made under the copyright law, transfers from other government agencies, exchange arrangements, and gifts. In time it has become one of the greatest libraries in the world.

11. Secretary Adams requested federal district attorneys to provide the departmental library with complete sets of the statutes of the States and to keep these files current, and he asked State Governors to supply the Department with copies of laws enacted at each session of the State legislatures. Although the Library of Congress had been created, the Department of State still served as a repository of books and records that eventually became the responsibility of the National Archives, created by law in 1934. Initially, therefore, the State Department served as the precursor of both the Library of Congress and the National Archives.

12. For more detail, see Stuart, *The Department of State*, pp. 53–58.

13. Also see n.4. For the full text of this report, see James F. Hopkins and Mary W. M. Hargreaves, eds., *The Papers of Henry Clay* (Lexington: University Press of Kentucky, 1973), vol. 5, pp. 109–12.

14. Andrew Jackson, appointed Minister to Mexico, declined the offer; presidential nominations for John J. Appleton (to Portugal) and William Short (to Russia) were rejected by the Senate; nominations were withdrawn by the President before commissioning for John Hamm (to Guatemala) and John Prevost (to Peru); two appointees died en route to their posts—William Miller (Guatemala) and Emanuel J. West (Peru); William B. Rocherster returned from Guatemala without presenting his credentials; and the remaining four did not serve for other reasons.

Although Appleton was not confirmed by the Senate for appointment as Chargé d'Affaires to Portugal, he nevertheless served as Chargé d'Affaires ad interim from June 1820 until mid-1821. In addition, the Senate rejected the nomination of two others. John Quincy Adams was nominated as Minister to Russia in March 1809, which was rejected, but he was renominated in June and was confirmed; and Jonathan Russell was nominated as Minister to Sweden in May 1813, which was rejected by the Senate, and he was renominated in January 1814, which was approved. In addition, when William Pinkney was commissioned to Great Britain in 1806 to take James Monroe's place while he served on a special diplomatic mission, the British Government declined to accept Pinkney's letter of credence, but it dealt with him informally until he was recommissioned and reaccredited.

15. Thus, Adams was appointed sequentially to Russia and Great Britain, Alexander H. Everett to the Netherlands and Spain, Albert Gallatin to France and Great Britain, Christopher Hughes to Sweden and the Netherlands, Samuel Larned to Chile and Peru, William Pinkney to Great Britain and Russia, and Jonathan Russell to France and Great Britain. In addition, John J. Appleton served as Chargé d'Affaires ad interim in Portugal, 1820–1821, and later was sent as Chargé d'Affaires to Sweden (1826–1830). James A. Bayard was appointed to France in 1801 by President John Adams and in 1815 was nominated as Envoy Extraordinary and Minister Plenipotentiary to Russia, but he did not serve in either of these appointments. George W. Erving held two appointments to Spain, as Chargé d'Affaires ad interim (October 1805–February 1810) and as Minister Plenipotentiary (August 1814–May 1819).

16. In addition to John Quincy Adams, this may be said of Albert Gallatin, Rufus King, James Monroe, William Pinkney, and William Short.

17. These included ten of the original thirteen States (not including Connecticut, New Jersey, and New Hampshire) and six new States (Illinois, Kentucky, Louisiana, Ohio,

Tennessee, and Vermont). The largest numbers were appointed from Massachusetts (eleven), New York (six), Virginia (six), Rhode Island (five) and South Carolina (five).

18. The European countries were Denmark, France, Great Britain, the Netherlands, Portugal, Russia, Spain, and Sweden; the Latin American states included Argentina, Brazil, Chile, Colombia, Guatemala, Mexico, and Peru.

19. The shortest lapses between nomination and reception of diplomats, approximately two months, were experienced by Robert R. Livingston (to France), William Pinkney (to Great Britain), and Richard Rush (to Great Britain). The lapse ranged between two to four months for many appointees to France and Great Britain. The longest timelag ran to twelve to sixteen months and, in the case of George Erving's accreditation to Spain, to more than two years.

20. At times the President nominated the succeeding envoy months before the preceding emissary's mission terminated. More frequently, the lapse of time between diplomats temporarily left the United States without representation. The transition from Rufus King to Albert Gallatin in Great Britain in 1826 amounted to a little more than two months. In other cases, the delay in succession lasted two years or more. The longest hiatus was the transition from Charles Pinckney to George Erving in Spain. Pinckney present his recall in October 1804, and his successor, James Bowdoin, did not proceed to his post, so that Erving served as Chargé d'Affaires ad interim from October 1805 to February 1810 and was nominated as Minister Plenipotentiary in August 1814 but did not present his credentials until two years later (August 1816), thus leaving a hiatus at the ministerial level of nearly twelve years.

21. Among these were Caesar R. Rodney, commissioned to Argentina, who presented his credentials in December 1823 and served only six months before he died; James Cooley, who after only nine months also died at his post in Peru; and Jonathan Russell, whose service in London was limited to less than nine months because of the outbreak of the War of 1812. Four others also died at their posts. In some cases, such as that of Samuel Larned, tenure was limited because of transfer; after only eleven months in Chile he was accredited to Peru.

22. Illustrating the special case of multiple appointment, however, John Quincy Adams served for a combined total of more than twelve years—in Russia and Great Britain plus earlier service in the Netherlands and Prussia.

23. In 1829, after more than four years as Envoy Extraordinary and Minister Plenipotentiary, Joel R. Poinsett, the first American to serve as envoy to that country, Mexico requested his recall because of alleged interference in its internal affairs, and he left his post on January 3, 1830.

24. Rufus King, appointed in May 1796, remained for another two years, till mid-May 1803, after President Jefferson nominated James Monroe to replace him. Similarly, in the case of Spain, President Jefferson nominated Charles Pinckney early in June 1801 to replace David Humphries, who, however, did not leave his post until that December. More significantly, presidents did not nominate replacements to the Netherlands and Portugal; and the lapse for Prussia ran for more than three decades.

25. In the 1820s the President sought to appoint four Chargés d'Affaires to Guatemala, of whom only one served and then for only one year. Three Ministers were appointed to Mexico, one of whom declined appointment, and another failed to proceed to his post. The President also nominated four Chargés to Peru; one was not commissioned and had his nomination withdrawn before the Senate acted on it, another died en route to his

post, and another died at his post after serving for a year, but the fourth, Samuel Larned, appointed in 1828, served for more than seven years.

26. The first diplomats to be nominated as Envoys Extraordinary and Ministers Plenipotentiary were John Quincy Adams (Great Britain), James A. Bayard (Russia), William Eustice (the Netherlands), and Albert Gallatin (France). Eustice was nominated in December 1814, and the others were appointed in February 1815.

27. Of these nineteen Envoys Extraordinary, three did not serve in these appointments, including Andrew Jackson, who, named as the first U.S. envoy to Mexico, declined the appointment.

28. The revival of the use of the Minister Resident rank for some fifteen countries commenced in 1854, when William L. Marcy was Secretary of State, and Franklin Pierce was President. The former rank of Minister Plenipotentiary was superseded by that of Envoy Extraordinary.

29. The sole exception was Turkey, to which the United States sent a Minister Resident in 1839, following two earlier Chargés d'Affaires, and continued to appoint Ministers Resident until the early 1880s.

30. Exceptions, where the United States continued to use the Minister Resident rank beyond the early 1880s, were Haiti (until 1897), Iran and Korea (1901), and Liberia (1931).

31. These countries included Brazil, Chile, France, Germany, Great Britain, Italy, Mexico, Peru, Russia, Spain, and such additional countries as China and Japan.

32. In other words, the appointee must be persona grata to the receiving government. Rejection is rare. Earlier, Charles C. Pinckney was rejected as Minister Plenipotentiary to France in 1796, but relations between the two countries had so deteriorated that it was unlikely that any American appointee would have been acceptable to the French regime at that time. The issue also arose in the early nineteenth century, when Don Luis de Onis, who had been seeking acceptance as the Minister of Spain to the United States since 1809, was not accepted by the President until late in 1815, because of his interference in American internal affairs. Secretary Adams concluded the Florida cession treaty with him several years later.

33. The appointment of Ambassadors was authorized by both the Articles of Confederation (Article 18) and the Constitution (Article 2, section 2, clause 2), but the United States refused to appoint diplomats at that elevated rank for more than a century after it went into effect.

34. This formula does not deal with lesser ranks, such as commissioners, agents, attachés, and others.

For the text of the rules established by the Vienna Convention on Diplomacy, signed on March 19, 1815, and accepted by all of the major European powers, see Moore, *A Digest of International Law*, vol. 4, pp. 430–31. For the original French text, see Clive Parry, ed., *The Consolidated Treaty Series* (Dobbs Ferry, N.Y. Oceana, 1969), vol. 64, pp. 2–3.

For additional commentary and documentation, see Barnes and Morgan, *The Foreign Service of the United States*, pp. 146–47; Moore, *A Digest of International Law*, vol. 4, pp. 732–36; Plischke, *Conduct of American Diplomacy*, 3d ed., pp. 602–603; and Stuart, *American Diplomatic and Consular Practice*, pp. 126–28.

35. These were Graham (Minister Plenipotentiary to Portugal), Prevost (Chargé d'Affaires to Peru), and Rodney (Minister Plenipotentiary to Argentina).

36. Beginning at the time of the French Revolution, when recognition policy was

founded on the concept of legitimacy, and amplified at the time of the Latin American revolutions, early in the nineteenth century the United States adopted its de facto recognition policy for both new states and governments. For a comprehensive historical study on American recognition practice, see Galloway, *Recognizing Foreign Governments: The Practice of the United States*, especially Chapter 1.

37. Eventually, Richard C. Anderson, first Minister Plenipotentiary to Colombia, and John Sargeant of Philadelphia were appointed as Ministers to the "Assembly of American Nations at Panama." But Anderson died en route, and Sargeant, having started so late, failed to reach Panama in time for the sessions.

38. These included George W. Erving (Turkey, 1831, nominated but not commissioned), Alexander H. Everett (China, 1845, his third diplomatic appointment), John Hamm (Chile, 1830), Christopher Hughes (Sweden, 1830, and the Netherlands, 1842, his third and fourth appointments), and Richard Rush (France, 1847).

39. These Secretaries of the Treasury included Gallatin (1801–1814) and Rush (1825–1829); sequentially, the Secretaries of War were William Eustis, John Armstrong, James Monroe, William H. Crawford, James Barbour, and Joel R. Poinsett; and William Pinkney, Caesar R. Rodney, and Richard Rush served as Attorneys General.

40. In addition to Adams, Clay, Gallatin, Livingston, and Monroe, each of whom signed three or more treaties for the United States, these included John J. Appleton, James A. Bayard, Rufus King, Henry Middleton, Charles Pinckney, Joel R. Poinsett, Richard Rush, Jonathan Russell, and William Tudor. Also see the section on treaties.

41. The latter were located in China (Canton), India (Calcutta), the Dutch East Indies (Batavia), and South Africa (Capetown).

42. Such as James L. Cathcart, Consul consecutively at Tunis, Madeira, and Cadiz (1799–1817).

43. For example, John Murray Forbes served as Consul at Hamburg (1802–1816), Chargé d'Affaires ad interim to Denmark (1812–1816), Consul General at Copenhagen (1816–1818), Commercial Agent at Buenos Aires (1820–1823), and Secretary of Legation and later Chargé d'Affaires at Buenos Aires (1825–1831). Similarly, George W. Erving functioned as Consul at London (1801–1805), Secretary of Legation at Madrid, Special Minister to Denmark for the settlement of American claims, and Minister Plenipotentiary to Spain, where he served for several years (1816–1819). Erving was unique in that he held both consular and diplomatic appointments.

44. Barnes and Morgan, *The Foreign Service of the United States*, p. 65. For additional information on the administration of the consular service, its expansion, length of tenure of consular officers, multiple appointments, and commentary on the deficient administration and supervision of the system, see pp. 60–65.

45. In the annals of American treaty making, this was a unique executive agreement in that, although the Senate gave its approval ten days in advance of the signing of the diplomatic notes, there was no formal ratification or exchange of ratifications, but the President issued an official proclamation to put it into effect. Because the British government was skeptical as to whether such an agreement would be binding on his successors, President Monroe submitted it to the Senate for its advice and consent, which normally is not required for agreements concluded under presidential authority.

46. These treaties were signed at London (seven of them), Algiers (three), Paris (three), and St. Petersburg, Stockholm and Tripoli (two each), as well as Honolulu, Madrid, Mexico City, and Rio de Janeiro.

47. These American Ministers included Robert Livingston (France), Joel R. Poinsett

(Mexico), Albert Gallatin (Great Britain), Henry Middleton (Russia), Jonathan Russell (Sweden), Rufus King (Great Britain), and Charles Pinckney (Spain). In two cases the signers were Chargés d'Affaires, and the Treaty of Peace and Amity with Tripoli was signed by the American Consul General Tobias Lear, accredited to Algiers. Two treaties with Algiers and the commercial agreement with Hawaii were signed by American naval officers.

48. The Senate refused to confirm Gallatin to the first three-member treaty commission because he was then Secretary of the Treasury, but when he resigned this office, he was reappointed to the five-member commission.

49. The Articles of Confederation, Article 9, provided that "the United States in Congress assembled" shall be the last resort for all "disputes and differences now subsisting or that hereafter may arise between two or more states concerning boundary jurisdiction, or any other cause whatever" and that the agency for resolution was to consist of seven to nine "commissioners or judges," whose determination would be "final and conclusive." Technically, this constituted an adjudication, rather than a conciliation or arbitral process.

Under the Constitution and international law, the American States are constituent members of the Federal Union, not independent nations. Therefore, under Article 3, section 2, clause 2 of the Constitution, all disputes between the States, "as to both law and fact," are to be decided by the Supreme Court, which possesses "original jurisdiction" in such cases. Although clearly a matter of peaceful settlement, this also constitutes an adjudicative process.

50. Characteristic of the differences among these peaceful settlement processes, in cases of mediation and good offices a third party interposes diplomatically, through suggestion and advice, to induce the disputing parties to negotiate a settlement themselves. For conciliation, arbitration, and adjudication, normally, the disputing governments submit their conflict to a third party or agency for resolution. In conciliation the agency or commission agreed upon either files a report as to the facts at issue or, if so authorized, makes recommendations to resolve the problem. Arbitration and adjudication, the most sophisticated of these procedures, involve either a preestablished agent, agency, or court, or one prescribed by special treaty or agreement—called a *compromis d'arbitrage*—whose determination is binding on the disputing governments. For additional explanation of these terms, see Gamboa, *Elements of Diplomatic and Consular Practice: A Glossary*, and Plischke, *Conduct of American Diplomacy*, Glossary.

51. A commission consisting of two arbiters from each party met at Hartford, Connecticut, which rendered a determination fixing the boundary of the Dutch territory.

52. Deliberations were held by a "court of commissioners" consisting of five members of the Continental Congress at Trenton, New Jersey, commencing on November 12, 1782, with the decision rendered on December 30. See *Journals of the Continental Congress*, 1783, 24: 6–32.

53. In the St. Croix River arbitration, the commission met in 1798 and agreed upon the river location in favor of Great Britain. But extension of the northeast boundary of the United States under the Peace Treaty of 1783 required additional adjustment, and despite the negotiation of a separate convention signed in 1803, the Senate rejected one of its articles. The issue, therefore, remained unsettled by the time of the War of 1812, and the Peace Treaty of Ghent, signed in 1814, provided for new commissions to mark the American boundary from the Atlantic Ocean to the Lake of the Woods.

The commission on debts owed by the United States, which met at Philadelphia, failed to reach a judgment, and in 1802 the American government agreed to pay a lump-sum indemnification of 600,000 pounds sterling.

The commission on spoliations, which met at London, produced its determination in 1804, awarding more than $10 million to American claimants. From the perspective of the development of international law and procedure for peaceful settlement, this third commission established a number of important precedents concerning the legality of capture and condemnation of ships and cargoes of neutral nations in time of war and compensation to be awarded to their owners for their losses.

So far as the peaceful settlement mechanisms were concerned, the agency established to deal with the St. Croix issue consisted of one commissioner from each country, who together agreed on a third, neutral party. The other two commissions comprised two commissioners selected by each government who unanimously selected the fifth, with the understanding that if they failed to agree on a neutral party, the fifth would be chosen by lot.

54. These territorial disputes concerned the northeastern boundary of the United States from the St. Croix River to the St. Lawrence River and the boundary at the Lake of the Woods, under Articles 5 and 7 of the Treaty of Ghent. Both issues were assigned to mixed commissions, which failed to agree. The northeastern boundary question was then turned over to the King of the Netherlands, whose award was rejected by the United States. Eventually, both of these matters also were resolved by direct negotiation and embodied in the Webster–Ashburton Treaty.

55. Because this claims dispute was not resolved under the Treaty of 1822 by two commissioners and two arbiters (one each from the United States and Great Britain), who met at Washington in 1823, the two governments, therefore, decided to negotiate a settlement directly.

56. By December 1818 additional claims were presented, and, consequently, the Spanish–American treaty of 1802 was annulled and was superseded by the Transcontinental Treaty of 1819, in which the two governments reciprocally renounced their claims. But the United States established a national commission of three members to determine indemnifications to be paid to Spain—not exceeding a total of $5 million—in accordance with international law and the stipulations of the Pinckney Treaty.

57. Article 1 of the Louisiana Cession Treaty of 1803 nebulously defined the boundary of the Louisiana Territory as ''the said territory with all its rights and appurtenances as fully and in the same manner as they have been acquired by the French Republic'' by the Treaty of San Ildefonso.

4

Transition Period—Extension and Stabilization, 1829–1861

In this period from the end of the Democratic–Republican years to the inauguration of Abraham Lincoln, significant changes materialized. These involved the expansion of the territory and population of the United States, the growth of the number of States constituting the American Union, the nature and turnover of political leadership, and the role played by the United States in international affairs.

Sometimes this period, called the "democratic era," is characterized as emphasizing American continental affairs and domestic governmental crystallization. However, it also represents the time when international interests mounted, when Congress and the Department of State focused on departmental reorganization and structural refinement, when the diplomatic and consular services and the negotiation of treaties and agreements expanded geographically and increased both substantively and numerically, and when the handling of the State Department's domestic and other extraneous functions peaked, and Congress finally commenced to transfer some of them to other Executive Departments and agencies.

ORGANIZATION AND MANAGEMENT

During the four decades prior to the inauguration of Andrew Jackson, six Presidents were elected, of whom four served double terms, and they appointed nine Secretaries of State, who provided considerable stability in the management of foreign affairs. By comparison, in the next thirty-two years nine Presidents were elected. Of these only Jackson served two terms, and Martin Van Buren, James K. Polk, Franklin Pierce, and James Buchanan held office for four years. All of them were Democrats. The Whigs did not fare as well. William Henry

Harrison and Zachary Taylor, the first Presidents to die in office,[1] were succeeded, respectively, by John Tyler (for nearly four years) and Millard Fillmore
(for some two and one-half years).

Secretaries of State

These Presidents appointed thirteen Secretaries of State, who served fourteen
incumbencies during the three decades from 1829 to 1861. As indicated in Table
4.1, sequentially, these included Martin Van Buren (of New York, 1829–31),
Edward Livingston (Louisiana, 1831–33), Louis McLane (Delaware, 1833–34),
John Forsyth (Georgia, 1834–41), Daniel Webster (Massachusetts, 1841–43),
Abel P. Upshur (Virginia, 1843–44), John C. Calhoun (South Carolina, 1844–
45), James Buchanan (Pennsylvania, 1845–49), John M. Clayton (Delaware,
1849–50), Daniel Webster (second appointment, 1850–52), Edward Everett
(Massachusetts, 1852–53), William L. Marcy (New York, 1853–57), Lewis Cass
(Michigan, 1857–60), and Jeremiah S. Black (Pennsylvania, 1860–61). All of
these, except Webster, Upshur, Calhoun, Clayton, and Everett, served in Democratic administrations, and during this period Webster was the only Secretary
of State to be given two separate appointments, by different Presidents, which
was rare in American history and was regarded as a signal honor, although others
have held the office for longer periods.

Bridging short periods between appointments, nine officials—a relatively
large number—functioned as Secretary of State ad interim (see Table 4.1). These
included one designated as Acting Secretary (James A. Hamilton),[2] four Cabinet
members—Attorneys General Hugh S. Legare and John Nelson, Secretary of
War Charles M. Conrad, and Secretary of the Navy Abel P. Upshur, pending
his immediate appointment as Secretary of State—and three departmental Chief
Clerks—Jacob L. Martin, William S. Derrick and William Hunter, III, who was
appointed twice, in 1853 and 1860. The Chief Clerks served for only two to
four days, whereas several other interim Secretaries functioned from twelve days
to more than a month. The longest gap occurred between Secretaries Webster
and Upshur, which ran for more than two and one-half months, during which
three successive interim Secretaries were appointed—including Attorney General Legare, who served in a dual capacity for forty-three days.

Presidents and Their Secretaries of State

President Jackson made no pretense at appointing his Cabinet members for
reasons other than personal relationships and political considerations. He appointed four Secretaries of State. These included Van Buren (then Governor of
New York), Livingston (brother of the first Secretary for Foreign Affairs during
the Confederation and then Senator from Louisiana), McLane (then Secretary
of the Treasury), and Forsyth (then Senator from Georgia). Forsyth also re-

Table 4.1
Department of State Secretaries, 1829–1861

Name	Appointed	Entry on Duty	Termination of Appointment
* James A. Hamilton (N.Y.) (Acting Secretary)	Mar. 4, 1829		Mar. 27, 1829
Martin Van Buren (N.Y.)	Mar. 6, 1829	Mar. 28, 1829	Mar. 23, 1831
Edward Livingston (La.) [1]	May 24, 1831	May 24, 1831	May 29, 1833
Louis McLane (Del.)	May 29, 1833	May 29, 1833	June 30, 1834
John Forsyth (Ga.)	June 27, 1834	July 1, 1834	Mar. 3, 1841
* Jacob L. Martin (N.C.) (Chief Clerk, Dept. of State)	Mar. 4, 1841		Mar. 5, 1841
Daniel Webster (Mass.)	Mar. 5, 1841	Mar. 6, 1841	May 8, 1843
* Hugh S. Legare (S.C.) (Attorney General)	May 9, 1843		June 20, 1843
* William S. Derrick (Pa.) (Chief Clerk, Dept. of State)	June 21, 1843		June 23, 1843
* Abel P. Upshur (Va.) (Sec. of Navy)	June 24, 1843		July 23, 1843
Abel P. Upshur (Va.)	July 24, 1843	July 24, 1843	Feb. 28, 1844
* John Nelson (Md.) (Attorney General)	Feb. 29, 1844		Mar. 31, 1844
John C. Calhoun (S.C.)	Mar. 6, 1844	Apr. 1, 1844	Mar. 10, 1845
James Buchanan (Pa.)	Mar. 6, 1845	Mar. 10, 1845	Mar. 7, 1849
John M. Clayton (Del.)	Mar. 7, 1849	Mar. 8, 1849	July 22, 1850
Daniel Webster (Mass.)	July 22, 1850	July 23, 1850	Oct. 24, 1852
* Charles M. Conrad (La.) (Sec. of War)	Oct. 25, 1852		Nov. 5, 1852
Edward Everett (Mass.)	Nov. 6, 1852	Nov. 6, 1852	Mar. 8, 1853
* William Hunter (R.I.) (Chief Clerk, Dept. of State)	Mar. 4, 1853		Mar. 7, 1853
William L. Marcy (N.Y.)	Mar. 7, 1853	Mar. 8, 1853	Mar. 6, 1857
Lewis Cass (Mich.)	Mar. 6, 1857	Mar. 6, 1857	Dec. 14, 1860
* William Hunter (R.I.) (Chief Clerk, Dept. of State)	Dec. 15, 1860		Dec. 16, 1860
Jeremiah S. Black (Pa.)	Dec. 17, 1860	Dec. 17, 1860	Mar. 5, 1861

*Indicates Secretary of State ad interim.
[1] Livingston was commissioned when the Senate was in recess. He accepted the office on April 20, and on May 24 he entered upon his duties.

mained Secretary of State throughout the Van Buren Administration until March 1841.

Van Buren had assisted in electing Jackson as President. He was on friendly terms with the President, who wished to have him as his successor in the presidency. When Van Buren decided to resign as Secretary in 1831, he was appointed as Envoy Extraordinary and Minister Plenipotentiary to Great Britain. On his recommendation, President Jackson next appointed Livingston, who had no training in foreign affairs. He resigned on May 29, 1833, and was immediately accredited as Envoy Extraordinary to France. His successor, McLane, resigned his office suddenly in June 1834, because of policy disagreements with the President concerning both domestic and foreign issues and for being by-passed for appointment to the Supreme Court. After some years of business engagements, in 1845 he was appointed as Envoy Extraordinary to Great Britain. President Jackson next recruited Forsyth, who had both political and diplomatic experience and who had supported the foreign policy of both former President Monroe and Secretary of State John Quincy Adams. When Van Buren was elected President, he retained Forsyth as his Secretary for another four years.

William Henry Harrison was elected as the first Whig President. He offered Webster the choice of commissioning as either Secretary of State or Secretary of the Treasury, and Webster opted for the Department of State. The President died within a month, on April 4, 1841. He was succeeded by President John Tyler, and Webster continued as Secretary for more than two years. When he resigned on May 8, 1843, the President appointed Upshur, whose tenure was cut short by his untimely death on February 28, 1844,[3] and then commissioned Calhoun, an eminent statesman who had previously been John Quincy Adams' and Andrew Jackson's Vice President for nearly eight years and also a member of Congress for many years, and he continued as Secretary throughout the remainder of President Tyler's Administration.

James K. Polk, a Democrat, was inaugurated in 1845, and he made Buchanan his Secretary of State. Originally a Federalist, Buchanan became a Democrat. He was better qualified for the office by background and experience than his immediate predecessors, and he served creditably for four years despite what one of his biographers calls "lamentable lack of harmony" with the President. Buchanan had previously been appointed Envoy Extraordinary to Russia, and subsequently he was accredited as Envoy Extraordinary to Great Britain.

When Zachary Taylor became President in 1849 and sought to establish a Whig Administration, he first offered the position of Secretary of State to John J. Crittenden (then the elected Governor of Kentucky), who declined. He next tendered the post to Clayton, who accepted immediately and served until mid-1850. He had assisted in securing Taylor's election and had previously been considered for a Cabinet post in the Harrison Administration, but he had little interest in foreign affairs. His tenure of approximately fifteen months was terminated when Vice President Fillmore succeeded to the presidency.

Fillmore, also a Whig, decided to commission Webster to his second appointment as head of the Department of State. However, his tenure ended with his death on October 24, 1852, and he was succeeded for four months by Everett, who was a close friend of both the President and Secretary and who previously had been commissioned as Envoy Extraordinary to Great Britain.

The remaining three Secretaries during this period were Marcy, Cass, and Black, who served during the Pierce and Buchanan Administrations. President Pierce first offered the position to John A. Dix, former Senator from New York, but, because of political opposition, the offer was withdrawn, and the President considered appointing Senator Robert M. T. Hunter, but he declined. Then the

President turned to Marcy, who had served as Secretary of War for four years and as a member of the Mexican Claims Commission for two years. He held the office throughout the Pierce Administration.

Having previously represented the United States as Envoy Extraordinary to two major European countries and also having been Secretary of State, Buchanan was elected President in 1857. He determined to play the leading role in the conduct of foreign affairs. He appointed Cass, who had a military background and headed the War Department (1831–36) and served as Envoy Extraordinary to France for nearly six years (1836–42). He headed the Department of State for nearly four years and resigned late in 1860 because of differences with the President over domestic policy issues. Black, who was appointed after Abraham Lincoln had already been elected as the next President, held the office of Secretary for less than three months. Late in his Administration President Buchanan nominated Black to the Supreme Court, but the Senate ignored the nomination. Subsequently, Black was made reporter to the Supreme Court and published two volumes of its *Reports*.

Among the noteworthy factors that influenced presidential appointment of these departmental leaders were geographical representation, political orientation, and professional background and qualifications. As indicated in earlier chapters, five of the earliest nine Secretaries of State were from Virginia, and the rest were from Kentucky, Maryland, Massachusetts, and Pennsylvania. During this period two were appointed from Delaware, Massachusetts, New York, and Pennsylvania, and the remaining five were from Georgia, Louisiana, Michigan, South Carolina, and Virginia. This denoted a wider geographic distribution and included appointment from some of the newer States. It is not clear whether this was by design, except in the case of Secretary Cass, when it was deemed necessary to accommodate representation from the "West."[4]

President Jackson is reputed to have introduced the spoils system—which has been called the sublegal prerequisite of election—into the Federal Administration. Despite President Washington's counsel to prefer those who possessed the greatest fitness for public office, political patronage originated early in American public affairs, especially in the States, and it also permeated the Federal Government beginning in 1829. Among other things, Jackson was motivated by fear of developing a bureaucracy that perpetuated itself and its hold on the government. He preferred rotation in public office. Some also allege that he desired to punish political opponents by removing them and their followers from administrative posts, characterized by the notion that "to the victor belong the spoils." In many ways it permeated American public life, including the personnel engaged in the management of the Department of State and in the Diplomatic and Consular Corps, until after the Civil War and eventually was replaced by the merit system.[5]

To review the matter of political orientation of Secretaries of State, whereas from 1789 to 1801 they consistently served Federalist Presidents, and for the next twenty-eight years they were all appointed by Democratic-Republican Presidents, during the three decades from 1829 to 1861 they vacillated between Democratic and Whig Administrations. For twenty years the Presidents, representing the Democratic Party, appointed eight of the thirteen Secretaries of State,[6] and the remaining five were appointed by Whig Presidents.[7] This political affiliation factor naturally produced frequent changes in the leadership of the Department of State and affected its foreign policy and administrative development.

More important, however, were the personal qualities and prior experience of the Secretaries and other staff members, including both domestic and diplomatic service. Several Secretaries had previously held other Cabinet posts. In addition to McLane, who had been Secretary of the Treasury (1831–33), Black had been Attorney General (1857–60), and three of them had been appointed as Secretary of War—Calhoun (1817–25), Cass (1831–36), and Marcy (1845–49). In addition, Upshur served as Secretary of the Navy (1841–43), was named Secretary of State ad interim in 1843, and was then nominated and confirmed as Secretary.

Seven of the Secretaries also had diplomatic experience. Three were accredited as Minister Plenipotentiary prior to their appointment to head the Department. These included Forsyth (Spain, 1819–23), Everett (Great Britain, 1841–45), and Cass (France, 1836–42). While stationed in London, Everett also was designated Commissioner to China, but he declined the appointment. More unusually, following their service as Secretary of State, Van Buren was accredited to Great Britain (1831–32), and Livingston was sent to France (1833–35). Even more exceptionally, two of them held major diplomatic assignments both before and after they served as Secretary. These were McLane (Great Britain, 1829–31 and 1845–46) and Buchanan (Russia, 1832–33, and Great Britain, 1853–56). All of these appointments were at the rank of Envoy Extraordinary and Minister Plenipotentiary, except for Forsyth, who was commissioned simply as Minister Plenipotentiary. Also, all of them were accredited to major European powers, and except for the appointments of Cass, Everett, and Forsyth, they were for relatively short periods. Only six of them had no prior or subsequent diplomatic appointments.[8] Collectively, therefore, these Secretaries represented substantial diplomatic and administrative experience.

On the matter of longevity in office as Secretary, by comparison with earlier administrations, when two Secretaries remained for eight years (James Madison and John Quincy Adams), and two-thirds of the Secretaries held office for four years or longer, during this period from 1829 to 1861 less than half served for similar periods. Thus, whereas Forsyth served both Presidents Jackson and Van Buren for nearly seven years, and Buchanan, Marcy, and Cass remained approximately four years, all the rest held appointments for two years or less. The shortest tenure was provided by Upshur (seven months), Everett (four months), and Black (only eleven weeks). This frequent turnover reflected not only more changes in the presidency but also intensification of political partisanship and greater concern with domestic issues and policies.

In summary, during this period each of the thirteen Secretaries held a single appointment except for Webster, who was commissioned twice, by Presidents William Henry Harrison and Fillmore. Only three of them served throughout a presidential administration of four years, with Forsyth bridging two administrations from 1834 to 1841, and five Secretaries held office for merely thirteen months or less. Eight were appointed by Democratic and five by Whig Presidents. They represented nine different States, and not more than two were from any single state. In the intermediate periods between regular Secretaries, eight other officials functioned ad interim, of which half then held other Cabinet posts.

All of these Secretaries were lawyers, except for Everett, who was a member of the clergy, a respected orator, the recipient of the Ph.D. degree from Goettingen University in Germany, a Professor of Greek and later also President of Harvard College, and editor of the *North American Review*. In addition, seven held State legal and juridical offices.[9] Three Secretaries had military experience. Livingston functioned as Aide to General Andrew Jackson during the Battle of New Orleans, Marcy was a captain in the Army during the War of 1812, and Cass was commissioned in 1813 as a Brigadier General in the military.

As a group, they had extensive experience as members of Congress, seven in the House of Representatives and eleven in the Senate. The only exceptions were Upshur and Black. Some were reelected for long terms, such as McLane and Everett, who were members of Congress for a decade, and Buchanan and Webster for more than twenty years. Several also held important State and other public offices, including members of State legislatures (Van Buren, New York; Buchanan, Pennsylvania; Clayton, Delaware; and Cass, Ohio); State Governors (Everett, Massachusetts; Marcy, New York; and Van Buren, New York); State Comptroller (Marcy, New York); and Mayor of New York City (Livingston); and Cass was named both Governor of the Michigan Territory and its Superintendent of Indian Affairs, in which capacity he negotiated nineteen treaties with the Indians.

Prior to appointment as Secretary of State, six held other Cabinet assignments for a combined total of approximately thirty years. Even more impressive, both Calhoun and Van Buren were elected as Vice Presidents, respectively, in 1825 and 1833, and after serving as Secretary of State, both Van Buren and Buchanan were elected as President, continuing the precedent set by Thomas Jefferson, James Madison, James Monroe, and John Quincy Adams.[10]

Despite the application of the spoils system, the obvious role played by partisanship and political affiliation and leadership, the significance of personal friendships, and, in several cases, presidential appointment of second or third choices, such as Clayton and Marcy, overall these thirteen Secretaries represented a broad and respectable spectrum of political and administrative qualities and experience in public office, including prior diplomatic assignments. Naturally, because of differing international problems and national interests and needs with which they were concerned, they varied in their performance and achievements. Inasmuch as more than half of them had diplomatic experience, there was substantial bridging of service in the office of Secretary and as diplomats in the field, evidencing a degree of diplomatic professionalization during this period.

These Secretaries were appointed for a variety of reasons. In addition to support in electing the President and other political considerations and endorsement of presidential policies, either domestic and/or foreign, these included personal friendships, professional relations, and individual background and experience. For example, political factors and personal friendship played a significant role in the selection of Secretaries Van Buren, Forsyth, Calhoun, Clayton, Marcy, and Cass. On the other hand, professional qualifications and prior public service were decisive in the selection of Buchanan and Webster.

Termination of service of the Secretaries was attributed to four main reasons. Not unexpectedly, they were replaced on the election of each new President, except in the case of Forsyth, President Jackson's fourth Secretary, who remained in office throughout the Buchanan Administration. A change also was made at the beginning of Jackson's second Administration. Thus, Forsyth, Calhoun, Buchanan, Everett, Marcy, and Black were replaced by new presidential administrations. Secretaries Upshur and Webster died in office, whereas Van Buren, Livingston, McLane, Clayton, and Cass elected to formally resign the office, largely because of policy disagreements with the President. Although difficult to determine cause and effect, the first two of President Jackson's Secretaries—Van Buren and Livingston—were immediately appointed to diplomatic positions.[11]

Biographers and historians emphasize diverse special features of these Secretaries. Thus, during Jackson's presidency, Van Buren was regarded as particularly successful in managing the many responsibilities of the office, and he was a master of the art of political management. Livingston, who had established an international reputation as a notable reformer of criminal law, was overshadowed by Jackson's personal involvement in the conduct of foreign relations. McLane's principal contribution was the first major departmental reorganization and reform, discussed later. Forsyth is remembered for additional departmental realignment and for bridging the administrations of both Presidents Jackson and Van Buren and, therefore, for holding the office longer than any other Secretary during this period.

Subsequently, Upshur's service has been characterized as providing the assertiveness of a special pleader. Calhoun's participation in President Tyler's Cabinet was as much political as diplomatic, and he was accessible to, and cooperative with, Congress, especially the House Committee on Foreign Affairs. Buchanan is reputed to have been especially well qualified for the office of Secretary and to have appointed an able corps of diplomats to major European countries.[12] Clayton's philosophy was that Congress would settle domestic policy and that he would handle the conduct of foreign affairs, but he learned that President Taylor would choose to play that role himself. Everett, though a disciple of Webster and a candidate for Vice President, excelled more as an acknowledged orator than in administering the Department.[13] Marcy, although regarded as less well prepared by training and experience than other Secretaries during this period, was skilled in understanding and dealing with international problems and became the spokesman for President Pierce on foreign policy matters. Cass and Black were overshadowed by President Buchanan in the management of foreign relations. Reputedly, Cass was a figurehead whose appointment was viewed as a political necessity, and, during his short tenure, Black was largely an interim Secretary.

Webster held two separate appointments (the only Secretary to have this distinction, except for James G. Blaine, who was appointed in 1881 and 1889) and served three Presidents—William Henry Harrison, Tyler, and Fillmore. He has been extolled as a great orator, an expositor of doctrines of international law expressed with convincing lucidity, an accomplished negotiator, and a national statesman. Aside from achieving fame as a liberal and enlightened political leader, it is said that he confronted critical political situations with acute intellectual power and inspired confidence in others, even his political opponents. Diplomatic historian Samuel Flagg Bemis has written that he "towered above" any other Secretary of State between John Quincy Adams and William H. Seward and that his dignified, consistent, and conciliatory spirit "mark him one of our greatest Secretaries of State."[14]

The potentiality and accomplishment of each of these Secretaries were influenced not only by personal qualities, preparation, the course of events, and the needs and opportunities of the times but also by the role assumed by the President. Technically and pragmatically, the President is the principal executive officer for foreign policy making, and the Secretary is the chief adviser and administrator. In addition to exercising the role of policy maker, during this period both Presidents Jackson and Buchanan also deliberately sought to be their own Secretaries of State. Buchanan, like Thomas Jefferson and John Quincy Adams, was especially well equipped to assume this function. Formerly Envoy Extraordinary to Russia for a year and Secretary of State for four years, during which he negotiated and signed four treaties with Austria, Great Britain, and Switzerland, he was convinced that he could and should serve as his own Secretary.[15] As a consequence, this posture of Jackson and Buchanan affected the attitudes and performance of the first four and the last two Secretaries during this period.

STAFFING AND REORGANIZING THE DEPARTMENT

At the deputy level of management in the Department of State, the Chief Clerk continued as the principal surrogate of the Secretary until the mid-1850s, when this office was superseded by the Assistant Secretary, reminiscent of the Under Secretaries elected during the Confederation years. Unlike the Chief Clerk, the Assistant Secretary was commissioned when appointed. Nevertheless, on August 26, 1842, Congress defined the authority and responsibility of the Chief Clerks of all the departments as supervising "under the direction of his

Table 4.2
Other Department of State Officers, 1829–1861

Chief Clerks [1]

Name	Appointed	Termination of Appointment
Daniel Brent (Va.)	Sept. 22, 1817 [2]	Aug. 22, 1833
Asbury Dickins (N.C.)	Aug. 23, 1833	Dec. 12, 1836
Aaron Ogden Dayton (N.J.)	Dec. 13, 1836	June 25, 1838
Aaron Vail (N.Y.)	June 26, 1838	July 15, 1840
Jacob L. Martin (N.C.)	July 16, 1840	Mar. 5, 1841
Daniel Fletcher Webster (Mass.)	Mar. 6, 1841	Apr. 23, 1843
William S. Derrick (Pa.)	Apr. 24, 1843	Apr. 9, 1844
Richard K. Cralle (Va.)	Apr. 10, 1844	Mar. 10, 1845
William S. Derrick (Pa.)	Mar. 11, 1845	Aug. 27, 1845
Nicholas P. Trist (Va.)	Aug. 28, 1845	Apr. 14, 1847
William S. Derrick (Pa.)	Apr. 15, 1847	Jan. 25, 1848
John Appleton (Me.)	Jan. 26, 1848	Apr. 25, 1848
William S. Derrick (Pa.)	Apr. 25, 1848	May 15, 1852
William Hunter, III (R.I.)	May 17, 1852	July 27, 1866 [3]

Assistant Secretaries of State [4]

Name	Appointed		Termination
Ambrose Dudley Mann (Ohio)	Mar. 23, 1853		May 8, 1855
William Hunter, III (R.I.)	May 8, 1855	May 9, 1855	Oct. 31, 1855
John Addison Thomas (N.Y.)	Nov. 1, 1855	Nov. 1, 1855	Apr. 3, 1857
John Appleton (Me.)	Apr. 4, 1857	Apr. 4, 1857	June 10, 1860
William H. Trescott (S.C.)	June 8, 1860	June 11, 1860	Dec. 10, 1860

[1]The office of Chief Clerk, as second ranking member of the Department of State, who was designated but not commissioned, continued until 1853. This office, though not as second ranking member of the Department, continued until 1939, was revived in 1942, and was abolished in 1944. In 1853 the Assistant Secretary of State became the second ranking member of the Department.

[2]Daniel Brent was continued in this position from Secretary of State Henry Clay's administration.

[3]William Hunter continued as Chief Clerk after the appointment of A. Dudley Mann as the first Assistant Secretary of State. He continued as Chief Clerk until he was appointed as the initial Second Assistant Secretary of State on July 27, 1866.

[4]Unlike Chief Clerks, Assistant Secretaries of State were commissioned officers.

immediate superior, the duties of the other clerks therein, and see that they are faithfully performed.''

Daniel Brent, inherited from Secretary Clay's administration, held the post of Chief Clerk for sixteen years, from September 22, 1817, to August 22, 1833, which provided valuable continuity. To 1860 he was succeeded by ten others, of whom William S. Derrick received four appointments between 1843 and 1852. Ambrose Dudley Mann was commissioned the first Assistant Secretary of State in 1853, and this position as chief deputy to the Secretary continued until 1927, although a series of higher-level offices were created in the meantime. Two other former Chief Clerks—John Appleton and William Hunter III— were later also appointed as Assistant Secretaries during this period. See Table 4.2.

Several Chief Clerks also held other positions. Like Brent in 1825, three functioned as Secretary of State ad interim—Jacob L. Martin (1841), Derrick (1843), and Hunter (1853 and 1860). Later, in 1866, Hunter was designated Second Assistant Secretary when that office was created. Three Chief Clerks were subsequently also accredited to diplomatic posts. These included Appleton—Chargé d'Affaires to Bolivia (1848–49) and Envoy Extraordinary and Minister Plenipotentiary to Russia (1860–61); Martin—first Chargé d'Affaires commissioned to the Papal States (1848); and Aaron Vail—who served as Chargé d'Affaires in both Great Britain (1832–36) and Spain (1840–42). In addition, Nicholas P. Trist, who was a Clerk in the Department for eight years, Chief Clerk from 1845 to 1847, and Consul to Havana, was later appointed as a special "Commissioner and Plenipotentiary" to negotiate a peace treaty with Mexico.

Staff of Secretaries Van Buren and Livingston, 1829–1833

When he became Secretary of State in 1829, Van Buren was disposed to apply the spoils system and was beleaguered by many applicants for appointment. He encouraged several of the clerks to resign, some of whom had served for five or more years.[16] However, he retained Brent as Chief Clerk, as well as some other clerks who had long experience, including John Martin Baker, Andrew T. McCormack, and Josiah Wilkins, which provided some degree of staff stability. Secretary Livingston, who was not favorable to the spoils system, made few changes in the departmental staff.

Secretary McLane's Reorganization and Forsyth's Realignment, 1833–1841

Inspired by President Jackson's concern with reducing the Department of State's domestic duties and with "so organizing that Department so that its Secretary may devote more time to our foreign relations," Secretary McLane instituted major reforms—what Professor Graham H. Stuart has called "the first over-all reorganization of the Department since its establishment in 1789."[17] In view of expanding departmental business, the Secretary submitted a memorandum to the President in August 1833, in which he reported that he had urged staff members to survey their functions and to suggest improvements in departmental organization and management. Based on the results, McLane prepared a series of recommendations, that he sent to the President for approval, who acquiesced in them and ordered their implementation.

By administrative order, McLane elevated the Chief Clerk to function as an "Acting Under Secretary of State" in charge of seven functional bureaus. Two of these, the Bureaus of Diplomatic Affairs and Consular Affairs, manned by five clerks, handled the business of American diplomats and consular officials stationed abroad and those accredited to the United States. The three clerks assigned to diplomatic matters were made responsible for individualized geographic areas. Derrick serviced France, Great Britain, the Netherlands, and Russia; Aaron Ogden Dayton handled other missions in Europe to which, three years later, certain countries in Asia and Africa and consular establishments in Morocco and the Barbary powers were added; and Hunter was made responsible for the Western Hemisphere.

The issue of structuring this dichotomy of interrelating functional and geographic responsibilities became more acute as the diplomatic relations of the United States increased. This reform also specified in some detail the duties to be performed by this Bureau, such as the preparation and indexing of instructions and communications, registering and filing the dispatches received, producing letters of credence, and preparing treaties for ratification. It also had responsibility for surveying the status and activities of each American diplomatic mission abroad and for maintaining a current record of the arrival of foreign diplomats and consuls in the United States.

The Consular Bureau was given similar functions respecting consular correspondence, keeping indexes and summaries of the state of relations with American consulates, and issuing and recording exequaturs issued (which was transferred to the Home Bureau the following year). Francis Markoe, Jr., and Benjamin C. Vail were originally assigned to this Bureau, and a third clerk, T. W. Dickins, was added by 1836. Consular assignments were also structured on a threefold geographic basis.

The Home Bureau, managed by Andrew T. McCormic and Lewis Randolph, dealt primarily with filing and registering domestic correspondence with the Department, authenticating certificates issued under the departmental seal, and keeping a register of seamen and the arrival of passengers from abroad. Other domestic functions were ascribed to the Bureau of Archives, Laws, and Commissions and the Bureau of Pardons, Remissions and Copyrights. The first of these prepared and recorded commissions issued by the Federal Government; cared for, published, and distributed copies of laws enacted; and distributed messages of the President and reports issued by the heads of other Departments. These tasks were performed by Thomas P. Jones, formerly Superintendent of the Patent Office, assisted by George Hill. The Bureau of Pardons, Remissions, and Copyrights, headed by Arthur Shaaff, exercised its functions as they had been in the past and was also made responsible for the State Department Library and for collecting and maintaining a record of the statutes enacted by the States. Because its activities were so diversified, this bureau was abolished in 1834. The handling of pardons, remissions, and copyrights was turned over to the Home Bureau, and the maintenance of the Library was ascribed to the departmental Translator and Librarian.

To manage financial matters, the Disbursing and Superintending Bureau made purchases and disbursements, under the direction of the President and the Secretary of State, kept a record of correspondence concerning money transactions, and arranged for payments. Edward Stubbs headed this Bureau, and he also had custody of both the Great Seal of the United States and the departmental seal. The Translating and Miscellaneous Bureau provided for translating and filing communications and documents, the preparation of personal and special passports, and the maintenance of correspondence related to them, as well as miscellaneous correspondence. Robert Greenhow served as Translator. Finally, no substantial change was made in the Patent Office, which remained a separate responsibility of the Department and was administered as a special function, with Henry W. Ellsworth in charge, and, beginning in 1835, he was assisted by three clerks.[18]

This internally devised reorganization systematized the structuring of the Department of State staff, allocated jurisdictions and functions more precisely, and improved efficiency without materially altering its prescribed responsibilities. It was accompanied by directives to improve operational aspects of staff functions[19] and required the maintenance of confidentiality of diplomatic papers.[20]

On the other hand, the small number of clerks authorized to service the Bureaus responsible for Diplomatic and Consular Affairs, recognized as the chief functions of the Department, was manifestly insufficient to provide emissaries and consuls in the field with adequate and often necessary guidance and direction. This was especially the case with consular officers, who were obliged to exercise considerable discretion in performing their official duties.

At that time, although the total departmental staff remained small, during the period from 1829 to 1835, at least two dozen different persons served as staff members at one time or another. More important, several of them continued in their appointments for extended periods and eventually became professional staff members. These included Andrew T. McCormick, appointed in 1818, and William S. Derrick, William Hunter, Thomas P. Jones, and Edward Stubbs, who were appointed in the 1820s, two of whom (Derrick and Hunter) also were later appointed Chief Clerk and served as Secretary of State ad interim.

After Forsyth was appointed Secretary in 1834, he issued an order in October by which he realigned several departmental functions. He expanded the duties of the Home Bureau to include exequatur, commissions, passport, pardons and remissions, copyright, custody and application of seals, and other services. The Bureau of Pardons, Remissions, and Copyright and the Bureau of Archives, Laws, and Commissions were abolished, and the Office of Keeper of the Archives was created to have custody of departmental records and the rolls of the laws, as well as responsibility for the distribution of public documents. The Disbursing and Superintending Bureau was redesignated and alloted a Disbursing Agent, and the maintenance of the departmental Library was ascribed to the Translator.

As a result, the seven Bureaus were reduced to three, of which the Home Bureau was the largest and functionally most comprehensive. Subsequently, in November 1836, Secretary Forsyth also transferred the administration of the departmental Library to the Home Bureau and issued more extensive directions concerning the operations of the bureaus and the maintenance of security and confidentiality. In effect, Forsyth's action was more concerned with readjusting functions than with basic structural reform, so that the manifold division of functions continued, administered by the remaining three bureaus, the Patent Office, and a number of individualized staff agents, such as the Disbursing Agent, the Keeper of the Archives, and the Translator-Librarian. He did this without increasing the size of the existing departmental staff. Except for minor changes, this basic structuring of the Department was maintained for nearly four decades, until Secretary Hamilton Fish undertook to reform the Department.

As of 1836, when Asbury Dickins was Chief Clerk, the departmental staff consisted of thirteen clerks and the Superintendent of the Patent Office assisted by three clerks—totaling eighteen. The combined salary budget of the Department of State amounted to $29,500, including the Secretary, whose salary was $6,000, and the Patent Office, whose combined salary was $4,300.[21]

During the Administration of President Jackson and Secretary Van Buren the Department was saddled with two additional domestic functions. Complying with a Senate resolution, the Secretary was burdened with filing a report on the number of suits on the dockets of the Federal District and Circuit Courts and a report on the mileage traveled by each Justice of the Supreme Court performing judicial circuit proceedings. More laboriously, the Secretary was involved in the preparation of the sixth decennial census of the United States. In his report of December 1839, Secretary Forsyth noted discrepancies in the existing census law, the problems experienced by Federal Marshals in making the enumeration, and the difficulties of the Department in compiling, condensing, and printing them, and he submitted suggestions for improving the process. Eventually, however, by law enacted May 23, 1850, the seventh decennial census was turned over to the Department of the Interior, which had been created the preceding year.

Simultaneously, in 1849 the Department of State was relieved of responsibility for the Patent Office. Previously, Dr. William Thornton, in charge of the patent system, bore the courtesy title of Superintendent of Patents, which had not been recognized by law until April 23, 1830. The patent system was modified by statute on July 4, 1836, which created the office of Commissioner of Patents, under the Department of State, and which required the Secretary of State to sign all patents, substantiated by the countersignature of the Commissioner. When the Department of the Interior was created, the Patent Office was transferred to it.[22] Thus, with these changes, Congress commenced the process of relieving the Department of State of some of its most incongruous and time-consuming functions.

Staff of Secretaries Webster, Upshur, and Calhoun, 1841–1845

When Webster became Secretary of State in 1841, he appointed Daniel Fletcher Webster, his son—who had no previous experience on the departmental staff—as his Chief Clerk. In April the following year, Secretary Webster filed a report on the organization and functioning of the Department, specifying the duties of the Chief Clerk (including some additional functions not embodied in the realignment of 1836, such as drafting letters for the Secretary, reviewing and revising letters prepared by the departmental bureaus, superintending the operations of the Department, and assuming the duties of the Secretary during his absence).

At this time the Diplomatic Bureau had four clerks—Derrick to handle correspondence with the major European governments; Markow for other European countries, Asian and African governments, and Hawaii; and Hunter for Mexico, Central and South America, and Texas. The fourth prepared ceremonial letters and treaties, kept the secret journal of the Department, and handled letters of credence, full powers, and exequaturs. Similarly, Benjamin C. Vail, James S. Ringold, and Robert S. Chew performed correlative duties for the Consular Bureau.

The Home Bureau, the principal agency for the manifold departmental domestic affairs, was manned by seven clerks. These included the Disbursing Agent (Edward Stubbs, who also was Superintendent of the North East Executive Building), the Translator and Librarian (Robert Greenhow), Keeper of the Archives (Asbury Dickins), three clerks who handled other Home Bureau functions (Derrick, Horatio Jones, and McCormick), and a copying clerk (George Hill). Of these fourteen regular clerks, nine had been staff members for some time,[23] and only a few were recruited after 1836.

Supplementary staff members were employed for special, temporary tasks, such as producing a comprehensive report to Congress. These and the regular clerks, together with the Chief Clerk, messengers, watchmen, laborers, and agents engaged in forwarding departmental communications, totaled approximately thirty. Secretary Webster justified this growth of staff by stressing the increase in the number of foreign governments with which the Department was dealing and the amount of correspondence flowing back and forth, together with the burden of its many domestic functions. In a letter to the House of Representatives Ways and Means Committee, December 24, 1842, he argued for more regular clerks, or, alternatively, if they were not provided, he proposed increasing the employment of temporary assistants for special purposes.[24]

During his short term as Secretary of State, Upshur made no significant changes in either departmental organization or personnel. His successor, as Secretary ad interim, John Nelson, then Attorney General, filed a comprehensive report with the Senate, listing the names, nationality, and fees of American consuls serving the United States as of February 1844.

Calhoun became Secretary of State in March 1844, and he appointed Richard K. Crallé as his Chief Clerk, and Derrick, who had been a member of the departmental staff since 1827, reverted to the status of senior clerk in the Diplomatic Bureau. In a report on the Department early the following year Calhoun joined the litany of complaints of departmental understaffing and the necessity of recruiting temporary help. A month later, he also complained that between

1818 and 1845 only four regular, full-time clerks had been added to the Department. He stressed that during more than a quarter of a century the number
of American diplomatic missions and consular offices had nearly trebled and
that the duties of the departmental staff had quadrupled. He recommended that,
to comply with the Act of August 16, 1842, to produce an annual report on
foreign governments' commercial systems, a permanent Statistical and Miscellaneous Bureau be established and properly manned to replace the previous use
of supplementary or temporary clerks for this purpose.[25]

Secretary Buchanan's Management of the Staff, 1845–1849

On the appointment of Secretary Buchanan, Chief Clerk Crallé resigned and
was succeeded by Derrick as interim Chief Clerk, his second appointment to
this position. After only five months he was replaced by Nicholas P. Trist, who
had previously been a departmental clerk and for eight years served as Consul
to Havana. He held the office for less than two years, until April 14, 1847, when
he was appointed "Commissioner Plenipotentiary" to Mexico to negotiate a
peace treaty. Derrick was then reappointed as Chief Clerk, who was succeeded
by John Appleton early in 1848. After only three months, he was superseded
by Derrick, appointed to this position for the fourth time.

Dissatisfied with the understaffing of the Department, in 1846 Secretary Buchanan also filed a report on the matter, sent to the House of Representatives
Judiciary Committee. He complained that only three clerks in the Diplomatic
Bureau and only two in the Consular Bureau at that time were insufficient to
handle correspondence with what he described as "all the nations of the world,"
that he was the only departmental officer who could decide on foreign relations
matters and sign any departmental papers, and that, because of his manifold
administrative responsibilities, he was forced to neglect proper study and understanding of the host of American foreign interests and policies. He emphasized that in twenty-eight years the accumulation of the Secretary's diplomatic
responsibilities had increased by 236 percent and for consular affairs by 153
percent, whereas the departmental staff had been expanded by only 36 percent.
He added that, by comparison, the British Foreign Office, which had no domestic
functions, engaged a staff or more than two and one-half times that of the United
States.

To relieve some of his administrative difficulties, Buchanan also proposed
that the rank of the Chief Clerk be elevated to the position of Assistant Secretary,
with responsibility to manage the functions of the Department, other than diplomatic relations, leaving these in the hands of the Secretary. He also recommended that the salary of this new office be increased to $3,000, that three
clerks be added to the Diplomatic Bureau and two to the Consular Bureau, and
that the Patent Office be transferred to the Attorney General. It was not until
1853, however, when Everett was Secretary, that the office of Assistant Secretary of State was authorized by law.

One of Buchanan's recommendations bore fruit when, in 1848, Congress provided for the appointment of a clerk to deal with the claims of Americans against foreign governments brought to the Department of State, and in October Hunter, who had been a departmental clerk since 1829, was selected to assume this duty on an acting basis. The following March he was elevated to the position of Claims Clerk and was succeeded by Abel French on April 1, 1853, when Marcy was Secretary of State. Hunter and French were the only appointees as Department of State Claims Clerks, because this office was later retitled Examiner of Claims.[26]

Staff of Secretaries Clayton, Webster, and Everett, 1849–1853

In 1849 Secretary Clayton inherited Derrick as Chief Clerk, who was serving his fourth term in this office and remained until the spring of 1852, when he died.[27] Hunter continued as Claims Clerk. A number of other longtime clerks—including Robert S. Chew, Robert Greenhow, George Hill, and Francis Markoe, Jr.—continued as departmental staff members, all of whom had been appointed in the early 1830s. According to a House of Representatives report of February 21, 1850, Secretary Clayton increased the size of his staff substantially to embrace twenty-four clerks, one messenger and two assistant messengers, two special clerks, and others (such as several packers and one laborer).[28]

When Clayton resigned, in July 1850 President Fillmore commissioned Webster to his second appointment as Secretary of State. Shortly before he died in October 1852, he also filed a report on the matter of staffing the Department. He reiterated the need for an Assistant Secretary, with a salary of $3,000 (equal to that of the assistant Secretary of the Treasury). Later he also recommended increasing the salary of the Translator and Librarian and the appointment of an assistant translator. He deplored that, as of 1851 the Department had only nineteen regular clerks and that most were underpaid, inasmuch as only the Chief Clerk and the Clerk of Claims received annual salaries of $2,000, that only two others had salaries over $1,600, and that the rest received even less compensation. Because of Webster's declining health, in the fall of 1852 Chief Clerk Hunter performed many of the Secretary's duties until October 25, when Charles M. Conrad, then Secretary of War, assumed the role of Secretary of State ad interim.

Everett held the office of Secretary for only four months. He also felt the pressure of the tasks incumbent on his office and its staff and joined the ranks of his three predecessors who had proposed the creation of the Office of Assistant Secretary.[29] Only two weeks before he was succeeded by Secretary Marcy, he wrote President Fillmore, arguing that "the time is near at hand when the Department can hardly get on" without this new office. He recommended that Congress be petitioned to take this action, which was done, and the next Appropriations Act authorized its establishment in 1853.[30]

Reform and Staff Changes by Secretary Marcy, 1853–1857

Although Marcy is reputed to have authored the expression "to the victors belong the spoils,"[31] he did not apply it to appointments to his departmental staff. Because both President Pierce and Secretary Marcy lacked experience in matters of foreign affairs, in March 1853 they decided to appoint Ambrose Dudley Mann as the first Assistant Secretary, who was regarded as a "special diplomat" and a consular officer in that he had served more than ten years in Germany, Hungary, and Switzerland.[32] This marked a noteworthy change in departmental management in that Mann bridged diplomatic and administrative service, as did several of his successors in this office.

The President and Secretary also retained Hunter as Chief Clerk, who had nearly twenty-five years of experience as a departmental clerk, and two years later, in May 1855, he was temporarily advanced to the rank of Assistant Secretary, but he remained in this position for less than six months. He was succeeded on November 1 by General John Addison Thomas, who had been appointed as an American agent on the British-American Claims Commission. He held the office until April 1857 following the election of President Buchanan.

While Marcy was Secretary, Congress enacted major reform acts in 1855 and 1856 to regularize the Diplomatic and Consular Services, as noted later. The second of these enactments mandated considerable change in departmental personnel. The position of Superintendent of Statistics was formally created, although a statistical unit had been establishment two years earlier to prepare reports on foreign commercial systems, as required by an Act of 1842. Secretary Webster had assigned an extra clerk to this function, and later Secretary Calhoun promoted the notion of creating a departmental Statistical Bureau.

Secretary Marcy also introduced a new classification for departmental staff, based on salary levels. Aside from the Secretary, Assistant Secretary, Chief Clerk, the Disbursing Officer, the Superintendent of Statistics, and several other officers, the regular clerks were grouped into four salary categories: Class 4 (eight clerks, each at $1,800 per annum), Class 3 (ten clerks at $1,600), Class 2 (three clerks at $1,400), and Class 1 (four clerks at $1,200)—totaling thirty officers and staff members. They were supplemented with an additional twenty-seven special and temporary clerks, messengers, and others, thus aggregating more than fifty-five in addition to the Secretary in 1856.

Staff of Secretaries Cass and Black, 1857–1861

Shortly after Cass became Secretary of State in March 1857, he replaced John Addison Thomas with John Appleton as his Assistant Secretary. Appleton had previous experience as Chief Clerk for three months in 1848, as Chargé d'Affaires to Bolivia for four months in 1849 (the first American diplomat accredited to that country), and as Secretary of Legation in London in the early

1850s, and later he served as Envoy Extraordinary and Minister Plenipotentiary to Russia, 1860–61. Early in June 1860 he was succeeded as Assistant Secretary by William H. Trescott, who remained for six months and resigned on December 10. The staff of the Department remained relatively unchanged, except that the position of Disbursing Clerk, which had been abolished by law in March 1855, was revived two years later as the Disbursing Agent, was retitled several times, and continued into the twentieth century as expanded into the Bureau of Accounts.

When, in mid-December 1860, Black was commissioned as the last Secretary during this period, he had little opportunity or inclination to introduce any major innovations. The principal staff change contemplated at the time was the replacement of Trescott as Assistant Secretary. Secretary Black sought to recruit Thomas F. Bayard, but he declined,[33] so the post remained vacant, and the staff continued to function under the direction of Chief Clerk Hunter.

Reflections on Departmental Staffing

In addition to the growth and major reorganization of the Department and its staff and functions and the creation of the office of Assistant Secretary, it may be concluded that during these three decades eleven Chief Clerks and five Assistant Secretaries were appointed as senior staff members, and some thirty other regular clerks served to administer its functions.[34] A few of these had been appointed before 1829, such as Daniel Brent, William Derrick, Thomas P. Jones, Andrew McCormick, and Thomas Thurston. Some senior staff members received more than a single appointment, including Derrick (four appointments) and Hunter and Appleton (two each). The total number of senior, other regular, and temporary staff members from 1829 to 1861 approximated sixty. They were supplemented with additional temporary and special appointees of various types.

Individuals varied in their length of service. As a group the Assistant Secretaries averaged only 1.4 years in their appointments, and Chief Clerks averaged 1.85 years. On the other hand, representing longevity, Brent held the position of Chief Clerk for seventeen years (1817–33), Derick was a staff member and Chief Clerk for more than a quarter century, and William Hunter was a clerk, Chief Clerk, and Assistant Secretary for fifty-seven years (1829–86), and several others served for a decade and longer. On the other hand, some, such as Chief Clerk Daniel Fletcher Webster and Assistant Secretary Ambrose Dudley Mann, held office for approximately two years, and Assistant Secretary William H. Trescott remained for only six months.

As a consequence, staff appointments apparently reflected both the spoils system and, occasionally, nepotism but also, in some cases, stability and developing professionalism. Certain staff members became functional specialists in such matters as diplomatic and consular affairs, copyrights, patents, translation, and archives management. Interchange of individuals applied to both specific types of duties and assignments to departmental bureaus and, at times, to promotion to senior positions in the Department. A few staff members also were given diplomatic and consular appointments abroad.[35]

These developments denoted the virtue and necessity of building on past experience and the desirability of incremental structural innovation and administrative improvement. This also laid the basis for future expansion, reorganization, and, with the relocation of certain responsibilities to other Executive Departments and agencies, the commencement of relief from the burdens of a number of domestic and otherwise extraneous functions.

HOME OF THE DEPARTMENT

The Department of State was housed in the Treasury Building—also called the Northeast Executive Building—located at the corner of Pennsylvania Avenue and Fifteenth Street, to the east of the White House throughout this period and until 1866. This two-story, brick edifice was later described by Secretary of State Seward as substantial, neither stately nor imposing, but serviceable and convenient.[36] The Department of State was located on the second floor. Two rooms in the northeast corner served as the headquarters of the Secretary, one for his office and the other for receiving American and foreign officials. Across the hall were the facilities of the Assistant Secretary, the Chief Clerk, and staff members, and messengers were located nearby. Originally, these accommodations were adequate, but in time, as departmental responsibilities and staff expanded, they proved to be insufficient, especially for the housing of proliferating archives, other records, and the departmental Library. Nevertheless, unlike the preceding decades, the Department was finally able to enjoy a relatively stable headquarters site throughout this period and for nearly half a century. In addition, to accommodate the needs of dealing with patents, in 1828 Congress legislated for additional quarters for the Patent Office, and in 1836 it authorized the construction of a separate Patent Office building.

EXTRANEOUS AND DOMESTIC DEPARTMENTAL
FUNCTIONS—ALLOCATION AND TRANSFER

During this period preceding the Civil War, the burden and number of extraneous functions of the Department of State peaked. Many of them might have been handled by other Federal Government agencies, had they existed at the time, such as a Presidential Secretariat or Executive Office, a Congressional Secretary or Administrative or Servicing Agency, or a Home Department, or by other Departments that were later created. The Department of State continued as the prime residual administrative agency, and, as the country expanded territorially, its population increased, and the Federal Government's functions accelerated quantitatively, its nonforeign relations responsibilities mushroomed. However, this period also marked the commencement of the transfer of some of these activities to other Departments and agencies as Congress decided to establish them.

Because Congress still declined to create a Home Office, the Department of State continued to be saddled not only with the comprehensive national management and administration of foreign relations activities but also with the stewardship of many domestic functions. Naturally, it was responsible for issuing, publishing, indexing, and maintaining custody of the records pertaining to diplomats, foreign commissioners, consuls, and commercial agents abroad, including departmental instructions, credentials, correspondence, and the texts and documents concerning the negotiation of treaties and agreements. But it was also directed to serve in a similar capacity with respect to the resolutions, enactments, and other actions of Congress, presidential orders and proclamations, commissions, and other documents that concerned Federal domestic officials and affairs. In addition, it acted as the continuing agency for several major and minor residual responsibilities that were extraneous to the normal duties of the other Departments and the Attorney General.

Categories of Extraneous Department of State Duties

In his history of the Department of State, Gaillard Hunt designates some of these as "occasional duties" and "sometimes duties." Though necessary and important, often they were time-consuming and, in some cases, difficult to integrate logically into the developing structure of the Department of State and the conduct of foreign affairs. They may be grouped in four general categories— constant or continuing domestic functions, occasional domestic obligations, servicing domestic activities concerned with external ramifications, and domestic responsibility for compiling and publishing foreign affairs documentation.

One of the continuing domestic functions was the handling of executive appointments, dismissals, resignations, and suspensions of Federal officials. These included applications, recommendations, appointments, and other documents, not only for diplomatic and consular officers but also for other public officials. The documents, addressed to, and issued by, the Secretary of State, became part of the Department's archives. Thus, it was the preparation agency for many of them and the archival depository for most of them.

A related duty was to issue official commissions to various officials to authenticate their appointments. Beginning in 1789, these were prepared by the Department of State, signed by the President, authenticated by the Secretary of State and by the application of the Great Seal. This procedure applied to all civil officers appointed by the President with the approval of the Senate, which included diplomatic, consular, and domestic appointees. Archival commissioning records were maintained by the Department. For more than two centuries, responsibility for the custody and use of the Great Seal remained and continues with the Department of State.[37]

Initially, to implement Article 1, section 8, of the Constitution, Congress passed an act on April 10, 1790, that authorized the Secretaries of State and War and the Attorney General to issue patents on behalf of the United States. The Attorney General was required to examine letters of patent, and, if they qualified, they were certified to the President and were recorded by the Secretary of State's office, the seal of the United States was affixed, and they were then returned to the patentee. In February 1793 Congress revised this procedure by ascribing the granting of patents to the Secretary of State, subject to confirmation by the Attorney General that the letters patent conformed with the law. The Patent Office was launched as a separate division in the Department of State in 1802, with Dr. William Thornton in charge. He was unofficially regarded as "Superintendent of Patents" and served in this capacity until he died on March 28, 1828.[38] He was succeeded by Thomas P. Jones, who, in turn, was followed by Dr. John D. Craig in 1830, at which time the title of Superintendent was officially recognized by law.[39]

Because the issuing of patents was regarded as a special function of the Department of State, new legislation was passed in 1836. It reorganized the patent system and raised its status to that of a separate Bureau in the Department and created the Office of the Commissioner of Patents. It also required that all patents were to be signed by the Secretary of State and countersigned by the Commissioner,[40] who was empowered to appoint a Chief Clerk, patent examiners, and other assistants to service this function. This provided a staff of full-time professionals, and the Act of 1836 also authorized an appropriation for a library of scientific works and periodicals, both American and foreign. Congress viewed this function as warranting special facilities, so in 1836 it also ordered the construction of a separate Patent Office building. For some time the implementation of the patent service operated independently of the Department of State, and eventually, in 1849, when the Department of the Interior was established, the Patent Office and its records were transferred to its custody.

By comparison, the Department of State was not saddled with correlative authority to administer the American trademark system. Trademark administration is not mentioned specifically in Article 1, section 8, of the Constitution. It was not prescribed by statute until March 3, 1881, which was modified by subsequent legislation. It was superseded by the Lanham Act, adopted in 1946, which also has been subsequently amended several times. At the outset trademarks were administered by the Patent Office, located in the Department of the Interior.[41] The principal role of the Department of State has been to negotiate both international and inter-American trademark conventions.

The Constitution, Article 1, section 8, paragraph 8, coupled copyright protection and management with patents, which also became an early responsibility of the Department of State. The original Copyright Act of May 31, 1790, provided that to obtain a copyright of books and other materials, applicants would need to deposit each title in the Clerk's office of the U.S. District Court where the applicant resided, that public notice of the matter would be made, and that a copy of the publication would be deposited in, and preserved by, the Department of State. Therefore, it became the original repository of both copyright returns and copyrighted materials, which augmented its archival and library functions. It held this responsibility until an Act of February 5, 1859, transferred them to the Librarian of Congress.[42]

Similarly, the Department of State was given custody as repository of valuable American historical documents. These included the Declaration of Independence, Revolution archives, the records of the Continental Congress and the Constitutional Convention, the original copies of the Constitution, early diplomatic records and the original copies of treaties, the papers of early Presidents and other leaders, and similar archives. In the Department these were in the custody of the clerks concerned with archives and the departmental Library. By act of Congress, February 25, 1903, most of these were transferred to the Librarian of Congress.

Among the most extraneous, continuing duties of the Department was the role it was required to play in the handling of what was called "pardons and remissions." Although the office of the Attorney General was established in 1789, without the status of an executive Department, initially, the incumbent served only part-time as an adjunct of the Department of State. Federal judges, marshals, and attorneys communicated with, and received instructions from, the Secretary of State. In 1818 the Attorney General was provided with an independent office, but the marshals and attorneys continued to correspond with the Secretary of State until 1870, when the Department of Justice was created.

Of greater significance, throughout these decades and until 1893 the Department of State also exercised responsibility for the execution of presidential pardons and commutations of sentences. To 1850 the Secretary of State received petitions for pardons, examined them, made recommendations with the concurrence of the Attorney General, and presented the papers to the President for decision. In that year the President directed that this matter was to be administered entirely by the Attorney General. Thereafter, the Department of State acted largely in an administrative capacity, for preparing warrants, which were sent to the President for signature and countersignature by the Secretary of State. By executive order, in June 1893 the preparation of warrants was also transferred to the Department of Justice, and the Attorney General was required to execute this function and apply the Department of Justice seal to such documents.

In addition, the Department of State was engaged in compiling, forwarding, and, in some cases, publishing a variety of reports, many of which did not pertain to foreign relations. For example, as American continental "territories" were acquired and politically organized, because there was no Federal agency for their national management, their Governors and other leading officials communicated with the Federal Government through the Secretary of State.[43] Only by the Act of March 1, 1873, was this activity shifted to the Interior Department.

The Department of State also exercised other continuing functions, which had some relationship to external affairs but might have been the responsibility of a Home Department. These included the filing of reports on lists of passengers on ships that arrived in the United States and on the handling of immigration matters,[44] as well as the publication of reports entitled *Commercial Relations of the United States*[45] and the *Biennial Register* or *Blue Book*, which provided lists of all American officers and agents in the service of the American government.[46]

The second major category, consisting of occasional departmental extraneous functions, embraced participation in the publication of the decennial American census, the handling of Electoral College returns for electing the President and Vice President, assisting in the process of action to approve constitutional amendments, and servicing American participation in international exhibits and world fairs. The first three were solely domestic concerns, whereas only the fourth had relevance to foreign affairs.

The Department's involvement in preparing and publishing census reports to 1820 has already been discussed.[47] During this period, 1829–61, it was responsible for publishing the fifth and sixth census reports for 1830 and 1840.[48] By the Act of May 23, 1850, however, this task was transferred to the newly established Department of the Interior, and it was reassigned to the Department of Commerce and Labor in July 1903 and later to the Department of Commerce, to be supervised by the Director of the Census.

A strange and purely internal servicing function of the Secretary and Department of State was the recording of documents pertaining to the quadrennial elections of the President and Vice President. The Constitution, Article 2, section 1, stipulated that the votes of the State Electors were to be certified and transmitted "to the seat of the Government of the United States, directed to the President of the Senate." The Twelfth Amendment, adopted in 1804, changed the voting process, but neither stipulation prescribed the transmittal link between the Federal Government and the States. However, an Act of March 1, 1792, amended in January 1845, ascribed a number of contingency monitoring, transmission, and acknowledgment functions to the Secretary of State. Not until 1951 was this role transferred to the Administrator of General Services and in 1984 to the National Archivist.[49]

The Act of 1792 also made the Secretary of State responsible for communicating with State Governments concerning an Electoral College special balloting in the event that the country would be without both a President and Vice President. Later, the Presidential Succession Act of January 19, 1886, provided for automatic succession without such a special election.[50] In addition, the original Act of 1792 prescribed that, if the President or Vice President declined to serve or resigned from office, the only valid evidence certifying to this action was to be a signed, written instrument delivered to the Secretary of State. Such unusual action was first taken by Vice President John C. Calhoun, who resigned on December 28, 1832, to free him to serve in Congress as a Senator from South Carolina. Similar action was taken nearly a century and a half later by Vice President Spiro T. Agnew, on October 10, 1973. The only President to resign the office was Richard M. Nixon, who tendered his resignation on August 9, 1974.[51]

Another interesting internal servicing function of the Secretary involved certain procedures for amending the Constitution. It does not specify how amendments passed by both houses of Congress (which do not require executive involvement) were to be submitted to the States for ratification and how the States were to inform the Federal Government of their approval. Initially, the Secretary of State and the Governors of the States served as the conduit for this process. Reports on State action were sent to the President, who notified Congress of each ratification and transmitted the State messages to the Secretary of State for safekeeping.

Subsequently, in the absence of a law governing this matter, proposed amendments passed by Congress were communicated by the Secretary of State to the States for ratification, and approval and rejections were sent directly to the Secretary for transmittal and custody. In 1818 Congress regularized this practice, so that the Department of State became the customary conduit and transmittal agency for this purpose and also for proclaiming them when constitutional amendments came into effect. Later this duty was transferred, first to the General Services Administration and then to National Archives.[52]

Similarly, representing one of the Department's lesser activities, the Secretary became the communications agent for the United States with respect to American participation in international exhibitions and world fairs, but the Department has not been responsible for either managing or establishing regulations respecting them. Naturally, their initiation and national or other participation vary for those held abroad or in this country, but official international communications respecting them, at least through the nineteenth century, were interchanged through the Department of State.[53]

The third category of extraneous departmental responsibilities consists of continuing domestic responsibilities that relate to specific aspects of foreign relations. The first of these has involved the Department in the issuance of letters of marque and reprisal. Prior to the Mexican War, that is, during the conflict with France in the 1790s, those with Tripoli and Algiers in the early nineteenth century, and the War of 1812, the Secretary of State was authorized to issue such letters to arm private American vessels to attack and seize enemy vessels on the high seas. In 1863 this function was transferred to the Navy Department.[54]

As chief agent for foreign affairs, the Secretary of State has been charged with the role of dealing with other governments in cases of international extradition, which is the mutual process of surrendering individuals to the custody of another nation when they are accused or convicted for a criminal offense committed outside its own jurisdiction. In early American history this was handled by the Governors of the States. After the Constitution went into effect, this procedure continued, subject to the approval of the Secretary of State, and, in time, this became the exclusive function of the Federal Government.

Under international law and practice, such surrender of criminal fugitives must be based on statute and/or treaty, normally the latter, which creates a reciprocal obligation. The first international extradition commitment of the

United States was embodied in the Jay Treaty dealing with Amity and Commerce, signed with Great Britain in November 1794. It applied solely to the crimes of murder and forgery. A new treaty was concluded with Great Britain in 1842, known as the Webster–Ashburton Treaty, which dealt with several subjects, including extradition.[55] Some sixteen other bilateral extradition treaties were concluded by the United States during this period, 1829–61, as discussed later in the section on treaty making. This has become common international practice. Nevertheless, in 1933 the United States also participated in concluding a multipartite Inter-American Extradition Treaty.[56]

Aside from the task of negotiating such treaties, the Secretary and Department of State have been involved in administering the domestic process of extraditing specific individuals. Beginning in 1853, the normal process has involved three stages, which in the United States are known as the issuance of a request for arresting the individual concerned (often called a warrant of arrest), a warrant for surrender, and, in cases that involve fugitives from American justice, the President's warrant empowering American agents to go abroad to bring a surrendered criminal to this country for trial and punishment. To 1860 the warrant of arrest of an alleged criminal in the United States was signed by the President, and subsequently, being an intergovernmental document, it was signed by the Secretary of State. The application by legal authorities in the United States to have a fugitive who is located abroad extradited to this country has also been signed by the Secretary. The President's warrant to bring an arrestee back to the United States is signed by the President and countersigned by the Secretary. The Secretary continues to transmit and receive international extradition documents at the intergovernmental level.[57]

The issuance of passports by the United States, described as one of the ''manifestly proper functions'' of the Federal Government, has been and remains a continuing responsibility of the Department of State. Prior to the Constitution passports were issued by State and local authorities. However, in 1856 Congress enacted a statutory prohibition on this procedure and empowered the Secretary of state to issue them, under such rules as the President prescribed. Passports identify their holders as Americans entitled to protection abroad by the U.S. Government. Only the Department of State is authorized to issue them. They are of three types—diplomatic, special, and ordinary passports. Congress enacted a series of passport laws, beginning in April 1790 and June 1796, that were revised and updated in 1834, 1856, and 1926.[58] To administer this function, under Secretary Forsyth's reform its management was assigned to the Home Bureau. Subsequently, in 1870, under the reforms of Secretary Hamilton Fish, a separate Passport Bureau was created, headed by a Passport Clerk,[59] and this service continues to be provided by the Department of State.

Finally, as an important domestic function, the Department was responsible for the production and publication of a number of special compilations and reports concerning various aspects of American foreign relations. Examples include Jonathan Elliot, ed., *Diplomatic Code of the United States: Embracing a Collection of Treaties and Conventions between the United States and Other Powers from the Year 1778 to 1828* (Washington, D.C.: Editor, 1827)[60] and Jared Sparks, *The Diplomatic Correspondence of the United States of America from the Signing of the Treaty of Peace, 10th September, 1783, to the Adoption of the Constitution, March 4, 1789*, in 7 volumes (Washington, D.C.: Francis Preston Blair, 1833). These served as predecessors of a host of later departmental publications, such as brief histories of the Department, compilations of diplomatic papers, lists of Department and Foreign Service personnel, biographic registers, digests of international law as developed and interpreted by the United States and of arbitrations engaged in by the American Government, collections of the texts of treaties and lists of treaties currently in force, and reports on many specialized topics, to mention a few. Many of these and other publications are discussed or listed in later chapters.[61]

Transfer of Extraneous Responsibilities—Summary

Over time, most of these twenty-two extraneous activities of the Department have been transferred to other Federal Departments and agencies. During this period, 1829–61, three major responsibilities were assigned to the Department of the Interior, including patents (1849),[62] the census (1850), and copyrights (1859). Later, in 1870 the copyright function was reassigned to the Library of Congress. These actions relieved the Department of some of the most time-consuming duties of the Secretary and Department of State.

This led the way for the transfer of five more major extraneous activities by the end of the nineteenth century. These embraced the compilation and publication of the *Biennial Register* (to the Interior Department, 1861), the issuing of letters of marque and reprisal (Navy Department, 1863), the administration of continental territories (Interior Department, 1873), the filing of reports with Congress on passengers arriving at ports in the United States (Department of the Treasury, 1891), and the handling of presidential pardons and remissions (Department of Justice, 1893).

Soon thereafter, the task of coping with reports on the commercial relations of the United States was turned over to the Department of Commerce and Labor, established in 1903, and custody of the accumulated historical documents and records was shifted to the Library of Congress that same year. Subsequently, immigration administration was consigned to the Department of Justice in 1940, and the servicing of Presidential Electors' reports to the General Services Administration in 1951 and then to the National Archives in 1984. All of these actions constituted total transfers.

In addition, departmental involvement in the process of electing a new President if both the presidency and vice presidency were vacant was superseded by the Presidential Succession Act of 1886. Departmental obligation for at least three more tasks was partly shifted to other agencies. These pertained to the handling of appointments and dismissals of Federal officials, the preparation of commissions for them, and certain aspects of the extradition process.

This left the Department responsible for only a few remaining domestic extraneous tasks, some of which may be regarded as normal foreign relations administration. These embraced the processing of certain Federal commissions,[63] the production and publishing of compilations and other foreign affairs studies, the servicing of intergovernmental relations concerning international exhibits and world fairs, and the custody and application of the Great Seal—which burgeoned during the twentieth century. As a consequence, the Department of State was becoming a genuine Department of Foreign Affairs.

International Conventions and Organizations to Coordinate Such Functions

A correlative aspect of some of these functions is the action of the Department of State in negotiating international treaties and conventions, both bilateral and multilateral, concerned with them. Although some aspects of this matter are dealt with in the section on treaty making, especially extradition, to summarize, in addition to the multipartite convention to standardize weights and measures concluded at Paris in May 1875 (which is dealt with in Chapters 2 and 3), beginning in the 1880s the United States became a party to such conventions concerned with the protection of industrial property (both patents and trademarks) concluded in 1883,[64] the international exchange of official documents in 1886,[65] and the international publication of customs tariffs in 1890.[66]

Previously, the United States had already joined other nations in concluding a postal convention in 1863 to facilitate the international transmission of mails. Subsequently, the Department of State also participated in concluding conventions to align policy and provide for institutionalized cooperation respecting a great many other matters, such as atomic energy, civil aviation, development, education, fisheries (including seals and whales), human rights, hydrography, maritime affairs, meteorology, migration and refugees, mutual defense, outer space, peaceful settlement of disputes (including conciliation, arbitration, and adjudication), public health, radio, statistics exchange, telecommunications, and tourism, as well as global and regional banks and even legal metrology and epizootics.

Concomitantly, the United States became a joiner of a group of multipartite international organizations and other agencies to provide for cooperation in coordinating, monitoring, and, in some cases, regulating a variety of these subjects. Initially, these included the Universal Postal Union (joined in 1874), the International Bureau of Weights and Measures (1878), the International Union for the Protection of Industrial Property (1884), the International Center for the Exchange of Publications (1889 and 1968), and the International Union for the Publication of Customs Tariffs (1891).

Prior to World War II, the United States also joined such additional general international organizations as the International Institute of Statistics (joined in 1885), the International Penal and Penitentiary Commission (1896), the International Council of Scientific Unions (1919), the International Hydrographic Bureau (1921, succeeded by the International Hydrographic Organization in 1970), the International and, later, the World Meteorological Organization (1930 and 1949), the International Criminal Police Commission (INTERPOL, 1938), and the International Telecommunication Union (1934).

After World War II, the United States became a party to the General Agreement on Tariffs and Trade system (1948) and affiliated with the Bureau of International Expositions (1968), the Customs Cooperation Council (1970), the World Intellectual Property Organization (1970), and the International Center for the Study of the Preservation and Restoration of Cultural Property (1971), as well as the United Nations and its specialized agencies. In addition, the United States has participated in similar Western Hemisphere agencies, including the Inter-American Trademark Bureau (1912), the Inter-American Statistical Institute (1942), and the Inter-American Cultural and Trade Center (1966).

To conclude, originally, the United States was reluctant to become committed to such international conventions and organizations unless they were conceived as being important and advantageous to its commercial and national interests and did not impinge on its political independence and security. However, except for its initial cooperation respecting international postal affairs, not until the 1880s did the American government begin to participate in global and inter-American conventions and agencies, and after World War II it became a prime initiator in generating many such arrangements. Eventually, these affiliations numbered more than 200.[67]

On the other hand, it should be noted that, for dealing with the alignment of American copyright interests, laws, and procedures with those of other countries, the United States delayed in undertaking multipartite commitments concerning them. In March 1891 Congress passed an act to amend American statutes to support mutual international copyright relations, but only under prescribed conditions. Thereafter, several approaches were employed, including presidential proclamations concerning American practice in dealing with particular countries[68] and, commencing late in the nineteenth century, the conclusion of bilateral agreements, largely by means of exchanges of diplomatic notes with individual countries. These exchanges simply provided for mutual recognition and respect for the national laws of the signatory countries.[69]

In the meantime, other countries joined to negotiate a multipartite Copyright Convention, signed at Bern in 1886, to which the United States did not adhere.[70] However, the Department of State did participate in concluding two inter-American copyright conventions, at Mexico City on January 27, 1902 (ratified by the President in 1908), and at Buenos Aires on August 11, 1910 (ratified the following year).[71] Eventually, a new global convention was signed at Geneva in 1952, which was ratified by the United States in 1954 and proclaimed the following year and which provided for an Intergovernmental Committee to administer it.[72] It took another three decades before Congress enacted a long-awaited revision of the American Copyright Law in 1988, although American legislation had been codified in the 1947 *U.S. Code*, Title 17, which was updated in 1976.[73]

DIPLOMATIC AND CONSULAR REPRESENTATION

This period of three decades prior to President Lincoln's inauguration also produced significant changes in the nature, organization, and management of the Diplomatic and Consular Corps and their activities. William Barnes and John Heath Morgan in their study of *The Foreign Service of the United States* stress the significance of applying the spoils system to diplomatic and consular appointments, and they conclude that this practice endured for eighty years. Although able emissaries were recruited, appointments frequently were determined by political and financial considerations, and many American representatives were temporary appointees who did not compare with the traditional professional diplomats of other leading countries.

Acts of 1855 and 1856

Movement to reform the spoils system originated in the early 1830s, and the first American Civil Service Act was enacted in 1883, but it did not apply to the Diplomatic and Consular Services. In the meantime, Congress enacted separate legislation in the mid-1850s to establish the first comprehensive organic structure for foreign representation.

On March 1, 1855, when Marcy was Secretary of State, Congress passed a detailed, innovative law that prescribed diplomatic and consular posts, ranks, compensation, and consular functions. It also specified that the President "shall appoint no other than American citizens" as diplomats or consuls, their assistants, and other workers, and it discontinued "outfits and infits"—that is, henceforth, compensation begins when the appointee reaches the assigned post and enters upon official duties and ceases the day a successor takes over the duties of the office. It regulated the location and the days and hours of functioning of legations and consulates, standardized and prohibited absence of emissaries and consular officers from their posts for more than ten days without previous approval of the President, and disallowed pay for such absences. It also prescribed a variety of specific functions to be performed by consular officials.

By applying to only Envoys Extraordinary and Ministers Plenipotentiary, Secretaries of Legation, and one Commissioner, in dealing with diplomats it disregarded the ranks of Ministers Resident (following the promotion of many envoys to that rank in 1854) and also Chargés d'Affaires and thereby appeared to automatically advance them to the status of Ministers Plenipotentiary. Of special significance, it put consular officers and commercial agents on a salary basis and required that the fees they collected be turned over to the U.S. Treasury.

This act was regarded as revolutionary and constituted an attempt to rectify the disorder that previously permeated the Diplomatic and Consular Services. However, Secretary Marcy disagreed with several of its provisions, especially the requirement that all Ministers Resident be promoted to the rank of Envoy Extraordinary and Minister Plenipotentiary and to provide them with Secretaries of Legation. He viewed such actions as unconstitutional because they impinged upon the discretionary authority of the President. He posed a number of queries to Attorney General Caleb Cushing,[74] who prepared an opinion, dated May 5, in which he informed President Pierce that Congress could not prescribe the power, rank, numbers, time, or place of diplomatic envoys or automatically elevate Ministers Resident to the status of Ministers Plenipotentiary. As a consequence, a number of the enactment's provisions were not implemented.

The following year, therefore, Congress passed a superseding law on August 18, that was more detailed and expansive and that made a number of important changes.[75] It reiterated some of the policies and administrative regulations of the 1855 Act but incorporated many additional specifications. It recognized and included Chargés d'Affaires and introduced the notion of presidential appointment of ''consular pupils'' to be selected on the basis of prior examination and training.[76]

It established rules to govern situations in which a diplomat served in two appointments simultaneously, a Secretary of Legation functioned as a Chargé d'Affaires ad interim, and a consular officer performed diplomatic functions during the absence of a diplomat. It also prescribed certain restrictions on diplomatic and consular officers. For example, they were required to maintain secrecy regarding public affairs,[77] and were prohibited from recommending ''any person, at home or abroad, for any employment of trust or profit under the government of the country'' to which they were accredited or assigned and from requesting or accepting for themselves or other persons ''any present, emolument, favor, office, or title of any kind, from such government.'' This Act of 1856 was so carefully framed that its essentials were not superseded until the twentieth century.

Unlike the treatment of consular functions, noted later, this enactment did not define the nature and responsibilities of diplomatic envoys and attendant personnel, except for such matters as the issuance of passports abroad. Presumably, this lack of prescribing diplomatic functions was due to the fact that their activities were governed by traditional international practice, comity, and law, and their concrete tasks were prescribed by the policies of the President and the individual instructions of the Secretary of State.

So far as the structuring of American foreign representation was concerned, this 1856 Act, like that of 1855, combined stipulations concerning the allocation of diplomatic and consular representatives with their ranks and their compensation, to encompass the totality of the Foreign Services of the United States.

It created six categories of officials: (1) diplomatic officers, consisting of three classes, each with a prescribed annual salary level, (2) Consuls General, (3) major Consuls, (4) Commercial Agents, (5) lesser Consuls, and (6) unsalaried consular officers. It also specified maximum diplomatic salary levels in each category for individual countries and other territories. To accommodate variation according to each individual diplomat's title and rank, it provided that Ambassadors,[78] Envoys Extraordinary and Ministers Plenipotentiary, and Ministers Resident would receive the full compensation specified, and lesser envoys would be paid smaller amounts as described later. Additional provisions were made for a few special types of appointees, such as an interpreter in China and a dragoman in Turkey.

Of historic administrative importance, the Act of 1856 empowered the President "to prescribe such regulations, and make and issue such orders and instructions, not inconsistent with the Constitution or any law of the United States, in relation to the duties of all diplomatic and consular officers, . . . and it shall be the duty of all such officers to conform to such regulations, orders, and instructions." This provision had the effect of giving the force of law to executive orders and other regulations of the President, which introduced the practice of executive control over the Diplomatic and Consular Services and became the basis of subsequent Department of State regulations.

Diplomatic Corps

From 1829 to March 1861 the number of U.S. diplomatic missions more than doubled, from fifteen to thirty-four.[79] In 1829 the Department of State maintained eight missions in Europe (Denmark, France, Great Britain, the Netherlands, Portugal, Russia, Spain, and Sweden) and seven in Latin America (Argentina, Brazil, Chile, Colombia [New Granada], Guatemala, Mexico, and Peru). By 1860 some nineteen new missions were established, seven in Europe (Austria, Belgium, the Holy See [the Papal or Pontifical States], Italy, Prussia, Switzerland, and the Two Sicilies), seven in Latin America (Bolivia, Costa Rica, Ecuador, El Salvador, Honduras, Nicaragua, and Venezuela), two in Asia (China and Japan), and three others (Egypt, Hawaii, and Turkey). The former Two Sicilies was incorporated into the new Kingdom of Italy.

The President made 252 diplomatic nominations during these thirty-two years, averaging nearly eight per year. As indicated in Table 4.3, some 211 served in their appointments, thirteen nominees declined to serve, the Senate failed to approve five of them, two died en route to their posts, six were nominated but not commissioned, and fifteen did not serve for other reasons. Thirteen diplomats were inherited by President Jackson and Secretary Van Buren in 1829. Several of these were replaced within a year, such as James Barbour (Great Britain), James Brown (France), Alexander Hill Everett (Spain), Christopher Hughes, Jr. (Netherlands), Samuel Larned (Chile),[80] Joel R. Poinsett (Mexico, whose recall had been requested), and William Tudor, who died at his post in Brazil in 1830.

Table 4.3
American Diplomats, 1829–1861

Country	Years to 1861	Appointed	Served	Declined appointment	Senate not approve	Died en route	Not Commissioned	Not serve for other reasons
Argentina *	1829-	11	7	1	1		2	
Austria-Hungary	1838-	8	8					
Belgium	1832-	8	7	1				
Bolivia	1848-	6	5					1
Brazil *	1829-	8	8					
Chile *	1829-	9	8					1
China	1843-	12	8	3				1
Colombia *	1829-	10	9				1	
Costa Rica	1853-	4	2	1				1
Denmark *	1829-	9	8					1
Ecuador	1848-	5	5					
Egypt	1848-	3	3					
El Salvador	1853-	2	0	1				1
France *	1829-	11	9		2			
Germany (Prussia) [1]	1835-	6	6					
Great Britain *	1829-	11	11					
Guatemala *	1829-	12	4	1	1	1	1	4 [2]
Hawaii	1853-	2	2					
Holy See [3]	1848-	3	3					
Honduras	1853-	4	1	1			1	1
Italy [4]	1840-	7	6	1				
Japan	1859-	1	1					
Mexico *	1829-	12	11					1 [5]
Netherlands *	1829-	8	8					
Nicaragua	1851-	7	5	1			1	
Peru *	1829-	5	5					
Portugal *	1829-	8	8					
Russia *	1829-	14	12	1				1
Spain *	1829-	11	9	1		1		
Sweden/Norway *	1829-	5	5					
Switzerland	1853-	1	1					
Texas	1837-45 [6]	6	6					
Turkey	1831-	6	5		1			
Two Sicilies [7]	1831-60 [7]	10	8					2
Venezuela	1835-	7	7					
Total 35		252	211	13	5	2	6	15 [8]

*Indicates countries to which American diplomats were accredited prior to 1829.

[1] Previously, John Quincy Adams served in Prussia, 1797–1801.

[2] William E. Venable died at post before presenting credentials.

[3] Envoys were commissioned to the "Papal States" or the "Pontifical States."

[4] Envoys were commissioned to Sardinia (capital at Turin) prior to 1861.

[5] John Slidell was appointed after Mexico had severed diplomatic relations with the United States, so that he did not present his credentials.

[6] Diplomatic representation to Texas was terminated when it was annexed in 1845.

[7] American legation was terminated in 1860, when the Two Sicilies was incorporated into the Kingdom of Italy.

[8] These envoys did not proceed to post or proceeded to post but did not present their credentials.

On the other hand, Larned, who had been accredited simultaneously to Chile and Peru, remained at his post in Peru until March 1837, Henry Wheaton remained in Denmark until the end of May 1835, and Thomas L. L. Brent left his post in Portugal at the end of November 1834.[81]

These diplomatic envoys represented a broad spectrum of the thirty States and the District of Columbia from which they were appointed. Of the individuals nominated by the President, some 128, or roughly half, came from the original thirteen States.[82] Seven or more were appointed from several other States, such as Alabama, Indiana, Kentucky, Louisiana, Maine, and Ohio. A smaller number were recruited from the more recently admitted States and the District of Columbia.[83]

A substantial number of these diplomats received multiple appointments. They are of two types, the more common sequential and the relatively unique simultaneous appointments. The sequential appointees include those who combined service as Department of State officials and as diplomats and those who held two or more nonconcurrent appointments to foreign governments. Seven diplomats also were appointed as Secretary of State and four as Secretary ad interim.[84] Four departmental Chief Clerks[85] and two Assistant Secretaries of State[86] also received diplomatic commissions. The rest fell into two subgroups, those who were given multiple sequential appointments to a single foreign country,[87] and nearly thirty envoys who were accredited sequentially to more than a single country.[88]

On the other hand, the practice of commissioning envoys to simultaneous diplomatic assignments, which was not exceptional in earlier times, was rare during this period. Samuel Larned, referred to earlier, was commissioned to Chile in February 1828 and presented his credentials in November and was also appointed to Peru in December and presented his credentials there in 1829. He served the two countries temporarily and was recommissioned and remained in Peru for nearly a decade. In the late 1840s Ambrose Dudley Mann was designated as a special Commissioner to negotiate simultaneously with a number of the German States.

The practice of appointing individual envoys to simultaneous assignments was attempted primarily in Central America, but without much success. At least a dozen were nominated for such joint positions. In the 1820s and early 1830s seven were commissioned to "Central America," of which only two actually served—John Williams and Charles G. DeWitt.[89] In 1853 John Slidell and Solon Borland[90] were also appointed to "Central America," but even though their rank had been raised from Chargés d'Affaires to Envoys Extraordinary, they also did not serve.[91] Later, in the 1850s, Beverly L. Clarke was accredited to both Guatemala and Honduras (1858–60), and Mirabeau B. Lamar and Alexander Dimitry were commissioned to both Nicaragua and Costa Rica (1858–61). Thus, only five of these twelve appointees actually held such dual missions.

The American Government had introduced the new rank of Envoy Extraordinary and Minister Plenipotentiary in 1814 and 1815,[92] and during the period from 1820 to the mid-1850s it virtually eliminated the ranks of both Minister Plenipotentiary and Minister Resident, except for Turkey.[93] However, in 1853, when Pierce was President, and Marcy was Secretary of State, the United States revived the rank of Minister Resident and applied it to Theodore S. Fay, the first American diplomat accredited to Switzerland. The following year it was reestablished as the common rank below that of Envoy Extraordinary and was simultaneously applied to sixteen countries.[94] At that time, this represented an advancement from the rank of Chargé d'Affaires, except for the Central American Republics. Shortly thereafter, however, the envoys commissioned to Costa Rica, El Salvador, and Honduras, as well as Hawaii and Japan, were also accredited as Ministers Resident. During this period, therefore, the superior titles of Envoy Extraordinary and Minister Resident were widely employed, and the rank of Chargé d'Affaires virtually disappeared.[95]

To summarize, of the 252 diplomatic appointments, eighty-four were at the rank of Envoy Extraordinary, thirty-two were Ministers Resident, and 121, or nearly half, were Chargés d'Affaires. Twelve, accredited solely to China and Hawaii, were designated as Commissioners, and three emissaries sent to Egypt bore the rank of Agents/Consuls General. More than half of the Envoys Extraordinary were appointed to such major European countries as France, Prussia, Great Britain, Russia, and Spain,[96] some thirty-one were appointed to eight Latin American countries,[97] and a few were named to Austria, China, and the Netherlands.[98] However, as of 1861, the United States was accrediting such Envoys Extraordinary to only twelve countries.[99]

Despite the discontinuance of appointing envoys as Chargés d'Affaires after 1885, numerically, this was the most commonly used rank during these three decades. It was employed in three ways: as the initial rank preceding later advancement to that of Minister Resident or Envoy Extraordinary,[100] as a fallback rank after commencing diplomatic relations at a higher level and then deliberately reducing the rank for extended periods[101] and as an interim or temporary rank for particular individuals.[102]

When the decision was made to renew the Minister Resident rank in 1854, a substantial number of Chargés d'Affaires were promoted to this higher status. Consequently, prior to the Acts of 1855 and 1856 American foreign representation had stabilized with nine Envoys Extraordinary, eighteen Ministers Resident, two commissioners (China and Hawaii), and one Agent/consul general (Egypt). In the next four years diplomatic relations were also initiated at the Minister Resident level with four more countries.[103]

The president and Department of State experienced considerable difficulty in establishing diplomatic representation in Central America. Prior to 1854, beginning in 1825, the president nominated fourteen envoys to this area, of whom only three served as chargés d'affaires in Guatemala and one in Nicaragua. The first of these, John Williams, was accredited as Chargé to Guatemala in 1825 (succeeded by Charles G. De Witt in 1833 and Elija Hise in 1848), and John B. Kerr was commissioned as Chargé to Nicaragua in 1851. To resolve its problem in this area the United States decided to appoint multiple representatives, accrediting them simultaneously to "the Central Republic of America," "the Federation of the Centre of America," "the Republic of Central America," simply "Central America," or "the Central American States."[104] Not until 1854, however, did the President begin to nominate particular envoys to the five individual states of Costa Rica, El Salvador, Guatemala, Honduras, and Nicaragua.[105] Thereafter, representation to these countries was established at the Minister Resident rank, in keeping with then-current American practice.

Finally, constituting a special case, between 1843 and 1857, the President appointed ten envoys to China, all of whom were designated as Commissioners. In keeping with the changes in the 1850s, William B. Reed was accredited at the senior rank of Envoy Extraordinary and Minister Plenipotentiary in 1857. Similarly, the first three envoys sent to Hawaii were designated as Commissioners from 1853 to 1863, when James McBride was commissioned as Minister Resident. Although it was exceptional to designate regularly accredited American diplomats simply as Commissioner, it was more unique to denominate representatives as "Agent and Consul General," which was the case in appointing the first twenty-four emissaries to Egypt, beginning in 1848 and continuing until 1922, when the British Protectorate came to an end.[106]

Of the 211 diplomats who represented the United States abroad, only thirty served in individual assignments for more than five years. Those who remained in their appointments for the longest periods included Christopher Hughes, Jr., who initially held appointment as Chargé d'Affaires to Sweden and Norway for more than five years (1819–25), was recommissioned in March 1830, and continued for an additional eleven years (1830–41), totaling more than seventeen years in this post; John R. Clay, Chargé d'Affaires and later Envoy Extraordinary to Peru for nearly thirteen years (1847–60), when the United States suspended diplomatic relations with that country; David Porter, first Chargé d'Affaires to Turkey for more than eleven years (1831–43); and Henry Wheaton, Chargé d'Affaires and later Envoy Extraordinary to Prussia for nearly eleven years (1835–46).[107] Ten others held appointments for seven to ten years,[108] and sixteen for five to seven years. One of these, Auguste G. Davezac, held two separate appointments as Chargé d'Affaires to the Netherlands in the 1830s and 1840s, which combined, totaled nearly thirteen years.

On the other hand, illustrating one of the disconcerting problems of manning American diplomatic missions, nearly forty emissaries served in their appointments for less than a year, of whom four died at their posts. Wilson Shannon had his tenure of less than five months terminated by Mexico, when it severed diplomatic relations with the United States on March 28, 1844. Others served for even shorter periods, of four months or less, and the briefest tenures were held by Robert M. McLane, Commissioner to China for less than six weeks; by Tilghman A. Howard, Chargé to Texas, who was nominated by President Tyler on June 11, 1844, presented his credentials on August 12, and died fourteen days later; and Jacob L. Martin, who presented his credentials as Chargé d'Affaires to the Papal States (Holy See) on August 19, 1848, and died seven days later.

As was previously the case, most diplomats left their posts for such customary reasons as change in the presidential administration or determination by the Department of State to transfer an emissary from one post to another. In addition to Tilghman A. Howard, twelve envoys died in service. In two cases foreign governments requested the recall of American diplomats. These were Joel R. Poinsett, whose recall was requested by Mexico on October 17, 1829, and Anthony Butler, who had served in Mexico for nearly six years, whose recall was requested on October 21, 1835, because of his intrigues for the United States to acquire Texas, but he did not leave his post until his successor arrived in January 1836.

When Mexico severed diplomatic relations with the United States on March 28, 1845, Wilson Shannon, then Envoy Extraordinary, left his post and was replaced in January the following year, and John Forsyth, Envoy Extraordinary to Mexico, was relieved of his post when the United States "suspended" the political relations of its legation in June 1858. Similarly, John R. Clay, Envoy Extraordinary to Peru, notified its government in October 1860 that the United States was suspending diplomatic relations with it, which were not renewed until 1862, although recognition of the Peruvian government was delayed for several more years.

At the time of the transition from President Buchanan to President Lincoln in March 1861, a preponderant number of envoys continued to serve the new administration in their foreign missions. Those of Texas and the Two Sicilies had been terminated,[109] And American diplomatic posts in five countries were vacant at the time.[110] All the rest of the American emissaries continued in their posts into 1861, several as long as November, and, though exceptional, Robert H. Pruyn remained as Minister Resident to Japan until April 1865.

Compensation of Diplomats

Major reforms respecting the compensation of diplomats were instituted by the Acts of 1855 and 1856. Early in the Marcy administration, the ten highest diplomatic salaries were fixed at $9,000 a year, with an additional $9,000 during the first year of service for what was called "outfit." In accordance with traditional practice, Congress could determine the use of categories of diplomatic ranks and the compensation of diplomats, the President could appoint particular individuals to diplomatic posts with the approval of the Senate, and the Secretary of State could recommend nominees for appointment and their diplomatic status. Congress continued to exercise considerable control through the appropriations process. From 1853 to 1857 it considered several notions for remodeling and regulating certain aspects of diplomacy, and in the mid-1850s it systematized salary arrangements for both diplomats and consular officers.

The Act of 1855 stipulated the maximum annual salaries for Envoys Extraordinary and Ministers Plenipotentiary for twenty-eight countries.[111] These ranged from $7,000 per year for sixteen envoys,[112] to a maximum of $15,000 for diplomats accredited to China and France and $17,000 for Great Britain.[113] These compensation levels were based entirely on the location of diplomatic missions, but because the act fixed maximums allowed, the President and Secretary of

State were afforded some flexibility for variation.[114] If all the envoys were paid the maximum permitted under this plan, the total amounted to $267,000 for Envoys Extraordinary. Similarly, the law provided for the salaries of Secretaries of Legation for twenty-six countries, ranging from $1,000 to $2,500, totaling $44,000. Congress also authorized a Commissioner for Hawaii to be compensated at the rate of $6,000, an interpreter for China at $2,500, and a dragoman for Turkey at $2,500. All told, these salaries aggregated $322,000.

The Act of 1856 modified this arrangement by employing a clever, flexible, and more equitable formula that combined the specification of countries and salary levels with diplomatic ranks. Instead of periodically legislating salary levels or amounts for all individual legations and monitoring changes as additional countries were added to the diplomatic roster, as new emissaries were appointed, and as their diplomatic ranks changed, it enabled the Department of State to provide specific salaries for all envoys. However, Congress could change the categories of countries and the amount of salaries applicable to particular diplomatic ranks.

This act distinguished three categories of countries: (1) France and Great Britain, at the maximum annual salary level of $17,500[115]; (2) seven countries (Austria, Brazil, China, Mexico, Prussia, Russia, and Spain) at $12,000; and (3) all other countries at a maximum of $10,000. It also provided for six classes of diplomatic ranks—Envoys Extraordinary and Ministers Plenipotentiary, Ministers Resident, Chargés d'Affaires, Commissioners, Secretaries of Legation, and others. It mandated that salaries for Envoys Extraordinary would be at the full amount of the prescribed salary, Ministers and Commissioners at 75 percent of such amounts, Chargés d'Affaires at 50 percent,[116] Secretaries of Legation at 15 percent, and the Chinese interpreter and the dragoman in Turkey were ascribed specific salaries.

Diplomatic Ceremonial Dress

The matter of diplomatic court dress and uniforms emerged as a troublesome issue during this period. By way of background, differing from past practice, in 1817, during the administration of Secretary Monroe, the Department of State issued a circular that prescribed the wearing of a blue coat lined with white silk, a gold-embroidered cape, white breeches with gold knee buckles, white silk stockings, gilt shoe buckles, and a three-cornered hat, smaller than the French but larger than the British, and a ceremonial sword. This was to conform with established usage at European courts. During President Jackson's Administration, when Van Buren was Secretary, this was "democratized" to the wearing of a black coat with a gold star on each side of the collar, a three-cornered hat with a white cockade and a gold eagle, and a sword in a white scabbard—which was regarded as representing the simplicity of existing American institutions.

A quarter century later, on June 1, 1853, Secretary Marcy, electing to promote even greater democratic restraint, issued a revised "Dress Circular," prescribing the diplomatic attire to reflect the American citizen but authorizing that, if the occasion necessitated it, emissaries could wear a costume that allowed a minimum of elegance. The typical garb, therefore, was to be the conventional evening clothes usually worn in the United States on formal social occasions. Because the circular was loosely written, it left the individual envoy with considerable discretion. Nevertheless, because the American typical evening dress, it has been said, resembled the costume worn by waiters, servants, and funeral directors, the resulting problems of nonprotocolary attire at court receptions resulted in serious, embarassing developments.[117] American diplomats have frequently advocated the adoption of an American diplomatic uniform, but Congress has refused to authorize it.

Concerned with the furor over the matter, the Senate decided to debate the issue. During the Lincoln Administration, on March 27, 1867, it passed a resolution that stipulated that "all persons in the diplomatic service of the United States are prohibited from wearing any uniform or official costume not previously authorized by Congress." Eighty years later the Foreign Service Act of 1946, section 1001, reiterated that "no officer or employee" of the Foreign Service was to "wear any uniform except such as may be authorized by law."[118] In the absence of such legislative permission, these actions, therefore, categorically prohibited the wearing of formal diplomatic uniforms.[119]

Presidential Special Diplomatic Envoys

As in earlier times, presidential special envoys or executive agents were employed occasionally for certain types of diplomatic relations—for handling communications and negotiations prior to recognition and the exchange of traditional representatives, for the negotiation of treaties and agreements, and for other purposes. Examples of the first type applied to dealing with the Ottoman Empire (1830), Cochin China (Vietnam) and Siam (Thailand, 1833), Greece (1837), Sardinia (1838), Switzerland (1850), Japan (1854), Persia (Iran, 1856), and a number of German States (*Laender*), as well as for several island groups.

Special envoys also were commissioned to negotiate some thirty-six treaties and agreements with twenty-five different countries and other territories.[120] Six of these were concluded in the 1830s, eleven in the 1840s, and nineteen in the 1850s, evidencing a progressive increase. These treaties and agreements were of two basic types. Nearly half were negotiated by emissaries then accredited to other countries.[121] The rest were handled by special envoys specifically commissioned to represent the United States for this purpose, including several naval and military officers.[122]

Among the best-remembered executive agents are Ambrose Dudley Mann, Nicholas P. Trist, and Commodore Matthew C. Perry. Mann, who was later appointed as the first Assistant Secretary of State in 1853, was sent as a Special Commissioner to the German States, as a secret agent to Hungary to deal with Lajos Kossuth, the nationalist leader, with authority to recognize Hungary's independence if conditions warranted it, and as a special agent to Switzerland in 1850, where he concluded a Treaty of Friendship and Extradition, leading to the formalization of diplomatic relations three years later.

Of quite a different nature, during the Mexican War President Polk initiated a remarkable venture when he sent Trist, Chief Clerk of the Department of State, along with U.S. military forces under General Winfield Scott, as a presidential confidential agent, clothed with full powers to conclude a Peace Treaty with the Mexican government. On February 2, 1848, he signed the Treaty of Guadalupe Hidalgo, which ceded extensive territory to the United States.

During the following decade, President Fillmore decided to attempt the opening of Japan to Occidental contact, trade, and diplomatic relations. He appointed Commodore Perry to command a naval expedition to visit the island empire and, as a special presidential envoy, to negotiate a treaty for the United States. Perry sailed into Tokyo Bay, and in 1854 he signed a treaty and two executive agreements, which served as the opening wedge in Japanese relations with the outside world and paved the way for the persuasive negotiations of Townsend Harris that followed.

Often overlooked are the earlier exploits of Edmund Roberts, who undertook the earliest missions to Asia. He was an American trader in the Indian Ocean area and later a consular officer, who was commissioned by President Jackson to explore and conclude treaties with Cochin China (Southern Indochina), Siam (Thailand), Muscat (Oman), and Japan. Viewing his mission to Japan as his final, rather than his primary, responsibility, he negotiated treaties with both Siam and Muscat in 1833 but was unsuccessful in Cochin China. Two years later he returned to exchange ratifications of the two treaties and was directed by the Department of State to proceed to Japan to consummate his special diplomatic mission, but he died en route.

Consular Affairs

The Acts of 1855 and 1856 were even more revolutionary and detailed for consular officers than they were for diplomats. Among the main problems were the existing haphazard appointment to consular posts, the lack of previous training for the service, the compensation system founded not on fixed salaries but on the collection of service fees, the attendant disparity of such fees, and the general lack of professionalism.

Widespread complaints resulted in initiatives for reform, focused especially on the fee system. The Senate became involved as early as 1830, when it requested Secretary Van Buren to report on the matter. He acknowledged the deficiencies of consular practice and noted the lack of statutory regulation and reports from the field. To assist him, consular officers at some of the main foreign ports were directed to file reports on their activities and problems. These were reviewed by Daniel Strobel, American Consul at Bordeaux who was in Washington at the time and who proposed a plan of reform. His report, submitted to the Senate in February 1831, recommended the principle of full-time officers, more guidance and direction from the Department of State, and other changes. But no action was taken by Congress.

Two years later Secretary Livingston filed a carefully prepared review of the subject with President Jackson. It defined the duties of consular officers, criticized the fee system, and suggested major changes, but Congress still took no action. Subsequently, additional proposals for improvement were produced, both in and outside Congress, including one devised by the House of Representatives Commerce Committee in 1846, and Secretary Buchanan approved measures being considered by the House of Representatives and added recommendations of his own. Again Congress failed to legislate reform.[123]

Not until the enactment of the Acts of 1855 and 1856, therefore, was the consular system subjected to major overhaul and stabilization. That of 1856 was comprehensive, precise, and demanding. Congress authorized the establishment of some 125 consular establishments throughout the world, with specific salary amounts ranging from $500 to $7,000 per year, which introduced a major renovation in the compensation system for many, but not all, consular officers.

Congress specified the location and compensation of four categories of consular officials, ranging from Consuls General to lesser Consuls, but not for unsalaried consular officials. Consuls General were authorized to be maintained in seven locations with maximum annual salaries ranging from $3,000 to $6,000.[124] Some eighty-two Consuls were individually specified for thirty-two wide-ranging countries and other territories.[125] The largest number were located in British territory (nineteen), followed by Spain (seven), France (six), China (five), and Russia (four). Their salaries were fixed at $1,000 in Amsterdam, Munich, Prince Edward Island, and Stuttgart, to as high as $5,000 for Paris, $6,000 for Le Havre, and $7,000 for Liverpool and London. The preponderant majority, however, were set at from $1,500 to $2,500. Only three Commercial Agents were included, with salaries fixed at $1,500 and $2,000.[126] Finally, thirty-three lesser Consuls were authorized for twenty-three countries and islands, with salaries ranging from $500 to $1,000.[127] If all consular officials in these four categories were paid the maximum salaries, the total amounted to more than $800,000.

Congress also recognized a fifth category, consisting of additional consular officials. Without specifying their number, rank, location, and salary levels, the Act of 1856 stipulated that they would be entitled, as compensation, to continue to collect fees for their services as prescribed by law. The number of such unsalaried officials in service throughout the world exceeded those placed on a prescribed compensation basis. According to the Department of State, the aggregate number of consular posts increased from 141 in 1830, to 152 in 1841, 197 in 1851, and, following the Acts of 1855 and 1856, to 480 by 1860.[128] This meant that the actual number of consular posts was nearly four times the number identified in the Act of 1856, so that a preponderant majority continued under the original fee system. Nevertheless, it set a pattern for salaried consular officers that could be applied in subsequent congressional salary authorization legislation.

Aside from these categories of consular officials, the Act of 1856 empowered the President to appoint Vice Consuls and Vice Commercial Agents and Deputy Consuls and Deputy Commercial Agents. But no separate compensation was allowed for their services, so that they were to be paid out of the salaries of the "principal consular officer in whose place such appointment shall be made." To clarify the titles of those engaged in consular affairs, the Act defined distinctions among types of consular officers as denoting "full, principal, and permanent" Consuls General, Consuls, and Commercial Agents, as distinguished from "subordinates and substitutes," such as Deputy Consuls and Consular Agents, whereas Vice Consuls and Vice Commercial Agents were defined as those who temporarily filled the places of consular officers when they were absent or relieved of their duty.

To enhance the professional nature of the Consular Service, the Act of 1856 introduced an additional category of consular officials. It empowered the President, "whenever he shall think that the public good will be promoted thereby," to appoint up to twenty-five American citizens as "consular pupils," each to be compensated at not more than $1,000 annually, and to assign them to consulates abroad. This stipulation introduced the novel principle of appointment based on examination to establish "qualifications and fitness for the office." It was the first to introduce the merit principle involving prior examination for appointment and training of consular officers, which was intended to move toward a corps of qualified and experienced consular officers.[129] However, this section of the law was repealed the following year, but a limited number of such appointments again were authorized by Congress in 1864.

Under the Act of 1855, Secretary Marcy issued a set of consular regulations, which set a precedent for his successors. As modified in 1856, the law created greater disciplinary control of the Consular Service and sought to eliminate abuse and corruption. It empowered the President to define official consular services and to prescribe fees for them. It also required that annual reports be filed with Congress, that the tariff of fees be publicly posted, that receipts be provided for fees paid, that a register of fees collected be maintained, and that consular officials render accounts to the Secretary of the Treasury of fees collected. To validate these arrangements, consular officers were required to enter into bonds to the United States—amounting from $1,000 to $10,000, or up to the annual salary of the individual—which bonds were subject to forfeiture for malfeasance, abuse, or corruption.

The 1856 Act also prescribed that no consular official was to exercise diplomatic functions or engage in correspondence or relations with a foreign national government unless expressly authorized to do so by the President and that he shall define the location and extent of consular and commercial districts. Furthermore, it specified their functions respecting the issuance of passports and the administering of oaths and prescribed responsibilities for handling the affairs of stranded seamen and deceased Americans abroad.

Although this enactment possessed the advantage of establishing a necessary framework for the administration of consular affairs, it did not replace political appointment with a viable merit or dependable career system. Many consular officials remained dependent on fees and engagement in private business or trade. It has been said that this act, so far as consular officers were concerned, was often honored in the breach more than in its observance and that the yearly income of some consuls exceeded the salary of the President. As a result, legislating in keeping with existing financial needs and resources left little room for perfecting a career service founded strictly on merit, which was not realized until the twentieth century.

Emissaries Remembered

Aside from those who served for exceptionally lengthy periods in their foreign assignments, such as John R. Clay, Christopher Hughes, Jr., David Porter, and Henry Wheaton, American emissaries are remembered for a variety of reasons. Seven of them were appointed Secretary of State, and five were commissioned as Chief Clerks and Assistant Secretaries of State.[130]

Not surprisingly, it is held that the key diplomatic positions at London and Paris were filled with a number of distinguished envoys. Louis McLane was named Envoy Extraordinary and Minister Plenipotentiary to Great Britain twice (1829–31 and 1845–46). Others of note who served in London during this period include Van Buren (1831–32), Aaron Vail (1832–36), Edward Everett (1841–45), eminent American historian George Bancroft (1846–49), and Buchanan (1853–56). McLane and Buchanan negotiated with the British government on the Oregon question, and later Secretary of State Buchanan signed the Oregon Treaty in Washington in 1846. Vail, although commissioned as Chargé d'Affaires, enjoyed the confidence of both President Jackson and the British Government and was later appointed as Chargé to Spain (1840–42). Bancroft was later given four commissions to Prussia and the German Empire (1867–74).

American Ministers to France included Edward Livingston and Lewis Cass, both of whom also were appointed Secretary of State, and William C. Rives and Richard Rush. Rives held two appointments as Envoy Extraordinary to Paris (1829–32 and 1849–53), and he concluded an important Claims Settlement Treaty with the French Government in 1831. Rush had previously served as Secretary of State ad interim in 1817 and as Envoy Extraordinary to Great Britain (1817–25), and during his service in France (1847–49) he had to deal with the Revolution of 1848.

Among the ablest diplomats was Henry Wheaton, who served continuously in Europe for more than eighteen years as America's first emissary, at the rank of Chargé d'Affaires, in Denmark (1827–35) and then as the first envoy to Prussia since John Quincy Adams. He was accredited to Berlin as a Chargé d'Affaires in 1835 and was promoted to Envoy Extraordinary two years later, where he remained until July 1846. He concluded a Claims Convention with Denmark in 1830 and treaties with six of the German States between 1840 and 1846, which he signed in Berlin.[131] His treaty work among the German States was later continued by special envoy Ambrose Dudley Mann.

Remembered for their special diplomatic exploits with Mexico are Nicholas P. Trist and James Gadsden. Trist, departmental Chief Clerk (1845–47), commissioned as a special presidential envoy, concluded the Peace Treaty of Guadalupe Hidalgo. Five years later Gadsden, Envoy Extraordinary and Minister Plenipotentiary to Mexico, signed a boundary treaty whereby the so-called Gadsden Territory was ceded to the United States, for which he is remembered.

Especially impressive for their diplomatic achievements as special envoys in Asia and the Pacific were Edmund Roberts, Caleb Cushing, Commodore Matthew C. Perry, and Townsend Harris. Roberts was the first American emissary to Asia, who concluded treaties with Siam (Thailand) and Muscat (Oman) in the early 1830s. Cushing, accredited as Commissioner to China (1843–44), whose status was somewhat confused,[132] negotiated a Treaty of Commerce with China at Wanghia in 1844. Perry concluded a treaty and two executive agreements with Japan at Kanagawa and Shimoda and also an agreement with the Loochoo (Ryukyu) Islands in 1854. As Consul General to Japan, and before he was accredited as American Minister Resident, Harris also was successful in negotiating three treaties with the Japanese government (1857–58), as well as a Treaty of Amity and Commerce with Siam (Thailand) in 1856. Diplomatic historian Thomas A. Bailey has memorialized him in his ''Hall of Fame for American Diplomats.'' These emissaries played a major role in initiating Japanese diplomatic relations with the United States and the Western world.

Others who served creditably were Commodore David Porter, John Porter Brown, and Andrew Jackson Donelson. After a distinguished career in the Navy and a short period of service as Consul in Algiers, Porter was commissioned as Chargé d'Affaires to Turkey in 1831 and promoted to Minister Resident in 1839, serving in that country for twelve years until he died in 1843. Brown has the distinction of serving in the American Legation in Turkey for forty years, as dragoman, as Chargé d'Affaires ad interim on several occasions, and as a commissioned Secretary of the Legation beginning in 1858, which position he held until he died in 1872. His value was enhanced by his knowledge of the Arabic and Turkish languages. Donelson, related to President Jackson by marriage, served as his private secretary when Jackson was President and was later appointed by President Tyler as Chargé d'Affaires to Texas (1844–45). He played a significant role in persuading the Texas Government to accept annexation to the United States. In 1846 he was appointed to succeed Wheaton in Prussia, where, as Envoy Extraordinary, he remained until 1849.

Also remembered, but in a different way, was Pierre Soulé, who was accredited as Envoy Extraordinary to Spain (1853–55), who has been called "a most undiplomatic diplomat," and who experienced "one of the stormiest diplomatic tours in the annals of the Department of State."[133] As a vocal promoter of U.S. annexation of Cuba, which he evidenced in a series of questionable actions in Spain, he impaired his usefulness as an emissary. He was a joint author, with American envoys to Great Britain and France, of the notorious "Ostend Manifesto," which recommended the purchase of Cuba from Spain and the forced seizure of the island if purchase failed. This was rejected by the United States, obliging him to resign his post in December 1854.

Among the luminaries appointed during this period were two distinguished American authors. Washington Irving, one of the most famous Americans representing the United States abroad at the time, was appointed as Secretary of Legation at Madrid from 1826 to 1829, where he wrote *The Conquest of Granada* and *The Alhambra*. From there he went to Great Britain, and in 1832 he returned to America after an absence of seventeen years. Ten years later he was accredited as Envoy Extraordinary and Minister Plenipotentiary to Spain, where he served until August 1842. Nathaniel Hawthorne, a close friend of President Pierce, published a biography entitled *The Life of Franklin Pierce* and helped him to be elected, and was rewarded with appointment as Consul at Liverpool in 1853. This was the most lucrative post in the Consular Service at the time. He produced a detailed account of his experiences, which was published as *Our Old House*, portions of which divulged his consular activities, and he resigned his post in 1857, then spent nearly two years in Italy and returned to the United States in 1860.[134]

TREATY MAKING

Evidencing growing concern with foreign affairs, due to the increasing number of countries with which it maintained diplomatic and consular relations and the expansion of its international interests, the American Government signed a great many more treaties and agreements than it did prior to 1829. During the preceding four decades American negotiators concluded a total of fifty-six with seventeen foreign governments, whereas in these three decades the United States concluded nearly 130 new treaties and agreements—averaging more than forty per decade—with fifty-three countries and other territories. Only one of them was a multipartite agreement.[135] See Table 4.4.

These treaties and agreements dealt not only with such traditional subjects as peacemaking, territorial expansion and boundary settlement, amity and commerce, navigation, consular affairs, claims indemnification, and peacekeeping arrangements but also with such matters as extradition, postal affairs, maritime rights in time of war, inheritance rights of private individuals, and even the construction of a Central American isthmian canal.

Other changes introduced were the negotiation and signing of a substantially increased number and percentage of executive agreements, the consummation

Table 4.4
Treaties and Agreements, 1829–1861

Country	No.	T or A		Washington	Abroad	1829-39	1840s	1850-60
				Bipartite				
Argentina	2	2			2			2
Austria	3	3		3		1		2
Belgium	3	3		2	1		1	2
Bolivia	1	1			1			1
Brazil	1	1			1		1	
Chile	2	2			2	1		1
China	4	4			4		1	3
Colombia	4	4		2	2		2	2
Costa Rica	2	2		1	1			2
Denmark	2	2		1	1	1		1
Ecuador	5	1	4		5	1	1	3
El Salvador	1	1			1			1
Fiji Islands	2		2		2		1	1
France	5	5		4	1	1	2	2
Germany								
Baden	1	1			1			1
Bavaria	2	2			2		1	1
Bremen	1		1		1			1
Brunswick-Luneburg	1	1		1				1
Hannover	3	3			3		2	1
Hanseatic Republics	1	1		1				1
Hesse	1	1			1		1	
Mecklenburg-Schwerin	2	1	1		2		1	1
Nassau	1	1			1		1	
Oldenburg	2		2		2		1	1
Prussia	1	1		1				1
Saxony	1	1			1		1	
Schaumburg-Lippe	1		1		1			1
Württemberg	2	1	1		2		1	1
Great Britain	10	7	3	7	3		4	6
Greece	1	1			1	1		
Guatemala	1	1			1	1		
Hawaiian Islands	2	1	1	1	1		1	1
Iran (Persia)	1	1			1			1
Japan	6	3	3		6			6
Lagos (Nigeria)	1		1		1			1
Loochoo (Ryukyu) Islands	1	1			1			1
Mexico	7	6	1	1	6	3	3	1
Muscat (Oman)	1	1			1	1		
Netherlands	3	3		2	1	1		2
Nicaragua	1		1		1			1
Ottoman Empire	1	1			1	1		
Paraguay	2	2			2			2
Peru[1]	7	5	2		7	1	1	5
Portugal	1	1		1				1
Russia	2	2		1	1	1		1
Sardinia	1	1			1	1		
Spain	1	1			1	1		
Sweden and Norway	1	1		1				1
Switzerland	2	2		1	1		1	1
Texas	2	2		1	1[2]	2		
Thailand (Siam)	2	2			2	1		1
Two Sicilies	4	4			4	1	1	2
Venezuela	10	2	8		10	1	5	4
				Multipartite				
Samoa	1	1			1	1		
Totals	129	96	33	32	97	23	34	72

[1]One treaty (1836) applied to the Peru-Bolivian Confederation.
[2]One treaty with Texas was signed in Houston, which then was foreign territory.

of pickaback arrangements largely by means of Declarations of Accession to preexisting treaties, and the conclusion of more claims settlements. These were supplemented with experimental procedures for handling postal conventions, treaties and agreements with not only Prussia but also thirteen other German States (*Laender*) and the Hanseatic Republics and several unusual treaty ratification and implementation arrangements.

Treaty Record

More than forty countries and other territories were added to the American treaty list. These ranged from twenty in the European area[136] and twelve in Latin America,[137] to six in Asia and the Pacific, three in the Mideast, one in Africa, and the newly independent State of Texas.[138] These supplemented and in some cases superseded preexisting treaties with such countries as France, Great Britain, several other European and Latin American states, and Morocco and the Barbary regencies.

In terms of constitutional procedure, whereas ninety-six were formal treaties, requiring Senate approval prior to presidential ratification, surprisingly thirty-three (or 25.6 percent) of them were executive agreements, evidencing both interest in consummating international arrangements without resorting to the more cumbersome American treaty process and coping with certain subjects that did not require legislative implementation or involve other nations that lacked full international status.[139] More than half of the executive agreements concerned claims settlements, and others dealt with such matters as amity and commerce, the maritime rights of neutrals in time of war, the joint occupation with Great Britain of the San Juan Islands, and the suspension of hostilities to terminate the Mexican War. Five of these agreements were in the nature of simple exchanges of diplomatic notes.[140]

An interesting procedural innovation was introduced in dealing with the separate German States. One executive agreement with Oldenburg was in the nature of a Declaration of Accession to a commercial treaty with Hannover, and five were Declarations of Accession to a Convention on Extradition with Prussia.[141]

So far as titles are concerned, a great many were simply designated as treaties or agreements. However, a goodly number were called conventions, especially those that provided for claims settlements but also those that dealt with consular, extradition, private inheritance, and postal affairs. A few bore such titles as simple declaration (of policy and general commitment), declaration of accession, exchanges of notes, and regulations. The only other designations employed were compact and protocol. These represent a majority of the titles used in modern diplomacy.

As in the past, most treaties and agreements—nearly 100—were concluded and signed abroad by American emissaries. At the outset it was unusual to have them consummated in the United States. The first to be signed in this country was a Commerce Treaty with Great Britain concluded at Philadelphia in 1796

and signed by Secretary of State Timothy Pickering, and during the first three
decades under the Constitution, only eight were signed in Washington.[142] The
pace increased substantially during this period, when thirty-four of them were
signed in the American capital.[143]

Some treaties and agreements were negotiated abroad by such consular officers as Townsend Harris, who signed four with Asian countries before he was
promoted to the rank of Minister Resident to Japan in 1859, and Consul J. C.
Williams, who joined U.S. Naval Officer Charles Wilkes in signing the tripartite
Samoan agreement in 1839. A few were negotiated and signed by special presidential envoys. These included James B. Bowlin (who signed two treaties with
Paraguay in 1859), Ambrose Dudley Mann (three with German States in 1846
and 1847 and one with Switzerland in 1850), Nathaniel Miles (a Treaty of Amity
and Commerce with Sardinia in 1838), and Edmund Roberts (who signed treaties with Muscat and Siam in 1833). Others were concluded by naval and military officers.

Most unusually, six Declarations of Accession by German States dealing with
commerce and extradition and one such Declaration by Hawaii to subscribe to
the principles of maritime neutral rights, which were in the nature of executive
agreements, were not signed by any American emissaries. Also uniquely, the
Commercial Agreement with Lagos (Nigeria) was signed by Commodore William K. Mayo aboard the USS *Constitution* off the coast of Africa in 1854.

Occasionally, treaties were negotiated and signed by more than one American
emissary. For example, a Commerce and Navigation Treaty with the Ottoman
Empire was signed in 1830 by Charles Rhind, Commodore James Biddle, and
David Offly; two treaties with Argentina were signed by Robert C. Schenk,
Envoy Extraordinary to Brazil and Chargé d'Affaires John S. Pendleton; and
the Mexican Suspension of Hostilities Agreement 1848 was signed by Major
General W. J. Worth and Brigadier General Persifor F. Smith and then ''rati-
fied'' by Major General W. O. Butler.

Whereas most treaty and agreement signers employed their full names, it is
interesting to note that some Secretaries of State used initials or such abbreviations as Lew Cass, W. L. Marcy, A. P. Upshur, M. Van Buren, and Dan (or
Danl.) Webster. Similarly, others signed as C. Cushing, Alex Dimitry, J. Holt,
and M. C. Perry. More unusual were the signatures of Jn° Hamm, Robt C.
Schenck, and Jn° H. Wheeler.

Due, in part, to slowness and difficulties of communications between envoys
and the Department of State in Washington and delay for Senate consideration
and approval, the time lag between signature and implementation of some treaties was protracted. However, twenty went into force on signature, most of
which were executive agreements,[144] a substantial number became effective in
less than a year, and several went into force in a month or two. On the other
hand, though exceptional, the Treaty of Friendship, Commerce, and Extradition
with Switzerland took nearly five years to be implemented, and a Claims Convention with Peru took even longer, and both of these received double ratifi-

cation.[145] It is noteworthy that, whereas certain treaties and agreements expired upon fulfillment of their terms, many were later superseded or formally terminated, and a few endured for long periods, in some cases for more than a century.[146]

It may be noted that some treaties, negotiated and signed, failed to be ratified. During the half century from 1825 to 1874, of those submitted to the Senate for approval, only six were formally rejected, and nineteen others failed to be acted upon. Of these unratified treaties, nearly half were negotiated with European countries and most of the remainder with Latin American states. Four unapproved treaties with Mexico concerned a claims settlement (1843), extradition (1850), transit and commerce (1859), and U.S. intervention rights (1859). In addition, treaties with Texas signed in 1842 and 1844 dealing, respectively, with commerce and annexation and a treaty with Hawaii signed in 1855, providing for commercial reciprocity, also failed to be implemented.

Treaty Subjects

These treaties and agreements dealt with an increasing variety of subjects, grouped in three categories, as illustrated in Table 4.5. The preponderant majority (approximately 70 percent) were concerned with five traditional subjects. The largest number, amounting to at least one-third, provided for amity, commerce, and navigation,[147] twenty of which were signed in the 1850s, so that by 1860 the United States had concluded such arrangements with some forty-six countries and other territories. The Commerce and Navigation Treaty with the Ottoman Empire (1830)—addressed to "the Sublime Porte of perpetual duration"—was unique in several respects, including an appended secret article to provide the Ottoman Empire with seagoing ships.[148] The second largest number were claims conventions with 18 countries, which are discussed separately later. Others dealt with consular affairs, the acquisition of territory, and the settlement of boundaries.

Four treaties and agreements with Great Britain concerned territorial and boundary issues. That of 1842 provided for a process to resolve remaining issues concerning the northeastern boundary of the United States. Four years later the Oregon Treaty extended the 49th parallel of north latitude from the Rocky Mountains westward to the middle of the channel between the continent and Vancouver Island through the Straits Juan de Fuca to the Pacific Ocean. This treaty, which left all of Vancouver Island to Great Britain, specified that the whole of the straits, channel, and Columbia River was to be navigable by both nations.[149]

Following the War with Mexico, when the United States and Great Britain were competing for rights to construct a Central American isthmian canal to join the Atlantic and Pacific Oceans, by the Clayton–Bulwer Treaty, signed in 1850, they agreed that neither would unilaterally construct and exercise exclusive control over a ship canal through any part of Central America. That same

Table 4.5
Treaty and Agreement Subjects, 1829–1861

Basic Subjects	No.
Amity, friendship, commerce, and navigation	46
Claims	34
Acquisition of territory by United States, and boundaries	7
Consular affairs (duties, rights, privileges, and immunities)	4
Peace Treaty, Mexico, 1845	1

New General Subjects	
Extradition	16
Abolition of droit d' aubaine and taxes on emigration [1]	5
Rights of neutrals at sea	5
Postal affairs	3

Specialized Subjects	
Discontinuance of sound duties, Denmark, 1857	1
Disposal of personal property, Switzerland, 1847	1
Fisheries in North America, Great Britain, 1854	1
Inheritance, Brunswick-Luneberg (Germany), 1854	1
Navigation of Parana and Uruguay Rivers, Argentina, 1853	1
Port regulations, Japan (Shimoda), 1854	1
Reciprocal personal rights and activities of citizens, Switzerland, 1850	1
Regulation of trade, China, 1858	1
Rights of Americans, Japan, 1857	1
Ship canal (in Nicaragua), Great Britain, 1850 (Clayton-Bulwer Treaty)	1
Slave trade, Great Britain, 1842	1
Suspension of hostilities, Mexico, 1848	1
Total	133 [2]

[1]These dealt with the abolition of "every kind of droit d'aubaine, droit de retraite, and droit de detraction or tax on emigration." This unique type of treaty was negotiated solely with five German states.

[2]Because of multiple subjects combined in certain treaties, this total differs from the total number of treaties and agreements.

year, by means of an executive agreement, the two governments signed a protocol produced by a conference in London, that provided for the construction of a lighthouse at the outlet of Lake Erie and, to facilitate this purpose, for the cession of Horseshoe Reef to the United States.

By the Peace Treaty of Guadalupe Hidalgo, signed on February 2, 1848, Mexico ceded to the United States the extensive territory between the Rio Grande River and the Pacific Ocean,[150] in return for which the United States agreed to pay $15 million ($3 million immediately on Mexican ratification) and assumed the claims of Americans against the Mexican government in the amount of $3,250,000. This treaty, plus the prior annexation of Texas in December 1845, rounded out U.S. contiguous continental territory, except for a small triangular section of land desired by the United States to construct its American southern transcontinental railway. This additional territory was acquired by the Gadsden Purchase Treaty concluded in 1853—which diplomatic historian Thomas A. Bailey calls "The Gadsden Aftergulp." Under its terms Mexico sold 19 million acres of desert land south of the Gila River to the United States for $10 million payable in two installments. It also defined its boundary and provided for a joint commission to survey and mark it.

The second major category, consisting of nearly thirty treaties and agreements, introduced new subjects into the American treaty complex. More than half of these dealt with mutual extradition of alleged criminals for trial and judgment. American interest in dealing with international extradition began as early as the negotiation of the Jay Treaty, signed in 1794, but it began to burgeon during this period. All of these were concluded with fourteen European governments, including Prussia and eight other German States.

Unlike earlier treaties that specified only a few extraditable crimes, such as murder and forgery, the treaties with France (1843, 1845, and 1850), in addition to murder, applied to assault with intent to murder, arson, burglary, counterfeiting (of both paper money and coins), embezzlement (of both public and private funds), forgery, rape, and robbery. By and large, the extradition treaties with Switzerland (1850), Austria (1856), and Sweden and Norway (1860) included the same crimes but also added piracy. The pickaback Declarations of Accession to the Extradition Treaty with Prusia signed in 1852 applied to the same extraditable crimes but did not include burglary and rape.

Two unusual topics were introduced into treaty making, dealing with the rights of neutral states in time of war and subscription to the principle of what was entitled the abolition of "droit d'aubaine." Similar to the system used for the German States in subscribing to extradition, in the case of neutral rights the United States concluded basic bilateral treaties on the subject with Russia (1854), the Two Sicilies (1855), and Peru (1856). These were supplemented with executive agreements with Hawaii and Nicaragua in 1855, which were pickaback declarations of accession to the treaty signed with Russia.[151]

Of special historic significance, at the International Congress convened in France following the Crimean War, which was not attended by the United States, seven European nations subscribed to the Declaration of Paris.[152] It affirmed four basic principles to govern freedom of the seas and maritime neutrality in time of war, which the United States had supported from the outset and which provided the following: "privateering is and remains abolished" as a maritime practice; a "neutral flag" covers or protects immunity from seizure and confiscation of an "enemy's goods, with the exception of contraband of war"; neutral goods, with the exception of contraband, "are not liable to capture under enemy's flag''; and naval blockades, in order to be binding, ''must be effective,'' that is, ''maintained by a force sufficient really to prevent access to the coast of the enemy.''

Subsequently, several dozen other governments subscribed to these rules, but the United States, although it favored the general concept and most of its applications, did not accede to the Declaration because it did not go far enough to satisfy American objectives and national interests as a major maritime neutral during Europe's wars.[153] Eventually, the matter was dealt with in detail by the codification of international law on the rules of land and naval warfare agreed to at the Hague Conferences of 1899 and 1907 and embodied in comprehensive multilateral conventions, which were signed and ratified by the United States.

Designed to benefit persons who emigrated to the United States, in the mid-1840s the Department of State concluded some unusual conventions with several German States (Bavaria, Hesse, Nassau, Saxony, and Württemberg) to abolish ''every kind of droit d'aubaine, droit de retraite, and droit de detraction,'' thereby eliminating emigration taxes, recognizing the right of emigrant citizens to inherit property in the territory from which they migrated, and acknowledging freedom to dispose of property to the citizens of the other signatory.[154]

Finally, intending to facilitate the international transmission of mails, the United States also commenced to negotiate detailed, bilateral postal conventions to stabilize and regulate the procedure and postage for posting, transmission, and delivery of letters, newspapers, periodicals, pamphlets, and other materials. The first bilateral Postal Convention was signed by Chargé d'Affaires William M. Blackford with New Granada (Colombia) in March 1844. This was followed by the conclusion of such conventions with Great Britain by Envoy Extraordinary George Bancroft in December 1848, and with Belgium by Postmaster General Joseph Holt in 1859.

These postal conventions were regarded as formal treaties, ratified by the President. However, while the Colombian and British conventions were approved by the Senate before presidential ratification, the Belgian convention was ratified by the President without submitting it to the Senate for approval. This introduced an important, extraconstitutional deviation from the normal treaty process in 1859, so far as both negotiation and signing by the Postmaster General and the approval procedure were concerned, and set a precedent for future postal conventions.[155]

Claims and Settlement of Disputes

Approximately one-fourth of the treaties and agreements dealt with claims settlements with eighteen countries and other territories.[156] These included eighteen formal treaties and sixteen executive agreements. Twenty-four of them determined indemnification of the United States for a variety of claims, in many cases for the seizure and condemnation of American merchant vessels but also for the confiscation or destruction of American property and the mistreatment of Americans.[157]

In all but two of these settlements the other signatories agreed to pay for damages to the United States. In a treaty with France (1831) the United States committed itself to pay the French government 1,500,000 francs and France to pay the United States a lump sum of 25 million francs in six installments for distribution to Americans entitled to compensation. The Anglo-American treaty of 1845, to deal with the mutual claims of the United States for indemnification for excess British actions on "parcels of rough rice imported into England" and the claims of the British government for the refunding of excess American duties levied on goods imported into the United States under the Commercial Convention of 1815 also provided an interesting settlement. These claims were eventually offset, both governments agreeing that they acted in error, so that each was to review and verify the amounts claimed by its citizens, and the other government would pay the amount then decided upon.

The remaining ten claims settlement treaties and agreements were concerned with arrangements for the resolution of international conflicts by means of either joint or mixed commissions or by third-party arbitration. In the cases of disputes dealt with by treaties with Mexico (1839), Great Britain (1853), New Granada (Colombia, 1857), Paraguay (1859), and Costa Rica (1860), the treaties mandated the establishment of joint commissions (consisting of either one or two Commissioners from each country) appointed by the two governments. The Commissioners were directed to meet at a given place to resolve the dispute, and, if they failed to agree, they were to be joined by a third-party arbiter or umpire. Their determination would be final and conclusive.[158] An agreement with Ecuador (1857) differed in that it provided for a mixed commission of three Commissioners, one from each of the signatories, plus "a Foreign Gentleman resident at Guayaquil selected by the other two."

On the other hand, peaceful settlement treaties with Chile (1858) and Portugal (1851) differed in that they established the process of settlement solely by third-party arbiters. The Chilean dispute was required to be decided by the King of Belgium and that with Portugal by the "Sovereign, Potentate, or Chief of some other nation" to be selected by the two governments.[159]

CONCLUSION

This period evidenced a combination of both major internal and extensive external issues and developments. Highlighting the purely domestic were such matters as the rise of the spirit of the common person, political competition of Democrats and Whigs and the launching of the Republican Party in the presidential campaign of 1856, and the Lincoln election four years later. These were paralleled by the rise of nationalism, emphasis on national advancement, and the emergence of a sense of mission to promote the concept of democratic

republics abroad; Jacksonian democratization of political power, public participation, and administrative management; and employment of the spoils system.
Other factors of consequence were the increase of U.S. population from less
than 13 million in 1830 to more than 31 million by 1860, westward migration,
and the settlement, organization, and development of contiguous territories and
the admission of ten new States into statehood.

Also of importance were the domestic wars with the Black Hawk and Sem-
inole tribes in 1832 and 1836–46, the War with Mexico, the growth and realignment of sectionalism, and the events presaging the Civil War. These
included conflict over States' rights, nullification, slavery and the admission of
slave States and nonslave States into the Union, secession, and the preservation
of national integrity. Some issues bridged internal and external policies and
action, especially the secession of Texas from Mexico, its independence, annexation, and acceptance into statehood, and the transfer of certain State Department extraneous functions to other Federal Departments and agencies.
Others that involved both domestic and foreign relations concerned the handling
of extradition; the issuance of passports; issues of expatriation, naturalization,
and citizenship; and tariff policy, enactments, and administration.

In the international and diplomatic arena, the United States continued its policy of abstinence from European politics and insisted upon exercising its neutral
rights in time of war, while advancing its foreign commerce and consular interests beyond Europe and the Barbary emirates and counteracting the European
Doctrine of Mercantilism. In the Western Hemisphere it continued to apply and
refine the Monroe Doctrine and invoke it in recognizing the independence of,
and dealing with, Central and South American countries and the Caribbean islands.

It also expounded and applied its policy of ''Manifest Destiny,'' first coined
in 1845, which diplomatic historian Samuel Flagg Bemis calls ''Manifest Opportunity'' and diplomatic historian Wayne S. Cole calls ''Geographical Predestination.'' It represented a popular conviction that the United States would
expand territorially by peaceful process and extend its republican form of government throughout North America. Expansionist ferver reached its peak under
Democratic President Polk and Secretary Buchanan, which was modified by
periods of conciliation and friendly adjustment during the administrations of
Presidents Tayler and Fillmore and Secretaries Clayton and Webster, but it became more aggressive again when they were succeded by President Buchanan
and Secretary Cass.

The United States not only annexed Texas but also engaged in the Mexican
War, expanded its territory in the Southwest and Oregon Territories, rounding
out its contiguous continental domain, and disarmed its northern boundary. The
government also was concerned with European commercial and territorial interests in Central America and the West Indies, including Cuba and other islands,
and it recognized and established diplomatic and consular relations with individual countries as they gained their independence. It also evidenced early con-

cern with the potentiality of naval bases in the area and the construction of an isthmian canal in Central America. On the other hand, it opposed intervention in Hawaii and other Pacific Islands.

By law the United States created a new office of Assistant Secretary of State and in the mid-1850s reformed and systematized its Diplomatic and Consular Services, including specific salary arrangements and consular functions. It modified the ranking of American diplomats, elevating most envoys to the status of Envoys Extraordinary and Ministers Resident, and virtually eliminated that of Chargé d'Affaires. Foreign representation was expanded substantially, in Europe and Latin America and also extended to diplomatic relations in Asia and the Pacific, the Middle East, and Africa. And the Secretary of State and Congress fussed over diplomatic ceremonial attire.

Technically, the Diplomatic and Consular Services remained unprofessional, the spoils system was applied to presidential appointments, and some nepotism pertained,[160] but a few individual diplomatic and consular officers served for long periods and in various assignments, and they matured into professionals. In 1856, suggesting the initiation of professionalism in the Consular Service, Congress provided for the appointment of a limited number of trainees based on prior examination and experience, but this was short-lived. Some appointees served in both administrative posts in Washington and in diplomatic and consular assignments abroad, thereby providing for a degree of interchange. However, although the Diplomatic and Consular Services remained separate, a few individuals bridged the gulf and served in both capacities.

The United States also extended its treaty making considerably, both territorially and substantively, by adding thirty-six more countries and other territories to its treaty roster and by extending its treaty concerns to include extradition, personal inheritance, postal affairs, isthmian canal construction, and other matters. All but one of these treaties and agreements were bilateral, and, although the United States was a primary exponent of neutral rights, it refused to accede to the Declaration of Paris (1856). It also experimented with alternative treaty ratification procedures and tailored them in particular cases to bridge constitutional prescriptions with the needs of the times, which influenced subsequent practice. But it was not yet ready to participate freely in multipartite international conferencing.

In short, despite major concern with domestic issues and responsibilities during these three decades, the United States was becoming globally involved in terms of commercial and other nonpolitical matters, diplomatic and consular representation, and treaty making. As a consequence, the Secretary and Department of State were burdened with increasing duties and responsibilities.

NOTES

1. William Henry Harrison served as President for only thirty-one days, and Zachary Taylor for sixteen months.

2. James A. Hamilton of New York, who served in the New York Militia during the War of 1812 and on President Jackson's "Appointing Council," was a friend of Secretary-Designate Van Buren, and he served as Secretary ad interim for some three weeks.

3. Secretary Upshur and other notables, including President Tyler, the Secretary of the Navy, and others were guests aboard the battleship *Princeton* on the Potomac River on February 28, 1844. A large, new cannon, called the "Peacemaker," was fired several times without mishap. After lunch, on what was to be the last charge, the gun exploded, and Upshur, the Secretary of the Navy, and others were killed instantly, and many others were seriously injured.

4. Care must be exercised in assessing this factor. The initial nine Secretaries of State (1789–1829) were all from the original thirteen States, except for Henry Clay, who, although born in Virginia, twenty years later moved to Kentucky, from which he was appointed Secretary. During the following three decades all of the Secretaries were also born in the original thirteen States. Edward Livingston was born in New York in 1764 and moved to Louisiana four decades later, and Cass was born in New Hampshire in 1782 and served in the military in Michigan, where he settled after the War of 1812. Thus, it may be said that prior to the Civil War all Secretaries of State hailed from the original thirteen States, and only three were appointed from other States to which they subsequently moved.

In the meantime, between 1789 and 1800 three new States were admitted into the Union, from 1801 to 1828 some eight were added, and another nine were admitted between 1829 and 1860—totaling twenty new States and extending the American Union to thirty-three constituent States. As a consequence, from a geographical perspective, to the 1860s the corps of Secretaries of State were almost entirely recruited from the original thirteen States and therefore represented a small segment of the United States.

5. Although President Jackson did not originate the spoils system, he was responsible for transplanting it from the States to national politics. As a result, an "office-seeking class" emerged as part of the democratization of the Federal Government. Van Buren, Jackson's successor, more than anyone else applied to national politics the principles of political patronage that had been developed in New York, his home State, and yet, in March 1831, he resigned from the Cabinet because he regarded it as improper to remain Secretary of State while he was popularly regarded as a candidate for Vice President.

6. These included Van Buren, Livingston, McLane, Forsyth, Buchanan, Marcy, Cass, and Black.

7. Secretaries Webster, Upshur, Calhoun, Clayton, and Everett were appointed by Presidents Harrison, Tyler, Taylor, and Fillmore.

8. The six Secretaries who had no prior diplomatic appointments were Webster, Upshur, Calhoun, Clayton, Marcy, and Black.

9. These included Van Buren, New York Attorney General; Livingston, U.S. District Attorney in New York; Forsyth, Attorney General in Georgia; Upshur, Judge on the General Court of Virginia; Clayton, Chief Justice in Delaware; Marcy, Associate Justice on the New York Supreme Court; and Webster, who handled several cases before the U.S. Supreme Court.

10. In addition, McLane, Webster, Calhoun, Clayton, Marcy, and Cass aspired to become President; McLane, Forsyth, Clayton, and Everett to be elected Vice President; and McLane and Black to be appointed to the Supreme Court.

11. On the other hand, when Polk was elected President, he offered to appoint Secretary of State Calhoun as Envoy Extraordinary to Great Britain, but he declined. Although both McLane and Buchanan held diplomatic appointments after serving as Secretary of State, these were neither immediate nor related to their departure from the Department of State.

12. These emissaries were George Bancroft (appointed to Great Britain, who also served later in Germany), Richard Rush (accredited to France, who also was previously commissioned to Great Britain), and Henry Wheaton and Andrew J. Donelson (appointed to Prussia, where Wheaton served for seven years, and Donelson for more than three years). Wheaton previously was Chargé d'Affairs in Denmark, and Donelson was previously Chargé d'Affairs in Texas.

13. It has been written that Everett was adept at "taking a great idea or principle" and "could so clothe it in words as to make it live in the minds and hearts of men." As evidence of his oratorical ability, he embarked on a tour for several years throughout the country, lecturing on "The Character of Washington," and later, recognizing the greatness of Abraham Lincoln, he delivered a two-hour oration that "served as the foil for Lincoln's Gettysburg Address." See Foster Stearns, "Edward Everett: Secretary of State," in *The American Secretaries of State* series, vol. 6, pp. 137, 139–40.

14. Preface to *The American Secretaries of State and Their Diplomacy* series, vol. 4, p. viii.

15. As a diplomat Buchanan also negotiated and signed a Commerce and Navigation Treaty with Russia (1832) and two with German States (in the mid-1850s). Throughout his career he concluded seven treaties.

16. In his first Annual Message to Congress, December 8, 1829, President Jackson acknowledged that, because of Congressional reluctance to create a Home Department to relieve the Department of State of its burden of domestic functions, he was not "disposed to revive" the issue. See James D. Richardson, *Messages and Papers of the Presidents*, vol. 2, pp. 1024–25.

17. Stuart, *The Department of State*, p. 78.

18. For additional information on Secretary McLane's reorganization and duties of the bureaus and staff members, see Hunt, *The Department of State of the United States*, pp. 203–7, and Stuart, *The Department of State*, pp. 77–81.

19. For example, the McLane reforms provided that business hours were to run from 10:00 A.M. to 3:P.M., during which no clerk was to be absent without special permission; that all business was to be acted upon and disposed of within a day unless this was impracticable; and that all leaves of absence for a period longer than twenty-four hours would have to be requested of the Secretary in writing.

20. Thus, no copies of departmental papers relating to diplomatic and consular affairs were to be furnished to any outsider without express direction of the President or the Secretary of State, and no one was to write any letters relating to departmental business without the Secretary's advance approval.

21. For a listing of departmental clerks, as of 1836, with their individual dates of appointment and salaries, see Stuart, *The Department of State*, p. 83. For a comparison with those as of 1820, see Hunt, *The Department of State of the United States*, p. 201.

22. In effect, the patent function had gradually become an independent subagency of the Department of State. To 1836 the Secretary filed an annual report with Congress, listing patents granted, and from 1836 to 1842 this responsibility was ascribed to the Commissioner of Patents, which, after 1849, was transferred to the Department of the

Interior. Also see the section on the Department of State's Extraneous and Domestic Functions.

23. McCormick had been appointed in 1818; Derrick, Hunter, Markoe, and Stubbs in the 1820s; and Chew, Dickins, Greenhow, and Vail in the early 1830s.

24. Secretary Webster pointed out that in a decade responsibility of the Department for U.S. diplomatic missions had been increased from thirteen to twenty-one, and, most impressive, American consulates had mushroomed from approximately 130 to more than 160. For additional complaints of Secretary Webster, see Stuart, *The Department of State*, p. 92.

25. This Act of 1842 specified that "it shall be the duty of the Secretary of State to lay before Congress, annually, at the commencement of its session, in a compendious form, all such changes and modifications in the commercial systems of other nations, whether by treaties, duties on imports and exports, or other regulations as shall have come to the knowledge of the Department" (5 Stat. 507).

26. Abel French served as Claims Clerk until mid-1855. This office was superseded by the Examiner of Claims, created by law in July 1866 and abolished in June 1869. It was reestablished the following May and placed under the Department of Justice by the act creating that Department, approved on June 22, 1870. However, by an act of March 31, 1891, its title was changed to Solicitor for the Department of State.

27. William S. Derrick, who was a member of the departmental staff for more than a quarter century, died on May 15, 1852. He was first appointed March 3, 1827, as a clerk at the salary of $800, which eventually reached $2,000 when he became Chief Clerk, in which capacity he served in four separate appointments between 1843 and 1852. He also functioned briefly as Acting Secretary of State twelve different times, and the Department of State lists him as serving as Secretary ad interim for three days in 1843. After his death his widow petitioned the government for the difference in salary between that of Chief Clerk and Secretary of State for the 263 days he functioned as Secretary, amounting to nearly $2,900, but her request was denied. See Stuart, *The Department of State*, p. 116, who resents the reasons for this denial.

28. The House of Representatives report is cited in Stuart, *The Department of State*, p. 110, n.2.

29. For commentary on Secretary Buchanan's plea for an Assistant Secretary of State, see Stuart, *The Department of State*, p. 105; for Webster's plea, see p. 115; and for Everett's plea, see p. 117.

30. In his letter to the President, Secretary Everett acknowledged that this action would enhance the patronage of his successor but maintained that, despite this political disadvantage, it was "incontestably desirable for the dispatch of public business." For the text of Everett's letter and commentary, see Foster Stearns, "Edward Everett," in *The American Secretaries of State and Their Diplomacy* series, vol. 6, p. 138.

31. In a speech to the Senate, January 1832, Marcy had claimed: "They see nothing wrong in the rule that to the victor belong the spoils of the enemy."

32. Formerly an American consul in Bremen, in 1846 Ambrose Dudley Mann was sent as a bearer of dispatches to Berlin and on a special mission to the German States of Hannover, Mecklenburg-Schwerin, Mecklinburg-Strelitz, and the Grand Duchy of Oldenburg. Three years later, in June, while in Paris as an attaché to the American legation, he was appointed a secret agent to Hungary to review the possibility of recognizing its independence from the Austrian Empire, with discretionary authority to recognize Hungary and, if warranted, to negotiate a commercial treaty with its government.

33. A quarter of a century later Bayard was appointed Secretary of State by President Cleveland (1885–89).

34. Comparing this period with those that preceded it, during which only seven Chief Clerks were appointed, the turnover of senior staff, including sixteen Assistant Secretaries and Chief Clerks, accelerated significantly, denoting a degree of fluidity in senior departmental management.

35. These included Appleton, Mann, Martin, Trist, and Aaron Vail.

36. Quoted in Frederick William Seward, *Seward at Washington, as Senator and Secretary of State* (New York: Derby and Miller, 1891), vol. 2, p. 519.

37. After the Constitution went into effect in 1789, Roger Alden was responsible for the Great Seal, as noted in Chapter 2. In 1808 Stephen Pleasanton executed all civil commissions. Under the McLane reorganization, in 1833 this was turned over to the departmental Bureau of Archives, Laws, and Commissions, and the following year, when Secretary Forsyth enlarged the Home Bureau, he transferred this function to it. In 1841 it was committed to the care of a Commission Clerk, where, under changing designations, it remained for several decades. This position was held for nearly half a century by George Bartle, from 1852 to 1899, when he died.

38. An interesting historical development had occurred during the War of 1812, when Superintendent Thornton persuaded the British forces to spare the American Patent Office from destruction. Unfortunately, however, in 1836 its records and models were lost in a fire. See Bruce W. Bugbee, *Genesis of American Patent and Copyright Law* (Washington, D.C.: Public Affairs Press, 1967), p. 150.

39. The first American patent was issued in July 1790. In forty-five years, by late 1835, more than 9,000 patents had been granted under existing statutes.

40. For nearly half a century, 1790–1836, the Secretary of State also filed an annual report with Congress listing the patents conferred, and from 1836 to 1842 this was the responsibility of the Commissioner of Patents.

41. Trademarks became a major international treaty issue in the 1870s and 1880s. The United States provided for reciprocal registration and protection in international commerce in several bilateral treaties concluded in the 1870s, such as those with Austria-Hungary (November 25, 1871), Brazil (September 24, 1878), and Germany (December 11, 1871). Late in the 1880s the United States also adhered to the Paris multipartite convention, which dealt with both patents and trademarks, as noted later. See Bevans, *Treaties and Other International Agreements of the United States of America*, vol. 1, pp. 80–88 (hereafter cited as Bevans, *Treaties*).

For discussion on American international trademark relations with other countries in the 1870s–1890s, see Moore, *A Digest of International Law*, vol. 2, pp. 34–44 (hereafter cited as Moore, *Digest*). For current American trademark law, see *U.S. Code*, Title 15, Chapter 22, which deals with such subjects as applications, registration, certification, classification, legal and jurisdical protection, and infringement of trademarks.

42. In 1870 Congress passed a comprehensive copyright statute, that reconfirmed the assignment of authority for granting copyrights to the Librarian of Congress, who was made responsible for receiving and maintaining copyright records. The Library of Congress also became the depository for copyright documents previously maintained by the U.S. District Courts. Many of the old records were destroyed during the Civil War or were otherwise lost because of fire or negligence, but some 170,000 pre-1870 records had survived. After 1870 the copyright laws were revised or superseded many times; for current law, see *U.S. Code*, Title 17, Chapter 7, which concerns the Copyright Office.

43. Subsequently, in some cases, as noncontiguous territories were acquired by the United States, the Secretary of State also became the agent through whom communications were exchanged concerning them. Similarly, the Secretary was the Federal Government's channel for exchanges dealing with the sale of public lands in these American territories.

44. By the Act of March 2, 1819, as each vessel arrived in American ports, its officers were required to file a report listing all passengers. These reports were submitted to the local customs collector, who was directed to send quarterly returns, including ships' manifests, to the Secretary of State, who transmitted them to Congress. Beginning in 1874 these reports were transmitted to the Secretary of the Treasury.

Moreover, in 1864 Congress passed an Immigration Act, which authorized the President to appoint a Commissioner of Immigration to function under the Secretary of State. Four years later this arrangement was abolished, but when it was revived in 1891, it was assigned to the Treasury Department. Later it was transferred to the Department of Commerce and Labor when it was established, then to the Department of Labor, and eventually, in 1940, to the Department of Justice.

45. This was an annual compilation composed of reports of American consuls, consisting of "Commercial Digests," "Comparative Tariffs," and "Consular Relations." These were mandated by the Act of August 18, 1856 (11 Stat. 60) and were submitted to Congress until 1903, when this requirement was turned over to the Department of Commerce and Labor. These reports were supplemented with special trade reports prepared by American consular officers. For additional commentary, see Hunt, *The Department of State of the United States*, pp. 144–52.

From 1779 to 1812 the Secretary of State was also required by law to furnish Congress, at the commencement of each session, with an annual report based on information provided by collectors of customs on the impressment of American seamen by foreign governments.

46. This *Biennial Register*, required by Congressional resolution of April 27, 1816, listed all current officers and agents, civil and military, compiled and published under the direction of the Secretary of State. It was amplified by law in July 1832, and in 1861 this duty was assigned to the Department of the Interior.

47. The four decennial census reports of 1790–1820 are discussed in the section on the functions and responsibilities of the Department of State in Chapter 3.

48. Because the census report for 1830 was so poorly printed, Congress directed the Secretary of State to correct and republish it, and the two versions were bound and released together. The 1840 census consisted of four segments—a general compendium, an enumeration of inhabitants, a compilation of U.S. statistics, and a census of pensioners who had been engaged in military service, specifying their names, ages, and places of residence. It aggregated more than 1,450 pages. See Hunt, *The Department of State of the United States*, pp. 127–28.

49. The current practice is that Electors file six sets of election certificates by registered mail. See *U.S. Code*, Title 3, secs. 9–11.

50. For earlier reference, see Chapter 2, n.3.

51. Such resignation notification was transmitted by Vice President Calhoun late in December 1832, which was not acknowledged by Secretary of State Edward Livingston, so that Calhoun wrote a follow-up letter early in January 1833, which was then confirmed by the Secretary. In his initial letter, Calhoun wrote: "Having concluded to accept a seat in the Senate, to which I have been elected by the Legislature of this State [South

Carolina], I hereby resign the office of Vice President of the United States." See Clyde N. Wilson, *The Papers of John C. Calhoun* (Columbia: University of South Carolina Press, 1978), vol. 11, p. 685. A similar action was taken by Vice President Spiro T. Agnew when he resigned in October 1973.

Following an address to the nation on August 8, 1974, concerning his resignation, President Nxon wrote Secretary of State Henry Kissinger on the following day: "I hereby resign the office of President of the United States." See *Public Papers of the Presidents of the United States: Richard Nixon*, 1974, p. 633.

52. For additional commentary and for copies of representative instruments employed to implement this constitutional amendment process, see Hunt, *The Department of State of the United States*, pp. 168–78. For current law, see *U.S. Code*, Title 1, sec. 106b.

53. On the other hand, much of the administration and management, including international communications concerning international exhibitions and fairs, was handled by private agencies and persons for those that were held abroad, and the degree of those held in the United States has varied. For current law, see *U.S. Code*, Title 22, Chapter 40 on "International Expositions," which deals with Federal recognition, Federal participation, establishment of standards, and the like.

54. For earlier reference to letters of marque and reprisal, see Chapter 3, and for examples of a petition to obtain such a letter and of regulations for the conduct of privateers, see Hunt, *The Department of State of the United States*, pp. 154–57.

55. In Article 27 the Jay Treaty provided that "on mutual Requisitions" the two governments "will deliver up to Justice, all Persons who being charged with Murder or Forgery committed within the Jurisdiction of either, shall seek an Asylum within any of the Countries of the other, Provided that this shall only be done on such Evidence of Criminality as according to the Laws of the Place, where the Fugitive or Person so charged shall be found, would justify his apprehension and commitment for Tryal, if the offence had there been committed."

By the Webster–Ashburton Treaty, nearly half a century later, which was concerned with boundaries, slave trade, and extradition, the United States and Great Britain reconfirmed this extradition commitment and procedure. However, it expanded the list of crimes to include arson, piracy, and robbery. For the texts of these stipulations, see Bevans, *Treaties*, vol. 12, pp. 30, 88.

56. This unique multipartite Inter-American Extradition Treaty, signed at Montevideo on December 26, 1933, by twenty Western Hemisphere countries, defined the obligations, procedure, responsibility for costs, and forms of documentation for extradition among the signatories. However, it did not specify the crimes covered but merely stated that it applied to persons "who are accused or under sentence" according to the "laws of the demanding and surrendering States" that prescribe "a minimum penalty of imprisonment for one year." See Bevans, *Treaties*, vol. 8, pp. 152–60.

57. For examples of nineteenth-century extradition warrants, see Hunt, *The Department of State of the United States*, pp. 405–13, and for a comprehensive early analysis of American practice concerning the nature and process of extradition, with illustrative documentation, see Moore, *A Digest of International Law*, vol. 4, Chapter 14, pp. 240–424, and Whiteman, *Digest*, vol. 6, pp. 727–1122, which deals with actions under treaty and without a treaty, offenses, jurisdiction, surrender, procedure, evidence, conviction in absentia, and expenses; hereafter cited as Whiteman, *Digest*. For current U.S. law, see *U.S. Code*, Title 18, Chapter 209.

58. For illustrations of pertinent early legislation, the texts of various passports, rules

governing and instructions for issuing them, see Hunt, *The Department of State of the United States*, pp. 350–82, and for a table of the number of passports issued by each Secretary of State from 1810 to 1911, see p. 360. For a brief statement of passport work abroad by diplomatic and consular officers, see Barnes and Morgan, *The Foreign Service of the United States*, p. 198, and for the legal aspects of the subject in the nineteenth century, see Moore, *Digest*, vol. 3, pp. 855–1022; also see Whiteman, *Digest*, vol. 8, pp. 194–347, which deals with types, authority to issue, eligibility, renewal, denial, and alternative travel documents.

59. This Passport Bureau was abolished three years later, and in 1894 the passport service was assigned to a division of the Bureau of Accounts, still manned by a Passport Clerk. Later, in 1902, it was reestablished as the Passport Bureau, which in time was designated the Passport Office. For current law and practice, see the *U.S. Code*, Title 22, Chapter 4, and Chapter 38, sec. 2662.

60. This compilation was later republished as *The American Diplomatic Code . . . 1778–1834*, 2 vols. (Washington, D.C.: J. Elliot, Jr., 1834).

61. For a comprehensive compilation of Department of State publications, see Table 7.14, section on Diplomatic Documents and Publications; Plischke, *U.S. Foreign Relations: A Guide to Information Sources*, Chapter 22, especially pp. 549–68; and the Bibliography.

62. The management of issuing trademarks, generally associated with patents, was not assigned by law to the Department of State. By the time Congress passed the first act on the subject in 1881 and ascribed its administration to the Patent Office, it had already been moved to the Department of the Interior.

63. Currently, the law specifies that, with certain exceptions, such as the Defense Department, judicial officers, and some others, the Department of State remains responsible for issuing a good many Federal commissions. The law stipulates that the Secretary of State "shall make out and record, and affix the seal of the United States to, the commission of an officer appointed by the President." This is based on laws enacted in 1966 and 1975. See *U.S. Code*, Title 5, sec. 2902.

64. The Paris Convention for the "Protection of Industrial Property" was concluded on March 20, 1883, by eleven European and Latin American countries, to which the United States was not an original signatory but to which it adhered four years later, on March 29, 1887. It was amended and superseded from time to time, in 1891 (at Madrid), 1900 (Brussels), 1911 (Washington), 1925 (The Hague), 1934 (London), and 1958 (Lisbon). For the texts of these conventions, see Bevans, *Treaties*, vol. 1, pp. 80–88, 183–84, 296–301, and 791–803; vol. 2, pp. 524–41; and vol. 3, pp. 223–41; and Department of State, *United States Treaties and Other International Agreements*, 1962, vol. 13, pp. 1–46, hereafter cited as *UST*.

In July 1962 a revised convention was concluded at Stockholm. The President ratified it on May 25, 1970, except for Articles 1–12, which the United States could not ratify until it enacted new national implementing legislation. This was achieved in 1972, and the American Patent Office revised and published its new regulations on April 13 the following year. See *U.S. Code*, Title 35, Chapter 35. This was supplemented by a global trademark convention concluded at Nice in June 1957 to classify goods and services for purposes of trademark registration, which was replaced by the Geneva Convention of May 13, 1977, which came into force for the United States in February 1984. See *UST*, 1972, vol. 23, pp. 1336–1438, and Department of State, *Digest of United States Practice in International Law*, 1977, pp. 789–91, and 1979, pp. 1495–97. The United States also

participated in concluding regional inter-American trademark conventions, signed at
Buenos Aires on August 20, 1910, at Santiago on April 28, 1923, and at Washington on
February 20, 1929. For their texts, see Bevans, *Treaties*, vol. 1, pp. 767–79, and vol. 2,
pp. 395–405 and 751–74.

65. On March 15, 1886, the United States and seven European countries signed the
first convention, at Brussels, on the International Exchange of Official Documents. It
created a commitment to exchange national official parliamentary, executive, and administrative records and to establish national bureaus to manage this program. The same
day they also signed an additional convention for the immediate exchange of published
official journals, parliamentary annals, and related documents. Similarly, on January 27,
1902, at Mexico City, the United States and sixteen Latin American countries concluded
an inter-American convention that provided for a more comprehensive coverage of published official documents. It was superseded by a new convention, signed at Buenos
Aires on December 23, 1936, by twenty-one American republics, which made the national libraries of each country responsible for implementing this service. For their texts,
see Bevans, *Treaties*, vol. 1, pp. 107–11, 335–38, and vol. 3, pp. 378–82.

Under the auspices of the United Nations Educational, Scientific, and Cultural Organization, December 3, 1958, a new global convention for the exchange of publications
was concluded at Paris. See *UST*, 1968, vol. 19, pp. 4449–91.

66. An international Convention for the Publication of Customs Tariffs was concluded on July 5, 1890, and subscribed to by the United States and approximately sixty
other countries by the time of World War II, and eventually by approximately eighty
countries. On May 3, 1923, the United States also signed an inter-American convention
to provide publicity concerning national customs documents, including all ''laws, de-
crees, and regulations that govern the importation or the exportation of merchandise.''
The global convention of 1890 was supplemented in December 1949, when a protocol
negotiated at Brussels established the International Union for the Publication of Customs
Tariffs, to which the United States adhered in 1957. See Bevans, *Treaties*, vol. 1,
pp. 172–82; vol. 2, pp. 420–23; vol. 4, p. 864; and *UST*, 1957, vol. 8, pp. 1669–98.

67. Collectively, these numbered some 275 to 300. For discussion of subsequent and
current U.S. membership in international organizations, see secs. on international conferences and organizations in Chapters 5–7 and Tables 6.10 and 7.12.

68. For commentary on the process of achieving bilateral cooperation on copyright
by means of presidential proclamations, see Moore, *Digest*, vol. 2, pp. 45–55. Later the
United States informed the United Nations that, as of the 1960s, this country had applied
this procedure more than fifty times with some thirty-six countries. See Whiteman, *Digest*, vol. 13, p. 943.

69. Prior to World War II such diplomatic notes were exchanged sequentially with
Italy (1892 and 1915), Spain (1895 and 1902), China (1911), and Argentina (1934) and
later with Great Britain (1944), France (1947), the Philippines (1948), and Australia
(1949). Strangely, the only such bilateral arrangement consummated by means of a formal convention was concluded with Austria-Hungary in 1912.

70. The American representative to a conference held at Bern in 1885 did not sign
the resulting copyright convention concluded on September 18. A follow-up conference
was convened at Bern in September 1886, which concluded a definitive international
code on copyright, which also was not signed by the American government. It was
amended and supplemented in 1896 (Paris), 1908 (Berlin), 1914 (Bern), 1928 (Rome),
1948 (Brussels), 1967 (Stockholm), and 1971 (Paris), which entered into force for the

United States in 1989. See Moore, *Digest*, vol. 2, pp. 44–45, and Whiteman, *Digest*, vol. 7, pp. 913–14. Also see Department of State, *Treaties in Force*, Appendix.

71. For their texts, see Bevans, *Treaties*, vol. 1, pp. 339–43, 758–62.

72. For the text of this 1952 Universal Copyright Convention, see *UST*, 1955, vol. 6, pp. 2731–2828, and for commentary, see Whiteman, *Digest*, vol. 7, pp. 907–20. For a detailed description and analysis of American practice concerning copyright legislation, presidential proclamations, agreements, and conventions, listing the nature of bilateral and multilateral commitments, the individual foreign countries concerned, the dates of relevant documents and their effectiveness, and statutory citations, see Department of State, annual vol. on *Treaties in Force*, Appendix.

73. For additional commentary on U.S. practice concerning copyrights, patents, and trademarks, see Bruce W. Bugbee, *Genesis of American Patent and Copyright Law*; Levin H. Campbell, "Patent System of the United States: A History," *Official Gazette*, vol. 12, no. 5; *Everyone's Guide to Copyrights, Trademarks, and Patents* (Philadelphia: Running Press, 1990); P. J. Frederico, ed., *Outline of the History of the United States Patent Office*, Centennial No. of the *Journal of the Patent Office Society*, 18 (July 1936); Stephen P. Ladas, *Patents, Trademarks, and Related Rights*, 3 vols. (Cambridge: Harvard University Press, 1975); Emerson Root Newell, *Patents, Copyrights, and Trade Marks* (New York: Cooke and Fry, 1900); *Patent System of the United States So Far As It Relates to the Granting of Patents: A History* (Washington, D.C.: McGill and Wallace, 1891); L. Ray Patterson and Stanley W. Lindberg, *The Nature of Copyright* (Athens: University of Georgia Press, 1991); George Haven Putnam, comp., *The Question of Copyright*... (New York: Putnam, 1891); and U.S., Department of Commerce, Patent Office, *The Story of the American Patent System, 1790–1952* (Washington, D.C.: Government Printing Office, 1953).

74. Caleb Cushing previously had served as Envoy Extraordinary to China (1843–44) and later as Envoy Extraordinary to Spain (1874–77).

75. For the 1855 and 1856 Acts, see 10 *Stat.* 619–26, and 11 *Stat.* 52–65.

76. Section 7 of the 1856 Act authorized the President to appoint such "consular pupils" for assignment to prescribed posts and assignments. It specified that for appointment, candidates would need to qualify "by examinations or otherwise," certified to the Secretary of State for transmittal to the President. Also see section on Consular Affairs.

77. Section 19 of the 1856 Law specified: "... nor shall any diplomatic or consular officer correspond in regard to the public affairs of any foreign government with any private person, newspaper, or other periodical, or otherwise than with the proper officers of the United States."

78. It is interesting that the Act of 1856 should include the rank of Ambassadors, even though Congress had not yet authorized the appointment of diplomats at that level, and none would be appointed until 1893.

79. In the case of two countries, the United States also had earlier diplomatic relations—Germany (1797–1801) and Guatemala (1825–27).

80. Samuel Larned was simultaneously accredited to both Chile and Peru in 1828. He left Chile on October 29, 1829, but remained in Peru until 1837.

81. Larned served in his post in Peru for nearly seven years, Wheaton for more than eight years, and Brent for more then ten years.

82. These included Pennsylvania (twenty-six), New York (twenty-two), Virginia (eighteen), Massachusetts (twelve), Maryland (twelve), Georgia (seven), North Carolina (seven), South Carolina (seven), New Jersey (five), Connecticut (four), Delaware (four),

Rhode Island (three), and New Hampshire (one). It is noteworthy that all appointees to Great Britain, Portugal, and Spain and most of those to Denmark, France, Italy, the Netherlands, Russia, and Sweden—all European powers—were from the original thirteen States.

83. For example, four nominees were from Arkansas; three from Illinois, Missouri, Texas, and Vermont; two from Iowa; one from California, Michigan, and Wisconsin; and two from the District of Columbia.

84. As noted earlier, those who served as Secretaries of State and as diplomats were James Buchanan, Lewis Cass, Edward Everett, John Forsyth, Edward Livingston, Louis McLane, and Martin Van Buren, whereas Hugh S. Legare, Jacob L. Martin, John Nelson, and Richard Rush served as Secretaries of State ad interim and as diplomats. Most of these represented the United States to France and Great Britain.

85. These were John Appleton, who was accredited to Bolivia in 1848 and Russia in 1860; Jacob L. Martin, to the Papal States (Holy See) in 1848; and Aaron Vail, commissioned to Great Britain in 1832 and Spain in 1840. Also Nicholas P. Trist served as presidential special Envoy to Mexico in the 1840s.

86. These included Assistant Secretaries John Appleton and Ambrose Dudley Mann, who was commissioned as a presidential special envoy. Appleton served in three capacities, as Chief Clerk, Assistant Secretary, and diplomatic envoy.

87. Including recommissioning and promotion, those who held multiple sequential appointments were August Belmont (the Netherlands), Lewis Cass (Papal States), John W. Dana (Bolivia), John M. Daniel (Sardinia), Auguste G. Davezac (the Netherlands, 1831 and 1845), Charles Eames (Venezuela), William Hunter, Jr. (Brazil), John Leake Marling (Guatemala), John L. O'Sullivan (Portugal), Robert D. Owen (the Two Sicilies), James A. Peden (Argentina), William C. Rives (France, 1829 and 1849), Francis Schroeder (Sweden and Norway), and John Jacob Seibels (Belgium). Except for Davezac and Rives these were continuous appointments.

88. Examples of the nearly thirty emissaries who served in sequential multiple appointments to more than a single country include John James Appleton, George Bancroft, John R. Clay, Caleb Cushing, Andrew Jackson Donelson, George W. Erving, Alexander H. Everett, Christopher Hughes, Jr., Henry R. Jackson, Robert M. McLane, and Henry Wheaton.

89. Those who did not serve for various reasons were John Hamm, William N. Jeffers, William Miller (who died en route to his post), William B. Rochester, and James Shannon (who also died en route).

90. Solon Borland was the first to be commissioned to the individual republics as well as to ''Central America.''

91. Similarly, in the 1870s and 1880s individual envoys were accredited to ''the Central American States.''

92. By the 1850s the American emissaries to nine countries—France, Great Britain, and Russia (since 1815), Mexico (since 1823), Spain (since 1825), Germany (since 1837), Brazil (since 1841), Chile (since 1849), and Peru (since 1853)—had the title Envoy Extraordinary and Minister Plenipotentiary.

93. Ministers Resident were appointed to Turkey beginning in 1839, which continued until 1882.

94. These included Argentina, Austria, Belgium, Bolivia, New Granada (Colombia), Denmark, Ecuador, Guatemala, the Papal States (Holy See), Italy, the Netherlands, Nicaragua, Portugal, Sweden and Norway, the Two Sicilies, and Venezuela.

95. The principal exceptions after 1853 were the continued use for a short time of the Chargé d'Affaires rank for two Central American Republics (Costa Rica and El Salvador); for a few pro tem appointments to Austria, Finland, and Hungary following World War I (1921–22) and to Thailand following World War II (1946); and for the initial diplomatic representatives to such countries as Ghana (1957), Greece (1876–79), Kuwait (1961–62), Maylasia (1957), Romania (1880–82), and Sudan (1956).

When diplomatic relations with the Holy See (Papal States or Pontifical States), which ceased in 1867, were informally revived during World War II, Harold H. Titman, Jr., represented the United States as Chargé d'Affaires from 1941 to 1944.

Most exceptional, however, was the temporary demotion of the diplomatic rank from Minister Resident to Chargé d'Affaires in several countries, such as Denmark, Portugal, and Switzerland—from 1876 to 1882—during the Administrations of Presidents Grant, Hayes, and Garfield.

96. The only other appointees to these five countries were ranked as Chargés d'Affaires, who served for short interim periods. One of these, Henry Wheaton, in Prussia, was promoted to Envoy Extraordinary and Minister Plenipotentiary in less than two years.

97. Aside from Mexico, to which ten of twelve envoys were accredited at this rank, Envoys Extraordinary were also appointed to Brazil, Chile, Costa Rica, El Salvador, Guatemala, Honduras, and Nicaragua. Several of these, however, did not serve in their appointments.

98. In the case of Austria, America's first two envoys were ranked as Envoys Extraordinary (1838–45) and the next five were designated Chargés d'Affaires (1845–54), when Henry R. Jackson was promoted to the status of Minister Resident, and four years later, in 1858, American envoys were again ranked as Envoys Extraordinary.

99. These included France, Germany, Great Britain, Russia, and Spain in Europe, to which Austria, Brazil, Chile, China, Italy, Mexico, and Peru were added between 1829 and March 1861.

100. For example, the rank of Chargé d'Affaires was used initially when the United States established diplomatic relations with such countries as Denmark, Ecuador, the Papal States (Holy See), Italy, Texas, Turkey, the Two Sicilies, and Venezuela.

101. Although diplomatic representation commenced at a higher rank, it was changed to the Chargé d'Affaires level for extended periods, especially during the 1830s and 1840s, in the case of such countries as Argentina (1825–54), Belgium (1832–54), the Netherlands (1831–54), Portugal (1825–54), and Sweden and Norway (1819–54). All of these were changed again when it was decided to revive the Minister Resident rank in 1854.

102. Illustrations of accrediting specific individuals with the rank of Chargé d'Affaires for short periods include Levett Harris (France in 1833), John Randolph Clay (Russia, 1836–37), and Aaron Vail (Spain, 1840–42). Such appointments were in keeping with earlier short-lived appointments as Chargé d'Affaires in the case of Jonathan Russell to France for a few months in 1811, followed by seven months in Great Britain, 1811 to 1812, which was terminated by the outbreak of the War of 1812.

103. These were Costa Rica, El Salvador, Honduras, and Japan.

104. To illustrate this confusing and disappointing situation, eight emissaries were nominated for appointment to Guatemala between 1825 and 1853, and two to Nicaragua between 1851 and 1853. These were at the rank of Chargé d'Affaires. Only two of them, John Williams and Charles G. De Witt, served in Guatemala (1825–26 and 1883–89,

respectively), and John B. Kerr served in Nicaragua (1851–53). All the rest were not commissioned, did not proceed to their posts, or died en route.

In March 1853 the President changed tactics and appointed John Slidell as Envoy Extraordinary and Minister Plenipotentiary to Costa Rica, El Salvador, Guatemala, Honduras, and Nicaragua, embracing all five Central American republics, but he declined the offer. The following month the President appointed Solon Borland as Envoy Extraordinary to all of Central America, who did not present his credentials to any of these republics.

105. These were John Leake Marling (to Guatemala) and John H. Wheeler (to Nicaragua) in 1854; Beverly L. Clarke (to Honduras) and Mirabeau B. Lamar (to Costa Rica) in 1858; and James R. Partridge (to El Salvador) in 1863.

106. The use of the title "Agent and Consul General" was attributed more to the international status of Egypt than to the qualifications of individual emissaries. For example, Charles Hale later became an Assistant Secretary of State; Eugene Schuyler had previously served in Romania, Serbia, and as Assistant Secretary of State; Frederick C. Penfield later became Envoy Extraordinary to Austria-Hungary; John W. Riddle later became Envoy Extraordinary to Romania and Serbia and Ambassador to Russia and Argentina; Peter Augustus Jay later became Envoy Extraordinary to El Salvador and Romania and Ambassador to Argentina; Hampson Gary later became Envoy Extraordinary to Switzerland; and Joseph Morton Howell was promoted to Envoy Extraordinary to Egypt. Two of them—Riddle and Jay—also acquired career Foreign Service status.

107. Wheaton was the first envoy to Prussia since John Quincy Adams (1797–1801). He also previously served as Chargé d'Affaires in Denmark for more than eight years, thus totaling more than eighteen years in the American Diplomatic Service.

108. Among these, for example, were William Hunter, Jr. (Brazil, nine years), Lewis Cass, Jr. (Papal States or Holy See, nine years), and Theodore S. Fay (Switzerland, eight years).

109. That of Texas was ended in 1845, and the Legation accredited to the Two Sicilies ended in November 1860, in anticipation of the ascendancy of King Victor Emmanuel in Italy.

110. The posts in China, El Salvador, Guatemala, Honduras, and Peru were vacant at the time of transition. In the case of Guatemala and Honduras the American envoys had died and had not yet been replaced. No separate emissary had yet been appointed to El Salvador, and diplomatic relations with Peru remained ruptured at that time.

111. The Act of 1855 ranked all of these as Envoys Extraordinary but made no reference to Ministers Plenipotentiary, Ministers Resident, or Chargés d'Affaires and did not allow for a Commissioner to Hawaii and lesser officials.

112. These included envoys to Belgium, Denmark, Italy (both Rome and Naples), the Netherlands, Portugal, Sardinia, Sweden, and Switzerland in Europe, and seven Latin American states.

113. The Act of 1855 also allowed $12,000 for envoys accredited to Austria, Brazil, Mexico, Prussia, Russia, and Spain; $10,000 for Peru; and $9,000 for Chile and Turkey.

114. In addition, this Act of 1855 allowed for a Commissioner to Hawaii. However, this list made no provision for representation to Egypt, the Papal States or Holy See, Central America (except for Guatemala and Honduras), the two Sicilies, or New Granada (Colombia).

115. This maximum annual salary level of $17,500 remained in effect into the twentieth century.

116. Thus, hypothetically, Envoys Extraordinary and Ministers Plenipotentiary accredited to France and Great Britain would receive the full $17,500, whereas a Minister Resident would receive $13,125 (75 percent), and a Chargé d'Affaires would receive $8,750 (50 percent). An Envoy Extraordinary to Mexico would receive $12,000, a Minister Resident would receive $9,000, and a Chargé would receive $6,000; and an Envoy Extraordinary to Denmark, Portugal, or Venezuela would receive $10,000, whereas a Minister Resident would receive $7,500, and a Chargé would receive $5,000.

117. According to historian Henry Barrett Learned, this circular constituted a series of instructions, cautious rather than explicit, to guide American diplomats. Recognizing that an envoy "might wish to conform to the customs of the country to which he was accredited and to dress according to the rules of etiquette there prescribed," it allowed the envoy "to exercise his judgment in the matter." Nevertheless "the Secretary of State desired to encourage every diplomatic official, as far as practicable without impairing his usefulness to his country, to appear at court 'in the simple dress of an American citizen.'" *William Learned Marcy*, in Bemis, ed., *The American Secretaries of State and Their Diplomacy*, vol. 6, p. 264.

118. Stuart, *American Diplomatic and Consular Practice*, p. 215, adds that, inasmuch as Congress had already permitted Army and Navy officers to wear their uniforms, diplomatic envoys who had served in these services could wear their military dress uniforms. This further confused the issue of diplomatic dress.

119. For additional commentary, with discussion of diplomatic interchanges and instructions and specific embarassing experiences regarding diplomatic dress, see *William Learned Marcy* in Bemis, *The American Secretaries of State and Their Diplomacy*, vol. 6, pp. 263–68; Foster, *The Practice of Diplomacy*, pp. 130–41; Plischke, *Conduct of American Diplomacy*, pp. 16–17; Moore, *Digest*, vol. 4, pp. 761–73; Stuart, *American Diplomatic and Consular Practice*, pp. 214–16, and *The Department of State*, pp. 119–20; Thayer, *Diplomat*, pp. 236–38; and Trask, *A Short History of the U.S. Department of State*, p. 6.

For a discussion of this subject from the international perspective, see Wood and Serres, *Diplomatic Ceremonial and Protocol*, Chapter 10 on "Ceremonial Dress and Decoration," which includes a table of diplomatic attire for official ceremonies on p. 152, specifying details for several types of functions—official ceremonies, morning functions, mourning ceremonies, and informal occasions.

120. These bilateral treaties and agreements were negotiated and signed by special envoys with Argentina (two), Ecuador (one), Fiji Islands (one), Greece (one), Japan (six), Lagos (Nigeria, one), Loochoo (Ryukyu) Islands (one), Mexico (two), Ottoman Empire (one), Paraguay (two), Persia (Iran, one), Sardinia (one), Switzerland (one), and Siam (Thailand) (two). Moreover, the United States also concluded eleven such bipartite treaties and agreements with nine German States and joined Great Britain in negotiating a bilateral agreement to jointly occupy the San Juan Islands and a multipartite agreement with the Samoan Islands.

To these thirty-six treaties and agreements may be added a bipartite Postal Convention signed with Belgium in 1859 by Joseph Holt, the American Postmaster General, who was later appointed Secretary of War.

121. To illustrate, James Buchanan and Henry Wheaton, Envoys Extraordinary, respectively, to Great Britain and Prussia, signed seven treaties with various German States; Robert C. Schenk, Envoy Extraordinary to Brazil, signed two with Argentina; Carroll

Spence, Minister Resident to Turkey, signed one with Persia (Iran); and Andrew Stevenson, Envoy Extraordinary to Great Britain, signed one with Greece.

122. For example, Commodore James Biddle, David Offley, and Charles Rhind signed a treaty with the Ottoman Empire in 1830; Charles Wilkes, American naval officer and explorer, concluded the commercial agreement with Samoa and Great Britain in 1839; Major General W. J. Worth and Brigadier General Persifor F. Smith signed the Suspension of Hostilities Agreement with Mexico in 1848; Commodore H. T. Mayo signed an agreement with Lagos (Nigeria) in 1854; Commodore Matthew C. Perry signed a treaty and two agreements with Japan and a treaty with the Loochoo (Ryukyu) Islands in 1854; and General Winfield Scott signed an agreement with the British Governor of the Vancouver colony in 1859 for the joint occupation of the San Juan Islands.

123. Childs, *American Foreign Service*, p. 6, blames "the politicians of the times" for the lack of Congressional action. For additional information see Barnes and Morgan, *The Foreign Service of the United States*, pp. 82–86; and Stuart, *American Diplomatic and Consular Practice*, pp. 85–87.

124. These were located in British North America (Quebec), Cuba (Havana), Egypt (Alexandria), Hanseatic and Free Cities of Germany (Frankfurt am Main), India (Calcutta), Japan (Shimoda), and Turkey (Constantinople).

125. Consuls were provided for such major European cities as Amsterdam and Rotterdam, Antwerp, London, Moscow and St. Petersburg, Paris, and Vienna. Eleven were allocated for Latin America, including Buenos Aires and Rio de Janeiro. Others were authorized for Asia and the Pacific (including Canton, Hong Kong, Honolulu, and Singapore), the Mideast (Beirut and Jerusalem), and the Barbary emirates (Tangier, Tripoli, and Tunis).

126. One of these Commercial Agents was assigned to Nicaragua, and two to Santo Domingo.

127. These were allocated to such places as Athens, Capetown, Montevideo, Tampico, and Venice and such islands as the Cape Verdes, Cyprus, the Falklands, Fiji, St. Croix, Tahiti, and Zanzibar.

128. See Barnes and Morgan, *The Foreign Service of the United States*, p. 350.

129. Barnes and Morgan, *The Foreign Service of the United States*, p. 110, declare, "The framers of the act intended this provision to be the beginning of a permanent corps of consular officers composed of men of experience who had grown up with the work."

130. These included John Appleton, Ambrose Dudley Mann, Jacob L. Martin, Nicholas P. Trist, and Aaron Vail. Also see notes 85 and 86.

131. Prior to his diplomatic service, Henry Wheaton was a Reporter for the Supreme Court, 1816–27. In 1842 he published *Elements of International Law* in Berlin, 3d ed. (Philadelphia: Lea and Blanchard, 1846), and in 1845 he published *History of the Law of Nations in Europe and America* (New York: Gould and Banks, 1845; reprinted New York: Garland, 1973), both of which were completed while he served in Prussia.

132. Caleb Cushing was given two separate commissions on May 3, 1853, as both Commissioner and Envoy Extraordinary, during a recess of the Senate, but after confirmation he was recommissioned solely as Commissioner.

133. Trask, *A Short History of the U.S. Department of State*, p. 10.

134. For commentary on Nathaniel Hawthorne's consular experiences, see Barnes and Morgan, *The Foreign Service of the United States*, pp. 99–106.

135. This multipartite agreement was negotiated with a British Consul and Samoan Islands leaders, signed in 1839, which dealt with commerce, consular rights, and navi-

gation. The only previous multipartite agreement, signed in 1826, dealt with the creation of an international cemetery in Algiers.

136. This number included the thirteen German States other than Prussia, as well as Sardinia and the Two Sicilies. This meant that at the time the United States had treaty relations with all of the European countries.

137. Aside from eight South American states, these included four of the individual Central American countries (except for Honduras).

138. The Asian and Pacific countries embraced China, Japan, Siam (Thailand) and the Fiji, Loochoo (Ryukyu), and Samoan Islands. The list also included the Ottoman Empire (Turkey), Muscat (Oman), and Persia (Iran) in the Mideast, and Lagos (Nigeria) in Africa, as well as Texas.

139. Precedents for such executive agreements commenced as early as the Declaration on the Cessation of Hostilities with Great Britain (1783), the agreement with Great Britain to limit naval forces on the Great Lakes (1817), and a commercial agreement with Hawaii (1826), discussed in earlier chapters. The agreement with Fiji (1840) was unusual in that it consisted of "regulations" to govern commerce, consular rights, and shipping, which was signed but not formally approved or ratified.

140. These exchanges of notes included claims settlements with Venezuela (1844), Great Britain (1845), and Peru (1851), a commercial agreement with Lagos (Nigeria) (1854), and the arrangement for joint British-American occupation of the San Juan Islands (1859).

141. These Declarations of Accession were with the German States of Bremen, Mecklenburg, Oldenburg, Schaumburg-Lippe, and Württemberg.

142. These eight treaties and agreements were signed by Acting Secretary of State Richard Rush (one) and Secretaries John Quincy Adams (two) and Henry Clay (five).

143. These thirty-four treaties and agreements were signed by Secretaries of State Van Buren (one), Forsyth (three), Webster (six), Upshur (one), Calhoun (one), Buchanan (seven), Clayton (three), Everett (one), Marcy (five), and Cass (five), as well as by Postmaster General Joseph Holt (one).

144. Twelve of these executive agreements were claims settlements. Others included an agreement with Great Britain providing for the cession of Horseshoe Reef to the United States (1850), with Nicaragua on the rights of neutrals at sea (1855), and three with Japan dealing with commercial affairs (1854 and 1859).

Some treaties were unique in that they also became effective on signature, even though they were regarded as formal treaties and required presidential ratification. These included two treaties with China signed at Shanghai on November 8, 1858, which became effective on that date but were not approved by the Senate until March 1, 1859, and ratified by the President two days later; and the Treaty with the Loochoo (Ryukyu) Islands signed on July 11, 1854, which went into effect that day but was not ratified and proclaimed until March 9, 1855.

145. The treaty with Switzerland was signed at Bern on November 25, 1850, was ratified by the President the following March but was amended and then reapproved by the Senate and reratified by the President on November 8, 1855, and went into effect two days later. Also unusual, the Claims Settlement Convention with Peru was signed at Lima on March 17, 1841, ratified by the President and provisionally by the Peruvian government in 1843, and proclaimed by the President in February 1844, but was amended and reratified by the President and Peru in 1846, and finally went into force at the end of October 1846.

Another unique procedure applied to the Treaty of Amity and Commerce with Muscat (Oman), which was signed on September 21, 1833, approved by the Senate on June 30, 1834, and became effective on that date but was not ratified by the President until the following January, and ratifications were not exchanged until September 30, 1835.

146. For example, the Treaty of Amity and Commerce with Mexico endured for half a century (1831–81) and that with Hawaii for nearly half a century (1850–98); the Extradition Treaty with France (1843–1909) and the multipartite agreement with Samoa (1839–99) and the Amity and Commerce Treaty with Thailand (1856–1920) for more than sixty years; the Treaty of Friendship and Commerce with Persia (1856–1928) for more than seventy years, and the Treaty of Commerce and Navigation with Greece for nearly eighty-five years (1837–1921). The Amity and Commerce Treaty with Thailand survived for sixty-five years (1856–1920). In addition, several treaties and agreements with the individual German States continued in effect until World War I.

The Treaty of Friendship and Commerce with Austria, signed in 1853, was revived for Austria and Hungary after World War I, and, although it was superseded by a new treaty with Austria in 1930, it was continued and revived for Hungary after World War II.

Even more impressively, the original Treaty of Wanghia with China, signed in 1844, was supplemented and revised in 1858, continued in force by a treaty of 1903, and was not superseded until after World War II, thus surviving for more than a century. Similarly, the Treaty of Commerce and Navigation with the Ottoman Empire, signed in 1830, survived for more than a century, until it was replaced by a treaty with Turkey in 1933.

147. Most of these Amity, Commerce, and Navigation Treaties were with European and Latin American countries, although eleven of them also applied to Asia, the Mideast, Pacific Islands, and Africa (Lagos).

148. This 1830 treaty with the Ottoman Empire consisted of nine short, substantive articles devoted to explaining the reasons for the treaty and a ''Separate Act Containing a Secret Article'' concerned with the building of Ottoman seagoing ships in the United States. The Senate approved the treaty but not the secret article, and the President ratified it in October 1831.

The only previous attempt at treaty secrecy occurred in 1778, prior to the Constitution, when a treaty was signed with France providing Spain with the right of accession to the Franco–American Treaties of Amity and Alliance, discussed in Chapter 1.

149. Moreover, initiated by the United States, by an exchange of nine notes in 1859, agreement was reached with Great Britain to jointly occupy the San Juan Islands lying in the Georgia Strait between the mainland and Vancouver Island.

150. This cession comprised the territories of the States of Arizona, California, Nevada, New Mexico, a corner of Wyoming, and Western Colorado. The treaty also defined the boundaries between Mexico and the United States and provided for joint boundary demarcation.

The territory ceded to the United States, together with Texas, exceeded the Louisiana Territory in size and comprised approximately half of the Mexican domain, it provided the United States with the major Pacific harbors at San Francisco and San Diego, and it converted the United States into a major continental, two-ocean nation.

151. Several features of these treaties and agreements on neutral rights warrant consideration. As a neutral in early nineteenth-century European wars, the United States had long been a leader in promoting maritime neutral rights, as was Russia. It was natural, therefore, that the first of these treaties would be concluded with the Russian Government,

but none were signed with any other major European power. Moreover, these were the only such treaties and agreements concluded by the United States. Second, one might wonder why they were signed with Peru and Nicaragua and no other Latin American country. Third, although the executive agreements with Hawaii and Nicaragua were declarations of accession, they incorporated the full language of the treaty with Russia.

152. These European signatories included Austria, France, Great Britain, Prussia, Russia, Sardinia, and Turkey.

153. For additional commentary on the Declaration of Paris and neutral rights, see Moore, *Digest*, vol. 7, pp. 562–83; Hackworth, *Digest of International Law*, vol. 6, pp. 598–605 and all of vol. 7; Winfried Baumgart, *The Peace of Paris, 1856: Studies in War, Diplomacy, and Peacemaking*, trans. Ann Pottinger Saab (Santa Barbara, Calif.: ABC Clio, 1981); and Carlton Savage, *Policy of the United States toward Maritime Commerce* (Washington, D.C.: Government Printing Office, 1934 and 1936).

154. Only one additional treaty of this type, with the German State of Hannover, was subsequently concluded, on November 6, 1861. However, a Disposal of Property Convention was also signed with Switzerland in 1847, and an Inheritance Convention was concluded with the German State of Brunswick-Luneburg in 1854.

155. By an act of June 8, 1872, the Postmaster General was given authority to enter into money-order agreements with postal departments of foreign governments and, by and with the consent of the President, to conclude postal conventions (without requiring the consent of the Senate). This changed the treaty process and eliminated the Department of State from negotiating such conventions, and in the 1890s practice changed to concluding multilateral postal agreements.

156. The European countries included Denmark, France, Great Britain, Portugal, Spain, and the Two Sicilies. Those in Latin America embraced Brazil, Chile, Costa Rica, Ecuador, Mexico, New Granada (Colombia), Paraguay, Peru, and Venezuela. Claims treaties and agreements were also concluded with China, Fiji, and Texas.

157. For example, in 1852 Peru undertook to pay Samuel Franklin Clay, a U.S. citizen, in the amount of $26,560 in two installments for losses sustained, and in 1859 Venezuela agreed to indemnify the United States in the amount of $130,000 for evicting Americans from Aves Island.

158. In keeping with earlier experience, the arbiter usually was agreed upon by the Commissioners. However, in the case of the treaty with New Granada (Colombia, 1857), it was specified that this umpire would be designated by the Minister of Prussia accredited to the United States, in the Mexican treaty (1839) it was mandated that the arbiter would be the King of Prussia or someone appointed by him, and in the Paraguayan treaty (1859) it was provided that the arbiter would be the diplomatic envoys of Prussia and Russia who were accredited to Washington. In such cases the process amounted to third-party conciliation.

159. The remaining two peaceful settlement treaties were supplementary. That with Mexico (1843) simply established the method of payment by Mexico (but it was absolved from this responsibility by the Peace Treaty of 1848). That with Great Britain (1854) merely extended the time limit for determining claims settlement under the basic treaty of 1853.

160. Several officials who served as President, as Secretary of State, and in the Diplomatic and Consular Corps were related. For example, Andrew Jackson Donelson, a nephew by marriage of President Jackson, was commissioned to represent the United States as Chargé d'Affaires in Texas during its independence (1844–45) and was later

appointed as Envoy Extraordinary to Prussia/ Germany (1846–49). James K. Polk's brother William was accredited by President Tyler as Chargé d'Affaires to the Two Sicilies in 1845, where he remained for two years. Edward Livingston, the brother of former Secretary for Foreign Affairs Robert R. Livingston, was appointed Secretary of State during the Jackson Administration, and Secretary Edward Everett's brother Alexander Hill Everett had a successful diplomatic career as Chargé d'Affaires to the Netherlands (1818–24), Envoy Extraordinary to Spain (1825–29), and Commissioner to China (1845–47).

The sons of three Secretaries of State also received diplomatic appointments. These were Lewis Cass, Jr., who was sent as Chargé d'Affaires and later as Minister Resident to the Papal States (1849–58); James Brown Clay, son of Henry Clay, who was sent as Chargé d'Affaires to Portugal (1849–50); and Lewis McLane's son Robert, who served as Commissioner to China (1853–54), Envoy Extraordinary to Mexico (1859–60), and eventually Envoy Extraordinary to France (1885–88). William Hunter, Jr., who served as Chargé d'Affaires and later as Envoy Extraordinary in Brazil (1834–43), was the father of William Hunter III, who was commissioned as Chief Clerk (1852–55), Assistant Secretary of State (1855), and Second Assistant Secretary of State (1866–86). Combined, they held office for more than thirty-two years.

Others who bore similar names include John Appleton and John James Appleton, Daniel Brent together with Thomas L. L. Brent, and William Brent, Jr., Secretary Henry Clay and Cassius and John Randolph Clay, Caleb Cushing and Courtland Cushing, Levett and Townsend Harris, Henry Rootes Jackson and Isaac R. Jackson, and Van Brugh Livingston. Most unique was the appointment of two unrelated John Forsyths, who must not be confused—the Secretary of State during President Jackson's Administration and the American Envoy Extraordinary commissioned to Mexico by President Pierce (1856–58).

PART III

1861–1945

5

The Road to Becoming a Great World Power—Amplification, Innovation, and Renovation, 1861–1913

Many changes, both internal and external, in the development of the United States and its government affected the management of its foreign affairs, the evolvement of its foreign policy, and the functioning of the Department of State. Fourteen new States were added to the Federal Union,[1] bringing the total to forty-eight, which encompassed the entire contiguous continental territory of the Union. The population of the country nearly tripled, increasing from 31.4 million in 1860 to 92.2 million in 1910 (including nearly 23 million immigrants admitted during these five decades), and by the time of World War I this population exceeded that of all of the European countries except Russia. New Federal Departments were created—including Justice (1870),[2] Agriculture (1889), and Commerce and Labor (1903).[3]

The United States fought two major wars—the Civil War (1861–65) and the Spanish-American War (1898). Three Presidents—Abraham Lincoln, James A. Garfield, and William McKinley—were assassinated, Andrew Johnson was impeached but not convicted, and an attempt was made to assassinate former President Theodore Roosevelt in 1912. This country subscribed to the gold standard, was the leading manufacturing country in the world, experienced the Industrial Revolution, which affected American exports, suffered acute economic panics and depressions,[4] endured political controversy over high tariffs and enacted major tariff legislation, and launched Civil Service reform based on the merit system, beginning with the Pendleton Act in 1883.

Formal diplomatic relations, previously maintained with thirty-three governments, were extended to nineteen additional foreign countries. By the time of World War I, although temporarily discontinued with several of them, such as the Holy See and Korea, diplomatic representation applied to virtually all recognized, independent members of the family of nations.

The American government purchased Alaska from Russia in 1867 (acquiring its first noncontiguous territory); established a protectorate over, and in 1898 annexed, Hawaii; and, following the Spanish–American War, acquired the Philippines, Guam, and Puerto Rico by treaty in 1898. It had gone to war with Spain to gain independence for Cuba and, under the Platt Amendment of 1901, the island was rendered a virtual protectorate. At a tripartite conference in 1889 it joined Great Britain and Germany in establishing a joint protectorate over Samoa and ten years later signed a partition treaty that divided the islands between Germany and the United States. Boundary issues arose with Great Britain (respecting the Alaska–Canadian boundary) and Mexico (concerning the Rio Grande River and water rights). Early in the twentieth century President Theodore Roosevelt became involved in the construction of an isthmian canal, linking the Atlantic and Pacific Oceans, and in 1906 he undertook the first presidential summit trip abroad when he sailed to inspect and hasten the completion of the Panama Canal.

The traditional American policies–isolation (or abstention from Europe's politics and wars) and the Monroe Doctrine (for the Western Hemisphere)—remained in effect. But, although the United States did not become entangled in the Franco–Prussian War (1870–71) or major wars in Asia and South Africa, abstentionism did not prevent American involvement in international economic and other matters, and the Monroe Doctrine was reinterpreted by the Olney Corollary of 1895 and the Roosevelt Corollary of 1904.[5] In addition, the United States continued to apply de facto recognition to new countries and governments, to espouse freedom of maritime navigation and international trade, to expand its Manifest Destiny or "geographic predestination" expansionist policy in the Caribbean and Pacific areas, to apply its neutrality policy in certain foreign wars, and to insist on the rights of expatriation and naturalization. Other policy developments of consequence were the commencement of Pan-Americanism for Latin America in 1889 and the Open Door for the Far East at the turn of the century,[6] President Roosevelt's "Big Stick" strategy for Latin America enunciated early in the twentieth century,[7] President Taft's "dollar diplomacy" and territorial expansionism beyond the North American Continent, and commitment to become a major naval power.[8]

Evidencing its proliferating interests and actions in world affairs, the United States commenced to promote Western Hemisphere integration and to participate in a series of global international conferences and the establishment of general and regional international organizations and administrative agencies. In addition to concluding an increased number of bilateral treaties and agreements, it also participated in negotiating many multilateral conventions and other arrangements. It also joined other governments in agreeing to define the laws of war and neutrality and to resolve international disputes by arbitration and other means of pacific settlement, including the fabrication of advance arrangements such as the Hague Permanent Court of Arbitration and the Root arbitrations treaties.

Illustrated by these and other developments, the United States was rapidly emerging in the twentieth century as a world power, and by the time of World War I as a Great Power. Its growing status and influence were appreciated at home and respected by others, epitomized as domination in the Western Hemisphere, cooperation in Asia and the Pacific, and political abstention in Europe prior to the outbreak of war in 1914. Naturally, these factors influenced the growth and role of the Department of State, its leadership and staffing, its diplomatic and consular emissaries, and its negotiations and the conclusion of treaties and agreements.

PRESIDENTS, THEIR SECRETARIES, AND SENIOR DEPARTMENTAL STAFF

During this period of more than half a century, from Abraham Lincoln to Woodrow Wilson, called the "Republican Era," eleven Presidents were elected, who made seventeen appointments of Secretaries of State. James G. Blaine held two separate appointments, under Presidents James A. Garfield and Benjamin Harrison. Political constancy permeated presidential politics. All of the Presidents from Lincoln to William Howard Taft were Republicans,[9] except for Grover Cleveland, elected as a Democrat, who served two nonconsecutive terms in the 1880s and 1890s.

Despite the facts that Presidents Lincoln, Garfield, and McKinley were assassinated and superseded by their Vice Presidents and that Secretaries Walter Q. Gresham and John Hay died in office, the average length of service of both Presidents and their Secretaries exceeded slightly the tenure of those who preceded them.[10] On five occasions Acting Secretaries ad interim were designated between the terms of Secretaries. They served for short periods, running from ten to twenty-six days. Unlike earlier times, when approximately two-thirds of such Acting Secretaries were of Cabinet rank, these were all Assistant Secretaries of State. William F. Wharton was twice appointed in this capacity, in June 1892 and February 1893.[11]

As indicated in Table 5.1, President Lincoln appointed William H. Seward as his Secretary in March 1861. Seward had spent twelve years as a Senator from New York (1849–61) and was Lincoln's rival for President in the Republican nominating convention. A lawyer and professional politician, he continued as Secretary throughout the Lincoln and Andrew Johnson Administrations.

When Ulysses S. Grant became President, he nominated Elihu B. Washburne, one of his political supporters, on March 5, 1869, who entered upon his duties as Secretary the same day. He has the distinction of resigning five days after his appointment and served for only twelve days, until March 16, and the following day he was nominated to become Envoy Extraordinary and Minister Plenipotentiary to France (1869–77).[12] The President then considered appointing John Lothrop Motley, historian, who had been Minister Plenipotentiary in Austria for nearly six years, but changed his mind. Instead, he replaced Washburne

Table 5.1

Department of State Principal Officers, 1861–1913

Secretaries of State

Name	Appointment	Entry on Duty	Termination of Appointment
William H. Seward	Mar. 5, 1861	Mar. 6, 1861	Mar. 4, 1869
Elihu B. Washburne	Mar. 5, 1869	Mar. 5, 1869	Mar. 16, 1869
Hamilton Fish	Mar. 11, 1869	Mar. 17, 1869	Mar. 12, 1877
William M. Evarts	Mar. 12, 1877	Mar. 12, 1877	Mar. 7, 1881
James G. Blaine	Mar. 5, 1881	Mar. 7, 1881	Dec. 19, 1881
Frederick T. Frelinghuysen	Dec. 12, 1881	Dec. 19, 1881	Mar. 6, 1885
Thomas F. Bayard	Mar. 6, 1885	Mar. 7, 1885	Mar. 6, 1889
James G. Blaine	Mar. 5, 1889	Mar. 7, 1889	June 4, 1892
* William F. Wharton (Assistant Sec.)	June 4, 1892		June 29, 1892
John W. Foster	June 29, 1892	June 29, 1892	Feb. 23, 1893
* William F. Wharton (Assistant Sec.)	Feb. 24, 1893		Mar. 6, 1893
Walter Q. Gesham	Mar. 6, 1893	Mar. 7, 1893	May 28, 1895
* Edwin F. Uhl (Assistant Sec.)	May 28, 1895		June 9, 1895
Richard Olney	June 8, 1895	June 10, 1895	Mar. 5, 1897
John Sherman	Mar. 5, 1897	Mar. 6, 1897	Apr. 27, 1898
William R. Day	Apr. 26, 1898	Apr. 28, 1898	Sep. 16, 1898
* Alvey A. Adee (2nd Assistant Sec.)	Sep. 17, 1898		Sep. 29, 1898
John M. Hay	Sep. 20, 1898	Sep. 30, 1898	July 1, 1905
* Francis B. Loomis (Assistant Sec.)	July 1, 1905		July 18, 1905
Elihu Root	July 7, 1905	July 19, 1905	Jan. 27, 1909
Robert Bacon	Jan. 27, 1909	Jan. 27, 1909	Mar. 5, 1909
Philander C. Knox	Mar. 5, 1909	Mar. 6, 1909	Mar. 5, 1913

Assistant Secretaries of State

Name	Appointment	Entry on Duty	Termination of Appointment
Frederick W. Seward	Mar. 6, 1861	Mar. 6, 1861	Mar. 4, 1869
J. C. Bancroft Davis	Mar. 25, 1869	Apr. 1, 1869	Nov. 13, 1871
Charles Hale	Feb. 19, 1872	Feb. 19, 1872	Jan. 24, 1873
J. C. Bancroft Davis	Jan. 24, 1873	Jan. 25, 1873	Jan. 30, 1874
John L. Cadwalader	June 17, 1874	July 1, 1874	Mar. 20, 1877
Frederick W. Seward	Mar. 16, 1877	Mar. 21, 1877	Oct. 31, 1879
John M. Hay	Nov. 1, 1879	Nov. 1, 1879	May 3, 1881

Name	Appointment	Entry on Duty	Termination of Appointment
Robert R. Hitt	May 4, 1881	May 4, 1881	Dec. 19, 1881
J. C. Bancroft Davis	Dec. 19, 1881	Dec. 20, 1881	July 7, 1882
John Davis	July 7, 1882	July 8, 1882	Feb. 23, 1885
James D. Porter	Mar. 20, 1885	Mar. 21, 1885	Sep. 10, 1887
George L. Rives	Nov. 19, 1887	Nov. 21, 1887	Mar. 5, 1889
Eugene Schuyler	(Nomination withdrawn)		
William F. Wharton	Apr. 2, 1889	Apr. 11, 1889	Mar. 20, 1893
Josiah Quincy	Mar. 20, 1893	Mar. 21, 1893	Sep. 22, 1893
Edwin F. Uhl	Nov. 1, 1893	Nov. 11, 1893	Feb. 11, 1896
William Woodville Rockhill	Feb. 11, 1896	Feb. 14, 1896	May 10, 1897
William R. Day	May 3, 1897	May 11, 1897	Apr. 27, 1898
John Bassett Moore	Apr. 27, 1898	Apr. 28, 1898	Sep. 16, 1898
David J. Hill	Oct. 25, 1898	Oct. 25, 1898	Jan. 28, 1903
Francis B. Loomis	Jan. 7, 1903	Feb. 9, 1903	Oct. 10, 1905
Robert Bacon	Sep. 5, 1905	Oct. 11, 1905	Jan. 27, 1909
John Callan O'Laughlin	Jan. 27, 1909	Jan. 28, 1909	Mar. 5, 1909
F. M. Huntington Wilson	Mar. 6, 1909	Mar. 6, 1909	Mar. 19, 1913

Second Assistant Secretaries of State

Name	Appointment	Entry on Duty	Termination of Appointment
William Hunter, III	July 27, 1866	July 27, 1866	July 22, 1886
Alvey A. Adee	Aug. 3, 1886	Aug. 6, 1886	June 30, 1924

Third Assistant Secretaries of State

Name	Appointment	Entry on Duty	Termination of Appointment
Benjamin Moran		(Not commissioned)	
John A. Campbell	Feb. 24, 1875	Feb. 24, 1875	Nov. 30, 1877
Charles Payson	June 11, 1878	June 22, 1878	June 30, 1881
Walker Blaine	July 1, 1881	July 1, 1881	June 30, 1882
Alvey A. Adee	July 18, 1882	July 18, 1882	Aug. 5, 1886
John Bassett Moore	Aug. 3, 1886	Aug. 6, 1886	Sep. 30, 1891
William M. Grinnell	Feb. 11, 1892	Feb. 15, 1892	Apr. 16, 1893
Edward H. Strobel	Apr. 13, 1893	Apr. 17, 1893	Apr. 16, 1894
William Woodville Rockhill	Apr. 14, 1894	Apr. 17, 1894	Feb. 13, 1896
William Woodward Baldwin	Feb. 24, 1896	Feb. 29, 1896	Apr. 1, 1897
Thomas Wilbur Cridler	Apr. 8, 1897	Apr. 8, 1897	Nov. 15, 1901
Herbert H. D. Peirce	Nov. 15, 1901	Nov. 16, 1901	June 22, 1906
F. M. Huntington Wilson	June 22, 1906	July 2, 1906	Dec. 30, 1908
William Phillips	Jan. 11, 1909	Jan. 11, 1909	Oct. 13, 1909
Chandler Hale	Sep. 15, 1909	Oct. 14, 1909	Apr. 21, 1913

*Indicates Secretary of State ad interim.

with Hamilton Fish, who was a member of Congress for eight years and had supported Grant's election but whom the President knew only slightly. Initially, Fish declined the offer, even though the President had already sent his nomination to the Senate. Although he expected to resign after the current Congress adjourned, he remained until March 1877 and therefore was the only Secretary during this period, except for Seward, to hold the office for eight years.

Before his election as President, Rutherford B. Hayes prepared a list of his potential Cabinet members and opted for William M. Evarts as Secretary of State. He was a prominent attorney, regarded as one of the most brilliant minds of the day, who previously had been appointed as Assistant U.S. Attorney for the Southern District of New York (1849–53), chief counsel for President Johnson during his impeachment trial in 1868, Attorney General in Johnson's Cabinet, and a member of the commission that represented the United States before the Geneva Arbitration Tribunal to resolve the *Alabama* controversy with Great Britain (1871–72). He remained Secretary for four years (1877–81).

For personal and political reasons President James A. Garfield turned to James G. Blaine, a lawyer and press editor who had spent nearly a quarter century in legislative politics (in the Maine House of Representatives for four years and twenty years in Congress) and was a prominent Republican leader. When Garfield was assassinated in September 1881 and was succeeded by Chester A. Arthur, Blaine remained Secretary only until December, thus serving for less than ten months. He was succeeded by Frederick T. Frelinghuysen, a conservative lawyer who, in addition to holding local and state offices, had spent ten years as a U.S. Senator. Together these three—Evarts, Blaine, and Frelinghuysen—headed the Department of State for eight years, until 1885.

A major political change began on March 4, 1885, when Grover Cleveland was inaugurated as the first post–Civil War Democratic President. He considered Thomas F. Bayard, a professional politician, for appointment as Secretary of either the State or the Treasury Department and selected him for the former. He had been U.S. District Attorney for Delaware (1853–54), was elected to the Senate for sixteen years (1869–85), and was an unsuccessful candidate for the Democratic presidential nomination in 1876, 1880, and 1884. He had no prior training, experience, or interest in foreign affairs but remained Secretary of State throughout the first Cleveland Administration.

The next President, Benjamin Harrison, appointed two consecutive Secretaries of State. James G. Blaine was commissioned a second time, served for more than three years (1889–1892), and, because of ill health, was away from the Department from March to October 1891, and he resigned abruptly on June 4, 1892. The President then selected John W. Foster, who, although he remained Secretary for less than eight months, had extensive diplomatic experience, both before and after serving as Secretary of State.

During President Cleveland's second term, he also appointed two Secretaries. In keeping with his desire for "career officers" in his Cabinet, although it was thought that he might reappoint Bayard, he first selected Walter Q. Gresham, a lifelong Republican who had previously been Postmaster General (1883–84) and briefly Secretary of the Treasury (1884) in President Arthur's Cabinet, U.S. Circuit Judge (1884–93), and successful candidate for the Republican presidential nomination in 1888. He remained Secretary of State for somewhat more than two years. When he was stricken with pneumonia and died in May 1895, the President turned to his Attorney General, Richard Olney, a corporate lawyer and strong supporter of the Democratic Party, to head the Department of State for the remainder of his administration. During Gresham's illness, the President had assigned a number of diplomatic duties to Olney, and he was called upon for additional foreign relations service after he left the State Department.

President William McKinley appointed three Secretaries of State. The first two—John Sherman and William R. Day—held office for relatively short periods, especially Day, who served for less than five months. Sherman, a professional politician, originally was a Whig who became active in the National Republican Party, and he served as a member of Congress for more than two decades. He was appointed Secretary in March 1897, when he was advanced in age, apparently in order to have him vacate his Senate seat to make room for the designation of Mark Hanna as Senator from Ohio. He was succeeded in April 1898 by Day, a lawyer and former judge who had been commissioned Assistant Secretary of State in 1897 and was promoted to the office of Secretary the following April.

McKinley's third Secretary of State, John M. Hay, who studied law in the office of Abraham Lincoln, served as his private secretary in the early 1860s and spent twenty years as an author and poet. He also held several diplomatic and Department of State administrative appointments, including that of Secretary of Legation at Paris (1865–67) and Madrid (1869–70), Chargé d'Affaires ad interim at Vienna (1867–68), Assistant Secretary of State (1879–81), and Ambassador to Great Britain (1897–98). He began his career as Secretary of State in September 1898. When McKinley was reelected to a second term and was assassinated in September 1901, Hay continued as Secretary for another four years, until his death in July 1905. Having devoted nearly three decades to the diplomatic profession, he has been regarded as a career foreign relations officer.

President Theodore Roosevelt considered two prominent lawyers and active political leaders as Hay's successor—William Howard Taft and Elihu Root, who had preceded Taft as head of the War Department. Roosevelt wanted to have both of them in his Cabinet. He decided to appoint Root to head the Department of State, where he remained for more than three years and was then elected to the Senate (1909–15), and he later held several important diplomatic and arbitral commissions. He recommended the nomination of Robert Bacon, a banker and financier, as his successor, whom President Roosevelt appointed on January 27, 1909. Bacon had previously served as Assistant Secretary of State (1905–9) and as Acting Secretary when Root attended the Third Pan-American Conference at Rio de Janeiro in 1906. Bacon's tenure as Secretary was short-lived, from late January to March 5.

When Taft was inaugurated as President in 1909, he appointed Philander C. Knox as the last pre–World War I Secretary of State. However, desiring to retain Bacon in the Department, Taft introduced a bill in Congress to create a new office of Under Secretary of State to accommodate him, but Congress failed to enact it. The President then appointed Bacon as Ambassador to France (1909–12). Knox had spent twenty-four years in the legal profession and served as Assistant U.S. Attorney in Pennsylvania (1876–77), President of the American Bar Association (1897), Attorney General in the Cabinets of Presidents McKinley and Roosevelt (1901–4), Senator from Pennsylvania (1904–9), and unsuccessful candidate for the Republican presidential nomination in 1908. He remained Secretary for the full term of four years, until the inauguration of Woodrow Wilson.

Corps of Secretaries

Naturally, these sixteen Secretaries of State (see Table 5.1) varied in their qualifications, interests, and achievements. Pertinent factors include the States from which they were appointed, their age on appointment, their length of service, their professional training, their prior diplomatic, Congressional, other Cabinet, and additional public service, their personal qualities and their qualities for the office, their relations with the Presidents under whom they served, and the contributions for which they are remembered.

Five Secretaries were appointed from New York—Bacon, Evarts, Fish, Root, and Seward; two each from Indiana and Ohio; and one from the States of Delaware, Illinois, Maine, Massachusetts, New Jersey, and Pennsylvania. Hay was the first Secretary to be appointed from the District of Columbia. This geographic distribution pattern differed from that of earlier times. Prior to 1861 Virginia was the preferred State (especially during the initial years prior to 1829), and only three Secretaries were appointed from States other than the original thirteen. However, from 1861 to 1913 the largest number were from New York, only four others were from other original States (Delaware, Massachusetts, New Jersey, and Pennsylvania), and the rest came from four of the newer States (Illinois, Indiana, Maine, and Ohio) and the District of Columbia.

All of these Secretaries were advanced in their careers when appointed. Most were in their upper fifties and early sixties, Secretaries Bacon and Day were only in their late forties, Blaine (at the time of his second appointment) was seventy-one, and Sherman was already seventy-four years of age. Their length of service was affected primarily by politics, changes in the presidency (including the assassination of Presidents Lincoln, Garfield, and McKinley), and the health and, in rare cases, the age and the death of the Secretary. Seward and Fish, like former Secretaries James Madison and John Quincy Adams, bear the distinction of holding office for eight years (during the 1860s and 1870s), and Hay served for nearly seven years at the turn of the century. Evarts, Bayard, and Knox remained for four years, Blaine for more than four years (for his two appointments combined), and Frelinghuysen and Root for more than three years. These nine provided substantial continuity in the office. The rest served for briefer periods, with Foster, Day, and Bacon for less than a year and Washburne for only a few days. The tenure of several Secretaries was cut short, primarily by change in presidential administrations and for Gresham and Hay by their death in office.

The Secretaries differed in their professional background and interests. All, except Bacon, were trained in the law, several were practicing lawyers, and Foster was a renowned expert on international law. Many were professional politicians, of whom nine had experience in Congress before becoming Secretary, six of whom held congressional office for ten years or longer. Those with the longest records were Sherman (twenty-two years), Blaine (twenty years), and Washburne and Bayard (sixteen years each).[13]

Six Secretaries also were commissioned to other Cabinet posts before they headed the State Department. Thus, Evarts (1868–69), Olney (1893–95), and Knox (1901–4) served as Attorney General; Gresham (1884, for two months) and Sherman (1877–81) as Secretaries of the Treasury; Root as Secretary of War (under Presidents McKinley and Roosevelt (1899–1904); and Gresham as Postmaster General (1883–84).[14] Several also were elected or appointed to State political offices, usually before they became active in the national arena,[15] and four held a number of Federal and State judicial positions.[16] Eight had presidential aspirations or were promoted for running for election as Chief Executive.[17]

Of critical significance as preparation for appointment as Secretary of State was the matter of prior foreign relations experience. Only six Secretaries—Evarts, Foster, Day, Hay, Root, and Bacon—had the benefit of such prior responsibility.[18] On the other hand, more Secretaries were subsequently commissioned to diplomatic missions. Washburne was rewarded with immediate appointment as Envoy Extraordinary and Minister Plenipotentiary to France (1869–71), and Evarts, Bayard, Foster, Olney, Day, Root, and Bacon were later appointed to various diplomatic, peacemaking, and peaceful settlement responsibilities.[19] Thus, nine of the sixteen Secretaries provided prior and/or subsequent foreign relations service in a variety of capacities.

Aside from the political reasons for their appointment, most of these Secretaries had amicable relations with the Presidents they served. For example, although a rival for the Republican nomination for the presidency, Seward not only enjoyed an intimate professional relationship with President Lincoln but was also virtually acknowledged as his "Prime Minister." Blaine and President Garfield regarded each other with confidence and esteem, and later Blaine and President Harrison had cordial relations. Bayard ranked among the foremost of President Cleveland's Cabinet officers during his first administration, and it was said that a Cabinet without him "was unthinkable." Root worked closely and harmoniously with President Roosevelt. Knox was a friend and classmate of Roosevelt at Harvard University, and President Taft thought highly of him. Good relations also permeated the relations of Secretary Day with President McKinley and Secretary Hay with both Presidents McKinley and Roosevelt, although Hay was not particularly happy in the role of Secretary of State. On the other hand, even though he was a strong pillar of President Grant's Administration, Fish disagreed with him on several diplomatic appointments, and Secretary Sherman resented it when President McKinley invited Assistant Secretary Day to accompany him in Cabinet meetings.

Biographers, historians, and other analysts have stressed many qualities and characteristics of these Secretaries. To mention a few, Seward has been regarded as a master of compromise, a "political wizard," and an adept political manager; Fish as having a natural aptitude for administrative detail and supervision of subordinates; Evarts, in whom the lawyer dominated the statesman, as one of the most brilliant minds of his day and as a diplomat by nature, possessing an international reputation; Blaine as resourceful and dynamic—a man of action; Bayard as courteous and possessing a sense of fair play; Foster, recognized as a leading expert on international law and diplomacy, as devoted to civic duty and service; Olney as a practical decision maker and a strong-willed leader; Sherman as peace-oriented despite the events that led to the War with Spain; Day as inexperienced in world affairs but blessed with able and reliable assistants; Hay and Bacon as widely traveled and knowledgeable concerning international relations; Root as noted for his keen interest in public affairs, for having an international reputation, and for being a trustworthy confidant of Presidents, Cabinet members, and Senators; and Knox as an able and decisive organizer and administrator, with ability to conciliate. Evarts, Frelinghuysen, and Knox were also reputed to be accomplished orators, and Hay was a recognized author, biographer, and poet.

Individual Secretaries have also been publicly acknowledged and are remembered for specific foreign affairs contributions and achievements. To illustrate, Fish, Root, and Knox are noted for Department of State and Diplomatic and Consular Service reform. Olney introduced the practice of producing Secretary of State annual reports and amplified the Monroe Doctrine with his corollary in 1895. Blaine was appointed Secretary twice and served under three Presidents, and he promoted Pan-American unity and cooperation. Seward played a major role in negotiating the treaty for the purchase of Alaska in 1867, Day assisted President McKinley in negotiating the annexation of the Philippine Islands in 1898, and Hay was instrumental in negotiating treaties respecting the construction of the Panama Canal early in the twentieth-century. In a public address Hay also declared the "Golden Rule" to be the cardinal principle of American diplomacy and was an avid promoter of the Open Door policy. Knox contributed to the Taft Administration development of "dollar diplomacy." Secretaries Hay and especially Root are noted for their negotiation of a series of arbitration treaties in 1905 and 1908–9, and Washburne is remembered as the Secretary who served for the shortest period, for less than two weeks in 1869.

It has been written by Claude G. Bowers and Helen Dwight Reid that, as of

1928, "The United States has never had a Secretary of State better qualified by temperament and social gifts for the lighter side of diplomacy" than William M. Evarts; by Chauncey Depew that Foster was "the handyman of the Department of State"; by Montgomery Schuyler that as Secretary of State, Olney "will stand for a long while as one of the most vigorous, resolute and independent men who have ever held the office"; and by James Brown Scott, discussing Elihu Root as an "Elder Statesman," that he was "an outstanding figure of his generation." Graham Stuart has declared that, as of 1949, if one assesses Secretaries of State on the organization and work of the Department, Knox "would surely rate among the top half dozen." Stuart also has concluded that Foster's fame rests more on his overall record as a diplomat and a writer on diplomatic history, practice, and procedure than on his service as Secretary of State, and James Bryce, providing the highest accolade, regarded Foster as "the most distinguished diplomat of our time."

Assistant Secretaries

With the creation of the positions of Second and Third Assistant Secretaries of State, respectively, in 1866 and 1875, the Secretary was assisted by a senior staff of four officials—three Assistant Secretaries and the Chief Clerk. From 1861 to 1913, the President and Secretary of State commissioned twenty Assistant Secretaries (called the "First Assistant Secretary"),[20] two Second Assistant Secretaries, fourteen Third Assistant Secretaries, and eight Chief Clerks (see Table 5.1). The Assistant Secretaries were commissioned as presidential appointees, with Senate confirmation, and they functioned as the Secretary's immediate deputies, whereas the Chief Clerk, not a commissioned officer, was an administrative manager in charge of departmental Clerks and other employees.

Providing a degree of continuity, of the three dozen individuals who served as Assistant Secretaries, John M. Hay, William R. Day, and Robert Bacon were later appointed as Secretaries of State. Five of the Third Assistant Secretaries were subsequently promoted—Alvey A. Adee to Second Assistant Secretary, and John Bassett Moore, William Phillips, William W. Rockhill, and F. M. Huntington Wilson to the rank of First Assistant Secretary. Four Assistant Secretaries—Adee, Francis B. Loomis, Edwin F. Uhl, and William F. Wharton—also functioned as Secretary of State ad interim. Phillips acquired the unusual record of serving as Third Assistant Secretary twice (1909 and 1914–17) before being commissioned as First Assistant Secretary (1917–20), and he was the only Assistant Secretary to later become a member of the career Foreign Service, and eventually he was appointed as Under Secretary of State (1933–36) and as ranking diplomat to several foreign governments.

Three First Secretaries—J. C. Bancroft Davis, David J. Hill, and Huntington Wilson—and four of the Third Assistant Secretaries—Adee, Moore, Thomas W. Cridler, and Herbert H. D. Peirce—served for more than four years.[21] Frederick W. Seward, who was commissioned First Assistant Secretary twice (1861–

69 and 1877–79) held this office for more than ten years. William Hunter III, who, in addition to long service as Chief Clerk, also became the initial Second Assistant Secretary for twenty years, and Adee, his successor, held the offices consecutively as Third and Second Assistant Secretaries for nearly half a century. Thus, Hunter and Adee provided remarkably high-level stability in the management of the Department of State for a span of more than seven decades. On the other hand, a number of First and Third Secretaries remained for less than a year.[22]

Evidencing interchange, at least fifteen appointees bridged service as Assistant Secretaries in Washington with diplomatic and consular assignments abroad. Charles Hale was named Agent/Consul General to Egypt (1864–70), and Francis B. Loomis was accredited as Minister Plenipotentiary to Venezuela (1897–1901) and to Portugal (1901–2) before they became Assistant Secretaries. Between his appointments as Third and First Assistant Secretary Huntington Wilson was commissioned as Minister Plenipotentiary to Rumania and Serbia and as Diplomatic Agent to Bulgaria in December 1908 and as Minister Plenipotentiary to Argentina in January 1910, but he did not proceed to either of these posts because he was promoted to the rank of First Assistant Secretary.

On the other hand, twelve other Assistant Secretaries received diplomatic appointments following their Department of State assignments. After he became First Assistant Secretary (1905–9) and then Secretary of State (1909), Robert Bacon was commissioned as Ambassador to France (1909–12). Bancroft Davis was made Minister Plenipotentiary to Germany (1874–77) between his two appointments as First Assistant Secretary. After his service as Third and then First Assistant Secretary, William W. Rockhill was accredited as Minister Plenipotentiary sequentially to Greece, Rumania, and Serbia (1897–99), China (1905–9), Russia (1909–11), and Turkey (1911–13). The most impressive record was held by William Phillips. In addition to serving as Third and later as First Assistant Secretary, he became Minister Plenipotentiary to the Netherlands and Luxembourg (1920–22), Under Secretary (1922–24), Ambassador to Belgium (1924–27) and Canada (1927–29), Under Secretary for the second time (1933–36), and Ambassador to Italy (1936–41).[23]

Chief Clerks

The role of the Chief Clerk was modified as the senior level of State Department organization and administration was amplified by the creation of new Assistant Secretaries and as their responsibilities were legally prescribed. The Act of August 26, 1842, which defined the administrative functions of the Chief Clerk, remained in effect throughout this period.

President Lincoln and Secretary Seward inherited William Hunter III as Chief Clerk, who served in this capacity for fifteen years, until he was promoted to the rank of Second Assistant Secretary in July 1866, when that position was created. During the following four and one-half decades he was succeeded as

Chief Clerk, respectively, by Robert S. Chew (1866–73), Sevellon A. Brown (1873–92), William W. Rockhill (1893–94, when he was promoted to Third Assistant Secretary), Edward I. Renick (1894–97), William H. Michael (1897–1905), Charles Denby (1905–7), Wilbur J. Carr (1907–9), and William McNeir (1909–13). Several of these Chief Clerks provided the Department of State with administrative continuity, especially Brown, who held office for nearly twenty years, Chew and Michael, each of whom served for approximately eight years, and McNeir, who remained for four years. Beginning in the 1890s, however, except for Michael and McNeir, Chief Clerks held their positions for relatively short periods.

As a group these nine Chief Clerks constituted a remarkable corps of departmental administrators. Hunter, appointed as a clerk in 1829, was promoted to the position of Chief Clerk in 1852 and to Second Assistant Secretary in 1866, and he died in office twenty years later, after serving the Department for nearly six decades. Five others—Chew, Brown, Renick, Carr, and McNeir—were promoted from clerkships and other Departmental positions. Carr was later made Director of the Consular Service and then Assistant Secretary (1924–37). Rockhill had a successful Departmental and diplomatic career following his service as Chief Clerk, and Denby was commissioned as Consul General in China. McNeir later became Chief of the departmental Bureau of Accounts, was a member of the American Secretariat at the World War I Peace Conference, and retired from the Department of State in 1937, after more than fifty-five years of service.

COMPOSITION, REORGANIZATION, AND MANAGEMENT

In general, while other administrative departments and agencies of the Federal Government were created for the purpose of carrying out the enactments of Congress, it has been said that the primary function of the State Department was to implement the will of the President in dealing with foreign governments and that this involved not only what should be done but also how it should be accomplished.[24] Nevertheless, Congress continued to control the establishment of new positions, the number of departmental clerks and other staff members, budgets, and salaries.

The structure of the Department of State was subject to review and modification not only by the Secretary of State but also by Congress, which controlled developments through appropriations, other enactments, and legislative procedures. Major reorganization was undertaken by Secretary Fish beginning in 1869 and by Secretaries Root and Knox early in the twentieth century. Among the principal reforms were the introduction of administrative divisions to supplement departmental bureaus, agencies, and other individuals and geographic as well as functional or servicing units and agents. Both of these innovations continued for some time, especially geographic structuring for the management of overseas affairs.

When Seward became Secretary and served during both the Lincoln and Johnson Administrations, he made few organizational alterations but changed some departmental personnel. His principal assistants were his son Frederick W. Seward, who was named Assistant Secretary and held this position for eight years (1861–69),[25] and William Hunter, the veteran Chief Clerk, who continued in this capacity for another five years. The Secretary also replaced all Secessionists.

Congress legislated two administrative changes in the 1860s. An Act of July 4, 1864, authorized the President to appoint a Commissioner of Immigration to serve under the direction of the Secretary. This proved to be temporary and was abolished in less than four years. Of greater significance, an Act of July 25, 1866, created the office of Second Assistant Secretary of State, to which Hunter was promoted two days later. In addition, a temporary Bureau was established to care for Civil War political prisoners and for rebel correspondence, under the direction of E. D. Webster. The regular clerks were supplemented with the appointment of temporary assistants when they were needed, who from time to time varied from five to twenty-five.[26]

Secretary Fish's Reorganization, 1869–1877

Secretary Fish instituted the first major post–Civil War departmental reorganization in 1870. The number of clerks had gradually increased, but Congress mandated reduction of this staff from forty-eight to thirty-one, beginning July 1, 1869. Secretary Fish filed objections with both the Speaker of the House and its Foreign Affairs Committee, complaining that this action reduced departmental personnel by more than one-third. Nevertheless, he devised his reorganization on the basis of thirty-one staff members, grouped in thirteen units, consisting of nine Bureaus, two agencies, one Translator, and one Telegrapher. The largest unit under this arrangement was titled the Chief Clerk's Bureau, comprising Chief Clerk Robert S. Chew and five clerks, who were responsible for archives and rolls, receipt and distribution of correspondence, indexing records, and related duties.

The four principal functional units consisted of two Diplomatic and two Consular Bureaus. The First Diplomatic Bureau was under the direction of First Assistant Secretary J. C. Bancroft Davis, with Henry D. J. Pratt in charge, assisted by two clerks who were responsible for eleven European countries and China and Japan.[27] The Second Diplomatic Bureau was headed by Robert S. Chilton under the superintendence of Second Assistant Secretary William Hunter, assisted by two clerks. It handled relations with seventeen Latin American countries, as well as three remaining European countries[28] and the Barbary States, Egypt, the Hawaiian Islands, Liberia, and Turkey, totaling more than two dozen foreign countries and other territories.[29] The First and Second Consular Bureaus were responsible for relations with the same countries as the respective Diplomatic Bureaus. The First Consular Bureau was headed by Jasper Smith, assisted by three clerks, also under First Assistant Secretary Bancroft Davis, and the Second Consular Bureau was under A. H. Clements, assisted by two clerks, supervised by Second Assistant Secretary Hunter.

The Law Bureau coped with the examination of legal questions submitted to it by the Secretary and Assistant Secretaries and was administered by E. Pershine Smith. He was known as the Examiner of Claims, a position created by Congressional resolution of May 27, 1870, who, it is interesting to note, functioned under the jurisdiction of the Department of Justice. The Passport Bureau was headed by Thomas C. Cox, the Passport Clerk, who issued and recorded passports and collected the revenue tax imposed on them. The Statistical Bureau, responsible for the care of printed books, pamphlets, and prepared commercial reports, was administered by Charles Payson, the Librarian, assisted by a temporary clerk. The Bureau of Accounts, manned by the Disbursement Clerk, George E. Baker, managed the custody and disbursement of all State Department funds, as well as the Department's headquarters building and property.

Two additional units, called agencies, dealt with commissions, pardons, and domestic records. The first of these was responsible for processing applications for Federal appointments and the preparation of presidential commissions and pardons, handled by George Bartel with the help of one assisting clerk. The agency concerned with domestic records consisted of a single clerk, Edward Haywood, under the direction of the First Assistant Secretary. It handled correspondence with territorial officers and other communications that did not relate to diplomatic and consular affairs. At that time Henry L. Thomas was Translator, and Thomas Morrison was Telegrapher, both of whom served the Secretary of State, the Assistant Secretaries, and in some cases the Chief Clerk.

An innovative feature of this arrangement was that it prescribed specific administrative assignments to the First and Second Assistant Secretaries, placing the First Diplomatic and Consular Bureaus under the former and the Second Diplomatic and Consular Bureaus under the Second Assistant Secretary. This prescribed principal deputies of the Secretary of State for particular geographic areas and structured the Department on a geographic as well as a functional basis.[30]

Although this remained the basic organizational pattern for nearly four decades, personnel and modest organizational changes were made from time to time. In 1872 the Domestic Records Agency was retitled the Territorial and Domestic Records Agency. The following year a Bureau of Indexes and Archives was created with a principal officer and three clerks. It had the task of opening mail, indexing it, preserving the archives, and responding to calls for papers and information. This relieved the Chief Clerk of such duties so that he could concentrate on supervising the clerks and other employees of the Department. When Congress, by the Act of March 3, 1873, formally reorganized six Bureaus—two Diplomatic, two Consular, Accounts, and Indexes and Archives—technically the Statistical, Domestic Records, and Passport Bureaus were abolished,[31] and departmental responsibilities for American territories were transferred to the Department of the Interior.

As a consequence of the enactment of this act, beginning in 1873 the heads of the bureaus named in the law were provided with commissions, signed by the Secretary of State. The following year, however, the question arose as to whether the bureau chiefs, like the Secretary and Assistant Secretaries, required presidential nomination and appointment subject to Senate confirmation. On June 26, 1875, the departmental law office ruled that they, not regarded as "clerks," were presidential appointees subject to Senate confirmation, and on July 1 the President provided them with formal commissions. This afforded them a special status superior to that of the Chief Clerk and other clerks. However, after these initial presidential appointments of bureau chiefs, none were made for nearly two decades, during which they were made by the Secretary of State, until Secretary Gresham reinvoked the practice in 1894. Secretary Olney referred this status issue to the U.S. Attorney General for an opinion in 1896, who ruled that the heads of bureaus were clerks and therefore were entitled only to departmental commissions, signed by the Secretary of State.[32]

By its Act of June 20, 1874, Congress reduced the number of legally recognized bureaus to five, by allowing only one chief for the combined Diplomatic Bureau and one for the Consular Bureau and formally recognizing the Bureau of Rolls and Library in addition to the Bureaus of Accounts and of Indexes and Archives.[33] The budgetary Act of August 15, 1876, reconfirmed the recognized bureau chiefs as numbering five. But the Act of June 19, 1878, reduced the number to four by dropping the Bureau of Rolls and Library and designating a departmental clerk as Librarian with the same functions as those previously ascribed to the chief of this bureau. This congressional action reduced the Department to the lowest level of formally authorized bureaus.

A major top-level addition was made when, by the Act of June 20, 1874, Congress established the office of Third Assistant Secretary, and John A. Campbell was commissioned on February 24 the following year. Thus, by 1875 the Secretary of State was provided with three commissioned Assistant Secretaries and the Chief Clerk as his ranking managerial team.

Secretary Fish also prescribed a series of regulations to administer the Department and expedite its performance. He fixed the office hours, running from 9:30 A.M. to 4:00 P.M., or later if business required, and he ordered at least one clerk in each bureau to remain until the mail for the day was signed.[34] A record was made of the absence of staff members throughout each day. They were also prohibited from furnishing outsiders with information concerning departmental business. Secretary Fish insisted that dispatches be copied promptly. To facilitate and systematize procedure, he instituted a revised procedure for registering correspondence in a set of index volumes for diplomatic, consular, and other correspondence and for binding volumes of miscellaneous documents.

Secretaries Evarts to Hay, 1877–1905

During the administrations of the Secretaries from Evarts to Hay, they instituted no basic structural and few administrative changes. By the early 1880s, when Frelinghuysen was Secretary, the official number of bureaus was increased to seven, including the combined Diplomatic and Consular Bureaus, plus the Accounts, Indexes and Archives, Law, Rolls and Library, and Statistics Bureaus. The Passport Bureau was reestablished in 1902, with Gaillard Hunt as its chief, and five years later it was retitled the Bureau of Citizenship. During the Sherman Administration the Statistics Bureau was retitled the Bureau of Foreign Commerce, which, in 1903, was converted into the Bureau of Trade Relations. Later, it was ascribed new duties imposed on the Department of State by the Tariff Act of 1909, and it was provided with additional staff, including two commercial advisers. Consequently, by the end of the Hay Administration in 1905, the Department of State consisted of nine functional and administrative bureaus.

Other departmental units, called bureaus, though not so recognized by Congress, were established. For example, the Bureau of Pardons, Remissions, and Copyright, previously created by Secretary McLane, abolished by Secretary Forsyth, and reestablished by Secretary Fish as the Bureau of Commissions and Pardons, was converted into the Bureau of Appointments in 1896. Three years earlier, in 1893, by executive order, responsibility for preparing presidential pardons had been transferred to the Department of Justice. Also, the Passport Bureau, which had been created in 1870 and abolished three years later, was reestablished in 1902.

Several additional institutional changes were made. The Office of the Librarian was converted into that of Chief of the Bureau of Rolls and Library in 1875[35]; the Chief Clerk was given responsibility as Superintendent of the Department of State building in 1882; the title of the Examiner of Claims was changed to Solicitor by the Act of March 3, 1891; the office of Appointment Clerk, to head the Bureau of Appointments, was created in 1896 to consider applications for appointment to public office and the preparation of commissions, exequaturs, and warrants for extradition and to have custody of, and apply, the Great Seal of the United States; during the Olney Administration a Departmental Board of Promotion was established, with the Chief Clerk at its head; an Assistant Solicitor was provided in April 1900; and a second Translator was added that same year, as was a confidential clerk to assist the Secretary of State's private secretary.

Turning to senior officials, Frederick W. Seward was reappointed First Assistant Secretary (1877–79). He was succeeded by fourteen other appointees prior to the commissioning of Secretary Root in 1905. They averaged approximately two years of service. Some were promoted from lesser positions in the Department, a few held prior or subsequent diplomatic or consular appointments, and two of them—William R. Day and John M. Hay—later became Secretary of State. During these years only Alvey A. Adee, promoted in August 1886, to succeed William Hunter, was commissioned as Second Assistant Secretary, and he held the office until 1924. Beginning with the appointment of John A. Campbell in February 1875, some eleven officers served as Third Assistant Secretary. Adee had held this post before he was promoted to the rank of Second Assistant

Secretary, and both William W. Rockhill and John Bassett Moore were promoted from Third to First Assistant Secretary.

Secretary Root's Reforms, 1905–1909

Early in the twentieth century Secretary Root launched the second major post–Civil War organizational reform of the Department. Huntington Wilson, then Third Assistant Secretary, assumed leadership in managing this revision. He devised a plan to establish separate geographic divisions to manage diplomatic and consular affairs for Western Europe, Latin America, and the Far East, each to be administered by an experienced officer of the Diplomatic or Consular Service. Oversight would be provided by the First Assistant Secretary, who was to function as an Under Secretary of State. Although reluctant to institute such a revolutionary change, Secretary Root authorized Wilson to establish a Far Eastern Affairs Division on an experimental basis, with the assistance of William Phillips, Second Secretary of the American Legation in Peking, and Percival Heintzleman, who had five years of field experience in the Consular Service in China. This geographic division arrangement, formalized in March 1908, proved to be sufficiently successful to induce Secretary Knox to adopt it in March 1909 for the management of all diplomatic and consular relations.[36]

To facilitate classification and arrangement of documents, Secretary Root decided to modernize the existing system consisting of folio index books established in 1870 and utilized for thirty-five years and to centralize archival functions in the Bureau of Indexes and Archives. Based on his earlier experience with War Department records management, in 1906 he recruited David A. Salmon from that Department and consigned three State Department staff members to it to familiarize them with its procedures. Secretary Root issued an order to institute a system of numerical subject classification and filing for State Department documents, which began to be implemented in 1909.[37] This reform proved to be so useful that Salmon was kept in charge of departmental files and was subsequently elevated to the rank of Chief of the Bureau of Indexes and Archives.

Gaillard Hunt, Chief of the Passport Bureau, reported to Secretary Root in April 1907 that all communications to the State Department concerned with citizenship and the protection of Americans abroad became the responsibility of that bureau, which had authority to act on them. The following month the Secretary retitled the Passport Bureau as the Bureau of Citizenship.[38]

Secretary Knox's Reorganization, 1909–1913

Secretary Knox, with the assistance of Huntington Wilson, then First Assistant Secretary, masterminded the next major departmental reorganization in 1909.[39] At the senior level the First Assistant Secretary, regarded as an Under Secretary of State, comparable to a Vice Minister of Foreign Affairs in other governments, remained the Secretary's principal deputy. As Second Assistant Secretary, Adee continued to exercise general direction over all functional aspects of departmental responsibilities, and the Third Secretary was prescribed purely administrative direction of the Diplomatic and Consular Services, international conferences, ceremonial matters, and approval of expenditures.[40] To accommodate increased needs, the office of Solicitor was expanded to embrace three assistants and several law clerks to handle issues of international law and diplomacy, including the legal aspects of asylum, citizenship, claims, expatriation, extradition, extraterritoriality, naturalization, neutrality, passports, and similar matters.

Several new positions were established. The office of Counselor was created in 1909 and given responsibility to investigate, report, and counsel the Department on various issues that required uninterrupted technical and international legal attention, such as managing the negotiation of trade agreements and American participation in international conferences on maritime and other matters. Henry M. Hoyt, former Solicitor General of the United States, was the first appointee, and he was succeeded by Chandler P. Anderson, who had previously served as special counselor to Secretary Root.

The position of Resident Diplomatic Officer was introduced to assist Secretary Knox in formulating and executing foreign policy and to provide him with advice from the perspective of those who served abroad, as well as a Director of the Consular Service to systematize the operation of consular affairs and to supervise the Consular Bureau. Thomas C. Dawson, who had diplomatic experience in Brazil, Chile, Colombia, and Santo Domingo and who was also Chief of the Division of Latin American Affairs, became the first Resident Diplomatic Officer. He was succeeded by H. Percival Dodge in 1910, and the office was discontinued three years later. Wilbur Carr, who had served in the Department for seventeen years and had been Chief of the Consular Bureau, was made the first Director of the Consular Service.

The most notable organizational change instituted by Secretary Knox was the complete restructuring on a geographic basis of the combined diplomatic and consular departmental components and elevating them to division status. Having experimented with the Far East Division, new Divisions of Western European, Middle Eastern, and Latin American affairs were added. At the time the Far Eastern Division was responsible for all major countries and territories in the Asian area, including not only China and Japan but also French Indochina, Hong Kong, India, Siam, and Siberia, as well as Borneo, the East Indies, and the Straits Settlements. The Division of Latin American Affairs, established by departmental order in November 1909 and placed under the direction of the Resident Diplomatic Officer, was charged with administering relations with Mexico, Central America, South America, and the West Indies. The Division of European Affairs, created by departmental directive the following month, was supervised by the Third Assistant Secretary to monitor relations with ten European countries, the British colonies, Morocco, Liberia, and the Congo. The Division of

Middle Eastern Affairs, authorized by the same departmental order, managed relations with several Central and Eastern European countries (Austria-Hungary, the Balkan states, Germany, Greece, Italy, and Russia, and their colonial territories), together with Abyssinia (Ethiopia), Egypt, Persia, and Turkey.

Another innovation of historic consequence was the establishment of a Division of Information. By means of publishing an "Information Series," headed initially by Philip H. Patchin, the Department of State advised American missions abroad concerning contemporary developments and negotiations, and it provided current news summaries for distribution to senior officers and the heads of departmental divisions and bureaus. It also was given the task of preparing and publishing the *Foreign Relations of the United States* compilations of American diplomatic documentation, discussed later.

Other departmental agencies were also modernized. As a result of increased responsibilities under the Tariff Act of 1909, two commercial advisers were added to the Bureau of Trade Relations, established in 1903, to which was allocated a substantial clerical staff of thirteen. Its functions bridged the handling of trade reports, corresponding with diplomatic and consular officers respecting trade and tariff matters, compiling commercial data, and promoting American foreign business. The Bureau of Indexes and Archives modified its files, switching from a chronological to a more convenient and useful decimal classification system. The Bureaus of Citizenship, Rolls and Library, and Appointments remained relatively unchanged structurally, but they experienced increased workloads, and in some cases they received additional staff. The Bureau of Accounts required updating, and in 1911 Secretary Knox informed Congress of the need for procedural change, but this was impossible until legislation was enacted to change the Department's legal requirements and duties.

Organization as of 1913

The organization of the Department had mushroomed by 1913 to consist of some two dozen units and individual officers.[41] In addition to the Secretary, three Assistant Secretaries, and the Chief Clerk, these embraced five Divisions, nine Bureaus, and six other individual agencies or agents, evidencing considerable structural proliferation by the time of World War I. The Second and Third Secretaries and nine of these units were created after 1861, including the four Geographic Divisions, the Division of Information, the Bureau of Trade Relations, the Resident Diplomatic Officer, the Director of the Consular Service, and the Counselor. The Bureaus of Appointments, Citizenship, Law, and Rolls and Library were reorganized or retitled. Only six bureaus and agents remained unchanged.[42]

Departmental Staff and Budget

As Department of State functions and responsibilities expanded, its staff and budget also increased. The domestic staff grew substantially during the years between the war with Spain and World War I. It increased from fewer than thirty members in the late 1850s, to eighty by 1880, and to ninety-one by 1900 and grew to 234 by 1910. Aside from the five senior officers, this included thirty other ranking officials, 135 clerks, twenty-eight messengers, and service personnel, such as telephone operators, laborers, clerical staff, a porter, and others.[43]

The annual salary of the Secretary of State was raised from $8,000 to $10,000 in 1873, reduced back to $8,000 the following year, and increased to $12,000 in 1911. Compensation of Assistant Secretaries, clerks, and others varied on the basis of experience and length of service.[44] The overall salary budget for the departmental staff increased from approximately $118,000 in 1898, to $191,000 by 1905 and to more than $228,000 by 1908. The total Department of State annual expenditures, combining departmental staff and the Diplomatic and Consular Services overseas rose from approximately $1.3 million in 1860, to somewhat less than $3.4 million in 1900, to $4.9 million in 1910.[45]

Origin of the *Foreign Relations of the United States* Series

Another major innovation of this period, in 1861, during Seward's Administration, the Department of State began to publish annual compilations of American diplomatic documents and other materials.[46] Initially, one or two volumes were produced each year, except for 1869, but later the number of yearly volumes increased considerably. At the outset the production of these volumes was assigned to the Division of Information, headed by Philip H. Patchin. They contained a variety of selected documents and other materials, including diplomatic communications, exchanges of notes, instructions and reports, and other official papers relating to the conduct of foreign relations and the diplomacy and consular affairs of the United States. Thus, with this historic, voluminous world-famous collection, coupled with the systematic publication of U.S. treaties and agreements, Department of State in-house studies, and various lists, guides, registers, and other compilations, the United States established and maintained a remarkably open system of its foreign relations documentation.[47]

Spoils and Tentative Launching of the Merit Principle in the State Department

One of the critical management and personnel issues of this half century was changing from the spoils to the merit system for recruiting, appointing, and promoting officials and employees in the Executive Branch of the American Government, including the Department of State. Inasmuch as the Secretary and Assistant Secretaries were presidential appointees, initially, the merit system was applicable primarily to departmental clerks and other staff members.

The spoils system, involving political patronage, which permeated executive appointments, beginning in the 1830s during the Andrew Jackson Administration, became especially pronounced during and after the 1840s and continued throughout the nineteenth century. Reform to institute the merit principle as a basic personnel formula was promoted by certain Presidents, members of Congress, the Department of State, and others, such as the Civil Service Reform League, established in 1881. The Pendleton Civil Service Act—called the Magna Charta of Civil Service reform—to manage the corps of executive employees was passed on January 16, 1883.[48] It laid the foundation for the American Civil Service System, administered by the Civil Service Commission. But the State Department, regarded as the "President's Office," was generally exempted, as were the Diplomatic and Consular Services, to be dealt with separately by a series of Congressional acts and executive orders. Early departmental personnel reform was more concerned with preventing abuses than with guaranteeing efficient administration by unpolitical staff members.

In the foreign relations arena dominance of a single political party from 1861 to 1913 assured a degree of stability and expertise in certain departmental positions. Post–Civil War reforms focused especially on such matters as eliminating the evils of the spoils system, political privilege, wealth as a standard for appointment (including the post–Civil War nouveau riche), property ownership, nepotism, and what has been branded "the baneful influence of politics" and "the meddlesome political interference with the Department of State."

Reform of personnel in both the State Department and the Diplomatic and Consular Services was achieved slowly and separately from the general Civil Service. The Secretary and Assistant Secretaries remained political appointees, subject to Senate confirmation. Several of them served for long periods, some were promoted from lesser positions, and a few—such as Alvey A. Adee, Sevellon A. Brown, Wilbur J. Carr, Thomas W. Cridler, William Hunter, John Bassett Moore, William Phillips, William W. Rockhill, Sydney Y. Smith, and Huntington Wilson—became virtual testimonials to a career service.

Despite the lack of the application of Civil Service regulations to the Department of State, President Arthur, previously a New York spoilsman, gave Secretary Frelinghuysen a free hand to keep the spoils system out of the Department. In some cases, despite political change in the presidency, little change was made in the staff of clerks and other personnel for political reasons, even when President Cleveland, a Democrat, took office in 1885 and 1893, because he was an advocate of Civil Service reform and the retention of qualified personnel.[49]

Domestic and Extraneous Functions, Transfer, and Denouement

As indicated in Chapter 4, the quantity of Department of State domestic and other nonforeign relations functions, which Gaillard Hunt, in his history of the Department, calls "sometime duties," peaked during the period prior to the Civil War. Some of these responsibilities were transferred to the Department of the Interior, created in 1849, which satisfied the earlier pressure to establish a Department of Home Affairs. During this half century additional extraneous functions were turned over to other Departments, the National Archives, the

Library of Congress, and other agencies. Consequently, complaints addressed to the President and Congress concerning the burden of fulfilling domestic responsibilities declined.

Beginning in 1861 additional transfers were made. These, for example, included responsibility for administering the process of presidential succession (made automatic under the Presidential Succession Act, 1886); issuing letters of marque and reprisal (to the Navy Department, 1863); handling American territorial papers (to the Department of the Interior, 1873); filing of reports with Congress on passengers arriving at U.S. ports (to the Treasury Department, 1891); dealing with presidential pardons and commutations (to the Justice Department, 1893); preparing reports on the foreign commercial relations of the United States (to the Department of Commerce and Labor, 1903); and custody of accumulated historical documents and records (to the Library of Congress, 1903).

Thus, the Department of State was gradually relieved of the burden of serving as a Department of both Foreign and Home Affairs, and it was converted into a purely foreign relations ministry. However, it continued to be saddled with some residual domestic functions, such as custody and application of the Great Seal, issuing passports in the United States and abroad, servicing intergovernmental relations for international exhibits and world fairs in the United States, and preparing and publishing various reports and documents. During the Knox Administration the latter was ascribed to the departmental Division of Information.

New Home of the Department

In 1866, during Seward's Administration, the Department of State had to change its domicile in the District of Columbia to make room for the expanded Treasury Department, with which it had been sharing office space.[50] Because no adequate public facility was then available, it was moved temporarily into the Washington Orphan Asylum, which was then being constructed at 14th and S Streets. Recognizing the need for more office space, in 1869 Congress set up a commission to recommend a site and submit plans for a new executive building to house the Department. Two years later it passed an act to construct this new building, located at Pennsylvania Avenue and 17th Street, immediately to the west of the White House, which came to be called the State, War, and Navy Building. It was built in five sections over a period of seventeen years. Although the State Department began to move into its south wing in July 1875, the building was not completed until January 1888. Its exterior consisted of hand-hewn granite, it contained five floors in addition to its basement and subbasement, and it cost more than $10 million.

This was the first imposing headquarters of the Department of State. Upon completion, described as a ''grand Renaissance building,'' it was then reputed to be the largest and finest office building in the world. The esthete derived satisfaction from the change of domicile from the Orphan Asylum (which perhaps caused more ridicule and adverse comment than any other edifice in Washington) to the new facility. Nevertheless, it has been described as ornamented with "jimcracks and spizzerinktums," and, when told that it was fireproof, General William T. Sherman (who was later to become Secretary of State) is reputed to have responded: "What a pity."

When the State Department moved into this facility, it did not occupy the entire building. The unused space was taken over by the Navy and War Departments so that it came to be known as the State–War–Navy Building. State Department quarters were adequate until the 1890s. In his annual report of 1896, Secretary Olney complained that the Department was in dire need of expanded or new facilities. In time, the Navy and War Departments moved to new quarters, and the departmental Bureaus of Trade Relations, Citizenship, and Accounts, the Solicitor and the Translator were transferred to other buildings. By congressional action, on July 3, 1930, the facility was renamed the "Department of State Building," and it served as the State Department's headquarters for six decades, until 1947.[51]

DIPLOMATIC AND CONSULAR REPRESENTATION

Major reforms in the Diplomatic and Consular Services were embodied in a series of congressional acts and executive orders during this period. One historic change was instituted in the Diplomatic Corps when, in 1893, Congress authorized the creation, under limited conditions, of the rank of Ambassador, and two executive orders, issued in 1905 and 1909, began to introduce the merit system for certain members of the Diplomatic and Consular Services. Most of the reforms applied to the Consular Service. An Act of 1874, superseding that of 1856, classified consular posts for salary purposes, and three decades later, by an Act of 1906, Congress legislated a significant modification, designed to reclassify consular establishments, apply the merit principle, and create a Consular Inspection Corps.

It is worthy of note that, while Congress focused primarily on matters of diplomatic and consular allocation, ranks, classification, and compensation, the President, by means of a series of executive orders, began to apply the merit system to the appointment and promotion of consular and lower-ranking diplomatic officers. Not until 1915, however, did Congress formally institute the merit principle on a statutory basis for both diplomatic and consular officers, as described later. Prior to the early twentieth century, therefore, with certain exceptions, appointments and promotions were largely influenced by politics, tenure in office was often short, turnover of personnel was substantial, and many individuals could not count on remaining in office beyond the presidential administration that appointed them.

Creating the Rank of Ambassador, 1893

In preconstitutional times American foreign envoys were usually titled "Commissioner." However, when John Adams was presented to the King of Great Britain in 1785, he was called "Ambassador Extraordinary from the United States of America." Contemplating the accreditation of diplomatic emissaries, the Constitutional Convention specified, in Article 2, section 2, that the President possessed authority, by and with the advice and consent of the Senate, to "appoint Ambassadors, other public Ministers, and Consuls." Therefore, although the President legally had the power to accredit Ambassadors, and the Department of State acceded to the rules concerning diplomatic rank adopted at the Congress of Vienna in 1815, not until 1893 did Congress legally authorize the commissioning of American diplomats at this rank, and none were designated as Ambassadors until that year. In the meantime, for more than a century, this rank had been regarded as reflecting the international conception of superior emissaries who directly represented the "person" of the "sovereign" rather than the government or the people, as too ostentatious and aristocratic for the emissaries of a democratic republic, and it was generally identified with monarchical and imperial governments.

Late in the nineteenth century American Ministers complained that they, as envoys of the second and third rank, were not only inconvenienced but also often humiliated, which impaired their work. Several Secretaries of State were reluctant to recommend to Congress that it authorize appointment at the highest rank. Secretary Frelinghuysen, former Minister Plenipotentiary, held that the United States could not, in justice to American Ministers, raise them to the level of Ambassadors with existing salaries, and he appealed to Congress to provide them with compensation commensurate with this higher rank. In 1885, when Edward J. Phelps, the American Minister Plenipotentiary to Great Britain, requested that his mission be raised to embassy status, Secretary Bayard disapproved the appeal on the grounds that it was unwarranted.[52] Yet, a few years later, in 1893, he was destined to become the first American envoy appointed at that rank.

Commenting on this matter in 1900 and agreeing with Bayard, former Secretary Foster, who had previously also served as Minister Plenipotentiary to Mexico, Russia, and Spain, concluded that creating the position of Ambassador would produce a pseudoaristocratic social class, unbefitting American democratic pretensions and traditions, and would create serious and often embarrassing problems of social status, demeanor, and protocol in Washington public affairs. He also contended that the American Diplomatic Service had previously "won deserved honor and distinction" without requiring "the bauble of a title to give its envoys greater standing or efficiency," and he questioned whether the absence of the ambassadorial rank had "ever prevented any really able minister of the United States from rendering his country a needed service." To resolve the issue of diplomatic classification, he proposed "the abolishment of all rank in the diplomatic body," contending that the international issue of diplomatic status would not be resolved "until all class distinctions and privileges are abolished, and a single grade is established in all the capitals of the world." He regarded the attitude that Ambassadors possessed the special capacity to personally represent their Head of State to foreign governments as not being applicable to Ministers, as emanating from Medieval practice, and as "pure fiction" in modern times.[53]

The action taken to create the rank of Ambassador was peculiar in several respects. On March 1, 1893, Congress legislated: "Whenever the President shall be advised that any foreign government is represented, or is about to be represented, in the United States by an ambassador . . . he is authorized, in his discretion, to direct that the representative of the United States to such government shall bear the same designation."[54] The process and the text of the law were unique in that this stipulation did not overtly create the rank but merely acknowledged it; it appended this action as a rider to a regular diplomatic and consular appropriations bill without discussion or comment[55]; while Congress recognized the principle of automatic reciprocity and comity for diplomatic grades, it left the initiative to "any foreign government" irrespective of its importance; and for purposes of administration, it did not relate specifically to salary levels. Nevertheless, Congress still controlled diplomatic appointments through its appropriations legislation, and, because no advanced salary levels were legislated, only the wealthy could afford appointment as Ambassadors to major posts and maintain requisite accommodations and lifestyles.

Great Britain was the first country to designate its envoy to Washington as an Ambassador in 1893, followed that same year by France, Germany, and Italy and in 1898 by Mexico and Russia. During the following decade, the United States elevated its diplomatic representation to only four additional countries— Austria (1902), Brazil (1905), and Japan and Turkey (1906). To regain control of American diplomatic representation, Congress passed an act on March 2, 1909, that restricted presidential action by providing that "hereafter no new ambassadorships shall be created unless the same shall be provided for by an act of Congress." In 1913 Spain was added to the list, which raised the total to eleven of the nearly fifty countries with which the United States then maintained diplomatic relations.[56] Thus, representation at the ambassadorial rank developed slowly, and it did not become common practice until the 1940s.

Diplomatic Corps

As indicated in Table 5.2, the United States appointed diplomats to fifty-two countries during this period, of which nineteen were additions to the American diplomatic list, primarily in the 1860s (four), 1880s (six), and especially after 1900 (eight). Diplomatic relations with Hawaii ceased in 1898, when it was annexed, and they were temporarily suspended with Ethiopia (1910–28), the

Table 5.2
American Diplomats and Missions, 1861–1913

Country	Years to 1913	Appointed	Served	Declined appointment	Senate not approve	Not commissioned	Not serve for other reasons
Argentina *	1861-	19	16		1		2
Austria *	1861-	28	17	1	7	1	2
Belgium *	1861-	18	16	1	1		
Bolivia *	1861-	22	19	1	1		1
Brazil *	1861-	16	15		1		
Bulgaria	1901-	7	4				3
Chile *	1861-	17	15		1		1
China *	1861-	15	11				4
Colombia *	1861-	20	18	1	1		
Costa Rica *	1861-	14	12		2		
Cuba	1902-	4	4				
Denmark *	1861-	16	12	1	1		2
Dominican Rep.	1883-	10	10				
Ecuador *	1861-	18	11		3	2	2 a
Egypt *	1861-	17	16	1			
El Salvador *	1861-	15	14		1		
Ethiopia	1908-1910	1	1				
France *	1861-	15	15				
Germany *	1861-	17	17				
Great Britain *	1861-	17	13	2	2		
Greece	1868-	17	15	1	1		
Guatemala *	1861-	17	16	1			
Haiti	1862-	13	11		1		1
Hawaii *	1861-1898	13	11		2		
Holy See *	1861-1867	4	3	1			
Honduras *	1861-	21	15	2			4
Iran (Persia)	1883-	15	10	1	1	1	2
Italy *	1961-	15	12	2			1
Japan *	1861-	15	14	1			
Korea	1883-1905	8	7	1			
Liberia	1864-	20	16	2	1		1
Luxembourg	1903-	4	4				
Mexico *	1861-	19	17	1			1
Montenegro	1905-	4	4				
Morocco	1906-	3	3				
Netherlands *	1861-	18	14	2		1	1
Nicaragua *	1861-	17	15		1		1
Norway	1905-	3	3				
Panama	1903-	7	7				
Paraguay	1861-	14	12	1		1	
Peru *	1861-	15	14				1
Portugal *	1861-	20	19				1
Romania	1881-	16	13	1			2
Russia *	1861-	28	23		3	1	1
Spain *	1861-	23	20	1	2		
Sweden *	1861-	13	11		1		1
Switzerland *	1861-	18	16				2
Thailand (Siam)	1882-	7	6	1			
Turkey *	1861-	18	16	1	1		
Uruguay	1867-	15	12	1	2		
Venezuela *	1861-	22	19		1		2
Yugloslavia	1882-	16	12	1			3
Total 52		764	646	30	39	7	42

*Indicates countries to which American diplomats were accredited prior to 1861.
aOne envoy to Ecuador died en route.

Holy See (1867–1941), and Korea (1905, when Japan assumed control over the country, to 1949). Put another way, when Lincoln became President, the United States maintained envoys to thirty-three foreign countries,[57] and by the end of the Taft Administration this increased to fourty-eight—twenty in both Europe[58] and Latin America, three in both the Middle East and Asia, and two in Africa. This embraced virtually all of the recognized independent members of the society of nations at that time.[59]

From 1861 to 1913, also indicated in Table 5.2, Presidents made a total of 764 diplomatic appointments. The largest numbers—20 or more—were made to nine countries.[60] On the other hand, those who actually served in their appointments numbered 646, or approximately 85 percent of those nominated. The largest numbers of these were accredited to eight European countries, ten Latin American countries, and three in the Middle East and Africa.[61] A few who were appointed were not commissioned or formally accredited, but most of the 118 who did not serve either were not approved by the Senate (thirty-nine), declined their appointments (thirty), were renominated but not commissioned (seven), or did not serve for other reasons (forty-two).[62]

At times diplomatic relations with individual countries were temporarily suspended. The most serious interruption occurred when the Spanish government severed relations with the United States on April 21, 1898. Minister Plenipotentiary Stewart L. Woodford left his post on that day, and Congress declared war on Spain four days later. Normal relations were not resumed until June 1899, when Bellamy Storer presented his credentials. In several cases the United States was reluctant to recognize changes in the governments of such countries as Peru (November 1865–May 1866 and September 1881–April 1884), China (February 1912–November 1913), and Mexico (February 1913–March 1917). Especially interesting, Allan A. Burton, appointed Minister Resident to Colombia in 1861, who did not present his credentials until March 1864, notified its government on December 10, 1866, that he "would have no further relations with it."

The length of individual tenure at a given post varied considerably. Whereas many envoys served for brief periods, before the creation of the professional Foreign Service of the United States, providing for transfer from post to post and between the Diplomatic and Consular Services, it was possible for a substantial number of diplomats to remain at a single post for more than five years. At least seventy remained at individual posts for six or more years.[63] Henry C. Hall represented the United States to the five Central American Republics for nearly seven years. Similarly, Whitelaw Reid was Ambassador to Great Britain for seven years but had his service cut short by his death. Both Elihu B. Washburne and Horace Porter served in France for eight years, as did Henry S. Sandford in Belgium and Ernest Lyon in Liberia, and Irving B. Dudley in Peru for more than nine years. Four envoys—Ebenezer Bassett, John M. Langston, William Frank Powell, and Henry W. Furniss—represented the United States in Haiti for a period of twenty-eight years.

However, those who held their tenure for the longest periods were Maurice F. Egan (Denmark, ten years), Thomas O. Osborn (Argentina, eleven years), John A. Bingham (Japan, twelve years), John Randolph Clay (Peru, nearly thirteen years), Charles Denby (China, thirteen years), William L. Merry (Costa Rica, fourteen years) and, most impressive, George P. Marsh (Italy) and Edwin V. Morgan (Brazil), each for more than twenty years. Marsh might have continued even longer, but he died at his post on July 23, 1882, and, together with his previous appointment to Turkey, he served in the Diplomatic Corps for nearly a quarter century, and Morgan held six diplomatic appointments over a period of nearly thirty years.

Due to political turnover, the launching of new missions that the United States established in additional countries and territories, the severance of diplomatic relations, the outbreak of war with Spain, or the death of the emissary, a good many envoys held short diplomatic appointments. For example, Benjamin P. Avery (China) and William T. Coggeshall (Ecuador) died at their posts in less than a year, as did John T. Croxton in Bolivia after one year of service. Between 1882 and 1893 four American Ministers Plenipotentiary also died at their posts in Liberia after serving less than a year. All told, approximately fifty accredited diplomats served for less than twelve months.

Nearly thirty envoys died at their posts in eighteen different countries; of these envoys Whitelaw Reid, Ambassador to Great Britain for more than seven years, who died in December 1912, ranks among the most prominent. Several appointees died before commencing their service, including Thomas Biddle, commissioned as Minister Resident to Ecuador, who died at Guayaquil in 1875 before his official reception, and Charles Allen T. Rice, who took the oath of office as Minister Plenipotentiary but died in the United States before proceeding to Russia in 1889.

Among the shortest tenures were those of Larz Anderson (Japan, some forty days, terminated by the inaugural of Woodrow Wilson), Lambert Tree (Russia, twenty-nine days in 1889), and Person C. Cheney, who established a record of serving only four days in Switzerland in January 1893, presaging Cleveland's second administration. Most strange, Marcus Otterbourg, minister Plenipotentiary to Mexico, appointed on July 1, 1867, immediately following the end of the Maximilian fiasco during which the United States was represented by a Chargé d'Affaires, presented his credentials on August 19, but he informed the Mexican Government by note the previous day that "he considered his mission terminated," and he left his post before the end of September, so that it may be said that he did not serve at all.

Two major changes were made in the ranking of American diplomats. In addition to the introduction of ambassadorships, the United States revived and later again eliminated the rank of Minister Resident.[64] Beginning in 1893, noted in Table 5.3, the President appointed fifty-one Ambassadors, who were commissioned to 10, largely European countries, but, to the end of the Taft Administration, this rank was still exceptional. By far the largest contingent, amounting

Table 5.3
American Diplomatic Appointees, 1861–1913

(Number of Appointments by Ranks)

Country	AE/P	EE/MP	MR	MR/CG	CdA	CdA/CG	Dip/Agt	Agt/CG	Comm	Comm/CG	Total
Argentina		11	8								19
Austria	4	24									28
Belgium		10	8								18
Bolivia		8	7	7							22
Brazil	4	12									16
Bulgaria		2					5				7
Chile		17									17
China		15									15
Colombia		12	8								20
Costa Rica		7	7								14
Cuba		4									4
Denmark		5	6	3	2						16
Dominican Rep.		1		3	6						10
Ecuador		7	11								18
Egypt								17			17
El Salvador		8	7								15
Ethiopia				1							1
France	6	9									15
Germany	6	11									17
Great Britain	4	13									17
Greece		11	4	2							17
Guatemala		11	6								17
Haiti		2		10						1	13
Hawaii		4	8						1		13
Holy See			4								4
Honduras		13	8								21
Iran (Persia)		5		9		1					15
Italy	9	6									15
Japan	4	8	3								15
Korea		2		6							8
Liberia				18						2	20
Luxembourg		4									4
Mexico	4	15									19
Montenegro		4									4
Morocco		3									3
Netherlands		7	10		1						18
Nicaragua		10	7								17
Norway		3									3
Panama		7									7
Paraguay		6	5		3						14
Peru		15									15
Portugal		9	5	6							20
Romania		14		2							16
Russia	7	21									28
Spain		23									23
Sweden		5	8								13
Switzerland		11	3	2	2						18
Thailand (Siam)		2	1	4							7
Turkey	3	8	7								18
Uruguay		6	6		3						15
Venezuela		11	10	1							22
Yugoslavia		14	2								16
Total 52	51	436	157	76	17	1	5	17	1	3	764

Code: AE/P=Ambassador Extraordinary and Plenipotentiary; EE/MP=Envoy Extraordinary and Minister Plenipotentiary; MR=Minister Resident; MR/CG=Minister Resident and Consul General; CdA=Chargé d'Affaires; CdA/CG=Chargé d'Affaires and Consul General; Dip/Agt=Diplomatic Agent; Agt/CG-Agent and Consul General; Comm-Commissioner; and Comm/CG-Commissioner and Consul General.

to 436 (57 percent) of the nominees, were designated as Envoys Extraordinary and Ministers Plenipotentiary.[65] The rank of Minister Resident, discontinued in 1820, was reinstated in 1853–54 and, during the following four decades, was applied to more than 230 envoys (30 percent) accredited to thirty-two countries.[66] It was discontinued for six of them in 1882 and for all the rest by 1893, except for Haiti (discontinued in 1897), Korea and Iran (1901), Thailand (1903), and eventually also Liberia (not until 1931) and Ethiopia (1943). It may be said, therefore, that the United States virtually ceased to employ the Minister Resident rank by the mid-1890s. The lesser ranks of Chargé d'Affaires, Diplomatic Agent, and Commissioner were rarely employed.[67]

Presidents continued to make simultaneous, multiple appointments to certain countries, especially when commencing diplomatic representation and usually as interim arrangement for proximate countries. In Europe such multiple emissaries were accredited to nine of twenty-one countries-the Balkans (from the 1880s till World War I), as well as to Greece,[68] to the Netherlands and Luxembourg,[69] and to Sweden and Norway.[70] In the Western Hemisphere they were made to eleven of twenty Latin American countries, especially the Central American Republics.[71]

Not surprisingly, a good many envoys were commissioned to sequential, multiple diplomatic missions, in most cases to different countries. These ranged from two to as many as ten appointments. Exclusive of those who became Secretary of State, such as Bacon, Foster, and Hay, approximately forty-five individuals received three or more assignments. James R. Partridge received six appointments, William W. Rockhill received seven, and John Brinkerhoff Jackson set a record by receiving nine, largely to Balkan countries.[72] Most unique, however, was William Phillips, initially commissioned as Third Assistant Secretary of State in 1909, who received ten appointments and wound up his career as Ambassador to Italy in October 1941, shortly before that country declared war on the United States.[73]

Early American diplomatic missions possessed a minimum of subordinate staff members to assist and relieve accredited envoys. Some diplomats employed their own private secretaries to aid them in their work. By the early 1880s only twelve missions had Legation Secretaries provided at public expense.[74] In 1881 Secretary Blaine proposed a plan for the systematic appointment of a small corps of diplomatic clerks to serve in those missions that lacked Legation Secretaries, to be appointed on the basis of examination, who could later be promoted to this grade. Congress failed to adopt the plan, but, during the following decade, by March 1892, it provided for twenty-seven such Secretaries (including three interpreters), which still left nearly half of the American missions without these assistants.[75]

Evidencing that diplomats are agents of Presidents and serve at their pleasure, some diplomats were recalled, which terminated their service. For example, when John Lothrop Motley, Minister Plenipotentiary to Great Britain, violated his instructions from Secretary Fish regarding the handling of the *Alabama* claims issue (discussed later) in 1870, President Grant asked him to resign. When Motley refused, the President ordered him to turn his functions over to the Legation Secretary in London. In the meantime the President nominated Frederick T. Frelinghuysen (who later became Secretary of State) and then Oliver Morton, both of whom declined, and eventually, Robert C. Schenk was nominated on December 22 and took over on June 23, 1871.

Early in the twentieth century Herbert W. Bowen, Minister Plenipotentiary in Venezuela (where he served 1901–5 and had previously been Minister Resident/ Consul General to Persia, 1899–1901), who reputedly had revealed confidential information to the press, was offered a transfer by President Theodore Roosevelt, which he declined. He was then recalled and dismissed, and he left his post on May 1, 1905. Four years later President Taft, for personal reasons, requested the resignation of Henry White, then American Ambassador to France, who had been in the American Diplomatic Service for some thirty years, had previously served as Ambassador to Italy (1905–7), and was regarded highly as a capable diplomat. The President dismissed him, and he left France on November 3, 1909.

Especially interesting was the recall of Cassius M. Clay and Bellamy Storer. Clay, briefly Minister Plenipotentiary to Russia during Lincoln's Administration, who was appointed on March 28, 1861 and presented his credentials on July 14, was requested by Secretary Seward to resign. However, Clay agreed to resign only on the arrival of his successor. So he remained in St. Petersburg until June 25, 1862, and his successor, Simon Cameron, presented his credentials to the Russian Government that same day. However, Clay was reappointed to Russia in 1863 and served until 1869. Storer, formerly Minister Plenipotentiary to Belgium (1897–99) and Spain (1899–1902) and Ambassador to Austria-Hungary (1902–6), was recalled by President Roosevelt because his wife had used the status of the American Embassy to promote a particular candidate for appointment as a Catholic Cardinal. Storer was summarily recalled in 1906, which Graham Stuart regards as the ''most striking example of summary recall by the home Government in the annals of American diplomacy.''[76]

Occasionally, American envoys are held to be persona non grata by receiving governments. In the case of Thomas Russell, Jr., Minister Resident to Venezuela, its Minister of Foreign Affairs notified him on January 29, 1877, that it was breaking off relations with him because one of his confidential dispatches to the Department of State, which criticized the Venezuelan Government, had been made public in the United States. Russell was ''handed his passports'' and left Venezuela on February 17. However, he returned to Caracas on March 17, 1878, to present his letter of recall but left again two days later because the Venezuelan Government refused to receive it. In March 1901 Venezuela also requested the United States to recall Francis B. Loomis, Minister Plenipotentiary since October 1897, and he left his post early in April and was subsequently appointed to Portugal (1901–2) and later as Assistant Secretary of State (1903–5).

In accordance with diplomatic etiquette, it usually is sufficient to allege that envoys are persona non grata to secure their recall. However, in 1891 the Chilean envoy in Washington notified Secretary Blaine that his government declared that Patrick Egan, who had been appointed Minister Plenipotentiary at Santiago in 1889, was no longer acceptable and should be replaced and that Chile had an international right to request his recall. The Department of State demurred. Secretary Blaine acknowledged this right, provided the request for recall specified an acceptable reason for such action. Apparently, Chile opted not to press the matter further, and the American Minister remained at Santiago until July 1893. In 1891 President Harrison nominated Henry W. Blair, former Senator from New Hampshire, to become Minister Plenipotentiary to China, which objected that he "had bitterly abused China in the Senate" and had participated in passing Chinese exclusion legislation so that sentiment in China opposed the appointment. Even though Blair had taken the oath of office, he was recalled before he set sail for the Orient.

One of the most celebrated cases in which an American diplomat was held to be persona non grata was that of Anthony M. Keiley, appointed by President Cleveland as Minister Plenipotentiary to Italy and then to Austria-Hungary in 1885. The Italian Government rejected his appointment because he had made a speech in 1871 in which he protested against the invasion and spoliation of the domain of the Catholic Church by King Victor Emmanuel as violating existing treaties. Secretary Bayard acknowledged Italy's prerogative in objecting to the appointment, and, when Keiley tendered his resignation, the President nominated John B. Stallo to represent the United States in Italy and appointed Keiley to Austria-Hungary. Its government also found him to be persona non grata on the grounds that "the position of a foreign envoy wedded to a Jewess by civil marriage would be untenable and even impossible in Vienna." Secretary Bayard rejected this position and requested reconsideration by the Austrian Government, which then switched its rejection to the same objections that had been raised by Italy, and Keiley decided to tender his resignation. The President delayed in appointing a successor to Austria for two years and left the American Legation in Vienna under the care of a Chargé d'Affaires ad interim.

Of a different nature, Charles A. Washburn, first U.S. Minister Resident to Paraguay (1861–68), who provided asylum for a number of foreigners and members of the overthrown government, was charged by President F. S. Lopez, who assumed dictatorial powers, threatened to imprison the American diplomat, and finally ordered him to leave the country. To afford him refuge the U.S. Government dispatched a naval vessel to rescue him, and he left Paraguay in September 1868. Friendly relations were resumed, and Martin T. McMahon, who was selected to succeed Washburn, was received by the Paraguayan Government in December.[77]

When Woodrow Wilson succeeded President Taft, the United States maintained diplomatic missions to forty-eight countries.[78] Six posts were vacant at the time of Wilson's inaugural (including the Ambassadorship to Great Britain, where Whitelaw Reid died at his post on December 15, 1912), and thirty-four envoys remained in their diplomatic positions for short periods ranging from

March to the end of 1913. A few continued into the following year, including Myron T. Herrick, Ambassador to France, who was not replaced until the end of November. Moreover, Henry P. Fletcher was retained in Chile and promoted to the rank of Ambassador and remained until March 1916. Similarly, Maurice Francis Egan, appointed Minister Plenipotentiary to Denmark in 1907 continued at Copenhagen until December 1917.

Consular Affairs

The Consular Service of the United States had been the subject of much criticism for several decades, and a number of attempts were made to secure Congressional action for its reform. Several Presidents and Secretaries of State urged the enactment of legislation for reorganization and improvement, including provisions for bringing more consular officers under a government salary plan, increasing compensation levels, placing appointment and promotion under the merit system, and providing stability of tenure. During this period Congress passed two major laws, the first to revise the classification and salary arrangement legislated in 1856 and the second to expand classification, update compensation, and cope with the evils of the fee system.

By the Act of June 11, 1874, enacted when Grant was President and Fish was Secretary of State, Congress reclassified consular positions and salaries. In general, it continued the same formula specified in the Act of 1856, relating salary to location or post rather than to the qualities and experience of individual appointees. This new law dealt with more than 180 consular offices. It prescribed eighteen Consul General positions, listed in six annual salary groups ranging from $2,000 at Mexico City and St. Petersburg to $6,000 at Havana, Liverpool, London, Paris, and Rio de Janeiro. Consulates, numbering 160, were grouped in seven classes, based on salaries ranging from $1,000 to $4,000.[79] These were supplemented with five commercial agencies, located at lesser posts, for which no salary was prescribed. In addition, the law authorized the use of clerks for hire,[80] ascribed to consular officers stationed at thirty of the principal consular posts, whose salaries ran from $1,500 to $3,000,[81] supplemented with ten interpreters for China and Japan with salaries of $500 to $2,000. This enactment prescribed no rules to ameliorate either the evils of appointment and promotion based on political considerations or the fee compensation system that prevailed for those consular officers who were not specified in the law.

In an interesting innovation of this Act of 1874, to manage travel time reimbursement, Congress directed the Secretary of State to determine and publish "as soon as practicable" the "length of time actually necessary" to transit, "by the shortest and most direct mode of conveyance" between Washington and both diplomatic and consular posts and vice versa, as well as between Washington and the place of residence of individual officers. Secretary Fish produced a table of "maximum amount of time actually necessary" for such transit between Washington and forty-four foreign countries and islands (such as the Fiji,

Friendly, and Society Islands) and for more than fifty colonial possessions and individual ports throughout the world.

The Department of State and Presidents Cleveland and Roosevelt sought legislation to rectify and improve the fee system applied by the Consular Service. A report of the Consular Inspector, published in 1882, castigated the fee system and the conduct and performance of certain consular officers, but reports of congressional committees in 1884 and 1886 to remedy the situation were not acted upon. As a result, consular reform was initiated by executive orders to introduce the merit system.

Major consular reorganization was provided in the Act of April 5, 1906, when Roosevelt was President and Root was Secretary of State. It regraded the classification of consular posts, again relating them to salary levels but extending their application. Seven classes of Consuls General were specified for fifty-six cities and ports, with salary categories ranging from $3,000 to $12,000.[82] Consuls, grouped in nine classes, were provided for more than 250 locations around the globe, with salaries varying from $2,000 for Class 9 to $8,000 for Class 1.[83] The Offices of Vice Consuls General, Deputy Consuls General, Vice Consuls, Deputy Consuls, and Consular Agents were recognized, without specifying either their number, their location, or their salaries. However, the Office of Commercial Agent was abolished.

To monitor the Consular Service, this act provided for five Inspectors of Consulates, appointed by the President with the consent of the Senate, to be commissioned as "Consuls General at Large," each paid annual salaries of $5,000 plus their travel expenses. They were required to inspect each consular office at least once every two years and report to the Secretary of State. The President was also empowered to authorize them to suspend consular officers for cause and to administer the agencies temporarily. Consular officers paid $1,000 or more were prohibited from engaging in business, either directly or indirectly, or to practice as a private lawyer. They were also directed to charge fixed fees for services rendered, which were required to be accounted for and paid into the Treasury of the United States (except for Consular Agents, who could retain half of the fees they collected, up to a maximum of $1,000 per year).

It is noteworthy that this act failed to require either qualifying examinations for appointment to the two lowest grades in the Consular Service or for promotions based on merit, even though these matters were embodied in the original legislative proposals. However, they were dealt with by President Roosevelt in Executive Orders number 367 of November 10, 1905, and number 469 of June 27, 1906. The first of these extended the merit system to all consular officers who received annual salaries of more than $1,000, and the second prescribed regulations governing certain appointments and promotions in accordance with Civil Service provisions.

In 1860 the United States had 282 primary consular posts (not including Consular Agencies), which grew to 323 by 1890 and declined to 304 by 1910.

The number of Consular Agencies, which numbered 198 in 1860, increased to 437 by 1890, declined to 262 by 1910, and then suddenly dropped to less than 100. One of the reasons for the increase in the number of Consular Agencies between 1860 and 1890 was that consular officers who depended on fees below the annual $1,000 level were inclined to subdivide their services to produce greater personal income.[84] Comparing the growth of consular establishments with resident diplomatic missions, whereas diplomatic posts increased steadily but slowly, the total number of consular posts grew from 480 in 1860, to more than 600 in 1870, and to 760 by 1890, dropped to 566 by 1910, and thereafter declined considerably.

During the period from 1890 through World War I, the functions and activities of consular officers expanded. In the early years they focused primarily on serving the American merchant marine. After the Civil War their responsibilities also included such matters as monitoring and handling customs revenues, bills of health for ships sailing to American ports, the promotion of exports to foreign lands and providing information for the production of trade reports, and caring for the interests of Americans who traveled overseas.[85]

Movement toward Merit and Professionalism of Diplomats and Consuls

One of the principal defects in the management of appointing and promoting diplomatic and consular officials, as well as State Department officers, was the spoils system. Not until the last quarter of the nineteenth century did Congress manage to pass Civil Service legislation.[86] However, beginning in the 1880s various leaders and groups also began to promote the concept of professionalism of diplomatic and consular officers, based on the view that diplomacy is not only an art but also a science, a business, and a career that must be learned and nurtured to be effective and productive. The route to major diplomatic and consular personnel reform prior to World War I was tentative. Early action dealt separately with the two services, initially with consular officers and later with diplomatic staffs. It exempted Ambassadors and Ministers on the grounds that, like Cabinet members, they are Presidential appointees who, although subject to Senate confirmation, are the principal agents of the President in dealing with Chiefs of State, Heads of Government, and the Foreign Offices of other countries.

Following the enactment of the Organic Act of 1856, the Treasury Department, responsible for the accounts of consular officers, began to send agents abroad to inspect consular financial operations. They uncovered serious abuses and recognized that, with some exceptions, the average level of efficiency and honesty was questionable, and, on comprehensive review of the situation, an officer of the Treasury Department reported that the principal cause was the spoils system employed for appointment, tenure, and transfer of consular officials and their inadequate compensation.

During the Arthur Administration, under the direction of Secretary Frelinghuysen, in 1884 the Department of State sent Congress a comprehensive report proposing consular reform, which proposed tentative changes in the Act of 1856. It suggested not only salary increases but also placing the entire Consular Service on a salaried basis, coupled with remission to the Treasury Department of all fees collected, the establishment of a periodic inspection system, and abolition of the use of Consular Agents. A reform bill, approved by the House Foreign Affairs Committee, failed to pass. During his first administration, President Cleveland also advocated reorganization of the Consular Service, but no action was taken, and, beginning with his annual message to Congress in December 1893, at the end of the first year of his second administration, he reiterated his earlier recommendations and called for removing consular officials from politics, but again Congress failed to act.[87]

Although consular reorganization was provided by the Acts of 1874 and 1906, initial action for personnel reform was initiated by a series of Executive Orders between 1895 and 1909. The first of these, issued by President Cleveland on September 20, 1895, specified that consular positions bearing salaries from $1,000 to $2,500 a year were to be filled either by transfer or promotion of qualified officers of the Department of State or by candidates selected on the basis of written and oral examinations. This applied to nearly two-thirds of consular positions. The President reported at the end of 1896 that twenty-eight appointments were made in accordance with this change. President McKinley left the executive order unchanged, but it was circumvented when he recalled 259 of the 320 consular officers then in service, and they were replaced with new appointees.

Before Theodore Roosevelt became President, in 1894 he declared that he favored a career Foreign Service, and in his first inaugural address he suggested reforming the Consular Service by testing candidates for fitness, promoting officers on the basis of performance, and preserving tenure against the inroad of partisan considerations. Later, he also maintained that fees should be replaced by public salaries. It is not surprising, therefore, that he issued Executive Order No. 367 on November 10, 1905, extending the scope of President Cleveland's Executive Order of 1895 by applying the merit principle to appointments to all consular positions bearing annual compensation of more than $1,000. This formula was introduced into Congress in December and was incorporated into the Reorganization Act of April the following year.

On November 10, 1905, President Roosevelt also issued Executive Order No. 368, which provided for the appointment of Diplomatic Secretaries on a merit basis, with vacancies to be filled by transfer or promotion or by appointment after oral and written examinations. Secretary Root immediately created an Examining Board to determine candidates' qualifications. The following year, on June 27, President Roosevelt carried the process further by promulgating Executive Order No. 469, to rectify deficiencies in the consular Reorganization Act of April 5, 1906. It prescribed regulations to govern both appointments and promotions in the Consular Service in accordance with the Civil Service Act of 1883.[88]

Several years later, on November 26, 1909, President Taft issued another Executive Order, No. 1143, which extended the merit principle for appointments to, and promotions in, the Diplomatic Service for officers below the rank of Ministers. It stipulated that the Board of Examiners, consisting of five members (including four designated Department of State officers and a representative of the Civil Service Commission), was responsible for preparing and administering written and oral examinations for the appointment of Legation Secretaries. It also required that in making appointments attention be paid to proportional representation among the States and other territories of the United States, and it prohibited consideration of the political affiliation of candidates.[89]

This Taft order also required that "efficiency records" be maintained for "every officer" of the Diplomatic Service to be used for considering promotion and retention of officers and prescribed that diplomatic secretaryships be graded according to importance and other factors, that appointment to higher classes be filled by promotion from lower classes, and that transfers from "one branch of the foreign service to another" be based on examination (but that Department of State employees paid $1,800 or more were exempted from this stipulation). In effect, after nearly a century and a quarter this presidential mandate instituted the rudiments of a systematic system for appointment, promotion, retention, and transfer of diplomatic officers below the ambassadorial and ministerial levels.

These actions introduced certain aspects of the merit system and professionalism into the Diplomatic and Consular Services. But they dealt largely with appointment and only minimally with promotion and tenure, and they fell short of providing statutory validation of the merit principle. Furthermore, not until 1915 was this rectified by Congress, 1924 that the Diplomatic and Consular Services were amalgamated into the career Foreign Service of the United States, and 1946 that a basic organic act of a modern American Foreign Service was enacted.[90]

Presidential Special Diplomatic Envoys

To facilitate the management of foreign relations, American Presidents also appointed occasional special diplomatic emissaries for various purposes. However, when approving a treaty of amity, commerce, and navigation with Korea in 1882, the Senate declared that "it does not admit or acquiesce in any right or constitutional power in the President to authorize or empower any person to negotiate treaties or carry on diplomatic negotiations with any foreign power unless such person shall have been appointed for such purpose or clothed with such power by and with the advice and consent of the Senate."[91]

Subsequently, in 1894, during an investigation of Hawaiian affairs, the Senate Committee on Foreign Relations reviewed the matter of the President's commissioning of James H. Blount as his personal representative. The leader of the committee, John T. Morgan, reported: "Many precedents could be quoted to show that such power has been exercised by the President on various occasions without dissent on the part of Congress. These precedents also show that the Senate of the United States, though in session, need not be consulted as to the appointment of such agents." Although the minority of the committee held that the appointment of Blount "was an unconstitutional act," in 1906 John W. Foster, former Secretary of State, concluded that the weight of precedents "seems to sustain the right of the President to make appointments of special commissioners and plenipotentiaries independent of the Senate."

Commenting on this practice in 1936, Professor Benjamin H. Williams, in his study of American diplomacy, observed that technically, "from a strictly legal standpoint" such special diplomatic missions may be extraconstitutional, but "the overwhelming demand made upon the President to conduct negotiations without undue delay" necessitated a practice "that is at variance with the written Constitution." Nevertheless, Henry M. Wriston, who published a special study on executive agents, after examining congressional opinion on the matter in some detail, concluded in 1929 that Senators have rarely raised objections except when motivated by political bias and that by the late 1920s protests in Congress had virtually ceased. Graham Stuart concluded in 1952 that "the President does possess the power to appoint special diplomatic agents without senatorial confirmation," and he reported that between 1789 and 1888 Presidents had appointed 438 persons to negotiate with foreign governments without formal Senate consent.[92] Prior to the creation of the ambassadorial rank, at times the President may have preferred to commission American representatives as such envoys in order to clothe them with special status and dignity for their missions and to expedite their utility.

Theoretically, Congress could block the appointment of unconfirmed special envoys by refusing to provide funding for their salaries and expenses. Aside from those who currently hold public office and are commissioned as special emissaries, it is incumbent on the President to provide funds for these missions. However, because diplomatic representation is such an important and sometimes critical matter, Congress has not withheld its funding. Realizing that future events and obligations cannot be anticipated with precision, Congress provides the President with an Executive Contingent Fund for extraordinary and emergency purposes.

Normally, special agents—especially if their duties and responsibilities are not clearly defined, and if they are made principal negotiators with individual foreign governments or at international conferences, thereby bypassing or superseding resident emissaries—are objected to by the Diplomatic Service. If such personal envoys are appointed to give the President greater personal direction over foreign relations, as they may be recruited in times of crisis or to achieve important goals outside the traditional diplomatic bureaucracy, they are likely to be resented by its members.

The practical use of special envoys was facilitated in the nineteenth century by major improvements in the means of communications and transportation. With the invention and refinement of magnetic and, later, wireless telegraphy, the Morse code, and the laying of the transatlantic cable in 1858, the President and Department of State were able to communicate with special agents and resident diplomats with greater facility. As the speed, certainty, and comfort of overland and seagoing travel improved—with the development of rail systems and, later, the automobile, the invention and improvement of the steamship, and aircraft—it became easier for the President to send and rely on such special envoys.

Occasionally, Presidents appoint such special representatives to ceremonial missions. Captain G. V. Fox, Assistant Secretary of the Navy, sailed to Russia in 1866 in an American ironclad Civil War ship, to carry a joint resolution of Congress congratulating the Emperor on his escape from assassination. Whitelaw Reid, former Minister Plenipotentiary to France, was sent as an Ambassador Extraordinary on a special mission in 1897 to congratulate Queen Victoria on the sixtieth anniversary of her accession to the British throne. In 1910 former President Theodore Roosevelt, who was in Europe at the time of the death of King Edward VII of Great Britain, was recruited by President Taft to represent the U.S. Government at his funeral. Two years later President Taft dispatched Secretary Knox to attend the funeral of the Emperor of Japan. These set a precedent for many later ceremonial and courtesy missions.

Other special missions were designed to provide diplomatic representation prior to the establishment of traditional relations. William T. Buchanan, who previously represented the United States in Argentina for five years, was appointed as Minister Plenipotentiary on a special mission to Panama late in 1903, and he received new regular accrediting credentials only a few days before he was to depart, thus acting as a special emissary until he left his post early in February 1904. Eugene Schuyler, commissioned as Diplomatic Agent/Consul General to Romania in June 1880, delivered his credentials in a private audience in December but was not officially received. However, the Romanian Foreign Ministry indicated in August its willingness to provisionally enter into relations with him. Appointed as diplomatic Agent to Bulgaria in April 1901, while the Senate was in recess, Charles M. Dickinson was also assigned as Consul General to Constantinople, where he resided. Apparently, he represented American interests to Bulgaria without presenting his credentials, and his appointment terminated at the end of June 1903.

Also important, at times the President or Secretary of State appoints special agents to investigative diplomatic missions. Secretary Seward, with the approval of President Lincoln, sent Archbishop Hughes and Bishop McIlwaine as confidential agents to Europe in 1861 to report on the opinions and actions respecting the American Civil War. Ten years later President Grant commissioned B. F. Wade, Andrew D. White, and S. G. Howe to go to Santo Domingo to make inquiries concerning local conditions and assess possible annexation by the United States. In November 1881 President Garfield appointed William Henry

Trescot, former Assistant Secretary of State, as his Minister Plenipotentiary on a special mission to Bolivia, Chile, and Peru to investigate relations between them "so far as this government may deem it judicious to take action," with the understanding that his mission did not interfere with the traditional duties of the resident American Ministers in those countries.

Of a more critical nature, President Cleveland appointed a special envoy in 1886 to investigate the arrest of A. K. Cutting in Mexico, bypassing Minister Plenipotentiary Henry R. Jackson, an experienced diplomat who had previously served in Austria for nearly five years. Cutting was arrested for publishing an article in a Texas newspaper in 1886, which was regarded as violating the Mexican penal code. A series of high-level exchanges ensued, and Jackson, affronted by his treatment, resigned in October. During the Venezuelan dispute with Great Britain, 1895–96, Secretary Olney recruited Henry White (former Legation Secretary in London and later to be made Ambassador to Italy and France, 1905–9) to return to Great Britain in a semiofficial role to assist Ambassador Thomas F. Bayard in clarifying American policy and averting a serious conflict with the British Government.

A notable example of a special mission was that of James H. Blount, an avowed anti-imperialist, who was accredited by President Cleveland in March 1893 to investigate and report on the situation in Hawaii following a revolt supported by John L. Stevens, the American Minister Plenipotentiary, who had previously held several diplomatic appointments. Stevens ran up the American flag, and Sanford B. Dole formed a provisional government in Honolulu. Blount's letter of credence declared him to be "paramount" in matters affecting U.S. relations with Hawaii, and Stevens was requested to continue, until further notice, to perform his diplomatic duties as long as they were not inconsistent with those of the special emissary. He relinquished his post on May 18, nine days after Blount was nominated to succeed him as Minister.

Most frequently, the President appoints special envoys to negotiate with foreign governments, often leading to the conclusion of treaties and agreements. To illustrate, in 1868 George Bancroft, Minister Plenipotentiary to Prussia (1867–74), was also specially accredited to the German states of Baden, Bavaria, Hesse, and Wuerttemberg to negotiate naturalization treaties with them. That same year George F. Seward, Consul General in Shanghai, was empowered to negotiate a commercial and claims convention with Korea. However, Commodore R. W. Shufeldt, who had previously led an unsuccessful expedition to investigate the destruction by Koreans of the American schooner *General Sherman*, was commissioned by President Garfield in November 1881 to conclude a Treaty of Amity and Commerce, which was signed the following May. This was Korea's first treaty with the Western World and opened that country to foreign relations.

Similarly, in August 1882 General U. S. Grant and William Trescot were appointed to negotiate a commercial treaty with Mexico; George H. Bates was sent to the Society Islands (French Polynesia) in July 1886 to negotiate a treaty with Tonga; and Bartlett Tripp was selected by President McKinley in April 1899 to conclude a settlement with British and German commissioners concerning pending issues in their relations with the Samoan Islands. Shortly after his inauguration, to implement an act of Congress, in April 1897 President McKinley appointed Charles J. Paine, Adlai E. Stevenson, and Edward O. Wolcott as special agents to seek to negotiate an international agreement on bimetallism with France and Great Britain, which the British Government rejected.

At the turn of the century President McKinley also appointed William W. Rockhill, former Assistant Secretary of State and Minister Plenipotentiary to Greece, Romania, and Serbia, to examine and report on the Boxer Rebellion in China and the siege upon the foreign legations at Peking. Initially, he was to serve as "counselor and adviser" to Edwin H. Conger, the resident American Minister Plenipotentiary. However, when the latter was absent on a leave of absence, Rockhill was commissioned by presidential telegraphic instructions to continue negotiations directly with the representatives of China and other powers. He remained in this capacity until the Peking Protocol was signed in September 1901, and later he became Minister Plenipotentiary to China (1905–9).

Also in keeping with earlier practice, some special envoys were recruited to participate in international joint commissions to negotiate treaties for the settlement of disputes. President Grant selected Secretary Fish to head a delegation of five to serve on a British-American Joint Commission to resolve issues that had arisen during the Civil War. They concluded the historic Treaty of Washington (1871), discussed later. It provided for the resolution of the *Alabama* claims controversy, which was submitted to an Arbitration Tribunal convened at Geneva from December 1871 to June 1872. The American delegation to Geneva consisted of Charles Francis Adams (former Minister Plenipotentiary to Great Britain) as the American arbitrator, J. C. Bancroft Davis (former Assistant Secretary of State) as the American agent, and Caleb Cushing (former Commissioner to China), William M. Evarts (who later became Secretary of State), and Morrison R. Waite as counselors.

Another such Joint High Commission, which met in Washington, undertook to resolve the long-standing thorny Northeast fisheries controversy with Great Britain. In November 1887 President Cleveland named Secretary Bayard, Judge William L. Putnam, and James B. Angell, who negotiated with Joseph Chamberlain (British Minister in Washington) and the Canadian Prime Minister, and they concluded a treaty on February 15, 1888. A decade later, in 1898, a third Anglo-American Joint High Commission, consisting of six representatives from the United States and from Great Britain, convened to resolve pending issues in Canadian–American relations. American members of such commissions were generally accredited as Ministers Plenipotentiary or Commissioners Plenipotentiary. These and other cases that dealt with peaceful settlement are discussed in the section on the American Arbitration Record.

Additional special envoys were used for unusual missions. During the Civil War Robert J. Walker (former Secretary of the Treasury) was dispatched to

Europe to assist in the financial operations of the Union Government. In 1867 General D. E. Sickles was sent by President Andrew Johnson to Colombia to join Peter J. Sullivan, American Minister Resident, to arrange for the transit of American troops across the Isthmus of Panama. In March 1873, under direction of President Grant, Secretary Fish appointed Colonel A. B. Steinberger, an adventurer and soldier of fortune, to promote American relations with Samoa. He united the Samoan tribes, organized a government with himself as its leader, and then resigned as special agent. The United States disavowed official relations with him, and he was deported on a British cruiser.

Occasionally, American diplomats may be recruited as third-party intermediaries to represent the interests and affairs of other countries to the governments to which they are accredited. In the 1870s John W. Foster, Minister Plenipotentiary to Mexico after the downfall of Maximillian, unofficially handled the relations of eight foreign governments with the Mexican Foreign Ministry. U.S. practice has permitted its diplomats, at the request of friendly foreign powers and with the consent of the local national government and the approval of the Department of State, in accordance with the principle of good offices, to provide such third-party services of a temporary nature. In 1874 the German Consul General in Guatemala left his post before his successor arrived, and George M. Williamson, the American Minister Resident, took over responsibility for managing the interests of German nationals. For some time a similar service was provided for Swiss subjects when the Swiss Government was unrepresented in Guatemala City.

Quite unusually, at the outbreak of the Franco-Prussian War in 1870, Elihu B. Washburne, previously Secretary of State for a few days and then Minister Plenipotentiary to France, was the only diplomatic representative of a major power remaining in Paris. Requested by the German Ambassador and with the authorization of the Department of State, he took over the German Embassy, raised the American flag, and agreed to protect the interests of the North German Confederation and the South German States, and he served as the communications link of German authorities with the French Government.

Finally, it is not surprising that those who become Secretary of State also have been appointed as presidential special envoys. Some were recruited for such service before they became Secretary. Thus, Evarts was commissioned as a member of a special mission to Great Britain during the Civil War to assist Minister Plenipotentiary Charles Francis Adams in dealing with legal issues (1863–64) and as counsel to the American delegation at the Geneva Arbitration Tribunal (1871–72), established to resolve the *Alabama* claims controversy with Great Britain. Later, Evarts was also named as special plenipotentiary to negotiate reciprocity agreements (1890–91) and as the agent of the United States in the Bering Sea Fur-Seal Arbitration at Paris, which convened in 1892. Secretary Root, together with Senator Henry Cabot Lodge and former Senator George Turner, was chosen as a member of the Alaskan Boundary Tribunal, 1903.

Also, beginning as early as 1866, occasionally, Secretaries have also engaged personally in ministerial diplomacy abroad. These include Secretaries Seward, Hay, Root, and Knox, who traveled overseas for a variety of purposes, principally to consult with foreign leaders but also to attend international conferences, as described in Chapters 6 and 7. More commonly, however, former Secretaries of State have also been assigned to such special diplomatic functions. For example, Evarts was appointed a delegate to the International Monetary Conference at Paris in 1881; Foster was commissioned a special Ambassador to Great Britain and Russia in 1897, and he served as the American agent before the Alaska Boundary Tribunal in 1903; Olney was made the American member of the Permanent International Commission under the Bryan–Jusserand Treaty of 1914 with France; and Day, who headed the American Commission to conclude the Peace Treaty with Spain in 1898 and, while serving as Associate Justice of the Supreme Court, was called upon to be the umpire in the Mixed Commission of the United States and Germany, 1922–23, for adjudicating the claims of American citizens against Germany during World War I.[93]

Foreign Mission Buildings Program

For a century and a quarter Congress was remiss in providing funding for the offices and residences of American diplomats and consular officers stationed in foreign countries. Not until it passed the Lowden Act on February 17, 1911, did it authorize Secretary of State Knox to acquire sites and purchase or erect buildings abroad, at a total of not more than $500,000 in any fiscal year, with expenditures for any single facility not to exceed $150,000.

At that time the United States possessed diplomatic office buildings in only four capitals—Bangkok, Constantinople, Peking, and Tokyo—and legation quarters in the International Zone of Tangier, together with a few American-owned consular premises in Amoy, Seoul, Tahiti, and Yokohama. Most of these facilities, except for those in Constantinople and Peking, were unimpressive. Progress in inplementing the foreign buildings program was dilatory, in part because appropriations to implement the Lowden Act were not made until 1914. However, action accelerated after World War I and was facilitated by the Foreign Service Buildings Act passed in 1926, which remedied some of the defects in the Lowden Act.[94]

Emissaries Remembered

Aside from those diplomats who served in single assignments for extended periods—George P. Marsh (Italy) and Edwin V. Morgan (Brazil)—American diplomats are remembered for many reasons. A few may be recognized for the number of sequential appointments they received, such as James P. Partridge (six), Lewis D. Einstein, Henry P. Fletcher, and William W. Rockhill (seven each), John Brinkerhoff Jackson (eight), and William Phillips (ten). Some had long diplomatic careers. In addition to Morgan (nearly three decades) and Marsh (nearly a quarter century), these included Einstein, Jackson, Partridge, and Frederick Van Dyne, who served for periods ranging from fifteen to more than twenty-five years, Henry P. Fletcher and Rockhill for approximately thirty years each, and William Phillips for nearly forty-five years.

Additional diplomats and consular officers are regarded as members of the first generation of professionals. These are represented by Arthur M. Beaupre, William I. Buchanan, and Thomas C. Dawson, who jointly served in six Latin American countries and at several Inter-American Conferences, and William J. Calhoun, Edwin H. Conger, and William W. Rockhill, who represented the United States in China. Three others—Eugene Schuyler, William L. Scruggs, and Henry White—also had a talent for diplomacy and jointly held positions in at least a dozen European, Latin American, and other countries. White was also involved in the settlement of the Alaskan boundary and Venezuelan disputes, and he advised Secretary Hay on the Boxer Revolt and the Open Door policy with China. Some would add Lloyd C. Griscom and F. M. Huntington Wilson to this list, as well as Einstein and Phillips, who held office during the transition years in the early twentieth century. Others who were highly regarded were George Bancroft, Charles Denby, Edward J. Phelps, and Elihu B. Washburne, who represented the United States to such major countries as France, Germany, and Great Britain in Europe and to China.

The first American diplomats to be commissioned as Ambassadors in 1893 were Thomas F. Bayard (Great Britain), James B. Eustis (France), Isaac W. MacVeagh (Italy), and Theodore Runyon (Germany). Four professional diplomats, who began their careers in the early twentieth century, were incorporated into the career Foreign Service of the United States after it was created by law in 1946. These were Henry P. Fletcher, Hoffman Phillip, William Phillips, and John W. Riddle, all of whom served into the post–World War I period.

Of all the diplomatic and consular officers who served during these fifty-two years, only Charles Francis Adams and Anson Burlingame have been commemorated in historian Thomas F. Bailey's American diplomatic "Hall of Fame." Adams, son of John Quincy Adams and grandson of John Adams, had the virtue of being born and raised in a diplomatic environment, and he became the third generation in the Adams family to represent the United States in Great Britain (1861–68). He served valiantly and effectively during the trying and critical time of the Civil War. He induced the British Government to halt the delivery of war vessels (such as the *Alabama* and *Florida*) to the Confederacy in violation of what the Union regarded as the laws of war, and he helped to avert British intervention and the outbreak of war with the United States. Characterized as an able, dedicated, and persistent, but also reasonable, sincere, honest, and credible, emissary, it has been said: "No other minister of the United States has ever passed through so long a period of excitement and critical responsibility. He displayed diplomatic skill of the highest order, and a patriotic spirit unsurpassed by his fathers." In Bailey's list of six most memorable American diplomats, he lists Adams as number three, after Benjamin Franklin and Albert Gallatin.

Burlingame, listed as number five by Bailey, who held only one diplomatic appointment, has been described as magnetic, candid, and tolerant. Accredited to China (1861–67) immediately after the Anglo–French War with China, he became the leader of the foreign diplomatic corps during this period of East–West tension. By peaceful persuasion and negotiation he played a leading role in averting the partition of China and staving off foreign encroachment on its sovereignty, and he managed to establish freer commercial and political relations of other powers with that country. He was so highly regarded by the Chinese Government that, following his service in Peking, it commissioned him as its plenipotentiary to the outside world, including the United States. To his credit, the American rule prohibiting the reception of one of its own citizens as a diplomatic representative of a foreign power was waived. As a member of a Chinese imperial mission to the principal Western powers, in 1868 he negotiated a treaty with Secretary Seward, known generally as the ''Burlingame Treaty,'' which added several articles to the Sino-American Treaty of Tientsin, concluded in 1858. He has been called ''the ablest representative of the United States in China since [Caleb] Cushing, and one of the most notable products of American 'militia diplomacy.' ''

Diplomats are also remembered for other reasons. Thomas C. Dawson, who had served as American emissary to four Latin American countries, was appointed as the first departmental Resident Diplomatic Officer, and Huntington Wilson was selected to manage the Knox reorganization of the State Department and headed the Board of Examiners to implement the merit system. Elihu Washburne valiantly persevered in Paris at the time of its siege by German forces during the Franco–Prussian War, as did Conger in China at the time of the Boxer Rebellion.

Several diplomats distinguished themselves by their extensive treaty making, such as George Bancroft, Whitelaw Reid, and William W. Rockhill. John A. Kasson represented the United States at the Berlin Conference in 1885, which negotiated the Berlin Act, signed by the representatives of most major European powers, Turkey, and the United States, to deal with the disposition of African territory, but it was withheld from Senate approval by President Cleveland. Kasson, as a special agent, also concluded Commercial Treaties with several European powers at the turn of the century, as well as a number of treaties providing for reciprocal tariffs for European dependencies in the Western Hemisphere—known as the ''Kasson Treaties''—which the Senate rejected for economic reasons.

Rockhill is also noted for contributing to devising the Hay Open Door notes to five major European powers and Japan to provide free trade relations with China. William L. Scruggs, Minister to Colombia in 1873, negotiated a settlement of American claims and also served as arbiter in a claims case between the British and Colombian Governments. William I. Buchanan, American Minister to Argentina in the 1890s, also provided American good offices to that country and Chile, and he was invited to serve as umpire on the mixed Boundary Commission to settle their territorial dispute. On rare occasions an American emissary was so highly reputed in a foreign country that he was recruited into its diplomatic service. As Burlingame became the diplomatic envoy of China in the 1860s, former Minister and Secretary of State John W. Foster represented China in negotiating the Peace Treaty with Japan in 1895, and Scruggs was appointed in 1894 as legal adviser and special agent of the Venezuelan Government during its boundary dispute with Great Britain.

On the other hand, some diplomats are remembered less for their diplomatic service than for other reasons. Carl Schurz, German immigrant and military officer during the Civil War, Senator, Secretary of the Interior, and Minister Plenipotentiary to Spain for a few months, became famous for his political and other writings and his newspaper work, and he was commemorated by the Carl Schurz Memorial Society.

Some diplomats were accorded special accolades and honors. For example, Joseph F. Choate was reputed to have gained such popularity for his frequent and witty speeches in Great Britain that he was deemed to be "a sort of ambassadorial lecturer to the English nation," and he was honored by election as the first non-British subject to be made an "honorary bencher" of the Honorable Society of the Middle Temple. Caleb Cushing, first American envoy to China, Attorney General, and Minister Plenipotentiary to Spain in the 1870s, was heralded by Ralph Waldo Emerson as the "most eminent scholar of his day." Charles Denby, as Minister to China for nearly thirteen years, acquired "unusual prestige and influence in Peking and won Chinese favor for his efforts to end the Sino–Japanese War of 1894–95." Henry Vignaud, serving continuously for thirty-four years in Paris, came to be regarded "as virtually indispensable" and acquired "an almost legendary reputation" in the Diplomatic Service, and the French Government named him to the rank of Grand Officer in the Legion of Honor. Henry White "did much to promote the Anglo–American *rapprochement* which began at the time of the Spanish–American War," and Theodore Roosevelt declared that he was "the most useful man in the diplomatic service during my presidency, and for many years before." White and Rockhill were characterized by Secretary Hay "as the best American diplomats of the time."[95]

Finally, note must be taken that a remarkable number of Department of State, diplomatic, and consular officers published an extraordinary library of volumes that dealt with a broad spectrum of subjects. Some produced one or two volumes, but a good many contributed ten or more, and, surprisingly, a few produced as many as thirty to nearly 100 volumes. Collectively, some 160 officers published more than 1,000 memoirs and biographies,[96] collections of papers and documents, histories and legal tomes, travelogues and studies on foreign lands and peoples, general and technical monographs, novels and short stories, plays and collections of poetry, and other literary works. Secretaries Bacon, Foster, Hay, and Washburne and nine Assistant Secretaries collectively published more than seventy volumes, of which at least thirty concerned American diplomacy and foreign affairs. An additional forty-five diplomatic and consular officers, including renowned authors like James Russell Lowell and Lew Wallace, and others such as John Russell Coryell, Bret Hart, and Lorin A. Lathrop rank among those who were widely published.[97]

TREATY MAKING

In managing foreign affairs, as the United States expanded its relations with additional countries during the half century from 1861 to 1913 and extended the breadth of its treaty interests, it concluded some 480 treaties and agreements, both multilateral and bilateral, averaging more than nine per year. Supplementing the traditional categories of earlier treaty processes and subjects, the Department of State augmented its treaty making in several ways—by concluding bilateral arrangements with additional countries and other territories, by broadening the sphere of treaty concerns, by experimenting with new treaty processes, and by associating with foreign governments in concluding dozens of multilateral treaties and agreements and establishing joint and collective institutions to regularize certain common international interests and functions.

Bilateral Treaties and Agreements

To be expected, the Department of State expanded its treaty making incrementally with respect to the countries, other territories, and islands with which it dealt, the subjects encompassed, and the quantity of treaties and agreements it concluded. As indicated in Table 5.4, the United States signed nearly 400 new bilateral treaties and agreements with sixty foreign governments. Whereas from 1789 to 1861 some 168 were concluded with fifty-three foreign authorities, the United States added twenty new countries and other lands and islands to its treaty roster[98] and negotiated no new treaties and agreements with more than a dozen, some of which were superseded, such as eight of the German States, Sardinia, the Two Sicilies, and Texas (which had been annexed).

The new treaty package consisted of 264 formal treaties and 133 executive agreements. This reflected increasing Department of State action not only to stabilize contractual international political and legal relationships and to conclude commitments with a widening circle of foreign governments but also to deal with many issues by the simpler executive agreement process.[99] In international terms, a substantial majority (70 percent) were titled conventions (159), treaties (eighty), and agreements (thirty-nine). Others were in the form of exchanges of notes (fifty-two) and supplementary protocols (forty-two). The remainder were designated as declarations (ten), acts or additional acts (nine), memorandums of agreement (three), conference minutes (two), or simply an article (one).

Illustrating growing American involvement, bilateral treaty making acceler-

Table 5.4
Bilateral Treaties and Agreements, 1861–1913

Country	No.	T	A	Washington	Abroad	1860s	1870s	1880s	1890s	1900s	1910-13
Argentina	1	1			1				1		
Austria	1		1	1		1					
Austria-Hungary	5	5		3	2		2			2	1
Belgium	12	11	1	6	6	5	2	3		2	
Bolivia	1	1			1					1	
Brazil	5	4	1	1	4		1		1	3	
Chile	5	3	2	2	3				3	2	
Colombia	2	2		1	1	1		1			
Congo	2	1	1	1	1			1	1		
Costa Rica	3	2	1	2	1						3
Cuba	9	7	2	6	3					9	
Denmark	12	7	5	9	3	2	1	2	2	5	
Dominican Republic	8	3	5	1	7	1			2	5	
Ecuador	5	5		2	3	1		2		1	
El Salvador	8	7	1	2	6			4		3	1
Ethiopia	1	1			1					1	
France	14	8	6	11	3	2		3	1	6	2
Germany											
Baden	1	1			1	1					
Bavaria	1	1			1	1					
Hanover	1	1			1	1					
Hesse	1	1			1	1					
North Germ. Conf.	1	1			1	1					
Wuerttemberg	1	1			1	1					
German Empire	7	3	4	4	3		1		1	5	
Great Britain	57	33	24	46	11	3	10	4	13	21	6
Greece	2	1	1		2					1	1
Guatemala	6	4	2	3	3				2	4	
Haiti	11	5	6	8	3		1	4	1	5	
Hawaii	2	2		2			2				
Honduras	4	3	1	1	3	1				3	
Italy	17	11	6	14	3	4	2	3	1	5	2
Japan	14	12	2	8	6	1	1	2	3	6	1
Korea	1	1			1			1			
Liberia	1	1			1	1					
Luxembourg	2	2			2			1		1	
Madagascar	2	2			2	1		1			
Mexico	38	30	8	33	5	4	5	10	11	8	
Netherlands	8	5	3	7	1			1	3	4	
Nicaragua	10	5	5	4	6	1	1		1	7	
Norway	3	3			3					1	2
Orange Free State	2	2		1	1			1	1		
Ottoman Empire	3	2	1		3	1	2				
Panama	6	2	4	2	4					5	1
Paraguay	1	1			1					1	
Peru	12	10	2	9	3	3	3	1		3	2
Portugal	6	3	3	6					2	3	1
Romania	2	2			2			1		1	
Russia	9	5	4	5	4	2	1	2	1	3	
Samoa	1	1		1			1				
San Marino	1	1		1						1	
Spain	30	9	21	16	14	4	11	6	9		
Sweden and Norway	1		1	1		1					
Sweden	4	3	1	3	1				1	1	2
Switzerland	4	2	2	3	1			1	1	2	
Thailand (Siam)	2	1	1	1	1	1		1			
Tonga	1	1		1				1			
United Arab Republic	1	1			1	1					
Uruguay	3	3		2	1	1				3	
Venezuela	10	5	5	4	6	2		2	1	5	
Yugoslavia	3	3			3			2		1	
Zanzibar (Muscat)	4	4		3	1			1		3	
Total 60	397	264	133	234	163	47	47	65	62	153	23

Note: Austria became Austria–Hungary in 1867. Norway separated from Sweden in 1905, although individual treaties with Norway were concluded as early as 1893.

ated from less than fifty in both the 1860s and the 1870s, to more than sixty in the 1880s and the 1890s and peaked in the period from 1900 to 1913, when more than 175 (44 percent) were concluded. Also significant, denoting greater U.S. international stature and Department of State initiative, whereas previously three-fourths of the treaties and agreements were signed abroad, during this period 234 (or nearly 60 percent) were signed in the United States. Most notable examples were Great Britain, which signed forty-six of fifty-nine in Washington, followed by Mexico (thirty-three of thirty-eight), Italy (fourteen of seventeen), France (eleven of fourteen), and Denmark (nine of twelve), and all six concluded with Portugal were signed in Washington.[100]

Of those signed in this country, 210 bear the signature of Secretaries of State.[101] The most treaties were signed by Secretaries Hay (forty-five), Root (thirty-four), and Fish and Frelinghuysen (eighteen each), followed by Secretaries Seward (sixteen), Bayard (fifteen), Knox (fourteen), Evarts and Blaine (nine each), Olney (eight), Bacon (seven), and Gresham (six). The fewest were signed by Sherman and Day (four each) and Foster (three), who served for short periods, and Washburne signed none.

More unusually, introducing a new feature, at least twenty-five of the treaties and agreements concluded in the United States were signed by other officials. These included President Theodore Roosevelt, who signed an executive agreement with Cuba in 1903 providing for the leasing by the United States of lands for a coaling station at Guantánamo. This was the first time that the President personally signed an international treaty or agreement for the United States, which later became a common aspect of summit diplomacy.[102]

Others, commissioned as special envoys, who also signed treaties and agreements in this country included other Cabinet members—Caleb B. Smith, Secretary of the Interior (who signed an executive agreement with Denmark concerning West Indies colonization in 1862), William Howard Taft, Secretary of War (who signed an exchange of notes with Panama in 1904 concerning its legal tender, coinage, and monetary system), and General U. S. Grant and William Henry Trescot, former Assistant Secretary of State (who jointly signed a basic commerce treaty with Mexico in 1883). On a few occasions commissions of emissaries concluded treaties and agreements. To negotiate the general treaty with Great Britain in 1871—known as the Treaty of Washington—Secretary Fish headed an American delegation of five members,[103] and Secretary Knox captained a delegation to confer with British delegates on the matter of fishing rights, which convened in Washington in 1911 and produced two sets of conference minutes in the nature of executive agreements.[104]

In addition, several Assistant Secretaries of State—Alvey A. Adee, Robert Bacon, John Davis, William F. Wharton, and Huntington Wilson—signed treaties and agreements as Acting Secretary of State,[105] and a Fisheries Arbitration Treaty with Great Britain (1912) was signed by Chandler P. Anderson, Counselor of the Department. John A. Kasson, former Minister Plenipotentiary to Austria-Hungary and Germany, signed a series of Commerce Treaties with

France, Italy, and Portugal (1898–1900) in Washington, and he, together with Secretary of State Foster, also signed a Treaty of Amity with Great Britain concerning relations with Canada (1898).

Most exceptional, the exchange of notes signed by Secretary of War Taft in Washington in 1904 was signed for Panama by its Special Commissioner, who was in New York City. Similarly, in 1907 Robert Bacon, then First Assistant Secretary, participated as the Acting Secretary in an exchange of notes with the British government. His notes emanated from Washington, whereas the British notes were signed at Intervale, New Hampshire. These notes created an executive agreement by which the United States acquiesced in administration by the British North Borneo Company of certain islands leased to the United States off the coast of Borneo.

The preponderant majority of treaties and agreements concluded abroad were signed in foreign capitals by resident American diplomats, mostly Ambassadors and Ministers, but occasionally by Chargés d'Affaires and consular officers,[106] and, in some cases, by special envoys. Those who signed the largest number abroad were William W. Rockhill (seven), George Bancroft and Whitelaw Reid (six each), S. R. Gummere and Henry S. Sanford (four each), and Eugene Schuyler (three).[107] Illustrating those concluded by special envoys commissioned for this purpose, Secretary of War Taft negotiated an exchange of notes with Panama in 1904, known as the Taft Agreement, concerning American canal rights in that country. Other special envoys were commissioned to conclude Amity and Commerce Treaties with a number of countries, especially those that were newly added to the American treaty roster,[108] and to negotiate with Panama concerning the Canal and with Venezuela respecting claims settlements.[109]

The Department of State also enlarged its roster of bilateral treaty subjects, as indicated in Table 5.5. Some of the basic topics were traditional, such as those concerned with the acquisition of territory and the fixing of boundaries, amity and commerce, arbitration, claims and their settlement, commercial reciprocity, consular affairs, customs and revenues, and peacemaking. Other subjects, some of which had been dealt with previously, included extradition, fisheries and the preservation of fur seals, naturalization, and the construction of an isthmian canal. A few were added that treated both bilaterally and miltilaterally such matters as copyright, patent and trademark protection, and postal affairs.

Several aspects of these bilateral treaty subjects warrant special attention. Because the United States became involved in only one foreign war, the sole peace treaty was signed with Spain at Paris in 1898. In addition to restoring peace, the Spanish government relinquished sovereignty over Cuba and ceded the Philippines, Guam, and Puerto Rica to the United States, which paid Spain $20 million. To promote amity, trade, and shipping, the United States continued to conclude an array of treaties concerned with commercial relations and reciprocity. In more than a dozen cases, the first treaty negotiated with a foreign country dealt with these matters.[110] Other popular treaty subjects were claims

Table 5.5
Bilateral Treaty and Agreement Subjects, 1861–1913

Basic Subjects	No.
Amity, friendship, commerce, and navigation	59
Extradition	51
Arbitration	50
Claims and claims settlements	47
Acquisition of territory by United States and boundaries	32
Commercial relations and reciprocity	16
Consular affairs	14
Customs and revenues	5
Peace treaty and protocol for establishing peace	2

Additional Major Subjects

Patents and trademarks	37
Naturalization	24
Fisheries	15
Bering Sea fur seals	11
Isthmian canal	6
Copyright	5
Immigration (China)	2
Nationality (Philippines)	1
Postal affairs (Mexico)	1

Specialized Subjects

Mutual rights to pursue Indians across boundary, Mexico	6
Disposition of real and personal property, Great Britain and Guatemala	2
Export of tobacco, Austria and France	2
Extraterritorial rights, Italy and Zanzibar	2
Corporations and other commercial organizations, Russia, 1904	1
Deserters from merchant vessels, recovery of, Great Britain, 1892	1
Exemption of salesman's samples from customs inspection, Great Britain, 1910	1
Harbor dues, Zanzibar, 1903	1
Legal tender and coinage, Panama, 1904	1
Letters rogatory, Spain, 1901	1
Measurement certificates for vessels, Russia, 1884	1
Naval warfare, Spain, 1898	1
Policy—Root-Takahira Agreement, Japan, 1908	1
Protection of literary and artistic property in China, France, 1911	1
Real property, right to hold (Ottoman Empire, 1874)	1
Shipwreck expenses, Japan, 1880	1
Spirituous liquors, traffic in, Thailand, 1884	1
Transit of United States troops, Panama, 1912	1
Total	404 *

*Because of multiple subjects treated in certain treaties and agreements, this total differs from the total number of treaties and agreements.

settlement and arbitration of disputes. Some of the treaties and agreements concerned with claims constituted negotiated resolutions of disputes, but many provided for subsequent submittal to settlement by arbitration and other peaceful processes. Nearly 100 treaties and agreements were devoted to these matters. Those that provided for arbitration as the method of resolution were of two types. As in the past, many agreed to the institution of the arbitral process for specific existing disputes, whereas others created a new bilateral advance commitment to arbitrate when disputes subsequently arose.

By way of background, in the 1880s the United States initiated systematic international action to arbitrate international disputes. In November 1881 Secretary Blaine, on behalf of President Garfield, extended an invitation to independent Western Hemisphere countries to participate in an international conference held at Washington to discuss methods of preventing war. This conference did not convene until 1889, and it adopted a plan for arbitration as a principle of international law, but it failed to achieve governmental approval.

The following year Congress authorized the President to negotiate peaceful settlement arrangements with other governments. The first such advance arbitration convention was signed in 1897 by Secretary Olney with Sir Julian Pauncefote of Great Britain—known as the Olney–Pauncefote Treaty—which failed to gain the necessary two-thirds vote in the Senate. Two years later the Hague Peace Conference produced a general treaty providing for both mediation and arbitration as universal methods of peaceful settlement. At the Second International Conference of American States, which met in Mexico in 1901, the participants signed two instruments, a Protocol for adhesion to the Hague Convention, signed by all delegates (except Chile and Ecuador) and a treaty to arbitrate pecuniary claims, in which the United States did not participate.

Influenced by the Hague Peace Conference of 1899, which created the Permanent Court of Arbitration, in 1905 Secretary Hay negotiated a number of basic bilateral arbitration treaties, providing for the submittal of each dispute with a foreign government under a *compromis d'arbitrage*, which specified the matter to be arbitrated. However, the Senate insisted upon the substitution of the term "treaty" for the "*compromis*," thereby assuring itself that the standard American treaty procedure would have to be applied not only to the basic treaty but also to each individual case, but President Roosevelt rejected this requirement.

Secretary Root, an avid supporter of arbitration who had served as a member of the Alaska Boundary Tribunal in 1903, undertook the negotiation of twenty-five such basic arbitration treaties in 1908 and 1909, primarily with European and Latin American countries but also including China and Japan. They were originally intended to remain in effect for five-year terms, and some were renewed periodically and remained in effect for about twenty years. Subsequently, they either expired or have been superseded. They stipulated that international differences not resolved by diplomacy were to be referred to the Permanent Court of Arbitration for resolution, with the debilitating condition that such differences did not "affect the vital interests, the independence, or the honor" of the contracting states.[111] Most of these were signed by Root in Washington, a few arbitrations were held under them, and in 1912 Root was awarded the Nobel Peace Prize, the second American (Theodore Roosevelt was the first in 1906) but the first American Secretary of State to be so honored.

President Taft and Secretary Knox sought to conclude additional, more sweeping bilateral arbitration treaties in 1911. They accepted the Senate dictum for the limiting arbitration *compromis* but provided for the arbitration of all "justiciable" issues, even those involving vital interests, and for the submittal of disputes to commissions of inquiry merely by executive agreement. Once more the Senate demurred and proceeded to amend—some say mutilate—them, causing President Taft to refuse ratification.

In keeping with earlier practice, during this period the Department of State concluded fifty-one new extradition treaties with thirty-four governments, including the Republic of San Marino. In several cases multiple treaties were concluded with individual countries. The Department also broadened the scope of crimes specified, which ranged from ten to as many as twenty-four. The most inclusive treaties applied to such crimes as abortion, arson, assault on ships, bigamy, breaking into government offices, burglary, counterfeiting of money and securities, crimes at sea, embezzlement, falsification of official acts, forgery, fraud or breach of trust, housebreaking, kidnapping, larceny, manslaughter, murder and attempted murder, mutiny, obtaining funds under false pretenses, perjury and subordination of perjury, piracy, rape, receiving stolen goods or money, robbery, wrongfully sinking or destroying a vessel at sea, and even the destruction of railroads.

Unique was the conclusion of treaties and agreements concerned with such new subjects as naturalization (twenty-four, which implemented the American policy of expatriation),[112] the construction of a Western Hemisphere isthmian canal (six), immigration (two with China), and the special problem of preserving the Bering Sea furbearing seals (ten with Great Britain and one with Russia). Other specialized subjects—ranging from the payment of harbor dues, shipwreck expenses, and the disposition of private property abroad, to the matter of legal tender and coinage and the protection of literary and artistic treasures—are listed in Table 5.5.

Many of these treaties and agreements were important, and some were critical to the welfare and development of the United States. These would include the Peace Treaty ending the Spanish–American War (1898) and those providing for the purchase of Alaska (1867) and other territories, the Treaty of Washington with Great Britain (1871), and the Taft–Katsura and Root–Takahira Agreements with Japan (1905 and 1908). To these may be added the packages of treaties and agreements that dealt with amity, commerce, and reciprocity; claims settlements; arbitration, including the Root treaties; boundary settlements with Great Britain and Mexico; and the construction of an isthmian canal, as well as international extradition and fishing rights.

A number of special features, reflecting State Department bilateral treaty management, may be noted. Despite the Senate's jealously guarded constitutional approval role, one-third were in the nature of executive agreements, which influenced future procedure. Normally, certain subjects, such as amity and commerce, arbitration, claims settlement, extradition, peacemaking, and territorial cession, were dealt with in formal treaties. Treaty making emerged as one of the Department of State's major achievements, reflecting the growing function of both implementing American foreign policy and managing negotiations by diplomats.

At times long gaps occurred between the negotiation of treaties and agreements with certain countries. Thus, none were concluded with Portugal for nearly half a century (1851–99) and, most remarkably, with Sweden for 110 years (1783–1893). Many treaties and agreements were brief, consisting of only a few paragraphs, but others, especially those concerned with amity and commerce, extradition, and peacemaking, were comprehensive and detailed, some running as long as fifteen to twenty or more printed pages.

Prior to the establishment of the German Empire in 1871 the United States concluded separate treaties and agreements with individual German States and the North German Confederation. Twelve of those negotiated with Spain concerned Cuba and other Spanish territorial possessions. In nearly twenty cases the United States concluded only a single treaty or agreement with a foreign government. On the other hand, those with Great Britain dealt with twenty different subjects, ranging from arbitration, boundaries, commerce, and extradition, to the exemption of salesman's samples from customs inspection. The preponderant majority of those negotiated with France, Great Britain, Italy, Mexico, and other countries were signed in Washington.

Multilateral Treaties and Agreements

A major innovation was the conclusion of dozens of multilateral treaties and agreements. Whereas the United States signed only two multilateral agreements prior to 1861, beginning with four in the 1860s and accelerating in the 1890s and especially in the years from 1900 to 1913, the United States concluded nearly ninety such treaties and agreements, as indicated in Table 5.6. These consisted of eight tripartite, three quadripartite, sixteen inter-American, and, most surprisingly, sixty global treaties and agreements. More than forty of the latter may be considered as of general applicability, and the rest were of restricted substantive concern.

In international parlance, some fifty-five (63 percent) were titled "conventions," most of which created legal, political, economic, and other commitments. Eight were called "protocols," which supplemented earlier arrangements, only two were titled "treaties," and seven were designated as "agreements." Four that dealt with the Pan-American Union constituted "resolutions" passed by the International Conferences of American States, and the remainder had such titles

Table 5.6
Multilateral Treaties and Agreements, 1861–1913

Titles and Categories

United States

Treaties	62
Agreements	25

International

Conventions	55
Treaties	2
Agreements	7
General Acts	5
Protocols	8
Declarations	4
Resolutions (Inter-American)	4
Arrangements	2

Number of Participating Governments

Tripartite	8
Quadripartite	3
Inter-American	16
Global—General	43
Limited	17

Decades Treaties and Agreements Signed

1860s	4	1890s	16
1870s	5	1900s	38
1880s	9	1910-13	15

Location Where Signed

Washington	8		
Europe			
Berlin	3	London	1
Bern	2	Madrid	2
Brussels	9	Paris	10
Geneva	2	Rome	3
The Hague	18	Vienna	1
Lisbon	1		
Latin America			
Buenos Aires	5	Rio de Janeiro	4
Mexico City	5		
Asia and Pacific			
Apia	3	Yedo	1
Peking	4	Yokohama	1
Seoul	1		
Others			
Algeciras	1	Exchange of	
Tangier	1	Notes	1

Treaty and Agreement Subjects

Global Organizations and Agencies

Agriculture	1
Hague Tribunal	3
Patents and Trademarks	6
Postal Affairs	6
Public Health	4
Publication of Tariffs	1
Seismology	1
Telecommunications	2
Weights and Measures	1

Inter-American

Pan American Union	4
Commission of Jurists	1

Other Subjects

Cape Spartel Lighthouse	1
Claims and Arbitration	7
Commerce and Tariffs	2
Copyright	2
Exchange of Publications	3
Hospital Ships	1
Laws of War and Neutrality	13
Obscene Publications	1
Patent Drugs	1
Peaceful Settlement—Inter-American	2
Red Cross	2
Salvage at Sea	1
Submarine Cables	3
White Slave Traffic	1

Specific Geographic Areas and Countries	17 *

*These included Africa (three), China (three), Korea (one), Latin America (two), Morocco (two), Northern Pacific (preservation of fur seals, one), and Samoa (five).

as "acts" or "declarations." Two were simply called "arrangements."[113] So far as American constitutional practice is concerned, twenty-five (approximately 30 percent), were executive agreements, reflecting a remarkable use of this process, which bypassed formal Senate approval.[114] In six cases the United States did not participate in negotiating the treaties but later acceded or adhered to them. Two of the agreements consisted of exchanges of notes.[115]

Most unique in the management of the treaty process was the handling of international postal arrangements. Early in the 1870s, during the formative years of American participation in multilateral international agencies, the United States instituted a special process for dealing with the international transmission of mails. When multilateral postal conventions were concluded, they were ratified by the Postmaster General with the approval not of the Senate but of the President. This procedure was authorized in 1872, when Congress passed an act that empowered the Postmaster General "by and with the advice and consent of the President" to conclude such agreements.[116]

The significance of this arrangement is that, to facilitate the management of international mail administration, the Postmaster General (later, the Postal Service), rather than the President or the Department of State, not only negotiates postal conventions but also ratifies them without the consent of either the Senate by two-thirds vote or by both houses of Congress by simple majority vote. Based on the precedent established in the 1870s for handling these conventions, which differs from both the constitutionally mandated treaty process and the normal executive agreement procedure, Congress prescribed an extraordinary, if not "extraconstitutional," scheme for creating and joining international postal agencies to facilitate not only the international transmission of ordinary mail but eventually also for the handling of money orders, parcel post, express mail, and similar materials.

These multilateral treaties and agreements dealt with a broad spectrum of subjects,[117] concluded at global, regional, and more limited international conferences. Some may be grouped as "packages," either by clustering related topics or by associating basic documents with revisions and amplifications. Of those concerned with specific subjects, eighteen were devoted to peacekeeping and the rules of war and neutrality; sixteen pertained to inter-American affairs; eleven established international organizations, in addition to the Pan-American Union and the Hague Tribunal; eight pertained to copyright, patents, and trademarks; seven provided for claims settlements, arbitration, and indemnities; six governed the Universal Postal Union; and four related to public health and sanitation. In addition, multiple treaties and agreements were concluded to deal with Samoa (five), the protection of submarine cables (three), and the Red Cross, telecommunications, and the Chinese Whangpoo Conservancy (two each).[118]

Only nine of these treaties and agreements were concluded in Washington, three of which were signed by Secretary of State John Hay.[119] Except for an exchange of notes constituting an agreement with four European powers and Japan on commercial relations with China (1899–1900), the rest were signed abroad in foreign capitals and other cities.[120] As was to be expected, more than forty were signed by resident American emissaries, mostly by ranking diplomats, and a few by consular officers.[121]

In some cases they were concluded and signed by special envoys. These are represented by William W. Rockhill, who participated in negotiating the Boxer Protocol at Peking in 1900 and was appointed Minister Plenipotentiary to China five years later; by John W. Garrett, who signed a treaty concerning the exemption of hospital ships from taxation at The Hague in 1904 and who was later appointed Minister Plenipotentiary to Venezuela, Argentina, the Netherlands, and Luxembourg and also as Ambassador to Italy; by Arthur Bailly-Blanchard, who signed the Paris Treaty on the Repression of the Circulation of Obscene Publications in 1910 and who subsequently was appointed Minister Plenipotentiary to Haiti; and by Charles Nagel, the Secretary of Commerce and Labor, who, with Chandler P. Anderson, who became Counselor of the Department of State, signed the Bering Sea Fur Seals Convention in Washington in 1911.

In a good many cases the President and Department of State appointed joint commissions to conclude these treaties and agreements. To illustrate, such delegations participated in concluding and signing seventeen inter-American treaties and agreements in Washington, Mexico City, Buenos Aires, and Rio de Janeiro and five Postal Conventions, as well as the Act for the Protection of Industrial Property (Brussels, 1900), two International Public Health and Sanitary Conventions (Paris, 1903 and 1912),[122] a Red Cross Convention (Geneva, 1906), the Telecommunication Conventions (Berlin, 1906, and London, 1912), and the Assistance and Salvage at Sea Convention (Brussels, 1910). The largest delegations consisted of eight diplomats and experts who signed the Inter-American Copyright Convention of 1910 and twelve technical experts who signed the Telecommunication Convention at London in 1912.

Although exceptional, on occasion executive agreements were unsigned. Thus, a revised Convention on the International Association of Seismology, dated August 15, 1905, though unsigned, became effective in April the following year, and Congress authorized American participation on June 30. Also, the Whangpoo Conservancy Agreement of 1912, though not formally signed, was approved "by the diplomatic body" in Peking.[123]

Historically, among the most important of these multilateral treaties and agreements were those that resolved political and territorial disputes and pretensions, established bodies of law and regulations, and created institutions to provide and coordinate international services. Aside from some thirty that created and modified international organizations, illustrations include the Hague Conventions on pacific settlement of disputes and on the laws of war and neutrality (1899 and 1907), the Declaration of London concerning the rights and duties of belligerents and neutrals in time of war (1909),[124] the Red Cross Conventions (1864 and 1906), the Declaration for the Open Door in China (1899–1900), the Protocol to settle claims against Portugal (1891), the Protocols with Germany and Italy to resolve the matter of claims against Venezuela (1903), the treaties and agreements to cope with the Samoan issue (1879, 1880, 1889, and 1899), the Boxer Protocol (1900), the General Act of Algeceiras to settle the Moroccan question (1906), the Treaty of Washington to resolve the international dispute concerning the Bering Sea fur seal controversy (1911), and the treaties concluded to establish common policy and practice concerning copyrights, patents, and trademarks.

Treaties and Territorial Expansion

During the half century from the Mexican to the Spanish-American War, the United States acquired extensive territory in the North and Central Pacific and the Caribbean areas. It became a two-ocean country when it acquired the California and contiguous territory from Mexico by the Treaty of Guadelupe Hidalgo in 1848. By means of a series of subsequent treaties, protectorates, annexations, and effective occupation, it became a major naval power in the Pacific basin and Caribbean areas, under the leadership of such Presidents as Grant, Benjamin Harrison, McKinley, and Theodore Roosevelt, Secretaries Seward and Hay, Admiral Alfred T. Mahan, and others.

To summarize, prior to 1861, for purely economic reasons (guano mining), in 1857–58 the United States appropriated a number of islands in the mid-Pacific—Baker, Christmas, Howland, and Jarvis. A decade later, in 1867, by treaty with Russia, the United States purchased Alaska and the Aleutian Islands, which constituted its only noncontiguous North American territory and provided an extensive archipelago across the northern Pacific. That same year the United States took possession of the uninhabited Midway Islands, northwest of Hawaii in the mid-Pacific. For years, beginning in the 1830s, Germany, Great Britain, and the United States were interested in possessing the Samoan (formerly the Navigator) Islands, lying within the Polynesian Archipelago. By treaty with Germany in 1878, the United States acquired title to Tutuila, with its potential naval base at Pago Pago, together with the Manua group, Swains, and other islands. This extended American naval power into the South-Central Pacific.

In the mid-1850s an American Commissioner negotiated an abortive treaty for the annexation of the Hawaiian Islands, and a second such treaty, signed in 1893, was aborted by President Cleveland. Eventually, President McKinley promoted the negotiation of a new annexation treaty, signed on June 16, 1897, but when approval languished in the Senate, he urged annexation by means of a joint resolution of Congress, which he signed on August 12, 1898. It provided for jurisdiction over all of the main Hawaiian Islands and also the southern islet of Palmyra and gained the major naval base at Pearl Harbor in the Central Pacific.

Following the Spanish-American War, by the Treaty of Paris, in 1898 Spain ceded to the United States the Philippine Archipelago, with its potential naval base at Manila in the Western Pacific, as well as Guam, one of the main islands in the Mariannas that then was also regarded as a possible naval base and a cable station. A year later the United States annexed unpopulated Wake Island, located in the mid-Pacific west of Hawaii, for possible use as a naval and transpacific cable station.

Paralleling these acquisitions, in the Caribbean area, by the Treaty of Paris, in 1898 Spain also ceded Puerto Rico to the United States and conferred independence upon Cuba, over which the United States established a protectorate under the Platt Amendment to an Army appropriation bill. In 1902, also by treaty, the United States acquired the right from Cuba to establish a major base in Guantanamo Bay, which served as its primary naval facility in that area. Earlier that year the American Government, which had been interested in acquiring the Virgin Islands from Denmark since the Grant Administration, negotiated a purchase treaty, which was rejected by the Danish Parliament. Not until 1917, therefore, was a new purchase treaty concluded and ratified. To these developments must be added American isthmian diplomacy that resulted in the treaty of 1903 with Panama, providing for the construction, operation, and defense of the Panama Canal, U.S. jurisdiction over it "in perpetuity," and a protectorate over Panama.

Thus, in little more than three decades, the American advance into the Pacific Ocean area and the Caribbean encompassed the acquisition of not only such major territories as Alaska and the Aleutians, the Philippines, and Puerto Rico but also Guam, Midway, Samoa, Wake, the Virgin Islands, the Pacific Guano and other lesser islands. This provided the United States with substantial territories in the Caribbean and the North, Central, and Western Pacific and some lesser holdings. Largely through the treaty process, therefore, the United States became the paramount naval power in the Caribbean and a major naval power in the Pacific. With hindsight, these achievements constituted one of the most significant features of American diplomatic progress and of the treaty work of the Department of State during this period.

Aborted Treaties

Some treaties and agreements were negotiated but failed to be ratified or were otherwise aborted, which illustrates some of the difficulties permeating executive-legislative relations in the treaty process. For example, shortly after the Civil War, Secretary Seward attempted to buy the Danish West Indies (Virgin Islands) to provide the United States with a naval-base harbor on St. Thomas. A purchase treaty for $7,500,000 was signed in October 1867, the cession to be subject to a favorable vote of the local inhabitants. The House of Representatives opposed it and passed a resolution declaring that it had no obligation to approve the funding, and the treaty languished and died in the Senate in 1869. Later, the treaty of 1902 was rejected by Denmark. President Grant also became interested in annexing the Republic of Santo Domingo, then a bankrupt and revolution-rent country. It was favored by American naval leaders to provide a Caribbean base at Samana Bay. A treaty was signed in 1869 that, when voted on by the Senate, failed to achieve the necessary two-thirds majority.

Similarly, early attempts to annex Hawaii failed to materialize. An annexation treaty, negotiated in 1854, was rejected by the Senate, in part because it contained an article that provided for immediate American statehood. A Reciprocity Treaty was concluded in 1855, which the Senate also failed to approve, as was another Reciprocity Treaty negotiated during the Seward Administration in 1867. Subsequently, such a treaty was finally approved in 1875, which was supplemented by another treaty in 1884, approved three years later, which secured for the United States the use of Pearl Harbor as a naval station. In 1893 another annexation treaty was signed during the Benjamin Harrison Administration and sent to the Senate, which Cleveland withdrew when he became President. Hawaii was finally annexed in 1898 by a congressional joint resolution.

Despite growing American interest in the construction of an isthmian canal and the conclusion of a series of treaties dealing with the matter, not all of them became effective. Thus, a treaty negotiated with Nicaragua in 1884, known as the Frelinghuysen–Zavala Treaty, provided for joint ownership and was violative of the Clayton-Bulwer Treaty with Great Britain (1850). When the Cleveland Administration came to power, the treaty was doomed. Later, the Hay–Herran Treaty with Colombia, signed in January 1903, failed to be ratified. Colombian instructions to Thomas Herran, which directed him not to sign, arrived after he had already done so, and, although the Senate of the United States had given its approval, the Colombian Senate rejected it in August.

John A. Kasson, newly appointed Minister Plenipotentiary to Germany, as directed by Secretary Frelinghuysen, represented the United States at the Berlin Conference of 1884–85, convened by Bismarck to deal with the territory of the African Congo, which Belgium sought to acquire to develop its empire. The resulting treaty—known as the General Act of Berlin—among other matters, adopted the principle of ''effective occupation'' to establish legal title to landed territory. Although Kasson signed the treaty, when Cleveland succeeded President Arthur in March 1885, he refused to submit it to the Senate for approval.

Some treaties with Great Britain also failed to become effective. An arrangement for a joint U.S.–British Fisheries Commission, the Bayard–Joseph Chamberlain pact of February 1888, constituted a compromise to settle a century-old dispute over fishing rights, was rejected by the Senate. Later, in January 1897 Secretary Olney concluded a general Arbitration Treaty with Great Britain, which had the support of President McKinley. It provided that all pecuniary claims that did not individually exceed £100,000 were to be submitted to an Arbitration Tribunal consisting of one arbitrator from each country who would jointly select an empire, with their decisions to be made by a majority. It also provided for a separate Tribunal, consisting of three American and three British Judges, to decide disputes concerning territorial claims. This was a landmark treaty in that it projected a continuing process for the resolution of major categories of international disputes between the two countries. The British Parliament approved it, but the Senate withheld its consent.

Arbitration Record

As an alternative to direct negotiations, the customary method of resolving international problems and crises during the nineteenth century by means of arbitration became an acceptable, if not conventional, alternative process for peaceful settlement, especially in Anglo–American relations. Approximately 300 arbitration treaties were concluded worldwide, all providing for some form, mostly ad hoc, of arbitral machinery. A preponderant majority of these were bilateral, but some, such as the Hague Conventions, also provided for multilateral commitments and the Permanent Court of Arbitration. Well over 200 formal arbitrations were decided, with the United States participating in sixty-nine to 1914, exceeded only by Great Britain, which engaged in seventy-one. During this period the United States employed arbitration to resolve disputes concerning pecuniary claims indemnifications, territorial and boundary allocation, fishing rights, and the preservation of fur seals.

Most American arbitrations were with Great Britain (twenty-two), but they were also achieved with Colombia, Costa Rica, Denmark, Ecuador, El Salvador, Haiti, Nicaragua, Paraguay, Peru, Portugal, Santo Domingo, Siam (Thailand), and Venezuela. In addition, the President acted as arbitrator between other nations in five cases, and American diplomats or others designated by the United States served as arbitrators or umpires in nine settlements.

In terms of the import of the subject and the seriousness of the dispute, given sequentially, the following are the most memorable of these arbitrations. During the Civil War, the Confederate steamship *Alabama*, built in Great Britain, preyed on American commerce and destroyed nearly seventy-five ships before the Union Navy sank it. Following the war, the Department of State levied claims for damages against the British Government, claiming that it failed to prevent the building of the *Alabama, Florida*, and other Confederate ships and that it permitted them to be supplied in British ports. The Treaty of Washington (1871) provided for submittal to an Arbitration Tribunal consisting of five arbitrators appointed by the United States, Great Britain, Brazil, Italy, and Switzerland to convene in Geneva to adjudicate the claims, deciding issues by majority vote. Its determination of September 1872 ruled that Great Britain had violated its international responsibility for exercising "due diligence," as required by international law and prescribed in the treaty, so it awarded the United States $15,500,000.[125]

After the United States acquired Alaska in 1867, American policy sought to protect the furbearing seals inhabiting and breeding in the Pribilof Islands located in the Bering Sea. The Department of State negotiated treaties with both Russia and Great Britain (on behalf of Canada), which sought to forbid the killing of female and young seals and to limit the number taken annually. It argued that the United States possessed proprietary rights within the closed Bering Sea, founded on an earlier Russian pretension. This issue involved the American seizure of vessels that allegedly violated American jurisdiction, based on the doctrine of *mare clausum* (or the closed sea), which ran counter to its own traditional policy of freedom of the seas. A treaty was signed with Great Britain in 1892 that provided for submittal of the dispute to a mixed Arbitration Tribunal comprising seven members who met at Paris the following year. The Tribunal rendered its judgment against the United States and prescribed seven rules to govern future sealing. In a separate arbitration, agreed to by another treaty in February 1896, the United States paid nearly $475,000 for the seizure of Canadian sealers. Later, in 1911 the United States, Great Britain, Japan, and Russia signed a multilateral convention to regulate the sealing industry in the North Pacific, to prohibit pelagic sealing, and to share the profits.

One of the most serious disputes involved a long-standing controversy over the boundary line between Venezuela and British Guiana. The issue for the United States was British advancement of territorial claims and expansion in violation of the Monroe Doctrine, which interdicted European colonization in the Western Hemisphere. Both Venezuela and the Department of State recommended arbitration, and Venezuela severed diplomatic relations with Great Britain in 1877. In July 1895 Secretary Olney, supported by President Cleveland, sent a strong note to the British Government demanding to know whether it would arbitrate, and it propounded his Corollary to the Monroe Doctrine, in which he asserted American paramountcy in the Western Hemisphere. This converted the British dispute with Venezuela into a conflict with the United States, especially when the British response presumed to define the Monroe Doctrine for the United States.

Eventually, an Arbitration Treaty was signed by Great Britain and Venezuela at Washington in February 1897. It provided for the submission of the dispute to an Arbitration Tribunal consisting of two members designated by the Supreme Court of the United States, two members determined by the British Supreme Court, and a fifth to be agreed upon by the four arbiters or, if they could not agree within three months, to be selected by the King of Sweden and Norway. The Russian jurist, F. F. de Martins, was selected as the fifth arbiter. The award was delivered on October 3, 1899, the crisis was averted, arbitration was consecrated as the preferred method of peaceful settlement and was embodied in the Hague Convention of 1899, and the international credence of the Monroe Doctrine was enhanced.

The Pious Fund arbitration with Mexico is notable because it was the first case settled under the Hague Permanent Court of Arbitration. It concerned pecuniary claims of prelates of the Roman Catholic Church brought against the Mexican Government by the United States. An executive agreement, dated May 1902, stipulated in detail the issues and format of an international Tribunal, consisting of two arbitrators named by the United States and two by Mexico, plus an umpire, to resolve the issue of financial compensation. Their decision, rendered in October, awarded the United States nearly $1,500,000 Mexican, plus some $43,000 Mexican annually thereafter.[126]

When the United States purchased Alaska, it acquired the islands adjacent to its panhandle, the inner boundary of which, prescribed in a treaty between Russia and Great Britain (1825), was in dispute. Secretary Hay negotiated a treaty with Great Britain in 1903, providing for the settlement of differences by a mixed Arbitration Tribunal consisting of three American arbitrators and three British arbitrators, to meet in London to decide the matter by a majority of at least four. The award, determined by the Americans and one British arbitrator in 1903, compromised the competing interests, which proved to be less extensive than demanded by the United States. It also awarded Canada two of the four disputed uninhabited islands in the southern part of the panhandle.

Fishery rights in the North Atlantic off the coast of Canada, a frequently contested problem in Anglo-American relations, came to a head when the stipulations of the Treaty of Washington (1870) expired. Under a Treaty of Arbitration, concluded by Secretary Root in 1909, the matter was submitted to an International Tribunal under the aegis of the Permanent Court of Arbitration. Its decision, awarded the following year, also established a compromise, which was reconfirmed, with some modifications, in the Anglo-American Fisheries Treaty of 1912. It created Permanent Mixed Fishery Commissions for the United States and Canada to resolve future disputes whenever they arose.

INTERNATIONAL CONFERENCES AND ORGANIZATIONS

Evidencing the proliferation of U.S. foreign interests and active participation in both global and Western Hemisphere relations, during this period, in addition to accelerating its bilateral negotiations and conferencing, the United States joined other governments in a number of multilateral international conferences and participated in creating multilateral international organizations and other agencies. These and related innovations paved the way to becoming a major world power and, despite its traditional policies of abstentionism respecting Europe's political and jurisdictional issues and neutrality during its wars, portended widespread involvement in world affairs.

The international conference has been defined as the diplomatic process that, in its most elemental form, consists of the representatives of two or more states meeting to deal with matters of common concern. Usually applied in a more advanced or sophisticated form, the concept denotes a meeting of the delegates of two or more states to negotiate mutual agreements to coordinate policy, establish common objectives, procedures, and programs, settle differences, and resolve disputes.

Previously, the Department of State engaged in traditional bilateral peacemaking, treaty negotiations, and international congresses, conferences, and meetings.[127] During the half century prior to World War I, reflecting the growth of the family of nations, the desire for regulating and administering selected aspects of foreign relations, and producing a network of institutionalized systems of mutual cooperation, multilateral international conferences provided the vehicle for initiating and promoting these developments. It was natural, therefore, that the Department of State would be cloaked with responsibility for managing American participation in this evolving diplomatic process. As a consequence, the United States evidenced a growing spirit of cooperation and became an active participant in the evolution of a growing range of collective developments.

The objectives of international conferences vary according to their type and the subjects under consideration. A peacemaking conference is usually convened at a neutral site. Sometimes a third power may be involved, as was the case when President Theodore Roosevelt initiated and monitored the Portsmouth (New Hampshire) Conference in 1905 to negotiate the treaty terminating the Russo-Japanese War. The objectives of peacetime conferences are more diverse, ranging from preliminary or preparatory planning for future negotiations, to the conclusion of treaties and agreements and the production of constitutive acts creating temporary or continuing international organizations.

Studies of international conferences categorize them in many ways. The most obvious differentiations are between ad hoc and regularized, bilateral and multilateral, or peace settlement and peacetime conferences, and among congresses, conferences, and meetings. Or they may be classified as global, hemispheric (such as inter-American or European), and regional (such as Central American or Middle Eastern), or as public or intergovernmental, semipublic, and private, or, relying on the level of representation, as summit, ministerial, diplomatic, and administrative conferences. Most frequently, however, for descriptive purposes, they are categorized functionally as peacemaking, peacekeeping, law- and regulation-creating, constitutive (creating international agencies), political, economic, humanitarian, scientific, social, technical, and other types.[128]

According to the Department of State, so far as timing is concerned, in the nineteenth century the United States participated in 100 conferences, the preponderant majority of which were bilateral. During the next quarter century, to 1925, it was represented at some additional 180 conferences, and thereafter the number increased markedly. A substantial number of these produced signed treaties and agreements. This indicates that, at the outset, the American Government exhibited some, but by no means complete, reluctance to join other governments at the conference table. After the Civil War it also began to parallel bilateral with multilateral conferencing, but prior to the Lincoln Administration the United States attended none of what are historically regarded as the major general or global international conferences. From 1861 to 1913, however, the United States joined other governments in at least twenty-five, or one-fourth, of the most important conclaves, not counting arbitrations.

Nevertheless, overall, during the half century prior to World War I, it attended more than 100 multilateral conferences, consisting of eight inter-American, six major European, seventeen global and regional constitutive,[129] and more than seventy other conferences. Participation began modestly in the 1860s and 1870s, and accelerated in the 1880s and 1890s, and more than half of these conferences were convened in the early years of the twentieth century. The preponderant majority were held in European capitals, and only eight were hosted by the Department of State in Washington.

Illustrating U.S. practice, at the hemispheric level, Secretary Blaine convened the first International Conference of American States, which met in Washington in 1889. Later these were called Pan-American and then Inter-American Conferences, which met in Mexico City (1901–2), Rio de Janeiro (1906), and Buenos Aires (1910). On the other hand, the global or general conferences consisted of three basic types. Aside from those that were constitutive, which produced treaties and agreements to create international organizations and agencies to deal with particular international issues and practices, they consisted of those that concerned similar international matters without establishing multilateral machinery and those that focused on more specific issues.[130]

A survey of the subjects treated by these multilateral conferences reveals that, while none of them served to produce a major peace treaty, and they did not deal with certain matters treated by many bilateral treaties and agreements, such as citizenship, consular rights, extradition, immigration, and naturalization, they covered a variegated range of international subjects. In addition to a few that were devoted to peacekeeping (such as those that produced the Hague Conventions of 1899 and 1907), they were concerned with agriculture, claims settlement, commerce and trade, copyright, exchange of official documents and other materials, fisheries and fur seals, laws of war and neutrality, navigation and maritime law, patents and trademarks, postal affairs, the prime meridian, private international law, public health and sanitation, the Red Cross, salvage at sea, submarine cables, tariffs and dues, and territorial disposition, occupation, and jurisdiction. A few also dealt with more specialized matters, including the African liquor traffic, opium and other drug control, the slave trade and white slavery, and unification of pharmaceutical formulas for patent drugs.[131]

The constitutive conferences produced a series of multilateral international organizations, some of which have been modified and remain in existence. Listed chronologically, they include such agencies as the Universal Postal Union (1874), Permanent International Bureau of Weights and Measures (1878), International Union for the Protection of Industrial Property (patents and trademarks, 1883), the Hague Tribunal (Permanent Court of Arbitration, 1899 and 1907), Commercial Bureau of the American Republics and the Pan-American Union (1890), International Bureau for the Publication of Customs Tariffs (1890), Permanent International Association of Navigation Congresses (1885, 1894, and 1898), Pan-American Sanitary Bureau (1902), International Association of Seismology (1905), Whangpoo Conservancy Board (1905 and 1912), Inter-American Commission of Jurists (1906), International Bureau of the Telegraphic Union (1906), International Office of Public Health and Sanitation (1907 and 1912), Permanent International Association of Road Congresses

(1908), and the Inter-American Union for Trademarks (1910).[132] Also see Table 6.10, Part A.

By comparison with subsequent practice, the aggregate and types of American participation in international conferences and organizations prior to World War I were noteworthy but not remarkable, particularly with regard to political and critical world diplomatic matters. Wariness was due, in part, to concentration on internal problems and development, the traditional policy of avoiding foreign entanglements, and, in certain respects, the relatively limited power posture of the United States in world affairs, at least until the last decade of the nineteenth century. International involvement of the United States also was affected by the necessity of realigning the thinking, policy, and action by the President, Congress, and the Secretary and Department of State to determine the feasible American role and the advantages and costs of involvement. As far as conference administration is concerned, early American practice tended to be primarily ad hoc, dealing with the issues of each gathering as it occurred. In the course of time, however, the Department of State perfected elements of standardization that facilitated its international conference participation.[133]

CONCLUSION

During this half century, the Department of State and the Diplomatic and Consular Services underwent material changes, and the United States emerged as a major world power. Departmental modulation reflected both volitional innovation and shifts due to foreign permutation and influence. These produced modification of the Department, increase of diplomatic and consular staffing and functions, extension of American foreign relations, negotiation of new treaties and agreements, and the commencement of involvement in multilateral international conferencing and the joining of international organizations.

Former basic foreign policies continued to dominate the attention of the Department. They were supplemented with expansionism into noncontiguous territories, the promotion of reciprocal trade benefits, the establishment of the Open Door policy, especially in the Far East, reinterpretation of the Monroe Doctrine by the Olney and Theodore Roosevelt Corollaries, advance arbitration commitments, mutual acceptance of the right and legal validity of naturalization, multilateral negotiations, treaties, and international organizations, and others. Such policy mutations affected both the functions and practices of the Department and the Diplomatic and Consular Services.

The Department instituted significant organizational and administrative modifications, especially during the Fish, Root, and Knox Administrations. The senior administrative staff was amplified by the addition of Second and Third Assistant Secretaries and the creation of a number of specialized officers. Although diplomatic and consular management remained separate, the Department was restructured into a more systematic organization of geographic and functional bureaus and other agencies and officials. Only a few alterations were made to change the nature and personnel of the Diplomatic Service, except for the creation of the ambassadorial rank and the virtual elimination of the position of Minister Resident, so that by the time of World War I, the principal diplomatic oficers, generally commissioned as Ambassadors and Ministers Plenipotentiary, were accorded the two highest diplomatic titles. The Consular Service was subjected to more substantial reforms. These included reclassification of posts, closer regulation of consular activities, and adoption of a salary basis for part of the consular corps. Transfer from the spoils to the merit system was dilatory, applied primarily to consular officers, and reform depended largely upon executive orders.

The President and Secretary of State increased their use of special envoys, which, although contested by Congress, became common practice. Several individual diplomatic and consular officers emerged as professionals. By virtue of performance and extended service, some became careerists, even though diplomacy had not yet been legislated as a formal career service of the American Government. Later, a few were inducted into the Foreign Service of the United States.

Treaty-making practice indicates that the Department was prepared to conclude bilateral treaties and agreements with more countries and other territories, including those in Africa, the Mideast, the Orient, and Pacific Islands. More than half were executive agreements, and nearly three of every five were signed at Washington. While concluding many new bilateral commerce and reciprocity claims, consular, extradition, and territorial acquisition conventions, the Department also added such subjects as the construction of an isthmian canal, copyright protection, fisheries, naturalization, pacific settlement, and other more specialized subjects to its treaty record.

More important historically, however, the Department launched a substantial program of participation in multilateral international conferencing, the negotiation of treaties and agreements with groups of foreign governments, and the joining of a series of nonpolitical, administrative, technical, and other international organizations. The American Government thereby became committed to collective handling of arbitration, copyright, patents and trademarks, postal affairs, public health and sanitation, and other matters.

The United States fought the tragic Civil War but remained united. It also engaged in the war with Spain, which resulted in important territorial concessions. They were supplemented by the purchase of Alaska, the acquisition of additional territories in the Caribbean and the Pacific areas, and the possession of major naval bases in Guantánamo, Manila, Pearl Harbor, and elsewhere, as well as the construction of the Panama Canal. These actions produced a new international posture for the United States based on primary naval power status in the Western Hemisphere and major power ranking in the Pacific Basin.

Such developments required changes and improvements in central departmental organization and management, capable leadership, qualified and experienced personnel, and flexibility of administration and procedures. They were influenced and constrained by such factors as congressional legislation, the direction, foreign relations interests, partisanship, and turnover of Presidents, the qualities and experience of the Secretaries and Assistant Secretaries of State, and the attendant political and policy considerations, financing, and nepotism.

Nevertheless, a goodly number of able individuals were appointed to administrative, diplomatic, and consular positions. Some of them served creditably both in the Department and abroad, and many remained in service for lengthy periods and became genuine professionals. Whereas the Department, its staff, and the Diplomatic and Consular Services had their functional and personnel weaknesses, as a whole they were maturing into an agency attuned to the demands of active promotion of American policies and interests abroad as the United States moved into the twentieth century and approached the era of World War I.

NOTES

1. Sequentially, these additional States included West Virginia (1863), Nevada (1864), Nebraska (1867), Colorado (1876), Montana (1889), North Dakota (1889), South Dakota (1889), Washington (1889), Idaho (1890), Wyoming (1890), Utah (1896), Oklahoma (1907), Arizona (1912), and New Mexico (1912). No additional States were added until 1959, when Alaska and Hawaii were admitted into the Union.

2. The office of Attorney General was established by law in September 1789. The Attorney General headed the Department of Justice when it was created in 1870.

3. In 1913 Congress divided this department into separate Departments of Commerce and Labor, each headed by a Secretary.

4. The economic depressions occurred in 1866, 1873, 1882, 1890, 1900, and 1907. The major tariff legislation included the McKinley (1889), Wilson (1894), Dingley (1897), and Payne–Aldrich (1909) Tariff Acts. These were followed in 1913 by the Underwood Tariff.

5. The Olney Corollary boasted: "Today the United States is practically sovereign on this continent [the Western Hemisphere], and its fiat is law upon the subjects to which it confines its interposition."

The Roosevelt Corollary stipulated that Latin American countries that conducted themselves responsibly, maintained order, and paid their debts could count on American friendship, but if they were guilty of impotence and chronic wrongdoing, foreign intervention might become necessary.

6. The Open Door notes of 1899 and 1900, sent by the United States to Great Britain, Germany, Russia, France, Japan, and Italy, were intended to serve the interests of Americans in China and to preserve Far Eastern peace. They were devised by William W. Rockhill, an "old China hand" who was the Far Eastern adviser of Secretary of State John Hay, for presentation to President McKinley, and they were transmitted to the foreign governments by Secretary Hay. They helped to establish and maintain an "Open Door" commercial policy in China.

7. President Theodore Roosevelt was credited with endorsing the slogan "speak softly and carry a big stick" in U.S. relations with Latin America.

8. Beginning with the Civil War but expanded in the following half century, sup-

porters of a big navy sought to enhance America's trade and security and its international stature. The movement was sparked by Navy Captain Alfred T. Mahan, who contended that to be a Great Power, it was necessary for the United States to be a great naval power, and to be a great naval power it was essential to control the major sea-lanes and foreign naval bases. He influenced American expansionists like President Roosevelt. Eventually, by the time of World War I the United States possessed control of not only the Panama Canal Zone but also naval bases in Guantánamo Bay (Cuba), Honolulu, Manila, and Pago Pago (Samoan Island of Tutuila).

9. The Republican Party was founded in 1854, and Lincoln was its first President.

10. Prior to 1861, for seventy-two years some twenty-three Secretaries of State were appointed by fifteen Presidents, the Secretaries serving an average of 3.13-year terms, whereas from 1861 to 1913 they increased the average to 3.76 years.

11. In most cases each Secretary remained in office until a successor was confirmed by the Senate and assumed the responsibilities of the office. Only in the 1890s and 1905 were there breaks in continuity requiring the designation of the Acting Secretaries, necessitated, in part, by the death of Secretaries Gresham and Hay.

12. It has been reported that President Grant appointed Washburne as Secretary for a mere twelve days so that he could enjoy the prestige of having served in that distinguished position when he became America's diplomatic emissary to France. See Trask, *A Short History of the U.S. Department of State*, pp. 15–16.

13. In addition, both Secretaries Evarts and Knox were elected to the Senate after serving as Secretary of State. Secretaries Foster, Gresham, Olney, Day, Hay, Root, and Bacon had no congressional experience.

14. Also of relevance contributing to their background, Foster, Gresham, and Sherman served in the Union Army during the Civil War. Later, during World War I, Bacon went to France in August 1914 to work with the American Ambulance Corps and, commissioned a Major, was assigned to General John J. Pershing's staff in 1917; the following year, promoted to the rank of Lt. Colonel, he headed the American Military Mission to the British General Headquarters.

15. For example, Seward was a member of the New York State Senate (1830–34) and Governor of New York (1838–42), Fish was elected Lt. Governor and Governor of New York (1848–50), Blaine served in the Maine House of Representatives (1859–62) and was elected its Speaker (1861–62), Gresham became Indiana's financial agent in New York City (1867–69) and declined the Republican nomination for Governor of Indiana in 1880, and Olney was a member of the Massachusetts House of Representatives in 1874.

16. Evarts was chief counsel for President Andrew Johnson during his impeachment trial in 1868, and some supported him to be appointed Chief Justice of the United States; Gresham was both the U.S. District Judge for fifteen years in Indiana (1869–83) and later Circuit Judge for ten years (1884–93); Day was later appointed to the U.S. Court of Appeals (1899–1903) and as Associate Justice of the Supreme Court (1903–22); Root was a U.S. Attorney for the Southern District of New York (1883–85) and later served as counsel for the United States in an arbitration (1910), became a member of the Hague Permanent Court of Arbitration, and was a member of the Committee of Jurists, which planned the League of Nations Permanent Court of International Justice.

17. Those who ran unsuccessfully or were otherwise supported for Republican nomination for the presidency included Seward (1860), Washburne (1880, after he was Secretary of State), Fish (who was supported but was not interested), Blaine (1876 and 1880),

Bayard (1876, 1880, and 1884), Gresham (1888, and transferred to the Democratic Party in 1892), Sherman (1880, 1884, and 1888), and Knox (1908).

18. Foster had the most prior diplomatic experience, including more than a decade of assignments in both Latin America and Europe, having been commissioned as Minister Plenipotentiary to Mexico (1873–80), Russia (1880–81), and Spain (1883–85), as special plenipotentiary to negotiate reciprocity agreements (1890–91), and as special agent in the Bering Sea Fur-Seal Arbitration (1892–93).

Hay was recruited as Secretary of Legation at Paris (1865–67), Chargé d'Affaires ad interim at Vienna (1867–68), Secretary of Legation at Madrid (1869–70), Assistant Secretary of State (1878–81), and Ambassador to Great Britain (1897–98).

Day and Bacon were appointed Assistant Secretaries of State, from which they were elevated to become Secretary, respectively, by Presidents McKinley and Roosevelt in 1898 and 1909. While Assistant Secretary, Bacon was also sent, with Secretary of War William Howard Taft, as special agents appointed by President Roosevelt, to restore peace in Cuba.

Evarts was sent as a special envoy to London (1863–64) to assist Charles Francis Adams, Minister Plenipotentiary, on several legal matters and served as Counsel for the United States in the *Alabama* claims controversy before the Geneva Arbitration Tribunal (1871–72).

Root was made a member of the Alaskan Boundary Tribunal (1903). In addition, President Grant nominated Frelinghuysen as Minister Plenipotentiary to Great Britain in July 1870, but he declined the appointment.

19. Evarts was a delegate to the International Monetary Conference on bimetallic standards convened at Paris in April 1881. Bayard was commissioned as Ambassador to Great Britain (1893–97), and Bacon served as Ambassador to France (1909–12). Day, who was Secretary of State during the Spanish–American War and participated in preparing the draft of the American peace settlement, was immediately appointed as a special envoy to head the American delegation to negotiate the Peace Treaty with Spain in 1898. Later, in 1922 President Harding appointed him as umpire for the mixed U.S.-German Claims Commission.

Olney was later offered an Ambassadorship to Great Britain by President Woodrow Wilson, which he declined, and was appointed as the American member of the Permanent International Commission under the Bryan–Jusserand Treaty of 1914 with France (1915–17).

Most impressive were the records of Foster and Root. Foster served on special missions to Great Britain and Russia (1897) and as the U.S. agent before the Alaska Boundary Tribunal (1903), as well as being appointed the Commissioner of China in the negotiation of a peace treaty with Japan (1895) and the representative of China at the Second Hague Peace Conference (1907). Similarly, Root was the U.S. counsel in the North Atlantic Fisheries Arbitration (1910), chief of a special mission to Russia following its revolution and the establishment of a provisional government (1917), adviser to the American delegation at the World War I Paris Peace Conference in 1919, member of the Committee of Jurists to plan a draft Statute for the League of Nations Permanent Court of International Justice (1920), and delegate to the Washington Conference on the Limitation of Armaments (1921–22).

20. Of the twenty-four nominations for the position of First Assistant Secretary, that of Eugene Schuyler in 1889 was not consummated. Frederick W. Seward received two

nonconsecutive appointments, and J. C. Bancroft Davis was commissioned three times, in 1869, 1873, and 1881.

21. J. C. Bancroft Davis, who held three appointments as First Secretary, served for more than four years. In addition, William F. Wharton remained First Secretary for nearly four years.

22. These included First Secretaries Charles Hale, Robert R. Hitt, Josiah Quincy, William R. Day, and John Bassett Moore and Third Secretaries Walker Blaine, Edward H. Strobel, and William Phillips.

23. Other Assistant Secretaries who received diplomatic appointments included John M. Hay, Ambassador to Great Britain (1893–98) before he became Secretary of State; David J. Hill, Minister to Switzerland (1903–5) and the Netherlands and Luxembourg (1905–8); Benjamin Moran, Minister Plenipotentiary to Portugal (1875–76) and Chargé d'Affaires to Portugal (1876–82); Charles Payson, Chargé d'Affaires to Denmark (1881–82); Herbert H. D. Peirce, (Minister Plenipotentiary to Norway (1906–11); James D. Porter, Minister Plenipotentiary to Chile (1893–94); Edward H. Stroebel, Minister Plenipotentiary to Ecuador (1894) and Chile (1895–97); and Edwin F. Uhl, Ambassador to Germany (1896–97).

24. See Hackworth, *Digest of International Law*, vol. 4, p. 623.

25. Frederick W. Seward was later reappointed as Assistant Secretary (1877–79) and therefore served for more than ten years.

26. It should be noted that in 1861, during Secretary Seward's Administration, the Department of State began to publish the comprehensive and invaluable official *Foreign Relations of the United States* series, which is described later.

27. The European countries included Austria, Belgium, Denmark, France, Great Britain, the Netherlands, North Germany, Portugal, Spain, Sweden and Norway, and Switzerland.

28. The Latin American countries included Argentina, Bolivia, Brazil, Chile, Colombia, Costa Rica, Ecuador, Guatemala, Haiti, Honduras, Mexico, Nicaragua, Paraguay, Peru, El Salvador, Venezuela, and Uruguay, and the European countries were Greece, Italy, and Russia.

29. It is interesting to contemplate this arrangement. One may wonder why all European and Middle Eastern countries were not grouped in one bureau and the Latin American and Asian countries and the Hawaiian Islands in another bureau, with the Middle East and African states placed in either to provide an acceptable balance.

30. For a more detailed description of Secretary Fish's reorganization, see Hunt, *The Department of State of the United States*, pp. 222–24, and Stuart, *The Department of State*, pp. 142–45.

31. However, the bureaus that had not received formal congressional recognition remained in existence but were headed by Clerks rather than bureau Chiefs.

32. See Hunt, *The Department of State of the United States*, pp. 227–28.

33. When the Diplomatic and Consular Bureaus were consolidated into single departmental units, the new Diplomatic Bureau was divided into three geographic segments, each dealing with specific sets of foreign countries based on the subdivision previously established and subsequently modified to embrace additional countries. The same geographic breakdown applied to the unified Consular Bureau.

Whereas this geographic principle had been introduced in the 1830s by Secretary Louis McLane, not until the administration of Secretary Knox did it begin to dominate diplomatic and consular segmentation in State Department organization.

34. Congress also addressed this matter of work hours. An Act of June 20, 1874, ascribed authority to the respective Federal Departments, and an Act of March 3, 1883, required a workday of at least seven hours, which for twenty years was defined as running from 9:00 A.M. to 4:00 P.M. In 1904 President Theodore Roosevelt extended this to 4:30 P.M. See 18 Stat. 109 and 22 Stat. 563.

35. In 1875 Department of State Library holdings were reduced by transferring materials not particularly relevant to its functions to the Library of Congress or to other departments. In 1882 the State Department Library maintained a collection of approximately 18,000 works. By the time of the Knox Administration, this had expanded to 70,000 volumes, plus the originals of laws, proclamations, executive orders, and treaties and agreements, plus original manuscript records and papers.

For additional commentary on the State Department Library, its development and holdings, including historical manuscripts and the papers of leading officials, as well as a variety of relics, see Hunt, *The Department of State of the United States*, pp. 322–26.

36. This Root reform launched two crucial changes in the organization of the State Department—the concentration of management and coordination of amalgamated diplomatic and consular affairs on a geographic basis, and the establishment of departmental units at the division level as primary structural components.

37. This new system of indexing and filing consisted of nine primary classes of documents, ranging from 0 to 8, as follows: Class 0—General; 1—Administration, government of the United States; 2—Extradition; 3—Protection of American interests; 4—Claims; 5—International conferences, congresses, and treaties; 6—Commerce and commercial relations; 7—Political relations; and 8—Internal affairs of the States. Using a decimal system similar to a modern library cataloging arrangement, each of these classes was divided into specific subject fields. For a detailed description of this classification system, see Hunt, *The Department of State of the United States*, pp. 418–23.

38. For the text of Hunt's message to Secretary Root and the latter's order to implement this change, see Hunt, *The Department of State of the United States*, pp. 240–42.

39. Following seven years of diplomatic experience, to supervise the Consular Bureau, in 1906 Huntington Wilson was appoint Third Assistant Secretary of State, and, although he was nominated to become Minister Plenipotentiary to Argentina, he was promoted to First Assistant Secretary in March 1909.

40. Shortly before he became Secretary of State, in January 1909 Knox, then a Senator from Pennsylvania, proposed an amendment to the State Department Appropriations Act, in which he recommended that an Under Secretary of State and a Fourth Assistant Secretary be added to the senior staff of the Department. Even though approved by the Foreign Relations Committee and by the Senate, it was rejected by the House of Representatives.

41. To summarize, in addition to the Senior staff, these were the four Geographic and Information Divisions and in addition to the Diplomatic and Consular Bureaus, the Bureaus of Appointments, Citizenship, Indexes and Archives, Law, Rolls and Library, and Trade Relations. Other functions were the responsibility of the Resident Diplomatic Officer, the Director of the Consular Service, the Counselor, the Solicitor, the Translator, and the Telegrapher.

42. Hunt, *The Department of State of the United States*, pp. 245–47, summarizes the structure of the Department as provided in appropriations acts preceding World War I as consisting of the Secretary and First Assistant Secretary as chief officers; ''adminis-

trative officers'' as including the Second and Third Assistant Secretaries, Director of the Consular Service, and the Chief Clerk; the ''Advisory Officers''—the Counselor, Solicitor, and Foreign Trade Advisers; and ''other administrative officers''—Chiefs of the Geographic and Information Divisions, the Diplomatic, Consular, and other Bureaus; and other agencies and individuals, such as assistant chiefs and classified clerks.

Hunt adds that in 1913 other modifications were made in congressional appropriations legislation, which abandoned this classification and ranked individuals on the basis of their salaries and importance, led by the Secretary, the Counselor, the Solicitor, the three Assistant Secretaries, the Director of the Consular Service, the Chief Clerk, the Foreign Trade Advisers, the division heads, bureau chiefs, and others.

43. Calculations vary in counting messengers, laborers, and a few other types of workers. For additional commentary on the State Department staff size, see Stuart, *The Department of State*, pp. 124, 155, 173, 184, 201, 212, 219, and Trask, *A Short History of the U.S. Department of State, 1781–1981*, pp. 21, 42.

44. Salaries of Assistant Secretaries were fixed at $3,500 annually in 1873 and subsequently varied with the individual up to $8,000. As of 1909 the Counselor and Resident Diplomatic Officer received $7,500, the Chiefs of the Geographic Divisions $3,000 to $4,500, clerks $900 to $1,800, messengers $720 to $840, and laborers $600 a year or $1.50 per day.

45. For more detail on budgets and salaries, see Stuart, *The Department of State*, pp. 145, 155, 191–92, 201, 212, 213, and 219, and Trask, *A Short History of the U.S. Department of State*, pp. 12, 21, 37.

46. Initially, these volumes were titled *Papers Relating to Foreign Affairs*, which, in 1870, was changed to *Papers Relating to the Foreign Relations of the United States*, and in 1932 to *Foreign Relations of the United States: Diplomatic Papers*. Following World War II the subtitle was dropped, so that currently the series is simply known as *Foreign Relations of the United States* (FRUS).

47. For a comprehensive description of the *Foreign Relations* series, see Chapter 7, section on ''*Foreign Relations of the United States* Series.'' For additional information, see Hunt, *The Department of State of the United States*, pp. 220–21; Stuart, *The Department of State*, pp. 217, 243, 260, 296; and Plischke, *Contemporary U.S. Foreign Policy*, pp. 1–20, especially pp. 16–20. For a general listing of Department of State publications, see Plischke, *U.S. Foreign Relations: A Guide to Information Sources*, pp. 549–68.

48. The Pendleton Act of 1883 provided for selection and appointment of Federal employees based on open competitive examinations, guarantees to executive employees against solicitation for funds for partisan purposes, against coercion by political leaders and parties, and against allocation of appointments to the States and other territories based on proportional representation—to be administered by the Civil Service Commission. The President was given authority to determine, by executive order, the classification of positions subject to Commission jurisdiction. From time to time Congress enacted additional legislation to modify and improve the system, such as the Lloyd–LaFolette Act of 1912, the Civil Service Retirement Act of 1920, the Hatch Act of 1939, and others. Also see note 86.

49. For additional information on the spoils and merit systems, as applied to the Diplomatic and Consular Services, see the section on ''Spoils and Tentative Launching of the Merit Principle in the State Department.''

50. The two-story brick Treasury Building located on Pennsylvania Avenue east of the White House was razed to make room for a new Treasury Building.

51. When completed this new building provided ten acres of floor space and somewhat less than two miles of corridors twelve feet wide. For additional information on the nature and construction of the State, War, and Navy Building, with photographic depictions, see Gerber, *The Department of State of the United States*, pp. 5–6; Plischke, *Conduct of American Diplomacy* (3d ed., 1967), pp. 167–68; Spaulding and Blue, *The Department of State of the United States*, pp. 49–50; Trask, *A Short History of the U.S. Department of State*, pp. 18–19; and especially Hunt, *The Department of State of the United States*, pp. 429–37.

52. Responding to the request of Phelps, Secretary Bayard observed that the question of sending and receiving Ambassadors, under the existing authorization of the Constitution and existing statutes, had been given consideration, ''but I cannot find that at any time the benefits attending a higher grade of ceremonial treatment have been deemed to outweigh the inconveniences which, in our simple social democracy, might attend the reception in this country of an extraordinary foreign privileged class.''

53. Foster, *The Practice of Diplomacy*, pp. 21–26. Foster also discusses several specific experiences and problems concerning the application of diplomatic ranking experienced by the United States. Also see Moore, *The Principles of American Diplomacy*, pp. 434–37, Stuart, *American Diplomatic and Consular Practice*, pp. 136–38, and Williams, *American Diplomacy*, pp. 457–58.

54. 27 Stat. 497.

55. Foster maintained that if the significance of this stipulation had then been realized, ''it is extremely doubtful that it would have secured the approval of Congress.'' *The Practice of Diplomacy*, p. 23.

56. In eight of these eleven cases the existing resident American diplomat was promoted to the ambassadorial rank. Only in the case of Great Britain, Italy, and Japan were they new appointees.

57. Diplomatic relations with Texas had ceased when it was annexed in 1845, and those with the Two Sicilies had ended in 1860.

58. American emissaries to Austria were accredited to Austria-Hungary from 1875 to 1913, those to Germany were accredited to Prussia till 1871, those to the Holy See were accredited as ''Ministers Resident at Rome,'' 1858–67, and those to Norway were simultaneously accredited to Sweden, from 1814 to 1905, and they resided in Stockholm.

59. Envoys to Thailand were accredited to Siam till 1940. Those to Iran were accredited to Persia until 1933. Hoffman Phillip was accredited to Abyssinia, 1908–10, but subsequent emissaries, beginning in 1927, were commissioned to Ethiopia.

60. These included Austria and Russia (twenty-eight each), Spain (twenty-three), Bolivia and Venezuela (twenty-two each), Honduras (twenty-one), and Columbia, Liberia, and Portugal (twenty each). Of these 204 nominees, some 35 did not serve for various reasons, including ten appointments to Austria, seven of which were rejected or tabled by the Senate during the Lincoln and Johnson Administrations.

61. These included Russia (twenty-three), Spain (twenty), Bolivia, Portugal, and Venezuela (nineteen each), Colombia (eighteen), Austria, Germany, and Mexico (seventeen each), Argentina, Belgium, Egypt, Guatemala, Switzerland, Turkey, and Liberia (sixteen each), and Brazil, Chile, Greece, Honduras, and Nicaragua (fifteen each).

62. The thirty-nine nominees who were not approved by the Senate are listed by the Department of State as being tabled, rejected, or ''not confirmed by the Senate.'' The

forty-two appointees categorized as not serving for other reasons are listed as having their nominations withdrawn from the Senate by the President, as failing to proceed to the posts to which they were assigned or to present their credentials, or simply as "did not serve."

63. Of these, fifteen remained at their posts for at least six years, fourteen for at least seven years, sixteen for at least eight years, and five for at least nine years.

64. Illustrating this change, in 1861 the President accredited only twelve of thirty-three emissaries (thirty-six percent) as Envoys Extraordinary and Ministers Plenipotentiary, together with eighteen (55 percent) as Ministers Resident, and three as Commissioners. In 1913, by comparison, thirty-six of forty-eight (75 percent) bore the rank of Envoy Extraordinary and Minister Plenipotentiary, whereas ten were Ambassadors (21 percent), and only one was denominated as a Minister Resident/Consul General (Liberia) and one as Diplomatic Agent (Egypt).

65. To indicate the commonality of the Minister Plenipotentiary rank, all emissaries to such countries as Chile, China, Peru, and Spain, as well as other countries with which diplomatic representation was initially established in the early twentieth century, including Cuba, Luxemburg, Norway, and Panama, were at this rank.

66. One-third of these were appointed in the dual capacity of Minister Resident and Consul General, in such countries as Denmark, Persia, Portugal, Switzerland, Thailand, and Yugoslavia.

67. Only eighteen appointees were at the rank of Chargé d'Affaires, often of an interim nature, whereas twenty-two were designated as Diplomatic Agents (five to Bulgaria from 1901 to 1910 and seventeen to Egypt who were accredited jointly as Agents and Consuls General, which continued until 1922). The remaining appointees were accredited as Commissioners serving as initial envoys to Haiti, Hawaii, and Liberia.

68. Generally, the envoys to Balkan countries resided at Athens (1883–1902), as did those accredited to Montenegro (1905–20), and for a time those accredited to Bulgaria resided at Constantinople (1901–3), and those sent to Romania, Serbia, and Bulgaria resided at Bucharest (1907–13).

69. Seven envoys to the Netherlands, resident at The Hague, were also accredited to Luxembourg from 1903 to 1922.

70. Prior to 1905 American emissaries were accredited to Sweden and Norway, who resided at Stockholm; from 1905 to 1906 Charles H. Graves was accredited individually to the two countries; and beginning in August 1906 the Department of State maintained separate representation to Norway, resident at Oslo.

71. In addition to the five Central American Republics, these embraced Argentina and Uruguay (three envoys, resident at Buenos Aires, 1866–70), Haiti and Santo Domingo (five envoys, 1883–1909), and Paraguay and Uruguay (eight envoys, 1882–1914). During the period from 1873 to 1909 some fourteen envoys held simultaneous appointments to the Central American Republics in various combinations, such as Costa Rica, El Salvador, and Nicaragua; El Salvador and Honduras; and Guatemala and Honduras. Five of them, however, were accredited to the "Central American States," 1873–91.

72. James R. Partridge's appointments ran from 1862 to 1883, William Rockhill's from 1884 to 1913, and John Brinkerhoff Jackson's from 1902 to 1913. Rockhill's career combined appointments as Third and First Assistant Secretaries of State as well as diplomatic service abroad.

73. Phillips' diplomatic service began during this period, spanned more than three

decades, and eventually resulted in induction into the Career Foreign Service of the United States.

74. Such Secretaries were provided for four "first-class" Legations (Berlin, London, Paris, and St. Petersburg), seven "second-class" missions (Madrid, Mexico City, Peking, Rio de Janeiro, Rome, Tokyo, and Vienna), and the Legation at Constantinople, where the Consul General served ex officio in this capacity. See Barnes and Morgan, *The Foreign Service of the United States*, pp. 129–31.

75. Some of these Secretaries of Legation were provided for such additional countries as Argentina, Chile, Colombia, Guatemala, Korea, Peru, Turkey, and Venezuela. In time the staff hierarchy of Embassies and Legations consisted of first, second, and third Secretaries, the First Secretary being regarded as "The Secretary." The Office of Diplomatic Secretary, viewed under international law and practice as a diplomatic representative, was empowered to assume the duties ad interim of the Chief of Mission. For additional comment, see Foster, *The Practice of Diplomacy*, pp. 205–8.

76. Stuart, *American Diplomatic and Consular Practice*, p. 266.

77. For additional commentary on the recall and rejection of American diplomats, including the Keiley case, see Barnes and Morgan, *The Foreign Service of the United States*, pp. 141–42; Foster, *The Practice of Diplomacy*, pp. 40–45, 180–83; Moore, *A Digest of International Law*, vol. 4, pp. 473, 480–84, 535–36; Plischke, *Conduct of American Diplomacy*, pp. 293–95; and Stuart, *American Diplomatic and Consular Practice*, pp. 142–43, 264–66.

For information on the American requests for the recall of foreign representatives from the United States, including the Lord Sackville-West case in 1888 involving his alleged intervention in a presidential election, see Foster, *The Practice of Diplomacy*, pp. 187–89; Moore, *A Digest of International Law*, vol. 4, pp. 536–48; Plischke, *Conduct of American Diplomacy*, pp. 303, 313–14; and Stuart, *American Diplomatic and Consular Practice*, pp. 196, 268–70.

78. U.S. diplomatic relations with Korea had been suspended when Japan assumed direction of its foreign relations in November 1905, and they were not revived until after World War II. Although Hoffman Philip served as Minister Resident/Consul General in Ethiopia (1909–10), no successor was appointed to that country until 1927. Diplomatic relations with the Holy See were suspended in August 1867 until the time of World War II, and they were terminated with Hawaii when it was annexed in August 1898.

79. Hong Kong and Honolulu were placed in Class 1, which received annual salaries of $4,000, and such locations as Batavia, Ceylon, Milan, Tahiti, Venice, and Zanzibar were listed in Class 7, which were paid $1,000.

80. Although a decade earlier, by the Act of June 20, 1864, the President had been authorized to appoint, on the basis of examination, thirteen consular clerks who were to have permanent tenure during good behavior and to be paid $1,000 per annum, no appropriations for their hire were provided prior to the Act of 1874.

Congress increased allowances for additional clerks as well as their stipends from time to time. In 1872 this was included in a general fund for clerkships. The number of clerks was raised to fifty in 1881 and to eighty-four in 1896. Moreover, the plan to establish consular pupils, provided for in the Act of 1856, the number of whom was reduced from twenty-five to thirteen in 1864, who were to be recruited on the basis of an examination with the expectation that they could be promoted to higher consular positions, was far from successful. Of the sixty-four consular clerks appointed from 1864 to 1896, only eight were promoted to consulships. See Barnes and Morgan, *The Foreign Service of the United States*, pp. 122–23.

81. For example, the $3,000 annual salary applied to Havana and Liverpool; $2,000 to London, Paris, and Shanghai; and $1,500 to Belfast, Berlin, Dresden, Naples, Vienna, and the rest.

82. Consuls General were grouped as follows: Class 1 (two Consulates General), Class 2 (six), Class 3 (eight), Class 4 (eleven), Class 5 (seventeen), Class 6 (nine), and Class 7 (three). The salary levels for Consuls General were fixed at $3,000, for example, for Athens and Copenhagen (Class 7); at $4,500 for Buenos Aires, Rome, and Singapore (Class 5); at $8,000 for Berlin, Hong Kong, and Rio de Janeiro (Class 2); and the highest for London and Paris at $12,000 (Class 1).

83. Thus, the salary levels for Consuls ranged from $2,000 for such places as Cartagena, Saigon, Stavanger, and Tuxpam, to Class 2 at $6,000 for Manchester, and to Class 1 at $8,000 for Liverpool.

84. According to the Department of State, the number of Consulates General increased each decade from eight in 1860 to sixty-three by 1910, Consulates grew from 226 in 1860 to 269 by 1870, and dropped to 241 by 1910, and Commercial Agencies grew from twenty-four in 1860 to fifty-one by 1880, thereafter declined to twenty-three by 1900, and were subsequently disestablished. In addition, lesser establishments called vice consulates, which dated back to the eighteenth century, were dropped from the consular roster for several decades, were revived in the mid-nineteenth century, but were used only sparingly.

85. For information on consular intelligence-gathering activities in Europe during the Civil War and some illustrations of the quality of consular officers, see Barnes and Morgan, *The Foreign Service of the United States*, pp. 116–17 and 157–58. For more comprehensive discussion of consular duties at of the end of this period, see Foster, *The Practice of Diplomacy*, pp. 222–36; Schuyler, *American Diplomacy*, Chapter 2; and Stuart, *American Diplomatic and Consular Practice*, Chapter 18.

86. The tortuous road to adoption of the merit system took several decades. Congress attempted to deal with the matter, beginning in 1853, when legislation was introduced to require candidates for certain Federal positions to be selected by examination, but it was foredoomed to failure. Two decades later, Congress passed a bill, in 1871, directing the President to take remedial action, and that same year President Grant appointed the Civil Service Commission to draft a code for Federal hiring procedures, but Congress withdrew its financial support in 1873, before the Commission completed its program.

Not until 1883 did Congress adopt the Pendleton Act (22 Stat. 403), creating the foundation of the American Civil Service system. It provided for open, competitive examinations, for a three-member bipartisan Civil Service Commission empowered to frame rules and regulations to administer the program, and for guarantees to employees against solicitation for funds or help for and against coercion by political parties. Subsequently, its application was extended and eventually covered a substantial majority of such appointments. From time to time Congress enacted supplementary legislation to expand and improve the system. These included the Lloyd–LaFollette Act (1912), the Civil Service Retirement Act (1920), the Hatch Act (1939), the Veterans' Preference Act (1944), and others. Also see n.48.

87. See Barnes and Morgan, *The Foreign Service of the United States*, pp. 148–50. Stuart, *American Diplomatic and Consular Practice*, pp. 90–91, notes that it was much later that President Cleveland came to be regarded as the progenitor of consular reform.

88. This Executive Order No. 469 of June 27, 1906, stipulated that appointment to consular Classes 8 and 9 under the Act of April 1906 be filled either by promotion of Vice Consuls, Deputy Consuls, and Consular Agents who had been appointed by virtue of examination or by new appointees who passed a qualifying examination; that vacancies in Classes above 8 and 9 be filled by promotion based on performance and conduct; that the Board of Examiners, including a representative of the Civil Service Commission, handle the examinations and that these examinations cover a specified, but broad, spectrum of subjects, including international, commercial, and maritime law.

89. Among other matters, this Executive Order of November 1909 prescribed in detail the subjects to be covered by examinations, the scale for weighing written, oral, and physical examinations, age, character, and habits, other requisite qualifications of candidates, and the maintenance of an eligibility list for appointment purposes.

90. For additional analysis and commentary on diplomatic relations and transition to the merit system, see Barnes and Morgan, *The Foreign Service of the United States*, Chapter 16 and pp. 124–26, 148–49, 150–51, 163–68; Blancké, *The Foreign Service of the United States*, pp. 15–17; Childs, *American Foreign Service*, pp. 5–10; Foster, *The Practice of Diplomacy*, pp. 239–42; Ilchman, *Professional Diplomacy in the United States*, Chapters 2–3; Plischke, *Conduct of American Diplomacy*, pp. 229–31; Schulzinger, *The Making of the Diplomatic Mind*, pp. 40–46 (which emphasizes training); Schuyler, *American Diplomacy*, Chapter 3; Stuart, *American Diplomatic and Consular Practice*, pp. 90–94; Werking, *The Master Architects: Building the United States Foreign Service, 1890–1913*; and West, *The Department of State on the Eve of the First World War*, pp. 21–23.

91. Malloy, *Treaties, Conventions, International Acts, Protocols and Agreements between the United States and Other Powers*, vol. 1 (1910), p. 430.

92. See, respectively, Williams, *American Diplomacy*, pp. 422–23; Wriston, *Executive Agents in American Foreign Relations*, Chapter 4; and Stuart, *American Diplomatic and Consular Practice*, p. 138.

93. For additional commentary and consideration of these and other special missions and envoys, see Foster, *The Practice of Diplomacy*, pp. 195–201; Moore, *A Digest of International Law*, vol. 4, pp. 452–57; Plischke, *Conduct of American Diplomacy*, pp. 48–49, 92–94; Stuart, *American Diplomatic and Consular Practice*, pp. 138, 201–3; Williams, *American Diplomacy*, pp. 422–24; Wriston, *Executive Agents in American Foreign Relations*, Chapter 4.

94. For additional commentary, see Barnes and Morgan, *The Foreign Service of the United States*, pp. 154, 174–77, 221–22, 337; Stuart, *American Diplomatic and Consular Practice*, p. 47, and *The Department of State*, p. 289.

95. Barnes and Morgan, *The Foreign Service of the United States*, pp. 141, 146, 178–79, 181; Boyce and Boyce, *American Foreign Service Authors: A Bibliography*, pp. 80–81; and Stuart, *American Diplomatic and Consular Practice*, p. 221.

96. These memoirs were produced by such diplomats as Charles Francis Adams, Caleb Cushing, Maurice F. Egan, Benjamin Moran, William Phillips, Carl Schurz, Oscar S. Straus, Bayard Taylor, Elihu B. Washburne, Andrew Dickson White, Henry Lane Wilson, and Huntington Wilson; consular officers included Henry Boernstein, Lucius Fairchild, G. Henry Horstmann, George Horton, William Dean Howells, Charles Edwards Lester, Luigi Monti, John Singleton Mosby, and William James Stillman.

97. For additional information on the writings of diplomatic and consular officers, see Boyce and Boyce, *American Foreign Service Authors: A Bibliography*, and Plischke,

United States Diplomats and Their Missions, Chapter 7, and "American Diplomats as Authors," *Society for Historians of American Foreign Relations NEWS-LETTER* 15 (December 1984): pp. 1–20.

98. These additions included the Congo territory, Cuba, Dominican Republic, Ethiopia, Italy, Korea, Liberia, Luxemburg, North German Confederation, Norway, Orange Free State, Panama, Romania, Samoa, San Marino, Tonga, United Arab Republic, Uruguay, Yugoslavia, and Zambia.

99. Whereas the use of executive agreements dates back to 1826, during the seven decades from 1789 to 1861 the United States concluded thirty-four such agreements (approximately one-fourth of its treaties and agreements). During this half century, 1861–1913, however, the ratio of executive agreements increased to more than one-third.

100. Others included the Netherlands (with seven of eight treaties and agreements), Japan (with eight of fourteen), Haiti (with eight of eleven), Cuba (with six of nine), Russia (with five of nine), Spain (with sixteen of thirty), and Belgium (with six of twelve), signed in Washington.

101. One of these, a series of exchanges of notes on naval warfare with Spain in 1898, bridged the incumbencies of two Secretaries of State, signed in part by Secretary Sherman and subsequently by Secretary Day.

102. Earlier, in 1891, in establishing commercial relations with Cuba and Puerto Rico, President Benjamin Harrison also became indirectly involved in treaty making. He issued a proclamation that was embodied in an executive agreement consisting of an exchange of notes with Spain, which were signed by Secretary Blaine.

103. The other delegation members were Robert C. Schenck (newly appointed Minister Plenipotentiary to Great Britain), Samuel Nelson (Justice of the Supreme Court), Ebenezer R. Hoar (Attorney General in President Grant's Administration), and George H. Williams (Senator from Oregon).

104. Secretary Knox was accompanied by Chandler P. Anderson, who was special Counselor to Secretary Root and became Counselor of the Department of State in 1912.

105. These Assistant Secretaries signed the following treaties and agreements: Adee (exchange of notes with Spain, involving both Secretary Hay and Assistant Secretary Adee, 1895), France (1902), Great Britain (1905), and Mexico (1905); Bacon with Denmark (1907) and Great Britain (1908); Davis with Spain and Switzerland (both in 1883); Wharton with Great Britain (1891) and Italy (exchange of notes, 1892); and Huntington Wilson with Portugal (exchange of notes, 1910).

106. Examples of such consular officers were Frederick M. Cheney (Zanzibar, 1833), N. D. Comanos (Cairo, United Arab Republic, 1884), John Goodnow (China, 1903), J. H. Hood (Thailand, 1867), W. W. Robinson (Madagascar, 1881), and Benjamin F. Whitten (Haiti, 1885), as well as Samuel R. Gummere (Germany, respecting Tangier, 1901; Great Britain, respecting Morocco, 1895; and Italy, respecting trademarks in China, 1903). In 1907, as a special agent accredited as an American Minister, Gummere also signed an agreement with Great Britain concerning the protection of patents in Morocco. In addition, Major John P. Finkelmeier, an American commercial agent, signed a Commerce Treaty with Madagascar in 1867.

107. Thus, Rockhill, Minister Plenipotentiary to China, signed a series of agreements with other foreign emissaries stationed in Peking that concerned the protection of trademarks in China. Bancroft, Minister Plenipotentiary to Prussia, signed a variety of treaties and agreements with German States and later the German Empire. Reid signed the Peace Treaty with Spain in 1898 and five treaties and agreements with Great Britain. Gummere

signed agreements with Italy, Germany, and Great Britain concerning relations with China, Morocco, and Tangier. Sanford, Minister Resident in Belgium, signed four treaties and agreements with that country. Schuyler, Chargé d'Affairs in Yugoslavia, signed three commercial and consular treaties with Romania and Yugoslavia in 1881.

At least fifteen others signed multiple treaties and agreements abroad, such as George H. Boker (Minister Resident in the Ottoman Empire), William I. Buchanan (High Commissioner and special agent in Venezuela), Powell Clayton (Ambassador in Mexico), John Jay II (Minister Plenipotentiary in Austria), Elliott Northcott (Minister Plenipotentiary in Nicaragua), and Caleb Cushing, John W. Foster, and Bellamy Storer (Ministers Plenipotentiary in Spain).

108. These special envoys who concluded such Treaties of Amity and Commerce included George H. Bates (Tonga, 1886), General Tasker H. Bliss (Cuba, 1902), Willard E. Edcomb (Orange Free State, 1871), Commodore R. W. Shufeldt (Korea, 1882), and Robert R. Skinner, who signed such a Treaty with King Mendik II of Ethiopia (1903).

109. General George W. Davis, American Governor of the Panama Canal Zone, signed a boundary agreement in 1904, and William I. Buchanan, as American High Commissioner, signed a claims agreement with Venezuela in 1909.

110. Such initial, general Treaties of Amity and Commerce were concluded with Bolivia, the Congo, Cuba, Dominican Republic, Haiti, Korea, Liberia, Madagascar, Orange Free State, Ottoman Empire, Thailand, Tonga, United Arab Republic, and Yugoslavia. The rest were superseding or revisory treaties. In some cases they were paralleled or supplemented with separate treaties and agreements to provide for commercial reciprocity or consular relations.

111. It has been said that the exceptions specified in these Root Arbitration Treaties exempted virtually all significant international disputes and that, in any case, the special *compromis* would still have to surmount the hurdle of Senate treaty approval. For additional information, see World Peace Foundation Pamphlets, *Arbitration and the United States*, vol. 9 (Boston: World Peace Foundation, 1926). A list of Arbitration Treaties is given on pp. 587–61.

112. These twenty-four naturalization treaties were concluded with twenty-one countries and German States—Austria-Hungary, Belgium, Brazil, Costa Rica, Denmark, Ecuador, El Salvador, Great Britain, Haiti, Honduras, Mexico, Nicaragua, Peru, Portugal, Sweden and Norway, Uruguay, and the German States of Baden, Bavaria, Hesse, the North German Confederation (the only treaty signed with it), and Wuerttemberg.

113. These "arrangements" provided for the creation of the International Office of Public Hygiene (Paris, 1908) and a Treaty for the Repression of the Circulation of Obscene Publications (Paris, 1910).

114. These executive agreements included, for example, six Postal Conventions, four inter-American conference resolutions creating and organizing the Pan-American Union (1890, 1902, 1906, and 1910), the Protocol to settle the Boxer revolt in China (1900), and two agreements to establish the Whangpoo Conservancy in that country (1905 and 1912).

115. These exchanges of notes laid down regulations for the maintenance of Samoa as a neutral territory (1880) and the Declaration providing for the Open Door in commercial relations with China (1899).

116. Subsequently, many multilateral and bilateral postal conventions were negotiated and ratified by this procedure. In 1970 the statute simply specified that the Postal Service "with the consent of the President, may negotiate and conclude postal treaties and con-

ventions . . . between the United States and other countries.'' Public Law 91–375, dated August 12, 1970; 84 *Stat.*, 724; 39 *U.S. Code* 407.

117. Table 5.6 for a list of subjects.

118. Of the eighty-seven multilateral treaties and agreements more than thirty created, amended, and amplified multilateral international organizations and other agencies for the administration of a variety of international programs.

119. Secretary Hay signed two Samoan treaties (1899) and a package of protocols concerning claims against Venezuela (1903). The remaining five signed in Washington, though not by the Secretary of State, included the resolution of 1890 creating the Pan-American Union, the Postal Convention of 1897, the Inter-American Sanitary Convention (1905), the Inter-American Convention on the Protection of Industrial Property (1911), and the quadripartite convention to preserve the Bering Sea fur seals (1911).

120. As indicated in Table 5.6, the preponderant number of treaties and agreements concluded abroad were signed in European capitals, fourteen were signed in Latin America, ten in Asian and Pacific cities, and the remainder in other locations.

121. These included three Ambassadors, thirty-one Ministers Plenipotentiary, three Ministers Resident, one Chargé d'Affaires, two Consuls General, and three Consuls.

122. Signers of public health and sanitation conventions usually held medical-administrative positions. Thus, the signers of the Sanitary Convention of 1903 were Frank Anderson (Medical Inspector of the Navy) and H. G. Giddings (Assistant Surgeon General), and those who signed the Inter-American Sanitary Convention of 1905 were the Surgeon General, the Assistant Surgeon General, and four other doctors.

123. This same procedure of approval by the diplomatic corps was employed for a supplementary agreement on the Whangpoo Conservancy in 1915.

124. The Declaration of London, which codified maritime policy and practice, superseded the Declaration of Paris (1856) and benefited the neutral interests of the United States and other small maritime powers. The Senate opposed ratification, and the British House of Lords failed to approve it, so that the President did not ratify it, and it was not in effect at the time of World War I.

125. The Treaty of Washington laid down the international law precepts to be applied by the Tribunal to a "neutral" power in time of hostilities and specified that if it failed to reach agreement on the amount of the award, a three-member Board of Assessors was to be appointed, consisting of individuals named by the United States, Great Britain, and the Italian diplomat stationed in Washington to fix the amount of compensation.

This Treaty of Washington also provided for three additional arbitrations. It designated the German Emperor as the arbitrator of the long-standing San Juan Islands maritime boundary dispute. These islands are located in the Georgia Strait between the State of Washington and Vancouver Island. In October 1872 the German Emperor's award upheld the American contention that the islands were within American jurisdiction. A mixed commission was provided for the adjudication and payment of all other existing claims of American citizens and British subjects. Consisting of three individuals, this commission met in Washington, 1871–73 and awarded the British Government nearly $2 million in damages. Another mixed commission, to meet at Halifax, Nova Scotia, was created to determine the amount to be awarded to Great Britain for American inshore fishing rights in British North American waters. It awarded the British Government $5,500,000 in 1877.

126. Of the fifteen arbitrations handled under the Hague Tribunal system to the time of World War I, the United States was a party to only three others—Venezuelan pref-

erential claims (1904), the North Atlantic fisheries controversy with Great Britain (1910), and the Orinoco Steamship Company claims dispute with Venezuela (1910). For the text of these cases and awards, see George Grafton Wilson, *The Hague Arbitration Cases* (Boston: Ginn, 1915).

127. International conferencing dates back to ancient times but accelerated considerably in the second half of the nineteenth and the twentieth centuries. The term "conference" is used both generically and technically. Some were called "congresses" in the eighteenth, nineteenth, and early twentieth centuries, such as that held in Panama in 1826 (for which U.S. delegates arrived too late to participate) and those convened at Vienna (1814–15), Aix-la-Chapelle (1818), Paris (1856), Berlin (1878 and 1884–1885), and Algeciras (1906). The term "congress" was reserved for those that were deemed to be more important, formal, and august. But this distinction has disappeared since World War I, except for the semipublic gathering or for the technical or administrative conference concerned with scientific, legal, or sometimes other nonpolitical matters, particularly in inter-American affairs. Also, in time, the differentiation between a "conference" and a "meeting" has come to be founded primarily on the number of participants, and the latter is normally applied to those that are bilateral and less formal.

128. In his study entitled *The Public International Conference*, Hill, for example, grouped his analysis in five categories—peacemaking, peacetime, League of Nations, other permanent organizations, and semipublic conferences. Currently, one would need to add United Nations conferences, as well as those of the inter-American system, the European Union, and other regional organizations. On the other hand, some analyses merely distinguish between the major or more important and other international conferences.

129. These constitutive conferences established continuing or permanent international organizations and other agencies, such as the Hague Tribunal or the Permanent Court of Arbitration, the Universal Postal Union, the Pan-American Union (later the Organization of American States), and others.

Some analysts refer to the function of engaging in international organizations as "consensus diplomacy." Applied to conferencing and the creation of international organizations and subsequently to the operation of these agencies, this evokes both positive and negative reactions. Multilateralism, while useful for discussion and the achievement of agreement, may also produce risks or disadvantages if resulting determinations violate national preferences and vital interests. This applies particularly to those agencies that deal with political and territorial, as distinct from technical, issues.

130. The following, given chronologically, are illustrative of the more important international conferences attended by the United States prior to World War I (not including peace conferences and those that created international organizations and other agencies):

Red Cross (Geneva, 1864; The Hague, 1904; and Geneva (1906)

Samoa (Apia, 1879, followed by conferences in 1880, 1889, and 1899)

Public Health and Sanitation (Washington, 1881; Paris, 1903; Rome, 1907; and Paris, 1912)

Prime Meridian (Washington, 1884)

Africa, governance of the Congo (Berlin, 1884–85)

Maritime (Washington, 1889)

Inter-American (Washington, 1889–90, followed by conferences in 1901–2, 1906, and 1910)

Peace, Arbitration, and Laws of War and Neutrality (The Hague, 1899 and 1907)

Slave Trade (Brussels, 1890)

Boxer Rebellion (Peking, 1900)

White Slavery (Paris, 1904)

Morocco, jurisdiction in (Algeciras, 1906)

Fisheries (Washington, 1908)

Naval—Freedom of the Seas, Declaration of London (London, 1908–9)

Economic (London, 1909)

Opium Control (Shanghai, 1909; and The Hague, 1911–12)

Assistance and Salvage at Sea (Brussels, 1910)

Fur Seals, North Pacific (Washington, 1911)

131. Aside from integration and the establishment of the Pan-American Union, the inter-American conferences were concerned with copyright, the exchange of official documents, pacific settlement of disputes, public health and sanitation, patents and trademarks, and other matters.

132. In addition, several organizations created during this period were later joined by the United States, such as the International Institute of Statistics, established in 1885 but not joined until 1924, and the Central Bureau of the Map of the World on the Millionth Scale, established in 1891 and joined by the United States in 1926.

133. For additional commentary on international conferencing, see Simeon E. Baldwin, ''The International Congresses and Conferences of the Last Century as Forces Working Toward Solidarity of the World,'' *American Journal of International Law* 1 (1907): 808–29; Dunn, *The Practice and Procedure of International Conferences*; Hankey, *Diplomacy by Conference*; Hill, *The Public International Conference*; Kaufmann, *Conference Diplomacy*; Pastuhov, *A Guide to the Practice of International Conferences*; Plischke, *Conduct of American Diplomacy*, pp. 469–523 and Appendix IV-A; and Satow, *A Guide to Diplomatic Practice* (1957, Chapters. 25–27).

6

United States Becomes a Superpower—Expansion, Reorganization, and Career Consolidation, 1914–1945

The years from 1913 to April 1945 proved to be a critical period of U.S. development and involvement in world affairs, which launched what has been called "the American Century" and the era of "the new diplomacy" and which affected the organization, management, and functioning of the Department of State and the conduct of diplomacy in many ways. By way of background, the American population grew by nearly 40 percent, including an estimated 10 million new immigrants (although this represented a declining rate of admissions). Agricultural and industrial production and foreign trade increased, and by the early 1920s the United States became both a leading economic power and the principal international creditor nation. As American trade expanded, the Department of State shifted from concluding conditional to unconditional most-favored-nation commercial treaties and agreements.

But the stock market crash of October 1929, followed by the Great Depression, affected foreign trade and resulted in increased tariffs (evidenced by the Smoot-Hawley Tariff Act of 1930) and eventually, in a series of new reciprocal trade agreements. The changing financial and economic status of the United States was reflected in the creation of the Federal Reserve system in 1913 and the dropping of the gold standard and launching of President Franklin D. Roosevelt's New Deal twenty years later. During World War II, however, the United States became the principal supplier of both the anti-Axis Allies and the redeemed former occupied powers. It also contributed to the development and expansion of the intercontinental air age and, with the invention of atomic energy, the nuclear age.

President Woodrow Wilson suffered a stroke in October 1919, which invalided him for months, President Warren G. Harding became ill as he returned from a trip to Alaska and died in San Francisco on August 2, 1923, and was succeeded by Vice President Calvin Coolidge, and, when Franklin Roosevelt died in office on April 12, 1945, early in his fourth term, he was succeeded by Vice President Harry S. Truman. At the Cabinet level, no new Departments were created, but the Department of Commerce and Labor was divided into two separate agencies in March 1913. The Department of State increased in size and modified and augmented its domestic structure and foreign representation, and Congress converted its personnel into a genuine professional Foreign Service of the United States.

Having previously acquired the Central American isthmian territory, the United States constructed the Panama Canal, bridging the Atlantic and Pacific Oceans, which began operating in 1914, facilitated transoceanic commerce, enhanced American naval power, and was ranked as one of the great engineering feats of the day. The only new territory acquired was the Virgin Islands, purchased from Denmark for $25 million in 1917 to supplement U.S. defense interests in the Caribbean.

In the foreign affairs arena, this country became involved in World Wars I and II and emerged from both a greater world power. In the meantime it left its traditional isolationist/noninvolvement policy in 1917 when it joined the Allied and Associated Powers in the war against the Central Powers, returned to isolationism following World War I, rejected involvement in the League of Nations, enacted four Neutrality Acts between 1935 and 1939, and, during and following World War II, emerged as the primary exponent of global cooperation in the United Nations system. It also increased substantially its participation in international conferencing and treaty and agreement making, not only bilateral but also multilateral, and it promoted consultation, negotiation, and agreement at the Presidential and Secretary of State levels, initiating the era of summit and ministerial diplomacy.

The United States modified its international recognition policy, undertook action to crystallize Western Hemisphere integration, and, led especially by Secretaries of State William Jennings Bryan and Frank B. Kellogg, assumed leadership in concluding advance commitments to resolve international disputes by peaceful means. Other major American policy propositions included President Wilson's Fourteen Points (1918), J. Reuben Clark's Memorandum on the Monroe Doctrine (1928), the Hoover-Stimson nonrecognition policy concerning the Far East (1932), major power naval arms limitation during the interwar period, and President Roosevelt's Four Freedoms, Atlantic Charter, and United Nations Declaration (1941 and 1942).

The Department of State encountered serious economic, political, and military difficulties, principally with Germany and Japan but also in Latin America. Among others, these included the preserving of China's territorial integrity and stabilizing territorial possessions in the Pacific in the early 1920s, China's civil war in 1927, and Japanese annexation of Manchuria in 1931. In the Western Hemisphere these problems involved a small "legation guard" intervention in Nicaragua (1912–33), intervention in Mexico and nonrecognition of its government (1913–17), intervention in, and military occupation of, Haiti (1915–34), and a short-term occupation of the Dominican Republic (1924). Most serious, however, were Germany's attack on American shipping during World War I and Japan's attack on Pearl Harbor, resulting in American participation in two World Wars.

During these three decades, as the United States converted into a major world power and then into a superpower and the primary nuclear power, the Department of State became a leading global foreign ministry. Led by several capable Secretaries and a good many assistants, the personnel was molded into a professional administrative, diplomatic, and consular service. As the Department broached the post–World War II era, it had changed from a modest agency to a leader in the conduct of worldwide foreign affairs.

PRESIDENTS AND THEIR SECRETARIES OF STATE

During this period the American Government was headed by five Presidents. Sequentially, these were Woodrow Wilson (Democrat, two terms, 1913–21), Warren G. Harding, Calvin Coolidge, and Herbert Hoover (Republicans, 1921–33), and Franklin D. Roosevelt (Democrat, 1933–April 12, 1945), who was succeeded by Vice President Harry S. Truman (Democrat). Wilson suffered a stroke late in September 1919, following the Paris Peace Conference and Senate rejection of the Versailles Treaty, and Presidents Harding and Roosevelt died in office, which brought Vice Presidents Coolidge and Truman into the presidency.

They appointed a succession of eight Secretaries of State, as indicated in Table 6.1. Secretaries William Jennings Bryan, Robert Lansing, and Bainbridge Colby served President Wilson; Charles Evans Hughes, Frank B. Kellogg, and Henry L. Stimson were Secretaries during the twelve years of the Harding, Coolidge, and Hoover Administrations; and Secretaries Cordell Hull and Edward R. Stettinius, Jr., held the position during the Roosevelt years and the early months of the Truman Administration.

When Wilson appointed Bryan, a staunch Democrat who helped turn the tide in nominating him for the presidency but who had little qualification for the office of Secretary of State by virtue of background, experience, or temperament, he did so with considerable trepidation. Two years later, when Bryan resigned, the President considered appointing his personal confidant, Colonel Edward M. House, who was in poor health, but he decided, rather, to promote Robert Lansing to the office. The son-in-law of former Secretary of State John W. Foster, Lansing had been Counselor of the State Department from April 1914 to June 1915. This was the first time that the second-ranking officer in the Department was directly advanced to the position of Secretary. Shortly thereafter, in order to guarantee continuity in the management of foreign affairs in the event that he was defeated in the presidential election of 1916, Wilson devised a novel scheme for immediately succeeding Lansing with the newly elected President prior to his inauguration the following January.[1]

Table 6.1

Department of State Principal Officers, 1913–1945

Name	Appointment	Entry on Duty	Termination of Appointment
Secretaries of State			
William Jennings Bryan	Mar. 5, 1913	Mar. 5, 1913	June 9, 1915
* Robert Lansing (Counselor)	June 9, 1915		June 23, 1915
Robert Lansing	June 23, 1915	June 24, 1915	Feb. 13, 1920
* Frank Lyon Polk (Under Secretary)	Feb. 14, 1920		Mar. 14, 1920
Bainbridge Colby	Mar. 22, 1920	Mar. 23, 1920	Mar. 4, 1921
Charles Evans Hughes	Mar. 4, 1921	Mar. 5, 1921	Mar. 4, 1925
Frank B. Kellogg	Feb. 16, 1925	Mar. 5, 1925	Mar. 28, 1929
Henry L. Stimson	Mar. 5, 1929	Mar. 28, 1929	Mar. 4, 1933
Cordell Hull	Mar. 4, 1933	Mar. 4, 1933	Nov. 30, 1944
Edward R. Stettinius, Jr.	Nov. 30, 1944	Dec. 1, 1944	June 27, 1945
* Joseph C. Grew *	June 28, 1945		July 3, 1945
Under Secretaries of State			
Frank Lyon Polk	June 26, 1919	July 1, 1919	June 15, 1920
Norman H. Davis	June 11, 1920	June 20, 1920	Mar. 7, 1921
Henry P. Fletcher *	Mar. 7, 1921	Mar. 8, 1921	Mar. 6, 1922
William Phillips *	Mar. 31, 1922	Apr. 26, 1922	Apr. 11, 1924
Joseph C. Grew *	Mar. 7, 1924	Apr. 16, 1924	June 30, 1927
Robert E. Olds *	May 19, 1927	July 1, 1927	June 30, 1928
J. Reuben Clark, Jr.	Aug. 17, 1928	Aug. 31, 1928	June 19, 1929
Joseph P. Cotton	June 7, 1929	June 30, 1929	Mar. 10, 1931
William R. Castle, Jr.	Apr. 1, 1931	Apr. 2, 1931	Mar. 5, 1933
William Phillips *	Mar. 3, 1933	Mar. 6, 1933	Aug. 23, 1936
Sumner Welles *	May 20, 1937	May 21, 1937	Sep. 30, 1943
Edward R. Stettinius, Jr.	Oct. 4, 1943	Oct. 4, 1943	Nov. 4, 1944
Joseph C. Grew *	Dec. 20, 1944	Dec. 20, 1944	Aug. 5, 1945
Assistant Secretaries of State 1913-1924			
First Assistant Secretaries			
John E. Osborne	Apr. 21, 1913	Apr. 21, 1913	Dec. 14, 1916
William Phillips *	Jan. 24, 1917	Jan. 25, 1917	Mar. 25, 1920
Fred Morris Dearing *	Mar. 11, 1921	Mar. 15, 1921	Feb. 28, 1922
Leland Harrison *	Mar. 31, 1922	Apr. 4, 1922	June 30, 1924
Second Assistant Secretary			
Alvey A. Adee	Aug. 3, 1886	Aug. 6, 1886	June 30, 1924
Third Assistant Secretaries			
Dudley Field Malone	Apr. 21, 1913	Apr. 22, 1913	Nov. 22, 1913
William Phillips *	Mar. 13, 1914	Mar. 17, 1914	Jan. 24, 1917
S.M. Breckinridge Long	Jan. 24, 1917	Jan. 29, 1917	June 8, 1920
Van Santvoord Merle-Smith	June 21, 1920	June 24, 1920	Mar. 4, 1921
Robert Woods Bliss *	Mar. 15, 1921	Mar. 16, 1921	May 3, 1923
J. Butler Wright *	Jan. 30, 1923	June 11, 1923	June 30, 1924
Assistant Secretaries of State, 1924-1944			
Leland Harrison *	(1)	July 1, 1924	Apr. 1, 1927
Alvey A. Adee	(1)	July 1, 1924	July 5, 1924
J. Butler Wright *	(1)	July 1, 1924	Apr. 17, 1927

Wilbur J. Carr	July 1, 1924	July 1, 1924	Mar. 6, 1933
John Van A. MacMurray *	Nov. 18, 1924	Nov. 19, 1924	May 19, 1925
Robert E. Olds	Oct. 1, 1925	Oct. 5, 1925	June 30, 1927
Francis White *	Feb. 26, 1927	Apr. 27, 1927	July 2, 1933
William R. Castle, Jr.	Feb. 26, 1927	Apr. 2, 1927	Dec. 13, 1929
Nelson T. Johnson *	Aug. 9, 1927	Aug. 15, 1927	Dec. 26, 1929
William R. Castle, Jr.	June 4, 1930	July 1, 1930	Apr. 1, 1931
James Grafton Rogers	Feb. 27, 1931	Mar. 10, 1931	Mar. 6, 1933
Harvey H. Bundy	June 10, 1931	July 13, 1931	Mar. 4, 1933
Wilbur J. Carr	Mar. 6, 1933	Mar. 7, 1933	July 28, 1937
Raymond C. Moley	Mar. 6, 1933	Mar. 7, 1933	Sept. 7, 1933
Sumner Welles *	Apr. 6, 1933	Apr. 6, 1933	Apr. 28, 1933
Harry F. Payer	June 13, 1933	June 19, 1933	Nov. 26, 1933
Jefferson Caffery *	July 11, 1933	July 12, 1933	Dec. 4, 1933
R. Walton Moore	Sep. 19, 1933	Sep. 19, 1933	May 20, 1937
Francis B. Sayre	Nov. 17, 1933	Nov. 27, 1933	Aug. 7, 1939
Sumner Welles *	Dec. 12, 1933	Dec. 15, 1933	May 20, 1937
George S. Messersmith *	July 9, 1937	July 26, 1937	Feb. 15, 1940
Hugh R. Wilson *	July 9, 1937	Aug. 23, 1937	Jan. 17, 1938
Adolf A. Berle, Jr.	Mar. 5, 1938	Mar. 7, 1938	Dec. 19, 1944
Henry F. Grady	Aug. 7, 1939	Aug. 8, 1939	Jan. 15, 1941
S. M. Breckinridge Long	Jan. 16, 1940	Jan. 23, 1940	Dec. 15, 1944
Dean G. Acheson	Jan. 31, 1941	Feb. 1, 1941	Aug. 15, 1945
G. Howland Shaw *	Feb. 21, 1941	Mar. 4, 1941	Dec. 14, 1944

Other Officers

Assistant Secretary for Administration

Julius C. Holmes *	Dec. 20, 1944	Jan. 29, 1945	Aug. 17, 1945

Assistant Secretary for American Republic Affairs

Nelson A. Rockefeller	Dec. 20, 1944	Dec. 20, 1944	Aug. 17, 1945

Assistant Secretary for European, Far Eastern, Near Eastern, and African Affairs

James C. Dunn *	Dec. 20, 1944	Dec. 20, 1944	Nov. 11, 1946

Assistant Secretary for Economic Affairs

William L. Clayton	Dec. 20, 1944	Dec. 20, 1944	Aug. 16, 1946

Assistant Secretary for Congressional Relations and International Conferences

Dean G. Acheson	Dec. 20, 1944	Dec. 20, 1944	Aug. 15, 1945

Assistant Secretary for Public and Cultural Affairs

Archibald MacLeish	Dec. 20, 1944	Dec. 20, 1944	Aug. 17, 1945

Counselor

John Bassett Moore	Apr. 21, 1913	Apr. 23, 1913	Mar. 4, 1914
Robert Lansing	Mar. 27, 1914	Apr. 1, 1914	June 23, 1915
Frank L. Polk	Aug. 30, 1915	Sep. 16, 1915	June 30, 1919
R. Walton Moore	May 20, 1937	May 21, 1937	Feb. 8, 1941

Legal Adviser

Green H. Hackworth	July 1, 1931	July 1, 1931	Mar. 1, 1946

*Before name indicates Secretary of State ad interim or Acting Secretary.

*After name indicates those officers who had or later achieved Foreign Service career status.

[1]Leland Harrison, Alvey A. Adee, and J. Butler Wright were not recommissioned but continued to serve under their previous appointments as numbered Secretaries of State.

Because Lansing, like Bryan, disagreed with the President on several matters of importance, and the President relied more heavily on Colonel Edward M. House in planning the League of Nations and negotiations at the World War I Paris Peace Conference, and because Wilson resented Lansing's convening of the Cabinet while he was ill during the fall and winter of 1919–20, he demanded Lansing's resignation. The President then considered appointing either Newton D. Baker, his Secretary of War, or financier Bernard Baruch. When Lansing resigned, Under Secretary of State Frank L. Polk (who was promoted from the rank of Counselor, in which he served for nearly four years) became Acting Secretary, and it was speculated that he would become the next Secretary. However, although he had not sought the appointment, Bainbridge Colby, whom the President admired and with whom he enjoyed a political and spiritual kinship and who had supported Wilson in the presidential election of 1916, was nominated, and, after a delay of a month, during which the Senate considered his acceptability, he was finally confirmed.[2]

When Harding was inaugurated in March 1921, he first considered selecting Colonel George Harvey as his Secretary, who had supported him in his election, but Harvey did not feel that he should be appointed. The President decided, rather, to appoint Charles Evans Hughes, who, although he was inexperienced in foreign relations, had a long record of public service and was regarded as acceptable to competing Republican factions. His appointment was widely applauded. When Harding died early in August 1923, and Coolidge succeeded him, he retained Hughes during the remainder of his first term, so that Hughes served as Secretary for a full four years as head of what he regarded as his "Department of Peace." He campaigned for Coolidge's reelection, but, although the President wished to have him remain as his Secretary, he had secretly informed the President that immediately after the election he wished to resign in order, after twenty years of public service and older than sixty years, to return to private pursuits. In 1925, therefore, Coolidge decided to appoint Frank B. Kellogg, then American Ambassador to Great Britain. He also served for a full four years, and, at President Hoover's request, he remained for several additional weeks, awaiting the return of his successor from the Far East.

President Hoover considered three possibilities for appointment as Secretary of State—William E. Borah (who chaired the Senate Foreign Relations Committee), career diplomat Henry P. Fletcher (then Ambassador to Italy), and Dwight W. Morrow (banker, whom Secretary Kellogg had considered for appointment as Under Secretary of State and who had become Ambassador to Mexico in 1927). The President offered the position to Borah, who declined, and Morrow was unavailable, so he then decided to offer the position of either Attorney General or Secretary of State to Colonel Henry L. Stimson, who preferred the latter. He was recommended for the position by both former Secretaries Root and Hughes and had previously been Secretary of War during the Taft Administration (1911–13) but was not immediately available because he was then serving as Governor of the Philippines. This explains why Secretary

Kellogg remained in office for several additional weeks. Stimson remained throughout the Hoover Presidency.

On the return of the Democratic Party to power, President Roosevelt considered six possibilities for the office—Newton D. Baker (former Secretary of War, 1916–21, and later member of the Permanent Court of International Justice); Robert W. Bigham (publisher of the Louisville *Courier Journal*); Cordell Hull, Key Pitman, and Joseph T. Robinson (longtime members of Congress then serving in the Senate); and Owen D. Young (financier who produced the Young Plan for dealing with international debt settlement). The President preferred Hull or Young, and prior to his inauguration, he offered the position to Hull, who accepted with the understanding that he would be responsible for more than merely handling diplomatic correspondence and that his authority would include foreign policy making, with the assistance of departmental officers subject to the President's direction and approval, to which Roosevelt acceded. Hull remained Secretary for nearly thirteen years—longer than any other in American history—when, because of illness, he felt obliged to resign.

Edward R. Stettinius, Jr., former head of the U.S. Steel Corporation and the War Resources Board and the Administrator of the Lend-Lease program, was made Under Secretary of State in 1943 and advanced to succeed Hull the following year. Although at the time he failed to meet the traditional requisites for the position of Under Secretary, especially prior departmental or diplomatic service at a high level, in view of his organizational and managerial experience, the President selected him for this appointment. Later, because of his experience in the Department at the highest level in association with Secretary Hull in planning and negotiating on matters of post–World War II relations and especially the creation of the United Nations, Roosevelt felt justified in promoting him to succeed Hull as Secretary.

The President had considered others following the election of 1944, including career diplomat Norman Armour, James F. Byrnes (who later became President Truman's Secretary of State), Sumner Welles (former Assistant and later Under Secretary of State and Ambassador to Cuba), and Henry Wallace (former Secretary of Agriculture and Vice President). Roosevelt opted for Stettinius, in part because he intended to be his own Secretary of State on many matters and believed he could rely on Stettinius to implement presidential policy without friction. When Roosevelt died, and Truman succeeded him, he retained Stettinius as Secretary for another two months to enable him to complete the negotiation of the United Nations Charter, which was signed at San Francisco on June 26, 1945. The following day he resigned, and a few days later the President nominated James F. Byrnes to succeed him.[3]

Relations of Presidents and Their Secretaries

As in all official affairs, the relations of individuals vary. Usually these Presidents and their Secretaries had amicable relations. Those of Secretary Colby with President Wilson, Secretaries Hughes, Kellogg, and Stimson with Presidents Harding, Coolidge, and Hoover, and those of Secretaries Hull and Stettinius with President Roosevelt were generally cordial. In Colby, it has been said, Wilson finally found a Secretary whose mind ran in the same channel as his own. President Harding (and others) had confidence in, and respect for, Hughes, who was regarded as a reliable and competent associate on whom he could rely. Coolidge and Secretary Kellogg had friendly relations and were temperamentally congenial, and the President regarded foreign relations as significantly improved under his administration. Stimson, believed by some to be an "unknown quantity" when appointed, had the advantage of serving a President who had more interest in, and was better acquainted with, foreign affairs than his immediate predecessors. His relations with President Hoover were equable not only in dealing with diplomatic issues and developing certain foreign policies but also in improving the organization, management, and financing of the Department of State.

Although Secretary Hull endured some difficulties with President Roosevelt, who clearly intended in many respects to be his own Foreign Minister and who served during the critical years of the Great Depression, World War II, and the fabrication of the postwar peacekeeping organization, they generally enjoyed amicable relations. The President relied upon and respected his Secretary, who enjoyed a high degree of independence in managing the Department and conducting diplomatic relations. But Hull resented not so much President Roosevelt's summit diplomacy as his use, without consulting him, of personal confidants and envoys like Harry Hopkins, W. Averell Harriman, Sumner Welles, and others, which interfered with regular diplomatic representation abroad. Hull also was displeased with Roosevelt's bypassing departmental channels when he consulted directly with Under Secretary Welles, who sometimes failed to inform the Secretary on such matters,[4] and with Roosevelt's dealing directly with politically appointed American diplomats abroad.

Exhausted from his many obligations and in ill health, Hull elected to resign on November 30, 1944. Stettinius took over the reins of Secretary the following day, but when he submitted his courtesy resignation at the end of Roosevelt's third term, he was retained. He continued as chief of foreign relations during the final months of the Roosevelt Administration and the early weeks of the Truman Administration.

Extension of Summit Diplomacy

During this period both Presidents Wilson and Roosevelt contributed to the intensification of summit diplomacy involving not only policy making but also conferencing with foreign leaders at the Head of Government level and dealing directly with foreign representatives, appointing personal confidants and other special envoys to diplomatic missions, and personally negotiating and signing international treaties and agreements, thereby supplementing, sometimes by-passing, and occasionally ignoring the Secretary and Department of State.

As chief of state and head of government, foreign policy determination and enunciation are the President's legal and political prerogative. Moreover, al-though precedents existed for some elements of presidential diplomacy, such as undertaking ceremonial and diplomatic trips abroad, and especially the use of special agents, all aspects of summitry mushroomed during the Wilson and Roo-sevelt Administrations. The resulting issue in the relations of the President and his Secretary became a matter of the degree and the manner in which the Pres-ident assumed this role without using or even consulting the Secretary and De-partment of State.

President Wilson often relied on personal emissaries, especially Colonel House, and let him create a separate ad hoc planning agency in New York of experts, called "The Inquiry," to parallel the Department of State in planning for the World War I settlement and peace treaty and the League of Nations, and he took House to the Paris Peace Conference in 1918 to serve as his principal and intimate adviser.[5] Both Secretaries Bryan and Lansing were bothered by the President's summiteering, but Secretary Colby proved to be more amenable to such presidential action. Except for the appointment of some special envoys, Presidents Harding, Coolidge, and Hoover were less inclined to engage in sum-mitry.

However, President Roosevelt became even more highly involved in summit practices. He relied on a number of personal advisers and special emissaries, including Hopkins (who was a longtime associate and became his intimate con-fidant), Vice President Wallace, Secretary of the Treasury Henry Morgenthau, Jr., and Under Secretary of State Welles. Roosevelt also engaged in an extensive personal correspondence with foreign heads of government, especially Winston Churchill, and undertook widespread, high-level consultation with him and other government leaders both in the United States and abroad. He also participated personally in more than twenty bilateral and trilateral summit meetings and conferences in five years, including those held at Quebec, Casablanca, Cairo, Tehran, Malta, and Yalta. Meanwhile, Secretary Hull and the Department of State managed day-to-day policy making and administering foreign trade and other matters and led in planning for the postwar United Nations.

The significance of these developments for the management and functioning of the Department of State is that they launched the era of American summit diplomacy, which subsequently became common presidential practice. As ex-ecutive instruments the Secretary and Department of State serve both the Pres-ident and the foreign interests and welfare of the nation, and during this period the Secretary also intensified personal involvement in ministerial diplomacy. The issue in the relations of the President and Secretary of State is primarily a matter of the way in which and the extent to which the President becomes personally involved and therefore disaffects the status, responsibility, functioning, morale, and the performance of the Secretary and the Department of State.[6]

Corps of Secretaries

The eight Secretaries of State differed substantially in their background, qualifications, experience, and achievements. All of them were trained and practicing lawyers, with Lansing specializing in international law and Hughes serving as a professor of law at Cornell University in the early 1890s. Several also held public legal offices and juridical positions of importance.[7] As in the previous half century, the largest number were appointed from New York, including Lansing, Hughes, Kellogg, and Stimson, who were born there. Kellogg later moved to Minnesota, and Colby moved to New York from St. Louis, as did Stettinius, who was born in Chicago. Only Bryan (born in Illinois, who moved to Nebraska) and Hull (born in Tennessee) were not New Yorkers. However, several had become Washingtonians by the time of their appointments as Secretary. By this time Secretaries were recruited from twenty States and the District of Columbia, with the largest numbers coming from New York (eleven), Virginia (seven), Pennsylvania (four), and Massachusetts (three). Only three Under Secretaries—Robert Lansing, Frank L. Polk, and Joseph C. Grew—served briefly as interim Secretaries between the resignation of Secretaries Bryan, Lansing, and Stettinius and the commissioning of their successors.

In the broadest sense, all of them except Lansing and Stettinius were politicians. Three were elected to Congress, including Bryan (1891–95), Kellogg (1916–22), and Hull for a quarter century (1907–21 and 1923–33). Some were active in national politics,[8] and Bryan and Hughes aspired to the Presidency—Bryan as the Democratic nominee in 1896, 1900, and 1908 and Hughes as Republican nominee in 1916, who lost to Wilson. Colby was supported as a presidential candidate for the Progressive Party in 1916, but he declined. Several were otherwise active in national party politics, and some held State political offices.[9]

Bryan had journalistic ambitions and experience. He edited the Omaha *World-Herald* (1894–96) and founded a weekly newspaper, *The Commoner*, in 1901. Bryan and Hull had served in the Spanish–American War, Bryan as a Colonel and Hull as a Captain. Stimson, who signed up with the National Guard during the war with Spain but was not sent into action, later served as an Army Colonel in France (1917–18).

Several Secretaries had other previous and subsequent high-level government experience. Stimson was Secretary of War for both Presidents Taft (1911–13) and Roosevelt (1940–45), and he became Governor of the Philippines (1927–29), immediately before he became Secretary of State. During World War I Colby was a member of the U.S. Shipping Board (1917–19) and a Trustee and Vice President of the Emergency Fleet Corporation (1918). During World War II Stettinius held a series of important administrative posts (1939–43) prior to his appointment to the Department of State.[10]

Of special relevance, unlike some earlier Secretaries, only Kellogg, who served as a delegate to the Fifth Pan-American Conference at Montevideo (1923) and as Ambassador to Great Britain for a year (1924–25), had traditional diplomatic assignments prior to becoming Secretary. However, four others had some departmental or related diplomatic experience. Lansing participated in a number of international arbitrations and counseled the Chinese and Mexican legations in Washington, and he had been Counselor of the Department.[11] Colby was a member of the American Mission to the Inter-Allied Conference at Paris (1917), Stimson served as special representative of President Coolidge to Nicaragua (1927), and Stettinius was appointed Under Secretary in 1943, prior to becoming Secretary.

Bryan was considered to be a sagacious political strategist, and he and Colby possessed a rare talent for oratory. Hull was recognized as a successful, experienced, and respected politician. Stimson proved to be an effective administrator and a master of public relations, and he, Hull, and others were regarded as devoted public servants. Biographers and historians note and, in some cases, laud Bryan as a ''legendary figure''; Lansing as an able and reputable international lawyer and yet a stern realist; Colby as politically courageous and adept at drafting documents; Kellogg as sincere, kindly, trustworthy, and respected by his subordinates; Hughes as an accomplished jurist, possessing not only ability and a judicial temperament but also technical skill, personal and professional integrity, and a sense of obligation to respect basic principles in promoting justice; Stimson as broad-gauged, forthright, and dedicated to public service but also liberal concerning issues of protocol and procedure; Hull as principled, sincere, devoted to the ideal of decent human conduct and to the cause of justice, which made him widely endeared and respected; and Stettinius as widely experienced, good-willed, and an able organizer and administrator. Hull also was viewed as a realist who maintained that the United States should ''make no threat without having the power and the will to back it up, and make no promise that could not be fulfilled.''

These Secretaries were confronted with many international problems and crises. Bryan, Lansing, and Colby had to deal with the Mexican Revolution and governmental recognition, the Tampico incident, German submarine attacks, the sinking of the *Lusitania*, World War I, peace negotiations, and Senate action on the Versailles Treaty. Hughes, Kellogg, and Stimson wrestled with such issues as World War I reparations and international debt settlement, recognizing the Communist Government of Russia, naval arms limitation, the worldwide Great Depression, joining the Permanent Court of International Justice, the Manchurian Crisis, and avoiding war with Japan. Hull coped with the depressed world economic situation and trade revival, the Spanish Civil War, inter-American integration, and especially World War II, and he and Stettinius played a central role in planning for its consequences and the formulation of the United Nations Charter.

Colby's explanation and interpretation of the Monroe Doctrine in December 1920 have been called both an enlightened statement and an oratorical achievement that made it possible for Latin American countries to accept it. The J.

Reuben Clark, Jr., Memorandum on the Monroe Doctrine, issued in December 1928, when he was Under Secretary, redefined American policy and repudiated both Secretary Richard Olney's anticolonization dictum of 1895 and the Theodore Roosevelt corollary of 1904 regarding U.S. intervention in Latin America. Other important policies associated with the Secretaries of State include the Stimson Non-Recognition Doctrine regarding the Japanese aggressive position in Korea and Hull's policies for easing relations with Latin America and promoting global tariff reduction and international commercial reciprocity.

Major treaty developments associated with particular Secretaries are represented by the Bryan–Chamorro Treaty with Nicaragua for an interoceanic canal (1914), the Bryan "Cooling Off" Pacts, the Lansing Treaty of 1916 to purchase the Danish West Indies, the Lansing–Ishii Agreement of 1917 concerned with Japan's relations with China, and the Kellogg–Briand Pact and Kellogg's bilateral arbitration and conciliation treaties. Certain Secretaries are also noted for their personal involvement in international conferences and meetings, both in the United States and abroad. Epitomizing the growth of ministerial diplomacy, from 1921 to 1945 they participated in more than fifteen, most notably, several arms limitation conclaves, the tripartite Moscow Ministerial Conference of 1943, and the Dumbarton Oaks and San Francisco Conferences to negotiate the United Nations Charter in 1945.[12]

The performance of these Secretaries varied with the issues of the times, the Presidents under whom they served, their relations with Congress and their departmental subordinates and other government agencies, and their decision-making prowess and managerial skill. Hughes was in charge when the Rogers Act was passed by Congress to amalgamate the Diplomatic and Consular Services and create the Foreign Service of the United States, discussed later. Stimson improved departmental morale and was the first Secretary to appoint a personal military aide, who functioned largely as his social secretary and sounding board. Kellogg and especially Stettinius are noted for their reorganization of the Department of State. Hull not only held the office of Secretary of State for the longest period but also signed the largest number of treaties and agreements.

Several of these Secretaries have been extolled for their character and achievements. It has been claimed that Colby must be assigned a high rank among our great Secretaries because he had to deal with international matters of great difficulty, complexity, and vexation, but it may be questioned whether those faced by Secretaries Lansing, Hull, and others were not equally or even more pressing and serious. Bryan was known as "The Great Commoner," Kellogg has been called a "world statesman," and Stimson has been regarded as an "elder statesman" whose government service spanned half a century.

Some of the most impressive accolades were accorded to Secretary Hull. It has been noted that he is remembered for four things—his nonpartisan foreign policy during World War II, the Good Neighbor policy for Latin America, the reciprocal trade agreements program to lower national tariffs and improve international trade relations, and the creation of the United Nations. His promotion of trade reciprocity has been credited as one of the most enduring changes of American foreign affairs during the twentieth century. He also has been called the "Father of the United Nations" by President Roosevelt and others, for which he won world renown. Graham Stuart assesses him as "a great Secretary of State, a great statesman, but, above all, a great man," and diplomatic historian Samuel Flagg Bemis has written: "There will never be another Secretary of State like Cordell Hull."

Recognizing their contributions, as was President Wilson in 1919, both Kellogg and Hull were awarded Nobel Peace Prizes, Kellogg in 1929 and Hull in 1945 (who had also been nominated for this honor in 1937, 1938, and 1939). Kellogg also was the recipient from the French Government of the Grand Cross of the Legion of Honor and honorary doctorates from Oxford and Harvard Universities. Honorary degrees were also conferred upon Hughes by the Universities of Brussels and Louvain. Stimson received the Distinguished Service Medal presented to him by President Truman on his retirement from the War Department in September 1945, and Truman also conferred the Medal of Merit with an oak-leaf cluster (with two citations) on Secretary Hull in 1947. If a Hall of Fame for leading American Secretaries of State were established, there is little doubt that Hull would be a deserving contender.

Ministerial Personal Diplomacy Abroad

Supplementing policy making, negotiation, conferencing, and treaty and agreement signing in Washington, during the twentieth century the Secretary of State also became involved in the conduct of foreign relations and a series of diplomatic ventures abroad. Secretary Seward initiated this practice as early as mid-January 1866, when he spent two weeks meeting with Danish and Spanish officials in the Virgin Islands and Cuba and with the Presidents of the Dominican Republic and Haiti. However, in the 1890s Secretaries John W. Foster and William R. Day resigned as Secretaries of State in order to undertake diplomatic and arbitral duties in Europe.

Beginning with Secretary Hay in 1905, to the end of World War II, all Secretaries of State, except Bacon and Bryan, ventured abroad on official business. During these four decades ten Secretaries averaged approximately 2.3 foreign visits per year. Secretaries Hay, Root, and Knox took seven trips abroad between 1905 and 1912 and made twenty-seven visits to Great Britain and other European countries, Canada, Newfoundland, Latin America, and the Virgin Islands. From 1913 to 1945 Secretaries Lansing to Stettinius undertook twenty-six trips and made sixty-six individual foreign visits.

Secretary Lansing served as a member of President Wilson's delegation to the World War I Paris Peace Conference. Secretary Colby visited three Latin American countries and the islands of Barbados and Trinidad late in December

1920 and January 1921. Secretary Hughes visited Canada, Bermuda, Brazil, and four European countries. Secretary Kellogg's schedule took him to Canada (twice), Cuba, France, and Ireland. Secretary Stimson broadened his itinerary to include Canada, Great Britain (three times), France, Italy, Germany, the Netherlands, and Switzerland. Secretary Hull established a record by undertaking twenty-nine foreign visits during the decade from June 1933 to November 1943, mostly to Latin American countries and Trinidad twenty-one, but also including Toronto, London, Moscow, and four Middle East and North African cities (Casablanca, Algiers, Tehran, and Cairo). He also accompanied President Roosevelt to the summit meeting at Quebec in 1943. On a single trip from January 26 to March 9, 1945, Secretary Stettinius traveled to ten countries in preparation for, attending, and returning from, summit conferences and meetings at Malta, Yalta, and Cairo, and he participated in the Chapultepec Inter-American Conference on the Problems of War and Peace.

In addition to such major ventures as the World War I Peace Conference, summit conferences and meetings during World War II, and the Moscow Foreign Ministers meeting in 1943 attended by Secretary Hull, these Secretaries also participated in a memorable series of other significant events. Thus, Secretary Kellogg negotiated and signed the historic treaty on the Renunciation of War (Kellogg–Briand Pact) at Paris in August 1928; Secretaries Root and Kellogg attended inter-American conferences, respectively, at Rio de Janeiro (1906) and Havana (1928); Secretary Stimson attended the London Naval Conference (1930), the conference on the German economic crisis (London, 1931), and the Geneva Disarmament Conference (1932); Secretary Hull attended the London Monetary and Economic Conference (1933) and four International Conferences of American States at Montevideo (1933), Buenos Aires (1936), Lima (1938), and Havana (1940); and Secretary Stettinius attended the Chapultepec and chaired the San Francisco Conferences (both in 1945).

Undertaking this new form of ministerial diplomacy, overall these eleven Secretaries traveled to thirty-four countries and island territories. They embraced eighteen of the Latin American countries (all except Bolivia, Paraguay, and Santo Domingo) for forty-nine visits, ten European powers (not including Austria-Hungary, Norway, Portugal, Spain, and Sweden) for thirty-four visits, Canada for seven visits, the Middle East (Egypt, Iran, and Morocco) for five visits, and Japan and Liberia, each for a single visit. The largest number of visits was made to Great Britain thirteen, Canada seven, France seven, Brazil six, Cuba five, and Panama five. Only a single visit was made to more than ten countries, including Belgium, Ireland, the Netherlands, and Switzerland in Europe; Costa Rica, El Salvador, Honduras, Nicaragua, and Venezuela in the Western Hemisphere; and Iran, Liberia, and Japan. Chronologically, four such foreign visits were made in 1866, twenty-eight during the period from 1905 to 1919, fifty-five from 1920 to 1944 (twenty-nine by Secretary Hull), and the remaining ten in 1945 by Secretary Stettinius.

These ventures in ministerial diplomacy abroad may be grouped in the following manner:

Secretaries of State (no. of visits)		Categories	
Seward	4	Accompanied President	3
Hay	4	Ceremonial	4
Root	10	Official visits	8
Knox	13	En route/stopover	6
Lansing	1	"Met with" foreign officials	50
Colby	5	"Discussed with" foreign officials	2
Hughes	7	International conferences and meetings	13
Kellogg	5	Inter-American	7
Stimson	9	Other conferences	5
Hull	29	Foreign Ministers meeting	1
Stettinius	10	Signed treaty	1
		Personal	4
		Vacation	6
TOTAL	97	TOTAL	97

The nature of most of these categories suggested in a Department of State study is self-evident. Those designated as "met with" and "discussed with" generally involved conferral, consultation, and sometimes negotiation with foreign leaders. Elucidating several other categories, Secretaries Lansing and Hull, respectively, accompanied Presidents Wilson and Roosevelt to three international conferences and summit meetings. The "ceremonial" visits included the attendance of four Secretaries at such special events as the funeral ceremony for Japanese Emperor Mutsuhito (Knox, Tokyo, 1912), commemorating the centenary of Brazilian independence (Hughes, Rio de Janeiro, 1922), dedication of the "Peace Bridge" between Buffalo and Fort Erie (Kellogg, 1927), and dedication of the "Peace Monument" at Toronto (Stimson, 1930).

The items listed as "personal" consisted of Secretary Hughes' address to the Canadian Bar Association (Montreal, 1923), attendance at an international law convention (London, 1924), a visit with French international lawyers (Paris, 1924), and the conferral of honorary degrees upon him in Belgium and France (1924). Those labeled "vacation" embraced four consecutive visits by Secretary Hay, for health reasons, to Italy, Germany, France, and Great Britain for two months, from April 3 to June 7, 1905; Secretary Root to Newfoundland and Labrador in August 1905 (to gather information on the fisheries question); and Secretary Hughes to Bermuda in 1922.

Historically, the Seward trip to the Caribbean as early as 1866 was important in that it initiated this new diplomatic practice. The most important ventures

during this period included the Paris Peace Conference of 1918–19, the negotiation and signing of the Treaty for the Renunciation of War by Secretary
Kellogg in 1928, the inter-American conferences that contributed to the development of the Western Hemisphere cooperative system, the international conferences concerned with disarmament and world economic and monetary
problems in the early 1930s, Hull's participation in the Quebec Summit Meeting
and the Moscow Foreign Ministers Conference, both in 1943, and Stettinius'
attendance at the Malta, Yalta, and Cairo summit conferences in 1945. Also of
interest, six Secretaries undertook extended foreign tours for official reasons,
beginning with Root's trip to six Latin American countries in 1906, followed
by Stimson's trip to five European countries in 1931, Hull's three tours to Latin
American in 1933–34, 1936, and 1938–39, and Stettinius' trips to ten countries
and other territories at the time of the Yalta Conference in 1945.

This experiment with, and these experiences in, ministerial diplomacy reflected the paralleling of the level of diplomatic action abroad with that generally
undertaken in Washington. It also evidenced the desire to elevate international
representation, consultation, and negotiation; the preference occasionally for
high-level ceremonial and consultative participation; and the need for, and value
of, Secretary of State personal conferencing, especially during the World War
II years and times of international crisis, as well as the physical perfection of
travel facilities. They also came to render this practice commonplace and portended an even greater degree of reliance on this medium of diplomatic relations
following World War II. The ascendance of ministerial diplomacy in the 1930s
and early 1940s is evidenced by the fact that Secretary Hull accounted for nearly
one-third (30 percent) of such foreign visits, and Stettinius spent half of his
seven months as secretary attending international conferences (including the
Dumbarton Oaks and the San Francisco Conferences in 1945).

MANAGEMENT, REORGANIZATION, AND MODERNIZATION

As the United States mutated from an important to a major world power and
emerged as a superpower, the Department of State underwent considerable
growth and change. Many forces affected its development, especially World
War I, the Great Depression, and World War II. Due to the expansion of the
international community, American foreign interests, and Department of State
involvement, the structure, management, funding, and personnel changed dramatically. New positions were created at the senior and other levels during this
era of evolution, both the Department's resources and staffing increased significantly, and, by the time of World War II, the Department outgrew its office
accommodations.

Acts of 1924 and 1931

In 1909 President Taft sought to provide a high-level deputy in the Department of State, titled Under Secretary, which was rejected by Congress. Ten years later, on March 1, 1919, Congress authorized the creation of this office, and on July 1 Frank L. Polk, who was then serving as Acting Secretary following Secretary Lansing's resignation, became the first Under Secretary. Congress also passed two major acts that affected departmental management. The Rogers Act of 1924, which applied primarily to the Foreign Service and is discussed later, contained a few provisions concerning the organization of the Department. It specified, in section 22, that the titles "Second" and "Third" Assistant Secretaries were abolished, established a fourth Assistant Secretary and eliminated numerical distinction among them. The four Assistant Secretaries, therefore, were equalized in rank and were subsequently distinguished primarily on the basis of function and geographic area of responsibility. Twenty years later, Acting Secretary of State Stettinius recommended the authorization of two additional unnumbered Assistant Secretaries, increasing their number to six, which Congress approved on December 8, 1944. The Rogers Act also abolished the position of Director of the Consular Service, which had been established by the Knox departmental reorganization of 1909.

The Moses–Linthicum Act of 1931, sections 30 and 32, made several additional changes. It created the Office of the Legal Adviser to replace the Solicitor, and prescribed the functions of the departmental Division of Foreign Service Personnel. In both of these acts—section 14 of the Rogers Act and section 21 of the Moses–Linthicum Act—Congress specified that Foreign Service careerists could be "assigned for duty in the Department of State . . . for a period of not more than three years." However, if the public interest demanded it, such assignment could be extended "for a period not to exceed one year." This encouraged interchanges of personnel for duty overseas and in the Department, but it also resulted in greater turnover in departmental service.

As in the past, other congressional enactments, especially appropriations legislation, also modified departmental staffing. In addition to creating the senior position of Under Secretary of State in 1919, changes were made in the status, designation, and functions of Assistant Secretaries, the office of Counselor, Legal Adviser, Economic Adviser, other special advisers, and the Chief Clerk. In time, however, constituting a major administrative modification, many such developments and modifications were specified in departmental directives, except for personnel matters requiring Senate approval.

Management, 1913–1933

Prior to 1914 the Department was headed by the Secretary, three ranked Assistant Secretaries, and the Chief Clerk, and it consisted of nine Bureaus, five

Divisions, and six other officers, including the Counselor, Solicitor, Resident Diplomatic Officer, and Director of Consular Services. Dozens of changes were instituted during the next two decades, including the creation of many new units and officers, retitling some of them, and, in certain cases, amalgamating, separating, and disestablishing them. Modification was generally instituted incrementally. However, modest reorganization was introduced by Secretary Kellogg late in the 1920s, and major reorganizations were undertaken during the Hull administration in 1938 and 1944. As a result, the Department emerged from World War II a much expanded and far more intricate mechanism designed to handle the burden of modern international responsibilities of a leading world power.

Some changes were made in both departmental staff and agencies during the Wilson Administration. Franklin Lyon Polk was appointed as the first Under Secretary in June 1919. He was succeeded by Norman H. Davis in June 1920 and by careerist Henry P. Fletcher in March 1921, followed by ten other officers, as indicated in Table 6.1. Whereas Alvey A. Adee continued as Second Assistant Secretary throughout these years, John E. Osborne, appointed First Assistant Secretary in 1913, was succeeded by William Phillips in January 1917, who served in this capacity until March 1920 and was succeeded by Fred Morris Dearing the following year and by Leland Harrison in 1922. Dudley Field Malone, William Phillips, Breckinridge Long, Van Santvoord Merle-Smith, Robert W. Bliss, and J. Butler Wright successively served as Third Secretaries. Of these eleven numbered Assistant Secretaries, six eventually became career Foreign Service Officers. Personnel changes were also made in the Offices of Counselor and Solicitor and other ranking positions.

Except for temporary organizational changes to handle special functions, few new agencies were created during the World War I years. When the war broke out in 1914, a Welfare and Whereabouts Section was added to the Consular Bureau to assist Americans who were stranded in the war zone. It was headed by Nathaniel P. Davis, and eventually it employed a staff of ninety persons. After the war it declined, and its residual functions were turned over to the Division of Foreign Intelligence, which had been established during the Knox Administration as the Division of Information. It was enlarged and retitled in 1917 and was then headed by Philip H. Patchin, who was succeeded by careerist Hugh S. Gibson.[13] To cope with issues resulting from the Mexican Revolution, in July 1915 Secretary Lansing created a separate Division of Mexican Affairs, headed by Leon J. Canova, who had been Chief of the Division of Latin American Affairs. The following year Secretary Lansing also organized a temporary Secret Intelligence Bureau, headed by careerist Leland Harrison.

Naturally, the Department of State expanded its staff to handle its increased workload during World War I. Chief Clerk Ben G. Davis, who succeeded William McNeir (who had served in the Department since 1881 and as Chief Clerk since 1909), declared that the Department's workload increased 400 percent during the first six weeks of the war. It was also reported, by Wilbur J. Carr, former Chief Clerk and Director of the Consular Service, that in a week to ten days, departmental personnel grew by at least 150.[14] To handle its additional wartime responsibilities, many diplomatic and consular officers were assigned duty in the Department, so that its stateside personnel more than doubled from some 200 in 1914 to 440 by 1918.[15]

To provide adequate accommodations, by 1918 the Department expanded its office quarters to several additional nearby buildings, and, regarded as essential to maintain security and confidentiality, special passes were required to enter Department of State buildings. Public information was handled by the Secretary of State at daily press conferences or by the Division of Information, and top-secret documents were restricted to only a few upper-level and other responsible officers. In order to assist in the relief and transportation of American citizens located in war zones, in 1914 Congress provided the Department with special funds amounting to $2,750,000, to be administered by American diplomats abroad.

At the outbreak of the war most belligerent governments turned the protection of their diplomatic and other representation in the warring powers and the administration of their affairs over to the United States, and the Department of State became the hub of the exchange of communications between belligerents. Later, when the United States entered the war in 1917, a number of Allied diplomatic missions came to Washington for consultation, and arrangements for military, naval, and financial affairs were funneled through the Department of State.

Other departmental changes were made during Lansing's tenure as Secretary between 1915 and early 1920. For example, in 1916 a new agency, titled the Office of the Adviser on Commercial Treaties, was established. Several agencies were augmented, including the addition of three Assistant Solicitors in 1916, and twenty-nine temporary clerks were added to the Bureau of Citizenship, which was retitled the Division of Passport Control in 1918, a separate Visa Office was assigned to it, and the following year, in November, it was elevated to office status and made responsible for visa control.

Prior to 1918 the Bureau of Indexes and Archives was the largest departmental agency, with a staff of 143, and the Bureau of Citizenship followed with a staff of sixty, and supplementary passport agencies were established in New York and San Francisco. A few days before Lansing resigned as Secretary, on February 6, 1920, a new Division of Political Information was created, headed by Prentiss B. Gilbert, to collect and coordinate information and supply it to principal departmental officers. The following year its functions were broadened, and its title was changed to the Division of Political and Economic Information.

During these years several women were appointed or promoted to important administrative posts. These included Margaret M. Hanna (Chief of the Correspondence Bureau), Anna A. O'Neill (law clerk), Nina G. Romeyn (Division of

Latin American Affairs), Ruth B. Shipley (Correspondence Bureau, who later became Chief of the Passport Division), and Natalia Summers (Division of Near Eastern Affairs).

To manage certain functions, during the war President Wilson established a number of special administrative agencies. These included the Committee on Public Information, the Emergency Fleet Corporation, the U.S. Shipping Board, the War Industries Board, the War Trade Board, and others. Some of them sent staff abroad and set up contingents outside the Diplomatic and Consular Services.

Most exceptionally, however, bypassing the Department of State, President Wilson appointed Colonel House to organize and head "The Inquiry." It consisted of outside "experts," mostly college professors, to assemble a mass of economic, ethnographic, geographic, historical, and political information for use at the Paris peace negotiations in 1919.[16] An ad hoc agency, unrelated to the Department of State, assembled in New York City, it was responsible directly to the President. Although he later appointed Lansing as a member of his peace commission, where he served on the Committee of Ten, the Secretary and Department of State personnel played a small part in negotiating the Versailles Treaty.

The Armistice of November 11, 1918, did not produce an immediate reduction in the tasks of the Department. Actually, its workload increased when it inherited some of the duties of the temporary wartime agencies, including the War Trade Board, incorporated as an agency of the Department in July 1919. Shortly before he resigned, in a letter to Congressman John Jacob Rogers, January 21, 1920, Secretary Lansing recommended a thorough reorganization of the Department and the Diplomatic and Consular Services, which resulted in the enactment of the Rogers Act several years later, but no major departmental reorganizations were undertaken until 1938 and 1944.

During the last years of the Wilson Administration, when Colby was Secretary of State, several additional changes were made in the upper echelons of administration. Norman H. Davis was appointed Under Secretary and Van Santvoord Merle-Smith became Third Assistant Secretary, both in June 1920. Thus, by early 1921 the senior departmental management staff consisted of Under Secretary Davis, Assistant Secretaries Adee and Merle-Smith, Fred K. Nielsen as Solicitor, and Ben G. Davis as Chief Clerk. The positions of First Assistant Secretary and Counselor were vacant, awaiting appointment.

To be expected, when Harding became President, and Hughes was appointed Secretary, following eight years of Democratic administration, additional personnel and some structural changes were made. Largely by routine promotion and transfer, in some cases due to retirement of officers, careerists Henry P. Fletcher, William Phillips, and Joseph C. Grew were successively appointed Under Secretary. Similarly, careerists Fred Morris Dearing and Leland Harrison became First Assistant Secretaries, Adee continued as Second Assistant Secretary, and careerists Robert Woods Bliss and J. Butler Wright served as Third Assistant Secretaries.

When the Rogers Act was passed in 1924, which discontinued the numerical distinction among Assistant Secretaries and added a fourth Assistant Secretary, Harrison and Wright, as well as Adee, were terminated in their existing positions on June 30. But Adee,[17] Harrison, and Wright were immediately reappointed as regular (unnumbered) Assistant Secretaries in July, and later Wilbur J. Carr and John Van A. MacMurray were appointed as new Assistant Secretaries. Of these ten Under and Assistant Secretaries, all became Foreign Service Officers except Adee, but he had already become a longtime careerist. When, after eleven years, Ben G. Davis retired from his position as Chief Clerk, Secretary Hughes selected E. J. Ayers to succeed him, and he held this office until his death in April 1931.

Several administrative changes were instituted while Hughes was Secretary. In October 1922 the Division of Russian Affairs, established a few years earlier, was renamed the Division of Eastern European Affairs, to also embrace Estonia, Finland, Latvia, Lithuania, and Poland. The Rogers Act of 1924, discussed later in the section on "Diplomatic and Consular Representation," established the position of Director of the Consular Service. The Diplomatic and Consular Bureaus, which had been in existence since the McLane reorganization in the 1830s, were replaced by a new Division of Foreign Service Administration, headed by Herbert C. Hengstler, who had been in charge of the Consular Bureau since 1907. To handle increased departmental correspondence, in 1924 Secretary Hughes created an Office of Coordination and Review, which filled an essential need previously furnished by the Correspondence Bureau during the Wilson Administration.

By March 1925, Secretary Hughes' principal assistants included the Under Secretary (who functioned as his principal deputy, especially concerned with important policy issues), three unnumbered Assistant Secretaries (who specialized, respectively, in economic and financial matters, political and international law issues, and administration), and a Chief Clerk (who supervised the departmental clerical staff and handled property matters). These were supplemented by the Solicitor, an Economic Adviser, and the Director of Consular Services, who also functioned as Budget Officer. The basic structure of the Department then consisted of a series of bureaus, offices, and divisions, including the Geographic Bureaus, the Diplomatic and Consular Bureaus, the Bureau of Accounts, the Office of Coordination and Review, and units that dealt with Foreign Service administration, passports, publications, visas, and other functional and servicing components.

After Kellogg became Secretary in 1925, Robert E. Olds, promoted from the position of Assistant to Under Secretary, succeeded Grew in July 1927, and J. Reuben Clark, Jr., who had served as Assistant Solicitor for seven years, replaced him in August 1928. New Assistant Secretaries were also appointed in 1927—Nelson T. Johnson and Francis White, who held career Foreign Service status, and William R. Castle, Jr. No appointment as Counselor was made between June 1919 and May 1937. However, Lester H. Woolsey had retired as Solicitor in 1920 and was succeeded by Fred K. Nielsen, and he was followed by Charles Cheney Hyde and, in 1925, by Green H. Hackworth. The title of the office was changed to Legal Adviser by act of Congress passed in February 1931, and Hackworth remained in this position until early 1946.[18] In keeping with the spirit of the Rogers Act, Secretary Kellogg, who supported careerism, interchanged careerists in senior departmental posts and made no political appointments to important positions in the departmental bureaucracy.

Several organizational and administrative changes were made while Kellogg was Secretary, which were referred to as Kellogg's reorganization. Early in 1926 the Division of Passport Control, still the second largest departmental unit, was renamed the Passport Division, headed by J. Klar Huddle, who was assisted by three Foreign Service Officers and a staff of sixty clerks. By departmental order, in February 1928, the Secretary elevated the Ceremonial Officer, established in 1919 (who then came under the Third Assistant Secretary), to full divisional status. This office was given charge over matters of *agréation* and the reception of American diplomats abroad and foreign envoys in the United States, ceremonies at White House and Department of State functions, advance preparation for international Conferences, and related matters. The following year its title was changed to the Division of International Conferences and Protocol.

Also in 1928 the Translating Bureau was recognized as the successor to the Translating and Miscellaneous Bureau, which had been established by Secretary McLane in 1833, and Emerson B. Christie was put in charge.[19] To manage the increase in treaty and agreement making following World War I, by departmental order a separate Treaty Division was also created in April 1928, headed by Charles M. Barnes, who had served in the Department since 1912 and had been named Assistant Solicitor in 1920.

Additional personnel but few structural changes were instituted by Secretary Stimson, 1929–33. Joseph P. Cotton, who had previously served in the Food Administration of Herbert Hoover, was appointed Under Secretary in June 1929, and he was followed by William R. Castle, Jr., in April 1931, who was promoted from his post as Assistant Secretary. In addition to Castle, the President appointed two new Assistant Secretaries—James Grafton Rogers and Harvey H. Bundy. They, together with Carr (appointed Assistant Secretary in 1924) and Francis White (appointed in 1927) resigned in 1933 following the election of President Roosevelt. Of these officers, only White was a Foreign Service Officer, but Carr and Castle had extensive previous experience in the Department of State. On the other hand, Allen T. Klots, a political appointee, served the Secretary as his personal Special Assistant.

Less than a month before Stimson became Secretary, the Division of Publications was converted into the Office of the Historical Adviser, and Dr. Taylor Dennett, Historian and Chief of the Division of Publications since 1924, was named Historical Adviser on February 19, 1929. Five years later this office was divided into the Office of the Historical Adviser, held by David Hunter Miller (who had served as a legal adviser to Secretary Lansing at the Paris Peace Conference) and the Division of Research and Publication, headed by Dr. Cyril Wynne.[20]

Secretary Stimson also made a number of other personnel changes. When Arthur N. Young resigned as Economic Adviser in 1929, Dr. Herbert Feis was appointed as his successor. Chief Clerk Ayers died on April 30, 1931, after seven years of service, and he was temporarily succeeded by Harry A. McBride and subsequently by Percy F. Allen until January 1, 1932, when Clinton E. MacEachran was made Chief Clerk and Administrative Assistant, who served for several years until he was transferred to consular duties in Canada.

Secretary Stimson also made a number of structural changes in 1931. On January 1 the Bureau of Indexes and Archives was converted into the Division of Communications and Records, with David A. Salmon as its chief. Staffed by more than 150 employees, it held the distinction of being the largest departmental agency. In mid-September the Division of International Conferences and Protocol was divided, with James C. Dunn as Chief of International Conferences and Warren D. Robbins in charge of protocol, both of whom were career officers. Stimson also terminated the "Black Chamber," the secret code-breaking agency engaged in cryptography for sixteen years.[21]

Roosevelt's Senior Departmental Staff

Aside from the personnel shifts in senior Department of State positions attributable to transition from twelve years of Republican to Democratic rule, a host of individual organizational changes were made during the Roosevelt Administration. These were caused by, and reflected, the natural expansion of functions, the lack of systematic departmental reorganization since that of Secretary Kellogg, many individual modifications and three major reorganizations, and the length of Secretary Hull's tenure. In addition to personnel transfers and turnover, the management of the Department was affected by such matters as the attempt to prevent the outbreak of war and, later, the policies and actions taken to wage and win the war, planning for postwar peace, which produced new diplomatic requirements and challenges, President Roosevelt's inclination to serve as his own Foreign Minister in dealing with many matters, and intensification of international conferencing and the escalation of many meetings and conferences to the ministerial and summit levels. They also resulted in paralleling normal departmental and diplomatic functions with extraordinary responsibilities, departmental policy and administrative agencies, interdepartmental coordinating facilities, and multilateral institutions.

As indicated in Table 6.1, between March 4, 1933 and April 12, 1945, when President Roosevelt died, he appointed Secretaries Hull and Stettinius, four Under Secretaries of State—William Phillips (1933–36), Sumner Welles (1937–43), Edward R. Stettinius, Jr. (1943–44), and Joseph C. Grew (1944–45). Except for Stettinius they were of Foreign Service career status. Robert Walton Moore was named Counselor (1937–41),[22] and Hackworth, commissioned as the first Legal Adviser in 1931, continued to hold this office throughout these years, until March 1, 1946, following his election as a Judge on the International Court of Justice.

Between 1933 and 1945, some fourteen persons were appointed to the four regular offices of Assistant Secretary, including Sumner Welles, who was appointed twice, in April and December 1933, and was named Under Secretary in 1937, and Dean G. Acheson, appointed in 1941, who later became President Truman's Secretary of State. Five of these were Foreign Service Officers—Jefferson Caffery, George S. Messersmith, G. Howland Shaw, Sumner Welles, and Hugh R. Wilson. Adolf A. Berle, Jr., Wilbur J. Carr, Henry F. Grady, Breckinridge Long, and Francis B. Sayre, though noncareerists, were rated as highly qualified and able Assistant Secretaries. Several served for short periods, especially early in the Hull Administration, such as Raymond C. Moley, Harry F. Payer, and Jefferson Caffery, each of whom held the office for less than a year.

During Secretary Stettinius' reorganization of the Department in December 1944, referred to later, the President also began to appoint specialized or functional Assistant Secretaries. The first to be commissioned, on December 20, 1944, were William L. Clayton (Assistant Secretary for Economic Affairs), Archibald MacLeish (Assistant Secretary for Public and Cultural Affairs), and Nelson A. Rockfeller (Assistant Secretary for American Republic Affairs). Shortly thereafter Julius C. Holmes was made Assistant Secretary for Administration. The fifth, Dean G. Acheson, although appointed as one of the four regular Assistant Secretaries on February 1, 1941, had his title changed to Assistant Secretary for Congressional Relations and International Conferences on December 20, 1944. This modification set a precedent, and no new general Assistant Secretaries were appointed after December 1941.

In 1937 Edward Yardley succeeded Clinton E. MacEachran as Chief Clerk, and he held this office until 1939. Although it was then discontinued, it was revived in 1942 as the Chief Clerk and Administrative Assistant, to which Millard L. Kenestrick was appointed.

Roosevelt's First Administration, 1933–1937

When Cordell Hull became Secretary of State, he was determined to retain meritorious officers as heads of departmental units, so that few shifts were made in Division Chiefs and similar positions.[23] However, due to the requirement specified in the Rogers Act, limiting tenure of Foreign Service Officers to three consecutive years in stateside departmental appointments, the Chiefs of at least five of the Divisions were changed by late 1937.[24] Several other personnel and administrative changes were made. William C. Bullitt was made Special Assistant to the Secretary, and he later became one of President Roosevelt's closest advisers. Norman H. Davis, former Under Secretary (1920–21), who represented the United States at the Disarmament Conference sponsored by the League of Nations, was made American Ambassador at Large in 1933 to head the American delegation at Geneva. This special ambassadorial rank, to provide high-level international representation and negotiation, was not formally established until 1949.

To assist with current policy issues, by departmental order in 1933, Secretary Hull created a Division of Research and Publication, headed by Dr. Cyril Wynne, a former Assistant Solicitor. Implementing those provisions of the Philippine Independence Act of March 1934 that involved the Department of State, Secretary Hull also established a special Office of Philippine Affairs, with Joseph E. Jacobs as Chief. When the Trade Agreements Act was passed by Congress in June 1934, authorizing the Department of State to negotiate reciprocal trade agreements based on the most-favored-nation principle, President Roosevelt formed an interdepartmental Executive Committee on Commercial Policy. It consisted of representatives of the Departments of State, Agriculture, Commerce, and Treasury, and other federal agencies, headed initially by Under Secretary William Phillips and later by Assistant Secretary Francis B. Sayre. To manage the trade agreements program, in May 1935, Secretary Hull also added a Division of Trade Agreements, with Henry F. Grady as Chief, who was succeeded by Harry C. Hawkins the following year.

Similarly, when, in August 1935, to maintain American neutrality, Congress legislated to prohibit the export of arms and implements of war to belligerent countries, the President created an interdepartmental National Munitions Control Board, consisting of the Secretaries of State, Commerce, Navy, and War. Secretary Hull appointed Joseph C. Green to head a departmental Office of Arms and Munitions Control to administer this mission. Its responsibilities embraced registering manufacturers, importers, and exporters of arms and military matériel and issuing requisite licenses for trading in them.

Like other government agencies, the Department of State was confronted with retrenchment at the time of the Great Depression. Although, under the Economy Act of June 1932, some 170 clerks were dropped in American diplomatic and consular establishments abroad, Secretary Hull introduced a number of measures to forestall similar departmental staff reduction. By January 1936 the Department consisted of thirty-three divisions, offices, and bureaus, manned by more than 750 officers and employees, of whom 719 were permanent, and thirty-four were temporary.

Roosevelt's Second Administration, to Pearl Harbor, 1937–41

The Department of State had undergone no major overhaul since that of Secretary Knox in 1909–13. During the critical five years from the beginning of Roosevelt's second term to Pearl Harbor, it underwent many administrative changes to cope with the continuing depression and the outbreak and spread of World War II. George S. Messersmith, a career Foreign Service Officer and former Consul General to Berlin and then Assistant Secretary of State (July 1937 to February 1940), instituted a piecemeal, but comprehensive, reorganization and expansion of the Department.

Several new offices and other agencies were created. An Office of Fiscal and Budget Affairs, responsible directly to the Secretary, was established in 1937 to prepare and justify the departmental budget and handle all other budgetary matters. The following year, in July, a Division of Cultural Relations was added to stimulate international intellectual cooperation, followed in August by a Division of International Communications, consisting of separate sections to deal with aviation, shipping, and telecommunications.

One of the most significant innovations involved the administrative determination to have selected, ranking officers focus on long-term policy making. Several new positions were provided to serve this purpose, such as an Adviser on International Economic Affairs (Dr. Herbert Feis) and a number of Regional Political Affairs Advisers—James C. Dunn for European Affairs, Stanley K. Hornbeck for Far Eastern Affairs, Laurence Duggan for American Republics Affairs, and Wallace Murray for Near Eastern Affairs. Each of these officers had previous experience as chiefs of agencies concerned with these respective geographic agencies. Also, the position of Counselor was reestablished to deal with legal issues, to which R. Walton Moore was appointed.

That same year the Divisions of Mexican and Latin American Affairs were amalgamated and designated the Division of American Republics, headed by Laurence Duggan, the Western European and Eastern European Divisions were also combined, headed by James C. Dunn, and the Division of Protocol and Conferences (which had combined these two functions in 1929, were divided in 1931, and again rejoined in 1933) was again separated into two agencies, with the Division of Protocol headed by George T. Summerlin, and the Division of Conferences, which was also made responsible for international civil aviation, headed by Richard Southgate.

Other revisory actions were taken to facilitate State Department implementation of congressional legislation concerned with neutrality, the arms embargo, and "cash and carry" regulations to deal with the imminent war in Europe, the Italian invasion of Ethiopia, the Spanish Revolution, and the Japanese invasion of Manchuria. To control traffic in arms and implements of war, the Office of Arms and Ammunition Control was expanded and, in November 1938, was converted into the Division of Controls. Its staff was enlarged, and its functions were expanded to include policy initiation as well as administration, and Joseph C. Green remained its Chief.

Also in 1938, David Hunter Miller, who headed the Office of the Historical Adviser, was given the title Editor of Treaties, and other duties of the office were transferred to the Division of Research and Publication, which included the departmental Geographer. The archival documents in the custody of the Historical Adviser were turned over to the Chief Clerk and later transferred to the National Archives, which finally ended Department of State responsibility for this domestic function. Later, in 1944, the office of the Editor of Treaties was abolished, and its functions were also ascribed to the Division of Research and Publications.[25]

During the years from 1939 to December 1941, the Department modified its structure to cope with the outbreak and expansion of World War II in Europe. After Germany invaded Poland, Secretary Hull established a "Special Division," headed by Breckinridge Long, then Special Assistant to the Secretary, to assist and repatriate Americans who were in Europe.[26] Shortly thereafter, a Representation Section was added to this Special Division. Through American missions abroad, prior to Pearl Harbor, as third-party protecting power, it handled the protection of the interests of Allied powers in Germany and took custodial charge of the official property, missions, and documents of the protected governments and furnished financial assistance and repatriation services to their nationals seeking to return to their homelands. It also provided protection of prisoners of war and civilian internees. These functions ended after Pearl Harbor when the United States became a belligerent.

One of the new agencies created during this period was the Division of Commercial Treaties and Agreements, established in July 1940 as a successor to the Trade Agreements Division, headed by Harry C. Hawkins, which was retitled the Division of Commercial Policy and Agreements in October the following year. Another new agency, called the Division of Foreign Activity Correlation, was an intelligence-gathering facility, created in November 1940 to acquire information regarding the interests of foreign leaders and to monitor the purposes, nature, and activities of foreign groups visiting the Department. When the United States and Great Britain established the bilateral Anglo-American Caribbean Commission, as an intergovernmental advisory and consultative agency, in March 1942, to collaborate on economic, social, and security matters in the Caribbean, the Department of State established a separate Caribbean Office, headed by Coert du Bois, to administer the Commission's determinations.

Other departmental agencies were modified or retitled, such as a consular commercial unit, responsible for promoting and protecting American commerce and agricultural interests abroad, which, in February 1940, was converted into the Division of Commercial Affairs, headed by James J. Murphy, Jr. At the time a great deal of attention was devoted to economic matters involving cooperation with such American interdepartmental agencies as the Board of Economic Warfare (procurement of strategic materials), Economic Defense Board (exports), Lend-Lease Administration (financial assistance), Maritime Commission (shipping), National Munitions Board (munitions), and War Production Board (industrial production). The principal State Department cooperating agencies included the Board of Economic Operations, the Division of Commercial Treaties and Agreements, changed to the Division of Commercial Policy and Agreements, which facilitated the implementation of wartime economic agreements, the Division of Defense Materials, Division of Exports and Defense Aids, the Division of Studies and Statistics, and the Foreign Funds and Financial Division, which was split into the Financial Division and the Foreign Funds Control Division.

The Passport and Visa Divisions acquired special functions and responsibilities at the time, which increased their activities and necessitated the provision of suboffices. New regulations were issued to govern the foreign travel of Americans and entry into, and departure from, the United States of both citizens and aliens. Transition from protection of Americans to matters of national security resulted in changing the format and color of American passports and the establishment of subsidiary passport offices in Boston, Chicago, New York, and San Francisco. Beginning in 1928, Ruth B. Shipley managed the Passport Division for more than two decades. Also for security reasons, a new visa procedure had to be instituted, and an interdepartmental advisory committee, consisting of representatives of the Departments of State and Justice, military intelligence agencies, and the Federal Bureau of Investigation, was formed to decide on problem cases. Avra M. Warren, a careerist, served as Chief of the Visa Division, 1941–42, who was later accredited as Minister Plenipotentiary or Ambassador to a succession of six countries. She was succeeded by Howard K. Travers, also a careerist, who subsequently was sent as Ambassador to Haiti.

Exercising prescient foresight, as early as 1940, Secretary Hull appointed a high-level departmental committee to compile information and plan for both immediate and long-range programs for the consequences of the war. This launched the beginning of the long, critical, and complex process of designing a peace settlement and the postwar United Nations system. This Advisory Committee on Problems of Foreign Relations, chaired by Under Secretary Welles, included careerist Hugh Wilson (Special Assistant to the Secretary, as vice chairman) and thirteen other high-ranking departmental officers. R. Walton Moore, George Rublee, and Leo Pasvolsky headed its three subcommittees. The deliberations of this committee system produced the genesis of the plans that became the basis of the Dumbarton Oaks Proposals and the Charter of the United Nations.[27]

As of December 1941 the senior departmental staff consisted of the Under Secretary and four Assistant Secretaries. Secretary Hull also had an assistant to help with office routine and four functional Special Assistants. The Under Secretary had three Special Assistants to deal with political and economic policy coordination, petroleum issues, and export control. They were in charge of, and assisted by, several advisers, the Counselor, and the various traditional and wartime offices, divisions, and individual functional officers. The total departmental staff numbered approximately 1,000 permanent and 600 temporary employees.[28] The budget of the Department (not including overseas operations) ran to more than $3,300,000, of which salaries accounted for at least 80 percent.

The War Years, December 1941–1945

The Department of State underwent its greatest transformation during the World War II years, December 1941 to 1945. Organizational and administrative change occurred in three ways—by ad hoc alteration of its basic units, major reorganizations, and modifications to meet emergency needs to deal with wartime contingencies and postwar planning.

A number of new offices and other agencies were established to serve special needs. These included a Liaison Office, located in the office of the Under Secretary to coordinate issues involving both political and military considerations[29]; a Committee on Political Planning, consisting of the departmental Political and Economic Advisers and other officers, chaired by Political Adviser James C. Dunn, to advise the Secretary and Under Secretary on plans for American political activities; a Committee of three, comprising of the Under Secretary and two Assistant Secretaries, to consider plans that necessitated the use of non-State Department officials overseas, with the Division of Foreign Service Administration to handle arrangements for their foreign missions; a Division of Departmental Personnel, whose chief, John C. Ross, was designated as Executive Officer of the Department; and an Office of Foreign Territories, concerned with civil governance of occupied foreign territories, headed by Paul Appleby, recruited from the Department of Agriculture.

Several other administrative changes were made. The Office of Chief Clerk—established in 1789 and held by some half dozen officers for some thirty years, including William McNair, Ben G. Davis, E. J. Ayers, Clinton E. MacEachran, and Herbert O. Yardley—was discontinued in 1939. It was reestablished in August 1942, with the title Chief Clerk and Administrative Assistant, to which Millard L. Kenestrick was appointed, who had previously served in the Department for more than a decade. An Office of Foreign Relief and Rehabilitation Operations was created in November 1942, headed by Herbert H. Lehman, former Governor of New York, to plan, coordinate, and arrange for administering the relief of liberated territory under Allied occupation.

In June 1943 the Department added an Office of Foreign Economic Coordination, comprising several preexisting divisions, whereupon the Office of Foreign Territories and the Board of Economic Operations were abolished. The Division of Communications and Records absorbed the Division of Commercial Affairs in August 1943, which was headed by careerist Raymond H. Geist. Its records branch was gradually reorganized on a functional basis, a records retirement program was introduced, and a new system was instituted to maintain a running register of the disposition of papers. When Herbert Feis resigned in October 1943, who had served as Economic Adviser since 1931, this office was abolished.

To implement President Roosevelt's plan for dealing with liberated territories, Secretary Hull established two interdepartmental committees, one for policy consideration and the other for coordination. They consisted of representatives of the State, Navy, Treasury, and War Departments, plus such other agencies as the Board of Economic Warfare and the Lend-Lease Administration. Both of them were placed under Assistant Secretary Acheson, and separate subcommittees were provided for various European regions, with their chiefs and secretariats furnished by the Department of State.[30]

Simultaneously, Secretary Hull and the Department of State assumed a leading role for postwar planning, which, unlike President Wilson's independent "Inquiry," functioned as a type of "special department" within the Department of State. As early as 1939, prior to the Japanese attack at Pearl Harbor, Leo Pasvolsky, Governor of New York, was appointed as Special Assistant to the Secretary. He, together with his deputy, Dr. Harley Notter, of the office of Under Secretary Welles, prepared exploratory studies concerning forty-seven foreign neutral governments, focusing primarily on economic matters and the limitation of armaments.

A Division of Special Research was established in February 1941, with Pasvolsky as Chief and Notter as his Assistant Chief for political security, territorial, and armaments matters, Henry J. Wadleigh for economic affairs, and Charles W. Yost for administration. In January 1943 this agency was separated into Divisions for Political Studies and for Economic Studies, both of which came under Pasvolsky, with Notter heading the Political Division and Leroy D. Stinebower as Chief of the Division of Economic Studies. These two agencies contained nine Assistant Chiefs and some 130 staff members. By the end of 1943 they prepared tentative drafts of a host of studies, paying special attention to postwar international organization, thus contributing to the framing of the organic acts of the United Nations and other international organizations.

Paralleling these actions, after Pearl Harbor, late in December 1941, on the suggestion of Secretary Hull, President Roosevelt appointed a top-level Advisory Committee on Postwar Foreign Policy to formulate plans based on major policy pronouncements, such as the Four Freedoms and the Atlantic Charter. This committee, chaired by the Secretary, included Under Secretary Welles, Assistant Secretaries Acheson and Adolf A. Berle, Economic Adviser Feis, Legal Adviser Hackworth, the Chiefs of the Divisions of Commercial Policy and Special Research, and several eminent outsiders, including the President of the Council on Foreign Relations and the editor of *Foreign Affairs*. Additional participants were recruited from Congress, and the Navy, War, and other Departments and agencies, eventually numbering nearly fifty persons, of whom one-fifth represented the Department of State. This combination of the Secretary's Advisory Committee and Department of State special research divisions provided a massive resource for wartime and postwar policy planning.[31]

Secretary Hull resigned on November 30, 1944, and President Roosevelt promoted Under Secretary Stettinius to take his place. As indicated in Table 6.1, the President also appointed Joseph C. Grew as the new Under Secretary (his second appointment to this office), and William L. Clayton as Assistant Secretary for Economic Affairs, Archibald MacLeish as Assistant Secretary for Public and Cultural Relations, and Nelson A. Rockefeller as Assistant Secretary for American Republic Affairs. Assistant Secretary Acheson remained to handle relations with Congress and departmental participation in international conferences. When two additional Assistant Secretaries were authorized by Congress in December 1944, James C. Dunn, to be in charge of several geographic offices, and Julius C. Holmes, to handle departmental administration, were appointed. Of the senior officers, only Grew, Dunn, and Holmes were career Foreign Service Officers, but several others, such as Acheson, Clayton, Rockefeller, and Stettinius, also had considerable prior foreign relations experience, and Mac-Leish had previously been Librarian of Congress.

While he was Under Secretary, in January 1944, Stettinius undertook to reorganize the Department, which for several years had been mutating piecemeal. Previously, in November 1943 he convened a staff group to consider departmental realignment, and he decided to regroup related responsibilities and to establish an integrated chain of command. To achieve this and to interrelate policy making and implementation, minimize the overlap of functions, and strengthen the management of long-range planning, the following January, by departmental order, he mandated major reorganization.

For example, financial and economic matters were joined under the jurisdiction of Assistant Secretary Acheson, and administrative and public information functions were ascribed to G. Howland Shaw, who had been appointed Assistant Secretary in March 1941. The Office of Controls (including the Passport, Visa, Special War Problems, and Foreign Activities Correlation Divisions) and the Office of Transportation and Communications (including aviation, shipping, and telecommunications) came under Assistant Secretary Adolph A. Berle, Jr., who had been named to this office in 1938. S. M. Breckinridge Long, appointed Assistant Secretary in January 1940, handled liaison with Congress.

Administrative functions were grouped in twelve Offices, each headed by a Director and a Deputy Director, with the Divisions grouped under them. The Directors of the four Geographic Offices of American Republic Affairs, European Affairs, Near Eastern and African Affairs, and Far Eastern Affairs, as well as the Office of Special Political Affairs were responsible directly to the Under Secretary. Economic matters were confined to two Offices concerned with traditional Economic Affairs and special Wartime Economic Affairs. The field of administration and public information consisted of three Offices dealing, respectively, with Departmental Administration, Foreign Service Administration, and Public Information. The Office of Departmental Administration consisted of three Divisions—Administrative Management, Departmental Personnel, and Budget and Finance, which replaced the former Office of Fiscal and Budgetary Affairs and the Division of Accounts. The Office of Foreign Service Administration comprised separate Divisions of Foreign Service Personnel and Foreign Service Administration.

No Office encompassed more than six or fewer than two Divisions. The four Geographic Offices were in charge of nineteen Divisions, six of which came under the Director of the Office of Inter-American Affairs. The positions of special Economic and Political Advisers and the Chief Clerk and Administrative Assistant were abolished, whereas those of Counselor and Legal Adviser continued. As a matter of departmental structuring, it is worthy of note that by this time the title ''Bureau,'' which had been ascribed to primary departmental agencies since the early 1830s when Louis McLane was Secretary, was eliminated, and basic departmental units were titled "Offices."

To fulfill a crucial need, long-range planning became the responsibility of two separate, high-level agencies, a departmental Policy Committee and a Committee on Postwar Programs, both chaired by the Secretary with the Under Secretary as his Deputy. The membership of both committees included the four Assistant Secretaries, the Legal Adviser, and the Secretary's Special Assistant Leo Pasvolsky, and the twelve Directors of Offices were made ex-officio members.[32]

Prior to his appointment as Secretary, during 1944 Under Secretary Stettinius and his advisers prepared a second major reorganization plan, which was issued on December 20. He considered four alternative structure designs and chose a moderate version that modified and extended the reorganization of January. His major changes at the senior coordinating level included two primary committees. The former Policy Committee and Committee on Postwar Programs were replaced by a single Staff Committee to advise the Secretary on current and long-range policy. It consisted of the Secretary, Under Secretary, the six Assistant Secretaries, the Legal Adviser, and a Special Assistant for International Organization.

A lower-level Coordinating Committee, comprising the Under Secretary, the Directors of the twelve Offices, and the Special Assistant for Press Relations, was designed to provide initial consideration of policy issues and deal with interagency relations. To facilitate operations, the Secretary also created a Joint Secretariat to assemble and coordinate information and materials on important matters of policy and procedure, to advise departmental representatives serving on interdepartmental agencies concerned with foreign affairs, to monitor implementation by the operating agencies of the Department, and to file reports on actions taken.

In addition to realigning the departmental superstructure, this second reorganization was largely a continuation and refinement of that of January. It continued to combine similar functions within individual Offices and grouped related offices under specific Assistant Secretaries of State. Nevertheless, major changes were made in administration, economic and financial affairs, public information, and relations with international, private, and other organizations.

Assistant Secretary for Administration Holmes supervised three Offices—for Departmental Administration, Controls, and the Foreign Service. That concerned with departmental administration, then the largest office, consisted of eight Divisions, which dealt with Management Planning, Departmental Personnel, Budget and Finance, and Central Services, as well as such more specialized matters as Coordination and Review, Protocol, International Conferences, and Cryptography.[33] The Office of Controls embodied four units—the Passport, Visa (and immigration), Foreign Activity Coordination, and Special War Problems Divisions.

The Office of the Foreign Service, responsible for stateside management of the expanding diplomatic and consular career system, was reorganized in April

1945. Three new agencies were created. These embraced a Division of Foreign Service Planning to provide recommendations concerning, and to prescribe the functions and activities of, the Foreign Service, a Division of Training Services, to furnish orientation and advanced training, and a Division of Foreign Reporting Services to manage the dissemination of information received from abroad. A Division of Foreign Service Personnel, established in January, was retained, and few changes were instituted respecting recruitment and promotion of personnel.[34]

In the economic field, the Offices of Economic Affairs and Wartime Economic Affairs were replaced by an Office of Commercial Policy, which was later renamed the Office of International Trade Policy. The latter embraced the Commodities, War Areas Economic, Petroleum, and Commercial Policy Divisions, plus a Division of Labor, Social, and Health Affairs. Early in 1945 the Office of Financial and Development Policy had jurisdiction over the Financial Affairs, Foreign Economic Development, Lend-Lease and Surplus War Property, and Economic Security Controls Divisions.

To handle public affairs, the Office of Public Information, headed by Assistant Secretary MacLeish, was changed to the Office of Public Affairs. It consisted of the Divisions of Public Liaison, Cultural Cooperation (concerned with art, education, and science), Motion Pictures and Radio, International Information, and Telecommunications.

At that time, two Assistant Secretaries headed the Geographic Offices. Those concerned with European, Far Eastern, and Near Eastern and African Affairs came under the jurisdiction of Assistant Secretary Dunn and consisted of fourteen Divisions. The Office of American Republic Affairs, composed of six regional Divisions, was headed by Assistant Secretary Rockefeller. A supplementary agency, the American Republics Analysis and Liaison Division, had been added in May 1944 to provide information on, and assessment of, Latin American countries.

In addition, the Office of Special Political Affairs, created early in 1944 and headed by Pasvolsky, was retained. However, its Division of International Security and Organization was superseded by three separate divisions concerned with International Security, International Organization Affairs, and Dependent Areas. The Division of Territorial Studies was terminated in March 1945. Those agencies concerned with international security and international organizations played a major role in planning for the United Nations and other international organizations.

By 1945, therefore, the top-level organization for Department of State management consisted of the Secretary, the Under Secretary, and six Assistant Secretaries. Stettinius, who served as Secretary for only seven months, resigned on June 27, the day after the San Francisco Conference adjourned, at which he chaired both the American delegation and the conference. His short tenure was unique in several respects. He spent much of his time attending international conferences (including the summit conferences at Malta and Yalta, and the

United Nations Conference at San Francisco), at which time Under Secretary
Grew served as Acting Secretary. His tenure as Secretary was cut short by
President Roosevelt's death. Third, to adjust the organization of the Department
to the needs of the immediate post–World War II era, he may be credited with
designing the first overall reorganization of the Department since that of Secretary Fish in 1870, as subsequently modified by Secretaries Knox and Kellogg
and Assistant Secretary Messersmith.

Reviewing the assisting staffs of senior officers illustrates the extensive
growth of the Department of State. At the time the immediate office of Secretary
Stettinius consisted of a Liaison Officer to the White House (Charles E. Bohlen),
an officer to execute special assignments (Morris N. Hughes), and an Information Officer (Robert Borden Reams), who were all Foreign Service Officers and,
to review outgoing correspondence prior to the Secretary's signature, Blanche
R. Halla, Chief of the Division of Coordination and Review. They were supplemented by a corps of specialists to handle particular services, such as Leo
Pasvolsky (Chief of the Office of Political Affairs), Michael J. McDermott (for
press relations), George T. Summerlin (Protocol Officer), and Hamilton Fish
Armstrong, Isaiah Bowman, Henry P. Fletcher, Joseph C. Green, Charles B.
Rayner, and Charles W. Tausig (Special Advisers), of whom Fletcher and Sum-
merlin were careerists.

Under Secretary Grew was assisted by a staff of eight, headed by careerist
Frances E. Willis. The staffs of the six Assistant Secretaries also burgeoned.
Thus, Assistant Secretary Acheson had a personal staff of sixteen Special Assistants, other assistants, and clerks, Clayton had forty-seven, Dunn had eight,
Holmes had seven, MacLeish had nine, and Rockefeller had sixteen, which
totaled more than 100. Of these principal officers roughly half were career officers.

This reorganization of 1944 modernized the Department of State and prepared
it for the important role the United States was to play in post–World War II
affairs. It "marked the dividing line between the old Department of State and
the present agency" and, concluded the Department of State Historian: "The
new Department of State emerged from World War II better prepared to play a
leading role in the foreign policy process and fully aware that the tasks ahead
loomed more difficult than any encountered in earlier years."[35]

Department of State Organization as of 1945

As this era came to an end, in addition to these ranking officers, the Department consisted of some twenty Offices and more than fifty Divisions, plus a
group of Special Assistants, structured as indicated in Table 6.2. To these must
be added such agencies and officers as the Central Translating Division, the
Geographer, the Historian, the Legal Adviser, the Editor of Treaties, and a group
of special advisers and other assistants. However, the Office of Chief Clerk,
discontinued in 1939 but reestablished in August 1942, to which Millard L.

Table 6.2
Principal Agencies of the Department of State, 1945

General and Coordinating Agencies

Staff Committee   Policy Committee
Coordinating Committee   Problems Committee
Joint Secretariat

Offices and Divisions

Principal Officers/Offices	Offices	Divisions
Liaison with Congress and International Conferences (Asst. Sec. Dean G. Acheson)	Liaison and Conferences	
Geographic (Asst. Sec. James C. Dunn *)	Europe	4
	Far East	8
(Asst. Sec. Nelson A. Rockefeller)	Near East and Africa	2
	American Republics	7
Public Affairs (Asst. Sec. Archibald MacLeish)	Public Affairs	5
Administration (Asst. Sec. Julius C. Holmes *)	Departmental Administration	8
	Controls	4
	Foreign Service	4
Economic Affairs (Asst. Sec. William L. Clayton	Commercial Policy	5
	Financial and Development Policy	4
Special Political Affairs (Leo Pasvolsky)	Special Political Affairs	3
Others		
Special Assistant (Michael J. McDermott *)	Press Relations	
Counselor (vacant till October, 1945)	Counselor	
Geographer	Geography	
Historian	Historian	
Legal Adviser (Green H. Hackworth)	Legal Affairs	
Translation	Translation	
Special Assistant (George T. Summerlin *)	Protocol	1
Chief Clerk and Administrative Assistant (abolished)	Chief Clerk	1
Editor of Treaties (abolished)		
Total	20	56

Table 6.2 (continued)

Departmental Divisions, 1945

Geographic

    Europe
        British Commonwealth
        Eastern Europe
        Northern Europe
        Western Europe

    Far East
        China
        East Indies
        French Indochina
        India
        Japan
        Philippines
        Siam
        Siberia

    Near East and Africa
        Africa
        Near East

    American Republics
        American Republics Analysis
            and Liaison
        Bolivia
        Brazil
        Caribbean and Central America
        Mexico
        River Plate
        West Coast

Public Affairs

    Public Affairs
        Cultural Cooperation
        International Information
        Motion Pictures and Radio
        Public Liaison
        Telecommunications

Protocol

    Chief of Protocol
    International Conferences

Administration

    Controls
        Foreign Activity Coordination
        Passports
        Special War Problems
        Visas

    Departmental Administration
        Budget and Finance
        Central Services
        Coordination and Review
        Cryptology
        Departmental Personnel
        International Conferences
        Management Planning
        Protocol

    Foreign Service
        Foreign Property Services
        Foreign Service Personnel
        Foreign Service Planning
        Training Services

Economic Affairs

    Commercial Policy
        Commercial Policy
        Commodities
        Labor, Social, and Health Affairs
        Petroleum
        War Areas

    Financial and Development Policy
        Economic Security Control
        Financial Affairs
        Foreign Economic Development
        Lend-Lease and Surplus Property

Special Political Affairs

    Special Political Affairs
        Dependent Areas
        International Organization
        International Security

*Indicates officers who had or later achieved Foreign Service career status.

Note: By the 1940s the designation of Department of State agencies as "bureaus," common in earlier times, had disappeared, and the principal subunits were called "offices" and "divisions."

Kennestrick was appointed, was again abolished by the reorganization of January 1944.[36] Two additional developments are of note. The former structural agencies designated as bureaus had been eliminated. With the passage of the Rogers Act and the professionalization of the Foreign Service, increasingly, appointees to senior positions below the rank of Secretary were experienced members of the career Foreign Service.

It needs to be added that Department of State officers also served on, or cooperated with, a variety of interdepartmental wartime and post-hostilities agencies and their subsidiaries.[37] In addition, the Department represented the United States in a good many international World War II temporary commissions, committees, councils, and other agencies,[38] as well as dozens of other more permanent international institutions, which are discussed later in the section on "International Organizations and Other Agencies."

The evolution and organization of the Department of State were influenced by major needs and significant domestic and international developments. These included congressional legislation, the expansion of American interests and relations abroad, changes in foreign policy, and external forces. By the end of 1945 some agencies and officials reflected the waging and the aftermath of World War II and were subsequently changed or eliminated, but most of them remained essential to the continuing management of American foreign affairs.

Professionalization of Management

Considerable change from the spoils to the merit system was achieved during this period. Presidents and their Secretaries of State varied in their attitude concerning political appointments, as applied primarily to the top-level departmental positions. By this time the clerical force was under Civil Service regulations. When the Rogers Act was passed in 1924, it provided, in section 14, that career Foreign Service Officers could be assigned to stateside duty in the Department of State for periods of up to three consecutive years, and the Secretaries of State were persuaded to appoint many such experienced officers to important departmental posts. These developments resulted in large-scale professionalization of the staff of the Department.

Under the Constitution and congressional legislation, Presidents continued to select their Secretaries of State, and together they appointed departmental Under Secretaries, Assistant Secretaries, and certain other top-level officers. Major changes of appointees, therefore, were to be expected when political shifts occurred in the presidency, as when Presidents Wilson, Harding, and Roosevelt were elected. Similarly, changes may be made when such senior officers resign and whenever Presidents are inaugurated, even when they succeed themselves.

Partisanship continued to dominate the appointment of a few senior officers. In addition to the Secretaries and some Under Secretaries, only a few Assistant Secretaries were clearly political appointees, such as John E. Osborne and Dudley Field Malone, commissioned in 1913, and Raymond C. Moley, Robert

Walton Moore, Harry F. Payer, and Francis B. Sayre (President Wilson's son-in-law), appointed in 1933. Practice with respect to lesser departmental officials depended more on professional qualifications and experience for the Chiefs of Offices, Divisions, and other leading posts. Despite the inundation by many office seekers at the time of change in presidential administrations, a corps of primary officials and other longtime officers and staff members had been developing to manage particular functions.

The first of these categories includes such officers as Dean Acheson, Alvey A. Adee, Wilbur J. Carr, William R. Castle, Jr., Joseph C. Grew, S. M. Breckinridge Long, William Phillips, Sumner Welles, and Francis White. All of them became professionals and served as Assistant and/or Under Secretary for at least four to eight years, which illustrates an increasing desire by the Presidents and their Secretaries to professionalize the senior service.[39]

A good many others, at lesser ranks, also served for lengthy periods in departmental administrative posts and may be regarded as careerists. A sample would include Blanche R. Halla, Green H. Hackworth, Herbert C. Hengstler, Stanley K. Hornbeck, John Bassett Moore, Harley A. Notter, Leo Pasvolsky, Dr. C. Easton Rothwell, David A. Salmon, Ruth B. Shipley, and Sydney Y. Smith. Many of such longtime officers and other staff members are rarely recognized in histories of American foreign relations. Examples of others who not only served in departmental administration but also were appointed as career Foreign Service Officers embrace Nathaniel P. Davis, James C. Dunn, Margaret Hanna, Julius C. Holmes, George S. Messersmith, Wallace S. Murray, G. Howland Shaw, and Frances E. Willis.

Department Personnel

During these three decades the personnel of the Department (not including overseas staff) increased substantially, advancing at the time of World War I, expanding somewhat during the 1930s despite the Great Depression, and burgeoning during World War II. According to State Department figures, the number grew from 234 in 1910, to 708 in 1920, declined below 600 during the years 1921–23, leveled off to 714 by 1930, rose to 974 by 1939, reached 1,128 by 1940, and then more than tripled by 1945, amounting to 3,767. Prior to 1920 the overseas staff traditionally was larger than that in Washington, sometimes numbering as much as twelve to fifteen times that of the Department, but in later decades, through World War II, the departmental staff exceeded that of the diplomatic and consular services abroad.[40]

Women Officers and Staff Members

An important departmental personnel change occurred with the appointment of more women to important administrative positions. Although women had been recruited earlier, mostly as clerks, this practice of assigning them to more responsible administrative posts increased beginning during World War I and continued in following decades. To illustrate, Blanche R. Halla, after twenty years' service in the Department, was made Assistant Chief and in 1937 was promoted as Chief of the Office of Coordination and Review, and she later became Executive Assistant to Secretary Stettinius. Margaret M. Hanna was made Chief of the Correspondence Bureau and later, after serving as Chief of the Office of Coordination and Review for thirteen years, became a Foreign Service Officer, and Secretary Hull assigned her to Geneva. Shortly before this appointment, with the collaboration of Alice M. Ball, she prepared the Department of State Correspondence Manual.

Also, in 1917, during the Wilson Administration, Marion Letcher, a Foreign Service Officer, was made Chief of the Office of the Foreign Trade Adviser, with a staff of eighteen. Ella A. Logsdon became Assistant Chief of the Office of Fiscal and Budget Affairs and was promoted to head it in 1940. Ruth B. Shipley served as Assistant Chief of the Office of Coordination and Review and was appointed Chief of the Passport Division in 1928, an office that she held for many years into the 1950s. Natalia Summers, previously employed in the Division of Near Eastern Affairs, became departmental Archivist and was transferred to the National Archives Building in 1938. Frances E. Willis, who had more than seventeen years' experience abroad and in the Department, became Under Secretary Grew's primary assistant in 1944 and Chief of the Western European Affairs Division three years later. She was the highest-ranking feminine Foreign Service Officer and spent most of her career in diplomatic and consular appointments abroad, mostly in Europe.

Other women who held positions of prominence include Madge M. Blessing, who handled Welfare and Whereabouts Division work for more than twenty years; Helen Daniel and Sarah Moore, who served in the Division of Communications and Records; Virginia Hartley who was appointed to the political section of the Division of Special Research, concerned with post–World War II planning; Amy C. Holland, who rose from the position of clerk to divisional assistant in the Division of Near Eastern Affairs and became the first woman to achieve this rank of a policy officer; Marion A. Johnston, who was recruited as Under Secretary Grew's office director; Margaret H. Potter, who became a member of the economic staff of the Division of Special Research; and Nina G. Romeyn, who served in the Division of Latin American Affairs. Several women also were members of the staff of the Legal Adviser, such as Katherine B. Fite, Anna O'Neil, and Marjorie M. Whiteman. Whiteman had previously been assistant to the Solicitor and later assistant to the Legal Adviser, and she is remembered for editing and publishing the fifteen-volume *Digest of International Law* (1969–73).

Department of State Budgets and Funding

With the increase in domestic and overseas staff of the Department of State, its budgets and expenditures mushroomed. Total departmental expenditures, including both stateside and overseas services, grew from $4,909,558 in 1910, to

$13,590,289 in 1920, due largely to World War I and its aftermath, to
$13,986,173 by 1930, nearly doubled to $24,003,329 by 1940, and then more
than doubled again by 1945, when it reached approximately $50 million, after
which it grew even more substantially. Thus, evidencing increased U.S. involvement in foreign affairs, the financial cost of the Department grew from less than
$5 million a year to ten times that amount within the space of thirty-five years.
Nevertheless, allowing for credits for income derived from passport, consular,
and other fees, the actual expenditures from the treasury for the State Department amounted to only 8 to 12 percent of its total budget in some years.

However, only a small portion of these expenditures was used by the domestic
staff of the Department of State. These ranged from $1,185,033 in 1923, to
$1,313,515 two years later, rose to $2,502,118 by 1932, then dropped somewhat
the following two years, and increased to $3,318,440 by 1942, of which ap-
proximately 82 percent was allocated for salaries and allowances.[41]

Building Expansion

Because of its increased duties and staff size the Department required additional office space during World War I and especially at the time of World War
II. During the first war, by 1918, the Department had expanded to auxiliary
quarters in the National Savings and Trust Building and other nearby facilities
on Pennsylvania and New York Avenues in Washington. By the time of World
War II the Navy and War Departments had moved out of the State, War, and
Navy Building adjacent to the White House, and in 1930 its title was changed
to the Department of State Building. However, Presidential Assistants, the Bureau of the Budget, and the National Resources Planning Board moved into the
space previously occupied by the Navy and War Departments.

By the fall of 1941 the Department of State again expanded its offices to such
nearby facilities as a portion of the Commerce Building, the Winder Building
on 17th Street, the annex to the American Institute of Architects Building on
New York Avenue, the Metropolitan Club Annex on H Street, the Hill Building
at 17th and I Streets, an apartment building on 22d Street, and another building
on 21st Street. Thus, the needs of the department continued to exceed the space
provided in the headquarters building it occupied since 1875.[42] Eventually, when
the War Department moved from its building on Virginia Avenue in "Foggy
Bottom" to the Pentagon (known as the world's largest office building), the
Department of State began to move into that building, as indicated in Chapter 7.

State Department Courier Service

The problem of handling the transmittal of official written communications
and documents between the United States and its missions abroad dates back to
the beginning of American diplomacy. The earliest American courier, Peter Par-

ker, was commissioned by the Continental Congress in July 1776 to convey messages to France. Initially, the American Government relied solely on ad hoc "bearers of dispatches." Overseas Chiefs of Missions were authorized to recruit special messengers when needed, usually to convey signed copies of treaties to the Department of State.

Over the years various means were employed for this service, ranging from the use of special agents, to reliance on ordinary mail services or employing any convenient and reliable American who was going abroad or returning to the United States. In the twentieth century attention was paid to adopting a more systematic arrangement. During World War I a courier service was temporarily established, using American military personnel as transmittal agents. Late in 1914 American Embassies in London and Paris were the first posts to hire full-time couriers. Following the war the Department of State resumed the use of ordinary mails, supplemented with convenient travelers as ad hoc couriers. Shortly after he became President, Franklin Roosevelt had the Department of State create its own courier service, beginning with a single agent allotted to American embassies in London and Paris. When war broke out in Europe, it was expanded and improved, and by 1941 the United States also maintained foreign courier bases in China and Japan.[43]

DIPLOMATIC AND CONSULAR REPRESENTATION

Major legislative and administrative changes were made to reform and improve the diplomatic and consular services, the overseas personnel was revised, professionalized, and modernized, and the career Foreign Service was created. Representation was extended to more than fifteen additional countries, some diplomats were appointed to higher ranks, most diplomatic appointees served in their appointments, and the consular system was expanded and regularized. Special problems arose in the management of diplomatic and consular affairs, and more duties were added to the responsibilities of the Department of State and its foreign representatives during World Wars I and II. However, diplomatic relations were interrupted with certain countries during these wars and because American policy shifted from de facto to de jure recognition of foreign states and governments. Difference of opinion emerged respecting the appointment of careerist and noncareerist diplomats to senior departmental posts and as ranking emissaries, women were appointed to senior departmental posts and foreign assignments, and some Presidents, especially Woodrow Wilson and Franklin Roosevelt, were disposed to rely on a corps of special envoys for a greater variety of assignments.

Acts of 1915, 1924, and 1931—Reform and Professionalization

Congress enacted three major acts to reform and convert the Diplomatic and Consular Services to the merit system. The Act of February 5, 1915, concerned largely with diplomatic secretaries, Consuls General, and Consuls, provided that they were to be consummated "by commissions" to these ranks and "not by commission to any particular post," as had previously been the practice, and that such officers "shall be assigned to posts and transferred from one post to another by order of the President as the interests of the services may require." It also authorized their assignment for duty in the Department without loss of grade, class, or salary for a period not to exceed three years unless required in the public interest and that none of these officers were to be "promoted to a higher class except upon the nomination of the President, with the advice and consent of the Senate." This act also established five salary classes of diplomatic secretaries, five classes of Consuls General, and nine classes of consuls, and it defined the nature of various types of consular officials and the term "diplomatic officers."

In addition, this act dealt with the matter of diplomatic secretaries who lawfully functioned as Chargé d'Affaires ad interim, compensation levels for diplomatic secretaries, Consuls General, and Consuls, and recommendations by the President and Secretary of State for promotion and transfer of such officers, as well as those who qualify by examination for appointment to the lower grades of the Foreign Service. Finally, it prohibited all diplomatic officers from engaging in, or transacting, business as a merchant or agent.[44]

On June 4, 1920, Congress amended this act to create a new diplomatic rank—that of Counselor of Embassy or Legation—to serve as deputy chief of the foreign mission, and it empowered the President to designate any diplomatic secretary of class 1 to this position. This amendment also reduced the number of classes of diplomatic secretaries to four and raised their compensation levels. Despite the initial legislative use of the title "Foreign Service," the improvements respecting both diplomatic officers who ranked below Chiefs of Mission and consular officers, and the fixing of classes and salary levels, the Act of 1915, as amended, did not provide for the union of the Diplomatic and Consular Services and their personnel. Although the expression "Foreign Service" was used informally, this title was not officially established until later.[45] In the meantime, by Executive Order No. 3987, dated April 4, 1924, President Coolidge required administrative cooperation abroad, to integrate the activities of the Department of State with those of other Departments and agencies. It prescribed periodic meetings, the exchange of information and reports, and joint special investigations.

The Rogers Act, passed by Congress on May 24, 1924, the first genuine organic act of the Foreign Service, constituted a landmark in amalgamating the Diplomatic and Consular Services into a professional "Foreign Service of the United States." It instituted a sweeping reorganization of positions and personnel in a unified career agency,[46] and it removed the Foreign Service from politics, established it as a permanent and professional career service, and applied merit to all appointments and promotions.

Aside from formally creating and titling an integrated Foreign Service and rendering its members interchangeable in diplomatic and consular assignments, this act removed all professional officers from the spoils system. It established nine classes of Foreign Service Officers, plus "unclassified officers," with salaries and percentages of personnel fixed for each class. Salaries ranged upward from $1,500 to $3,000 for unclassified officers and to a maximum of $9,000 for those in class 1. It stipulated that new Foreign Service Officers may be appointed and commissioned as secretaries in the Diplomatic Service, as consular officers, or as both, with the approval of the Senate, that such appointments be made after examination and a period of probation as an "unclassified officer" or by transfer after five years of continuous service in the Department of State, that candidates must be American citizens, and that, as under the Act of 1915, all appointments be by commission to a specific class rather than a particular post.

Furthermore, the Rogers Act established regulations for promotion, transfers, and periodic inspection and for special representation and transportation allowances, bonding of officers, and handling of fees collected. It authorized assignment of Foreign Service officers for duty in the Department of State, statutory leave of absence after three years of continuous service abroad, temporary recall of retired officers in the event of a public emergency, and appropriations for private secretaries of ambassadors. The most comprehensive section of the law dealt with the establishment of a Foreign Service retirement and disability program, Administered under the direction of the Secretary of State. Finally, it provided that previous legislation not inconsistent with this act remained applicable to Foreign Service Officers.[47]

This act was immediately supplemented by a number of presidential and departmental orders. Executive Order No. 4022, dated June 7, 1924, contained rules to govern promotion from lower positions to Classes 1–9 of the Foreign Service on the basis of "ability and efficiency." It also created a Foreign Service Personnel Board to manage personnel matters, a Board of Examiners to formulate rules and administer oral and written examinations for commissioning into the Foreign Service and to maintain an eligibility list of qualified candidates for appointment, and a Foreign Service School for instructing new appointees. Secretary Hughes also published two Department of State orders on June 9 to create an Executive Committee of the Personnel Board to handle personnel files and efficiency records, to recommend assignments and transfers of Foreign Service Officers, and to formulate regulations for the management and operation of the Foreign Service School.

To rectify deficiencies in the Rogers Act,[48] on February 23, 1931, Congress enacted the Moses–Linthicum Act. Constituting a revised, comprehensive, organic act for the Foreign Service, although it reiterated much of the Rogers Act, it ranked Foreign Service officers in eight regular classes, plus unclassified officers, increased their salaries ranging from $3,500 to $10,000 annually, and provided for annual leaves, sick leaves of absence, and other details concerned with commissioning and retirement arrangements.

Innovative in two major respects, it reorganized the Foreign Service Personnel

Board and modified arrangements respecting the overseas clerical staff. It formulated elaborate regulations to govern the Personnel Board's composition, authority, and functions concerning matters of compiling and appraising efficiency reports of officers and maintaining confidentiality of their correspondence and records (except for the President, the Secretary of State, and Board members). It supplemented these matters with specifications pertaining to automatic within-grade salary increases, special allowances, and improvements in the retirement program. It also revised and regularized the system of diplomatic clerks, organizing them in two categories consisting of senior clerks arranged in five classes and junior clerks in three classes, with annual salaries ranging from $2,750 to $4,000, and it dealt with their appointment, advancement, and special living expenses.[49]

The Moses–Linthicum Act also updated and improved the organization and management of the Foreign Service. Assessing this revision, in 1934 Assistant Secretary Wilbur Carr, who played a major role in devising the substance of the Acts of 1924 and 1931 and who has been called the ''Father of the Foreign Service,'' observed that ''the Foreign Service had finally attained the goal for which Presidents, Secretaries of State, and the businessmen of the country had striven for years.''[50]

Congress and the President made several additional changes between 1931 and 1945. By Executive Order of November 1936, President Roosevelt declared that future Foreign Service Officers who wished to marry an alien were required to request permission, accompanied by the applicant's resignation for such action as might be taken in the circumstances. Although such marriages had previously been allowed, they had resulted in difficulties in the assignment and use of the officers.[51] To develop a corps of specialists to handle certain functions, from 1937 to 1941 Congress authorized annual funding to provide a year of advanced training for junior officers at selected academic institutions. This program was suspended during World War II but was later reinstated. Paralleling the Foreign Service in the late 1920s and early 1930s Congress empowered the Departments of Commerce and Agriculture and the Bureau of Mines of the Interior Department to appoint their own representatives to foreign countries, and the Treasury Department maintained a number of foreign customs agents.

On May 3, 1945, Congress also legislated to authorize a new category of administrative, fiscal, and clerical Officers, assistants, and clerks to exercise administrative duties abroad. The objective of this change was to relieve Foreign Service officers from such managerial duties and to improve the classification and salary arrangements for administrative personnel. This act also eliminated the percentage specification for the number of Foreign Service officers in each class that had been stipulated in the Rogers Act. These actions produced greater flexibility respecting appointments and promotions and enabled the Department of State and other government agencies to temporarily interchange personnel for up to four years.

Organization and Management of Overseas Missions

Before Congress enacted the Rogers Act, overseas diplomatic and consular missions were administered separately, but in the 1930s the Department of State combined them in single establishments in most foreign capitals. This integrated Foreign Service personnel in single establishments generally housed in the same building. Such combined missions were normally headed by the Chief and Deputy Chief of Mission and embodied a political section led by a Diplomatic Secretary, an economic section under a Commercial Attaché, and an administrative and consular section under a Consul General or Consul. Consular officers not located in foreign capitals remained separate but were linked with the Chief of the Embassy or Legation Consular Section, who functioned as supervisory consular officer for the entire country.

By the time of World War II five State Department agencies were responsible for administering the Foreign Service. The Board of Foreign Service Personnel, under the President and Secretary of State, handled the assignment, transfer, promotion, and disciplining of Foreign Service Officers and exercised related duties, such as preparing recommendatory lists of those qualified for designation as Chiefs of Mission. The Division of Foreign Service Personnel recommended personnel actions to the Personnel Board and had custody of confidential personnel files. The Board of Examiners, headed by the Assistant Secretary of State for Administration, constituted the oral examining board, graded candidates who passed the written examination, and prepared the eligibility list of candidates for appointment. The Division of Foreign Service Administration was responsible for implementing appointments, leaves of absence, promotions, transfers, and related matters. The Budget Officer of the Department, who served as Assistant Secretary for administration and also Chairman of the Board of Foreign Service Personnel, compiled the budget for the Department, including the Foreign Service.

American foreign diplomatic missions increased from approximately fifty in 1910 to nearly sixty by 1940.[52] To be more precise, as indicated in Table 6.3, the United States was diplomatically represented to sixty-eight countries during the period from 1913 to 1945, some two-thirds of which continued on the American diplomatic roster throughout this period. Between World War I and 1945 some twenty countries were added, including eleven in Europe, three in Africa, and three in the Middle East, plus Afghanistan, Canada, and New Zealand. These were new additions except for the Holy See, with which formal relations were suspended in 1867 and temporarily reestablished in 1941.[53] However, the American diplomatic community was reduced to merely fifty-one by 1945, largely as a consequence of World War II. In addition, relations with Montenegro ended in 1918, when it was absorbed by Yugoslavia, and Harold H. Tittmann, Jr., the American Chargé d'Affaires representing the United States to the Vatican (who was neither formally accredited nor commissioned), served de facto only from December 1941 to July 1944.

Table 6.3
American Diplomats and Missions, 1913–1945

Country	Years to 1945	Appointed	Served	Declined appointment	Senate not approve	Not commissioned	Not serve for other reasons
Afghanistan	1935-	4	4				
Albania	1922-1939	5	5				
Argentina *	1913-	6	6				
Austria *	1913-1937	7	7				
Belgium *	1913-	10	10				
Bolivia *	1913-	12	11				1
Brazil *	1913-	3	3				
Bulgaria *	1913-1941	7	6				1
Canada	1927-	9	8		1		
Chile *	1913-	7	7				
China *	1913-	7	7				
Colombia *	1913-	9	9				
Costa Rica *	1913-	11	9			2	
Cuba *	1913-	10	10				
Czechoslovakia	1919-1939	9	9				
Denmark *	1913-	9	9				
Dominican Rep. *	1913-	10	10				
Ecuador *	1913-	8	7				1
Egypt *	1913-	9	9				
El Salvador *	1913-	10	10				
Estonia	1922-1940	6	5				1
Ethiopia	1927-1936	2	2				
Finland	1920-	7	6				1
France *	1913-	8	8				
Germany *	1913-1941	7	7				
Great Britain *	1913-	10	10				
Greece *	1913-	10	9			1	
Guatemala *	1913-	9	8				1
Haiti *	1913-	8	8				
Holy See *	1941-1944	2	1			1	
Honduras *	1913-	7	7				
Hungary	1922-1941	6	6				
Iceland	1941-	3	3				
Iran (Persia) *	1913-	8	8				
Iraq	1931-	4	4				
Ireland	1927-	5	5				
Italy *	1913-1941	8	8				
Japan *	1913-1941	9	9				
Latvia	1922-1940	6	5				1
Lebanon	1942-	1	1				
Liberia *	1913-	9	6	1			2
Lithuania	1922-1940	5	5				
Luxembourg *	1913-	16	13				3
Mexico *	1916-	8	7		1		
Montenegro *	1913-1918	2	2				
Morocco *	1913-	4	4				
Netherlands *	1913-	10	10				
New Zealand	1942-	4	3			1	
Nicaragua *	1913-	10	10				
Norway *	1913-	7	7				
Panama *	1913-	10	9				1
Paraguay *	1913-	9	8			1	
Peru *	1913-	8	8				
Poland	1919-1939	10	8			1	1
Portugal *	1913-	8	7			1	
Romania *	1913-1941	7	7				
Russia * 1	1913-	8	7	1			
Saudi Arabia	1939-	4	4				
South Africa	1929-	4	4				
Spain *	1913-	9	9				
Sweden *	1913-	8	8				
Switzerland *	1913-	6	6				
Syria	1942-	1	1				
Thailand *	1913-1942	13	11			1	1
Turkey *	1913-	7	7				
Uruguay *	1913-	11	9				2
Venezuela *	1913-	6	6				
Yugoslavia *	1913-	8	8				
Total 68		500	470	2	2	9	17

*Indicates countries to which American diplomats were accredited prior to 1913.

1Russia was converted into the Soviet Union following World War I.

During World Wars I and II diplomatic relations with more than twenty countries were interrupted because of declarations of war, annexation or military occupation, and the severance of relations. For example, at the time of World War I, the United States severed relations with, and declared war on, Germany and Austria-Hungary, and Turkey severed relations with the United States in 1917. They were not revived with Germany and Austria until 1921 and with Turkey in 1927.

In the interwar period, Italy annexed Ethiopia in 1936, but relations were revived with it in 1943. During World War II Austria was annexed by Germany in March 1938. The following year Germany and the Soviet Union invaded Poland, Nazi forces occupied Belgium, Czechoslovakia, Denmark, Greece, Hungary, Luxembourg, the Netherlands, Norway, and part of France, Italian forces occupied Albania, and Japan invaded and occupied extensive colonial territory in the Far East and Pacific, as well as Thailand. The Soviet Union annexed the Baltic States of Estonia, Latvia, and Lithuania in June 1940, and Germany occupied Yugoslavia in April 1941. Japan, Germany, Italy, Hungary, and Romania declared war on the United States in December 1941, as did Thailand in June 1942. Finland also severed relations with the United States in June 1944. The governments of most of the countries occupied by Germany fled into exile, and the Department of State continued diplomatic relations with them, primarily in Great Britain and Canada for Western European countries and in Egypt for Greece and Yugoslavia. Traditional relations with Japan, Germany, and Italy were not resumed until peace treaties were concluded.

Diplomatic representation abroad was also interrupted for a variety of other reasons. Turnover of diplomatic appointees was most prevalent when political shifts occurred in the American Presidency. When Wilson was inaugurated in 1913, and Bryan became Secretary of State, and the Democratic Party returned to power after an interval of sixteen years, their new diplomatic team consisted of ten officers who had been Ambassadors and Ministers at previous posts, eighteen who were promoted from other diplomatic and consular positions, and thirteen (or less than one-third) who lacked prior diplomatic experience. The President replaced such experienced diplomats as William W. Rockhill (Ambassador to Turkey), Arthur M. Beaupre (Minister to Cuba), H. Percival Dodge (Minister to Panama), and John B. Jackson (Minister to Romania, Serbia, and Bulgaria). But he retained Edwin V. Morgan (Ambassador to Brazil), Henry P. Fletcher (Ambassador to Chile), and Arthur Bailly-Blanchard (promoted to Minister to Haiti), who were careerists, and he appointed Walter Hines Page as Ambassador to Great Britain, James W. Gerard III, as Ambassador to Germany, Paul S. Reinsch as Minister to China, Thomas Nelson Page (Ambassador to Italy), Henry Van Dyke (Minister to the Netherlands and Luxembourg), Brand Whitlock (Minister to Belgium), and others who were noncareerists.

When Republicans returned to power in 1921, President Harding and Secretary Hughes, who sought to rely on more careerists as Chiefs of Mission, retained Edwin V. Morgan as Ambassador to Brazil, Hugh S. Gibson as the first

Ambassador to Poland, and Ira N. Morris as Minister to Sweden. They also appointed such career officers as Fred Morris Dearing (Portugal), Henry P. Fletcher (Belgium), Joseph C. Grew (Switzerland), Peter Augustus Jay (Romania), Hoffman Philip (Uruguay), and Charles S. Wilson (Bulgaria), all of whom had held previous senior appointments. Several former diplomats were also brought back into service, including Lewis D. Einstein as Minister to Czechoslovakia, Myron T. Herrick as Ambassador to France (his second appointment in this capacity), John W. Riddle as Ambassador to Argentina, and Laurits S. Swenson for his second appointment as Minister to Norway.

In 1933, after twelve years of Republican rule, President Roosevelt and Secretary Hull made many changes in diplomatic appointments, but they relied substantially on career officers. One-third of their initial appointments of Ambassadors and nearly half of the Ministers were Foreign Service Officers. For example, they retained Fred M. Dearing in Peru, Joseph C. Grew in Japan, Nelson T. Johnson in China, Edwin V. Morgan in Brazil, and Hugh R. Wilson in Switzerland, and they named Hugh S. Gibson as Ambassador to Brazil, Robert P. Skinner to Turkey, and Alexander W. Weddell as Ambassador to Argentina, all of whom were careerists. When the United States decided to recognize the revolutionary Soviet government, in 1933 they commissioned William C. Bullitt, a noncareerist, as first post–World War I Ambassador to Moscow, who was transferred to Paris in 1936. President Roosevelt also appointed the first women ranking diplomats in 1933 and 1937.

Thus, despite such major political changes in the presidency and the facts that diplomatic careerism was not legislated until 1915 and that the Foreign Service Act was not passed until 1924, Presidents frequently appointed or transferred experienced emissaries to many diplomatic posts, denoting a substantial shift respecting diplomatic professionalism. During the period from 1913 to 1945 nearly 45 percent of those nominated as chiefs of mission were careerists. On the other hand, more than half were noncareerists.

Ordinarily, the diplomatic missions of individuals are terminated by resignation, recall, supersession, or dismissal. In U.S. practice supersession is facilitated by the long-standing practice that when a President is inaugurated, all Ambassadors and Ministers tender their resignations—often called "courtesy resignations"—and it is up to the President to accept or reject them, but regular members of the Foreign Service whose resignations are honored retain their career status and are shifted to other positions. This affords newly inaugurated Presidents flexibility in selecting their American diplomatic teams. Even if such courtesy resignations were not filed, the President could simply nominate preferred replacements.[54] Or diplomats may resign, particularly if they had held their posts for lengthy periods, or, in the case of noncareerists, they desire to return to other pursuits. Or they may resign because they disagree with the President or the Secretary of State on matters of policy or, at times, because they find the expenses of their office too burdensome.

In specifying the common reasons for the termination of individual diplomatic missions, the Department of State reports that during this period the preponderant majority of Chiefs of Mission simply left their posts or their countries of assignment without specifying the reasons. In more than twenty cases they were viewed as having "presented their recall," and in several instances they are recorded as having their "recess appointment expired" (Paul Knabenshue, Iraq in 1933, and F. Lammot Belin, Poland in 1933) or simply as "termination of appointment" (John L. Caldwell, Iran in 1921, Fred Morris Dearing, Sweden in 1938, and Charles H. Sherrill, Turkey in 1933). Occasionally, missions were terminated because "normal relations were interrupted."

However, Charles J. Vopicka, a noncareerist, appointed as Minister Plenipotentiary to Bulgaria, Romania, and Serbia in 1913, bears the distinction of being "relieved of active functions" in Bulgaria and Serbia in December 1918, but he continued to serve in Romania until 1920. In the case of Charles E. Mitchell, accredited as Minister to Liberia in the early 1930s, he did not present his credentials because the Liberian Government requested his recall prior to his official reception. Thomas Sambola Jones, commissioned as Minister Plenipotentiary to Honduras in 1918, was held to be person non grata on January 1, 1920. He was the only American emissary to be dismissed for this reason during this period. Moreover, some fifteen emissaries died at their posts, and Alexander P. Moore, nominated as Ambassador to Poland in 1930, died in the United States before taking the oath of office.

As indicated in Table 6.3, Presidents appointed 500 diplomats during these three decades, of whom all but thirty served in their appointments. Whereas previously (1861–1913), some 15 percent of the appointees failed to serve, this ratio was reduced to only 6 percent (1913–45). Only two candidates declined their appointments, two did not receive Senatorial confirmation, and nine, though approved, were not commissioned. For most of the forty countries with which the United States maintained diplomatic representation throughout this period, the number of emissaries who served averaged between seven and ten.[55] Luxembourg was the exception, to which thirteen were commissioned. On the other hand, only three envoys were accredited to Brazil, and four were appointed to Morocco.

Marking the shift to professionalism, between 1913 and 1945 some 216 (more than 43 percent) of the diplomatic nominees were careerists. As indicated in Table 6.4, no career diplomats were appointed to Great Britain and Russia, and very few were commissioned to France, Germany, Japan, Mexico, the Netherlands, and Portugal. However, all envoys accredited to Ethiopia, the Holy See, Iraq, Lebanon, and Syria were careerists, as were the preponderant majority of the emissaries sent to eleven other countries.[56] Among the reasons for the increase in the number of careerist Chiefs of Mission appointed in the 1930s and 1940s were the professionalization of the Foreign Service and the resulting availability of more experienced diplomats, and, when Cordell Hull became Secretary of State, he favored a 50–50 formula for career officers and outsiders. Ultimately, the choice was the prerogative of the President, and when Roosevelt

Table 6.4
American Diplomatic Appointees, 1913–1945 (Number of Appointees by Ranks)

Country	C	NC	AE/P	EE/MP	MR/CG	CdA	Dip/Agt	Agt/CG	Total
Afghanistan	3	1		4					4
Albania	2	3		5					5
Argentina	5	1	6						6
Austria	2	5	1	5		1			7
Belgium	4	6	10						10
Bolivia	5	7	2	10					12
Brazil	2	1	3						3
Bulgaria	4	3		7					7
Canada	5	4	1	8					9
Chile	2	5	7						7
China	3	4	3	4					7
Colombia	6	3	3	6					9
Costa Rica	5	6	2	9					11
Cuba	4	6	8	2					10
Czechoslovakia	2	7	2	7					9
Denmark	3	6		9					9
Dominican Republic	9	1	3	7					10
Ecuador	3	5	2	6					8
Egypt	3	6	1	5				3	9
El Salvador	8	2	2	8					10
Estonia	5	1		6					6
Ethiopia	2				2				2
Finland	2	5		6		1			7
France	1	7	8						8
Germany	1	6	6			1			7
Great Britain		10	10						10
Greece	3	7	3	7					10
Guatemala	2	7	2	7					9
Haiti	7	1	2	6					8
Holy See	1	1				2			2
Honduras	3	4	1	6					7
Hungary	2	4		5		1			6
Iceland	2	1		3					3
Iran (Persia)	4	4	2	6					8
Iraq	4			1	2	1			4
Ireland	1	4		5					5
Italy	4	4	8						8
Japan	1	8	9						9
Latvia	5	1		6					6
Lebanon	1			1					1
Liberia	1	8		2	7				9
Lithuania	3	2		5					5
Luxembourg	9	7		15		1			16
Mexico	2	6	8						8
Montenegro		2		2					2
Morocco	3	1					2	2	4
Netherlands	3	7	8	2					10
New Zealand	2	2		4					4
Nicaragua	6	4	2	8					10
Norway	2	5	2	5					7
Panama	5	5	4	6					10
Paraguay	3	6	2	7					9
Peru	3	5	7	1					8
Poland	3	7	7	3					10
Portugal	2	6	1	7					8
Romania	4	3		7					7
Russia[1]		8	8						8
Saudi Arabia	2	2		3	1				4
South Africa	2	2		4					4
Spain	3	6	9						9
Sweden	5	3		8					8
Switzerland	2	4		6					6
Syria	1			1					1
Thailand	3	10		13					13
Turkey	3	4	7						7
Uruguay	9	2	1	10					11
Venezuela	1	5	1	5					6
Yugoslavia	3	5	3	5					8
Total 68	216	284	177	296	12	8	2	5	500

Code: C=Foreign Service Career status and NC=Non-Foreign Service Career status. AE/P=Ambassador Extraordinary and Plenipotentiary; EE/MP=Envoy Extraordinary and Minister Plenipotentiary; MR/CG=Minister Resident and Consul General; CdA=Chargé d'Affaires; Dip/Agt=Diplomatic Agent; and Agt/CG=Diplomatic Agent and Consul General.

[1]Russia was converted into the Soviet Union following World War I.

was first elected, he appointed such outsiders as Robert W. Bingham (London), Claude G. Bowers (Madrid), William C. Bullitt (Moscow), Josephus Daniels, Jr. (Mexico City), William E. Dodd (Germany), and Jesse I. Straus (Paris).

Diplomatic Corps

Another major change concerned the ranking of diplomats. Whereas prior to 1913 less than 7 percent were accredited as Ambassadors, during this period 177 of 500, or 35.4 percent, held that rank. Previously, Ambassadors were appointed to only ten countries—seven in Europe (Austria, France, Germany, Great Britain, Italy, Japan, and Russia), two in Latin America (Brazil and Mexico), and Turkey. By 1945 the United States exchanged Ambassadors with forty-one countries, more than quadrupling representation at the highest rank. Two-thirds of these advancements to the level of Ambassador occurred between 1940 and 1945.[57] When the United States emerged from World War II as a superpower, most of its Chiefs of Mission had been raised to ambassadorships, reflecting American regard of the important diplomatic role it was to play in the postwar era.

Also reflecting this change in attitude, the rank of Minister Resident was discontinued except for a few envoys who were nominated as combination Ministers Resident and Consuls General and assigned to Ethiopia, Iraq, Liberia, and Saudi Arabia. However, the largest number, 296 or more than 59 percent, were designated as Envoy Extraordinary and Minister Plenipotentiary. In addition, eight nominees were assigned the rank of Chargé d'Affaires, six of whom served as the first envoys at the commencement of American diplomatic relations with Finland, Hungary, and Iraq or to renew diplomatic relations following World War I and to provide special relations with the Holy See and Luxembourg during World War II. Seven others were designated as Diplomatic Agents, and the rank of Commissioner was dropped. This revised rank distribution and the breadth of its diplomatic representation also reflected U.S. advancement into the ranks of the great world powers.

At least thirty-five mission chiefs enjoyed extended diplomatic careers with five or more such appointments, some of which extended beyond 1945. The preponderant majority were Foreign Service Officers, several of whom held as many as eight appointments (such as Joseph C. Grew, Harrison F. Matthews, and Avra Milvin Warren), nine appointments (Norman Armour and George Wadsworth II), and even ten appointments (William Phillips)—all of whom were careerists. Anthony J. Drexel Biddle, Jr., who also held ten appointments, was the only noncareerist with such a lengthy career. More than half of these served as Mission Chiefs for twenty years or longer, several of whom continued in such assignments for more than thirty years, including Boaz W. Long (thirty-one years), William Phillips (thirty-two years), Jefferson Caffery (thirty-three years), and James C. Dunn (thirty-four years).

However, of the 470 emissaries who served in their appointments, more than sixty held their positions for less than one year, including three of those commissioned to Austria, Denmark, and Thailand and four assigned to Japan and Luxembourg. Three died within a year—Grenville T. Emmett after only twelve days in Austria in 1937, William W. McDowell after fourteen days in Ireland in 1934, and Edgar A. Bancroft after eight months in Japan in 1925. Edmund Albright, appointed Minister Plenipotentiary to Costa Rica in 1937, took the oath of office but died in the United States before proceeding to his post.

Cornelius Van Hemert Engert, named Minister Resident/Consul General to Ethiopia, had the shortest tenure—merely five days—when Italian forces occupied Addis Ababa in 1936. Others had their service cut short by the severance of diplomatic relations and the outbreak of World Wars I and II. Those whose service was interrupted by war included Abram I. Elkus, Ambassador to Turkey in 1917; John Cudahy, Ambassador to Belgium and Minister to Luxembourg in 1940; and Willys R. Peck, Minister Plenipotentiary to Thailand in 1941. The truncation of service due to the severance of diplomatic relations applied to Henry Lane Wilson in Mexico in 1913, Edward J. Hale in Costa Rica and David R. Francis in Russia in 1917, Edward Capps in Greece in 1920, Benton McMillin in Guatemala in 1922, Charles B. Curtis in El Salvador in 1932, and Sumner Welles in Cuba in 1933. Some of these had served in their assignments for only two months or less.

The preponderant majority of American diplomats remained from two to four years, and nearly eighty continued at their posts for five to nine years.[58] Records were set by ten emissaries who held their posts for ten years or longer. These included Nelson T. Johnson (China, eleven years), Lincoln MacVeagh (Greece, more than eleven years, in two appointments, interrupted when Germany invaded that country), Claude G. Bowers (Chile, fourteen years), Maxwell Blake (Morocco, sixteen years), and, most exceptionally, Edwin V. Morgan (Brazil, twenty-one years from 1912 to 1933, extending from the time of President Wilson to Franklin Roosevelt).[59] Three of these—Blake, Johnson, and Morgan—were career officers.

Relating turnover in the Presidency and length of service, more than twenty of President Wilson's appointees remained for five to eight years. When Harding became President, seventeen served for five to nine years. But when Roosevelt took office, only eight held their posts for five to nine years, indicating not only an actual and relative decline in the length of diplomatic tenure in individual posts but also the shift of more careerists from one post to another.

Some 113, or 24 percent, of the emissaries received sequential multiple appointments.[60] Eighty were commissioned two or three times, and thirty-three received four or more appointments. More than half of these were careerists, ten of whom were accredited to six to nine missions. In addition to Biddle, Grew, and Phillips, these included Henry P. Fletcher, Hugh S. Gibson, Leland Harrison, Arthur Bliss Lane, Reymond H. Norweb, and Joshua B. Wright.

Equally impressive is the record of those emissaries who held simultaneous multiple appointments, which were of two types. The normal use of this technique has been to accredit a single envoy to two or more generally adjacent or nearby countries. In earlier times the United States used this technique primarily for representation to the Central American Republics, to Haiti and Santo Domingo, and to Greece, Romania, and Serbia. During these three decades John W. Garrett, William Phillips, and Henry Van Dyke were accredited simultaneously to both the Netherlands and Luxembourg, resident at The Hague (1913–22); and Fletcher, Phillips, Gibson, John Cudahy, Joseph E. Davies, and Dave Hennen Morris served as Ambassadors to both Belgium and Luxembourg, resident at Brussels. Similarly, Charles J. Vopicka was commissioned simultaneously to Bulgaria, Romania, and Serbia, resident at Bucharest (1913–18); Edward Capps was accredited as Minister to Greece as well as to Montenegro, but he did not serve in the latter capacity (1920–21); and a series of emissaries, including Frederick W. B. Coleman, Arthur Bliss Lane, and John C. Wiley, were commissioned as Ministers to Estonia, Latvia, and Lithuania, resident at Riga (1922–37).

Subsequently, Bert Fish and Alexander C. Kirk, sent as Ministers Plenipotentiary to Egypt, resident at Cairo, were also accredited to Saudi Arabia (1941–43); Lewis G. Dreyfus, Jr., and William H. Hornibrook were appointed to Iran and Afghanistan, stationed at Tehran (1934–43); and George Wadsworth II, assigned as Minister Plenipotentiary to Lebanon, stationed at Beirut, also served as envoy to Syria (1942–47).

The alternative use of simultaneous multiple appointments was made during World War II to maintain relations with governments in exile. The most remarkable of such plural representation, Ambassador Biddle, representing the United States in Poland, left Warsaw in September 1939 and followed the Polish Government first to France and then to Great Britain, where, 1941–43, he served simultaneously as Ambassador or Minister to eight governments in exile—Poland and Belgium, Czechoslovakia, Greece, Luxembourg, the Netherlands, Norway, and Yugoslavia—while John G. Winant represented the United States to Great Britain.

For a time others also handled relations with several governments in exile. Rudolph E. Schoenfeld, Chargé d'Affaires, stationed in Great Britain, preceded Biddle in representing the United States to Belgium, the Netherlands, Norway, and Poland, beginning in 1940, to which Yugoslavia was added in 1944. Similarly, Ray Atherton, Minister Plenipotentiary to Denmark in 1939, was transferred to Canada in 1943, where he also represented the United States to Denmark and Luxembourg, stationed at Ottawa, and he remained in Canada until 1948. Alexander C. Kirk, accredited as Minister Plenipotentiary to Egypt (1941–44) temporarily represented the United States to the governments of Greece and Saudi Arabia at Cairo, and Lincoln MacVeagh, Ambassador to Greece, also dealt with the governments of Yugoslavia and Egypt, stationed at Cairo, until the Yugoslavian Government transferred to London and the American mission was returned to Athens. Thus, Cairo, Ottawa, and especially London became the centers of American wartime multiple diplomacy, and a good many such appointees on simultaneous missions—such as Atherton, Kirk, and Schoenfeld—were career Foreign Service Officers.

To review the status of the American diplomatic establishment at the end of World War II, when President Roosevelt died on April 12, 1945, the United States maintained a corps of diplomatic officers stationed in fifty countries. These were headed by thirty-six Ambassadors, thirteen Ministers Plenipotentiary, and a Chargé d'Affaires on duty at the Holy See. Some of these were accredited to European governments in exile. Diplomatic representation had been suspended in twelve countries due to the war and was temporarily in abeyance with four other countries pending transition to new appointees. Harry Truman, therefore, had an early opportunity to fill sixteen vacant diplomatic posts. However, in the case of Germany, Italy, and other Axis belligerents, new appointments were deferred until peace was restored, but in more than twenty other cases the tenure of envoys was terminated, and President Truman commissioned replacements by mid-1946.

Women had been eligible for appointment to the career Foreign Service since 1924, but for two decades the number who applied and passed the Foreign Service examinations was minuscule. For example, three were appointed in the 1920s, and six in 1930, of whom only two remained in 1931. However, Lucile Atcherson became the first woman Foreign Service Officer in 1922, and she was sent to Berne and later transferred to Panama City. In 1927 Frances E. Willis was commissioned as Vice Consul to Valparaiso, Chile, held a variety of other posts both in the Department of State and in the field, served as Ambassador to Switzerland beginning in 1953 and later to Norway, and in the 1960s was promoted to the distinguished rank of Career Ambassador.

In the meantime, President Roosevelt appointed the first women Chiefs of Mission. Ruth Bryan Owen (daughter of former Secretary Bryan), who had previously served in Congress, was accredited as the first woman Minister Plenipotentiary, and was sent to Denmark in 1933, where she served for more than three years. President Roosevelt also appointed Florence Jaffray Harriman, who had been active in the Democratic National Committee and campaigned actively for Roosevelt's election. She was commissioned as Minister Plenipotentiary to Norway in 1937, where she remained until the German occupation of that country in April 1940.

Caretaking Missions for Other Governments

Another interesting feature of diplomatic relations occurred during World Wars I and II, before the United States became a belligerent. From 1914 to 1917, while this country remained neutral, the American Embassy at Paris, headed by Ambassadors Myron T. Herrick and William G. Sharp, serving as a third party, handled the affairs of Germany, Austria-Hungary, and Turkey, and in Berlin Ambassador James W. Gerard serviced the interests of the British, Japanese, Italian, Romanian, and Serbian governments, and from 1913 to 1917

Ambassador Henry Morgenthau had charge of the interests of France, Great Britain, Russia, and other Allied nations in Turkey. When the United States broke off relations with Germany in 1917, American interests were entrusted to the care of the Spanish Embassy at Berlin, while German affairs in this country were assumed by the Swiss Legation.

During World War II, prior to Pearl Harbor, the Department's "Special Division" was created to handle not only the affairs of Americans located in belligerent countries but also those of various belligerent governments seeking such assistance. Consequently, the Department of State and American foreign missions took over the interests of Australia, Canada, France, Great Britain, and New Zealand in Germany and offered its services to other governments in the event that the war would spread. Eventually, such assistance was also supplied to Belgium, Luxembourg, and Egypt, as well as to Costa Rica, Haiti, and Panama at Berlin. Also, Ambassador William C. Bullitt remained in Paris, despite the flight of the French Government in 1940, in order to turn the French capital over to invading German forces.

By May the following year, as a neutral power, the United States had assumed the capacity of protector of the interests of belligerent states in twenty-five countries. For example, this country temporarily represented the welfare and affairs of ten states in Bulgaria, nine in Italy, eight each in Germany and the Netherlands, and seven each in Belgium, Denmark, and Norway. In France, the American Embassy had the unique experience of representing seven Allied powers at Paris (occupied France). In this manner the Department of State and American diplomats assumed the massive responsibility for an aggregate of nearly seventy governments in eight different countries.

Conversely, following Pearl Harbor, Japan left its Washington Embassy in charge of the Spanish Ambassador until March 1945 and then turned it over to the Swiss Government. The United States transferred most of its diplomatic establishments in belligerent countries to the Swiss Government. Thus, the Swiss represented the United States in Bulgaria, Denmark, France, Germany, Hungary, Indochina, Italy, Japan, Romania, Thailand, and occupied China. Switzerland also represented Bulgaria, Germany, Italy, and Japan in the United States, and Sweden handled the affairs of Hungary and Romania in Washington.

In undertaking such third-party administration of the diplomatic affairs of other countries, the Department of State and its foreign missions affording good offices had to be careful not to compromise this government as a neutral or to disaffect its amicable relations with the governments concerned. In addition to exercising the customary responsibilities for the Department of State, American envoys usually take over the custody of the diplomatic mission of the country represented, raise the American flag, assist its diplomatic corps to leave the country at war, secure the archives, and then care for the nationals and interests of that country and also distribute whatever relief is provided by the belligerent government on whose behalf such action is taken.[61]

Subordinate Staffs

As noted in Chapter 5, Congress procrastinated in providing American diplomatic missions with subordinate staff members. During the twenty years from
1898 to the end of World War I, the number of diplomatic secretaries increased
from twenty-four to ninety-seven during the war years and to 122 by 1918. By
Executive Order No. 1143 of November 26, 1909, certain principles concerning
appointment, promotion, transfer, and retention embodied in Civil Service regulations were applied to such diplomatic secretaries. The Act of February 5,
1915, specified that all secretaries in the Diplomatic and Consular Services were
to be made by commissions to specific offices rather than to particular posts
and that such officers should be careerists assigned to posts and transferred from
one to another as required. This act also provided for the grading of diplomatic
secretaries abroad in five classes, with salaries ranging from $1,200 to $3,000,
and officially recognized them as "diplomatic officers." The following year
their salaries were increased: from $2,500 to $4,000.

The Rogers Act of 1924 reconfirmed these mission secretaries as Foreign
Service Officers, reduced the number of classes from five to three, and fixed
their salaries by class in the Foreign Service. These provisions were reconfirmed
by the Moses–Linthicum Act of 1931, with some modification of salary ranges.
It also authorized appropriations for the salaries of *private* secretaries of American Ambassadors. Due to the low salary scale for diplomatic secretaries, however, appointments were generally restricted to young persons of wealthy
families who had the resources to finance themselves abroad. In 1916 Congress
also created the rank of Counselor of Embassy or Legation, which ranked next
to that of Ambassador or Minister and above that of mission secretaries.

For more than a century and a half routine administrative functions of American embassies, legations, and consular offices were the responsibility of regular
commissioned officers and hired clerks. However, in May 1945 Congress
amended the Moses–Linthicum Act to provide a separate category of administrative, fiscal, and clerical personnel in the Foreign Service. This consisted of
administrative officers, administrative assistants, and clerks, with salaries ranging from $2,900 to $5,600. The advantage of this arrangement was that it relieved Foreign Service Officers from ordinary administrative duties, including
such matters as office management, budget and accounting services, and the
care of citizenship, immigration, and shipping duties. But this new category was
short-lived, until November 1946, when it was incorporated into a new corps
of Foreign Service Staff Officers.[62]

Attachés

To ease its shortage of mission secretaries and staffing, early in the nineteenth
century the Department of State authorized the extralegal appointment of unpaid
attachés. In those early days they possessed independent incomes, performed

the functions of Secretaries of Legation, and sometimes served in the absence of the official Diplomatic Secretary, but usually only for short periods. Congress began to take action in 1855 to abolish the use of these general attachés, and the acts of 1855 and 1856 disallowed such appointments, which was reconfirmed by official regulations in 1874 and 1897.

Aside from those officers who served as Secretaries of Embassies and Legations, who were responsible to the Department of State, in some missions functional attachés were appointed by other Departments and agencies to serve in diplomatic missions. Administratively, they were under the Chief of Mission but functioned as experts and advisers in their respective fields and reported to their own Departments or agencies.

The earliest action taken by Congress to authorize the appointment of such functional attachés in September 1888 provided for the commissioning of Military and Naval Attachés to American diplomatic missions abroad. The initial appointees were stationed at Berlin, London, Paris, St. Petersburg, and Vienna in 1889, and others were subsequently added, assigned to Rome (1890), Brussels (1892), Madrid (1893), and Tokyo and Mexico City (1894). During the Spanish-American War the number was increased to sixteen, which was reduced to ten at the end of the war, but by 1914 the number had risen to twenty-three Military Attachés and eight Naval Attachés. By the time of World War I they had become a standard feature of American diplomatic missions, and Air Attachés were added in the 1920s. The total number of American attachés stationed abroad rose to thirty-four by 1936 and to sixty by 1940.

Until the 1920s the Diplomatic and Consular Services were the only official agencies that represented the United States abroad. However, in 1927, to deal with the American foreign commerce boom, Herbert Hoover, then Secretary of Commerce, persuaded Congress to create a separate Foreign Commerce Service. It consisted of a group of Commercial Attachés and Trade Commissioners to function under the supervision of the American diplomatic establishment abroad. Three years later Congress also empowered the Department of Agriculture to launch a similar Foreign Agricultural Service, and in 1935 the Bureau of Mines of the Department of the Interior followed suit. Designated as attachés, these foreign agents performed specialized functions not normally handled by the regular Foreign Service, and they reported directly to their own Departments.

Difficulties of coordination and duplication of activities weakened American representation abroad so that, under the Reorganization Act of 1939, President Roosevelt consolidated the Commercial and Agricultural Attachés with the diplomatic Foreign Service, as were Bureau of Mines foreign agents in 1943. At the time President Roosevelt held that overseas representation and reporting in these fields should be a part of a single, integrated foreign relations establishment. However, the Treasury Department maintained a number of customs officials abroad who functioned as Treasury Attachés, and, when the amalgamation of 1939 was put into effect, they were exempted.

Nevertheless, by the time of World War II, the roster of such specialized agents embraced primarily Agricultural, Commercial, Civil Air, Labor, Military, Naval, and Treasury Attachés, as well as Financial and Press Attachés. The latter differed in that they, respectively, functioned in the diplomatic mission much as a financial reporter and statistician and a director of public relations in a government bureau. During the war the list was expanded to also include such specialists as Petroleum and Telecommunications Attachés. These developments paved the way for further expansion of the attaché system during the postwar era.[63]

Presidential Special Diplomatic Envoys

The presidential use of special diplomatic envoys accelerated considerably during this period, especially during the Wilson and Roosevelt Administrations. These may be grouped in several general categories—ceremonial, fact-finding, investigatory and reporting, consultative, negotiatory, mediatory, and administrative. Such appointments at the highest level bypassed or complemented regular diplomatic representation, and sometimes these were resented by the Department of State.

Ceremonial representation functions were ascribed to both special appointees and resident emissaries commissioned specifically for such functions. To illustrate, Presidents appointed Ambassador Charles MacVeagh, resident Ambassador, to attend the enthronement ceremony of the Japanese Emperor in 1928 and H. M. Jacoby (rather than the resident Minister Plenipotentiary/Consul General Addison E. Southard) to participate in the coronation festivities of the Ethiopian Emperor in 1930. Similarly, American Ambassadors and Ministers attended the inauguration of the Bolivian President in 1917, the wedding of the King of Yugoslavia in 1922, the marriage of the Crown Prince of Belgium in 1926, the second inaugural of the President of Chile in 1929, the national centennial of Uruguay in 1930, the inaugural of the Spanish President in 1936, and similar ceremonies.

Illustrating presidential special mediatory emissaries, in May 1917 President Wilson sent a diplomatic mission of nine members, headed by former Secretary of State Root, designated as "Envoys Extraordinary of the United States on Special Mission," to counteract Germany's efforts to conclude a separate peace with Russia. Twenty years later, President Roosevelt commissioned Francis (Frank) P. Corrigan, who served as Minister Plenipotentiary successively to El Salvador, Panama, and Venezuela, 1934–47, to provide good offices to facilitate a pacific solution of a controversy between Venezuela and Costa Rica. During Mexico's revolutionary period, 1910–20, President Wilson also dispatched several special envoys to Mexico to induce its leaders to establish an acceptable constitutional government, including William Bayard Hale and Reginald del Vale, but John Lind, former Governor of Minnesota, was most noteworthy, commissioned as his "personal spokesman and representative."

At the outbreak of World War I the President recruited Herbert Hoover, a successful mining engineer who was then living in Europe, to organize and direct the American Relief Committee to aid in repatriating Americans in Europe, and he was later made head of the Belgian Relief program.[64] During the war President Wilson sent John Gardner Coolidge, former Minister to Nicaragua, as a special agent to Paris and Henry Morgenthau and Felix Frankfurter on a special mission to Egypt to discover whether it was possible to detach Turkey from the Central Powers and to investigate the status of the people in Palestine. He also dispatched Frank E. Anderson, ostensibly an agent of an American industrial firm, to undertake a confidential investigation of constitutional reforms in Central Europe and to promote American trade with the Central Powers.

Following the Armistice President Wilson headed a personal executive delegation to the Paris Peace Conference, consisting of Secretary of State Lansing, Colonel Edward M. House, the president's personal adviser, Henry White (former Ambassador to Italy and France), and General Tasker H. Bliss. They were regarded as unique in that they served as special presidential envoys without Senate confirmation. During the conference, the President also sent a delegation, headed by author and journalist William C. Bullitt, to Russia to ascertain whether possible terms of agreement between its revolutionary government and the Allies were feasible. Later, he intended to have the United States represented on the Allied Reparations Commission, but, when the Senate Foreign Relations Committee demurred, the President sent a special agent to attend as observer.

During the interim between the two World Wars, the appointment of special envoys declined until the election of President Roosevelt and the world economic and political crises of the 1930s. However, President Coolidge sent Henry L. Stimson, former Secretary of War who later became Secretary of State, to Nicaragua in 1921 to assist its government to reform its electoral machinery and to supervise its election. Norman H. Davis, who had previously been appointed Under Secretary of State in 1920, served on a number of special missions. Several Presidents appointed him to represent the United States at disarmament conferences sponsored by the League of Nations, and he was the first American emissary to be called "Ambassador at Large."[65]

One of the most colorful military officers employed in such special presidential diplomatic missions was Major General Frank R. McCoy, who held several such assignments over a period of more than thirty years. He had been appointed by President Theodore Roosevelt as a peace commissioner in Cuba, headed a military commission to Armenia after the World War Armistice of November 1918, was sent to Tokyo in 1923 to assist the Japanese following a devastating earthquake and fire, and was sent to supervise Nicaraguan elections in 1927 and, two years later, to resolve the dispute between Bolivia and Paraguay over the Gran Chaco. Several years later, in 1932, he was selected as the American member of the Lytton Commission, sent by the League of Nations to investigate and report on Japanese intervention in Manchuria. Subsequently, late in 1945, following the Japanese surrender, President Truman named him as the U.S. envoy on the eleven-member Far Eastern Commission in Washington to coordinate military occupation policy for Japan.

President Franklin D. Roosevelt, however, set a record-breaking precedent for personal diplomacy—both personal participation in international meetings and conferences and the appointment of special diplomatic emissaries to function as his surrogates. To cite some of the more important special missions, he sent William C. Bullitt as special agent to the Soviet Union in 1933 in advance of American recognition of its Communist government, which was formalized by an exchange of notes, and Bullitt was accredited as American Ambassador in November; Sumner Welles, then Under Secretary of State, to go to Europe early in 1940 as an observer and listener to learn whether the principal belligerents could be induced to accept a peaceful settlement before the war spread throughout the continent[66]; Foreign Service Officer Robert D. Murphy, Counselor of the American Embassy in France, to negotiate the Murphy-Weygand Agreement of February 1941 for General Dwight D. Eisenhower, to support resistance by the Free French to German intrusion in North Africa and later also to pave the way for Allied landings in 1943[67]; and Colonel William J. Donovan to Yugoslavia in 1941 to report on how that country would withstand Nazi diplomatic and military pressures.

President Roosevelt also sent Vice President Henry A. Wallace on several diplomatic assignments in 1944, including a critical mission to China and the Soviet Union to try to improve their cooperation and to induce the warring factions in China to combine their efforts in fighting Japan. This was the first such mission for these purposes, which was followed by that of Major General Patrick J. Hurley in August 1944. When Allied forces liberated the countries of Western Europe, the President sent Judge Samuel I. Rosenman to ascertain their pressing food needs. Instead of utilizing a senior member of the American Embassy in London, in September 1944 he appointed Hamilton Fish Armstrong as his personal representative with the rank of Minister to go to London to assist Ambassador John G. Winant in his work on the European Advisory Commission, which was engaged in major power negotiations on the treatment of European enemy states. Of quite a different nature, Roosevelt revived U.S. diplomatic relations with the Holy See, suspended in 1867, by sending Myron C. Taylor, a steel magnate, as his special agent and personal representative with the rank of Ambassador to Pope Pius XII in 1939, where he remained until 1950, even though Harold H. Tittman, Jr., was appointed American Chargé d'Affaires in December 1941, who served in this capacity until mid-1944.

At times the President and Secretary of State also employ regular members of the Diplomatic and Consular Services on such special missions. For example, in 1917 President Wilson commissioned Basil Miles as special representative to Russia to assist Ambassador David R. Francis in representing the interests of foreign powers at Petrograd. In 1922 President Harding commissioned Brigadier

General John H. Russell as High Commissioner to represent him in Haiti, while the United States was formally represented there by interim Chargé d'Affaires James C. Dunn. That same year Sumner Welles, who later became Ambassador to Cuba, was accredited as Commissioner to the Dominican Republic. Prentiss Gilbert, American Consul at Geneva, was deputed by Secretary Stimson in 1931 to attend the public sessions of the League of Nations and report to Washington.

Some special envoys were appointed to serve at various international conferences and agencies. In addition to Norman Davis, Prentiss Gilbert, Frank Mc-Coy, and members of the Paris Peace Conference delegation, these included General Charles G. Dawes and businessman and financier Owen D. Young, who produced master World War I reparations plans and headed successive international Reparations Commissions in the 1920s to deal with World War I occupation costs and compensation funding by defeated Germany.[68] Myron Taylor, in addition to representing the United States to the Vatican and serving on several American postwar planning agencies, in 1943 chaired the American delegation to the Anglo-American and Canadian-American ''conversations'' on postwar economic relations and commercial policy.

Most impressive, however, were the diplomatic exploits of Colonel Edward M. House, Harry L. Hopkins, and W. Averell Harriman. Although they were not career diplomats by profession, Presidents called upon them for many diplomatic assignments, and they enjoyed the personal confidence of the those they served. All three rank among the President's four-star personal emissaries.

House, a Texas Colonel, widely traveled, became President Wilson's close friend, confidant, and personal policy adviser who came to have considerable influence on the President. Actually, his policy counseling role was greater than his diplomacy, but he did serve as the President's personal plenipotentiary on five important missions to Europe and represented the United States on the Supreme War Council of the Allied and Associated Powers. In 1914 he sought to act as mediator in the deteriorating European power struggle, hoping to avert the outbreak of hostilities. After Europe became engulfed in war, in 1915 and 1916 he attempted to bring the belligerent governments to the conference table to negotiate a peace settlement, but these missions were foredoomed. When House returned to Europe in 1918, after the United States joined the Allies, his task changed to persuading the warring sides to accept an armistice founded on Wilson's historic Fourteen Points. His final diplomatic venture took him to Paris as a key member of Wilson's peace conference delegation, which was the first time he held a formal diplomatic status. The President returned to the United States during the conference, and he left House in charge, but when Wilson returned to Paris, he felt that his deputy had betrayed his policy.

A generation later, Hopkins represented the alter ego of President Roosevelt and worked closely with him for twelve years as speechwriter, member of the President's ''Brain Trust,'' intimate adviser, ''minister without portfolio,'' and personal envoy. He was constantly at the President's side and served as sounding board and counselor but eschewed the drive for personal political power and prestige. He and the President established a close bond of mutual respect and affection, and he served as the President's principal summit surrogate.

His chief diplomatic responsibilities were twofold—to represent Roosevelt as his personal envoy with Prime Minister Winston Churchill and Marshal Joseph V. Stalin and pave the way for the President to work directly and closely with them at the Head of Government level and to accompany Roosevelt to the wartime summit conferences and meetings. He undertook several missions to Europe and was at Roosevelt's side at virtually all of the major summit conclaves, from the Argentia (Atlantic) meeting to the Yalta Conference. When, on Roosevelt's death, Truman suddenly succeeded to the presidency, he sought Hopkins' advice respecting Roosevelt's relations with Churchill, Stalin, and other world leaders and asked him to return to Moscow as his personal envoy to discuss plans for voting in the United Nations Security Council, which was Hopkins' last journey to the Soviet capital. For years he had served as Roosevelt's eyes, ears, and voice and became, as Roosevelt put it, "the perfect Ambassador for my purposes."

During the generation from World War II to the Vietnam War Harriman achieved one of the most remarkable, varied, and distinguished careers in the annals of American diplomacy. Less of a behind-the-scenes, day-to-day intimate adviser than either House or Hopkins (although sometimes he played this role), he was especially effective as a roving ambassador and troubleshooter at the center of the diplomatic stage in a good many important matters. Perhaps more than any previous presidential personal envoy, he personified the successful noncareerist professional. He was sent to represent the United States in a variety of diplomatic capacities and was recognized as being concerned more with results than with formalities, procedures, and channels.

Harriman joined the Roosevelt Administration in 1933. In some respects he was to Hopkins what the latter was to the President. In 1941, at the request of the British Prime Minister, the President sent him to London to expedite Lend-Lease assistance. In 1942 he attended the Churchill–Stalin talks in Moscow, he was accredited as Ambassador to the Soviet Union in 1943, where he served till 1946, he was later commissioned as Ambassador to Great Britain by President Truman in 1946, he then became Secretary of Commerce, he headed the Marshall Plan to Europe in 1948 and became Director of the Mutual Security Program three years later, and he served as "Special Assistant to the President" for Foreign Affairs in 1950–51 and as the President's personal envoy on several special missions. From 1942 to 1945 he accompanied President Roosevelt to all of the summit meetings and conferences except the Second Quebec Conference in 1944. Later, he also served creditably at high levels in various offices and diplomatic missions during the Truman, Kennedy, and Johnson Administrations, thus bridging the administrations of four Presidents over a period of more than two decades.[69]

Thus, by the time of the Roosevelt Administration, the practice of appointing and commissioning presidential special envoys had become commonplace. Even though the Senate objected to this procedure as being extraconstitutional, if not unconstitutional, the overwhelming demands made on the President to conduct diplomatic relations, often without delay and sometimes with confidentiality, have long been viewed as necessitating and justifying such appointments. Senatorial objections have been motivated more by political than by legal considerations, and analysts have come to focus more on the issue of the President's relations with his Secretary and Department of State and, when outsiders are recruited for such service, on the deleterious effects on the morale of the career Foreign Service.

Consular Affairs

The Act of April 5, 1906 marked the commencement of the consular system, and the Rogers Act converted consular and diplomatic officers into Foreign Service Officers and rendered them interchangeable in their assignments. The notorious fee system was abolished, except for consular agents. The functions of consular officers increased in both type and quantity.

To structure the consular system, the Act of February 5, 1915 grouped Consuls General in five classes with annual salaries ranging from $4,500 for those in Class 5 to $12,000 for those in Class 1, and nine classes of Consuls, with salaries for Class 9 set at $2,000 and those in Class 1 at $8,000. It also defined the status and position of Consuls General and Consuls as "full, principal, and permanent consular officers" as distinguished from "subordinates and substitutes," such as consular agents and vice consuls, all of which were regarded as "consular officers."

When the Rogers Act of 1924 amalgamated the Consular and Diplomatic Services into the Foreign Service of the United States, its members were assignable to either diplomatic or consular duties as required. Therefore, those who served in both diplomatic and consular assignments came under a uniform system so far as examination, appointment, promotion, salary and allowances, assignment, transfer, treatment, and retirement were concerned. It also devised a formula for the initial incorporation of existing consular officers.[70] These arrangements were not revised by the Moses–Linthicum Act of 1931.

The number of separate American consular posts peaked at 713 in 1900, dropped dramatically to 566 in 1910, and to 412 in 1921, 362 in 1930, and 293 in 1940, and subsequently continued to decline. During those years the number of Consulates General vacillated from forty-three in 1900, to sixty-three in 1910, forty-eight in 1921, sixty-six in 1930, rose to sixty-nine in 1940, and declined following World War II. The number of Consulates remained relatively constant from 1900 to 1921, when it reached 256, but dropped significantly by 1930, numbered only 192 in 1940, and declined rapidly after the war. The small number of vice consulates dropped to only three in 1940, and thereafter they were discontinued; the number of consular agencies, the preponderant type of consular establishment in the 1880s, declined steadily from 395 in 1900 to only 28 by 1940; and commercial agencies, which also peaked in 1880, were discontinued after 1910.[71] Thus, by the time of World War II, the consular system was consolidated almost entirely in two categories—Consulates General and Consulates, plus a few consular agencies.

To systematize consular relations internationally, during the second half of the nineteenth century a series of international law experts published comprehensive codes that dealt with the duties, jurisdiction, rights, and privileges of consular officers.[72] In 1896 the Institute of International Law and in 1925 the American Society of International Law produced short codes that focused largely on consular privileges and immunities. Later, the League of Nations established a committee to study the legal status and functions of consular officers, and the Inter-American Commission of Jurists, meeting at Rio de Janeiro in 1927, devised an encompassing code of consular affairs, which was adopted at the Sixth International Conference of American States at Havana in 1928 and was signed by twenty American republics.

Alternatively, from the outset the United States adopted the practice of prescribing and regularizing consular relations by means of bilateral consular conventions. Beginning with the Franco-American Treaty of Amity and Commerce (1778), which provided for consular establishments, as did similar conventions with the Netherlands (1782) and Morocco (1787), the United States undertook to formalize commercial and consular relations by these conventions, and the first such treaty under the Constitution was concluded with France in 1788, consented to by the Senate the following year, and became effective in January 1790. Since then scores of such conventions were concluded by American emissaries. Prior to 1913, the United States signed nineteen purely consular conventions and nearly ninety treaties of amity, commerce and navigation, which generally involved some aspects of consular affairs. By 1945 more than fifty new and supplementary treaties were added, even including one multilateral consular convention.[73]

The basic functions of those commissioned to consular duty remained relatively constant, but they were supplemented with additional responsibilities as the shipping and commercial interrelations of governments expanded, especially during World Wars I and II. At the beginning of World War I consular as well as diplomatic officers were required to systematically file reports on political, economic, financial, and commercial developments, summaries of local press accounts, and biographic analyses on foreign leaders and to telegraph information on German submarine activity. Following the war they also handled increased passport and visa demands, the administration of public health and quarantine regulations, various legal actions for Americans abroad, and special cooperative services for other Departments and agencies.

In summary, by the time of World War II the gamut of consular functions embraced such traditional responsibilities as promoting and protecting American trade interests, settling trade disputes, certifying invoices for the shipment of foreign goods to the United States, providing protection and assistance to seamen, exercising jurisdiction over shipwrecks and stranded vessels, and furnishing protection to, and servicing, American nationals abroad, including citizenship, passport, and visa matters. They also involved assistance to Americans to cope with accidents, illness, cases of distress, and violation of local laws, to locate missing persons and lost articles, to handle funerals and shipment of deceased Americans to the United States and disposal of their effects, to perform marriages for Americans, to serve subpoenas issued by Federal courts applicable to Americans abroad, to authenticate documents and administer oaths, to leave troubled or war-torn areas, and to provide a great many services to American tourists.[74] But normally, consular officers do not perform diplomatic duties.

Salaries and Allowances

The Rogers Act, which established the Foreign Service system, prescribed the salary levels of nine classes of Foreign Service Officers,[75] with fixed percentages allowable for individual classes and with specified annual salary levels ranging from $3,000 to $9,000.[76] Nearly half of the officers were required to belong to the lower Classes 7 to 9. In addition, unclassified officers, the lowest category, were to be paid from $1,500 to $3,000. By Executive Order of June 7, 1924, President Coolidge ruled that all new recruits were to be appointed as unclassified officers. The Moses–Linthicum Act of 1931, retaining the percentage/salary formula, provided for eight salary brackets, varying from $2,500 to $3,400 for unclassified officers to a maximum of $9,000 to $10,000 for those in Class 1.[77] This arrangement allowed for both variation of salary and higher maximums within each class. It eliminated Class 9 but retained the existing percentage figures. It also established salary levels for five classes of senior clerks amounting to $3,000 to $4,000 and for three classes of junior clerks with salaries of less than $2,500 to $2,750.

In 1915 Congress also legislated salary brackets for five classes of diplomatic or mission Secretaries (to be distinguished from clerks who performed secretarial services), which ranged from Class 5 at $1,200 to Class 1 at $3,000 per year,[78] and stipulated that such Secretaries who acted as Chargés d'Affaires at interim would be paid their regular salaries plus the difference between these salaries and those provided for the Ambassador or Minister at their respective posts. It also authorized additional compensation for ''special duty'' outside Washington, not to exceed $5.00 per day for a maximum of sixty days unless the Secretary was assigned to an international conference or congress. In 1920 the number of classes of these Secretaries was reduced from five to four, and their salaries were increased to range from $2,500 to $4,000. The Moses–Linthicum Act also fixed salaries of senior clerks at $3,000 to $4,000 and junior clerks at $2,750 or less, which in 1945 was increased to a maximum of $2,900 for administrative clerks.

To subsidize the costs of various financial burdens of diplomats and consuls, Congress also provided for certain special allowances. In 1906 it supplied funds to cover official transportation to and from foreign posts at the rate of five cents per mile. In 1919 this allowance was extended to include their families. To deal with increased living costs during World War I, especially in Europe, at the request of the Department of State, in 1916 Congress appropriated $150,000 to supply supplementary compensation for officers stationed in belligerent and contiguous countries. These special appropriations were increased in succeeding years to 1924. Secretary Stimson persuaded Congress in 1930 to add additional allowances for rent, heat, and light for the living quarters of American employees abroad. To accommodate high living costs and to improve Foreign Service employability, this special allowance arrangement became a permanent feature of Foreign Service financing.[79]

The Rogers Act also introduced the payment of "representation allowances" to diplomatic missions, to cover official entertainment, public relations and personal appearances, and the like. However, not until 1931 did Congress actually appropriate such funds, amounting to $92,000, increased to $125,000 the following year. Under the Moses–Linthicum Act such post and representation allowances were authorized for both Chiefs of Mission and Foreign Service Officers.

During the Great Depression several congressional economy acts not only reduced salaries by 15 percent but also abolished representation, post, and other allowances and reduced them for such matters as rent, heat, and light. These reductions, accompanied by the depreciation of the dollar, cut the income of officers by 30 percent, so that they were hard-pressed to meet their financial burdens. However, Congress passed an Exchange Bill in March 1934 to allow payment to American officials stationed abroad in currency equivalent to an approximate conversion value, and it took other actions so that late in 1935 Foreign Service Officers regained the salary and allowance levels contemplated by the Moses–Linthicum Act.[80] Not until 1946, however, was this special allowance arrangement amplified to cover additional expenses.

Foreign Mission Buildings Acquisition

The enactment of the Lowden Act in February 1911, providing a maximum of $500,000 annually for the acquisition of buildings for American diplomatic and consular purposes abroad, resulted in a modest program to improve the physical facilities for the conduct of foreign affairs. By 1924 only nine embassy and legation buildings had been acquired—in Havana, London, Mexico City, Oslo, Panama City, Paris, San José, San Salvador, and Santiago, plus a site for the construction of a building in Rio de Janeiro—at a cost of more than $1,669,000. Both lack of funding and the absence of departmental requisite administrative machinery inhibited the progress of this program.

However, in May 1926 Congress passed the Foreign Service Buildings Act, which empowered the Secretary of State, with the direction of a Foreign Service Buildings Commission, to acquire property and buildings and to repair and furnish facilities for diplomatic and consular representatives. At the time, a Foreign Service Building Fund was established, providing $10 million, of which not more than $2 million could be spent in a single year, administered by a Foreign Service Buildings Office, which was converted into the Division of Foreign Service Buildings Operations in 1944. In 1935 and 1938 Congress authorized additional funding for this purpose in the amount of more than $6,500,000. As a consequence, by 1946 the number of American office buildings increased to thirty-one, and the residences of foreign representatives numbered eighty-three.[81]

Emissaries Remembered

Among those emissaries who are remembered because they are frequently quoted are Charles G. Dawes, who, sent as Ambassador to Great Britain during the Hoover era, reportedly claimed that "American diplomacy is easy on the brain but hell on the feet." Experienced careerist Henry P. Fletcher, who served as Under Secretary of State and Minister or Ambassador to six countries, wittily responded, "It depends on which you use."

Others are remembered for many different reasons and accomplishments. For example, a few of those diplomats who served as foreign emissaries or in lesser departmental positions and were appointed as Secretaries of State included Robert Lansing, who first held the position of departmental Counselor (1914–15), and Edward R. Stettinius (Under Secretary of State, 1943–44). Some held positions as Secretaries of other government Departments, such as Henry L. Stimson (Secretary of War, 1911–13 and 1940–45), Josephus Daniels (Secretary of the Navy, 1913–21, and later, Ambassador to Mexico, 1933–41), Andrew W. Mellon (Secretary of the Treasury, 1921–32, when he was named Ambassador to Great Britain, 1932–33), and Patrick J. Hurley (Secretary of War, 1929–33, and later, Minister to New Zealand and Ambassador to China, 1942 and 1945). Others who were commissioned not only as emissaries abroad but also as Under Secretary of State included Henry P. Fletcher, Joseph C. Grew (twice), William Phillips (twice), and Sumner Welles, and a dozen were also appointed as Assistant Secretaries[82]—all of whom were careerists.

Those worthy of note for their lengthy and varied diplomatic duties would embrace Foreign Service Officers Norman Armour, Jefferson Caffrey, James C. Dunn, Henry P. Fletcher, Hugh S. Gibson, Joseph C. Grew, Loy W. Henderson, H. Freeman Matthews, George S. Messersmith, William Phillips, and Avra M. Warren. Of these, all except Gibson and Warren also held high-ranking administrative positions in the Department of State.

Prominent noncareerists who warrant special note include William C. Bullitt, wealthy Philadephian, who was sent as special envoy to Russia twice (in 1918 and 1933) and who later served as Ambassador to the Soviet Union and to France; James W. Gerard, a wealthy New York lawyer, Ambassador to Germany

(1913–17); Myron T. Herrick Ambassador to France (twice, 1912–14 and 1921–29, who died at his post); Frank B. Kellogg, former Senator from Minnesota, Ambassador to Great Britain (1924–25, who then became Secretary of State); Dwight W. Morrow, Ambassador to Mexico (1927–30, who, despite his short tenure, helped to reestablish favorable relations and to settle a number of disputes over American oil and other property rights in that country); and Walter Hines Page, editor and partner in Doubleday and Page publishing firm, Ambassador to Great Britain (1913–18).

Two such noncareerists are remembered as the first American women chiefs of mission—Ruth Bryan Owen, Minister to Denmark from 1933 to 1936, and Florence Jaffray Harriman, Minister to Norway from 1937 to 1939, when the Nazis invaded that country. Lucile Atcherson became the first Foreign Service Officer in 1922. Other women of note were Margaret M. Hanna and Alice M. Ball, who prepared the Department of State Correspondence Manual; Ruth B. Shipley, who has been recognized for her long service as a departmental administrative officer, including many years as chief of the Passport Division; and Frances E. Willis, who not only held important posts in the Department but later also held diplomatic assignments abroad as Ambassador to three countries (Switzerland, Norway, and Ceylon/Sri Lanka, 1953–64) and was the first woman to be promoted to the rank of Career Ambassador in 1962.

More unusually, a few non-Foreign Service Officers spent most of their careers in Department of State administration but also held brief appointments as Chiefs of Missions abroad. These are illustrated by such old hands as Wilbur J. Carr and William R. Castle, Jr. Carr held a number of posts in the Department for forty-five years (1892–1937), principally as Director of the Consular Service and Assistant Secretary when, in 1937, President Roosevelt named him Minister to Czechoslovakia, where he served for eighteen months (September 1937 to March 1939), when Germany occupied that country. Castle, who had a fruitful and lengthy career in the Department, including heading the Bureau of European Affairs and serving as Assistant Secretary and Under Secretary (1921–33), was also appointed Ambassador to Japan in 1930, where he remained only four months. He resigned as Under Secretary when Roosevelt became President, and he was succeeded by careerist William Phillips. Special attention must also be paid to Alvey A. Adee, Assistant Secretary from 1882 to 1924, when he died, and Green H. Hackworth, Solicitor and later, Legal Adviser (1931–46), who produced the eight-volume *Digest of International Law* (published 1940–44) and was later elected a judge of the International Court of Justice.

James Rives Childs, career Foreign Service Officer who published *American Foreign Service* in 1948, has called Congressman John J. Rogers, whose name is identified with the Foreign Service Act of 1924, the ''Father of the Modern American Foreign Service.'' However, in view of his initiation, contribution, and influential support, Carr must be equally acknowledged as the progenitor of the combined Foreign Service of the United States.

Other prominent noncareerists who functioned as special presidential emissaries, in addition to Bullitt, Averell Harriman, Harry Hopkins, and Colonel House, included Henry Morgenthau and Felix Frankfurter, who undertook a critical mission to Egypt during World War I; Herbert Hoover, who headed the American relief program in Europe following that war; Frank R. McCoy, who was recruited for a number of special missions to Latin America and the Far East; and Myron Taylor, who had the distinction of serving as the personal envoy of both Presidents Roosevelt and Truman throughout World War II and until 1950.

Some diplomats had a previous military background. These are represented by Charles G. Dawes (Ambassador to Great Britain), Patrick J. Hurley (Minister to New Zealand and Ambassador to China), Admiral Alan G. Kirk (Chargé d'Affaires to Germany and Minister or Ambassador successively to Egypt, Saudi Arabia, Greece, and Italy), and Admiral William D. Leahy (Ambassador to France). In addition to Dawes and Major General McCoy, Colonel William J. Donovan was recruited as a presidential special envoy.

More than a dozen academicians also were appointed to a variety of diplomatic assignments. Jacob Gould Schurman, President of Cornell University, was accredited as Minister to Greece, Montenegro, and China and as Ambassador to Germany. Howard Lee Nostrand, Professor and President of Yale University, served at the Paris Peace Conference following World War I and as Cultural Attaché in Peru. Others who were commissioned as diplomats include historian William E. Dodd of the University of Chicago as Ambassador to Germany, Carlton J. H. Hayes, historian, as Ambassador to Spain; Paul S. Reinsch, political scientist, as Minister to China; Frederic J. Stimson, lawyer and professor, as Ambassador to Argentina; and Henry Van Dyke of Princeton University, as Minister to the Netherlands and Luxemburg. In addition, Claude A. Buss, political scientist, served in Peking and Nanking; Herbert Feis, economist, and Ellery C. Stowell, professor of international law, at a number of international conferences; James L. McCamy, political scientist, as economic adviser in Austria; and Graham Stuart, political scientist, Minister to Tangier.

All of these also authored collections of volumes numbering from four to six (Nostrand, McCamy, Schurman, and Stowell) to twenty or more (Feis, Hayes, and Stimson) and, in the case of Henry Van Dyke, nearly forty volumes of his sermons, poetry, and other literary productions. To these must be added several well-known authors who were appointed to diplomatic posts, illustrated by Stephen Vincent Benet, clerk in the American Embassy at Paris in 1918, who published some eighteen novels, short stories, and volumes of poetry; Claude G. Bowers, Ambassador to Spain (1933–39) and Chile (1939–53), who authored fifteen biographies, memoirs, histories, and commentaries; Thomas Nelson Page, Ambassador to Italy (1913–20), who produced twenty-two novels and volumes of poetry; and Brand Whitlock, Minister and later, Ambassador to Belgium (1913–21), who published at least twenty biographies, histories, and analyses.

Although not necessarily critical to performance but sometimes an advantage, a few emissaries were members of what diplomatic historian Thomas A. Bailey branded the "millionaire's club." Among them he lists Robert W. Bingham (Ambassador to Great Britain, 1933–37), Charles G. Dawes (Ambassador to Great Britain, 1929–31), Averell Harriman (Ambassador to the Soviet Union, 1943–46, and later also to Great Britain, 1946, and Ambassador at Large), Joseph P. Kennedy (Ambassador to Great Britain, 1938–40), and Andrew W. Mellon (Ambassador to Great Britain, 1932–33).[83] To these may be added other diplomats of considerable means, such as Norman Armour, William C. Bullitt, Herbert Hoover, Henry Morgenthau, Dwight W. Morrow, Walter Hines Page, Edward R. Stettinius, Myron C. Taylor, Owen D. Young, and others. Of these, only Armour was a diplomatic careerist, and only he and Harriman had other extensive diplomatic duty and experience.

Few diplomats are memorialized for, or identified historically with, major foreign policy developments. However, J. Reuben Clark, Jr., who served as Under Secretary of State (1928–29) and as Ambassador to Mexico (1930–33), is remembered for his Memorandum on the Monroe Doctrine, and Charles G. Dawes and Owen D. Young, for their development of post–World War I reparations policy and treaty plans. Whereas some treaties or agreements are historically identified with American Secretaries of State who sign them, such as the Bryan–Chamoro, Clayton–Bulwer, Hay–Pauncefote, Rush–Bagot (Rush was acting Secretary), and Webster–Ashburton Treaties, or with the place of signature (such as the London, Paris, Versailles, and Washington Treaties), or with specific subjects (such as peace treaties and the Alaska and Louisiana Territory purchase treaties), during this period few are identified with the names of American diplomats. However, though highly exceptional, the World War II compact with the French in North Africa is remembered as the Murphy–Weygand Agreement of 1941.

Also memorialized, but for different reasons, Major Robert W. Imbrie, American Vice Consul in Persia, was beaten to death in 1924 by a mob of fanatics, and J. Theodore Marriner, Consul General in Beirut, was murdered in 1937, both of whom were commemorated by the Department of State.[84] Also, in 1932 Culver B. Chamberlain and Arthur R. Ringwalt, consular officers stationed in Mukden and Shangai, were attacked by Japanese, and J. Hall Paxton, Second Secretary of the American Embassy at Nanking, narrowly escaped injury or death when Japanese planes bombed and sank the U.S. gunboat *Panay* on the Yangtze River in 1937.

Also, other diplomats are remembered for their heroic service under critical conditions. Like Myron T. Herrick, Ambassador to France, who refused to leave Paris in the face of the German advance during World War I, Ambassador William C. Bullitt remained in Paris during World War II, even after the flight of the French Government, in order to manage the affairs of the French city for a few hours and ultimately to turn it over to the Nazi occupiers. Meanwhile, Ambassador John G. Winant stayed in London despite the "little blitz" and the V-bomb campaign of the Nazis, 1943–45, while over a million persons, including some high-level British Government officials, were evacuated to places of greater safety.

The Constitution specifically forbids employees of the Federal Government to accept any presents, offices, or titles from foreign governments without the consent of Congress. The Foreign Service *Regulations* affirm similar restrictions but authorize envoys to apply to Congress for permission to accept them when they are offered. Congress has generally been reluctant to grant such approval, although it relented somewhat at the end of World War I.[85]

During this period the British Government wished to express its gratitude to Ambassador Myron T. Herrick, accredited to Paris, for the services he rendered after the French Government and the British Embassy left the French capital during World War I. Following the war and after Herrick returned to private life, so that the American restrictions no longer applied to him, the British Government presented him with an English silver service, the French Government bestowed on him the Grand Cross of the Legion of Honor, and the City of Paris issued him a gold medal. On the other hand, when Walter Hines Page, Ambassador to Great Britain (1913–18), was chosen as President of the Birmingham and Midland Institute, regarded as an outstanding honor (which had previously been bestowed upon James Russell Lowell and Joseph Choate), this was viewed as an unofficial, but exceptional, honor lying beyond the application of the American restriction and was therefore permitted. His successor, Ambassador John W. Davis, was made an honorary bencher of the Honorable Society of the Middle Temple and also a Senior Warden of the Grand Lodge of Freemasons, which had not previously been conferred on any foreigner.

Other American diplomats have been recognized and made the recipients of special recognition and honors. James C. Dunn, Loy W. Henderson, H. Freeman Matthews, and Robert Murphy, careerists who served during this period and into the 1950s, were the first to be appointed to the superior rank of Career Ambassador in 1956. For his frequent and valued service as a presidential special envoy, Norman Davis was unofficially called Ambassador at Large, as was William C. Bullitt, presaging the formal establishment of this distinguished diplomatic rank in 1949.

Dwight W. Morrow, lawyer and banker, a gifted amateur who, it has been said, became a professional diplomat overnight, although he served briefly as Ambassador to Mexico, was awarded the Distinguished Service Medal, and he has been honored by inclusion in diplomatic historian Thomas A. Bailey's Diplomatic Hall of Fame.[86] Colonel House, Harry Hopkins, and Averell Harriman are regarded as four-star presidential noncareerist special envoys, and General Frank McCoy is also remembered for his manifold service as such a special emissary. Stephen Vincent Benet, best known as a novelist and poet, who served briefly as a clerk in the American Embassy at Paris, was awarded the Pulitzer Prize for poetry in 1929, and for his contribution to deal with the World War I reparations issue, Charles G. Dawes became the fourth American to be awarded the Nobel Peace Prize.[87]

TREATY AND AGREEMENT MAKING

As the United States continued to extend its relations with the international community and other governments and expanded the breadth of its treaty interests, during the period from 1913 to 1945 it concluded a great many new treaties and agreements. The relative ratio of multilateral to bilateral treaties and agreements remained fairly constant, amounting to 17 to 18 percent. However, the ratio of executive agreements to formal treaties changed dramatically, increasing from less than 33 percent to more than 70 percent. Moreover, during this period these were supplemented by dozens of international conference agreements, as well as unilateral American declarations of policy, such as President Wilson's Fourteen Points, changes in recognition policy, and President Roosevelt's Good Neighbor, Quarantining of Aggressors, Four Freedoms, Lend-Lease, and Unconditional Surrender policy pronouncements and the Atlantic Charter.

These actions both reflected and portended greater activity as a leader in mutual and cooperative involvement in world affairs, the inter-American system, and the creation of the United Nations and its affiliates. The Department of State not only cooperated in stabilizing legal, political, economic, and social relations with other governments, but by the treaty process the United States also assumed the vanguard in leading the rest of the world.

In 1882, while Frelinghuysen was Secretary of State, the Senate had resolved that "it does not admit or acquiesce in any right or constitutional power in the President to authorize or empower any person to negotiate treaties or carry on diplomatic relations with any foreign power unless such person shall have been appointed for such purpose or clothed with such power by and with the advice and consent of the Senate." However, by 1913 and during this period the Executive Branch, principally the Department of State with the authorization of the President, negotiated many treaties and agreements and certainly carried on scores of "diplomatic relations" with dozens of foreign governments around the globe without overt prior Senate advice and consent for the designation of American negotiators for this purpose.

International Policy Declarations and Proclamations

In addition to concluding international treaties and agreements, the American government, principally the President and the Secretary and Department of State, issued or otherwise subscribed to a good many foreign policy declarations, statements, acts, international conference resolutions (especially in the inter-American system), and other pronouncements. Some asserted that unilateral American policy and others constituted bilateral and multilateral propositions. Most of those dating from the late 1930s to 1945 were concerned with the conduct, conclusion, and aftermath of World War II.

As originally propounded, they were expressions of guiding principles of policy and action, usually regarded as valid until changed or rescinded, which, therefore, played a prominent role in the development of American foreign relations. When initiated, they represented interests and action taken under executive authority, although some—such as the Hoover World War I debt moratorium in 1931, the reciprocal trade and most-favored-nation principles expressed by President Roosevelt and expanded by Secretary Hull in 1936, and the World War II Lend-Lease program—were endorsed by subsequent legislation. Others constituted or resulted in the negotiation of executive agreements, represented by those concluded to implement the Atlantic Charter of 1941 and the United Nations Declaration of 1942, and a few, including President Wilson's Fourteen Points of 1918, the unconditional most-favored-nation principle espoused by Secretary Hughes in 1923, and the World War II Doctrine of Unconditional Surrender and the Dumbarton Oaks Proposals, resulted in the consummation of formal treaties.

The practice of issuing unilateral, joint, and multilateral pronouncements and declarations was not unfamiliar in American foreign relations. This was evidenced by President Washington's Neutrality Proclamation in 1793, Secretary Hay's Open Door notes respecting China in 1889–90, the resolutions adopted at inter-American conferences, and the policy declarations to promote arbitration and other forms of pacific settlement of international disputes. However, it accelerated markedly during the period from World War I through World War II. The most important are listed chronologically in Table 6.5. These policy declarations, pronouncements, and other statements provided a useful prelude to the conclusion of formal treaties and executive agreements in the development and management of American foreign affairs and amplified leadership of the President and Department of State in the conduct of diplomatic relations as the United States emerged as a great world power.

Bilateral Treaties and Agreements

Due to the broadening of U.S. international interests and involvements, its ascendance as a leading world power, the enlargement of the community of nations, the pressing exigencies of World Wars I and II, and the establishment of the United Nations, this country experienced a marked increase not only in the number of treaties and agreements concluded but also in the variety of subjects treated. During these thirty-three years the Department of State negotiated 1,363 new treaties and agreements of all types, more than twice as many as those that were signed and ratified during the preceding century and a quarter, and attained an average of more than forty per year. Of these 1,127 were bilateral, and 236 involved three or more foreign governments.

Surprisingly, whereas 296 constituted formal treaties, 831 were regarded as executive agreements in the American constitutional system. This characterized a substantial shift in treaty practice. Prior to 1913 more than 70 percent were subject to formal Senate approval and presidential ratification. During this period the numbers were reversed in that at least seven of every ten were handled as

Table 6.5
International Policy Declarations and Other Pronouncements, 1913–1945

De Jure Recognition Policy, statement, President Wilson, March 1913

Open Door Policy for Commerce with China, statement, Secretary Bryan, March 1915

Lansing-Ishii Agreement, exchange of notes, United States and Japan, November 1917

Fourteen Points, pronouncement, President Wilson, January 1918

Unconditional Most-Favored-Nation Principle, confidential directive, Secretary Hughes, August 1923

Memorandum on Monroe Doctrine, Under Secretary J. Reuben Clark, December 1928

Rejection of De Jure Non Recognition Policy, statement, Secretary Stimson, February 1931

World War I War Debt Moratorium, President Hoover, June 1931

Non-Recognition of Territorial Acquisition by Force, applicable to Japan, identical notes to China and Japan, President Hoover and Secretary Stimson, January 1932 (Hoover-Stimson Doctrine)

General Disarmament Principles, President Hoover, submitted to Disarmament Conference, June 1932

Return to De Facto Recognition Policy, statement, President Roosevelt, 1933

American Interests in World Events, Secretary Hull, address, February 1935

Reciprocal Trade Arrangements, address, Secretary Hull, April 1936

Good Neighbor Policy, declaration, President Roosevelt, August 1936

Inter-American Solidarity and Cooperation, Declaration of Principles, Inter-American Conference, Buenos Aires, December 1936

Quarantining Aggressors, address, President Roosevelt, October 1937

Fundamentals of American Foreign Policy, pronouncement, Secretary Hull, March 1938

Declaration of Lima, Inter-American Ministerial Consultation for Defense of Peace, Security, and Territorial Integrity, December 1938

Declaration of Panama on Inter-American Neutrality, American Foreign Ministers Conference, October 1939

Act of Havana, Inter-American peaceful settlement of disputes, July 1940

Ogdensburg (N.Y.) Agreement, joint U.S.–British statement, President Roosevelt and Prime Minister Churchill, August 1940

Destroyers-Bases Arrangement, U.S. and Great Britain, message, President Roosevelt, September 1940

Arsenal for Democracy, pronouncement, President Roosevelt, January 1941

Four Freedoms, pronouncement, President Roosevelt, January 1941

American Bases in Greenland, statement, Department of State, April 1941

Exchange of Defense Materials with Canada, Hyde Park Declaration, President Roosevelt and Prime Minister Mackenzie King, April 1941

American Base in Iceland, message, President Roosevelt, July 1941

Atlantic Charter, joint U.S.–British pronouncement, President Roosevelt and Prime Minister Churchill, Argentia/Atlantic meeting, August 1941

Proposal for Peace in the Pacific, draft mutual declaration of policy, presented to Japanese government by Secretary Hull, November 1941

Continental Solidarity, declaration, Inter-American Conference, Rio de Janeiro, January 1942

Good Neighbor Policy, declaration, Inter-American Conference, Rio de Janeiro, January 1942

Severing Diplomatic Relations with Axis Aggressors, declaration, Inter-American Conference, Rio de Janeiro, January 1942

Lend-Lease Declaration, report to Congress, President Roosevelt, June 1942

American Objectives in World War II, radio address, Secretary Hull, July 1942

Unconditional Surrender Doctrine, President Roosevelt and Prime Minister Churchill, Casablanca Conference, January 1943

Cairo Declaration on Japan, President Roosevelt and Prime Minister Churchill, November 1943

Declaration on Austria, Foreign Ministers Conference, Secretary Hull, Moscow, November 1943

Declaration on German Atrocities, Foreign Ministers Conference, Secretary Hull, Moscow, November 1943

Declaration on Italy, Foreign Ministers Conference, Secretary Hull, Moscow, November 1943

Four Nation Declaration on General Security, Foreign Ministers Conference, Secretary Hull, Moscow, November 1943

Declaration on Iran, Tehran Conference, President Roosevelt, Prime Minister Churchill, and Marshal Stalin, December 1943

Declaration to Win the War with Germany and Cooperate in Peace, Tehran Conference, President Roosevelt, Prime Minister Churchill, and Marshal Stalin, December 1943

Dumbarton Oaks Proposals, for United Nations Charter, October 1944

Agreement regarding Soviet Entrance into War with Japan, Yalta Conference, President Roosevelt, Prime Minister Churchill, and Marshal Stalin, February 1945

Declaration on Liberated Europe, Yalta Conference, President Roosevelt, Prime Minister Churchill, and Marshal Stalin, February 1945

Post–World War II Treatment of Poland, declaration, Yalta Conference, President Roosevelt, Prime Minister Churchill, and Marshal Stalin, February 1945

Protocol on German World War II Reparations, Yalta Conference, President Roosevelt, Prime Minister Churchill, and Marshal Stalin, February 1945

Act of Chapultepec, Inter-American Conference, Mexico City, March 1945

Proclamation on War in Asia, Potsdam Conference, President Truman, Prime Minister Churchill, and concurred in by Generalissimo Chiang Kai-shek, July 1945

Table 6.5 (continued)

U.S. Initial Post-Surrender Policy for Japan, Department of State jointly with Departments of War and Navy, September 1945

World Trade and Employment, proposal, Assistant Secretary William L. Clayton, December 1945

Note: To these may be added dozens of resolutions and other policy actions taken at regular and special inter-American conferences.

executive agreements, indicating greater executive latitude and Department of State flexibility in the management of international affairs and reducing the Senate's role in the treaty-making process.

The United States added twenty-four foreign states and the League of Nations to its bilateral treaty roster and dropped six former treaty partners.[88] As indicated in Table 6.6, the largest number of treaties and agreements was concluded with Brazil (35), Canada (100), France (49), Great Britain (64), Haiti (48), Mexico (52), Panama (31), and Peru (31).[89] On the other hand, only one executive agreement was signed with the League of Nations, and one or two with Afghanistan, Austria-Hungary, the Belgo-Luxembourg Economic Union, Liechtenstein, Monaco, Palestine, San Marino, and Saudi Arabia.

So far as international titles are concerned, a majority of those dealt with by the United States as formal bilateral treaties were also internationally designated as treaties, whereas some 100 were denominated conventions, and thirty-four were called agreements. These titles, though sometimes confusing, are less material to American constitutional procedure than to the nature of their subjects and the significance of their content and application. Thus, lawmaking instruments, such as those dealing with customs revenues, double taxation, extradition, fishing rights, smuggling, and even the rights of foreign traveling sales representatives, were called conventions.

On the other hand, in some cases it is difficult to determine the distinction between the titles "treaty" and "agreement" in international usage. However, usually those concerned with basic friendship and commerce, extraterritorial rights, naturalization, and advance arrangements for arbitration and conciliation (including those pertaining to the promotion of peace) were titled treaties. Similarly, those that focused on certain aspects of military cooperation during World War II and an impressive series of reciprocal trade arrangements, were internationally known as agreements, or, as in the case of Lend-Lease commitments, they simply constituted "exchanges of notes."

The American executive agreement process was employed in 831 cases. Of these, 214 were formally designated as "agreements," whereas, surprisingly, 569—or 50 percent of all treaties and agreements—consisted of "exchanges of notes." This represented a material shift in Department of State treaty practice, not only the widespread employment of executive agreements but also to the simpler, more flexible method of agreement by exchanging diplomatic communications to deal with a broad spectrum of issues.[90] Most of the remaining

Table 6.6
Bilateral Treaties and Agreements, 1913–1945

Country	No.	T or A		Washington	Abroad	1913-19	1920s	1930s	1940-45
*Afghanistan	2		2		2			1	1
*Albania	7	4	3	2	5		4	2	1
Argentina	8	1	7	3	5			3	5
*Australia	6	2	4	4	2			1	5
*Austria	11	7	4	4	7		5	6	
Austria-Hungary	1		1	1		1			
*Belgo-Luxembourg Economic Union	1		1	1				1	
Belgium	24	6	18	14	10	2	9	6	7
Bolivia	8	1	7	4	4	1			7
Brazil	35	1	34	18	17	1	4	9	21
*Bulgaria	8	5	3	3	5		5	3	
*Canada	100	16	84	50 [1]	48		9	27	64
Chile	17	2	15	8	9	1	2	7	7
China	11	5	6	8	3	2	2	3	4
Colombia	17	2	15	9	8	1	2	4	10
Costa Rica	13	3	10	6	7	2	3	1	7
Cuba	18	5	13	6	12		4	7	7
*Czechoslovakia	16	5	11	9	7		8	6	2
Denmark	16	5	11	10 [2]	5	2	6	5	3
Dominican Republic	14	3	11	6	8		3		11
Ecuador	21	2	19	13	8	1		4	16
Egypt	8	2	6	3	5		2	5	1
El Salvador	15	2	13	5	10	1	2	1	11
*Estonia	11	5	6	6	5		8	3	
Ethiopia	5	3	2	1	4	1	2		2
*Finland	13	6	7	10	3		7	6	
France	49	14	35	18	31	8	15	15	11
Germany	22	7	15	10	12		12	9	1
Great Britain	64	23	41	43	21	10	17	11	26
Greece	18	7	11	9	9	1	5	7	5
Guatemala	24	3	21	12	12	4	3	3	14
Haiti	48	1	47	8	40	9	6	8	25
Honduras	13	3	10	4	9	1	3	1	8
*Hungary	8	4	4	6	2		6	2	
*Iceland	10	1	9	4	6		2	2	6
*India	3		3	1	2			3	
Iran	7		7	1	6		3		4
*Iraq	5	2	3	1	4			3	2
*Ireland	5		5	2	3			4	1
Italy	22	7	15	16	6	7	6	6	3
Japan	13	5	8	8	5	3	8	2	

Table 6.6 (continued)

Country	No.	T	or A	Washington	Abroad	1913-19	1920s	1930s	1940-45
* Latvia	9	5	4	3	6		4		5
* League of Nations	1		1		1				1
Liberia	12	5	7	0 [2]	11		2	5	5
* Liechtenstein	2	1	1		2		1	1	
* Lithuania	12	5	7	8	4		6		6
Luxembourg	5	3	2		5		2	2	1
Mexico	52	21	31	19	33		9	14	29
* Monaco	1	1			1			1	
Netherlands	28	9	19	23	5	4	9	8	7
* New Zealand	6	2	4	4	2			1	5
Nicaragua	17	2	15	8	9	1	3	4	9
Norway	26	10	16	22	4	4	8	7	7
* Palestine	1		1	1					1
Panama	31	8	23	14	17	6	4	11	10
Paraguay	9	3	6	6	3	4			5
Peru	31	2	29	16	15	1	4	3	23
* Poland	21	6	15	14	7		8	10	3
Portugal	10	5	5	4	6	3	4		3
Romania	10	4	6	5	5		6	4	
San Marino	1	1		1				1	
* Saudi Arabia	1		1		1			1	
* South Africa	8	1	7	4	4			4	4
Soviet Union [3]	13	1	12	7	6	3		6	4
Spain	16	4	12	8	8	5	8	1	2
Sweden	26	9	17	18	8	4	5	15	2
Switzerland	11	5	6	4	7	1	2	4	4
Thailand (Siam)	4	3	1	1	3		3		1
Turkey [4]	16	3	13	1	15		9	5	2
Uruguay	6	2	4	4	2	2			4
Venezuela	16	3	13	4	12	2	1	3	10
Yugoslavia	8	2	6	5	3		5	1	2
Total 72	1,127	296	831	555	572	99	276	312	440

*Denotes addition to the U.S. treaty list during period 1913–1945.

[1] In addition, two were signed in Ogdensburg and Hyde Park, New York.

[2] One was signed in New York City.

[3] Russia was converted into the Soviet Union following World War I.

[4] Formerly the Ottoman Empire.

executive agreements were denominated memorandum of conversations, agreement, or understanding (twelve), protocol (eleven), aide memoir (four), and joint statement (three) or bore such titles as additional act, arrangement, exchange of letters, or executive decree. Although highly exceptional, two exchanges with El Salvador concerning a military academy were labeled contracts.

The most memorable executive agreements by means of exchanges of notes included the Lansing–Ishii Agreement with Japan (1917) and its subsequent cancellation five years later,[91] the recognition of the Soviet government and the establishment of normal diplomatic relations with it (1933), the commitment to register American treaties and agreements with the League of Nations (1934),[92] the Bases–Destroyers Agreement with Great Britain (1940),[93] and a series of notes, consisting of more than a dozen exchanges providing for most-favored-nation commercial treatment as well as a few concerned with reciprocal trade and Lend-Lease (although most of the latter were embodied in regular formal executive agreements).

Several unusual procedural developments illustrate flexibility in the treaty process in order to accommodate particular needs. Some treaties, conventions, and agreements were accompanied by exchanges of notes to amplify or clarify them. Usually, executive agreements that dealt with World War I debt funding, while not regarded as formal treaties by the United States, were nevertheless approved by acts of Congress, but they were not officially ratified by the President. Similarly, two exchanges of notes with Canada pertaining to water control for the Niagara River were approved by the Senate, whereas an executive agreement of 1929 with Belgium providing for the handling of World War I battle monuments, signed by General John J. Pershing, was legitimated by a congressional act followed by presidential ratification.

Continuing the practice of concluding bilateral treaties and agreements in the United States, during this period 551 were signed in Washington and four elsewhere in this country,[94] whereas 572 were signed abroad. Of those consummated in Washington, evidencing a marked increase in the personal involvement of the Secretary of State in ministerial diplomacy, the preponderant majority (nearly 350) were signed personally by Secretaries of State, led by Secretaries Hull (more than 150), Kellogg (55), Lansing and Hughes (each 36), and Bryan (35). The least were concluded by Secretaries Stimson (19), Stettinius (8), and Colby (who signed a single Commerce Treaty with China in 1920).[95] Also, Under Secretary Welles signed a surprising number (more than 50) between 1937 and 1943, and approximately 25 other Under Secretaries and Assistant Secretaries who were designated as Acting Secretaries (led by Adolf A. Berle, Wilbur J. Carr, William R. Castle, Goseph C. Grew, R. Walton Moore, William Phillips, Frank L. Polk, and G. Howland Shaw) served as signers of more than eighty treaties and agreements.

In addition, President Roosevelt personally signed a joint statement and three exchanges of notes,[96] at least twenty-five Debt Funding Agreements were signed by Secretaries of the Treasury Andrew W. Mellon and Ogden L. Mills, half a dozen by the Secretary or Acting Secretary of Agriculture, one each by Harry

T. Woodring, the Secretary of War and the chief of the Foreign Economic Administration, and several were signed by military officers and others.[97] Surprisingly, it should be noted that some thirty-five executive agreements were unsigned. These were generally in the nature of *aide memoirs, notes verbale*, and other exchanges of communications between American diplomatic missions and the Foreign Offices of other governments.

Treaties and agreements concluded abroad were normally signed by resident American diplomats and, occasionally, consular officers at the national capitals of other governments, although a few were signed in neutral places, such as London and Paris. At times other sites were used, as in the care of a treaty with Turkey signed at Lausanne (Switzerland) in 1923, a modus vivendi with France signed at Algiers in 1943, executive agreements with Liberia signed at New York City and with Great Britain at Quebec in 1943, an exchange of notes with Iceland signed at Copenhagen in 1925, and joint statements with Canada signed at Ogdensburg and Hyde Park, New York, in 1940 and 1941.

By comparison with earlier times, the repertoire of U.S. bilateral treaty and agreement subjects not only confirmed earlier American interests but also proliferated to encompass a host of new subjects, as indicated in Table 6.7. Some 420 (or nearly 40 percent) involved such traditional matters as diplomatic and consular relations, commerce, pacific settlement of disputes and the maintenance of peace, claims arrangements,[98] extradition,[99] Lend-Lease and foreign assistance, and, to a lesser extent, territorial issues and national boundaries, customs, and taxes.

The twenty treaties and agreements concerned with territory and boundaries included those that governed the cession of the Danish West Indies (Virgin Islands) to the United States (1916), the specification of American rights in the pre–World War I German (later, Japanese-mandated) islands in the Pacific (1922), arbitration with the Netherlands for the possession of Palamas Island lying between the Philippines and the Dutch East Indies (1925), fixing of the boundary between the Philippines and British North Borneo (1930), and arranging for the joint U.S.-British administration of Canton and Enderbury Islands (in the Phoenix Islands in the mid-Pacific, 1939). Others dealt with boundary issues with Mexico and the Panama Canal Zone and ten treaties and agreements with Canada concerning settlements for Lake Superior and the Lake of the Woods, the development of the St. Lawrence Seaway, water rights and levels, and naval forces on the Great Lakes.

Nevertheless, substantial changes were introduced in the fields of commercial relations and pacific settlement of disputes. Although more than two dozen treaties of amity, commerce, and navigation were negotiated, primarily at the commencement of diplomatic relations, these were accompanied or supplemented by nearly ninety additional treaties and agreements, many of which provided for reciprocal trade and most-favored-nation commercial treatment.

The second major modification, the most dramatic substantive change, concerned the promotion of institutionalized peacekeeping. It involved several dis-

Table 6.7
Bilateral Treaty and Agreement Subjects, 1913–1945

Basic Subjects

Peaceful settlement of disputes	107	Extradition	53
Arbitration (48)		Claims and claims settlements	38
Advancement of peace (40)		Relations: amity, commerce, and navigation	26
Conciliation (19)		Territory, waters, and national boundaries	20
Commerce, tariffs, reciprocal trade,		Consular affairs	18
and most-favored-nation	88	Customs, revenues, and taxes	14
Lend-Lease and foreign aid	56		

Additional Major and General Subjects

World Wars I and II	150	Cooperation in educational programs	
Military missions (53)		(Latin America)	20
Military cooperation (52)		Smuggling of intoxicating liquors	20
Military overflights (13)		International highways (Alaska, Canada,	
Debt funding (32)		Pan American, and Trans-Isthmian	17
Visas and visa fees for		Radio broadcasting and communications	17
non-immigrants	64	Rights of Americans in foreign territories	11
Civil aviation	52	Fisheries	10
Commodities	34	Commercial representatives and samples	7
Health and sanitation (Latin		Canol petroleum pipeline project (Canada)	7
America)	29	Isthmian canal (Panama)	7
Double taxation (on incomes,		Agricultural experiment stations (Latin	
estates, and shipping profits)	27	America)	6
Maritime, shipping and load lines	27	Jurisdiction over captured prizes (vessels)	6
Administration and financing of		Copyright, patents, and trademarks	5
Haiti	26	Dual nationality	5
Exchange of official publications	25	Disposition of real and personal property	4
Narcotic drug control	25	Migratory workers	4
		Naturalization	3

Specialized Subjects (Selections)

Anthropological research (Mexico and Peru, 1943 and 1944)
Atomic energy development (Great Britain, 1943)
Boundary changes of occupation zones in Germany (Soviet Union, 1945)
Currency and coinage (Panama, 1930 and 1931)
Exchange of liberated prisoners of war, World War II (Soviet Union, 1945)
Exemption of pleasure yachts from navigation dues (Sweden, 1930)
Extraterritorial rights (China, 1943)
Great Lakes-St. Lawrence Seaway (Canada, 1940)
Joint administration of Canton and Enderbury Islands in Pacific (Great Britain, 1939)
Mapping project (Peru, 1942)
Motion picture films (Czechoslovakia, 1938)
National Guard, establishment (Nicaragua, 1927)
Naval forces on Great Lakes (Canada, 1939)
Parcel post (Palestine, 1943)
Personal status and family law (Iran, 1928)
Prevention of disease in livestock (Mexico, 1924)
Protection of birds and mammals, conservation (Great Britain, 1916, and Mexico, 1936)
Reparations, World War I (Germany, 1926)
United States evacuation and end of occupation (Dominican Republic, 1924)
War memorials and battle monuments (France, 1924, and Belgium, 1929)

tinct attempts to fabricate bilateral treaties to produce advance commitments for the resolution of international disputes by the pacific means of arbitration and conciliation. These supplemented the multilateral Hague Conventions of 1899 and 1907, the Permanent Court of Arbitration, and various inter-American treaties and agreements,[100] and they superseded some of the Root Arbitration Treaties of 1908 and 1909, discussed in Chapter 5. This treaty development consisted of four aspects. The first consisted of some two dozen treaties that extended the applicability of the Root treaties, which ran for five years and were periodically renewed for ten countries, some until the late 1920s.

Another aspect was characterized by the conclusion of new bilateral conciliation treaties. Initiated by Secretary Bryan in 1913 and 1914 and continued by Secretaries Stimson and Hull, forty basic treaties (some with ancillary exchanges of notes) were concluded with twenty-seven countries.[101] Although officially called "Treaties for the Advancement of Peace" by the Department of State, they were short conciliation commitments, popularly known as "cooling-off pacts." They provided for five-member Commissions of Inquiry to investigate and report, pending which the signatories agreed to refrain from resorting to hostilities or declarations of war for at least one year following the Commission's report. These treaties remained in effect for five years and thereafter until twelve months after one of the signatories gave notice of termination.[102]

The third aspect, instituted by Secretary Kellogg in 1928, involved nearly forty-five advance pacific settlement treaties, twenty-five dealing with arbitration and nineteen with conciliation. Many of these were negotiated with governments other than those that had signed Bryan cooling-off pacts.[103] The general Arbitration Treaties provided for international dispute settlement by the Hague Permanent Court of Arbitration or by some other competent tribunal agreed to by the parties in a separate, special treaty. This process was restricted to "justiciable issues" that were "susceptible of decision by the application of the principles of law or equity." The Kellog Conciliation Treaties were similar to the earlier Bryan treaties, except that they had no five-year applicability stipulation.

In addition, the Department of State negotiated a few treaties to submit specific disputes to arbitration. The principal illustration that raised issues of international law as applied to territorial acquisition was a treaty with the Netherlands, signed by Secretary Hughes in 1925, to submit a jurisdictional dispute to the Hague Tribunal. The issue was "whether the Island of Palmas (or Miangas) in its entirety forms a part of territory belonging to the United States of America or of Netherlands territory," to be determined by an arbiter from the Permanent Court of Arbitration. He was required to render an award within three months, the determination of which the two governments agreed in advance to honor.[104] The decision, delivered by Max Huber of Zurich in April 1928, awarded the island to the Netherlands.

In summary, during less than four decades, the Department of State concluded some 130 such advance pacific settlement treaties with nearly fifty foreign governments. More than half of these were signed with European countries, a dozen with Latin American nations, and a few with Canada and African, Asian, and Mideast governments. The principal exceptions were some of the newer states (Morocco, Thailand, and Saudi Arabia), Turkey, and several Central and South American republics, but many of the latter were covered by multilateral inter-American arrangements. By the time of World War II most of the bilateral arbitration treaties and thirty-five of the conciliation pacts remained in effect, but none of them had ever been put into action, although some of them may have served to moderate international tensions.

Bilateral treaties and agreements varied considerably in their generality and specificity, as well as their length and detail. Some consisted of only a few sentences or paragraphs, such as the agreement to establish the U.S.–Canadian Permanent Joint Board on Defense, several financial agreements with Haiti, and the Murphy–Weygand agreement to deal with U.S.–French relations in North Africa during World War II. Others were comprehensive and detailed, including those concerned with commerce and consular affairs, the exchange of official publications (which listed them by individual agencies and titles), extradition, debt funding (providing annual payment schedules), and reciprocal trade, as well as World War I Peace Treaties with Germany (Versailles, 218 pages, 1919, not ratified by the United States), Hungary (126 pages, 1921), and Austria (120 pages, 1931).

Several treaties and agreements served as constitutive acts for bilateral international agencies. In addition to various arbitration and conciliation claims commissions, illustrations include agreements for joint U.S.-British administration of Canton and Enderbury Islands in the Pacific (1939) and the creation of the Canadian-American Permanent Joint Board on Defense (1940) and their Joint Committee on Economic Cooperation (1941).

A few were widely known by popular titles. Examples include the Bryan Cooling-Off Pacts, the Kellogg Arbitration and Conciliation Treaties, the World War I Debt Funding Agreements, the Hull Trade Agreements, the Lend-Lease Agreements, the Bases-Destroyers Agreement, and the Lansing–Ishii and Murphy–Weygand Agreements.

Aside from the categories of basic subjects and some of those listed as other major categories in Table 6.7, several individual bilateral treaties and agreements may be noted as of special or historic significance. In addition to those concerned with the recognition of new states and those signed at Algiers that concerned the American role in North Africa during World War II, listed chronologically these include the Bryan–Chamorro Treaty with Nicaragua, concerned with the isthmian canal (1914), the cession of the Danish West Indies (Virgin Islands) to the United States (1916), the Lansing–Ishii Agreement with Japan (1917), the World War I peace treaties with Germany and Austria (1921), the post–World War I disposition of the former German islands in the Pacific and the establishment of the Japanese mandate (1922), the evacuation of the Dominican Republic (1924), the evacuation of Haiti (1934), the agreement to register American treaties and agreements with the League of Nations (1934), the Bases-Destroyers

Agreement with Great Britain (1940),[105] the creation of the Permanent Joint Board on Defense with Canada (1940), the Great Lakes–St. Lawrence Seaway with Canada (1940), the development of atomic energy with Great Britain (1943), and perhaps the construction of the Alaskan and Pan-American Highways.

It may be concluded that the Department of State became responsible for a greatly expanded role in treaty making with an enlarged number of foreign governments on an expanded number and enriched variety of issues. It was negotiating for more executive agreements, including exchanges of notes, than formal treaties, blanketing the globe not only with those that dealt with traditional treaty subjects but also with a host of others, and concluding an increasing number in Washington. This enabled the Secretary of State to engage in more personal diplomacy, which enabled him and his Under and Assistant Secretaries to manage the treaty process more intimately and effectively at the ministerial level.

Multilateral Treaties and Agreements

Whereas the United States concluded eighty-nine multilateral international treaties and agreements prior to 1913, as indicated in Table 6.8, this mounted to more than 236 during this period through 1945. Only ninety-five of these were regarded as formal treaties, and 141 were viewed as executive agreements in American constitutional practice.[106] To 1912, multilateral treaties outnumbered executive agreements, but during this period they declined to approximately 40 percent. Internationally, they consisted of seventy-one conventions, forty-three agreements, thirty-one protocols, nineteen resolutions of international conferences, seventeen declarations of policy and commitment, and fifteen formal treaties, and forty carried other titles, such as arrangements, communiqués, exchanges of notes, and related designations.[107]

Some of these treaties and agreements were tripartite or quadripartite, but the preponderant majority were subscribed to by more governments. Sixty of the latter were inter-American commitments, and 121 were of greater widespread application, of which more than half were generally regarded as universal compacts, such as postal conventions and the constitutive acts of global international organizations and other agencies.

Only twenty were signed between 1913 and 1920, and sixty-three in the 1920s. The majority (153) were concluded during the fifteen years from 1931 to 1945, most of which (112, or nearly half of the total) were consummated during the Roosevelt administration.[108] Evidencing increased treaty importance of the United States in world affairs, more than forty-five were signed in this country, primarily in Washington.[109] However, the most were signed in Europe (108, in more than twenty cities) and Latin America (fifty-four, in eight cities).[110]

Of the treaties and agreements concluded at the highest levels in Washington, President Hoover signed a Telecommunications Convention in 1927, and Pres-

Table 6.8
Multilateral Treaties and Agreements, 1913–1945

Titles and Categories		Number of Participating Governments		Where Signed	
United States				Washington	39
Treaties	95	Tripartite	37	Elsewhere in U.S.	8
Agreements	141	Quadripartite	18	Europe	108
TOTAL	236	Inter-American	60 [1]	Latin America	54
				Mideast	12
International		Global		Asia and Pacific	7
Conventions	71	General	58	Others	8
Agreements	43	Limited	63		
Protocols	31			When Signed	
Resolutions	19			1913-15	4
Declarations	17			1916-20	16
Treaties	15			1921-25	31
Exchanges of notes	7			1926-30	32
Instruments of surrender	6			1931-35	21
Arrangements	3			1936-40	44
Communiques	3			1941-45	88
Others	21				

Principal Subjects (Examples)		Specialized Subjects
Armistice and Surrender Instruments	17	Aliens, Status of
Arms Limitation	8	Artistic Exhibitions
Commerce, Tariffs, and Trade	7	Atomic Energy—Peaceful Use of
Commercial Aviation	6	Automotive Traffic
Commodities [2]	12	Drug Control—Opium, Narcotic Drugs
Consular Affairs	1	Dual Nationality—Military Obligations
Cultural Affairs	2	Interchange of Publications
Extradition	1	Load Lines (Ships)
Food and Agriculture	4	Most-Favored-Nation Treatment
Inter-American System	48	Nationality of Women
International Organizations and Agencies	27	Pan American Highway
Laws of War and Neutrality	4	Prisoners of War
League of Nations	1	Protection of Wildlife
Merchant Marine and Shipping	7	Renunciation of War
Monetary Affairs	3	Safety of Life at Sea
Patents and Trademarks	2	Slave Trade—Suppression of
Peace Keeping and Peaceful Settlement	17	Statistics on Causes of Death
Peace Treaties	2	Submarine Warfare
Postal Affairs	19	Whaling
Railways	2	War Criminals—Treatment of
Renunciation of War	1	Specific Territories
Reparations	4	Africa—Revision of General Act
Rights and Duties of States	1	China—Military Forces, Railways,
Sanitary and Quarantine	6	Expropriation, Extraterritoriality
Telecommunications	11	Danzig—Allied Forces in
Trademarks	2	Egypt—Abolition of Capitulations
United Nations System	9	European Waters—Mine Clearance
Weights and Measures	1	Spitzbergen—Status of
World War II (Allied) Declarations to Wage and Win the War	31	Venezia Giulia—Administration of
		Western Hemisphere—Wildlife

[1]These do not include the Postal Union of the Americas and Spain, which are incorporated into the global/limited category.

[2]Commodities included coffee (two), gold (one), industrial diamonds (one), rubber (one), silver (one), sugar (four), and wheat (two).

ident Roosevelt signed both the United Nations Declaration in 1942 and the agreement to create the United Nations Relief and Rehabilitation Administration in 1943. Secretaries of State signed twenty in Washington, including Hughes (nine), Kellogg (three), Hull (five), Stettinius (two), and Dean G. Acheson (one), and Under Secretary Welles also signed two executive agreements there. Furthermore, two additional executive agreements (on North American broadcasting and international trading in wheat) were signed by other officials in Washington, and eight important constitutive treaties and agreements were concluded at Bretton Woods, Chicago, and San Francisco in 1944 and 1945.

On the other hand, most treaties and agreements concluded abroad were signed by resident or special emissaries. However, President Wilson signed the Versailles Treaty in 1919, Secretary Hughes signed five treaties negotiated at the Havana Inter-American Conference in 1928, Secretary Kellogg signed the Pact for the Renunciation of War as an instrument of national policy for settling international disputes at Paris in 1928, Secretary Stimson signed the Naval Arms Limitation Treaty at London in 1930, and Secretary Hull signed nine treaties and agreements at the Buenos Aires Inter-American Conference in 1936. In addition, many that dealt with policy and commitments respecting World War II, which grew out of a series of summit and ministerial tripartite and quadripartite conferences and meetings held at Moscow, Cairo, Tehran, Yalta, and Potsdam, were signed by Presidents Roosevelt and Truman and Secretary Hull.

Not only the number but also the variety of subjects of these multilateral treaties and agreements increased markedly, evidencing active and broad-scale U.S. involvement in international cooperation in world affairs. During the period from 1861 to 1913 these included some two dozen categories (see Table 5.6), but important new subjects were added. These embraced such matters as arms (especially naval) limitation; automotive traffic, commercial aviation, and highways; commodities; the League of Nations, the United Nations system, the International Court of Justice, and other international organizations and agencies; merchant marine and shipping; monetary affairs; multilateral peace treaties; peacekeeping and peaceful settlement; postwar reparations; surrender instruments and armistices; trademarks; treatment of prisoners of war and war criminals; and even the nationality of women, the protection of Western Hemisphere wildlife, and the compilation of statistics of the causes of death.

Some of these treaties and agreements were comprehensive in their coverage and treatment. Aside from the Versailles Treaty, examples include those that served as the constitutive acts of the United Nations and its specialized agencies, the postal unions, and general conventions that dealt with aerial and maritime sanitary affairs, the protection of industrial property (patents and trademarks), limiting the processing and regulating the distribution of narcotic drugs, telecommunications, the protection of nature and wildlife in the Western Hemisphere, and some commodity agreements, as well as four wartime and postwar agreements on Allied supplies for the Soviet Union. These also tended to be among the lengthiest documents, often running some forty to more than sixty printed pages. Others were remarkably short instruments of one or two pages, sometimes consisting of only three or four paragraphs.[111] Some were of historic significance, illustrated by the World War I Peace Treaty, signed at Versailles in 1919 (which also included the Covenant of the League of Nations and the Statute of the Permanent Court of International Justice),[112] the Kellogg–Briand Pact, the United Nations Charter and the organic acts of other postwar global organizations, and the series of World War II collective defense, armistice, and surrender instruments.

In addition to the Kellogg–Briand Pact, some bear special popular titles. These include the Wilson–Lloyd George Agreement of 1919, dealing with disposal of shipping tonnage following World War I; the Four Power Treaty of 1921, concerning insular possessions in the Pacific; the inter-American Gondra Treaty, 1923, to prevent international conflicts; the inter-American Saavedra Lamas Treaty, 1933, for nonaggression and conciliation; the Declaration of Lima, 1938, promoting inter-American solidarity; the Declaration of Panama, 1939, establishing inter-American neutrality in the European war; the Act of Havana, 1940, for the provisional administration of European colonies and possessions in the Americas; the Atlantic Charter, 1941, stipulating the eight objectives of the Allies during World War II (comparable to President Wilson's memorable Fourteen Points at the time of World War I); the United Nations Declaration, 1942, pledging the World War II Allies to cooperate by employing their resources to wage and win the war and not to sign a separate peace with the enemy; and the Act of Chapultepec, 1945, providing for inter-American reciprocal assistance and solidarity during World War II.

Several interesting features of these multilateral treaties and agreements warrant special mention. One of these concerns ratification. It is customary that all treaties, whatever their international titles, require Senate approval prior to presidential ratification. It is common knowledge that the Versailles Treaty failed to receive Senate approval and therefore was not ratified.[113] It also is well known that usually, executive agreements do not require or receive formal ratification. However, the extraconstitutional practice established by Congress early in the 1870s, described in Chapter 5, was continued for dealing with nearly twenty additional universal and inter-American postal conventions that were ratified by the Postmaster General, subject to the approval of the President.

Also of interest is the degree to which a good many treaties and agreements may be grouped in clusters or packages of two types. On one hand, as indicated in Table 6.8, on the basis of the subjects treated, several groups of ten or more deal respectively, with World War II armistices and surrender instruments (seventeen), commodities (twelve), international organizations and other agencies (twenty-seven), peacekeeping and peaceful settlement (seventeen), postal affairs (nineteen), and telecommunications (eleven). The largest aggregates concern World War II Allied declarations and other instruments to wage war and defeat the Axis powers (thirty-one) and deal with inter-American organization and substantive interrelations (forty-eight). To these may be added the development of the United Nations system (nine).

On the other hand, many were concluded at international conferences and meetings, such as those held at Washington on China's affairs in 1922, at Geneva in 1929, Madrid in 1931, Geneva again in 1936, Chicago, Dumbarton Oaks, London, and San Francisco in 1945, and also the World War II summit and ministerial gatherings at Moscow, Cairo, Tehran, Yalta, and Potsdam. The same applies to a series of regular and special inter-American conferences. Historically, the amplification of the inter-American and the establishment of the global international organization systems, the network of arrangements for peacekeeping and the peaceful settlement of disputes, and the formulation of the association of World War II Allies to deal with the Axis powers rank among the most impressive multilateral treaty developments produced by means of international conferencing.

Third is the matter of secrecy. It may be boasted that since 1789 the United States has never signed a secret treaty, but it has concluded confidential military and political arrangements in time of war. During this period, according to the Department of State, it concluded two important executive agreements, called protocols, at the Moscow Foreign Ministers Conference on November 1, 1943. The first, labeled "secret," constituted an agreement on plans and machinery to manage and shorten the war in Europe. Each of eight subjects treated, including the creation of the European Advisory Commission, was supplemented with a carefully crafted annex. The second, labeled "most secret," concerned preparations for the invasion of Western Europe by the United States and Great Britain and for other strategic actions. Surprisingly, although Secretary Hull headed the American delegation, Averell Harriman, then Ambassador to the Soviet Union, signed both of them, and they were later published by the Department of State.[114]

Fourth, most unusually, a surprising number of agreements were not formally signed. In a few cases the United States was not an original signatory but later filed instruments of accession or adherence.[115] More frequent was the practice of adopting international conference and meeting determinations as binding without signature. This procedure was especially common for inter-American conference resolutions, regarded by the United States as executive agreements.[116] However, it was also utilized for other executive agreements such as the Atlantic Charter in 1941, the Cairo Conference communiqués, the Tehran Conference Declarations in December 1943, and the London agreement of the Allied governments in August 1945 for the prosecution and punishment of Axis major war criminals, including the original Charter of the International Military Tribunal.[117] Especially irregular as a matter of treaty procedure, however, at a general conference at Geneva in 1936, the members of the International Labor Organization adopted three conventions that, though unsigned, were nevertheless treated by the United States as formal treaties, and they were approved by the Senate and ratified by the President.

Finally, two additional special aspects of the multipartite treaty process warrant attention. One of these, unique to this period, was the package of more than a dozen armistices and surrender instruments concluded with the Axis powers, 1943–1945. The other was the quantity of arrangements concluded at the summit and ministerial levels, many of which related to the conduct of World War II and its aftermath. Of these, twelve treaties and agreements were signed by Presidents—two by Wilson (including the Versailles Treaty), seven by Roosevelt (all executive agreements, including the United Nations Declaration and the organic act of the United Nations Relief and Rehabilitation Administration), and three by Truman (also all executive agreements, including the terms of the Japanese surrender and the creation of the Council of Foreign Ministers in 1945). Secretaries and Under Secretaries of State also signed nearly forty, all but six of which were formal treaties and most of which were signed by Secretaries Hughes (eleven) and Hull (eighteen).[118]

Aborted Treaties

In view of the failure of the Senate to approve the World War I Versailles Treaty, opinion has been widespread that the American treaty process is seriously flawed. Reviewing the development of treaty making and Senate approval, during nearly half a century, from 1900 to 1944, of the 645 treaties sent to the Senate for acceptance, 477 (or 74 percent) were approved as submitted, and eighty-eight (or 14 percent) were approved as amended. At the same time sixty-nine were not finally acted upon by the Senate, eight were withdrawn, and only three were formally rejected.

Illustrating Senate interpretation of a treaty by amendment or reservation, it insisted that a Treaty of Friendship, Commerce, and Consular Rights with Germany, signed in 1923, was to have no effect on American immigration control and legislation. In the case of the multilateral London Naval Arms Limitation Treaty of 1930, the Senate granted its consent subject to the explicit understanding that there were no secret documents, arrangements, or agreements in any way modifying its provisions.

The classic, most widely debated treaty action was the congressional handling of the World War I Versailles Treaty late in 1919 and 1920. The Senate deliberated on it for several months and voted on it in several versions. The Foreign Relations Committee reviewed it and considered nearly fifty amendments and reservations. Realizing that it was unfeasible to reconvene the Paris Peace Conference to acquire general acceptance of such wholesale revision, the Senate decided to modify the application of the treaty by means of adding American reservations. Initially, it rejected the treaty with the addition of fourteen so-called Lodge Reservations (named after Senator Henry Cabot Lodge, Republican majority leader of the Senate, who chaired the Foreign Relations Committee), in which version the treaty was voted on and disapproved. The Senate also voted down a version with five reservations, as well as the treaty without any reservations—described as in all its pristine purity. Because of popular support of both a treaty to legally end the war with Germany and to establish the League of Nations, the treaty was reconsidered with fifteen reservations in March 1920, which the Senate again rejected.

Eventually, Congress passed a resolution on July 2, 1921, that declared the end of the state of war with Germany and reserved to the United States the rights that would have accrued to this country under the Versailles Treaty or by the peace treaties with the remnants of the Austro–Hungarian Empire. The following month the United States signed separate, short peace treaties with Germany, Austria, and Hungary that, promptly approved by the Senate and formally ratified, provided this country with the rights, privileges, reparations, and other advantages insisted upon by Congress.

The other two treaties that failed to obtain Senate approval were a Claims Convention with Norway and a Consular Treaty with Lithuania, signed, respectively, on March 28 and May 20, 1940. The treaty with Norway involved individual claims of Christopher Hannevig and George R. Jones. The U.S. Court of Claims held that Norway had no valid claim upon the United States on behalf of Hannevig, and, by diplomatic note in 1952, the American Government informed Norway that it would no longer pursue the claim on behalf of Jones. The Lithuanian Consular Treaty became redundant when the Soviet Union occupied the country in June 1940.

Contrary to the prevailing impression, the number of treaties formally rejected by the Senate by unfavorable vote was minuscule, amounting to less than .005 percent. However, during this period from 1900 to 1944, some sixty-nine, or nearly 11 percent, failed to be approved by the Senate simply by inaction, deliberate or inadvertent, which also amounted to approval failure and lack of ratification. In addition, a few signed treaties were withdrawn by the White House and required no Senate action.[119]

INTERNATIONAL CONFERENCES AND MEETINGS

Traditionally, through Senate approval of commissioned diplomats to represent the United States abroad, Congress exercised some control over American participation in international conferences and meetings and in approving the treaties and agreements they produced. Although the United States had previously participated in scores of bilateral and multilateral conferences and meetings convened both in Washington and abroad, as indicated in Chapter 5, attempting to regularize its control, in March 1913, Congress declared: ''Hereafter the executive shall not extend or accept any invitation to participate in any international congress, conference, or like event without first having specific authority of law to do so.''[120]

Except for congressional authorization respecting the unique method of negotiating, signing, and ratifying postal conventions, prior practice of Congress in this regard is unclear. In any case, while presidential–congressional relations pertaining to treaty making were constitutionally mandated, there is no stipulation in the Constitution that restricts the powers of the President to authorize American representation at international conferences and meetings. Commenting on this matter, President Wilson called this congressional action of 1913 excessive and "utterly futile." Professor Graham Stuart branded it "an unconstitutional infringement upon the President's control of foreign relations and as such has been violated with impunity by subsequent presidents," and Benjamin Williams observes that Congress cannot "restrict the President with regard to one of the powers with which he is most clearly endowed by practice, *i.e.*, that of treaty negotiation."[121]

The use of international conferencing as a vital supplement to traditional bilateral diplomatic negotiation mushroomed during the period from World War I to World War II. Employed by the President and the Department of State to coalesce the interests, plans, and conduct for collective waging of war and concluding subsequent peace settlements, it became a primary means for dealing with a great many international political, legal, economic, social, arms limitation, and other issues, especially those that required multilateral consensus. Expansion of both the community of nations and matters of common interest and jurisdiction accelerated preference for, and reliance on, the conference process. Despite its long-standing policy of isolationism and noninvolvement in Europe's political affairs, the United States became an avid proponent of, and often a leader in, conference participation.[122]

To provide for Department of State management of certain aspects of the preparation for, and administration of, international conferences and meetings, in February 1928 Secretary Kellogg decided to establish a Division of Protocol (originally, the Ceremonial Officer) to handle both protocol and international conference affairs. The following year the Secretary changed its title to the Division of International Conferences and Protocol, headed by careerist James C. Dunn, while Charles Lee Cooke continued as Ceremonial Officer. Two years later, in 1931, it was divided into two separate units, with Dunn continuing in charge of conferences and Warren D. Robbins as head of the Division of Protocol, assisted by Cooke as Ceremonial Officer. In 1933 the two agencies were reunited, but in July 1937, because of the increased work in both fields, they were separated again. Richard Southgate headed the reborn Division of Conferences, and George T. Summerlin became Chief of Protocol. The conference duties of the Department increased throughout this period, culminating in the San Francisco Conference of 1945, which has been called the most elaborate and perhaps the most important conference in which the United States ever participated.

Supplementing the discussion of international conference types in the preceding chapter, as the United States became more highly involved in this diplomatic process, additional analysis of their categories warrants attention. For descriptive purposes they may be grouped according to their composition, formality, subject matter, and objectives. Based on the character of participants, public or intergovernmental conferences, at which official government delegations convene to consider and settle international matters and usually conclude treaties and agreements, need to be distinguished from semipublic and private gatherings.[123] Distinctions among the intergovernmental types include the congress, the conference, and the meeting. Whereas the title "congress" had previously been employed to differentiate those that were regarded as more significant and dignified than the conference, that were convened to consummate a major peace settlement or territorial disposition and represented an especially important occasion, and that involved a greater number of powers than a conference, this distinction has since become less critical.[124]

Of greater significance is the distinction between conferences and meetings. To the time of World War II these expressions were regarded as interchangeable. Subsequently, the term "conference" ceased to be used by the Department of State for bilateral gatherings or regularized sessions of permanent agencies (such as the United Nations, the Organization of American States, the North Atlantic Treaty Organization, and similar agencies), which are customarily called meetings or sessions. The term "conference," therefore, has come to be applied to those gatherings that are generally multilateral and ad hoc.

Aside from the obvious differentiation between the bilateral, tripartite, quadripartite, and other multilateral gatherings, they may also be distinguished on the basis of three primary levels of participants. These are commonly called diplomatic (consisting of commissioned diplomatic representatives), ministerial (involving the Secretary of State), and summit (participated in personally by the President) conferences and meetings. Or they may be distinguished as to whether, so far as purpose is concerned, they are largely cooperative-discussion, policy-aligning, treaty-negotiation, peacemaking, peacekeeping, law-or rule-creating, administrative, or constitutive (creating international organizations and other agencies) conferences and meetings. Sometimes they are identified simply as formal or informal and occasionally as preparatory or pickaback gatherings when they lead to, or grow out of, other conferences and meetings.

In earlier times the United States was represented at international conferences and meetings by resident or special emissaries when they were convened abroad and by the Secretary of State or his deputy when they were held in this country. This practice has continued, but during this period the President and Secretary of State became more personally involved in summit and ministerial conference participation abroad as well as in Washington.

It should be noted, however that, during World War I President Wilson began the practice of sending unofficial, sometimes called "silent," observers to sessions of the Allied Supreme War Council, whom French Premier Georges Clemenceau called an ear but not a mouth. In the course of time American collaboration with the Council increased virtually to the point of complete partnership. As the United States returned to isolation and noninvolvement following the war, for some years Presidents relied on this practice of using unofficial observers at international gatherings more consistently than any other major power. Under President Harding, for example, such observers were sent to meetings of the Allied Supreme Council, the Conference of Ambassadors, and the Reparations Commission. Americans were sent in a similar capacity to sessions of the League of Nations, its committee meetings, and other conferences and meetings, some of which were held under its auspices. However, by the time of World War II the United States had completely reversed its attitude.

Evidencing increasing U.S. conference participation, whereas it was represented at 179 during the quarter century from 1901 to 1925 (averaging 7.2 per year), during the next two decades, to 1945, this rose to 818 (averaging nearly forty-one per year). On the other hand, the United States attended only ten major international conferences during the period from the 1880s to 1913, such as the two Hague Conferences (1899 and 1907), the London Naval Conference (1908–9), and four International Conferences of American States (1889–1910). However, following World War I, American participation and often leadership increased markedly. Demonstrating this change, American representatives participated in some eighty such important conferences and meetings between 1919 and 1945.[125] These consisted of twenty-five global multilateral, eleven inter-American, and two bilateral diplomatic-level, as well as 126 summit and seventeen ministerial conferences and meetings, as indicated in Table 6.9.[126]

Between 1913 and 1945 the World War I Allied and Associated Powers negotiated the Versailles Treaty at Paris and produced the League of Nations Covenant, eleven conferences dealt with a variety of inter-American affairs, four concerned naval arms limitation, two held at Geneva focused on traffic in arms and general disarmament, and two were devoted to producing a moratorium on World War I intergovernmental debts and coping with world economic conditions.

However, the majority of these conferences and meetings—constituting a unique diplomatic experience—were concerned with the waging and winning of the war against the Axis powers and creating the United Nations and several of its specialized agencies. President Roosevelt participated personally in at least eighteen wartime summit conferences and meetings, beginning at Ogdensburg, New York, in 1940, and continuing to the historic Yalta Conference in February 1945. He met, consulted, and negotiated with Prime Minister Mackenzie King of Canada three times, with Prime Minister Winston Churchill in bilateral meetings ten times, in tripartite meetings with the British Prime Minister and Marshal Stalin of the Soviet Union at Tehran late in 1943 and at Yalta in February 1945. He and Churchill also conferred with Generalissimo Chiang Kai-shek of China and with the President of Turkey, and he held a bilateral courtesy meeting with the Shah of Iran on November 30, 1943.

Subsequently, in July 1945 President Truman conferred with Prime Minister Churchill (and when he was defeated in the British parliamentary election that

Table 6.9
International Conferences and Meetings, 1913–1945[1]

Major Multilateral—International

1919	Paris	World War I Peace and League Of Nations *
1921-22	Washington	Naval Arms Limitation and Far East
1924-25	Geneva	Second Opium
1925	Geneva	Traffic in Arms
1927	Geneva	Naval Arms Limitation
1930	London	Naval Arms Limitation
1931	London	Moratorium on World War I Intergovernmental Debts
1932-34	Geneva	General Disarmament
1933	London	Second World Monetary and Economic
1935	London	Naval Arms Limitation
1937	Montreux	Revision of Capitulatory Regime in Egypt
1937	Brussels	Nine Powers on "War" in Far East
1938	Evian (France)	Political and Racial Refugees Outside Germany
1941	Washington	Draft United Nations Declaration
1943	Hot Springs (VA)	United Nations on Food and Agriculture *
1943	Washington	U.N., Food and Agriculture Organization (FAO) *
1943	Atlantic City	U.N., Relief and Rehabilitation Organization (UNRRA) *
1944	Philadelphia	International Labor Organization (ILO) *
1944	Bretton Woods	U.N., Monetary and Financial (IB and IMF) *
1944	Dumbarton Oaks	Principles for Postwar International Organization *
1944	Montreal	2nd U.N. on Relief and Rehabilitation (UNRRA) *
1944	Chicago	U.N., Civil Aviation (ICAO) *
1945	Washington	U.N., Statute of International Court of Justice *
1945	San Francisco	United Nations Charter *
1945	London	U.N., Education, Science, and Culture (UNESCO) *

Major Inter-American [2]

1922-23	Washington	Central American Arms Limitation
1923	Santiago	General, Fifth Inter-American
1928	Havana	General, Sixth Inter-American
1929	Washington	Conciliation and Arbitration
1933	Montevideo	General, Seventh Inter-American
1936	Buenos Aires	Maintenance of Peace
1938	Lima	General, Eighth Inter-American
1939	Panama City	First Foreign Ministers—Neutrality
1940	Havana	Second Foreign Ministers—Economic and Financial
1942	Rio de Janeiro	Third Foreign Ministers—Technical Economic Cooperation
1945	Chapultepec (Mexico City)	Problems of War and Peace

Major Bilateral

1941	London	U.S. and Great Britain—Refugees and Relief
1943	Hamilton (Bermuda)	U.S. and Great Britain—Refugees

Summit Conferences and Meetings
World War I

1919	Paris	Wilson	World War I Peace and League of Nations Covenant

Inter-War Period

1921-22	Washington	Harding **	Naval Arms Limitation
1928	Havana	Coolidge **	6th Inter-American
1936	Buenos Aires	Roosevelt **	Special Inter-American
1938	Kingston, Canada	Roosevelt and MacKenzie King	

World War II

1940, Aug. 18	Ogdensburg, N.Y.	Roosevelt and MacKenzie King
1941, Apr. 20	Hyde Park, N.Y.	Roosevelt and Churchill
1941, mid-August	Atlantic/Argentia	Roosevelt and Churchill
1941-42, Dec. 22-Jan. 14	Washington (1st)	Roosevelt and Churchill
1942, June 19-25	Hyde Park and Washington (2nd)	Roosevelt and Churchill
1943, Jan. 14-25	Casablanca	Roosevelt and Churchill
1943, May 12-15	Washington (3rd)	Roosevelt and Churchill
1943, Aug. 14-24	Quebec (1st) and Hyde Park	Roosevelt, Churchill, and MacKenzie King
1943, Sep. 1-11	Washington (4th)	Roosevelt and Churchill
1943, Nov. 22-26	Cairo (1st)	Roosevelt, Churchill, and Chiang Kai-shek
1943, Nov. 27-Dec. 2	Teheran	Roosevelt, Churchill, and Stalin
1943, Nov. 30	Teheran	Roosevelt and Shah of Iran **
1943, Dec. 2-7	Cairo (2nd)	Roosevelt and Churchill
1943, Dec. 4-7	Cairo (2nd)	Roosevelt, Churchill, and President of Turkey
1944, Sep. 13-16	Quebec (2nd)	Roosevelt, Churchill, and MacKenzie King
1944, Sep. 18-19	Hyde Park	Roosevelt and Churchill
1945, Jan. 30-Feb. 3	Malta	Roosevelt and Churchill
1945, Feb. 4-11	Yalta	Roosevelt, Churchill, and Stalin
1945, April 25	San Francisco	Truman **
1945, July 17-Aug. 2	Potsdam/Berlin	Truman, Churchill and Atlee, and Stalin

Ministerial Conferences and Meetings

1921-22	Washington	Hughes	Naval Arms Limitation
1922-23	Washington	Hughes	Central American Arms Limitation
1929	Washington	Kellogg	Conciliation and Arbitration
1930	London	Stimson	Naval Arms Limitation
1931	London	Stimson	1st World Monetary and Economic
1932	Geneva	Stimson	General Disarmament
1933	Montevideo	Hull	7th Inter-American
1933	London	Hull	2nd World Monetary and Economic
1936	Buenos Aires	Hull	Inter-American, Maintenance of Peace
1938	Lima	Hull	8th Inter-American
1939	Panama City	Hull	1st Inter-American Foreign Ministers
1940	Havana	Hull	2nd Inter-American Foreign Ministers
1942	Rio de Janeiro	Hull	3rd Inter-American Foreign Ministers
1943	Moscow	Hull	Big Four—Prepare for Anti-Axis Summit Conferences
1944	Dumbarton Oaks	Hull[3]	Principles for Postwar International Organization
1945	Chapultepec/ Mexico City	Stettinius	Problems of War and Peace
1945	San Francisco	Stettinius	United Nations Charter

*Denotes constitutive conference.

*Indicates the President participated in a ceremonial capacity.

[1] List does not include conferences, meetings and sessions of regularized World War II agencies such as the Combined Chiefs of Staff, the European Advisory Commission, and the Far Eastern Commission. Nor does it include all summit and ministerial conferences and meetings, which are listed separately. The United States was also "unofficially represented" at such conferences as those held at Portorose (Austria-Hungary succession states for cooperation, 1921), Genoa (Soviet Expropriation Reparations, 1922), Lausanne (Peace Treaty with Turkey to supersede Treaty of Sevres, 1923), and London (Reparations, 1924).

[2] The regularized general inter-American conferences began in Washington (first, 1899), followed at Mexico City (second, 1901–2), Rio de Janeiro (third, 1906), and Buenos Aires (fourth, 1910). The ninth was held at Bogotá (1948), and the tenth at Caracas (1954). In the meantime the Organization of American States superseded these conferences.

[3] Secretary Hull was accompanied by Under Secretary Stettinius; Hull dealt with policy, and Stettinius headed the American delegation for negotiations.

year and was replaced by Clement R. Attlee) and Stalin at Potsdam. At these conferences and meetings Presidents Roosevelt and Truman planned and agreed on military, naval, and air strategy, the liberation of Axis-occupied territories, postwar political, economic, territorial settlements, and the United Nations organization, and they dealt with other issues.

Ministerial conferencing also became commonplace during this period, not only in Washington but also abroad. During the 1920s and early 1930s Secretaries Hughes and Kellogg presided over three conferences held in Washington, and Secretary Stimson represented the United States at three conferences at London and Geneva dealing with arms limitation and world monetary and economic affairs. Setting a record, Secretary Hull participated in at least nine ministerial conferences, including the Second World Monetary and Economic Conference (London, 1933), six inter-American conferences, of which half were general gatherings of Western Hemisphere Foreign Ministers, and the most critical at Moscow in October 1943 to prepare the way for the Tehran and Cairo summit conclaves and at Dumbarton Oaks the following year to plan the postwar global international organization.

In the meantime, at more than a dozen separate diplomatic conferences, the wartime United Nations negotiated treaties and agreements to devise international plans for dealing with political and racial refugees outside Germany and at twelve conferences to establish a series of international organizations. These dealt with the fields of civil aviation (International Civil Aviation Organization), financial affairs (International Bank and International Monetary Fund), education, science, and culture (United Nations Educational, Scientific, and Cultural Organization), food and agriculture (Food and Agricultural Organization), labor (International Labor Organization), and relief and rehabilitation (United Nations Relief and Rehabilitation Organization). At the Dumbarton Oaks and San Francisco Conferences they also created the United Nations to supersede the League of Nations and the International Court of Justice to replace the former Permanent Court of International Justice (World Court).

These two critical diplomatic ventures—waging and winning the war with the Axis powers and establishing the postwar United Nations system within five years—involving twenty summit conferences and meetings and many ministerial and diplomatic-level negotiations, constituted a monumental task and resulted in remarkable achievement. Nevertheless, one of the critical political issues flowing from the frequent personal participation of the President not only in the management of policy but also in attendant conference negotiations was the degree to which the Secretary and Department of State were bypassed.

During the war military planning also required conference participation by Army and Navy officers. Therefore, it was natural that large military, naval, and air staffs, consisting of dozens of officers, led by Admiral William D. Leahy (Chief of Staff to the President), and General George C. Marshall, Admiral Ernest J. King, and General Henry H. Arnold (Chiefs of Staff), accompanied the President to these wartime summit conferences. They convened in many sessions of the American Joint Chiefs of Staff at the major summit conferences at Washington, Casablanca, Cairo, Tehran, Malta, Yalta, and Potsdam, and they also held many Combined Chiefs of Staff sessions with British military leaders.

On the other hand, whereas Secretary Hull headed the American delegation to important Foreign Ministers conferences, he did not accompany President Roosevelt to most of the wartime bilateral and trilateral summit conferences and meetings. He was made a member of the President's delegations to three of the early meetings with Prime Minister Churchill at Washington (1941–43) and the First Quebec Conference in August 1943. (However, when President Truman went to the Potsdam Conference in July 1945, he took Secretary James F. Byrnes and a corps of some two dozen Department of State officers and diplomats with him, including three Assistant Secretaries.)[127]

The most egregious example of presidential departure from normal practice in appointing his assistants and advisers on his summit team occurred at the time of the Second Quebec Conference in September 1944. The first aberration was to bypass the Department of State entirely and to take with him Secretary of the Treasury Henry Morgenthau, Jr., as his principal Cabinet-level adviser, accompanied by his assistant Harry Dexter White. The second mistake was the President's acceptance of the "Morgenthau Plan" for the postsurrender treatment of Germany, which was unalterably opposed by Secretary of State Hull and Secretary of War Stimson, neither of whom was at the conference.

This plan proposed not only the disarming of Germany, the destruction of the German armament industry, and the removal or destruction of other key industries, restitution and reparations, and punishment of war criminals but also the political partitioning of Germany, ceding German territory to Poland and France, and political decentralization—amounting to "deindustrializing and agriculturalizing" future Germany. Though supported by the President and reluctantly endorsed by Prime Minister Churchill, much of the plan was later rejected. This unfortunate incident illustrates one of the risks of engaging in summitry as a diplomatic process without Department of State guidance, review, and approval.[128]

Nevertheless, these experiences introduced a revolutionary trend in the conduct of American foreign relations and the role and functions of the Department of State. The era of reluctance to join in international conferences and meetings anywhere on the globe had ended. Rather, the day of full U.S. cooperation with other governments around the conference table had arrived, portending virtually the total panoply of international affairs, ranging from peacekeeping, peacemaking, and collective security, to cooperation respecting a variety of both general and technical matters.[129]

To summarize, in earlier times the United States was represented at international conferences and meetings largely by the Secretary of State when they were convened in Washington and by resident emissaries when they were held abroad. This practice has continued, but during this period the President and Secretary of State became more personally involved in summit and ministerial conference participation, both in America and abroad.

INTERNATIONAL ORGANIZATIONS AND OTHER AGENCIES

Prior to World War I the United States was reluctant to join with other governments in permanent and continuing international organizations to coordinate and regularize the administration of mutual affairs. The principal exceptions, numbering nearly fifteen, were the Hague Tribunal (Permanent Court of Arbitration), the Pan-American Union, and agencies to deal with postal affairs, health and sanitation, meteorology, patents and trademarks, telegraphic communication, weights and measures, and a few other nonpolitical matters.

During this period the American Government joined at least thirty-five additional major agencies, so that by the end of World War II, it held membership in approximately fifty such international organizations, as indicated in Table 6.10. This represented an accelerating degree of multilateral involvement in this aspect of the conduct of foreign relations. It also characterized willingness to sponsor the creation of such agencies and to host their headquarters and, with the establishment of the United Nations with its headquarters in New York, a revolutionary policy of leading in the management of global affairs. If the temporary, wartime agencies are added, the United States became the progenitor of, and participant in, a massive complex of international organizations and agencies, evidencing that the United States had become an avid joiner.

After the Senate rejected the Versailles Treaty, the League of Nations Covenant, and the Statute of the Permanent Court of International Justice, during the following two decades the United States joined twelve new major international organizations, including a few Inter-American agencies. However, during the Roosevelt Administration it affiliated with twenty-three additional organizations. These embraced the United Nations, the International Court of Justice, six United Nations specialized agencies,[130] and the wartime United Nations War Crimes Commission, most of which were established at international conferences convened in the United States. Except for several Inter-American agencies, most others were created at foreign capitals. To appreciate the full extent of this conversion of the United States, however, it is necessary to add at least three dozen multilateral and some fifteen temporary wartime military bilateral planning, coordinating, and administrative agencies.[131]

As of 1945 these new, major organizations and agencies may be grouped in three major categories—the United Nations system (eleven), the Inter-American system (ten), and other fields of cooperative interest (fourteen). Functionally, these and the older organizations were concerned with a broad range of international cooperation, embracing not only general policy making and administration (including the United Nations and the Pan-American Union) and peaceful

Table 6.10
International Organizations and Other Agencies, 1913–1945*

A. Earlier Organizations Still in Existence

Central Bureau of the International Map of the World on the Millionth Scale, 1913
International Bureau for the Publication of Customs Tariffs, 1890
International Bureau of Weights and Measures, 1875 and 1921
International Institute of Statistics, 1885
International Meteorological Organization, 1878
International Office of Public Health, 1907
International Union for the Protection of Industrial Property, 1883
Interparliamentary Union, 1899
Pan American Sanitary Bureau, 1902
Pan American Union, Washington, 1889-90
Permanent Court of Arbitration, 1899 and 1907
Permanent International Association of Navigation Congresses, 1885, 1894, and 1898
Permanent International Association of Road Congresses, 1908
Universal Postal Union, 1874

B. International Organizations and Agencies Created 1913-1945

United Nations System and Specialized and Other Agencies

Food and Agriculture Organization (FAO), Hot Springs, Va., 1943
International Bank for Reconstruction and Development (IB), Bretton Woods, N.H., 1945
International Civil Aviation Organization (ICAO), Chicago, 1944
International Court of Justice (ICJ), San Francisco, 1945
International Labor Organization (ILO), Paris, 1919, and Philadelphia, 1944
International Monetary Fund (IMF), Bretton Woods, N.H., 1945
International Telecommunication Union (ITU), Madrid, 1932
United Nations (UN), San Francisco, 1945
United Nations Educational, Scientific, and Cultural Organization (UNESCO), London, 1944
United Nations Relief and Rehabilitation Administration (UNRRA), Washington, 1943
United Nations War Crimes Commission, London, 1943

Inter-American

American International Institute for the Protection of Childhood, Santiago, 1924
Emergency Advisory Committee for Political Defense, Rio de Janeiro, 1942
Inter-American Coffee Board, Washington, D.C., 1940
Inter-American Commission of Women, Havana, 1928
Inter-American Indian Institute, Mexico City, 1940
Inter-American Institute of Agricultural Sciences, Washington, 1940
Inter-American Juridical Committee, Panama City, 1939, amplified 1940 and 1942
Inter-American Statistical Institute, Washington, 1940
Office of Inter-American Telecommunications, Rio de Janeiro, 1945 (replaced Inter-American
    Radio Office)
Pan American Postal Union, Buenos Aires, 1921, converted into Postal Union of the Americas
    and Spain, 1931

Others[1]

Allied Commission on Reparations, Yalta, 1945 (tripartite, US, U.K., and Soviet Union)
European Central Inland Transport Organization, London, 1942
Intergovernmental Committee on Refugees, Evian, 1938
International Cotton Advisory Committee, Washington, 1939
International Council of Scientific Unions, Brussels, 1931
International Criminal Police Commission, Vienna, 1924
International Hydrographic Bureau, London, 1920
International Seed Testing Association, Cambridge (Great Britain), 1924
International Sugar Council, London, 1937
International Technical Committee of Aerial Legal Experts, Paris, 1925
International Tin Committee, London, 1931 and 1933
International Wheat Council, Washington, 1942
Permanent Central Opium Board, Geneva, 1925
Rubber Study Group, 1944 (tripartite, U.S., Great Britain, and the Netherlands)

*Location and dates indicate where and when treaties and agreements were concluded to establish
    the international organizations and other agencies.

[1]For additional World War II temporary commissions and other agencies, see n.38.

settlement and adjudication (including the Permanent Court of Arbitration and the International Court of Justice) but also such fields as agricultural, commercial and financial, commodity, drug control, educational and cultural, health and sanitation, labor, postal, scientific, social, transport and communications affairs, and a variety of more specialized matters.[132]

Paralleling its traditional bilateral diplomacy, this development augmented American leadership as a superpower and increased the burden and responsibilities of the Department of State in the management of world cooperation. These organizations and agencies were founded on either treaties and agreements or international conference resolutions and, in rare cases, by means of joint press announcements for some of the World War II temporary agencies. As a result, the United States moved from its earlier position of selective international integration (not including involvement in global, particularly European, political affairs represented by the League of Nations) to a policy of active internationalism. This broadened the responsibilities of the Department of State so that, in the reorganization of December 1944, Secretary Stettinius created a special Division of International Organization Affairs to coordinate departmental service and activities in dealing with this matter.[133]

PUBLICATIONS OF THE DEPARTMENT OF STATE

To satisfy growing public and scholarly interest in the way the American Government, especially the Department of State, conducts American foreign relations, efforts were made to increase the production of publications and related materials. The Bureau of Rolls and Library was reorganized in May 1921 as the Division of Publications, headed by Gaillard Hunt, who had entered the Department as a clerk in 1897 and published his history of the Department in 1914. A few years later the Division of Publications was converted into the Office of the Historical Adviser, under Tyler Dennett, a notable historian, who was succeeded in 1931 by David Hunter Miller, which produced the *Foreign Relations* series and to which the preparation of a collection of American treaties and agreements was added. In 1933 this office was divided, and Cyril Wynn became chief of a new Division of Research and Publication, which handled the preparation, editing, and distribution of departmental publications, except those produced by the Historical Adviser. By Stettinius' reorganizations these functions were ascribed to the Historical Adviser and the newly created Office of Public Affairs. In addition to the production of the *Foreign Relations of the United States* series, the Department of State has issued a considerable variety of publications, listed in Table 7.14.[134]

CONCLUSION

These years from 1913 to 1945 proved to be a revolutionary period for the Department of State. In certain respects, as a force in international affairs, the

United States was recognized as a great world power from the outset. This status was confirmed by the role it played during and following World War I, and its global stature was elevated to that of a superpower at the time of World War II, from which it emerged as the sole nuclear power. It achieved this status without the acquisition of significant additional territory, except for the purchase of the Danish West Indies in 1916.

American participation, leadership, and posture were evidenced by the creation of the departmental rank of Under Secretary and the augmentation of the number of Assistant Secretaries and other ranking officers, by increases in the number of overseas diplomatic and consular missions, the elevation of two-thirds of American diplomatic posts to the ambassadorial rank, the professionalization of departmental, diplomatic, and consular personnel, the creation and amalgamation of the career Foreign Service of the United States, and experimenting with the creation of the special rank of Ambassador at Large. Modernization and change were also embodied in major departmental reorganizations instituted by Secretary Kellogg, Assistant Secretary Messersmith, and Under Secretary and, later, Secretary Stettinius. Also noteworthy were the intensification of diplomatic relations and negotiations at the summit and ministerial levels and the use of presidential personal envoys to supplement traditional diplomatic and consular representation.

Department of State functions and activities mushroomed in two respects. They increased in both kind and quantity. This amplification applied not only to representation, negotiation, and servicing American public interests and nationals abroad but also to the number of international policy declarations that were issued, the quantity of treaties and agreements concluded, the international conferences and meetings attended, and the international organizations and other agencies with which the United States affiliated. Also denoting change, the Department of State concluded a great many more executive agreements than formal treaties, increased the number negotiated and signed in Washington, and accelerated considerably the pace of treaty and agreement making in the period from 1940 to 1945.

Of special importance, whereas the United States led in negotiating the Covenant of the League of Nations during the Wilson Administration, it reverted to traditional isolationism and noninvolvement during the 1920s and much of the 1930s. But it assumed leadership during the Roosevelt Administration in consummating the United Nations system in the 1940s, which involved commitment to the doctrine of collective security and cooperation in political and defense fields as well as many other subjects of mutual concern at international conferences and by expanding American membership in several dozen additional international organizations and other agencies.

The Department of State and its overseas missions became responsible for implementing major innovations in American foreign policy. Among others, these included modification in the recognition of new states and governments, the Stimson Non-Recognition Doctrine, the moderation and subsequent continentalization of the Monroe Doctrine (including the Clark Memorandum of 1928), isolationism and neutrality, the aberrant Morgenthau Plan for the post–World War II treatment of Germany, World War I and II reparations, mutual arms limitation, and especially President Wilson's Fourteen Points and President Roosevelt's Arsenal for Democracy, Atlantic Charter, Four Freedoms, Good Neighbor, Lend-Lease, Reciprocal Trade, and other policy pronouncements.

These developments and changes evidenced the dynamic nature of the diplomatic process and portended and prepared the United States for what has been called "the new diplomacy." Sir Harold Nicolson, well-known British diplomat, in his analysis of the evolution of diplomatic method, discusses the Greek, Roman, and Italian (fifteenth and sixteenth centuries), the French (seventeenth to nineteenth centuries), and the American (twentieth century) systems of diplomacy.

Beginning with World War I, fundamental changes in diplomatic style, referred to as the "American method," emerged, which have been characterized as "the new diplomacy." It consists primarily of "parliamentary diplomacy" practiced in international organizations such as the United Nations and its specialized agencies, "conference diplomacy" utilized in bilateral and multilateral conclaves and meetings, "personal diplomacy" resorted to by political leaders and their Foreign Ministers and special emissaries, and "open diplomacy." In some respects it denotes what some denominate as "democratic" or "democratized" diplomacy, portrayed by increased responsiveness to the people, less government confidentiality, and popularization in the sense of reposing less emphasis on aristocratic or formal protocol, attire, demeanor, and procedure.[135]

NOTES

1. This unique scheme of President Wilson to have his successor succeed him immediately following the presidential election of 1916, conveyed to Secretary Lansing in a confidential letter, provided that, if Charles Evans Hughes was elected President, Secretary Lansing would resign at once, and Wilson would appoint Hughes as Secretary. Then President Wilson and Vice President Thomas R. Marshall would also resign, and, under the Presidential Succession Act, Hughes would succeed to the presidency immediately. This arrangement would avoid the hiatus in foreign affairs that normally occurs during the months of November to early March, pending the inauguration of a new President. See Stuart, *The Department of State*, pp. 241–42. However, inasmuch as Wilson won the election, such action was unnecessary.

2. This appointment was critical because both the President and the Vice President were in poor health, so Henry Cabot Lodge, who headed the Senate Foreign Relations Committee, took a month to investigate and approve Colby because, under the Presidential Succession Act, the Secretary of State was next in line for the presidency. As a consequence, the new Secretary would be confronted with a series of critical issues— serving during the last year of Wilson's second term, the failure of the Senate to approve the Versailles Treaty and the consequences for U.S. world leadership, the realignment of nations in Central Europe, the Communist upheaval in Russia and its invasion of Poland, and Japan's annexation of Sakhalin Island.

3. Roosevelt had considered Byrnes as his running mate in the election of 1944, but, due to strong labor objections, he switched to Truman as his vice presidential candidate. Had Byrnes been elected as Vice President, he rather than Truman could have succeeded to the Presidency following Roosevelt's death. As Secretary of State, Byrnes still was next in line for the Presidency until the 1948 presidential election. Later, as noted in Chapter 7, Byrnes became President Truman's Secretary of State.

4. As early as January 1935 Secretary Hull issued an order to his Under Secretary and Assistant Secretaries not to go to President Roosevelt without having appointments made through the office of the Under Secretary.

For some time Secretary Hull and Under Secretary Welles had not been compatible, and the gulf between them grew steadily. When Hull was ill, and Welles served as Acting Secretary, he did not keep Hull adequately informed on important matters, did not consult him when it seemed essential to Hull, and disregarded Hull's instructions to be applied at an inter-American conference at Rio de Janeiro in 1942; their relations were so strained that President Roosevelt finally decided that one of them had to leave, and he accepted the resignation of Welles in 1943. Both the President and Secretary Hull sought to appoint Welles as a roving ambassador or as a special envoy to Russia, which he declined.

5. President Wilson's Paris Conference delegation, in addition to himself, consisted of Colonel House, Secretary Lansing, General Tasker H. Bliss (member of the Supreme War Council in Paris), and career diplomat Henry White (former Ambassador to Italy and France, 1905–9). Later, Wilson was faulted for not including any leading Republicans, such as former President Taft or former Secretary Root.

6. For comprehensive studies on presidential personal diplomacy at the summit, see Plischke, *Summit Diplomacy: Personal Diplomacy of the President of the United States, Diplomat in Chief: The President at the Summit*, and "World War II Summits" in John W. McDonald, Jr., *U.S.-Soviet Summitry: Roosevelt through Carter*, pp. 1–15; Weihmiller and Doder, *U.S.-Soviet Summits: An Account of East-West Diplomacy at the Top, 1955–1985*.

7. For example, Lansing represented the United States in more international arbitrations than any previous American, and he was involved in the founding of the American Society of International Law (1906) and establishing the *American Journal of International Law* (1907).

Colby was a Special Assistant to the U.S. Attorney General in anti-trust proceedings (1917), and he later returned to the practice of law with Woodrow Wilson in New York City (1921–23).

Hughes was a Special Assistant to the U.S. Attorney General in a coal investigation (1906), Associate Justice of the Supreme Court (1910–16), and subsequently a member of the Permanent Court of Arbitration (1926–30), Judge on the Permanent Court of International Justice (1928–30), and Chief Justice of the U.S. Supreme Court (1930–41).

Kellogg was a government delegate to the Universal Congress of Lawyers and Jurists at St. Louis (1904), special counsel for the government to prosecute antitrust suits, President of the American Bar Association (1912–13), and Judge on the Permanent Court of International Justice (1930–35).

In addition, Stimson served as U.S. Attorney for the Southern District of New York (1906–9) and U.S. District Attorney for New York City; Hull became a judge of the fifth Judicial Circuit of Tennessee (1903–7).

8. Bryan was a delegate to the Democratic National Convention on five occasions

(1896, 1904, 1912, 1920, and 1924), Colby participated in founding the Progressive Party and attended its conventions in 1912 and 1916 as a delegate, Kellogg was a member of three Republican National Conventions (1904–12), and Hull chaired the Democratic National Committee (1921–24).

9. Bryan attended the Nebraska Democratic State Convention (1888), Colby served in the New York State Assembly (1901–2), Hughes was counsel to a New York legislative committee (1905–6) and Governor of New York (1907–10), Kellogg was appointed City Attorney of Rochester, Minnesota (1878–81), Stimson became a delegate at large to the New York State Constitutional Convention (1915), and Hull was a delegate to the Tennessee Democratic Convention (1890).

10. Stettinius chaired the War Resources Board (1939), was a member of the advisory committee to the Council of National Defense (1940), chaired the Priorities Board and became the Director of the Priorities Division of the Office of Production Management (1941), Lend-Lease Administrator and member of the Canadian-American Joint Defense Production Board (1941–43), and a member of the Board of Economic Warfare (1942–43).

11. Lansing had participated in the Bering Sea Arbitration (1892–93), the Bering Sea Claims Commission (1896–97), the Alaskan Boundary Tribunal (1903), the North Atlantic Coast Fisheries Arbitration at The Hague (1908–10), and the British-American Claims Arbitration (1912).

12. Also see the sections "Treaty and Agreement Making" and "International Conferences and Meetings" later in this chapter.

13. The duties of the Division of Foreign Intelligence included sending information to American diplomatic and consular officers abroad, preparing news items for the press, handling departmental publicity, and providing information to members of Congress and the public, as well as producing the volumes of the *Foreign Relations* series.

14. Much of the Department's personnel expansion during World War II entailed temporary staff members engaged to handle the upsurge of repatriation and welfare functions.

15. The principal added wartime responsibilities of the Department of State during World War I embraced action to deal with problems resulting from American neutrality, the protection of American citizens and their interests and welfare, passport and visa services, assistance to war relief agencies, including the Red Cross, negotiations respecting economic cooperation with the Allies, third-party representation of the interests of belligerent countries, and related special or emergency functions.

16. Among the members of the Inquiry were such academic experts as Charles H. Haskins, Charles Seymour, Stanley Hornbeck, James Brown Scott, James T. Shotwell, and David Hunter Miller, and Dr. Sidney Mezes was made Director, and Walter Lippman served as its secretary.

17. Alvey A. Adee, who was recommissioned on July 1, 1924, and died a few days later, on July 4, when he was eighty-two, had become a legend in the Department of State. He was a remarkable reservoir of diplomatic information and an able linguist who served for more than a half century under nineteen Secretaries of State.

18. To review the development of the position of Legal Adviser, the Claims Clerk was appointed in 1848, changed to Examiner of Claims in 1870, was designated as Solicitor in 1887, and headed the departmental Law Bureau, which was retitled the Office of Legal Adviser in February 1931. It dealt with such matters as extradition, recognition, boundary settlements, treaties, and especially claims settlements.

19. Over the years, the office of Translator had been held by a small, but remarkable, group of linguists. According to Graham Stuart, Robert Greenhow, appointed in 1831, was succeeded by Henry Livingston Thomas, appointed in 1870, who knew almost all important ancient and modern languages, including Greek, Hebrew, and Latin, and could speak and write in many of them. At the time the principal languages employed by emissaries accredited to the United States were French, German, Italian, and Spanish, supplemented with Danish, Dutch, Greek, Hebrew, Portuguese, and Swedish. Thomas was succeeded by Wilfred Stevens, who served for approximately twenty years and allegedly had a working knowledge of some thirty languages. He was succeeded by John S. Martin, who served for twenty-four years as Assistant Translator and later as Translator. When Emerson B. Christie became Chief of the Translating Bureau in 1928, he had a staff of four Assistant Translators and one clerk. See Stuart, *The Department of State*, pp. 80, 82, 144, 173, 289–90.

20. The Historical Adviser was made responsible for the publication of many documents and compilations issued by the Department of State, including the annual *Foreign Relations* volumes. The departmental library and archives to August 1906 were also placed under the jurisdiction of this office.

21. The story of American code and cryptographic work during and immediately after World War I is recounted by Yardly in *The American Black Chamber*. Also of relevance are Gaines, *Cryptanalysis: A Study of Ciphers and Their Solution*; Laffin, *Codes and Ciphers*; Moore and Waller, *Cloak and Cipher*; Pratt, *Secret and Urgent— The Story of Codes and Ciphers*; and Wrixon, *Codes and Ciphers*. Also see Stuart, *American Diplomatic and Consular Practice*, pp. 51–52, and Thayer, *Diplomat*, pp. 139–52.

22. No Counselors were commissioned during the periods from June 30, 1919, when the office of Under Secretary was created, to May 1937 and during the World War II years from February 8, 1941, to October 11, 1945.

23. For example, the following remained in their posts: Herbert Feis (Economic Adviser) to 1943, Green H. Hackworth (Legal Adviser) to 1946, Margaret M. Hanna (Chief, Office of Coordination and Review) to 1937, when she was assigned to Geneva, Stanley K. Hornbeck (Far Eastern Affairs and Political Adviser) to 1944, when he was made Special Assistant, Herschel V. Johnson (Mexican Affairs) to 1941, when he became Minister Plenipotentiary to Sweden, Albert F. Kelly (Eastern European Affairs) to 1937, Michael McDermott (Chief, Division of Current Information) to 1944, David Hunter Miller (Historical Adviser) to 1938, when he was made Editor of Treaties, Jay Pierrepont Moffat (Western European Affairs), who was appointed Minister Plenipotentiary to Canada in 1940 and died at his post in January 1943, Wallace Murray (Near Eastern Affairs) to 1942, when he became an Adviser on Political Relations, Ruth B. Shipley (Chief of the Passport Division) through the 1940s, and Edwin C. Wilson (Latin American Affairs) to 1944, when he became Director of Far Eastern Affairs.

24. Thus, James C. Dunn replaced Jay Pierrepont Moffat as Chief of the Division of Western European Affairs, Edward L. Reed replaced Herschel V. Johnson as Chief of the Division of Mexican Affairs, Laurence Duggan replaced Edwin C. Wilson as Chief of the Division of Latin American Affairs, John Farr Simmons replaced A. Dana Hodgdon as Chief of the Visa Division, and Richard Southgate replaced James C. Dunn as Chief of the Division of Protocol and Conferences. All of those replaced were career officers.

25. David Hunter Miller compiled and edited a major collection of *Treaties and*

Other International Acts of the United States of America, 8 vols., published by the Government Printing Office, 1931–48. It contains the texts of treaties and agreements, with commentary, for the period 1776 to 1863. A number of other early treaty compilations have been published, such as that produced by William M. Malloy, C. F. Redmond, and Edward R. Trentwith, entitled *Treaties, Conventions, International Acts, Protocols, and Agreements Between the United States of America and Other Powers*, 4 vols., published as Senate Documents in 1910, 1923, and 1938.

26. For a description of this Special Division, see Stuart, *The Department of State*, pp. 340–42, 358.

27. This Advisory Committee on Problems of Foreign Relations, in turn, had several subcommittees. For a detailed account of these initial developments to cope with World War II diplomatic planning, see Department of State, *Postwar Foreign Policy Preparation, 1939–1945*, Chapters 1 and 2.

28. Of these departmental agencies, the Division of Communications and Records, the largest departmental unit, for example, consisted of a records section composed of seven functional units with a staff of nearly 270, a telegraph section with more than 110, and fifteen telephone operators—totaling nearly 400 members.

29. This Liaison Office bridged relations of the State Department with the Navy and War Departments, as well as the Inter-American Defense Board. Departmental Advisers on Political Affairs also coordinated work with the President's Administrative Assistant, the Joint Chiefs of Staff, the Lend-Lease Administration, the Board of Economic Warfare, and other agencies concerned with censorship, psychological warfare, and other wartime activities.

30. When serious problems of functional jurisdiction and field operations arose in 1943, the President created the Foreign Economic Administration in September, which merged the functions of several wartime agencies. It was headed by Herbert Lehman, bearing the title of Special Assistant to the President.

31. For additional information on this presidential Advisory Committee on Postwar Foreign Policy, see Stuart, *The Department of State*, pp. 378–81, and Department of State, *Postwar Foreign Policy Preparation, 1939–1945*, Chapters 2–7, especially pp. 58–59, 63–65.

32. For analysis of the weaknesses of this reorganization plan of January 1944, see Stuart, *The Department of State*, pp. 393–96.

33. The functions of most of these administrative divisions are self-evident. The Division of Central Services, then the largest departmental Division, absorbed the Division of Administrative Services and the Division of Communications and Records. It handled communications, the maintenance of records and files, procurement, supply, and office space.

34. For additional information concerning the responsibilities of these Foreign Service Divisions, see Barnes and Morgan, *The Foreign Service of the United States*, pp. 251–53.

35. Trask, *A Short History of the U.S. Department of State, 1781–1981*, p. 30.

36. By way of comparison, describing the organizational structure of the Department of State below the level of Secretary, Deputy Secretary, and Assistant Secretaries, as of 1936, see Spaulding and Blue, *The Department of State of the United States*, pp. 10–23, who discuss twenty-one offices, divisions, and officers, and Williams, *American Diplomacy*, Chapter 24 on the "Machinery of Foreign Relations," who discusses twenty-eight of them. For a later organizational depiction, as of 1942, see Gerber, *The Department of*

State of the United States, who describes fifty-two offices, divisions, and officers, some of which were emergency wartime agencies. For analysis of the Department of State as of the early 1940s, see Bendiner, *The Riddle of the State Department* (1942).

All Chief Clerks were "designated," not "commissioned," officers, but they served as second-ranking Department of State officers until the mid-1850s, when the position of Assistant Secretary was established. For a list of the thirty-nine Chief Clerks who served from 1789 to 1939, see Spaulding and Blue, *The Department of State of the United States*, pp. 63–65.

37. Some of these interdepartmental wartime agencies were at the cabinet level, such as a Cabinet Committee on Germany, a Cabinet Committee on Inter-American Cooperation, the Office of Wartime Economic Affairs, the War Resources Board, and a Special Cabinet Committee (consisting of members of the Departments of State and Treasury, the Federal Reserve, the Board of Economic Warfare, and others).

Other interdepartmental agencies embraced the Advisory Committee on Postwar Economic Policy (with several subcommittees); Advisory Council on Post-War Foreign Policy; Board of Economic Warfare, succeeded by the Board of Foreign Economic Warfare and, later, by the Economic Warfare Administration; Committee on Coordination of Economic Policy Work; Economic Defense Board; Foreign Economic Administration, which merged the Lend-Lease Administration and several other agencies; Interdepartmental Neutrality Committee; Lend-Lease Administration; National Munitions Control Board; Office of Censorship; Office of the Coordinator of Information; Office of Strategic Services; Office of War Information; State-War-Navy Coordinating Liaison Committee, later, the Coordinating Committee; War Refugee Board; and others.

38. These World War II temporary international agencies included the Allied Commissions for Austria, Bulgaria, Hungary, Romania, and other countries; Allied Control Council for Germany; Allied Council for Japan; Allied Supply Council; Anglo-American Caribbean Commission; Caribbean Research Council; Combined Liberated Area Committee (United States and Great Britain); Emergency Advisory Committee for Political Defense (Inter-American); Emergency Economic Committee for Europe; European Advisory Commission; Far Eastern Advisory Commission; Inter-Allied Reparation Agency; Inter-Allied Development Commission; Inter-American Financial and Economic Advisory Board; Joint War Production Committee (United States and Canada); United Maritime Consultative Council; War Crimes Commission; and others. Also see the later section on "International Organizations and Other Agencies."

39. Moreover, those who also became career Foreign Service Officers included Joseph C. Grew, William Phillips, Sumner Welles, and Francis White.

40. See Stuart, *The Department of State*, pp. 275, 326, 414, and Trask, *A Short History of the U.S. Department of State, 1781–1981*, pp. 29, 42.

41. See Stuart, *The Department of State*, pp. 276, 307, 326, 351, 363, 414, and Trask, *A Short History of the U.S. Department of State, 1781–1981*, pp. 27, 29, 34, 37.

42. See Spaulding and Blue, *The Department of State of the United States*, pp. 49–50, and Stuart, *The Department of State*, pp. 363, 447–48.

43. For additional commentary on the American courier system, see Chapter 7, section on "Diplomatic Communications, the Courier System, and the Hot Line."

44. 38 *Stat.* 805. For additional commentary on the Act of 1915, see Barnes and Morgan, *The Foreign Service of the United States*, pp. 170–73.

45. See Barnes and Morgan, *The Foreign Service of the United States*, pp. 170–71, n.34.

46. Congressman John Jacob Rogers, who developed a keen interest in reforming the Diplomatic and Consular Services, introduced three bills in the House of Representatives in 1919 and another in 1921, but it was not until September 1, 1922, that he introduced a comprehensive bill, based on previous legislative proposals and the recommendations of Secretary of State Hughes and Assistant Secretary Wilbur J. Carr, which was passed by both houses of Congress in May 1924 and signed by President Coolidge on May 24. See Barnes and Morgan, *The Foreign Service of the United States*, p. 205.

47. 43 *Stat.* 140–46. For additional information on the Rogers Act, see Barnes and Morgan, *The Foreign Service of the United States*, pp. 203–15; Blancké, *The Foreign Service of the United States*, pp. 18–20; Ilchman, *Professional Diplomacy in the United States*, Chapters 4, 5; Lay, *The Foreign Service of the United States*, Chapter 11; Plischke, *Conduct of American Diplomacy*, pp. 183, 231–33, 281; Schulzinger, *The Making of the Diplomatic Mind*, pp. 7–8, 40, 47–57, 70–77, 116–18; Stuart, *American Diplomatic and Consular Practice*, pp. 99–103, and *The Department of State*, pp. 271–72, 287–88; Thayer, *Diplomat*, pp. 72, 265, 275; and Williams, *American Diplomacy*, pp. 460–62.

48. For discussion of the deficiencies of the Rogers Act, see Barnes and Morgan, *The Foreign Service of the United States*, pp. 210–14, and Stuart, *American Diplomatic and Consular Practice*, pp. 102–3, and *The Department of State*, pp. 287–88.

49. 46 *Stat.* 1207–17. For additional information on the Moses–Linthicum Act, see Barnes and Morgan, *The Foreign Service of the United States*, pp. 215–17; Ilchman, *Professional Diplomacy in the United States*, pp. 196–99; Plischke, *Conduct of American Diplomacy*, p. 233; Schulzinger, *The Making of the Diplomatic Mind*, pp. 122–23; and Stuart, *American Diplomatic and Consular Practice*, pp. 103–4.

50. Stuart, *American Diplomatic and Consular Practice*, p. 104.

51. Although such marriages of Foreign Service Officers to aliens had previously been allowed, this action was taken in 1936 because after 1922 an alien woman who married an American did not acquire her husband's nationality and could not automatically obtain an American passport, which created difficulties in transferring American officers from one post to another.

52. Barnes and Morgan, *The Foreign Service of the United States*, p. 349, indicate, decade by decade, that the number of missions varied from forty-nine in 1910, to forty-seven in 1920, fifty-eight in 1930, and fifty-nine in 1940. However, Trask, in *A Short History of the U.S. Department of State, 1781–1981*, p. 35, differs, giving the figures as forty-eight in 1910, forty-five in 1920, fifty-seven in 1930, and fifty-eight in 1940. For a map indicating the location of Foreign Service posts (embassies and legations) in 1936, see Spaulding and Blue, *The Department of State of the United States*, pp. 36–37.

53. The European states included Albania, Czechoslovakia, Estonia, Finland, the Holy See, Hungary, Iceland, Ireland, Latvia, Lithuania, and Poland. Those located in Africa were Ethiopia, Saudi Arabia, and South Africa, and those in the Mideast were Iraq, Lebanon, and Syria.

54. For additional commentary on courtesy resignations, see Plischke, *Conduct of American Diplomacy*, pp. 97–98, 265, and Stuart, *American Diplomatic and Consular Practice*, pp. 259–62. Stuart notes the distinction between courtesy resignations of noncareerist and careerist Ambassadors and Ministers. The careerists, especially after they become Foreign Service Officers, might be transferred but do not lose their career status when new Presidents are inaugurated. Noncareerists are expected to file courtesy resig-

nations to free the incoming President in making new appointments. In any case, the President can displace such diplomatic officers simply by appointing their successors.

55. Ten or more emissaries were accredited to Belgium, Bolivia, Cuba, Dominican Republic, El Salvador, Great Britain, Luxembourg, the Netherlands, Nicaragua, and Thailand.

56. These eleven countries included Afghanistan, Argentina, Brazil, Dominican Republic, El Salvador, Estonia, Haiti, Ireland, Latvia, Morocco, and Uruguay. On the other hand, a preponderant majority of the diplomats assigned to two dozen other countries (mostly European and Latin American) were noncareerists.

57. Ambassadors were first accredited to five foreign governments during the World War I period, five other countries were added in the 1920s and 1930s, and twenty-one more were added in the World War II period, especially in 1942 and 1943.

58. The seventy-nine envoys who served for five to nine years included twenty-five for five years, eighteen for six years, nineteen for seven years, twelve for eight years, and five for nine years.

59. Evidencing remarkable stability, only four emissaries served in Brazil from 1912 to February 1946.

60. These do not include officers who served only in departmental administrative appointments, those reappointed at higher rank (such as promotion from Minister Plenipotentiary to Ambassador at a given post), and ad interim appointees who were commissioned prior to April 1945 but continued into the post–World War II period.

61. For a comprehensive study on American diplomatic caretaker functions, see Franklin, *Protection of Foreign Interests: A Study in Diplomatic and Consular Practice.* Also see Plischke, *Conduct of American Diplomacy*, pp. 321–23; and Stuart, *American Diplomatic and Consular Practice*, pp. 202–4, and *The Department of State*, pp. 342, 358.

62. For additional information on foreign mission secretaries and staffs, see Childs, *American Foreign Service*, pp. 19, 60, 99, 103, 195, 214, 223, 246–47; Barnes and Morgan, *The Foreign Service of the United States*, pp. 170–73, 216, 253; and Lay, *The Foreign Service of the United States*, pp. 15, 105–6, 282.

63. Alfred Vagts, *The Military Attaché*, provides a comprehensive study on Military, Naval, and Air Attachés; for forerunners and nineteenth-century and early twentieth-century developments, see Chapters 1–5. Moore, *A Digest of International Law*, vol. 4, pp. 437–39, also notes the appointment of honorary attachés, interpreter attaché, and student attachés.

For additional information on attachés, see Barnes and Morgan, *The Foreign Service of the United States*, pp. 72–73, 189, 222–23; Blancké, *The Foreign Service of the United States*, pp. 21, 42–43, 166–68, 199–208; Childs, *American Foreign Service*, pp. 52, 55, 58–59, 60–63, 99–106, 130–41, 146–50, 154, 175, 195–96, 246–47; Lay, *The Foreign Service of the United States*, pp. 152–56, 159, 203; Plischke, *Conduct of American Diplomacy*, p. 157; and Stuart, *American Diplomatic and Consular Practice*, p. 106.

64. Also, after Herbert Hoover served as President, in 1946 President Truman appointed him to undertake a study of world food supplies to enable the American government to administer its relief program for more than three dozen war-damaged countries.

65. The rank of Ambassador at Large was not formally established by the United States until March 1949, to assist the Secretary of State in important international con-

ference attendance and other negotiations. See Stuart, *American Diplomatic and Consular Practice*, p. 42.

66. For commentary on how this European mission of Sumner Welles affected the relations of Secretary Hull and his Under Secretary, see Stuart, *The Department of State*, pp. 343–44.

67. Robert Murphy also became General Eisenhower's Political Adviser (POLAD) in Germany. Later, when Eisenhower became President early in the 1950s, Murphy became his principal diplomatic troubleshooter and was appointed Ambassador to Japan in 1952.

68. Charles G. Dawes also served as Ambassador to Great Britain, 1929–31, and he participated in the London Naval Arms Limitation Conference in 1930.

69. For additional commentary on presidential special diplomatic envoys and assessment of this process, see Wriston, *Executive Agents in American Foreign Relations*. Also see Barnes and Morgan, *The Foreign Service of the United States*, p. 227; Hackworth, *Digest of International Law*, vol. 1, pp. 255, 264–65 and vol. 4, pp. 412–14; Plischke, *Conduct of American Diplomacy*, pp. 48–49, 94–96, 154, *Diplomat in Chief*, pp. 78–80, 97–104, and *Summit Diplomacy*, Chapter 4, especially pp. 43–44; Stuart, *American Diplomatic and Consular Practice*, pp. 7–9, 133; and *The Department of State*, pp. 245–46, 343–44; and Williams, *American Diplomacy*, pp. 421–22.

70. For example, at the top of the list, diplomatic Secretaries of Class 1 designated as Counselors of Embassy or Legation and Consuls General of Classes 1 and 2 became Foreign Service Officers of Class 1 and so on, so that the lowest-level consuls of Class 8 and 9 became Foreign Service Officers of Class 9, and vice consuls of career, consular assistants, interpreters, and student interpreters became unclassified Foreign Service Officers. The position of consular assistant was abolished. Thereafter, all new appointments were as Foreign Service Officers.

71. See table in Barnes and Morgan, *The Foreign Service of the United States*, p. 350. According to Stuart, in 1931 the United States sent 870 and received 1,435 consular officials, compared with Great Britain, which sent 1,075 and received 1,605, and France, which sent 851 and received 1,566. The total number sent and received by all governments numbered 34,523. See his *American Diplomatic and Consular Practice*, p. 289.

72. Early maritime codes to govern international commercial affairs included the Rhodian Sea Law of the sixth century, the Tables of Amalfi of the eleventh century, the British Black Book of the Admiralty of the fourteenth century, and especially the *Consolato del Mare*, also of the fourteenth century.

In the seventeenth century states began to regulate consular missions by national legislation. The United States passed its first enactment of this type in 1792, and Consular Regulations of the United States were produced in 1888, 1896, 1924 and subsequently.

Well-known early publicists on international law and consular rules include J. K. Bluntschli, *Le Droit International Codife* (Paris, 1895), C. Calvo, *Le Droit International Theorique et Pratique*, 6 vols., (Paris, 1896), Ferdinand de Cussy, *Dictionaire di Diplomate et du Consel* (Leipzig, 1846), W. E. Hall, *International Law* (London, 1895), Frank C. Hinckley, *American Consular Jurisdiction in the Orient* (Washington, DC, 1906), J. L. Klueber, *Droit des Gens Moderne de l'Europe* (Paris, 1874), F. de Martens, *Traite de Droit International*, 3 vols. (Paris, 1883–87), R. Phillimore, *Commentaries upon International Law*, 3 vols. (London, 1879–89), P. Pradier-Fodere, *Cours de Droit Diplomatique*, 2 vols. (Paris, 1881), A. Rivier, *Principes de Droit des Gens*, 2 vols. (Paris, 1896), Henry Wheaton, *Elements of International Law*, 8th ed. (Boston, 1866), and T. D. Woolsey, *Introduction to the Study of International Law*, 5th ed. (New York, 1870).

Prior to World War I, these were followed by similar international law publications by Henry Bonfils (1912), F. Despagnet (1910), A. Merignhac (3 vols., 1905–12), John Bassett Moore (8 vols., 1906), Hannis Taylor (1901), John Westlake (1907), and George Grafton Wilson (1910).

Additional later volumes on consular affairs include Feller and Hudson, *A Collection of the Diplomatic and Consular Laws and Regulations, of Various Countries*, 2 vols. (Washington, DC, 1932), Alphonse de Heyking, *La Theorie et la Pratique des Services Consulaires* (Paris, 1928), and Stowell, *Le Consul* (Paris, 1909).

73. For all countries, it has been estimated that more than 200 treaties concerned with consular regulations were signed in the nineteenth century, and some 900 more were added by 1933. See Stuart, *American Diplomatic and Consular Practice*, p. 292.

74. For a comprehensive treatment of American consular functions, see Stuart, *American Diplomatic and Consular Practice*, Chapters 18–20. Also see Barnes and Morgan, *The Foreign Service of the United States*, pp. 157–58, 192–93, 197–200; Lay, *The Foreign Service of the United States*, Chapter 5; Moore, *A Digest of International Law*, vol. 5, Chapter 16; Plischke, *Conduct of American Diplomacy*, pp. 323–33; and Williams, *American Diplomacy*, pp. 470–73. Also see the studies of Clarence E. Gauss, Ellery C. Stowell, Chester L. Jones, Luke T. Lee, Ernest Lugwig, Eli T. Sheppard, Irwin Stewart, and David B. Warden listed in the bibliography.

75. See section on "Department of State Budgets and Funding" for overall departmental funding, and n.41.

76. The 1924 Foreign Service Officer salary scale created the following range: Class 9 at $3,000, Class 8 at $3,500, Class 7 at $4,000, Class 6 at $4,500, Class 5 at $5,000, Class 4 at $6,000, Class 3 at $7,000, Class 2 at $8,000, and Class 1 at $9,000.

77. The 1931 salary scale specified the following range for eight classes: Class 8 at $3,500 to $3,900; Class 7 at $4,000 to $4,400; Class 6 at $4,500 to $4,900; Class 5 at $5,000 to $5,900; Class 4 at $6,000 to $6,900; Class 3 at $7,000 to $7,900; Class 2 at $8,000 to $8,900; and Class 1 at $9,000 to $10,000.

78. The five classes of Mission Secretaries had their salaries fixed as follows: Class 5 at $1,200, Class 4 at $1,500, Class 3 at $2,000, Class 2 at $2,625, and Class 1 at $3,000.

79. These special allowances increased to $700,000 in 1917 and 1918, dropped in 1920 and 1921 to $600,000, and to $250,000 in 1922, to $200,000 in 1923, and to $150,000 in 1924, and later they increased to $664,000 in 1931 and $1,440,000 in 1932. Barnes and Morgan, *The Foreign Service of the United States*, pp. 195, 215.

80. For commentary on special allowances, see Barnes and Morgan, *The Foreign Service of the United States*, pp. 167, 195, 209, 215–17, 219, 261. Also see Stuart, *American Diplomatic and Consular Practice*, pp. 422–23.

81. Department of State, *Foreign Buildings Operations of the Department of State* (Washington, D.C.: Government Printing Office, 1952). Also see Barnes and Morgan, *The Foreign Service of the United States*, pp. 174–77, 221–22; Lay, *The Foreign Service of the United States*, Chapter 13; and Plischke, *Conduct of American Diplomacy*, pp. 280–82.

82. These diplomats who also served as Assistant Secretaries of State included Robert W. Bliss, Jefferson Caffery, Fred Morris Dearing, Leland Harrison (twice), Nelson T. Johnson, John V. A. Macmurray, George S. Messersmith, William Phillips (three

appointments), Sumner Welles (twice), Francis White, Hugh R. Wilson, and Joshua B. Wright (twice).

83. See Bailey's "A Hall of Fame for American Diplomats," *Virginia Quarterly Review* 36 (1960): 398–99.

84. On Imbrie and Marriner, see Barnes and Morgan, *The Foreign Service of the United States*, p. 228; also see Barnes and Morgan, p. 227, for a photographic reproduction of a State Department plaque honoring American diplomats who lost their lives under tragic circumstances. For an account of the shocking murder of Robert Imbrie, see Katherine Imbrie, *Data Relating to the Assassination of United States Consular Officer Robert Whitney Imbrie by the Military Police of Persia* (1924). Also see Plischke, *Conduct of American Diplomacy*, pp. 268–69, and Stuart, *American Diplomatic and Consular Practice*, pp. 379–80.

85. The story is told that when Whitelaw Reid was Ambassador to Great Britain (1905–12), he was asked what honors the United States conferred on Americans for distinguished public service. He replied that there were three options—in the North they were invited to present lectures, in the South they had conferred on them the honorary rank of Colonel or General, and if they entered politics and were elected to Congress, the country "let them take the consequences." Stuart, *American Diplomatic and Consular Practice*, p. 221.

86. See Bailey's "A Hall of Fame for American Diplomats," pp. 403–4, in which he discusses "the immortal six" worthy of grateful remembrance.

87. For additional information on diplomatic and consular relations, see Barnes and Morgan, *The Foreign Service of the United States*, Chapters 23–29; Blancké, *The Foreign Service of the United States*, especially Chapters 2–3, 8; Childs, *American Foreign Service*, Chapters 1–3; Ilchman, *Professional Diplomacy in the United States*, Chapters 4–5; Lay, *The Foreign Service of the United States*, Chapters 1, 4–5, 8–14; Plischke, *Conduct of American Diplomacy*, Chapters 8–10; Schulzinger, *The Making of the Diplomatic Mind*, Chapters 1–6; Stuart, *American Diplomatic and Consular Practice*, Chapter 6, and *The Department of State*, Chapters 20–33; Thayer, *Diplomat*, Chapters 6–16, 19–23; Williams, *American Diplomacy*, Chapter 24; West, *The Department of State on the Eve of the First World War*, Chapters 5–8.

88. Aside from the League of Nations, the states added embraced Afghanistan, Albania, Australia, Austria, the Belgo-Luxembourg Economic Union, Bulgaria, Canada, Czechoslovakia, Estonia, Finland, Hungary, Iceland, India, Iraq, Ireland, Latvia, Liechtenstein, Lithuania, Monaco, New Zealand, Palestine, Poland, Saudi Arabia, and South Africa. Those dropped were the Congo, Hawaii, Korea, Madagascar, Samoa, and Zanzibar.

89. Other countries with large numbers of treaties and agreements included Belgium (twenty-four), Ecuador (twenty-one), Germany (twenty-two), Guatemala (twenty-four), Italy (twenty-two), the Netherlands (twenty-eight), Norway (twenty-six), Poland (twenty-one), and Sweden (twenty-six).

90. To illustrate the growing facility and popularity of concluding agreements by means of exchanges of notes, this process was freely employed in relations with specific countries, such as those with Brazil (seventeen of thirty-five), Canada (seventy-eight of 100), France (twenty-six of forty-nine), Great Britain (thirty of sixty-four), Mexico (twenty-four of fifty-two), Panama (eighteen of thirty-one), and Peru (eighteen of thirty-one).

Examples of categories of agreement subjects treated in exchanges of notes embrace consular relations, cooperative educational programs, copyright, double taxation, exchange of official publications, health and sanitation, narcotic drugs, radio broadcasting, technical military matters during World War II, visa fees, and even the Alaska and Inter-American Highways, anthropological research in Mexico, and a mapping project in Peru.

91. The rather amorphous Lansing–Ishi Agreement with Japan (1917) recognized that "territorial propinquity creates special relations between countries" and provided that "Japan has special interests in China" but that the territorial sovereignty of China "remains unimpaired," that the signatories "deny that they have any purpose to infringe in any way the independence or territorial integrity of China," and that they will "always adhere to the principle of the so-called 'Open Door' or equal opportunity for commerce and industry in China."

92. This exchange of notes, the only official agreement of the United States with the League of Nations, provided for the international registration and publication of treaties and agreements. This notion was sponsored by President Wilson in his Fourteen Points, in point 1, of which he recommended: "Open covenants of peace, openly arrived at, after which there shall be no private international understanding of any kind, but diplomacy shall proceed always frankly and in the public view."

93. By this Bases-Destroyers Agreement the United States committed itself to provide Great Britain with fifty overage American destroyers in exchange for ninety-nine-year leases for naval and air bases in Newfoundland, British Guiana, and the six islands of Bermuda, the Bahamas, Jamaica, St. Lucia, Trinidad, and Antigua.

94. Two executive agreements with Canada in 1940 and 1941, called "joint statements," were concluded at Ogdensburg, New York (signed by President Roosevelt and Prime Minister Mackenzie King) and at Hyde Park, New York (which was unsigned). The third, a convention with Denmark (1916), by which it ceded the Virgin Islands to the United States, was signed by Secretary Lansing at New York City, and the fourth, an agreement with Liberia concerning Lend-Lease, was also signed at New York in 1943. Also, in 1928, an exchange of notes with Denmark concerning taxation was signed by the United States at Washington and by the Danish representative at Bar Harbor, Maine.

95. Secretary Byrnes, who signed five executive agreements later in 1945, is not included because he had only begun his administration.

96. The exchange of notes signed by President Roosevelt included those to recognize the Communist Government of the Soviet Union in 1953, the joint statement with Canada in 1940 to establish the Joint Permanent Board on Defense, an exchange of messages with the Prime Minister of Iceland in 1941 to provide American troops to defend that country during World War II, and an exchange of notes with the Emperor of Ethiopia concerning the gift of a Foreign Service facility to the American government in 1944.

97. To deal with posthostilities civil administration late in World War II, General Dwight D. Eisenhower signed executive agreements with Belgium, Luxembourg, and Norway in 1944, and other agreements were concluded by General John J. Pershing and other military officers. Of special interest, some were signed by such officials as the U.S. Governor of the Panama Canal Zone, the Commissioner of the Public Roads Administration, representatives of the Inter-American Educational Foundation, and the Institute of Inter-American Affairs.

Contrary to customary procedure, in 1929 a protocol providing for the exchange of official publications, which was unsigned, was approved by the Librarian of Congress, and a Parcel Post Agreement with Palestine, signed by the Acting Postmaster General in 1944, was "approved and ratified" by President Roosevelt.

98. As in the past, claims settlement arrangements, numbering thirty-eight, were of two types—those that created commissions to produce the settlement and those that constituted actually negotiated settlements. Some sixteen were formal treaties (generally called conventions) that required Senate approval, whereas the majority were executive agreements, some of which were simple exchanges of notes. These arrangements were concluded with sixteen countries—seven in Europe, six in Latin America, plus Australia, Canada, and Turkey. The largest numbers were negotiated with Mexico (ten), Canada (four), Turkey (four), Great Britain (three), and Panama (three).

Worthy of special note, in the case of Mexico, both general and special claims commissions were established, the latter to deal with claims arising from damages to Americans resulting from Mexican revolutionary actions from 1910 to 1920, and by the tenth treaty Mexico agreed to pay a lump sum of $40 million to settle all claims. By four executive agreements with Australia and Canada, it was agreed to waive all claims. So far as process is concerned, joint three-member commissions were established to resolve claims disputes with such states as Germany and Haiti, whereas single neutral arbitrators or commissioners were relied upon to resolve claims issues with Austria-Hungary, Guatemala, and the Netherlands.

99. Examination of more than fifty extradition treaties, many of which were new, but some of which simply added to the list of crimes covered by earlier treaties, reveals that most of them applied to more than twenty categories of crimes, in some cases mounting to nearly thirty. They applied to the following crimes: abduction of women for immoral purposes, abortion, assault aboard ships, arson, breaking into government buildings and offices, bribery, burglary and housebreaking, carnal knowledge of children under fifteen years, counterfeiting, crimes against bankruptcy laws, crimes against the laws for suppressing traffic in narcotics, embezzlement, forgery of papers and official acts, fraud or breach of trust, kidnapping, larceny, malicious wounding, murder and manslaughter (including infanticide and patricide), mutiny, obtaining money or securities under false pretense, perjury, piracy and other crimes at sea, rape, robbery, slavery and slave trading, willful desertion or nonsupport of children and other dependent persons, willful destruction of railroads, wrongfully sinking or destroying vessels at sea—and serving as accessory to these crimes.

100. During the 1920s and 1930s the United States participated in concluding more than a dozen inter-American treaties and agreements concerned with arbitration, conciliation, good offices and mediation, nonaggression, the prevention of conflicts, and other aspects of peacekeeping and peaceful settlement. For a general survey of American arbitration and conciliation treaty making, see Plischke, *Conduct of American Diplomacy*, pp. 437–41, 532, 537–39.

101. The countries with which Bryan Treaties for the Advancement of Peace were concluded embraced Argentina, Australia, Bolivia, Brazil, Canada, Chile, China, Costa Rica, Denmark, Ecuador, France, Great Britain, Guatemala, Honduras, Italy, the Netherlands, New Zealand, Norway, Paraguay, Peru, South Africa, Portugal, Spain, Sweden, Russia, Uruguay, and Venezuela.

102. These cooling-off pacts were formal treaties that provided for five-member Commissions to review the issues but not to hand down binding legal determinations. In 1915 and 1916 Secretaries Bryan and Lansing also concluded eleven supplementary treaties to briefly extend the time for establishing the Commissions. Because the original treaty

of 1913 with the Netherlands had not been ratified until 1928, that year Under Secretary J. Reuben Clark, Jr., signed an exchange of notes extending the establishment of the Commission for six months, and in 1931 Secretary Stimson concluded a revised Bryan-type conciliation treaty with Italy. Furthermore, in 1940 Secretary Hull signed five additional such cooling-off commitments with Argentina and four British dominions—Australia, Canada, New Zealand, and South Africa.

103. These twenty-five Kellogg arbitration treaties were signed with Albania, Austria, Belgium, Bulgaria, Czechoslovakia, Denmark, Estonia, Ethiopia, Finland, Germany, Greece, Hungary, Iceland, Italy, Latvia, Lithuania, Luxembourg, the Netherlands, Norway, Poland, Portugal, Romania, Sweden, the United Arab Republic (Egypt), and Yugoslavia. The nineteen Kellogg conciliation treaties were concluded with Albania, Austria, Belgium, Bulgaria, Czechoslovakia, Estonia, Ethiopia, Finland, Germany, Greece, Iceland, Hungary, Latvia, Lithuania, Luxembourg, Poland, Romania, the United Arab Republic (Egypt), and Yugoslavia. Noteworthy, except for Ethiopia and Egypt, is that they were all negotiated with European countries.

104. The United States alleged possession of Palmas Island, located between Mindanao (Philippine Islands) and the Dutch East Indies at the time, on the grounds of discovery (Spanish), and therefore it formed a part of the Philippine Islands, which passed to the United States as part of the archipelago in 1898 at the end of the Spanish–American War. This was contested by the Netherlands, which argued, on the basis of the principle of effective occupation, that it possessed and administered jurisdiction over the island as part of the East Indies since 1677.

105. It was written in 1955 that this Bases-Destroyers Agreement, a "mere exchange of notes," consummated an arrangement "far more important than most of the seven or eight hundred treaties that the Senate has ever ratified," that Secretary Hull secured from Great Britain a commitment that it would never surrender the British fleet containing these American destroyers, and that President Roosevelt, informing Congress of the exchange of notes, regarded the agreement as "the most important action in the reinforcement of our national defense that has taken place since the Louisiana Purchase." Samuel Flagg Bemis, *A Diplomatic History of the United States* (New York: Holt, 1955), pp. 853–55.

106. It is interesting to note that during the Wilson administration the United States signed three times as many executive agreements as treaties, during the Harding, Coolidge, and Hoover administrations it concluded more treaties than agreements, and during the Roosevelt administration through 1941 treaties continued to exceed agreements by a score of thirty-seven to twenty-six. However, during the war years to the end of 1945 the preponderant share of multilateral international commitments were executive agreements, in that the United States became a party to seventy-four executive agreements but only ten treaties.

107. These other titles included amendment to a convention, armistice, articles of agreement, charter (United Nations), constitution, joint note, memorandum, procès-verbal, proclamation, regulations, and statute (International Court of Justice and the International Bureau of Education).

108. Twenty treaties and agreements were concluded during the eight years of the Wilson Administration, sixty-nine during the twelve years of the Harding, Coolidge, and Hoover Administrations, 113 during the Roosevelt Administration, and thirty-four during the first nine months of the Truman Administration.

109. Of these forty-seven treaties and agreements, thirty-nine were concluded in

Washington, and the rest were signed elsewhere in the United States (Bretton Woods in New Hampshire, Chicago, and San Francisco).

110. In Europe the largest numbers were concluded at Geneva, London, Madrid, Moscow, and Paris. In Latin America the largest numbers were concluded at Buenos Aires, Havana, Lima, Mexico City, Montevideo, and Panama City.

111. Such very short instruments include the Kellogg–Briand Pact (1928), the tariff truce (1933), the conference resolution creating the Inter-American Defense Board (1942), and the Declaration on forced transfers of property in World War II enemy-controlled territory (1943). The historic Atlantic Charter and United Nations Declarations also were brief documents.

112. The only other peace agreement was concluded by the United States with Argentina, Brazil, Chile, Ecuador, and Peru in 1942, providing for friendship, peace, and a boundary settlement for Ecuador and Peru.

113. As a result, the United States never became a member of either the League of Nations or the Permanent Court of International Justice. Nevertheless, although the Constitution of the International Labor Organization, also embodied in the Versailles Treaty, was not ratified by the United States, it is noteworthy that by joint resolution and requiring the two-thirds Senate vote, in 1934 Congress authorized American acceptance of membership in this organization.

Other treaties that suffered at the hands of the Senate two-thirds rule include the Geneva Convention for the Supervision of International Trade in Arms, Ammunition, and Implements of War (1928) and the Protocol to join the Permanent Court of International Justice (1935).

114. However, these two executive agreements were not published in the customary serialized Treaties and Executive Agreement Series.

115. The process of accession applied to a treaty on international exhibitions, signed at Paris in 1928, which was acceded to by ratification forty years later, an agreement in 1929 to create the Inter-American Bureau of Education, which was approved by declaration in 1958, an International Labor Organization convention fixing professional qualifications for masters and officers of merchant ships agreed to at a Geneva Conference in 1936, which was ratified by the United States as a treaty two years later, an inter-American Radio-Communications Agreement signed at Santiago in January 1940 and acceded to by the United States the following June, and the Charter of the International Institute for the Unification of Private Law, signed at Rome in March 1940 and acceded to by the United States in March 1964.

116. This method of agreement making was employed for more than a dozen executive agreements embodied in inter-American conference resolutions approved at Santiago (1923), Mexico City (1926), Lima (1938), Panama City (1939), Havana (1940), Rio de Janeiro (1942), and Mexico City (1945). Of special importance, in 1942 the American Foreign Ministers provided for the creation of the Inter-American Defense Board, and in 1945 the American governments subscribed by this process to the Act of Chapultepec.

117. Other unsigned executive agreements included an armistice memorandum on the disposition of the Italian naval fleet in 1943; a Gold Policy Declaration on monetary stabilization issued in 1935 and published as an American Treasury Department release by Secretary Henry Morgenthau, Jr., in 1949; and a provisional agreement to create a European Central Inland Transport Organization in May 1945, which, however, was superseded by a formal, signed agreement in September that year.

118. In addition, it appears particularly strange that Henry A. Wallace, the Secretary

of Agriculture, signed a treaty for the Protection of Artistic and Scientific Institutions and Historic Monuments negotiated at Washington in 1935.

119. For treaty approval and rejection statistics from 1789 to 1944, with commentary, see Plischke, *Conduct of American Diplomacy*, p. 393, Table 4, and pp. 394–99. A comprehensive analysis of *Treaties Defeated by the Senate*, by Holt, was published in 1933, with Chapter 10 devoted to the Versailles Treaty, and a list of "unratified treaties" is provided in his index, pp. 326–27.

120. Presumably, the action of Congress respecting American attendance at international conferences to produce postal conventions beginning in the early 1870s and subsequently frequently revised or superseded was designed to provide such specific authority for this purpose.

In 1956 Congress liberalized this arrangement by authorizing the Secretary of State to provide for participation by the United States "in international activities" for which provision was not otherwise legally provided.

121. Stuart, *American Diplomatic and Consular Practice*, pp. 8–9, and Williams, *American Diplomacy*, pp. 398–400.

122. Illustrating the growth of international conferencing, Lord Maurice Hankey, secretary to the British Cabinet during World War I, who attended nearly 500 "international meetings" between 1914 and 1920, asserted that, in his opinion, "diplomacy by conference has come to stay." See his *Diplomacy by Conference*, p. 11. Norman Hill, *The Public International Conference*, pp. 15–18, observed that during and after World War I the conference system was not only "astounding" but also "of superlative importance in the conduct of international relations."

123. Semipublic international conferences and meetings may or may not be convened by governments, and, whereas official representation may be involved, delegates primarily represent quasi-official agencies, and end products usually are not formalized in instruments that become automatically binding on governments. Private international conferences and meetings are not intended for governmental purposes or participation, may be sponsored by nongovernmental organizations, and have no official significance unless governmental sanction is provided.

124. However, at times the term "congress" is still applied to international gatherings or technical and administrative meetings concerned with scientific, legal, or other nonpolitical matters, particularly in inter-American affairs.

125. While this represents a substantial increase in U.S. participation in major international conferences and meetings, evidencing American reluctance to become involved in many areas of European affairs, the Department of State did not participate in more than forty important conferences held in Europe during this period. Some of these constituted World War I peace settlements—Russia, Peace Treaty at Brest Litovsk (1917); Russia, expropriations and reparations at Genoa (1922); Turkey, Peace Treaty at Lausanne (1923); peace pacts guaranteeing Germany's Western European neighbors, Locarno (1925); Germany, World War I reparations, Lausanne (1932); and other wartime settlements.

Other conferences dealt with a variety of subjects of general worldwide concern, such as antiliquor smuggling (Helsingfors, 1924), arms limitation (Moscow, 1922–23, and Genoa, 1925 and 1932), child welfare (Geneva, 1925), customs formalities (Geneva, 1923), international economic and financial matters (Brussels, 1920, and Geneva, 1927), emigration (Rome, 1924), health and sanitation (Copenhagen and Rome, 1921, and Warsaw, 1922), international free trade (London, 1920), international police cooperation (Vienna, 1923), passports (Paris, 1920 and 1925), and wireless communication (Paris, 1921, and London, 1923).

Several conferences were concerned with the prelude to World War II, including those held at Nyon (1937) concerned with the submarine issue at the time of the Spanish Civil War and those convened at Berchtesgaden, Godesberg, and Munich in September 1938 to deal with the German annexation of Czechoslovakia.

126. Fifteen of these conferences and meetings are duplicated in the seven categories listed in Table 6.9. These embrace the Paris Peace Conference of 1919, the San Francisco Conference of 1945, five in which the President appeared in a ceremonial role, and the remainder, which are included under ministerial conferencing involving the Secretary of State.

127. Secretary Hull participated in President Roosevelt's summit meetings convened at Washington (December 1941, June 1942, and May 1943) and at Quebec (August 1943), but he did not accompany the President to the Casablanca, Cairo, Tehran, Second Quebec, Malta, and Yalta Conferences. However, Harry Hopkins accompanied the President to ten of these conferences and meetings, serving as Roosevelt's confidential adviser, and Averell Harriman, initially the personal representative of the President with the rank of Minister and later as Ambassador to the Soviet Union, participated in nine of them.

Nevertheless, other Department of State officers and American diplomats who were appointed to the President's principal delegations at these summit conferences and meetings included Under Secretary Welles; Assistant to the Secretary of State Wilder Foote; Assistant Secretary Charles E. Bohlen; Ambassadors (aside from Harriman) Ray Atherton, Alexander C. Kirk, Laurence A. Steinhart, and John G. Winant; Minister Louis G. Dreyfus, Jr.; and others, such as Adof A. Berle, Jr.; James C. Dunn, H. Freeman Matthews, and Robert D. Murphy.

128. Later, Secretary Hull wrote that the Morgenthau Plan "angered me as much as anything that happened during my career as Secretary of State." Although initially, Prime Minister Churchill opposed certain aspects of the Morgenthau Plan, apparently, President Roosevelt gained his acquiescence in return for a promise by Morgenthau of a substantial postwar subsidy to the British Government. In any case, President Roosevelt later acknowledged that he had approved the plan without giving it adequate thought (and without obtaining Department of State recommendation and endorsement), and he reversed his attitude on certain key provisions. Similarly, Prime Minister Churchill admitted that he regretted that he had initialed it.

For additional information and commentary on this matter, see Department of State, *Foreign Relations of the United States: The Conference at Quebec* (1944), especially pp. 101–8, 123–26, 128–31, 322–30, 342–44, 361–71, 390–91, 482–85; Bemis, *A Diplomatic History of the United States*, p. 891, n.1; Richard N. Current, *Secretary Stimson* (New Brunswick, N.J.: Rutgers University Press, 1954), pp. 216–18; Cordell Hull, *Memoirs of Cordell Hull* (New York: Macmillan, 1948), pp. 1602–22; Plischke, *Conduct of American Diplomacy*, p. 69, n.20, and p. 178; Henry L. Stimson and McGeorge Bundy, *On Active Service in Peace and War* (New York: Harper, 1948), pp. 568–83; and Stuart, *American Diplomatic and Consular Practice*, p. 11.

129. For additional information on U.S. international conference participation, see Hill, *The Public International Conference* (commentary on preliminary arrangements, participants, location, organization and procedures, limitations, value and accomplishments, and other subjects); Hulen, *Inside the Department of State*, Chapter 17; National

Archives, *Preliminary Inventory of the Records of U.S. Participation in International Conferences, Commissions, and Expositions*, compiled by H. Stephen Helton (1955); Plishke, *Conduct of American Diplomacy*, Chapters 15–16, and for a list of major international conferences pp. 596–99; Stuart, *American Diplomatic and Consular Practice*, pp. 200–201; Williams, *American Diplomacy*, pp. 95–100, 398–400.

130. These United Nations specialized agencies then included the Food and Agriculture Organization, International Bank, International Civil Aviation Organization, International Labor Organization, International Monetary Fund, and United Nations Relief and Rehabilitation Organization.

131. These temporary wartime agencies embraced such institutions as the Anglo-American Combined Chiefs of Staff, the European and Far Eastern Advisory Commissions, Allied Control Commissions for various European and Asian countries, Combined Civil Affairs and Liberated Areas Committees, Allied Reparations Agency, War Crimes Commissions, Inter-American Defense Board, and Inter-American Advisory Committee for Political Defense, of which there were more than thirty-five. Nor are more than fifteen important bilateral temporary wartime agencies included, such as the Anglo-American Caribbean Commission, the Canadian-American Joint Board on Defense, and the Joint Brazilian-U.S. Defense Commission, as well as more than forty bilateral Commissions of Inquiry for the peaceful settlement of disputes.

132. For example, the agricultural agencies include the Food and Agriculture Organization and the International Seed Testing Association; the commercial and financial include the International Bank, the International Monetary Fund, and the International Union for the Protection of Industrial Property; the commodities include coffee, cotton, rubber, sugar, tin, and wheat; drug control includes the Permanent Central Opium Board; education and cultural affairs includes the United Nations Education, Science, and Cultural Organization; health and sanitation includes the International Office of Public Health and the Pan-American Sanitary Bureau; labor includes the International Labor Organization; scientific includes the International Bureau of Weights and Measures, International Institute of Statistics, and International Meteorological Organization; social includes the Inter-American Commission of Women, Intergovernmental Committee on Refugees, and United Nations Educational, Scientific, and Cultural Organization; transport and communications includes the International Civil Aviation Organization, International Telecommunication Union, Pan-American Postal Union, and Universal Postal Union; and the more specialized include the Inter-American Indian Institute, the International Criminal Police Commission, and the Interparliamentary Union.

133. See Stuart, *The Department of State*, p. 407. For additional commentary, see Gerber, *The Department of State of the United States*, pp. 63–69; Spaulding and Blue, *The Department of State of the United States*, pp. 24–29 (provides list of thirty-four permanent international agencies as of 1936); and Plischke, *Conduct of American Diplomacy*, Chapter 17, especially pp. 529–42, "Evolution of Participation in International Organizations: The United States Experience," *Commonwealth* 5 (1991): 57–74, and "Joining International Organizations: The United States Process," *Commonwealth* 6 (1992–93): 48–77.

134. For additional information and listings, see Gerber, *The Department of State of the United States*, pp. 75–79, Spaulding and Blue, *The Department of State of the United States*, pp. 46–48. For a comprehensive list, see Plischke, *U.S. Foreign Relations: A Guide to Information Sources*, pp. 549–606.

135. For an early interpretation of this development, see Plischke, "The New Diplo-

macy: A Changing Process,'' *The Virginia Quarterly Review*, vol. 49, no. 3 (1973): 321–45, and *Conduct of American Diplomacy*, Chapter 2. Also see McCamy, *Conduct of the New Diplomacy*, Chapter 11, which focuses largely on change in the diplomatic process at the time of World War II and thereafter.

PART IV

1945– , AND THE FUTURE

7

United States as a Superpower— The Contemporary Era Since 1945

Following World War II many changes within the United States and in world affairs produced significant modifications in the Department of State, the Foreign Service, and American diplomacy. By way of background, the population of the country grew to more than 271,700,000 by 1999 (the third largest in the world), exceeded only by China and India and projected to increase to nearly 300 million in the next quarter century. Again it sustained a shift in the balance of payments, and it became a debtor nation, the stock market surged to exceed 11,000 in the 1990s, the United States became the world's greatest financial and economic power and continued to liberalize the international economic order by promoting free trade based on the most-favored-nation principle, and Alaska and Hawaii were granted statehood. John F. Kennedy was assassinated in 1963, and several other Presidents were attacked or shot, three Vice Presidents succeeded to the American Presidency, and several former members of Congress were appointed Secretary of State, as were the first career Foreign Service Officer and the first woman.

The United States annexed no additional territory, although in 1947 it acquired jurisdiction over Micronesia (the Mariana, Marshall, Caroline, and a few other islands in the northwest Pacific, formerly the Japanese Mandate), which it administered as a United Nations Trusteeship and most of which was later granted independence. The Philippines were granted their independence by the United States on July 4, 1946, which became the first of the postwar newly independent states.

On the making of foreign policy, to which the Department of State is a primary contributor, Assistant Secretary Harlan Cleveland declared: "The making of foreign policy is frequently like trying to nail jelly to the trunk of a tree," Under Secretary George W. Ball called the Department a "fudge factory," and

Under Secretary Nicholas DeB. Katzenbach observed: ''I have discovered that the foreign policy process is more like a taffy pull.'' Former Secretary of State Dean Acheson, responding to a question at a *Washington Post* book and author luncheon, stated: ''I think we can assume . . . that ignorance of foreign policy is no reason to disqualify one from talking about it,'' and referring to his host, he added that he ''offer[ed] the *Washington Post* as evidence of that.'' Commenting on foreign affairs, a Maryland gubernatorial candidate maintained that ''basically, all international problems develop out of our relations with other nations,'' to which the *New Yorker* responded, ''We love a straight thinker.''

The United States emerged from World War II as a superpower and acquired the advantages and responsibilities of world leadership, and it possessed the world's leading international industrial and trading systems. Since then the family of nations experienced its greatest modern decolonization and proliferation, nearly tripling the number of independent states with which the United States has dealt and currently deals diplomatically. This independence boom resulted in the dissolution of most of the Belgian, British, Danish, Dutch, French, German, Japanese, Portuguese, and Spanish empires. Recently, the Soviet Union, Czechoslovakia, and Yugoslavia have also been dissolved. This global disintegration movement resulted in dozens of new states in Africa, Asia, the Middle East, and the Caribbean and Pacific areas, as well as in Europe with the breakup of the Soviet Union and other European Communist states. For a time, it also involved American diplomatic relations with such divided states as China, Germany, Korea, and Indochina.

Remarkably, this massive proliferation of the community of nations was accompanied by an extensive integration of the United States and other nations in a great many new global and regional international organizations, represented by the United Nations system, the Organization of American States, the European communities, the North Atlantic Treaty Organization and other regional security arrangements, and a series of functional international institutions. This ostensibly antithetical phenomenon is regarded as one of the most extraordinary, yet an essentially natural, diplomatic development of the postwar era.

Although the world has been spared a third world war, during these years the community of nations underwent a good many regional and local military conflicts and international crises. In addition to the unique half-century Cold War with the Soviet Union, the United States was engaged in hostilities waged in Korea, Indochina (especially the eleven-year war with Vietnam—America's largest military encounter), and the Middle East war (Desert Storm) with Iraq in response to its invasion of Kuwait and brief military actions in Grenada and Panama.[1] It also endured mistreatment of American diplomatic hostages by Iran, the bombing of the American Embassy in Lebanon, the U-2 downing by the Soviet Union, and the Cuban missile and other international crises.

During these decades the United States engaged in what has been described as the ''New Diplomacy,'' consisting of the elevation of diplomatic relations to the summit and ministerial levels, shuttle diplomacy, and greater reliance on open diplomacy and multilateral interrelations at the international conference table and in international organizations, as well as the augmentation of technical diplomacy to supplement the traditional aspects of foreign affairs. Also relevant, American diplomacy has not only possessed the advantages of what diplomatic historian David F. Trask calls "the age of global leadership" by the United States but also needed to adjust to what may be denominated the air or aviation, outer space, nuclear, missile, and technological/computer ages. Simultaneously, the Department of State was obliged to deal with the spread and intensification of Communism and the emergence of autocracy in certain countries. For several decades relations with the Soviet Union and its allies were permeated by Cold War confrontational, nuclear diplomacy.

These events and developments affected the management, organization, personnel, and functioning of the Department of State and the Foreign Service. Major actions were taken to review and reform the leadership, structure, and administration of the Department and the amalgamation of Foreign Service and departmental officers. Attention was devoted to the integration and improvement of the structure and functioning of both the Department and the diplomatic and consular missions, advancement of the professionalization of the Foreign Service, increasing the number of women officers, coping with the burgeoning quantity of communications between the Department and its overseas missions, and coordination both in Washington and abroad of the Department with other U.S. agencies concerned with foreign affairs.

Additional departmental components were established, and some were reorganized to deal with various administrative, regional, and functional matters, and others were modified or discontinued. New positions and ranks of officers were created, including the Deputy Secretary of State, Career Ambassadors, and the Senior Foreign Service. While the quantity of American diplomatic missions increased substantially, the number of consular establishments decreased. Over the years diplomatic missions were universally elevated to embassy rank, and several lower-ranking classes of consular establishments were discontinued. As in the past, some emissaries have continued to be appointed to multiple, simultaneous assignments, and, with the amalgamation and professionalization of the Foreign Service, assignment to multiple sequential missions has become commonplace.

Aside from their traditional functions of representation, observation, reporting, negotiation, and protection and serving the interests of individuals abroad, to deal effectively with changing world conditions and problems, the Department of State and its foreign missions broadened their concerns and activities. In addition to such basic substantive matters as boundaries, claims settlement, commerce and trade, customs, extradition, peacekeeping and peacemaking, maritime matters, and general political, economic, financial, and national security matters, these were expanded to embrace civil and human rights, civil aviation, cultural property, energy, the environment and conservation, foreign aid, hijacking of aircraft, hostage taking, kidnapping of public officers, narcotic drugs, nuclear capability, pollution, the population explosion and handling of World War II and subsequent refugees, the seas and seabeds, telecommunications, weapons of mass destruction, missiles, land mines, and many other international affairs. Inasmuch as the Department of State was relieved of almost all of the extraneous domestic functions for which it was responsible in earlier times, it tended to become a genuine Department of Foreign Affairs or Relations.

Further evidencing that the United States changed from isolationism to international involvement and commitment, the Department of State negotiated a great quantity of new bilateral and multilateral treaties and agreements, a substantial number of which deal with new regional and functional subjects. Furthermore, Presidents and Secretaries of State have issued an increasing number of major American policy doctrines and declarations, and the United States became an ardent participant in international conferencing at all levels—the summit, ministerial, diplomatic, and technical—and in dozens of global and regional international organizations and other international agencies. Combined, these changes and improvements produced what some regard as the twentieth-century revolution in American diplomacy and others call "the American century." Thus, during five decades the United States became a prime actor in world affairs, presaging the needs and challenges of the twenty-first century.

THE NEW DIPLOMACY

One of the outstanding features of the conduct of foreign relations during the twentieth century, particularly after World War I, is the generation of what has become known as "the new diplomacy." On its emergence Sir Harold Nicolson, eminent British diplomatist and author of *The Evolution of Diplomatic Method*, identified five eras of diplomacy—the Greek, Roman, Italian (fifteenth and sixteenth centuries), and French (seventeenth to nineteenth centuries) methods, followed by the contemporary or American method. The latter he regards as a transition from the old—or classical—to contemporary diplomacy. In part, it is characterized by superimposing aspects of liberal democracy's domestic interests and processes upon the management of foreign relations.

Although this mutation had its origins during the nineteenth century, more recently, it was influenced by President Wilson's policies and practices, the creation of the League of Nations and changes in customary negotiation behavior, catering to the notions of active and vocal peoples, and major technological developments. Among the most important causes of the emergence and development of the new diplomacy are substantial changes in the perception of international and global affairs, the composition of the community of nations, the expanding quantity of interstate concerns, the improvement of modern communications, the objectives and uses of diplomacy, the relationships of governments to peoples, and the nature of warfare—which, combined, constitute a revolutionary era in world politics and in the role of the Department of State.

In both its conceptual and pragmatic versions, diplomacy—like most human institutions—is a dynamic process and changes with the times. In the twentieth century, after World War I and especially during and following World War II, the unfolding of events engendered significant modifications. Whereas in the past it was readily conceived as a unified, easily comprehensible subject, currently, consideration of the process to facilitate discriminating among its components and applications requires distinguishing various features based on differing criteria. For example, distinctions are sometimes founded on fundamental cultural and national characteristics.[2] More fundamentally, the literature is replete with allusions to particular brands of diplomatic practice that bear relationship to historical developments.[3] Beginning with World War I, however, the general conceptualization also came to denote fundamental alteration in diplomatic style and forums. In view of these changes, current perception of the new diplomacy is quite different from that of the 1920s, when the expression first came into use.

This new version of contemporary diplomacy—called the "corpus diplomaticum"—has been manifested in many ways. Among the most obvious are its participatory and substantive extension and multilateralization during the twentieth century. At the time of World War II the United States dealt with some fifty foreign governments, and diplomatic relations with fifteen more were temporarily suspended due to the war (including the Axis powers and the countries that were under Axis occupation). Since then, the community of nations has grown to embrace more than 165 countries. The subjects of primary diplomatic concern during the nineteenth century embraced amity, arms limitation, claims settlement, collective security, commerce and trade, conflict resolution, diplomatic and consular representation, economic and financial arrangements, peacekeeping and peaceful settlements, shipping and navigation, tariffs and customs, territorial acquisition and boundary delineation, and war and neutrality. To these have been added agriculture, arbitration, citizenship and naturalization, civil aviation, colonialism and self-determination, copyright, drug control, extradition, fisheries, health and sanitation, immigration, labor, patents and trademarks, propaganda, refugees, science, reparations, slavery and the slave trade, telecommunications, and many other matters.[4] Currently, diplomatic relations encompass the gamut of virtually all aspects of international concern and human relations.

Other major aspects of the new diplomacy are widely known as "open diplomacy" and "democratic diplomacy." Earlier diplomatic relations were confined to the actions of governments and were conducted in private when, it is alleged, chicanery and artful trickery often characterized relations between governments. Inasmuch as foreign policy was closely related to military policy and strategy, and because the latter was of such a nature that secrecy could be taken for granted, it was natural that foreign policy and diplomatic action were also held in confidence, at times resulting in the negotiation of secret alliances and sometimes in the outbreak of war. With the transition from monarchical and autocratic governments to the democratic system, executives were less able to engage in large-scale or long-range plans without legislative deliberation and popular support.

In 1918 President Wilson headed his historic Fourteen Points with the espousal of "open covenants . . . openly arrived at" and the conduct of diplomacy "in the public view," which he regarded as a solution to one of the causes of war. This principle was also incorporated into, and expanded in, the League of Nations Covenant. It provided in its Preamble that signatories accepted a commitment to "the prescription of open, just, and honorable relations between nations." Openness came to be applied to diplomatic end products—treaties and agreements—as evidenced by the increased and systematic publication of national treaty and agreement series and collections produced by the League and later by the United Nations.

However, as acknowledged by President Wilson, the concept of openness does not necessarily apply to all aspects of policy making and negotiation.[5] The policy-making process often needs to be conducted in confidence and generally is not publicized until the policy is determined. Furthermore, the publicizing of the details of policy positions and intergovernmental discussions and negotiations—which usually require compromise, especially on delicate and critical issues—is uncommon if they result in unwanted, nonnegotiable, frozen positions. Openness, therefore, has its obvious and inherent restrictions. But the concept of the new diplomacy postulated greater public disclosure—or less secrecy—than was previously practiced in the conduct of world relations, and in the twentieth century much American diplomacy and that of other democratic and free nations have exhibited greater openness.

The correlative aspect of openness is denominated "democratic diplomacy," also called "democratized diplomacy" or "popular diplomacy." In general it suggests increased influence by, or actual participation of, representative bodies such as Congress, pressure groups, and other participants in the formulation of policy and the administration of foreign relations. In its extreme form it means the utilization or influence of "representatives of the people," greater employment of organized public relations agencies and techniques, direct and immediate popular support of policy and negotiations, and general insistence in the name of the people on not only "a right to know" but also a "right to participate," directly or indirectly.

All of these evoke aspects of popular support of the government but also considerable criticism by serious-minded observers. Questions are raised concerning premature revelation, utilization of nonprofessionals and politically motivated participants, the validity of actions of formal voting processes in international conferences and organizations that equate minor nations with the major powers, which has been called "the vice of the majority," and the diffusion of responsibility and subordination of principle to expediency, substituting the vague for the precise and superseding the most beneficial and rewarding for the subsidiary and those most susceptible to immediate, popular approval.

The challenge of statesmanship is for the President, Congress, and the Department of State to strike a realistic and equitable balance between the authority and responsibilities of those who espouse the public interest and welfare and those who represent the mass of the people or their vocal exponents.

Equally impressive is the intensification of "multilateral diplomacy" in its two versions of "conference diplomacy" and "parliamentary diplomacy." These feature the growth of the conduct of foreign relations *among* as well as *between* governments. The Department of State maintains that during the twentieth century "perhaps no greater change has occurred than the increased emphasis on multilateral diplomacy and the employment of the international conference as a medium for co-operative action among governments." Since World War II this applies equally to deliberations and negotiations in public international organizations and similar agencies.

International conferencing at both the customary diplomatic and the highest levels, overseas as well as in Washington, accelerated remarkably during and since World War II. In addition to diplomatic appointees to represent the United States, the Secretaries of State and their representatives, other Cabinet members, chiefs of other administrative agencies, and sometimes even the President have participated personally in international conferences, meetings, and sessions of continuing international agencies, both in the United States and overseas, which are discussed in the sections on summit meetings, ministerial diplomacy abroad, international conferences, and international organizations.

Personal participation at the highest levels—called "summit diplomacy" and "ministerial diplomacy"—which career diplomat George F. Kennan branded as diplomatic dilettantism, was exceptional prior to World War I, and since the Paris Peace Conference of 1918 the President and Secretary of State have increasingly engaged in personal diplomatic practice. However, the same may be said of their functional experts, specialists, and technicians serving both as members of American diplomatic teams and as primary negotiators. As a consequence, these cadres of American officials have come to engage concurrently and continuously in scores of multilateral as well as bilateral consultations, deliberations, and negotiations on a broad menu of issues. At times the President and, more consistently, the Secretary of State assumed the role of peripatetic and even itinerant emissaries for many special missions, ranging from ceremonial and goodwill undertakings to multilateral negotiations and even treaty-making ventures.

"Parliamentary diplomacy," regarded as a non sequitur by Harold Nicolson and eminent British diplomat Lord Vansittart, a currently prevailing mutation of multilateral diplomacy and a concomitant of "conference diplomacy," and called "institutionalized conferencing," is pursued in permanent political agencies founded on formal constitutive acts. In this guise, much international conferencing and negotiation are pursued within fixed and continuing forums, and decision making is reduced to a consensus or usually a formal voting process, which former American Foreign Service Officer Charles W. Thayer deplored as "diplomacy by ballot" and Professor Hans J. Morgenthau described as "the vice of the majority decision."

Such diplomacy is employed in the United Nations and its specialized agencies, the Organization of American States, and a host of other regional and functional public international organizations in which the United States holds membership. Since its rejection of the League of Nations the United States has become an avid "joiner," participating in virtually every international conference and organization in which it has an interest and from which it is not otherwise excluded.

A related aspect of this new diplomacy has been designated "multiple diplomacy," which may be ascribed differing meanings. For example, this concept is applicable to dealing simultaneously or sequentially with international issues at several levels—the technical, diplomatic, ministerial, and summit—for discussion, negotiation, and administration within different, overlapping agencies—functional, geographic, and global—and to varying forms of participation—bipartite, areal, and universal forums. So far as matters of program development, regulatory control, or policy coalescence are concerned, questions of jurisdiction and competence are readily resolvable. When they are critical, however, "secondary diplomacy" may be needed to resolve issues of alternative diplomatic procedures and to determine the responsible or acceptable diplomatic institutions. To manage this problem, complex networks of potentially competing negotiatory and peacekeeping diplomatic facilities have been established, which provide a range of readily available facilities. At times, if governments disagree over the diplomatic agency to be employed, direct negotiations or mutually acceptable ad hoc processes may be devised.

To manage serious substantive disputes, the new diplomacy also features what is known as "crisis diplomacy," or what former Assistant Secretary of State Harlan Cleveland denominated "crisis management." This entails both the matter of escalating the level of participants and the creation of special agencies for crisis resolution. In the twentieth century, Secretaries of State and Defense, the Director of Central Intelligence, and their representatives have increasingly become involved as participants in disputes in which the United States is a primary party or as mediators and conciliators of disputes between other countries. Increasingly, the Secretaries of State and their deputies have ventured abroad for this purpose, often undertaking extensive "shuttle diplomacy" or initiating and monitoring the negotiations of other governments.

Upper levels of the government, including the Secretary of State, devote their energies and time to this task because there is no other way for them to fulfill their responsibilities for making crucial decisions on critical matters, to maximize and master the complexities inherent in dealing rapidly and effectively with such issues, and to engage in advance contingency planning to cope with them. This requires greater attention to gaining the confidence of foreign disputants and possesses, or at least may be viewed as evidencing, qualities of equity, justice, and often resilience and determination but also dignity, probity, and the ability to depolarize policy issues and conflicting national interests.

Finally, some of these aspects coalesce in what is called "total diplomacy." Some years ago Chester B. Bowles—noncareerist who served as Ambassador to India and Nepal and as Ambassador at Large and Under Secretary of State—wrote that "foreign relations in today's world call for a total diplomacy." This concept also bears differing connotations. On one hand, it applies to dealing with the totality of related subjects of mutual concern and the expansion and interrelation of multilateral, parliamentary, multiple, and high-level personal diplomacy. However, with its rise to a position of international paramountcy following World War II, its assumption of responsibility for worldwide interests and leadership, and its position as an epicenter of world power, the United States also became actively engaged in every corner of the globe, resulting in a wholesale magnification and complication of its diplomatic relations and the functions of the Department of State.

At the same time, modern diplomats, at whatever level, are confronted with issues that encompass virtually all aspects of human life, because every feature of contemporary existence possesses some international dimensions. These include the totality of such matters as political, economic, social, scientific, cultural, and educational development and public relations, as well as intelligence and propaganda. They also entail the interrelations of the executive and legislative branches of the Government, requiring Department of State liaison with them, the occasional appointment of legislators to representation missions and conference delegations, and the involvement of other Departments and agencies in the affairs of the Department of State. Furthermore, they necessitate the forging of a coherent and unified national policy and cooperation of the Department of State with other American agencies in providing coordinated overseas missions with clearly established leadership, lines of responsibility, and channels of communication with, and reporting to, Washington.

From another perspective, technological advancements in travel and communications enabled the government to engage in a massive increase in diplomatic exchanges of the White House, Department of State, and other public agencies with foreign governments and field missions. Transmission was expedited by means of telephone, telegraph, airgram, faxing, "telecons" (or "teleconferences"), "hot lines," and other facilities, radio hookups, transoceanic cables, encoding and decoding mechanisms, computer-based terminals, and the traditional couriers and mail pouch service to handle the worldwide flow of messages, some of which are bounced off space satellites. This updated communications system enables the Department of State to maintain constant and instantaneous, long-range communications throughout the world, and it produces a prodigious quantity of incoming and outgoing messages and other documents.[6]

Thus, the new diplomacy reflects the changing needs, personnel, and processes of the contemporary conduct of foreign relations and the functioning of the Department of State and Foreign Service. These modifications not only affected the nature and quality of diplomatic practice but also required the development of new management and administrative facilities, reorientation of personnel, and the alignment of generalists and specialists. It has been said that to deal with contemporary foreign relations, the ideal "new diplomat" not only must be skilled in traditional diplomacy and consular relations but also must be prepared to handle such matters as cultural programs, economic and trade development, educational exchanges, foreign aid and assistance of various types, intelligence operations, international terrorism, measures to counter insurgence movements, political action, and others mentioned earlier. To cope effectively with these requirements and innovations, the Secretary and Department of State must adapt and modulate their policies and actions.

The true test of statesmanship lies in neither outright rejection nor slavish endorsement of innovation, which, in any case, may be inevitable, but rather in molding the process of American diplomacy to blend the best of both the old and the new to produce the better—or at least the most creditable and livable—results. Whatever emerges as a new diplomacy in any era, nevertheless, will itself be mutable, will change with the times, and unfortunately, is unlikely to approximate the status of perfectibility.[7]

SUMMIT AND MINISTERIAL DIPLOMACY

Following World War II, personal diplomacy at the summit and ministerial levels, as components of the new diplomacy, indicated in Figure 7.1, not only continued but also accelerated and became global and commonplace. Both of these types of diplomatic practice mushroomed since 1945, especially that engaged in by the Secretary of State, which has elevated a good deal of representation, consultation, and negotiation to the highest levels, often to deal with the most pressing and critical issues of contemporary foreign relations.

Summit Diplomacy

Continuing and expanding the engagement in personal diplomacy at the summit undertaken by President Franklin D. Roosevelt during the 1930s and early 1940s, all subsequent Presidents have participated in a variety of summit relations with foreign Chiefs of State and Heads of Government. These include personal communications, the commissioning of presidential special envoys, hosting summit visits to the United States by foreign leaders, presidential trips abroad, and summit conferences and meetings.

President Eisenhower confessed that for centuries personal correspondence between government leaders "has been an extremely valuable channel of communication when the normal diplomatic channels seemed unable to carry the full burden." Diplomatic communications at the summit are frequently employed and have become a widely accepted instrument of diplomatic exchange. Influenced by their personal persuasions, their interpretation of their constitu-

Figure 7.1
Summit and Ministerial Diplomatic Participation

New Diplomacy	Personal Diplomacy	
Bilateral Diplomacy	*Summit*	*Ministerial*
Policy Making	*	*
Representation		*
Reporting		*
Conferring	*	*
Negotiation	*	*
Conferencing	*	*
Multilateral Diplomacy		
Conferences and Meetings		
Ad Hoc[1]	*	*
Occasional[2]	*	*
Recurrent[3]	*	*
Regularized[4]	*	*
International Organizations and Agencies		
Global		
General[5]	*	*
Specialized[6]		*
Regional		
General[7]	*	*
Specialized[8]		*
Security Agencies[9]	*	*

[1]Such as the San Francisco Conference (1945, United Nations Charter), World War II Peace Conference (Paris, 1946), Manila Conference (1966), Vietnam War Peace Conference (Paris, 1973), and Cancun North-South Meeting (1981).

[2]Such as U.S.–Soviet and China summit and ministerial meetings at Washington and Camp David, Beijing, Geneva, Glassboro, Helsinki, Moscow, Reykjavik, Vienna, and elsewhere.

[3]Such as East-West Big-Four and Western Big-Four, and Inter-American summit and ministerial conferences and meetings.

[4]Such as annual Economic Summit Meetings of major industrialized powers and the Post-World War II Council of Foreign Ministers meetings.

[5]Such as the United Nations.

[6]Such as the Organization for Economic Cooperation and Development (OECD).

[7]Such as the Pan-American Union and the Organization of American States.

[8]Such as the Council of Foreign Ministers Meetings.

[9]Such as ANZUS, ASEAN, Baghdad Pact, CENTO, CSCE, NATO, and SEATO summit and ministerial meetings.

Source: Based on Plischke, *Diplomat in Chief: The President at the Summit*, p. 16.

tional powers, the counsel of their staffs, their historic sensitivity, and the events of their times, Presidents differ in their degree of usage of this form of summitry. In some cases they are dauntless initiators, in others they become willing respondents, and sometimes they become reluctant or even unhappy participants. The means they employ range from written messages, the most common, to telegraphic, telephonic, and more sophisticated exchanges, including the "telecon" (or teleconference hookup introduced during World War II to consult with Allied leaders) and the "hot line" initiated with the Soviet Union in the early 1960s.

It is essential to distinguish between summit communications that are private and those that are official as well as between those that are personal in intent and those that are personal in form. Some messages are prepared by the State Department and diplomatic staffs and are simply transmitted at the presidential level to imbue them with special significance. Others are more genuinely at the summit, prepared by the President personally or by his White House staff. Certain traditional formal transmissions, such as accreditations of diplomats, certifications of negotiators' authority, and ratifications of treaties, have historically been signed by the President and communicated at the summit level as formal documents.

Summit communications may be grouped in six general categories. These include ceremonial and other formal messages to foreign leaders, such as messages of congratulation and condolence; presidential exchanges designed to serve as a prelude to later extensive negotiations at other levels; communications to afford an extensive exchange of intimate or formal, but official, views on policy and relations; presidential personal interposition in a mediatory capacity in a major international dispute or crisis between foreign governments; personal participation of the President in crisis diplomacy involving the United States as a primary participant; and other communications that do not readily fall into the other groupings.

The primary advantage of communication at the summit is that it involves political principals—those most directly responsible as decision makers in the conduct of foreign relations. The attendant hazards are circumvention of the Department of State and the regular diplomatic establishment, resultant inconsistency or discord with traditional channels and the work of resident diplomats, and top-level intrusion in matters best left to Secretaries of State and their envoys. While a good many criticisms are directed at presidential "meddling" in the diplomatic process of summit communications, the post–World War II trend is not likely to be reversed. Each President will deal directly and personally with other world leaders as frequently and extensively as deemed desirable or necessary.

At times, but with increasing frequency, the President appoints diplomatic representatives as his personal surrogates to supplement regular resident emissaries in order to keep the White House informed, negotiate on its behalf, and extend the President's vicarious influence and responsibility abroad. At the outset they were called "secret agents," and early in the nineteenth century they were sufficiently rare to be readily identified in the chronicles of diplomacy, but they have come to be so freely used that news commentator Waverly Root branded their use as "troubleshooting diplomacy." Initially appointed only on special occasions and for particular purposes, although sometimes for extended periods, this practice has extended to cover virtually any type of diplomatic assignment the President wishes to handle outside conventional channels and to represent and be responsible directly to the White House.

Prior to World War II some 500 to 600 were commissioned, and subsequently more than two dozen have been accredited in a single year. While the total number of their missions can only be surmised, it is likely that they aggregate several thousand. Currently, they bear such generic titles as "executive agents," "special representatives," extraordinary "personal emissaries," and "presidential envoys," but technically they may be designated as having "the personal rank of Ambassador" or "Ambassador at large." Those appointed may include the Secretary of State and other senior Department of State officers, the National Security Adviser and other Cabinet members, Senators and Congressmen, experienced diplomats assigned to the field and former diplomats, and occasionally even such subsummit emissaries as former Presidents, the Vice President, and the First Lady.

So far as their assignments are concerned, they may be categorized as ceremonial agents to represent the President personally at an important function, such as an independence or anniversary ceremony, a coronation, wedding, or funeral, dedication or commemorative celebration; the goodwill emissary who visits foreign lands primarily for purposes of popular appeal and the promotion of favorable relations; the special messenger to convey presidential communications, policy views, or proposals; the conference commissioner or delegate to negotiate; the troubleshooter or special negotiator; the mediator, who offers the good offices of the United States to ameliorate or resolve an international policy dispute or military conflict; the extraordinary resident envoy, such as Myron Taylor in his mission to the Vatican; and the Ambassador at large, a position that was formally established in 1949. Occasionally, it may be added, such special missions to initiate political relations with countries with which the United States previously maintained no political contacts are assigned to unrecognized, emergent states. Some of these special envoys vary from the norm in that they serve under the direction of the Secretary of State, and internationally, they are viewed as little different from regular diplomats.[8]

Hundreds of foreign chiefs of state, heads of government, and other ranking dignitaries have come to the United States on official and unofficial visits. The increased tempo in recent decades of pilgrimages to Washington by emperors, kings, presidents, premiers and princes, presidents-elect, prime ministers, leading officials of international organizations, and others has become routine. In peak months there may be as many as five to ten such visits, and at times they may number more than twenty. From 1945 to the mid-1980s there were more than 900 such summit visits to the United States, with the largest number credited to the Johnson, Nixon, and Reagan Administrations. Overall, they average approximately twenty-three per year, and during President Reagan's first term he hosted more than forty-five per year, or nearly four per month, but in some weeks there were eight or ten. These do not include private or personal visits or transit through the United States, nor do they include those of former political leaders, presidents-elect, vice presidents, or leaders of international organizations. However, sometimes many foreign leaders simultaneously visit the United States as a group.

The primary types of these visits embrace official (or official working), informal or unofficial, private, and formal state visits, supplemented with occasional visits to attend such events as President Truman's memorial service, President Eisenhower's funeral, and President Nixon's dinner for approximately thirty foreign leaders to commemorate the twenty-fifth anniversary of the United Nations. At times summit visitors also come to the United States to attend international meetings, including a Caribbean Heads of Government Meeting (1984) and the President's important bilateral meetings with the leaders of China and the Soviet Union. These foreign leaders have represented approximately 140 countries, of which 100 were new states that acquired their independence since World War II.

When foreign dignitaries come to the United States on summit visits, their reception and treatment are determined by their official and personal rank, the purpose of the visit, and the nature of the invitation. The primary distinctions among the types of such visits are based on the status of the guest, whether the visit is "official" or "unofficial" (determined by the invitation and advance arrangements), and whether it is intended to be a "formal state visit" or an "informal visit" for purposes of discussion and negotiations.

At times these visits are regarded as unnecessary pomp and ostentation. It is hazardous to generalize too sweepingly respecting their objectives and especially their results because, despite erroneous implications suggested by developing commonality of protocol and procedure, each visit has its own peculiarities. Nevertheless, a number of broad conclusions may be drawn respecting their merits. Most of them are intended in some way to promote goodwill, understanding, and favorable relations, which have come to be taken for granted.

One obvious motivation is the desire of national leaders to get to know one another personally—to meet face-to-face—and to enhance mutual understanding. Another motivation, particularly among leaders of newly independent countries, is to achieve acceptance by the United States and other nations. More sanguine are the summit meetings of both allies and adversaries in times of crisis. Most common, however, are the summit discussions of policies and issues of mutual concern to build a friendly and effective fraternity for the accommodation of national interests.

Nevertheless, these visits of foreign leaders are time-consuming, it is difficult to strike a proper balance between underscheduling and overscheduling, and, as the quantity increases, there is some risk that they may become so routine that government leaders and the public tire of them. Furthermore, their costs, direct and indirect, may amount to hundreds of thousands of dollars per year and, in some cases, such as the visit of the Chinese Vice Premier in 1979, cost the United States more than $1 million.

Conversely, American Presidents have increasingly undertaken a variety of trips and visits abroad. Using Department of State designations, they consist of five basic types: formal state visits, official visits (sometimes called official working visits during the Reagan and Bush administrations), informal visits, "met with" visits involving particular individuals, and international conferences and meetings. Beginning with President Truman in the late 1940s to the time of George Bush, Presidents were received abroad in approximately forty-five formal state visits (especially by Presidents Nixon and Reagan). These were supplemented with more than thirty official visits, nearly twenty informal visits, some sixty-five "met with" visits, ten informal meetings with individual officials, eleven audiences with the Pope, various other visits (such as addressing foreign parliaments, visiting American troops abroad, an occasional private visit, and several stopover, refueling, and rest or vacation stops. In many ways, the thirty most important presidential foreign trips involved attendance at international meetings and conferences.

Whereas President Truman undertook only four trips abroad involving six visits, President Eisenhower relished and institutionalized American participation by making sixteen trips entailing thirty-six visits of various types but was received in only two formal state visits. Presidents Kennedy and Johnson increased the ratio of state visits, which set a precedent for their successors. Presidents Nixon and Ford set a record of more than sixty visits on twenty foreign trips during eight years. From 1945 to 1990 such foreign ventures aggregated 105 presidential trips and approximately 225 separate visits, thus averaging approximately five visits per year. However the pace is uneven.[9] Normally, these foreign visits are brief, some lasting a single day or part of a day and most continuing for two to four days. However, President Truman's participation in the Potsdam Conference in 1945 lasted eighteen days, and others have lasted for seven to nine days.[10]

The apparent consequences of presidential foreign trips differ, to some degree, with the objectives sought, and in this respect, they are essentially of three types. Some have no negotiatory purposes, in which case the results most frequently cited are achievement of understanding and goodwill and an opportunity for political leaders to get to know and understand one another. Usually, formal state visits and goodwill tours and often official and informal visits achieve these objectives. The second group has a distinct negotiatory purpose, serving either as the means of producing understanding and consensus on mutual interests and problems or as the forum for consummating one or more stages in the agreement-making process. The third type is the relatively short visit of limited purpose, such as exchanging greetings and public addresses, attending a national ceremony, honoring a political leader or event, or pausing while en route to some other country. They may be of little diplomatic consequence, although they may serve as a facade for serious discussions.[11]

In making such foreign summit trips and visits, the President needs to balance the benefits anticipated against the costs and time spent preparing for, undertaking, and recuperating from them. Although price tags are kept in confidence, it has been estimated that some such ventures cost millions of dollars. Despite the exhilaration and euphoria they may engender, Presidents are burdened by so many hours or days of strenuous theatrics, maintaining such loaded schedules, waving to so many crowds, shaking so many hands, making so many speeches, eating so many official dinners, drinking so many toasts, communicating through so many interpreters, coping with so many problems, and losing so much sleep. There also are the hazards that flow from the nature of the presidential office, the character of the trip, the location of the ceremony or meeting, and sometimes the manner of official and public performance. The greater the public contact and exposure and the popular enthusiasm or contention, the greater are the hazards and possible personal security.

The matter of constitutionality of such foreign ventures, challenged especially during the Grant, Taft, Theodore Roosevelt, Wilson, and Franklin Roosevelt Administrations, was ameliorated in certain respects by the Presidential Succession Acts.[12] Nevertheless, due in part to the spread of terrorism, the matter of personal security while the President travels abroad is paid special attention, and during such presidential foreign trips the Vice President remains in the United States, usually in Washington.

The fifth and, in many ways, the most important aspect of contemporary summitry is the summit conference and meeting, which focus most directly on policy accommodation, negotiation, and mutual agreement. Following the precedents of Woodrow Wilson at Paris in 1919 and Franklin Roosevelt during World War II, all recent Presidents have engaged in many international meetings and conferences, as listed later in Table 7.11, Part A. This type of summitry generally receives the greatest amount of official, journalistic, scholarly, and popular attention. Dean Acheson has claimed that there are fashions in most societal relations so that, while humankind has experienced ways of behavior respecting the horrors of warfare, there also are fashions in remedies to avert holocaust, including, in recent years, the meeting at the summit.

For descriptive purposes summit conferences and meetings often are grouped in categories according to their composition (bilateral and multilateral), subject matter, objectives, and other differentiating factors (such as ad hoc, occasional, recurrent, and regularized), some of which may be further refined as summit conferencing associated with the establishment and functioning of international organizations and related agencies. Roughly 60 percent of summit conferencing has been bilateral, and it is generally ad hoc. North Atlantic Treaty Organization and Inter-American Heads of Government Meetings and those that involve the East-West Big Four in the 1940s and 1950s and the Western Big Three and Big Four may be regarded as occasional. Bilateral meetings with the leaders of Canada, France, Germany, Great Britain, and Mexico, as well as China and especially the Soviet Union, numbering more than seventy, are deemed to be recurrent. The annual multilateral meetings of the President with the leaders of the major economic/ industrialized powers exemplify the regularized category, which is exceptional.

Because these summit ventures often lack formal titles, one of the most difficult distinctions to draw is between summit "conferences" and "meetings." The preponderant majority of such gatherings are clearly informal, without systematized advance preparations, and consist largely of discussions in an improvised forum, which are regarded as meetings. Others may be meticulously planned and highly structured, such as Potsdam and the other World War II conferences and meetings. Later examples include the Conference on Security and Cooperation in Europe (CSCE, Helsinki, 1945), the Organization of American States Conference at Punta del Este (1967), and the global Conference on the World Environment (Earth Summit, Rio de Janeiro, 1992), but such formal conferences at the summit are rare, and in such cases the President generally plays a minor role.

On the basis of past practice it may be concluded that within a single generation presidential involvement in summit conferencing became a widely used technique of contemporary diplomacy to supplement that engaged in at the traditional level and that, although its use is not apt to decline, it is equally unlikely to increase significantly. Assessing summit diplomacy in general, there is little doubt that it is not only a useful but also a necessary foreign relations technique. The manner and frequency with which it is employed, the type and form utilized, and its effectiveness vary according to the circumstances of the times and the ability and judgment of the President.

As a major diplomatic technique, summit diplomacy, which has been branded "pinnacle diplomacy" and "ambulatory diplomacy," merely supplements other levels and processes provided by the State Department, its use varies with Presidents and prevailing circumstances, and it possesses distinct advantages but also entails risks (both substantive and physical), limitations, and disadvantages. It tends to generate overexpectations and overestimation and must not be extolled as a foreign relations panacea, and even though the President is America's diplomat in chief, resort to the summit should be restricted to only those functions that cannot be better handled by the Secretary and Department of State and their diplomats abroad.[13]

Ministerial Diplomacy Abroad

As an accompaniment of summit diplomacy and to that undertaken by the Secretary of State in the United States, the practice of ministerial diplomacy abroad—the Secretaries of State often serving as their own ambassadors—introduced in 1866 proliferated at a dizzying pace since World War II and came to demand a great deal of attention and time. As air travel expanded and improved, all Secretaries since Byrnes became extensively involved in official foreign ventures in the pursuit of their overseas personal diplomacy as well as in

Washington. Several of them, notably, Secretaries Dulles, Rusk, Rogers, Kissinger, Vance, Shultz, and subsequent Secretaries, became peripatetic, if not itinerant, diplomatic emissaries.

Between the end of World War II and 1990, the Secretaries aggregated nearly 1,170 foreign visits, as indicated in the following table[14]:

Byrnes	9	Rusk	116	Haig	53
Marshall	14	Rogers	119	Shultz	270
Acheson	22	Kissinger	216	Baker	85
Dulles	117	Vance	113		
Herter	22	Muskie	10	TOTAL	1,166

It should be stressed that this extensive and time-consuming burden of ministerial diplomacy overseas supplemented the traditional stateside duties of the Secretary of State—reporting to, and consulting with, the President and Congress, foreign policy making and coordination, managing the Department of State and Foreign Service, supervising the activities of American diplomatic and consular missions, and directing participation in treaty making, international conferencing, and representation and negotiation in international conferences and organizations.

Of those who achieved the most active records during this period, Secretary Rusk averaged approximately 14.5 foreign visits per year, which Dulles increased to 18.6, Rogers to 24.8, and Vance to 33.2. Records were set, however, by Shultz, who averaged 41.5 each year or more than three per month, and Kissinger, who served as Secretary for only forty months, achieved the remarkable average of nearly sixty-four per year, or more than five every month.

During the early post–World War II years the number of such foreign visits varied annually from only three or four (Byrnes in 1946 and Acheson in 1949 to 1951) to twelve (Acheson in 1952). Subsequently, these ranged from fewer than ten to as many as fifty or more in a single year. In the 1950s and 1960s they rarely exceeded twenty per year (only in 1952, 1953, 1955, and 1969). The largest annual number of visits was achieved by Secretaries Kissinger (fifty-nine in 1975, fifty-one in 1976, and eighty in 1974) and Shultz (seventy-three in 1988). When Kissinger undertook the phenomenal number of eighty foreign visits in a single year, he engaged in four extended tours of shuttle diplomacy to promote the Middle East peace process, prepared for, and participated in, the Moscow summit meeting in 1974, and briefed the major European powers concerning its consequences.

On these trips, the Secretaries visited 109 foreign countries and other territories. Not surprisingly, they undertook sixty-six visits to immediate neighbors Canada and Mexico. They paid 565 visits to twenty-five European countries and Vatican City, 206 to fourteen Middle East countries, 178 to twenty-six Far East and Pacific countries (including the two Chinas), eighty-nine to eighteen Latin

American countries and eleven to five Caribbean islands (Barbados, Grenada, Jamaica, St. Lucia, and Trinidad and Tobago), and fifty-one to eighteen African countries. Thus, nearly two-thirds of their foreign personal diplomacy was devoted to Europe and the Middle East.

The largest number of visits was made to Great Britain (102), France (ninety-one), Germany (sixty-eight—which included the Federal Republic, the Democratic Republic, and the Republic of Germany), and Belgium (fifty-nine). Others with high numbers were Israel (forty-five) and Egypt (forty-two), largely because of Middle East crises and the peace process, and neighboring Canada (thirty-four) and Mexico (thirty-two). These eight countries accounted for more than 40 percent of such ministerial visits. Next most frequently visited were Italy (thirty-one) and Japan (thirty), followed by Switzerland (twenty-seven) and several additional countries involved in the Middle East peace process, such as Jordan (twenty-six) and Syria (twenty-six).

Only one or two visits were made to some thirty-four countries. These embraced Bulgaria and Czechoslovakia in Europe, Haiti and Paraguay in Latin America, Burma and Mongolia in Asia, Iraq and Kuwait in the Middle East, and Ethiopia and Zimbabwe in Africa, as well as Jamaica and St. Lucia in the Caribbean and Fiji and Western Samoa in the Pacific. It also should be noted that approximately forty other countries and island groups were not included in the itineraries, mostly African and Asian nations, such as Cambodia, Madagascar, Nigeria, and Somalia, but also Cuba.

The most frequently visited cities were Paris (eighty-five visits), London (seventy-seven), Bonn and West Berlin (sixty), Brussels (fifty-nine), Jerusalem and Tel Aviv (forty-five), Cairo (thirty-five), and Rome (thirty, not including eleven visits to Vatican City). Also favored were Tokyo (twenty-eight), Damascus (twenty-six), Geneva (twenty-eight), Moscow (twenty-four), Ottawa (twenty-four), Amman (twenty-three), and Mexico City (nineteen). The reason for the popularity of Paris and London as traditional international centers of diplomacy is obvious, Bonn and West Berlin were preferred for dealing with the post–World War II German issue, many NATO meetings were held at Brussels, which also was the city to which Secretaries flew at the commencement of some of their European tours, and Geneva was generally valued as a neutral site for deliberations and negotiations. Jerusalem and Tel Aviv, Cairo, Damascus, and Amman were centrally involved in the Middle East peace process. Others with interesting records were Seoul (nineteen), Manila (eighteen), Tehran (thirteen), Helsinki (twelve), New Delhi (eleven) and, surprisingly, Hong Kong (eight) and Kuala Lumpur and Nairobi (each with five).

Ministerial visits and trips varied in duration and frequency. Many were short, lasting from one to three days, often only part of a day. On a trip to the Middle East and Europe in April 1981, Secretary Haig traveled to nine countries in nine days, in 1988 Shultz shuttled for seventeen visits in thirteen days, and early the following year, in a whirlwind tour, Baker flew to thirteen European countries and Turkey in only seven days, often visiting two and even three of them in a single day. On the other hand, some individual visits lasted for several weeks. When Secretary Marshall went to attend the fourth session of the Council of Foreign Ministers in 1947, he remained in Moscow for a month and a half (March 10–April 25), and Herter spent forty-one days (May 4–June 20) in Geneva to attend the Big Four Conference on the German and Berlin issues in 1959. Several other meetings of the Council of Foreign Ministers remained in session for three to more than four weeks.

A remarkable record had been set by Byrnes, the first post–World War II Secretary, who, during his short tenure of 18½ months, spent 213 days, or approximately seven months, largely in negotiations at critical international conferences and meetings. During the period from April 25 to October 15, 1946, he spent 135 days or nearly twenty weeks at Paris, attending sessions of the Council of Foreign Ministers and the World War II Peace Conference. His participation in the latter lasted eighty days or nearly three months, from July 28 to October 15, plus travel time.

A good many tours and other extended trips consisting of multiple visits lasted from two to nine weeks. Among the lengthiest was Secretary Marshall's attendance at the third session of the United Nations General Assembly at Paris in 1948, which, with side visits to Athens, London, and Rome, took sixty-four days (September 20–November 22). Kissinger's shuttle mission in the spring of 1974, which took him to Geneva for discussions with the Soviet Foreign Minister and entailed nine visits to Middle East nations, lasted thirty-four days; and Secretary Shultz took a twenty-day trip in June 1987, which encompassed Venice, Reykjavik, and four Asian and Pacific states. Earlier, in March 1956 Secretary Dulles circled the globe, visiting Great Britain and ten Asian countries—including the Philippines, the Republic of China, South Korea, and Japan—in seventeen days.

Illustrating the rapid pace of some foreign ministerial diplomacy, in 1954 Secretary Dulles attended a Big Four Meeting in Berlin (January 22–February 18) and an Inter-American Conference at Caracas (February 28– March 13) and made a trip to Great Britain and France (April 11–14), followed by another trip to Europe (April 21–May 3) to attend a meeting of the North Atlantic Treaty Organization and a Geneva Conference on Indochina and Korea and to visit the Italian Prime Minister, amounting to sixty days plus travel time in less than three and one-half months. Even more impressive, Secretary Kissinger undertook four foreign trips between April 28 and July 9, 1974, on which he made twenty-four official visits and attended a North Atlantic Treaty Organization session in fifty-nine days, plus travel time, during a period of only two months and twelve days.

Often during such intensive schedules the turnaround time between trips amounted to only a few days. In 1974 Kissinger accompanied President Nixon to Austria, Germany, and four Middle East nations and then attended a North Atlantic ministerial meeting at Ottawa (June 10–19), and only five days later he accompanied the President to a North Atlantic Heads of Government Meeting at Brussels and on a summit trip to Moscow and then visited seven other European powers (June 25–July 4). The following year he went to four Asian countries (December 1–8) and with only three intervening days flew to Europe to visit several European countries (December 11–17). In 1982 Haig accompanied President Reagan on a trip to four Latin American countries (November 30–December 4), and with only two days of turnaround time he set out for a thirteen-day trip to seven European countries (December 7–19). In 1990 Baker had only a single day between a trip to visit five European countries and Canada (February 6–13) and his trip to Colombia to accompany President Bush to an Inter-American Drug Summit Conference (February 15).

One of the most significant aspects of ministerial diplomacy is its purposes and functional types. According to the Department of State, these may be grouped in the following categories:

Accompanied the President	161
Ceremonial	44
Official visits	19
En route/stopover	24
"Met with" foreign leaders	440
"Discussed with" foreign leaders	101
"Briefed" foreign leaders	37
"Conferred with" foreign leaders	10
"Reviewed the Middle East peace process with" foreign leaders	25
Negotiated	17
Signed treaties and agreements	21
Attended Foreign Ministers meetings	21
International conferences	26
International organization sessions	173
Personal or private	1
Vacation	7
Others	39
TOTAL	1,166

Secretaries of State accompanied Presidents on a variety of summit missions abroad. Some of these were ceremonial, largely to attend the funerals of foreign leaders and dedication ceremonies.[15] Many involved presidential tours to four or more countries, including several goodwill missions,[16] although sometimes these were keyed to such special events as presidential state visits and summit meetings[17] and a few treaty-signing proceedings. When Secretary Kissinger accompanied President Ford to the Economic Summit convened at Rambouillet,

France, in 1975, this set the precedent for joint President–Secretary of State participation in such annual meetings.

Illustrating the extended tours of Presidents with their Secretaries of State, in 1960 President Eisenhower and Secretary Herter undertook a goodwill tour to four Latin American countries, in 1970 President Nixon and Secretary Rogers visited five European countries, in 1975 Secretary Kissinger also accompanied President Ford to four European countries and Vatican City, late in 1977 and early 1978 President Carter and Secretary Vance journeyed to six European and Middle East countries, in 1982 President Reagan and Secretary Haig flew to six European countries, and in 1985 President Reagan and Secretary Shultz made a tour of four European countries, as did President Bush and Secretary Baker in 1989.

Except for Byrnes and Marshall, the Secretaries of State also undertook forty-four foreign ceremonial visits on their own. Secretary Shultz led with sixteen, Secretary Rusk followed with eight, and most of the rest made only one or two. More than half of these visits were to attend the inauguration of Latin American Presidents and the funerals of such officials as King George VI of Great Britain (1952), Pope Pius II (1958), and Prime Minister Winston Churchill and President Anwar Sadat (1981). Other ceremonial visits by the Secretaries on their own involved six anniversary celebrations. These included Secretary Herter's attendance at the 150th anniversary of Mexican independence (Mexico City, 1960), Shultz's participation in a commemorative ceremony for the Marshall Islands (Majuro, 1988), and several anniversary celebrations of the Austrian State Treaty and the treaty establishing the Council on Security and Cooperation (CSCE) in Europe, and Secretary Baker was present at the Namibian independence ceremonies at Windhoek in 1990.

More uniquely, Secretary Marshall laid a wreath at the tomb of France's Unknown Soldier (1947), Acheson spoke at the cornerstone laying for the American Memorial Library in West Berlin (1952), Rusk dedicated a memorial to former Secretary George C. Marshall in Frankfurt, Germany (1963), and attended the dedication of Mexico's new Foreign Office building (1966), Kissinger was awarded the city's Gold Medal for Distinguished Native Citizens by Fuerth, Germany (1975), Haig addressed the Berlin Press Association in 1981, and Shultz presented an address and signed its Golden Book at West Berlin (1985). Most unusually, Secretary Herter was the personal representative of President Eisenhower at the wedding of King Baudouin of Belgium in 1960.

It is somewhat surprising that only seventeen foreign ventures of the Secretaries are labeled "negotiation" visits by the Department of State. The first of these occurred when Secretary Kissinger undertook his shuttle negotiations and participated in concluding a Mideast Egyptian–Israeli–Syrian disengagement agreement in 1974. In many cases visits designated as "met with," "conferred with," "discussed with," and "briefed" foreign leaders, which generally are self-explanatory, also involved negotiations, in some of which the Secretary served as broker or mediator in international disputes. These include most of the visits related to the Middle East wars and subsequent peace negotiations by Secretaries Rogers, Kissinger, Vance, Haig, and Shultz. Often negotiations also were involved in Foreign Minister meetings and ministerial sessions of the inter-American, North Atlantic, and other regional international agencies.

Seven of these Secretaries personally signed more than twenty treaties, agreements, and similar instruments while on their foreign travels. Among the most important, listed chronologically, were the Southeast Asia Collective Defense Treaty (Manila Pact, Dulles, 1954), the Austrian State Treaty (reestablishing post–World War II peacetime relations, Vienna, Dulles, 1955), the Nuclear Test Ban Treaty (Moscow, Rusk, 1963), the Vietnam Peace Agreement (Paris, Rogers, 1973), and the Convention on the Prohibition of Military or Any Other Hostile Use of Environmental Techniques (Geneva, Vance, 1977).

Others of interest include agreements for West German membership in the North Atlantic Treaty Organization and the European Defense Community (Bonn, Acheson, 1952) and a Protocol to the North Atlantic Treaty regarding the European Defense Community (Paris, Acheson, 1952). Still others embraced the Korean Mutual Defense Treaty (Seoul, Dulles, 1953), the Space Cooperation Agreement with Japan (Tokyo, Rogers, 1969), the Great Lakes Water Quality Agreement with Canada (Ottawa, Vance, 1978), the Lajes Bas Agreement with Portugal (Lisbon, Vance, 1979), the Nuclear Cooperation Agreement with Canada (Ottawa, Vance, 1980), and the Arctic Cooperation Agreement with Canada (Ottawa, Shultz, 1988). Vance also attended the exchange of ratifications of the Egyptian–Israeli Peace Treaty in 1979.

All of these Secretaries, except Acheson, Muskie, and Haig, also personally represented the United States at more than two dozen major international conferences of several types convened abroad. Substantively, four of these focused on ending wars in Europe, Vietnam, and the Middle East,[18] several dealt with arms control and disarmament,[19] and others pertained to economic development and cooperation.[20] Secretaries also represented the United States at inter-American conferences convened abroad,[21] and some focused on individual countries or other territories.[22] In addition, introducing a new and unique element into international conferencing, beginning in 1955 Secretaries Dulles, Rusk, Rogers, Kissinger, Vance, and Shultz held occasional special intra-American meetings with groups of American Chiefs of Mission abroad in such places as Manila (1955), Paris (1957 and 1958), Taipei (1958), Geneva (1965), Kinshasa (Zaire, 1970), Tokyo (1970 and 1973), London (1973, 1978, and 1985), and Hong Kong (1983).

Especially impressive, the Secretaries participated personally in nearly 175 sessions of international organizations and similar agencies convened abroad. The most highly involved were Secretaries Shultz (thirty-nine), Rusk (twenty-nine), Dulles (twenty-two), and Rogers (twenty), and those who participated the least were Secretaries Byrnes and Marshall (one each), Muskie (four), and Herter (six). Secretary Kissinger was so extensively concerned with Middle East shuttle diplomacy and the peace process that he attended only eleven such sessions.

The first and third sessions of the United Nations General Assembly were attended by Secretaries Byrnes at London in 1946 and Marshall at Paris in 1948, and Secretary Acheson attended the sixth session at Paris in 1951. Of the remaining such sessions, ninety-seven were meetings of the North Atlantic Treaty Organization (NATO), and approximately seventy-five involved other, largely regional international agencies.[23] Secretary Dulles also attended two sessions of the Baghdad Pact powers (consisting of the "northern tier" of Middle East countries—Iran, Iraq, Pakistan and Turkey, with the added membership of Great Britain—which convened at Ankara and London, both in 1958.

To these must be added the immediate post–World War II Council of Foreign Ministers (CFM) meetings (Byrnes four, Marshall two, and Acheson one), the so-called Big-Four Powers Foreign Ministers meetings (Dulles two), Western Foreign Ministers meetings (Herter three), Inter-American Foreign Ministers meetings (Rusk two), "Two plus Four" Foreign Ministers meetings on German reunification (Baker four), and several ad hoc ministerial meetings.[24]

In addition to such engagement in the deliberations of multilateral international organizations, beginning with Secretary Rusk in 1961, the Secretaries attended approximately twenty sessions of bilateral standing international committees and commissions. These were the Joint U.S.–Canadian Commission on Trade and Economic Affairs, the U.S.–Indian Joint Commission, the U.S.–Irani Joint Commission, the U.S.–Japan Joint Committee, the U.S.–Mexican Binational Commission, and the U.S.–Spanish Council, as well as the Egyptian–Israeli Political Committee.

Illustrative of those foreign visits listed as "others," on their foreign travels Secretaries Rogers and Kissinger, respectively, announced the restoration of American diplomatic relations with Yemen (Sana'a, 1972) and Egypt (Cairo, 1974). In 1948 Secretary Marshall met with Pope Pius XII, setting a precedent, so that beginning with Dulles in 1958 all of the Secretaries except Herter and Rusk had eleven formal audiences with the Pope at Vatican City; the visits of Rogers, Muskie, and Haig were in accompaniment with the President. Dulles and Shultz took vacations in the Caribbean (Bahamas, Jamaica, and Nassau), Rogers spent three days vacationing in Cozumel, Mexico, in 1971, and Kissinger spent three vacation days in Deauville, France, in 1976. Also, Secretary Rogers addressed the Belgo-American Association at Brussels in 1969 and the Organization of African Unity at Addis Ababa in 1970, Haig spoke to the Berlin Press Association in 1981, Shultz presented an address at a special meeting of the North Atlantic Foreign Ministers at Brussels (1985), and Baker delivered addresses at Charles University in Prague and the International Affairs Committee of the Supreme Soviet in Moscow (both in February 1990).

Other such visits abroad were more unique. Thus, Secretary Dulles announced the return of the Amami Islands to Japan (Tokyo, 1953) and attended the opening of the Austrian State Opera (Vienna, 1955). Rusk received an honorary degree from Oxford University (1962) and attended the dedication of a memorial to John F. Kennedy in Great Britain (1965). Kissinger honeymooned at Acapulco, Mexico, for eleven days (1974, when he also met with senior Mexican officials), addressed the World Food Conference at Rome (November 1974), attended a banquet in honor of British Foreign Secretary James Callaghan at Cardiff (March 1975), and addressed the Berlin House of Representatives (May 1975) and the American Bar Association on international law at Montreal (August 1975). Vance returned the Crown Jewels of St. Stephen to Budapest (January 1978), delivered President Carter's invitation to President Sadat of Egypt and Prime Minister Begin of Israel (August 1978) to convene with him at Camp David to work out a Middle East peace settlement, and addressed the Royal Institute for International Affairs at London (December 1978). Haig deposited the American instrument of ratification of the Treaty for the Prohibition of Nuclear Weapons in Latin America (Mexico City, 1981). Shultz attended the signing of an agreement for the withdrawal of Soviet forces from Afghanistan (Geneva, 1988) and was awarded an honorary degree by the Weizman Institute in Israel (1987).

One of the impressive features of ministerial diplomacy is the role played by Secretaries of State in mediation and brokering the resolution of international crises and their participation in other peaceful settlements. In addition to many trips and visits of the Secretaries concerning the German and Berlin questions following World War II, Dulles attended the Geneva Conference on Indochina and Korea (1954), and he participated in three London conferences dealing with the Suez Canal settlement (August and September 1956), Haig shuttled between London, Buenos Aires, and Caracas on five visits in his attempt to resolve the Falkland/Malvinas Islands crisis (1982), and Shultz attempted to negotiate the withdrawal of foreign forces from Lebanon (1983).

Most remarkable, however, was the American diplomatic attempt to resolve Middle East crises by brokering negotiations in implementing the peace process. Secretaries Rogers, Kissinger, Vance, Haig, and Shultz made 166 visits to Israel (forty-three), Egypt (thirty-six), Jordan (twenty-five), Syria (twenty-five), Saudi Arabia (nineteen), Lebanon (nine), and other Middle East states (nine) on these trips. Secretary Kissinger alone accounted for seventy-one such shuttle visits, followed by Shultz with forty-nine, Vance with thirty-three, and Haig and Rogers with thirteen during a period of eighteen years. Most of these visits were short, usually for a day or two, although negotiations leading to the Egyptian–Israeli disengagement agreement in May 1974 lasted for thirty days. This aspect of ministerial service was also continued by subsequent Secretaries.

Other memorable achievements in which the Secretaries were involved abroad included the launching of the United Nations General Assembly (1946–48); the many sessions of the post–World War II Council of Foreign Ministers (CFM); the developing inter-American system, the North Atlantic Treaty Organization (NATO) and other regional security, economic, and development agencies; the signing of the Paris World War II treaty and arms limitation and other treaties and agreements; the periodic economic summits; and a variety of goodwill and other protracted trips and visits. Historically, perhaps most significantly, these

and similar ventures in ministerial diplomacy energized and exalted the inter-
national role of the Secretary of State and generated and enhanced U.S. and
Department of State leadership and influence in world affairs following World
War II.

Despite the value of such ministerial diplomacy, its chief disadvantage is the
absence of the Secretary of State from Washington and the effect of the distances
they travel. In their foreign ventures, Secretary Dulles traveled 560,000 miles
(more than the distance of a round trip to the moon) in little more than six years,
Rusk traveled more than 600,000 miles in approximately 375 days, or more than
one of his eight years as Secretary, Kissinger traveled 555,000 miles (not including his earlier extensive foreign trips as National Security Adviser), and
Baker set a new record with more than 700,000 miles, or the equivalent of
twenty-eight trips around the globe, in four years.[25]

Put another way, since World War II, American Secretaries spent a great deal
of time participating in international conferences and meetings and conferring
with foreign leaders. Following Secretary Hull, who expended 22 percent of his
long tenure away from his desk in Washington, Stettinius consecrated an amaz-
ing 67 percent of his short tenure of approximately 120 days as Secretary to
this purpose, nearly half of which was devoted to attending summit meetings at
Malta, Yalta, and Cairo and the Inter-American Conference at Chapultepec,
Mexico, on the Problems of War and Peace and chairing the historic San Francisco Conference to consummate the United Nations Charter.

During the Truman Administration, Hull and Stettinius were followed by
Secretaries Byrnes (62 percent abroad), Marshall (47 percent), and Acheson (25
percent, when Ambassador at Large Philip C. Jessup and Presidential special
envoy John Foster Dulles relieved the Secretary of many high-level representation responsibilities abroad). Subsequently, in terms of days, those Secretaries
who engaged in the most personal diplomacy away from Washington included
Shultz (440 days, or more than a year), Dulles (360 days, nearly a year), Kissinger (348 days), Rusk (335 days), Rogers (252 days), and Vance (223 days).
On the other hand, so far as the percentage of their time is concerned, beginning
in the early 1950s, aside from Herter (during his short tenure, 64.9 percent),
they range from Kissinger (28.6 percent), Shultz (19.8 percent), Haig (18.9 percent), Vance (18.7 percent), Dulles (15.8 percent), and Rogers (15 percent), to
Rusk (11.5 percent) and Muskie (9.8 percent). Such arduous schedules mean
that recent Secretaries must frequently be absent, sometimes for lengthy periods,
from their duties in the Department of State.

Because of such intensive involvement of Secretaries of State in ministerial
diplomacy abroad, domestic and foreign pressures to deal diplomatically with
foreign governments at the highest level, and their frequent and often extended
absence from Washington, Department of State administrative practices and personnel changes were warranted. On one hand, in 1949 the Office of Ambassador
at Large was established on an experimental basis, which was regularized in the

early 1960s with appointees assigned to deal with particular functional subjects or geographic areas. Even more crucial, in 1972 a new Office of Deputy Secretary of State was created, largely to captain the Department during the absence of Secretaries and to relieve them of some stateside and overseas responsibilities. Although these actions failed to reduce the pace of overseas ministerial diplomacy, they freed the Secretary to continue and even expand this practice.

The allegation that resort to the summit and ministerial levels necessarily results in the decline of conventional diplomacy and disaffects the Department of State presumes not only that this is true but also that it is pernicious. Actually, the changing role of traditional State Department and diplomatic functions in recent decades reflects more fundamental changes and intensification in the conduct of foreign affairs at their levels, and analytical studies recognize their primacy. Professional diplomats criticize the growing use of such personal diplomacy, contending that top-level officials should establish basic policy and manage the foreign affairs mechanism, whereas representation and especially negotiation, in addition to reporting and other customary diplomatic services, should be left to those who devote their careers to dealing with foreign governments. However, its defenders support its use when appropriate and necessary, especially when issues can best be handled and resolved most readily at the highest levels.

PRESIDENTS AND THEIR SECRETARIES OF STATE

During the half century following Franklin Roosevelt's death, ten Presidents have held the presidency. Five were Democrats—Harry S. Truman, John F. Kennedy, Lyndon B. Johnson, Jimmy (James Earl) Carter, and William (Bill) Clinton—and five were Republicans—Dwight D. Eisenhower, Richard M. Nixon, Gerald R. Ford, Ronald Reagan, and George Bush.

Vice President Truman succeeded to the presidency on the death of Roosevelt, Johnson succeeded Kennedy when he was assassinated, and Ford succeeded Nixon when he resigned the presidency. Four succeeded from the vice presidency—Truman, Johnson, Ford, and Bush—and Nixon had previously also served as Eisenhower's Vice President. Only four—Eisenhower, Nixon, Reagan, and Clinton—were elected to two terms. Six—Truman, Kennedy, Johnson, Nixon, Ford, and Bush—had previous experience as members of Congress. In addition to Kennedy, Presidents Truman, Ford, and Reagan were subjected to assassination attempts.

Several had engaged personally in foreign relations while serving as Vice President—especially Johnson, Nixon, Ford, and Bush—but only Bush was appointed to the important office of American Representative to the United Nations (1971–73) and as head of the U.S. Liaison Office to China at Beijing (1974–75). Eisenhower had considerable foreign relations experience as Commander in Chief of the Western Allied Forces in Europe during World War II. Two

Presidents—Kennedy and Nixon—evidenced inclination to serve as their own
Secretaries of State, but most of them intended to be responsible for foreign
policy determination.

Office of Secretary of State

Assessing the contemporary office of Secretary of State, former Secretary
Dean Rusk has said: "Previous experience will help, but there is no way to be
adequately prepared to become Secretary of State"; when Alexander Haig became Secretary, he defined his role as the nation's "vicar" for the framing and
articulation of foreign policy; and Secretary George P. Shultz has called the
office "the toughest, most demanding and yet potentially most exhilarating and
gratifying of jobs." Yet, Secretaries of State rarely define the nature of their
office. Often their memoirs recount developments and actions concerning foreign
policy, relationships, problems, and administrative arrangements without elucidating their conception of the essence of their profession.

Occasionally, historians and other analysts undertake this role. Thus, in analyzing John Foster Dulles as Secretary, Professor Hans J. Morgenthau has written: "A contemporary American Secretary of State must perform two basic and
difficult tasks: he must defend and promote the interests of the United States
abroad and he must establish and defend his position at home. Whereas the
former task is inherent in the office, the latter is the result of five interconnected
constitutional factors inherent in the American system of government," which
he prescribes as the President, Congress, other executive agencies, other member
of the Department of State, and public opinion, which affects the Secretary's
relation to the other four.

Assessing the office differently, diplomatic historian Samuel Flagg Bemis
declared: "The ideal Secretary of State should be an informed and loyal adviser
to the president, persuasive with Congress, on good terms with the press, a
compelling public speaker, an efficient and respected chief of his Department,
a sensitive and patient negotiator with foreign governments, and a philosopher
able to articulate the ultimate purpose of the nation's existence." Similarly,
Warren I. Cohen, describing Dean Rusk's view of the office, has said that he
is expected "to administer the Department, negotiate abroad, act as troubleshooter at the scene of crises, represent the United States at international conferences, appear as the nation's spokesman at the United Nations, and explain
and justify policy to Congress and the public," as well as devote considerable
energy in dealing with "complex negotiations within the executive branch of
government." On the other hand, Gaddis Smith, discussing Dean Acheson as
Secretary, has concluded that the Secretary commands no army to implement
foreign policy, has no political patronage to dispense, has no significant grants
or contracts to award, and subsists on only a tiny fraction of federal expenditures, whose power rests on the ability to persuade, the foundation of which

derives from the President, on which he builds relations with departmental staff, foreign leaders, other Departments, Congress, the press, and the public.[26]

Corps of Secretaries

The ten Presidents appointed sixteen Secretaries of State, half of whom served Democratic administrations, and half were appointed by Republican Presidents:

Truman (D)
  James F. Byrnes
  George C. Marshall
  Dean G. Acheson

Eisenhower (R)
  John Foster Dulles
  Christian A. Herter

Kennedy and Johnson (D)
  Dean Rusk

Nixon and Ford (R)
  William P. Rogers
  Henry A. Kissinger

Carter (D)
  Cyrus Vance
  Edmund S. Muskie

Reagan (R)
  Alexander M. Haig, Jr.
  George P. Shultz

Bush (R)
  James A. Baker, III
  Lawrence S. Eagleburger

Clinton (D)
  Warren M. Christopher
  Madeleine K. Albright

During the transition from one Secretary to another, Acting Secretaries serve temporarily, as listed in Table 7.1.[27]

Although their tenure averaged approximately three and one-half years, throughout this period Rusk was the only Secretary to serve for a full eight years,[28] exceeded previously only by Secretary Cordell Hull. Shultz held the office for nearly seven years, Dulles for more than six years, Rogers for nearly five years, Acheson and Christopher for four years, and Kissinger, Vance, and Baker for approximately three years, whereas the shortest tenure of two years or less was served by Byrnes, Marshall, Herter, Muskie, Haig, and Eagleburger.

Nine Secretaries were born in seven eastern states—Connecticut (Acheson), Georgia (Rusk), Maine (Muskie), New York (Rogers and Shultz), South Carolina (Byrnes), Pennsylvania (Haig and Marshall), and West Virginia (Vance). Others were born in the Midwest (North Dakota—Christopher, and Wisconsin—Eagleburger), Texas (Baker), and the District of Columbia (Dulles). Three were born abroad—Herter was born in Paris and lived in France for nine years before coming to the United States; Kissinger was born in Fuerth, Germany, in 1923, came to the United States as a refugee from the Nazis in 1938, and was naturalized in 1943; and Albright was born in Czechoslovakia and emigrated to the United States when she was a young teenager. Many of them were later regarded as residents of other states, especially New York and the District of Columbia, but there was no dominance of any particular States as in earlier times.

Although their appointments are regarded as political, few of these Secretaries

Table 7.1

Secretaries and Deputy Secretaries of State since World War II

Name	Appointment	Entry on Duty	Termination of Appointment
Secretaries of State			
* Joseph C. Grew (US) *	June 28, 1945		July 3, 1945
James F. Byrnes	July 2, 1945	July 3, 1945	Jan. 21, 1947
George C. Marshall	Jan. 8, 1947	Jan. 21, 1947	Jan. 20, 1949
Dean G. Acheson	Jan. 21, 1949	Jan. 21, 1949	Jan. 20, 1953
* H. Freeman Matthews (DUS) *	Jan. 20, 1963		Jan. 21, 1963
John Foster Dulles	Jan. 21, 1953	Jan. 21, 1953	Apr. 22, 1959
Christian A. Herter	Apr. 21, 1959	Apr. 22, 1959	Jan. 20, 1961
* Livingston T. Merchant (US) *	Jan. 20, 1961		Jan. 21, 1961
Dean Rusk	Jan. 21, 1961	Jan. 21, 1961	Jan. 20, 1969
* Charles E. Bohlen (DUS) *	Jan. 20, 1969		Jan. 22, 1969
William P. Rogers	Jan. 21, 1969	Jan. 22, 1969	Sep. 3, 1973
* Kenneth Rush (US) *	Sep. 3, 1973		Sep. 22, 1973
Henry A. Kissinger	Sep. 21, 1973	Sep. 22, 1973	Jan. 20, 1977
* Philip C. Habib (US) *	Jan. 20, 1977		Jan. 23, 1977
Cyrus Vance	Jan. 21, 1977	Jan. 23, 1977	Apr. 28, 1980
* Warren Christopher (DS)	Apr. 28, 1980		May 2, 1980
* David Newsom (US) *	May 2, 1980		May 3, 1980
* Richard N. Cooper (US)	May 3, 1980		May 3, 1980
* David Newsom (US) *	May 3, 1980		May 4, 1980
* Warren Christopher (DS)	May 4, 1980		May 8, 1980
Edmund S. Muskie	May 8, 1980	May 8, 1980	Jan. 18, 1981
* David Newsom (US) *	Jan. 18-20, 1981		Jan. 20-22, 1981
Alexander M. Haig, Jr.	Jan. 22, 1981	Jan. 22, 1981	July 5, 1982
* Walter J. Stoessel, Jr. (DS) *	July 5, 1982		July 16, 1982
George P. Shultz	July 16, 1982	July 16, 1982	Jan. 25, 1989
James A. Baker, III	Jan. 25, 1989	Jan. 25, 1989	Aug. 23, 1992
* Lawrence S. Eagleburger *	Aug. 23, 1992		Dec. 8, 1992
Lawrence S. Eagleburger *	Dec. 8, 1992	Dec. 8, 1992	Jan. 19, 1993
Warren M. Christopher	Jan. 20, 1993	Jan. 20, 1993	Jan. 17, 1997
Madeleine K. Albright	Jan. 17, 1997	Jan. 23, 1997	
Deputy Secretaries of State			
John N. Irwin, II	July 13, 1972	July 13, 1972	Feb. 1, 1973
Kenneth Rush	Feb. 2, 1973	Feb. 2, 1973	May 29, 1974
Robert S. Ingersoll	June 30, 1974	July 10, 1974	Mar. 31, 1976
Charles W. Robinson	Apr. 7, 1976	Apr. 9, 1976	Jan. 20, 1977
Warren M. Christopher	Feb. 25, 1977	Feb. 25, 1977	Jan. 16, 1981
William P. Clark	Mar. 25, 1981	Mar. 25, 1981	Feb. 9, 1982
Walter J. Stoessel, Jr. *	Feb. 10, 1982	Feb. 11, 1982	Sep. 22, 1982
Kenneth W. Dam	Sep. 23, 1982	Sep. 23, 1982	June 15, 1985
John C. Whitehead	July 8, 1985	July 9, 1985	Jan. 20, 1989
Lawrence S. Eagleburger *	March 17, 1989	Mar. 20, 1989	Aug. 23, 1992
Clifton R. Wharton, Jr.	Jan. 27, 1993	Jan. 27, 1993	Nov. 8, 1993
Strobe Talbott	Feb. 22, 1994	Feb. 23, 1994	

*Before name indicates Secretary of State ad interim or Acting Secretary
*After name indicates those officers who had or later achieved Foreign Services career status.
Code: DS = Deputy Secretary; DUS = Deputy of Under Secretary; US = Under Secretary.

were primarily professional politicians and longtime members of Congress, such as Byrnes, Herter, and Muskie. When Secretary Hull resigned in 1945, Byrnes was considered the leading contender, but President Roosevelt appointed Stettinius to lead in consummating the United Nations Charter. When Truman became President, he intended to leave foreign affairs to his Secretary of State. It was publicly speculated that Byrnes would be given any available post he desired, and the President immediately offered him the appointment as Secretary of State, but Byrnes persuaded him to defer his announcement while Stettinius was chairing the San Francisco Conference. At the time, because he had no Vice President, Truman gave serious consideration to the appointment of his Secretary of State, who might succeed him under the Presidential Succession Act of 1886. In view of their previous high-level experience, General Marshall and Assistant and Under Secretary of State Acheson, Truman's third and fourth Secretaries of State, were natural candidates for succession to the office.

When Eisenhower was elected President, among his candidates for the office were Allen Dulles, Paul Hoffman, Henry Cabot Lodge, and John J. McCloy, but he opted for John Foster Dulles, who had held several prior high-level diplomatic appointments. In 1959 he was succeeded by Herter, who had considerable congressional and some diplomatic field experience (1916–22, including attendance at the World War I Peace Conference and participation in the European Relief Council) and also two years as Under Secretary of State (1957–59), from which he was promoted to the position of Secretary.

President Kennedy expected, in many respects, to serve as his own Secretary of State and considered several candidates for the office, including David K. E. Bruce (former Under Secretary of State and Ambassador to both France and Germany), Robert Lovett (former Under Secretary of State and Secretary of Defense), and Senator J. William Fulbright. However, former Secretary Acheson recommended that Rusk (who had served as Assistant and Under Secretary of State and then as President of the Rockefeller Foundation) be considered, which was supported by Lovett and Ambassador Chester B. Bowles, and the President appointed him, and Rusk remained Secretary throughout the Kennedy and Johnson Administrations.

President Nixon, also intending to manage many important aspects of foreign relations himself and, some say, intending to serve as hs own Secretary of State, appointed William P. Rogers, who had been commissioned as Attorney General during the Eisenhower Administration and whom Nixon regarded as his mentor and had come to know well. However, Nixon paralleled Secretary Rogers with Henry Kissinger, whom he named as his National Security Adviser and on whom he relied for much foreign policy initiation, overall foreign relations strategy, diplomatic negotiations, and crisis management. Rogers had to compete with Kissinger as principal foreign policy adviser to the President, he differed with Kissinger on such issues as strategic arms limitation negotiations, "linkage strategy," and other matters, and he gradually lost interest and influence and relied heavily on Under Secretaries Elliot L. Richardson and John N. Irwin II.

When Kissinger sought to become Secretary of State, and Rogers was induced to resign, the President had little hesitation in naming him to this office. The issue as to whether Kissinger continued his arduous role as National Security Adviser or headed the Department of State was resolved temporarily by having him serve simultaneously in both offices for more than two years, which is the only example of such dual appointment. President Ford retained Kissinger as his Secretary of State, and in November 1975 he appointed Lt. Gen. Brent Scowcroft as his new National Security Adviser, ending the joint responsibilities of Kissinger.

When Carter became President, although he confessed that he intended to take charge of his own foreign policy, he realized that he needed an experienced policy adviser, team player, and negotiator as his Secretary of State. He considered three experienced possibilities—George Ball (former Under Secretary of State and Representative to the United Nations), Paul Warnke (who had served in the Defense Department during the Johnson Administration and later as Arms Control Director), and Cyrus Vance (who had experience as counsel for a Senate special committee, Secretary of the Army (1962–64), and Deputy Secretary of Defense (1964–67), and several missions as presidential special diplomatic representative (1967–69). The President chose Vance because he had such high-level administrative and diplomatic experience and was regarded as a successful lawyer in the National Capital, but he also paralleled Vance by appointing Zbigniew Brzezinski as his National Security Adviser, who played a major foreign relations role similar to that of Kissinger. When Vance resigned in 1980, the President changed his priorities and appointed Edmund Muskie, in part to serve as public spokesman and to ameliorate relations with the national Security Adviser. Both Vance and Muskie depended heavily on Deputy Secretary Warren Christopher.

Although President Reagan initially considered both Alexander Haig and George Shultz, he appointed Haig as his first Secretary of State in 1981. A professional military officer who retired from the Army in 1979, Haig spent much of his Army career in Washington in the Department of Defense, as Army Vice Chief of Staff, and as White House Chief of Staff, but he also served abroad in the Vietnam War and as Supreme Commander of the NATO forces. He had also previously functioned as military adviser to Kissinger when he was the National Security Adviser (in which capacity Haig was called ''Kissinger's Kissinger''). In 1981 President Reagan also named Vice President Bush to head his National Security Crisis Committee. In mid-1982 Haig was succeeded as Secretary of State by Shultz, former senior staff economist during the Eisenhower Administration, and later Secretary of Labor (1969–70), Director of the Office of Management and Budget (1970–72), and Secretary of the Treasury (1972–74), for which he came to be known as a veteran of the Nixon Administration. While attending a business conference at London, President Reagan telephoned him to announce that Haig was resigning and to offer him the office of Secretary of State.

President Bush also appointed two Secretaries of State. The first, James A. Baker III, was Bush's vice presidential campaign manager (1979–80), senior adviser to the Reagan-Bush Committee (1980–81), and Secretary of the Treasury (1985–88), and he chaired Bush's presidential campaign (1988). Two days before he was elected Bush offered Baker the office of Secretary of State if he won the election, and Baker accepted. Later, when Baker became the Chief of Staff and senior White House Counselor in 1992, at the President's request, he recommended that he be succeeded by careerist Lawrence S. Eagleburger, who joined the Department of State in 1957 and who served as Ambassador to Yugoslavia and as senior State Department administrator in several capacities.

Similarly, President Clinton appointed two Secretaries of State. In 1993 he recruited Warren M. Christopher, who previously served as Deputy Attorney General during the Johnson Administration (1967–69), Deputy Secretary of State during the Carter Administration (1977–81), and Acting Secretary twice in 1980. He held the office for four years and was succeeded by Madeleine Albright, who previously served as legislative aide to Senator Muskie (1976–78), a member of the National Security Council staff (1978–81), and head of the Georgetown University Center for National Policy and who held the position of U.S. Permanent Representative to the United Nations for four years in the 1990s.

As is traditional, during this period, automatic resignations of the Secretaries of State at the end of a four-year term or of the administration of the Presidents under whom they served applied to Secretaries Marshall, Acheson, Herter, Rusk, Kissinger, Muskie, Shultz, Eagleburger, and Christopher. Dulles was the only Secretary to die in office. He was operated on for cancer in 1956, two years later he had an attack of diverticulitis and underwent a hernia operation early in 1959, and when he was diagnosed as having incurable cancer later that year, he dictated his resignation, which President Eisenhower rejected, and he died in May. As noted earlier, Rogers and Baker resigned during a presidential administration.

At times, however, the President and Secretary of State have serious differences over policy or decisions on the conduct of foreign relations. For example, President Truman was offended that Secretary Byrnes and the State Department failed to keep him informed concerning developments at the Moscow Foreign Ministers Meeting in December 1945. Throughout the following year it was understood that Byrnes would resign whenever the President decided on a successor, and President Truman appointed General Marshall in January 1947, when he returned from his special diplomatic mission to China. Disagreeing with Presidential Adviser Zbigniew Brzezinski and the National Security Council over the decision to undertake the helicopter mission to rescue the American diplomatic hostages held by Iran, which was decided by President Carter without consulting him while he was out of town, Secretary Vance, who suffered severe back pains, submitted his resignation on April 21, 1980, which the President accepted a week later.

More unique, in 1982 relations between President Reagan and Secretary Haig deteriorated so that the President privately handed his Secretary a letter accepting what Haig called his "nonexistent resignation." The Secretary had no alternative but to submit his letter of resignation, so his term as Secretary lasted only eighteen months and ended on July 5. Haig had high political ambitions, and he reports that he owed his loyalty to the people and U.S Constitution, not to his superior.

On the other hand, also illustrating the competition of the Secretary of State and the President's National Security Adviser, on several occasions Shultz wanted to resign over the issue of being bypassed, but President Reagan assured him that he was indispensable. Similarly, in 1986 President Reagan and Secretary Shultz differed over the draft of a speech concerning the handling of antiapartheid developments in South Africa. Shultz presented his letter of resignation, but President Reagan refused to accept it.

So far as background and professional interests are concerned, these Secretaries vary considerably. Except for Secretary Byrnes, they were all college and university graduates.[29] Several also took advanced graduate studies. These included Eagleburger (M.S., University of Wisconsin), Haig (M.A., Georgetown University), Kissinger (M.A. and Ph.D., Harvard University), and Shultz (Ph.D., Massachusetts Institute of Technology); Dulles spent a year in advanced studies at the Sorbonne (Paris); and Rusk became a Rhodes Scholar for three years at Oxford University. Several Secretaries also had college and university teaching and administrative experience.[30] Most of them published their memoirs and, as a group, more than thirty other volumes, most of them dealing with foreign affairs.[31]

Reminiscent of earlier times, legal training and experience continued to characterize the professional background and interest of half of these Secretaries. Byrnes, the only one who was trained in the earlier manner, left school when he was fourteen years of age to work in a law office, served as a court stenographer, and passed the bar exam in 1904, practiced law (1925–31 and also later, 1947–50), and was appointed Associate Justice of the Supreme Court (1941–42). Nearly half of them were graduates of law schools[32] and practiced or taught law. Acheson also served as secretary to Supreme Court Associate Justice Louis D. Brandeis, and Vance became President of the New York Bar Association. Following their tenure as Secretary of State, Acheson, Baker, Byrnes, Dulles, Muskie, and Rogers returned to practicing law, and in 1969 Rusk began to teach international law at the University of Georgia.

Only four of these Secretaries—Byrnes, Dulles, Herter, and Muskie—served in Congress.[33] Several—Byrnes, Herter, and Muskie—held State and various other political and administrative offices.[34] Byrnes was considered by President Roosevelt as a possible nominee for Vice President in the campaign of 1944, Herter was interested in the Vice Presidency if Nixon would not be a candidate in 1956, and two other Secretaries—Muskie and Haig—had presidential ambitions.

Most remarkably, two-thirds of these Secretaries had military training and experience. Marshall and Haig were professional soldiers. Marshall, who served in World Wars I and II, had forty-five years of military service, served as Chief of Staff, and achieved the five-star rank of General of the Army. Haig, who served in World War II and the Korean War, was Deputy Commandant of West Point and Supreme Commander of the North Atlantic Forces and achieved the rank of Major General. Dulles, Rusk, and Eagleburger also served in the Army; Acheson, Christopher, Muskie, Rogers, and Vance served in the Navy; and Baker and Shultz were Marines. Although Kissinger did not serve in the military, he was recruited as a consultant and agent to undertake military missions for the Army Department and other military agencies. Only Albright, Herter, and Rogers lacked military experience.

Similarly, nearly two-thirds of the Secretaries also had prior government administrative experience, in some cases including Cabinet appointments. To illustrate, aside from senior Department of State positions, these included Rogers (Attorney General, 1957–61), Vance (Secretary of the Army, 1962–64, and Deputy Secretary of Defense, 1964–67), Shultz (Secretary of Labor, 1969–70, and Secretary of the Treasury, 1972–74), and Baker (Secretary of the Treasury (1985–88). After he headed the State Department, when the Korean War Broke out, President Truman appointed Marshall as his Secretary of Defense (1950–51).

In addition, Byrnes, called the "Assistant President on the Home Front" during World War II, served as President Roosevelt's chief executive assistant and Director of the Office of Economic Stabilization and the Office of War Mobilization in the early 1940s, and later he headed the Arms Section of the Permanent Joint Defense Board (1947–48). Acheson was appointed Under Secretary of the Treasury (1933); Rusk became a Special Assistant to the Secretary of War (1946); Rogers was designated a member of the President's National Commission on Law Enhancement and the Administration of Justice (1965–67); Vance served as General Counsel of the Department of Defense (1961); Haig was appointed Military Assistant to the President's National Security Adviser (1964) and his Deputy Assistant (1971), as well as Chief of the White House Staff (1973); Shultz became Director of the Office of Management and Budget (1970–72), Assistant to the President (1972–74), and head of the Economic Policy Advisory Board (1981–82); Baker served as Under Secretary of Commerce (1975–76) and White House Chief of Staff (1981–85 and 1992–93); and Christopher held the office of Deputy Attorney General (1967–69).

Most relevant, however, were their prior Department of State and diplomatic experiences and accomplishments. Two Secretaries, Dulles and Vance, possessed the advantage of diplomatic heritage. Dulles' missionary grandfather John W. Foster was appointed Minister Plenipotentiary to Mexico (1873–80), Russia (1880–81) and Spain (1883–85) and Secretary of State (1892–93); his great uncle John Welsh served as Minister Plenipotentiary to Great Britain (1877–79); and later his uncle Robert Lansing was named Counselor of the State Department (1914–15) and Secretary of State (1915–20). Vance's heritage was less auspicious; his uncle John W. Davis, a lawyer, was named Ambassador to Great Britain (1918–21), and he was a Democratic candidate for the presidency (1924).

To illustrate prior diplomatic experience, Byrnes accompanied President Roosevelt to the Yalta Conference (1945), Marshall participated in the major World War II summit meetings and conferences from the Roosevelt–Churchill Meeting at Argentia Bay to the trilateral Potsdam Conference, and he was appointed President Truman's Special Representative to China with the rank of Ambassador (1945–47). Although he did not serve diplomatically in the field, Acheson had the advantage of nearly seven years of experience as Assistant and Under Secretary of State (1941–47). On the other hand, Dulles held more than a dozen diplomatic appointments, including attaché to the American Embassy in Berlin (1916–17), adviser to President Wilson and Secretary of the American Commission at the World War I Peace Conference (1919), and member of the Reparations Commission and the Supreme Economic Council (1919), and he served at the United Nations Conference at San Francisco (1945), as adviser to his four preceding Secretaries of State (Stettinius to Acheson), on delegations to the United Nations General Assembly for several years (1946–50), and, regarded as President Truman's Ambassador at Large (before the office was officially created), as Special Representative with the rank of Ambassador to negotiate the Japanese Peace Treaty (1950–51).

Herter and Rusk had extensive, early, high-level responsibilities in the Department of State and therefore, in a sense, were subsequently promoted to the rank of Secretary. In 1920 Herbert Hoover appointed Herter as a Special Assistant and Executive Secretary of the European Relief Council, and later, as he also worked for the American Relief Association, in 1922 he went to Russia to study and report on conditions following its 1921 famine. He also served as Under Secretary of State (1957–59), in which capacity he undertook a mission to Southeast Asia, where he visited nine countries (1957), and served as Acting Secretary when Secretary Dulles was away on many foreign trips and during his illness. Similarly, Rusk accompanied President Truman to Wake Island to consult with General MacArthur during the Korean War, served as Director or the State Department Office of Special Political Affairs (concerned largely with United Nations developments, 1947), Assistant Secretary for International Organization Affairs (1949), Deputy Under Secretary (1949–50), and Assistant Secretary for East Asian and Pacific Affairs (1950–51).

Kissinger's experience differed considerably in that his prior diplomatic concerns involved primarily his study, teaching, conference management, and publications on foreign policy and strategy, and his service as consultant to the National Security Council during the Kennedy and Johnson Administrations and as President Nixon's National Security Adviser, for which he came to be regarded as the "chief engineer" of what his biographers call "Henry's Wonderful Machine." In this capacity he was the President's special (sometimes confidential) emissary to at least twenty countries, functioning as troubleshooter, negotiator, and peace-seeker and peacemaker, for which he traveled abroad (occasionally, in the presidential jet) on dozens of diplomatic missions. Most unique, he continued in this role as National Security Adviser when he was appointed Secretary of State and thus wore two important hats for more than two years under two Presidents.

Vance undertook a number of foreign missions while he served in the Defense Department in the 1960s. As General Counsel he worked to obtain the release of the Bay of Pigs American military prisoners; as Secretary of the Army he was sent on a special mission to Panama at the time of the "flag crisis"; and he served as a member of a quadriumvirate to mediate and restore political stability in the Dominican Republic. Later, as Deputy Secretary of Defense, he participated in the attempt to resolve the Greek–Turkish conflict over Cyprus, as a member of a team of six he was sent by President Johnson to seek to resolve the *Pueblo* crisis with Korea, and subsequently he joined Averell Harriman as special emissaries to attempt to negotiate a settlement of the Vietnam War. Even though he held no major or formal diplomatic appointments, as a high-ranking military officer, Haig was a military assistant to the National Security Adviser and deputy assistant to the President for national security matters, in which capacity his functions often involved American diplomatic relations.

Eagleburger was unique in that he was the first career Foreign Service Officer to be named Secretary of State. He was appointed by the State Department in 1957 and devoted his career to diplomacy, serving in various junior capacities as a member of the National Security Council staff and Executive Assistant to the Secretary of State and eventually rising through the ranks to serve as Ambassador to Yugoslavia (1977–81) and Assistant and Under Secretary (1981–84), and eventually he was named Career Ambassador in 1984, prior to being appointed Secretary of State. Although he held no prior diplomatic appointments, Christopher served as Deputy Secretary of State for four years (1977–81) and briefly twice as Acting Secretary. Albright was appointed U.S. Representative to the United Nations, with the rank of Ambassador.

Therefore, only four of these Secretaries—Rogers, Muskie, Shultz, and Baker—had no prior Department of State or formal diplomatic experience, although Muskie had been a member of the Senate Foreign Relations Committee. Nevertheless, as a group these Secretaries of State were endowed with a rich background of academic, legal, administrative, military, some congressional, and, in most cases, also diplomatic experience, perhaps portending transition from basically partisan to a high level of professional standard for such appointments to manage the Department of State and the foreign relations of the United States.

It is exceptional for former Secretaries to be appointed to diplomatic assignments. Herter was an exception, however, in that in 1961 he chaired a Committee on Foreign Affairs Personnel, which issued its report in December the following year entitled *Personnel for the New Diplomacy*, and late in 1963 President Kennedy also made him his special Representative for Trade Negotiations, which continued until Herter died in December 1966.

Secretaries of State Remembered

Biographers, historians, journalists, and other analysts have credited these Secretaries with a variety of plaudits and accolades. Byrnes, who assumed the burdens of the office of Secretary at one of the most critical times in the nation's history, has been viewed as having defined the American role in an uneasy post–World War II world and initiating the American response to the vast power revolution in world affairs. Of Marshall it has been said that he was "not only the nation's most notable nonpolitical Secretary of State but also one of its most powerful," that few Secretaries of State were as conversant with the contemporary world political scene as he was when he assumed the office, that he was "worshiped" by President Truman and enjoyed great national and international respect, and that he is remembered for launching the Marshall Plan.

President Truman considered Acheson as indispensable, a realist who rendered the Department of State as paramount in the control of fundamental American foreign policy that laid the basis for U.S. behavior for two decades, led in the launching of the North Atlantic Treaty Organization, participated in preparing the Acheson–Lilienthal Report (which recommended the development of the hydrogen bomb), and presided over the San Francisco Conference to conclude the Japanese Peace Treaty. He was lauded by Alistair Cooke in the *Manchester Guardian* as "the most impressive Secretary of State since Elihu Root" and by the London *Economist* as "the best [Secretary of State] the United States has had in modern times." Diplomatic historian Norman A. Graebner has written: "No Secretary in living memory has commanded such respect abroad" while being "so thoroughly discredited at home" (by Congress, the media, and the public).

Dulles, who had the advantage of benefiting from President Eisenhower's "unprecedented prestige," was regarded by the President as "the greatest Secretary of State he had known," who handled the office "with greater distinction than any other man our country has known." He wielded great power over foreign affairs during an era of unprecedented economic, political, scientific, and social revolution, was called a peacemaker at heart in that he labored "to apply the virtue and might of a giant world power in a quest for world peace," and is remembered for initiating a "new look" in American foreign policy characterized by "liberation" to supersede "containment," "agonizing reappraisal" in Western Europe, "massive retaliation" in the face of challenges during the Cold War, and the "unleashing" of Chiang Kai-shek in China. Herter was the only appointee who was commissioned as Under Secretary and promoted directly to the Secretaryship. He has been described as a practical, patiently optimistic, consistently liberal-minded public servant and as a confirmed internationalist and supporter of the United Nations and the joint international security agencies who maintained good relations not only with the President but also with Congress, Department of State officers, and the Foreign Service.

Rusk, viewed as possessing a brilliant mind, is remembered for his ability to fashion a consensus and write lucid and succinct reports, his capability as a tactician, his *Foreign Affairs* article on "The President" (April 1960), chairing the panel that produced the Rockefeller Report on "The Mid-Century Challenge to U.S. Foreign Policy" (1959), producing the "Rusk Doctrine" committing the United States to oppose Communist aggression, direct or indirect, along the periphery of the Communist world, enduring the rigors of the office of Secretary for eight years during the Kennedy and Johnson Administrations, and defending the long and unpopular War in Vietnam, the handling of which was his greatest disappointment. His biographer has described him as "a better man, a wiser, more decent, humane, and moral man than either of the Presidents he served." Rogers is credited for initiating the "Rogers Plan" for peace for Middle East countries, which proved to be unacceptable to them, and he signed the Vietnam Peace Settlement at Paris in January 1973.

Kissinger has been described as a businesslike, charismatic, diligent, loyal, and persuasive officer, a demanding taskmaster who was distrustful of bureaucracy, a rare type of policy strategist and peripatetic Presidential special agent, National Security Adviser, and Secretary of State. He is remembered for espousing such policy and strategy concepts as Cold War détente, "forward strategy," "institutionalized policy," "linkage," and "preventive diplomacy." Biographers and commentators refer to him as "Nixon's Metternich," a "diplomatic phenomenon" who became an expert at "virtuoso diplomacy" and "master of the art of clandestine diplomacy," a "superstar of statecraft," the "Secretary of the World," "Professident of the United States," "the second most powerful man in the world," and "an extravaganza—all by himself." It has also been said that at the age of fifty-one, after only five years in Washington, he "emerged from the relative obscurity of a Harvard Professorship to become the most celebrated and controversial diplomat of our time."

Vance represented a combination of internationalism and idealism, political centrism, and a hopeful, but not utopian, outlook who was skilled as a policy analyst, had a "policy-oriented" rather than a "conceptual mind" in determining workable international choices, possessed skill and tenacity as an analyst and negotiator, and inspired his colleagues. He, it has been said, shared with President Carter espousal of a new "world order" based on human rights, self-determination, and the reign of international law, promoted "unlinkage" of arms control negotiations from Soviet actions in other fields, and came to be viewed by some as having "restored the diplomatic art to American statecraft."

Haig is remembered for seeking to resolve the Falkland Islands crisis in April 1982. Shultz signed an Arctic Agreement with Canada in January 1988, whom

National Security Adviser Colin Powell commended by saying that, in his view, the Secretary of State and head of the National Security Council had not gotten along so well since the days when Kissinger held both offices simultaneously.

All of the Secretaries beginning with Rogers engaged in shuttle diplomacy in their attempt to promote the peace initiative in the Middle East. Christopher, respected for his studied judgment, attention to detail, concern for human rights, and negotiating skills, is remembered for such achievements as the 1981 release of the U.S. hostages in Iran, changing the role of the North Atlantic Treaty Organization in the post–Cold War years, and advancing the Middle East peace process. Baker earned the reputation of being a shrewd, capable, pragmatic, and loyal administrator. Eagleburger, described as pragmatic, frank, and widely respected as a tough-minded problem solver and widely experienced in the craft of diplomacy, rose through the ranks to be described as ''a legend in the Foreign Service'' and later to be recruited as Secretary of State. Albright, who speaks several languages and is widely traveled, bears the distinction of possessing Cabinet status as U.S. Representative to the United Nations prior to becoming the first woman Secretary of State.

These Secretaries also were accorded many special honors. For example, Marshall and Kissinger (like earlier Secretaries Root, Kelllogg, and Hull) were awarded the Nobel Peace Prize. Other awards, medals, and special recognition included the Presidential Medal of Freedom (Acheson, Rusk, Rogers, Kissinger, Muskie, Baker, and Christopher), the Congressional Distinguished Service Award (Herter and Muskie), and many military recognition decorations, medals, and citations (Marshall and Haig). Scores of other awards and honors were also bestowed upon these Secretaries by nongovernmental institutions,[35] and many academic honorary degrees were conferred upon them.

To summarize, supporting the view that the Secretary of State ranks among the most carefully selected officials in the U.S. government, as a group these post–World War II Secretaries constitute a remarkable corps of highly educated, well-prepared, and widely experienced appointees. Several achieved the distinction of being recognized as honored American statesmen. All but one (Byrnes) graduated from various colleges, universities, and military academies, several took advanced degrees, including the Ph.D., and four also taught in colleges and universities. Eight were trained lawyers, most of whom practiced law, Rusk studied and taught international law, and Byrnes was appointed Associate Justice of the Supreme Court. Two were professional Army officers who attained the rank of General, and all of the rest, except for Byrnes, Herter, Rogers, and Albright, had some military experience. Five served as members of Congress or held other major political offices, but only three (Byrnes, Herter, and Muskie) may be described as committed politicians. Four held other Cabinet positions (Rogers, Vance, Shultz, and Baker) before becoming Secretary of State, and Marshall served as Secretary of Defense after he headed the State Department.

Most impressive, eleven had prior diplomatic experience as Ambassadors, presidential special emissaries, and senior State Department Deputy, Assistant, and Under Secretaries of State (especially Marshall, Dulles, Rusk, Kissinger, Christopher, who also served twice as interim Acting Secretary, and Eagleburger). Albright represented the United States as Ambassador to the United Nations. Eagleburger was the only professional Foreign Service Officer to devote his career to diplomacy and become Secretary of State. Moreover, Acheson, Dulles, Rusk, Kissinger, Christopher, and possibly Vance and several others may be regarded as foreign relations professionals when appointed as Secretary.

Most of these Secretaries served in critical times, especially those who held the office during the immediate post–World War II period, the Cold War, the Korean and Vietnam Wars, and a series of other major and minor international crises. Secretary Rusk served two Presidents for eight years, and three others held the office for four years (Rogers, Shultz, and Christopher). Nearly two-thirds were viewed as "establishment candidates" for the office of Secretary when they were appointed, and virtually all of them were deemed to be "Washington-wise prior to appointment." Finally, it needs to be remembered that three Secretaries were born abroad, of whom two (Kissinger and Albright) were foreign nationals who became American citizens, several were approved unanimously by the Senate (Marshall, Herter, Muskie, and Shultz), one died in office (Dulles), and three had Presidential aspirations (Byrnes, Muskie, and Haig) in which they were unsuccessful, but Byrnes might have been inaugurated under the Presidential Succession Act of 1886.

By way of conclusion, it is not unreasonable to suggest that the precedents being set, with greater experience of selecting Secretaries of State who possess a substantial degree of academic, legal, military, and especially prior diplomatic and high-level, particularly State Department, administrative experience, suggest the possibility of moving toward the professionalization of the office of Secretary of State.

Secretary of State Succession to the Presidency

As early as August 27, 1787, the framers of the Constitution considered the matter of presidential succession. In drafting the Constitution, in Article 2, section 1, clause 5, they provided that "Congress by law may provide for the case of the removal, death, resignation or inability of both the President and Vice President, declaring what officer shall then act as President . . . until the disability be removed, or a President shall be elected."

By law of March 1, 1792, Congress legislated that in such circumstances the President pro tempore of the Senate would succeed as President, and, if none is available, the Speaker of the House of Representatives would become Acting President, but only for the purpose of holding an election to choose a new President. Dissatisfied with this arrangement,[36] nearly a century later Congress passed the Presidential Succession Act of January 19, 1886, which stipulated that Presidential succession under these circumstances would rather devolve upon the Secretary of State, followed by the other Cabinet members in their traditional order of seniority. Thus, the Secretary of State became the ranking potential President.

When Harry Truman succeeded Franklin D. Roosevelt in April 1945, and the Vice Presidency was vacant, the hazards of long journeys, often abroad, by both the President and Secretary of State to participate in international conferences and meetings and other visits evoked grave concerns respecting continuity of the Presidency, and the apparent possibility that the President might be personally selecting his successor with neither electoral nor congressional approval disturbed political leaders. Viewed with hindsight, in the new era of nuclear destruction and the initiation of the Cold War, in January 1946 and February 1947 he recommended revision of the 1886 law. Congress enacted a new Presidential Succession Act in June 1947, joining the preceding arrangements. It provided that succession would pass to the Speaker of the House, then the President pro tempore of the Senate, both of whom are elected officials, followed by the Secretary of State and other Cabinet members in the order of their ascendancy.[37]

Although the Secretary of State has been included in the order of presidential succession since 1886, and these acts provide largely for statutory standby arrangements by which the Secretary might succeed to the Presidency, none has achieved the office in this fashion. Nevertheless, during the initial half century, five of the first eight Presidents had previously served as Secretary of State. These included Jefferson, Madison, Monroe, John Quincy Adams, and Van Buren, and later they were followed by Buchanan. At the time such succession came to be regarded as a stepping-stone to the Presidency, but since the 1850s no Secretary of State has subsequently been elected as President.[38]

Over the years, American history evidenced the need for a regularized system of Presidential succession. Beginning with the death of William Henry Harrison in 1841, eight Presidents, four of whom were assassinated, died in office, and beginning with George Clinton in 1812, seven Vice Presidents died in office, and Vice President Calhoun resigned his office in 1832 to become a member of the Senate.[39] The succession problem was compounded in that the death or resignation of the Vice President left eight Presidents without Vice Presidents to replace them, which in the case of Presidents Pierce, Cleveland, and Truman ran for more than three years.[40] Thus, by the mid-1960s nearly half of the Presidents served part of their tenure without Vice Presidents. Also relevant is the possibility of impeachment, illness, accident, and attempted assassination. Impeachment proceedings were launched against Presidents Andrew Johnson, Nixon, and Clinton; Presidents Wilson, Eisenhower, and others suffered serious and sometimes prolonged illnesses; and attempts were made to assassinate Presidents Truman, Ford, and Reagan. To summarize, of the forty-two elected Presidents, approximately one in five died in office, three were threatened with attempted assassination, two narrowly escaped removal from office by the impeachment process, one resigned, and several others suffered serious, debilitating illnesses.[41]

To deal with such contingencies and to facilitate presidential succession, the Twenty-Fifth Amendment was added to the Constitution in 1967. It provided a means for the appointment of a new Vice President when that office is vacant and for a process to have the Vice President act as President during the President's inability to carry out the functions and duties of the office,[42] which was first applied in the 1970s.[43] Together, this amendment and the Presidential Succession Act provide a comprehensive combination to govern the matter of presidential succession. However, it is unlikely that the Secretary of State will succeed to the Presidency under them, unless the country, especially Washington, sustains a catastrophe such as a disastrous epidemic or a massive nuclear attack, and the chief executive and congressional officers are simultaneously killed. Therefore, the Secretary of State's role has been reduced to the status of a standby, residual candidate for automatic succession to the Presidency.[44]

Acting Secretary of State

Prior to the twentieth century, during the occasional absence of the Secretary of State, the Chief Clerk served as Acting Secretary. For example, in the 1840s Chief Clerk William S. Derrick functioned briefly in this capacity twelve times. In the early 1860s, when Secretary William H. Seward and Assistant Secretary Frederick Seward were seriously injured in an accident, Chief Clerk William Hunter took charge of the Department of State. Five other Chief Clerks also acted in this capacity. Beginning in the 1890s Assistant or Under Secretaries usually played this role.[45]

However, as the Secretary became more involved personally in ministerial diplomacy abroad (discussed in the section on ministerial diplomacy) and in attendance at international conferences and meetings both in the United States and abroad, the matter of prescribing temporary replacements as Acting Secretary was regularized. Pursuant to law, President Eisenhower issued a series of Executive Orders, 1954–58, specifying particular Department of State senior officers to serve in this capacity. On November 28, 1958, in Executive Order No. 10791, he modified this arrangement by prescribing that in the case of the "death, resignation, absence, or sickness" of the Secretary and Under Secretary, "until a successor is appointed or until the absence or sickness" ceases to exist, the order of temporary succession would automatically devolve upon the Under Secretary for Economic Affairs, Deputy Under Secretary for Political Affairs, and Deputy Under Secretary for Administration, in this order.

Subsequently, on January 27, 1982, in Executive Order No. 12343, President Reagan empowered the Secretary to name his own temporary Acting Secretaries. It provided that during the absence or disability of the Secretary or the vacancy of the office of Secretary when neither the Secretary nor the Deputy Secretary is available to perform the duties of the office of Secretary, it would temporarily be handled by departmental officers "in such order as the Secretary of State may from time to time prescribe." This innovation accorded the Secretary authority to determine his order of succession. Nevertheless, only those officers are to be included who are Presidential appointees with Senate confirmation. Furthermore, if no order of succession is specified by a Secretary, it must conform with the descending order of rank prescribed in the *United States Code*.[46]

DEPARTMENT OF STATE MANAGEMENT

When President Truman took office in April 1945, the top-level staff of the Department of State consisted of eleven officers in addition to the Secretary. These included an Under Secretary and six Assistant Secretaries—concerned with Administration, Congressional Relations and International Conferences, Economic Affairs, Public Affairs, and two for geographic areas (one for American Republic Affairs and the other for combined European, Far Eastern, Near Eastern, and African Affairs)—plus the Counselor, the Legal Adviser, and Special Assistants for Public Relations and Protocol. Subsequently, most of these were modified, superseded, or supplemented. Lesser-ranked officials were the Geographer, Historian, Translator, and the Chiefs of the Divisions of Economic and Political Post–World War II Studies. The Secretary was also assisted by a number of general coordinating agencies, including a Joint Secretariat and Coordinating, Policy, Problems, and Staff Committees.[47]

Department of State Principal Officers and Agencies

Many changes were made during the Truman Administration. At the highest levels these embraced the creation of an Under Secretary for Economic Affairs (1946, which was renamed the Under Secretary for Economic and Agricultural Affairs in 1985), two Deputy Secretaries, one without a designated functional title (1949–53) and the other for Management (1949, which was elevated to the rank of Under Secretary in 1978). The two Assistant Secretaries for geographic areas were retitled and augmented. That for American Republic Affairs was retitled Secretary for Inter-American Affairs in 1949. That year the other countries were put under the jurisdiction of three new Assistant Secretaries—for European Affairs (1949, to which Canada was added in 1983), Far Eastern Affairs (1949, retitled East Asian and Pacific Affairs in 1966), Near Eastern and African Affairs (1949, which was renamed Near Eastern and South Asian Affairs in 1958), when an additional Assistant Secretary was also provided for African Affairs.

Other additions and modifications were made. The four preexisting functional Assistant Secretaries remained in existence, although the title of the Assistant Secretary for Congressional Relations was changed to Legislative and Intergovernmental Affairs in 1983 and to Legislative Affairs in 1987. Four additional functional Assistant Secretaries were created to deal with United Nations Affairs (1949, changed to International Organization Affairs in 1954), Occupied Areas (1946–49, held by only two persons), Political Affairs (1947–48, held by only one person), and Transportation and Communication (1947–49, also held by only one person). In addition, the Special Assistant for Protocol was advanced to the status of Chief of Protocol (1946, with the rank of Ambassador since 1961),[48] and four officers with the title Director were created. These were the Director General of the Foreign Service (1946–   ), and Directors of the Bureau of German Affairs (1950–52, held by only one person), the Foreign Service Institute (1947–   ), and the Policy Planning Staff (1947–   ). The new position of Ambassador at Large, regarded as ranking with State Department principal officers, was also established in 1949.

Thus, bridging the transition from World War II to the era of superpower international relationships, especially in the days of Secretaries Marshall and Acheson, the Truman Administration laid the basis for restructuring and stabilizing the principal officers of the Department of State. Nine preexisting officers were retained—the Under Secretary, four functional Assistant Secretaries, the Chief of Protocol (whose rank and title were changed), the Executive Secretary, the Counselor, and the Legal Adviser. Fifteen new officers were added, including a second Under Secretary, two Deputy Under Secretaries, four Assistant Secretaries for the Geographic Offices (which superseded the original two), four additional functional Assistant Secretaries, and four Directors (including those to head the Foreign Service and the Foreign Service Institute). However, three of the new Assistant Secretaries, appointed to head temporary postwar offices, were short-lived and were discontinued, leaving a corps of twenty-one principal officers to assist the Secretary of State. Their ranks and titles ranged from Under Secretary, Deputy Under Secretary, and Assistant Secretary, to General Director, Director, and Chief.

Since 1952 the Secretary has been provided with a new Deputy Secretary as his highest-ranking surrogate (1972–   ); three additional Under Secretaries for Management (1953–   ), Political Affairs (1959–   ), and Security Assistance, Science, and Technology (1972–   ); and two additional Deputy Secretaries for Economic Affairs (1955–72) and Political Affairs (1953–69). The greatest modification applied to the Assistant Secretary and other officers at equivalent levels. In addition to the Assistant Secretary for African Affairs, new functional Assistant Secretaries were provided for Consular Affairs (1962–   ), Diplomatic Security (1987–   ), Human Rights and Humanitarian Affairs (1976, later changed to Democracy, Human Rights, and Labor Affairs), Intelligence and Research (1957–   ), International Narcotics Matters (1979–   ), Oceans and International Environmental and Scientific Affairs (1975–   ), and Politico-Military Affairs (1969–   ). An Assistant Secretary for Educational and Cultural Affairs was also established in 1961, but it was terminated in 1978. The preexisting Assistant Secretary for Economic Affairs was retitled Assistant Secretary for Economic and Business Affairs in 1972, and the Assistant Secretary for Congressional Relations and International Conferences was retitled Assistant Secretary for Legislative and Intergovernmental Affairs in 1983 and was changed to Assistant Secretary for Legislative Affairs in 1987.

Table 7.2
Evolution of Department of State Principal Officers
(In addition to Secretary of State)*

Date	Deputy Sec.	Under Sec.	Deputy Under Sec.	Assistant Geographic	Secretary Functional	Director/ Coordinator[1]	Special Assistant[2]	Others[3]	Total
1945	0	1	0	2	4	0	2	2	11
1952	0	2	2	4	5	4	1	3	21
1960	0	2	2	5	6	3	1	3	22
1970	0	2	2	5	5	4	6	10	34
1980	1	4	0	5	9	4	7	7	37
1990	1	4	0	5	9	8	3	9	39
1998	1	5	0	6	14[4]	5	3	9	43

*The position of the Permanent Representative to the United Nations, responsible to the Secretary, is not included, nor is that of the Ambassador at Large, created in 1949, because the number of Ambassadors at Large varies from year to year.

[1]Directors have been responsible for administering such matters as Counterterrorism, Educational and Cultural Affairs, Foreign Buildings, the Foreign Service Institute, Intelligence and Research, Management Operations, Medical Service, Personnel, Refugee Programs, and others, and the title Coordinator has been applied to Policy Planning. Many of these have subsequently been elevated or changed.

[2]Special Assistants to the Secretary of State generally serve as personal assistants or advisers and often also as the Executive Secretary of the Department of State. Functional Special Assistants have been appointed occasionally to deal with such matters as liaison with State Governors, fisheries and wildlife, and other matters that were later elevated to the Assistant Secretary level.

[3]Those listed as "others" include such officers as Chief of Protocol, Chief of Staff, Comptroller, Counselor, Executive Secretary of the Department, and Inspector General, as well as such unique appointees as Bernard Kalb, who simultaneously served as "Spokesman of the Department" and Assistant Secretary for Public Affairs in the 1980s.

[4]The appointment of Deputy Assistant Secretaries has been rare. However, one was appointed to deal with Equal Employment Opportunity and Civil Rights in the 1990s.

Equally impressive is the creation of a series of additional officers of Assistant Secretary equivalency, the titles of which evidence the increasing number of more precise administrative and substantive functions and concerns of the Department. These are illustrated by the Executive Secretary (1961–), Comptroller (1979–), and the Directors of Refugee Programs (1979, later raised to the rank of Assistant Secretary for Population, Refugee, and Migration Affairs), Management Operations (1975–), Medical Services (1980–), Combating Terrorism (1976, later changed to the Coordinator for Counter-Terrorism), Foreign Missions, with the rank of Ambassador (1986–), and the Coordinator for International Communications and Information Policy (1984–).

The growth and modification of these principal State Department officers since World War II are illustrated and categorized in Table 7.2.

To summarize, since 1789, in addition to the Secretary of State, more than

Table 7.3
Current Department of State Principal Offices

SECRETARY OF STATE	**Assistant Secretary—Functional, cont.**
Chief of Staff	International Organization Affairs
Executive Assistant to the Secretary	Legislative Affairs
Special Assistant/Executive Secretary	Oceans and International Environmental and
	Scientific Affairs
Deputy Secretary of State	Politico-Military Affairs
	Population, Refugee, and Migration Affairs
Under Secretary	Public Affairs
Arms Control and International Security	Deputy Assistant Sec., Equal Employment
Economic and Agricultural Affairs	Opportunity and Civil Rights
Global Affairs	
Management	**Director/Coordinator**
Political Affairs	Director General of the Foreign Service
	Director, Foreign Service Institute
Assistant Secretary—Geographic Areas	Director, Medical Service
African Affairs	Director, Office of Foreign Missions
East Asian and Pacific Affairs	Director, Policy Planning Staff
European and Canadian Affairs	Coordinator, International Communications
Inter-American Affairs	and Information Policy
Near Eastern Affairs	Coordinator, Counter Terrorism
South Asian Affairs	
	Others
Assistant Secretary—Functional	Chairman, Foreign Service Grievance Board
Administration	Chief Financial Officer
Consular Affairs	Chief of Protocol
Democracy, Human Rights, and Labor	Civil Service Ombudsman
Diplomatic Security	Counselor
Economic and Business Affairs	Executive Sec., Board of the Foreign Service
Intelligence and Research	Inspector General
International Narcotics and Law Enforcement	Legal Adviser

fifty principal offices were created, some of which were retitled, and fifteen of them were superseded or discontinued.[49] Currently, the corps of senior management staff of the Department consists of some 45 senior officers, including the Secretary, as indicated in Table 7.3.

Most such principal officers are supported by a host of subsidiary officials, at times numbering more than 250, plus their staffs. Some individual ranking officers head corps of ten to twenty or more such auxiliary officers,[50] who bear a variety of ranks and titles.[51]

A number of additional features are worthy of note. Several pre-Truman offices remain in existence, although in some cases their titles have been changed.[52] Ten of those created during the Truman Administration also have survived.[53] Currently, as indicated in Table 7.3, aside from the Secretary the principal ranks and titles include the Deputy Secretary, Under Secretary, and Assistant Secretary (for both geographic and functional responsibilities). The rest bear various descriptive titles,[54] three of which serve in a diplomatic representational capacity—the Ambassador at Large and U.S. Representatives to the United Nations and the Organization of American States. Most of those who possess functional responsibilities are concerned with substantive (eighteen), servicing, (seventeen) and Foreign Service (eight) functions. Ambassadors at Large generally are commissioned with specific titles for particular functions.[55]

So far as the nature of appointment of these ranking officers is concerned, they are of two types. Most of them are formally appointed by the President and commissioned. On the other hand, liberalizing the process and reducing the burden on the White House and the Senate, many are appointed by the Secretary of State or are "designated" rather than commissioned. This has applied particularly to such officers as Director of the Foreign Service (prior to 1980), Director of the Foreign Service Institute, Director of Management Operations, Director of the Office for Countering Terrorism, Director of the Office of Medical Services, Director of the Policy Planning Staff, the Executive Secretary, Inspector of the Foreign Service (prior to 1981), and Protocol Officer (prior to 1946).

Of related interest is the number of appointees to these positions who are Foreign Service Officers, which varies with the rank and nature of the office. Over the years nearly half (47 percent) of those appointed to these ranking positions have been careerists, including Deputy Secretary Walter J. Stoessel, Jr. (1952), and approximately 30 percent of the Under Secretaries,[56] nearly 80 percent of the Under Secretaries for Political Affairs, 65 percent of Assistant Secretaries who head the Geographic Bureaus and nearly 45 percent of other Assistant Secretaries, and approximately three-fourths of the Executive Secretaries and the Directors of various offices. On the other hand, only a few Ambassadors at Large and Counselors and no Legal Advisers have been professional Foreign Service Officers.

Beginning with the appointment of Barbara M. Watson as Administrator of the Bureau of Security and Consular Affairs in 1968, at least thirty-five women were commissioned to approximately fifty appointments and served in at least two dozen of these ranking positions, with a substantial increase in the 1990s. She served twice in this capacity (1968–74 and 1977–80). Carol M. Laise also received two appointments, as Assistant Secretary for Public Affairs (1973–75) and Director General of the Foreign Service (1975–77), and Joan M. Clark served as Director of Management Operations (1977–79), Director General of the Foreign Service (1981–83), and Assistant Secretary for Consular Affairs (appointed in 1983). Both of them were career Foreign Service Officers, as were Rozanne L. Ridgway, commissioned as both Counselor and Assistant Secretary for European and Canadian Affairs, and Mary A. Ryan, as Assistant Secretary for Consular Affairs. Multiple appointments of women were also made to the positions of Assistant Secretary for International Narcotics Affairs and for Oceans and International Environmental and Scientific Affairs and as Coordinator for International Communications and Information Policy. The number of women appointees increased substantially in the 1990s.

The most women were appointed to the Office of Chief of Protocol, usually for short periods, including Marion H. Smoke (appointed in 1974), Shirley Temple Black, Edith H. J. Dobelle, Leonore Annenberg, Selwa Roosevelt, and Molly M. Raiser. Other women were commissioned as Under Secretaries for Arms Control and International Security Affairs, Economic and Agricultural Affairs, and Security Assistance, Assistant Secretaries for both two geographic and eight functional offices, and as Director of the Foreign Service Institute, Counselor, Inspector General, Civil Service Ombudsman, and others. In addition, Madeleine K. Albright, who later became Secretary of State, was commissioned to head the U.S. Mission to the United Nations, and Harriet C. Babbit and Gale W. McGhee were appointed as Permanent Representatives to the Organization of American States.[57]

Contemporary Structure of Department of State

Put another way, as illustrated by Figure 7.2, the Department of State currently consists of forty-two primary and subsidiary offices and other components,[58] headed by the Secretary and Deputy Secretary of State, to whom seventeen other officers and units are directly responsible. Some twenty-three of them are grouped under the five Under Secretaries for Arms Control and International Security, Economic and Agricultural, Global, Management, and Political Affairs. Of these, the most comprehensive deal with management (ten agencies), Political Affairs (seven agencies, including the six Geographic and International Organization Affairs), and Global Affairs (four agencies). The Under Secretary for Management is in charge of such matters as administration (general), administration of the Foreign Service, consular affairs and diplomatic security, finance and management policy, and personnel. The Under Secretary for Global Affairs administers four units concerned with Democracy and Human Rights, International Narcotics, Oceans and the International Environment, and Population, Refugees, and Migration.

Eleven other separate components are not responsible to the Under Secretaries. These include such officers as the Chief of Protocol, Chief of Staff, Executive Secretary, Legal Adviser, and Inspector General of the Department, as well as the Coordinator for Counterterrorism and the units concerned with Equal Employment Opportunity and Civil Rights, Intelligence and Research, Legislative Affairs, Policy Planning, and Public Affairs. The Counselor, Bureau of Communications and Information Policy, and the Office of Policy, Planning, and Budget are not included in the chart.

The principal components below the Offices of the Secretary, Deputy Secretary, and Under Secretaries are titled bureaus, of which there are six that deal with geographic areas, eighteen that concern functional responsibilities, and four offices, plus the Foreign Service Institute and the Policy Planning Council or Staff. Other units include the Offices of the Chief of Protocol, Chief of Staff, Counselor, Director of the Foreign Service, Executive Secretary, Inspector General, and Legal Adviser. Many of these components comprise lesser units, gen-

Figure 7.2
Department of State Organization

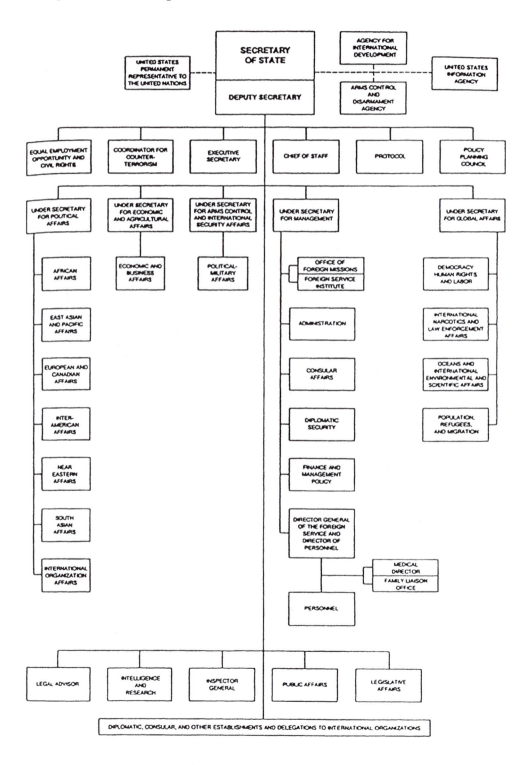

erally called divisions, which usually are headed by chiefs, directors, or special assistants. This fundamental structural pattern, which began to coalesce in the 1980s and was refined in the 1990s, is logical and is likely to prevail. But, as in the past, specific numbers, titles, functions, and allocation of individual components will change to satisfy developing departmental and international problems, needs, and responsibilities.

The functions of many of these officers, bureaus, and offices are obvious, such as those concerned with administration (general), counterterrorism, economic and business affairs, employee relations, finance and management policy, refugees and migration, and others. However, several require elucidation. The Office of the Secretary is described by the Department of State as embracing the Deputy Secretary, the Under Secretaries, Assistant Secretaries, Counselor, Legal Adviser, and Inspector General. The Chief of Protocol holds a unique position as adviser to the U.S. Government, the President, the Vice President, and the Secretary of State on matters of diplomatic propriety and procedure governed by law and international custom and practice. The Legal Adviser provides counsel and advice on international law matters to the President, the Secretary, and the American overseas posts. The Counselor is a special consultant and adviser on major policy and conducts special international negotiations as directed by the Secretary. The Inspector General arranges, directs, and conducts independent and systematic inspections, investigations, assessments, and audits of departmental bureaus and offices, U.S. foreign missions, and other American overseas posts.

The Office of the Director General of the Foreign Service and the Bureaus of Consular Affairs and Diplomatic Security are patently concerned with diplomatic, consular, and other personnel and their service abroad. That dealing with consular affairs handles shipping matters, the enforcement of American immigration and nationality laws, and the issuance of passports and visas, and it is also responsible for promoting the welfare of American citizens and interests abroad. The Office of Diplomatic Security, supported by an Overseas Security Advisory Council, is charged with providing a secure environment and personal security awareness for the conduct of American diplomacy abroad. The Office of Medical Services develops, manages, and staffs a worldwide health care system for U.S. officers, employees, and eligible dependents of the Department of State and fifty other foreign affairs agencies residing abroad.

The Bureau of Politico-Military Affairs affords guidance and coordinates policy formulation on national security issues, including such matters as nonproliferation of weapons of mass destruction and missile technology, weapons control and security assistance, and weapons export control. The Geographic Regional Bureaus are responsible for U.S. relations with individual countries and their regional interrelations, and the Assistant Secretaries who head them serve to chair the interdepartmental groups in the National Security Council system. The Bureau of International Organization Affairs manages U.S. participation in both international organizations and conferences and the development, coordination, and implementation of American multilateral policy. The Bureau of Oceans and Environmental and Scientific Affairs has primary responsibility for the Department's development and implementation of policies and proposals for the scientific and technological aspects of American relations with other governments and international organizations, including issues and problems pertaining to the environment, oceans, outer space, fisheries, and related matters.

Two agencies focus largely on domestic matters. The Bureau of Legislative Affairs (previously titled Congressional Relations) supervises and coordinates all legislative activities, except administrative matters, that affect Congress, the Department of State, and other Federal executive agencies. The Bureau of Public Affairs disseminates information on foreign relations to the American people, advises the Department on public concerns, produces and distributes publications of various types, including the *Foreign Relations* series, and serves in a liaison capacity with State and local officials. On the other hand, the Bureau of International Communications and Information Policy, not included in the chart, furnishes general and technical advice on multilateral and bilateral international telecommunications issues affecting American foreign affairs and national security, and it coordinates, with other U.S. Government agencies and the private sector, the framing and implementation of policies and practices relating to developing communications and information technologies.

As American foreign interests and needs evolve, and international issues emerge and change, and as Secretaries and other ranking members of the State Department determine, the structure, titles, and functions of departmental components will mutate, but the basic pattern of both their structure and relationship has been established and refined during the past half century. Self-assessment and review of these matters by the Department, the White House, and Congress will continue to influence future developments. These are more likely to pertain to details of configuration, elevating or restricting specific departmental components, or realigning particular offices, functions, or responsibilities. More serious are the degree to which other Executive agencies dealing with foreign affairs mesh or conflict with the State Department and the personnel factor involving the extent to which Presidents appoint outsiders to the upper levels of the Department that disaffect the professional Foreign Service.

Administration, Reorganization, and Reform

After Germany and Japan surrendered, ending World War II, the Department of State was confronted with the problem of realigning American policies, agencies, authorities, and personalities developed during the war years and with considerable criticism of the organization and management of the Department. Its problems were accentuated by the augmentation of ministerial diplomacy, which involved long periods of personal negotiations of the Secretary of State in the United States and abroad. The State Department needed to reorganize its structural mechanism for converting its wartime temporary expansion due to requirements for coping with World War II requirements (including many wartime, often uncoordinated agencies); for revising the host of agencies concerned with the conduct of foreign relations abroad; for realigning the Department's bureaus, offices, divisions, sections, and other units; for effecting an integrated relationship between traditional diplomatic and consular functions; for focusing responsibility and authority in the Department; for expediting means of achieving action; and for establishing closer amalgamation of State Department and Foreign Service personnel and more effective administrative direction of overseas personnel.

This extensive review and the reform that followed focused on a variety of substantive, structural, and procedural issues, practices, agencies and personnel. They concerned general matters of reform and reorganization of its management and administration; State Department relations with the President, Congress, the National Security Council, and other Departments and agencies concerned with foreign affairs; processes of liaison and coordination; the handling of policy making and implementation; creation of additional departmental agencies and services, including such separate units as an Executive Secretariat, a Policy Planning Staff, specialized Desks and Country Teams, and agencies to deal with public affairs and the media; and State Department, Foreign Service, and staffing personnel. In addition, attention was devoted to coping with such emerging matters as diplomatic security and terrorism, human rights, narcotics, and oceans and environmental and scientific affairs.

Although no new basic or organic laws were enacted to institute major structural and administrative reform of the State Department, changes were instituted piecemeal. For example, Acts of May 26, 1949 (63 Stat. 111) and August 5, 1955 (69 Stat. 536), respectively, increased the number of Assistant Secretaries to ten (two of whom might be designated as Deputy Under Secretaries) and later provided for three Under Secretaries. An Act of August 1, 1956 (70 Stat. 890), stipulated the fundamental authority of the Department and established its Working Capital Fund. Two years later, an Act of July 18, 1958 (72 Stat. 363), dealt with revising the senior organization and administration of the Department, providing for the Secretary, an Under Secretary, a second Under Secretary specifically for Economic Affairs, eleven Assistant Secretaries, and other senior officers. An Act of July 13, 1972 (86 Stat. 490), authorized the creation of the Office of Deputy Secretary of State, and a few years later an Act of October 7, 1978 (92 Stat. 963), redefined State Department organization and administration, providing for the Office of Deputy Secretary, three Under Secretaries (for Political, Economic, and Management affairs), thirteen Assistant Secretaries, and other principal officers, and it authorized the Secretary to promulgate rules and regulations to implement the functions and responsibilities of the Department. This structuring of the leadership of the Department was altered in the 1980s and 1990s. In addition, several Executive Orders, beginning in 1954, formalized the arrangement for a temporary Acting Secretary in case of the illness, absence, resignation, or death of the Secretary and in 1982 empowered the Secretary to specify the order of such succession of Acting Secretaries.

Other legislation dealt with the specific functional aspects of the Secretary and Department of State. For example, the Freedom of Information Act of July 4, 1966 (80 Stat. 250), authorized public access to certain official State Department documents. Later, the Diplomatic Security and Antiterrorism Act of August 27, 1986 (100 Stat. 853), established a Diplomatic Security Service to deal with international terrorism, multilateral cooperation to combat it, and criminal punishment of terrorists. Other acts dealt with such matters as the new home of the Department, funding the acquisition and maintenance of American diplomatic and consular offices and residential facilities abroad, the reception and disposition by American officials of gifts and decorations from foreign governments and institutions, the production and publication of the *Foreign Relations of the United States* series, and the creation of new agencies, such as the U.S. Institute of Peace for scholarly inquiry and research.

Modernization and improvement of the State Department were subjected to nearly fifty official and quasi-official, as well as many unofficial, studies on administrative and personnel reform of both the Department and the Foreign Service since 1945, but in some cases they also dealt with broader issues of organization, management, and Federal staffing, listed in Table 7.4, Part A. These studies evoked scores of formal reports and literary commentaries. In addition to those undertaken by the State Department, these were prepared by the Presidential Office and White House Staff, the Bureau of the Budget, the Senate and House of Representatives, and various private institutions, organizations, and individuals.[59] Many of these reform studies and proposals deal with the organization of the White House staff, interagency coordination, and personnel (both the Civil Service and Foreign Service and their interrelations), and others focus specifically on the State Department and Foreign Service. Table 7.4, Part B, lists the major official and unofficial analyses and commentaries pertaining to State Department organization, reorganization, management, administration, and personnel.

When Byrnes became Secretary of State in July 1945, he launched an extensive postwar review of the Department by requesting the Director of the Bureau of the Budget to provide him with an assessment of State Department problems and recommendations for modernizing its organization and administration. The following month the Director submitted his report, which focused largely on several personnel cleavages—that pertaining to the Departmental Service in Washington, staffed by Civil Service employees, and the Foreign Service, administered independently as a separate personnel system, and that within the Foreign Service, involving both career Foreign Service Officers and the wartime appointees constituting the Foreign Service Auxiliary. A second cleavage pertained to separate State Department agencies that administered these personnel systems, so that the Secretary possessed no single personnel or planning office

Table 7.4
Studies and Commentaries on Reorganization and Reform of the Department of State and Foreign Service since 1945

A. Studies on Management and Administration

Bureau of the Budget, Commission on Organization and Administration of State Department, 1945

State Department, Combining State Department and Foreign Service Personnel

State Department, Combining State Department and Foreign Service Personnel Gradually (Selden Chapin and Andrew B. Foster Report), 1945

State Department, Combining State Department and Foreign Service Personnel (O. L. Nelson), 1946

Congress, House of Representatives, Foreign Affairs Committee, Reorganization of the Foreign Service, 1946

State Department, Reorganization of the State Department (John E. Peurifoy), 1948

Brookings Institution, Governmental Mechanism for the Conduct of Foreign Relations (Leo Pasvolsky), 1949

Commission on the Organization of the Executive Branch of the Government (1st Herbert Hoover Commission), Task Force and general reports, 1949

Congress, House of Representatives, Committee on Foreign Affairs, Organization and Administration of the State Department, 1949

State Department, Secretary of State's Advisory Group on Amalgamation of the State Department and Foreign Service, 1949

State Department, Secretary of State's Advisory Committee on Personnel (James H. Rowe, Jr., Committee), 1950

Brookings Institution, Administration of Foreign Affairs and Overseas Operations (for Bureau of the Budget), 1951

Congress, House of Representatives, Committee on Foreign Affairs, State Department Personnel Improvement Plan, 1951

Congress, Senate, Committee on Government Operations, Overseas Activities of the Government, 1951

Woodrow Wilson Foundation, Organization and Control of Foreign Policy (William Y. Elliott), 1952

President, Advisory Committee on Government Organization (Nelson A. Rockefeller Committee), 1953

White House, Foreign Affairs Personnel Task Force, Foreign Affairs Personnel System (2d Hoover Commission), 1954

State Department, Public Committee on Personnel (Henry M. Wriston Committee), Toward a Stronger Foreign Service, 1954

White House, Task Force on Foreign Relations Personnel) Philip Young and Henry Dulton), 1954

Commission on the Organization of the Executive Branch of the Government, Personnel Management and Overseas Economic Operations (2d Hoover Commission), 1955

Congress, House of Representatives, Committee on Government Operations, Administration of Overseas Personnel, 1955

Congress, Senate, Report by Senator Alexander Wiley on Foreign Service Abroad, 1955

Table 7.4 (continued)

The American Assembly, Panels on Representation of the United States Abroad at 9th Assembly, 1956

President, Personnel Systems (Philip Young Proposal), 1957

President, Advisory Committee on Government Organization (Nelson A. Rockefeller Committee), 1957

Executive Office, Office of Personnel Management (Rocco C. Siciliano Proposal), 1959

Congress, Senate, Committee of Foreign Relations, Administration of State Department and Foreign Service, 1959

Syracuse University, Maxwell Graduate School, Operational Aspects of U.S. Foreign Policy (for Senate Foreign Relations Committee), 1959

Executive Office, Office of Executive Management (Nelson A. Rockefeller Proposal), 1960

Brookings Institution, Formulation and Administration of Foreign Policy (H. Field Haviland, Jr.), 1960

Congress, Senate, Committee on Government Operations, Subcommittee on Organization for National Security (Henry M. Jackson), 3 vols., 1961

State Department, ACCORD—Action for Organizations Development (William J. Crockett), 1961–67

State Department, Committee on Foreign Affairs Personnel, Personnel for the New Diplomacy (Christian H. Herter Committee), 1962

Carnegie Endowment for International Peace, six Foreign Service and Foreign Affairs Personnel Studies, 1964–66

Congress, Senate, Committee on Government Operations, Subcommittee on National Security Staffing and Operations (Henry M. Jackson), 1965

Brookings Institution, Making U.S. Foreign Policy (Burton M. Sapin), 1966

Task Forces on Coping with Overseas Problems and Interdepartmental Coordination (Maxwell D. Taylor), 1966

President, Task Force on Organization for Foreign Affairs (Heineman Task Force), 1967

American Foreign Service Association, Toward a Modern Diplomacy, 1967–68

President, Advisory Council on Executive Organization (Roy Ash Council), 1969

Institute of Defense Analysis, Management of National Security (Keith C. Clark and Lawrence J. Legere), 1969

State Department, Task Force on State Department Management Reform (William B. Macomber, Jr.), 1970

White House, President Richard M. Nixon, U.S. Policy for the 1970's: Report to Congress (4 vols.), 1970–73

Congress, Senate, Foreign Relations Committee, Foreign Service Grievance Procedures, 1972

State Department, Bureaucracy and Organization of the State Department (Donald P. Warwick), 1975

State Department, Commission on Organization of the Government for the Conduct of Foreign Policy (Robert D. Murphy), Report plus 7 vols. of Appendixes, 1975–76

Congress, House of Representatives, Committee on International Relations, Subcommittee on International Operations, Survey of Proposals to Reorganize Foreign Affairs Agencies (1951–75), 1977

State Department, Task Force to Produce a Revised Model for Managing Foreign Affairs, 1992

B. Selected Commentaries on Management and Administration

1. Official and Quasi-Official Commentaries

Bureau of the Budget, "The Organization and Administration of the Department of State," Aug. 15, 1945, unpublished memorandum at the request of Secretary James F. Byrnes.

Foster, Andrew B. "Examination of the Proposal to Combine the Foreign Service and the Department of State," Sept. 14, 1945, unpublished memorandum.

Chapin, Selden, "A Plan for a Single Service Under the Secretary of State," Oct. 31, 1945, unpublished memorandum.

Nelson, O. L., *Report on the Organization of the Department of State* (Wash.: Department of State, 1946), 89 p.

Congress, House of Representatives, Committee on Foreign Affairs, *Reorganization of the Foreign Service* (Wash.: Government Printing Office, 1946), 230 p.

Peurifoy, John E. "Reorganization of the Department of State," May 6, 1948, memorandum to Secretary George C. Marshall.

Brookings Institution, *Governmental Mechanism for the Conduct of United States Foreign Relations* (Wash.: Brookings Institution, 1949), 58 p.

Bundy, Harvey H., and James G. Rogers, *The Organizations of the Government for the Conduct of Foreign Affairs: A Report with Recommendations Prepared for the Commission on Organization of the Executive Branch of the Government* (Wash.: Government Printing Office, 1949), 134 p.

Commission on Organization of the Executive Branch of the Government (Hoover Commission), *Foreign Affairs: A Report to the Congress . . .* (Wash.: Government Printing Office, 1949), 77 p., and *Task Force Report on Foreign Affairs* (Appendix H), (Wash.: Government Printing Office, 1949), 134 p.

Congress, House of Representatives, Committee on Foreign Affairs, *To Strengthen and Improve the Organization and Administration of the Department of State* (Wash.: Government Printing Office, 1949), 80 p., and *Reorganization of the Department of State* (Wash.: Government Printing Office, 1949), 17 p.

State Department, *Facts and Issues Relating to the Amalgamation of the Department of State and the Foreign Service* (Wash.: Government Printing Office, 1949).

Secretary of State's Advisory Committee on Personnel, *An Improved Personnel System for the Conduct of Foreign Affairs* (Wash.: Government Printing Office, 1950), 43 p. and appendixes (Rowe Committee Report).

Brookings Institution, *The Administration of Foreign Affairs and Overseas Operations* (Wash.: Brookings Institution, 1951), 30 p.

Congress, House of Representatives, Committee on Foreign Affairs, *An Analysis of the Personnel Improvement Plan of the Department of State* (Wash.: Government Printing Office, 1951), 68 p.

State Department, "Directive to Improve the Personnel Program of the Department of State and the Unified Foreign Service of the United States" (Wash.: Department of State, 1951).

Congress, Senate, Committee on Government Operations, *Administration of Overseas Activities of the Government* (Wash.: Government Printing Office, 1951), 79 p.

Elliott, William, Y., et al., *United States Foreign Policy: Its Organization and Control* (N.Y.: Columbia University Press, 1952), 288 p., prepared by group of Woodrow Wilson Foundation.

State Department, *Toward a Stronger Foreign Service: Report of the Secretary of State's*

Table 7.4 (continued)

Public Committee on Personnel (Wash.: Government Printing Office, 1954), 70 p. (Wriston Committee Report).

White House Personnel Task Force, "A Foreign Affairs Personnel System" (Wash.: 1954), prepared by President's Adviser on Personnel Management Philip Young.

Commission on Organization of the Executive Branch of the Government (2d Hoover Commission), *Overseas Economic Operations* (Wash.: Government Printing Office, 1955), 854 p.

Congress, House of Representatives, Committee on Foreign Affairs, *The Foreign Service: Basic Information on Organization, Administration and Personnel* (Wash.: Government Printing Office, 1955).

Congress, House of Representatives, Committee on Government Operations, *Administration of Overseas Personnel* (Wash.: Government Printing Office, 1955), 4 parts in 2 vols.

Wiley, Alexander, *The United States Foreign Service* (Wash.: Government Printing Office, 1955), 23 p.

Congress, Senate, *Recruitment and Training for the Foreign Service*, Staff Study (Wash.: Government Printing Office, 1958).

State Department, *Career Opportunities in the Foreign Service* (Wash.: Government Printing Office, 1958).

State Department, *The Foreign Service of the United States* (Wash.: Government Printing Office, 1958).

Congress, Senate, Committee on Foreign Relations, *Administration of the Department of State and the Foreign Service* (Wash.: Government Printing Office, 1959), 240 p.

Syracuse University, Maxwell Graduate School of Citizenship and Public Affairs, *United States Foreign Policy: The Operational Aspects of United States Foreign Policy* (Wash.: Government Printing Office, 1959), 73 p., prepared at request of Senate Foreign Relations Committee.

Congress, Senate, Committee on Foreign Relations, *Administration of the Department of State* (Wash.: Government Printing Office, 1960).

Brookings Institution, *The Formulation and Administration of United States Foreign Policy* (Wash.: Brookings Institution, 1960), 191 p., prepared by H. Field Haviland, Jr., ed.

Congress, Senate, Committee on Government Operations, *Organizing for National Security* (Wash.: Government Printing Office, 1961), 3 vols., Senator Henry M. Jackson's subcommittee reports.

State Department, Committee on Foreign Affairs Personnel, *Personnel for the New Diplomacy* (Wash.: Carnegie Endowment, 1962), 161 p., Herter Committee Report.

Congress, Senate, Committee on Government Operations, *Administration of National Security* (Wash.: Government Printing Office, 1965), 600 p., Senator Henry M. Jackson's subcommittee reports.

Brookings Institution, *The Making of United States Foreign Policy* (Wash.: Brookings Institution, 1966 and N.Y.: Praeger, 1966), 425 p., prepared by Burton M. Sapin.

State Department, *A Management Program for the Department of State, Office of the Deputy Under Secretary for Administration* (Wash.: Department of State, 1966), summary of studies and reform launched by William J. Crockett.

President's Task Force on Government Administration (Wash.: unpublished report, 1967), prepared by Heineman Task Force.

American Foreign Service Association, *Toward a Modern Diplomacy* ... (Wash.: American Foreign Service Association, 1968), 185 p., prepared by committee chaired by Ambassador Graham Martin.

Clark, Keith C., and Laurence J. Legere, eds., *The President and the Management of National Security* (N.Y.: Praeger, 1969), 274 p., sponsored by the Institute for Defense Analysis.

State Department, *Diplomacy for the 70's: A Program of Management Reform for the Department of State* (Wash.: Government Printing Office, 1970), 610 p., prepared by Deputy Under Secretary William B. Macomber, Jr., at the request of Secretary Rogers.

Congress, Senate, Committee on Foreign Relations, *Background Material on Foreign Service Grievance Procedures* (Wash.: Government Printing Office, 1972), 89 p.

Commission on the Organization of the Government for the Conduct of Foreign Policy, *Commission on the Organization of the Government for the Conduct of Foreign Policy, June 1975* (Wash.: Government Printing Office, 1975–76), chaired by retired Ambassador at Large Robert D. Murphy, consisting of the report of 278 p. plus 7 vols. containing 24 Appendixes, totaling 2,724 p.

Congress, House of Representatives, Committee on International Relations, *Survey of Proposals to Reorganize the U.S. Foreign Affairs Agencies, 1951–1975* (Wash.: Government Printing Office, 1977), 70 p.

State Department, *State 2000: A New Model for Managing Foreign Affairs* (Wash.: Government Printing Office, 1992).

2. Other Commentaries

Acheson, Dean G., "The Eclipse of the State Department," *Foreign Affairs*, 49 (July 1971): pp. 593–606.

American Assembly, *The Representation of the United States Abroad* (N.Y.: Columbia University, Graduate School of Business, 1956), 217 p.

Barnes, William, and John Heath Morgan, *The Foreign Service of the United States* ... (Wash.: Department of State, 1961), 430 p.

Bolles, Blair, "Reorganizing the State Department," *Foreign Policy Reports*, 23 (Aug. 1947): 134–43.

Campbell, John Franklin, *The Foreign Affairs Fudge Factory* (N.Y.: Basic Books, 1971), 292 p.

Cheever, Daniel S., and H. Field Haviland, "Hoover Commission: A Symposium—Foreign Affairs." *American Political Science Review*, 43 (Oct. 1949): 966–78.

Childs, James Rives, *The American Foreign Service* (N.Y.: Holt, 1948), 261 p.

Elder, Robert E., *Overseas Representation and Services for Federal Domestic Agencies* (Wash.: Carnegie Endowment, 1965), 106 p.

Elliott, William Y., "The Control of Foreign Policy in the United States," *Political Quarterly*. 20 (Oct. 1949): 337–51.

Evans, A. E., "Reorganization of the American Foreign Service," *International Affairs* 24 (Apr. 1948): 206–17.

Fesler, James W., "Administrative Literature and the Second Hoover Commission Reports," *American Political Science Review*, 51 (Mar. 1957): 135–57.

Fielder, Frances, and Godfrey Harris, *The Quest for Foreign Affairs Officers—Their Recruitment and Selection* (Wash.: Carnegie Endowment, 1966), 63 p.

Goehlert, R. V., and Ed Hoffmeister, *The Department of State and American Diplomacy* (N.Y.: 1986).

Table 7.4 (continued)

Harr, John E., *The Anatomy of the Foreign Service—A Statistical Profile* (Wash.: Carnegie Endowment, 1965), 89 p.

———, *The Development of Careers in the Foreign Service* (Wash.: Carnegie Endowment, 1965), 104 p.

Jackson, Henry M., "Organizing for Survival," *Foreign Affairs*, 38 (Apr. 1960): 446–56.

Jones, Arthur G., *The Evolution of Personnel Systems for U.S. Foreign Affairs: A History of Report Efforts* (Wash.: Carnegie Endowment, 1964), 136 p.

Kennan, George F., "The Future of American Professional Diplomacy," *Foreign Affairs*, 33 (July 1955): 566–86.

Kennedy, Aubrey L., "Reorganization of the Foreign Service," *Quarterly Review* 566 (Oct. 1945): 397–413.

Laves, Walter H. C., and Francis O. Wilcox, "The Reorganization of the Department of State," *American Political Science Review* 38 (Apr. 1944): 289–301.

———, "Organizing the Government for Participation in World Affairs," *American Political Science Review* 38 (Oct. 1944): 913–30.

———, "The State Department Continues Its Reorganization," *American Political Science Review* 39 (Apr. 1945): 309–17.

McCamy, James L., *The Administration of American Foreign Affairs* (N.Y.: Knopf, 1950), 374 p.

———, *The New Diplomacy* (N.Y.: Harper and Row, 1964), 303 p.

Macmahon, Arthur W., "Administration and Foreign Policy," *University of Illinois Bulletin* 54, no. 44 (1957, entire issue).

Macomber, William B., Jr., "Change in Foggy Bottom: An Anniversary Report on Management Reform and Modernization in the Department of State," *Department of State Bulletin* 66 (Feb. 14, 1972): 206–12.

———, "Diplomacy for the Seventies: A Program of Management Reform for the Department of State," *Department of State Bulletin* 63 (Dec. 28, 1970): 775–93.

———, "Management Strategy: A Program for the Seventies," *Department of State Bulletin* 62 (Feb. 2, 1970): 130–41.

Maddox, William P., "The Foreign Service in Transition," *Foreign Affairs* 25 (Jan. 1947): 303–13.

Mosher, Frederick C., "Personnel Management in Foreign Affairs," *Public Personnel Review* 12 (Oct. 1951): 175–86.

Myers, Denys P., and Charles F. Ransom, "Reorganization of the State Department," *American Journal of International Law* 31 (Oct. 1937): 713–20.

Plischke, Elmer, *Conduct of American Diplomacy*, 3d ed. (Princeton: Van Nostrand, 1967), 677 p.

Saltzman, Charles E., "Progress Report on the Wriston Committee Recommendations," *Foreign Service Journal* 32 (Jan. 1955): 18–21, 42.

———, "The Reorganization of the American Foreign Service," *Department of State Bulletin* 31 (Sept. 1954): 436–44.

———, *The Reorganization of the American Foreign Service . . .* (Wash.: Government Printing Office, 1954), 446 p.

Schulzinger, Robert D., *The Making of the American Diplomatic Mind . . .* (Middletown, Conn.: Wesleyan University Press, 1975), 237 p.

Simpson, Smith, *Anatomy of the State Department* (Boston: Houghton Mifflin, 1967), 285 p.

———, *The Crisis in American Diplomacy* (North Quincy, Mass.: Christopher, 1980), 324 p.

Steiner, Zara S., *The State Department and the Foreign Service: The Wriston Report— Four Years Later* (Princeton: Princeton University Center for International Studies, 1958), 57 p.

Walker, Lannon, "Our Foreign Affairs Machinery: Time for an Overhaul," *Foreign Affairs* 47, (Jan. 1969): 309–20.

Walther, Regis, *Orientations and Behavioral Styles of Foreign Service Officers* (Wash.: Carnegie Endowment, 1965), 52 p.

Warwick, Donald P., *A Theory of Public Bureaucracy: Politics, Personality, and Organization in the State Department* (Cambridge: Harvard University Press, 1975), 242 p.

Note: For additional bibliographic listing, see Plischke, *U.S. Foreign Relations: A Guide to Information Sources*, pp. 174–78, 194– 214, 224–36, 547–48.

for the Department as a whole. Another distinction applied to the disparity between the geographic and functional units of the Department and their respective officers and staffs.

While the Budget Bureau did not prescribe solutions to these problems, it proposed that they be studied by the Department and that, in the interim, the Secretary achieve greater unity by consolidating managerial facilities and a unified system of personnel management, with an Under Secretary to serve as the Secretary's general surrogate at the highest level, and that a Deputy Under Secretary function as chief administrator of the Department. But it was not until 1947 that Assistant Secretary for Administration John E. Peurifoy was designated as Under Secretary for Administration, and the title of the office was not broadened to "Management" until 1971.

The next major study, undertaken by the Commission on Organization of the Government, headed by former President Herbert Hoover, provided for by law enacted in 1947, examined the entire machinery of the Executive Branch of the Government for the conduct of foreign affairs, with particular reference to the organization and administration of the State Department. Emphasizing the greatly expanded role of the United States in world affairs and noting that handling their administration had become the responsibility of the Government as a whole,[60] its report recommended in 1949 that, to reform and improve the foreign relations activities of American Executive agencies, the President should appoint Cabinet committees in crucial areas of external relations where issues transcended the responsibility of a single Department and where the President's consideration and/ or decision was necessary, subject to the reservation that the State Department remained the basic staff arm and coordinating agency of the President.[61]

So far as foreign relations are concerned, the Commission proposed that the State Department concentrate on the specification of foreign affairs objectives and the formulation of foreign policy and that it should coordinate overseas implementation of the functions of other Executive agencies but that it should not itself become a primary or sole operational agency abroad. It also sought to moderate the burdens placed on the Secretary and Under Secretary of State, reduce the number of organizational units, eliminate certain operational functions, simplify the assignment of work, target responsibility, and speed up action. On the critical matter of personnel it suggested that the permanent officers of the State Department in Washington and of the Foreign Service above a certain rank level be amalgamated during a short period of a few years into a single Foreign Affairs Service to serve both in Washington and abroad and that it be administered separately from the Civil Service. Based on this report, several changes were made to augment and regularize the staff of the State Department, as provided for by the Act of May 1949, and the authority of the Department's Geographic Offices was enhanced, administered by four separate units, each captained by an Assistant Secretary.

The Secretary of State's Committee on Personnel, chaired by James H. Rowe, Jr. (who had been a member of the Hoover Commission), was appointed in December 1949 to consider and report on the matter of amalgamating senior State Department and Foreign Service Officers. Known as the "Rowe Committee," it consisted of three members (including one career Foreign Service Officer, William E. DeCourcy) and reported to the Secretary by the end of July 1950. It recommended that there should be a single, flexible personnel system to replace the existing dual or separate arrangement of Civil Service and Foreign Service Officers. The report proposed that this unified system consist of two echelons, an officer corps embracing both generalists and specialists and a clerical and technical staff to provide supporting and auxiliary services, to be instituted gradually.

These proposals were supported by an independent survey of more than 2,000 State Department and Foreign Service members. In March 1951, Secretary Acheson issued a directive, called the Personnel Improvement Plan, which was intended to promote voluntary interchange of Department and Foreign Service personnel, stimulate for three years the personnel of other agencies to undertake lateral entry into the Foreign Service Reserve, and encourage State Department employees to serve abroad for two years while replacing them with the assignment of Foreign Service Officers for temporary duty in Washington. This program met with only modest success, and the situation was exacerbated by the application of a stringent reduction in force of both State Department and Foreign Service personnel.

Based on some of the recommendations of the Rowe Committee, in March 1951 the State Department issued a directive providing for a comprehensive Personnel Improvement Plan. It dealt with partial integration of Departmental and Foreign Service personnel and some interchange of headquarters and field assignments. It also provided for the systematic determination of personnel categories; identifying requirements for Foreign Service, Reserve, and Staff Officers; invigorating efforts for recruitment of junior Foreign Service Officers; establishing a lateral entry program; devising improved methods of assignment, development, and utilization of personnel; and instituting a process tailored to involve greater recognition of executive qualities among senior officers, including specialists as well as generalists. The implementation of this program was limited, in part, by lack of a sense of urgency and dedication to achieve its purposes and expectations.

A few years later, early in 1954, Secretary Dulles appointed a Public Committee on Personnel, headed by Dr. Henry M. Wriston, the President of Brown University, to examine the organization of the Department and Foreign Service and to make recommendations for improving the "professional service" to handle the increased foreign responsibilities of the United States. The committee included Donald Russell, former Assistant Secretary for Administration, and Charles E. Saltzman, Under Secretary for Administration, retired Ambassador Norman Armour, and Assistant Secretary Robert D. Murphy. It considered such issues as the decline in the number of Foreign Service Officers, the degenerating morale of the Foreign Service, the lack of various specializations, the inability to recruit entry-level Foreign Service Officers and insufficiency of later entry, the maintenance of a separate State Department personnel system, and a number of weaknesses of the Foreign Service Institute.

In addition to making recommendations to vitalize the Institute and creating a program of scholarships to recruit officers, the Committee's report, filed in May, proposed that the amalgamation and enlargement of the career Foreign Service embrace State Department Officers, Foreign Service Officers, and certain members of the Foreign Service Reserve and the Foreign Service Staff and that those in the Reserve should be specialists and those providing ordinary staff functions should be confined to clerical, custodial, and technical personnel of lower than officer rank. Thus, the report not only recommended amalgamation— or what came to be known as "Wristonization"—at the officer rank but also identification and retention of nonofficer personnel, regularized duty of Foreign Service Officers in the State Department in Washington, and contingents of specialists as well as generalists in a single Foreign Service corps.

In short, the significance of this development is that Foreign Service, Foreign Service Reserve, and Foreign Service Staff Officers were united in a single personnel system, members of which would be required to serve either at home or abroad in any assignment determined by the Secretary of State. Positions in both the State Department and American missions abroad were specifically designated to which members of the combined Service were to be appointed. Positions at posts abroad that lay outside the Foreign Service and Foreign Service Reserve categories were regarded as Staff Corps positions, the Foreign Service Reserve Corps remained intact, and residual State Department positions continued as Civil Service Officers and other employees. This major "Wristonization" reform was implemented during the following years, but serious administrative difficulties and impediments were encountered. Although in the long run the Foreign Service generally retained its esprit, and doubtless it benefited by the infusion of new blood, this amalgamation of personnel was not regarded as an unmixed blessing, and additional changes were envisioned as necessary to enable the Foreign Service to adjust to varying contemporary responsibilities and to provide essential specialized competence.

The second Hoover Commission on the Executive Branch of the Government, established in 1955, was concerned primarily with the Civil Service and overseas economic operations. Stressing matters of efficiency and economy, it sought to strengthen the position of American Chiefs of Diplomatic Missions in foreign countries, proposing that all personnel assigned overseas (except the military) be included in a unified personnel system. It also suggested that to achieve coordinated unity abroad, all overseas missions and their officers and staffs be incorporated as regular organizational units of American Embassies and Legations, subject to the authority of the Ambassador or Minister.

The next major Department of State study was undertaken in 1961, chaired by Christian A. Herter, former long-time Congressman and Under Secretary and Secretary of State. Designated the Committee on Foreign Affairs Personnel, it consisted of twelve members, including no State Department leaders and only one Foreign Service Officer. It was financed by the Carnegie Endowment for International Peace to study the American diplomatic establishment and its conduct of foreign relations. Its report, entitled *Personnel for the New Diplomacy*, unlike previous studies, focused, in part, on the environment in which diplomacy is conducted and emphasized such matters as organization and integration of the contemporary American diplomatic establishment. Stressing that the Secretary of State is responsible to the President for the administration of all U.S. activities abroad, it recommended that compatible foreign affairs services of the State Department and other agencies (including Civil Service employees) be amalgamated in a single Foreign Service and that it embody all attachés and specialists serving overseas. Presented to Secretary Rusk and published by the Carnegie Endowment in December 1962, apparently, this report produced no major reform movement.

Subsequently, the Herter Committee Report was supplemented by six special studies on the evolution of personnel systems in the United States, overseas representation and services for Federal domestic agencies, development of careers in the Foreign Service, the anatomy of the Foreign Service (presenting a statistical profile), orientations and behavioral styles of Foreign Service Officers, and recruitment and selection of foreign affairs personnel. These monographs were also published by the Carnegie Endowment, 1964–1966.

In the meantime, while Rusk was Secretary of State, careerist William J. Crockett, who joined the State Department in 1951 and a few years later attained Foreign Service Officer status, in which capacity he served for six years and was appointed Assistant Secretary for Administration in 1961 and Deputy Under Secretary for Administration two years later, undertook to produce major, multifaceted State Department reform during the 1960s. His concepts and actions constituted a significant effort to produce a major in-house reform and modernization program, developed independently from the Herter Committee report.

Relying on task forces and consultants, he promoted new and broadened approaches to management and operations, economy of time and personnel, and structural and personnel improvement.

The program he initiated, known as ACCORD—Action for Organization Development—sought to modernize State Department administration, involving progressive planning, programming, budgetary, and information processing techniques, both in Washington and in American missions abroad. He organized workshops to discuss and assess management performance. His primary objectives were to achieve major organizational reorientation, increase and advance methods and effectiveness of problem solving and decision making, and expose State Department and Foreign Service Officers to values and methods of team development. Specifically, he sought to attain administrative decentralization together with greater flexibility of operations abroad, create an office of Management Planning, introduce a rigorous and effective educational and training program for personnel, monitor the performance of personnel by administrative officers, and enhance relations of the Department and Foreign Service with the public. However, although remembered for the "Crockett reforms," he was confronted with considerable resistance to his reforms, failed to achieve enthusiastic support of more senior departmental officials, realized that the norms of his program came to be regarded as incompatible with the traditional Foreign Service culture, suffered decline of support on Capitol Hill, and therefore lacked the prospect of long-range change to serve as the foundation for incremental and permanent improvement.

Also active at this time, seeking to reform the Foreign Service, an unofficial Committee on Principles of the American Foreign Service Association engaged in an independent study and filed a preliminary report with the board of the Association in October 1967 and a final report in August 1968. The committee was composed of eight subcommittees, which were, respectively, concerned with foreign affairs personnel systems, manpower utilization and planning, personnel selection and development, training, openness of the Foreign Service, remuneration and benefits, organization and leadership, and technology and systems analysis. Its objective was to provide a more comprehensive study of modernizing the personnel of the State Department for the 1970s.

Its final report, entitled *Toward a Modern Diplomacy*, sponsored by its Board of Directors and published in 1968 by the Association, consists of a basic analysis of sixty pages, accompanied by eight "working papers" and several documents, a White House announcement, and several other papers concerning overseas interdepartmental matters, totaling 185 pages. It encompassed a comprehensive study of scores of organizational and personnel issues. It espoused the maintenance of a unified Foreign Service to handle the affairs of all foreign relations agencies and made seventeen major recommendations. These concern such matters as White House organization for the conduct of foreign affairs, providing two super-senior assistants to the Secretary of State, presidential mandating of the superior and controlling status of American Ambassadors over all

American agency activities in the countries to which they are accredited, clarifying the statutory independence, nature, and functions of the Board of the Foreign Service, creating manpower planning and utilization mechanism with budgeting responsibility, establishing a single salary schedule for various Foreign Service categories and a uniform system of benefits, and undertaking a thorough study of the applicability of new technologies to the conduct of international affairs.

Despite all the studies and ferment for reform and interagency cooperation and coordination, during the 1960s, some say that the basic components of the conduct of foreign relations remained fundamentally unchanged. Early in the 1970s President Nixon issued four annual White House reports, and the State Department undertook another major study on management reform. The Nixon reports, addressed to Congress, entitled *U.S. Foreign Policy for the 1970's*, published 1970–73 and containing approximately 850 pages, focused, respectively, on a new strategy for peace, building for peace, the emerging structure of peace, and shaping a durable peace. As their titles and subtitles illustrated, these deal primarily with substantive foreign policy matters related to maintaining international peace. They expound the thinking and plans of the President with respect to world affairs, including approximately twenty features providing a composite of goals, national interest, foreign policies, national and international interests and responsibilities.

Although they do not raise the issues of management, administration, and personnel or address the nature and operation of the State Department, the Foreign Service, or diplomatic missions, the President deals with the National Security Council system in the first and last of these reports, which involves the Secretary and Department of State and, more important, fixes the fundamental international goals and agenda of the United States to be pursued by them, for which their organization, administration, and personnel system are responsible during the post–World War II period. These reports are unique in that they laid out in some detail the expectations and the functional and geographic program of the United States in world affairs. Specifically, these include such matters as interdepartmental machinery and other agencies such as the United Nations and the North Atlantic Treaty Organization, international negotiations, economic interrelations and interdependence, conflict resolution and peaceful settlement, aircraft hijacking and sabotage, drugs and international narcotics controls, the global environment, outer space, population growth, disaster relief, and the new dimensions of diplomacy, including technology, the seas and territorial waters, and the exploitation of their resources—all of which involve the State Department and American diplomats.

Addressing itself directly to the matter of organization and staffing for the conduct of American foreign relations, William B. Macomber, Jr., noncareerist who became Assistant Secretary of State in 1957 and was later promoted to Deputy Under Secretary for Administration,[62] undertook a comprehensive and carefully structured in-house review of the State Department and its personnel to implement President Nixon's call for a decade of reform throughout the government. The resulting report, entitled *Diplomacy for the 70's: A Program of Management Reform*, was published in December 1970. It consists of a summary report of thirty pages addressed to Secretary Rogers, which contains a general statement concerning American diplomacy in a changing world, an agenda for reform, and recommendations for the management of foreign affairs, followed by thirteen substantial Task Force studies on a broad range of subjects.[63] These are supplemented by thirty appendixes, plus a general concluding appendix entitled "Management Strategy: A Program for the Seventies," many charts and tables, and a glossary, totaling 610 pages. Led by Macomber, approximately 265 professionals, including some Foreign Service Officers, participated in the project.

The Task Force reports stress management and administration analysis and improvement and deal with such matters as career development and assignment policies, an evaluation system, and management tools. Others are devoted to openness in the foreign affairs community, the roles and functions of diplomatic missions, the office of Country Director, and reorganization of the Foreign Service Institute. Nearly half of the topics reviewed emphasize staffing matters, including personnel requirements and resources, recruitment and appointment, training, performance appraisal, promotion policies, stimulation of creativity, and compensation, allowances, and perquisites.

Among the main conclusions drawn are that the Department of State did not necessitate a radical overhaul of the existing structure but required "the application of a number of practical measures to make the present structure function more effectively"; that its key decision-making levels (the Secretary and Assistant Secretaries) needed to be constituted as control centers in which management functions and the making of decisions are combined (accompanied by what the report calls Strategic Management Centers and supporting Bureau Management Centers); that the Department lacked the skills and essential managerial processes required for efficient contemporary administration; that it needed to advance its managerial capability and to establish and nurture officers to serve as modern "diplomatic managers"; and that for effective reform to succeed, a "new spirit" needed to be inculcated throughout the Department.

The Task Force studies present more than 500 recommendations for change and improvement, most of which the State Department adopted. In some cases they identify suggestions that required or did not require legislative action. Illustrating the many innovations proposed are the necessity to integrate personnel with functions, the importance of attitude and creativity of State Department and Foreign Service Officers, the need for more specialists to complement traditional generalists, the examination and prescription in detail of the role of Country Directors, and the clarification of the various categories of Foreign Service Officers, including those designated as Foreign Service Officers (FSOs), Foreign Service Information Officers (FSIOs), Foreign Service Reserve Officers (FSROs), Foreign Service Reserve Domestic Officers (FSR-DESs), Foreign Service Reserve—Unlimited Officers (FSRUs), and Foreign Service Staff Officers (FSSOs). The report also recommended that the Agency for International Development and the United States Information Agency should be completely integrated with the State Department.

One of the aspects for which the Macomber report is best remembered is its support and refinement of personnel "functional cones," consisting of specialists for administrative-managerial, political, economic-commercial, and consular responsibilities, supplemented by such auxiliary officers as scientists, doctors and nurses, security officers, and the like.[64] As envisaged by the report, assignment would normally extend to certain Foreign Service levels, with those in the highest officer categories recognized as "interfunctional," assigned to upper executive and program development positions.

Two years later, in its Foreign Relations Authorization Act of July 13, 1972 (86 Stat. 497), Congress legislated to establish a Commission on the Organization of the Government for the Conduct of Foreign Policy. It was instructed to study all Departments, agencies, independent establishments, and instrumentalities of the government that participate in the formulation and implementation of foreign policy and to file a comprehensive report, containing its findings and recommendations by June 30, 1974.

Chaired by retired Foreign Service Officer Robert D. Murphy (former Under Secretary of State, Career Ambassador, and member of the earlier Wriston Committee), the Commission consisted of former Senator James B. Pearson as Vice Chairman, ten other members (including three members of Congress and two members who had previous State Department administrative experience), and an Executive Director, Francis O. Wilcox, and a Deputy Executive Director, Fisher Howe. Known as the "Murphy Commission," it undertook a remarkable series of studies, produced a general report, and reviewed more than 450 projects grouped in twenty-four primary, interrelated areas of concern designated as appendixes, which are accompanied by more than 275 addenda, many of which are designated as annexes, and others consist of attachments, case studies, charts, tables, commentaries, and similar supplementary materials, plus occasional documents, interviews, diagrams, flowcharts, and similar materials. Some segments are footnoted or provide lists of sources. The composite package provides a massive study, published in 1975–76, totaling more than 2,700 pages.

Some segments are essays produced by individuals, but most are joint projects contributed by groups of participants under the direction of coordinators, and a few are studies produced by outside institutions, such as the Atlantic Institute for International Affairs and the National Academy of Public Administrations, whereas others are the handiwork of the Commission's own staff members. Aside from Commission participants, more than 150 persons were recruited to contribute to this venture. These consisted of State Department officers and diplomats,[65] members of Congress,[66] White House and National Security Council staff members, a great many academicians and technical experts, and others.[67]

Substantively, this comprehensive project examined, explained, analyzed, and assessed an extensive range of substantive, organizational, and procedural subjects. Only a portion of them concerned primarily the Department of State, the Foreign Service, and specific aspects of diplomacy. These subjects embraced the organization of State Department structural change and improvement, problems of coordination (especially in times of crisis), personnel for international affairs, foreign missions and posts, the role of the Ambassador, and field reporting. Among the more specific subjects treated are Chiefs and Deputy Chiefs of Mission, personnel employment and management, policy planning, overseas manpower systems, assignments abroad, multilateral diplomacy, international conferences and organizations, training and the Foreign Service Institute, and the Country Team.

However, much of this study dealt with broader subjects. To illustrate, these ranged from the nature of the international community, management of global issues, relations of Congress and the Executive, government organizational change and modernization, budgeting for foreign affairs, national security, foreign economic policies and relations, information and intelligence (including clandestine and covert operations), and ethical concerns to the National Security Council, the President's external advisers on foreign affairs and standing advisory bodies, Congressional use of appropriations to control foreign policy and relations, options and decision making, management of alliances, and computer technology as applied to policy making. Additional substantive issues considered varied widely, including international interdependence, arms control, the environment and pollution, nuclear power, population growth, science and technology, space satellites and communications, and international terrorism.

Early in the 1990s the Department of State established another Task Force, composed of Foreign and Civil Service Officers and outside experts to study and propose recommendations for improvement. Its report, entitled *State 2000: A New Model for Managing Foreign Affairs*, was published in 1992. It defined the three traditional roles of the Department as policy formulation respecting international issues, implementation of policy and the conduct of foreign relations, and coordination of major overseas programs and activities. It sponsored an improved interchange and coordinated interrelation of the President and Executive Office with Congress. It also urged a thorough reorganization of the internal structure of the State Department and the merger of the arms control function with the Department, discontinuing the Arms Control and Disarmament Agency.

Internally, the Task Force report espoused major functional restructuring of the Department's bureaus under a redesigned corps of five Under Secretaries for strategic management and program support, economics and the environment, global issues and programs, international security, and regional and multilateral diplomacy. Although the number of Under Secretaries was increased to five in the mid-1990s, their titles differed in that three of them continued to bear responsibility for Management, Economic and Agricultural, and Political Affairs, and the title of the fourth was broadened from International Security to Arms

Control and International Security Affairs. When the fifth was created, as recommended by the Task Force, it was put in charge of Global Affairs. The
position of Deputy Under Secretary had been discontinued by 1980, and by
1996 the relevant Assistant Secretaries and the bureaus they headed were placed
directly under the Under Secretaries.

Supplementing these studies and proposals, committees of Congress also undertook a number of studies, held hearings, and published reports on foreign
policy, modernizing the Department of State and reforming the conduct of foreign relations. A great many other studies, hearings, and reports were produced
and published by Congress. In 1978, for example, it issued *Congress, Information and Foreign Affairs*. Both the Senate and House of Representatives undertook a substantial number of independent investigations sponsored by the
Senate Committees on Foreign Relations and Government Operations and by
the House of Representatives Committees on Foreign Affairs, International Relations, and Government Operations. These are illustrated by the activities of
Senator Henry M. Jackson, who headed a series of Senate Subcommittees on
National Policy Machinery and National Security Staffing and Operations, which
produced a broad spectrum of materials that dealt with the affairs of the State
Department, diplomatic and overseas missions, and relations between Washington and the field. These included not only hearings but also staff studies and
anthologies of documents, essays, reports, and conclusions and recommendations.[68]

This comprehensive undertaking to review, reform, and modernize the Department of State and Foreign Service following World War II was to strengthen
and update them to cope more effectively and economically with postwar and
subsequent international affairs and prepare them for the twenty-first century.
This involved dozens of studies, many Congressional hearings and documents,
scores of official and other reports, hundreds of participants and commentators,
and tens of thousands of pages of published materials, providing a great many
suggestions and recommendations for modifications and improvements. As a
consequence important and minor changes were made in the structure and functioning of the Department, its relations with other Federal Departments and
agencies, and the foreign affairs personnel systems.

Nevertheless, many problems of structure, administration, and staffing continue, which will require future study and resolution. Some of these are common
to all political institutions, while others are unique to the State Department.
Examples of those that transcend the Department include balance between Presidential (political) and career appointments to senior departmental offices in
Washington and representational positions abroad and the coordination of other
governmental civil agencies in Washington and overseas. Those that lie within
the parameters of the State Department embrace such matters as integrating
foreign policy making and implementation, meshing of the nature and allocation
of its major units and subunits, blending of its substantive and management

responsibilites and agencies, allocation and assignment of generalists and specialists, interrelating geographic and functional agencies and their duties, and of diplomatic and consular functions and assignments, and handling such special problems as the status and duties of attachés and comparable American foreign representatives of other Departments and agencies.

Because of the large number of Executive Branch agencies having foreign relations responsibilities and programs, modification and improvement efforts need to focus on coordinating traditional Department of State functions and duties with those of other Departments and agencies. Options range from having the State Department conduct all American foreign affairs both in Washington and abroad, to restricting it to its traditional diplomatic and consular activities, subject to integration of policy matters primarily in Washington, or to some compromise of these extremes.

If the management of all foreign affairs, other than the military, were handled by the State Department, it would need to be converted into a genuine, full-fledged Department of Foreign Affairs, headed by a Secretary of Foreign Affairs who functioned at the Deputy Presidential or Prime Ministerial level in the foreign relations field. This would mean that the Department would need to become operational as well as representational and negotiatory, which has been rejected by some recent reform studies and the traditional attitude of the State Department and other Departments and independent agencies. Short of this conversion to complete integration, however, carefully crafted mechanisms for coordination are essential and must be systematized and monitored to render them workable, efficient, and effective.[69]

Country Desks and Country Directors

For the management of State Department relations with American diplomats abroad, a system of "Country Desks," headed by "Desk Officers," was established in the Geographic Bureaus. Originally, they constituted the base-level agencies for dealing with the panoply of issues relating to individual foreign governments. The work of these Desk Officers was coordinated by Directors of the respective Departmental Offices ranked under Assistant Secretaries, Under Secretaries, and so on up the chain of command to the Secretary of State.

By this arrangement decisions were frequently initiated at the desk level and were confirmed, modified, or rejected by higher ranks of authority, so that the geographic desks became the pivotal Departmental units for dealing with American Chiefs of Mission abroad. In time, this system was augmented with Deputy Assistant Secretaries for geographic subregions and Country Directors in charge of the Desk Officers. In day-to-day dealings the Assistant Secretary acted as the Ambassador's opposite number in the Department of State. Among the principal problems and weaknesses of this system were the relatively low rank of the country Desk Officers (generally midgrade Foreign Service Officers), the com-

plexity of layering of staff members and their varying authority, the need for
the State Department to deal effectively with the tripling of foreign governments,
and the requirement of coordinating geographic and substantive issues.

So far as the structuring of this arrangement is concerned, to elevate the
management of the Country Desks and reduce intermediate layering, the Country
Directorate system was inaugurated in the mid-1960s. It consists of a senior
officer (usually a top-grade Foreign Service Officer), called the Country Director, charged with the affairs of each foreign country, some of whom are responsible for related groups of countries. They may be assisted by one or more
deputies. The Country Director normally possesses prior experience in the geographic area concerned, has the authority and prestige of other Departmental
Office Directors, and is directly responsible to the Assistant Secretary of State.
This is designed to eliminate not only the layering of personnel that permeated
the earlier system but also the burdensome problems of intermediate clearance.
The primary goal and advantage of this innovation are the establishment of a
ranking and effective departmental base of operations upon which American
Chiefs of Mission and their Embassies can rely for policy guidance and program
devisement, direction, and implementation abroad.[70]

Department of State Appropriations

During this period since World War II, the financing of American foreign
relations also mushroomed. The overall expenditures of the Department of State
increased from approximately $24 million in 1940 to more than $350,855,000
by 1950 and then declined to $246,625,000 by 1960. According to *Congres-
sional Quarterly Almanac* annual reports, during subsequent years, departmental
appropriations mounted substantially each year, except for six years (fiscal years
1964, 1967, 1968, 1979, 1994, and 1996). They grew to nearly $400 million
by 1963, reached more than $.5 billion by 1973, and jumped to $1 billion four
years later. Eventually, they reached $1.5 billion by 1981, advanced to more
than $2 billion by 1984, $3 billion by 1990, and peaked at more than
$4,377,000,000 by 1993 but, when Congress became concerned with balancing
the federal budget, declined to less than $4 billion by 1996.

It must be understood that, while not all of these appropriations were devoted
to departmental operating expenses, the principal portion was designated for
personnel and administration. For the last thirty years the segment ascribed to
this purpose amounted to more than half of the departmental budget, varying
from 52.5 percent to approximately 78 percent. The principal matters encompassed in this category have included salaries and expenses (the preponderant
share), buildings abroad (second largest segment), representation allowances,
diplomatic and consular emergencies, and contributions to the Foreign Service
Retirement Fund.

The second largest category of departmental appropriations has been devoted
to Department of State funding for participation in international organizations

and conferences. This grew from $103,121,000 in the mid-1960s to more than $1.25 billion in the 1990s. It consists of contributions to the financing of international organizations and the costs of sending American missions to such organizations, international conferences, and international commissions.[71] The remaining expenditures have been devoted to boundary and claims settlements, special negotiations, and residual matters. In addition, separate appropriations are made occasionally to finance the American overseas Foreign Service buildings program, based on such acts as those of May 7, 1926 ($10 million), July 25, 1946 ($125 million), June 19, 1952 ($90 million), and August 17, 1977 ($90 million).

These Department of State expenditures do not represent the total cost of conducting American foreign relations. They need to be supplemented by the costs of such other agencies of the government as the Office of the United States Trade Representative (of the President's Executive Office) and various officials and agencies in other Cabinet Departments. To illustrate, aside from Department of Defense responsibilities, these include the Foreign Agricultural Service (Agriculture Department), the agencies that handle exports, patents and trademarks, and travel and tourism (Commerce Department), the Office of Assistant Secretary for Policy and International Affairs of the Energy Department, the Office of Insular Affairs (Interior Department),[72] the Bureau of Labor Affairs (Labor Department), the Aviation and Maritime Administrations and the St. Lawrence Seaway Development Corporation (Transportation Department), the Secret Service and Customs Service as well as an Under Secretary for International Affairs[73] and the Bureau of Public Debt (Treasury Department), and the agency responsible for National Cemeteries both abroad and in the United States (Veterans Administration).

The Department of Justice is also concerned with a number of important aspects of external relations. These are managed by an Office of International Affairs, which deals with matters of international law, such as extradition and mutual legal assistance treaties, and it coordinates international evidence gathering in cooperation with the Department of State. The Justice Department also encompasses a Foreign Claims Settlement Commission, a Drug Enforcement Administration (which operates abroad as well as in the United States), the Immigration and Naturalization Service, a Terrorism and Violent Crime Section, and a National Control Bureau, which serves as a link with the International Criminal Police Commission (INTERPOL).

To these must be added appropriations of other independent government agencies, some of which bear primary foreign relations responsibilities. In addition to the Agency for International Development (AID), Arms Control and Disarmament Agency (ACDA), and U.S. Information Agency (USIA), they have embraced the African Development Foundation, Central Intelligence Agency, Export-Import Bank, Federal Trade Commission, International Development Cooperation Agency, International Trade Commission (originally, the Tariff Commission), Mutual Security Agency, National Aeronautics and Space Administration, National Security Council, Overseas Private Investment Corporation, Panama Canal Commission, Peace Corps, Psychological Strategy Board, Trade Development Agency, U.S. Institute for Peace, and others. Except for the Export-Import Bank, Federal Trade Commission, and the Tariff Commission, these were established since World War II.

Nor do the Department of State expenditures include the vast appropriations for foreign aid, assistance, and development and other budgeted costs of international agencies. The primary purposes of U.S. generous financial support are to provide post–World War II relief and reconstruction, to enhance foreign economic and technological development, to promote containment during the Cold War, and to advance the cause of international security.

To illustrate, during the decade following World War II, as reported by the Department of State, the United States contributed nearly $11 billion for financing the European Recovery Program, more than $4 billion for government relief in foreign occupied areas, and nearly $3 billion for the United Nations Relief and Rehabilitation Administration. Other large amounts were provided to implement the Truman Doctrine to furnish aid to Greece and Turkey and Truman's Point Four Program to finance technical assistance to other countries, to support the United Nations Children's Emergency Fund and the International Refugee Organization, and to provide special assistance to individual countries, including the Philippines, China, and Korea. Combined, these totaled more than $22 billion.

Subsequently, massive expenditures were made to support multilateral and bilateral programs for foreign rehabilitation, military aid, mutual defense and security assistance, education and cultural exchange, the Western Hemisphere Alliance for Progress, and other programs. Substantial American contributions were also made to finance a group of global and regional banks and funds, grant and credit arrangements, and United Nations, inter-American, European, and other specialized agencies. Over the years, therefore, the United States appropriated many billions of dollars for these purposes.

Also noteworthy, comparing the level of appropriations for the Department of State with that of other Executive Departments, in the early 1960s the State Department had by far the lowest budget, amounting to less than $250 million, whereas the Defense Department, the most costly, received nearly $40 billion, the Post Office Department was allotted more than $4 billion, and the Department of Health, Education, and Welfare received more than $3,780,000,000. Other departmental budgets ranged from approximately $357 million to $832 million. At the same time, it is interesting to note that the President's Contingency Fund amounted to more than the State Department's appropriations, and the U.S. Information Agency and the military assistance and technical cooperation agencies combined were budgeted at more than $2 billion.

By the mid-1990s the Department of State continued to receive the smallest departmental authorization, except for the Energy Department.[74] Others that were accorded less than $10 billion were the Commerce and Interior Departments. Those that possessed the largest financial support were the Defense Department (more than $243 billion), Health and Human Services (nearly $209 billion), and Agriculture (approximately $69 billion). Both the Departments of Education and Housing and Urban Development were authorized budgets approximately six times that of the State Department. Moreover, the funding of such agencies as the Internal Revenue Service, National Aeronautics and Space Administration, Agency for International Development, and Environmental Agency was far higher than that of the State Department, and the Veterans Administration had a budget roughly eight times that of the State Department.

Despite its important responsibilities for formulating foreign policy, providing representation to several hundred foreign governments and international conferences and organizations, negotiating scores of treaties and agreements, servicing the interests of American nationals and institutions abroad, and maintaining the international status and leadership of the United States throughout the world, the Department of State receives relatively modest financial support. Although its annual appropriations increased since World War II, surprisingly, they currently amount to less than 7 percent of the total budget for the Executive Departments, of which only three-fourths is ascribed to departmental staffing, administration, and operations.

Current Home of the Department

As indicated earlier, over the years the Department of State was housed in various facilities but did not acquire an adequate and distinguished home of its own until 1875, when it began to move into the newly constructed State Department Building on Pennsylvania Avenue immediately to the west of the White House. But when the building was completed by 1888, the War and Navy Departments were also housed there, and in 1930 it was renamed the State-War-Navy Building. It served as the State Department domicile for more than six decades. When the War and Navy Departments required greater accommodations and moved, several White House agencies took over their space, and the State Department was obliged to rely upon a number of nearby annexes.

However, the War Department, which had moved farther west into its new edifice on Virginia Avenue shortly before Pearl Harbor, needed more space following World War II, and Congress authorized the construction of a new Defense Department facility across the Potomac River in Arlington, Virginia. The vacated War Department building on Virginia Avenue was then transferred to the State Department, into which it began to move in 1947. But Congress also enacted legislation to provide for its enlargement, its cornerstone was laid by President Eisenhower and Secretary Dulles on January 5, 1957, and it was finally completed and dedicated in 1961. Finally, the Department of State had its own gleaming, modern headquarters domicile, located between Virginia Avenue and C Street, and 21st and 23d Streets, which, because of its location, is familiarly known as ''Foggy Bottom''[75] and is formally called the ''New State Building.''

This development evoked a mixed reaction. It enabled the Secretary of State to bring more of the Department under a single roof and provided more serviceable and commodious accommodations. But some considered the new location as an affront to long-established tradition. The intimacy between the President and Secretary of State that is necessary and had previously existed by virtue of close physical proximity of the Department and the White House no longer was possible, it was claimed.

This current facility covers four square blocks (roughly three times the size of the original building), encompasses a total area of 2.5 million square feet, and consists of seven floors of office space and an eighth floor reserved for official functions, such as diplomatic receptions. When constructed, in addition to its many offices, it provided for a state dining room to accommodate more than 100 guests, an 800-seat auditorium where large press conferences and other gatherings could be held, a smaller international conference room with an attached lounge, and an extensive library. Later, as departmental functions and staff increased, requiring additional office space, it was again necessary to utilize a considerable series of supplementary annexes, including a nearby eight-story former apartment house for the Foreign Service Institute.

Diplomatic Communications, the Courier System, and the Hot Line

To possess an effective diplomatic and consular system, manage the implementation of American foreign policy and programs abroad, and facilitate representation at international conferences and organizations, the Department of State must possess a reliable global network of communications facilities. Whereas in earlier times this was limited largely to written messages and documents, they have subsequently also involved telegraph, teletype, cablegram airgram, telephone, radio, e-mail communications satellites, and other forms of messages, equipment, and means of transmittal. Post–World War II electronic communications not only transformed the means of conducting diplomacy by providing instant communications throughout the world but also introduced a series of new domestic and international issues, interests, and agreements with other countries. These include such matters as national policies, systems of communications facilities, continuing technological advancements, and legislation, treaties (both bilateral and multilateral), and international organizations.

The communications rooms of the Department of State, which form the hub of this critical service, are busy day and night receiving and dispatching communications throughout the year. In the 1960s a computer-based terminal system was established to modernize and enhance the handling of the constant flow, storage, retrieval, and display of information and intelligence. Incoming messages are routed to the responsible officers and units of the Department and other interested agencies for their information and action. Similarly, outgoing messages are disseminated to American diplomatic and consular missions abroad, both those to which they are addressed and others that also need to be informed. Thus, millions of official communications, often in cipher, are handled by the Department each year, numbering thousands each day. Only through the use of computers can it and current and future diplomats avoid being drowned by this massive sea of information and documentation that accumulates each day, and expeditiously retrieve those portions essential to dealing efficiently with matters of the moment.

In some respects the State Department also serves as a channel of communications with foreign governments for other Executive Departments agencies and has therefore been denominated "the Post Office" of the Government. Examples include cases involving trade (for the Commerce Department); immigration, citizenship, and the extradition of fugitives from justice (for the Justice Department); and delegations accredited to international conferences and international organizations; as well as the Agency for International Development, the Arms Control and Disarmament Agency, the U.S. Information Agency, the Peace Corps, and other agencies.[76]

Although he concedes that information is not merely important to the conduct of diplomacy, William B. Macomber, Jr., former Assistant and Deputy Under Secretary of State, maintains that "it is its life blood." On the matter of handling these communications and access of individual officers to them, however, he warns that "the need to know" principle must be zealously adhered to and that "sensitive information" must be confined to those officials who should be dealing with it. He also contends that a "natural law of bureaucracy" virtually guarantees that if such sensitive material spreads beyond the need-to-know circle, it is likely to ooze into the public domain and that, while diplomats recognize the importance of the need-to-know principle, "too many seem unable to master a psychologically conflicting personal need" not to appear "not in the know," which may affect their credibility with their colleagues.[77]

The matter of servicing the conveyance of official written communications and documents between the United States and its missions abroad dates back to the beginning of American diplomacy. Initially, the United States relied solely on ad hoc "bearers of dispatches." Overseas the heads of missions were authorized to employ special messengers when needed, usually to convey signed copies of treaties to the Department of State. Over the years various means were employed for this service, ranging from the use of special agents, to reliance on ordinary mail facilities or employment of any convenient and reliable American who was going abroad or returning to the United States. A worldwide system was established during World War II, and later, as the community of nations expanded and headquarters of several new international organizations were created, it was expanded to embrace the entire world. By the end of the 1950s more than sixty couriers and by the 1980s approximately seventy-five couriers transited the globe on their routes, emanating from Washington and a few foreign courier centers, such as Frankfurt, Panama, and Manila.

Eventually, a global courier network was perfected, comprising scores of individuals who travel from post to post by air, by ship, and by other means, bearing locked attaché cases constantly within reach. Collectively, they travel millions of miles each year, exceeding more than twenty round trips to the moon, each member averaging tens of thousands of miles while maintaining their vigil over their valuable pouches. According to the Department of State, the motto of this service is "none is swifter than these." Currently, although transmission of many communications is handled and expedited by alternative means, enhanced by technological advancements in telecommunications, many messages, documents, and other materials still require "safe-hand" personal delivery.

The corps of couriers consists of remarkable, adventurous, self-reliant, trustworthy, and usually young officers. Standards of appointment are rigorous; they commit themselves to remain for several years, and most serve for five years, although some remain longer, and John C. Grover, called the "courier's courier," served for twenty years. However, despite the fact that their task is arduous and debilitating, that they are required to devote outlandish hours to their travels governed by rigorous schedules, and that they live out of suitcases and often suffer from loss of sleep and sudden changes of climate, their morale remains high. Often they confront hazards of war, revolution, pestilence, shipwreck, and plane crashes, and several have lost their lives in the line of duty. Nevertheless, it has been reported that no diplomatic pouch or letter has ever been stolen from an American courier and that they are noted for "their outstanding record" for their expeditious and dependable delivery of their precious cargoes.[78]

In short, the courier service constitutes an essential, organized, official "mail system" to personally and safely convey communications and documents between the Department of State and American foreign diplomatic and consular missions and among American foreign missions throughout the world. Couriers serve solely to pick up and deliver packets of confidential materials. They carry special passports that identify their unique status. They and their pouches (which bear the State Department seal on identification tags to certify their official status) are inviolable, which may not be opened and searched while en route.

Furthermore, since World War II the nature and sanctity of the courier system have been formally recognized and guaranteed by international treaties. Thus, the multilateral Vienna Conventions on Diplomatic (1961, Article 27) and Consular (1963, Article 35) Relations, which have been signed and ratified by most nations, guarantee protection of "free communications" for "all official purposes," including the use of "diplomatic and consular couriers." These treaties also specify that they "shall be inviolable" and "shall not be liable to any form of arrest or detention." Currently, couriers usually are State Department employees or members of the armed services. The Foreign Service Act of 1946 provided that the Secretaries of War and the Navy are authorized, on the request of the Secretary of State, to assign or detail military and naval personnel for

State Department courier duty. Subsequently, this was broadened to include members of all the armed forces, to provide an "inter-agency courier service" on a nonreimbursable basis.[79]

In addition to the traditional systems of official communications, a major innovation known as the "hot line" was established in U.S.–Soviet relations during the Cold War. Because it took more than six hours to transmit messages between Washington and Moscow at the time of the Cuban missile crisis, it was decided that a more rapid and direct communications link was needed to deal with future crises. Initially, this hot line relied on written messages transmitted by means of a duplex telegraphic circuit routed from Washington, via London, Copenhagen, Stockholm, and Helsinki to Moscow, with a backup circuit via Tangier. Subsequently, this system was modernized. In the 1970s circuits that employed satellite facilities were added, in the 1980s a facsimile (fax) capability was developed, and eventually, the system consisted of computers and fax machines transmitting simultaneously via two satellites and an undersea cable, thereby providing instantaneous communications. With the decline of the Cold War, beginning in the 1990s, these facilities were supplemented by high-level conventional telephone exchanges.

Other Government Agencies Dealing With American Foreign Affairs

In earlier times the Department of State was not only responsible for the conduct of foreign relations but also burdened with many domestic functions, most of which were eventually transferred to other Executive Departments and agencies. Although the Secretary of State has retained a few domestic ceremonial and servicing responsibilities, during World War II and increasingly since 1945, as the United States assumed the role of a globally oriented superpower, this relationship was inverted in that most Federal Departments and a good many other agencies became involved in various aspects of external affairs. These mutate in number and types of responsibilities from time to time, and they range from those concerned largely with policy formulation and program management and some that function primarily abroad, to those that deal with the foreign affairs aspects of domestic functions and those that possess only limited responsibilities that impinge on external issues. This development has produced a conglomeration of agencies concerned with foreign relations and serious problems of jurisdiction, overlapping, competition, and the need for close cooperation and coordination.

This extra-Department of State involvement for handling aspects of foreign relations consists of three basic types—those agencies that apply to officers and components of the Executive Office of the President and other Executive Departments, those that have been structurally attached to the Department of State, and a host of what are generally regarded as independent and related agencies.

In addition to the Office of Management and Budget (formerly the Bureau of the Budget) to assist the President in preparing the national budget, three agencies located in the Executive Office exercise key foreign relations responsibilities. The National Security Council, created in 1947 to succeed the State-War-Navy Coordinating Committee and the State-Army-Navy-Air Force Coordinating Committee, of which the Secretary of State is a member, formulates and coordinates national priorities, considers policy choices, makes recommendations directly to the President, and reviews ongoing programs concerned with American security.[80] The Central Intelligence Agency, an adjunct of the National Security Council, acquires, evaluates, coordinates, and disseminates foreign intelligence and conducts counterintelligence operations within and outside the United States.[81] The third component is the Office of the Special Representative for Trade Negotiations. Created by the Trade Act of 1974; it is captained by the U.S. Trade Representative, who is of Cabinet rank and is responsible directly to the President. Combined, these agencies are headed by staffs of more than thirty-five principal officers, usually titled Special Assistant to the President, other Assistants, Directors and Deputy Directors, and the Executive Secretary of the National Security Council.[82]

Turning to the fourteen Executive Departments, all but those concerned with Energy and Veterans Affairs have some foreign relations interests and responsibilities, which are handled by a variety of principal officers and departmental components. Aside from the Departments of State and Defense, at least thirty-five departmental agencies have such functions. The Departments of Justice (eleven agencies), Commerce (six), and Transportation (five) head the list. The most common titles of these agencies are administration, agency, bureau, office, and service, which, combined, account for more than three-fourths of them.[83] Nearly half of these Departments possess basic components possessing overarching functions, which are generally called Bureau or Office of International or External Affairs.[84] Other agencies may be categorized as having important, but functionally more specific, responsibilities or, in some cases, narrowly restricted activities.

Some of these departmental agencies are well known. They include the Coast Guard (Treasury Department), Commodity Credit Corporation (Agriculture), Customs Service (Treasury), Federal Aviation Administration (Transportation), Federal Bureau of Investigation (Justice), Immigration and Naturalization Service (Justice), International Trade Administration (Commerce), Maritime Administration (Transportation), National Institutes of Health (Health and Human Services), Patent and Trademark Office (Commerce), and Secret Service (Treasury). In addition to the functional interests previously specified, they are concerned with agriculture, crime and racketeering, fish and wildlife, health, labor, oceanic and atmospheric matters, refugee settlement and repatriation, space transportation, terrorism and violent crime, travel and tourism, and other international affairs.

The principal officers of these departmental components, of whom there are more than 125, rank as high as Deputy Secretary (Treasury Department) and

Under Secretary (Agriculture, Commerce, and Treasury Departments). The preponderant number hold the positions of Deputy Under Secretary, Assistant Secretary, Deputy Assistant Secretary, and Director. Others are designated as Administrator (of such agencies as the Foreign Agricultural Service, the Drug Enforcement Administration, the Federal Aviation Administration, and the Maritime Administration), Chairman (of the Foreign Claims Settlement Commission), Commissioner (of the Customs Service and the Immigration and Naturalization Service), and Commandant (of the Coast Guard). The Treasury Department also has two Deputy Comptrollers for International Banking and Finance and for Multilateral Banking.

Several of the departmental agencies also have their own offices and staffs abroad. For example, the Foreign Agricultural Service staffs seventy-five posts overseas for the Agriculture Department, and the U.S. and Foreign Commercial Service of the Commerce Department mans more than 130 posts in sixty-eight foreign countries. Similarly, the Customs Service of the Treasury Department maintains twenty-one foreign field offices, the Immigration and Naturalization Service of the Justice Department has three foreign district offices, and the Travel and Tourism Administration of the Commerce Department has eight foreign offices.[85] Moreover, the Coast Guard of the Treasury Department establishes and maintains navigation guides in Europe, the Mediterranean, the Western Pacific, and elsewhere and also provides North Atlantic ice patrols and services Arctic installations, and, at times, members of the Secret Service of the Treasury Department venture abroad to provide protection and other services for American leaders and certain representatives performing special missions abroad.

In addition to these Departments, the former Post Office Department was converted into the U.S. Postal Service by the Postal Reorganization Act of 1970. It is headed by the Postmaster General, who is no longer a member of the President's Cabinet. A Deputy Postmaster General for International Affairs administers foreign postal matters for the United States.

The second major category of these government instrumentalities consists of a few independent agencies that are affiliated with the Department of State and whose leaders are responsible to the Secretary of State. The Peace Corps was established as an independent agency in 1961 to make available to newly developing countries, on their request, American volunteers to help their peoples meet their needs for skilled manpower. The volunteers engage, for short periods, in a program of teaching, building, working, and living in the foreign communities to which they are sent. The Corps is headed by a Director who was originally placed under the supervision of the Secretary of State. However, it is no longer regarded as an adjunct of the State Department, although it remains in existence as an independent foreign relations agency.

On the other hand, three separate, important agencies are currently attached to, or integrated into, the Department of State. The U.S. Information Agency (USIA), founded on the International Information and Education Exchange Act of 1948 and the Mutual Educational and Cultural Exchange Act of 1961, is an adjunct of the Department of State. Headed by an Administrator, it is implemented abroad by Foreign Service Officers and staffs assigned to American foreign missions. It services more than 200 posts in approximately 150 countries. Its overseas operations are generally administered by major U.S. embassy sections, or they may be a part of the public affairs section. The function of the Information Agency is to enhance mutual understanding between the people of the United States and other countries, authorize educational and cultural exchanges, sponsor participation in international fairs and expositions abroad, assist mass media in providing information concerning American policy and developments to audiences throughout the world, and ''sell America abroad.''

The Arms Control and Disarmament Agency (ACDA), created by an act of September 1961 and also located in the Department of State, is headed by a Director who is responsible to the Secretary of State and who is assisted by some twenty senior officers and their staffs. It serves to advise the President, Secretary of State, the National Security Council, and Congress on arms matters. It plays a significant role in formulating policy and basic positions on national security and strategy, negotiating international arms limitation treaties and agreements, and directing and participating in international arms control systems. It is claimed not only that was it essential to create such an agency during the critical post–World War II period but also that it is the first such coordinating instrumentality to be established by any government to serve this purpose.

The Agency for International Development (AID), initiated by the Foreign Assistance Act of 1961 and an Executive Order issued in November of that year, was established to succeed the International Cooperation Administration (ICA) when emphasis on American foreign ''aid'' was broadened to include ''development.'' It also constitutes a semiautonomous agency attached to the Department of State, is headed by an Administrator and is implemented by its own foreign missions or by sections within American Embassies, which consist of staffs of hundreds of overseas officers and other personnel throughout the world. This relationship enables the Secretary of State to provide foreign economic policy guidance and mesh the American foreign assistance program with the traditional functions of the State Department and the Foreign Service. It focuses on such matters as agriculture, education, health, housing, community development, public administration, and self-help and entails a program of both American grants and loans. Its purpose is to help the people of less developed countries to enhance the utilization of their human and economic resources, increase productive capacities, improve the quality of life, and promote economic and political stability.

Most astonishing, the third major category of Federal agencies concerned with a broad variety of aspects of American foreign affairs since World War II encompasses approximately 125 independent government agencies, listed in Table 7.5. Some of these are components of the Executive Office of the President and other Executive Departments. Most are titled administrations, agencies, boards,

Table 7.5

Independent and Other Federal Foreign Affairs Agencies (not including Department of State Components)

ACTION (Anti-poverty volunteer program)
African Development Foundation
** Agency for International Development
Air Coordinating Committee
Alliance for Progress
Arctic Research Council
** Arms Control and Disarmament Agency
Atomic Energy Commission
Board of Economic Warfare
* Board of Immigration Appeals
Board of International Broadcasting
* Bureau of Customs
Bureau of International Commerce
* Center for Disease Control
* Central Intelligence Agency
Central Intelligence Group
Civil Aeronautics Board
Civil and Defense Mobilization Board
* Coast Guard
Committee for Reciprocity Information
Committee on Foreign Investments in U.S.
Committee on Trade Agreements
Coordinator of Information
Coordinator of Inter-American Affairs
* Council of Economic Advisers
Council on Foreign Economic Policy
* Customs Service
* Defense Nuclear Agency
* Defense Security Agency
Displaced Persons Commission
* Drug Enforcement Administration
Economic Cooperation Administration
Economic Defense Board
Executive Committee for Commercial Policy
Export Control Review Board
Export-Import Bank
Federal Aviation Administration
* Federal Aviation Agency
* Federal Bureau of Investigation
Federal Communications Commission
* Federal Highway Administration
Federal Maritime Commission
Federal Radiation Council
Federal Trade Commission
* Food and Drug Administration
Foreign Agricultural Service
Foreign Claims Settlement Commission
Foreign Commercial Service
Foreign Economic Administration
Foreign Information Service
Foreign Operations Administration
* Immigration and Naturalization Service
Interagency Information Security Agency
Inter-American Foundation
Interdepartmental Regional Groups (IRS)
International Claims Commission of the U.S.
International Communications Agency
International Cooperation Administration
International Development and Coop. Agency
International Development Association
* International Trade Administration
Japan-United States Friendship Commission
Lend-Lease Administration

Marine Mammal Commission
* Maritime Administration
Migratory Bird Conservation Commission
* Mutual Security Agency
National Advisory Council on International Monetary and Financial Problems
National Aeronautics and Space Council
* National Aeronautics and Space Admin.
* National Institutes of Health
National Intelligence Authority
National Oceanic and Atmospheric Admin.
Nuclear Regulatory Commission
* National Security Agency
* National Security Council
* National Telecommunications and Information Administration
* Ocean Mining Administration
Office of Civil and Defense Mobilization
Office of Economic Opportunity
Office of Economic Warfare
Office of Educational Exchange
Office of Emergency Planning
Office of Export Control
Office of Foreign Economic Coordination
Office of Foreign Relief and Rehab. Ops.
Office of Information and Cultural Exchange
Office of International Information
* Office of International Security Affairs
* Office of National Control Policy
* Office of Special Rep. for Trade Negotiations
Office of Strategic Services
* Office of Territorial Affairs
Office of War Information
Operations Coordinating Board
Overseas Private Investment Corporation
Panama Canal Commission
Patents and Trademarks Office
Peace Corps
Permanent Joint Board on Defense (U.S. and Canada)
President's Foreign Intelligence Advisory Brd.
Psychological Strategy Board
* Public Health Service
* Secret Service
Senior Interdepartmental Group (SIG)
State-Army-Navy-Air Force Coord. Com.
State-War-Navy Coordinating Committee
Technical Cooperation Administration
Textile Trade Policy Group
Trade and Development Agency
Trade Agreements Committee
Trade Policy Committee
U.S. Information Administration
** U.S. Information Agency
U.S. Institute for Peace
U.S. International Trade Commission
U.S. Maritime Commission
U.S. Postal Service
U.S. Tariff Commission
U.S. Travel and Tourism Administration
War Claims Commission
War Relief Control Board
War Shipping Administration

*Indicates the agencies currently attached to the Executive Office of the President or one of the Federal Departments.

**Indicates the agencies currently attached to, or integrated into, the Department of State.

commissions, and offices; and others bear such designations as bureaus, committees, foundations, and services. A few were World War II residual agencies that were inherited by President Truman, which were later superseded or terminated.[86] Others that preexisted the Truman Administration remain in existence, such as the Bureau of Investigation, Customs Service (previously called the Customs Bureau), Export-Import Bank, Federal Communications Commission, Federal Maritime Commission, Federal Trade Commission, Immigration and Naturalization Service, Postal Service (previously the Post Office Department), and the Secret Service. A good many others have been superseded by, or amalgamated with, successor agencies. In some cases, multiple sequential agencies illustrate changing needs and administrative arrangements, illustrated by progressions in such fields as foreign aid and development, information and educational and cultural activities, and foreign intelligence.[87]

Often, the establishment of these administrative agencies was sparked by the issuance of major policy doctrines, declarations, and other proposals of the President, Secretary of State, and other leaders. President Roosevelt propounded the Arsenal of Democracy, Four Freedoms, Good Neighbor, Lend-Lease, quarantining of aggressors, and unconditional surrender concepts, and Secretary Hull added the Reciprocal Trade Agreements program. Some of these continued into the post–World War II period. Others that had an impact on the establishment of administrative agencies for their implementation embrace the Alliance for Progress, Atlantic partnership, Atoms for Peace, Cold War, collective and regional security, economic assistance, educational and cultural exchange, development loans, European Recovery from World War II, Food for Peace, Marshall Plan, Military Assistance, Mutual Defense Assistance, Peace Corps, and President Truman's Point Four (technical assistance) principles. All of these resulted in the creation of administrative agencies to implement them.

To summarize, these independent agencies deal with a remarkably comprehensive spectrum of functional aspects of U.S. foreign interests and programs. These embrace aeronautics and outer space, arms control and disarmament, atomic and nuclear, banking and investment, communications and telecommunications, customs and tariff, defense, displaced persons, drug enforcement, economic and commercial, foreign aid and development, foreign claims, health and disease, immigration and naturalization, information and intelligence, international claims, maintenance of peace, maritime and shipping, national security and defense, patents and trademarks, policy and program coordination, postal, psychological warfare, relief and rehabilitation, transportation, trade and commerce, and territorial matters, plus a variety of other more precise services programs and administrative coordination. The most common subject categories have been aid and development, defense and security, economic affairs, information and intelligence, and trade and commerce.

One of the major jurisdictional problems confronting the Department of State since the 1940s has been the matter of handling operational programs abroad. During World War II, when many administrative agencies with overseas responsibilities proliferated, the Department was confronted with the issue of distinguishing between its traditional diplomatic and consular functions and the operational activities of other agencies. When some of these established their own overseas branches and programs, it might have been expected that the State Department and Foreign Service would have undertaken their responsibilities abroad. However, following a conflict within the Department over the question whether it should assume such operational functions, under the influence of Secretary Hull it finally determined that its foreign missions would not assume this burden. Other, mostly independent, agencies were created to administer these functions. Except for a few that were attached to the Department of State, discussed earlier, this practice was continued into the post–World War II era. Although this determination preserved the Department of State from becoming the sole non-military administrative instrumentality of such foreign operational functions abroad, it produced serious problems of competition, duplication, confusion, and conflict.[88]

Several actions have been taken to stabilize interagency foreign relations. Recent Presidents have stipulated the preeminence of American Ambassadors within the countries of their assignment. Various stateside integration agencies have been established, such as the National Security Council system, the Central Intelligence Agency, the Senior Interdepartmental Group, and the Interdepartmental Regional Groups. Moreover, as the Geographic Bureaus were reorganized and standardized, the Department of State "Desk Officers" and "Country Directors" were created to specialize in dealing with individual countries and to provide concentrated interagency coordination responsibility respecting them. Overseas the concept of the "country team" was launched to meet the need for cooperation, coordination, and unified overall direction for the miscellany of American agencies functioning abroad.

In addition, there are the functional attachés stationed at American diplomatic missions abroad. Since World War II they have been appointed to represent agricultural, civil aviation, commercial, cultural, information, financial, labor, military (Army, Navy, and Air Force), minerals, petroleum, press, telecommunications, treasury, and other affairs, who are assigned to foreign posts to undertake their specialized tasks. Some are Foreign Service personnel, many of whom are not careerists who are assigned to an Embassy by other agencies. At times they may be incorporated into the Department of State. For example, in 1939 President Franklin D. Roosevelt transferred the activities and personnel of the Agriculture and Commerce Departments to the State Department on the assumption that overseas representation and reporting in those fields should be part of a single, integrated mechanism, but in 1953 President Eisenhower returned the Agricultural attachés to the Department of Agriculture.

The dichotomy of having the Department of State appoint various specialists to the Foreign Service to serve in these attaché positions or having other Departments and agencies recruit and assign their own attachés to American foreign missions is perplexing and is not easily resolved. On one hand, if they are

Foreign Service careerists who wish to advance in their rank and profession, they may be reluctant to remain such limited functional specialists. On the other hand, if they are specialists with primary responsibility to the Department or agency that recruits them, they remain adjuncts of the State Department and the Foreign Service. In any case, overseas they are made a part of the American Country Team, under the direction of the Ambassador.

Thus, the activities of the Department of State cut across the functions of most other government Departments and many independent administrative agencies that deal with matters transcending the national frontiers. In some respects it serves simply as a channel of communication with other Federal agencies and foreign governments. Because it provides this service, it has been called the "Post Office of the Government." Conversely, other Departments and agencies also assist the State Department in many respects. The Attorney General, for example, renders opinions interpreting municipal law that affect foreign relations, such as those that concern extradition, immigration, passport, visa, and similar issues, and the Justice Department defends the Department of State in suits brought against it and its personnel involving the execution of their official duties.

Nevertheless, the formulation and execution of foreign policy remain considerably decentralized, and most other Departments and a quantity of other agencies parallel and, in certain respects, compete with the Department of State, evidencing the need for carefully orchestrated coordination. Techniques to achieve this vary from integration at the President's level, as in the Cabinet, the National Security Council, and various functional committees and councils, and interdepartmental devices at or below the Cabinet level (as in the Central Intelligence Agency and the former Operations Coordinating Board, which was regarded as coordinator of coordinators),[89] to less formal interagency and liaison arrangements, a few special coordinators,[90] or resort to a "supercoordinator," which is rarely employed.[91]

Conversely, to achieve coordination by means of integration, theoretically, a super-Department of Foreign Relations might be fabricated, similar to aggregating the Departments of Army, Navy, and Air Force within the Department of Defense. Such an arrangement would be headed by a new Secretary of Foreign Relations, who would be of Cabinet rank and responsible for all or most foreign affairs and supported by the Secretary of State and other Secretaries for other foreign activities, responsibilities, and operational programs.[92] While such reorganization might have many advantages, it would not encompass overall and inclusive coordination of either policy making or operational implementation abroad unless all the other nonmilitary Departments and agencies were completely divested of their foreign affairs responsibilities.

Despite a great deal of organizational and administrative change that has been instituted with respect to staff, line, and coordinating agencies, since World War II the decentralization of many aspects of foreign affairs activities remains, sustained, in part, because of Department of State reluctance to become overburdened with overseas operational programs. As a consequence, it continues as the principal agency for dealing with foreign policy making and the traditional diplomatic and consular aspects of the conduct of American foreign relations, leaving many foreign administrative and technical programs to be managed by other agencies. The resolution of this matter, therefore, lies not in the absorption of the totality of the conduct of foreign affairs by the State Department but rather in providing and maintaining a cooperative system founded on well-designed and well-managed coordination.

DIPLOMATIC AND CONSULAR REPRESENTATION

Unauthorized Foreign Representation—The Logan Act Reiterated

Interestingly, the spirit and essence of the Logan Act of 1799, discussed in Chapter 2, remain extant but were updated on June 25, 1948, and September 13, 1994.[93] Currently, the act stipulates that any U.S. citizen who, without authority of the American Government, directly or indirectly "carries on any correspondence or intercourse with any foreign government or any officer or agent thereof, with intent to influence the measures or conduct of any foreign government" in relation to "any disputes or controversies with the United States, or to defeat the measures of the United States, shall be fined not more than $5,000 or imprisoned not more than three years, or both." However, this act does not abridge the rights of American citizens from applying for "redress of any injury which he may have sustained" from foreign governments or its agencies or subjects.

To summarize, the key components of the act are that they apply only to American citizens, who without government authority, indirectly as well as directly, carry on communications with a foreign government, with the objective of influencing it, respecting disputes and controversies, in order to disaffect the interests, goals, policies, negotiations, and actions of the United States. Experience has revealed that its practical applicability is far more restricted than may be presumed.

A number of Americans have represented diplomatically the interests of foreign governments in their relations with the United States. For example, in the 1920s Eldon R. James, an American, represented the Siamese Government on the Permanent Court of Arbitration and served as adviser on foreign affairs to the King of Siam and as his Minister Plenipotentiary. Under Secretary Joseph C. Grew approved such action, provided that no attempt was made to influence the Siamese Government in disputes or controversies with the United States.

Application of the Logan Act was suggested early in 1947, when former Secretary of Agriculture and Vice President Henry A. Wallace, on tour in Europe, spoke out sharply against the Truman Doctrine, which aroused the House of Representatives Un-American Activities Committee. Although no action was taken, public attention was focused upon the application of the act. Also, during the strained Soviet–American relations following World War II, atomic scientist Dr. Leo Szilard drafted an open letter to Premier Stalin in November 1947, urging him to meet with President Truman. Initially, he intended to send his letter directly to Stalin but failed to obtain permission from the Attorney General because such action was considered to violate the Logan Act. The following year Congress reiterated the act with slight modification.

Subsequently, other cases of possible violation evoked official and public attention. In October 1950 Harold Stassen, former Governor of Minnesota and unsuccessful contender for the Presidency, sent a letter to Premier Stalin requesting that he meet with several American "citizen" leaders, and again no action was taken under the act. Three years later Congressman Alvin E. O'Konski sent a letter to President Syngman Rhee of the Republic of Korea, congratulating him on freeing 23,000 North Korean prisoners of war and urging him to free an additional 27,000, which challenged established American policy and commitments, but Secretary of State Dulles took no action because it did not disturb U.S. relations with the Korean Government. In 1955, Congressman Adam Clayton Powell, an unofficial observer at an Afro-Asian Conference convened at Bandung, Indonesia, undertook to negotiate with the agents of the Chinese Communist Government regarding several American fliers imprisoned on charges of alleged espionage.

The issue of the application of the Logan Act was also raised in several cases involving American Senators and even a former President. In 1975 inquiries were raised as to certain activities of Senators John Sparkman and George McGovern concerning U.S.–Cuban affairs. Senator McGovern made it clear that he was not authorized to negotiate on behalf of the United States. In response, the Department of State observed that it appeared that nothing in the law restricts members of Congress "from engaging in discussions with foreign officials in pursuance of their legislative duties." The following year, when former President Nixon visited the Republic of China as a private citizen (and he made several such foreign trips), the Department of State took the position that it was up to "the Justice Department to make determinations of whether criminal statutes . . . have been transgressed and whether individuals should be prosecuted under them."

It appears that when the United States is faced with what may constitute a violation of the Logan Act, little is done because of the difficulty involved in determining judicially whether a foreign government is "influenced" by such actions, and, in some cases, the individuals concerned are members of the government. On the other hand, in 1962, James B. Donovan, a private citizen, apparently with government approval, successfully consummated two important "unofficial" negotiations with the Soviet Government providing for an exchange of a convicted Soviet spy for Francis Gary Powers, the American U-2 pilot shot down in Russia in 1960, and an exchange of some $50 million worth of medical supplies for the release of Fidel Castro's Cuban Bay of Pigs prisoners.

It may be concluded that this 200-year-old Logan Act, which has never been utilized to convict and punish anyone, continues to exist, although it is generally regarded as unenforceable, if not unconstitutional. Nevertheless, it remains an important protection of the welfare of the country and a constraint upon untoward acts by unofficial persons seeking to counter official policy and action.[94] Moreover, it appears that the United States also applies this principle in reverse. To illustrate, Georges Clemenceau, World War I Premier of France, then no longer possessing an official capacity, issued an open letter to President Coolidge, urging him to reduce or cancel the collection of war debts, thereby upsetting an agreement already concluded for their reduction. The President responded that the American Government will conduct its relations with foreign nations only "through their duly constituted authorities."

To regularize practice concerning the activities of representatives of foreign governments in the United States, Congress legislated that "[w]hoever, other than a diplomatic officer or attaché, acts in the United States as an agent of a foreign government without prior notification to the Attorney General . . . shall be fined not more than $75,000, or imprisoned not more than ten years, or both." It defined such "agents" as individuals "who agree to operate within the United States subject to the directions or control of a foreign government or official," other than regularly accredited and recognized diplomats and consuls, officially and publicly acknowledged and sponsored officials, and their staff members who are not American citizens.[95]

Modernization of the Foreign Service—Acts of 1946, 1980, and Others

Since 1945 the Foreign Service, consisting of both diplomatic and consular personnel, has undergone a major overhaul and crystallization. This was achieved by a series of Congressional acts, consisting of two basic organic statutes enacted by Congress in 1946 and 1980 and a series of supplementary and amendatory enactments.

Following World War II President Truman and Secretary Byrnes and their successors were confronted with the necessity of integrating certain temporary wartime agencies into the permanent structure of the Department of State, of systematizing the administration of American foreign affairs abroad, and of dealing diplomatically with an increased number of foreign governments and an expanded network of international conferences and meetings and global and regional international organizations. These and other developments, including the maturation of a professional Foreign Service, required its expansion and modernization to enable it to perform both its traditional and its added responsibilities. To deal with the immediate problem of insufficient staffing, Congress passed the Act of May 3, 1945 (59 Stat. 102) to establish a new category of administrative, fiscal, and clerical personnel within the Foreign Service, which was followed by the Act of July 3, 1946 (60 Stat. 426), known as the Foreign

Service Manpower Act, to provide a contingent of 250 additional Foreign Service Officers during the following two years, subject to demanding selection requirements.

Many State Department officials, including Secretary Byrnes, Foreign Service Officers, officials of other agencies, and members of Congress, combined to review, and recommend improvement of, the Foreign Service, which resulted in the enactment on August 13 of the Foreign Service Act of 1946 (60 Stat. 939). It was a comprehensive constitutive enactment of more than fifty printed pages, which superseded the earlier Rogers Act of 1924 and Moses-Linthicum Act of 1931.[96] Coterminous with the departmental reorganizations of Secretary Stettinius in 1944, this act was in preparation for two years, and, although approved by Congress, it nearly failed to be signed by President Truman due to objections raised by the Bureau of the Budget. It supplemented many aspects of earlier legislation and constituted a codification to govern the Foreign Service for the following thirty-five years. It provided a thoroughgoing renovation and synthesis of the basic legislation governing the Foreign Service, embodied changes based on the lessons learned over the years, and allowed more officers to benefit from training programs and increased salaries, especially those in the upper ranks of the Service.

The act specified nine basic goals. These included the determination to enable the Foreign Service to effectively serve the interests of the United States abroad, to provide a flexible and comprehensive framework for its direction in accordance with modern administrative practices, and to codify in a single act all provisions of law relating to its operation. It prescribed the general duties of Foreign Service Officers and employees and dealt with ten major aspects of the management of Foreign Service. These included appointments and assignments, categories of officers, career development, compensation, leaves of absence, management, medical services, promotion and retention, special allowances and benefits, and separation from service and retirement, plus several prohibitions.

To clarify the basic duties of Foreign Service Officers, it specified that they were to represent abroad "the interests of the United States" and to "perform the duties and comply with the obligations resulting from the nature of their appointments and assignments" prescribed by law, regulations issued by the President and Secretary of State, and international treaties and agreements. It also empowered the Secretary to amplify the law by issuing departmental regulations "not inconsistent with the Constitution and other laws of the United States" or with those prescribed by the President for the governance of the Foreign Service.

To stabilize and strengthen departmental management of the Foreign Service, as distinct from the officers of the State Department appointed by the President, it defined the roles of several officers and agencies concerned with the administration of the Foreign Service. For example, the Director General and Deputy Director General of the Foreign Service, to be appointed by the Secretary of State from among the upper classes of Foreign Service Officers, were made responsible for coordinating the activities of the Service with the needs of the Department and other Government agencies and for directing the performance of Foreign Service Officers and employees.

The Act also provided for two administrative agencies. The Board of the Foreign Service (which replaced the former Board of Foreign Service Personnel, created in 1924), headed by an Assistant Secretary in charge of administration, consisted of two other Assistant Secretaries, the Director General of the Foreign Service, and one member each from the Agriculture, Commerce, and Labor Departments. It was given responsibility for making recommendations concerning the functions of the Foreign Service; policies and procedures to govern the selection, assignment, rating, and promotion of Foreign Service Officers; policies and procedures for the administration and personnel management of the Foreign Service; and other specified duties. The other administrative agency, previously established by Executive Order in 1905, was the Foreign Service Board of Examiners, consisting of a mixture of members of the Foreign Service and others, constituted in accordance with regulations prescribed by the Secretary of State. It was put in charge of supervising and administering examinations for appointment of new Foreign Service Officers and for providing procedures to "determine the loyalty" of such officers "and their attachment to the principles of the Constitution."

Whereas previously, the Foreign Service consisted of several groups of officers and employees, this act established a new classification system, providing seven categories of Foreign Service personnel, with accompanying salary schedules. Although the appointment of Chiefs of Mission remained the prerogative of the President, it empowered the Secretary of State, on the recommendation of the Board of the Foreign Service, to furnish him with names of career officers qualified for appointment or assignment as Ambassadors and Ministers, arranged in four classes at annual salaries ranging from $15,000 to $25,000.[97] Prior to this act careerists were required to resign from the Foreign Service when they were appointed Chiefs of Mission. Under this new arrangement, they retained their career status and could later be named to succeeding missions at diplomatic and consular posts, usually at the level of Counselor of Embassy or Consul General. However, if they were not appointed to new missions, they were expected to retire. Foreign Service Officers were grouped in seven classes consisting of a new distinguished rank of Career Minister with a salary of $13,500 and six numbered classes, each of which carried several salary brackets. These ranged from a minimum of $3,300 to $4,400 for those in Class 6 to $12,000 to $13,500 for those in Class 1.

Another major innovation of the Act of 1946 was change in the composition of the Foreign Service Officer system. The Foreign Service Auxiliary, created in 1941 to help staff American missions abroad during World War II, was terminated.[98] It had constituted an auxiliary personnel category and eventually embodied nearly 1,000 officers, which actually exceeded the number of regular Foreign Service Officers. It was superseded by the creation of two new categories titled Foreign Service Reserve Officers (FSROs) and Foreign Service Staff Officers (FSSOs).

To accommodate the appointment of specialists, Foreign Service Reserve Officers could be drawn from the Government or outside to serve for temporary periods for a maximum of four years, which was increased to five years in 1955. Initially, it was contemplated that they would deal primarily with cultural, information, and labor affairs. When the amalgamation of State Department and Foreign Service Officers was undertaken, as recommended by the Wriston Committee Report of 1954 (discussed in the section on the reorganization and reform of the Department of State), these appointments were also extended to supply the Foreign Service with additional temporary specialists and provide a transition means for the appointment of Department of State and staff personnel to transfer into the Foreign Service Officer category and to accommodate other individuals who lacked the required number of years of service for lateral entry into the Foreign Service. However, such Reserve Officers were not eligible for promotion to the rank of Career Minister. The third category, designated Foreign Service Staff Corps, was established, provided for by the Act of May 3, 1945 (59 Stat. 102). It consisted of both officers and other employees who previously held administrative, fiscal, clerical, technical, custodial, and miscellaneous positions. Upper-ranking members were classified as Foreign Service Staff Officers (FSSSOs) by the Act of 1946.

For purposes of compensation, Foreign Service Officers and Foreign Service Reserve Officers were grouped in seven annual salary classes, each with five to seven subsidiary classes, ranging from a minimum of $3,300 to a maximum of $13,500. Foreign Service Staff Corps members were classified in twenty-two classes with precise salary levels for each class, which ranged from a minimum of $720 to $1,080 for Class 22 to $8,820 to $10,000 for Class 1. The middle and upper ranks of the Staff Corps consisted of senior administrative and fiscal personnel as well as some technical specialists, and the lower ranks included junior administrative personnel, clerks, couriers, and other employees.

The remaining categories of personnel pertained to alien clerks or employees, appointed by the Secretary of State, who were grouped together for administrative purposes, and consular agents. Their salaries were fixed by regulations prescribed by the Secretary of State. Officers temporarily serving as Chargés d'Affaires were also entitled to an additional salary differential for the duration of such service.

To summarize, this comprehensive personnel plan, therefore, provided for more than forty classes of officers and employees and some 225 prescribed salary brackets, as follows:

Positions	Classes	Salary Brackets
Chiefs of Mission	4	4
Foreign Service Officers	7	41

Positions	Classes	Salary Brackets
Foreign Service Reserve Officers	6	40
Foreign Service Staff Corps	22	141
Others	3	*
Total	42	226

*Salaries of Chargés d'Affaires, consular agents, alien clerks, and employees were fixed by the Secretary of State.

The major disadvantage of this cumbersome compensation arrangement was that, to maintain tight legislative control, Congress had to periodically review and modify this massive salary schedule, which was changed by the Act of 1980, as noted later.

The Act of 1946 also crystallized the appointment and assignment system and created a new promotion and retirement arrangement, characterized as a modified "promotion up or selection out" scheme. It specified that the President, with the consent of the Senate, would appoint not only Ambassadors, Ministers, and Career Ministers but also, at his discretion, Foreign Service Officers as Ministers Resident, Chargés d'Affaires, Commissioners, and diplomatic agents "as the public interest may require." To assist him, the Secretary of State, on the recommendation of the Board of the Foreign Service, was authorized to furnish the President with the names of Foreign Service Officers qualified for appointment as Chiefs of Mission and Career Ministers. Presidential appointments of individual Foreign Service Officers were required to be made to a class, not to a particular country or post. Candidates for appointment were required to pass written, oral, physical, and other examinations as prescribed by the State Department Board of Examiners.[99]

Similar arrangements were prescribed concerning the appointment, assignment, classification, reappointment, reassignment, and reinstatement of Foreign Service Reserve Officers, as well as appointments, assignments, and transfers of Foreign Service Staff Officers and employees, but these responsibilities devolved upon the Secretary of State. All Foreign Service, Reserve, and Staff Officers and employees serving the United States abroad were required to be American citizens, and they needed to be bonded before they entered upon their duties.

To deal with promotion and career development, the act required the Director General of the Foreign Service, under the supervision of the Foreign Service Board, to maintain confidential efficiency records on the ability, conduct, quality of work, industry, experience, dependability, and general usefulness of all Foreign Service Officers and employees. These became the basis of determination for promotion and separation from service. Promotion was required to be founded on merit. The Secretary was authorized to establish regulations respecting the minimum period that Foreign Service Officers, Reserve Officers, and Staff Officers needed to serve in each class in order to be eligible for promotion to a higher rank, to establish selection boards to evaluate performance, and to make recommendations to the President for promotion and in-class salary increases.

Superseding the Foreign Service School, created by Executive Order No. 4022 of June 7, 1924 (recommended by the Rogers Act), to furnish training and instruction to officers and employees of both the Department and Foreign Service, the Act of August 1946 stipulated that they were to be supplied by the Foreign Service Institute, headed by a Director appointed by the Secretary. Comparable to the military staff colleges to furnish in-service training to officers and employees at various stages in their careers, the Institute was made responsible for both planning and implementing instruction programs.

A separate section of the act dealt with special allowances and benefits. Previously established basic rent, cost of living, representation, and separation allowances were continued.[100] New allowances were added to defray expenses for the maintenance of official residences for Chiefs of Mission and to cover the costs of transfers from post to post and for special burdens of those assigned to duty in Washington. Eight categories of travel expenses were prescribed for Foreign Service Officers and members of their families and for the costs involved in the transit of their automobiles by water, rail, or air. Emergency commissary or mess services were also authorized to meet temporary contingencies. Salary differentials were allowed for those individuals assigned to posts "at which extraordinarily difficult living conditions or excessive physical hardships prevail or at which notably unhealthful conditions exist."

Various types of leaves of absence were specified, including annual leave (not to exceed sixty calendar days), of which a portion could be accumulated for succeeding years, and sick leave, at the rate of fifteen days per year, which also could be accumulated up to a total of 120 days. To "re-Americanize" members of the Foreign Service stationed abroad, they were required to return to the United States for not less than three years during the first fifteen years of service, and both officers and employees were required to return to the United States on statutory leave on the completion of two years of continuous service abroad or as soon thereafter as possible.

Dealing with separation from the Foreign Service and retirement, the act distinguished among categories of officers. Career Ministers (unless they were then serving as Chiefs of Mission) were to be retired when they reached the age of sixty-five, except if they were needed in an emergency, when their tenure could be extended for a period of not more than five additional years. Other Foreign Service Officers were to be retired at the age of sixty, with a possible extension of five years if needed in an emergency. The Secretary of State was authorized to establish regulations governing officers in Classes 2–6 respecting the maximum period they could remain in the Service without promotion. Voluntary retirement was made available for officers who were at least fifty years of age and had rendered at least twenty years of service. In addition, the act specified rules to govern separation from the Service, for both unsatisfactory performance of duty and misconduct or malfeasance in office.

A separate Foreign Service Retirement and Disability System was provided, handled by the Retirement and Disability Fund administered by the Treasury Department. This Fund had originally been established under the Rogers Act of 1924. The 1946 Act contained comprehensive stipulations concerning participants, annuitants, compulsory member contributions, computation of retirement, benefits accruing to those retired with disabilities or incapacities, computation of retirement benefits, financing the system, and other payments to retirees.

At the discretion of the Director General, any officer or employee of the Foreign Service could be assigned or detailed for duty in the Department of State or any other Government agency for periods of not more than four years. They also could be assigned to participate in international conferences and meetings held in the United States or abroad or in international organizations.

Although the provisions concerning the Foreign Service apply to consular as well as diplomatic officers, several provisions of the act pertain specifically to consular affairs. Thus, the Secretary of State was empowered to define the limits of consular districts; on the recommendation of the Secretary, the President may commission staff officers or employees to serve in a consular capacity, and the Secretary may also appoint consular agents under such regulations as may be prescribed; when any Foreign Service Officer or any consul or vice consul who is not a Foreign Service Officer is temporarily in charge of a Consulate during the absence or incapacity of the principal officer, such temporary surrogate is to receive additional compensation; and dealing with consular compensation, the act stipulated that salaries of consular agents were to be fixed by the Secretary in accordance with regulations determined by the Department on the basis of the classification of positions. Furthermore, the Secretary, in accordance with prescribed regulations, was empowered to separate from service consular agents for unsatisfactory performance, misconduct, or malfeasance.

Other traditional matters in the 1946 Act pertained to regulations concerning the appointment and treatment of alien clerks and employees; the maintenance of "efficiency records" and the production of "efficiency reports" on the performance of officers and employees and the preservation of their confidentiality under regulations prescribed by the Secretary of State; the bonding of officers and employees; and medical treatment and expenses, including periodic physical examinations, inoculations, and hospitalization. Finally, a few specifications dealt with prohibitions. The wearing of special uniforms, the acceptance of presents and titles from foreign governments without the specific consent of Congress, the transaction of business or engagement for profit in any profession in the foreign countries to which officers and employees are assigned were proscribed. They also were prohibited from engaging in personal correspondence concerning the public affairs of foreign governments. The act also empowered the Secretary to delegate to other officers and employees holding positions of responsibility in the Department or the Foreign Service the powers conferred upon the Secretary to the extent to which this served "the interests of the efficient administration of the Service."[101]

Between 1946 and 1980 Congress legislated a number of changes to supplement the Act of 1946 by means of additions and amendments. It authorized the appointment of 500 additional Foreign Service Officers at other than the minimum salary for the classes to which such appointments were made (Act of August 13, 1954—68 Stat. 1051); created the Foreign Agricultural Service (Act of August 28, 1954—68 Stat. 897); and prescribed legislative rules governing the disposition of gifts and decorations received by American officials from foreign governments (Acts of September 11, 1967—81 Stat. 195, and August 17, 1977—91 Stat. 844). Of notable significance, the Act of August 5, 1955 (69 Stat. 536), provided for the creation of the distinguished new rank of Career Ambassador.

Congress also updated the Act of 1946 by issuing several amendatory laws. The Act of April 5, 1955 (69 Stat. 24), provided that up to 1,250 additional Foreign Service Officers might be appointed from the Civil Service and Foreign Service Reserve and Foreign Service Staff Corps, authorized hardship post salary differentials for certain officers, home service transfer allowances, and educational allowances, granted credit for prior military service toward retirement, clarified and revised the basis for the selection-out system for forced retirement, and other changes. The amendatory Act of July 28, 1956 (70 Stat. 704), dealt with salary increases for Chiefs of Mission and Career Ministers; liberalizing the retirement system, medical services, and hospitalization; increasing the number of Foreign Service classes from six to eight to provide more rapid progression of careerists; broadening lateral entry into the Foreign Service from several other Government agencies; and the integration of qualified Foreign Service Reserve Officers into the Foreign Service. The amendments contained in the Act of September 8, 1960 (74 Stat. 831), stipulated the foreign language proficiency requirements for Chiefs of Mission and Foreign Service Officers, liberalized in-class salary increases and the retirement system, provided discretionary authority to appoint candidates directly to Class 7 (second from the lowest) for a limited number of candidates, and extended the retirement age for Career Ambassadors and Ministers. The Vietnam Amendments Act of December 23, 1967 (81 Stat. 671), provided special arrangements for American officers and employees stationed at high-risk posts and for other purposes.

On October 17, 1980, Congress enacted a new organic act for the Foreign Service (94 Stat. 2071–2175). It constituted an updated basic and comprehensive prescription, also applicable to both diplomatic and consular officers and personnel. Aside from stipulating that the career Foreign Service, "characterized by excellence and professionalism, is essential in the national interest to assist the President and the Secretary of State in conducting the foreign affairs of the United States" and that it "should be representative of the American people," it specified that it "must be preserved, strengthened, and improved in order to carry out its mission effectively in response to the complex challenges of modern diplomacy and international relations." The basic objectives for legislating a new Foreign Service Act were prescribed, embracing the merit principle; admission by means of an updated and rigorous examination system; producing more efficient, economical, and equitable personnel administration; improving

Foreign Service managerial flexibility and effectiveness; increasing efficiency and economy by promoting maximum compatibility among the agencies authorized by law to use the Foreign Service personnel system; and providing the highest caliber of representation in handling the foreign affairs of the United States.

In addition to such goals and general provisions, the act consists of nearly 160 sections grouped in fifteen chapters, constituting 100 printed pages. Among the major topics treated are management of the Foreign Service; appointments; compensation; classification of positions and assignments; promotion and retention; the Foreign Service Institute, career development, training, and orientation; retirement and disability; travel, leave, and other benefits; labor–management relations; grievances; transition arrangements; and provisions concerning relations with other Government agencies concerned with foreign affairs. Much of this act is based on, and updates and refines, the basic act of 1946 supplemented by intervening amendments and additions. It pays special attention to such new subjects as management of the Foreign Service, labor–management relations, and the handling of personnel grievances, and greater attention is paid to the nature and functions of the Foreign Service Institute. The few stipulations that refer to consular affairs are similar to those contained in the Act of 1946.

Stressing the matter of management, this act makes the Secretary of State responsible for the administration of the Department of State and other government agencies that use Foreign Service members (such as the Departments of Agriculture and Commerce) and empowers the Secretary to prescribe regulations deemed necessary to implement its provisions. It also stipulates that Chiefs of Mission serving abroad possess "full responsibility" for the administration of all Government officers and employees (other than the military) stationed in foreign countries and defines the roles, authority, and functions of the Inspector General of the Department, the Director General of the Foreign Service, the Board of the Foreign Service and its companion Board of Examiners, the Foreign Service Labor Relations and Grievance Boards, and other departmental agencies.

Dealing with Foreign Service personnel, this act details regulations respecting a host of matters concerned with appointments (limited to American citizens, except those appointed for service abroad as consular agents and foreign national appointees); commissions for both diplomatic and consular officers; promotion based on determination by Selection Boards and retention in the Service; retirement (mandatory and voluntary), reemployment, disability, and death in service; labor–management relations (including management and employer rights and conflict resolution); and the right of Foreign Service members to bring grievances and the facilities and methods of handling them.

Other more specific matters relating to personnel, updating earlier laws, embrace appointment of Foreign Service Officers based on performance in written, oral, physical, foreign language, and other examinations and the obligation of Foreign Service members to serve abroad "for substantial portions of their careers" as well as in the United States normally for not more than eight years. This act of 1980 also introduced a system for the conferral of special awards, commendations, and medals in "recognition of outstanding contributions to the Nation," presented by the President and the Secretary for "performance in the course of or beyond the call of duty" and involving "distinguished, meritorious service," including "extraordinary valor in the face of danger to life or health" (discussed more fully in the section on "Recognition and Awards" in Chapter 8).

Among the more crucial changes are specifications concerning the classification of Foreign Service Officers and personnel and their compensation. The most senior appointees, in terms of their personal rank, appointed by the President with the advice and consent of the Senate, include Chiefs of Mission, Ambassadors at Large, Career Ambassadors, and career members of the Senior Foreign Service. In terms of the positions they hold, senior appointees include those commissioned as Ambassadors and Ministers. The rank of Career Minister, established by the Act of August 13, 1946, was supplemented with the rank of Career Ambassador by the Act of August 5, 1955, and was dropped in the Act of 1980. The Secretary of State is ascribed authority to classify other Foreign Service positions held in the Department of State and abroad at diplomatic and consular posts. Such classifications levels are required to be related to assignment to particular posts and tours of duty, not to exceed four years, and include service as Chargés d'Affaires and individuals on assignment to other Government agencies functioning abroad, or to attend international conferences or participate in international organizations. In addition, subject to certain conditions, the President is authorized to appoint individuals, including members of the career Foreign Service, with "the personal rank of Ambassador or Minister" to undertake special missions of a temporary nature, not exceeding six months in duration.

To govern the matter of compensation, a new system was created. Instead of stipulating specific Foreign Service salary amounts, the Act of 1980 simply provides that various categories of officers and personnel be compensated in accordance with a number of salary schedules, with specific amounts fixed by separate periodic laws and Executive Orders. Thus, salaries of Chiefs of Mission and Senior Foreign Service Officers are ascribed by the President, and those of other Foreign Service Officers are assigned by the Secretary of State. The specific amounts within these categories have since been defined and periodically modified by a series of Executive Orders. Those pertaining to the Department of State are prescribed in four general categories, titled "Executive Schedule," "Senior Executive Service Schedule," "General Schedule," and "Foreign Service Schedule."

The highest salary levels are provided in the Executive Schedule, which consist of five levels, with mid-1990s annual amounts ranging from $108,200 to $148,400, and in the Senior Executive Service Schedule composed of six levels ranging from $92,900 to $115,700. The General Schedule, more detailed and complicated, embraces fifteen GS categories (GS 1 being the lowest, and GS 15 the highest), each with ten salary stages, with salary levels ranging from $12,141 to $15,183 for the lowest class to $67,941 to $88,326 for the highest. While these schedules and classes tend to be stable, specific amounts are periodically increased by Executive Orders rather than statutory enactments.

The separate professional Foreign Service Schedule is composed of nine classes, each of which consists of fourteen categories called "steps," producing more than 125 different salary levels. For example, in the mid-1990s those of Foreign Service Officers in Class 9 (the lowest) range from $18,707 to $27,472 and those in Class 1 (the highest) range from $67,941 to $88,326. Thus, overall, the extremes vary considerably from $18,707 to $88,326. Within-class salary raises are generally automatic, based on length of time in, and quality of, service, but also for especially meritorious service as determined by the Secretary of State. The specific class salary amounts are usually increased annually by Executive Orders, which obviates the earlier practice of periodically modifying them by new or amendatory acts of Congress. Promotion of Foreign Service, Foreign Service Reserve, and Foreign Service Staff Officers from class to class, as well as in-class promotions, are automatically accompanied by not only advancement in grade rank but also salary increases.

In practice, Chiefs of Mission are compensated according to the salary levels specified in the upper four levels of the Executive Schedule, which in 1995 ran from $115,700 to $148,400, and Senior Foreign Service Officers receive salaries prescribed for the six levels prescribed in the Senior Executive Service Schedule. Other members of the Foreign Service—including Foreign Service Officers, Foreign Service Reserve Officers, and officers and other personnel of the Foreign Service Staff Corps—are salaried according to the Foreign Service Schedule, whereas others, such as staff employees, are compensated according to the General Schedule.[102]

Additional or supplementary compensation is also provided for by the Act of 1980. These embrace such matters as special performance pay (lump-sum additions to basic pay to a limited number of members of the Senior Foreign Service for "especially meritorious or distinguished service," as recommended by the Secretary of State); special increases for officers who serve temporarily as head of a Foreign Service post abroad during the absence or incapacity of the principal officer; special differentials to complement basic compensation for those required to perform extra work on a regular basis in substantial excess of normal requirements; and special gratuities to surviving dependents of Foreign Service Officers and employees who die as a result of injuries sustained in the performance of duty abroad (amounting to one year's salary). Others include representation expenses for attendance at official receptions and entertainment for official purposes, travel expenses for the performance of official duties, training grants for members of the families of officers and employees who participate in Foreign Service Institute programs, and pay benefits for those in transition, pending the full implementation of legislation.

Finally, this Act of 1980 also deals with many other matters, some of which are carried over from earlier acts. For example, it specifies that the Foreign Service is required to be administered in such a way as to assure maximum compatibility with all Government agencies authorized to use its personnel system. The nature and functions of the Foreign Service Institute have been reformed and updated, including programs of education in foreign languages, personnel training, and career development and counseling. Others pertain to commissioning of all diplomatic and consular officers (including Vice Consuls) to specific missions; providing extra credit for service at specific unhealthful posts so that each year counts for a year and a half for purposes of retirement computation; authorizing the recall and reemployment of retired career members of the Foreign Service, for limited appointments up to four years, and the employment of former Government employees under special circumstances; furnishing special compensation for imprisoned foreign national employees who are incarcerated as a result of employment by the United States; preserving the confidentiality of records of individual officers used in matters of promotion and retention (except for those concerned with the handling of funds); and accessing by individuals concerned of their records in cases of grievance proceedings. Supplementing earlier statutory prohibitions and restrictions, to preserve the prerogatives of Congress, the act specifies that, except in the case of the appointment of Career Ambassadors, no individual may be designated as an Ambassador or Minister or appointed to serve in any position bearing these titles without the advice and consent of the Senate.[103]

Since 1980, aside from periodic authorization and appropriations measures, Congress passed several amendatory and supplementary acts. For example, the Foreign Missions Act of August 24, 1982 (96 Stat. 282), provides legal controls governing the establishment, location, and other matters regarding the diplomatic missions and facilities of foreign governments in the United States and for establishing an Office of Foreign Missions in the Department of State to implement it; the Act of October 19, 1984 (98 Stat. 2649), created a Department of State independent, nonprofit Institute of Peace for scholarly inquiry and research respecting American diplomatic affairs; and the Omnibus Diplomatic Security and Antiterrorism Act of August 27, 1986 (100 Stat. 853), established a Diplomatic Security Service to deal with international terrorism, multilateral cooperation to combat it, diplomatic security abroad, and punishment for terrorist acts, including those directed against American diplomats and their facilities.

Thus, founded on past experience and several decades of post–World War II refinement, the Act of 1980 constitutes an inclusive complex to govern the nature and operation of the contemporary Foreign Service. It contains scores of primary and secondary, traditional and innovative aspects of the essence and functioning of a unique American career service to handle contemporary diplomacy. While legal regulations have been stabilized in many respects, specific details have been subsequently modified and will in the future be changed by amendatory and supplementary legislation, Executive Orders, and departmental regulations. Designated as America's peacetime "first line of defense" by Dean Acheson in 1946 and as "the road builders along the way to peace" by historian William A. Williams, the Foreign Service has been and will in the future need to be continuously and incrementally renovated to deal effectively with the diplomatic relations of the United States as a superpower.

Diplomatic Missions

Since World War II the United States has undergone a remarkable expansion of its diplomatic community, tripling the foreign representation responsibility of the Department of State. In 1945 American diplomatic missions were maintained at fifty-six foreign capitals, but not in the Axis powers, their satellites, the countries they occupied, and the Baltic states occupied by the Soviet Union. As a consequence of the historic independence boom that followed, more than 125 missions were added throughout the world, commencing during the half decade from 1946 to 1949 and peaking in the mid-1990s, due largely to the breakup of the Soviet Union, Czechoslovakia, and Yugoslavia and the revival of the independence of the Baltic states.

This expansion of American diplomatic representation manifests an interesting dichotomy of ready recognition of new states and establishing formal diplomatic relations with them and, on the other hand, a complex, incremental process for the Department of State. Whereas in earlier times the United States was inclined to be selective in recognizing the independence of foreign countries, following World War II it extended its diplomatic representation to all of them, even to several city-states.

Since 1945 the Department of State has maintained regular diplomatic missions accredited to 189 individual countries and to a number of international organizations and other continuing agencies, totaling more than 200, as listed in Table 7.6, Part A.[104] President Truman inherited a diplomatic establishment of fifty-six such missions in 1945. In the next two years relations with Austria, Bulgaria, Hungary, Romania, and Thailand, which had been severed during the war years, were revived, and by 1950, beginning with the Philippine Republic on July 4, 1946 (the first postwar country to gain independence and American recognition), the United States rapidly revived relations with Korea (which had been discontinued in 1905) and added eight new countries (primarily Asian but also including Israel and Yemen) to its diplomatic community, raising the total to 71. Thereafter, as noted in the table, it grew each decade and currently numbers more than 175.[105] To summarize, fifteen states were added from 1945 to 1949,[106] twelve during the 1950s, thirty-seven during the 1960s, twenty-eight during the 1970s, fifteen during the 1980s, and twenty-six during the 1990s (to 1998). Notably, the most substantial increases occurred during the 1960s and 1970s and, remarkably, twenty-three in the single year 1995.

One of the major complexities encountered centered on rectifying the diplomatic disruption caused by World War II, when relations were severed not only

Table 7.6
American Diplomatic Representation since 1945

A. Countries

Country	Capital	Diplomatic Representation							Current Rank
		1945	1950	1960	1970	1980	1990	1998	
* Afghanistan	Kabul	x	x	x	x				--
Albania	Tirana						(1995)	x	A
Algeria	Algiers			(1962)	x	x	x	x	A
Angola	Luanda						(1993	x	A
Antigua & Barbuda	St. Johns					(1982)	x	x	A
* Argentina	Buenos Aires	x	x	x	x	x	x	x	A
Armenia	Yerevan						(1995	x	A
* Australia	Canberra	x	x	x	x	x	x	x	A
* Austria	Vienna	(1946)	x	x	x	x	x	x	A
Azerbaijan	Baku						(1995	x	A
Bahamas	Nassau				(1973)	x	x	x	A
Bahrain	Manama				(1972)	x	x	x	A
Bangladesh	Dhaka				(1974)	x	x	x	A
Barbados	Bridgetown			(1967)	x	x	x	x	A
Belarus	Minsk						(1995)	x	A
* Belgium	Brussels	x	x	x	x	x	x	x	A
Belize	Belize City					(1983)	x	x	A
Benin (Dahomey)	Cotonou			(1960)	x	x	x	x	A
* Bolivia	La Paz	x	x	x	x	x	x	x	A
Bosnia & Herzegovina	Serajevo						(1995)	x	A
Botawana	Gaborone				(1971)	x	x	x	A
* Brazil	Brasilia/Rio de Janeiro	x	x	x	x	x	x	x	A
Brunei	Bandar Seri/ Begawan					(1984)	x	x	A
* Bulgaria	Sofia	(1947)	x	x	x	x	x	x	A
Burkina Faso	Oaugadougou			(1960)	x	x	x	x	A
Burma	Rangoon	(1947)	x	x	x	x			--
Burundi	Bujumbura			(1963)	x	x	x	x	A
Cambodia	Phnom Penh		(1950)	x	x	x	--	x	A
Cameroon	Yaounde			(1960)	x	x	x	x	A
* Canada	Ottawa	x	x	x	x	x	x	x	A
Cape Verde	Praia				(1976)	x	x	x	A
Central African Rep.	Bangui			(1961)	x	x	x	x	A
Chad	N'Djamena			(1961)	x	x	x	x	A

Key

*	Indicates countries with which the U.S. had diplomatic relations prior to 1945.
x	Indicates applicability at the time.
(Dates)	Indicate year when post World War II diplomatic relations commenced.
A	Indicates Ambassadorial rank, generally Ambassador Extraordinary & Plenipotentiary.
C	Indicates Consular Office in 1998.
N	Indicates there no Embassy or Consular Office in 1998, but serviced by diplomat from nearby territory.
S	Indicates special status of representation.
T	Judicates that diplomatic relations were terminated.
--	Indicates diplomatic relations suspended as of 1998.

Country	Capital	Diplomatic Representation							Current Rank
		1945	1950	1960	1970	1980	1990	1998	
* Chile	Santiago	x	x	x	x	x	x	x	A
* China (Original)	Canton	x	x	x	x				T
China (People's Rep.)	Beijing				(1979)	x	x	x	A
China (Taiwan)	Taipei				(1979)	x	x	x	S
* Colombia	Bogota	x	x	x	x	x	x	x	A
Comoros	Moroni					(1982)	x	x	N
Congo (Rep. of)	Brazzaville			(1960)	x	x	x	x	A
* Costa Rica	San Jose	x	x	x	x	x	x	x	A
Cote d'Ivoire	Abidjan			(1960)	x	x	x	x	A
Croatia Zagreb							(1995)	x	A
* Cuba	Havana	x	x	x					--
Cyprus	Nicosia			(1960)	x	x	x	x	A
Czech Republic	Prague						(1995)	x	A
* Czechoslovakia	Prague	x	x	x	x	x	x		T
* Denmark	Copenhagen	x	x	x	x	x	x	x	A
Djibouti	Djibouti				(1977)	x	x	x	A
Dominica	Roseau				(1979)	x	x	x	N
* Dominican Republic	Santo Domingo	x	x	x	x	x	x	x	A
* Ecuador	Quito	x	x	x	x	x	x	x	A
* Egypt	Cairo	x	x	x	x	x	x	x	A
* El Salvador	San Salvador	x	x	x	x	x	x	x	A
Equatorial Guinea	Malabo			(1968)	x	x	x	x	A
Eritrea	Asmara						(1995)	x	A
* Estonia	Tallinn						(1995)	x	A
* Ethiopia	Addis Ababa	x	x	x	x	x	x	x	A
Fiji	Suva				(1972)	x	x	x	A
* Finland	Helsinki	x	x	x	x	x	x	x	A
* France	Paris	x	x	x	x	x	x	x	A
Gabon	Libreville			(1961)	x	x	x	x	A
Gambia	Banjul			(1965)	x	x	x	x	A
Georgia	Tbilisi						(1995)	x	A
Germany, Dem. Rep.	Berlin				(1974)	x	x		T
* Germany, Fed. Rep.	Bonn		(1955)	x	x	x	x	x	A
Ghana	Accra		(1957)	x	x	x	x	x	A
* Greece	Athens	x	x	x	x	x	x	x	A
Grenada	St. George				(1975)	x	x	x	N
* Guatemala	Guatemala City	x	x	x	x	x	x	x	A
Guinea	Conakry		(1959)	x	x	x	x	x	A
Guinea-Bissau	Bissau				(1976)	x	x	x	A
Guyana	Georgetown			(1966)	x	x	x	x	A
* Haiti	Port-au-Prince	x	x	x	x	x	x	x	A
* Holy See (Papal States)	Vatican City					(1984)	x	x	A
* Honduras	Tegucigalpa	x	x	x	x	x	x	x	A
Hong Kong	Hong Kong						(1994)	x	C 1
* Hungary	Budapest	(1946)	x	x	x	x	x	x	A
* Iceland	Reykjavik	x	x	x	x	x	x	x	A
India	New Delhi	(1947)	x	x	x	x	x	x	A
Indonesia	Jakarta	(1949)	x	x	x	x	x	x	A

[1] After 99 years as a British Crown Colony, returned to china in July 1997.

Table 7.6 (continued)

Country	Capital	Diplomatic Representation 1945	1950	1960	1970	1980	1990	1998	Current Rank
* Iran	Tehran	x	x	x	x				--
* Iraq	Baghdad	x	x	x			x		--
* Ireland	Dublin	x	x	x	x	x	x	x	A
Israel	Tel Aviv	(1949)	x	x	x	x	x	x	A
* Italy	Rome	x	x	x	x	x	x	x	A
Jamaica	Kingston			(1962)	x	x	x	x	A
* Japan	Tokyo		(1952)	x	x	x	x	x	A
Jerusalem	Jerusalem					(1980)	x	x	A
Jordan	Amman		(1950)	x	x	x	x	x	A
Kazakhstan	Almaty						(1995)	x	A
Kenya	Nairobi			(1964)	x	x	x	x	A
Kiribati	Parawa					(1980)	x	x	N
* Korea	Seoul	(1949)	x	x	x	x	x	x	A
Kuwait	Kuwait			(1961)	x	x	x	x	A
Kyrgyz	Bishkek						(1995)	x	A
Laos	Vientiane		(1950)	x	x	x	x	x	A
* Latvia	Riga						(1995)	x	A
* Lebanon	Beirut	x	x	x	x	x	x	x	A
Lesotho	Maseru				(1971)	x	x	x	A
* Liberia	Monrovia	x	x	x	x	x	x	x	A
Libya	Tripoli		(1952)	x	x	x	x		--
* Lithuania	Vilnius						(1995)	x	A
* Luxembourg	Luxembourg	x	x	x	x	x	x	x	A
Madagascar (Malagasy)	Antananarivo			(1960)	x	x	x	x	A
Malawi	Liongwe			(1964)	x	x	x	x	A
Malaysia	Kuala Lampur		(1957)	x	x	x	x	x	A
Maldives	Malé			(1965)	x	x	x	x	N
Mali	Bamako			(1960)	x	x	x	x	A
Malta	Valletta			(1965)	x	x	x	x	A
Marshall Islands	Majuro					(1987)	x	x	A
Mauritania	Nouakchott			(1960)	x	x	x	x	A
Mauritius	Port Louis			(1968)	x	x	x	x	A
* Mexico	Mexico City	x	x	x	x	x	x	x	A
Micronesia	Kolonia					(1987)	x	x	A
Moldova	Chisinau						(1995)	x	A
Mongolia	Ulaanbaatar					(1987)	x	x	A
* Morocco	Rabat	x	x	x	x	x	x	x	A
Mozambique	Maputo				(1976)	x	x	x	A
Namibia	Windhoek						(1995)	x	A
Nauru	Yaren				(1974)	x	x	x	N
Nepal	Kathmandu	(1948)	x	x	x	x	x	x	A
* Netherlands	The Hague	x	x	x	x	x	x	x	A
* New Zealand	Wellington	x	x	x	x	x	x	x	A
* Nicaragua	Managua	x	x	x	x	x	x	x	A
Niger	Niamey			(1960)	x	x	x	x	A
Nigeria	Abuja			(1960)	x	x	x	x	A
* Norway	Oslo	x	x	x	x	x	x	x	A
Oman	Muscat				(1972)	x	x	x	A

Country	Capital	Diplomatic Representation							Current Rank
		1945	1950	1960	1970	1980	1990	1998	
Pakistan	Islamabad	(1948)	x	x	x	x	x	x	A
* Panama	Panama City	x	x	x	x	x	x	x	A
Papua New Guinea	Port Moresby				(1976)	x	x	x	A
* Paraguay	Asuncion	x	x	x	x	x	x	x	A
* Peru	Lima	x	x	x	x	x	x	x	A
Philippines	Manila	(1946)	x	x	x	x	x	x	A
* Poland	Warsaw	x	x	x	x	x	x	x	A
* Portugal	Lisbon	x	x	x	x	x	x	x	A
Qatar	Doha				(1972)	x	x	x	A
* Romania	Bucharest	(1947)	x	x	x	x	x	x	A
Russian Federation	Moscow						(1993)	x	A
Rwanda	Kigali			(1963)	x	x	x	x	A
St. Kitts and Nevis	Basseterre					(1984)	x	x	N
St. Lucia	Castries				(1979)	x	x	x	N
St. Vincent & Grenadines	Kingstown					(1981)	x	x	N
Sao Tomé & Principe	Sao Tomé				(1976)	x	x	x	N
* Saudi Arabia	Riyadh	x	x	x	x	x	x	x	A
Senegal	Dakar			(1960)	x	x	x	x	A
Seychelles	Victoria				(1976)	x	x	x	A
Sierra Leone	Freetown			(1961)	x	x	x	x	A
Singapore	Singapore			(1966)	x	x	x	x	A
Slovak Republic	Bratislava						(1995)	x	A
Slovenia	Ljubijana						(1995)	x	A
Solomon Islands	Honiara				(1978)	x	x	x	A
Somalia	Mogadishu			(1960)	x	x	x	x	A
* South Africa	Cape Town	x	x	x	x	x	x	x	A
* Spain	Madrid	x	x	x	x	x	x	x	A
Sri Lanka (Ceylon)	Colombo	(1949)	x	x	x	x	x	x	A
Sudan	Khartoum		(1956)	x	x	x	x	x	A
Suriname	Paramaribo				(1976)	x	x	x	A
Swaziland	Mbabane				(1971)	x	x	x	A
* Sweden	Stockholm	x	x	x	x	x	x	x	A
* Switzerland	Bern	x	x	x	x	x	x	x	A
* Syria	Damascus	x	x	x	x	x	x	x	A
Tajkistan	Dushanbe						(1995)	x	A
Tanzania (Tanganyika)	Dar es Salaam						(1995)	x	A
* Thailand	Bankok	(1946)	x	x	x	x	x	x	A
Togo	Lomé			(1960)	x	x	x	x	A
Tonga	Nuku'alofa				(1972)	x	x	x	N
Trinidad & Tobago	Port-of-Spain			(1962)	x	x	x	x	A
Tunisia	Tunis		(1956)	x	x	x	x	x	A
* Turkey	Ankara	x	x	x	x	x	x	x	A
Turkmenistan	Ashgabat						(1995)	x	A
Tuvalu	Funafuti					(1980)	x	x	A
Uganda	Kampala			(1963)	x	x	x	x	A
Ukraine	Kiev						(1995)	x	A
* USSR/Soviet Union	Moscow	x	x	x	x	x	x		T
United Arab Emirates	Abu Dhabi				(1972)	x	x	x	A

Table 7.6 (continued)

Country	Capital	Diplomatic Representation							Current Rank
		1945	1950	1960	1970	1980	1990	1997	
* United Kingdom	London	x	x	x	x	x	x	x	A
* Uruguay	Montevideo	x	x	x	x	x	x	x	A
Uzbekistan	Tashkent						(1995)	x	A
Vanuatu (New Hebrides)	Port Via					(1987)	x	x	N
* Venezuela	Caracas	x	x	x	x	x	x	x	A
Vietnam	Saigon		(1950)	x	x				--
Western Samoa	Apia				(1971)	x	x	x	A
Yemen	Sanaa	(1946)	x	x	x	x	x	x	A
* Yugoslavia	Belgrade	x	x	x	x	x	x		T
Zaire (Congo)	Kinshasa			(1960)	x	x	x	x	A
Zambia	Lusaka			(1965)	x	x	x	x	A
Zimbabwe	Harare					(1980)	x	x	A
TOTAL 189		71	83	120	145	157	182	177	

B. Missions to International Organizations

		1945	1950	1960	1970	1980	1990	1997	
European Communities	Brussels			(1961)	x	x	x	x	A
International Atomic Energy Agency	Vienna		(1957)	x	x	x	x	x	A
International Civil Aviation Org.	Montreal	(1947)	x	x	x	x	x	x	A
North Atlantic Treaty Org.	Brussels		(1952)	x	x	x	x	x	A
Org. for Economic Coop. & Dev.	Paris			(1961)	x	x	x	x	A
United Nations	New York	(1946)	x	x	x	x	x	x	A
U.N. (European Ofc.)	Geneva			(1958)	x	x	x	x	A
U.N. Educational Scientific and Cultural Org.	Paris			(1961)	x	x			N
U.N. Industrial Development Org.	Vienna			(1968)	x	x	x	x	A
United Nations Ofc.	Vienna					(1983)	x	x	A
Food & Agr. Org.	Rome					(1983)	x	x	A
Office for Arms Reduction Neg.	Geneva					(1985)	x	x	A
Org. of American States	Washington	(1948)	x	x	x	x	x	x	A

Note: For a historical listing of the commencement of American diplomatic representation to foreign nations, in chronological order to 1960, with brief descriptions, see Barnes and Morgan, *The Foreign Service of the United States*, Appendix 3, pp. 339–48, and for current annual lists, see the *United States Government Manual*.

with Germany (1938–55) and Japan (1941–52) but also with Austria (1938–46), Bulgaria (1941–47), Hungary (1941–46), Italy (1941–45), Romania (1941–47), and Thailand (1941–46). Regular relations with the major Axis powers were not revived until the 1950s, and those with Axis allied and occupied states were resumed in 1946 and 1947. In the case of Albania, which became a member of the Communist orbit following the war, they remained in abeyance from 1939 to 1995.[107] These were paralleled by the postwar initiation of diplomatic exchanges with newly independent Burma, Cambodia, India, Indonesia, Israel, Jordan, Laos, Nepal, Pakistan, the Philippines, Sri Lanka, Vietnam, and Yemen—all 1946 to 1950, plus the renewal of relations with Korea, which had been annexed by Japan in 1905. Except for Israel, Jordan, and Yemen, these were all Asian nations.

Another major development involved the substantial breakup of the former British, Dutch, French, Italian, Japanese, Portuguese, and Spanish empires; the dissolution in the 1990s of the Soviet Union into twelve states, Yugoslavia into three states, and Czechoslovakia into two states[108]; special diplomatic arrangements with the Holy See, Hong Kong, and Jerusalem[109]; and the postwar political changes in Germany and China. Germany was occupied by the United States, the United Kingdom, the Soviet Union, and France and eventually was divided into the West German Federal Republic, to which the United States accredited an Ambassador beginning in 1955, and the German Democratic Republic, to which the Department of State sent an Ambassador commencing in 1974, and they were reunited in October 1990.

Especially interesting is the manner in which the Department of State handled the matter of representation with China. Following World War II it continued to maintain an Embassy at Taipei, but when mainland China came under Communist rule, the Department also established a Liaison Office at Beijing from May 1973 to March 1979. That year the United States recognized the People's Republic of China and transferred its Embassy to Beijing. However, when the Nationalist Government of China was established in Taiwan, the Department created a special diplomatic arrangement for dealing with it. Under the Taiwan Relations Act of 1979, technically, the Department continued to deal with the Government of China located in Taiwan on a ''nongovernmental basis'' through its American Institute in Taiwan, a nonprofit District of Columbia corporation that the Department has described as constituting ''neither recognition of the Taiwan authorities nor the continuation of any official relationship'' but with which the United States continues to maintain treaty relations, including some concluded since 1979. The official Taiwan counterpart agency is designated as the Coordination Council for North American Affairs.

More common are the interruption or severance of diplomatic relations. Temporary suspensions were instituted by the formal severance of relations by the United States or the foreign country, the closing of the American Embassy, or the withdrawal of American diplomatic personnel with at least fifteen foreign governments, which were later revived. Such ''interruptions'' or ''suspensions'' of normal relations were instituted by the Department of State with Bolivia (1980–81), Bulgaria (1950–60), Dominican Republic (1963–64), and Peru (1962–63); "withdrawals" of American diplomatic personnel were instituted with Congo (1965–77) and Uganda (1973–79); and the American Embassy was "closed" in Chad (1980–83). Conversely, interruptions were initiated by foreign governments, including the recall of American diplomats accredited to Burundi (1955–68) and Haiti (1963–64) and, more seriously, by the formal severance of relations by Algeria (1967–75), Egypt (1967–74), Iraq (1967–85), Mauritania (1967–71), Sudan (1967–72), and Syria (1967–74). Such actions initiated in 1967 resulted from the Israeli Six-Day War with Egypt and other Arab countries. Many of these lapses lasted for years, sometimes for more than a decade. Moreover, in several cases the United States reduced its representation level to missions headed by Chargés d'Affaires (often ad interim) rather than ranking diplomats. These included Afghanistan (1979–), China (1950–53), Hungary (1957–67), Libya (1972–80, when the American Embassy was formally closed), Madagascar (1975–80), Poland (1983–87), and Yemen (1962–72).

Most crucial have been the long-term suspensions of normal relations with Afghanistan (following the assassination of the American Ambassador in 1979); Cambodia (in which the American Embassy was closed in April 1975 and was not revived until the early 1990s); Cuba (where the Department of State severed relations in January 1961); Iran (where the American Embassy was forcibly seized, whereupon the United States severed relations in April 1980); Iraq (which severed relations with the United States on June 7, 1967, which were revived in November 1984, only to be severed again in the early 1990s); Libya (where the American Embassy was closed in May 1980), in which relations were not revived by the late 1990s; and Vietnam (where the American Embassy was closed, and U.S. personnel were evacuated on April 29, 1975, and post–Vietnam War relations were not established by the late 1990s. Moreover, although diplomatic representation was terminated in Estonia, Latvia, and Lithuania when they were occupied by the Soviet Union in June 1940, they were formally revived by 1995, following the dissolution of the Soviet Union.[110]

Turning to the matter of geographic distribution, since 1945 the largest number of American diplomatic missions listed in Table 7.6 has been located in Africa (forty-nine), followed by Europe (thirty-nine), Asia (thirty-two), Latin America (twenty-two), the Mideast (fourteen), Oceania (fourteen), the Caribbean (thirteen), the Indian Ocean (five), and Canada. In time, additional states will become independent and need to be accommodated. Keeping in mind that several current diplomatic partners have populations of less than 50,000, namely, St. Kitts and Nevis (41,000), Burundi (28,000), and Nauru (only 10,000) and Vatican City (1,000), theoretically, future possibilities might include such territories as the European principalities of Andorra (with a population of more than 60,000), Liechtenstein (31,000), Monaco (30,000), and San Marino (25,000).

Aside from additional fragmentation of existing countries, other hypothetical possibilities might include such continental territories as French Guiana, North Korea, Tibet, the West Bank and Gaza Strip (Palestine), Inner Mongolia, Manchuria, Taiwan, Tibet, and a good many individual islands and island groups. In addition to the breakup of the Indonesian Islands, illustrations include such American possibilities as Puerto Rico (with a population of 3,600,000, which on several occasions has considered becoming independent or opting for American statehood as an alternative to its commonwealth status), American Samoa (47,000), Guam (133,000), Northern Marianas (43,500), Palau (15,122), and the Virgin Islands (102,000). Foreign potentialities, having populations exceeding 100,000, embrace the Azores (Portugal), Corsica (France), French Polynesia, Guadelupe (France), Hong Kong (China), Macao (Portugal), Madeira (Portugal), Martinique (France), New Caledonia (France), the Netherlands Antilles, Sardinia (Italy), Sakhalin (Russia), and Sicily (Italy), several of which have populations exceeding 1 million.[111] If all of these became independent, the State Department would need to add another thirty to its diplomatic community.

The Embassy diplomatic mission headed by an Ambassador was created by law in 1893, and in 1945 some forty of the fifty-six (71 percent) American missions were of this rank. Since then, after the United States achieved superpower status, it has become common to maintain Embassies in foreign countries regardless of their location, size, or population and to accredit its emissaries at the Ambassadorial rank. Since 1945 the State Department has raised its existing missions, primarily from that of Legations headed by Ministers (largely, Envoys Extraordinary and Ministers Plenipotentiary) to Embassy rank in thirty additional foreign countries.[112] For virtually all of the rest, numbering more than 100, the rank of Ambassador has been accorded at the outset of diplomatic relations.[113] As a consequence, the primary contemporary diplomatic ranks have been reduced to two—the Ambassador and occasional temporary or transitional Chargés d'Affaires.

However, occasionally, emissaries are temporarily given special titles for unique functions. For example, in Vietnam, 1964–73, five envoys were appointed as Deputy Ambassadors to supplement the regularly commissioned Ambassadors; from 1973 to 1979 four envoys to Communist China were accredited to head the U.S. Liaison Office in Beijing pending the transfer of the American Embassy from Taipei, and for a time the American mission to Saudi Arabia was regarded as a Liaison Office, which was raised to the rank of Embassy in 1984; on the revival of diplomatic relations with Cambodia in the 1990s an "American Representative" served briefly pending the appointment of an Ambassador; and for some years in the 1990s the Department of State was represented by a "Director" of a special mission to Angola. Also, an American "Interests Section" was maintained in the Belgian Embassy in Iraq, 1972–84, manned sequentially by seven diplomatic emissaries, and in the mid-1990s the United States began to maintain a special "Interests Section" in Cuba.

To conclude, currently, the Department of State maintains some 175 "Diplomatic Offices" to represent it to foreign governments, consisting of 166 Embassies, several other missions of various types, and an Interest Section in Cuba—all headed by Ambassadors. To these must be added the Chiefs of Mission, which generally bear the title "Representative" or "Permanent Representative" of the United States, with the rank of Ambassador Extraordinary and Plenipotentiary, to a number of international organizations, listed in Table 7.6, Part B.

Thus, whereas in earlier times it was American practice to grant its foreign missions modest diplomatic ranks, since World War II virtually all regular emissaries are accorded the highest status. Inasmuch as they are mutually agreed to on the basis of the principle of mutual equivalency or *agreation*,[114] as a characteristic of the new diplomacy, the United States now enjoys the advantages of being represented abroad and maintaining its foreign missions at the highest diplomatic level, and the scale of rank precedence is minimized, if not eliminated, for contemporary American envoys.[115] Because this escalation to the Ambassadorial/ Embassy level has become universal, internationally, the United States no longer suffers from the appointment of lesser-ranked diplomats, and differentiation among American Ambassadors has come to be based not on rank and precedence but rather on personal Foreign Service status for those who are careerists and the particular countries to which they are accredited.

Multiple Simultaneous Appointments

The Department of State practice of assigning individual emissaries to simultaneous missions was continued for assignments throughout the world, except for European and Latin American continental countries. Often such multiple accreditations were made at the outset of diplomatic relations, which were later converted into separate missions. Whereas most of these envoys were commissioned as Ambassadors, even those appointed to small islands, a few initial appointees were designated as Chargés d'Affaires.

More than ninety emissaries held such simultaneous assignments commissioned to some fifty nations. Less than thirty were continental countries (Australia, fifteen in Africa, three in Asia, and eight in the Mideast). The rest were individual islands and island groups. Approximately half of the diplomats who held such assignments were career Foreign Service Officers, of whom eleven were women. Such appointees represented the United States to from two to as many as eight countries simultaneously. These ranged from Jamaica, Madagascar, New Zealand, Sri Lanka, and Papua New Guinea (with populations esceeding 2 million), to such ministates as Antigua and Barbuda, Grenada, Kiribati, the Marshall Islands, and Tonga (all with less than 100,000 population) and such microstates as Nauru (10,000) and Tuvalu (12,000).

These simultaneous diplomatic missions involved logical, sometimes interesting, and varying combinations. For example, in the Caribbean area, with headquarters at Bridgetown (Barbados), envoys were simultaneously assigned to such additional island countries as Antigua and Barbuda, Dominica, Grenada, St. Kitts and Nevis, St. Lucia, and St. Vincent and the Grenadines.[116] In the

Mideast they were appointed simultaneously to such groupings as Egypt or Saudi Arabia and Yemen, and Ambassador William A. Stoltzfus, Jr., stationed at Kuwait, also represented the United States to Bahrain, Oman, Qatar, and the United Arab Emirates (1972–76). Six American Ambassadors accredited to India, resident at New Delhi, also represented the Department of State to Nepal,[117] and Ambassador Donald R. Heath was commissioned simultaneously to Vietnam, Cambodia, and Laos (1950–54), resident at Saigon. Nine Ambassadors, stationed in Sri Lanka (Ceylon), also served as diplomatic agents to the Maldives, and an Ambassador stationed at Madagascar also serviced the island of Mauritius. Similarly, in Oceana at least six Ambassadors accredited to Papua New Guinea also handled diplomatic relations with the Solomon Islands; several assigned to New Zealand similarly serviced Fiji, Tonga, and Western Samoa; those stationed in Australia customarily manage affairs with the tiny island of Nauru; and those resident at Fiji generally also service Tonga and Tuvalu.

Most complex and comprehensive was the treatment of African countries. Since World War II approximately two dozen emissaries, stationed in Botswana, Cameroon, Congo, Côte d'Ivoire, Gabon, Kenya, and Senegal, have handled diplomatic relations in various groupings with nine additional countries (Benin, the Central African Republic, Chad, Equatorial Guinea, Mauritania, Niger, São Tomé and Principe, Sechelles, and Swaziland), which changed from time to time.

At least ten of these American diplomats represented the Department of State to four or more countries simultaneously. Those who held the largest number of such multiple concurrent missions included Jeanette W. Hyde (seven), Thomas H. Anderson (six), Paul A. Russo (six), Milan D. Bish (five), Sally A. Shelton (five), and William Stoltzfus (five). Some fifteen envoys had the distinction of receiving four or more Department of State and foreign appointments of various types (counting their multiple assignments as single appointments), all but four of whom were career Foreign Service Officers, and several of them also held senior State Department offices, served as Ambassadors at Large, or were designated as Career Ambassadors.

By the mid-1990s most of these simultaneous combinations were superseded by separate appointments to individual countries, except for the continued grouping of the Caribbean islands of Barbados with Antigua and Barbuda, Grenada, and St. Kitts and Nevis, Australia with Nauru, and the Pacific Islands of Tonga with Kiribati and Tuvalu. For the sake of economy, conserving manpower, and convenience, some of these remaining groupings are likely to persist, and as additional small and adjacent states emerge, this practice of simultaneous diplomatic appointments is bound to continue.[118]

Diplomatic and Consular Functions

Although diplomatic and consular officers have been merged into a single Foreign Service and are interchangeable in their individual assignments, they perform different, often complementary functions. Those of diplomats may be variously defined. Their traditional primary responsibilities are said to consist of representation, observation, negotiation, reporting, and protection. The first three bring diplomats into direct contact with receiving, host governments and are easily comprehended, even though representation, which some regard as the highest or purist aspects of diplomacy, must be understood as also serving as the principal channel of communications between governments. However, observation, reporting on political, economic, social, and other matters, and protection of American interests are services performed on behalf of the sending government, as is the protection of the welfare of American nationals residing in, or visiting, the country. Customarily, these are governed by the Vienna Convention on Diplomatic Relations of 1961, applicable to the United States in 1972, and U.S. law and regulations. Occasionally, these basic functions are supplemented with ceremonial and social responsibilities and with third-party representation, mediation, and handling the concerns of nationals of other countries.

Another way of distinguishing diplomatic activities is to differentiate administrative and substantive functions. The administrative encompass the management of American diplomatic missions abroad, their principal officers and organizational structure, communications with the Department of State, coordinating relations with other, usually nearby, American diplomatic missions, integrating diplomatic missions with consular establishments within the country or region, and such other matters as financing, housing, transportation, health, and similar services. This category also encompasses program planning, direction, and implementation, which usually are handled by Chiefs of Mission, their deputies, and their senior officers.

The substantive units and duties, though they differ in number and size with the importance and location of individual missions, generally fall into the following categories. The traditional and most common embrace political and economic affairs, both of which are usually handled by Chiefs of Mission and their senior deputies. Political affairs involve American foreign policies and international interests and the political forces, parties, and events in the host country and reporting on them to the Department of State. The economic responsibility involves the implementation of American economic policy and developments in the host country, as well as detailed reporting by means of a regularized departmental Current Economic Reporting Program.

Other substantive functions include commercial affairs, concerned largely with trade and commerce promotion and protection, which may be handled separately or encompassed by those that deal with economic affairs; educational and cultural activities throughout the world in accordance with policies and interests of the United States and promoting educational and cultural exchange; information and intelligence concerned with a broad spectrum of reporting to inform policymakers in the Department of State, although technically, national security intelligence is handled by the Central Intelligence Agency and the Department of Defense; international organization affairs, concerned with handling a variety of multilateral substantive and functional activities, which is largely in the nature of an operational responsibility, and also with those American missions assigned to specific international organizations, such as the United Nations, the European Union, the North Atlantic Treaty Organization, the Organization of American States, and the Organization for Economic Cooperation and Development; and public affairs, concerned with providing information to both the American people and the public of foreign countries, although much of the latter is handled by the U.S. Information Agency since its establishment in 1953 (as successor to the Office of War Information).

Other, in some cases more recently established, substantive functions that apply multilaterally as well as bilaterally in particular cases include an array of subjects. These embrace agriculture, aviation, claims, conservation, copyright, customs, energy, the environment, extradition, fisheries, humanitarian affairs, intellectual and other property, international scientific affairs, international terrorism, maritime matters, meteorology, narcotic drugs, patents and trademarks, population and refugees, publications, satellites, smuggling, telecommunications, taxation, trademarks, and similar matters. Additional subjects, such as arms control and limitation (including nuclear), outer space, and the seas and seabeds are usually the responsibility of special missions, and others are handled by the attachés assigned to diplomatic missions.

On the other hand, consular missions—both those embodied within diplomatic establishments in the capitals of foreign countries and separate agencies located in selected foreign cities (usually, ports and other places that are important to American shipping, commercial, immigration, and other concerns)—deal with more limited, but also important, matters. Currently, consular missions are usually designated as Consulates General, Consulatees, and Consular Agencies, depending on the importance and location of the particular mission. They are headed by Consuls General, Consuls, and Consular Agents, depending on the importance of the particular mission (former Commercial Agencies and Vice Consulates were discontinued prior to 1950). Like diplomats, these officers are commissioned by the President and are assigned to posts by the Department of State. Consular missions are normally established with the consent of the host government, but consular officers are not regarded as official intergovernmental representatives.

Unlike diplomats, consular officers deal mostly with individuals and often handle the affairs of American nationals in accordance with the laws and regulations of the United States, more than seventy-five bilateral consular conventions and other agreements with the host countries, and the multilateral Vienna Consular Convention of 1963. Where there are several American consular offices in cities outside the local capital, a Counselor of Consular Affairs may be assigned to the diplomatic mission to assist in supervising and coordinating them. The Department of State defines the extent of their consular districts. Usually, Consuls General are Foreign Service Officers of Class 1 (the highest), Consuls are of Class 3, and Consular Agents are of Class 8.

Much of the responsibility of consular officers is devoted to serving the interests and welfare of American citizens abroad, both residents and tourists. Traditionally, they perform two types of functions. Those of a general nature consist of trade promotion and protection, including such matters as facilitating American exports to their consular districts, filing commercial and financial reports on marketing opportunities, certifying shipping invoices for goods destined for the United States, handling and certifying shipping papers of American merchant vessels located in foreign ports, and arbitrating or otherwise resolving disputes between masters and crews of American commercial vessels.

However, most consular duties are devoted to assisting individual Americans. These include such functions as maintaining a record of Americans residing abroad; registering the birth of American children; assisting Americans to be married or who are stranded, ill, injured, or who die abroad, and then taking custody of their property for eventual disposition; providing assistance in other emergencies; issuing, extending, renewing, and amending American passports and providing visas to foreigners coming to the United States; protecting the lives and welfare of Americans who are confronted with serious or threatening conditions in hazardous areas; representing the causes of those who are apprehended to see that they are given prompt and fair trials; and providing many other services or benefits.[119]

Coordination of Diplomatic and Other Responsibilities Abroad and the Country Team

Following World War II the problem of coordinating the functions, responsibility, and authority of diplomatic missions with those of other American government agencies abroad plagued the White House and Department of State. To deal with the matter, Presidents have issued a series of Executive Orders and letters to govern this relationship. They focused on the control and coordinating role of American chiefs of diplomatic missions in the countries to which they are accredited. In Executive Order No. 10338 of April 4, 1952, President Truman initiated the process in which he specified that the chief of the American diplomatic mission in each foreign country "as the representative of the President and acting on his behalf, shall coordinate the activities of the United States representatives of other agencies" and "shall assume responsibility for assuring unified development and execution" of American programs in that country.

Similar action was taken by subsequent Presidents, evidencing several progressions and changes. In form they mutated from basic executive orders, to Presidential communications addressed to chiefs of government agencies, to Presidential letters sent directly to American Ambassadors in the field. Concerning functions they varied from simple "coordination," to "coordination and supervision," to "oversight and coordination," to "direction and coordination," and to "direction, coordination, and supervision" of all "Executive branch U.S. officers and personnel" in the foreign country. So far as responsibility and authority are concerned, they changed from "responsibility," to "authority and responsibility," to "full responsibility."

In the 1990s President Bush introduced exceptions applied to overseas personnel under the jurisdiction of an American area military commander, under the authority of another U.S. Chief of Mission or detailed to duty on the staff of an international organization. He also emphasized that the Secretary of State has responsibility "not only for the activities of the Department of State and the Foreign Service, but also, to the fullest extent provided by law, for the overall coordination and supervision of United States Government activities abroad."[120]

Another new technique was developed to enhance geographic coordination of American diplomats abroad. Also beginning in the 1950s, Secretaries of State have personally participated in occasional brief intra-American diplomatic conferences with Chiefs of Mission accredited to major geographic areas. These, almost invariably appended to foreign trips of the Secretary, often extend to visits to several foreign governments and North Atlantic Treaty Organization and other meetings. These conferences are generally of short duration, usually of one to three days, depending on the Secretary's schedule. They are held at such centers as London and Paris for European countries, Geneva for the Middle East, Kinshasa (Congo) for Africa, and Hong Kong, Manila, Taipei, and Tokyo for Asia and the Pacific.

Furthermore, as American diplomatic missions abroad increased in size, complexity, and responsibilities, and the number of U.S. agencies with foreign responsibilities multiplied, their integration and coordination required systematic management. The concept of a unifying arrangement emerged to facilitate executive and administrative teamwork in planning, consultation, assignment of duties, instituting a spirit of cooperation, and other functions of American Embassies.

As a result, another post–World War II innovation, called the "Country Team," was introduced in the 1950s. It is applied to individual American diplomatic missions headed by the resident Ambassador and Deputy Chief of Mission. Broadly defined, it is composed of all the principal components of the American mission in each foreign country. It is described as a management agency—a council of senior officers—to consolidate the heads of diplomatic mission segments. Institutionally, the teams vary with the interests and responsibilities of their members, the number of functional programs involved, and their methods of operation.

Periodic sessions—unofficially called Chancery meetings—with principal representatives of diplomatic and consular embassy units and other American agencies convene to integrate policies and programs in individual foreign countries. Said to have been initiated by the Department of State, without legislative mandate, this development represents an evolutionary, rather than a revolutionary, modification. Such teams are designed to amalgamate diplomatic, consular, political, economic, public relations, administrative, nation building, and other affairs. Their meetings facilitate orientation, rapid interchange of consultation, the exchange of views, determination of action on American interests, policies, recommendations, strategies, and tactics in the field, and the elimination of conflicting reports to Washington.

In practice the Country Team may vary in composition, procedure, and effectiveness, depending on the personal modus operandi of the Ambassador, the number and type of American agencies and programs involved, the qualities and disposition of their senior officers, and the nature of problems considered, especially in times of crisis. It was established to handle the proliferation of post–World War II foreign relations needs and has been developed and modified incrementally as an important administrative device and to mollify the competitive status of the agents of American operational programs overseas.[121] Those who implement it recognize that the Ambassador, the President's personal representative to the leaders of the host government, is the senior American officer in each foreign capital and therefore heads the team. As a result, the role of Ambassadors has been modified in recent decades to include participation in administering operational programs, in addition to maintaining traditional diplomatic relations devoted primarily to representation, negotiation, and serving as listening and information-gathering facilities.

Inasmuch as U.S. relationships with each foreign country are unique, the functioning of the Country Teams varies, depending on the preference of the Ambassador and the nature of American interests in, and policy toward, individual countries. Usually, the Ambassador manages it personally, but some prefer to delegate this to the Deputy Chief of Mission. In large American Embassies, it may consist of the Ambassador, the Deputy Chief, the heads of major sections, corps of various specialized attachés, the supervising Consul General if there are a number of American consular officers in the country, and the chiefs of all such functional agencies as the Agency for International Development, the Central Intelligence Agency, the Military Assistance Advisory Group, the Peace Corps, the U.S. Information Agency, and other agencies if they exist in the particular mission. The only exceptions are U.S. military commands stationed abroad and American missions to international organizations. The timing of meetings also varies from periodic, usually weekly, to special emergency sessions. Some Ambassadors also utilize subsidiary committees, subcommittees, and task forces to deal with special substantive matters, emerging problems, and major crises. However, care must be exercised that the Country Team process does not degenerate into a system of "decision by committee," which debilitates the responsibility and authority of the Ambassador.

The Country Team constitutes the "Ambassador's cabinet," which may function as an advisory body, a forum for discussion and consultation, and a means of instilling a spirit of coordination respecting objectives and priorities. Under the Ambassador's leadership it may also serve as a planning body to analyze local developments and devise courses of action to deal with them and as an executive agency to distribute tasks to be performed, to monitor their implementation, and to pool resources for their achievement. Equally important, it may recommend policy to the Department of State, but to achieve the most desirable results, systematized cooperation of the State Department and other Departments and agencies needs to be paralleled in Washington. Normally, the Ambassador's channel of responsibility flows via the departmental Country Director to the appropriate Geographic Assistant Secretary of State.

So far as competing interests and decision-making authority are concerned, other Departments and agencies generally defer to the State Department, but care needs to be exercised that the conduct of foreign affairs is not usurped by a series of "foreign offices" operating independently either in foreign countries or in Washington. Legally and practically, the State Department is the sole official foreign ministry of the United States and serves as the hub of the Country Team system, possesses the most extensive professional personnel resources, and alone can instruct the Chief of Mission. Therefore, the Ambassador is "commander in chief" in the field and possesses authority to dominate intergovernmental rivals, and all Embassy officers and other personnel are subject to the Ambassador's jurisdiction.

Thus, there is no sacrosanct design for the composition, structure, or method of operation of the Country Team and the interdepartmental system, and it is subject to continued modification and improvement. But, to fulfill its purposes, it must encompass members of all the Departments and agencies whose interests and programs are concerned, and it must be led by the officers of the diplomatic mission. As former Deputy Under Secretary of State William B. Macomber, Jr., has put it, "The Department which commands the commander is in a strong position in relation to its rivals."[122] This was epitomized by recent Presidents who formally annunciated that Ambassadors are in charge of the entire U.S. diplomatic missions and that these include not only the personnel of the Department of State and the Foreign Service but also the representatives and officers of all other American agencies that have programs or activities in the countries of their assignment.

Foreign Service Institute

As Department of State and Foreign Service personnel multiplied, their functions and responsibilities broadened in scope and became more specialized, and officers and staff members were frequently shifted from one agency or post to another, a comprehensive program of in-service training became imperative. The State Department had experimented with a variety of programs, and an Executive Order of June 7, 1924, authorized the creation of a Training School, which became the forerunner of the Foreign Service Institute.[123]

Following World War II, the need for systematic instruction and training of both officers and other personnel intensified. The Foreign Service Act of 1946, sections 701–7, provided for the establishment of the Institute to furnish training

and instruction in the field of foreign relations to both officers and other employees of the Department of State and Foreign Service throughout their careers,
as well as to other personnel of the American Government. It specified that this
Institute was to be headed by a Director, appointed by the Secretary of State,
to manage its operations and programs, under the direction of the Secretary-
General of the Foreign Service and in accordance with prescribed rules and
procedures. It was the intent of Congress that the Director should be an educational leader of distinction. The act was implemented by Departmental Regulations issued by Secretary Marshall in March 1947, and it also encouraged
the assignment of officers and employees to outside cooperating institutions of
higher learning.

Since its inception the Institute has sought to secure its objectives through a
thoroughgoing educational system, functioning largely ''at the graduate school
level,'' supplemented with a broad spectrum of technical instruction. It provides
a unique system of programs tailored to meet the requirements of a competent,
modern Foreign Service. It determines the needs of the Department of State and
Foreign Service, formulates appropriate plans, and administers the programs
when they are established. It is staffed by experienced Foreign Service Officers,
full-time professional instructors, and visiting lecturers from other government
agencies, universities, and the business world.

Initially, the Institute consisted of four Schools, each headed by an Assistant
Director, to furnish both basic and advanced (graduate-level) officer programs,
management and administrative training, and instruction in thirty-six foreign
languages. The appointment of faculty and the pattern of instruction were intended to be flexible to meet a variety of needs. It has offered programs of full-
time instruction for short periods up to six months, part-time instruction for
varying periods, organized on-the-job training within the State Department, assignment to other government agencies and outside educational institutions, and
programs maintained by the Institute at Foreign Service posts abroad, as well
as extension courses for employees abroad.

By 1949 the Institute provided an extensive menu of instruction, consisting
of nearly sixty subjects and projects, of which more than forty concentrated on
management and administration topics, evidencing the need for greater expertise
in this field. These ranged from Foreign Service indoctrination, diplomatic and
consular practice, American orientation seminars, selected problems in foreign
relations, and power factors in world affairs, to such management topics as
personnel and fiscal administration, responsibilities of security officers, international conference leadership and procedures, communications and cryptology,
and even instruction in office effectiveness and document-filing practices. Many
of these programs lasted only a few hours or days, others ran full-time for
several weeks or months, and longer programs entailed assignment of upper-
class officers to universities and the American War Colleges. The languages
taught have embraced not only Chinese, German, Italian, Japanese, Russian, and

Spanish but also Albanian, Arabic, Bengali, Finish, Hindustani, Icelandic, Persian, Pidgin English, and many others.

Later, the Institute was reorganized to consist of two primary components—a School of Foreign Affairs and a School of Languages and Area Studies. It conducts programs for thousands of students each year, most from the Department of State and Foreign Service but also many from other government agencies. New programs are established as needed. These are represented by interdepartmental and special regional seminars, advanced area studies, and training in additional languages, including African languages such as Iglo, Hansa, Twi, and Yoruba.

Currently, the Institute services the personnel of forty government agencies in addition to the Department of State and Foreign Service and offers more than 300 programs, including courses in some sixty foreign languages. It promotes successful performance in foreign relations assignments, enhances leadership in policy making and implementation and management capabilities, and facilitates adjustment of officers and staff members to foreign countries and cultures.

In the 1960s thought was also devoted to creating a National Academy of Foreign Affairs for more advanced training, to supplement the Foreign Service Institute. In 1961 a special committee submitted a report to Secretary Rusk, which recommended the establishment of such an Academy for additional training at the highest level, to include instruction, research, and leadership for all governmental education programs and to deal with "the delicate dynamic of democratic strategy." Legislation was introduced in 1963 to provide for the Academy, but it languished in Congress, following hearings in the Senate Foreign Relations Committee.

However, in 1982 the State Department established a Center for the Study of Foreign Affairs as an adjunct of the Foreign Service Institute. It was designed to enrich traditional Foreign Service training by bringing government officials in many agencies abreast of emerging foreign concepts and developments. It provides a program consisting of conferences, research exercises and simulations, and publications dealing with a variety of functional and procedural subjects.[124]

Inspection System

To monitor the activities of consular officers, especially their financial affairs, in April 1906 Congress established a Consular Inspection Corps of five officers to be headed by a Consul General at Large, with responsibility for inspecting each consular officer every two years. The Rogers Act of 1924, which amalgamated Diplomatic and Consular Services, created the office of Foreign Service Inspector to perform this service for all American foreign missions. Following World War II, the Act of 1946 authorized the Secretary of State to detail Foreign Service Inspectors to examine and review all diplomatic and consular establishments every year or two. They were given authority to suspend any officer serving abroad, except for Chiefs of Mission, and by 1954 this group was headed by a Chief Inspector.

The Act of 1980 formalized the current inspection system. It created a special Inspector General of the Department of State, to be appointed by the President "from among individuals exceptionally qualified for the position by virtue of their integrity and their demonstrated ability in accounting, auditing, financial analysis, law, management analysis, public administration, or investigations, or their knowledge and experience in the conduct of foreign affairs," to serve directly under, and report to, the Secretary of State. This was the first congressional enactment to define the authority and functions of the inspection program, which broadened its applicability to both the Department and foreign missions, and it required such inspections every five years. Generally, these Inspectors General have been experienced Foreign Service Officers. The law authorizes them to undertake not only inspections and audits but also investigations for "efficiency, effectiveness, and economy" and to check for fraud, abuses, and deficiencies, and they are required to file annual reports with the Secretary of State.

Women in Contemporary American Diplomacy

As noted in earlier chapters, initially, women served largely in clerical positions in the Department of State and the diplomatic service abroad. Shortly after World War II, when Acheson was Secretary, of the fifty senior departmental offices, none were held by a woman. Meta K. Hannay was the first woman to take the examinations for appointment to the Diplomatic Service in 1921 but failed to pass both the written and oral tests. Lucile Atcherson was the first to pass the examinations, in 1922, and be appointed as a Foreign Service Officer. She was followed by Pattie H. Field, the first to be appointed as a Foreign Service Officer following the enactment of the Rogers Act, followed by Frances E. Willis in 1927, Margaret Warner and Nelle B. Stogsdall in 1928, and Constance R. Harvey in 1929. Of these both Willis and Harvey remained in the Foreign Service for more than thirty years. Also, after nearly forty-two years in the Department of State, in 1937 Margaret M. Hanna was the first woman to become a Foreign Service Officer by means of lateral entry. Not until 1945 did six more women pass the examinations—Katherine W. Bracken, Betty A. Middleton, Helen R. Nicholl, Anne M. Oehm, and Mary S. Olmsted—and become Foreign Service Officers. Thereafter, some women were also assisted by a series of special arrangements—much as the Manpower Act of July 3, 1946, the Department of State exchange program for Civil Service personnel in 1949, the Rowe Committee Plan of 1951, and the Wristonization program of the 1950s— all of which provided for appointment to the Foreign Service by lateral entry.

By 1953 there were forty-three women Foreign Service Officers, and since then the number has steadily increased. During the 1960s official recruiting policy was made identical for the appointment of both women and men. By 1963 the number of women increased to 310 Foreign Service Officers, fifty-eight Foreign Service Reserve Officers, and approximately 2,175 Foreign Service Staff Officers and clerical employees. The overseas corps of women Foreign Service Officers then consisted of one Ambassador (Frances E. Willis, Sri Lanka), twenty-nine Counselors or First Secretaries of American diplomatic missions, 220 Second Secretaries, and sixty Third Secretaries. At that time nearly 5,400 women served in the Department and the Foreign Service, and there were more women in the upper-level positions of the State Department than in any other American Government agency.

After World War II women became a major component of the senior personnel corps of the Department of State and the diplomatic service. Prior to 1945 their appointment to major administrative offices and representational posts was rare. Exceptions were limited to Ruth Bryan Owen as Minister to Denmark (1933–36) and Florence Jaffray Harriman as Minister to Norway (1937–40), and a few held important positions in the State Department. Several women also had entered the career Foreign Service, such as Lucille Atcherson, appointed Third Secretary in the American Legation in Switzerland (1922, and later sent to Panama City), and Frances E. Willis, appointed in 1927, who served abroad at Brussels, Luxembourg, Madrid, Santiago, Stockholm, and Valparaiso prior to World War II. Some also served on the American delegation to the United Nations Conference at San Francisco in 1945. Virginia C. Gildersleeve, Professor and Dean at Barnard College, was a member of Secretary Stettinius' eight-person delegation. Other women functioned in a variety of other capacities, including Marjorie M. Whiteman as a technical expert from the Office of the Legal Adviser of the Department, and more than thirty others represented various departmental agencies, more than ten of whom were from the State Department Division of International Organization Affairs.

During the past half century, however, a substantial number of women were appointed to both principal Department of State and chief of diplomatic mission positions. Thus, some twenty were commissioned to ten ranking departmental offices. These included Secretary of State (Madeleine Albright, 1997), Under Secretary for Security Assistance, Science, and Technology (Lucy W. Benson, 1977), Counselor of the Department (Rozanne L. Ridgway, 1980), Assistant Secretary (ten), Chief of Protocol (five), Coordinator for International Communications and Information Policy (two), Director of the Foreign Service (two), and Director of Management Operations (one). Those who had more than one of these assignments were Joan M. Clark, Caroline C. Laise, Ridgway, and Barbara M. Watson.[125]

A good many others also held other departmental administrative positions, some of substantial responsibility. For example, Katherine W. Bracken, who became a clerk in the State Department in 1940, entered the Foreign Service six years later and served in missions abroad in Eastern Europe, the Mideast, and Asia, as a Consul, and she headed the Agean Division of the Department.

Ethel B. Dietrich held several posts abroad, became a Foreign Service Reserve Officer in 1952, headed the American negotiating teams at several international conferences, and eventually served in the U.S. mission to the North Atlantic Treaty Organization. More uniquely, Ruth B. Shipley became a clerk in the Department in 1914 and was appointed as Chief of the Passport Division in 1928, in which capacity she served for nearly a quarter century, and she was followed by Frances G. Knight, who, after serving in the Army (1943–45), entered the Department of State as a foreign affairs specialist in 1948 and became Director of the Passport Office in 1955, a post that she also held for many years. Whiteman, trained in the legal profession, joined the staff of the Department of State Solicitor in 1929 and rose to the rank of Assistant Legal Adviser by 1950, and she produced the comprehensive fifteen-volume third edition of the *Digest of International Law*, succeeding those prepared by John Bassett Moore (1906) and Green H. Hackworth (1940–44). Virginia C. Westfall entered the Department as a foreign affairs specialist in 1950, became a Foreign Service Officer in 1960, and was appointed the Deputy Director of the Office of International Administration.

Many more women served in a diplomatic representational capacity. Some eighty-five were accredited as chiefs of mission, of whom the preponderant number were commissioned to foreign governments, and a few to international organizations. The first group consisted of thirty-six Foreign Service Officers and forty-four noncareerists. Combined, they received nearly 100 appointments.

Of the careerists, Frances E. Willis is noted for the precedent she set. She was the first Foreign Service Officer to be commissioned as a Chief of Mission, to hold the rank of Ambassador, to function as emissary to three countries (Switzerland, Norway, and Ceylon over a period of twelve years, from 1953 to 1964), and to achieve the highest honorary ranks in the Foreign Service. She was succeeded by Clare H. Timberlake (the first woman Ambassador to the Congo, 1960–61), Margaret J. Tibbetts (Norway, 1964–69), Laise (Nepal, 1966–73), and Eileen R. Donovan (Barbados, 1969–74)—all appointed in the 1960s.

Ten more careerists were commissioned in the 1970s, and the number rapidly increased to thirteen in the 1980s and to sixteen from 1992 to 1996, portending considerable subsequent growth. Of these, several were given more than one Chief of Mission assignment. They included Aurelia E. Brazeal (Kenya and Micronesia), Patricia M. Byrne (Burma and Mali), Mary A. Casey (Algeria and Tunisia), Nancy V. Rawls (Côte d'Ivoire and Togo), Ridgway (Finland and the German Democratic Republic), Terisita C. Schaeffer (Maldives and Sri Lanka), Theresa A. Tull (Guyana and Laos), and Melissa F. Wells (Cape Verde and Guinea Bissau). Of these, only Ridgway was sent to European countries.

On the other hand, nearly sixty noncareerists were accredited as diplomatic mission chiefs to foreign governments throughout the world. The earliest after World War II were Eugenie Anderson (Denmark, 1949), Perle Mesta (Luxembourg, also 1949), and Clare Boothe Luce (Italy, 1953). Thereafter, the record of appointing women to representational positions increased each decade—four in the 1960s, eleven in both the 1970s and the 1980s, and nearly thirty from 1990 to 1997. A few received more than one appointment, such as Anderson (also to Bulgaria, 1962), Luce (also to Brazil, 1959, which she declined), and also Shirley Temple Black (Ghana, 1974, and Czechoslovakia in the early 1990s), Cynthia S. Perry (Sierra Leone, 1986, and Burundi, 1991), Mabel M. Smythe (Cameroon, 1977, and Equatorial Guinea, 1979), and Faith R. Whittlesey (Switzerland twice, 1981 and 1985). All of them were at the rank of Ambassador except those of Anderson to Bulgaria and Mesta to Luxembourg, who were at the rank of Minister Plenipotentiary. Initially, Harriet W. Isom was designated as Chargé d'Affaires ad interim to Laos in 1986, which was advanced to Chargé d'Affaires the following year, and she was later named Ambassador to Benin and then to Cameroon.

However, the preponderant number of noncareerists received single appointments (a few to major powers), such as Anne L. Armstrong (United Kingdom), Ann C. Chambers (Belgium), Carol B. Hallett (Bahamas), Pamela Harriman (France), Margaret M. O. Heckler (Ireland), Anne F. Holloway (Mali), and Marquita M. Maytag (Nepal). Other such single appointees were Elizabeth F. Bagley (Portugal), Loret M. Ruppe (Norway), Jean K. Smith (Ireland), Helene A. Von Damm (Austria), and Katherine White (Denmark).

Occasionally, women have also been commissioned to represent the United States on multiple assignments to several countries simultaneously. The earliest was Mary S. Olmsted (Papua New Guinea and the Solomon Islands, appointed in 1978), followed by Ann Clarke Martindell (New Zealand and Western Samoa, 1979), Sally A. Shelton (Barbados, Dominica, Grenada, and St. Lucia, 1979), M. Virginia Schafer (Papua New Guinea and the Solomon Islands, 1981), and Patricia G. Lynch (Comoros and Madagascar, 1986). In the early 1990s these also included Della Newman (New Zealand and Western Samoa), Evelyn Teegan (Pacific Islands of Fiji, Kiribati, Tonga, and Tuvalu), and Jeanette W. Hyde (the Caribbean Islands of Antigua and Barbuda, Barbados, Dominica, Grenada, St. Kitts and Nevis, St. Lucia, and St. Vincent and the Grenadines). Of these, only Olmsted and Schafer were careerists.

Over the years, women were appointed to represent the United States to at least seventy-five countries, including eighteen in Europe, sixteen in the Western Hemisphere, many in Africa, and a few in Asia, the Mideast, and the Indian and Pacific Oceans. These countries spanned the globe, ranging from Austria, France, the German Democratic Republic, Italy, and the United Kingdom in Europe, to Bagladesh and Burma in Asia; Guatemala and Guyana in Latin America; New Zealand and Micronesia in the Pacific; and Kenya, Zaire, and Swaziland in Africa. At least two women were accredited to each of sixteen countries,[126] and three to Barbados, Cameroon, Grenada, Nepal, and Sierra Leone. The most popular, however, was Luxembourg, beginning with the appointment of Perle Mesta in 1949, who set a precedent, followed by Patricia R. Harris (1965), Ruby R. Farkas (1973), Rosemary L. Ginn (1976), and Jean B. Gerard (1985)—all noncareerists.

Of special interest, in the mid-1990s women were also accredited as the first American Ambassadors to the new Soviet Republic of Kyrgyz (Eileen A. Malloy) and Moldova (Mary C. Pendleton). Although in the early 1990s Ambassador William C. Harrop was commissioned to Israel, stationed at Tel Aviv, which the United States recognized as its capital, Molly Williamson also represented the State Department at Jerusalem for several years. In addition, beginning early in the 1970s, a few noncareerist women were accredited as resident Ambassadors to several international organizations. These included the United Nations at New York (Jeane J. Kirkpatrick, 1981–85, and Madeleine Albright, 1993–97), the International Civil Aviation Organization (Betty R. Dillon, 1971–77), the United Nations Educational, Scientific and Cultural Organization (Barbara W. Newell, 1979–81), and the United Nations Agencies for Food and Agriculture (Millicent Fenwick, 1983–87).

Some women are historically noteworthy for a variety of reasons. Those remembered as ''firsts,'' to name a few who held State Department administrative offices, include Albright as Secretary of State, Lucy W. Benson as Under Secretary, Rozanne Ridgway as Counselor, Marion H. Smoak as Chief of Protocol,[127] Carol Laise as Assistant Secretary of Public Affairs and Director General of the Foreign Service, and Joan M. Clark as Director of Management Operations. Some are noted for receiving the largest number of appointments as principal officers. These are exemplified by Shirley Temple Black (three), Clark (four), Laise (three), Ridgway (four), and Barbara M. Watson (four). Others are noted for representing the United States to the largest number of countries simultaneously, including Shelton (four), Teegan (four), and Hyde (seven). In addition to the matters mentioned earlier, Frances Willis, with thirty-five years as a Foreign Service Officer, achieved distinction by being honored as the first woman to be accorded the ranks of Career Minister (1955) and Career Ambassador (1962).

Thus, whereas in the United States, as in most other countries prior to World War II, women were generally excluded from, or limited in their, participation in the centers of diplomatic affairs, this has changed considerably since 1945. Initially, there were reservations concerning the ability of women to endure the trials and vicissitudes of duty overseas, which hindered their acceptance in such assignments. Subsequently, however, both as Foreign Service Officers and noncareerists, they have increasingly been appointed to principal Department of State offices and as Chiefs of Mission. With a few exceptions, they have been recruited to fill the most senior departmental posts, such as Secretary, Under Secretary, and Assistant Secretary in charge of the geographic and certain other offices, for which political appointees are generally recruited by the President.

On the other hand, women have been increasingly accredited as diplomatic emissaries to a broad range of foreign countries and to some international organizations, currently almost invariably at the highest diplomatic rank. Restraint on their appointment to these positions is due less to their gender than to other factors. It appears that the countries to which they are not commissioned is determined largely by the cultural attitudes, values, and sensitivities of the host governments and peoples of the countries to which they are sent. As a consequence, while some contend that women have merely begun to make slow progress entering and progressing in the domain of foreign relations, the gender factor appears to be in perceptible decline.[128]

Emissaries Remembered

Many American diplomats have achieved distinction and are recognized for their special achievements as emissaries and for their appointments to and service as senior Department of State officers. Some of them are remembered as "firsts," paving the way for those who followed, for the extended duration of their diplomatic service, for their contribution to Department of State management reform, for their service on special missions, for being honored by promotion to the distinguished rank of Career Ambassador, or for their unique achievements as Ambassadors at Large. Many are also acknowledged as publicists and authors and, in special cases, for the special honors bestowed upon them. On the matter of Department of State special recognition citations and awards, see Chapter 8.

Evidencing increased professionalism and emerging stability of ranking members of the American Diplomatic Service and reflecting the expansion of the U.S. diplomatic community, during the period since World War II, whereas most emissaries were accredited to one or two foreign missions, well over 200 received three or more sequential appointments, many of whom also held senior Department of State assignments. Of this total number of diplomats, more than 70 percent were given three or four appointments, and the rest, with five to ten assignments, may be regarded as exemplars of contemporary multiple sequential diplomatic appointees. A substantial number of these major appointees (43 percent) were commissioned only to representational assignments (accredited mainly to foreign governments but also to a few international organizations), whereas occasionally, they were assigned solely to Department of State administrative offices (less than 4 percent). The majority held combinations of both types of assignments (53 percent).

Approximately 80 percent of these officers were members of the career Foreign Service, manifesting the fruition of a growing and stable professional corps of experienced diplomats. The preponderant number of their representational commissions were as Ambassadors, although in earlier years following the war, as new countries were added as diplomatic partners, some appointments were initially at the Minister Plenipotentiary or Chargé d'Affaires rank. A few also held additional pre–1946 diplomatic assignments.[129] A small, but increasing, number of these emissaries were women.[130]

Many career Foreign Service Officers may be cited for their years of creditable performance and are historically remembered for their diplomatic records. Examples of those acknowledged largely for their sequential accreditation as representatives to five or more foreign governments and international organizations include Willard L. Beaulac, Philip W. Bonsal, Ellis O. Briggs, Cavendish W. Cannon, William Dawson, Jr., John G. Dean, William L. Eagleton, Jr., Donald R. Heath, James S. Moose, George Wadsworth II, Avra M. Warren, and Charles W. Yost. On the other hand, very few careerists held solely three or more Department of State administrative positions, such as Robert E. Lamb and Joseph J. Sisco.

Most numerous, however, are those who served in a series of combination appointments, as both foreign emissaries and principal State Department officers. Approximately sixty careerists held four or more such mixed assignments. Those who received the highest number of these commissions—six to ten—are represented by such Foreign Service Officers as:

George V. Allen	Loy W. Henderson	Thomas R. Pickering
Norman Armour	Deane R. Hinton	William J. Porter
Charles E. Bohlen	U. Alexis Johnson	William M. Rountree
Henry A. Byroade	Douglas MacArthur II	Harry W. Shlaudeman
John M. Cabot	Thomas C. Mann	Ronald I. Spiers
Selden Chapin	H. Freeman Matthews	Walter J. Stoessel, Jr.
Nathaniel Davis	Livingston T. Merchant	Terence A. Todman
James C. Dunn	Robert D. Murphy	
Raymond A. Hare	David D. Newsom	

Hare was commissioned ten times, followed by Armour, Johnson, and Porter. Armour held nine appointments, three of which were issued after 1945, and both Henderson and Murphy held six. Others also prominent in the annals of American diplomacy are:

Alfred L. Atherton	Arthur W. Hummel, Jr.	G. Frederick Reinhardt
Lucius D. Battle	George F. Kennan	Robert M. Sayre
William G. Bowdler	Robert E. Lamb	Llewellyn E. Thompson
Ellis O. Briggs	Walter P. McConaughy, Jr.	George S. Vest
William W. Butterworth	Richard W. Murphy	Edward T. Wailes
Gerald A. Drew	John E. Peurifoy	Frances E. Willis
Lawrence S. Eagleburger	Christian M. Ravndal	Charles W. Yost
Charles B. Elbrick	James W. Riddleberger	
Thomas O. Enders	Rozanne L. Ridgway	

Many of these had five or six appointments to ranking positions.

The most commonly held ranking Department of State administrative positions occupied by these Foreign Service Officers were Assistant Secretary (seventy-three appointments, which accounted for more than 70 percent of such appointees), Under Secretary (fourteen), and Deputy Under Secretary (thirteen). Individual careerists also served as Deputy Secretary of State (Stoessel),[131] Acting Secretary ad interim, Executive of the Department, Counselor, Chief of Protocol, Director General of the Foreign Service, Inspector General of the Department of State (initially called the Inspector General of the Foreign Service), and Director of the Foreign Service Institute. Others were designated as Directors of the Bureau of German Affairs, the Policy Planning Staff, and the Offices of Consular Affairs, Counterterrorism, Diplomatic Security, Intelligence and Research, Management Operations, and Politico-Military Affairs. Some were appointed to particular offices more than once, especially as Assistant Secretary.[132]

Several officers specialized in representing the United States to particular countries or geographic areas. For example, Allen held Ambassadorial posts to five East European and Mideast countries and as Assistant Secretary for Near Eastern Affairs; Byroade was accredited as Ambassador to four Asian countries but also served as Director of the Bureau of German Affairs (the only appointee to this position); Hare was commissioned twice to both Egypt and Saudi Arabia; Mann was Ambassador to both El Salvador and Mexico; Merchant was sent to Canada twice; and Stoessel became Ambassador successively to Poland, the Soviet Union, and Germany. After serving at Tehran, Jidda, Aden, Baghdad, and the National War College, Herman F. Eilts was accredited as Ambassador to both Saudi Arabia (1966–70) and Egypt (1974–79). Robert D. Murphy, who, as personal representative of the President, secretly gained the support of the Free French in North Africa during World War II, became Political Adviser to the Commandant of the U.S. Forces in Europe in the 1940s and participated in the session of the Council of Foreign Ministers at Paris before he was accredited as Ambassador to Belgium in 1949 and to Japan in 1952, and he later served as Assistant and Under Secretary of State. Although Porter received four appointments to Mideast countries, he was also commissioned to Canada, Korea, and Vietnam and as Under Secretary for Political Affairs.

Other careerists specialized in Department of State administration. Thus, in the 1980s Lamb held appointments as Assistant Secretary for Administration, Coordinator of the Office of Security, and Assistant Secretary for Diplomatic Security. In addition to his appointments as Ambassador to Canada, Merchant served as Assistant Secretary twice, Deputy Under Secretary, Under Secretary, and Secretary of State ad interim. Sisco received two appointments as Assistant Secretary and later became Under Secretary for Political Affairs. Vest was commissioned as Director General of the Foreign Service, Director of Politico-Military Affairs, and Assistant Secretary, as well as Representative to the European Communities. Eagleburger is unique in that, although he was accredited as Ambassador to Yugoslavia (1977–81), he served primarily in ranking State Department positions as Assistant Secretary, Deputy Under Secretary, and

Under Secretary, and he became the only career Foreign Service Officer to be appointed Secretary of State.

Also worthy of note, Allen, in addition to his appointment as Ambassador to five countries, was also named Director of the Foreign Service Institute and Assistant Secretary twice. Bohlen served successively as Ambassador to the Soviet Union, the Philippines, and France and as Secretary of State ad interim, Deputy Under Secretary, and Counselor twice. Johnson, over a period of two decades, was commissioned to four foreign governments, as Under Secretary twice and as Ambassador at Large. Kennan was the first Director of the Policy Planning Staff (1947–49) before he became Counselor and Ambassador to the Soviet Union and to Yugoslavia. Newsom was accredited as Ambassador to Indonesia and the Philippines, was appointed Under Secretary, and served as Acting Secretary ad interim three times.

Achieving special distinction, since 1956 some of these members of the career Foreign Service, usually late in their careers, were officially recognized and promoted to the special rank of Career Ambassador. These, referred to earlier, have included:

Allen	Henderson	Pickering
Atherton	Hinton	Riddleberger
Bohlen	Hummel	Spiers
Briggs	Johnson	Stoessel
Butterworth	MacArthur	Thompson
Dunn	Matthews	Vest
Eagleberger	Merchant	Willis
Elbrick	Richard Murphy	Yost
Hare	Robert Murphy	

The first awardees of this eminent personal diplomatic rank were Dunn, Henderson, Matthews, and Robert Murphy, who were so recognized on March 7, 1956. Other careerists so honored also embrace Walworth Barbour, Winthrop G. Brown, Walter C. Dowling, Arthur A. Hartman, and Foy D. Kohler. This crowning title, created by Act of Congress on August 5, 1955 (69 Stat. 536), is conferred only upon experienced Foreign Service Officers "in recognition of especially distinguished service over a sustained period" (previously specified as a minimum of "fifteen years in a position of responsibility in a Government agency."[133]

Some noncareerists also are recognized for their distinguished diplomatic service since 1945. Examples of those with extensive representational appointments include Ellsworth Bunker (Ambassador to five countries and Representative to the Organization of American States), Henry Cabot Lodge, Jr. (Ambassador to two countries—Germany and Vietnam twice, Presidential personal representative to the Vatican, and Ambassador to the United Nations), and Robert Strauss-Hupe (Ambassador to five countries and Representative to the North Atlantic Treaty Organization). Anthony Drexel Biddle, Jr., was unique in that prior to 1945 he received eight diplomatic appointments to nine foreign governments but also was later accredited to Spain in 1961.

Those noncareerist emissaries who also held senior Department of State administrative positions were David K. E. Bruce (Ambassador to France, Germany, and Great Britain, Liaison Officer to China—Peking, Representative to the North Atlantic Treaty Organization, and Under Secretary of State); Clarence D. Dillon (Ambassador to France and three appointments as Under Secretary); Angier Biddle Duke (Ambassador to four countries and Chief of Protocol twice); John N. Irwin II (Under Secretary, Deputy Secretary, and Ambassador to France); William B. Macomber, Jr. (Ambassador to two countries, Assistant Secretary twice, and Deputy Under Secretary twice); George C. McGhee (Ambassador to two countries, Director of the Policy Planning Staff, Assistant Secretary, and Under Secretary); and Gerard C. Smith (Representative to the International Atomic Energy Agency, Director of the Policy Planning Staff, and Assistant Secretary twice). W. Averall Harriman served as presidential personal emissary on several missions, Ambassador to both the Soviet Union and the United Kingdom, and later as Assistant Secretary, Under Secretary, and Ambassador at Large twice. After World War II John H. Hilldring and Charles E. Saltzman were the only Assistant Secretaries for Occupied Areas (1946–49).

Usually, those appointed as Deputy Secretary of State have been political appointees, and often they had no prior or subsequent diplomatic or State Department administrative experience. Exceptions were Warren M. Christopher, Robert S. Ingersoll, John N. Irwin II, and Kenneth Rush, all of whom were noncareerists and early appointees (1972–77). However, Foreign Service Officer Stoessel, a careerist, was exceptional in that he held a series of representational and ranking Department of State administrative offices before he served briefly as Deputy Secretary in 1982.

Several noncareerists were especially unique in that they were commissioned to senior State Department positions prior to becoming Secretary of State, notably, Dean Acheson (Assistant Secretary twice and Under Secretary), Warren M. Christopher (Deputy Secretary), Christian A. Herter (Under Secretary), and Dean Rusk (Assistant Secretary twice and Deputy Under Secretary). Several others had considerable diplomatic and other foreign relations experience but held no traditional Ambassadorial or State Department offices prior to appointment as Secretary of State. These included John Foster Dulles, Henry A. Kissinger, George C. Marshall, and Cyrus R. Vance. Unlike Eagleburger, a careerist who previously held several high-level Department of State posts, Madeleine Albright, a noncareerist, spent four years as Ambassador to the United Nations immediately before she was appointed Secretary of State in 1997. Also, former Vice President Walter F. Mondale was accredited as Ambassador to Japan in the 1990s, and George H. Bush served as U.S. Representative to the United

Nations (1971–73) and chief of the American Liaison Office at Peking, China (1974–75), before he was elected as Vice President and later as President, both of whom also were noncareerists.

Also noteworthy, more than thirty officers have been appointed by the President for special service as Ambassadors at Large since March 1949. Only a few of these top-level personal envoys have been careerists, such as Alfred L. Atherton, Jr. (1978–79), L. Paul Bremer III (1986), U. Alexis Johnson (1973–77), Robert J. McCloskey (1974–75), Henry D. Owen (1978–81), Harry W. Shlaudeman (1984–86), Gerard C. Smith (1977–80), and Llewellyn E. Thompson (1962–66). Most such appointees have been noncareerists, including Philip C. Jessup (the first Ambassador at Large, 1949–53, who later became a member of the International Court of Justice), Chester B. Bowles (1961–63), Ellsworth Bunker (twice, 1966–67 and 1973–78), Howard E. Douglas (1982–86), Arthur J. Goldberg (1977–78), W. Averell Harriman (twice, 1961 and 1965–69), Henry Cabot Lodge, Jr. (1967–68), George C. McGhee (1968–69), Elliott L. Richardson (1977–80), and Vernon A. Walters (1981–85). Certain Ambassadors at Large have specialized in dealing with important areal or functional matters. They embrace such matters as counterterrorism, cultural affairs, economic summit coordination, law of the sea negotiations, nonproliferation and nuclear energy, refugee affairs, security cooperation in Europe, and even liaison with State and local governments. Authorized by law, these ranking emissaries are appointed primarily to relieve the President and Secretary of State of top-level, extended diplomatic negotiations and international conference attendance and therefore are worthy of special recognition.

Certain officers are remembered as "firsts" to serve in particular diplomatic capacities or as State Department administrative chieftains. At the highest administrative levels, Lawrence Eagleburger was the first Foreign Service Officer to become Secretary of State, and Madeleine Albright was the first woman to be appointed to this office. The initial Deputy Secretary, John N. Irwin II, and the first post–World War II Under Secretary, Dean Acheson, were both noncareerists. On the other hand, the first persons appointed as Chief of Protocol by the President (Stanley Woodward, 1946–50), Executive Secretary of the Department (Lucius D. Battle), Inspector General of the Department (Raymond C. Miller), Director General of the Foreign Service (Selden Chapin), and Directors of the Bureau of German Affairs (Henry A. Byroade), Management Operations (Earl D. Sohn), and Policy Planning Staff (George F. Kennan) were all Foreign Service Officers. Llewellyn Thompson was the first careerist Ambassador at Large, Charles E. Bohlen was the first careerist Counselor of the Department, Rozanne L. Ridgway, also a careerist, was the first woman Counselor, and Frances E. Willis was the first woman Career Minister and Career Ambassador.

Similarly, the first noncareerist women appointed to represent the United States in international organizations included Jeane J. Kirkpatrick (United Nations), Barbara W. Newell (United Nations Educational, Scientific and Cultural Organization), and Millicent Fenwick (United Nations Agencies for Food and Agriculture). The first post–World War II women Ambassadors accredited to European countries were appointed to Austria (Helene A. Von Damm), Belgium (Anne C. Chambers), Czechoslovakia (Shirley Temple Black), Denmark (Eugenie Anderson), Finland (Rozanne Ridgway), Italy (Clare Boothe Luce), Luxembourg (Perle Mesta), Norway and Switzerland (Frances E. Willis), and the United Kingdom (Anne L. Armstrong), of whom only Ridgway and Willis were Foreign Service Officers.

Other women may be remembered historically as "firsts." They consist of two categories. For example, those who became Foreign Service Officers include Meta K. Hannay, the first woman to take the diplomatic examinations but failed to be appointed (1921); Lucile Atcherson, the first woman to pass the Foreign Service examinations and be appointed (1922); and Margaret M. Hanna, the first woman to enter the Foreign Service by means of lateral entry (1937). On the other hand, aside from those already mentioned, several are remembered as firsts to be appointed as Chiefs of Mission abroad and as ranking State Department officers. Thus, Frances E. Willis was the first woman careerist to rise to the level of Ambassador (Switzerland, 1953), and Mary S. Olmsted was the first woman to be appointed to multiple, simultaneous diplomatic missions. On the other hand, Lucy W. Benson was the first woman Under Secretary of State (for Security Assistance, 1977), Marion H. Smoak served as the first of a series of women to be appointed Chief of Protocol (1974); Barbara M. Watson was the first woman Assistant Secretary of State (for Consular Affairs, 1968); and Caroline C. Laise was the first woman to become Director of the Foreign Service (1975). In addition, Marjorie M. Whiteman is remembered for compiling and publishing her fourteen-volume *Digest of International Law*.

Since World War II approximately three dozen diplomats are remembered for having their missions terminated by death or assassination or because they were declared to be persona non grata, or their recall was requested by the governments to which they were accredited. Customarily, diplomatic missions are terminated by what the Department of State describes as "left post" to which assigned, "presented their recall," "relinquished charge" of a foreign mission, or simply having their appointments terminated by the United States. On occasion diplomats are appointed but not commissioned, and sometimes their nominations by the President are withdrawn before the Senate confirms them.

Occasionally, Chiefs of Mission, though appointed and confirmed, died before taking the oath of office or proceeding to their posts. Others died in office, half of whom were Foreign Service Officers, including Monnett B. Davis, John G. Erhardt, William S. Howell, Jr., Henry A. Hoyt, Jay P. Moffat, Albert F. Nufer, John E. Peurifoy, Arnold L. Raphel, and Samuel Z. Westerfield, Jr., and such noncareerists as Kenneth B. Keating, William R. Rivkin, and Laurence A. Steinhardt (who served as Chief of Mission to six countries, 1933–50).

More serious, the rise of terrorism as a political threat upon American diplomats has resulted in attacks, kidnappings in Brazil, Jordan, and Zaire, and worse, several assassinations. Thus, Barbara A. Robbins was killed in the bomb-

ing of the American Embassy in Vietnam in 1965, and careerist Ambassador
John G. Mein was assassinated in Guatemala (in 1968—the first American Chief
of Mission to be murdered in the line of duty), followed by Cleo A. Noel, Jr.
(Sudan, 1973), Roger P. Davies (Cyprus, 1974), and Adolph Dubs (Afghanistan,
1979). They, together with diplomatic officers who died "under heroic or tragic
circumstances" as a result of earthquakes, volcanic eruptions, and other trage-
dies, are memorialized by a plaque located in the diplomatic lobby of the Department of State, dedicated by the Foreign Service Association in 1933 and
supplemented with a second plaque forty years later. To deal with personal
protection of diplomatic officials abroad after World War II, the State Department entered into an agreement with the Navy in 1948 to provide Marine de-
tachments assigned to diplomatic posts abroad, which grew to a protective force
of hundreds of Marines stationed at Embassies and Legations throughout the
world. In 1987 careerist Robert E. Lamb was appointed the first Assistant Secretary for Diplomatic Security to manage this responsibility.[134]

One of the most egregious and inflammatory diplomatic crises suffered by
the United States occurred when the American Embassy at Tehran was attacked
by a large band of Iranian militants on November 4, 1979. They marauded and
seized the diplomatic compound, and, although a few hostages were released,
despite the attempts by the United States to negotiate their release, intervention
of several intermediaries, including the United Nations, the application of diplomatic and economic sanctions, pleading of the American case before the International Court of Justice at The Hague, which handed down a unanimous
decision demanding their release, and an attempted, but aborted, ninety-man
American commando helicopter rescue attempt, Ayatollah Khomeni and his revolutionary regime held fifty-two American diplomatic hostages in violation of
the sanctity of traditional privileges and immunities of diplomatic personnel.
More than a year later, after the Iranian government stabilized, and an agreement
for the release of the hostages was finally brokered by the Algerian Government
and for the arbitration of the matter by an international commission to settle
American financial claims against Iran, the hostages were finally released to the
United States on January 25, 1981. At the time of the attack the American
Embassy was headed by Chargé d'Affaires L. Bruce Laingen; and the United
States severed relations with Iran on April 7, 1980.

Diplomats also are remembered because they were held to be unacceptable,
or their recall was requested by the governments to which they were accredited.
Following World War II a veritable battle of attrition on diplomatic staffs accompanied the Cold War between East and West. American chiefs of mission
formally declared to be persona non grata were Selden Chapin (Hungary, 1949),
Donald R. Heath (Bulgaria, 1950), and George F. Kennan (Soviet Union, 1952),
all career officers. Hungary contended that Chapin cooperated with Cardinal
Mindzenty, who was tried and sentenced to life imprisonment for alleged treason, and Bulgaria's action against Heath led to the severance of diplomatic
relations for a decade (January 1950–March 1960).

One of the most celebrated cases was that involving Ambassador Kennan, accredited to Moscow. On October 3, 1952, the Soviet Government informed the Department of State that on September 19, at Tempelhof Airport in West Berlin, he made remarks to the press paralleling the situation of members of the American diplomatic mission in Moscow with what he allegedly experienced when he was interned in Germany by the Nazis during 1941 and 1942. The Soviet Union regarded his statements as "slanderous attacks" and "a rude violation of generally recognized norms of international law," and therefore it found him to be persona non grata and demanded his immediate recall.

Other emissaries declared to be persona non grata included Ambassadors Vincent W. de Roulet (Jamaica, 1973), Deane R. Hinton (Zaire, 1975), and Herbert J. Spiro (Equatorial Guinea, 1976). For half a dozen other Chiefs of Mission foreign governments to which they were accredited requested their "departure" or "recall." Furthermore, when Walter L. Cutler was appointed as Ambassador to Tehran in May 1979, he did not proceed to his post because the Iranian Government refused to receive him, which left Chargé d'Affaires Laingen in charge of the American mission when the hostage imbroglio erupted.

Many members of the American diplomatic establishment and officers of the Department of State have published an extensive library of volumes on a broad series of subjects since 1945. Some of these officials are remembered for specific publications, and others are known for the quantity or quality of their literary production. Within a few decades more than 300 members of American diplomatic staff produced more than 1,250 books and monographs. Two-thirds of these authors were members of the Foreign Service—mostly Foreign Service Officers but also including Foreign Service Auxiliary, Reserve, and Staff Officers. The rest were noncareerists. A few of these authors bridged earlier years, some were well-known diplomats or Department of State senior officers, and a substantial number did not hold ranking positions. Occasional volumes were coauthored, published in foreign languages, translations, or edited compilations. Some constituted novels, plays, and collections of poetry.

The noncareerist authors represented a variety of professional backgrounds. These include a number of acknowledged statesmen and members of Congress, the military, the legal profession, banking and business, journalism and publication, and other professions.[135] The largest number, however, numbering in the dozens, was recruited from educational and advanced academic institutions. Examples of the latter include James B. Conant, Herbert Feis, John Kenneth Galbraith, Thorsten V. Kalijarvi, Henry A. Kissinger, James L. McCamy, Dana G. Munro, Edwin O. Reischauer, Graham H. Stuart, and Willard L. Thorp.[136] Although some are recognized as distinguished scholars and eminent authors, few are reminiscent of such earlier literati as Stephen Vincent Benet, James Fenimore Cooper, Nathaniel Hawthorne, William D. Howells, Washington Irving, James Russel Lowell, James G. Thurber, and Henry Van Dyke or such popular writers as John Russell Coryell (Nick Carter) or Brett Harte, who also became involved in American diplomacy.

A good many of the authors produced one or two volumes, but a substantial number proved to be prolific authors. More than thirty (10 percent) published ten or more volumes. This included Foreign Service Officers James Rives Childs, William Giloane, George F. Kennan, and Charles W. Thayer and Foreign Service Auxiliary and Reserve Officers Cyril E. Black, Paul H. Bonner, John L. Brown, John C. Caldwell, Herbert Feis, Arthur Goodfriend, and Alice R. Hager. Of these, Childs, Caldwell, Feis, and Goodfriend were the most prolific. On the other hand, Adolph A. Berle, Claude G. Bowers, James B. Conant, John Kenneth Galbraith, and Adlai E. Stevenson, who served as chiefs of mission to foreign countries, and Eleanor Roosevelt (who represented the United States to the United Nations) and Hamilton Fish Armstrong (who served as attaché to Serbia and in the Department of State) were the noncareerists with the largest publication production.

Many officers published their memoirs. These are represented by such well-known careerists as Willard L. Beaulac—*Career Ambassador* and *Career Diplomat*; Charles E. Bohlen—*Witness to History*; Ellis O. Briggs—*Farewell to Foggy Bottom*; Winthrop G. Brown—*Wartime Diary*; James Rives Childs—*Foreign Service Farewell*; Nathaniel P. Davis—*Few Dull Moments*; George F. Kennan—*Memoirs* (two volumes); Robert D. Murphy—*Diplomat among Warriors*; William Phillips—*Ventures in Diplomacy*; Karl L. Rankin—*China Assignment*; and Robert Strausz-Hupe—*In My Time*.

Other memoirs were produced by noncareerists, such as Arthur A. Ageton—*Admiral Ambassador to Russia*; Claude G. Bowers—*My Life* and *My Mission to Spain*; Chester B. Bowles—*Ambassador's Report* and *Promises to Keep*; Spruille Braden—*Diplomats and Demagogues*; William B. Conant—*My Several Lives*; Josephus Daniels, Jr.—*Shirtsleeve Diplomat*; John Kenneth Galbraith—*Ambassador's Journal*; W. Averell Harriman—*America and Russia in a Changing World: A Half Century of Personal Observations*; William D. Leahy—*I Was There*; Perle Mesta—*Perle—My Story*; DeLesseps S. Morrisons—*Latin American Mission*; Francis B. Sayre—*Glad Adventure*; Walter Bedell Smith—*My Three Years in Moscow*; William H. Standley—*Admiral Ambassador to Russia*; and John G. Winant—*Letter from Grosvenor Square: An Account of Stewardship*.[137]

Reflecting the desire to publish their views, many volumes produced by these officers—careerists and noncareerists—were devoted to the practice of diplomacy, the Foreign Service, the conduct of international relations, and foreign policy. These are illustrated by William Barnes and John Heath Morgan—*The Foreign Service of the United States*; Andrew Berding—*Foreign Affairs and You* and *The Making of Foreign Policy*; Adolph Berle—*The Tides of Crisis: A Primer of Foreign Relations*; William W. Blancké—*The Foreign Service of the United States*; Ellis O. Briggs—*Anatomy of Diplomacy*; John F. Campbell—*The Foreign Affairs Fudge Factory*; James Rives Childs—*American Foreign Service*; John Patton Davies—*Foreign and Other Affairs*; Robert F. Delany—*Your Future in the Foreign Service*; Glen H. Fisher—*Public Diplomacy and the*

Behavioral Sciences; John E. Harr—*The Anatomy of the Foreign Service* and *The Professional Diplomat*; Ralph Hilton—*Worldwide Mission: The Story of the United States Foreign Service*; Henry A. Kissinger—*The Necessity for Choice: Prospects of American Foreign Policy and Diplomacy;* Richard A. Johnson—*The Administration of United States Foreign Policy*; George F. Kennan—*American Diplomacy, 1900–1950* and *Realities of American Foreign Policy*; James L. McCamy—*The Administration of Foreign Affairs* and *Conduct of the New Diplomacy*; Elmer Plischke—*Conduct of American Diplomacy, Contemporary U.S. Foreign Policy: Documents and Commentary, Modern Diplomacy: The Art and the Artisans*, and *United States Diplomats and Their Missions*; Smith Simpson—*Anatomy of the State Department* and *The Crisis in American Diplomacy*; E. Wilder Spaulding—*Ambassadors Ordinary and Extraordinary*; Graham H. Stuart—*American Diplomatic and Consular Practice* and *The Department of State*; Charles W. Thayer—*Diplomat*; Henry S. Villard—*Affairs at State* (on the Foreign Service); Sumner Welles—*Seven Major Decisions*; and Charles W. Yost—*The Conduct and Misconduct of Foreign Affairs*.[138]

Dozens of others have published several hundred volumes that deal with a surprisingly broad variety of additional, often surprising and sometimes titillating subjects. These embody analyses that deal with economic, political, social, and legal matters; national security, intelligence, and military affairs; trade and commerce; geographical areas and particular countries; religion and morality; sports, entertainment, and travel; and other matters, as well as fiction, plays, and poetry.[139] In time, as new members join the diplomatic corps, doubtless many more volumes will be produced to swell this library of studies on foreign affairs and the Department of State.

In the aggregate these volumes constitute a rich and varied resource for understanding and improving the diplomatic process. Combined, its authors provide substantial commentary and analysis on its challenges, functioning, mutations, needs, strengths and weaknesses, and achievements and failures. Some volumes provide probing insights into its quality and versatility in dealing with other countries on an array of issues and processes, for which their authors will be remembered.[140]

TREATY MAKING

Inasmuch as the principal functions of the Department of State are foreign policy advice and formulation, representation abroad, participation in international conferences, and bilateral and multilateral negotiation with foreign governments, the crowning end product of its mission may be measured, to a large extent, by the treaties and agreements concluded. The anatomy of the American treaty system produced by the Department of State consists of an aggregate of international policy commitments in the nature of Presidential doctrines and proclamations, national and joint declarations, and other pronouncements, many of which have binding legal effect, a host of regular bilateral and multilateral treaties and agreements, a variety of supplementary, subsidiary, and related agreements, and a good many treaty amendments and extensions. Analysis of the current treaty/agreement process evidences growing, widespread, and continuous involvement by the United States—handled primarily by the Department of State—in establishing and maintaining wholesale American cooperation in the foreign affairs of the world.

The development of this system evidences considerable enlargement and change since World War II respecting the types and quantity of treaties, agreements, the variety of their subject categories, and the breadth of coverage throughout the international community. As the United States mutated from a colonial dependency to a minor and later a major world power and, following the Second World War, a superpower, its role and leadership as an international treaty partner steadily increased both quantitatively and functionally.

By way of background, following the negotiation of thirteen treaties and two executive agreements with six countries prior to 1789, during the first century and a quarter (1789–1913) the United States negotiated 654 treaties/agreements (565 bipartite and eighty-nine multipartite). During the next three decades (1913–45) its treaty participation more than doubled with the conclusion of an additional 1,363 treaties/agreements (1,127 bipartite and 236 multipartite) with some 100 foreign governments.[141] In the next half century (1946–96) the United States added more than 6,900 regular treaties/agreements (6,303 bilateral and 599 multilateral), tripling its previous treaty record, evidencing its readiness not only to engage in, but also to exercise considerable leadership in, treaty relations with 200 other governments and fifty-six international organizations and other agencies.

This post–World War II development reflected the desire of the Department of State to continue to reduce many traditional foreign relationships and issues to formal legal commitments in both bilateral and multilateral treaties. It also evidences the necessity of coping with the consequences of World War II, expanded treaty involvement with dozens of new states that emerged, and the proliferation of international matters of mutual concern.

Treaty Making Process

By the time of World War II, American treaty and agreement making had been refined into a workable executive-legislative process, with the central negotiating, approval, and processing roles well established. However, because of the increase in summit and ministerial diplomacy, the involvement of other government agencies in foreign affairs, and especially the enormous extension of treaty making and the quantity of international commitments undertaken by the United States as a superpower, new issues arose in the relations of the executive and legislative branches of the government.

Treaty making is bifaceted in that both international requisites and domestic constitutional and political requirements must be satisfied. Five major steps are customarily involved: (1) negotiation and signature; (2) legislative approval subject to Senate "advice and consent" by a two-thirds vote; (3) ratification by the President as Chief of State by means of formal approval and signature; (4) exchange of instruments of ratification, generally entailing a protocol or *proces verbal* handled by the Department of State and American diplomats; and (5) executive proclamation or promulgation (which determines legal effectuation of private rights and responsibilities of individual citizens and of government agencies).

Article 2 of the Constitution recognizes only formal "treaties" and does not acknowledge other types of international compacts. Over the years the United States also became party to many executive agreements, the conclusion and implementation of which do not conform with the regular treaty process. They are of two types, those having and those not having congressional approval. Some are concluded under prior legislative authorization or are subsequently approved by enactments of both houses of Congress, which are called "congressional-executive agreements." Those not possessing legislative authorization or approval are designated "presidential agreements" or "pure executive agreements," sometimes called "sole executive agreements." A third type, negotiated in accordance with prior treaty stipulations, may be regarded as "treaty authorized or implementing agreements."

The Department of State has observed that it is well recognized that an executive agreement cannot alter existing law and must conform with it, although it may augment or explicate statutory enactments. A formal treaty that is ratified as required by the Constitution becomes the "law of the land" and takes precedence over prior statutory law. Furthermore, the Supreme Court has held that, in certain respects, executive agreements "have a similar dignity" to that of formal treaties.

Domestic controversies arising over the legitimacy of such understandings usually pertain to those concluded under exclusive Presidential authority. However, those made under Presidential responsibility as Commander in Chief, such as wartime military cooperation agreements, surrenders, and armistices and post-hostilities occupation arrangements, normally are uncontested. However, executive agreements negotiated under the President's general diplomatic or foreign relations authority, which are both numerous and diverse, sometimes evoke disagreements with Congress, especially when they produce important commitments or major foreign policy developments or changes, create obligations to submit international disputes to arbitration or to settle claims against the United States, or require U.S. funding.

The American treaty-making process—involving treaties, executive agreements, and postal and other conventions—developed incrementally and served the international interests and constitutional requirements of the United States for nearly a century and a half. To 1945 by far the largest number of treaties submitted to the Senate was approved without change (72 percent), some were amended or subjected to reservations, a few were withdrawn from Senate consideration, and only fourteen were rejected. However, since 1913 and especially during and since World War II, many American international commitments, including military matters and the establishment of bilateral and multilateral international agencies, have been embodied in executive agreements. To surmount the Senate veto or modification, the President and Department of State developed methods of persuasion to achieve Senate approval, of substituting joint congressional action for the treaty procedure,[142] and of utilizing Senators as negotiators to achieve subsequent implementation and appropriations legislation.

In the early 1950s a major movement was launched in Congress to amend the treaty clause of the Constitution. Four major issues dominated the debate that ensued. These flowed from the reaction to wartime and postwar political commitments undertaken by Presidents Roosevelt and Truman at the summit meetings held at Casablanca, Cairo and Tehran, Malta and Yalta, and Potsdam (1943–45), to certain undertakings negotiated within the United Nations system, to the *Fuji vs. California* case in 1950, in which a California court invalidated a State law on the grounds of incompatibility with the United Nations Charter, and to the earlier case of *Missouri vs. Holland* (1920), which raised the issue as to whether the National Government should be able to accomplish by treaty what it lacks normal legislative authority to handle under the division of powers in the absence of a treaty.[143]

Senator John W. Bricker led the movement, beginning in 1951, to amend the Constitution to curb the treaty-making authority of the Executive, which included the Department of State. He introduced amendatory proposals regularly until he was defeated for reelection in 1958. His proposals sought to specify that a provision of a treaty that conflicts with the Constitution shall have no force and effect, that a treaty shall become effective as internal law only through legislation that would be valid in the absence of a treaty, that Congress shall have power to regulate all executive and other agreements with foreign governments and international organizations, and that such agreements shall be subject to the limitations imposed on treaties. President Eisenhower and Secretary Dulles opposed such action on the grounds that presidential treaty-making authority would virtually be emasculated and would invalidate or exceed the intent of the framers of the Constitution.[144]

Another wave of controversy emerged in the late 1960s and 1970s. On one hand, attention was paid to defining and assessing the authority of the Executive to conclude not only formal treaties requiring Senate approval by two-thirds' vote but also executive agreements. The Department of State declared that international arrangements brought into force without Senate advice and consent had become common practice and that they were binding upon the United States, and in October 1974 it issued Circular 175, which prescribed the details of American practice in defining and handling both treaties and agreements.

In the meantime, in August 1972 Congress enacted the Case Act (named after

Senator Clifford P. Case), which mandated that the Secretary of State transmit to it the texts of all international agreements, other than treaties, within sixty days. However, those for which immediate public disclosure, in the opinion of the President, would ''be prejudicial to the national security of the United States'' should rather be transmitted to the Senate Foreign Relations and House Foreign Affairs Committees ''under an appropriate injunction of secrecy to be removed only upon due notice by the President.''

Moreover, in 1978 the Senate considered the Treaty Powers Resolution to define its role and procedure in the treaty process. It declared that ''no international agreement which in the judgment of the Senate should be submitted as a treaty will be implemented by the Senate without its prior advice and consent to ratification of that agreement.'' It also stated that the requirement for such Senate action had in recent years been circumvented by the use of ''executive agreements'' and specified that the Senate could ''refuse to consider legislative measures to authorize or appropriate funds to implement those international agreements which, in its opinion, constitute treaties to which the Senate has not given its advice and consent to ratification.'' But the Senate failed to pass this resolution, and it substituted an alternative to require the President, in determining whether a particular agreement should be submitted to the Senate as a treaty, to obtain the advice of the Senate Foreign Relations Committee through agreed procedures established by the Secretary of State.

To further restrain executive treaty authority, the Senate also initiated action to be involved in the termination of treaties. Following the transfer of American diplomatic recognition as the sole Government of China from the Republic of China (Taiwan) to the People's Republic of China (Beijing), effective January 1, 1979, and notification of the termination of the 1954 Mutual Defense Treaty between the United States and the Republic of China, also effective on January 1, 1979, a treaty termination resolution was introduced into Congress on March 8. It stipulated that treaties, subject to certain exceptions, could not be terminated or suspended by the President without the concurrence of Congress. The Department of State objected to this resolution and argued that Presidents had previously exercised this power, which had generally been recognized by legal authorities. This resolution also failed to pass the Senate, and a broadened substitute resolution was introduced to provide guidelines for such presidential action.[145]

So far as the publication of American treaties and agreements is concerned, the Secretary of State is required by law to furnish copies of all treaties, including postal conventions, to the Public Printer ''as soon as possible'' following ratification and proclamation, so that they may be published. Cumulative collections of them began to be published as early as 1815. In the twentieth century, in 1908, the Department of State undertook the systematic publication of the texts of individual treaties in the *United States Treaty Series*. A separate *Executive Agreement Series* was launched in 1929, and later, in 1945, these were combined and superseded by the *Treaties and Other International Acts*

Series. In addition, for more than a century, the texts of treaties and certain executive agreements were also published annually in the *United States Statutes at Large.* However, this practice was discontinued in 1951, when the State Department launched the publication of annual volumes of the current series entitled *United States Treaties and Other International Agreements.*

The Department of State also published a complete twelve-volume cumulative collection, compiled by Charles I. Bevans, entitled *Treaties and Other International Agreements of the United States of America, 1776–1949.* Moreover, since World War I the United States also registered for the publication of its treaties and agreements in the *League of Nations Treaty Series* (1920–44), created in accordance with the first of President Wilson's Fourteen Points, and following World War II this was superseded by the *United Nations Treaty Series.*[146]

International Policy Doctrines, Proclamations, Declarations, and Other Major Pronouncements

By way of background it is useful to note that in previous centuries both international doctrines and declarations were promulgated and regarded as binding instruments, even though they were not embodied in formal treaties, and some of them were founded on natural law. They tend to be given more attention in treatises on international law and, to some extent, on philosophical analyses, rather than contemporary diplomatic histories.[147] In more recent times, however, these concepts have come to be applied primarily to national and multilateral professions of policy regarding foreign affairs.

Since 1945, accelerating its previous practice considerably, the United States participated in propounding many new international policy doctrines, declarations, and other pronouncements as important instruments of foreign policy and relations. The doctrines were promulgated by the President, as were unilateral foreign relations proclamations and some declarations and comparable policy propositions. Bilateral and multilateral declarations, generally consummated by the Secretary of State or American diplomats, constitute mutual professions of purpose, intent, and policy, which, with few exceptions, are neither treated or regarded as formal treaties or agreements. However, some of these pronouncements are subsequently implemented by legal action, many are supplemented by additional policy statements and engender diplomatic consideration and negotiations, and others prove to be of limited duration.

Presidential Doctrines

International doctrines, unless confirmed by statute or embodied in international treaties or agreements, lack the formal commitment of binding law but are more compelling than ordinary policy statements, and they may have important political impact. They are of two types. A few historic international doctrines—also called rules—that have become widespread in the relations of nations exceed the interest solely of the United States. For example, the "Doctrine of State Responsibility" has been regarded as requiring governments to act in accordance with international law, violations of which are imputable to national governments; the "Doctrine of Continuous Voyage" has been concerned with shipping, cargoes, and contraband during wartime; the "Doctrine of the Two Spheres" has provided that the wars of European countries would not extend to their overseas colonies and, conversely, that conflicts between their colonies would not spread to continental Europe; and the more recent "Doctrine of Implied Powers" has predicated that permanent agencies of international organizations have the legal right to interpret their constitutive acts so as to justify implied authority for action flowing from their expressed powers and objectives. In addition, the "Doctrine of Self-Determination" has encompassed the principles of liberty, independence, and popular choice of a system of governance in accordance with the will of the people, and the "Doctrine of Non-Intervention" of one nation in the domestic affairs of another has been embodied in the principle of decolonization since World War II.

American national doctrines, on the other hand, are major policy statements applied largely as a general U.S. philosophy, aspiration, or goal, which may be concretized as specific objectives and plans of action. Not usually so designated by their initiators, they are subsequently labeled doctrines by historians, publicists, or the media. They were rarely issued prior to World War II.

Of special importance in American history is the Monroe Doctrine, enunciated in 1823. It embodied a unique combination of foreign relations precepts, including noninvolvement, noninterference, nonintervention, and nonextension of nonindigenous systems of governance by foreign powers in the Western Hemisphere. Virtually sacrosanct, it was frequently reiterated and refined, sometimes reinterpreted, multilateralized, and subsequently reaffirmed by President Truman in 1945 and President Kennedy in 1962.[148] The Hoover–Stimson Non-Recognition Doctrine of 1932 was more limited in both scope and duration.

After World War II, beginning with President Truman, it became common practice—some call it "doctrine mania"—to credit Presidents with individualized foreign policy doctrines, as listed in Table 7.7, Part A. Like the Monroe Doctrine, most of these focused on particular geographic areas—the Western Hemisphere (Presidents Johnson and Reagan), Europe (Truman), the Middle East (Eisenhower and Carter), and Asia and the Pacific (Johnson, Nixon, and Ford). A few also acquired broader connotations or application, such as the Truman Doctrine, which encompassed the principle of containment during the Cold War, and the Nixon Doctrine of 1971, which was readily transmuted into a change in attitude respecting American global commitments and shared responsibilities. Except for President Nixon's Doctrine on new forms of partnership and President Ford's "New Pacific Doctrine," none were originally enunciated as presidential doctrines, but this appellation was applied by others.[149]

Table 7.7
Presidential Doctrines, International Policy Declarations, and Other Pronouncements since 1945

A. Presidential Doctrines

Truman Doctrine—U.S. Aid to Greece and Turkey, Mar. 12, 1947

Eisenhower Doctrine—Protect Inviolability, Integrity, and Independence of Middle East Nations, Jan. 5, 1957

Johnson Doctrine (1)—End Communist Subversion and Aggression in Southeast Asia, Aug. 5, 1964

Johnson Doctrine (2)—Prevent Communist Subversion in Dominican Crisis, May 2, 1965

Nixon Doctrine (1)—Basic Policy in Asia and Pacific following War in Vietnam, July 25, 1969

Nixon Doctrine (2)—New Forms of Partnership, Commitments, and Shared Responsibility to Meet Change in International Strategic Relationships, Feb. 25, 1971, reiterated May 3, 1973

Ford Doctrine—Maintain Stable United States Balance of Power in Pacific Area, Dec. 7, 1975

Carter Doctrine—Regarding Attempt by Outside Force to Gain Control of the Persian Gulf Region as an Assault on the Vital Interest of the United States to Be Repelled by Any Means Necessary, Jan. 23, 1980, and reiterated Feb. 19, 1980

Reagan Doctrine (1)—Caribbean Basin Initiative Against Spread of Communism, Feb. 24, 1982, reiterated Apr. 17, 1983 and Feb. 25, 1986

Reagan Doctrine (2)—Preservation of Democracy, Free Economy, and National Self-determination in Central America, June 24, 1986

B. International Policy Declarations and Other Pronouncements*

Quadripartite Declaration on Defeat of Germany and Assumption of Allied Supreme Authority, by United States, France, Soviet Union, and United Kingdom, June 1945

Quadripartite Final Act, Reestablishment of International Regime of Tangier, United States, France, Soviet Union, and United Kingdom, Aug. 1945

Quadripartite Potsdam Declaration to Implement the Cairo Declaration of 1943, Aug. 1945

Declaration on Initial American Postwar Policy concerning Japan, President Truman, Sept. 1945

Proclamation on Natural Resources of Subsoil and Seabed of Continental Shelf, President Truman, Sept. 1945

Declaration on Fundamentals of American Foreign Policy, President Truman, Oct. 1945

Proclamation Implementing United Nations Charter and Statute of International Court of Justice, President Truman, Oct. 1945

Tripartite Declaration on International Control of Atomic Energy, President Truman, Prime Minister Attlee, and Prime Minister MacKenzie King, Nov. 1945

Declaration on African Denuclearization, U.N. Gen. Assembly, Dec. 1945

Proclamation of Independence of Philippine Islands, President Truman, July 4, 1946

Declaration Accepting Compulsory Jurisdiction of the International Court of Justice, President Truman, Aug. 1946

American Postwar Policy concerning Germany, Secretary Byrnes, Sept. 1946, and Secretary Acheson, Apr. 1949

Marshall Plan for European Recovery Program, June 1947

Inter-American Declaration on Rights and Duties of Man, Bogotá Conference, 1948

Note, United States Protest of Soviet Blockade of Berlin, Secretary Marshall, July 1948

Universal Declaration of Human Rights, U.N. General Assembly, Dec. 1948 (to implement Presidential Truman's proposal for an International Bill of Rights, 1945) called the first United Nations Law-making Act

Point Four Program, Technical Assistance to Underdeveloped Areas, President Truman, Jan. 1949

Tripartite Declaration on Allied Policy toward Germany, United States, France, and United Kingdom, May 1950

Tripartite Declaration on Negotiation of Austrian State Treaty, United States, Great Britain, and Soviet Union, May 1950

Tripartite Declaration regarding Armistice Borders Between Arab States and Israel, United States, France, and United Kingdom, May 1950

Uniting for Peace Resolution, U.N. General Assembly, Nov. 1950

Tripartite Declaration on Inclusion of Germany in European Community, United States, France, and United Kingdom, Sept. 1951

Proclamation on Termination of State of War with Germany, President Truman, Oct. 1951

Proclamation on Termination of State of War with Japan, President Truman, Apr. 1952

Quadripartite Declaration of Allied Kommandatura on Policy in Berlin, May 1952

Tripartite Declaration on New Relationship with Germany by United States, France, and Great Britain, May 1952

Joint Declaration on Policy toward Korea, Assistant Secretary of State Walter S. Robertson and President of Republic of Korea, July 1953

Inter-American Declaration of Caracas Providing for Solidarity, Preservation of Political Integrity, and Prevention of Communism, Mar. 1954

Tripartite Declaration on Status of East Germany, United States, France, and United Kingdom, Apr. 1954

Declaration of Common Principles of Anglo-American Policy—Potomac Charter, June 1954

Joint Statements for Distant Early Warning Systems—"Pine Tree Line," "Mid-Canada Line," and "Dew Line," United States and Canada, Apr. and Sept. 1954

Pacific Charter to Maintain Peace and Security in Southeast Asia and the Pacific, Sept. 1954

Final Act of London Nine-Power Conference on Security and Integration of the Western World in the Atlantic Community, Oct. 1954

Joint Declaration on Trademark Protection, United States and Vietnam, Nov. 1953 and Oct. 1954

Tripartite Declaration on Allied Policy Toward Berlin, United States, France, and Great Britain, Oct. 1954

Tripartite Declaration on Germany, Austria, and European Security, United States, France, and Great Britain, Apr. 1955

Tripartite Proclamation of Allied High Commission for Germany, Terminating Occupation Regime, May 1955

Tripartite Declaration on Germany and European Security, United States, France, and Great Britain, Nov. 1955

Declaration of Washington on Self-Government and Independence of All Nations, President Eisenhower and Prime Minister Eden, Feb. 1956

Table 7.7 (continued)

Joint Declaration of Washington on the Origin of Man and His Destiny, President Eisenhower and Prime Minister Eden, Feb. 1956

Four-Power Declaration on Disarmament, United States, Canada, France, and United Kingdom, May 1956

Inter-American Declaration on Education and Literacy, May 1956

Declaration on Neutralism, President Eisenhower, June 1956

Inter-American Declaration of Principles, Conference of Presidents, Panama City, July 1956

Tripartite Declaration on Nationalization of the Suez Canal Company, United States, France, and United Kingdom, Aug. 1956

Declaration on Establishment of Suez Canal Users Association, Sept. 1956

Multilateral Declaration on Abolition of the International Regime of Tangier, Oct. 1956

Declaration Reaffirming Mutual United States–Vietnam Friendship and Support, President Eisenhower and President Ngo Dinh Diem, May 1957

Joint Declaration on Maintaining Peace and Freedom, President Eisenhower and Chancellor Adenauer, May 1957

Quadripartite Declaration on German Reunification, United States, France, West Germany, and United Kingdom, July 1957

Joint Declaration of Common Purposes, President Eisenhower and Prime Minister of United Kingdom, Oct. 1957

Declaration of NATO on Liberty, Human Rights, Peace, Unity, and Security, Dec. 1957

Joint Declaration of NATO Heads of Government Concerning Purposes of the Alliance, Dec. 1957

Tripartite Declaration on Preparatory Work for an East–West Summit Conference, United States, France, and United Kingdom, Mar. 1958

Declaration of London of Baghdad Pact Powers on Maintaining Collective Security, July 1958

Declaration on United States Cooperation in the Security and Defense of the Baghdad Pact Nations, Secretary Dulles, July 1958

Declaration of Washington on Inter-American Economic Cooperation, Dec. 1958

Declaration on Berlin, NATO Council, Dec. 1958

Proclamation on Importation of Petroleum and Petroleum Products into the United States, President Eisenhower, Mar. 1959, and modification, Apr. 1959

Inter-American Declaration on Peace, Solidarity, Human Rights, and Representative Democracy, Santiago, Aug. 1959

Inter-American Declaration on Principles of Democracy, Santiago, Aug. 1959

Quadripartite Declaration on Methods of Advancing Disarmament Negotiations, Big Four Foreign Ministers, Aug. 1959

Declaration on the Rights of the Child, UN General Assembly, Nov. 1959

Joint Declaration on Relations, Montevideo, United States and Uruguay, Mar. 1960

Inter-American Declaration Condemning Extracontinental Intervention in Western Hemisphere, San José, Aug. 1960

Inter-American Declaration on Endangerment of Intervention from Outside the Hemisphere, San José, Aug. 1960

Act of Bogotá on Inter-American Economic Cooperation, Sept. 1960

Declaration on Granting Independence to Colonial Countries and Peoples, U.N. General Assembly, Dec. 1960

Declaration to Exclude Cuba from Participation in the Inter-American System, Jan. 1961

Inter-American Declaration and Charter of Punta del Este to Establish the Alliance for Progress, Aug. 1961

Declaration on General and Complete Disarmament, U.S. Delegation to United Nations General Assembly, Sept. 1961

Joint Declaration on Reexamining Commercial Relations, United States and representatives to the European Economic Community, Mar. 1962

Declaration and Protocol on the Neutrality of Laos, July 1962

Proposed Declaration of Interdependence with a United Europe, President Kennedy, July 1962

Proclamation to Interdict Delivery of Offensive Weapons to Cuba, President Kennedy, Oct. 1962

Declaration on Permanent Sovereignty over Natural Resources, U.N. General Assembly, Dec. 1962

Declaration on Rights of States to Dispose of Their Wealth and Resources, U.N. General Assembly, Dec. 1962

Declaration of Central America and Panama on Economic and Social Development, San José, Mar. 1963

Inter-American Declaration on Central America, San José, Mar. 1963

Joint United States-Panamanian Declaration to Resolve Crisis and Reestablish Diplomatic Relations, Apr. 1964

Tripartite Declaration on Soviet–East German Plan for Treatment of Germany, United States, France, and United Kingdom, June 1964

Inter-American Declaration Establishing Sanctions against Cuba, Washington, July 1964

Tonkin Gulf Resolution to Protect American Armed Forces in Southeast Asia, Aug. 1964 (in lieu of a declaration of war or of national emergency)

Act of Washington—Procedure for Admission of New Members Into the Organization of American States, Dec. 1964

Tripartite Declaration on Resolving the German Reunification Issue, United States, France, and United Kingdom, May 1965

Inter-American Declarations on Peaceful Settlement in Dominican Republic, Santo Domingo, June and Aug. 1965

Act of Rio de Janeiro to Modify Charter of the Organization of American States, Nov. 1965

Declaration of Honolulu on Defense of South Vietnam against Aggression, President Johnson and Prime Minister Nguyen Cao Ky, Feb. 1966

Declaration of Manila on Peace and Progress in Asia and the Pacific, Oct. 1966

Declaration against Intervention in the Domestic Affairs of States and Protection of Their Independence and Sovereignty, U.N. General Assembly, Nov. 1966

United States Fourteen Points for Peace in Southeast Asia, Secretary Rusk, Feb. 1967

Inter-American Declaration of American Presidents on Latin America, including common market, Punta del Este, Apr. 1967

Proclamation on War in Vietnam, President Johnson, May 1967

Declaration of Presidents on United States–Mexican Boundary, Ciudad Juarez, Oct. 1967

Declaration on Elimination of Discrimination against Women, U.N. Gen. Assembly, Nov. 1967

Table 7.7 (continued)

Declaration on Principles of International Law concerning Friendly Relations and Co-operation among States, U.N. Gen. Assembly, Oct. 1970

Declaration on Basic Principles of Mutual Relations, President Nixon and Premier Brezhnov, May 1972

Declaration on Environmental Protection, U.N. Conference, Stockholm, June 1972

Declaration on New International Economic Order, U.N. Gen. Assembly, Jan. 1974 (rejected by United States)

Declaration on Atlantic Relations, 25th Anniversary of NATO, reaffirming the Alliance and its purposes, June 1974

Joint Statement on Relations, United States and Jordan, Amman, June 1974

Multilateral Declaration of Principles on Security and Cooperation in Europe, July 1974

Aide-Memoire on Continuing Negotiations on Nuclear Arms, President Ford and Premier Brezhnev, Nov. 1974

Charter of Economic Rights and Duties of States, U.N. Gen. Assembly, Dec. 1974

Charter of the Rights and Duties of States, U.N. Gen. Assembly, Jan. 1975

Declaration and Plan on Industrial Development and Cooperation, Mar. 1975

Helsinki Declaration to Implement Final Act of Conference on Security and Cooperation in Europe, Aug. 1975

Declaration on Protection of Persons from Torture and Other Cruel, Inhumane or Degrading Punishment, U.N. General Assembly, Dec. 1975

Joint Declaration on Economic Interdependence and Development, Economic Summit Meeting, Dorado Beach, Puerto Rico, June 1976

Joint Declaration to Economic Challenges of the Future, Economic Summit Meeting, London, May 1977

Joint Declaration on Antiqua and Barbuda, United States and United Kingdom, London, Oct. 1977

Joint Declaration on Public Policy, United States and India, Jan. 1978

Joint Declaration on Mutual Relations, President Carter and President Ceausescu of Romania, Apr., 1978

Proclamation on Establishment of Commonwealth of Northern Mariana Islands (in union with the United States), President Carter, May 1978

Joint Declaration on Restoring the International Economy, Economic Summit Meeting, Bonn, July 1978

Joint Statement on Economic Relations, Economic Summit Meeting, Bonn, July 1978

Joint Statement on International Terrorism, Economic Summit Meeting, Bonn, July 1978

Joint Declaration on Energy Conservation, Economic Summit Meeting, Tokyo, June 1979

Proclamation on Nondiscriminatory Treatment of Chinese Products, President Carter, Oct. 1979

Proclamation Prohibiting Petroleum Imports from Iran, President Carter, Nov. 1979

Joint Declaration on Mutual Economic Needs and Responsibilities, Economic Summit Meeting, Venice, June 1980

Joint Statement on Hijacking, Economic Summit Meeting, Venice, June 1980

Joint Statement on Problem of Refugees, Economic Summit Meeting, Venice, June 1980

Joint Delcaration on Settlement of Claims concerning Detention of 52 American hostages held by Iran, United States and Iran, Algiers, Jan. 1981

Joint Statement with Hungary on Development of Agricultural Trade and Cooperation, Washington, May 1981

Declaration on Economic Relations, Economic Summit Meeting, Ottawa, July 1981

Declaration on Terrorism, Economic Summit Meeting, Ottawa, July 1981

Joint Statement on Economic Relations, Economic Summit Meeting, Versailles, June 1982 (accompanied by Joint Communiqué)

Manila Declaration on Peaceful Settlement of International Disputes, U.N. Gen. Assembly, Nov. 1982

Caribbean Basin Initiative, President Reagan, Dec. 1982

Proclamation on Establishment of Exclusive Economic Zone of the Contiguous United States Coastal Sea, President Reagan, Mar. 1983

Declaration on World Economic Recovery, Economic Summit Meeting, Williamsburg, May 1983

Joint Statement on Shared Commitment on Security Issues, Economic Summit Meeting, Williamsburg, May 1983

Memorandum of Agreement concerning Military Bases, United States and Philippines, June 1983

Inter-American Agreement on Bases for International Understanding, Caracas, Sept. 1983

Inter-American Declaration of Twenty-one Points for Peace in Central America, Panama City, Sept. 1983 (also resolution of Organization of American States, Nov. 1983)

Declaration for Comprehensive Political Dialogue and Cooperation with the Soviet Union, NATO Council, Dec. 1983

Proclamation Proscribing Imports of Petroleum and Petroleum Products From Libya, President Reagan, Dec. 1983

Note on Modification of Declaration of 1946 Accepting Compulsory Jurisdiction of the International Court of Justice, Secretary Shultz, Apr. 1984

Declaration on Democratic Values, Economic Summit Meeting, London, June 1984

Declaration on East–West Relations and Arms Control, Economic Summit Meeting, London, June 1984

Declaration on Economic Affairs, Economic Summit Meeting, London, June 1984

Declaration on International Terrorism, Economic Summit Meeting, London, June 1984

Declaration on Population and Development, International Conference on Population, Mexico City, Aug. 1984

Declaration Reaffirming Purposes of Environmental Modification Convention, Sept. 1984

Declaration on Right of Peoples to Peace, U.N. Gen. Assembly, Nov. 1984

Declaration on Determination to Cooperate for Prosperity, Economic Summit Meeting, Tokyo, May 1986

Joint Statement, Looking Forward to a Better Future, Economic Summit Meeting, Tokyo, May 1986

Proclamation on United States Relations with Northern Mariana Islands, Micronesia, and Marshall Islands, President Reagan, Nov. 1986

Joint Declaration with Soviet Union on Guarantees Regarding Settlement of Afghanistan War, Geneva, April 1988

Declaration on Economic Affairs, Economic Summit Meeting, Toronto, June 1988

Proclamation on Suspension of Cuban Immigration into United States, President Reagan, Aug. 1988

Proclamation on Territorial Sea of United States, President Reagan, Dec. 1988

Proclamation to Implement United States–Canada Free Trade Agreement, President Reagan, Dec. 1988

Declaration on Economic Affairs, Economic Summit Meeting, Paris, July 1989

Declaration on Economic Development, Coordination, and Efficiency, Economic Summit Meeting, Paris, July 1989

Table 7.7 (continued)

Declaration on Human Rights, Economic Summit Meeting, Paris, July 1989

Quadripartite Declaration on Illicit Drugs, Cartagena, Feb. 1990

Final Document of Bonn Conference on Security and Cooperation in Europe (CSCE) Providing for a New Order of Peace, Stability, and Prosperity, Apr. 1990

Declaration on Advancing and Securing Democracy, Economic Summit Meeting, Houston, July 1990

Declaration on Democracy and Economic Development, Economic Summit Meeting, Houston, July 1990

Declaration on Major Transformation of NATO Alliance, London, July 1990

Declaration of National Emergency Regarding Iraq, President Bush, Aug. 1990

Quadripartite Declaration Suspending Rights and Responsibilities in Germany, New York, Oct. 1990

Charter of Paris for a New Europe, Conference on Security and Cooperation in Europe (CSCE), Nov. 1990

Declaration of Twenty-five Parties to the Treaty on Conventional Armed Forces in Europe, Paris, Nov. 1990

Declaration on Principles of a United States–European Community Partnership, Nov. 1990

Declaration on Arms Transfers and Nuclear, Biological, and Chemical Weapons Proliferation, Economic Summit Meeting, London, July 1991

Declaration on Building World Partnership, Economic Summit Meeting, London, July 1991

Declaration on Strengthening the International Order, Economic Summit Meeting, London, July 1991

Declaration on Environment and Development (27 principles), U.N. Conference, Rio de Janeiro, 1992

Proclamation on Extending United States Copyright Protection to Works of People's Republic of China, President Bush, Mar. 1992

Declaration on State of the World Environment, U.N. Conference, Nairobi, May 1992

Declaration on Shaping the New Partnership, Economic Summit Meeting, Munich, July 1992

Declaration on World Economy, Economic Summit Meeting, Munich, July, 1992

Proclamation on Implementing Compact of Free Association with Republic of Palau, President Bush, Sept. 1994

*This list is confined to selected Presidential proclamations and national and international policy declarations and other comparable pronouncements, listed chronologically, some of which are designated as acts or resolutions of international conferences and organizations, charters, exchanges of notes, or joint policy statements. At times Congress enacts declarations of foreign policy in the form of joint resolutions. Sometimes these are ignored or vetoed by the President or modified by the Secretary of State, or they may provide guidance in the shaping of policy. Occasionally, executive declarations evolve from the crystallization of public sentiment. Some declarations are regarded as binding law and are listed in Department of State, *Treaties in Force.*

Whereas these doctrines have constituted presidential prescriptions for executive intent, policies, and actions, most of them required legislative implementation, Department of State explication and application, and/or confirmation by negotiation and incorporation into statutes, treaties or agreements, or action by international organizations or other agencies. They possess several common characteristics. Cast and justified as transcendent precepts, or virtually "articles of faith," as a group their purposes characteristically reflect fundamental, often traditional American political values, such as democracy, freedom, national security, peace, self-determination, and the will of the people, as well as the promotion of human rights and welfare. Even if not formally implemented by legislation, executive orders, treaties, or agreements, they exceed ordinary policy goals by specifying, reiterating, generating, or at least implying legal principles, which appeal to the American law-oriented disposition, and by extolling the approximation of the "rule of law." Except for the Monroe Doctrine and, in some respects, perhaps the Nixon Doctrine of 1971 and the Carter Doctrine of 1980, they tend to be short-lived or otherwise limited, although some have potential durability.

Although rare in American history, it has been alleged that Nixon, while Vice President during the Eisenhower Administration, propounded a corollary to the policy of massive retaliation during the Cold War. Called the "Nibble to Death Doctrine," in response to the Communist Soviet Union and Chinese Democratic Republic strategy of nibbling to death the United States and its allies with challenges and limited wars in Europe, the Far East, and elsewhere, the American Government would rely on massive retaliatory power and nuclear response. It also has been suggested that certain methods of diplomatic practice may be reduced to permeative doctrines. Thus, Secretary Kellogg regarded the principles embodied in the Logan Act (discussed in the section on unauthorized foreign representation) as axiomatic doctrine requiring diplomacy to be handled solely by official emissaries.

Presidential Proclamations and American and International Policy Declarations

Also historically noteworthy are Presidential proclamations, national and international declarations, and other comparable enunciations concerning foreign affairs, listed in Table 7.7, Part B. Presidents issue dozens of proclamations each year, but only a few concern foreign relations. They have the force of law for the United States, which may be confirmed or annulled by legislative action but may not violate existing law, and they set direction and boundaries for the behavior of both private individuals and the American Government. They differ from executive orders, which are issued to, and binding solely upon, American Government agencies. Proclamations also differ from national and international declarations, most of which constitute important policy pronouncements, short of formal national and international commitments, but are historically more significant than the thousands of ordinary policy statements of Presidents, Secretaries of State, and other officials. They generally establish aspirations and future courses of action that emphasize American foreign interests and, in some cases, provide specifications for future international conduct. More than two-thirds of these are designated as declarations, approximately 10 percent are denominated proclamations, and the rest bear other titles, such as acts or final acts, charters, resolutions, or statements.[150]

Like those documents that establish or sever diplomatic relations, declare the going to war, or affirm neutrality in time of hostilities, international pronouncements designated as proclamations are rarely issued.[151] In principle, they usually are reserved for the establishment of international rights and duties, status, or actions binding on the governments concerned. Since World War II they have been applied unilaterally by the President to such matters as instituting the United Nations Charter and the Statute of the International Court of Justice, providing independence to the Philippines, terminating World War II with Germany and Japan, instituting American sanctions against particular foreign countries, suspending Cuban immigration into the United States, denominating an exclusive economic zone within American coastal waters, and determining the status of relations with former Pacific Trusteeship territories. Exceptional was the tripartite proclamation 1955 issued by the Allied High Commission to terminate the occupation of West Germany. Additional proclamations, not included, apply to more specific items, such as specifications concerning imports of various products, temporary suspension of most-favored-nation treatment of individual countries, and changes in American tariff schedules.

On the other hand, reminiscent of President Wilson's historic Fourteen Points (January 1918) and President Roosevelt's pronouncements of the Atlantic Charter in August 1941 and the concept of the Arsenal for Democracy, the Four Freedoms, and the Good Neighbor and Lend-Lease programs the following year, more recent Presidents and Secretaries of State propounded a number of similar major unilateral propositions called declarations. These are represented by President Truman's unique Twelve Fundamentals of Foreign Policy (October 1945),[152] the Marshall Plan for the European Recovery Program (June 1947), Truman's Point Four Program for technical assistance to underdeveloped countries (January 1949), and Eisenhower's Declaration on Neutralism (June 1956).

Since World War II some 165 instruments regarded as declarations or comparable documents were issued. Only a few were unilateral U.S. pronouncements, which dealt with such matters as confirming and modifying acceptance of the compulsory jurisdiction of the International Court of Justice (1946 and 1984), the congressional Gulf of Tonkin Resolution on Southeast Asia (1964), and President Bush's Declaration of a National Emergency Regarding Iraq (1990). Approximately one-fourth were bilateral, tripartite, and quadripartite,[153] and nearly 60 percent were subscribed to by more than four governments, of which most were United Nations and inter-American,[154] or involved periodic Economic Summit Meetings[155] begun in 1975 (also called Transatlantic Economic Conferences), and others were issued by the North Atlantic Treaty Organization and ad hoc international conferences.

Although the titles of most declarations specify their subjects of concern, a few are historically identified with the location of issuance, represented by the Inter-American Act of Chapultepec (1945), the Declarations of Panama (1956), Washington (1956 and 1958), Honolulu (1966), Manila (1966 and 1982), and Helsinki (1975), the Shanghai Communiqué (1972), and the Charter of Paris (of the Conference on Security and Cooperation in Europe, 1990). The Tonkin Gulf Resolution (1964) served in lieu of a declaration of war or national emergency. Several declarations were regarded as comparable to formal treaties or executive agreements, such as the Quadripartite Declaration on the Assumption of Allied Authority in Germany (1945), the Tripartite Declaration on Atomic Energy (1945), the Pacific Charter to Maintain Peace and Security in Southeast Asia and the Pacific (1954), the Declaration on United States Cooperation with the Baghdad Pact Nations (1958), the Inter-American Charter to Establish the Alliance for Progress (1961), the Declaration on the Neutrality of Laos (1962), and the Inter-American Declaration Establishing Sanctions Against Cuba (1964).

To be expected, as a group these multilateral declarations concern a broad spectrum of functional subjects. They embrace such international issues as arms control, atomic energy regulation, economic assistance and cooperation, hemispheric solidarity, international hijacking and terrorism, managing relations with the defeated World War II Axis powers, maritime jurisdiction, mutual friendship, national security, nuclear-age defense, peace and security, peaceful settlement, and trade and commerce. They also focus on domestic matters, including the application of sanctions against certain countries, democratic values, education and literacy, energy conservation, freedom and nonintervention, human rights, population development, protection of natural resources, and territorial disposition.

Some have been applied to particular geographic areas or specific countries. Europe and Latin America were accorded the greatest degree of attention, whereas Africa received the least. So far as participation in joint and multilateral declarations are concerned, the United Kingdom joined the United States in more tripartite and quadripartite arrangements than any other country, although more than a dozen also involved France, and several, concerned primarily with Germany and Berlin affairs, also included the Soviet Union. Of the general or universal multilateral declarations, those emanating from the United Nations have included a Declaration of Human Rights (1948), supported independence for colonial countries and peoples (1960), opposed foreign intervention in another country's domestic affairs (1966), and endorsed general and complete disarmament (1961), permanent sovereignty over natural resources (1962), the rights of children (1959), and other matters.

Evidencing substantial increase in the quantity and variety of national and multilateral policy declarations as well as Presidential Doctrines, engendered by the proliferation of American foreign relations interests and the extension of participation in international conferences and organizations, this practice is likely to continue. However, assessing this aspect of the conduct of contemporary American foreign affairs, whereas many of them were deemed to be important at the time of their enunciation, few have achieved the historical significance of the Monroe Doctrine, President Wilson's Fourteen Points, President Truman's Fundamentals of American Foreign Policy following World War II, or the Act of Chapultepec, the Marshall Plan, and the Point Four Program. Nevertheless, they may be expected to evoke the negotiation of more conventions, treaties, and agreements, concerned with such matters as airspace and outer space, arms limitation, decolonization, economic cooperation and assistance, energy (including nuclear), human rights, nonintervention, peaceful settlement, the seas, terrorism, and trade, thereby increasing the burden of the Secretary and Department of State.[156]

Anatomy of the American Bilateral Treaty Complex

Currently, the United States is a party to more than 6,000 regular bilateral treaties and agreements with some 194 foreign governments and fourteen of their dependencies, as indicated in Table 7.8, of which some 5,350 were concluded during the half century since 1945. In addition to the countries referred to in previous chapters, such treaty relations apply to approximately 125 additional treaty partners throughout the world. Most of these were formerly African, Asian, Caribbean, Mideast, and Pacific dependent territories of major world powers. For example, in some cases they resulted from the breakup or amalgamation of such European states as Czechoslovakia, the Soviet Union, and Yugoslavia[157]; from the two Chinas following World War II; from the independence of Singapore from Maylasia in 1965; from the independence of Eritrea from Ethiopia in 1993; from the breakup of French Indochina into Cambodia, Laos, and Vietnam; from the independence and subsequent merger of the two Yemens in 1990; and from the independence of the former Pacific Trust Territories of the Marshall Islands, Micronesia, and Palau in the 1990s. The treaty family also includes the European principalities of Liechtenstein, Monaco, and San Marino, with which the United States concluded treaties/ agreements prior to 1946. Hong Kong, the British dependency for nearly a century, reverted to China in 1997, which affected its subsequent treaty status.

The United States is a signatory to merely one or two treaties/agreements with only a few of these new states.[158] The countries with which it has the largest number—exceeding 125—include Canada (250), United Kingdom (209, plus twenty-two for its eight dependencies), Mexico (186), the Soviet Union (108, plus 196 for its twelve newly independent republics), Germany (150), France (121, plus five for its four dependencies), and Japan (141). Another twenty-eight countries are each party to from fifty to 100. Combined, these thirty-five treaty partners (or approximately 17 percent) account for more than

Table 7.8
Bilateral Treaties and Agreements in Force

A. Countries and Other Territories

Column groups: **Totals** (Cat, T&A); **International Titles** (C, T, A, M, O); **U.S. Titles** (TIAS, T, EA, EN); **Dates Signed** (Pre-1946, 1946-1949, 1950s, 1960s, 1970s, 1980s, 1990s)

Countries	Cat	T&A	C	T	A	M	O	TIAS	T	EA	EN	Pre-1946	1946-1949	1950s	1960s	1970s	1980s	1990s
Afghanistan	12	19			19			9		1	9	2		6	6	5		
Albania	11	16	3	12	1			9	3		4	5	2					9
Algeria *	7	8		7	1			7	1						1		4	3
Angola *	2	2			2			1			1							2
Antigua and Barbuda *	14	19	4	1	10	1	3	9	3	1	6		3	2	5	3	5	1
Argentina	33	64		5	46	12	1	40	1	4	19	9		9	8	8	14	16
Armenia *	5	5			5			4	1									5
Australia	33	78	8	2	54	7	7	41	6	2	29	7	5	11	10	11	21	13
Austria	25	45	5	5	32	1	2	20	6	5	14	13	7	12	4	4	4	1
Azerbaijan *	2	2			2			1			1							2
The Bahamas *	16	40	3	2	31	2	2	21	3	2	14	8	2	6	4	7	12	1
Bahrain *	6	9			9			3		1	5					2	2	5
Bangladesh *	9	19		1	14	4		13	3	3						8	8	3
Barbados *	15	22	5	1	13	1	2	4	7	4	7	6		1	3	2	10	
Belarus *	7	12			12			9		1	2							12
Belgium	30	65	7	5	40	7	6	31	7	8	19	16	3	12	11	6	15	2
Belize *	15	24	3	1	16	2	2	10	3	3	8	4		1	4	4	8	3
Benin *	6	10			10			2		2	6					4	3	3
Bhutan *	1	1			1			1										1
Bolivia	22	53		4	46	2	1	35	3	2	13	4	2	9	12	4	15	7
Bosnia-Herzegovina *	2	2			2						2							2
Botswana *	8	12			10	1	1	6	1		5				1	3	7	1
Brazil	32	76	2	3	55	11	5	40	4	6	26	9	2	7	17	11	22	8
Brunei *	6	6	1	1	3		1	3	2	1		2	1	1		1		1
Bulgaria	14	22	3	6	14	1	1	10	5	5	5	9				3	1	12
Burkina Faso *	6	7			6		1	1		2	4				3	1	2	1
Burma *	14	16	3	1	11		1	5	5		6	4	4	3	2	1	2	
Burundi *	5	5			5					1	4				1	1	3	
Cambodia *	9	11			10	1		7		1	3				1	1	5	4
Cameroon *	7	13		1	11	1		7		1	5			3	1		3	6
Canada	60	250	18	23	148	19	42	100	27	12	111	58	15	30	18	48	60	21
Cape Verde *	4	11			11			8		2	1					7	2	2
Central African Rep. *	5	9			9			5		1	3				2	5	2	
Chad *	7	9			9			2		1	6				2		5	2
Chile	29	60	2	3	46	9		31	4	3	22	8	1	10	9	10	12	10
China (Peoples Rep.)	22	46	1		32	9	4	30		4	12					5	30	11
China (Taiwan) *	15	23	1	3	17	1	1	9	2	4	8	5	4	6	2	6		
Colombia	30	60	1	4	47	7	1	29	3	2	26	6	1	9	13	14	12	5
Comoros *	3	3			3						3						3	
Congo *	8	16	3	1	11	1		11		2	3	3	2	3			2	6
Cook Islands *	3	3	1		2			1			2						3	
Costa Rica	22	48	3	2	40	2	1	23	1	3	21	5	3	3	5	6	16	10
Cote d'Ivoire *	8	19			19			13		2	4				5	1	7	6
Croatia *	4	5			5			2		2	1							5
Cuba	20	36	4	4	22	1	5	13	7	2	14	13	3	13	1	2	1	3
Cyprus *	17	26	3	1	14	6	2	12	3	3	8	4	2	2	10	1	7	
Czech Rep. *	9	9	1		6	1	1	6		1	2							9
Czechoslovakia	20	36	2	6	25	1	2	14	5	7	10	10	3	1	2	4	7	9

Key to Symbols

*	Post-World War II independent countries and other territories

A	Agreements	EN	Exchange of Notes and Letters
C	Conventions	M	Memorandums of Understanding
Cat	Categories of T&A Subjects	T	Treaties
EA	Executive Agreements	TIAS	Treaties and Other International Acts
O	Others: Arrangements, Declarations, Procedures, Protocols, and Others		

Table 7.8 (continued)

A. Countries and Other Territories (cont.)

Countries	Totals		International Titles					U.S. Titles				Dates Signed						
	Cat	T&A	C	T	A	M	O	TIAS	T	EA	EN	Pre-1946	1946-1949	1950s	1960s	1970s	1980s	1990s
Denmark	29	57	11	4	34	4	4	17	7	5	28	18	5	13	5	3	10	3
Djibouti *	6	7			6	1		2		1	4					1	3	3
Dominica *	14	16	1	1	12	1	1	8	1		7	1		1	3	3	6	2
Dominican Rep.	22	45	2		39	4		27	2	2	14	4	1	5	13	5	9	8
Ecuador	23	50	1	4	42	2	1	25	5	3	17	6	4	6	10	4	10	10
Egypt	28	57	2	5	41	5	4	31	3	4	19	6	1	5	9	12	17	7
El Salvador	21	36	1	1	30	2	2	17	2	4	13	5	1	4	9	3	7	7
Equatorial Guinea *	3	3			3					1	2						2	1
Eritrea *	4	5			5			1		1	3							5
Estonia	16	22	7		14	1		6	5	4	7	11						11
Ethiopia	12	26		3	22	1		10		7	9	3	1	4	9	3	2	4
Fiji *	11	22	3	1	17		1	3	4	3	12	5		1	2	9	2	3
Finland	23	46	5	4	27	6	4	21	4	6	15	10	1	5	3	5	11	11
France	46	121	11	5	75	23	7	77	7	7	30	18	16	19	13	8	32	15
French Guiana	1	1	1								1	1						
Guadeloupe	1	1	1					1				1						
Martinique	1	2	1		1					2		2						
Society Islands	1	1	1								1	1						
Gabon *	6	9			9			5		1	3				1	1	5	2
The Gambia *	12	15	3	1	9		2	4	4		7	5		2	2	2	3	1
Georgia	6	6			6			3			3							6
Germany, Federal Rep.	41	150	2	7	99	36	6	95	5	3	47	7	1	40	15	32	32	23
Ghana *	17	29	2	1	24		2	14	3	2	10	5	2	6	4	4	5	3
Greece	31	72	5	4	54	2	7	34	5	6	27	15	6	16	8	9	7	11
Grenada *	14	24	3	2	18		1	8	4	3	9	6	1	1	4		9	3
Guatemala	23	38	5	2	29	1	1	15	5	2	16	10	1	6	7	4	8	2
Guinea *	9	22			22			13		1	8				12	2	7	1
Guinea-Bissau *	5	4			4					1	3						3	1
Guyana *	15	30	3	1	22	1	3	14	4	5	7	6	1	1	4	4	5	9
Haiti	19	29	1	1	27			9	2	1	17	5		7	3	4	6	4
Honduras	23	52	2	3	39	5	3	26	3	4	19	7		9	5	8	13	10
Hungary	28	46	5	3	33	1	4	22	5	6	13	9	1		1	13	10	12
Iceland	19	43	2	5	29	5	2	19	3	5	16	8	1	9	11	6	7	1
India *	28	58	3	1	47	4	3	33	6	2	17	6	3	9	18	13	8	1
Indonesia *	23	68	1		56	9	2	42		3	23	1	1	9	20	15	13	9
Iran	18	37		1	31	2	3	21		1	15	2		7	12	14	2	
Iraq	12	15		7	8			5	2		8	5		6	1		3	
Ireland	14	22	6	1	13		2	12	1	3	6	5	2	6	2	1	3	3
Israel *	31	82	2	1	62	13	4	52		3	27			15	17	16	25	9
Italy	40	95	6	6	55	19	9	43	5	4	43	16	8	18	9	9	22	13
Jamaica *	22	47	5	1	35	1	5	23	4	3	17	7		1	6	7	19	7
Japan	42	141	5	3	114	11	8	52	1	1	87	4	1	19	25	27	44	21
Jordan *	14	30		1	25	2	2	17		1	12			4	3	7	8	8
Kazakstan *	12	17		1	15		1	17										17
Kenya *	8	18		1	17			12		1	5	1	1	1	4	2	8	1
Kiribati *	8	9	1	2	5		1	5			4	1		1	2	4		1
Korea	33	102	2	2	70	19	9	70		4	28		6	13	20	14	26	23
Kuwait *	9	12	1		10		1	6		2	4			1	3	3	4	1
Kyrgyz Rep. *	8	10		1	9			7			3							10
Laos *	8	10			7	3		5		1	4			3	1	1		5
Latvia	15	22		5	15	2		10	6	5	1	9						13
Lebanon	11	23	2		21			7		1	15	3	1	3	5	6	4	1
Lesotho *	8	9	2	1	5		1	2	4	1	2	4			3		1	1
Liberia	23	49	2	2	41	3	1	20	5	5	19	9	2	10	9	5	14	
Libya *	1	3			2		1	2			1			2		1		
Liechtenstein	3	4		1	1		2		1		3	2	1			1		
Lithuania	17	24	1	4	15	2	2	7	4	5	8	9	2					13
Luxembourg	17	33	3	4	21	4	1	15	4	3	11	6	3	12	3		8	1
Madagascar *	9	17	1		16			9	2	1	5		4		2		9	2
Malawi *	7	11		1	10			4	1	1	5	1			2	1	6	1

Countries	Totals		International Titles					U.S. Titles				Dates Signed						
	Cat	T&A	C	T	A	M	O	TIAS	T	EA	EN	Pre-1946	1946-1949	1950s	1960s	1970s	1980s	1990s
Malaysia *	16	27	3	1	21	1	1	8	3	3	13	5	1	5	3	5	3	5
Maldives *	4	6			5		1	2		1	3						5	1
Mali *	10	15			14	1		7		2	6				7	2	3	3
Malta *	15	18	5	4	7		2	4	6	2	6	7	3	1	1	2	2	2
Marshall Islands *	7	11			11			5			6						8	3
Mauritania *	7	11			11			7		1	3				2	3	3	3
Mauritius *	11	14	3	2	8		1	4	4	1	5	4	2	1	1	3	1	2
Mexico	45	186	10	10	123	21	22	95	11	4	76	18	1	6	12	62	50	37
Micronesia *	7	8			8			4			4						6	2
Moldova *	6	7		1	6			6			1							7
Monaco	4	4		1	3				1		3	1	2	1				
Mongolia *	10	11			7	4		10			1						2	9
Morocco	20	41	2	2	35	1	1	27	1	2	11	1	1	1	11	3	20	4
Mozambique *	6	11			10	1		7		1	3					1	5	5
Namibia *	5	6			5	1		2	2	1	1							6
Nauru *	3	3		1	2				1	1	1	1		1				1
Nepal *	8	9			7		2	3			6		1	1	3	1	2	1
Netherlands	34	86	6	5	55	12	8	45	3	6	32	9	7	21	5	10	26	
Netherlands Antilles	2	4			4			1		3				1	1		1	1
New Caledonia *	1	1			1					1								1
New Zealand	25	36	5	3	23	5		12	4	4	16	6	3	4	7	4	8	4
Nicaragua	19	34		1	33			11	1	2	20	5		10	4	5		10
Niger *	6	16			16			9		1	6	1			3	1	8	3
Nigeria *	17	24	2	1	19		2	13	3	2	6	4	1	2		5	7	5
Niue *	1	1			1			1										1
Norway	32	72	5	6	45	12	4	35	6	5	26	12	9	13	5	8	17	8
Oman *	9	14		1	12	1		5		1	8			1		2	6	5
Pakistan *	25	57	4	2	32	15	4	32	5	3	17	5	4	20	6	6	14	2
Palau *	3	3			3			3									1	2
Panama	37	85	2	6	67	4	6	20	4	5	56	12	2	5	6	28	21	11
Papua New Guinea *	9	14	1	1	9	3		5	2	3	4	2	1		1	7	3	
Paraguay	18	39	1	4	34			21	3	2	13	4	3	2	16	8	2	4
Peru	29	66	3	3	53	4	3	34	5	3	24	8	1	12	9	7	18	11
Philippines *	32	99	4	2	87	2	4	39		3	57		8	21	32	10	19	9
Poland	35	78	5	5	56	8	4	49	9	1	19	13	3	6	10	10	16	20
Portugal	22	48	2	2	31	10	3	19	3	4	22	6	1	9	5	13	13	1
Macao	2	6			4	1	1			3	3					1	4	1
Qatar *	4	5			4	1		1		2	2						3	2
Romania	24	50	4	5	35		6	23	5	7	15	10	1		2	16	8	13
Russian Federation *	19	60	1		39	16	4	56			4							60
Rwanda *	6	6			6			2			4				1	1	3	1
Saint Kitts and Nevis *	13	15	4	1	9		1	7	3		5	3		2	1	1	7	1
Saint Lucia *	15	23	3	1	15	2	2	9	3	4	7	5	1	1	4	2	7	3
Saint Vincent and Grenadines *	14	19	3	1	14		1	5	3	3	8	5		1	2	3	6	2
San Marino	1	2	1	1					2			2						
Sao Tome and Principe *	3	3			3			1			2						2	1
Saudi Arabia	9	29			25	3	1	18		1	10	1		3	4	17	3	1
Senegal *	10	30		1	29			23		2	5				5	1	17	7
Seychelles *	10	11	1	1	8		1	3	2	1	5	2	1	2	2	1	1	1
Sierra Leone *	13	29	3	1	22	1	2	14	3	5	7	5	1	1	7	2	9	4
Singapore *	15	31	3	1	20	6	1	10	3	3	15	6		4	2	4	11	4
Slovak Rep. *	8	8	1		6	1		4		1	3							8
Slovenia *	3	3			3			1		1	1							3
Solomon Islands *	7	9		1	8			3	1		5	1	1	2	2	1		2
Somalia *	7	12			12			6		1	5				3	2	7	
South Africa	20	31	5	2	19	1	4	10	4	3	14	7	6	6			5	7
Spain	33	73	2	8	52	7	4	41	6	2	24	10	1	14	9	9	17	13
Sri Lanka *	19	33	2	2	26		3	15	4	3	11	5	1	8	6	2	5	6
Sudan *	6	27			26	1		19		1	7			3	4	6	13	1

547

Table 7.8 (continued)

A. Countries and Other Territories (cont.)

Countries	Totals		International Titles					U.S. Titles				Dates Signed						
	Cat	T&A	C	T	A	M	O	TIAS	T	EA	EN	Pre-1946	1946-1949	1950s	1960s	1970s	1980s	1990s
Suriname *	14	19	4	3	10	1	1	7	3	2	7	5	2	5		2	1	4
Swaziland *	7	11		1	9		1	4	1	1	5	1			1	4	5	
Sweden	25	49	9	2	26	5	7	25	5	3	16	14	4	2	5	3	12	9
Switzerland	20	45	4	5	29	2	5	25	5	2	13	9	3	5	3	10	13	2
Syrian Arab Rep.	8	14	1		13			6	1	2	5	3		2	4	4		1
Tajikistan *	2	2			2			2										2
Tanzania *	8	16	1	1	14			11	1	2	2	1		2	3	2	6	2
Thailand	23	43		4	32	6	1	24		3	16	1	2	7	8	10	9	6
Togo *	8	11		1	9		1	6		1	4			4	2	5		
Tonga *	7	9	1	2	5		1	3		3	3	3		1	1	1	2	1
Trinidad and Tobago *	18	29	4	1	20		4	11	4	4	10	6	2	3	4	3	7	4
Tunisia *	17	35	3	2	25	3	2	19	1	3	12	2	1	4	11	5	8	4
Turkey	24	64		5	53	4	2	31	2	5	26	6	4	18	7	6	18	5
Turkmenistan *	5	5			5			4			1							5
Tuvalu *	8	9	1	2	5		1	4		1	4	1		1	3	3	1	
Uganda *	6	11			11			5		1	5			2	1	7	1	
Ukraine *	38	64	3		49	9	3	45	2	3	14	5		3	9	7	40	
U.S.S.R./Soviet Union	47	108	6	6	64	17	15	81	6	4	17	11	1	2	4	31	33	26
United Arab Emirates *	6	8			5	2	1	4		1	3			1	5	2		
United Kingdom	50	209	15	16	123	37	18	89	31	13	76	48	15	20	25	27	47	27
Anguilla	3	3	1		2					1	2	1				2		
Bermuda	3	5			5			2			3	2			3			
British Virgin Isls.	1	1			1						1							
Gibraltar	1	1			1						1							
Hong Kong	4	6			6			1		2	3				1	1	2	2
Leeward Islands	1	1			1					1						1		
Montserrat	2	2	1		1					1	1			1			1	
Turks & Caicos Isls.	3	3		1	2			2			1					2	1	
Uruguay	18	31	2	3	26			15	3	1	12	3	2	5	6	4	6	5
Uzbekistan *	6	6			6			4		2								6
Vanuatu *	2	2		1	1			2										2
Vatican (Holy See)	1	1			1					1				1				
Venezuela	28	52	1	4	40	6	1	30	4	2	16	5		11	5	8	13	10
Vietnam *	17	35		1	33		1	19		1	15			10	18	3	1	3
Western Samoa *	5	6			6			2		1	3				1	1		4
Yemen *	7	12			12			6		2	4	1			3	6	2	
Yugoslavia	26	67	2	4	57	3	1	38	3	5	21	10	2	22	19	5	7	2
Zaire *	8	37		1	36			30		1	6		1		10	8	15	3
Zambia *	12	26	3	7	14		2	14	4	2	6	5	2	3	1	3	9	3
Zimbabwe *	13	15	3		8	3	1	8	3	1	3	3		1		1	6	4
TOTALS 208		6,163	360	363	4,509	555	376	3,077	432	451	2,203	810	250	774	846	931	1,465	1,087

B. International Policy Declarations and Other Pronouncements
(Treaties and Agreements)

Countries	Totals		International Titles					U.S. Titles				Dates Signed						
	Cat	T&A	C	T	A	M	O	TIAS	T	EA	EN	Pre-1946	1946-1949	1950s	1960s	1970s	1980s	1990s
African Development Bank (ADB)	2	2			2			2									1	1
Agency for the Safety of Air Navigation in Africa and Madagascar	1	1			1			1								1		
Asian Development Bank (ADB)	1	1			1			1								1		
Association of Southeast Asian Nations (ASEAN)	2	2			2			1	1								1	1
BENELUX (Belgium, Netherlands, Luxembourg)	1	3			3			2	1						2	1		
Caribbean Community Secretariat	1	1			1			1									1	

Countries	Totals		International Titles					U.S. Titles				Dates Signed						
	Cat	T&A	C	T	A	M	O	TIAS	T	EA	EN	Pre-1946	1946-1949	1950s	1960s	1970s	1980s	1990s
Central American Bank for Economic Integration	1	1			1			1								1		
Commission of the Cartagena Agreement (Andean Group)	3	3			1	2		3									2	1
Customs Cooperation Council	1	1			1			1										1
East African Common Services Organization	1	1			1			1							1			
European Atomic Energy Community (EURATOM)	1	8			6	1	1	8						1	1		5	1
European Community (EC)	3	16			14	2		11			5				2	5	5	4
European Space Agency	1	3				3		3									2	1
Food and Agriculture Organization (FAO)	2	2			2						2			2				
General Agreement on Tariffs and Trade (GATT)—Interim Commission	1	1			1			1									1	
Hague Conference on Private International Law	1	1			1			1										1
Inter-American Development Bank (IADB)	1	1			1			1							1			
Inter-American Institute for Cooperation on Agriculture	1	1			1			1										1
International Atomic Energy Agency (IAEA)	2	5			5			5						1		1	3	
International Centre for the Preservation and Restoration of Cultural Property	1	1			1						1					1		
International Civil Aviation Organization (ICAO)	1	1			1			1										1
International Coffee Organization	1	1			1						1					1		
International Cotton Advisory Committee	1	1			1						1					1		
International Hydrographic Bureau	1	1			1						1					1		
International Labor Organization (ILO)	2	2			2			1			1				1	1		
International Maritime Organization (IMO)	1	1			1			1										1
International Monetary Fund (IMF)	1	1			1						1					1		
International Natural Rubber Organization	1	1			1			1								1		
International Telecommunication Union (ITU)	2	2			2			1			1					1		1
International Telecommunications Satellite Organization	2	2			2			2								1	1	
International Tropical Timber Organization	1	1			1			1									1	
Inter-Parliamentary Union	1	1			1						1						1	

Table 7.8 (continued)

B. International Policy Declarations and Other Pronouncements (cont.)

Countries	Totals		International Titles					U.S. Titles				Dates Signed						
	Cat	T&A	C	T	A	M	O	TIAS	T	EA	EN	Pre-1946	1946-1949	1950s	1960s	1970s	1980s	1990s
Lake Chad Basin Commission	1	1			1			1								1		
Multinational Force and Observers	2	2			2						2						1	1
Mutual Aid and Loan Guaranty Fund of Council of the Entente States	1	2			2			2								2		
North Atlantic Treaty Organization (NATO)	7	11			7	2	2	10			1			3		1	3	4
NATO AEW&C Programme Management Organization (NAPMO)	1	1			1			1										1
NATO Maintenance and Supply Organization (NAMSO)	1	4			4			3			1			1			2	1
Organization for the Development of the Senegal River	1	2			2			2								2		
Organization for Economic Cooperation and Development (OECD)	2	2			1		1	2									2	
Organization of American States (OAS)	4	5			4	1		4			1			1	1	1	1	1
Palestine Liberation Organization (PLO)	1	1			1			1										1
Preparatory Commission for the Organization for the Prohibition of Chemical Weapons	1	1			1			1										1
South Pacific Commission (SPC)	1	1			1						1					1		
South Pacific Forum Fisheries Agency	1	1			1			1									1	
Supreme Headquarters Allied Powers Europe (SHAPE)	2	2			2			2									2	
United Nations (UN)	11	19			18	1		17			2		2	1	3	4	2	7
United Nations Children's Fund (UNICEF)	1	3			3			3								2	1	
United Nations High Commissioner for Refugees (UNHCR)	3	4			4			4								2	1	1
United Nations Industrial Development Organization (UNIDO)	1	1			1			1										1
Universal Postal Union (UPU)	1	1			1					1								1
World Food Program (WFP)	1	1			1			1								1		
World Health Organization (WHO)	1	1				1		1									1	
World Intellectual Property Organization (WIPO)	2	2			2			2									2	
World Meteorological Organization (WMO)	1	1			1			1									1	
World Tourism Organization	1	1			1						1						1	
TOTALS 56		140	0	0	123	11	6	113	0	3	24	0	2	10	14	33	49	32

half of these treaties and agreements.[159] Historically, the countries with which the most treaties/agreements were concluded prior to 1946 that remain extant are Canada (fifty-eight) and Great Britain and its dependencies (fifty-two), followed by Denmark, France, and Mexico (eighteen each) and then by Belgium and Italy (sixteen each), Greece (fifteen), Sweden (fourteen), and Austria, Cuba, and Poland (thirteen each).

So far as international titles are concerned, approximately three-fourths (4,509) are designated as "agreements." The rest consist of 360 "conventions," 363 "treaties," 555 "memorandums of understanding," and 376 that bear such other designations as "arrangements," "declarations," "protocols," and "others."[160] By comparison, using U.S. treaty designations, it is surprising that more than 2,200 (or more than one-third) are embodied in "exchanges of notes," rather than more formal treaties and agreements, which, prior to 1946, were customarily contained in the *United States Treaty Series* and the *Executive Agreement Series* and thereafter in the *Treaties and Other International Acts Series*. This extensive increase in reliance on simple exchanges of notes and letters denotes greater reliance on less formal arrangements, greater flexibility of the treaty/agreement process, and augmented informality. Such exchanges were concluded with all but twelve of the American treaty partners. More than twenty such exchanges were signed with twenty-seven different countries. The largest numbers involve Canada (111), Japan (eighty-seven), the United Kingdom and its dependencies (eighty-three), Mexico (seventy-six), the Philippines (fifty-seven), Panama (fifty-six), Germany (forty-seven), Italy (forty-three), the Netherlands (thirty-two), and France (thirty). They are employed for a variety of subjects, including boundaries and boundary waters, civil aviation, claims, defense, finance, trade, and many others, and they commonly apply to such matters as mutual security, narcotic drugs, and the Peace Corps.

Many of these bilateral treaties/agreements were signed in the United States. Of historic interest, more than 400, concluded with eighty-eight countries, dealing with nearly forty subjects, were signed in Washington and remain in effect. Overall, some 1,627 were concluded in Washington, an additional 332 were signed by the United States in Washington and by other parties in some foreign place, and ninety-two were signed in other American cities, especially New York and several cities in the Washington area, but occasionally also elsewhere in this country.[161] Combined, these amounted to more than 2,050, or approximately one-third of the total. In addition, forty-four treaties/ agreements with twenty international organizations, referred to later, were also signed in the United States. To illustrate, these included one with Benelux, two with the International Telecommunication Satellite Organization, three with North Atlantic Treaty Organization agencies, five with the Organization of American States, and seventeen with the United Nations.

Table 7.9 lists some 170 treaty/agreement subject categories (as utilized by the Department of State).[162] A great many are interrelated, such as those concerned with agricultural, boundary, cultural, defense, diplomatic and consular,

Table 7.9

Subject Categories of Contemporary Bilateral Treaties and Agreements[1]

Subject Categories	Countries and International Organizations	Number of Treaties & Agreements	Subject Categories	Countries and International Organizations	Number of Treaties & Agreements
Aerospace Disturbances	2	2	Fisheries	13	25
Agricultural Commodities	87	471	Forestry	2	2
Agriculture	27	42	Free Association with U.S.	2	2
Amity	7	11	Friendship	2	2
Arms Limitation	5	9	Fuels and Energy	1	1
Atomic Energy	54	158	General Relations	12	15
Automotive Traffic	3	12	Geodedic Survey	2	2
Aviation (Civil)	117	275	Grains	1	1
Boundaries	7	38	Headquarters (Inter. Orgs.)	3	6
Boundary Waters	2	34	Health	22	38
Canals	3	16	Highways	11	20
Canal Rights	1	1	Housing	5	6
Cemeteries	1	1	Humanitarian Assistance	1	4
Chemical Safety	1	1	Industrial Cooperation	2	2
Civil Emergency Management	1	1	Industrial Property	3	3
Claims	30	65	Information Media Guaranties	13	13
Climate Programs	1	1	Insular Possessions	1	1
Coffee	1	1	Intellectual Property	5	5
Commerce	51	74	Interest Sections (Diplomatic)	1	1
Conservation	5	10	Judicial Assistance	41	74
Consuls	66	76	Judicial Procedure	1	4
Copyright	12	15	Labor	4	6
Cultural Heritage	4	4	Lend-Lease	23	47
Cultural Property	7	7	Lend-Lease Settlement	5	16
Cultural Relations	26	31	Liquor	2	2
Customs	44	61	Mapping	47	66
Defense	164	906	Maritime Matters	31	57
Development Assistance	1	1	Marriage (Documentation)	1	1
Diplomatic Relations	4	4	Medical Assistance	2	2
Disaster Assistance	3	3	Meteorological Cooperation	2	2
Driver's Licenses	1	1	Meteorological Research	2	2
Drugs	1	1	Meteorology	4	5
Economic and Military Coop.	2	3	Migrants—Interdiction	1	1
Economic and Technical Coop.	145	247	Migration	2	4
Education	63	68	Migratory Workers	1	1
Embassy Sites	8	11	Military Cemeteries/Monuments	9	12
Emergency Preparedness	2	2	Military Missions	15	24
Employment of U.S. Dependents	59	62	Mutual Security	28	28
Energy	18	31	Narcotic Drugs	55	124
Environmental Cooperation	37	46	Narcotics (Money Laundering)	1	1
Evacuation	1	1	Nationality	7	7
Extradition	103	139	Naval Vessels	1	4
Finance	168	532	Navigation Cooperation	15	29
Fire Protection	1	3	North Atlantic Treaty Org.	4	4

Subject Categories	Countries and International Organizations	Number of Treaties & Agreements	Subject Categories	Countries and International Organizations	Number of Treaties & Agreements
Nuclear Material	1	1	Seismic Observations	8	8
Nuclear Test Limitation	1	2	Seismological Research	1	1
Nuclear War	1	4	Sewage Disposal System	1	1
Nuclear Weapons	1	1	Shellfish	5	5
Occupation Costs	1	1	Shipping	23	23
Occupied Territory	1	1	Smuggling	15	15
Oceanographic Research	1	1	Social Security	32	46
Oceanography	9	12	Space Cooperation	16	37
Pacific Settlement of Disputes	45	79	Space Research	2	2
Passports	1	1	Stolen Property (Recovery of)	1	1
Patents	20	34	Supplies (NATO)	1	4
Peace Corps	114	119	Surplus Property	11	19
Peace Treaties	5	7	Taxation	97	174
Peacekeeping	11	18	Technical Assistance	2	2
Petroleum	1	1	Technical Cooperation	2	2
Pipelines (oil)	1	2	Technical Missions	1	1
Police Equipment	1	1	Technology Transfer	1	1
Pollution	5	13	Telecommunication	94	198
Postal Matters	164	363	Television	1	1
Prisoner Transfer	9	9	Termination of Agreements	1	1
Prisoners of War	2	2	Territorial Acquisition	4	4
Privileges and Immunities	9	14	Territorial Sovereignty	1	1
Property	38	69	Territorial Status (Fisheries)	1	1
Property Transfer	2	7	Tourism	8	8
Publications	53	54	Tracking Stations (Spacecraft)	10	14
Refugee Relief	2	3	Trade and Commerce	92	257
Refugees	7	7	Trademarks	41	44
Relations (Diplomatic)	8	8	Transportation	2	2
Relief Supplies and Packages	25	25	Treaty Obligations	4	4
Remote Sensing (Atmosphere)	6	6	Treaty Succession	1	1
Rules of Warfare	4	4	Trusteeships (Pacific)	2	6
Sanctions (on Haiti)	2	2	Visas	82	105
Satellites (Space)	12	30	War Crimes	1	1
Scientific Cooperation	64	137	Weapons	5	26
Seabed Cooperation	1	2	Weather Modification	1	1
Seabed Operations	2	4	Weather Stations	16	18
Seabeds	4	4	Whaling	2	2

Unique Territorial Matters

Subject Categories	Countries and International Organizations	Number of Treaties & Agreements	Subject Categories	Countries and International Organizations	Number of Treaties & Agreements
Afghanistan War Settlement	2	2	Bering Straits Regional Comm.	1	1
Amani Islands	1	1	Bonin Islands	1	1
Antarctica	1	1	Roosevelt Campobello Park	1	1
Arctic	1	1	Ryukyu and Daito Islands	1	1

Totals Categories 170   Treaties and Agreements 6,244 *

[1]Table does not include Agency for International Development and other supplementary agreements or extensions of, or amendments to, treaties and agreements.

*This total differs from that in Table 7.8 because for certain countries no basic or regular economic and technical cooperation treaties or agreements are listed but includes only supplementary Agency for International Development and several other related agreements.

energy, fisheries, health and medical, maritime, outer space, property, refugee, seabed, territorial, trade and customs, and other matters. Several categories deal with various types of cooperation and assistance pertaining to economic development, disaster, humanitarian, Lend-Lease, military, Peace Corps, and scientific and technical subjects. Those that focus on peacekeeping and peacemaking encompass pacific settlement of disputes as well as a number of historic peace treaties. Nearly sixty, denominated peace, amity, commerce, navigation, consular, and protocol treaties and agreements, generally are embodied in basic and often initial diplomatic undertakings.

Aside from peace treaties following foreign wars, the pre–1946 traditional treaty/agreement subjects apply to amity and friendship, commerce and trade, consular, extradition, maritime matters and shipping, pacific settlement of disputes (the advancement of peace, arbitration, conciliation, and claims), the rules of war, and visa affairs.[163] Since World War II approximately 120 new subjects were added to the American treaty roster. To generalize, these embrace many treaties/agreements concerned with aerospace and outerspace, agricultural, energy and atomic energy, climate, conservation, cultural, defense, environmental, industrial, mapping, meteorological, migration, nuclear, oceanographic, passport, Peace Corps, pollution, property, refugee, seabed, seismological, Social Security, technical assistance, technological, telecommunication, territorial, and weather affairs. Other, more particularized subjects vary from diplomatic and consular privileges and immunities, disaster assistance, embassy sites, and juridical assistance, to such matters as driver's licenses, military cemeteries and monuments abroad, prisoner transfers, stolen property, tourism, the Washington–Moscow "hot line" communications link, and even a pipeline and a sewage disposal system.

Currently, the most popular subject categories are defense (more than 900 treaties/agreements), finance (more than 500), agricultural commodities (more than 470), and postal affairs (more than 360), followed by civil aviation (275), economic and technical cooperation and trade and commerce (each with approximately 250). Another dozen categories account, respectively, for fifty to 100 treaties/agreements. Examples include claims, commerce, consuls, customs, education, employment, judicial assistance, mapping, maritime matters, pacific settlement, property, and the exchange of official and other publications. Combined, these nineteen subject categories account for more than two-thirds of the total. This illustrates the degree of interest of the Department of State and the willingness of other countries to cooperate in dealing with these subjects. On the other hand, some sixty-five categories involved only one or two treaties or agreements.[164]

Although most of these subject categories are readily comprehensible, some require clarification. For example, the term "Aviation" applies not only to the many air transport service agreements but also to aeronautical facilities and navigation, air safety, air traffic control, airworthiness certificates, flight inspection service, pilot licensing, and related matters. "Education" applies primarily to financing educational and cultural exchange programs and the creation of joint educational commissions and foundations. Those designated "Employment" apply to the dependents of U.S. officials employed abroad. "Free Association" apply to the administration by the U.S. of former Japanese mandated islands in the Northwest Pacific and their subsequent free association with the United States. "Headquarters" agreements apply to the North Atlantic Treaty Organization facility at Norfolk, Virginia, the Organization of American States at Washington, and the United Nations at New York City. Similarly, "Military Cemeteries and Monuments" applies to facilities of the United States maintained in Belgium, France, Hungary, Italy, Luxembourg, the Netherlands, the Philippines, Romania, and the United Kingdom following World War II. "Mutual Security" applies to Cold War implementation of the Mutual Security Act of 1951. "Property" applies primarily to the tenure and disposition by Americans of real and personal property abroad. "Publications" applies principally to the mutual exchange of official publications (with more than fifty foreign givernments). "Smuggling" applies largely to alcoholic beverages, concluded in the 1920s to implement American Prohibition. "Social Security" applies to the payment by the United States of old-age, survivors, and disability benefits to American beneficiaries residing abroad. "Surplus Property" applies to the disposal of American government-owned excess and scrap property abroad. "Telecommunication" applies principally to radio broadcasting. "Weapons" applies to the safe and secure transportation, storage, destruction, and prevention of the proliferation of weapons of mass destruction and nuclear arms.

Special note may be taken of the pacific settlement, postal, and taxation categories. The nearly eighty pacific settlement treaties/agreements with forty-five countries that deal with the advancement of peace, arbitration, and conciliation, discussed earlier, remain extant as standby international commitments. Those concerned with taxation apply to such matters as double taxation, exemption of Americans from certain kinds of income and estate taxes abroad, relief from taxation of American Government expenditures in foreign countries, reimbursement of U.S. income taxes on staff members of the United Nations and other international organizations, and local taxation on American defense projects abroad. It should be understood that, although some treaty/agreement subjects are generally treated collectively and multilaterally, they are supplemented or implemented bilaterally. Thus, in the field of postal affairs, the United States not only is a party to multilateral postal arrangements but also has concluded more than 360 bilateral agreements with some 160 countries that deal primarily with express mail, money orders, parcel post, "collect-on-delivery" service, and the operations of INTELPOST, BUREAUFAX, and similar services.

The individual countries with which the United States has the largest treaty packages are Canada, Mexico, the United Kingdom and its eight dependencies, and the Soviet Union and its twelve successor republics. Each of these packages numbers more than 290 treaties/agreements, including their basic documents together with their amendments, extensions, and related agreements, as indicated in the following tabulation. Half of them bear the international title of basic "agreements," and one-fourth of them are in the nature of exchanges of notes and letters.[165]

Country	Basic Treaties/ Agreements	Supplementary Amendments/ Extensions	Related Agreements	Total Package	Number of Subjects
Canada	250	55	15	320	60
Mexico	186	133	7	326	45
Soviet Union	108	7	0	115	47
12 Republics	154	23	1	178	25
	262	30	1	293	
United Kingdom	209	62	4	275	50
	22	13	0	35	10
	231	75	4	310	
Total	929	293	27	1,249	

It is remarkable that many of these bilateral treaties/agreement subject categories parallel and supplement at least seventy multilateral categories, discussed later. It is even more surprising and noteworthy that more than half of the bilateral treaties/agreements complement the multilateral, including such quantitatively major matters as atomic energy, civil aviation, defense, economic and technical cooperation, extradition, finance, narcotic drugs, postal affairs, scientific cooperation, taxation, and trade and commerce.[166]

So far as timing is concerned, some 810 pre-1946 bilateral treaties/agreements with 116 countries remain in effect, and 250 were added during the immediate postwar years (1946–49), then increased each decade thereafter, peaking in the 1980s at 1,465 and the early 1990s at 1,087. This amounts to a surprising average of 123 regular treaties/agreements per year since 1946 and a remarkable average of some 385 a year, or more than one per day, since 1980. Moreover, over the years many others were also concluded, some of a temporary nature that became defunct or were superseded.

Assessing the contemporary bilateral American treaty/agreement aggregate, some are of historic significance. These include seven peace treaties concluding major wars beginning with that with Great Britain following the Revolutionary War (1783)[167]; four designated as territorial acquisition treaties, including the purchase of the Louisiana Territory from France (1803), Alaska from Russia (1867), and the Danish West Indies (1916)[168]; and many boundary settlements and the fixing of boundary waters, especially with Canada, Mexico, and Great Britain (concerning Canada), commencing in 1818, but recently also the settlement of maritime boundaries with Cuba (1977), Venezuela (1978), the Cook Islands (1980), and New Zealand (1980).

Other historic treaties/agreements still in effect are represented by those concerned with amity, commerce, and navigation that marked the commencement of diplomatic and consular relations with foreign governments, beginning in the late eighteenth century with that concluded by Great Britain and applied to Canada (1794) and with trade and commerce dating back to the early nineteenth century (Great Britain in 1815, France in 1822, Denmark in 1826, and Norway in 1827); and those that deal with pacific settlement, such as the Treaty of Washington with Great Britain (1871), intergovernmental claims, conventions, and agreements with some thirty foreign countries, and nearly sixty residual standby treaties for the advancement of peace, arbitration, and conciliation concluded in the early twentieth century, particularly in the late 1920s. Some would also regard as of potential, if not established, historic significance many of those concerned with claims settlement, the management of diplomatic and consular relations, national defense and mutual security, the alignment of policy, practice, and programs with other countries, restrictive and constraining controls of various matters, and the advancement and protection of the interests and welfare of Americans abroad.[169]

In addition to this complex of bilateral treaties/agreements with individual foreign countries, evidencing an important post–World War II innovation, the United States has concluded a series of 140 treaties/agreements with fifty-six international organizations and other agencies, as indicated in Table 7.8, Part B. The largest numbers were negotiated with the United Nations (nineteen), the European Community (sixteen), the North Atlantic Treaty Organization (eleven), the European Atomic Energy Community (eight), the International Atomic Energy Agency (five), and the Organization of American States (five). They apply to a variety of more than fifty subject categories, some of which are specialized. The most common deal with taxation, economic and technical cooperation, atomic energy, and the headquarters of international agencies, which, combined, account for approximately 45 percent of these arrangements. The preponderant majority are designated as agreements (91 percent), and many of the rest are exchanges of notes and understandings.

Supplementing these regular treaties/agreements, the United States also is committed to some 1,270 subsidiary agreements of two types with eighty-eight countries and five international organizations. Of these, 548 are Agency for International Development agreements to supplement basic instruments dealing with economic and technical cooperation. The second type consists of 723 "related agreements," the preponderant number of which (640) generally support agricultural commodities agreements, and the remaining eighty-three supplement those concerned with aviation, boundary waters, cultural relations, defense, energy, extradition, finance, judicial assistance, peacekeeping, and trade and commerce.[170]

To appreciate the totality of the contemporary American bilateral treaty/agreement complex, it is essential to understand the degree to which existing treaties and agreements have also been formally modified and/or extended.[171] Some 1,735 instruments of amendment and extension have been concluded with 141 countries and six international organizations.[172] They modify or continue expiring treaties/agreements and supplementary, related instruments. They deal with more than fifty-five subject categories, the largest numbers of which are concerned with agricultural commodities, civil aviation, defense, economic and technical cooperation, finance, and trade, which account for two-thirds of these instruments.[173] Other subjects with large numbers include atomic energy, education, military missions, and telecommunication.

Additional amendments/extensions apply to such varied matters as boundary waters, environmental cooperation, maritime matters, narcotic drugs, relief supplies, taxation, tracking stations, and visas, all of which number more than ten and in the case of narcotic drugs number eighty-five. Especially noteworthy are the substantial changes to treaties/agreements with Canada pertaining to boundary waters (twelve), Japan relating to defense (fifteen), Mexico concerning narcotic drugs (eighty) and telecommunication (thirty), and the United Kingdom (more than seventy involving at least a dozen subject categories). The largest number of amendments/extensions applies to Mexico (138), the United Kingdom (with dependencies, seventy-two), Canada (fifty-five), Korea (forty-seven), and Bangladesh (forty-four, all concerned with agricultural commodities).

Anatomy of the American Multilateral Treaty Complex

The United States is currently also a party to nearly 600 multilateral treaties and agreements, as indicated in Table 7.10, of which one of every five antedates 1946 and remains in effect, some of the earliest dating back to the nineteenth century.[174] Only a few bear the international title of "treaty"; approximately one-third are equally identified as "international conventions" and "agreements" (some of which are designated as "implementing agreements"), and the rest, numbering more than 180, bear a variety of other designations.[175] A majority were concluded since 1960, especially during the 1970s. Approximately 120 (20 percent) were signed in the United States, mostly at Washington, but also at New York City, Boston, Bretton Woods, Chicago, and San Francisco. Of those negotiated abroad, most were signed at Brussels, Berlin and Bonn, Geneva, London, Paris, Vienna, and Latin American cities, especially Buenos Aires.[176]

These multilateral treaties/agreements deal with 125 subject categories prescribed by the Department of State, as listed in the table. The largest numbers concern North Atlantic Treaty affairs (thirty-three), energy (thirty-two), trade and commerce (thirty-two), German affairs (thirty), telecommunication (twenty-four), maritime affairs (twenty-one), defense (twenty), and finance (nineteen), which, combined, amount to more than 35 percent of the total.[177] However, aside from the constitutive acts of international organizations and agencies, certain categories may be coupled, including defense and the North Atlantic Treaty system; energy, atomic energy, and nuclear materials; finance and financial institutions and funds; trade and commerce, the General Agreement on Tariffs and Trade, and customs; inter-American affairs; maritime matters, marine pollution, marine science, shipping, and containers; pacific settlement, arbitration, and peacekeeping; telecommunication and satellite communications; and warfare,

Table 7.10
Multilateral Treaties and Agreements In Force

Subjects	Total T&A	International Titles				U.S. Titles			Dates Signed						
		C	T	A	O	TIAS	T	EA	Pre-1946	1946-1949	1950s	1960s	1970s	1980s	1990s
Africa	4	2			2		4		4						
Agriculture	4	1		2	1	4			1				1	2	
Aliens	1	1					1		1						
Antarctica	1		1			1					1				
Arbitration	2	2				2					1	1			
Armistice	3			3				3	3						
Arms Limitation	1		1			1								1	
Astronauts	1		1			1						1			
Atlantic Charter	1				1			1	1						
Atomic Energy	11		9		2	11			1		2		4	1	3
Austria	2		1		1	2					2				
Automotive Traffic	4	4				4			1	1	2				
Aviation	10	5		4	1	8	1	1	2	1	2	1	3		1
Biological Weapons	1	1				1							1		
Cambodia	1			1		1									1
China (Taiwan)	1		1			1			1						
Claims	2	1	1			1	1		1	1					
Conservation	8	6			2	7	1		1		1		5		1
Consuls	3	2			1	2	1		1			2			
Containers	1	1				1							1		
Copper	1				1	1								1	
Copyright	4	4				3	1		2		1		1		
Cultural Property	2	1			1	2					1		1		
Cultural Relations	8	3	1	2	2	5	3		3	1	2		2		
Customs	12	11			1	10	2		2	1	3	2	3	1	
Defense	20	1	4	2	13	18	1	1	2	1	5		3	9	
Diplomatic Relations	2	1			1	2						2			
Economic Development	3	1		2		3						2		1	
Energy	32		29		3	32							27	5	
Environment	2	1		1		2									2
Environmental Modification	1	1				1							1		
Extradition	1	1					1		1						
Finance	19			13	6	18		1		9	9				1
Financial Institutions	10	1		9		10			2		2	2	1	2	1
Fisheries	10	7	1	1	1	10					2	2		4	2
Food Aid	1	1				1							1		
Food and Agriculture Org.	1			1		1			1						
Forrestry	1		1			1									1
Gas Warfare	1				1	1			1						
General Agreement on Tariffs and Trade	2			2		2				2					
Genocide	1	1				1	1			1					
Germany	30	2	1	18	9	29		1	4	3	15		2		6
Hague Conventions	2	2				2	2		2						
Health	10			1	9	8	2		2	1	1	3	2	1	
Human Rights	1				1	1				1					
Hydrography	1	1				1					1				
Industrial Property	4	3		1		2	2		3			1			
Insular Possessions	3	1	1	1				3	3						
Intellectual Property	1	1				1					1				
Inter-American Conventions	11	4	5		2	11			11						
International Civil Aviation	3	1			2	3			1			2			
International Court of Justice	1				1		1		1						
International Maritime Org.	1	1				1				1					
International Tracing Service	3			3		3						3			
Investment Disputes	1	1				1					1				
Judicial Procedure															
Inter-American	5	2			3	2	3		3					2	
Hague Conventions	4	4				4						2	1	1	

Key to Symbols

A	Agreements	T	Treaties
C	Conventions	TIAS	Treaties and Other International Acts
EA	Executive Agreements	O	Others: Accords, Acts, Charters, Constitutions, Protocols, Pacts, Statutes, etc.

Table 7.10 (continued)

Subjects	Total T&A	International Titles C	T	A	O	U.S. Titles TIAS	T	EA	Dates Signed Pre-1946	1946-1949	1950s	1960s	1970s	1980s	1990s
Jute	1		1			1								1	
Korea	4		3	1		4						4			
Labor	11	9	1		1	4	7		3	3	1		2	1	1
Laos	1			1		1									
Law—Private International	2				2	2			1		1				
Marine Pollution	8	5			3	8					1	1	3	2	1
Marine Science	1	1				1									1
Maritime Matters	21	16		2	3	19	2		2		4	8	5	2	
Migration	1				1	1					1				
Morocco	3	1			2	1	2		2		1				
Multilateral Funds	7		7			7						3	3	1	
Narcotic Drugs	6	3			3	6						2	1	1	2
Nationality	2	1			1		2		2						
North Atlantic Treaty Org.	33		1	10	22	33				1	6	4	8	8	6
Nuclear Accidents	2	2				2								2	
Nuclear Free Zone	2				2	2						2			
Nuclear Materials	1	1				1							1		
Nuclear Test Ban	1		1			1						1			
Nuclear Weapons—Non-Proliferation	1		1			1						1			
Oceanographic Research	1			1		1									1
Org. of American States	1				1	1				1					
Pacific Settlement of Disputes	12	6	4		2		12		12						
Pan American Highway	1	1				1			1						
Patents	10	1	2	3	4	10					2	1	3	4	
Peace Treaties	9		3	1	3	9					5	4			
Peacekeeping	1			1		1								1	
Phonograms	1	1				1							1		
Polar Bears	1			1		1							1		
Pollution	6	2			4	6							2	3	1
Poplar Commission	1	1				1					1				
Postal Affairs	10			2	8	10						4	2	4	
Prisoner Transfer	1	1				1								1	
Publications	10	6		1	3	5	5		5	1	2	1	1		
Racial Discrimination	1	1				1						1			
Red Cross	4	4				1				4					
Refugees	1				1	1					1				
Renunciation of War	1		1				1		1						
Reparations	6			2	4	5		1	1	5					
Rules of Warfare	13	11	1		1		13		13						
Satellite Communications	10	3		5	2	10					1	5	3	1	
Scientific Cooperation	2			1	1	2							1	1	
Seabeds	5		1	1	3	5							1	2	2
Slavery	3	2			1	2	1		1		2				
South Pacific Commission	1			1		1				1					
Space (Outer)	6	2		2	1	6						1	3	2	
Spitzbergen	1		1				1		1						
States—Rights and Duties	2	2					2		2						
Taxation	2	1		1		2								1	1
Telecommunication	24	5		5	14	21	3		4	1	3	3	6	7	
Terrorism	3	3				3							3		
Torture	1	1				1								1	
Tourism	1				1	1							1		
Trade and Commerce	32	3		24	5	31	1		1			1	11	1	18
Traffic in Women and Children	2			1	1	1	1		2						
Transportation (Foodstuffs)	1			1		1							1		
United Nations	3				2	1	1	1	2	1					
UN Industrial Development Org.	1				1	1							1		
Vietnam	1			1		1							1		
War Criminals	2			1	1	1		1	1	1					
Weapons	3	1			2	3								3	
Weights and Measures	3	3				1	2		2		1				
Whaling	3	2			1	2	1		1	1	1				
Wheat	2	1		1		2						1		1	
Wine	1			1				1	1						
Women—Political Rights	2	2				2					1	1			
World Heritage	1	1				1							1		
World Meteorological Org.	1	1				1			1						
World War II	4		1		3	1		3	4						
TOTALS 125	599	192	35	190	182	496	88	15	127	52	90	67	132	77	54

armistices, arms limitation, biological and gas warfare, the renunciation of war, reparations, the rules of warfare, war criminals, weapons, World War II and its peace treaties, and several nuclear treaties and agreements.[178] Combined, these account for more than half of these treaties/agreements.

From another perspective, it may be noted that, whereas most of them are concerned with functional subjects, some deal with individual countries or other territories, such as Africa, Antarctica, Austria, Cambodia, China (Taiwan), Korea, Spitzbergen, Vietnam, and especially Germany. On the other hand, other subject categories focus on the treatment of persons, including aliens, astronauts, extradition, health, human rights, migration, nationality, political rights of women, racial discrimination, refugees, slavery, torture, traffic in women and children, and war criminals.

The number of signatories varies, and these treaties and agreements may be grouped in four major categories—global in intent or universal in participation, regional (inter-American), functionally restricted, and simply tripartite or quadripartite. Dozens fall into the global-universal category, many of which have been signed by 175 or more countries. Those with the largest number of signatories are led by the Constitution of the World Health Organization (nearly 200), the Statute of the International Court of Justice, the Nuclear Non-Proliferation Treaty, the Constitution of the Universal Postal Union, the United Nations Charter, the Red Cross Convention, and the Articles of Agreement of the International Bank and the International Monetary Fund. Scores of others are also global in intent and virtually universal in participation.[179] Several signatory states are unique in that the United States maintains no regular diplomatic relations with them, they have ceased to exist, or they were otherwise modified.[180] Occasionally, international organizations are signatory parties.[181] Interestingly, whereas 105 signatories of the General Agreement on Tariffs and Trade are defined as ''contracting partners,'' it is also regarded as being ''applied de facto'' to twenty-six additional states.

Although most treaties/agreements are concluded and signed by diplomatic emissaries, occasionally, they are signed personally by the President or the Secretary of State in the United States or abroad. For example, in addition to the United Nations Charter signed by Secretary Stettinius at San Francisco in 1945, the Charter of the Organization of American States was signed by Secretary Marshall at Bogotá in 1948, the North Atlantic Treaty was signed by Secretary Acheson at Washington in 1949, the Austrian State Treaty was signed by Secretary Dulles at Vienna in 1955, the Nuclear Test Ban Treaty was signed by Secretary Rusk at Moscow in 1963, the Nuclear Non-Proliferation Treaty was signed by Secretary Rusk at Washington in 1968, the Vietnam Peace Agreement was signed by Secretary Rogers at Paris in 1973, the Convention on the Prohibition of Military Hostile Use of Environmental Techniques was signed by Secretary Vance at Geneva in 1977, and the Treaty on the Final Settlement of the German issue was signed by Secretary Baker at Moscow in 1990.

The number of signatories of inter-American treaties/agreements has varied from twelve countries for the Inter-American Convention on Extradition (1933)[182] to thirty-five for the Charter of the Organization of American States (1948). Other inter-American conventions deal with such matters as the status of aliens (1928), the nationality and political rights of women (1933 and 1948), the Pan-American Highway (1936), the Postal Union of the Americas and Spain (1971), and the rights and duties of states (1928 and 1933). Many other treaties/agreements are concerned with functional subject matters of concern to particular groups of signatories. These vary from the Austrian State Treaty (1955) and the post–World War II peace treaties with Bulgaria, Hungary, Italy, and Romania (1947) and with Japan (1951), to the continental shelf (1958), fishing (1958), international food aid (1986), the creation of an International Tracing Service (1955), private international law (1951), and the territorial seas and contiguous zone (1958). Some of these have more than fifty signatories, whereas others are more limited, such as an agreement on the conservation of polar bears and the agreement to create the International Development Law Institute, each signed by only five states. Surprisingly, the multilateral treaty complex also includes approximately sixty tripartite and quadripartite agreements. Most of these concern post–World War II German affairs, and others deal with energy, finance, narcotic drugs, satellite communications, and other matters.

In addition, these treaties/agreements have been supplemented with some 300 formal amendments, extensions, series of supplementary implementing protocols, special protocols, and procès-verbaux, as well as "certifications of change" to the General Agreement on Tariffs and Trade, which number eighty-eight, and a protocol to the Whaling Convention of 1956 was subjected to forty-seven "schedule amendments." The rest applied to more than thirty-five different subject categories, with the largest number of changes ascribed to such matters as Antarctica, financial institutions, the Food and Agriculture Organization, marine pollution, and other maritime matters. Moreover, three of the atomic energy agreements were supported by forty-four trilateral agreements between the United States, the International Atomic Energy Agency, and other specific countries.

Some of these multilateral treaties/agreements are deemed to be of historic significance. Aside from those treated in earlier chapters, such as the Atlantic Charter (1941), the Hague Conventions on Pacific Settlement (1899 and 1907), the Kellogg–Briand Pact (1928), and the Conventions on the Rules of Warfare (1854, 1904, and 1907), these deal with atomic and nuclear weapons, civil aviation, the Vienna Conventions on Diplomatic and Consular Relations, the General Agreement on Tariffs and Trade, and outer space. Most impressive is the series of constitutive acts of dozens of international organizations and other agencies, including the United Nations and its specialized agencies, the Organization of American States and its specialized organizations, the North Atlantic Treaty Organization and other regional security agencies, global and regional banks and funds, and a series of other international administrative, assistance, regulatory, and service agencies. Others of significance embrace such subjects as World War II peace settlements with European Axis powers and Japan and the establishment of the trusteeship system, atomic, biological, gaseous, and nuclear weapons, international terrorism, the adjudication of international disputes, and war crimes.

Of particular importance to the Department of State and the conduct of foreign relations are the two Vienna Conventions on Diplomatic and Consular Relations, the Convention on Crimes Against Internationally Protected Persons Including Diplomatic Agents, and implementing treaties/agreements concerned with peaceful settlement and the arbitration of international claims and with representation in international organizations and agencies, such as the United Nations, the Organization of American States, and the International Court of Justice.

To summarize, aside from its international commitments embodied in dozens of Presidential doctrines and proclamations and American and joint policy declarations, this contemporary U.S. treaty complex consists of 6,163 bilateral treaties/agreements with individual foreign governments and 140 with international organizations, supplemented by 723 related and 548 Agency for International Development agreements and 1,735 amendments and extensions, paralleled by 599 multilateral treaties/agreements, supplemented by 301 amendments and extensions, and forty-four trilateral atomic energy agreements signed by the United States, the International Atomic Energy Agency, and individual countries—totaling more than 10,250 applied to scores of subject categories. Some of these will expire or be augmented, modified, or superseded. But in time many additional treaties/agreements will be concluded, and new subject categories are bound to emerge, producing a monumental array of basic and supplementary international rights, commitments, and guarantees to be monitored and administered by the Department of State. It is not inconceivable that, at the current rate of increase, by the year 2000 the United States could become a party to an additional 1,200 basic treaties/agreements totaling more than 8,000.

Treaties Rejected and Deferred by the United States

It is rare for the United States to reject, or for the Senate to refuse to approve, treaties for ratification. However, the United States has rejected several major multilateral treaties since World War II. For example, the Havana Convention to establish the International Trade Organization was never ratified. On the recommendation of the United States, in February 1946, the United Nations Economic and Social Council convened a Conference on Trade and Employment, which provided for a Preparatory Committee composed of the representatives of eighteen countries to produce a preliminary draft treaty for the Trade Organization based on the American proposal. The resulting Havana Charter, signed on March 24, 1948, by fifty-four countries, specified that it would become effective if ratified by twenty countries by September 30, 1949, but that if it was not ratified by that time, the ratifying governments would determine whether and under what conditions the Charter would become effective. In the meantime, an Interim Commission for the Trade Organization was created to undertake preparatory work.

Because the Charter compromised many of the trade principles espoused by the United States and was so burdened with qualifications, reservations, and exceptions, no signatory ratified it by the due date. However, in the meantime the General Agreement on Tariffs and Trade (GATT) was concluded at Geneva in October 1947, became effective the following year, and then served as the basic multilateral vehicle for international trade relations. Several decades later, at Marakesh, in April 1994 the World Trade Organization (WTO) was finally created, supplemented by fifteen related agreements and understandings dealing with such matters as tariffs and trade, subsidies and countervailing arrangements, barriers to trade, and the settlement of trade disputes. This agreement went into force on January 1, 1995, and was ratified by 110 countries, including the United States.

Following nearly two decades of deliberations by the United Nations International Law Commission, the comprehensive Vienna Convention on the Law of Treaties, consisting of eighty-five articles, was signed in 1969 and came into effect in 1980. It deals with the conclusion and entry into effect, ratification, observance and interpretation, suspension and termination, and depositories and registration of treaties and agreements.

Whereas the United States has consistently pursued a policy of freedom of the seas, and Presidents Wilson, Franklin Roosevelt, and Truman espoused a generic freedom of the seas doctrine in their fundamental precepts of American foreign policy, respectively, in the Fourteen Points (1918), the Atlantic Charter (1941), and the Navy Day Address (1945), it rejected the United Nations Law of the Sea Convention of 1982. Traditionally, the Department of State has promoted such principles as freedom from interference with navigation, transit, fishing, and utilization of marine resources, subject to sovereign control over a contiguous belt of territorial waters and, recently, international cooperation respecting the conserving of marine resources, pollution, and establishing rights and international controls over the resources of the seabed and its subsoil.

Currently, the United States is a party to more than 300 bilateral and multilateral treaties/agreements concerned with the seas, seabed, fishing, navigation, pollution, shipping, and other maritime matters, including three major Conventions on the High Seas, the Territorial Sea and Contiguous Zone, and the Continental Shelf (concluded in 1958), as well as on Preventing Collisions at Sea (1972), Safety of Life at Sea (1974), and Search and Rescue at Sea (1979). It also participated in the lengthy negotiations sponsored by the United Nations resulting in the comprehensive Law of the Sea Treaty, which was approved by 130 in favor, four against (including the United States), and seventeen abstentions, and the resulting convention was formally signed by nearly 120 delegations in April 1982.

Although it contains many provisions endorsed by the United States, the Department of State and President Reagan withheld signature and approval. They objected particularly to the powers, functions, voting system, and financing of its seabed mining regime, inadequate guarantees to protect American interests, the requirement to transfer American technology to others without the legal approval of the United States, and stipulations allowing amendments to be negotiated and to enter into force for the United States without its approval.

The United States has been a leader in reducing and controlling nuclear weapons by the treaty process and has become a party to a series of multilateral treaties, including those banning nuclear tests in the atmosphere, in outer space, and underwater (Moscow, August 5, 1963); prohibiting nuclear weapons in Latin America (Mexico City, 1967); providing for nonproliferation of nuclear weapons (Washington, London, and Moscow, July 1, 1968); prohibiting the emplacement of nuclear weapons and other weapons of mass destruction on the seabed, on the ocean floor, and in the ocean subsoil (Washington, London, and Moscow, February 11, 1971); guaranteeing the physical protection of nuclear materials (Vienna, October 26, 1979); and requiring early notification of a nuclear accident (Vienna, September 26, 1986). These have been supplemented by at least a dozen bilateral nuclear treaties and agreements. However, the United States was reluctant to implement the Comprehensive Nuclear Test Ban Treaty, under negotiation by a sixty-one-member United Nations Disarmament Committee for two to three years and approved by a United Nations General Assembly vote of 158 to 3 on September 10, 1996. It was signed at New York on September 24 by China, France, Russia, the United Kingdom, and the United States, which had previously abandoned nuclear testing voluntarily, and was scheduled to go into effect when the forty-four nations with nuclear potential ratified it.

In the meantime, dealing with other instrumentalities of warfare, the United States became a party to multilateral conventions and treaties concerned with the limitation and prohibition of asphyxiating, poisonous, and other gases (Geneva, June 17, 1925, in force for the United States with reservations, April 10, 1975); genocide (Paris, December 9, 1948, in force with reservations for the United States February 23, 1989); bacteriological/biological and toxin weapons (Washington, London, and Moscow, April 10, 1972); and conventional weapons that are excessively injurious or have indiscriminate effects (Geneva, October 10, 1980, in force for the United States September 24, 1995). On the other hand, in dealing with the abolition of chemical weapons, including lethal nerve, blister, blood, and choking agents, as well as nonlethal disabling agents and tear gas, outlawed by a Geneva Protocol in 1925 (supplemented by a U.S.-Soviet Chemical Weapons Destruction Accord of June 1990), which was superseded by a universal Chemical Weapons Convention in 1992 (signed by more than 150 states, to become effective 180 days after being ratified by sixty-five of the signatories), it was not consummated by the mid-1990s, although the Senate approved it in April 1998.

In September 1995 the United States became bound, with reservations, by a Protocol providing for prohibitions and/or restrictions on the use of land mines, booby traps, and other devices, adopted at Geneva, October 10, 1980. Subsequently, at an international conference convened at Oslo, on September 18, 1997, when the delegates of eighty-nine countries approved a Convention on the Prohibition of the Use, Stockpiling, Production, and Transfer of Antipersonnel Mines and Their Destruction, the United States refused to sign it. Others that failed to sign this anti-land mine treaty included China, India, Iran, Iraq, Pakistan, and Russia—all states that regarded land mines as critical personnel security weapons. The United States contended that it could not be bound by a pact that compromised the safety of American troops then protecting South

Korea, sought but failed to delay the treaty's implementation for nine years, and indicated that in view of its international responsibilities, it was not prepared to become committed by the treaty until it could rely on an acceptable and effective defensive alternative.

Also, in July 1998, after nearly five weeks of final deliberations following years of preliminary negotiations, more than 150 nations signed a treaty to create a permanent International Criminal Court to bring perpetrators of genocide and crimes against humanity to justice and empowering it to indict, try, and punish global tyrants, mass murderers, and others guilty of the most serious crimes of international concern. In certain respects it was designed to supplement or supersede the Hague Tribunal, the International Court of Justice, and the post–World War II major war crimes trials held at Nuremberg and Tokyo. It remained open for signature until the year 2000. Although most nations supported the treaty, and the United States favored the basic goals of such a tribunal, it abstained from attending the signing ceremony largely because of the treaty's nebulous uncertainties, the possible surrender of American constitutional principles and guarantees, the absence of a veto power to restrain the Court's globalized assumption of priorities available by other means, excessive relinquishment of national control and the protection of American national interests, and the possibility of its being violated or ignored in many specific cases and the likelihood that the Senate would reject it.

Finally, relevant but of a different nature, is the domestic problem of "fast track authority" in executive-legislative relations respecting the General Agreement on Tariffs and Trade (GATT) and its successor, the World Trade Organization (WTO), the United States–Israel Free Trade Agreement (1985), and the United States–Canada Free Trade Agreement (1987). Fast-track trading authority provides that if the President consults with Congress during international trade negotiations, Congress agrees to consider final trade agreements expeditiously and without amending them. Such authority was granted to the President since the Gerald Ford Administration, but its renewal was objected to during the Clinton Administration. Supporters of this arrangement argue that complex trade agreements on nontariff matters are difficult to implement if they are subject to subsequent changes by Congress. Opponents of the fast-track authority process contend that Congress has the power to regulate commerce as specified in the Constitution, Article 1, section 8, clause 3, and that it, therefore, has not only the right but also the responsibility to review and, if it chooses, to modify draft trade agreements.

INTERNATIONAL CONFERENCES AND MEETINGS

Assessing international conference participation in 1929, Professor Norman L. Hill observed: "As a mechanism for the conduct of international relations the conference has secured wide recognition." Building on past experience and the intensification of American resort to bilateral and multilateral conferences and meetings during World War II, the United States was prepared to employ and extend this method of diplomacy during subsequent decades.

Legislative Control of American Participation

As noted in Chapter 6, in 1913 Congress sought to manage participation by mandating, in an appropriations act, that the Executive could not participate in any international conference without prior specific legal authority. Because funding for delegates to attend such gatherings in this country and abroad and for hosting those convened in the United States requires appropriations, it may be contended that Congress had the power and the right to legislate this constraint, but as a matter of constitutional propriety this 1913 injunction proved to be unenforceable.[183]

In practice, Presidents regarded this requirement as nugatory in that, in principle, costs could be provided by the Executive Contingent Fund, and the primary sanction applicable by Congress could be Senate refusal to approve treaties concluded at such conferences and meetings. Subsequent practice varied, with the President's seeking Congressional approval for hosting them in the United States and some other major gatherings abroad. Furthermore, as conference participation increased, such advance clearance would have crippled American attendance, constricted treaty negotiation, and impeded the pursuance of national interests and international cooperation.

In any case, in August 1956 Congress liberalized this arrangement by authorizing the Secretary of State to provide participation by the United States "in international activities which arise from time to time in the conduct of foreign affairs for which provision has not been made by the terms of any treaty, convention, or special act of Congress." However, the act stipulated that it was not to be construed "as granting authority to accept membership for the United States in any international organization" or to participate in the activities of such organizations "for more than one year without approval by the Congress."[184] By that time American conference attendance already exceeded 100 each year, and it continued to grow.

Quantity

Whereas the United States participated in only 100 international conferences to 1900 (averaging one per year), the rate of participation increased to nearly 180 during the next quarter century from 1901 to 1925 (or averaging 7.2 per year), to 818 from 1926 to 1945 (averaging almost forty-one per year), but by the late 1930s they mounted to 100 per year or nearly two a week. During World War II they increased even more. Following the war, during the decade from 1946 to 1955 the number of conferences and meetings jumped to 2,643 (averaging more than 260 per year), and by the 1960s representation amounted to well over 300 a year, approximating more than one new conference each working day. In 1965 the Department of State reported attendance at nearly 650, with American involvement in some fifteen to twenty each day. By the 1980s the number advanced to U.S. representation at some 900 to more than 1,000 conferences and sessions of international organizations each year.

International conferencing, therefore, became a major, full-time, yearlong responsibility of the Department of State. In the early 1960s, of the nearly 2,800 persons involved in a single year, roughly 40 percent represented the Department and Foreign Service, and most of the others were agents of other Federal Departments and agencies and members of Congress, serviced by the State Department. Currently, the annual costs of conference attendance amounts to millions of dollars.

See Table 7.11 for a representative list of some 500 important international conferences and meetings attended by the United States since 1945. It consists of four segments, dealing with those participated in by Presidents and Secretaries of State (listed separately), major inter-American conferences and meetings, and selected general, often universal assemblages. To these may be added special listings of those engaged in by such American officers as Vice Presidents, Special Assistants for National Security Policy, other Cabinet officers or administrative agency heads, and special presidential envoys.

Categories and Types

Much that has been said of conference types in earlier chapters also applies to those since 1945. However, it must be noted that the United States participates in a substantial number of constitutive conferences to create additional specialized agencies of the United Nations, the Organization of American States, other inter-American, regional security, and other international organizations.[185] A good many may be grouped by the level of representation—summit, ministerial, and traditional diplomatic, evidencing considerable growth of participation at the Presidential and Secretary of State levels. Other categories embrace those that are sponsored by the United Nations,[186] the Organization of American States, the North Atlantic Treaty Organization, and other regional agencies, which may be distinguished from ad hoc conferences and meetings. Other illustrations of packages embrace those that are differentiated on the basis of regional or functional concerns and those concerned with post–World War II occupation and peace treaty negotiations with Germany, Japan, and other Axis powers.

Additional elements of categorization include such factors as purposes (aside from constitutive, these include discussion, policy aligning, negotiation, peacemaking, peacekeeping, lawmaking and rule making, and international administration), composition or the number of participants (bilateral and multilateral), geographic involvement (universal or global, hemispheric, neighboring, and other relationships), and degree of formality (formal and informal). A few may be characterized as preparatory or pickaback conferences and meetings. Large

Table 7.11
International Conferences and Meetings since 1945

A. Summit Conferences and Meetings *

Truman

Potsdam	East-West Big Four Conference on Germany	1945
Washington	Tripartite Meeting on Atomic Energy	1945
Washington	Conference to Negotiate NATO Treaty (addressed)	1949
San Francisco	Conference to Draft Japanese Peace Treaty (addressed)	1951

Eisenhower

Bermuda	Meeting with British and French Leaders	1953
Geneva	East-West Big Four Heads of Government Conference	1955
Panama City	Inter-American Meeting of Presidents	1956
Bermuda	Meeting with British Prime Minister	1957
Paris	NATO Heads of Government Meeting	1957
Camp David	Meeting with Khrushchev	1959
Paris	Meeting with Leaders of France and Italy	1959
Paris	Conference with British, French and German Leaders	1959
Washington	Meeting with Khrushchev	1959
Paris	East-West Big Four Heads of Government Conference	1960

Kennedy

Vienna	Meeting with Khrushchev	1961
Bermuda	Meeting with British Prime Minister	1961
Nassau	Meeting with British Prime Minister	1962
San Jose	Conference with Presidents of Central American Republics	1963

Johnson

Honolulu	Meeting with Vietnamese Leaders	1966
Manila	Conference on Asia and the Pacific	1966
Punta del Este	Conference of Organization of American States Presidents	1967
Glassboro (NJ)	Meeting with Kosygin	1967
Guam	Meeting with Vietnamese Leaders	1967
Honolulu	Meeting with Korean Leaders (on Pueblo incident)	1968
San Salvador	Meeting with Presidents of Central American Republics	1968

Nixon

Midway Island	Meeting with Vietnamese Leaders	1969
Elmendorf Air Base	Meeting with Emperor Hirohito of Japan	1971
Beijing	Meeting with Mao Tse-tung and Chou En-lai	1972
Honolulu	Meeting with Emperor Tanaka of Japan	1972
Moscow	Meeting with Brezhnev and Kosygin	1972
Reykjavik	Meeting with French President	1973
Washington	Meeting with Brezhnev	1973
Washington	Meeting with Brezhnev	1973
Moscow	Meeting with Brezhnev and Kosygin	1974

* Based in part on Department of State, *Visits Abroad of the Presidents of the United States*. Does not include many additional bilateral meetings with foreign leaders in the United States and abroad, attendance at the ordinary sessions of the UN, NATO, and other international organizations and agencies, Presidential addresses to general diplomatic conferences convened in the United States, and bilateral inter-American conferences and meetings (listed in Part C of this Table).

Table 7.11 (continued)

Ford

Moscow	Meeting with Brezhnev	1974
Vladivostok	Meeting with Brezhnev	1974
Martinique	Meeting with French President	1974
Brussels	NATO Summit Meeting	1975
Helsinki	Conference on Security and Cooperation in Europe	1975
Rambouillet (France)	Economic Summit Meeting (first of annual meetings)	1975
Beijing	Meeting with Mao Tse-tung and Teng Deng Xiaoping	1975
Dorado Beach (Puerto Rico)	Economic Summit Meeting	1976

Carter

London	Economic Summit Meeting	1977
Washington	Meeting with Panamanian Leaders to sign Panama Canal Treaty package	1977
Washington	Meeting with Leaders of North Atlantic Powers	1978
Panama City	Meeting to sign protocol confirming ratification of Panama Canal Treaties	1978
Bonn	Economic Summit Meeting	1978
Camp David	Tripartite Meeting with Leaders of Egypt and Israel	1978
Washington	Meeting with Deng Xiaoping	1979
Guadeloupe	Meeting of Western Big Four	1979
Washington	Meeting with Leaders of Egypt and Israel to sign Peace Treaty	1979
Vienna	Meeting with Brezhnev to sign SALT II Treaty	1979
Tokyo	Economic Summit Meeting	1979
Venice	Economic Summit Meeting	1980

Reagan

Ottawa	Economic Summit Meeting	1981
Cancun	Meeting with Leaders of 12 countries on International Development	1981
Barbados	Meeting with Leaders of 8 Caribbean Islands	1982
Versailles	Economic Summit Meeting	1982
Williamsburg	Economic Summit Meeting	1983
Washington	Meeting with Zhao Ziyang	1984
Beijing	Meeting with Li Xiannian and Zhao Ziyang	1984
London	Economic Summit Meeting	1984
Bonn	Economic Summit Meeting	1985
Washington	Meeting with Li Xiannian and Li Peng	1985
Geneva	Meeting with Gorbachev	1985
Grenada	Meeting with Leaders of 13 Caribbean Islands	1986
Tokyo	Economic Summit Meeting	1986
Reykjavik	Meeting with Gorbachev	1986
Venice	Economic Summit Meeting	1987
Washington	Meeting with Gorbachev	1987
Brussels	NATO Summit Meeting	1988
Moscow	Meeting with Gorbachev	1988
Toronto	Economic Summit Meeting	1988
New York	Meeting with Gorbachev	1988

Bush

Ottawa	Meeting with Canadian Leaders	1989
Beijing	Meeting with Deng Xiaoping and Li Peng	1989
Brussels	NATO Summit Meeting	1989
Paris	Economic Summit Meeting	1989

Bush (cont.)

San Jose	Inter-American Meeting of Presidents	1989
Malta	Meeting with Gorbachev	1989
Cartagena	Four-Power Inter-American Drug Summit Meeting	1990
Helsinki	Meeting with Gorbachev	1990
Washington	Meeting with Gorbachev	1990
Houston	Economic Summit Meeting	1990
London	NATO Summit Meeting	1990
New York	Summit Meeting to Help Children	1990
Paris	CSCE Summit Meeting to Sign Treaty on Conventional Forces	1990
London	Economic Summit Meeting	1991
Moscow	Meeting with Gorbachev to Sign START Treaty	1991
Rome	NATO Summit Meeting	1991
New York	U.N. Security Council Summit Meeting	1992
Washington	Meeting with Yeltsin	1992
Rio de Janeiro	Conference on World Environment (Earth Summit)	1992
Munich	Economic Summit Meeting	1992
Moscow	Meeting with Yeltsin to sign START II Treaty	1993
Washington	Meeting with Leaders of Israel and Palestine	1993

Clinton

Tokyo	Economic Summit Meeting	1993
Seattle	Meeting of 12 Asia and Pacific Economic Cooperation Powers	1993
Washington	Meeting with Israeli and Palestinian Leaders	1994
Kiev	Meeting with Leaders of Russia and Ukraine	1994
Naples	Economic Summit Meeting	1994
Moscow	Meeting with Yeltsin	1995
Halifax	Economic Summit Meeting	1995
Washington	Meeting to Sign Arab-Israeli Peace Agreement	1995
Paris	Economic Summit Meeting	1996
Moscow	Economic Summit Meeting (hosted by Russian Government)	1996
Washington	Meeting with leaders of Israel and Palestine	1996
Helsinki	Meeting with Yeltsin	1997
Denver	Economic Summit Meeting	1997

B. Ministerial Conferences and Meetings *

Byrnes

Berlin	Potsdam Conference	1945
London	Council of Foreign Ministers Meeting	1945
Moscow	Council of Foreign Ministers Meeting	1945
Paris	Council of Foreign Ministers Meeting	1946
Paris	Council of Foreign Ministers Meeting	1946
Paris	World War II Peace Conference for 4 European Countries	1946

Marshall

Moscow	Council of Foreign Ministers Meeting	1947
Petropolis (Brazil)	Inter-American Foreign Ministers Conference	1947
London	Council of Foreign Ministers Meeting	1947
Bogota	Inter-American Conference (Charter of the Organization of American States)	1948

* Based in part on Department of State, *Foreign Travels of the Secretaries of State*. Does not include many additional, less formal, bilateral ministerial meetings in the United States and abroad, or attendance at many ordinary sessions of the United Nations, NATO, and other international organizations and agencies, bilateral international committees and commissions, shuttle negotiations to resolve disputes of other nations, and most summit conferences and meetings to which the Secretary of State accompanied the President.

Table 7.11 (continued)

Acheson

Paris	Council of Foreign Ministers	1949
Paris	Meeting of Foreign Ministers of 5 European Countries	1949
San Francisco	Drafting Japanese World War II Peace Treaty	1951
Washington	Inter-American Foreign Ministers Conference	1951
Bonn	Signing Meeting for West Germany's Membership in NATO	1952
Paris	Signing Meeting for European Defense Community	1952
Paris	NATO Ministerial Meeting	1952

Dulles

Seoul	Signing Meeting for Mutual Defense Treaty	1953
Berlin	Western Big Four Foreign Ministers Meeting	1954
Caracas	Inter-American Foreign Ministers Conference	1954
Geneva	Conference on Indochina and Korea	1954
Manila	Signing Meeting for Southeast Asia Collective Defense Treaty (Manila Pact)	1954
London	Nine-Power Conference on Germany	1954
Paris	Four- and Nine-Power Conferences on Germany	1954
Bangkok	SEATO Ministerial Meeting	1955
Vienna	Signing Meeting for Austrian State Treaty	1955
Paris	NATO Ministerial Meeting	1955
Geneva	Big Four Ministerial Meeting	1955
Paris	NATO Ministerial Meeting	1955
Karachi	SEATO Ministerial Meeting	1956
Paris	NATO Ministerial Meeting	1956
London	Tripartite Ministerial Conference on Suez Canal	1956
London	Twenty-Two Power Conference on Suez Canal	1956
London	Twenty-Two Power Conference on Suez Canal	1956
Paris	NATO Ministerial Meeting	1956
Canberra	SEATO Ministerial Meeting	1957
Bonn	NATO Ministerial Meeting	1957
London	Disarmament Conference	1957
Ankara	Baghdad Pact Ministerial Meeting	1958
Manila	SEATO Ministerial Meeting	1958
Copenhagen	NATO Ministerial Meeting	1958
London	Baghdad Pact Ministerial Meeting	1958
Paris	NATO Ministerial Meeting	1958

Herter

Paris	Western Foreign Ministers Meeting	1959
Geneva	Big Four Ministerial Meeting	1959
Geneva	Big Four Ministerial Meeting	1959
Santiago	Inter-American Foreign Ministers Meeting	1959
Paris	NATO Ministerial Meeting	1959
Tehran	CENTO Ministerial Meeting	1960
Istanbul	NATO Ministerial Meeting	1960
San Jose	Inter-American Foreign Ministers Meeting	1960
Paris	NATO Ministerial Meeting	1960

Rusk

Bangkok	SEATO Ministerial Meeting	1961
Ankara	Cento Ministerial Meeting	1961
Oslo	NATO Ministerial Meeting	1961
Geneva	Fourteen-Nation Conference on Laos	1961

Rusk, cont.

Paris	NATO Ministerial Meeting	1961
Paris	NATO Ministerial Meeting	1961
Punta del Este	Inter-American Foreign Ministers Meeting	1962
Geneva	Eighteen-Nation Disarmament Conference	1962
London	CENTO Ministerial Meeting	1962
Washington	Informal Inter-American Foreign Ministers Meeting	1962
Athens	NATO Foreign Ministers Meeting	1962
Paris	NATO Foreign Ministers Meeting	1962
Geneva	Conference on Laos	1962
Paris	NATO Foreign Ministers Meeting	1962
Karachi	CENTO Foreign Ministers Meeting	1963
Ottawa	NATO Foreign Ministers Meeting	1963
Moscow	Signing Meeting for Nuclear Test Ban Treaty	1963
Paris	NATO Foreign Ministers Meeting	1963
Manila	SEATO Foreign Ministers Meeting	1964
Washington	Inter-American Foreign Ministers Meeting	1964
The Hague	NATO Foreign Ministers Meeting	1964
Paris	NATO Foreign Ministers Meeting	1964
Tehran	CENTO Foreign Ministers Meeting	1965
Washington	Inter-American Foreign Ministers Meeting	1965
Rio de Janeiro	Special Inter-American Conference	1965
Paris	NATO Foreign Ministers Meeting	1965
Ankara	CENTO Foreign Ministers Meeting	1966
Brussels	NATO Foreign Ministers Meeting	1966
Manila	Seven-Nation Conference on Vietnam	1966
Paris	NATO Foreign Ministers Meeting	1966
Buenos Aires	Special Inter-American Conference	1967
Punta del Este	OAS Heads of State and Foreign Ministers Meeting on Vietnam	1967
Luxembourg	NATO Foreign Ministers Meeting	1967
Brussels	NATO Foreign Ministers Meeting	1967
Wellington	ANZUS and SEATO Foreign Ministers Meetings	1968
Wellington	Seven-Nation Foreign Ministers Meeting	1968
Reykjavik	NATO Foreign Ministers Meeting	1968
Brussels	NATO Foreign Ministers Meeting	1968

Rogers

Bangkok	Seven-Nation Foreign Ministers Meeting	1969
Tehran	CENTO Foreign Ministers Meeting	1969
Brussels	NATO Foreign Ministers Meeting	1969
Rome	NATO Foreign Ministers Meeting	1970
Manila	SEATO Foreign Ministers Meeting	1970
Saigon	Meeting of Foreign Ministers of Countries Contributing Forces to Vietnam War	1970
Brussels	NATO Foreign Ministers Meeting	1970
Ankara	CENTO Foreign Ministers Meeting	1971
Lisbon	NATO Foreign Ministers Meeting	1971
Paris	OECD Foreign Ministers Meeting	1971
Brussels	NATO Foreign Ministers Meeting	1971
Bonn	NATO Foreign Ministers Meeting	1972
London	CENTO Foreign Ministers Meeting	1972
Berlin	Foreign Ministers Meeting to sign Quadripartite Agreement on Berlin	1972
Brussels	NATO Foreign Ministers Meeting	1972
Paris	Signing Meeting for Vietnam Peace Agreement	1973

Table 7.11 (continued)

Rogers (cont.)

Paris	International Conference on Vietnam	1973
Copenhagen	NATO Foreign Ministers Meeting	1973
Helsinki	Conference on Security and Cooperation in Europe (CSCE)	1973

Kissinger

Brussels	NATO Foreign Ministers Meeting	1973
Geneva	Middle East Peace Conference	1973
Aswan/Luxor	Meeting to Negotiate Egyptian-Israeli Disengagement Agreement	1974
Mexico City	Inter-American Foreign Ministers Conference	1974
Ottawa	NATO Foreign Ministers Meeting	1974
Madrid	Meeting to Sign Joint Declaration of Principles on Security and Cooperation in Europe	1974
Moscow	Meeting with Brezhnev and Gromyko	1974
Brussels	NATO Foreign Ministers Meeting	1974
Vienna	Meeting with Gromyko Regarding the Middle East	1975
Ankara	CENTO Foreign Ministers Meeting	1975
Paris	International Energy Agency and Organization for Economic Cooperation and Development Ministerial Meetings	1975
Helsinki	Signing Ceremony for CSCE Treaty	1975
Jerusalem/Alexandria	Negotiation of Egyptian-Israeli Disengagement Agreements	1975
Beijing	Meeting with Mao Tse-tung and Foreign Minister Chiao	1975
Brussels	NATO Foreign Ministers Meeting	1975
Paris	Conference on International Economic Development	1975
Madrid	Signing Meeting for Treaty of Friendship and Cooperation	1976
Nairobi	UN Trade and Development Conference	1976
Oslo	NATO Foreign Ministers Meeting	1976
London	CENTO Foreign Ministers Meeting	1976
Brussels	NATO Foreign Ministers Meeting	1976

Vance

London	NATO Foreign Ministers Meeting	1977
Tehran	CENTO Foreign Ministers Meeting	1977
Geneva	Signing Meeting for Convention to Prohibit Hostile Use of Environmental Modification Techniques	1977
Paris	Conference on International Economic Development	1977
Paris	OECD Foreign Ministers Meeting	1977
Brussels	NATO Foreign Ministers Meeting	1977
London	CENTO Foreign Ministers Meeting	1978
Moscow	Meeting with Brezhnev and Gromyko (SALT negotiations)	1978
Paris	OECD Foreign Ministers Meeting	1978
Moscow	Meeting with Brezhnev and Gromyko	1978
Geneva	Meeting with Gromyko (SALT negotiations)	1978
Tel Aviv	Meeting for Exchange of Ratifications of Egyptian-Israeli Peace Treaty	1979
The Hague	NATO Foreign Ministers Meeting	1979
Vienna	Signing Meeting for SALT II Treaty	1979
Bali	ASEAN Foreign Ministers Meeting	1979
Brussels	NATO Foreign Ministers Meeting	1979

Muskie

Brussels	NATO Defense Planning Meeting	1980
Ankara	NATO Foreign Ministers Meeting	1980
Kuala Lumpur	ASEAN Foreign Ministers Meeting	1980
Brussels	NATO Foreign Ministers Meeting	1980

Haig

Rome	NATO Foreign Ministers Meeting	1981
Manila	ASEAN Foreign Ministers Meeting	1981
Cancun	North-South (Rich-Poor Countries) Meeting	1981
Brussels	NATO Foreign Ministers Meeting	1981
Brussels	Special NATO Foreign Ministers Meeting on Poland	1982
Geneva	Meeting with Gromyko	1982
Madrid	CSCE Meeting	1982
Luxembourg	NATO Foreign Ministers Meeting	1982

Shultz

La Sapiniere (Canada)	NATO Ministerial Meeting in Canada	1982
Brussels	NATO Ministerial Meeting	1982
Beijing	Meeting with Deng Xiaoping and Zhao Ziyang	1983
Paris	OECD Foreign Ministers Meeting	1983
Paris	NATO Foreign Ministers Meeting	1983
Madrid	CSCE Foreign Ministers Meeting	1983
Brussels	NATO Foreign Ministers Meeting	1983
Stockholm	CSCE Conference on Security and Disarmament in Europe	1984
Caracas	Meeting with Central American Foreign Ministers	1984
Jakarta	ASEAN Foreign Ministers Meeting	1984
Brussels	NATO Foreign Ministers Meeting	1984
Geneva	Meeting with Gromyko to Discuss Arms Limitation	1985
Lisbon	NATO Foreign Ministers Meeting	1985
Kuala Lumpur	ASEAN Foreign Ministers Meeting	1985
Perth/Canberra	ANZUS Foreign Ministers Meeting	1985
Brussels	NATO Foreign Ministers Meeting	1985
Brussels	NATO Foreign Ministers Meeting	1985
Brussels	Meeting with European Community Foreign Ministers	1985
Bali	ASEAN Foreign Ministers Meeting	1986
Halifax	NATO Foreign Ministers Meeting	1986
Manila	ASEAN Foreign Ministers Meeting	1986
Brussels	NATO Foreign Ministers Meeting	1986
Vienna	CSCE Foreign Ministers Meeting	1986
Brussels	NATO Foreign Ministers Meeting	1986
Beijing	Meeting with Deng Xiaoping and Zhao Ziyang	1987
Moscow	Meeting on Limitation of Intermediate Range Nuclear Weapons	1987
Reykjavik	NATO Ministerial Meeting	1987
Singapore	ASEAN Foreign Ministers Meeting	1987
Moscow	Meeting to Discuss Intermediate Nuclear Forces Limitations	1987
Brussels	NATO Foreign Ministers Meeting	1987
Geneva	Meeting with Shevardnadze	1987
Brussels	NATO Foreign Ministers Meeting	1987
Brussels	NATO Foreign Ministers Meeting	1987
Ottawa	Signing Meeting for Arctic Cooperation Agreement	1988
Moscow	Meeting with Gorbachev and Shevardnadze	1988
Brussels	NATO Foreign Ministers Meeting	1988
Rome	Signing Meeting for Scientific and Technological Cooperation Agreement	1988
Geneva	Signing of Agreement for Withdrawal of Soviet Forces from Afghanistan	1988
Geneva	Meeting with Shevardnadze	1988
Brussels	NATO Foreign Ministers Meeting	1988
Madrid	NATO Foreign Ministers Meeting	1988

Table 7.11 (continued)

Shultz (cont.)
Bangkok	ASEAN Foreign Ministers Meeting	1988
Guatemala City	Meeting with Central American Foreign Ministers	1988
Brussels	NATO and European Economic Community Ministerial Meetings	1988
Paris	Conference on Prohibition of Chemical Weapons	1989

Baker
Vienna	CSCE Ministerial Meeting on Conventional Armed Forces in Europe	1989
Moscow	Meeting with Gorbachev	1989
Brussels	NATO Foreign Ministers Meeting	1989
Bandar Seri (Brunei)	ASEAN Foreign Ministers Meeting	1989
Paris	International Conference on Cambodia	1989
Jackson (Wyoming)	Meeting with Shevardnadze	1989
Sydney	Conference on Pacific Area Economic Cooperation	1989
Brussels	NATO Foreign Ministers Meeting	1989
Brussels	Meeting of Group of 24 on Aid to Eastern Europe	1989
Moscow	Meeting with Soviet Leaders	1990
Ottawa	NATO and Warsaw Pact Foreign Ministers Meeting on Open Skies	1990
Brussels	NATO and European Community Foreign Ministers Meeting	1990
Bonn	Two-Plus-Four Foreign Ministers Meeting on German Reunification	1990
Moscow	Pre-Summit with Soviet Officials on Arms Reduction Negotiations	1990
Copenhagen	CSCE Foreign Ministers Meeting	1990
Turnberry (Scotland)	NATO Foreign Ministers Meeting	1990
Guatemala City	Meeting with Central American Foreign Ministers	1990
East Berlin	Two-Plus-Four Foreign Ministers Meeting on German Reunification	1990
Brussels	Meeting of Group of 24	1990
Paris	Two-Plus-Four Foreign Ministers Meeting on German Reunification	1990
Jakarta	ASEAN Foreign Ministers Meeting	1990
Singapore	Conference on Asia-Pacific Area Economic Cooperation	1990
Irkutsk	Meeting with Shevardnadze	1990
Moscow	Meeting with Shevardnadze	1990
Brussels	NATO Foreign Ministers Meeting	1990
Moscow	Meeting with Gorbachev and Shevardnadze	1990
Moscow	Two-Plus-Four Foreign Ministers Meeting on German Reunification (signed Treaty on Final Settlement with Germany)	1990
Washington	Meeting with Soviet Foreign Minister Bessmertnykh	1991
London	Meeting with Soviet Foreign Minister Bessmertnykh	1991

C. Inter-American Conferences and Meetings *

Petropolis (Brazil)	Conference on Maintenance of Continental Peace	1947
Rio de Janeiro	Special Inter-American Conference to Implement Act of Chapultepec of 1945	1947
Bogota	Inter-American Conference (Charter of the Organization of American States)	1948
Washington	Inter-American Foreign Ministers Conference	1951
Caracas	Inter-American Foreign Ministers Conference	1954
Panama City	Inter-American Summit Meeting	1956
Santiago	Inter-American Foreign Ministers Conference	1959
San Jose	Inter-American Foreign Ministers Conference	1960
Punta del Este	Inter-American Foreign Ministers Conference	1962
Washington	Informal Inter-American Foreign Ministers Conference	1962
San Jose	Summit Conference with Central American Presidents	1963
Washington	Inter-American Foreign Ministers Conference	1964

Washington	Special Inter-American Conference	1964
Washington	Inter-American Foreign Ministers Conference	1965
Rio de Janeiro	Special Inter-American Foreign Ministers Conference	1965
Buenos Aires	Special Inter-American Foreign Ministers Conference	1966
Mexico City	Conference to Establish Latin American Nuclear Free Zone	1967
Buenos Aires	Inter-American Foreign Ministers Conference	1967
Punta del Este	Inter-American Summit Meeting	1967
San Salvador	Summit Conference with Central American Presidents	1968
Mexico City	Inter-American Foreign Ministers Meeting	1974
San Jose	Inter-American Conference on Cuba and Panama	1975
Barbados	Summit Meeting with Leaders of 8 Caribbean Islands	1982
Caracas	Secretary of State Meeting with Central American Foreign Ministers	1984
Grenada	Summit Meeting with leaders of 13 Caribbean Islands	1986
San Jose	Inter-American Summit Meeting	1989
Cartagena	Four-Power Inter-American Drug Summit	1990
Guatemala City	Secretary of State Meeting with Central American Presidents	1990

D. Other Principal Conferences and Meetings **

London	Conference on Prosecution and Punishment of Major War Criminals	1945
Quebec	Conference to Establish Food and Agriculture Organization	1945
London	Conference to Establish UN Educational, Scientific, and Cultural Organization	1945
London	Conference to Establish International Refugee Organization	1946
Paris	Conference to Establish Inter-Allied Reparations Agency	1946
New York	Conference to Establish World Health Organization	1946
Paris	Conference on European Axis Powers Peace Treaties	1946
Montreal	Conference to Revise Constitution of International Labor Organization	1946
Canberra	Conference to Establish South Pacific Commission	1947
Paris	Meeting to Sign World War II European Axis Powers Peace Treaties	1947
Atlantic City	Conference to Establish International Telecommunication Union	1947
Geneva	Conference on Trade and Employment	1947
Washington	Conference to Establish World Meteorological Organization	1947
Havana	Conference to Establish International Trade Organization	1947-48
Geneva	Conference to Establish Maritime Consultative Organization	1948
Geneva	Conference on Freedom of Information	1948
Washington	Conference on Investment Disputes Between States and Foreigners	1948
Paris	Conference on Prevention and Punishment of Genocide	1948
Washington	Conference for Signing of North Atlantic Treaty (NATO)	1949

*   Some of these conferences and meetings were at the summit and ministerial levels, which are also included in Parts A and B of this Table. After the Organization of American States was established in 1948, much inter-American deliberation was conducted in its sessions, which are not included in this list.

** Most of these were general and some were global conferences and meetings. A few duplicate those listed in Parts A and B, a number were sponsored or endorsed by the United Nations, the Organization of American States, and other international organizations (which is not identified in this section), and sessions of such organizations and agencies are not included. Also excluded are conferences and meetings dealing with specific commodities, fisheries, and seals, and those concerned with the General Agreement on Tariffs and Trade (GATT) and with the drafting of a convention on the Law of the Sea, which are dealt with separately. Many of these conferences produced multilateral treaties and agreements.

577

Table 7.11 (continued)

Geneva	Conference on Protection of War Victims	1949
Geneva	Conference on Road Traffic	1949
New York	Conference on Conservation of Natural Resources	1949
Geneva	Conference on Rules of War	1949
Geneva	Conference on Refugees and Stateless Persons	1951
San Francisco	Conference to conclude World War II Peace Treaty with Japan	1951
San Francisco	Tripartite Conference for ANZUS Security Pact	1951
Brussels	Conference on Maritime Jurisdiction	1952
Brussels	Conference on Legal Metrology	1952
Geneva	Conference on Copyright Protection	1952
New York	Conference on Political Rights of Women	1953
New York	Conference on Opium Control	1953
Venice	Conference to Establish Intergovernmental Committee for Migration	1953
Washington	Conference to Establish Policy on Korea	1953
The Hague	Conference on Protecting Cultural Property During Armed Conflict	1954
London	Quadripartite Meeting on Free Territory of Trieste	1954
London	Conference on Pollution of Sea by Oil	1954
Washington	Conference to Establish International Finance Corporation	1955
Geneva	Conference on Peaceful Uses of Atomic Energy	1955
Vienna	Conference to Establish Independent and Democratic Austria	1955
Geneva	Conference on Abolition of Slavery	1956
New York	Conference to Establish International Atomic Energy Agency	1956
London	Disarmament Conference	1957
Brussels	Conference on Maritime Law	1957
New York	Conference on Enforcement of Foreign Arbitral Awards	1958
Geneva	Conference on Suspension of Nuclear Tests	1958
Geneva	Conference on Law of the Sea (First)	1958
Paris	Conference on International Exchange of Publications	1958
Paris	Conference on Exchange of Official Publications	1958
Washington	Conference to Establish Inter-American Development Bank	1959
Washington	Conference on Antarctica	1959
Washington	Conference to Establish International Development Association	1960
Geneva	Conference on Law of the Sea (Second)	1960
London	Conference on Safety of Life at Sea	1960
Paris	Conference to Establish Organization for Economic Cooperation and Development	1960
New York	Conference on Narcotic Drugs	1961
Vienna	Conference on Diplomatic Relations	1961
Washington	Nuclear Test Ban Talks	1963
Vienna	Conference on Consular Relations	1963
Moscow	Conference on Nuclear Test Ban	1963
Tokyo	Conference on Offenses Committed Aboard Aircraft	1963
Geneva	Conference on Trade and Development	1964
Vienna	Conference to Produce New Constitution for Universal Postal Union	1964
Copenhagen	Conference to Establish International Council for Exploration of the Sea	1964
London	Conference on Facilitation of International Maritime Traffic	1965
New York	Conference on Elimination of Racial Discrimination	1965
Manila	Conference to Establish Asian Development Bank	1965
New York	Conference on Human Rights—Civil and Political	1966
Washington	Conference on Exploration and Use of Outer Space	1967
Mexico City	Conference to Establish Latin American Nuclear Free Zone (U.S. not signatory, but subscribed to protocol in 1981)	1967
Stockholm	Conference to Establish World Intellectual Property Organization	1967

New York	Conference on Status of Refugees	1967
Washington	Conference on Non-Proliferation of Nuclear Weapons	1968
Washington	Conference on Patent Cooperation	1970
Monaco	Conference to Establish International Hydrographic Organization	1970
Mexico City	Conference to Establish World Tourism Organization	1970
The Hague	Conference on Unlawful Seizure of Aircraft (Hijacking)	1970
Paris	Conference on Prohibiting and Preventing Illicit Import, Export, and Ownership of Cultural Property	1970
Paris	Conference on Copyright Protection (revision)	1971
Washington	Conference on International Terrorism	1971
Washington	Conference on Prohibiting Emplacement of Nuclear Weapons on Seabed and Ocean Floor	1971
Strasbourg	Conference on Patent Classification	1971
Washington	Conference to Establish International Telecommunications Satellite Organization	1971
Montreal	Conference on Sabotage of Aircraft	1971
Santiago	Conference to Establish Postal Union of the Americas and Spain	1971
Washington	Conference on International Trade in Endangered Species of Flora and Fauna	1972
Washington	Conference on International Liability for Damage by Space Objects	1972
London	Conference on International Regulations to Prevent Collisions at Sea	1972
Paris	Conference on Protection of World Cultural and Natural Heritage	1972
Abidjan (Ivory Coast)	Conference to Establish African Development Fund	1972
Paris	Conference on Vietnam	1973
Geneva	Middle East Peace Conference	1973
New York	Conference on Law of the Sea (Third)	1973
Bucharest	Conference on World Population	1974
Rome	World Food Conference	1974
New York	Conference on Protection and Punishment of Crimes Against Internationally Protected Persons, Including Diplomats	1973
Bucharest	World Population Conference	1974
Paris	Conference to Establish International Energy Program	1974
New York	Conference on Registration of Objects Launched into Outer Space	1975
Mexico City	World Conference on Women	1975
Kyoto	Conference on Harmonization of Customs Procedures	1975
Nairobi	Conference on Trade and Development	1976
Stockholm	Conference on Human Environment	1976
Vancouver	Conference on Human Settlement (Habitat)	1976
Rome	Conference to Establish International Fund for Agricultural Development	1976
Paris	North-South (Rich-Poor Countries) Conference	1976
London	Conference to Establish International Satellite Organization	1976
Geneva	Conference on Prohibiting Military and Other Hostile Use of Environmental Modification Techniques	1977
Mar del Plata	Conference on Water	1977
Geneva	Conference on Arms Limitation and Disarmament	1978
Vienna	Conference to Establish UN Industrial Development Organization	1979
Hamburg	Conference on Maritime Search and Rescue	1979
Vienna	Conference on Physical Protection of Nuclear Materials	1979
Geneva	Conference on Long-Range Transboundary Pollution	1979
Geneva	Conference on Establishing Radio Regulations	1979
New York	Conference on Taking of Hostages	1979
Vienna	Conference on Contracts for Sale of Goods	1980

Table 7.11 (continued)

Geneva	Conference on Restricting Use of Conventional Weapons Which Are Excessively Injurious	1980
New York	Conference on Removing Vietnam Forces from Cambodia	1981
Geneva	Conference on Nuclear Weapons	1981
Geneva	Conference on Aid to Refugees	1981
Paris	Conference on Aid to Least Developed Countries	1981
Nairobi	Conference on Energy Resources	1981
Cancun	North-South (Rich-Poor Countries) Conference	1981
New York	Conference on Law of the Sea (Tenth Session)	1982
Nairobi	Conference on Telecommunications	1982
Vienna	World Assembly on Aging	1982
Strasbourg	Conference on Transfer of Sentenced Persons	1983
Mexico City	Conference on Population	1984
Washington	Conference to Establish Inter-American Investment Corporation	1984
New York	Conference on Torture and Inhumane Punishment	1984
Seoul	Conference to Establish Multilateral Investment Guarantee Agency	1985
Vienna	Conference on Early Notification of Nuclear Accidents	1986
Vienna	Conference on Illicit Traffic in Narcotic Drugs	1988
Paris	Conference on Control of Chemical Weapons	1989
Paris	Conference on Conventional Armed Forces in Europe	1990
Geneva	World Conference on Global Warming	1990
Rome	Conference on Unlawful Acts Against Safety of Life at Sea	1992
Nairobi	Conference on World Environment	1992
Rio de Janeiro	Conference on World Environment (Earth Summit)	1992
Washington	Conference to Establish North American Free Trade Association	1992
New York	Conference on Aging	1992
Vienna	World Conference on Human Rights	1993
Tokyo	Conference on African Development	1993
Marrakesh	Conference to Establish World Trade Organization	1994
Cairo	Conference on Population and Development	1994
Yokohama	World Conference on National Disaster Reduction	1994
Cairo	Conference on Population and Development	1994
New York	Conference on Families	1994
Naples	World Conference on Organized Transnational Crime	1994
Beijing	World Conference on Women	1995
Vienna	Conference on Prohibition or Restriction of Certain Weapons	1995
Geneva	Conference on Prohibition or Restriction of Certain Weapons	1996
Istanbul	Conference on Human Settlement	1996
Oslo	Conference on Banning and Destruction of Land Mines	1997
Kyoto	Conference on Global Warming (Limiting Emissions)	1997

gatherings, such as global and other inclusive conclaves, normally require a more formal treatment of organization and procedure. Finally, distinguished from the many ad hoc or individualized gatherings, many are periodic or regularized, including the series of North Atlantic heads of government and ministerial meetings, inter-American general and Foreign Ministers conferences, and annual Western Economic Summit Meetings, commenced in 1975.

Equally impressive is the broadening of the subjects treated. These are of two general types—those that are devoted to a single subject and those that are not so restricted. The latter have included most of the summit and ministerial conclaves. Others have focused on single subjects, represented by the following functional categories:

Aging	Law of the sea
Airspace	Migration
Alliance	Military occupation and civil affairs
Antarctica	Narcotic drugs
Arms limitation and disarmament	Natural resources
Atomic energy	North–South relations
Biosphere	Nuclear power and weapons
Commodities	Outer space
Conflict resolution	Patents
Copyright	Peace—establishment and maintenance
Cultural property and heritage	Peaceful settlement of disputes
Diplomatic and consular relations	Pollution
East–West relations	Population and refugees
Economic cooperation and development	Public international law
Education and culture	Racial discrimination
Energy (including atomic)	Rules of war
Environment	Seas and maritime affairs
Exchange of publications	Security and defense
Freedom of information	Slavery
Genocide	Space and space satellites
Global warming	Telecommunications
Health	Trade and employment
Hijacking and sabotage	Water resources
Human rights	Women's affairs
International terrorism	Others*

*Some subjects are more restricted in scope, such as collisions at sea, enforcement of arbitral awards, human settlements (habitat), internationally protected persons, safety of life at sea, and transfer of sentenced persons.

Thus, the breadth of conference subjects has been extended to embrace many new matters since World War II, to encompass virtually all major issues and problems of collective international concern. As a result the Department of State has needed to adapt itself to new, often critical policy positions and to negotiating or supporting and administering the involvement of a host of functional specialists representing the varied interests of the United States.

Location and Timing

The sites at which these conferences and meetings are convened are determined by host governments, by preliminary conferences or agencies (including the United Nations) that initiate them by agreement among participants, by participating governments if they are to meet periodically, or by contesting governments or victorious powers seeking a neutral negotiating site. Other factors include selection of a location that is felicitous, healthful, and safe from danger and international terrorism, that is conveniently located equidistant for participants, that has adequate aerial, communications, housing, and meeting room facilities, or simply to pass around the honor, burden, and cost.

Beginning with World War II, the United States has become one of the most popular conference hosts.[187] Aside from Washington in this country, Brussels, London, Geneva, and Paris rank among the most popular, with Moscow and Beijing hosting many of the bilateral summit and ministerial meetings of the United States with the Soviet/Russian and Chinese governments.

The location of conferences that produce the constitutive acts of international organizations has varied considerably. The Charters of the United Nations and the Organization of American States were negotiated, respectively, at San Francisco (1945) and Bogotá (1948). The organic acts of several United Nations specialized agencies were also concluded in the United States prior to 1946,[188] as was that of the World Meteorological Organization (Washington, 1947, successor to the International Meteorological Organization, created in the nineteenth century). A few specialized agencies were established by United Nations resolutions (the International Refugee Organization and the International Children's Emergency Fund, both in 1946), whereas others were created at international conferences, such as the International Labor Organization (established in 1919, which had its Constitution revised at a conference held at Montreal in 1946), the World Health Organization (New York, 1946), and the International Trade Organization (Havana in 1946, whose Charter was never ratified). Subsequently, between 1947 and 1994, more than fifteen additional major global international organizations were created at Washington, Atlantic City, and New York in the United States; at Geneva, London, Monaco, Rome, Stockholm, and Vienna in Europe; and at Mexico City, Marrakesh (Morocco), and Seoul (Korea). More than half of the conferences establishing the United Nations and other global international organizations were held in the United States, especially those concerned with financial affairs.[189] In addition, the North Atlantic Treaty Organization was created at a conference convened at Washington (1949), the ANZUS security organization at San Francisco (1951), the Southeast Asia Treaty Organization at Manila (1954), and the Central Treaty Organization at London (1958).

Most major inter-American conferences are convened at Washington (the headquarters of the Organization of American States) and the capitals of Latin American countries, but other meetings have been held in other places in the Western Hemisphere, including Cancún, Cartagena, Petropolis, Punta del Este, San Salvador, and such islands as the Bahamas, Barbados, Grenada, Guadeloupe, and Martinique. The quadripartite Council of Foreign Ministers (United States, France, Great Britain, and the Soviet Union) held its meetings at London, Moscow, and Paris. Of the security agencies Brussels and Paris have been the preferred sites for NATO summit and special ministerial meetings.[190] Those of SEATO, the Baghdad Pact and CENTO, and ASEAN are usually convened at major cities in member countries; conferences on Security and Cooperation in Europe (CSCE) have been held at Copenhagen, Madrid, and Vienna, as well as Helsinki; and ministerial meetings of the Organization for Economic Cooperation and Development (OECD) normally are convened at Paris.

Sometimes neutral sites have been utilized for conferences and meetings convoked to deal with crises and peace negotiations. During the Cold War, aside from Washington and Moscow, East–West summit meetings were held at Geneva and Vienna and occasionally also elsewhere, including Irkutsk, Malta, and Reykjavik. Others concerned with peacekeeping and peacemaking were frequently convened at Geneva, Paris, and Vienna, but for the Egyptian–Israeli conflict, the negotiators met at Aswan/Luxor, Jerusalem, and Tel Aviv in 1975 and 1976 and at Camp David and Washington in 1978 and 1979. Many of those sponsored by the United Nations and other conferences were deliberately convened at various other sites throughout the world.[191]

Uniquely, the first of the annual Summit Economic Meetings was held at Rambouillet (France) in 1975. Thereafter they often convened at the capitals of the original seven member countries according to a fixed, rotational schedule. However, those hosted by the United States have met sequentially at Dorado Beach (Puerto Rico), Williamsburg, Houston, and Denver. When Russia was added in 1997, it met at Moscow.

As in earlier times, some major conferences are remembered historically as identified with the places where they are held. These are represented by the San Francisco Conference, where the United Nations Charter was signed in 1945, the Bogotá Conference of 1948, where the Charter of the Organization of American States was negotiated, the Vienna conferences where the Conventions on Diplomatic and Consular Relations were concluded in 1961 and 1963, and the Geneva Conference on Disarmament of 1978.[192]

So far as timing is concerned, it may be noted that many conferences and meetings are ad hoc. However, for some time inter-American regular and special

Foreign Ministers Conferences were fairly regularized. Similarly, NATO Foreign Ministers Meetings have invariably been held in either May or June and in December (usually at Paris until 1967 and subsequently at Brussels), CENTO annual meetings normally in April or May, SEATO meetings annually in March or April, and ASEAN meetings in June or July. Since their inception Western Economic Summits are convened annually, usually in June or July.

Most bilateral and multilateral summit and ministerial meetings are of short duration (see sections on the new diplomacy and summit and ministerial diplomacy). Often, general conferences convene for several weeks or months. However, to negotiate the United Nations Charter, following two years of preliminary planning and the Dumbarton Oaks deliberations for more than six weeks, the San Francisco Conference lasted two months. Even more extended were the negotiations concerning the General Agreement on Tariffs and Trade (GATT) and the Law of the Sea negotiations (UNCLOS), which were unique in that they involved multiple conferences over several years.

The conferences creating the General Agreement on Tariffs and Trade, consummated initially by twenty-three countries at the Geneva Conference of October 30, 1947, have since been virtually in continuous session. Historians and economists brand its deliberations and negotiations as a series of ''rounds''— Geneva (1947), Annency (France, 1949), Torquay (Great Britain, 1950), Geneva (1956 and 1960–62), Dillon (named for C. Douglas Dillon, American Secretary of the Treasury, 1960–61), Kennedy (named for President Kennedy, 1962–67), Tokyo (1973–79), and Uruguay (1980s). By this process the original General Agreement has been reviewed, supplemented, and modified. Additions and changes were embodied in some eighty-five protocols, ''agreements to rectify'' specific stipulations, procès-verbaux, exchanges of notes, and other instruments, most of which were consummated at Geneva. Aside from two dozen protocols of accession, several changes were made in 1951, and most of the rest constituted major and minor modifications. To illustrate, whereas the original agreement of 1947 ran to fifty printed pages, the massive changes and addenda embodied in the protocol of 1967 following the Kennedy round ran to nearly 4,100 printed pages.[193] By 1996 some 105 countries were ''contracting members,'' and twenty-six others were denominated ''de facto participants.'' The principal exceptions are Afghanistan, China, Equador, Iran, Iraq, Panama, Soviet Union/Russia, Syria, and Vietnam.

Also noteworthy was the system of conferences devoted to negotiating the Law of the Sea Treaty. The first such conference met at Geneva in 1958, and a second conference was held at Geneva in 1960. Following five years of preparation by a United Nations General Assembly committee and a preparatory session in the summer of 1973, the initial session of the third Law of the Sea Conference (UNCLOS) met at New York in December 1973 to deal with conference organization, and the first substantive session was held at Caracas the next year, which lasted ten weeks. Eventually, approximately 150 governments were represented at ten such sessions (some call them separate conferences), usually convened at Geneva and New York, most of which lasted seven to ten weeks. The tenth session consisted of two segments in 1981, without reaching final consensus.

When, after fourteen years of deliberation, the eventuating text of the treaty was considered and voted on by the United Nations in April 1982, it was approved by 130 governments and disapproved by the United States, Israel, Turkey, and Venezuela, and seventeen delegations abstained. The treaty was finally opened for signature at Jamaica Bay (Kingston, Jamaica) in December 1982, where 118 governments signed the treaty.[194] This extended conference system, which lasted nearly ten years, failed to resolve the differences of the interests, policies, and practices of the developed and developing countries. The United States has refused to sign the treaty for various reasons, especially because of such matters as the extent of territorial waters, the arrangement for the powers and authority of the international management agency it established, its voting process based on equality, and the method of assessing the contributions of signatory governments.

Organization, Procedure, and Department of State Administration

Early American international conference administration was entirely ad hoc, dealing with the problems of each gathering as they arose. In the course of time, certainly by 1945, common procedures were developed, and eventually many aspects of conference management were standardized. The Department of State plays the key administrative role in managing the organization and procedure of all conferences and meetings hosted by the United States and of American delegations that attend those held abroad. This responsibility embraces such matters as officiating leaders, precedence of principal delegates, agenda, organization of American delegations and staffing, instruction to delegates, decision-making and voting processes, determination of American policy positions on issues raised, the form and nature of end products, and related matters. The extent to which these administrative factors are important to the functioning and success of each gathering depends on the degree of its formality and size. Figures 7.3, 7.4, 7.5, 7.6, and 7.7 illustrate the structure of the San Francisco Conference of 1945 (United Nations Charter), generic representations of conferences when the United States is the host government and when they are hosted abroad, and a general depiction of the flow of conference action.

Although the practice existed previously, in March 1979 the Department of State issued concrete guidelines concerning participation of private citizens as representatives of affected private sector interests to serve on American delegations to international conferences, meetings, and other negotiations. These specified criteria for inviting such participants and fixed the nature and limits of the role they would play.

Dealing with Department of State administration, although initially, in 1928

Figure 7.3
Conference Structure: San Francisco Conference, 1945

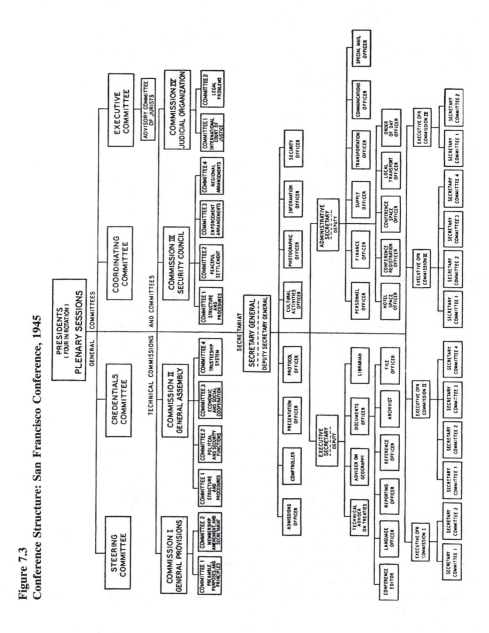

Figure 7.4
International Conference Procedure: Flowchart

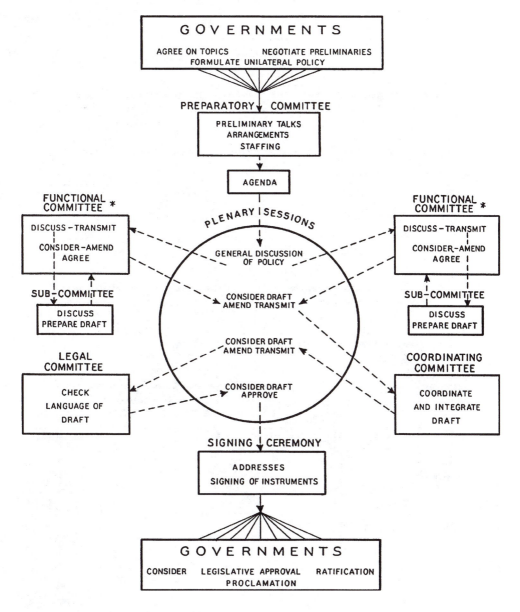

*There may be two or more functional committees, depending on conference organization.

Figure 7.5
Conference Delegation Structure: United States as Host State

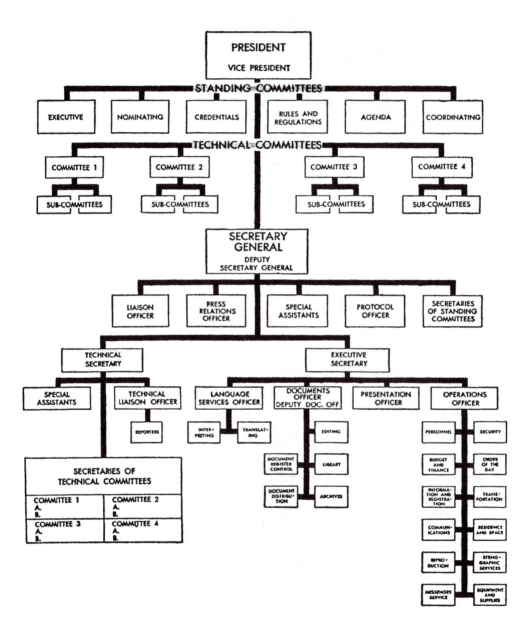

Figure 7.6
Conference Delegation Structure: U.S. Delegation Abroad

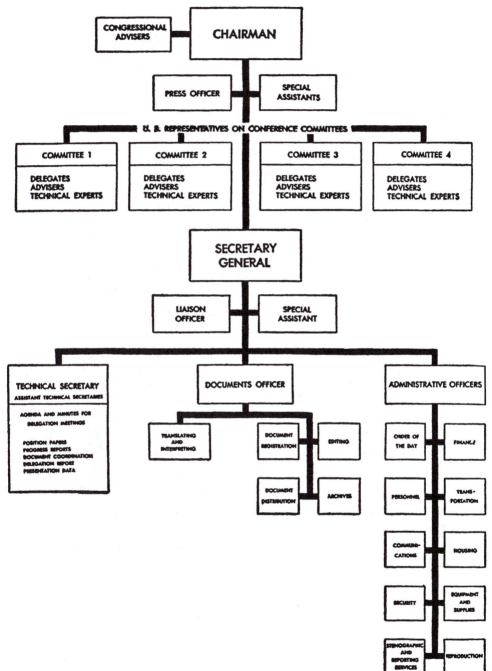

Figure 7.7
Typical International Conference Agenda

I. Conference Preliminaries

A. Initiation of conference
B. Selection of site
C. Invitation to participate
D. Governments appoint delegates
E. Convening of conference
   1. Opening session
   2. Adoption of rules of procedure
F. Credentials consideration
   1. Presentation of credentials
   2. Approval of credentials
   3. Report of credentials committee

G. Agenda
   1. Devisement of agenda
   2. Debate on agenda
   3. Adoption of agenda
H. Election of officers
   1. President of conference
   2. Vice President
   3. Rapporteur
   4. Secretary
   5. Other officers

II. Preparatory Action

A. Appointment of preparatory committee
   1. Preparatory committee deliberations
   2. Report of preparatory committee

B. Plenary statements of delegates
C. Deliberations of preparatory committee
D. Decision on final report of preparatory committee

III. Conference Plenary Deliberations

A. Committees and subcommittees
   1. Appointment of committees
   2. Deliberation of committees
   3. Presentation of committee reports
   4. Deliberation on committee reports
   5. Decision on committee reports
B. Conference resolutions
   1. Presentation of conference resolutions
   2. Debate on conference resolutions
   3. Decision on conference resolutions

C. Coordinating committee
   1. Appointment of coordinating committee
   2. Deliberation of coordinating committee
   3. Report of coordinating committee
D. Legal committee
   1. Appointment of legal committee
   2. Deliberation of legal committee
   3. Report of legal committee
E. Conference draft end-products
   1. Preparation of end-products
   2. Approval of end-products

IV. Final Conference Action

A. Preparing final end-product
B. Negotiating remaining differences
C. Plenary consideration and debate
D. Formal vote on final end-products

E. Termination of plenary deliberations
F. Formal signing of end-products
G. Transmittal of end-products to national governments
H. Termination of conference

V. Final Action by National Governments

A. Approval action by governments
   1. Ratification
   2. Reservations/declarations
   3. Deferred action
   4. Rejection

B. Registration with United Nations
C. Publication
   1. By United States
   2. By United Nations
   3. By others

VI. Implementation

it combined international conference management with protocol functions, these were divided into separate Divisions prior to the outbreak of World War II. In the late 1940s conference administration was incorporated as one of four Divisions in the Office of United Nations Affairs. Subsequently, by the early 1950s it was converted into an Office of International Administration and Conferences (together with three other offices) as part of the Bureau of United Nations Affairs. Later that decade it was relabeled the Office of International Conferences, which, together with four other offices, came under the Assistant Secretary in charge of the Bureau of International Organization Affairs. Currently, it continues as a component of this Bureau, which is headed by an Assistant Secretary of State, who serves under the Under Secretary for Political Affairs (who also has charge over the six Regional or Geographic Bureaus). This Bureau of International Organization Affairs provides guidance and support for U.S. participation in both international conferences and organizations and is responsible for the development, coordination, and implementation of American multilateral policy and negotiations.

Advantages, Limitations, and Assessment

As one of the principal diplomatic techniques, international conferencing enjoys a number of advantages. In 1946 Lord Maurice Hankey, British diplomat who personally attended nearly 500 conferences and meetings between 1914 and 1920, wrote: "Perhaps the most important result of conducting diplomacy by conference is the knowledge responsible statesmen acquire of one another." It enables conscientious political leaders and diplomats to know, understand, and respect each other. Often, it obviates extended exchanges of time-consuming written communications. The informality and sometimes intimacy of consultation and negotiation around the conference table are conducive to reducing or eliminating red tape and to expediting decisions, especially when time is crucial. They also may produce a degree of frankness and willingness to compromise that might otherwise be lacking, respecting such matters as the necessity of obtaining legislative approval and appropriations. Other possible advantages are elasticity of procedure, informality, and immediate interpretation and translation for the participants. In view of the interest engendered in the media, the conference also affords a greater share of openness concerning the progress of negotiations and especially the eventuating end products.

On the other hand, at times some of these factors may prove to be disadvantageous, and, as a diplomatic technique, it is scarcely a panacea and has its limitations. It is a deliberative, rather than a legislative or independent, law-creating process, and it requires advance State Department concurrence and subsequent Executive and Congressional approval, especially by ratification in the case of formal treaties. Nor does it ordinarily serve to arbitrate disputes by political means, and, if reconciliation is to be effected between governments, it must achieve this by means of voluntary pacification. It is not comparable to parliamentary bodies, such as international organizations, in the sense that, if decision making is based on principles of equality and unanimity, and a voting system is employed, individual governments can obstruct the taking of action, and if acceptable compromise or consensus is not achieved among the participants, governments may reject the outcome.

To conclude, the vast increase in the demands of coping with the conduct of relations in the contemporary community of nations, with their growing and diverse interests, issues, and problems affecting not only a few but many states, all of which seek mutually acceptable, if not favorable, arrangements, has necessitated greater dependence on conference diplomacy, both occasional or ad hoc gatherings, and increasingly also systematic and sometimes regularized conferences and meetings. Benefiting from previous experience, the United States utilizes such conferences to considerable advantage in recruiting qualified delegates and in relying on top-level principals and diplomats with authority to make decisions when necessary, rather than depending solely on local resident envoys who may have less specific, often technical experience concerning the matters under consideration. Popular support for the determinations produced is solicited among interested private American groups, aside purely from securing Senate approval. In some cases the overt prior authorization of Congress is obtained, thereby strengthening the negotiating position of commissioned delegates.

In short, conference diplomacy fulfills an important need in the conduct of contemporary foreign relations, supplementing both direct traditional bilateral and multilateral parliamentary diplomacy pursued through international organizations. Experience in recent decades evidences that the United States and other nations are prepared to handle an increasing amount of their collective interrelations at the conference table, and this is likely to continue at all levels— summit, ministerial, diplomatic, and technical. As a result, the burden of planning, representation, and administration by the Department of State and, in certain respects, by the policy officers and the Office of International Conferences has become a primary contemporary foreign relations function.[195]

PUBLIC INTERNATIONAL ORGANIZATIONS AND OTHER AGENCIES

Contrary to earlier popular belief, despite the failure to join the League of Nations and the Permanent Court of International Justice following World War I, the United States has been not only a joiner but also a major initiator of public international organizations and other agencies of various types. In less than a century and a quarter this country participated in nearly 300 such institutions. Some of these were short-lived, others were preparatory bodies that functioned pending the establishment of more permanent organizations, and many have been converted into successor agencies. More than fifty were World War I and

II temporary agencies, some of which served as transitional occupation and related administrations that have ceased to exist.

Currently, the United States is affiliated with all United Nations, all major inter-American, many European, and virtually all other global and a substantial number of regional and bilateral international institutions in which it possesses an interest and from which it is not excluded by virtue of geography or functional concerns. This development augments and complicates the means whereby the Department of State conducts contemporary American diplomacy.

Paralleling traditional direct representation, this feature of multilateral and parliamentary diplomacy has accelerated and expanded since 1945 and has become one of the principal, if not vital, means of conducting contemporary American foreign relations—launching the era of collective diplomacy by means of a network of durable international institutions. The preponderant majority of these are universal, although a respectable number have been quadripartite, tripartite, and bilateral. As elements of the international community of nations, they differ from both national governments that create them and international conferences in that, founded on their own constitutive acts, they possess their own individuality, international personality, constituencies, processes, and systems of governance.

Their purposes are manifold. In general, they are established by participating national governments to provide forums for international integration, negotiation, cooperation, and administration. More precisely, this development has been motivated by the gradual trend of forces for international coalescence to establish common policies, practices, and procedures, to formulate uniform rules and regulations, resolve differences, and prevent or alleviate crises, and to manage international programs. Naturally, the goals of each international organization vary according to the powers and responsibilities ascribed to it.

As viable institutions, these organizations perform both deliberative and administrative functions. Their principal internal activities, aside from policy devisement and negotiation and passing binding or recommendatory resolutions or producing operational agreements, are to perform such activities as implementing their operational structure, handling their funding and responsibilities, and providing custodial, secretariat, and staffing services. Their external functions embrace the servicing of incoming and outgoing communications and information, furnishing advisory and other services to national governments, and filing reports and other documents.

During the period from 1913 to 1945, as indicated in Chapter 6 and Table 6.10, the United States was a member of approximately fifty public international organizations. These were grouped as pre-1913 agencies, the United Nations system, inter-American, and other international agencies. Approximately thirty-five of these were established after World War I and remained in existence following World War II. Since the mid-1940s the United States affiliated with scores of new agencies, as listed in Table 7.12. These are arranged in four

Table 7.12
U.S. Participation in Public International Organizations and Other Agencies*

A. Multilateral Organizations and Agencies Since World War II [1]

Treaty or Agreement	Title of Organization	Title of Constitutive Act [2]	Date Effective for U.S.
A	African Development Bank (ADB)	Agreement	1983
A	African Development Fund (ADF)	Agreement	1976
A	Agricultural Development Fund (IFAD)	Arts. of Agr.	1977
A	American International Institute for the Protection of Childhood	Conf. Res.	1927
T	ANZUS Collective Security Organization	Treaty	1952
A	Asian Development Bank (ADB)	Arts. of Agr.	1966
	Baghdad Collective Security Alliance (see CENTO)		
T	Bureau of International Expositions	Convention	1968
A	Caribbean Commission	Agreement	1948
A	Caribbean Organization	Agreement	1961
A	Center for International Forestry Research (CIFOR)	Constitution	1993
A	Central American Tribunal	Protocol	1923
A	Central Bureau of the International Map of the World on the Millionth Scale	Conf. Res.	1921
A	Central Commission for Navigation of the Rhine	Notes	1945
T	Central International Office for the Control of Liquor Traffic in Africa	Convention	1929
A	Central Treaty Organization (CENTO/METO)	Conf. Declaration	1958
A	Colombo Plan Council for Southeast Asia	Constitution	1951
A	Combined Siam Rice Commission	Agreement	1946
A	Combined Tin Committee	Joint Com.	1945
T	Commission for the Conservation of Antarctic Marine Living Resources	Convention	1982
T	Committee of Control of the International Zone of Tangier	General Act	1906
		Protocol	1945
A	Council of Foreign Ministers (CFM)	Protocol	1945
T	Customs Cooperation Council (see also International Union for the Publication of Customs Tariffs)	Convention	1970
A	Emergency Advisory Committee for Political Defense (Inter-American)	Conf. Res.	1942
A	Emergency Economic Committee for Europe	Conf. Decision	1945
A	European Bank for Reconstruction and Development	Agreement	1990
A	European Coal Organization	Agreement	1946

*For comparison with pre–World War II American participation in international organizations and other agencies, see Table 6.10.

[1]This list is arranged alphabetically by titles of international organizations. U.S. commitments are designated as ''T'' (treaties) and ''A'' (agreements). The treaties are approved by the Senate in accordance with the constitutionally prescribed formal treaty process. Many of the agreements are formal executive agreements approved by both houses of Congress by normal legislative process. Some agreements, primarily embodied in conference resolutions (rather than formal agreements), are confirmed by legislation authorizing participation or providing for representation in the organization and/or financial support. The dates represent not the date of consummation or signature of a treaty or agreement but the date of effectiveness for the United States.

Many of these organizations and agencies are dealt with in the *U.S. Code*, Title 22, especially Chapters 7, 28–30, 35, 36, 45, and 47.

[2]The following abbreviations are employed: Arb. Rules (Arbitration Rules), Arts. of Agr. (Articles of Agreement), Conf. Com. (Conference Communiqué), Conf. Res. (Conference Resolution), Joint Com. (Joint Communiqué), and Notes (Exchange of Diplomatic Notes).

594

Multilateral Organizations and Agencies, cont.

A	European Coordination Group for Energy (see also International Energy Agency)	Conf. Com.	1974
A	European Space Research Organization (see also INMARSAT and INTELSAT)	Notes	1966
A	Far Eastern Commission	Conf. Com.	1945
A	Food and Agriculture Organization (FAO) (see also International Food Aid Committee and International Food Policy Research Institute)	Constitution	1945
A	General Agreement on Tariffs and Trade (GATT) system	Agreement	1948
A	Indo-Pacific Fisheries Council/Commission	Agreement	1948/1961
A	Indus Basin Development Fund	Agreement	1960
A	Inter-Allied Reparation Agency (IARA)	Agreement	1946
T	Inter-American Arbitration Tribunals	Treaty	1935
A	Inter-American Children's Institute	Statutes	1928
T	Inter-American Coffee Board	Agreement	1940
T	Inter-American Collective Defense Arrangement (Rio Pact)	Treaty	1948
A	Inter-American Commercial Arbitration Commission	Arb. Rules	1975
A	Inter-American Commission of Human Rights	Conf. Res.	1960
T	Inter-American Commission of Jurists (see also Inter-American Juridical Committee)	Convention	1908
A	Inter-American Commission of Women	Conf. Res.	1930
T	Inter-American Commissions of Inquiry	Convention	1925
A	Inter-American Committee on the Alliance for Progress	Charter	1961
T	Inter-American Conciliation Commissions	Convention	1929
A	Inter-American Cultural and Trade Center	U.S. Statute	1966
A	Inter-American Defense Board (IDB)	Conf. Res.	1942
A	Inter-American Development Bank (IDB)	Agreement	1959
A	Inter-American Development Commission	Conf. Res.	1940
T	Inter-American Indian Institute	Convention	1941
T	Inter-American Institute for Cooperation on Agriculture (see also Inter-American Institute of Agricultural Sciences)	Convention	1980
T	Inter-American Institute of Agricultural Sciences	Convention	1944
A	Inter-American Investment Corporation	Agreement	1983
A	Inter-American Juridical Committee (see also Inter-American Commission of Jurists)	Conf. Res.	1942
T	Inter-American Radio Office (OIR) (see also International Telecommunication Union)	Convention	1938
		Protocol	1942
		Agreement	1952
A	Inter-American Statistical Institute (IASI) (see also International Statistical Institute)	Statutes	1942
T	Inter-American Trade Mark Bureau (originally Inter-American Bureau for the Protection of Trade Marks; see also International Union for the Protection of Industrial Property)	Convention	1912
			1926
			1931
T	Inter-American Tropical Tuna Commission	Convention	1950
A	Intergovernmental Committee for European Migration (succeeded by International Organization for Migration)	Constitution	1954
T	Intergovernmental Maritime Consultative Organization (IMCO) (succeeded Maritime Consultative Council; succeeded by International Maritime Organization)	Convention	1958
A	Interim Commission for International Trade Organization (also see International Trade Organization)	Conf. Res.	1946
A	International Agency for Cancer Research	Statute	1965
T	International Atomic Energy Agency (IAEA)	Statute	1957
A	International Authority for the Ruhr (IAR)	Agreement	1951
A	International Bank for Reconstruction and Development (IB/IBRD) (World Bank)	Arts. of Agr.	1945

Table 7.12 (continued)

Multilateral Organizations and Agencies, cont.

A	International Bureau of Education	Statute	1958
T	International Bureau of Weights and Measures	Convention	1878
T	International Center for the Exchange of Publications	Convention	1889
		Convention	1968
T	International Center for the Settlement of Investment Disputes	Convention	1966
A	International Center for the Study of the Preservation and Restoration of Cultural Property (ICCROM)	Statutes	1971
T	International Civil Aviation Organization (ICAO)	Convention	1947
T	International Commission for the Conservation of Atlantic Tunas	Convention	1969
T	International Commission for the Northwest Atlantic Fisheries	Convention	1950
T	International Commission of the Cape Spartel Light	Convention	1867
A	International Copper Study Group	Terms of Ref.	1992
A	International Cotton Advisory Committee	Conf. Res.	1939
A	International Criminal Police Commission (INTERPOL)	Statute	1938
T	International Council for the Exploration of the Seas (ICES)	Convention	1973
A	International Council of Scientific Unions [3]	Conf. Res.	1919
T	International Court of Justice (ICJ) (see also Permanent Court of Arbitration)	Statute	1945
A	International Development Association (IDA)	Arts. of Agr.	1960
A	International Energy Agency (IEA) (see also International Atomic Energy Agency)	Agreement	1974
A	International Finance Corporation (IFC)	Arts. of Agr.	1956
T	International Food Aid Committee (see also Food and Agriculture Organization)	Convention	1980
A	International Food Policy Research Institute (see also Food and Agriculture Organization)	Agreement	1981
A	International Fund for Agricultural Development (IFAD) (see also International Institute of Agriculture and International Seed Testing Association)	Agreement	1977
A	International Fund for Ireland	Agreement	1986
A	International Hydrographic Bureau (succeeded by International Hydrographic Organization)	Regulations or Statutes	1921
T	International Hydrographic Organization	Convention	1970
A	International Institute for Cotton	Arts. of Agr.	1966
A	International Institute for the Unification of Private Law (UNIDROIT)	Statute	1964
A	International Institute of Agriculture (succeeded by Food and Agriculture Organization (FAO); see also International Fund for Agricultural Development, and International Seed Testing Association)	Convention	1906
A	International Jute Organization	Agreement	1991
A	International Labor Organization (ILO)	Constitution	1934
		Amendment	1948
T	International Maritime Organization (IMO) (succeeded Intergovernmental Maritime Consultative Organization)	Convention	1982
A	International Maritime Satellite Organization (INMARSAT)	Convention	1979
A	International Meteorological Organization (succeeded by World Meteorological Organization)	Statutes	1930

[3]The International Council of Scientific Unions constitutes a federation of some twenty agencies, such as the International Astronomical Union, International Geographical Union, International Scientific Radio Union, International Union of Biological Sciences (which consists of half a dozen subagencies), International Union of Chemistry, International Union of Crystallography, International Union of Geodesy and Geophysics, International Union of History of Science, International Union of Pure and Applied Physics, International Union of Theoretical and Applied Mechanics, and others.

A	International Military Tribunal (Europe)	Charter	1945
A	International Military Tribunal (Far East)	Charter	1946
A	International Monetary Fund (IMF)	Arts. of Agr.	1945
T	International North Pacific Fisheries Commission	Convention	1953/1983
T	International Office of Epizootics	Agreement	1975
T	International Office of Public Health (succeeded by World Health Organization, 1948)	Agreement	1908
T	International Organization for Legal Metrology	Convention	1972
A	International Organization for Migration (IOM), (see Intergovernmental Committee for European Migration)	Constitution	1989
A	International Penal and Penitentiary Commission	Notes	1896
A	International Refugee Organization (IRO) (see also Intergovernmental Committee for European Migration)	Constitution	1948
A	International Rice Commission	Constitution	1949
A	International Rubber Study Group	Press Announcement	1944
A	International Seed Testing Association (see also Food and Agriculture Organization and International Institute of Agriculture)	Conf. Res.	1925
A	International Statistical Institute (see also Inter-American Statistical Institute)	Regulations	1924
A	International Sugar Council	Agreement	1937
A	International Technical Committee of Aerial Legal Experts (CITEJA) (see also International Civil Aviation Org.)	Conf. Res.	1931
T	International Telecommunication Union (ITU)	Convention	1906
A	International Telecommunications Satellite Organization (INTELSAT)	Agreement	1973
A	International Tin Study Group	Agreement	1946
A	International Trade in Textiles Committee	Arrangement	1974
T	International Trade Organization (ITO) (also see World Trade Organization)	Charter	1948 [4]
T	International Union for the Protection of Industrial Property (see also Inter-American Trade Mark Bureau)	Convention	1884
T	International Union for the Publication of Customs Tariffs	Convention	1891
A	International Union of Official Travel Organizations (succeeded by World Tourism Organization, 1975)	Conf. Res.	1949
A	International Vine and Wine Office	Agreement	1984
T	International Whaling Commission (IWC)	Convention	1948
T	International Wheat Council	Agreement	1949
A	International Wool Study Group	Conf. Res.	1946
A	Interparliamentary Union	Conf. Res.	1935
A	Interparliamentary Union for the Promotion of International Arbitration	Conf. Res.	1989
	INTERPOL (see International Criminal Police Commission)		
T	Maintenance of Certain Lights in the Red Sea ("Arrangement for")	Agreement	1966
A	Maritime Consultative Council (succeeded United Maritime Consultative Council; succeeded by Intergovernmental Maritime Consultative Organization)	Agreement	1947
A	Multilateral Investment Guarantee Agency	Convention	1987
A	North American Development Bank	Agreement	1993
A	North Atlantic Ice Patrol	Agreement	1956
T	North Atlantic Salmon Conservation Organization	Convention	1983

[4]The Charter for the International Trade Organization provided for an Interim Commission. It also required approval by the signatory governments (by the treaty process in the United States), but no signatory government approved it by the due date, September 30, 1949. It was superseded by the General Agreement on Tariffs and Trade.

Table 7.12 (continued)

Multilateral Organizations and Agencies, cont.

T	North Atlantic Treaty Organization (NATO)	Treaty	1949
T	North Pacific Fur Seal Commission	Convention	1957
T	North Pacific Marine Science Organization	Convention	1992
A	Onchocerciasis Fund	Agreement	1975
T	Organization for Economic Cooperation and Development (OECD)	Convention	1961
A	Organization for European Economic Cooperation	Convention	1948
T	Organization of American States (OAS) (see also Pan American Union)	Charter	1951
T	Pan American Health Organization (PAHO)	Convention	1906
	(superseded by World Health Organization)	Convention	1925
		Protocol	1928
A	Pan American Institute of Geography and History (PAIGH)	Statutes	1929
A	Pan American Railway Congress Association	Charter	1948
T	Pan American Sanitary Organization	Constitution	1947
A	Pan American Union (PAU) (incorporated into the Organization of American States, 1951)	Conf. Res.	1890
T	Permanent Court of Arbitration (PCA) (see also International Court of Justice)	Convention	1900
		Convention	1910
A	Permanent International Association of Navigation Congresses	Regulations	1902
A	Permanent International Association of Road Congresses	Regulations	1926
T	Postal Union of the Americas and Spain and Portugal (see also Universal Postal Union)	Convention	1922
A	South Pacific Commission (SPC)	Agreement	1948
T	Southeast Asia Treaty Organization (SEATO)	Treaty	1955
A	Terbella Development Fund	Agreement	1968
A	United Maritime Authority (succeeded by United Maritime Consultative Council; see also International Maritime Organization)	Agreement	1945
A	United Maritime Consultative Council (succeeded United Maritime Authority, and succeeded by Maritime Consultative Council)	Agreement	1946
A	United Nations Institute for Training and Research (UNITAR)	UN Resolution	1963
A	United Nations International Children's Emergency Fund (UNICEF)	UN Resolution	1946
A	United Nations Relief and Rehabilitation Administration (UNRRA)	Agreement	1943
A	United Nations Trade and Development Board (UNCTAD)	Conf. Res.	1964
T	United Nations (UN)	Charter	1945
A	United Nations Educational, Scientific and Cultural Organization (UNESCO)	Constitution	1946
A	United Nations Industrial Development Organization (UNIDO)	Charter	1966
A	United Nations War Crimes Commission (see also International Military Tribunals)	Notes	1943
T	Universal Postal Union (UPU)	Convention	1874
	World Court (see International Court of Justice)		
A	World Health Organization (WHO) (see also International Office of Public Health and Pan American Health Organization)	Constitution	1948
T	World Intellectual Property Organization (WIPO)	Convention	1970
T	World Meteorological Organization (WMO) (succeeded International Meteorological Organization)	Convention	1950

T	World Tourism Organization (succeeded International Union of Official Travel Organizations)	Statutes	1975
T	World Trade Organization (WTO)	Agreement	1995 [5]

B. Additional Multipartite Organizations and Agencies
(Temporary, Suspended, Superseded, or Terminated by 1950)[6]

Allied Mission to Observe Greek Elections, 1945-46
Allied Occupation Control Commissions or Councils for Austria (1945-55), Bulgaria (1944-47), Hungary (1945-47), Germany (1944-49), Japan (1945--), and Romania (1945-47)
Combined Civil Affairs Committee, 1943-49
Combined Coal Committee, 1945-47 (superseded by European Coal Organization)
Combined Food Board, 1942-46 (superseded by Food and Agriculture Organization)
Combined Footwear, Leather, and Hides Committee, 1945-48
Combined Liberated Areas Committee, 1944-46
Combined Rice Commission, 1946-47
Combined Rubber Committee, 1945-46 (also see International Rubber Study Group)
Combined Textile Committee, 1945-46
European Central Inland Transport Organization, 1945-47
Far Eastern Advisory Commission, Aug.-Dec., 1945 (superseded by Far Eastern Commission)
Inter-American Development Commission, 1940-48
Inter-American Emergency Advisory Committee for Political Defense, 1942-48
Intergovernmental Committee on Refugees, 1938-48 (superseded by International Refugee Organization)
International Commission for the Decennial Revision of Lists of Diseases and Causes of Death, 1893-1948 (superseded by World Health Organization)
International Emergency Food Council, 1946-49 (superseded by Food and Agriculture Org.)
International Tin Committee, 1931-46
Tripartite Merchant Marine Commission, 1945-47

C. Other Organizations and Agencies Entitled To
Diplomatic Privileges and Immunities by the United States [7]

Border Environment Cooperation Commission, 1994
Commission for Environmental Cooperation, 1994
Commission for Labor Cooperation, 1994
Commission for the Study of Alternatives to the Panama Canal, 1986
Customs Cooperation Council, 1971
International Coffee Organization, 1965
International Committee of the Red Cross, 1988
International Development Law Institute, 1993
International Fertilizer Development Center, 1977
International Pacific Halibut Commission, 1962
International Secretariat for Volunteer Service, 1967
North Pacific Anadromous Fish Commission, 1994
North Pacific Marine Science Organization, 1994
Organization for European Economic Cooperation, 1950 (superseded by Organization for Economic Cooperation and Development)

[5] In December 1993 the General Agreement on Tariffs and Trade (GATT) system was liberalized and converted into the World Trade Organization.

[6] A few of these were tripartite agencies, such as the Combined Civil Affairs Committee and several commodity and other boards and committees; the Allied Control Commission for Austria and the Allied Control Council for Germany were quadripartite; and more than a dozen had more than four members. Only two of these temporary agencies—the post–World War II Allied Commission for Austria and the Allied Council for Japan—continued into the 1950s.

[7] As specified in the U.S. Code, Title 22, Chapter 7, Subchapter 18.

Table 7.12 (continued)

Other Organizations and Agencies, cont.

Organization of African Unity, 1974
Organization of Eastern Caribbean States, 1989
Pacific Salmon Commission, 1986
United International Bureau for the Protection of Intellectual Property, 1969

D. Bilateral Agencies [8]

Alaskan International Highway Commission—U.S. and Canada
American-Mexican Claims Commission
Anglo-American Rice Commission
British-American Interparliamentary Group
British-American Joint Patent Interchange Committee *
Canada-United States Interparliamentary Group
Claims Committee, U.S. and Spain *
Combined Chiefs of Staff, U.S. and United Kingdom *
Combined Civil Affairs Committee, U.S. and United Kingdom *
Commissions of Inquiry—with 44 other countries
Filipino Rehabilitation Commission—U.S. and Philippines
Conciliation Commissions—with 5 other countries
Great Lakes Fishery Commission—U.S. and Canada
International Boundary Commission—U.S. and Canada
International Boundary and Water Commission—U.S. and Mexico
International Fisheries Commission—U.S. and Canada
International Joint Commission—U.S. and Canada (for waterways)
Joint Agricultural Committee—U.S. and Canada *
Joint Aircraft Committee—U.S. and United Kingdom *
Joint Brazilian-United States Defense Commission *
Joint Hide Control Office—U.S. and United Kingdom *
Joint Mexican-United States Defense Commission *
Joint United States-Canadian Commission on Trade and Economic Affairs
Mexican-American Industrial Commission
Mexican-United States Agricultural Commission
Mexico-United States Interparliamentary Group
Munitions Assignments Board—U.S. and United Kingdom *
Permanent Joint Board on Defense—U.S. and Canada *
Trans-Isthmian Highway Board—U.S. and Mexico *
United States-Indian Joint Commission
United States-Irani Joint Commission
United States-Japan Joint Committee on Trade and Economic Affairs
United States-Mexican Binational Commission
United States-Mexico Border Health Commission
United States-Spanish Council
United States-St. Lawrence Advisory Committee—U.S. and Canada

[8]*Indicates temporary, World War II agencies.

Note: For a list of special voluntary international programs and agencies, including a series of specialized funds established by the United Nations and other international organizations, see the *United States Government Organization Manual.*

general categories—a cumulated list of multilateral organizations in existence since 1945, additional multilateral agencies that were temporary or were otherwise terminated, others that have been identified as entitled to possess diplomatic privileges and immunities under American law and presidential executive orders, and those that are bilateral in membership.

Other features distinguish among various types of organizations. In terms of participants, the majority are universal or global. Many are regional (including inter-American, European, and a few Middle East, African, and Asian), and some are bilateral (especially involving the United States and Canada, Mexico, and the United Kingdom). Functional types embrace those that are general or broad-scale (such as the United Nations and the Organization of American States) and those that are concerned primarily with policy making, regulating and rule making, administration, and servicing for common interests, programs, and clienteles, to which may be added those specialized institutions that deal with adjudication or peaceful settlement of claims and other disputes. Combined, they encompass a comprehensive network of political and operational instruments that supplement traditional diplomacy and international conferencing.

Contemporary International Organization System

Aside from the standby peaceful settlement agencies, during the half century following World War II the United States was a member of nearly 250 international organizations and other agencies, of which more than 190 were newly established. Of those listed in Part A of Table 7.12, the United States affiliated with nearly 30 percent during the 1940s. Only eight of these antedated the twentieth century, and ten were added between 1900 and 1918. Thereafter, the rate of affiliation increased, especially during the four decades from 1940 to 1979, and only a few were added in the early 1990s.

The titles of these organizations vary considerably. The title "United Nations" is unique in that historically, it has two meanings. During World War II it was used to identify the wartime Anti-Axis informal alliance, but currently it is understood to constitute an international organization.[196] The most common designation is "commission," applied to more than 100, followed by "organization" (forty-two), "committee" (twenty-six), "council" (sixteen), and "institute" (thirteen). Other titles are agency, association, board, bureau, center, office, group, and union. More descriptive titles, applied to financial institutions, are bank, fund, and corporation, and some adjudicatory agencies are designated as court or tribunal. Still other titles, rarely employed, are administration, alliance, mission, secretariat, and service. Some of these are logically applicable, whereas differences among others, such as agency, board, bureau, commission, committee, and council, are less apparent.

The titles of their constitutive acts also differ. The most formal and pretentious is "constitution," applied to only nine agencies, most of which were created prior to 1950, such as the Food and Agriculture Organization, International

Labor Organization, International Refugee Organization, United Nations Educational, Scientific and Cultural Organization, and the World Health Organization. Some half dozen are founded on constitutive acts called "charter," including the United Nations and the Organization of American States, and approximately fifteen are based on "statutes," including the International Court of Justice, International Atomic Energy Agency, International Criminal Police Commission, International Institute for the Unification of Private Law, and International Meteorological Organization.

By far the most common designations are international convention (forty-five) and agreement (forty, supplemented with half a dozen articles of agreement (used primarily for international banks and funds), whereas the title "treaty" is employed in only a few cases, primarily for defense and security agencies, such as the North Atlantic Treaty Organization. Other titles, descriptive of their sources, are simply denominated as conference communiqués or resolutions, declarations, and diplomatic exchanges of notes. Remaining titles range from general act to arrangement, regulations, and rules.[197] In many cases it is difficult to comprehend or justify the pragmatic use of these titles.

One of the interesting, but perplexing, features of American affiliation with international organizations is the flexibility of the constitutional process whereby the United States subscribes to their constitutive acts, which was liberalized considerably during this half century. Prior to 1900 it was common to undertake commitments to such agencies, even some of minor significance, by the formal treaty process. Similarly, of the international agencies joined between 1900 and 1918, all but one were founded on treaties.[198] However, in the twentieth century, as indicated in Part A of Table 7.12, more than 105, or nearly two-thirds, were joined by means of executive agreements, reflecting a major shift in executive-legislative relations.

To illustrate the bewildering history of the process of joining these organizations, the United States regarded the United Nations Charter and the constitutive acts of only eight of its specialized agencies as formal treaties. Similarly, those of the Permanent Court of Arbitration (Hague Tribunal), the International Court of Justice, and inter-American tribunals were deemed to be treaties, but the World War II military tribunals for Europe and the Far East and the Inter-American Juridical Committee were not. Moreover, all of the dozens of bilateral commitments providing for arbitration and conciliation agencies and commissions of inquiry were embodied in formal treaties, as was that of the International Center for the Settlement of Investment Disputes, whereas those of the Inter-American Commercial Arbitration Commission and the Interparliamentary Union for the Promotion of International Arbitration were regarded as executive agreements.

Understandably, affiliation with such defense and security agencies as North Atlantic Treaty Organization, the ANZUS collective security organization, the Southeast Asia Treaty Organization, and the Inter-American Collective Defense Arrangement (Rio Pact) was consummated by treaties, but the constitutive acts of the Inter-American Defense Board and the Inter-American Emergency Advisory Committee for Political Defense were not. On the other hand, the series of World War II commissions and councils established to deal with planning and administering military occupation of the defeated Axis powers, civil affairs, repatriation, and similar matters, which were regarded as temporary agencies and many of which embraced primarily military affairs, were all founded on executive agreements.[199]

Less comprehensible was the process of affiliation with more than twenty-five international banks, funds, and other important economic and financial, investment, and foreign aid and development agencies. Surprisingly, all of the articles of agreement, charters, conventions, and other instruments creating the fourteen banks and funds, entailing substantial funding, were treated as executive agreements.[200] On the other hand, evidencing high regard for important rights of nations and devotion to conservation, the constitutive acts of agencies concerned with fishing (including whaling and the capture of fur seals) were dealt with by the treaty process. Yet, of the twenty-three commodity agencies, only three of their constitutive acts were dealt with as treaties, whereas all but three of the twelve agencies concerned with agriculture were handled as executive agreements, including the Food and Agriculture Organization.

On balance, despite such apparent inconsistencies, the trend toward increased U.S. affiliation by instruments other than formal treaties is both comprehensible and defensible. In view of the liberalization of relations of the Executive and Congress, it has become easier for the United States to join a wider spectrum of such international agencies as an accompaniment of its leadership in promoting international cooperation in world affairs, and this is likely to continue.

These organizations and agencies differ considerably so far as their deliberation, policy making, and administration are concerned. The most sophisticated involve periodic conferences or plenary organs, an operational or administrative organ (often with its own substructure and personnel), and, in some cases, a conciliating or adjudicatory facility. The most comprehensive is the United Nations, comprising the General Assembly, Security Council, Economic and Social Council, Trusteeship Council, International Court of Justice, and Secretariat.[201] Its specialized agencies, which are autonomous, have their own constitutive acts, memberships, and organizational structure and usually are affiliated with the United Nations by "working agreements."[202] Other organizations with complex structures include the Organization of American States, the North Atlantic Treaty Organization and other security agencies, and others that function as continuing agencies and to which the United States assigns permanent representatives. The simpler international institutions generally consist of merely a deliberative body supported by a small servicing secretariat.

Most impressive is the extensive catalog of subjects handled by these organizations and agencies, which may be grouped in thirty-five categories, as listed in Table 7.13.[203]

The most numerous categories, each of which involves ten or more agencies, are peaceful settlement, followed by commodities, defense and security, economic and financial matters, fisheries, food and agriculture, foreign aid and assistance, legal affairs (including tribunals), the seas and maritime affairs (including navigation and shipping), trade and tariffs, and, not surprisingly, World

Table 7.13
International Organizations—Principal Subject Categories

General	2	Legal affairs (including tribunals, penal affairs, and war crimes)	11
Airspace and outer space	4		
Boundaries and borders (with Canada and Mexico)	4	Meteorology	2
		Patents and trademarks	3
Claims	2	Peaceful settlement (including Hague Tribunal and International Court of Justice) b	51
Commodities a	23		
Communications and transportation	6		
Defense and security	13	Population, migration, refugees, and rehabilitation	5
Economic, development, and financial	23	Postal affairs	2
		Reparations	1
Education and culture	5	Rivers and waterways	3
Energy (including atomic and nuclear)	3	Science and technology c	7
		Seas, shipping, maritime, and navigation	11
Environment	2		
Fisheries	14	Social affairs and human rights	6
Food and agriculture	12	Statistics	2
Foreign aid and assistance	15	Trade, customs, and tariffs	10
Health	5	Travel and tourism	2
Hydrography	2	Weights and Measures	1
Intellectual Property	2	World War II occupations, civil affairs, and administration (including war crimes)	14
Interparliamentary relations	4		
Labor	2		
		Others d	

aThe commodities include coal, coffee, cotton, leather and hides, jute, liquor, rice, rubber, sugar, textiles, tin, wheat, wine, and wool.

bThe peaceful settlement agencies include the Permanent Court of Arbitration, International Court of Justice, arbitration tribunals, commissions of inquiry, conciliation commissions, international military tribunals, and the International Center for the Settlement of Investment Disputes.

cIn addition to several other agencies, the International Council of Scientific Unions consolidates the interests of such agencies as the International Astronomical Union, International Geographical Union, International Union of Biological Sciences, International Union of Chemistry, International Union of Crystallography, International Union of Geodesy and Geophysics, International Union of the History of Science, International Union of Pure and Applied Physics, International Union of Theoretical and Applied Mechanics, and others.

dSome examples are listed in the statement on functionally unique international organizations.

War II military occupation and civil administration. The subjects with the lowest numbers, with three or fewer agencies, include the general organizations (United Nations and Organization of American States), claims, energy, environment, hydrography, intellectual property, labor, outer space, patents and trademarks, postal affairs, reparations, rivers and waterways, statistics, travel and tourism, and weights and measures.

In addition to the United Nations and the Organization of American States, their specialized organizations, the Permanent Court of Arbitration and International Court of Justice, the geographic security organizations, and the international and regional banks, funds, and aid and development agencies, this galaxy also encompasses a group of other basic institutions. These embrace the International Bureau of Weights and Measures, International Center for the Exchange of Publications, International Center for the Study of the Preservation and Restoration of Cultural Property, International Criminal Police Commission, International Energy Agency, International Maritime Satellite Organization, International Statistical Institute, International Union for the Protection of Industrial Property, and International Union for the Publication of Customs Tariffs—all important global agencies.

However, some organizations are functionally unique, most of which are highly specialized. At the global level these are exemplified by the Bureau of International Expositions, Commission for the Conservation of Antarctic Marine Living Resources, International Committee of the Red Cross, International Council for the Exploration of the Sea, North Atlantic Ice Patrol, and the World Tourism Organization. Others, more esoteric or limited geographically, are illustrated by the Alaskan International Highway Commission, Central Bureau of the International Map of the World on the Millionth Scale, Committee of Control of the International Zone of Tangier, Commission for the Study of Alternatives to the Panama Canal, International Commission of the Cape Spartel Light, International Commission for the Decennial Revision of Lists of Diseases and Causes of Death, International Fertilizer Development Center, International Office of Epizootics, International Organization of Legal Metrology, International Secretariat for Volunteer Service, and the Onchocerciasis Fund. The possibilities for such specialized agencies seems endless and are likely to be added in the future.

Department of State and International Organizations

Whereas previously, the matter of Department of State management and servicing of American relations with these international institutions was dealt with on an ad hoc basis, in January 1944 a Division of International Organization and Security was created as part of its Office of Special Political Affairs, which devoted its attention primarily to the evolution of the United Nations. Later that year it was superseded by a separate Division of International Organization, Security, and Dependent Areas Affairs. During the 1950s departmental responsibility was assigned to its Office of International Administration and Conferences, which was converted into a separate Bureau of International Organization Affairs (consisting of several divisions), which has since continued as the Department's primary administrative unit for managing American relations with international organizations. It provides guidance and support for American participation in them and for the development, coordination, and implementation of multilateral policy, although other departmental offices and bureaus also are concerned with certain areal and functional international agencies.

Responsibility for selecting American delegates to the plenary organ or con-

ference of international agencies frequently devolves upon the Department of
State. This has been the case even for some commodity agencies in which other
units of the National Government have a more direct and cogent interest. In
other instances it serves to coordinate the selection of delegates, and, in still
others, special arrangements are made for their designation. To mention a few,
the Commissioner of Patents has served as the American member at meetings
of the International Union for the Protection of Industrial Property, the Postmaster General has named delegates to the Universal Postal Union, and Congress
has selected delegates to attend the meetings of the Interparliamentary Union.

Whether it has a direct interest in the substantive affairs of the international
organization or not, the State Department usually exercises supervisory control
over the relations and communications of the U.S. Government with the agency.
However, some of them deal directly with other units of the American government. The technicians of the National Bureau of Standards coordinate with the
International Bureau of Weights and Measures, and to deal with international
bank and fund matters the Departments of State, Treasury, and Commerce coordinate their actions with the Chairman of the Federal Reserve and the President
of the Export-Import Bank. Such arrangements are essential for dealing with
some of the more important international organizations for which it is impossible
to rely solely upon unilateral State Department supervision.

Another important innovation was introduced by the Department of State to
deal with representation in certain international organizations. In many cases it
had assigned special teams to attend their occasional sessions. However, after
World War II it introduced the practice of appointing permanent chiefs of mission (with staffs) to represent the State Department on a continuing basis in a
number of organizations and to participate in other long-range negotiations. Beginning in December 1945 it appointed former Secretary of State Stettinius as
the first American Chief of Mission to the United Nations, bearing the title U.S.
Representative with the rank of Ambassador, stationed at New York City.

Since then similar permanent representatives have been designated to such
international agencies and offices as the European Office of the United Nations
(Geneva), the Food and Agriculture Organization (Rome), International Atomic
Energy Agency (Vienna), International Civil Aviation Organization (Montreal),
North Atlantic Treaty Organization (Brussels), Organization for Economic Cooperation and Development (Paris), Organization of American States (Washington), United Nations Educational, Scientific, and Cultural Organization (Paris),
the European Union (which amalgamated three preexisting Western European
Communities in 1967 and in which the United States is not a member, Brussels),
and the U.S. Office for Arms Reduction Negotiations (Geneva). Only a small
fraction of these appointees are career Foreign Service Officers.

At times the Department of State also sends ''observer missions'' to those
international agencies in which it has no formal membership but is concerned
with their activities. The principal function of such representatives is to report

to the Department, but they do not participate in discussions unless the organizations permit it, nor do they have the privilege of joining in the decision-making process. Nonmember observerships have become common practice for many international conferences and organizations since World War II. Branded "an ear without a mouth," they may be regarded as official or unofficial, and they rank below the representatives of regular members.

One of the serious problems of the Department of State is the matter of influencing voting and the financing of the United Nations and other international organizations and averting the United Nations system from presuming to assume the aura of a super-or world government. Illustrating the matter of financial contributions of the United States to these agencies, from 1946 to the mid-1990s, the regular annual budget of the United Nations, as approved by its General Assembly, mushroomed from approximately $19,400,000 to more than $2.5 billion.[204] When the United Nations was established, the United States was responsible for 39.89 percent of its annual budget. This was gradually reduced to 25 percent by 1974,[205] but still amounted to annual assessments of more than $.5 billion in the 1990s, not including additional massive "voluntary contributions" for costs of emergency programs, constabulary functions, or assessments for United Nations specialized agencies and other organizations.

Combined, American contributions to the United Nations, its specialized agencies, the inter-American system, and other global agencies, including both budgeted assessments and voluntary contributions, have soared since 1945 and are likely to continue to escalate. To these must be added the capitalization of international banks and funds and the financing of the North Atlantic Treaty Organization and its military establishment, as well as other regional institutions.

The United States derives many advantages from dealing multilaterally with other governments within the framework of these international forums. For example, it plays a leading role in initiating the creation of such organizations, possesses freedom in determining which agencies it wishes to join, and participates in designing their common goals and programs. Furthermore, instead of being bound by the process of decision making constrained by the rule of unanimity, which existed in the League of Nations, the formula for many contemporary international institutions is based on majority determination, including the United Nations, except for Great Power voting in the Security Council.

Often these organizations, especially those of a general nature, also serve as sparking agents for introducing new issues, plans, and the convening of international conferences. Most important, membership in these international agencies enables American diplomats to deal simultaneously and often continuously, bilaterally as well as multilaterally, with the representatives of many foreign governments at a neutral site. These forums differ in size, varying from a few, to nineteen members of the North Atlantic Treaty Organization, thirty-five in the Organization of American States, and more than 180 in the United Nations, some of its specialized agencies, and other global organizations. Collectively, therefore, they constitute a major supplement to traditional bilateral diplomatic representation and negotiation and enhance the role and responsibilities of the Department of State.

However, when assessments and contributions are related to decision making and voting power in a parliamentary international confederation like the United Nations, the United States is confronted with serious disadvantages. While it is assessed at the rate of one-fourth of the annual United Nations budget, in the General Assembly in which each member has an equal vote, the United States possesses no greater voting authority than some ninety other members, such as Afghanistan, Angola, Barbados, Chad, Fiji, Grenada, Haiti, Lebanon, Liberia, Malta, and Yemen—each of which contributes merely 0.01 percent of the budget. Consequently, on the United Nations budget and other issues decided by the General Assembly by simple majority vote, the United States can be outvoted by any two such states. In fact, these minimum contributors, which, combined, contribute less than only 1 percent of the assessment, wield approximately 50 percent of the total voting power.[206]

This inequity and the inflation of the administrative personnel and salaries at times have resulted in reluctance by the United States to pay its full assessment on time, which produced difficulties not only for the operation of the United Nations but also in American executive-legislative relations and public attitudes, with the Department of State caught in the difficult posture of compromising conflicting interests and positions. It may have been wiser, therefore, to equate voice and voting power with responsibility by requiring some form of unanimity for certain matters, such as determining budgets and financial contributions.

In summary, certain international organizations will be remembered for their longevity, including the Permanent Court of Arbitration, International Bureau of Weights and Measures, International Center for the Exchange of Publications, International Union for the Protection of Industrial Property, Pan-American Union, and the Universal Postal Union. Many are notable for their extensive or universal membership, represented by the United Nations and its specialized agencies, the International Court of Justice, the inter-American system, the International Criminal Police Commission, the International Meteorological Organization, and the International Union for the Publication of Customs Tariffs. A goodly number are recognized for their administration of extensive and worthy programs of assistance, development, and other services. Others are noted for sponsoring international conferences, producing common standards, or prescribing necessary regulations and rules. Finally, a few, especially the United Nations and the Organization of American States, are celebrated for their prominence and utility or, as in the case of the North Atlantic Treaty Organization and other regional security agencies, for their strategic significance.

As in the past, subjects of mutual concern that may be handled by such international organizations will be added unless they are politically too sensitive to be relegated to these agencies. Nevertheless, U.S. participation in multilateral and parliamentary diplomacy may be expected to continue to grow, requiring increased Department of State involvement and a greater burden of responsibility for representation, communication, deliberation, negotiation, and administration. Future changes, needs, interests, and growth of the international organization system are likely to require it to devote more attention, personnel, and funding to deal with their sessions and other activities. As these multilateral and bilateral institutions increase in number and variety and extend their programs, it is likely that the workload of the Department of State to manage American participation will increase, and more permanent representatives and missions will be appointed.[207]

DOCUMENTS AND PUBLICATIONS OF THE DEPARTMENT OF STATE

Despite the oft-repeated assertions concerning the people's right to know and secrecy enshrouding the Department of State, American foreign policy, and international relations, the quantity of documentary and literary materials published or otherwise publicly available is monumental, much of which is put into the public domain by the Department and private scholars. Although subjected to widespread debate and contrary to popular belief and the allegations of an insatiable media and others, the American Government pursues a liberal revelation and publication policy for its foreign affairs documentation, a practice initiated early in the nineteenth century. The inventory of regularized and ad hoc official publications on the Department and the conduct of American diplomacy, together with those on the formulation, essence, and implementation of policy, is massive, and the opening of diplomatic archival documentation, though sometimes not immediate, has been systematized and is comprehensive.

Foreign Relations of the United States Series

Among the most widely reputed and used American diplomatic publications is the *Foreign Relations of the United States* series. It was launched by Secretary of State William H. Seward in 1861, when he decided to publish his important foreign dispatches to provide a public record of then contemporary diplomacy. Initially designated *Papers Relating to Foreign Affairs Accompanying the Annual Message of the President to the Congress*, these were retitled *Papers Relating to the Foreign Relations of the United States* in 1870 and *Foreign Relations of the United States: Diplomatic Papers* in 1932, and they were abbreviated to their present title following World War II (1947). Currently, they are popularly known as *Foreign Relations*, or simply as *FRUS*.

This series has been published for more than 135 years (except for 1869). Originally, one or two volumes were produced each year, increased to five or more by 1932, and, due to the enormous expansion of annual American diplomatic documentation, since 1952 they are published for triyear cycles, numbering up to twenty or more volumes per three-year period. Since the early 1860s more than 350 volumes have been published. Called "the Historical Voice of America" by historian Samuel Flagg Bemis and denominated by political scientist Benjamin Williams as one of "the most valuable of all Department of State publications," this series is regarded as the most comprehensive and among the most current compilations of national diplomatic papers in the world.

The production of the *Foreign Relations* series has been regularized by the Department of State Basic Authorities Act of August 1, 1956, as amended on October 28, 1991. These laws require the continuing publication of these volumes, "which shall be a thorough, accurate, and reliable documentary record of major United States foreign policy decisions and significant United States diplomatic activity," and specify that they "shall be published not more than 30 years after the events recorded." They attribute responsibility for their preparation to the "Historian of the Department of State"; authorize the establishment of an "Advisory Committee on Historical Diplomatic Documentation" to review the records and provide advice and recommendations for the production of the volumes[208]; and require other government agencies to cooperate "by providing full and complete access to the records pertinent to United States foreign policy decisions and actions by providing copies of selected records, in accordance with the procedures developed," subject to certain exceptions. The acts also deal with the establishment of procedures for identifying records for the series, the process for declassifying them, and the relationship of this process to both the Privacy Act (to protect the sanctity of personal records) and the Freedom of Information Act.[209]

These *Foreign Relations* volumes contain the texts of diplomatic communications, exchanges of notes, reports, and other official papers relating to the foreign affairs and diplomacy of the United States, including those both originating with, and received by, the American Government. Materials are generally arranged by country and major events, grouped by geographic areas and by selected functional fields, sometimes arranged separately. Usually, each volume is individually indexed. The State Department characterizes them as containing "all documents needed to give a comprehensive record of the major foreign policy decisions within the range of the Department of State's responsibilities, together with appropriate materials concerning the facts which contributed to the formulation of policies." Documents in the files of the State Department are supplemented by papers from other government agencies involved in the matters treated. The volumes are compiled and edited by the Office of the Historian in accordance with the official guidance rules and procedures promulgated by Secretary Frank B. Kellogg on March 26, 1925, and individual documents are subject to review for declassification by a formal review process.

During the twentieth century the management of preparing and publishing the *Foreign Relations* was made the responsibility of a series of experienced, able chiefs, several of whom had previous State Department experience, a few who were recruited from academic institutions, and some who remained in charge for lengthy periods. These include Philip H. Patchin, a Journalist with foreign experience who served as Director of Information in the Department; Gaillard Hunt, who began his State Department career as a clerk, became Chief of the Passport Bureau and later the Citizenship Bureau, retired in 1908 after twenty-one years, became Chief of the Manuscript Division of the Library of Congress, published his comprehensive history of *The Department of State* in 1914, and returned to the State Department during World War I and was named Chief of its Division of Publications; Tyler Dennett, a historian with an acknowledged reputation, who succeeded as Chief of the Division of Publications, was designated as Historical Adviser in 1929, and resigned two years later; and David Hunter Miller, a lawyer who became Historical Adviser in 1931, who is remembered for producing his seminal eight-volume *Treaties and Other International Acts of the United States* (published 1931–48).

After World War II, they were followed by Dr. George Bernard Noble, Professor of Political Science who became a State Department careerist, served as Assistant Chief of Historical Policy Research and Publications, and later, in 1953, became Historical Adviser; Dr. David F. Trask, Professor of History at the State University of New York, recruited from the outside in 1976 and later titled Historian of the Department of State; and Dr. William Z. Slany, a State Department careerist since 1956 who served in the Historical Office and advanced up the ranks to be appointed the Historian.

Occasionally, the Department of State also publishes special volumes, appendixes, and supplements as components of the *Foreign Relations* series, dealing with a particular country, territory, event, or negotiation. Examples include volumes entitled *Affairs in Hawaii* (1895), *Whaling and Sealing Claims Against Russia* (1903), *World War I, 1914–1918* (nine volumes, 1928–1933), *Russia, 1918* (three volumes, 1931–32), *The Lansing Papers, 1914–1920* (two volumes, 1939), *Paris Peace Conference, 1919* (thirteen volumes, 1942–47), *Japan, 1931–1941* (two volumes, 1943), and *The Soviet Union, 1933–1939* (1952). Special volumes have also been published on World War II summit conferences and meetings entitled *Conferences at Washington, 1941–1942, and Casablanca, 1943* (1968), *Conferences at Washington and Quebec, 1943* (1970), *Conferences at Cairo and Tehran, 1943* (1961), *The Conference at Quebec, 1944* (1972), *The Conferences at Malta and Yalta, 1945* (1955), and *The Conference of Berlin (Potsdam) 1945* (two volumes, 1960). In 1966 the State Department also released the first volume devoted entirely to intelligence agencies and issues, entitled *Emergence of the Intelligence Establishment, 1945–1950*.

The major problems relating to the production and publication of the *Foreign Relations* volumes involve legislative and administrative authorization for their compilation and publication; the burgeoning volume of documentation that needs to be surveyed and the depth of penetration to be systematically published; distinguishing between information and documentation, preliminary and end-product documents, and release (rendering available) and formal publication of documents; secrecy versus openness, classification, and clearance for publication; the maintenance of an adequate and proficient staff to produce the increasing quantity of volumes; the time lag between the dates of publication and the years to which the volumes pertain; and the cost of both production and publication.

Initially, these volumes were published shortly after the years in which the documents were produced. The time lag reached twenty years by 1960, and by the early 1970s it exceeded twenty-five years. In 1960 the Secretary of State set the timing at twenty years, but this schedule was unattainable, largely because of the size of documentary resources, currently numbering hundreds of thousands of papers annually, and the extensive clearance requirement but also because of budgetary and personnel restrictions. In 1972 President Nixon issued a directive requiring a return to the twenty-year standard, but this also proved to be optimistic. As previously noted, the Act of 1991 fixed the maximum timing at thirty years.[210]

Other Department of State Publications

The Department of State also produces and publishes a great many other materials, a sampling of which is listed in Table 7.14. For catalogs of State Department unpublished records, beginning in 1789, for example, see *Preliminary Inventory of the General Records of the Department of State* (National Archives, Records Group 59, 1963); *List of Foreign Service Post Records in the National Archives* (Records Group 84, 1958); and *List of National Archives Microfilm Publications* (1968).

These publications and other materials embrace historical and contemporary collections, volumes, guides, indexes, commentaries, and records concerned with foreign affairs research resources; the Department of State, the Foreign Service, and diplomatic and consular missions and personnel; international conferences, meetings, and organizations and other agencies; treaty making and the nature and texts of treaties and agreements; foreign policy and relations respecting particular geographic regions and specific countries; topical and functional subjects; and a good many other matters.[211]

Table 7.14
Diplomatic Documents and Publications

The Department of State produces and publishes a prodigious quantity and a substantial variety of studies, collections, pamphlets, and other types of publications dealing with its activities, the diplomacy of the United States, and other aspects of American foreign policy and relations. Aside from the *Foreign Relations of the United States*, this table provides a sampling of such materials, giving their titles, their individual authors or editors where they are identified, and their dates of publication. Most of them are official publications, printed by the U.S. Government Printing Office, although some, including several earlier volumes, were privately printed. Arrangement is by category and thereunder alphabetically by titles, except where chronological sequence is noted. The preponderant majority were produced by the Office of the Historian. An asterisk identifies a number of relevant unofficial volumes and other materials.

Research Resources

The Availability of Department of State Records, William M. Franklin (1973).

Foreign Affairs Research: A Directory of Governmental Resources (1967), which was superseded by *Governmental Resources Available for Foreign Affairs Research* (1963 and revised in 1965).

*"The Future of the *Foreign Relations* Series," William M. Franklin, in *The National Archives and Foreign Relations Research*, ed. Milton O. Gustafson (Athens: Ohio University Press, 1974).

Government Publications and Their Use, Laurence F. Schmeckebier and Roy B. Eastin (2d ed., 1969).

Government Resources Available for Foreign Affairs Research, Linda Lowenstein, ed. (1965).

Public Availability of Diplomatic Archives (1963, rev. ed. 1976).

*"Research on the Conduct of American Foreign Relations," Elmer Plischke, *International Studies Quarterly* 15 (June 1971): 221–50.

Washington Sources in International Affairs, Genevieve C. Linebarger et al. (College Park: Bureau of Governmental Research, University of Maryland, 1951).

Guides to Publications

American Diplomacy: A Bibliography of Biographies, Autobiographies, and Commentaries, Elmer Plischke (College Park: Bureau of Governmental Research, University of Maryland, 1957).

American Foreign Relations: A Bibliography of Official Sources, Elmer Plischke (College Park: Bureau of Governmental Research, University of Maryland, 1966).

A Guide to Bibliographic Tools for Research in Foreign Affairs, Helen F. Conover, ed. (2d ed., 1958).

Guide to the Diplomatic History of the United States, Samuel Flagg Bemis and Grace Gardner Griffin, eds. (1935).

Major Publications of the Department of State: An Annotated Bibliography (pamphlet, initially published as *Publications of the Department of State* for 1929–52, 1953–57, and 1958–60 and, beginning in the 1960s, is updated and published periodically.

A Pocket Guide to Foreign Policy Information Materials and Services of the U.S. Department of State (1968, irregular).

Publications of the Department of State (3 vols., 1929–53, 1953–57, and 1958–60; subsequently publications listed in *Department of State Bulletin*).

U.S. Foreign Relations: A Guide to Information Sources, Elmer Plischke (Detroit: Gale Research, 1980).

Indexes to Historical Collections (Chronological)

Index to United States Documents Relating to Foreign Affairs, 1828–1861, Adelaide R. Hasse, ed. (3 vols., 1914–21).

General Index to the Published Volumes of the Diplomatic Correspondence and Foreign Relations of the United States, 1861–1899 (1902).

Papers Relating to the Foreign Relations of the United States: General Index, 1900–1918 (1941).

Table 7.14 (continued)

Basic Historical Collections (Chronological)

The Revolutionary Diplomatic Correspondence of the United States, Francis Wharton, ed. (6 vols, 1899).

The Diplomatic Correspondence of the United States of America, from the Signing of the Definitive Treaty of Peace, 10th September, 1783, to the Adoption of the Constitution, March 4, 1789 (7 vols, 1833–34; 2d ed, 1837, 7 vols; 3d ed, 1855, 3 vols.).

Foreign Relations in American State Papers: Documents, Legislative and Executive, of the Congress of the United States (1789–1828, 6 vols., published 1832–61).

Foreign Relations of the United States—FRUS (annual 1862– ; see separate discussion).

Basic Current Collections (chronological)

Peace and War: United States Foreign Policy, 1931–1941 (1943).

Postwar Foreign Policy Preparation, 1939–1945 (1949).

A Decade of American Foreign Policy: Basic Documents, 1941–1949 (1950).

American Foreign Policy, 1950–1955: Basic Documents (1957).

American Foreign Policy: Current Documents, 1956–1967 (annual, 1959–); also *American Foreign Policy: Basic Documents, 1977–1980* (1983).

*Contemporary U.S. Foreign Policy: Documents and Commentary, Elmer Plischke, ed. (Westport, Conn.: Greenwood, 1991).

Department of State

A. General Histories (chronological)

The Department of State of the United States: Its History and Functions (comprehensive, 1893).

History of the Department of State of the United States: Its Functions and Duties . . . , William H. Michael (comprehensive, 1901).

The Department of State of the United States: Its History and Functions, Gaillard Hunt (comprehensive, 1914).

*The Department of State: Its History and Functions, Gaillard Hunt (comprehensive, New Haven, CT: Yale University Press, 1914).

The Department of State of the United States (1933).

The Department of State of the United States, E. Wilder Spaulding and George Verne Blue (rev. ed., 1936).

The Department of State of the United States, William Gerber (1942).

*The Department of State: A History of Its Organization, Procedure, and Personnel, Graham H. Stuart (comprehensive, New York: Macmillan, 1949).

The Department of State Today (1951).

The Department of State, 1930–1955 (1955).

Department of State–1963: A Report to the Citizen (1963).

A Short History of the Department of State, 1781–1981 (Bicentennial, David F. Trask, with the assistance of David M. Buehler and Evan M. Duncan, 1981).

B. Others

Biographic Register of the Department of State—in 1950s, later changed to *The Biographic Register* (contains biographies of principal officers of the Department of State and other foreign relations agencies, members of the diplomatic service, Foreign Service, and Foreign Service Reserve, and Foreign Service Staff Officers (published occasionally since 1833; after 1974 issued only as classified editions with limited distribution).

Diplomacy for the 70's: A Program of Management Reform for the Department of State, William B. Macomber, Jr. (1970).

*The Economic Adviser of the Department of State, Ellery C. Stowell (Washington, D.C.: Digest Press, 1935).

Foreign Policy and the Department of State (1976).

Guidebook to Diplomatic Reception Rooms (in the Department of State, 1975).

Homes of the Department of State, 1774–1976, Lee H. Burke (1977).

An Improved Personnel System for the Conduct of Foreign Affairs . . . (1950).

*The Legal Adviser of the Department of State, Ellery C. Stowell (Washington, D.C.: Digest Press, 1936).

A Management Program for the Department of State, Office of the Deputy Under Secretary for Administration (1966).

The Organization and Administration of the Department of State (1945).

Outline of the Functioning of the Offices of the Department of State, 1789–1943, Natalia Summers (1946).

Principal Officers of the Department of State and United States Chiefs of Mission, 1778–1988 (1988). Successor to *United States Chiefs of Mission*, Richardson Dougall and Mary Patricia Chapman (1973) and *United States Chiefs of Mission, 1973–1974* (1975), and subsequent issues.

Report on the Organization of the Department of State (1946).

*"Research on the Administrative History of the Department of State," by Elmer Plischke, in *The National Archives and Foreign Relations Research*, ed. Milton O. Gustafson (Athens: Ohio University Press, 1974, pp. 73–102).

The Science Adviser in the Department of State (1960).

"The Seal of the Department of State," Richard S. Patterson, *Department of State Bulletin*, 21 (December 12, 1949): 894–96.

The Secretaries of State: Portraits and Biographical Sketches, Richard S. Patterson (1956), rev. ed., Lee H. Burke and Jan K. Herman, 1978).

Women in the Department of State: Their Role in American Foreign Affairs, Homer L. Calkin (2d ed. 1978).

Foreign Service (chronological)

The U.S. Foreign Service: A Career for Americans (published from time to time since the 1930s).

Reorganization of the Foreign Service (1946).

Facts and Issues Relating to the Amalgamation of the Department of State and the Foreign Service (1949).

The Foreign Service Institute (1949).

Some Facts about the Foreign Service: A Short Account of Its Organization and Duties Together With-Pertinent Laws (1950).

Toward a Stronger Foreign Service: Report of the Secretary of State's Public Committee on Personnel (1954).

The United States Foreign Service, Alexander Wiley (1955).

Career Opportunities in the U.S. Foreign Service (1958).

The Foreign Service of the United States (1958).

The People Who Wage the Peace: An Account of the History and Mission of the Foreign Service, Roy R. Rubottom, Jr. (1958).

Table 7.14 (continued)

The Foreign Service and the Panorama of Change, Charles E. Bohlen (1961).

The Foreign Service of the United States: Origins, Development, and Functions, William Barnes and John Heath Morgan (comprehensive, 1961).

*Personnel for the New Diplomacy (1962).

The Foreign Service Officer: A Career in the U.S. Department of State (1963).

The Foreign Service of the Seventies (1970).

Diplomatic and Consular Missions and Officials

*Ambassadors Ordinary and Extraordinary, E. Wilder Spaulding (Washington, D.C.: Public Affairs Press, 1961).

The American Agricultural Attaché (1967).

The American Ambassador (1957).

The American Cultural Attaché (1957).

*American Foreign Service Authors: A Bibliography, Richard Fyfe Boyce and Katherine Randall Boyce (Metuchen, N.J.: Scarecrow Press, 1973).

The Biographic Register (previously beginning in 1869 titled *Register of the Department of State*; revised periodically, and after 1974 issued as classified editions with limited distribution.

The Country Team: An Illustrated Profile of Our American Missions Abroad (1967).

Diplomatic Agents and Immunities, Amos S. Hershey (1919).

Diplomatic List (quarterly list of foreign diplomatic representatives in Washington), first issued in 1887 under the title *Foreign Legations in the United States*.

Employees of Diplomatic Missions (issued periodically, listing employees of foreign diplomatic representatives in Washington, 1948–   ).

Foreign Consular Officers in the United States (issued periodically since 1920, annually since 1941).

Foreign Services List, list of members of field staffs of American posts abroad, commencing in the 1820s under the title *List of Ministers, Consuls, and Other Diplomatic Agents of the United States in Foreign Countries* (1828–1975).

List of Documents Relating to Special Agents of the Department of State, 1789–1906, Natalia Summers (1951).

*Modern Diplomacy: The Art and the Artisans, Elmer Plischke, ed. (Washington, DC: American Enterprise Institute, 1979).

The Recall or Withholding of U.S. Ambassadors to Influence Other Governments or Express Disapproval of Their Actions: Some Specific Cases, Ernest S. Lent (1969).

Register of the Department of State (on American diplomatic representatives, 1789–1873, published in 1873). Also see *The Biographic Register* and *Principal Officers of the Department of State and United States Chiefs of Mission*.

United States Chiefs of Mission, 1778–1973, Richardson Dougall and Mary Patricia Chapman, comps. (1973).

*United States Diplomats and Their Missions: A Profile of American Diplomatic Emissaries since 1778, Elmer Plischke (Washington, D.C.: American Enterprise Institute, 1975).

World Diplomatic List, Franklin Roudybush (1943).

Conferences, Meetings, and International Organizations

A. General

American Delegations to International Conferences, Congresses and Expositions and American Representation on International Institutions and Commissions, with Relevant Data (annual, 1933–42).

Foreign Travels of the Secretaries of State, 1866–1990 (1990), consists of separate lists by secretaries and by individual countries visited.

International Agencies in Which the United States Participates (1946).

International Organizations in Which the United States Participates, 1949 (1950).

Participation of the United States Government in International Conferences (annual, 1947–62).

Presidential Diplomacy: A Chronology of Summit Visits, Trips, and Meetings, Elmer Plischke (Dobbs Ferry, N.Y.: Oceana, 1986).

Records of United States Participation in International Conferences, Commissions, and Expositions, H. Stephen Helton, comp. (1955, supplement, 1965).

Schedule of International Conferences (quarterly, 1963–   ).

United States Contributions to International Organizations (1953–   ).

Visits Abroad of the Presidents of the United States, 1906–1989 (1990, preceded by *Lists of Visits of the Presidents of the United States to Foreign Countries* (1962 and 1983); consists of separate lists by Presidents and by individual countries visited.

B. Major Post–World War II Conferences and Meetings (chronological)

The United Nations Conference on International Organization, San Francisco, April 25 to June 26, 1945: Selected Documents (1946).

International Health Conference, New York, N.Y., June 19 to July 22, 1946 . . . (1947).

Paris Peace Conference, 1946: Selected Documents, Velma H. Cassidy, ed. (1947).

International Telecommunication Conferences, Atlantic City, New Jersey, May–October, 1947 (1948).

Making the Peace Treaties, 1941–1947 (1947).

Ninth International Conference of American States, Bogotá, Colombia, March 30–May 2, 1948 (1948).

International Conference on Safety of Life at Sea, April 23–June 10, 1948 (1948).

Proceedings of the Inter-American Conference on Conservation of Renewable Natural Resources, Denver, Colorado, September 7–20, 1948 (1949).

Conference for the Conclusion and Signature of the Treaty of Peace with Japan, San Francisco, California, September 4–8, 1951: Record of Proceedings (1951).

Military Armistice in Korea and Temporary Supplementary Agreement: Agreement Signed at Panmunjom, Korea, July 27, 1953 (1953).

Tenth Inter-American Conference, Caracas, Venezuela, March 1–28, 1954 (1955).

The Korean Problem at the Geneva Conference, April 26–June 15, 1954 (1954–   ).

London and Paris Agreements, September–October 1954 (1954).

Termination of the Occupation Regime in the Federal Republic of Germany: Protocol Signed at Paris, October 23, 1954, With Related Documents (1956).

The Bangkok Conference of the Manila Pact Powers, February 23–25, 1955 (1955).

The Austrian State Treaty: An Account of the Postwar Negotiations Together with the Text of the Treaty and Related Documents (1957).

The Conference on Antarctica, Washington, October 15–December 1, 1959 (1960).

General Agreement on Tariffs and Trade, Analysis of United States Negotiations, 1960–1961 Tariff Conference, Geneva, Switzerland (3 vols., 1962).

Table 7.14 (continued)

Alianza El Progreso—The Record of Punta Del Este (1961).

United Nations Conference on Diplomatic Intercourse and Immunities, Vienna, Austria, March 2–April 14, 1961 (1962).

International Negotiations on Ending Nuclear Weapons Tests, September 1961–September 1962 (1962).

Safeguarding Our World Environment: The U.N. Conference on the Human Environment, Stockholm, June 1972 (1972).

Stockholm and Beyond, a Report of Secretary of State's Advisory Committee on the 1972 United Nations Conference on the Human Environment (1972).

Conference on Security and Cooperation in Europe: Final Act, Helsinki, 1975 (1975).

Treaties and Agreements

A. Lists and Catalog

List of Treaties Submitted to the Senate, 1789–1934 (1935).

List of Treaties Submitted to the Senate, 1935–1944 (1945).

List of Treaties Submitted to the Senate, 1789–1931, Which Have Not Gone into Force, October 1, 1932 (1932).

Numerical List of the Treaty Series, Executive Agreement Series, and Treaties and Other International Acts Series (1950).

United States Department of State Catalogue of Treaties, 1814–1918 (1919, reprint 1964).

*Also see Elmer Plischke, *U.S. Foreign Relations: A Guide to Information Sources* (Detroit: Gale Research, 1980), pp. 571–87.

B. Collections of Treaty and Agreement Texts (basic compilations, chronological)

**Diplomatic Code of the United States of America: Embracing a Collection of Treaties and Conventions between the United States and Foreign Powers, From the Year 1778 to 1827*, Jonathan Elliott, ed. (1827).

**The American Diplomatic Code: Embracing a Collection of Treaties and Conventions Between the United States and Foreign Powers from 1778 to 1834*, Jonathan Elliott, ed. (2 vols., 1834).

Treaties, Conventions, International Acts, Protocols, and Agreements between the United States and Other Powers, 1776–1909, comp. William M. Malloy (2 vols., 1910), 1910–23 by C. F. Redmond (vol. 3, 1923), and 1923–1937 by Edward J. Trentwith (vol. 4, 1938).

Treaties and Other International Acts of the United States of America, David Hunter Miller (8 vols., covers period 1776–1863, published 1931–48).

Treaties and Other International Agreements of the United States of America, 1776–1949, Charles I. Bevans (12 vols.—vols. 1–4 contain multilateral treaties/agreements and vols. 5–12 contain bilateral treaties/agreements, published 1968–74).

C. Treaty and Agreement Texts (individual treaties and agreements, chronological)

United States Treaty Series—(TS), includes individual treaties and agreements, numbered serially beginning in 1908 with number 489; prior to 1929 includes both treaties and agreements, after 1929 includes only treaties (published in pamphlet form, 1908–46).

Executive Agreement Series—(EAS), agreements numbered serially from 1 to 506, each agreement published in pamphlet form (1929–46).

Treaties and Other International Acts Series—(TIAS), combines the former Treaty Series and Agreement Series (numbered serially commencing with number 1501 (published in pamphlet form, 1945–   ).

United States Treaties and Other International Agreements—(UST), collection of volumes, numbered sequentially to supplement the *Treaties and Other International Acts Series* (1950–   ).

Also see *League of Nations Treaty Series*, 205 vols. and 9 index vols. (Geneva: Secretariat of League of Nations, 1920–44), and *United Nations Treaty Series* (New York: Secretariat of United Nations, 1945–   , indexed periodically).

D. *Treaties in Force: A List of Treaties and Other International Agreements of the United States in Force on January 1,*—— (published annually since 1956), consisting of two parts— bilateral by country and by subject thereunder and multilateral by subject; two earlier lists were published as of December 31, 1932 (published in 1933), and as of December 31, 1941 (published in 1944).

International Law

A. Digests (chronological)

A Digest of the Published Opinions of the Attorney General and the Leading Decisions of the Federal Courts, with Reference to International Law, Treaties, and Kindred Subjects, John L. Cadwalader, ed. (1877).

Digest of International Law of the United States, Francis Wharton, ed. (3 vols., 2d ed., 1887).

A Digest of International Law, John Bassett Moore, ed. (8 vols., 1906).

Digest of International Law, Green H. Hackworth (8 vols., 1940–44).

Digest of International Law, Marjorie M. Whiteman, ed. (15 vols., 1963–73).

Digest of United States Practice in International Law (annual, 1973–   ).

B. Others

American-Mexican Claims Commission: Report to the Secretary of State (1948).

Damages in International Law, Marjorie M. Whiteman, ed. (3 vols., 1937–43).

History and Digest of International Arbitrations to Which the United States Has Been a Party, John Bassett Moore, ed. (6 vols., 1898).

The International Law of Sovereign Immunity, Joseph M. Sweeney (1964).

Periodicals and Press Releases

Current Foreign Policy, 1972–   (2 per month).

Department of State Bulletin (weekly with semiannual index, 1939–89).

Department of State Newsletter, 1947–   (monthly).

Press Releases, 1912–   (irregular).

In-House Studies

The Office of the Historian (formerly the Historical Office) of the Department of State has produced hundreds of these studies and reports of two basic types: more fundamental and substantial "research projects" and less comprehensive, shorter "research memoranda." These are undertaken in response to specific needs and official requests from the White House, Congress, senior State Department Officers, or other government agencies. Some of them are security classified or are otherwise limited to internal governmental use. Occasionally, they are not made publicly available because they are in preliminary form. Still others become available, but on a limited basis, furnished on the

Table 7.14 (continued)

request of the outside researcher. Several are included elsewhere in this table. The following are illustrative examples:

Armed Actions Taken by the United States without a Declaration of War, 1789–1967 (1967).

Assaults on United States Diplomatic, Consular, and Information Installations Abroad, 1900–1965 (1965).

Office of the Counsellor of the Department of State (1961).

The Problem of Recognition in American Foreign Policy (1950).

The Protocol Function in United States Foreign Relations: Its Administration and Development, 1776–1968 (1968).

Others—Regions and Countries

Aid to Greece and Turkey: A Collection of State Papers (1947).

Allied High Commission Relations with the West German Government, Elmer Plischke (1952).

The Allied High Commission for Germany, Elmer Plischke (2d ed., 1953).

Boundaries of the Latin American Republics: An Annotated List of Documents, 1493–1943, Alexander Marchant (1944).

Documents on German Unity (4 vols., 1951–55).

Events in United States–Cuban Relations: A Chronology, 1957–1963 (1963).

The Far Eastern Commission: A Study in International Cooperation, 1945–52, George H. Blakeslee (1954).

A Historical Summary of United States–Korean Relations, with a Chronology of Important Developments, 1834–1962 (1962).

Inter-American Conferences, 1826–1933: Chronological and Classified Lists (1933).

International Transfers of Territory in Europe, With Names of Affected Political Subdivisions as of 1910–1914 and the Present, Sophia Saucerman (1937).

Non-recognition of Governments and Interruptions in Diplomatic Relations, 1933–1974 (1975).

Occupation of Germany: Policy and Progress (1947).

Occupation of Japan: Policy and Progress (1946).

Our Southern Partners: The Story of Inter-American Cooperation (1962).

The Record of Korean Unification, 1943–1960: Narrative Summary with Principal Documents (1960).

Records Relating to International Boundaries, Daniel T. Goggin, comp. (1968).

Revision of the Occupation Statute for Germany, Elmer Plischke (1952).

Termination of the Occupation Regime in the Federal Republic of Germany . . . (1956).

The United States and the Third World—A Discussion Paper, Ralph Stuart Smith (1976).

United States Policy Toward Latin America: Recognition and Non-recognition of Governments and Interruptions in Diplomatic Relations, 1933–1974 (1975).

United States Relations With China . . . 1944–1949 (1949).

For additional official geographic materials, see Plischke, U.S. Foreign Relations: A Guide to Information Sources, pp. 564–65, 598–606.

Others—Topical and Functional Subjects

The American Passport: Its History and a Digest of Laws, Rulings, and Regulations Governing Its Issuance by the Department of State, Gaillard Hunt (1898).

American Policy in Occupied Areas (1947).

Current Problems in the Conduct of Foreign Policy, George F. Kennan (1950).
Human Rights (7 documents, 1977).
Human Rights: Unfolding of the American Tradition (1968).
Landmarks in the History of the Cultural Relations Program of the Department of State, 1938–1976, J. Manuel Espinosa (1976).
Memorandum on the Postwar International Information Program of the United States, Arthur W. Macmahon (1945).
Peace and War, United States Foreign Policy, 1931–1941 (1943).
Policy of the United States toward Maritime Commerce in War, 1776–1918, Carlton Savage, ed. (2 vols., 1934 and 1936).
Protection of Foreign Interests: A Study in Diplomatic and Consular Practice, William M. Franklin (1947).
The Role of the Public in United States Foreign Relations, Harry Schuyler Foster (1961).
The State Department Policy Planning Staff Papers, 1947–1949, Anna Kastan Nelson, comp. (3 vols., New York: Garland, 1983), presents documents, including former top-secret papers, for first years of the Policy Planning Staff.
Technology and Foreign Affairs, T. Keith Glennan (1976).
United States Foreign Policy: The Operational Aspects of United States Foreign Policy (1959).
The United States Passport—Past, Present, Future (1976).

Note: To the documents and other materials listed in this table may be added many hundreds of official collections, studies, reports, and other publications on the Department of State, diplomatic and consular affairs, and American foreign policy and relations produced by the President, Congress and its committees, and other Departments and agencies, such as the Agency for International Development, the Arms Control and Disarmament Agency, the U.S. Information Agency, and others, as well as relevant unofficial documentary compilations and historical, descriptive, and analytical studies.

For a more comprehensive bibliographical compilation, including unofficial books, monographs, and journal articles, see Elmer Plischke, *U.S. Foreign Relations: A Guide to Information Sources* (Detroit: Gale Research, 1980, 715 pp. (contains some 8,000 citations, with official sources and resources given on pp. 503–670; Elmer Plischke, "Research on the Administrative History of the Department of State," National Archives and Foreign Relations Research, ed. Milton O. Gustafson, *National Archives Conferences*, vol. 4 (Athens:, Ohio: Ohio University Press, 1974) pp. 73–102; and Elmer Plischke, "United States Diplomats Since 1778: Bicentennial Review and Future Projection," *World Affairs* 138 (Winter 1975–1976): 205–18.

For illustrative facsimiles and other reproductions of principal diplomatic documents and for related charts, see Barnes and Morgan, *The Foreign Service of the United States*, pp. 360–63; Harmon, *The Art and Practice of Diplomacy: A Selected and Annotated Guide*, pp. 215–92; and Plischke, *Conduct of American Diplomacy*, 3d ed., pp. 600–623, and *International Relations: Basic Documents*, 2d ed., 1962.

NOTES

1. Other wars and hostilities, not directly involving American armed forces, include those waged by Croatia and Bosnia-Herzegovina, Great Britain, and Argentina over the Falkland Islands, India and Pakistan, Iraq and Iran, Israel and its neighboring Arab countries, and the Soviet Union's invasion of Afghanistan. Civil wars, bloody coups, Communist takeovers, and border skirmishes involved Angola, Cyprus, Ethiopia, Liberia, Libya, Rhodesia, Sudan, Yemen, Zaire, and other countries.

2. Differentiations are made between Occidental and Oriental, Western and Communist (or East and West), North and South, and totalitarian and democratic types of diplomacy, between that of developed and developing nations, and among Anglo-Saxon, Arab, Asian, European, Latin American, and other geobiological-cultural forms of diplomacy. Similarly, alliance and bloc diplomacy is compared with that of neutralist powers. To a large extent such ascriptions to establish qualities of distinction or change in defining the new diplomacy are associated less with distinguishable methods of procedure or form than with the participants or with the subjects of concern or treatment.

3. Reviewing U.S. historical experience, for illustrative purposes, early American practice acknowledges such forms as "colonial," "revolutionary age," "transcontinental," and "golden era" diplomacy. During the nineteenth century the substantively and procedurally oriented notions of "most-favored-nation diplomacy," "expansionist" or "manifestly destined diplomacy," "dollar diplomacy," "Open Door diplomacy," "gunboat diplomacy" and "shirtsleeve diplomacy" crept into American practices and consciousness.

Since the development of nuclear weaponry and the onset of the Cold War, additional types have been identified as "Cold War," "nuclear," and "preventive" diplomacy. One also encounters such recent expressions as "corridor," "hostage," "low profile," and even "instant" diplomacy. Many of these are less valid as significant types of diplomatic method than as reflections of the times, geopolitical power relations, or subjects of immediate concern. The use of additional adjectives renders the potential list of such mutations virtually endless.

4. Examples of these additional topics embrace atomic and nuclear energy and weapons and their control, the Berlin Wall and the division of Germany, common markets, education and cultural exchange, foreign aid and development, human rights, intelligence and espionage matters, outer space, particular commodities, the polar regions, propaganda, and self-determination and independence of colonial territories.

5. Confronted by the realities of the negotiation process, in June 1918 President Wilson moderated his position on open diplomacy and wrote to Secretary Lansing that, when he "pronounced for open diplomacy," he was proposing that no "secret agreements" should be concluded and that "all international relations, when fixed, should be open, aboveboard, and explicit," but not that "there should be no private discussions of delicate matters."

In an address to the American Legion in 1954, President Eisenhower reiterated this interpretation when he said that "much of the diplomatic work, particularly those efforts that are classed as preparatory toward the reaching of agreements, [should] be conducted in confidence," although on the broad objectives and purposes and on the acceptable methods for obtaining them, "the American people must be fully informed."

6. In addition to its own outgoing and incoming communications, the Department of State serves as the channel of transmission for other government agencies, so that it is known as the "Post Office" of the Government. Its current volume of diplomatic communication business is prodigious. Each year it handles millions of diplomatic messages, notes, reports, telegrams, and instructions to American diplomats abroad. To illustrate, Dean Rusk reported that during his eight years as Secretary of State, some 2,100,000 cables—or more than a quarter million per year—were transmitted over his signature alone. These did not include messages to other administrative agencies abroad, such as the Agency for International Development, the Peace Corps, and other Federal agencies. Also see section on "Diplomatic Communications."

7. For additional information on and analysis of, the new diplomacy, see Plischke,

Conduct of American Diplomacy, Chapter 2, and "The New Diplomacy: A Changing Process," *The Virginia Quarterly Review*, 49, (Summer 1973): 321–45 (reproduced in Plischke, *Modern Diplomacy: The Art and the Artisans*, pp. 54–72). Also see Mayer, *Political Origins of the New Diplomacy, 1917–1918*; McCamy, *Conduct of the New Diplomacy*, especially Chapter 11; Campbell, *The Foreign Affairs Fudge Factory*, pp. 20–31; Harr, *The Professional Diplomat*, pp. 28–33; and Department of State, *The Department of State Today* on "our new role in the world," pp. 1–10.

On secrecy and openness see Plischke, *Contemporary U.S. Foreign Policy: Documents and Commentary*, "Prologue: Foreign Relations Documentation—An Analysis," pp. 1–20, and on "Integrating Proliferation of Overseas Missions," pp. 100–101.

For additional consideration of various aspects of the new diplomacy, see Plischke, *Modern Diplomacy: The Art and the Artisans*, including Dag Hammarskjöld, "New Diplomatic Techniques in a New World," pp. 86–91; Elihu Root, "Requisite for the Success of Popular Diplomacy," pp. 102–8; Harry S Truman, "The People and American Foreign Relations," pp. 109–10; Monteagle Stearns, "Diplomacy vs. Propaganda," pp. 111–14; Andrew Berding, "Quiet vs. Unquiet Diplomacy," pp. 115–23; Hugh S. Gibson, "Secret vs. Open Diplomacy," pp. 124–35; William D. Blair, Jr., "Communication: The Weak Link," pp. 136–40; William M. Franklin, "Availability of Diplomatic Information and Documents," pp. 141–49; Inis L. Claude, Jr., "Multilateralism," pp. 188–98; Harlan Cleveland, "Crisis Management," pp. 199–208, in which he discusses five "lessons" for dealing with international crises; and Lincoln Gordon, "Expanded Foreign Relations Functions," pp. 346–49.

8. Examples of such special envoys include General Marshall, sent by President Truman to China for thirteen months (1946–47) to resolve the conflict between the Nationalists and Communists; John Foster Dulles, also recruited by President Truman for the important roving mission of negotiating the Japanese World War II Peace Treaty, signed at San Francisco in 1951; a series of special emissaries commissioned by Presidents Eisenhower, Kennedy, Johnson, and Nixon to promote negotiations to end the Vietnam War (1950s to the early 1970s); Career Foreign Service Officers Joseph J. Sisco and Philip C. Habib, sent, respectively, by Presidents Nixon, Carter, and Reagan to mediate conflict in the Middle East; New York Governor Nelson Rockefeller, former Assistant Secretary of State, accredited by President Nixon to undertake a major fact-finding mission to Latin America in 1969; and relied on by President Carter, a team of negotiators led by Deputy Secretary Warren Christopher to negotiate, indirectly under the auspices of the Algerian Government, a settlement of the Iranian hostage crisis early in 1981.

In the 1980s and 1990s Jeane J. Kirkpatrick and Madeleine K. Albright, U.S. Representatives to the United Nations, were sent by Presidents Reagan and Clinton on a variety of special missions.

Two such emissaries are recognized for their many exploits as distinguished four-star special envoys. W. Averell Harriman served in this capacity on a good many diplomatic missions for nearly three decades (1941–69) under Presidents Roosevelt, Truman, Kennedy, and Johnson. Later, Henry Kissinger, as National Security Adviser and Secretary of State under Presidents Nixon and Ford (1969–76), traveled some 560,000 miles to more than fifty countries, who devoted approximately eighty days in negotiations to resolve Middle East crises and pave the way for President Nixon's historic summit meetings at Beijing and Moscow. Both of them came to be regarded as presidential superemissaries.

9. During six years of the Truman Administration and also in 1954, 1965, and 1976 there were no presidential foreign trips, and in nine other years there were only one or two, whereas President Eisenhower made as many as eighteen in a single year late in

his administration (1959), Bush made seventeen in the first year of his administration (1989), Nixon made sixteen in the first year of his administration (1969), and Ford, Carter, and Reagan each made fourteen, respectively in 1975, 1978, and 1982.

10. Thus, President Eisenhower's attendance at the Geneva Big-Four Summit Conference lasted eight days in 1955, Nixon's ventures to Beijing and to Moscow in 1972 lasted eight and nine days, respectively, and the attendance of Presidents Carter and Reagan at Economic Summit Meetings at London lasted seven days each in 1977 and 1984 and that of President Reagan at Rome in 1987 lasted nine days.

11. Illustrating the variety of presidential trips abroad, President Truman visited Canada, Brazil, and Mexico in 1947; Eisenhower dedicated the Falcon Dam in Mexico in 1953 and joined Queen Elizabeth II in a ceremony opening the St. Lawrence Seaway (Montreal, 1959); President Kennedy met with the Soviet Premier at Vienna (1961); President Johnson attended Chancellor Adenauer's funeral (Bonn) and the Punta del Este Inter-American Summit Meeting (both in 1967); President Nixon addressed the West German Bundestag (Bonn, 1969), participated in memorial services for Charles de Gaulle (Paris, 1970), and held summit meetings with leaders of China (Beijing) and the Soviet Union (Moscow) in 1972; President Ford met with Soviet leaders at Vladivostok (1974) and attended the opening session of the Conference on Security and Cooperation in Europe (Helsinki, 1975) and the first of the annual Economic Summit Meetings (Rambouillet, 1975); President Carter undertook a series of state visits to seven countries in 1979 and attended a meeting to sign the protocol confirming the exchange of documents ratifying the new Panama Canal treaties (1978); President Reagan attended a summit Meeting on International Cooperation and Development (Cancun, 1981) and participated in a commemorative ceremony on the fortieth anniversary of the Allied landing in Normandy (1984); and President Bush attended the funeral of Japanese Emperor Hirohito (Tokyo) and an Inter-American Hemispheric Summit Meeting (San José), both in 1989.

12. Stipulations of the Constitution neither explicitly nor implicitly prohibit the President from leaving the National Capital of the country, but they do presume the unbroken continuance of executive functions and responsibility. So far as foreign trips and visits are concerned, the crucial legal issue is whether the President, because of physical location at a given time, is unable to ''discharge'' executive ''powers and duties.''

Major challenges to presidential absence from the seat of the government were raised initially during the Grant and Wilson administrations. However, modern technology to facilitate transportations and communications makes it possible for contemporary Presidents to handle many executive responsibilities while abroad and even while in flight, and if necessary they can return rapidly to Washington.

13. For more comprehensive analysis of summit diplomacy, see Plischke, *Summit Diplomacy: Personal Diplomacy of the President of the United States, Diplomat in Chief: The President at the Summit, Presidential Diplomacy: A Chronology of Summit Visits, Trips and Meetings, Conduct of American Diplomacy*, pp. 43–55, 292–93, 481–83, and 519; and journal articles listed in the bibliography. For a list of foreign presidential trips and visits, prepared by the Office of the Historian of the Department of State, see *Visits Abroad of the Presidents of the United States, 1906–1989*.

14. This analysis is based on Office of the Historian, Department of State, *Foreign Travels of the Secretaries of State, 1866–1990* (Washington, D.C.: Government Printing Office, 1990). Also see Plischke, *Conduct of American Diplomacy*, pp. 493–94, 510–13, and Henry M. Wriston, ''The Secretary of State Abroad,'' *Foreign Affairs*, 34 (July 1956): pp. 523–40. For a list of secretaries of State since World War II, see Table 7.1.

15. Although Secretaries of State also undertook ceremonial visits abroad on their own, on nine occasions they accompanied Presidents on such missions. For example, Secretary Rusk accompanied President Johnson to Mexico City to dedicate a statue of President Lincoln (1966), Secretary Rogers accompanied President Nixon to celebrate the tenth anniversary of the opening of the St. Lawrence Seaway (Montreal, 1969), and Secretaries Rogers, Muskie, Shultz, and Baker accompanied the President, respectively, to attend the funerals of former French President Charles de Gaulle (1970), Japanese Prime Minister Ohira (1980), Soviet President Chernenko (1985), and Japanese Emperor Hirohito (1989).

16. For example, President Eisenhower and Secretary Herter undertook a goodwill tour to four Latin American countries in 1960, President Nixon and Rogers visited five European countries in 1970, President Ford and Kissinger attended the Vladivostok U.S.–Soviet Summit and visited Peking, Seoul, and Tokyo late in 1974; visited four European countries and the Vatican in May 1975; and also attended the signing of the Final Act of the Conference on Security and Cooperation in Europe at Helsinki and visited four other Eastern European countries that same year. President Carter and Vance combined visits to six European and Middle East countries late in 1977 and early 1978 and later also flew to two Latin American and two African countries. President Reagan and Haig visited four European countries as well as West Berlin and the Vatican in 1982. President Reagan and Shultz visited four West European countries in 1985. President Bush and Baker made such joint trips in 1989, to the People's Republic of China, Korea, and Japan in February and to Belgium, Italy, Germany, the United Kingdom, and Vatican City in May.

17. These state visits and summit meetings included the Heads of Government Summit Conference, Geneva, 1955 (Eisenhower and Dulles); Meeting of the Presidents of the American Republics, Panama City, 1956 (Eisenhower and Dulles); Big Four Summit—France, Soviet Union, United Kingdom, and United States, at Paris, 1960 (Eisenhower and Herter); Bilateral U.S.–Soviet Summit Meeting, Vienna, 1961 (Kennedy and Rusk); Conference of Central American Presidents, San José, 1963 (Kennedy and Rusk); Bipartite U.S.–French Summit Meeting, Azores, 1971 (Nixon and Rogers); State Visit to Beijing, 1972 (Nixon and Rogers); State Visit to Moscow, 1972 (Nixon and Rogers); Bilateral U.S.–Soviet Summit Meeting, Vladivostok, 1974 (Ford and Kissinger); Conference on Security and Cooperation in Europe, Helsinki, 1975 (Ford and Kissinger); Bilateral U.S.–Soviet Summit Meeting, Geneva, 1985 (Reagan and Shultz); Bilateral U.S.–Soviet Summit Meeting, Reykjavik, 1986 (Reagan and Shultz); Bilateral U.S.–Soviet Summit Meeting, Moscow, 1988 (Reagan and Shultz); Western Hemisphere Summit Meeting, San José, 1989 (Bush and Baker); Bilateral U.S.–Soviet Summit Meeting, Malta, 1989 (Bush and Baker); Inter-American Drug Summit Meeting (Bolivia, Colombia, Peru, and United States), Cartagena, 1990 (Bush and Baker); Bilateral U.S.–Soviet Summit Meeting, Helsinki, 1990 (Bush and Baker).

18. These peace-settlement conferences included the Potsdam Summit Conference (President Truman and Secretary Byrnes, 1945), the World War II Paris Peace Conference at Paris (Byrnes, 1946), the Vietnam Peace Conference at Paris (Rogers, 1973), and the Middle East Peace Conference at Geneva (Kissinger, 1973).

19. The conferences on arms limitation and disarmament embraced the United Nations Disarmament Conference at London (Dulles, 1956), the Geneva Eighteen-Nation Disarmament Conference (Rusk, 1962), the Stockholm Conference on Confidence and Security Building Measures and Disarmament of Europe (Shultz, 1984, which established the Council on Security and Cooperation in Europe), and the Paris Conference on the Prohibition of Chemical Weapons (Shultz, 1989).

20. The conferences on economic development included the Paris Conference on International Economic Cooperation (Kissinger, 1975), the Paris Conference International Economic Development (Vance, 1977), the U.S.–Australian Conference on Asia-Pacific Economic Development convened at Sydney (Baker, 1989) and the Asia–Pacific Economic Cooperation Meeting at Singapore (Baker, 1990).

21. The inter-American conferences convened abroad at Petropolis, Brazil (Conference for the Maintenance of Continental Peace, Marshall, 1947), Bogotá (Ninth International Conference of American States, Marshall, 1948), Buenos Aires (Third Special Inter-American Conference, Rusk, 1967), Punta del Este, Uruguay (Conference of Inter-American Heads of State and Foreign Ministers, Rusk, 1967), and Tlatelolco, Mexico (Conference of Latin American Foreign Ministers, Kissinger, 1974).

22. The international conferences that focused on individual countries dealt with Cambodia (1989), Germany (1954), Laos (1961 and 1962), the Philippines (1989), Vietnam (1966 and 1973), and the Suez Canal (three conferences in 1956). In 1977 Secretary Kissinger also participated in a United Nations Trade and Development (UNCTAD) Conference convened at Nairobi, Kenya.

23. Aside from NATO, these regional international organizations included:

ANZUS: Australia, New Zealand, U.S. collective security organization (eight sessions)

ASEAN: Association of East Asian Nations (eleven)

CENTO: Central Treaty Organization (fourteen)

CSCE: Council on Security and Cooperation in Europe (six)

EEC: European Economic Community (one)

OAS: Organization of American States (thirteen)

OECD: Organization for Economic Cooperation and Development (six)

SEATO: Southeast Asia Treaty Organization (fifteen).

24. Illustrating these ad hoc ministerial meetings, Secretary Acheson met with the Foreign Ministers of Belgium, France, Luxembourg, the Netherlands, and the United Kingdom at Paris in 1949, Secretary Rusk convened with the Foreign Ministers of the NATO powers at Paris to discuss the Berlin question in 1961, and Secretary Rogers conferred at Saigon in 1970 with the Foreign Ministers of the countries contributing troops to wage the war in Vietnam.

25. Warren Christopher, who also served for four years, even transcended Secretary Baker's record.

26. See Hans J. Morgenthau, "John Foster Dulles," in Graebner, *An Uncertain Tradition: American Secretaries of State in the Twentieth Century*, p. 289; Bemis, *American Secretaries of State and Their Diplomacy*, vol. 19, Preface, p. iii; Warren I. Cohen, *Dean Rusk*, in *American Secretaries of State and Their Diplomacy* series, vol. 19, p. 92; and Gaddis Smith, *Dean Acheson*, in *American Secretaries of State and Their Diplomacy* series, vol. 16, p. 391.

More precisely, prescribing the responsibilities of the contemporary Secretary and Department of State, see Stuart, *American Diplomatic and Consular Practice*, pp. 23–25; McCamy, *Conduct of the New Diplomacy*, pp. 56–58; Plischke, *Conduct of American Diplomacy*, pp. 168–71, for a listing of nineteen functions of the Secretary, and pp. 198–219 for analysis of Department of State responsibilities; and Williams, *American Diplomacy*, pp. 450–52.

27. This occurred prior to the commencement of the service of such Secretaries as

Byrnes, Dulles, Rusk, Rogers, Kissinger, Muskie, Shultz, and others. Usually, these interim appointments last only a few days, pending the confirmation and entry on duty of a new Secretary. Occasionally they are more extended. For example, Under Secretary Grew served in this capacity for six days, between Secretaries Vance and Muskie five such interim appointees served for eleven days (some for only part of a day, with three holding this position sequentially on May 3, 1980), and the longest interim service occurred when Under Secretary Rush held this position for twenty days when Kissinger succeeded Rogers in 1973 and when Deputy Secretary Stoessel was Acting Secretary for twelve days when Secretary Shultz succeeded General Haig as Secretary. David Newsom held three such interim appointments in 1980–81, and most of them were career Foreign Service Officers.

28. Technically, Rusk is the only American Secretary of State to hold the office for a full eight years, during the Kennedy and Johnson Administrations. However, several earlier Secretaries also served during two sequential Presidential Administrations. These included James Madison (1801–1809), John Quincy Adams (1817–25), John Forsyth (1834–41), William H. Seward (1861–69), and Hamilton Fish (1869–77), each of whom served for nearly eight years.

29. These included Bates College (Muskie), Colgate University (Rogers), Davidson College (Rusk, who called it "the poor man's Princeton"), Harvard University (Herter and Kissinger), Princeton University (Baker, Dulles, and Shultz), University of Southern California (Christopher), University of Wisconsin (Eagleburger), and Yale University (Acheson and Vance). Marshall graduated from the Virginia Military Institute, and Haig from the U.S. Military Academy. Muskie and Herter graduated cum laude, Christopher graduated magna cum laude, and Kissinger achieved the status of summa cum laude, and Dulles and Kissinger were inducted into Phi Beta Kappa, and Christopher became a member of Phi Kappa Phi.

30. Herter lectured on international relations and organization at Harvard University (1929–30); Rusk taught for several years at Mills College (1934–40), where he also served as Dean of Faculty; Kissinger became Executive Director of the Harvard International Seminar, a member of the Department of Government (1958–69), and a faculty member of the Center for International Affairs at Harvard University; Shultz served on the faculty at the Massachusetts Institute of Technology (1949–57), the University of Chicago Graduate School of Business (1957–68) and Dean of the School (1962–68), and Stanford University (1974–82 and 1989–91), where he retired as Professor Emeritus in 1991; and Albright taught international affairs at George Washington University.

31. Illustrations of these publications include Byrnes, *Speaking Frankly* (1947); Acheson, *Administrative Procedure in Government Agencies* (1968), *A Citizen Looks at Congress* (1957), *The Korean War* (1971), *Sketches from Life of Men I Have Known* (1961), and *This Vast External Realm* (1973); Herter, *Toward an Atlantic Community* (1963); Dulles, *War, Peace, and Change*, 2d ed., (1942), *Six Pillars of Peace* (1943), and *War or Peace* (1950); Kissinger, *A World Restored: Castlereagh, Metternich, and the Problems of Peace, 1812–22* (1957), *Nuclear Weapons and Foreign Policy* (1957), *The Necessity for Choice: Prospects of American Foreign Policy* (1961), *Problems of National Strategy* (1965), *The Troubled Partnership: A Reappraisal of the Atlantic Alliance* (1965), and *Diplomacy* (1994); Muskie, *The Politics of Pollution* (with Clarence Davies, 1970) and *What Price Defense?* (1974); Haig, *Caveat: Realism, Reagan and Foreign Policy* (1984); Shultz, (with John A. Coleman, *Labor Problems*, 1959), *Guidelines, Informal Controls, and the Market Place* (1966), *Economic Policy beyond the Headlines*

(with Kenneth W. Dam, 1978); Baker, *The Politics of Diplomacy: Revolution, War, and Peace* (1995); and Christopher, *American Hostages in Iran* (1985).

In addition, for a time early in their careers Byrnes and Herter held journalism editorial positions.

32. These law schools included Cornell University (Muskie and Rogers), George Washington Law School (Dulles), Harvard University (Acheson), Stanford University (Christopher), University of Texas (Baker), and Yale University (Vance). Rusk also studied law at the University of California.

33. Byrnes represented South Carolina in the House of Representatives for fourteen years (1911–25) and in the Senate for ten years (1931–41); Dulles was appointed by the Governor of New York in July 1949 to fill the unexpired term of Senator Robert F. Wagner, but he was defeated for reelection; Herter represented Massachusetts in the House of Representatives (1943–52) and served as a member of its Foreign Relations Committee); and Muskie represented Maine in both the House and the Senate for two decades (1959–80).

34. For example, these included State Governorships (Byrnes, South Carolina, 1951–55); Herter, Massachusetts, 1953–57; Muskie, Maine, 1955–59); as well as State legislatures (Muskie, Maine House of Representatives, 1948–51, where he helped to build the Democratic Party).

In addition, Byrnes was a delegate to Democratic National Conventions (1920–40); Muskie was a member of the Democratic National Committee (1952–55); in addition his political roles mentioned earlier Baker was a member of the Reagan Transition Team (1980–81); and both Rogers and Vance served as counsel to various U.S. Senate committees.

35. To cite a few, Byrnes was recognized as "Man of the Year" by *Time* magazine; Marshall received the Four Freedoms Foundation Award; Rusk won the Cecil Peace Prize for an essay on the British Commonwealth and the League of Nations; Kissinger received the Medal of Liberty, the George Catlett Marshal Medal, and the Charles Evans Hughes Award; Baker and Christopher received the Jefferson Award presented by the American Institute for Public Service; and Shultz was appointed as a Distinguished Fellow at the Hoover Institute.

36. The main reasons for dissatisfaction with the 1792 law were that, if both the Presidency and the Vice Presidency became vacant, the office of President could pass to a member of another political party, thereby interrupting the continuity of executive policy, including foreign relations and negotiations. More significantly, if both offices became vacant during the time between the expiration of one Congress and the convening of the next, there might not be a President pro tempore of the Senate or a Speaker of the House of Representatives available to act as President, which was the case when Vice President Thomas A. Hendricks died in 1885.

37. This order of Cabinet Secretaries' precedence was amended from time to time to include the Secretaries of additional executive Departments as they were created, but the Secretary of State continued as the leading Cabinet member in the line of succession. For the current version of the law, see *U.S. Code*, Title 3, sec. 19.

38. Six former Secretaries of State were later elected President. In addition, Jefferson and Van Buren were also elected Vice Presidents before they became President. However, others who were appointed Secretary of State also had Presidential aspirations. Several former Secretaries were defeated for the office (Clay, Cass, Blaine [before his second term as Secretary], Bryan, and Hughes); some were considered for nomination but were

not selected (Seward, Bayard, Gresham, Sherman, and Knox); and a few were prominently mentioned as possible candidates for the Presidency (Webster, Olney, and Hull). On the other hand, Calhoun served as Vice President before he became Secretary of State. To the time of World War II, it has been said, some twenty, or nearly half of the Secretaries, "were close to the Presidency."

39. In addition to Harrison, the Presidents who died in office were Zachary Taylor (1850), Abraham Lincoln (1865), James A. Garfield (1881), William McKinley (1901), Warren G. Harding (1923), Franklin D. Roosevelt (1945), and John F. Kennedy (1963). Lincoln, Garfield, McKinley, and Kennedy were assassinated, and the others died of illness. Vice Presidents who died in office included George Clinton (1812), Elbridge Gerry (1814), William R. King (1853), Henry Wilson (1875), Thomas A. Hendricks (1885), Garret A. Hobart (1899), and James S. Sherman (1912).

40. These eight Presidents temporarily without a Vice President to succeed them included Jefferson, Madison, Jackson, Pierce, Grant, Cleveland, McKinley, and Taft.

41. President Andrew Johnson was impeached by the House of Representatives in 1868 but was not convicted by the Senate, and, when impeachment proceedings were initiated by the House of Representatives against Nixon in 1974, he resigned on August 9 and was succeeded immediately by Gerald Ford; and President Clinton was impeached by the House of Representatives in December 1998.

So far as serious illness and related disabilities are concerned, President Washington almost died of anthrax during his first few weeks in office, and shortly thereafter he nearly died of pneumonia; Jefferson suffered debilitating migraine headaches that rendered him virtually helpless in 1807 and 1808; after being shot in July 1881, President Garfield lingered for eighty days before he died; President Cleveland secretly underwent an operation for cancer in July 1883; President Wilson suffered a massive stroke in October 1919 that rendered him incapacitated for many months; Franklin D. Roosevelt suffered ill health for more than a year with an enlarged heart, hypertension, gallstones, cardiac failure, and other ailments before he died; between 1955 and 1957 President Eisenhower sustained a heart attack, an ileitis attack, and a mild stroke, and he was also invalided for months; and others have been hospitalized or bedridden with major and minor illnesses.

After World War II, Puerto Ricans attempted to shoot their way into Blair House, where President Truman was housed while the White House was being renovated, and an American guard was fatally shot; two attempts were made to assassinate President Ford in September 1975 shortly after he became President; and in March 1981 President Reagan was shot and seriously wounded and was incapacitated for several months.

42. The Twenty-Fifth Amendment stipulates that in the case of the removal of the President from office, death, or resignation, the Vice President shall become President. It also provides three courses of action to deal with Presidential disability: (1) if the President formally declares a state of disability to the President pro tempore of the Senate and the Speaker of the House of Representatives, the Vice President is made Acting President until the President notifies the leaders of the two chambers of Congress that the disability no longer exists; (2) if the President is unwilling or unable to declare such disability, the Vice President and a majority of the Secretaries heading the executive Departments or such body as the Congress may by law provide, transmit to the two leaders of Congress their written declaration that the President is unable to discharge the function of the office, the Vice President immediately assumes the role of Acting President until the President notifies the leaders of Congress that the disability has ended; and (3) if there is disagreement between the President and Vice President as to whether the disability no longer exists, Congress shall

immediately decide the issue by a two-thirds vote of both houses. The only role of the Secretary of State in these arrangements arises under the second and third alternatives, which, it appears, are rarely likely to be implemented.

43. To illustrate, when Vice President Spiro T. Agnew resigned in 1973 after pleading no contest to criminal charges, under this amendment President Nixon, with the concurrence of a majority of both houses of Congress, appointed Gerald R. Ford, minority leader in the House of Representatives, as his new Vice President. Later, in August 1974, when Nixon resigned the Presidency, Ford became President, and he, in turn, nominated former Governor of New York Nelson A. Rockefeller to become his Vice President. Thus, the gap in the Vice Presidency can readily be filled, and the continuity of the Presidency can be maintained.

44. For additional commentary, see Ruth C. Silva, *Presidential Succession* (Ann Arbor: University of Michigan Press, 1951); Arthur M. Schlesinger, Jr., "On Presidential Succession," *Political Science Quarterly* 89, no. 3 (September 1974): pp. 475–506; and Stephen W. Stathis, "Presidential Succession," *Encyclopedia of the American Presidency*, vol. 4, pp. 1413–16. Also see de Conde, *The American Secretary of State*, Chapter 4, and Hill, *Mr. Secretary of State*, pp. 132–37. Also see volumes on the Presidency, such as Edward S. Corwin, *The President* (New York: New York University Press, 1957), pp. 53–59, 64–68, 303, 344–46, 356–59; Joseph E. Kallenbach, *The American Chief Executive* (New York: Harper and Row, 1966), Chapter 6; Louis W. Koenig, *The Chief Executive* (New York: Harcourt, Brace, 1964), pp. 66–90; Sidney M. Milkus and Michael Nelson, *The American Presidency* (Washington, DC: Congressional Quarterly, 1990), pp. 37–38, 331, 372–73, 361–62, 366, 372; Richard M. Pious, *The American Presidency* (New York: Basic Books, 1979), pp. 116–19; and Clinton Rossiter, *The American Presidency* (New York: Harcourt, Brace, 1960), Chapter 7, entitled "The Firing, Retiring, and Expiring of Presidents." Additional citations on Presidential resignation, impeachment, and inability are contained in Silva, *Presidential Succession*, Bibliography, pp. 189–96.

45. Such temporary Acting Secretaries of State need to be distinguished from Secretaries of State ad interim, who normally serve for a few days during the interim between appointments when one Secretary succeeds another following a Presidential election and inauguration or when a Secretary resigns the office, pending the appointment and confirmation of a replacement.

46. For a list of Acting Secretaries of State, see Table 7.1.

47. By this time the Office of Chief Clerk, who earlier held a ranking Department of State position, and the numbered Assistant Secretaries, referred to earlier, had been disestablished.

48. Previously, the position of Chief of Protocol was held by a lesser-ranked officer, appointed by the Secretary of State, and was designated as Chief of the Division of International Conferences and Protocol and later as the Special Assistant to the Secretary of State and Chief of Protocol.

49. To illustrate, the initial categorization of Assistant Secretaries as First, Second, and Third Assistant Secretaries (1853–1944) was superseded by Assistant Secretaries bearing specific title designations, the position of Deputy Under Secretary was discontinued, the early Geographic Area Assistant Secretaries were retitled and changed, a few immediate post–World War II offices (including Occupied Areas and German Affairs) were terminated, and several others were modified.

50. For example, in 1960 the Assistant Secretary for Administration headed a staff

of more than forty Deputy and Special Assistants, Directors and Deputy Directors, Chiefs of Divisions, and Administrators and Deputy Administrators; in 1970 each of the Geographic Area Assistant Secretaries had staffs of sixteen to nineteen subsidiary officers, generally titled Deputy Assistant Secretary, Executive Director, Staff Director, or Adviser, and most of them were Directors for specific countries or groups of countries; and in 1980 the Legal Adviser had a staff of twenty-five assistants, including Deputy and Assistant Legal Advisers, plus a Counselor on International Law, an Executive Director, and an Attorney-Examiner General; and the five Geographic Area Assistant Secretaries headed a combined staff of eighty-five such officers.

51. The most common of these ranks and titles are Assistant, Director, Deputy Assistant or Deputy Director, and Chief of a Division or Staff. Others bear such titles as Executive Assistant, Executive Director, Executive Secretary, Staff Assistant, or Staff Director, and a few are designated Administrator, Adviser, Coordinator, Curator, Historian, or even "Spokesman for the Department."

52. These officers include the Assistant Secretaries for Economic and Business Affairs (though its title was changed), Inter-American Affairs (whose title also was changed), and Public Affairs and the Counselor and the Legal Adviser.

53. These officers include six Assistant Secretaries (three for the Geographic Areas) and those concerned with Administration, International Organization Affairs, and Legislative Affairs, plus the Ambassador at Large, the Chief of Protocol, and the Directors of the Foreign Service Institute and the Policy Planning Staff.

54. Illustrations of these titles, in addition to Ambassador at Large, include Chief Financial Officer, Chief of Protocol, Civil Service Ombudsman, Executive Secretary, Inspector General, Legal Adviser, and Representatives to the United Nations and the Organization of American States.

55. Ambassadors at Large have been commissioned with such titles as special representatives to particular countries or geographic areas, to participate in specified international conferences, for given policy subjects, or for certain liaison functions.

56. These Under Secretaries included such careerists as Michael H. Armacost, Lawrence S. Eagleburger (who later became Secretary of State), Henry P. Fletcher, Joseph C. Grew, Philip C. Habib, U. Alexis Johnson, Thomas C. Mann, Livingston T. Merchant, Robert D. Murphy, David D. Newsom, William Phillips, Joseph J. Sisco, and B. Sumner Welles.

57. Other women appointed as principal officers include Lucy W. Benson, Jacqueline L. Williams-Bridger, Catherine W. Brown, Eileen Claussen, Lynn E. Davis, Patricia M. Derian, Diana Lady Dougan, Sonia Landau, Barbara Larkin, Patsy T. Mink, Phyllis E. Oakley, Dixie Lee Ray, Robin L. Raphel, Joan E. Spero, and Ann B. Wrobleski.

58. This number does not include the Office of the Permanent Representative to the United Nations but does include that of the Counselor, which is not shown on the chart.

59. For additional listing of such reports and commentary, see Plischke, *U.S. Foreign Relations: A Guide to Information Sources*, pp. 224–36. Earlier similar interwar studies and reports are represented by National Civil Service Reform League, *Report on the Foreign Service* (1919, 322 p.); Commission of Inquiry on Public Service Personnel, *Better Government Personnel . . .* (1935, 86 p.); and President's Committee on Administrative Management, *Personnel Administration in the Federal Service* (1937).

60. The Hoover Commission noted that at the time at least forty-five executive agencies in addition to the State Department were involved in the administration of foreign affairs, that only 5 percent of funds expended for foreign activities abroad were ascribed

to the Department, and that only 11 percent of American civilian employees of the Government stationed abroad were attached to the Department and Foreign Service.

61. Inasmuch as Dean Acheson, former Assistant Secretary of State (1941–45), served as Vice Chairman of the Hoover Commission, it benefited by the wealth of his prior departmental experience and contributions, and its report was filed in 1949, when he was Secretary of State, so that it was well received, and most of the senior staffing changes proposed by the Commission were rapidly instituted.

62. A noncareerist, Macomber had previously been appointed Assistant Secretary of State for Congressional Relations (1957–61), Ambassador to Jordan (1961–63), and Assistant Secretary for Congressional Relations (1967–69); he was appointed Deputy Under Secretary for Administration (1969–71) and later Deputy Under Secretary for Management (1971–73) and ambassador to Turkey (1973–77).

63. Individual Task Forces were generally headed by a Chairman and an Executive Secretary, a substantial number of whom were career Foreign Service Officers, such as L. Dean Brown, Robert L. Brown, Winthrop G. Brown, Robert A. Hurwitch, Frederick Irving, Thomas W. McElhiney, Thomas R. Pickering, David E. Simcox, and James W. Spein—all of whom had already served as Ambassadors to foreign governments.

64. The functional cone system had previously been endorsed by both the Wriston Committee in 1954 and later by the Herter Committee, as applied to administrative, political, and economic affairs, to which consular specialists were added later.

65. Department of State officials and diplomats included such careerists as William O. Hall, Foy D. Kohler, Henry D. Owen, and Charles W. Yost and noncareerists Robert R. Bowie, Harlan Cleveland, Chester A. Crocker, Kenneth W. Damm, Richard N. Gardner, and John R. Schaetzel.

66. The members of Congress included Senators J. William Fulbright, Mike Mansfield, and Stuart Symington and Representative Clement J. Zablocki.

67. Others who played a major role heading panels or preparing separate reports included Graham T. Allison, Lincoln Bloomfield, McGeorge Bundy, William D. Coplin, Alexander I. George, William R. Harris, Richard E. Hayes, Louis Henkin, Robert O. Keohane, Abraham F. Lowenthal, M. Roger Majak, and Joseph S. Nye.

68. For listing of Senate and House of Representatives committee studies, see Plischke, *U.S. Foreign Relations: A Guide to Information Sources*, pp. 547–49, and its Index, especially pp. 709–11.

69. For additional comment on the future of the State Department and the Foreign Service, see Chapter 8.

70. For additional commentary, see Blancké, *The Foreign Service of the United States*, pp. 69–73; Harr, *The Professional Diplomat*, pp. 117, 123–24, 280, 302–7, 365; Macomber, *The Angels' Game*, pp. 91, 95; Plischke, *Conduct of American Diplomacy*, pp. 183, 195, 202; and Simpson, *Anatomy of the State Department*, pp. 19–21. Also see Macomber, *Diplomacy for the 70s*, pp. 341–59, for the basic functions of the Country Directors and approximately forty recommendations concerning them, which deal with organization of Country Directorates; relations with both regional and functional State Department Bureaus, senior Departmental officers, and other foreign affairs agencies; resources and personnel improvement; and other matters.

71. For commentary on U.S. contributions to international organizations, see the later section on International Organizations.

72. The Office of Insular Affairs is responsible for the Virgin Islands and in the

Pacific, American Samoa, Guam, the Marianna Islands, the Federated States of the Marshall Islands, Micronesia, the Republic of Palau, and others.

73. The Under Secretary for International Affairs of the Treasury Department is responsible for policy and guidance for international monetary affairs, trade and investment relations, international debt strategy and funding, and U.S. participation in international financial institutions.

74. The Post Office Department was converted into the U.S. Postal Service in 1971 and became self-supporting, with federal support of approximately $130 million in 1995.

75. It has been conjectured that "Foggy Bottom" might become a metonym in this country, comparable to its counterparts in London (Whitehall), Paris (the *Quai d'Orsay*), and Berlin (*Whilhelm Strasse*), and that some day the U.S. Department of State would be known simply as "Foggy Bottom" throughout the world. This, however, does not seem to be the case.

76. On diplomatic communications in general, also see Harr, *The Professional Diplomat*, pp. 127–28, 130, 297; Plischke, *Conduct of American Diplomacy*, pp. 99–100, 151–52, 207–209, 285–86; and Stuart, *American Diplomatic and Consular Practice*, p. 49. For recent analysis of American communications policy and transmission, with emphasis on electronic communications systems, development, and problems, see Wilson Dizard, Jr., "Communications Policy," *Encyclopedia of U.S. Foreign Relations*, vol. 1, pp. 296–300. For analysis of many legal aspects of international, including diplomatic, communications, also see Moore, *A Digest of International Law*, vol. 4, Chapter 7, pp. 686–726; Hackworth, *Digest of International Law*, vol. 4, Chapter 13, pp. 243–337; and Whiteman, *Digest of International Law*, vol. 7, pp. 174–252, 502–4. These deal with such matters as the use of codes, electrical communications (including submarine telegraphic cables), postal communications, radio, rights of official communications, inviolability of official exchanges, publication of correspondence, and similar issues.

77. Macomber, *The Angels' Game*, pp. 30–31.

78. For additional commentary on the courier system, see Department of State, *Department of State, 1963*, p. 67; Blancké, *The Professional Diplomat*, pp. 86–90; Foster, *The Practice of Diplomacy*, p. 212; Plischke, *Conduct of American Diplomacy*, pp. 208–209, 340; Stuart, *American Diplomatic and Consular Practice*, pp. 49–50, 238; Thayer, *Diplomat*, pp. 153–60; and Trask, *A Short History of the U.S. Department of State*, p. 24.

79. See Foreign Service Act of August 13, 1946, sec. 561 (60 Stat. 999), which was not reiterated in the Foreign Service Act of October 1980); also Act of August 10, 1956 (70A Stat. 33), Act of September 30, 1994 (108 Stat. 2649), and the *U.S. Code*, Title 10, secs. 713 and 2241.

80. The Assistant to the President for National Security, or National Security Adviser, who manages the National Security Staff, sometimes is used by the President for foreign policy advice, high-level foreign visits, and international negotiations, which may compete with, or bypass, the Secretary and Department of State.

81. The Office of Strategic Services (OSS), established during World War II to supplement military and combat intelligence, was disestablished following the surrenders of Germany and Japan. To deal effectively with American international commitments, it was deemed to be necessary to create a continuing coordinating intelligence agency, so that in 1945 the Office of Research and Intelligence was established in the Department of State. But in January 1946 President Truman launched the National Intelligence Authority to integrate and deal with foreign intelligence matters. It operated through a Central Intelligence Group consisting of officers from the Departments of State, War and

Navy. It was superseded by the Central Intelligence Agency (CIA), provided for by the National Security Act of 1947.

82. The Executive Office of the President also contains a series of other principal officers, including an Associate Director and a Deputy Associate Director for National Security and International Affairs in the Office of Management and Budget, an Associate Director for National Security and International Affairs in the Office of Technology, a Special Assistant for European Affairs, and the Special Representative for Trade Negotiations which possesses a staff of twenty-five high-level Assistants. Aside from its principal participants, the staff of the National Security Council also includes the Assistant to the President for National Security Affairs, the Assistant to the President for Economic Policy, and the Executive Secretary. The Central Intelligence Agency is headed by a Director and a Deputy Director.

83. Other titles of the departmental agencies range from commission and corporation to center, council, and institute.

84. These are located in the Commerce, Health and Human Services, Interior, Justice, Labor, and Treasury Departments.

85. The twenty-one Customs Service components, which implement more than 400 trade laws and regulations, are maintained at Bangkok, Beijing, Bonn, Brussels, Dublin, London, Mexico City, Ottawa, Panama City, Paris, Rome, Seoul, Singapore, Tokyo, and Vienna, and an attaché represents the Customs Service in the U.S. mission to the European Communities at Brussels. The three district offices of the Immigration and Naturalization Service are located at Bangkok, Mexico City, and Rome. The eight Travel and Tourism Administration foreign offices are stationed in Frankfurt, London, Mexico City, Milan, Paris, Sydney, Tokyo, and Toronto, in addition to using Miami to service a number of South American countries.

86. Examples of such independent agencies inherited by President Truman include the Foreign Economic Administration, Lend-Lease Administration, Office of Strategic Services, Office of War Information, and War Shipping Administration, which were liquidated in 1945 and 1946, although some of their functions were transferred to new agencies. President Truman also inherited the State-War-Navy Coordinating Committee (SWNCC or "Swink"), later expanded into the State-War-Navy-Air Coordinating Committee (SANACC), which remained in existence for some years.

87. Thus, World War II foreign aid programs administered by the Lend-Lease (1941) and Foreign Economic (1945) Administrations and other agencies were later succeeded by the Economic Cooperation Administration (1948), the Technical Cooperation Administration (1950), the Mutual Security Agency (1951), and eventually the Agency for International Development (1961).

The World War II information program involved the Office of War Information and the Office of Strategic Services (concerned with foreign intelligence), which were succeeded by the Department of State Offices of Information and Cultural Exchange and Information and Educational Exchange (1948), the U.S. International Information Administration (attached to the Department of State), and eventually, the U.S. Information Agency (1953).

The foreign intelligence programs consisted of the World War II Office of Strategic Services, which was succeeded late in 1945 by the Office of Research and Intelligence of the Department of State, the National Intelligence Authority supplemented by a Central Intelligence Group, and eventually, in 1947, by the Central Intelligence Agency.

88. This matter of interagency or superagency management of overseas operational

programs needs to be distinguished from the Department of State's own management facility. In 1961 it created an Operations Center within the departmental Secretariat to serve as a command and control instrumentality, which worked closely with the White House and other agencies. Also an Office of Operations handled a variety of services and other functions to support departmental substantive operations in Washington and overseas.

89. Other examples of such coordinating agencies include the Air Coordinating Committee (1946–60), the Committee for Information Reciprocity (1934–63), the Council on Foreign Economic Policy (1954–61), the Operations Coordinating Board (established in 1953 to handle advance consideration by the National Security Council and monitor implementation of decisions), and the Trade Agreements Committee (1934–63).

90. Such special coordinators are represented by the Coordinators of Information and of Inter-American Affairs.

91. The President is the obvious supercoordinator of foreign affairs. He could appoint a member of his Executive Office to function in the guise of a "Deputy President for Foreign Relations." In 1958 President Eisenhower proposed that there be two additional Vice Presidents, based on statutory authority, one of whom would serve as the "First Secretary for Off-shore Affairs," and the other would handle domestic matters.

92. This concept of clustering was recommended in a study produced by the Brookings Institution for the Senate Foreign Relations Committee in 1959.

93. 62 Stat. 744 and 108 Stat. 2147, *U.S. Code*, Title 18, sec. 953; and referred to in Title 50, sec. 34. For earlier citations, see Chapter 2, note 27. For commentary, see Frederick B. Tolles, *George Logan of Philadelphia* (New York: Oxford University Press, 1953), Chapters 7 and 14 on Logan's "missions" to Paris and London, and especially Chapter 10 on "Logan's Law"; Maureen Berman and Joseph E. Johnson, *Unofficial Diplomacy*, pp. 2–3 and, as applied to the Vietnam War, pp. 31–32; Hackworth, *Digest of International Law*, vol. 4, pp. 609–10; and Whiteman, *Digest of International Law*, vol. 7, p. 194.

94. Of a different character, Maureen R. Berman and Joseph E. Johnson, editors of *Unofficial Diplomats*, provide a series of case studies and commentary on what are called "diplomats without portfolios" or "unofficial go-betweens," who, though not accredited officials, may be recruited to serve as private intermediaries, may on their own initiative engage in preliminary explorations presaging official negotiations, may serve in a preparatory or supportive capacity, or may undertake projects to study given problems to lay the basis for official action. Usually, they are more concerned with assisting the American Government than with seeking to interject their influence upon foreign governments.

95. This enactment required the Attorney General to promulgate rules and regulations concerning requirements for such notification and to supply the Secretary of State with copies of these notifications. Early precedents were provided in the Acts of June 15, 1917 (40 Stat. 226) and March 28, 1940 (54 Stat. 80), and the current version is provided in the Acts of June 25, 1948 (62 Stat. 743) and January 12, 1983 (96 Stat. 2530); also see *U.S. Code*, Title 18, sec. 951.

96. The Department of State and Foreign Service Officers who contributed to this review included Assistant Secretary and careerist Julius C. Holmes (who captained the Division of Foreign Service Planning and integrated the views and proposals of career Foreign Service Officers); Selden Chapin (who became the first Director General of the Foreign Service); Monet B. Davis (former Minister to Denmark); Nathaniel P. Davis

(later appointed Ambassador to Costa Rica); Andrew B. Foster (Special Assistant to the Secretary of State and later Chief of the Division of Foreign Service Planning); Edmund A. Gullion (serving in the Department at the time); Alan N. Steyne (who had served abroad in many assignments), and Carl W. Strom (serving in the Department at the time).

97. Stuart, *American Diplomatic and Consular Practice*, p. 109, notes that these salaries could be augmented by representation and cost of living allowances, plus funding for an official residence.

98. Because the Foreign Service had insufficient personnel to handle many Department of State duties abroad during World War II, the Foreign Service Auxiliary was established without utilizing the normal admission examination system, to serve for the duration of the war. Initially, Auxiliary members were assigned primarily to Latin American posts, but later they were also sent to serve in various posts in Europe, the Middle East, and the Far East. By 1946 they outnumbered regular Foreign Service Officers.

99. With the consent of the Senate the President could also reappoint individual former Foreign Service Officers, and the Secretary of State was empowered to recommend the class to which each such reappointee was to be assigned, and in cases of emergency the Secretary could also recall retired Foreign Service Officers.

100. Separation allowances were provided to aid personnel stationed at dangerous posts abroad to support spouses and children who remained in the United States. This benefit had been established in 1941 to deal financially with family separation during the World War II years.

101. For additional commentary, see Congress, House of Representatives, *Reorganization of the Foreign Service*, Report (Washington, D.C.: Government Printing Office, 1946), and *The Foreign Service Act of 1946, as Amended to October 17, 1960* (Washington, D.C.: Government Printing Office, 1960); Barnes and Morgan, *The Foreign Service of the United States*, pp. 256–62 and Appendix 19; Plischke, *Conduct of American Diplomacy*, pp. 236, 255, 266, 284–85, 288, 289, and 314–15; Harold Stein, *The Foreign Service Act of 1946* (New York: Committee on Public Administration Cases, 1949); and Stuart, *American Diplomatic and Consular Practice*, pp. 108–12.

102. For current salary schedules, see *U.S. Code*, Title 5, sec. 5332, as amended.

103. For additional information on the Act of 1980 and the contemporary Foreign Service, see American Foreign Service Association, *American Diplomacy and the Foreign Service* (Washington, D.C.: American Foreign Service Association 1989); American Foreign Service Association and Diplomatic and Consular Officers, Retired, *The U.S. Foreign Service: A Global Mission* (Washington, D.C.: 1992); Henry E. Mattox, *Encyclopedia of U.S. Foreign Relations*, vol. 2, pp. 153–56; and Steigman, *The Foreign Service of the United States: First Line of Defense*.

For copies of replications of official U.S. diplomatic documents—such as commissions of appointment, letters of credence and recall, consular exequatur, letters of dismissal and resignation of a diplomat, full powers to negotiate a treaty or agreement, and similar records—see Barnes and Morgan, *The Foreign Service of the United States*, pp. 360–61; and Plischke, *Conduct of American Diplomacy*, pp. 603–14, and *International Relations: Basic Documents* (1962), pp. 13–23.

104. Some Department of State and other lists also include the four traditional European principalities of Andora, Liechtenstein, Monaco, and San Marino (which are not incorporated into this table). Usually, they are serviced by Consular Offices that provide both representational and consular functions.

105. During the past half century five states (original China, Czechoslovakia, German Democratic Republic, Yugoslavia, and the Soviet Union) have been superseded.

106. These fifteen states with which diplomatic relations were added, 1945–1949, included five revivals (with Austria, Bulgaria, Hungary, Romania, and Thailand in 1946–47); the new states included Burma, India, Indonesia, Israel, Nepal, Pakistan, Philippines, Sri Lanka, and Yemen (1946–49); and relations with postwar Korea were also initiated in 1949.

107. It should be noted, however, that the United States dealt with the Polish Government in exile (1939–45; Soviet forces occupied Estonia, Latvia, and Lithuania in mid-June 1940), and American informal diplomatic relations were handled with them in Washington; Thailand was occupied by Japan in December 1941, it declared war on the United States the following January, and relations were not revived until January 1946; and relations with other governments in exile during World War II, including Belgium, Denmark, Greece, Luxembourg, the Netherlands, Norway, Poland, and Yugoslavia were discussed in Chapter 6.

108. In the 1990s the Soviet Union was superseded by the Russian Federation, Armenia, Azerbaijan, Belarus, Georgia, Kazakhstan, Kyrgyz, Moldova, Tajikistan, Turkmenistan, Ukraine, and Uzbekistan; Yugoslavia was succeeded by Bosnia-Herzegovina, Croatia, and Slovenia; and Czechoslovakia was succeeded by the Czech and Slovak Republics.

109. American missions to the Holy See were originally accredited to the Papal States or the Pontifical States as Chargés d'Affaires and Ministers Resident. However, beginning in 1984 diplomacy was regularized, and American envoys were ranked as Ambassadors. The United States established a Consulate at Hong Kong in the mid-1990s, also at the Ambassadorial rank, and after ninety-nine years (1898–1997) as a British-leased territory designated as a Crown Colony, Hong Kong reverted to China in 1997, and the United States continued its consular office there. Although the Department of State established its Embassy to Israel at the Ambassadorial rank in 1949 stationed at Tel Aviv, in 1980 it also created a Consular Office headed by an Ambassador at Jerusalem, although the United States had not recognized it as the Israeli capital.

110. An earlier example of such a long-term break in diplomatic relations involved Korea, with which the United States had diplomatic relations from 1883 to 1905, when it was taken over by Japan, and they were not revived until 1949, when Korea regained its independence.

111. Other islands with populations exceeding 50,000 include Aruba (Netherlands), Bermuda (United Kingdom), Greenland (Denmark), and Mayette (France).

112. Examples of such traditional or longtime diplomatic partners for which American missions were elevated to the Embassy status following World War II include Denmark, Egypt, Ethiopia, Iraq, Korea, Liberia, South Africa, Sweden and Thailand, all in the 1940s, followed soon thereafter by Ireland, Luxembourg, Morocco, and Switzerland, in the 1950s.

113. In a few cases, however, diplomatic relations have been initiated by Chargés d'Affaires ad interim, but these positions were rapidly converted to that of Ambassador, as in the case of Algeria, Djibouti, Kuwait, Ghana, Malawi, Malaysia, Tunis, Sudan, and Vietnam.

However, when relations were commenced with former American territories, such as the Marshall Islands and Micronesia, the initial American envoys were designated as

"Representatives," and when they were launched with Angola early in the 1990s, they were handled by an American "Director."

In earlier times, by way of comparison, American diplomatic missions were often established at lower ranks, which were later elevated to higher levels. To illustrate, American emissaries to longtime diplomatic partners vacillated as follows: Egypt—Agt/CG (1849–1921), EE/MP (1922–44), and AE/P (1944–); Liberia—Comm/CG (1864–66), MR/CG (1866–1929), EE/MP (1935–49), and AE/P (1949–); Italy—CdA (1840–54), MR (1854–61), EE/MP (1861–94), and AE/P (1894–); Netherlands—MP (1782–88), MR (1792–1801), EE/MP (1815–18), CdA (1819–30), EE/MP (1830–31), CdA (1831–54), MR (1854–88), EE/MP (1888–1941), and AE/P (1942–); Russia/Soviet Union—MP (1809–14), EE/MP (1815–97), and AE/P (1898–); and Great Britain/United Kingdom—MP (1785–1808), CdA (1811), EE/MP (1815–89), and AE/P (1893–).

114. The traditional principle of *agreation*, provided for in the Vienna Convention on Diplomatic Relations of 1961 (Article 4) requires that the appointing government clear diplomatic appointees in advance in order to determine whether they are acceptable or persona grata to the receiving government, which also implies fixing the rank of the diplomatic mission.

115. The Congresses of Vienna (1815) and Aix-la-Chapelle (1918) provided for four basic diplomatic ranks—Ambassadors Extraordinary and Plenipotentiary and Papal Legates or Nuncios; Envoys Extraordinary, Ministers Plenipotentiary, and Papal Internuncios; Ministers Resident; and Chargés d'Affairs. The Vienna Convention of 1961, Article 14, provides for three "classes" of heads of mission—Ambassadors, Nuncios, or other Heads of Mission; Envoys, Ministers, and Internuncios; and Chargés d'Affairs. Those in the first two categories are accredited to Chiefs of State; those in the third category are accredited to Ministers of Foreign Affairs.

116. Thus, Sally A. Shelton, accredited as Ambassador to Barbados, Grenada, and Dominica in 1979 and as Minister Plenipotentiary to St. Lucia, was also appointed as Special Representative to St. Kitts-Nevis-Anguila and St. Vincent (resident at Bridgetown); and Milan D. Bish was accredited as Ambassador to St. Lucia, Antigua and Barbuda, Barbados, Dominica, St. Vincent and the Grenadines in 1981 and was also appointed as Special Representative to St. Kitts and Nevis, also resident at Bridgetown. These appointments as Special Representative were made before these islands were recognized as independent states.

117. These were the first six envoys accredited to India, including careerists George V. Allen and Loy W. Henderson and noncareerists Chester Bowles, Ellsworth Bunker, John Sherman Cooper, and Henry F. Grady—all distinguished American diplomats.

118. Conversely, although the Vienna Convention on Diplomatic Relations (1961), Article 6, provides that two or more states may accredit the same person as head of their diplomatic missions to another country, unless this is objected to by the receiving state, this practice has rarely been applied to the appointment of foreign diplomats to the United States.

119. For additional commentary on consular functions, see Department of State, *The American Consul* (Washington, D.C.: Government Printing Office, 1955), and *The Department of State, 1963* (Washington, D.C.: Government Printing Office, 1963), pp. 63–66; Barnes and Morgan, *The Foreign Service of the United States*, p. 303; Carol M. Crosswell, *Protection of International Personnel Abroad* (Dobbs Ferry, NY: Oceana, 1952); McCamy, *Conduct of the New Diplomacy*, pp. 191–93; Plischke, *Conduct of American Diplomacy*, pp. 323–33; Simpson, *Anatomy of the State Department*, pp. 108–

13, and *The Crisis in American Diplomacy*, pp. 151, 208–16); and Stuart, *American Diplomatic and Consular Practice*, pp. 302–75. For additional sources, see Plischke, *U.S. Foreign Relations: A Guide to Information Sources*, especially pp. 415–20. For tables of consular establishments, see Barnes and Morgan, p. 349, and Plischke, p. 263. On the matter of consular conventions, see also the section on Treaty Making and Tables 7.9 and 7.10.

120. For texts of, and commentary on, these Presidential orders and other documents dealing with the coordination and supervision responsibilities of the Secretary of State and chiefs of diplomatic missions over other government agencies, see Plischke, *Contemporary U.S. Foreign Policy: Documents and Commentary*, pp. 107–8, and *Modern Diplomacy, the Art and the Artisans* pp. 427–34. Also see *Papers of the Presidents*, Department of State, *American Foreign Policy: Basic Documents* and *Current Documents*, and *Digests of U.S. Practice in International Law*.

121. Blancké, *The Foreign Service of the United States*, pp. 138–39, reports that following World War II, a number of American government agencies sought to provide separate officers of ambassadorial rank to serve as their own regional representatives abroad, and the number of special emissaries proliferated, so that resident Ambassadors were often bypassed, and their status, authority, and prestige needed to be reaffirmed.

122. Macomber, *The Angels' Game*, p. 95. For additional information on coordination, see Department of State, *The Country Team*, especially pp. 5–9, which also discusses various substantive aspects of the concerns of country teams, including the foreign mission model concept, and it analyzes several specific diplomatic missions; Blancké, *The Foreign Service of the United States*, pp. 132–42, who also suggests the possibility of a ''A Country Team for Washington,'' as a counterpart of the Country Teams abroad, pp. 142–44; Briggs, *Anatomy of Diplomacy*, pp. 130–31; Harr, *The Professional Diplomat*, pp. 24–25, 237, 293–94, 297; Macomber, *The Angels' Game*, pp. 95–97 and *Diplomacy for the 70's*, pp. 449–523 on rules and functions of diplomatic missions; and Trask, *A Short History of the Department of State, 1781–1981*, p. 34. Also see Lincoln Gordon, ''Coordination of Overseas Representation,'' Chapter 6 of the American Assembly, *The Representation of the United States Abroad*, which deals with points of possible conflict, coordination at the country level, regional coordination, and coordination in Washington.

123. For example, Department of State language training was begun as early as 1895, with the assignment of officers as ''student interpreters'' to American legations in Korea, Persia, and Siam. In 1902 the State Department established ten student interpreter positions, and five years later it introduced a short, one-month training session for a few commissioned consular officers.

The Rogers Act of 1924 provided that new Foreign Service Officers would initially serve in the Department for a period of probation in an unclassified grade for purposes of instruction by a Foreign Service School prior to assignment abroad. In the 1930s this was renamed the Foreign Service Officer's Training School, and a Department of State Training Division was created to manage the program. This new division was intended to produce a basic program consisting of orientation and indoctrination courses for initiates, special courses in administrative functions, advanced specialized training, and language courses.

124. For additional commentary on developments of the Foreign Service Institute, see William P. Maddox, ''Foreign Service Institute of the Department of State,'' *Higher Education*, (October 15, 1947): 37–40; Department of State, *The Foreign Service Insti-*

tute, and *The Department of State*, pp. 89–91, and Barnes and Morgan, *The Foreign Service of the United States*, pp. 262, 274, 275, 285, 314–17, and 394–95.

Also see Plischke, *Conduct of American Diplomacy*, pp. 206, 252, 283, 284; Simpson, *Anatomy of the State Department*, pp. 11–12, 23, 129, 180, 194, 204, 217, 224, 227, and *The Crisis in American Diplomacy*, Chapters 7 and 8, and pp. 60–61, 77, 170, 205, 211, 224, 228, 229, 234, 254, 269, 303–5; and Stuart, *American Diplomatic and Consular Practice*, pp. 60–61, and *The Department of State*, pp. 452–53.

125. Clark served as Assistant Secretary for Consular Affairs, Director General of the Foreign Service, and Director of Management Operations; Laise as Assistant Secretary for Public Affairs and Director General of the Foreign Service; Ridgway as Counselor of the Department and Assistant Secretary for European and Canadian Affairs; and Watson as Assistant Secretary for Consular Affairs twice. Of these only Watson was a noncareerist.

126. These countries include Austria, Benin, Denmark, Dominica, Guatemala, Ireland, Kenya, Mali, Malta, New Zealand, St. Lucia, Solomon Islands, Sri Lanka, Switzerland, Togo, and Western Samoa.

127. Subsequently, a series of women, almost universally noncareerist, were appointed as Chiefs of Protocol, making this one of the most popular State Department agencies for women.

128. For a comprehensive history and analysis of the role of women as principal officers and in other capacities in the Department of State and American missions abroad, which provides valuable, detailed information concerning matters of policy, plans, regulations, and developments respecting appointments and other personnel factors, see Homer L. Calkin (longtime member of the Department of State), *Women in American Foreign Affairs* (Washington, D.C.: Department of State, 1977). In addition to his historical account, he appends more than thirty-five tables, charts, and appendixes. For additional studies, see Barnes and Morgan, *The Foreign Service of the United States*, pp. 220, 225–27, 325–26, 306; McCamy, *Conduct of the New Diplomacy*, pp. 206–7; and Stuart, *American Diplomatic and Consular Practice*, pp. 144–47.

129. For example, the ranking diplomats who held sequential appointments prior to 1946 included career Foreign Service Officers Norman Armour (five), James Rives Childs (one), Edmund A. Gullion (one), Loy W. Henderson (one), George Wadsworth, II (three), and Avra M. Warren (three), and noncareerists Anthony Drexel Biddle, Jr. (eight), and Lincoln MacVeagh (four).

130. Illustrative of the careerist women were Joan M. Clark, Caroline C. Laise, Rozanne L. Ridgway, Frances E. Willis, and Evelyn Teegan. Noncareerists included such celebrities as Shirley Temple Black, Ann Claire Booth Luce, and Perle Mesta, as well as Madeleine Albright, Anne L. Armstrong, Jean B. Gerard, Margaret M. Heckler, Jeane J. Kirkpatrick, and Katharine White.

131. This was a rare appointment; usually, Deputy Secretaries are noncareerists.

132. Examples include Mann (Assistant Secretary three times); Allen, Merchant, and Rountree (Assistant Secretary each twice); Johnson (Deputy Under Secretary twice), Bohlen (Counselor twice), and Newsom (Acting Secretary three times).

133. Other career Foreign Service Officers who also achieved the rank of Career Ambassador include Walworth Barbour, Winthrop G. Brown, Walter C. Dowling, Arthur A. Hartman, Foy D. Kohler, and Edwin M. Martin.

134. Robert E. Lamb had previously served as Coordinator of the Office of Security and Director of the Bureau of Diplomatic Security, beginning in 1985.

135. Illustrations of these professions embrace statesmen and members of Congress— John Foster Dulles, W. Averell Harriman, Christian A. Herter, Henry Cabot Lodge, Jr., Adlai E. Stevenson, and Arthur H. Vandenberg; military—Arthur A. Ageton (Navy), James M. Gavin (Army), William D. Leahy (Navy), George C. Marshall (Army), William H. Standley (Navy), Walter Bedell Smith (Army), and Maxwell D. Taylor (Army); legal profession—Adolph A. Berle, Philip C. Jessup, and Lee Merriweather; banking and business—Spruille Braden, Charles G. Dawes, John J. McCloy, Myron C. Taylor, and James J. Wadsworth; journalism and the media—Hamilton Fish Armstrong, Andrew H. Berding, Claude G. Bowers, Clare Boothe Luce, Nicholas Roosevelt, Lincoln MacVeagh, and William E. Warne.

136. Of these Kissinger was appointed Secretary of State, Kalijarvi and Thorp served as Assistant Secretaries of State, and Conant, Galbraith, Kalijarvi, and Reischauer were commissioned as Chiefs of Mission abroad.

137. Other memoirs produced by careerists are represented by John C. Caldwell— *American Agent*; Jefferson Patterson—*Diplomatic Duty and Diversion*; and Bartley F. Yost—*Memoirs of a Consul*; and by noncareerists William M. Collier—*At the Court of His Catholic Majesty* and Hallett Johnson—*Diplomatic Memoirs, Serious and Frivolous*.

138. Also of interest are Harlan Cleveland—*The Art of Overseasmanship*; Eliot B. Coulter—*Visa Work of the Department of State and the Foreign Service*; Seymour I. Nadler—*Life and Love in the Foreign Service*; Howard L. Nostrand—*The Cultural Attaché*; Jefferson Patterson—*Diplomatic Duty and Diversion*; Franklin Roudybush— *Foreign Service Training* (comparison of several countries); and Robert Strausz-Hupe—*A Forward Strategy for America* and *Geopolitics*.

139. Illustrative of those publications that bear unusual and intriguing titles are John L. Barnard—*Revelry by Night*; Eugene H. Bird—*The Generation Gap;* Niles W. Bond— *Arcanum* and *Elegos* (poetry); Paul H. Bonner—*SPQR* (fiction); John C. Caldwell—*Our Friends the Tigers*; Herbert Cerwin—*Famous Recipes by Famous People*; Morrill Cody—*The Favorite Restaurants of an American in Paris*; Barnaby Conrad—*Encyclopedia of Bullfighting*; Philip K. Crowe—*Sport Is Where You Find It*; Martin J. Hillenbrand—*Power and Morals*; John B. Martin—*Butcher's Dozen and Other Murders*; Harold H. Rhodes—*No "Four Letter" Words*; Paul C. Squire—*Fit To Print*; and Henry S. Villard—*The Great Road Races, 1894–1914*; as well as James Rives Childs' seven books on Casanova.

140. For additional commentary and listings, see Boyce and Boyce, *American Foreign Service Authors: A Bibliography*; Elmer Plischke, "American Diplomats as Authors," *Society for Historians of American Foreign Relations Newsletter*, 15 (December 1984): 1–20, and *U.S. Foreign Relations: A Guide to Information Sources*, especially Chapter 23.

141. Aside from the recognized foreign states with which the United States established diplomatic relations, these included such former entities as the Central American Federation, Hanseatic Republic, Orange Free State, and Prussia; Mid-East territories, including Algiers, Muscat, Ottoman empire, Palestine, Tripoli, Tunis, and the United Arab Republic; various islands such as Fiji, Loochoo (Ryukyu), Madagascar, Samoa, Tonga, and Zanzibar; and independent Hawaii and Texas, which were admitted into American statehood, but not the former German Laender.

142. For example, during World War II, fearing a repetition of the rejection by the United States of the League of Nations, the Department of State and leading members of Congress evolved what came to be called the "Green-Sayre formula" (championed

by Senator Theodore F. Green and Assistant Secretary Francis B. Sayre) to deal with
approval of an executive agreement, being negotiated by Secretary Hull, to create the
United Nations Relief and Rehabilitation Administration. In August 1943 a Senate subcommittee promised to recommend to the Senate that the agreement be approved by an
act of Congress providing the necessary appropriations to carry it into effect. This process
of legislating financial support implied acceptance of the agreement to participate in
UNRRA.

143. In the *Sei Fuji vs. the State of California* case in 1950, the District Court of
Appeals of California, by unanimous decision, held that the California alien land law
contravened the civil rights provisions of the Preamble and Articles 55 and 56 of the
United Nations Charter, concerning human rights and fundamental freedoms. This decision was later upheld by the California Supreme Court, which did so for other reasons,
relying rather on the equal protection clause of the Fourteenth Amendment to the American Constitution.

In the case of *Missouri vs. Holland* (1920), the Supreme Court of the United States
reversed an earlier decision that held a U.S. law to preserve various species of migratory
birds to be unconstitutional on the grounds that it invaded the powers reserved to the
States. Later, it upheld the validity of the Migratory Birds Act of 1918, which sought to
achieve the same goal, on the grounds that it was enacted to implement a prior treaty
with Great Britain, which was valid, and therefore the act was not deemed to be unconstitutional.

144. To curb the so-called Roosevelt–Truman treaty policy, in 1951 and 1952 several
proposals to govern executive treaty-making authority were introduced in both houses of
Congress, of which that of Senator Bricker received the widest attention, and the movement reached its peak in 1953 and 1954. This challenge to treaty-making authority proved
to be critical, with one version being defeated in the Senate by a scant margin of a single
vote. Apparently, as noted by the Department of State, the Congressional challenge was
founded on "fundamental distrust of the intelligence and integrity of both the President
and the United States Senate," as well as on "distrust of our courts."

145. For additional commentary on attempts by Congress to revise and restrain executive treaty authority and procedures, see Plischke, *Conduct of American Diplomacy*,
Chapter 12 (especially pp. 373–74, 380–86, and 399–414), and Chapter 13 (especially
pp. 419–22 and 428–29); and, *Contemporary U.S. Foreign Policy: Documents and Commentary*, pp. 132–43. For a short analysis of the constitutional aspects of the treaty
process, see Kenneth C. Randall, "Treaty-Making Power," *Encyclopedia of the American Presidency*, vol. 4, pp. 1487–90.

146. On the matter of the publication of American treaties and agreements, see Plischke, *Conduct of American Diplomacy*, pp. 452–53 and for current statutory requirements,
see *U.S. Code*, Title 1, secs. 112, 112a and b; Title 22, sec. 2660; and Title 44, secs.
709 and 711. For a comprehensive bibliographical listing of compilations of, and commentary on, official U.S., international, and other documents and volumes on American
treaties and agreements, see Table 7.14, section on Treaties and Agreements and Plischke,
U.S. Foreign Relations: A Guide to Information Sources, especially pp. 385–97 and 571–
87.

147. In addition to the well-publicized international Doctrines of Continuous Voyage
and Hot Pursuit, those dicta bearing these labels were ascribed to such international
matters as "dual nationality" or "double allegiance" (pertaining to citizenship), "necessity" (based on the fundamental right of nations to self-preservation, subject to certain

limitations), and "protection" (of individuals of one nationality traveling abroad within the jurisdiction of another country).

Pre–World War II declarations include a proposed Declaration of the Rights of Man (based on natural law, 1789), a Declaration of the Law of Nations (proposed by the Abbe Gregoire in 1795), the Declaration of St. Petersburg (to ban certain projectiles in warfare, 1868), the Declaration on Non-Alterating of Treaties (without the consent of other contracting states, London, 1871), and the well-known Declaration of Paris (1856) and the Declaration of London (1909), both regarded as treaties to codify maritime law in time of war. The Declaration of Paris prescribed four basic legal principles, whereas the Declaration of London, consisting of twenty-one articles, defined these relations in greater detail. The former was generally accepted by major European powers, but aspects of it were contested by the United States. The London Declaration was signed by ten (mostly naval) powers, including the United States, but none ratified it.

Examples of other such pronouncements include an unofficial Declaration on the Rights and Duties of States, consisting of six fundamental principles, adopted by the American Institute of International Law in 1916, which was later considered and adopted at the Havana Inter-American Conference in 1928. This was followed by the Inter-American Declarations of Lima (on American Principles, 1938), Panama (on Standards of Conduct of Neutrals during World War II, 1939), and Mexico City (on the Rights and Duties of Man, 1945, which was not signed until 1948, at Bogotá).

148. The Monroe Doctrine was unique in that it was later explained by President John Quincy Adams (1824), defined by President Polk (1845), applied to Central America by Secretary Clayton (1850), referred to by Secretary Seward (1861), supported by President Grant (1870), redefined by the Olney Corollary (1895) and the Theodore Roosevelt Corollary (1904), refined by President Wilson, who sought to Pan-Americanize it (1916), reasserted and clarified by the J. Reuben Clark Memorandum (1928), reserved from application of the Kellogg-type arbitration treaties (1928–   ), extended to Canada by President Franklin Roosevelt in the Hyde Park Declaration (1941), applied to the Soviet Union by Secretary Herter (1960), incorporated by President Truman as the ninth of his Fundamentals of American Foreign Policy (1945), and reaffirmed by the Department of State (1960), by President Kennedy (1962), and subsequently by other Presidents, including Nixon, Carter, and Reagan, and by Secretary Shultz.

It was also multilateralized by a series of multilateral declarations produced at inter-American conferences held at Buenos Aires (1936), Lima (1938), Havana (1940), Washington (1942), Chapultepec (Mexico City, 1945), Panama (1956), Santiago (1959), San José (1960), and others. The spirit of the Monroe Doctrine was also reflected and generalized in the United Nations General Assembly Declaration against Intervention in the Domestic Affairs of States and Protection of Their Independence and Sovereignty (1966).

For the texts of, and commentary on, such documents, see Ruhl S. Bartlett, ed., *The Record of American Diplomacy*, 4th ed. (New York, Knopf, 1964), pp. 181–83, 185–86, 201–3, 237–39, 245, 277, 312–14, 340–45, 539, 541–42, 546–51, 553–54, 561–62, 719–20, and 861–62; and Plischke, *Contemporary U.S. Foreign Policy*, pp. 160, 177–78, 182–83, 371, 426–29, 448, 762–68, 772–73, and 798.

For additional literature on the Monroe Doctrine, see J. Reuben Clark, *Memorandum on the Monroe Doctrine* (Washington, D.C.: Government Printing Office, 1930), also issued as Department of State publication no. 37); Donald M. Dozer, *The Monroe Doctrine: Its Modern Significance* (New York: Knopf, 1965); Thomas B. Edgington, *The Monroe Doctrine* (Boston: Little, Brown, 1905); Frederick Merk, *The Monroe Doctrine and American Expansionism, 1843–1949* (New York: Knopf, 1966); Ernest R. May, *The Making of the Monroe Doctrine* (Cambridge: Harvard University Press, 1975); Dexter Perkins, *The Monroe Doctrine, 1823–1826* (Cambridge: Harvard University Press, 1932); Armin Rappaport, ed., *The Monroe Doctrine* (New York: Holt, Rinehart, and Winston, 1964); Gaddis Smith, *The Last Years of the Monroe Doctrine, 1945–1993* (New York: Hill and Wang, 1994); David Y. Thomas, *One Hundred Years of the Monroe Doctrine, 1823–1923* (New York: Macmillan, 1923); Charles M. Wilson, *The Monroe Doctrine: An American Frame of Mind* (Princeton: Auerbach, 1971); and Arthur P. Whitaker, *The United States and the Independence of Latin America, 1800–1830* (Baltimore: Johns Hopkins University Press, 1941).

149. For the texts of recent Presidential Doctrines, see Plischke, *Contemporary U.S. Foreign Policy*, Chapter 7, pp. 177–205. For a comprehensive analysis of the subject, see Cecil V. Crabb, Jr., *The Doctrines of American Foreign Policy: Their Meaning, Role, and Future* (Baton Rouge: Louisiana State University Press, 1982).

150. Using Department of State expressions, policy declarations need to be distinguished from the thousands of other public pronouncements, diplomatic communications, and other documents designated by the President and the Department of State as addresses, announcements, communications, communiqués, determinations, exchanges of notes, memorandums, messages, proclamations, remarks, reports, and transcripts of exchanges and from such more formal or precise instruments identified as agreement, armistice, cease-fire, *compromis d'arbitrage*, concordat, final act, international statute, *modus vivendi*, pact, *proces verbal*, protocol, treaty, and truce.

The distinction among several of these designations is self-evident, and others have become well established in diplomatic practice, but some of them are not readily distinguishable from policy declarations.

A few listed in Table 7.7, Part B, as acts, charters, communiqués, memorandums, or resolutions of international conferences and organizations are more in the nature of policy declarations than binding international commitments. However, this list does not include the scores of additional traditional joint communiqué of summit and ministerial meetings or the thousands of international conference and organization resolutions, many of which prescribe international norms and standards of conduct and some of which are regarded as law-creating.

151. Since World War II only approximately twenty such proclamations were promulgated, all but one of which were unilateral American instruments. The exception was that of the Allied High Commission terminating the occupation of West Germany in 1955.

152. Although differing in detail, as essential aggregates of American policy objectives, President Truman's Twelve Fundamentals of United States Foreign Policy of 1945 is comparable, in many respects, to Wilson's Fourteen Points of January 1918 and the eight principles of the Atlantic Charter of August 1941.

All three extolled freedom of the seas, free trade, self-determination, arms limitation, and a peacekeeping international organization (which Wilson called "a general association of nations," the Atlantic Charter denominated "a wider and permanent system of general security," and Truman identified as the "United Nations Organization").

Wilson's "open covenants, openly arrived at" was later dropped. All three espoused democracy and self-determination in various versions, and Wilson's specification of the post–World War I treatment of particular countries was not repeated. The Atlantic Charter incorporated two of President Roosevelt's Four Freedoms—freedom from fear and want—and Truman's dictum included a third—freedom of expression, to which he added freedom of religion, and it also reiterated the essence of the Monroe Doctrine (which was not included by Wilson) and incorporated the "good neighbor" principle and the precept of nonaggression. Finally, Wilson's and Truman's declarations projected unilateral American policy postulates, whereas the Atlantic Charter was a bipartite declaration of President Roosevelt and British Minister Winston Churchill.

153. Examples of the bilateral, tripartite, and quadripartite declarations include many that dealt with the post–World War II treatment of Germany and Japan, Anglo–American attitudes on the origin and destiny of humankind, armistice borders between the Arab states and Israel, the Potomac Charter providing for common principles of Anglo–American policy, and bilateral arrangements concerning the U.S.–Mexican border and American bases in the Philippines.

154. Illustrations of inter-American declarations concerned the Alliance for Progress, the ideals of inter-Americanism and continental solidarity, education and literacy, peace and peaceful settlement in Central America and other countries, and sanctions against Cuba and its exclusion from the Organization of American States.

155. Economic Summit Meetings have dealt largely with economic interests and welfare but also involved advancing democracy and democratic values, arms transfers, elimination of nuclear and other weapons, energy conservation, human rights, international hijacking and terrorism, trade, and strengthening the international order.

156. For additional information on American foreign relations proclamations and declarations, see the *Public Papers of the Presidents* series; Department of State, *A Decade of American Foreign Policy: Basic Documents, 1941–49*; and Department of State, *American Foreign Policy: Current Documents* series; Bartlett, *The Record of American Diplomacy*; and Plischke, *Contemporary U.S. Foreign Policy: Documents and Commentary*, with a listing of declarations given on pp. 815–16. Additional bibliographical guidance is provided in Plischke, *U.S. Foreign Relations: A Guide to Information Sources*, pp. 555–58.

157. On December 31, 1992, Czechoslovakia was divided into the Czech and Slovak Republics; on December 31, 1991, the Soviet Union was broken up into twelve republics, including the Russian Federation and Armenia, Azerbaijan, Belarus, Georgia, Kazakstan, Kyrgyz, Moldova, Tajikistan, Turkmenistan, Ukraine, and Uzbekistan; and in 1992 Yugoslavia was dissolved into Bosnia-Herzegovina, Croatia, Slovenia, and the Federal Republic of Yugoslavia, consisting of Serbia and Montenegro.

158. These include such countries as Angola, Bhutan, New Caledonia, Niue, and Vanuatu, as well as San Marino and the Vatican.

159. These twenty-eight include European countries—Belgium, Denmark, Greece, Italy, the Netherlands, Norway, Poland, Romania, Spain, and Yugoslavia; Latin American—Argentina, Bolivia, Brazil, Chile, Colombia, Ecuador, Honduras, Panama, and Venezuela; and also Australia, Egypt, Indonesia, Israel, Korea, Pakistan, Philippines, Turkey, and Ukraine.

160. A substantial number of those listed as "others" are called "arrangements" (50 percent), followed by approximately 100 "declarations" and "protocols," and fifteen are listed as "procedures" (applied solely to judicial assistance arrangements). Others are identified as "accords," "acts," "basic principles," "frameworks," "joint communiqués," "minutes" (of boundary agreements with Mexico), "programs of cooperation," "projects," "settlements" (financial), and "undertakings."

161. Thus, thirty-five treaties/agreements were signed at New York City, including

fourteen with the United Nations. Some forty-six were signed elsewhere in the Washington area at Alexandria, Arlington, Fairfax, and Reston in Virginia and Bethesda, Gaithersburg, and Rockville in Maryland, more than half of which were signed at Reston. Others were signed at such other American places as Atlanta, Baltimore, Honolulu, Williamsburg, Lake Success and, strangely, Bar Harbor, Maine, and Jackson Hole, Wyoming.

162. Based on Department of State, *Treaties in Force* (1996).

163. Other subjects, some of which entailed substantial numbers of treaties/agreements prior to 1946, embrace civil aviation, commodities, customs, double taxation, education, exchange of official publications, fisheries, health, the isthmian canal, narcotic drugs, nationality and naturalization, the rules of warfare, smuggling, World War II military missions, the Lend-Lease program, and other matters.

164. Illustrating those subject categories limited to a single treaty/agreement are such varied matters as the creation of diplomatic interest sections of the United States and Cuba, respectively, in the Swiss Embassy in Havana and the Czech Embassy in Washington (1977), narcotic drug money laundering (Peru, 1991), passports for visitors to the Bering Strait region (Soviet Union, 1989), territorial sovereignty over the Swan Islands (Honduras, 1971), termination of certain bilateral agreements (Greece, 1995), treaty succession of Ukraine to bilateral treaties/agreements of the United States with the Soviet Union (1995), and contribution of personnel to the criminal tribunal for war crimes in Yugoslavia (with the United Nations, 1994).

Other interesting examples of single item treaty-agreement subjects embrace driver's licences (Mexico, 1991), interdiction of migrants (Haiti, 1981), marriage documentation of American citizens (Italy, 1964), and recovery of stolen property (vehicles and aircraft, Mexico, 1981).

165. Other countries with which the United States has substantial packages of more than 100 basic treaties/agreements are Germany (150), Japan (141), France and its dependencies (126), and Korea (102). These are followed by the Philippines (ninety-nine), Italy (ninety-five), the Netherlands with its dependency (ninety), and Panama (eighty-five).

166. To these subject categories may be added agricultural commodities, diplomatic and consular affairs, education and cultural affairs, energy, environment and pollution, outer space, peacekeeping, satellites, and tourism.

167. The other main bilateral peace treaties were concluded with Great Britain following the War of 1812 (1814), the Mexican War (1848), and the Spanish–American War (1899), supplemented with peace treaties with Morocco (1836) and Italy (two in 1951 following its World War II multilateral treaty).

168. Other territorial settlements include boundary arrangements with Great Britain concerning the American boundary in the Northeast and Midwest (Webster–Ashburton Treaty, 1842) and the Oregon Territory (Oregon Treaty, 1846), the cession of the Southwest and California Territory Treaty of Guadalupe Hidalgo at the conclusion of the Mexican War and the cession of the Philippine Islands following the Spanish-American War.

169. It is not inconceivable that in the future certain additional categories of treaties/agreements will be regarded as of historic significance, such as those concerned with atomic and nuclear energy and weapons, control of civil aviation, defense and mutual assistance, narcotic drug control, oceanic jurisdiction, outer space and satellites, the seas

and seabeds, the World War II Lend-Lease program, and the Peace Corps and other foreign assistance arrangements.

170. The Department of State simply lists these without detailed description or further identification in *Treaties in Force*.

171. The preponderant majority of these are simple "amendments," some are "agreed extensions," and the rest are combined "amendments/extensions."

172. These also include three dependencies—Monaco (Portugal) and Bermuda and Hong Kong (United Kingdom), as well as such international organizations as the African Development Bank, the European Atomic Energy Agency, and the United Nations.

173. Specifically, these embrace agricultural commodities (sixty countries, 499 amendments/ extensions), civil aviation (sixty-seven countries, 148 instruments), defense (thirty-four countries, 127 instruments), economic and technical cooperation (fifty countries, 133 instruments), finance (thirty-seven countries, sixty-six instruments), and trade (forty-three countries, 191 instruments).

174. The earliest of these multilateral treaties/agreements deal with the rights of neutrals at sea (1854), weights and measures (1875), right of protection in Morocco (1880), protection of submarine cables (1884), international exchange of official documents (1886), the laws of war on land (1889), the Hague Convention on the Settlement of Disputes (1899), relations with Samoa (1899), and customs (1890). In the early twentieth century these were supplemented by those on the suppression of the white slave traffic, inter-American pecuniary claims, industrial property, copyright, assistance and salvage at sea, and the laws of war. However, most of the pre-1946 treaties/agreements were concluded in the late 1920s, 1930s, and early 1940s.

175. Of these some sixty are designated as protocols, more than forty are memorandums of understanding, twenty are constitutive in nature (charter, constitution, covenant, and statute), and nearly as many are otherwise law-creating (accord, act or general act, code, pact, and regulations). Others are variously denominated as arrangements, declarations, programs, terms of reference, and procès-verbaux.

Exceptionally, the Vietnam War Settlement was designated the Act of the International Conference on Vietnam, which was signed at Paris on March 2, 1973, by twelve governments, including the United States, China, and the Soviet Union.

176. Other multilateral treaties/agreements were signed at more than thirty other places, including Algeciras, Budapest, Canberra, The Hague, Hamburg, Karachi, Locarno, Manila, Monaco, Moscow, Nairobi, Seoul, Strasbourg, Tokyo, Yalta, and others.

177. These are followed by fourteen other categories, each of which accounts for ten or more treaties/agreements. On the other hand, nearly one-fourth of the categories are represented by a single treaty or agreement, such as those concerned with Antarctica, extradition, gas warfare, genocide, human rights, phonograms, the renunciation of war, Spitzbergen, torture, tourism, and individual commodities. Some would regard some of these and certain other subjects as unique, including those concerned with aliens, environmental modification, polar bears, submarine cables, state and local taxation of foreign employees of public international organizations, and whaling.

178. Other individual subject categories also constitute treaty packages, such as those concerned with conservation, energy, Germany, civil aviation, patents, postal affairs, publications, taxation, telecommunication, and trade and commerce.

179. Representative examples include those with more than 100 signatures that are concerned with atomic energy, biological weapons, conservation of endangered species, consular and diplomatic affairs, copyright, food and agriculture, industrial development,

intellectual property, labor, narcotic drugs, nuclear testing, radio regulation, satellite communications, slavery, telecommunication, and the unlawful seizure of aircraft.

180. Examples include the Korean Democratic Republic, the former German Democratic Republic, former Czechoslovakia, Macedonia, the Soviet Union, and Yugoslavia, the European principalities (Andorra, Liechtenstein, Monaco, and San Marino), the two Yemens (subsequently amalgamated), and the Republic of China (Taiwan).

181. Most of these international organizations have been European agencies. Thus, the European Community signed an agreement for international cooperation in the field of energy (1974); the European Economic Community was a signatory of a series of treaties/agreements (mostly conventions) on the conservation of Antarctic marine living resources (1950), customs procedures (1973), cooperation in the field of energy (1974), outer space (1975), food aid (1986), wheat aid (1986), illicit traffic in narcotic drugs (1988), and climate change (1992); the European Space Agency subscribed to international instruments concerned with the rescue of astronauts (1968), international liability for damage caused by space objects (as did the European Telecommunications Satellite Organization, 1972), and the registration of objects launched into outer space (1975); the Commission for the European Communities signed four energy agreements (1977–78); and the European Energy Community became a party to three energy agreements (1977 and 1980) and a convention on the protection of nuclear materials (1979). Similarly, a convention concerning notification regarding nuclear accidents was signed by the Food and Agriculture Organization, the World Health Organization, and the World Meteorological Organization (1986); and several agreements on multilateral funds were signed by the International Bank, the International Development Association, and the African Development Bank (1960, 1972, and 1975).

182. It is worthy of note that there is no comparable global or universal extradition treaty. This matter is customarily dealt with bilaterally, as noted in the section on bilateral treaties.

183. Technically, advance legislative approval is unlikely if the United States wishes to issue or accept an invitation to attend conferences and meetings while Congress is not in session. Furthermore, Congress could scarcely by expected to act intelligently and expeditiously on the hundreds of conferences and meetings being convened, and, as a practical matter, the advance approval process would entail considerable additional, often unnecessary work for Congress, the White House, and the State Department.

184. Act of August 1, 1956 (70 Stat. 891); as amended by Act of August 24, 1982 (96 Stat. 282); *U.S. Code*, Title 22, sec. 2672.

185. Most of these constitutive conferences provided for the negotiation of the organic acts of more than thirty global and regional international organizations and similar agencies. More than one-third of the conferences were held immediately after World War II, during the short period from late 1945 to 1949. Two-thirds of them concerned global agencies, such as the International Atomic Energy Agency, Food and Agriculture Organization, International Development Association, International Finance Corporation, International Telecommunication Union, Multilateral Investment Guarantee Agency, United Nations Industrial Development Organization, and the International Trade Organization. The regional organizations included the Organization of American States, North Atlantic Treaty Organization and other regional security agencies, Council of Foreign Ministers, North American Free Trade Association, Postal Union of the Americas and Spain, and the South Pacific Commission.

186. The United Nations sponsors a substantial number of international conferences

that concern worldwide interests that, aside from those that create other international organizations and agencies to deal with specific problems, in some cases involve multiple conferences over the years. These embrace such matters as atomic and nuclear power and weaponry, the law of the sea, outer space, terrorism, trade and development, women's affairs, the world environment, and population and human rights.

187. More than thirty-five conferences and meetings listed in Table 7.11 convened at Washington, a dozen or more met in New York, and the others were held at Atlantic City, Camp David, Glassboro, Houston, San Francisco, and Williamsburg. Others held in American territory met in Alaska (Elmendorf Air Base), Guam, Hawaii, Midway, and Puerto Rico.

188. These pre-1946 United Nations specialized agencies include the Food and Agriculture Organization (Hot Springs, Virginia, 1943), the International Bank and International Monetary Fund (Bretton Woods, New Hampshire, 1944), the International Civil Aviation Organization (Chicago, 1944), and the United Nations Relief and Rehabilitation Administration (Washington, D.C., 1943, terminated in 1946). An early conference leading to the creation of the International Telecommunication Union was also held in Washington in 1927. However, the United Nations Educational, Scientific and Cultural Organization was created at London in 1945.

189. In addition to such financial agencies as the International Finance Corporation (1955), the International Development Association (1960), and the Multilateral Investment Guarantee Agency (1985), these included the International Atomic Energy Agency (1956), International Hydrographic Organization (1970), International Telecommunication Union (1947), United Nations Industrial Development Organization (1979), and the World Trade organization (1994).

190. However, NATO ministerial meetings have also been held occasionally at such places as Ankara, Bonn, Copenhagen, The Hague, Istanbul, Lisbon, London, Luxembourg, Madrid, Oslo, Ottawa, and Rome.

191. The conference and meeting sites listed in Table 7.11 number more than 100. In addition to those cited earlier, these include Denver, Honolulu, and Seattle (United States); Halifax, Ottawa, Quebec, and Toronto (Canada); Athens, Bucharest, Hamburg, Munich, Naples, Potsdam, Rambouillet, Strasbourg, Turnberry (Scotland), Venice, and Versailles (Europe); Barbados, Bermuda, Buenos Aires, Caracas, Guatamala City, Panama City, Rio de Janeiro, St. Georges, San José, and Tlatelolco (Latin America); Tehran (Middle East); Abijan and Nairobi (Africa); and Bali, Bandar Seri, Bangkok, Canberra, Jakarta, Karachi, Kiev, Kyoto, Perth, Saigon, Singapore, Sydney, Tokyo, Vladivostok, and Wellington (Asia and Far East). Some of these, such as Ankara, Bangkok, Caracas, Honolulu, Nairobi, and San José, hosted several of them, and the list of sites is likely to continue to grow.

192. Other conferences remembered as identified with sites at which they were held embrace those concerned with the World War II European Axis peace treaties (Paris, 1947), the peace treaty with Japan (San Francisco, 1951), the new Panama Canal treaties (Washington, 1977), North–South relations (Paris, 1976 and Cancun, 1981), and the world environment (Nairobi, 1992).

193. See Bevans, *Treaties and Other International Agreements of the United States*, vol. 4, pp. 639–88, and *United States Treaties and Other International Agreements*, vol. 19, parts 1–3, pp. 1–4,087. For additional commentary, see Susan M. Collins and Barry P. Bosworth, eds., *The New GATT: Implications for the United States* (Washington, D.C.: Brookings, 1994); Kenneth W. Dam, *The GATT: Law and International Organization*

(Chicago: University of Chicago Press, 1970); Kulwant R. Gupta, *A Study of the General Agreement on Tariffs and Trade* (Delhi: S. Chand, 1967); and John H. Jackson, *The World Trading System* (Cambridge: MIT Press, 1989).

194. The massive text of the Law of the Sea Treaty consists of 320 articles and three annexes. It deals with a host of details concerning free passage through the seas and coastal waters, gulfs, and straits, the extent of territorial waters and an additional exclusive economic zone, machinery to settle international disputes, national rights on the high seas, the nature and authority of an administrative agency to manage seabed mining, naval rights, pollution control, rights of landlocked countries, rules for fishing and shipping, principles governing the exploration and exploitation of seabed resources, scientific research, and creating a law of sea tribunal. For the text, commentary, a chronology, and other data, see *The Law of the Sea: Official Text of the United Nations Convention on the Law of the Sea* ... (New York: St. Martin's Press, 1983).

It should be noted that numerous aspects of U.S. interests in matters concerning the seas have also been treated at many additional conferences and meetings and have been embodied in some forty-five other multilateral conventions, treaties, agreements and protocols since 1945. These deal with fisheries and whaling (thirteen), marine science (one), marine pollution (seven), seabeds (four), and other maritime issues (twenty-one). The latter include such important subjects as collisions at sea, the continental shelf, exploration at sea, the high seas, maritime traffic, salvage at sea, safety of life as sea, search and rescue, and territorial waters and the contiguous zone. In addition, by 1995, the United States also was a party to bilateral treaties and agreements with some fifty other countries concerning the seas and maritime affairs. These included scores of treaties and agreements with more than thirty countries concerning maritime matters, with some two dozen countries concerning shipping and with fifteen or more countries concerned with both fisheries and navigation, as well as others dealing with maritime boundaries and boundary waters, canals, oceanography, naval vessels, seabeds, and related matters.

195. For additional commentary concerning international conferences and meetings, see Department of State, *American Delegations to International Conferences, Congresses, and Expositions* ... (annual vols. for 1931 to 1941), and *Participation of the United States Government in International Conferences* ... (1941–1960); Lay, *The Foreign Service of the United States*, pp. 57–58; Mathews, *American Foreign Relations*, p. 342 ff.; Stuart, *American Diplomatic and Consular Practice*, pp. 200–201; Williams, *American Diplomacy*, pp. 398–400; and Wriston, *Executive Agents in American Foreign Relations*, p. 128 ff.

Also see Hill, *The Public International Conference*, for analysis of American international conference participation to 1929, and Plischke, *Conduct of American Diplomacy*, Chapters 15 and 16 and Appendixes 20–22, for a comprehensive study of international conferences as a diplomatic process, which discusses such matters as their administration, agendas, categories, composition, decision-making processes, initiation, objectives, organization and procedure, participants, place and timing, problems, quantity, staffing, trends, and use, as well as an evaluation of the conferencing system. Also see Plischke, *International Relations: Basic Documents* (1962), pp. 38–50.

For legal analysis concerning American participation in international conferences and the negotiation of treaties and agreements, see Hackworth, *Digest of International Law*, vol. 5; Whiteman, *Digest of International Law*, vol. 14, pp. 1–510; and the annual *Digest of United States Practice in International Law*. They discuss such matters as adherence, amendments, constitutional limitations, denunciation, effective date, form as law, interpretation, as law of the land, modification, negotiation, power to conclude, procedure, proclamation, ratification, reservations, Senate action, signature, suspension, and other aspects of conferencing and treaty making.

For discussion and analysis of the President's participation in summit conferences and meetings, see Plischke, *Diplomat in Chief: The President at the Summit*, Chapters 6–8, *Presidential Diplomacy: A Chronology of Summit Visits, Trips and Meetings*, especially Chapter 5, *Summit Diplomacy: Personal Diplomacy of the President*, Chapter 6, and *Contemporary U.S. Foreign Policy*, pp. 235–50, 542–43, 569–71, 690–95.

196. When its Charter was signed in 1945, the title "United Nations" was co-opted for the postwar organization. It is necessary, when using this title, therefore, to recognize the difference between the wartime allies and the postwar international organization.

On the other hand, it is interesting to note that the twenty-two specialized agencies of the United Nations bear such titles as organization (eleven), fund (three), agency (two), union (two), administration (one), association (one), bank (one), and corporation (one).

197. To cite a few examples, the Central Treaty Organization was founded on a declaration, the Committee of Control for the International Zone of Tangier on a general act of an international conference, the Interparliamentary Union and the Pan-American Union on international conference resolutions, the International Statistical Institute on a set of regulations, and the Inter-American Commercial Arbitration Commission on a set of arbitration rules.

198. Of the eight pre-1900 organizations listed in Part A of Table 7.12, six were subjected to the formal treaty process, including the International Commission of the Cape Spartel Light (the earliest of these agencies joined by the United States, in 1867) and agencies concerned with the exchange of official publications, the protection of industrial property, the publication of customs tariffs, weights and measures, and the Universal Postal Union.

Early in the twentieth century the United States continued to rely on the treaty process when joining most international organizations, including the Permanent Court of Arbitration and the International Telecommunication Union, but it affiliated with the Permanent International Association of Navigation Congresses by means of an executive agreement.

199. These World War II temporary agencies embraced the Council of Foreign Ministers, Combined Civil Affairs Committee, Far Eastern Commission, Allied Occupation Control Commissions and Councils, and the Inter-Allied Reparation Agency.

200. These financial institutions included not only the International Bank for Reconstruction and Development and the International Monetary Fund but also eight regional banks and funds, the United Nations Children's Emergency Fund, and three other agencies. Only the International Center for the Settlement of Investment Disputes, which possesses adjudicatory powers, was regarded as a formal treaty.

201. Illustrating the substructure of the United Nations, the General Assembly, Security Council, and Economic and Social Council are supported by some 110 committees, commissions, special missions, bodies of experts, and other units. The Secretariat consists of more than seventy-five senior officers, headed by the Secretary-General and consisting of thirty-four Under Secretaries-General, seventeen Assistant Secretaries-General, ten Administrators, eight Directors of several ranks, and others called Officers in Charge, the Chief of Staff, Coordinator, Controller, and Special Advisers.

202. Since 1946 the following have been regarded as United Nations specialized agen-

cies (for their full titles, see the Glossary of Symbols; the asterisk identifies the original specialized agencies):

*FAO	*ICAO	IFC	*IMO	MIGA	UNIDO	*WHO
IAEA	IDA	*ILO	*IRO	UNESCO	*UNRRA	WIPO
*IB/IBRD	IFAD	*IMF	*ITU	*UNICEF	*UPU	*WMO
						WTO

The International Refugee Organization was superseded by the United Nations High Commission for Refugees; UNRRA was absorbed by the United Nations in 1948; and the World Trade Organization superseded the International Trade Organization, whose constitutive act was never ratified. It is interesting to note that the United States affiliated with fourteen of these specialized agencies by the executive agreement process.

Other basic international organizations have not formally affiliated with the United Nations, such as the International Bureau of Weights and Measures, International Criminal Police Commission, International Meteorological Organization, International Statistical Institute, and the International Union for the Protection of Industrial Property.

203. For an alternative categorization of the functional subjects with which international organizations are concerned, see Pitman B. Potter, who, in his early study entitled *An Introduction to the Study of International Organization*, 5th ed. (New York: Appleton-Century-Crofts, 1948), p. 140, lists ninety "Subject Matters of International Administration," grouped in five major categories.

204. The budget of the United Nations increased from $19,390,000 in 1946 to $27,740,000 the following year, approximated nearly $110 million by 1965, jumped to more than $606 million for the biennium 1974–75, exceeded $1 billion for 1978–79, doubled in amount by 1990–91, and rose to more than $2.5 billion by the mid-1990s.

205. The original American assessment percentage of 39.89 percent of the annual budget of the United Nations in 1946 was reduced gradually as new states were admitted to membership and reassessments were instituted. These amounted to 38.92 percent by 1950, 33.33 percent by 1954, 32.51 percent by 1959, 32.02 percent by 1963, 31.91 percent by 1966, and eventually 25 percent by 1974.

At the same time, the budget of the Organization of American States, far smaller by comparison, increased from $1 million per year prior to 1948 to more than $16 million by the 1960s, and the U.S. share of the contributions, originally amounting to 72 percent in 1949, was subsequently reduced to 66 percent.

206. This issue of financing international organizations is further exacerbated both by the increase in their number and by Article 17 of the United Nations Charter, which empowers the General Assembly to approve "financial and budgetary arrangements" of United Nations specialized agencies.

207. For additional information on many of these public international organizations and agencies, see *U.S. Code*, Title 22, Chapter 7, and Department of State, *International Agencies in Which the United States Participates* (1946), and *International Organizations in Which the United States Participates* (1949). Also see Elmer Plischke, "International Integration: Purpose, Progress, and Prospects," in *Systems of Integrating the International Community* (Princeton: Van Nostrand, 1964), pp. 1–25, "Reflections on International Integration: Problem of Organizational Institutionalization," *World Affairs* vol. 129 (April–June 1966): p. 20–27, "Evolution of Participation in International Organizations: The United States Experience," *Commonwealth: A Journal of Political Science* 5 (1991):

57–74, "Joining International Organizations: The United States Process," *Commonwealth* 6 (1992–93): 48–77, and *Conduct of American Diplomacy*, Chapter. 17–18.

Additional selected sources include David Armstrong, *The Rise of International Organization: A Short History* (New York: St. Martin's, 1982); Inis L. Claude, Jr., *Swords into Plowshares: The Problems and Progress of International Organization*, 4th ed. (New York: Random House, 1971); Edward S. Corwin, *The Constitution and World Organization* (Princeton: Princeton University Press, 1944); Norman L. Hill, *International Administration* (New York: McGraw-Hill, 1932), and *International Organization* (New York: Harper, 1952); Ruth C. Lawson, ed., *International Regional Organizations: Constitutional Foundations* (New York: Praeger, 1962); J. F. Meek and Louis W. Koenig, *The Administration of United States Participation in International Organizations* (Washington D.C.: American Society for Public Administration, 1950); Amos J. Peaslee, ed., *International Governmental Organizations: Constitutional Documents*, 3d ed., 5 vols. (The Hague: Nijhoff, 1974–79); Henry Reiff, *The United States and International Administrative Unions: Some Historical Aspects*, International Conciliation, no. 332, pp. 627–57; Giuseppe Schiavone, *International Organizations*, 2d ed. (Chicago: St. James, 1987); Laurence F. Schmeckebier, *International Organizations in Which the United States Participates* (Washington D.C.: Brookings Institution, 1935); and *Yearbook of International Organizations*, annual since early 1960s (Brussels: Union of International Organizations).

208. This Advisory Committee on Diplomatic Documentation is composed of nine members appointed by the Secretary of State "from among distinguished historians, political scientists, archivists, international lawyers, and other social scientists who have a demonstrable record of substantial research" pertaining to American foreign relations. Six of them are appointed from lists of individuals nominated by relevant associations and organizations. Members of the Advisory Committee serve for three years on a staggered basis, and they select their own chairperson. The committee has published periodic reports on its deliberations in major American professional journals.

209. See Act of August 1, 1956 (70 Stat. 890), as amended by Act of October 28, 1991 (105 Stat. 685–90; and *U.S. Code*; Title 22, secs. 4351–4357).

210. The preface to these *Foreign Relations* volumes indicate that they are prepared and edited by the Office of the Historian of the Department of State, that document texts are not altered, and that portions of them may be omitted for specified reasons. They are reviewed and cleared by the departmental declassification process and are coordinated with other units of the Department, and they identify the officers responsible for their preparation and editing.

211. For additional information on Department of State publications, see Department of State, Office of the Historian, periodic *Major Publications of the Department of State: An Annotated Bibliography*; E. R. Perkins, "Foreign Relations of the United States: Ninety-one Years of American Foreign Policy," *Department of State Bulletin* 27 (December 22, 1952): pp. 1002–7; Plischke, *Conduct of American Diplomacy*, pp. 37–38, 216–19, *Contemporary U.S. Foreign Policy: Documents and Commentary*, pp. 1–20, 109–21, and *U.S. Foreign Relations: A Guide to Information Sources*, especially pp. xxxiii–xlii, Chapter 21 and Chapter 22, pp. 549–68; David F. Trask and William Z. Slany, "What Lies Ahead for the *Foreign Relations* Series?" in *The Society for Historians of American Foreign Relations Newsletter* 9 (March 1978), 26–29; and Stuart, *The Department of State*, pp. 217, 243, 260, 296.

8

The Future

History is not only a review of the past but also the foundation and portender of the future. Commenting on past American experience, in the 1880s the Departments of State and the Treasury were described by Eugene Schuyler (former Minister to several European countries and nominated as Assistant Secretary of State) as the two ranking Cabinet Departments, because they could not only influence the foreign policy of the United States but also determine the welfare and the future of the country.[1] Two decades later John Bassett Moore (Assistant Secretary and Counselor of the Department) observed that American diplomacy was characterized by its practicality, which "sought to attain definite objects by practical methods," that it "exerted a potent influence upon the adoption of simple and direct methods in the conduct of negotiations," that American diplomats "usually relied rather upon the strength of their cause, frankly and clearly argued, than upon subtle diplomacy, for the attainment of their ends," that "American diplomacy in the main continued to be a simple, direct, and open diplomacy, the example of which has had much to do with shaping development of modern methods," and that "it may confidently invite a comparison as to the propriety of its speech and conduct with the diplomacy of other nations."[2]

Early in the twentieth century John W. Foster (former Minister to three countries and Secretary of State) noted that throughout its history the United States had a marked "influence in elevating the diplomatic intercourse of nations" and that it was "untrammeled by precedents and traditions," which made it easier "to discard the devious methods of the then existing diplomacy." At the time, however, American practice differed from the European, which had become a professionalized lifetime career system. Quoting former Secretary William H. Seward, who, referring to Chiefs of Mission, said that some American diplomats are sent abroad because they are needed abroad, and some are sent because they are not wanted at home,'' Foster added that this was more characteristic prior to the Civil War.[3]

According to Charles W. Thayer (former Foreign Service Officer): "The entry of the United States into world diplomacy after World War I was thus strongly influenced by the deep-seated American suspicion of diplomacy in general and by Congressional fears of entangling alliances in particular" and that this country "shambled self-conscious and diffident onto the diplomatic stage." He also speculates that this was puzzling to foreign commentators, such as Sir Harold Nicolson, who regarded American diplomats as suspicious "in the presence of continental diplomatists."[4]

More recently, in 1952 Professor Graham H. Stuart, analyzing what he calls the "curious anomaly" that exists "in the attitude towards diplomacy found in democracies," reasons that "it might be expected that inasmuch as the foreign office and its representatives abroad are the first line of defense against international trouble, public opinion would rally wholeheartedly to the support of such an organization; yet such is not the case. In fact, diplomacy, with its taboos and secrecy, its social trappings, and cast organization, is still regarded with skepticism or suspicion by the man in the street."[5] In 1964 Professor Frederick C. Mosher, speaking of American diplomats, remarked: "Having the right man in the right job at the right time and having him motivated to do that job to the best of his ability—these are the primary goals of personnel administrators in all organizations. . . . There is probably no other field of work so dependent upon the individuals who represent the nation's interests as the field of foreign affairs."[6]

In performing their day-to-day functions, the officers and staff of the Department of State and the Foreign Service are currently confronted with an almost immeasurable quantity of unfinished tasks in the pursuit of world betterment, peace, and justice. It has been said that never before in history have the problems of foreign policy making and implementation been more acute, complex, and widespread, and never before has it been so essential to resolve them by peaceful means during this era of an expanded and intricate community of nations in which each promotes its own national development and possesses its own diplomatic agenda; a massive population explosion, as well as political, economic, and social change; and advanced technology and nuclear weapons and instruments of mass destruction and annihilation.[7]

It is axiomatic that, although it is impossible to foresee the many problems and needs of dealing expeditiously and effectively with future international affairs, the foreign policy of the United States, the organization and management of the Department of State, and the nature and competence of the Foreign Service are bound to change in the next century. Past developments and achievements provided the basis for dealing with future needs. These may be categorized as the environment (both national and international), the State Department and other U.S. agencies concerned with foreign relations, and the Foreign Service to handle them abroad.

Their paramount responsibilities remain policy advisement and determination, representation to other nations and to international organizations, negotiation with foreign governments and at international conferences, and treaty making. Central to these are the devisement and pursuit of American national concerns and vital interests, fundamental purposes, goals, and objectives as related to national power, strategy and tactics, and international commitments. In addition to the general system of managing foreign affairs, these, in turn, entail processes of decision making, formulating and dealing with alliances and ententes, collective cooperation, crisis handling, conflict resolution, and the peaceful settlement of international differences and disputes. Some years ago Under Secretary of State and career Foreign Service Officer David D. Newsom summarized the well-known, essential qualities for the effective handling of American diplomacy, in the future as well as in the past, as requiring ''[A]n understanding of our own nation; a balanced sensitivity to other societies and peoples; a firm grasp of the subject matter of international relations; and the skill to bring this knowledge together in advancing both the interests of our country and the establishment of working understandings with others.''[8]

DOMESTIC AND INTERNATIONAL ENVIRONMENTS

The environmental component of the needs and developments of American diplomacy consists of both domestic and external features. One of the principal internal constituents is leadership, which centers primarily on future Presidents and Secretaries of State. While the Secretary continues as the President's principal adviser and implementer of foreign relations, the President also relies upon, and is assisted by, such executive agencies as the White House Office, the National Security Council, the Office of Management and Budget, the Office of Policy Development, and the Office of the Trade Representative. Leadership of the State Department involves the Secretary, Deputy Secretary, Under and Assistant Secretaries, and comparably ranked principal officers and their relations with the President and his staff, Congress and its committees, other agencies that deal with foreign affairs, and the public.

Moreover, especially during and since World War II, the conduct of traditional foreign relations has been overlaid with summitry and ministerial diplomacy. Although such escalation varies with the dispositions of Presidents (and their use of Ambassadors at Large and other special emissaries) and Secretaries of State (and their personal representatives), these have become commonplace and, in some cases, even regularized as major instruments of contemporary and future diplomacy. Whereas it may be contended that they bypass normal diplomatic relations, they are likely to continue as a valuable and sometimes preferred feature of American diplomacy.

On the other hand, the external factors, equally important but more complex and often less predictable, consist of both multilateral and bilateral institutional, legal, political, economic, and social components, which also are accompanied by current and future features. Fundamentally, they embrace customary elements of international relations, such as government-to-government representation, communications, agreements and disagreements, and wars. Some of these are embodied in multilateral conventions concerned with diplomats, consuls, and the treaty-making process and a host of bilateral treaties, agreements, and other understandings. In the future, as in the past, the United States will be viewed as the richest and most generous country and as being one of the primary policemen, peacemakers, and peacekeepers in the world.

Additionally, the United States must deal with an expanding quantity of international substantive and procedural matters. Illustrations of newer and future subjects include the expanding and revised community of nations and the increasing complexity of humanity; population growth and the handling of masses of refugees; disease, health, and sanitation; international financing through banks and other institutions; the seas, continental and riparian jurisdiction, and fisheries; outer space, satellites, and space stations; preserving and improving the global environment and maintaining access to, and conserving, global resources; international alignments, alliances, and ententes; international tensions, disagreements, and disputes; terrorism, kidnapping, hostage taking, and bombings; weapons proliferation and control, including land mines, bacteriological and gaseous agents, and weapons of mass destruction; and many others currently unforeseen. Among these, some analysts warn of the need to prepare for dealing with such shocking potentialities as the proliferation of international terrorism, involving not only that which utilizes explosives but also aberrant bioterrorism, chemical terrorism, and even nuclear terrorism. Others raise the specter of the massive clash of cultures or whole civilizations. Still others caution against insidious, creeping overglobalization of international relation and responsibilities at the expense of national concerns and welfare.

Given a diversified and changing environment, the issues and needs of future diplomacy will be dealt with incrementally, depending on the determinations of the Department of State and the influence of international agencies, including the United Nations. As William B. Macomber, Jr., former Ambassador and Assistant and Under Secretary of State, in what he calls his commentary on, and manual of requirements for, contemporary and future American diplomacy, has concluded, the achievement of our fundamental goal of engaging in amicable relations, cooperation, aligning of national interests, and pursuing the maintenance of peace in an often "selfish, predatory, dangerous, and explosive world" requires "a sustained, collective, resourceful, and, above all, hardheaded effort to deal with the world as it truly is," which is "unmasked by the deadly distortions of illusion and wishful thinking."[9]

THE DEPARTMENT OF STATE

The Department of State will continue to play a major future role in American foreign policy making. It provides cooperative and recommendatory assistance to the President and Congress and exercises a crucial function in devising many subsidiary policy and implementation plans and courses of action. This arrangement has been traditional in the American political system and is bound to continue, as influenced by the particular persuasions of Presidents and Secretaries of State. Historically, the State Department has been exceptional in many respects. It was the first executive Department to be created and enjoys a distinguished status in the American Government. It has been called America's bulwark in world affairs and the first among equals, and it serves as the Government's only agency concerned solely with the nation's manifold relations and international problems throughout the world. Moreover, the Secretary of State ranks above the heads of other Cabinet Departments and leads them in possible automatic succession to the Presidency.

Contemplating the State Department's strengths and weaknesses, the organization, machinery, operations, and functions as they have developed and matured over the years, since World War II they have been subjected to many reviews, appraisals, reforms, reorganizations, and refinements to update and improve it.[10] Future reassessments will be required, although the Department's general hierarchical structure, consisting of offices, bureaus, divisions, and other agencies and special officers, is likely to continue, subject to future adjustments and internal allocation. However, the basic distinction among geographic, functional, management, servicing, and other units may be supplemented or realigned. Some functional segments, such as those concerned with legislation, policy planning, diplomatic security, personnel, inspection, intelligence and research, international conferences and organizations, and legal, protocol, and public affairs, are also subject to future modification.[11] Caution will need to be exercised to avoid splintered compartmentalization, which occurred to meet temporary World War II needs, when the Department encompassed more than 100 units.

Among the major strengths of the Department is the elimination of the spoils system, one of the most criticized American practices, which permeated the appointment of both departmental and diplomatic and consular officers for many decades. The appointment of amateurs to provide them with diplomatic sinecures and lucrative consular positions for political or partisan purposes, which produced a deplorably low level of honesty and efficiency, was long condemned by objective analysts.[12] This must be distinguished from Presidential appointment of noncareerists to upper-level State Department positions and as chiefs of diplomatic missions, many of whom were competent and served creditably.

However, beginning with the Acts of April 1906 (applied to the Consular Service) and February 1915 (applied to both diplomatic and consular appointees), supplemented by Executive Orders, the merit system was gradually introduced. After World War II the organic Acts of August 1946 and October 1980 mandated the standardizing of the appointment, assignment, and promotion of Foreign Service members strictly on the basis of merit. This strengthened the personnel system of both the Department and foreign missions, including leadership positions both in Washington and overseas. Thus, although it took more than a century, the contemporary Foreign Service has been converted into a genuine professional system based solidly on the merit principle, whereas only the senior officers of the Department, the Chiefs of Mission, and a few Ambassadors at Large and other special emissaries remain political appointees, and even some of these positions are now filled with careerists.

An attendant strength is the quality of current departmental professional personnel. Assessing its quality, Macomber has declared that "its brainpower, integrity, and dedication" are "unexcelled anywhere" and that the leaders, officers, and staff members must continue to nourish a "systematic, competent, and aggressive" attitude to fulfill their responsibilities.[13] Modifications of the basic features of the personnel system—consisting of competitive examinations, appointment, classification, in-service training, assignment, promotion, compensation, retirement, and the like—have been legislatively prescribed, and they may be periodically reviewed and modified.

The need for balance and relationship of generalists, specialists, and servicing personnel has generally been stabilized but also will probably be modulated to deal with new developments and requirements in the United States and abroad. The current major specializations—managerial, administrative, political, economic, and consular—remain critical. For career development purposes, however, a degree of cross-specialization may be essential to extend the experiential basis of individual officers to enhance their professional value and advancement. One of the principal requisites for dealing with this factor is that care must be exercised to see that a corps of highly qualified generalists is available for senior departmental leadership and management positions while maintaining the necessary quantity of substantive, geographic, servicing, and other specialists and facilitating coordination among them and promoting their acquisition of the skills and experience that enable them to mature as generalists and emerge as proficient senior departmental and diplomatic officers.

Another major and historic change and benefit is that the Department of State has finally been relieved of the many extraneous and often diversionary and burdensome domestic functions with which it was saddled in earlier times. It may be said that it approaches the twenty-first century as a genuine Foreign Ministry. Although its current title is unlikely to be changed, it is not inconceivable that it could be legislatively reverted to the "Department of Foreign Affairs," as it was known prior to the Constitution.

On the other hand, in the past, historians and publicists and some members of the Department of State have deplored a variety of departmental weaknesses. Among the most egregious and continuing is its lack of a natural, well-defined, organized, and articulate public interest or pressure group to support it in Congress, the public forum, and the media. Most of the other Federal Departments and agencies—including those concerned with agriculture, commerce, defense and national security, education, energy, health and human services, transportation, and veterans affairs, as well as such other fields as civil rights, foreign trade, science and technology, and postal affairs—have the benefit and support of such groups, whereas those of the State Department and Foreign Service are limited to such agencies as the American Foreign Service Association, the American Academy of Diplomacy, and the Institute for the Study of Diplomacy.[14]

Sometimes certain Executive Departments and other administrative agencies serve as effective lobbies of various special interests in the deliberations of Congress, they receive the plaudits and support of those they represent, and the members of Congress are inclined to respect them. The Department of State lacks this advantage. Furthermore, it is sometimes criticized for American policies, which are determined by the President in collaboration with Congress, and often the functional interests of competing domestic pressure groups focus their criticism or dissatisfaction on the Department, even though the determination of that policy or its implementation abroad lies with other, sometimes competing government agencies.

It also needs to be noted that frequently, the American people are insufficiently motivated to bestir themselves—as do those with economic, commercial, educational, environmental, humanitarian, and other special interests—to engage and participate in action groups in support of the Department of State. Although a number of foreign relations action groups of a temporary or otherwise restricted nature emerge from time to time, they usually are limited to particular issues, emergencies, or crises. Attempts to organize similar national groups concerned with the promotion of sound general foreign relations programs and practices with the support of an effective Department of State and Foreign Service have usually been unsuccessful.[15]

Another serious problem of the Department of State, characteristic of most Foreign Offices, is that its action sometimes is slow, deliberate, and often cumbersome, for which it is publicly criticized. Frequently, delay is caused by the nature of the determination process and the necessity for consultation with other interested Departments and agencies. Or the Department's effective action is hindered by Congress, the President, or White House Executive Offices or is handled directly by unilateral Executive action taken without consulting the Department. In the past this matter has also been exacerbated by its deficiency of personnel and other resources. Occasionally, the Department may be ignored, as in Senate debate over the ratification of certain treaties.

There are other, more precise weaknesses, some of which are characteristic of many government agencies and several of which have been or are being addressed. Examples include the degree or balance of the appointment and turnover of senior-level political appointees and their qualifications for ranking departmental and Chief of Mission positions; the lack of overseas experience of many departmental officers, which has been modified by Congressional acts to require Foreign Service Officers to be appointed to State Department assignments and vice versa; tradition-bound and change-resistance proclivities, including an aura of superiority permeating some elements of the Department;

reluctance or opposition to receive advice from the outside, which is regarded as intervention; bureaucratic "layering" in the chain of authority and decision; and preserving confidentiality and averting leaks during negotiations.

In addition to these weaknesses and criticisms, occasionally, the Department of State is confronted with vicious attacks upon its personnel and action by unprincipaled political or other demagogues, which raises furor in the public media and weakens the credibility and prestige of the United States, undermines the morale of foreign relations personnel, and may militate against effective recruitment. One of the most aberrant post–World War II attacks was fomented by Senator Joseph R. McCarthy's bigoted search for Communist subversives in the Government, particularly the Department of State, early in the 1950s. His irresponsible allegations against, and attacks upon, individual officers, especially those concerned with Far Eastern affairs, even though unproven, resulted in damaging their reputations and forcing their departure and had a protracted, disruptive, and adverse effect upon the morale of the Department and Foreign Service.

Eventually, a member of the department's security staff concluded that "few people who lived through the McCarthy era in the Department of State can ever forget the fear, intimidation, and sense of outrage which permeated Foggy Bottom." Naturally, such scurrilous, unjustified incidents undermine the effectiveness of the Department. As Stuart has put it: "How can it be expected that the Foreign Service officer will report sincerely, objectively and fearlessly when his most confidential findings may be blazoned in the public press. . . . How will the United States obtain top-flight applicants for a service which is looked upon askance by the man in the street?"[16]

Among the problems that involve both the State Department and the Foreign Service is the matter of making unwise appointments. This generally is associated with political appointees to leading departmental positions or as Presidential personal envoys, Ambassadors at Large, and Chiefs of Mission, which is detrimental to both American interests and the reputation of the Department and Foreign Service. Although the number of cases is small, they tend to discredit not only the persons involved but also the quality of the American system, and they usually evoke unfavorable publicity and popular criticism. Since the reform and stabilization of the Foreign Service, there are carefully prescribed principles and procedures to guard against this risk for members of the career service, but it may still occur in the selection and assignment of principal officers.

This issue is complicated and entails more than politics, the persuasions of the President, the Senatorial confirmation process, and controlling laws governing the Department and its internal regulations. Some aspects are influenced by immemorial usage and international traditions, such as international protocol, the issuance of letters of credence and recall, and the principles of persona grata and persona non grata. Presidents may remove their appointees,[17] and the removal process for Foreign Service Officers has been specified in the Organic Acts of 1946 and 1980.

Furthermore, State Department, diplomatic, and consular officers may be reassigned. In the case of Chiefs of Mission, who are subject to the approval of receiving states, they may be disapproved or later dismissed by them when they become persona non grata. Naturally, senior Department of State Officers and Chiefs of Mission have the option of initiating their own resignations, and they are bound by the customary practice of filing courtesy resignations when one President succeeds another (or even if they succeed themselves), which incoming Presidents may accept or reject, and sometimes individuals may be "promoted" to some other post, making room for new candidates the President wishes to appoint.

Attention, now and in the future, needs to be paid to such continuing needs of the Department of State as integrating policy planning; providing efficient administrative support to overseas missions; security of American missions and personnel abroad and foreign diplomatic missions in the United States; constant modernization of worldwide diplomatic communications; upgrading computerization and advancement of technological facilities; centralizing budget and fiscal administration; dealing with the travel explosion of officers abroad; and reviewing and strengthening coordination of interdepartmental and interagency functions in Washington and abroad.

In summary, while the "Old Department" has been converted into the "New Department" during the World War II and Cold War eras, the matter of dealing with future developments in the United States and abroad remains a major and continuing responsibility. This requires periodic reviews of its strengths and weaknesses, involving constructive departmental and outside oversight, an effective inspection system, maintaining close cooperation with the President's Executive Office and Congress, and, above all, attracting and maintaining qualified, dedicated, and efficient personnel. New tasks, some of great magnitude, and incessant challenge continue to confront the Department. New programs and changing leadership, personnel, and organizational arrangements must be accommodated rapidly and effectively. Leadership must be statesmanlike. Adjustment to these demands of the times remains one of the most pressing problems confronting the Department, and it has no alternative but to continue to meet this challenge.[18]

THE FOREIGN SERVICE

Although it took more than two centuries, at least 100 Congressional acts (not including periodic financial enactments) and Executive Orders, scores of departmental rules and regulation, separate fundamental treaties on diplomatic and consular relations, and many traditional diplomatic practices, which produced incremental development of the American diplomatic system, the essence, roles, responsibilities, and functions of the Foreign Service—both diplomats and consular officers—have matured and remain relatively constant.

As former Assistant Secretary Dean Acheson and others have put it, the For-

eign Service possesses the crucial obligation of serving as America's first line
of defense. Some years ago it was said by Tracy H. Lay, who served as Consul
General: "There is no loyal American who will not admit the desirability of
fostering cordial and friendly relations with other nations, not for selfish but for
altruistic reasons; there is no practical American who cannot see the importance
of the same attitude, not for altruistic but for selfish reasons. Both our idealism
and our practical judgment are involved in the formula of neighborly esteem
and good will."[19] At the vanguard of the maintenance of such relations stands
the Foreign Service.

Many legal aspects of contemporary diplomatic and consular practice are now
governed by international conventions and agreements, especially the fundamental Vienna Treaties on Diplomatic Relations (1961) and Consular Relations
(1963), both of which are universally applicable. These are supplemented by
several additional multilateral and some eighty bilateral treaties and agreements
concluded with dozens of foreign countries. Combined, these fix the parameters
and prescribe detailed determinants of contemporary American diplomatic practice and the Foreign Service in conducting future foreign affairs.

Throughout its history the Foreign Service (and previously, the Diplomatic
and especially the Consular Services) has been subjected to criticism within the
Department and by outsiders. Some of these have applied to the personnel of
both the Department and the Foreign Service. These include such matters as
political appointments and especially the spoils system, aggregate and personal
relations with Congress and the public, the deliberate and dilatory consultation
process, integrating relations with other Departments and agencies concerned
with foreign affairs, interrelations of generalists and specialists, dual service of
individuals in the Department and abroad, managerial and coordination skills,
and secrecy during the policy-making process and international negotiations.[20]

Directed more particularly at the Foreign Service, weaknesses and censure
have been widespread, in some cases long-standing, and sometimes unjustified.
One of these is that, while stationed abroad, Foreign Service Officers are regarded as members of an elite and sacrosanct profession. This is attested to by
historical precedent, current treaties and regulations concerning the extraterritoriality pertaining to individuals, their families, staffs, official facilities and
residences; their personal inviolability; and their unique and extensive privileges
and immunities, applying to themselves, their work, and their archives and communications, even including certain exemptions from local jurisdiction, customs
duties, and taxes.

While these are regarded as essential to the performance of the diplomatic
profession and are recognized and honored throughout the world, combined,
they tend to produce an attitude of professional and personal superiority and
snobbishness. This, in turn, tends to kindle what some call a unique and permeative diplomatic elitist psychology, or what has been called "the Foreign
Service Culture," which has evoked one of the severest criticisms of some
members of the Foreign Service.[21] Nevertheless, the factors upon which it is

founded, it is contended, are essential to maintaining international diplomatic respectability and esprit de corps, whereas without them the Foreign Service would cease to be an elite.

However, this attitude contributes to the perception that diplomats are not only special but also above the law. In some respects they are, but when exceeded or violated, this image evokes public disapproval and may provoke international crises. Because they are guests in the countries to which they are assigned, while they possess various rights, exemptions, and privileges, this does not accord them free license. They have the obligation of scrupulously observing the letter and spirit of local laws and regulations, which most of them do.

Generally overlooked in the development of this diplomatic psychology, which applies only to diplomatic Chiefs of Mission, is the traditional manner of addressing them. Whereas in all countries they are titled by their professional rank, currently as Ambassador or formerly as Minister, they are personally addressed as "Your Excellency." This distinguished title is also applied to some high foreign political personalities, even in countries where they do not use such official designations. This manner of address has applied to American Chiefs of Diplomatic Missions throughout its history, even before 1789.

It is essential to understand, however, that when the Constitution of the United States was being devised at Philadelphia in 1787, the draft produced by its Committee on Detail specified that the proposed President be titled "Your Excellency," which was not debated Constitutional at the Convention. However, when the draft was later submitted to the Convention Committee on Style and Arrangement to prepare its final version, this stipulation was deleted, again apparently without Convention debate. After the Constitution went into effect, this matter was raised in the first session of Congress, before Washington was inaugurated. Senate members preferred to address the President as "Your Excellency" (or by some alternative distinguished designation such as "His Highness"), but when the House of Representatives demurred, the matter was submitted to a conference committee, and it was not reraised.

As a consequence, American Presidents have since been addressed simply as "Mr. President." However, the Vice President while serving as President of the Senate, the Speaker of the House, and the President-elect and former Presidents, as well as members of Congress, the Supreme Court and other Federal courts, Cabinet Secretaries, and State and local government officials have come to be addressed as "the Honorable." What makes this most unique and significant is that for more than two centuries only ranking American diplomats serving abroad as Chiefs of Mission are addressed by the distinguished title "Your Excellency," which puts them in an elite class of their own in American public affairs.

Related to these matters is the criticism that American diplomatic performance is bound by an exceptional and, in some respects, archaic international and national system of etiquette, protocol, and other formalities and proprieties. These embrace the formality of precedence, ceremonious treatment at royal courts, formal reception and departure ceremonies, special holiday celebrations, ceremonial dress, format and treatment of official and informal correspondence and other communications, manner of preparation and format of documents, and similar matters. Some of these, while they may be essential to the profession, nevertheless are regarded in the United States as strange, affected, clannish and pretentious, if not un-American. Associated with them are pomp and ritualistic and stylized practices, including the use of stilted language, participation in lavish and ostentatious social functions, and pompous or exaggerated manners and formality, most of which are not likely to be changed, although they contribute to the popular perception that some diplomats are dilettantes, and they are disparaged as snobs, stuffed shirts, "cookie-pushers," or what has been ridiculed as a "starched futility" corps.[22]

Another criticism concerns the nature and manner of reporting to the Department of State. While this is one of the primary duties of diplomatic and consular officers, cynics contend, it sometimes results in either underreporting or overreporting. Discriminating, accurate, and objective reporting is essential and expected by the Department. However, the attitude that the performance of officers and staff members is judged by the number of file-cabinet inches of reports they produce, attesting to their value, reflects an abnormal perception of their utility.

Though not definable as a weakness, Foreign Services Officers have been disparaged for the deceit attributed to the practice of diplomacy, which characterized it for several centuries but still emerges in contemporary relations and which has been euphemistically called "refined concealment" respecting policy goals and diplomatic procedures. Whereas most diplomats find it to be to their advantage to foster honesty, credibility, and integrity in their dealings with the Foreign Ministries of other countries, there still are situations in which some emissaries employ equivocating language or "double-talk" at times to maintain advantage or occasionally to deliberately mislead or confuse other governments. Concerning such equivocation and understatement, Macomber reports that it was the trademark of diplomacy in earlier times, which was parodied as:

If a diplomat says "yes," he means "perhaps."
If a diplomat says "perhaps," he means "no."
If a diplomat says "no," he is no diplomat.[23]

However, analysts generally put integrity at the head of a diplomat's essential qualities, without which mutual confidence suffers. Unfortunately, the lack of credibility and the use of artful deception and what have been called the "patriotic lie," "moral inaccuracies," or "sharp practices" are still practiced by some governments and, therefore, remain in the popular characterization of diplomacy.

Diplomats are naturally subject to official censure if they exceed or violate their authority in negotiating international commitments. Technically, these are known as "sponsions," to which their governments cannot rightly be bound, and, therefore, they usually deem them to be violable, if not automatically null and void. In earlier times such situations occurred, especially with respect to military surrender agreements. This principle has also been applied to commitments subscribed to by diplomats who are not appropriately commissioned or who exceed their instructions. Prior to the current treaty ratification procedure, when communications were slow and uncertain and when diplomats enjoyed discretion in their discussions and negotiations, the home government required the safeguard of not being bound by what was detrimental to its welfare or in excess of its intent. However, since the acceleration of international communications, which enable the Department of State to maintain direct, immediate, and constant management of the actions of its emissaries and the adoption of the current ratification process, which provides an opportunity for approval *ad referendum*, this has ceased to be a serious problem for ordinary negotiations or the consummation of treaties, agreements, and other international commitments.[24]

Despite these criticisms, however, the contemporary Foreign Service has been modernized, institutionalized, strengthened, and perfected. It is now a professionalized, first-rate service, encompassing both diplomatic and consular officers who bear fixed ranks and titles, function as generalists and specialists, and serve primarily abroad but periodically also in the Department of State in Washington. Since World War II it has been governed by comprehensive Organic Acts as amended, which stipulate the manifold details concerning careers in the service. Its membership and competence have been broadened to embrace not only traditional diplomatic and consular functions but also skills in such fields as budgetary and fiscal work, foreign trade, international finance, labor relations, and science and technology. Most important, it is founded on the merit principle applied to appointment, assignment, classification, advancement, promotion, compensation, retirement, and other factors.

The contemporary and future Foreign Service enjoys the advantage of substantial opportunity for able and dedicated officers to rise to top-level positions in both the Department and the expanded list of Ambassadorships. Among the continuing and future major problems and needs, aside from coping with archaic usages (some of which are no longer useful) include recruiting and maintaining the highest caliber of personnel; developing and enhancing both the core personnel qualities and skills and the art of representation, reporting, and negotiation; satisfying the need for thorough familiarity with not only U.S. interests and policies but also those of the host countries in which they serve and their relations with other countries; eschewing the attitude by American diplomatic officers that they possess a monopoly of wisdom respecting the matters with which they are concerned; encouraging those serving in mundane assignments, including routine consular and administrative posts, and not penalizing these officers in the pursuit of their advancement; monitoring and enhancing the morale of officers and staff members, especially those at lower ranks and those assigned to less desirable posts; guarding against, or at least ameliorating, the personal physical risks of American missions and their personnel abroad; and succumbing to either "localitis" or "the malady of clientitis" (by which diplomats and their staff members view policy and developments from the perspective of the host country to which they are assigned rather than from that of the United States or assuming the role of advocate for the host country vis-à-vis their own), which is sometimes designated as "going native" or acting like "foreign expatriates," and "capitalitis" (by which they remain in the capital of the host country without gaining an understanding of the rest of the nation to which they are accredited).

CONTEMPORARY AND FUTURE DIPLOMACY

Following World War II, as noted in Chapter 6, Sir Harold Nicolson, in *The Evolution of Diplomatic Method*, identified five basic or historical systems of diplomacy as the Greek, Roman, Italian, French, and American (twentieth-century), with various subtypes. Others characterize them as epochal classifications—ancient, medieval, Renaissance, early modern, and contemporary and future—evidencing that diplomacy has changed and will continue to mutate, respecting its essence, as a process, its participants, and its subjects of concern. Its basic goals and end products, such as prescribing rights and responsibilities, producing mutually beneficial arrangements, resolving conflicts and preventing and ending wars, and its concerns and methods have expanded and changed throughout the centuries and will continue to do so in the future.

Many commentators and analysts have produced complex paradigms of former, current, and future categories of diplomacy. In terms of timing for the United States, these may be described by broad historical periods, such as the colonial, Confederation, postindependence, Federalist, post-Federalist, Civil War, World Wars I and II, and contemporary and other periods. Or they may include more specifically time-oriented versions, identified with particular leaders, such as nineteenth-century Prince Bismarck, Viscount Castlereagh, and Prince Metternich, and twentieth-century Adolf Hitler, Benito Mussolini, and Josef Stalin, and in the United States with individual Presidents and Secretaries of State. Other time-related eras for the United States are well known as expansionist, wartime (Revolutionary War, Civil War, Spanish–American War, Mexican War, and World Wars I and II), Cold War, global leadership, and superpower eras.

Another general category focuses on areally-oriented diplomacy respecting the Western Hemisphere, Europe, the Mideast, Africa, and the Far East and Pacific basin. At times American diplomacy also specializes on individual and groups of countries, such as the Barbary Powers, Canada, China, Japan, Germany, Mexico, the Soviet Union, the United Kingdom, and others, as well as the polar regions, the Central American isthmian canal, and the Vatican. Other basic variations distinguish types of diplomacy as applied to particular national and cultural factors, including monarchical versus republican, democratic versus dictatorial societies, and Christian, Muslim, and Jewish powers.

So far as diplomacy as a process is concerned, distinctions are made on the basis of confidentiality—open (public) and private (quiet, discreet, or secret); the number of participants—universal or restricted (Great Powers, allies, developing states, or regional groups) or bilateral and multilateral; the level of participants—standard or traditional (involving regularly accredited diplomats), exceptional (involving ad hoc special emissaries), ministerial (involving the Secretary of State), and summit (involving the President); the forum employed— ad hoc and institutionalized (parliamentary, as practiced in international conferences and organizations); the nature of communications (traditional person-to-person discussion, written correspondence, and special processes such as the "hot line"; and attitudinal persuasions—defined as idealistic, realistic, and pragmatic diplomacy; flexible and stereotyped or doctrinaire diplomacy; ostentatious, ceremonious, or quiet and unpretentious diplomacy; and friendly, conciliatory, unfriendly, hostile, devious, and unprincipled diplomacy. Still others are more esoteric, denominated as Big-Stick, cold-fist, dollar, fast-track, gruff-tough, imperialistic, push-button, Open Door, relaxed, shirtsleeve, and other brands of diplomacy.

Often diplomacy is also characterized on the basis of functional and substantive matters of concern. Illustrations embrace such broad areas as political, economic and commercial, security, social, and legal affairs. More specific types are illustrated by the tables on treaties and agreements, international conferences and meetings, and international organizations provided in earlier chapters.

Most of these types of diplomacy are addressed in biographical and historical accounts and other analyses, and some of them are treated in detail in separate studies. Collectively, they evidence not only the essence but also the complexity and mutability of the diplomatic process. Many of these categories of contemporary diplomacy will continue into the future, some will decline or disappear, others will increase in usage and importance, and new types are likely to emerge to meet changing needs and persuasions. However, the time-tried essence of the diplomatic process, so essential to the beneficial conduct of international affairs, is bound to continue to serve the mutual interests and goals of the United States in its future relations with other governments and international institutions.

RECOGNITION AND AWARDS

A longtime weakness of the Department of State and Foreign Service has been the lack of a systematic process for recognizing, honoring, and rewarding officers and other personnel for exceptional performance. Lacking knighthoods and other prestigious recognition and titles that carry no duties, common in some countries in earlier times, for many decades the principal American system of political and diplomatic awards to individuals was embodied in the spoils system, supplemented by the appointment of wealthy individuals to ranking diplomatic positions. Although the Foreign Service has been professionalized, the United States has been dilatory in recognizing and rewarding individuals for past diplomatic service. At the highest professional levels this was ameliorated by the creation of the ranks of Career Minister in 1946 and Career Ambassador in 1955.

By comparison, a host of global and national awards, prizes, and medals was established in the twentieth century to recognize and reward those who excel in a broad array of achievements. Examples embrace the Nobel Prizes in six fields; the American Pulitzer Prizes in approximately twenty fields such as meritorious journalism, letters, music, biography, history, and public service; as well as scores of awards and prizes in the fields of sports and athletics, entertainment, motion pictures, and many others, supplemented by a variety of "Halls of Fame."

Aside from memorializing those American diplomatic and consulor officers who were killed or died in service abroad by inscribing their names retroactively on a Department of State plaque established in 1933, only recently has the Department of State launched a systematic process of recognizing and rewarding its officers and personnel. These consist of awards specifically designated for "Distinguished Service," "Superior Service," "Meritorious Service," and "Commendable Service," as well as certain "cash performance," "suggestion awards," and other honors and tributes, including a special Secretary of the Year Award providing a significant tax-free cash prize for its annual recipient. This matter of Department of State awards was not formally legislated by Congress until the passage of the Organic Act of 1980.[25]

FUTURE DEVELOPMENT AND PROBLEMS

If change is "the law of life," as it has been called, among others it governs the future of peoples, nations, and governments. Continuing and future issues and problems, to recapitulate, concern the environment, the Department of State, and the Foreign Service in the conduct of American diplomacy. Of these, the environment, both domestic and international, is among the least predictable. The addition of new states may expand the community of nations, a few may merge to form new entities, additional alliances may be created, new subjects of mutual concern will emerge, and more diplomatic relations are likely to be handled at international conferences and meetings or by international organizations and similar agencies.

Based on past experience, the Department of State will need to adjust to handle these additional subjects of national and mutual international concern. Its bureaus, offices, divisions, and other organizational components may have to be refocused, retitled, and realigned. Although in the past its basic structure was frequently reorganized, its current organization appears to be serviceable, and some existing units may be augmented, shifted, or amalgamated. However, the basic patterning of functional and geographic components, complemented by management, administrative, and servicing units, is bound to remain, whereas their subunits may be supplemented, restructured, or realigned.

Its principal continuing and future problems and needs embrace such matters as (1) accommodating continuing political appointments of senior departmental officers and diplomatic mission chiefs, which the Department can influence but not control; (2) dealing effectively with Congress and its committees; (3) adapting to widespread and increasing diplomacy at the summit and ministerial levels; (4) managing relations and coordinating with other Departments and agencies having important responsibilities and programs abroad and minimizing their rivalry and counteraction; and (5) participating in extended and continuous parliamentary diplomacy, international conferencing, and treaty making. Moreover, in the twenty-first century the United States will need to adjust to the creeping and burgeoning globalization of world affairs, including international institutionalization and, in some cases, governance of such matters as global population explosion and movement, health and epidemics, conservation of resources, economic production and trade, currency and banking, investments and inflation, terrorism and criminal justice, and peaceful settlement and peacemaking, which in some cases transcends or even violates American national interests and objectives.

Other persisting matters pertain to the affairs of both the Foreign Service and the State Department. Some of the most obvious are (1) applying an effective decision-making system for formulating foreign policy, utilizing the options analysis and/or bureaucratic processes[26]; (2) resolving the dichotomy of, and integrating, the devisement and implementation of policy and handling operational foreign relations programs abroad; (3) minimizing overbureaucratization, not only in terms of structure but especially with respect to process and procedure in order to maintain effective management of foreign relations; (4) balancing the quantity and use of generalists and specialists in both the Department and Foreign Service; (5) interchanging personnel for service in Washington and abroad to achieve the greatest benefit to the Department, the foreign missions, and individual officers and also exchanging them with other Departments and agencies; (6) expediting the flow of documents, messages, and information provided by the Department and missions abroad; and (7) selecting deserving individuals for special recognition and awards. To these may be added the lack of, and need for, departmental clearance for appointments, especially for Presidential appointees, utilizing the counsel and recommendations of outside professional agencies and qualified institutions.

"WHAT IS PAST IS PROLOGUE"—ASSESSMENTS

This expression, coined by Shakespeare as used in *The Tempest* and emblazoned on the National Archives building in Washington, characterizes the future of the Department of State and the conduct of American foreign relations. The essence and practical implications of such conduct are complex and difficult to comprehend and assess and are usually colored by subjective predispositions. In 1976, in a pamphlet entitled *United States Foreign Policy*, the Department of State observed that no nation can choose the timing of its fate, that the tides of history take no account of the fatigue of the helmsman, and that posterity will regard not the difficulty of the challenge but only the adequacy of the response. Based on years of experience, Henry Kissinger warned that each foreign relations success only buys an admission ticket to a more vexatious problem.

Simply put, about the relationship of foreign policy and the conduct of foreign affairs in the past and the future, James Rives Childs, career Foreign Service Officer and Chief of Mission to several Middle Eastern countries, has written: "The art of diplomacy consists of making the policy of one government understood and if possible accepted by other governments. Policy is thus the substance of foreign relations; diplomacy proper is the process by which policy is carried out."[27] Analyzing the nature of diplomacy in greater depth, Newsom disputes the attitude that it is unpolitical. He contends that it is an intensely political process in which diplomats, espousing the national interests of their governments, seek to persuade host countries to make political decisions that will be least damaging to the countries they represent. Moreover, he believes that Americans have historically viewed diplomacy as "a mixture of ignorance of its details, suspicion of its objectives, contempt for its importance, and fascination with its romance" and that they have always had difficulty "accepting the styles and conventions of diplomacy." He also concludes that it "is neither a capricious luxury nor an outmoded anachronism," that it "is and must remain vital to the security of the nation" and that the skills and advice of diplomats "are an indispensable insurance against disaster."[28]

As U.S. participation in world affairs intensified, the disparity between domestic and foreign policy and relations diminished. Whereas previously, policies, laws, and agencies dealt with either internal or external affairs, many of these distinctions evanesced. Consequently, the making and implementation of foreign policy now involve not only the President, Congress, and the Department of State but also the Commerce, Defense, Treasury, and most other Departments, the intelligence community, and the foreign assistance, information, and other agencies, some of which are represented abroad by their own attachés, agents, and staffs. This proliferation generated serious problems of coordination and control among these Departments and agencies, both in Washington and abroad, which are not likely to be fully resolved.

Operating in an atmosphere of criticism, distrust, and resentment, often rendered inevitable by the very nature of diplomatic practice, Macomber has noted: "The defining of altered responsibilities in a changing environment has been, and from now on is likely always to remain, one of the most difficult problems facing the modern diplomat." Addressing himself to the key function of diplomacy, he contends that the predominant responsibilities "of all true diplomats" is to preserve the national interests, security of the American people, and peace, which requires a lifetime of dedication "to the strengthening of the fabric of fair and peaceful settlements" and which "all true diplomats honor," whereas, if war comes, it "represents the ultimate failure of the diplomat." Even then, the diplomat is obliged "to contain the fighting and bring it to an acceptable conclusion as soon as possible" and "to guide events in such a way that postwar conditions will not undermine a future peace."[29] This is regarded as the universal First Commandment of the diplomatic profession.

Prescribing his view of the basic function of diplomacy, Thayer has written: "Diplomacy mediates not between right and wrong but between conflicting interests. It seeks to compromise not between legal equities but between national aspirations. . . . Furthermore, a nation's interests, aspirations, and the power to satisfy them vary from year to year, indeed from day to day. What yesterday was satisfactory may tomorrow be intolerable and unenforceable."[30] Smith Simpson, a former Foreign Service Officer, adds that diplomacy "can be both a nursery and an instrument of law and order, with diplomats serving not simply the needs of their governments but also those of the community of nations," and that they play a "civilizing, ethical role, contributing constructively to the evolution of the world community."[31]

More comprehensively, Under Secretary of State and Ambassador at Large Chester B. Bowles, in an address at the National Press Club in 1962, envisioned an all-encompassing diplomacy when he declared: "We are also coming to realize that foreign operations in today's world call for a total diplomacy that reflects the dynamic phases of our own American society—from our industrial capacity and military defense to our education system and our dedication to the rights of the human individual," and American diplomats "can no longer be content with the wining and dining, reporting, analyzing, and cautiously predicting. They must act as administrators and coordinators, responsible for the effective operations of all U.S. Government activities in the countries of their assignment."[32]

Contemporary and future diplomacy differs substantially from that of earlier times. Analysts of the need to accommodate to changes in the conduct of foreign relations identify a host of matters, such as: (1) the revolution in world politics; (2) enlargement of the society of nations and future political fragmentation, additional decolonization, and actual and potential integration; (3) rivalry among competing blocs of nations; (4) conflict of nationally and internationally oriented forces and movements; (5) the permeative role of competing ideologies; (6) frequent if not endemic, international crises; (7) rapid obsolescence of aspects of foreign policy; (8) speed of events requiring rapid responses and negotiations; (9) multiplication and convolution of subjects of international concern; (10) increase in the role of the military in foreign affairs; (11) intensification of complexity of the conduct of foreign affairs; (12) decline of formality in diplomacy; (13) application of diplomatic intercourse not only with foreign leaders but also with whole populations; (14) increasing need for an admixture of substantive and procedural policy making, qualities and skills of personnel, and management and administrative competence; (15) improved availability of forms of, and increase in, the speed of communications, rendering them virtually instantaneous; (16) the paramount role of the United States in world affairs and nearly total involvement in international relations; (17) augmentation of American interventionist and activist methods of diplomacy; (18) escalation of personal diplomacy of Presidents, Secretaries of State, and their special emissaries and negotiators; (19) greater impact of domestic concerns and public pressures and lessening of the distinction between American domestic and foreign national interests and policy; and (20) influence of the media on the conduct of foreign relations.[33]

Early in the eighteenth century, discussing the role of diplomats, François de Callières claimed simply that they have two principal duties, namely, to conduct the business of their masters and to discover the business of others. Contemplating the current situation, Macomber observed that no current or future diplomats can be effective or lay legitimate claim to the title unless they have mastered the personal "core qualities" and the professional "core skills" that the modern profession requires. Otherwise, regardless of how profoundly they may be committed to the nation's interests and the cause of peace, they remain "ineffective in any positive sense" and might even become "a menace on the international scene."[34]

Analyses differ on the official and personal interrelations of Presidents and their Secretaries of State. One simple version, based on past practice, distinguishes three fundamental types of relationship: (1) the predominant President, (2) the predominant Secretary of State, and (3) the compromise relationship in which they participate jointly. The first two usually produce functional and procedural difficulties, and the joint relationship raises the issue of fixing the dividing line respecting the authority and responsibility of the Secretary of State. However, few Secretaries regard themselves as Prime Ministers who, with the indulgence of the President may be allowed to exercise more than their normally ascribed prerogatives.[35]

Put in terms of relationship patterns, another analyst also identifies three general categories: (1) the Secretary who functions primarily as a "clerk" when the President chooses to be his own Foreign Minister; (2) the Secretary who serves largely as a "figurehead" when the President prefers to be his own Foreign Secretary in many respects but relies on the Secretary to gain and maintain support for his Administration's foreign policy and programs; and (3) the Secretary who assumes the role of the President's "Prime Minister" and becomes the chief formulator of foreign policy and manager of diplomatic relations.[36]

Focusing on the importance of the components of this interrelationship, designed to service the President, an alternative formulation stresses such matters as who is located most closely to the President and confers with him with the greatest of ease and frequency (which may be sacrificed if the Secretary spends much of his time in negotiations abroad), who is in charge of advising the President most freely on foreign relations, who briefs the President first on issues, who briefs him last on making decisions, who drafts the final version of recommendations that require the President's determinations, who makes the most salutary case for the good of the nation, and who is able to persuade the President as to what is best politically for his Administration.[37]

Another version is concerned with defining a series of declaratory precepts for the Secretary in this relationship. It specifies that the Secretary must be an ardent defender of the Presidential prerogative in foreign relations, must serve as the principal information channel to the President on international affairs, must be the President's chief adviser on foreign policy and the conduct of American diplomacy, must act as arbiter between the Executive and the Department of State, must participate actively in the preparation of Presidential foreign affairs speeches, and must prevent overinstitutionalization of the policy process, while also serving personally as an effective diplomat.[38]

In short, the Secretary of State remains not a responsible, elected Foreign Minister but rather "the representative of the President—and not of the people directly"—when implementing foreign policy, whereas "the President—not the Secretary—is responsible to the people." It is an unwritten rule that Secretaries who do not agree with the President are nevertheless expected to implement the President's policies faithfully, or they need to resign.[39] In some cases an effort may be made at the outset by Presidents and their Secretaries to agree on principles to guide their relationship and joint effort and the role to be played by the Secretaries. However, as Professor Norman Hill notes, usually the nature of personalities and the exigencies of the times rather than such understandings "map the areas" in which they relate and operate, individually and jointly.[40]

On the matter of leadership in the Department of State, former Secretary Dean Acheson has been quoted as saying, "Nobody has been able to run the Department in a hundred and fifty years."[41] Put another way, Dean Rusk acknowledged that the Secretary cannot run American foreign relations by himself. "He must delegate the overwhelming bulk of decision making to hundreds of Foreign Service Officers, authorized to act on his behalf. The world has become so complex . . . that junior officers in the State Department now make decisions which before World War II would have been made by the Secretary," to which he added, "Fortunately the Secretary of State is backed up by a professional diplomatic service second to none in the world," which must "ensure that the wishes and policies of the President and Secretary of State are carried out. That process is very complex, but the system works."[42] Commenting on his relations with the President when he became Secretary, James A. Baker revealed that he "intended to be the President's man in the State Department, not the State Department's man at the White House."[43]

Once Secretaries of State assume their office, they must perform three critical functions: the corporate role of managing and administering the State Department; the policy-making role, providing guidance and participating personally in the policy process; and a representative role, presenting the Department's corporate recommendation and interests in the larger policy-making arena of the national Government.[44] Related are the Secretary's responsibilities for interagency and interdepartmental coordination and integration.

Assessing the burden of responsibilities of the contemporary Secretary of State, Senator Henry M. Jackson's subcommittee reported: "The modern Secretary of State is thus adviser, negotiator, reporter of trouble, spokesman, manager, and coordinator. This is all too much. Yet somehow he must handle it. He cannot take any one piece of his job. He has to do the best he can with all his several duties. None can be sacrificed—or wholly delegated to others. As a result some duties are bound to be shortchanged. Some things that need doing by him, will be left to others—or left undone, for they will not have sufficient priority to crowd other things off his schedule."[45] This problem was later ameliorated somewhat by the creation of the office of Deputy Secretary of State. Nevertheless, the value and greatness of future Secretaries of State will depend on such factors as their personal qualities and actions, the challenges and exigencies of the times, the lasting benefits to the nation they manage to produce, and the assessments of history.

Prior to World War II Professor Benjamin H. Williams concluded that the Department of State and Foreign Service serve as the epicenter of the United States for maintaining friendly relations with other countries and as "the roadbuilders along the way to peace." The role the United States plays throughout the world "will be determined not only by policymakers in the White House and the halls of Congress but also by hundreds of men engaged in the day to day routine of the Department of State and of the embassies, legations, and consulates spread over the earth. The wise and discriminating protection of citizens, treaty making, arbitration, legislative preparations in committees and conferences, the administrative work of international commissions, and many other aspects of international contact, all depend upon a well-trained personnel which can give advice and apply policies wisely in conformity with the public interest."[46]

Shortly after the war Professor Stuart observed: "In a world of ruthless power politics it is vital that the Department of State be made an efficient and responsible agency capable of formulating and carrying out foreign policy which will maintain, strengthen, and improve the status of the United States in world affairs" and that if this were done, it "would add materially to the stature of the Department of State as the most important Department in the government."[47]

Commenting on his experience as head of the Department, former Secretary Cyrus Vance has written: "Although it is small in number of personnel and budget, the State Department contains probably the most able and dedicated professional group in the federal government," which is "peopled with extraordinarily able and devoted men and women who are not adequately appreciated by many of our citizens."[48] In his valedictory address to his State Department staff, Baker confessed, "Any success that we may have achieved is due in considerable part to the hard work, spirit, professionalism, and commitment of all of you.''[49]

Dr. Henry M. Wriston, notable for the amalgamation of the personnel of the Department of State and the Foreign Service—known as ''Wristonization''—later observed in a lecture at the Associated Claremont Colleges: ''The Foreign Service Officer corps has been virtually invisible throughout the larger part of its half century or more of history. This is not peculiar or abnormal. Most of the officers are stationed abroad; they are out of the public eye except upon relatively rare occasions. . . . But their effectiveness is in almost inverse ratio to their conspicuousness. It is not only bad form, it is bad diplomacy, for them to win 'victories.' Such 'triumphs' are hollow, for they are bound to injure domestically the government with which the diplomat has to deal, and make future relationships and negotiations more difficult, needlessly.''[50]

Subsequently, William Barnes and John Heith Morgan, Foreign Service Officers, in their comprehensive history of the Foreign Service, wrote: ''Henceforth the Diplomatic and Consular Services were to be known as the Foreign Service of the United States, and the designation 'Foreign Service officer' was to denote permanent officers'' below the rank of Chiefs of Mission, who were subject to ''assignment to either the diplomatic or the consular branch of the Service.'' They concluded their volume: ''For the young man or woman who seeks interesting and challenging work providing broad and varied experience, the advantages and opportunities of a career in the Foreign Service far outweigh the hardships and handicaps.''[51]

In his study on American diplomatic practice, Professor Stuart concluded that ''no service today is more important to the nation than the Foreign Service'' and that ''in organization and personnel'' it ''now stands second to none.'' Quoting a career diplomat's advice concerning the rewards that might be anticipated, he cautions: ''You must expect neither financial rewards nor the rewards of prestige extended officers of the Army or Navy; expect no appreciation of your services from the public nor from the Government; all that you can expect is the reward springing from the consciousness of duty faithfully performed in the service of your country.''[52]

More recently, W. Wendell Blancké, former Ambassador and retired Foreign Service Officer, looking to the future, concludes his analysis: ''Assuming the continuing need for a select career group to serve as keystone for the U.S. effort abroad, it should be recognized—without dishonor to those who have served so well in the past—that the Foreign Service of the future must maintain standards of intellect and expertise considerably beyond those once found acceptable. To attract and hold the people needed for great and difficult tasks, the Service must be so organized that its officers not only are trained to be part of a highly professional corps but are also consistently provided, at all levels, with highly professional work to do.''[53]

''An ambassador is an honest man sent to lie abroad for the good of his country.'' This is the classic and oft-repeated definition of a diplomat offered by Sir Henry Wotton early in the seventeenth century. It expresses the essence of the chicanery and deception indulged in by states in the conduct of their foreign relations at the time that modern diplomacy was developing. Each country, intent upon satisfying its own self-interests, participated in the complicated international chessboard politics of the day through diplomats who served simply as paid agents in the struggle for the triumvirate of patrimony, power, and prestige.

However, modern diplomatic practice is far different from what it was in the seventeenth century. It is influenced considerably by the advances made in social customs, popular thought, political institutions, and legal requirements and restrictions. The usages, the forms, and the rules that govern it vary less with the countries and their governments than with the times, and its character changes ceaselessly in accordance with the modifications introduced into legal commitments and political and social customs of the community of nations.

It has been reported that Secretary Cordell Hull required four things of his Ambassadors, namely, to report honestly what is going on, to represent the United States before foreign governments and publics, to negotiate U.S. Government business, and to look after American lives and property abroad.[54] Overseas, according to Blancké, as Chief of Mission the Ambassador, like the President he serves, remains the "chief executive of a large and complex establishment, the active interpreter of policy and director of programs abroad," and he is "the President's man and the Number One official American in the country of his accreditation, not just a chairman of the board." Summarizing the need for the future, he concludes: "In the golden age of American diplomacy, our pioneer diplomats were among the best the times had to offer; the cause of our struggling new nation could afford no less. The developing course of human events today demonstrates clearly, once again, that we cannot afford anything short of the best. . . . The pace of events is too rapid; the problems, too complicated—and the stakes, far too high—to permit of anything else."[55]

It may be taken for granted as an organizational imperative, as Secretary Baker has put it, that Foreign Service Officers generally hope to become Ambassadors, which represents the peak of their diplomatic careers and which may be exceeded by becoming Dean of the Diplomatic Corps in a particular foreign country. Yet there are those who caution them to regard their status as the elite among elites strictly in a positive sense. Thus, Macomber has warned that embassies tend to remain, with respect to their structure and the manner of handling their affairs, "as their nation's last outposts of feudalism," in which authority "is notably centered in the person of the ambassador," who is accorded "a marked degree of protocol . . . both outside and inside his embassy." There is always, therefore, "the danger that this combination of deference and authoritarianism will stultify creative thinking."[56]

Summarizing the past, in his short bicentennial history of the Department of State, David F. Trask, then Department's Historian, has written:

After two centuries the Department of State—its offices and its people—comprise one of the world's nerve centers of world affairs. During the earliest days of the Republic, it made indispensable contributions to the preservation of our independence. . . . Across the twentieth century, as Americans came to accept the responsibilities of leadership, the Department, like the nation it serves, has experienced remarkable growth in size, influence, and function. . . . For more than two centuries the men and women of the Department have chosen this form of public service because they are deeply committed to the search for solutions to the problems of tomorrow. Throughout the world they daily face the threat of disease, terrorism, war, kidnapping, and death. Along with these hazards come the normal demands of day-to-day problemsolving, decisionmaking, and coping with life at home and abroad. All things considered the people of the United States have been well served.[57]

Thus, since 1789 the Department of State has constituted the epicenter of the growing and mutating foreign affairs of the United States and has evolved into one of the world's leading political and administrative agencies for the conduct of diplomacy and the search for contemporary and future solutions to international issues and the amelioration of conflicts. It continues to possess the primary administrative responsibility for international problem solving, decision making, and promoting American interests and welfare in world affairs. During and following World War II the United States assumed an active world leadership role, not only in American foreign policy making but also in the promotion of, and participation in, diplomatic relations, multipartite organizations, and international conferencing, which it will continue to bear in the twenty-first century.

NOTES

1. Schuyler, *American Diplomacy and the Furthering of Commerce*, pp. 4–7; for a description of early Department of State functions and activities, also see pp. 7–40.

2. Moore, *The Principles of American Diplomacy*, pp. 425–27.

3. Foster, *The Practice of Diplomacy*, pp. 1, 7, 13.

4. Thayer, *Diplomat*, p. 72.

5. Stuart, *American Diplomatic and Consular Practice*, p. 417. On this subject, he also quotes Mowrer, *Our Foreign Affairs*, p. 193, and adds that, on the other hand, citizens in democracies appreciate the value of armies and navies dealing with foreign affairs. Peter L. Szanton, focusing on the past, suggests: "Critics of military planning have remarked that in time of peace generals prepare to win the previous war" and "Critics of diplomacy have added that in time of peace diplomats attempt to avoid the previous war." See Robert Murphy, *Commission on the Organization of the Government for the Conduct of Foreign Policy*, Appendixes, vol. 1, Appendix A, p. 5.

6. Introduction to Harr, *The Development of Careers in the Foreign Service*, p. xiii.

7. See Stuart, *The Department of State*, p. 466.

8. Quoted in Trask, *A Short History of the U.S. Department of State, 1781–1981*, p. 37.

9. Macomber, *The Angels' Game: A Handbook of Modern Diplomacy*, p. 191.

10. The World War II supplementary agencies concerned with foreign relations responsibilities have been eliminated, absorbed, or otherwise modified, although some, in different versions, have been retained, a few of which have been incorporated into, or attached to, the Department of State.

11. The matter of reform and reorganization of the State Department following World War II is discussed in Chapter 7, section on Department of State Management.

12. See Barnes and Morgan, *The Foreign Service of the United States*, pp. 124–27, in which they list many major and minor abuses performed by consular officers and discuss the merit system. Also see Macomber, *The Angels' Game*, pp. 133–38, in which he discusses the appointment of noncareerists and what he calls "subprofessionals." On the other hand, for discussion of what he calls "the myth" that all political appointees are amateurs, see McCamy, *Conduct of the New Diplomacy*, pp. 233–45.

13. Macomber, *Diplomacy for the 70's*, pp. 588–89.

14. These agencies are in a much different relationship with Congress and the White House than are scores of other organizations, such as the American labor unions, American Association of Retired Persons, American and National Bar Associations, American Farm Bureau Federation, American Legion, American Medical Association, National Education Association, National Organization for Women, Urban League, the U.S. Chamber of Commerce, and scores of others.

15. For general commentary on this problem, see Knappen, *An Introduction to American Foreign Policy*, Chapter 6, especially, pp. 201 ff. on "Citizenship Education"; McCamy, *The Administration of American Foreign Affairs*, Chapter 14; and Plischke, *Conduct of American Diplomacy*, pp. 83–88. On the other hand, often foreign governments employ lobbyists, largely Americans, as their "public relations counselors," to lobby on their behalf; see Simpson, *Anatomy of the State Department* (Boston: Houghton Mifflin, 1967), pp. 165–66.

16. On Senator Joseph R. McCarthy and McCarthyism, see John F. Anderson, *McCarthy: The Man, the Senator, the "Ism"* (Boston: Beacon, 1952); Cedric Belfrage, *The American Inquisition, 1945–1960: A Profile of the "McCarthy Era"* (Indianapolis: Bobbs-Merrill, 1973); Roy M. Cohn, *McCarthy* (New York: New American Library, 1968); Albert Fried, ed., *McCarthyism: The Great American Red Scare–A Documentary History* (New York: Oxford University Press, 1997); Richard M. Fried, *Nightmare in Red: The McCarthy Era in Perspective* (New York: Oxford University Press, 1990); Owen Lattimore, *Ordeal by Slander* (Westport, Conn.: Greenwood, 1971); Thomas C. Reeves, *The Life and Times of Joe McCarthy* (New York: Stein and Day, 1982); Richard H. Rovere, *Senator Joe McCarthy* (New York: Harper and Row, 1969). Also see J. Garry Clifford, "McCarthyism," in *Encyclopedia of American Foreign Relations*, vol. 3, pp. 118–23; Stuart, *American Diplomatic and Consular Practice*, pp. 420–21; and Trask, *A Short History of the Department of State*, p. 34.

17. The matter of Presidential appointments with the consent of the Senate that are later revoked has evoked disagreement between the two branches of the Government. The Tenure of Office Acts of 1867 and 1869, by which the Senate sought to participate in Presidential removals from office, were repealed in 1886. But it was not until 1926 that the Supreme Court ruled that it was not constitutionally proper for Congress to restrict the President's right of removal from office of political appointees.

18. For general conclusions regarding the Department of State, see Plischke, *Conduct of American Diplomacy*, pp. 220–22; Simpson, *Anatomy of the State Department*, Chap-

ters 11 and 12, and *The Crisis in American Diplomacy*, Chapter 20; and Stuart, *The Department of State*, p. 466.

19. Lay, *The Foreign Service of the United States*, pp. 378–79.

20. On the matter of secrecy versus. openness respecting American diplomatic documentation, see Plischke, *Contemporary U.S. Foreign Policy*, pp. 1–20.

21. The term "elite," as applied to Ambassadors and Foreign Service Officers, is used in two ways. In the positive sense it acknowledges the necessity and reasons for many of the privileged aspects of their status and treatment. However, it also is used in a pejorative sense when other aspects of their profession, such as their extraterritoriality, inviolability, and dilettantism, are emphasized.

For commentary on the criticism of diplomatic snobbishness, see Stuart, *American Diplomatic and Consular Practice*, pp. 419–20; for general commentary on American prejudice against elites, see Thayer, *Diplomat*, p. 282; and for ten aspects of the "Foreign Service Culture," see the Murphy Commission Report, vol. 6, Appendix P, pp. 199–200.

22. National attitudes concerning precedence vary widely. Whereas some countries prescribe their own schedules of precedence, the United States has no officially determined listing for this matter, preferring to adapt both treatment and precedence to specific events and circumstances. Consequently, it is flexible, for which guidance is provided by the Department of State's Protocol Office. On precedence and proper protocol, see Childs, *American Foreign Service*, pp. 84–86, and for a comparison of precedence ranks of U.S. diplomatic and military officers, see pp. 246–47.

On the matter of archaic and stilted language, it must be remembered that at one time Latin was the common language of diplomacy of the Occidental world, and it was used in both oral and written communications and agreements. With the rise of the modern state system, the French language gradually achieved ascendancy into the nineteenth century, when English gained prominence. As a consequence, certain earlier terms were carried over into contemporary practice. Aside from various universally used legal terms, examples include such expressions as *ad referendum, agréation,* aide-memoire, *casus foederis,* communiqué, *compromis d'arbitrage, corps diplomatique,* détente, despatch/dispatch, doyen (dean of the diplomatic corps), modus vivendi, *note diplomatique,* note verbal, process verbal, persona grata and persona non grata, and rapporteur. In addition, antiquated or stilted expressions, sometimes understatements, are used, such as "accept, Excellency, assurances of my highest consideration," "an unfriendly act," "view with concern," "I have the honor to report," and "Your Excellency's obedient servant." For additional commentary, see Macomber, *The Angels' Game*, pp. 141–43; Plischke, *Conduct of American Diplomacy*, pp. 17–20; Thayer, *Diplomat*, pp. 99–102; and for examples of diplomatic notes that illustrate such usage, see Plischke, *Conduct of American Diplomacy*, pp. 604–14, and *International Relations: Basic Documents*, especially Chapter 2; and Williams, *American Diplomacy: Policies and Practice*, pp. 463–66.

23. Macomber, *The Angels' Game*, p. 142.

24. An interesting situation occurred in 1945, for example, when a brief, unconditional surrender with Germany was negotiated in the field and signed at Reims, France, on May 7, and a "ratification meeting" took place at Berlin the following day. This constituted an executive agreement, consummated under the President's authority as Commander in Chief. The first surrender of May 7 was signed at 2:41 A.M. by representatives of the United States and Great Britain, and was certified by a Soviet liaison officer, which applied solely to the German forces in the West.

However, the single capitulation of all German forces on both the Western and Eastern fronts had previously been discussed at the Potsdam Conference and was under negotiation for months at London by the tripartite European Advisory Commission (consisting of high-level representatives of the American, British, and Soviet Governments), the text of which had their advance approval and was intended to be used as a tripartite surrender instrument. When the Soviet Government objected to the Reims agreement, it was declared that it was merely a "preliminary surrender," and a second "official surrender" was signed in Berlin on May 8 by three German military officers and two representing the Western Allied and Soviet forces.

For an excellent account of what he calls a "bungling affair" that was "covered up" by this dual surrender process, see Robert D. Murphy (Political Adviser to General Eisenhower), *Diplomat among Warriors* (Garden City, N.Y.: Doubleday, 1964), pp. 240–42; also see Plischke, *Conduct of American Diplomacy*, pp. 425–26.

25. This Act of 1980 (section 613) authorized the President to establish a "system of awards to confer appropriate recognition of outstanding contributions to the Nation by members of the [Foreign] Service," to consist of "medals or other suitable commendations for performance in the course of or beyond the call of duty which involves distinguished, meritorious service to the Nation, including extraordinary valor in the face of danger to life or health."

26. This problem of the nature of the decision-making process permeates the thinking and analysis of participants from the Secretary of State down the chain of responsibility, often is determined by individual participants, and sometimes is confused or ignored. For analysis of the decision-making systems, see Elmer Plischke, *Foreign Relations Decisionmaking: Options Analysis*, which contains a table of the principal steps in the decision-making process, a table of fifteen principal query analysis points, cosmographic options analysis configurations, and substantive foreign policy options determination hypothetical models, and Plischke, *Foreign Relations: Analysis of Its Anatomy*, Chapter 9, which contains similar listings and graphic depictions.

27. Childs, *American Foreign Service*, p. 64.

28. Newsom, *Diplomacy and the American Democracy*, pp. 6, 26, 219.

29. Macomber, *The Angels' Game*, pp. 19, 24–25.

30. Thayer, *Diplomat*, p. 252.

31. Simpson, *The Crisis in American Diplomacy*, p. 66.

32. Chester B. Bowles, address, March 23, 1962, in Department of State, *American Foreign Policy: Current Documents, 1962*, p. 990.

33. Based on Harr, *The Professional Diplomat*, pp. 28–33, and Newsom, *Diplomacy and the American Democracy*, pp. 2–6.

34. Macomber, *The Angels' Game*, p. 26.

35. See Hill, *Mr. Secretary of State*, pp. 36, 43.

36. See Stupak, *The Shaping of Foreign Policy*, pp .108–10.

37. See Newsom, *Diplomacy and the American Democracy*, pp. 28–29.

38. See Stupak, *The Shaping of Foreign Policy*, pp. 83–89.

39. See DeConde, *The American Secretary of State*, pp. 32–33.

40. Hill, *Mr. Secretary of State*, pp. 34–35. On the relations of the President and Secretary of State, also see Price, *The Secretary of State*, Chapter 2, especially pp. 43–50 on the Secretary's working relations with the President; Plischke, *Conduct of American Diplomacy*, pp. 178–80; and Stuart, *American Diplomatic and Consular Practice*, pp. 24–25.

41. Quoted in McCamy, *Conduct of the New Diplomacy*, p. 7, and Stupak, *The Shaping of Foreign Policy*, p. 66.

42. Dean Rusk, *As I Saw It* (New York: Norton, 1990), p. 525.

43. James A. Baker III, *The Politics of Diplomacy* (New York: Putnam, 1955), pp. 29–30.

44. See Stupak, *The Shaping of Foreign Policy*, p. 67.

45. *The Administration of National Security: The Secretary of State*, 88th Cong., 2d Sess., 1964, p. 3.

46. Williams, *American Diplomacy: Policies and Practice*, p. 473.

47. Stuart, *The Department of State*, p. 466.

48. Cyrus Vance, *Hard Choices* (New York: Simon and Schuster, 1983), pp. 39–40.

49. Baker, *The Politics of Diplomacy*, p. 27.

50. Wriston, *Diplomacy in a Democracy*, pp. 3–4.

51. Barnes and Morgan, *The Foreign Service of the United States*, pp. 205–6, 330.

52. Stuart, *American Diplomatic and Consular Practice*, pp. 424–25.

53. Blancké, *The Foreign Service of the United States*, pp. 254–55.

54. Noted in Thayer, *Diplomat*, p. 81. Put in substantive terms, on the other hand, the Department of State has specified that the contemporary and future conduct of foreign relations is "everybody's business, because it affects everyone." Among the Ambassador's principal goals and responsibilities are (1) the achievement of security through strength, to deter or defeat aggression at any level; (2) progress through partnership, to promote the prosperity and security of the free world, including aid to less developed areas; (3) revolution of freedom, to help less advanced nations achieve modernization without sacrificing their independence or the pursuit of democracy; (4) world community under law, largely through integration by means of global and regional international organizations; and (5) peace through perseverance, by ending the arms race and reducing the risk of war. See *Department of State, 1963: A Report to the Citizen*, pp. 8–15.

55. Blancké, *The Foreign Service of the United States*, pp. 99, 255. On the matter of an Ambassador's authority and responsibility, he discusses their lines of communication with the State Department, their independent judgment in the field, their personality as communicator (both as sender and receiver), and their capacity as Chiefs of Mission (which he denominates as functioning in loco parentis, pp. 98–101, and he analyzes the role of Deputy Chiefs of Mission, pp. 101–4.

56. Macomber, *The Angels' Game*, pp. 146–47.

57. Trask, *A Short History of the U.S. Department of State, 1781–1981*, p. 41.

Appendix I

Principal Statutes and Executive Orders concerning the Department of State and the Foreign Service

Not including periodic Department of State fiscal authorization and appropriations acts or acts concerning the domestic functions of the Department of State and their transfer to other agencies of the U.S. Government.

Act of July 27, 1789 [First Constitutive Foreign Affairs Statute] (1 Stat. 28)—Establishing the Department of Foreign Affairs and the Office of Secretary of the Department of Foreign Affairs, which had previously been created by resolution of the Continental Congress on Jan. 10, 1781 (*Journals of the Continental Congress*, 19: 43).

Act of Sept. 15, 1789 [Department of State Creation Act] (1 Stat. 68)—Establishing the Department of State and the Office of Secretary of State, to supersede the Department and Secretary of Foreign Affairs; continuing the use of the Great Seal previously employed by the Continental Congress; making the Secretary of State responsible for the custody of, and affixing, the Great Seal of the United States to important U.S. documents (which, under the Confederation, had been the responsibility of the Secretary of the Continental Congress); and authorizing the devisement, subject to the approval of the President, of a Department of State seal for its documents.

Act of July 1, 1790 (1 Stat. 128)—Authorizing the sum of $40,000 annually for the expenses of foreign intercourse, fixing the salaries of diplomatic officers, and authorizing Secretaries for American Ministers abroad.

Act of Apr. 14, 1792 (1 Stat. 254)—First organic enactment defining the powers and functions of consular officers.

Act of Jan. 30, 1799 [Logan Act] (1 Stat. 613)—Prohibiting unauthorized citizens from assuming diplomatic functions, amended by Act of June 25, 1948 (62 Stat. 744) and Act of Sept. 13, 1994 (108 Stat. 2147); *U.S. Code*, Title 18, sec. 953.

Acts of Feb. 28, 1803, Apr. 20, 1818, and Mar. 1, 1823 (2 Stat. 202 and 433, and 3 Stat. 729)—Enlarging the duties and functions of consular officers.

Act of May 1, 1810 (2 Stat. 608)—Prohibiting American consuls from engaging in trade abroad and authorizing appointment of Secretaries of diplomatic missions abroad.

Act of Aug. 26, 1842 (U.S. Revised Statutes, sec. 173)—Defined the administrative functions of the Chief Clerk to supervise the administrative functioning of the Department of State.

Act of May 23, 1850 (9 Stat. 428)—Transferring responsibility for taking the U.S. census from the Department of State to the Department of Interior.

Act of Mar. 3, 1853 (10 Stat. 212)—Authorizing the appointment of the First Assistant Secretary of State, to which the Second Assistant Secretary was added by the Act of July 25, 1866, the Third Assistant Secretary was added by the Act of June 20, 1874, and the numbering of these Assistant Secretaries was eliminated by the Rogers Act of May 24, 1924 (43 Stat. 140).

Act of Mar. 1, 1855 (10 Stat. 619)—Remodeling the Diplomatic and Consular Systems, prescribing grades, posts, and salaries in the Diplomatic and Consular Services, and authorizing the appointment of one secretary to each American legation overseas. (Repealed by Act of Aug. 18, 1856.)

Act of Aug. 18, 1856 (11 Stat. 52)—Establishing an organic framework for the Diplomatic and Consular Systems, with provisions fixing new salary rates for diplomatic officers, classifying consular posts according to method of compensation (salary or fees), and establishing regulations to govern the exercise of consular duties. Also authorized the Department of State to issue passports in foreign countries by diplomatic and consular officers under rules prescribed by the President.

Act of June 22, 1860 (12 Stat. 72)—Providing for the exercise of extraterritorial judicial functions by diplomatic and consular officers in certain countries.

Act of June 20, 1864 (13 Stat. 139)—Authorizing the appointment of thirteen consular clerks to have permanent tenure during good behavior.

Act of July 4, 1864 (13 Stat. 385)—Authorizing the President to appoint a Commissioner of Immigration to serve under the Secretary of State, which was abolished by the Act of Mar. 30, 1868 (15 Stat. 58), and was not revived until the Act of Mar. 3, 1891 (26 Stat. 1084), as a Bureau of Immigration and placed under the Treasury Department, and it was later transferred to the Labor Department when it was established.

Act of June 8, 1872 (17 Stat. 304)—Authorizing the Postmaster General, subject to Presidential approval, to conclude postal conventions (differing from the normal treaty process). Postal arrangements had originally been authorized by statute in 1792 (1 Stat. 239). For current law, see Act of Aug. 12, 1970 (84 Stat. 724), by which the Post Office Department was superseded by the U.S. Postal Service, under which the Postmaster General exercises the same unusual treaty authority. Updated by Act of Aug. 12, 1970.

Act of June 11, 1874 (18 Stat. 66)—Reclassifying consular posts according to salary and providing allowances for clerks hired at certain consulates, and establishing rules governing travel time to foreign posts.

Act of June 20, 1874 (18 Stat. 88)—Requiring that copies of all treaties and postal conventions be submitted by the Department of State to the Public Printer for publication; amended and updated periodically, including the Act of Oct. 19, 1984 (98 Stat. 2268).

Act of June 20, 1874 (18 Stat. 109)—Authorizing the Secretary of State to fix the working hours of Department of State clerks.

Act of Mar. 3, 1875 (18 Stat. pt. 3, p. 483)—Increasing the salaries of diplomats.

Act of Sept. 30, 1878 (92 Stat. 808)—Known as the ''Diplomatic Relations Act,'' implementing the Vienna Convention on Diplomatic Relations, concerned primarily with privileges and immunities.

Act of Jan. 16, 1883 [Pendleton Civil Service Act]—Providing for the appointment by means of competitive examinations for recruiting members of the classified Civil Service personnel, which later served as the basis of reform of the Department of State staff and the Foreign Service.

Act of Mar. 3, 1883 (22 Stat. 563)—Specified that Department of State staff members daily spend at least seven hours at their work, which was interpreted to run from 9:00 A.M. to 4:00 P.M. with one-half hour for lunch.

Act of Jan. 19, 1886 [Presidential Succession Act] (24 Stat. 1)—Providing that if both the offices of President and Vice President are vacant, the Secretary of State would succeed to the Presidency (followed by the other Secretaries in their order of precedence; superseded the Presidential Succession Act of 1792, and was later superseded by the Presidential Succession Act of July 18, 1947).

Act of Mar. 1, 1893 (27 Stat. 497)—Providing for the appointment of Ambassadors on a reciprocal basis; the first American Ambassadors were appointed following this enactment.

Act of July 26, 1894 (28 Stat. 142)—Authorizing the appointment of the first Secretaries of Embassies.

Executive Order of Sept. 20, 1895—Providing for appointments on a merit basis to consular offices with annual compensation of from $1,000 to $2,500.

Act of Mar. 22, 1902 (32 Stat. 76, 78)—Providing for the first student interpreters for overseas missions.

Executive Order No. 367 of Nov. 10, 1905—Extending the merit system of appointment to all consular offices with annual compensation of more than $1,000.

Executive Order No. 368 of Nov. 10, 1905—Providing for appointments of diplomatic secretaries on a merit basis.

Act of Apr. 5, 1906 (34 Stat. 99)—Providing for the reorganization of the Consular Service, including the reclassification of consular officers, periodic inspections of consular posts by Consular Inspection Corps, other administrative provisions, and the merit system for appointments.

Act of June 16, 1906 (34 Stat. 288)—Authorizing appropriations for official transportation expenses of diplomatic and consular officers, and augmented to cover travel expenses of their families by Act of Mar. 14, 1919 (40 Stat. 1325).

Executive Order No. 469 of June 27, 1906—Prescribing regulations governing appointments and promotions in the Consular Service in accordance with Civil Service provisions.

Act of March 2, 1909 (35 Stat. 672)—Restricting appointment of new ambassadorships to creation by congressional act.

Executive Order No. 1143 of Nov. 26, 1909—Prescribing regulations governing appointments and promotions in the Diplomatic Service in accordance with Civil Service provisions.

Act of Feb. 17, 1911 [Lowden Act] (36 Stat. 917)—First Act authorizing the purchase of building sites and the purchase, construction, repair, and furnishing of buildings for American diplomatic and consular establishments abroad, with expenditures limited to $500,000 annually and to $150,000 in any one place.

Act of Mar. 4, 1913 (37 Stat. 913)—Providing that the Executive, including the Department of State, could not extend or accept any invitation to participate in any international congress, conference, or international organization without having the specific authority of law to do so; superseded by Act of Aug. 1, 1956.

Act of Feb. 5, 1915 [Act to Improve the "Foreign Service"] (38 Stat. 805)—Establishing the merit system in the Diplomatic and Consular Services on a statutory basis; providing for appointments to classes rather than to posts; and reclassifying diplomatic and consular officers. This was the first act to formally use the term "Foreign Service" as applied to the Diplomatic and Consular Services.

Act of July 1, 1916 (39 Stat. 252)—Establishing the Office of Counselor of Embassy or Legation as the second-ranking officer of American diplomatic missions.

Act of June 15, 1917 (40 Stat. 226)—Providing legal requirements for the registration of "foreign agents" in the United States, other than accredited diplomatic and consular personnel, and for punishment of such agents acting without registration; amended and updated periodically, including the Act of Sept. 13, 1994 (108 Stat. 2147).

Act of Mar. 1, 1919 (40 Stat. 1224)—Authorizing the appointment of an Under Secretary of State as second-ranking officer of the Department. Subsequently, additional Under Secretaries were authorized, and beginning in 1946 they were appointed with functional titles, such as Political Affairs, Economic Affairs, Management, and Security Assistance.

Executive Order No. 3987 of Apr. 4, 1924—Establishing a system of cooperation among the missions of the Department of State and other Departments of the United States abroad, requiring their leaders to meet periodically.

Act of May 24, 1924 [Rogers Act] (43 Stat. 140)—Amalgamating the Diplomatic and Consular Services into the Foreign Service of the United States, establishing the Service on a career basis with provision for a more adequate scale of salaries and allowances and a retirement system, and creating the Office of Foreign Inspectors.

Executive Order No. 4022 of June 7, 1924—Prescribing regulations governing the reorganized Foreign Service, including the appointment of all new recruits as unclassified officers. Implemented by Departmental Orders 295 and 296. Also provided for a Training School for new Foreign Service Officers.

Act of May 7, 1926 [Foreign Service Buildings Act] (44 Stat., pt. 2, p. 403)—Authorizing the Secretary of State, subject to the direction of a Foreign Service Building Commission, to purchase or construct, alter, repair, and furnish buildings for diplomatic and consular purposes and establishing a Foreign Service Building Fund of $10 million of which not more than $2 million could be spent in one year. Periodically amended and supplemented.

Executive Order No. 5189 of Sept. 11, 1929—Providing for transfer of officers and employees with five years of continuous experience in the State Department to the Foreign Service by means of the lateral entry process.

Act of June 26, 1930 (46 Stat. 818)—Providing for allowances for rent, heat, and light for living quarters of American officers and employees abroad.

Act of Feb. 23, 1931 [Moses–Linthicum Act] (46 Stat. 1207)— Establishing the office of Legal Adviser (formerly the Solicitor), empowering the Secretary of State to recommend the promotion of Foreign Service Officers to the position of Minister, and providing for a more liberal system of allowances, ingrade salary increases, improved personnel administration, and the classification of Foreign Service clerks.

Act of Mar. 26, 1934 [Exchange Act] (48 Stat. 466)—Providing for payment of American officials abroad in dollar equivalents to their conversion value before the United States went off the gold standard.

Executive Order No. 7497 of Nov. 17, 1936—Banning the marriage of aliens by members of the Foreign Service.

Executive Order of July 1, 1939—Under the Reorganization Act of 1939, transferring to the Foreign Service the foreign activities and personnel of the Departments of Commerce and Agriculture.

Act of May 3, 1945 (59 Stat. 102)—Establishing a new category of administrative, fiscal, and clerical personnel within the Foreign Service, which later became the Foreign Service Staff Officer Corps.

Act of July 3, 1946 [Foreign Service Manpower Act] (60 Stat. 426)—Providing for the lateral appointment of up to 250 Foreign Service Officers with special experience and qualifications (emergency measure for two years).

Act of July 25, 1946 (60 Stat. 663)—Authorizing the expenditure of $125 million (of which $110 million was in foreign currencies) on the Foreign Service buildings program.

Act of Aug. 13, 1946 [Foreign Service Organic Act] (60 Stat. 999)—The basic organic act of the Foreign Service, replacing the Rogers Act of 1924. Provided for new personnel structure, increased salaries and allowances, new promotion and retirement systems, and establishment of the Foreign Service Institute for in-service training; also created the rank of Career Minister.

Act of July 18, 1947 [Presidential Succession Act] (61 Stat. 380)—Amending the Act of Jan. 19, 1886, by providing that if both the offices of President and Vice President are vacant, then the position of President would be filled by the Speaker of the House of Representatives, the President pro tempore of the Senate, followed by the Secretary of State and then the other Secretaries in their order of seniority; superseded the Act of Jan. 19, 1886.

Act of June 25, 1948 (62 Stat. 744)—Providing for reiteration and updating of the Logan Act of 1799.

Act of May 26, 1949 (63 Stat. 111)—Providing for ten Assistant Secretaries of State, two of whom might be designated as Deputy Under Secretaries, and transferring to the Secretary of State the powers given under the Foreign Service Act of 1946 to the Assistant Secretary for Administration and the Director General of the Foreign Service.

Act of Oct. 22, 1951 (65 Stat. 599)—Providing that no representative of the United States Government shall make any commitment requiring the appropriation of American funds in excess of 33 1/2 percent of the budget of any international organization without the consent of the Appropriations Committees of the U.S. Senate and House of Representatives.

Act of June 19, 1952 (66 Stat. 140)—Authorizing the expenditure of $90 million in foreign currencies on the Foreign Service buildings program.

Executive Orders of Apr. 30, 1954, Apr. 23, 1955, Sept. 14, 1956, No. 10791 of Nov. 28, 1958, and No. 10839 of Sept. 30, 1959—Providing temporary arrangement for an Acting Secretary of State in the case of the death, resignation, absence, or sickness of the Secretary of State.

Act of Aug. 13, 1954 (68 Stat. 1051)—Authorizing the increase of 500 additional Foreign Service Officers and specifying their salaries.

Act of Aug. 28, 1954 (68 Stat. 897)—Providing for the establishment of a separate Foreign Agricultural Service.

Act of Apr. 5, 1955 (69 Stat. 24)—This act, known as the "Foreign Service Act Amendments of 1955," provided, among other things, for the payment of salary differentials not exceeding 25 percent to all Foreign Service personnel assigned to hardship posts; for a system of educational allowances for Foreign Service personnel; and for various changes in the provisions governing selection-out and lateral entry of Foreign Service Officers.

Act of Aug. 5, 1955 (69 Stat. 536)—Providing for three Deputy Under Secretaries and ten Assistant Secretaries and for the establishment of a new class of Career Ambassador and stipulating the requirements for appointment to this rank.

Act of July 28, 1956 (70 Stat. 704)—This act, known as the "Foreign Service Act Amendments of 1956," provided for (1) increased salaries for Chiefs of Mission; (2) an increase in the number of classes of Foreign Service Officers to ten classes, including the classes of Career Minister and Career Ambassador; (3) authority to establish Government commissary and recreation facilities at posts abroad; and (4) various medical and hospital benefits for Foreign Service personnel and their dependents.

Act of Aug. 1, 1956 (70 Stat. 890)—Providing certain "Basic Authority for the Department of State," concerned largely with authorization for payment for specified responsibilities and functions, and establishing a departmental Working Capital Fund (not restricted to specific fiscal years); also provides authority and responsibility for the Department of State, specifically the Office of the Historian, to produce and publish the *Foreign Relations of the United States (FRUS)*, superseded by the Act of Oct. 28, 1991.

Act of Aug. 1, 1956 (70 Stat. 891)—Authorizing the Secretary of State to provide participation of the United States in "international activities" (including international conferences), for which provision was not made under any treaty, convention, or special act of Congress; amended the earlier Act of Mar. 4, 1913.

Act of July 18, 1958 (72 Stat. 363)—Establishing organization and administration of Department of State, headed by the Secretary, an Under Secretary, an Under Secretary for Economic Affairs, eleven Assistant Secretaries, a Counselor, and a Legal Adviser, and authorizing the Secretary to promulgate rules and regulations to implement the functions of the Department of State.

Executive Orders No. 10791 of Nov. 28, 1958, and No. 12343 of Jan. 27, 1982— Providing for succession to the office of Secretary of State during the absence or disability of the Secretary.

Act of Sept. 8, 1960 (74 Stat. 831)—This act, known as the "Foreign Service Act Amendments of 1960," added a number of provisions liberalizing the Foreign Service Retirement and Disability System, set forth a significant statement of policy regarding the language and area qualifications of Chiefs of Mission and Foreign Service Officers, and provided for other changes of a technical, clarifying, or perfecting nature.

Act of July 4, 1966 [Freedom of Information Act] (80 Stat. 250)—Providing for public access to certain official documents; supplemented by Executive Order No. 11652 of Mar. 8, 1972.

Act of Sept. 11, 1967 (81 Stat. 195)—Prescribing rules governing the receipt and disposition of gifts and decorations received by American officials from foreign governments; supplemented by Department of State Regulation 108.556 of Apr. 28, 1967, and superseded by Act of Aug. 17, 1977.

Act of Dec. 23, 1967 (81 Stat. 671)—Known as the "Vietnam Amendments Act," providing for special arrangements for employees stationed at high-risk posts, and for other purposes.

Senate Resolution 205 of Sept. 25, 1969—Specifying basic principle regarding the recognition by the United States of foreign governments.

Act of Aug. 12, 1970 (84 Stat. 724)—Providing renewed version of procedure for negotiating and concluding postal conventions and agreements.

Executive Order No. 11652 of Mar. 8, 1972—Revising the State Department documents classification system (replacing the previous classification process).

Act of July 13, 1972 (86 Stat. 490)—Authorizing the appointment of a Deputy Secretary of State, as the new second-ranking officer of the Department of State.

Act of Aug. 22, 1972 (86 Stat. 619)—Requiring Department of State to transmit to Congress the text of international agreements (including oral agreements) other than treaties within sixty days, unless public disclosure is prejudicial to national security.

Department of State Circular 175 of Oct. 25, 1974—Stipulating State Department procedures for negotiating, signing, publishing, and registering treaties and other international agreements of the United States.

Act of Oct. 8, 1976 (90 Stat. 2000)—Providing for the protection and security of foreign officials while in the United States, including diplomatic and consular officers, and official guests of the United States; amended by Act of Oct. 24, 1978 (88 Stat. 1070).

Act of Aug. 17, 1977 (91 Stat. 844)—Prescribing updated rules governing the receipt and disposition by American officials of foreign gifts and decorations; superseded Act of Sept. 11, 1967.

Act of Aug. 17, 1977 (91 Stat. 845)—Revising the Foreign Service Buildings Act of May 7, 1926 (as amended), adding amounts not to exceed $90 million for this purpose.

Act of Oct. 7, 1978 (92 Stat. 963)—Redefining organization and administration of the Department of State, providing for the Secretary, a Deputy Secretary, three Under Secretaries for Political and Economic Affairs and for Management, thirteen Assistant Secretaries, the Counselor, and the Legal Adviser, and authorizing the Secretary to promulgate rules and regulations to implement the functions of the Department of State.

Act of Oct. 17, 1980 [Foreign Service Organic Act] (94 Stat. 2071)—Revised basic organic act of the Foreign Service, superseding the Act of Aug. 13, 1946; provided for a Senior Foreign Service category and authorized the personnel rank of Career Ambassador and the rank of Ambassador at Large, and prescribed principles for the management of the Foreign Service, including appointment, assignment, and promotion procedures, compensation, allowances and benefits, retirement and disability, travel, health care, career development, labor–management relations, grievances, and the administration of the Foreign Service. It also provided for an Inspector General and a systematic inspection system for both the Department and the Foreign Service, and authorized a system of recognition awards.

Executive Order No. 12343 of Jan. 27, 1982—Authorizing the Secretary of State to specify the order of succession of Acting Secretaries of State in case of the absence, disability, or vacancy of the Office of Secretary of State.

Act of Aug. 24, 1982 [Foreign Missions Act] (96 Stat. 282)—Providing legal controls to govern the establishment, location, and other matters regarding foreign government missions and facilities in the United States, and establishing an Office of Foreign Missions in the Department of State.

Act of Oct. 19, 1984 (98 Stat. 2649)—Establishing a Department of State independent, nonprofit U.S. Institute of Peace for scholarly inquiry and research.

Act of Aug. 27, 1986 (100 Stat. 853)—Known as the "Diplomatic Security and Antiterrorism Act," providing for the establishment of a Diplomatic Security Service to deal with international terrorism, multilateral cooperation to combat it, and criminal punishment for terrorist acts.

Act of Oct. 28, 1991 (105 Stat. 685–90)—Providing authority and responsibility of the Department of State, specifically the Office of the Historian, to produce and publish the *Foreign Relations of the United States (FRUS)*; superseded the Act of Aug. 1, 1956.

Act of Apr. 30, 1994 (108 Stat. 402)—Providing for updated changes in the organization of the Department of State, including specification of its principal officers and other modifications.

Act of Sept. 13, 1994 (108 Stat. 2147)—Providing for modernization of the Logan Act of 1799 as amended in 1948.

For a comprehensive compilation of current *Legislation on Foreign Relations Through* [year], see Congress, Committees on Foreign Relations (Senate) and Foreign Affairs (House of Representatives), Joint Committee Print, prepared by the Library of Congress and published periodically in several volumes by the Government Printing Office. See especially sections on the "Department of State," which include current authorization and appropriations legislation, international claims settlement legislation, legislation authorizing U.S. Participation in Interparliamentary Conferences, and directives concerning operations of the U.S. Government overseas. Current law is provided in the *U.S. Code*, as described in Appendix II.

Appendix II

U.S. Law on the Conduct of American Foreign Relations

For the current, comprehensive codification of American statutes on the Department of State, the Foreign Service, and other aspects of the conduct of foreign relations, see the *U.S. Code*. It is structured in fifty Titles, which are organized in Chapters, in some cases also Subchapters, and specific numbered sections. Currently, the *U.S. Code* consists of fifty Titles, contained in more than twenty volumes, accompanied by six index volumes.

PRINCIPAL SEGMENTS OF STATUTORY LAW—THE DEPARTMENT OF STATE AND THE FOREIGN SERVICE

The most pertinent statutory segments of the *Code* are coalesced in Title 22, a comprehensive compilation entitled "Foreign Relations and Intercourse." It consists of seventy-one Chapters that run for nearly 1,300 printed pages. The primary segments are Chapter 38, which focuses on the "Department of State," and Chapter 52, which concerns the "Foreign Service."

Chapter 38 consists of sections 2651 to 2724. It covers the establishment of the Department of State, its top-level officers, management and administration of foreign affairs, various aspects of funding, appropriations, and expenditures, criteria for the selection and confirmation of Ambassadors, certain reporting requirements, custody of official seals and property, servicing of copies of treaties and agreements for printing, diplomatic telecommunications, services and facilities for employees abroad, acceptance of gifts on behalf of the United States, dealing with terrorism and undertaking counterterrorism, maintaining reception areas of the Department of State building, and many other, related departmental responsibilities and functions.

Chapter 52, on the Foreign Service, is composed of fourteen Subchapters (sects. 3901 to 4226), which deal with the following matters:

I. General Provisions
II. Management of the Foreign Service

Other Chapters of Title 22 apply to various related functions. Thus, Chapter 8 is devoted entirely to the "Foreign Service Buildings" cumulative program, including the purchase, leasing, construction, renovation, maintenance, and furnishing of diplomatic and consular facilities abroad. Chapter 23 is concerned with the protection of American citizens abroad and guarantees naturalized as well as native-born citizens protection of their persons and property in foreign lands, including fair and equitable treatment by the U.S. government with respect to citizenship, progeny, taxation, voting rights, Social Security compensation, veterans support, and other rights and benefits. Chapter 53B specifies in detail the legal prescriptions for the compilation and publication of the *Foreign Relations of the United States* series. Chapter 58 provides for, and assures the security of, "diplomatic operations in the United States and abroad" and defines Department of State responsibility for coordinating actions and evacuations of persons in cooperation with other Federal agencies.

On the other hand, several chapters of Title 22 are devoted to the affairs of foreign diplomats and consuls in the United States. Chapter 6, entitled "Foreign Diplomatic and Consular Officers," concerns the number, status, privileges and immunities, accommodations, facilities, travel, and similar matters respecting foreign diplomatic and consular officers serving in the United States. Chapter 53, on the "Regulation of Foreign Missions," makes the Secretary of State responsible for determining the location of foreign missions in the District of Columbia, the acquisition of official property, privileges and immunities, travel restrictions, and physical protection of foreign diplomatic and consular personnel within American jurisdiction, as well as for defining American responsibility toward United Nations employees. In addition, Chapter 11 provides for the prescription of rules and regulations to govern the registration of "Foreign Agents and Propagandists" in this country, the filing and labeling of political propaganda, and transmittal of reports to Congress concerning the implementation of such stipulations, and it authorizes the enforcement of these rules and the application of penalties (including deportation) for their violation.

Chapter 7 contains statutory law governing U.S. participation in multipartite international organizations, congresses, bureaus, commissions, and other institutions, including the United Nations and its specialized agencies, and the privileges and immunities of such agencies and their personnel in the United States. Chapter 40 applies to American participation in international expositions held in the United States, recognition by the President when this is regarded as being "in the national interest," and authorization of appropriations for such involvement.

Several Title 22 chapters apply to other, related Federal agencies and programs that have responsibilities abroad. Aside from the military services and agencies, these embrace Chapter 32, entitled "Foreign Assistance," which applies to the Agency for International Development (AID) and American agricultural, population planning and health, education and human resources, energy, and other programs, as well as international development and military assistance; Chapter 18, which specifies the law respecting "United States Information and Educational Exchange Programs"; Chapter 33, which provides for the "Mutual Educational and Cultural Exchange Program" (and deals with its purpose, authorization of its activities, grants and contracts, international agreements and organizations, and administration by the Bureau of Education and Cultural Affairs of the United States Information Agency [USIA]; Chapter 34, which concerns the American "Peace Corps," for furnishing an American volunteer service in newly developing nations at their request; Chapter 35, which pertains to the "Arms Control and Disarmament Agency" (ACDA); and Chapter 71, which stipulates the law on "United States International Broadcasting," including such programs as *Radio Free Asia, Radio Free Europe, Radio Liberty, Radio and TV Marti*, and the *Voice of America*. Also related are Chapter 29 (on "Cultural, Technical, and Educational Centers"), Chapter 30 (on "International Cooperation in Health and Medical Research"), and Chapter 57 (on the "United States Scholarship Program for Developing Countries").

A number of other, disparate Title 22 segments of the *Code* also warrant mention. These include Chapter 4 on "Passports"; Chapter 10 on "Hemispheral Relations"; Chapters 21 on the "Settlement of International Claims" and 21A on "Settlement of Investment Disputes"; Chapter 37, which restricts American diplomats, consuls, and members of their families and households from accepting personal gifts and decorations from foreign governments (and which is related to a more comprehensive treatment of this subject in Title 5, Chapter 73, Subchapter IV); and Chapters 61 and 64, which are devoted to "Anti-Terrorism" and "United States Response to Terrorism Affecting Americans Abroad." Also of interest is Chapter 56, which concerns the establishment by October 19, 1984, of the U.S. Institute of Peace as an independent, nonprofit corporation to engage in scholarly inquiry and research and to award an annual Medal of Peace (with a cash award not to exceed $25,000).

RELATED U.S. STATUTORY LAW

Other segments of the *U.S. Code* that concern important aspects of the conduct of foreign affairs and involve the Department of State and the Diplomatic and Consular Services include the following Titles:

4. United States Flag and Seal (Chapter 4 of which is devoted to the nature of the Great Seal and its custody by the Secretary of State)

8. Aliens and Nationality

9. Arbitration

15. Commerce and Trade

17. Copyrights

19. Customs Duties

33. Navigation and Navigable Waters

35. Patents

39. Postal Service

44. Public Printing and Documents

46. Shipping

47. Telegraphs, Telephones, and Radiotelegraphs

48. Territories and Insular Possessions

50. War and National Defense (which, among other matters, deals with the Central Intelligence Agency (CIA), especially Chapters 15 on National Security and 36 on Foreign Intelligence Surveillance

In addition, other segments of the *Code* also deal with aspects of foreign affairs. Thus, portions of Title 18 on "Crimes and Criminal Procedure" are especially relevant. For example, Chapter 41, section 878, concerns the prevention of, and punishment for, crimes against foreign officials (including diplomatic and consular personnel), official foreign guests, and internationally protected persons in the United States, and Chapter 45, entitled "Foreign Relations," contains legal prescriptions concerning such matters as Americans acting illegally as agents of foreign governments (sec. 951), diplomatic codes and correspondence (sec. 952), correspondence of private individuals with foreign governments (sec. 953), conspiring to injure the property of foreign governments in the United States (sec. 956), and protection of the property of foreign governments and international organizations located in the United States, including Embassies, Consulates, and international organization headquarters and other offices (sec. 970). Other Chapters of Title 18 deal with espionage and censorship (Chapter 37), genocide (Chapter 50A), piracy and privateering (Chapter 81), sabotage (Chapter 105), and terrorism (Chapter 113B). To these should be added the updating of the Logan Act of January 30, 1799 (1 Stat. 613), amended by the Acts of June 25, 1948 (62 Stat. 744), and September 13, 1994 (108 Stat. 2147); also see *U.S. Code*, Title 18, sec. 953.

It is worthy of note that the *U.S. Code* contains no separate Title on treaty making and publication. However, this subject is treated in several ways. For example, the *Code* index refers to a number of specific treaties, agreements, and conventions, which are listed separately or according to functional subjects, and to elements of the treaty process, such as the use of the official U.S. seal to certify their authenticity, printing and publication, and adjudication. Thus, Title 4, section 42 (note) and Executive Order 10347 of April 18, 1952, as amended, authorizes the Secretary of State to affix the Seal of the United States, without any special warrant, to various official foreign relations documents, including full powers to negotiate treaties, instruments of ratification, Presidential proclamations pertaining to treaties, and exchanges of ratification instruments. Title 39, section 407, prescribes the unique method of concluding postal treaties and conventions, which, when approved by the President (not confirmed by the Senate), are transmitted to the Secretary of State for forwarding to the Public Printer for publication. Title 22, section 2660, requires the Secretary of State to furnish copies of all treaties and agreements to the Public Printer for publication, which is confirmed by Title 44, sections 711 and 712, providing for the printing and publication of all treaties and agreements (including postal conventions), and section 728 on the distribution of printed copies of treaties and other international agreements.

CURRENT COMPILATIONS OF LEGISLATION

For periodic, updated, and current compilations of the texts of laws on the foreign relations of the United States, see *Legislation on Foreign Relations Through*——[year], prepared by and for the Senate Foreign Relations and House Foreign Affairs Committees, with the cooperation of the Department of State, and published since 1957 by the Government Printing Office. Originally, it was titled *Legislation on Foreign Relations—With Explanatory Notes*, published in single volumes. This was changed to its current title and has subsequently been published in three volumes, of which volumes 1 and 2 contain the texts of legislation and related documents and are revised and republished annually, whereas volume 3 is revised and republished occasionally and contains the texts of selected treaties and related documents.

The volumes of legislation are organized in functional categories, such as the Department of State, agricultural commodities, arms control and disarmament, aviation and space, energy and natural resources, financial institutions, foreign economic policy—tariffs and trade, information and cultural affairs, law of the seas and selected maritime matters, the Peace Corps, the United Nations and other international organizations, war powers, collective security, and other legislation. The section on the Department of State includes legislation on budgetary authorizations and appropriations, organization and administration, Foreign Service buildings, foreign gifts and decorations, passport regulations, refugee assistance, and the like. The section on other legislation pertains to such matters as the registration of foreign agents and international claims settlements.

Appendix III

U.S. Territorial Expansion

Territory	Date	From Whom Acquired	Nature of Acquisition	Gross Area (Sq.Mi.)	Status
Continental U.S.					
Original Territory	1783	Great Britain	Peace Treaty	891,364	Statehood
Louisiana Territory	1803	France	Purchase Treaty	831,321	Statehood
Floridas	1819	Spain	Cession Treaty	69,866	Statehood
Texas	1845	Texas (Independent)	Joint Resolution	384,958	Statehood
Oregon Territory	1846	Unoccupied; resolution of claims with Britain	Treaty	283,439	Statehood
California and Southwest	1848	Mexico	Cession Treaty	530,706	Statehood
Gadsden Territory	1853	Mexico	Purchase Treaty	29,640	Statehood
Caribbean Territories					
Puerto Rico	1898	Spain	Cession Treaty	3,515	Unincorporated
Panama Canal Zone	1904	Panama	Treaty Lease	647	Unincorporated
Virgin Islands	1917	Denmark	Purchase Treaty	132	Unincorporated

Pacific Territories and Dependencies

Alaska	1867	Russia	Purchase Treaty	591,004	Statehood
Hawaii	1898	Hawaii (Independent)	Joint Resolution	6,471	Statehood
Pacific Islands*	1898, 1850s, and later	Unoccupied	Effective Occupation	50	Unincorporated
Guam	1898	Spain	Cession Treaty	209	Unincorporated
Philippines	1898	Spain	Cession Treaty	115,000	Independent
American Samoa	1900	Unoccupied; agreement with Germany	Treaty	77	Unincorporated
Pacific Trust Territory	1947	Japanese Mandate; Treaty with UN	Trusteeship Treaty	717	Trust Territory**

* Includes Baker, Howland, Jarvis, Ocean, Midway, Palmyra, Wake, and others.

**By the mid-1990s the Trust Territory was converted into the Commonwealth of the North Marianas (U.S.), and the independent Federated States of Micronesia, the Republic of the Marshall Islands, and the Republic of Palau. In addition, the Ryukyu Islands (south of Japan) were taken by the United States during World War II, and their administration was ceded by Japan to the United States by the Peace Treaty of 1952. Some islands reverted to Japan in 1953 and 1968, and the rest were returned to Japan in 1972, but the United States retained a military base in Okinawa.

Bibliography

This bibliography consists of five sections, presenting basic bibliographical and research guides to literature, major histories of the Department of State, volumes on international law related to American foreign relations, collections or series of volumes of treaty texts, and a comprehensive listing of books, collections, pamphlets, and essays concerned with the Department of State and Foreign Service, the conduct of American foreign relations, the diplomatic process, diplomatic and consular affairs, negotiations, treaty and agreement making, U.S. participation in international conferences and organizations, and crisis handling, peaceful settlement of disputes, arbitration, and adjudication. It does not include general American histories, biographies and memoirs, or foreign-language literature, such as the classics on diplomacy and consular relations produced by such authors and compilers as Jean Dumont, Louis J. D. Ferand-Giraud, Guillaume de Garden, Charles de Martens, August H. Meisel, A. Pecquet, Paul L. E. Pradier-Fodere, and others.

For a list of studies and commentaries on the reorganization and reform of the Department of State and the Foreign Service since 1945, see Table 7.4, and for commentary on Department of State documents and publications and a listing of its publications, see Chapter 7, section on Documents and Publications and Table 7.14.

For guidance to memoir and biographical literature, see Barnes and Morgan, *The Foreign Service of the United States: Origins, Development, and Functions*, pp. 410–12; Boyce and Boyce, *American Foreign Service Authors: A Bibliography*; and Plischke, *U.S. Foreign Relations: A Guide to Information Sources*, pp. 613–70.

BIBLIOGRAPHICAL AND RESEARCH GUIDES

Beers, Henry P., ed. *Bibliographies in American History: Guide to Materials for Research*. 2d ed. New York: Wilson, 1942.

Bemis, Samuel Flagg, and Griffin, Grace Gardner. *Guide to the Diplomatic History of the United States*. Washington, D.C.: Government Printing Office, 1935.

Besterman, Theodore, ed. *A World Bibliography of Bibliographies*. 4th ed. 5 vols. Geneva: Societies Bibliographica, 1965–67.

Boehm, Eric H., ed. *Bibliographies in International Relations and World Affairs: An Annotated Directory*. Santa Barbara, Calif.: Clio Press, 1965.

Boyce, Richard F., and Boyce, Katherine Randall. *American Foreign Service Authors: A Bibliography*. Metuchen, N.J.: Scarecrow, 1973.

Brown, John C., and Rieg, Michael B. *Administration of United States Foreign Affairs: A Bibliography* 2d ed. University Park: Pennsylvania State University Library, 1972.

Burns, Richard D. *Guide to American Foreign Relations since 1700*. Santa Barbara, Calif.: ABC-Clio, 1982.

Carlsen, Charles. *Bibliography: The Generalist and the Specialist in the United States Foreign Service*. Processed, 1965.

Conover, Helen F., comp. *Current National Bibliographies*. Washington, D.C.: U.S. Library of Congress, 1955.

———, ed. *A Guide to Bibliographic Tools for Research in Foreign Affairs*. 2d ed. Washington, D.C.: U.S. Library of Congress, 1958.

Coulter, Edith M., and Gerstenfeld, Melanie. *Historical Bibliographies: A Systematic and Annotated Guide*. Berkeley: University of California Press, 1935.

Council on Foreign Relations series:

Langer, William Leonard, and Armstring, Hamilton Fish. *Foreign Affairs Bibliography: A Selected and Annotated List of Books on International Relations, 1919–1932*. New York: Harper for Council on Foreign Relations, 1933.

Woolbert, Robert Gale. *Foreign Affairs Bibliography: A Selected and Annotated List of Books on International Relations, 1932–1942*. New York: Harper for Council on Foreign Relations, 1945.

Roberts, Henry L. *Foreign Affairs Bibliography: A Selected and Annotated List of Books on International Relations, 1942–1952*. New York: Harper for Council on Foreign Relations, 1955.

———. *Foreign Affairs Bibliography: A Selected and Annotated List of Books on International Relations, 1952–1962*. New York: Bowker, 1964.

———. *Foreign Affairs Bibliography: A Selected and Annotated List of Books on International Relations, 1962–1972*. New York: Bowker, 1976.

Dexter, Byron, ed. *The Foreign Affairs 50-Year Bibliography . . . 1920–1970*. New York: Council on Foreign Relations, 1972.

Encyclopedia of U.S. Foreign Relations, 4 vols. New York: Oxford University Press, 1997.

Graebner, Norman A., comp. *American Diplomatic History before 1900*. Arlington Heights, Ill.: A H M, 1978.

Gustafson, Milton O., ed. *The National Archives and Foreign Relations Research*. Athens: Ohio University Press, 1974.

Harmon, Robert B., ed. *The Art and Practice of Diplomacy: A Selected and Annotated Guide*. Metuchen, N.J.: Scarecrow, 1971.

Hart, Albert Bushnell. *The Foundations of American Foreign Policy, with a Working Bibliography*, New York: Macmillan, 1901.

Holler, Frederick L. *The Information Sources of Political Science*. 2d ed. 5 vols. Santa Barbara, Calif.: ABC-Clio, 1975.

Johnson, Harold S., and Singh, Baljit. *International Organization: A Classified Bibliography.* East Lansing: Michigan State University, 1969.

Lakos, Amos. *Modern Diplomacy: A Bibliography.* Monticello, Ill.: Vance, 1985.

Linebarger, Genevieve C., comp. *Washington Sources on International Affairs: A Guide to Some Research Facilities in the District of Columbia.* College Park, Md.: Bureau of Public Administration, University of Maryland, 1951.

Lowenstein, Linda, comp. *Government Resources Available for Foreign Affairs Research.* Office of External Research, Department of State. Washington, D.C.: Government Printing Office, 1965.

Palmer, Norman D., ed. *A Design for International Relations Research: Scope, Theory, Methods, and Relevance.* Philadelphia: American Academy of Political and Social Science, 1970.

Platig, E. Raymond. *International Relations Research: Problems of Evaluation and Advancement.* Santa Barbara, Calif.: Clio Press, 1967.

Plischke, Elmer. *American Diplomacy: A Bibliography of Biographies, Autobiographies, and Commentaries.* College Park: Bureau of Governmental Research, University of Maryland, 1957.

———. "American Diplomats as Authors." *Society for Historians of American Foreign Relations NEWSLETTER*, 15 (December 1984): pp. 1–21.

———. *American Foreign Relations: A Bibliography of Official Sources.* College Park: Bureau of Governmental Research, University of Maryland, 1955. Reprinted by Johnson Reprint Corporation, New York, 1966.

———. "Bibliography on Conduct of Foreign Relations" and "Bibliography of Autobiographies, Biographies, Commentaries, and Memoirs." In Smith Simpson, ed., *Instruction in Diplomacy: The Liberal Arts Approach*, Monograph 13, American Academy of Political and Social Science, 1972, pp. 290–342.

———. "Research on the Administrative History of the Department of State." In Milton O. Gustafson, ed., *The National Archives and Foreign Relations Research.* Athens: Ohio State University Press, 1974, pp. 73–102.

———. "Research on the Conduct of United States Foreign Relations." *International Studies Quarterly* 15 (June 1971): 221–50.

———. *U.S. Foreign Relations: A Guide to Information Sources.* Detroit: Gale Research, 1980.

Trask, David F., Meyer, Michael C., and Trask, Roger R., eds. *Bibliography of United States–Latin American Relations since 1810: A Selected List of Eleven Thousand Published References.* Lincoln: University of Nebraska Press, 1968.

United States, Department of State. *Executive-Congressional Relations and Foreign Policy: A Bibliographical Survey.* Washington, D.C.: Government Printing Office, 1949.

———, Historical Office. *Public Availability of Diplomatic Archives in the United States and Certain Foreign Countries.* Washington, D.C.: Department of State (processed), 1961 (earlier ed., 1958).

———, Library of Congress. *A Directory of Information Resources in the United States: Social Sciences.* 2d ed. Washington, D.C.: Government Printing Office, 1973.

———. *Organizing for National Security: A Bibliography.* 86th Cong., 1st Sess. Washington, D.C.: Government Printing Office, 1959. Also contained in *ibid., Organizing for National Security* 2 (1961): pp. 27–111.

———, Senate, Committee on Foreign Relations. *Strengthening Free World Security . . . A Collection of Excerpts and Bibliographies.* Prepared by Library of Congress. Washington, D.C.: Government Printing Office, 1960.

———, Senate, Committee on Government Operations. *Administration of National Security: A Bibliography.* 87th Cong., 2nd Sess. Washington, D.C.: Government Printing Office, 1963.

Wasserman, Paul, and Silander, Fred S. *Decision-Making: An Annotated Bibliography.* Ithaca, N.Y.: Graduate School of Business and Public Administration, Cornell University, 1958.

Zawodny, Janusz K., ed. *Guide to the Study of International Relations.* San Francisco: Chandler, 1966.

MAJOR COMPREHENSIVE HISTORIES OF THE DEPARTMENT OF STATE (CHRONOLOGICAL)

Michael, William H. *History of the Department of State of the United States.* Washington, D.C.: Government Printing Office, 1901.

Hunt, Gaillard. *The Department of State of the United States: Its History and Functions.* New Haven, Conn.: Yale University Press, 1914.

Stuart, Graham H. *The Department of State: A History of Its Organization, Procedure, and Personnel.* New York: Macmillan, 1949.

INTERNATIONAL LAW AND ARBITRATION COMPILATIONS (CHRONOLOGICAL)

Cadwalader, John L., ed. *A Digest of the Published Opinions of the Attorneys-General, and of the Leading Decisions of the Federal Courts, with Reference to International Law, Treaties, and Kindred Subjects.* Washington, D.C.: Government Printing Office, 1877.

Wharton, Francis, ed. *Digest of the International Law of the United States.* 2d ed. 3 vols. Washington, D.C.: Government Printing Office, 1887.

Moore, John Bassett, ed. *A Digest of International Law.* 8 vols. Washington, D.C.: Government Printing Office, 1906.

Hackworth, Green H., ed. *Digest of International Law.* 8 vols. Washington, D.C.: Government Printing Office, 1940–44.

Whiteman, Marjorie M., ed. *Digest of International Law.* 15 vols. Washington, D.C.: Government Printing Office, 1963–73.

Digest of United States Practice in International Law. Comp. Legal Adviser's Office of the Department of State. Washington, D.C.: Government Printing Office, 1973–.

Moore, John Bassett, ed. *History and Digest of International Arbitrations to Which the United States Has Been a Party.* 6 vols. Washington, D.C.: Government Printing Office, 1898.

Whiteman, Marjorie M., ed. *Damages in International Law.* 3 vols. Washington, D.C.: Government Printing Office, 1937–43.

TREATIES AND AGREEMENTS—COMPILATIONS, SERIES, LISTS, AND INDEXES

A. Official U.S. Compilations (Chronological)

Elliott, Jonathan, ed. *Diplomatic Code of the United States: Embracing a Collection of Treaties and Conventions between the United States and Foreign Powers, from the Year 1778 to 1827.* Washington, D.C.: Editor, 1827.

————, ed. *The American Diplomatic Code: Embracing a Collection of Treaties and Conventions between the United States and Foreign Powers from 1778 to 1834.* 2 vols. Washington, D.C.: Editor, 1834.

Davis, J. C. Bancroft, ed. *Treaties and Conventions Concluded between the United States of America and Other Powers since July 4, 1776.* Washington, D.C.: Government Printing Office, 1871.

Haswell, John H., ed. *Treaties and Conventions Concluded between the United States of America and Other Powers since July 4, 1776.* Washington, D.C.: Government Printing Office, 1889.

Malloy, William M., Redmond, C. F., and Trentwith, Edward J., comps. *Treaties, Conventions, International Acts, Protocols, and Agreements between the United States and Other Powers.* 4 vols. Washington, D.C.: Government Printing Office, 1910–38.

Miller, David Hunter, comp. *Treaties and Other International Acts of the United States of America.* 8 vols. Washington, D.C.: Government Printing Office, 1931–48.

Bevans, Charles I., ed. *Treaties and Other International Agreements of the United States of America, 1776–1949.* 12 vols. Washington, D.C.: Government Printing Office, 1968–76.

B. Contemporary U.S. Series (Chronological)

United States Treaty Series (UST). Washington, D.C.: Government Printing Office, 1908–46.

Executive Agreement Series (EAS). Washington, D.C.: Government Printing Office, 1929–46.

Treaties and Other International Acts Series (TIAS). Washington, D.C.: Government Printing Office, 1945– .

United States Treaties and Other International Agreements. Washington, D.C.: Government Printing Office, 1950– .

C. Lists and Indexes (Chronological)

A Tentative List of Treaty Collections. Washington, D.C.: Government Printing Office, 1919.

United States Department of State Catalogue of Treaties, 1814–1918. Washington, D.C.: Government Printing Office, 1919; reprinted, New York: Oceana, 1964.

List of Treaties Submitted to the Senate, 1789–1931, Which Have Not Gone into Force, October 1, 1932. Washington, D.C.: Government Printing Office, 1932.

List of Treaties Submitted to the Senate, 1789–1934. Washington, D.C.: Government Printing Office, 1935.

List of Treaties Submitted to the Senate, 1935–1944. Washington, D.C.: Government Printing Office, 1945.

Numerical List of the Treaty Series, Executive Agreement Series, and Treaties and Other International Acts Series. Washington, D.C.: Government Printing Office, 1950.

D. Treaties in Force for the United States (Chronological)

Bryan, Henry L., comp. *Compilation of Treaties in Force*. Washington, D.C.: Government Printing Office, 1899.

A List of Treaties and Other International Acts of the United States of America in Force on December 31, 1932. Washington, D.C.: Government Printing Office, 1933.

A List of Treaties and Other International Acts of the United States of America in Force on December 31, 1941. Washington: Government Printing Office, 1944.

Treaties in Force: A List of Treaties and Other International Agreements of the United States in Force on January 1,—. Washington, D.C.: Government Printing Office, annual since 1956.

E. Unofficial Collections

American Bar Association. *The Commercial Treaty Index*. 2d ed. Lexington, MA: Lexington Books, 1975.

Bridgman, Raymond L. *The First Book of World Law: A Compilation of the International Conventions to Which the Principal Nations Are Signatory, with a Survey of Their Significance*. New York: Garland, 1972.

Davenport, Francis G., ed. *European Treaties Bearing on the History of the United States and Its Dependencies*. 4 vols. Washington, D.C.: Carnegie Endowment, 1917–37.

Deak, Francis, and Jessup, Philip C., eds. *A Collection of Neutrality Laws, Regulations and Treaties of Various Countries*. 2 vols. Washington, D.C.: Carnegie Endowment, 1939.

Diamond, Walter H., and Diamond, Dorothy B., eds. *International Tax Treaties of All Nations: A Collection and Retrieval Source*. 10 vols. Dobbs Ferry, N.Y.: Oceana, 1977.

Fischer, Peter, ed. *Concessionary Agreements: A Collection of Concessionary and Related Agreements between States and Nationals of Other States*. 16 vols. Dobbs Ferry, N.Y.: Oceana, 1975.

Gamble, John K., ed. *Index to Marine Treaties*. Seattle: University of Washington Press, 1972.

Grenville, John. *Major International Treaties, 1914–1973*. New York: Stein and Day, 1974.

Habicht, Max, ed. *Post-War Treaties for the Pacific Settlement of International Disputes*. Cambridge: Harvard University Press, 1931.

Hill, Charles E., ed. *Leading American Treaties*. New York: Macmillan, 1931.

Hudson, Manley O., ed. *International Legislation: A Collection of Multipartite Inter-*

national Instruments of General Interest. 9 vols. Washington: Carnegie Endowment, 1931–50.

Israel, Fred L., ed. *Major Peace Treaties of Modern History, 1648–1967.* 4 vols. New York: McGraw-Hill, 1967.

Myers, Denys P. *Manual of Collections of Treaties and of Collections Relating to Treaties.* Cambridge: Harvard University Press, 1922.

Parry, Clive, comp. *Consolidated Treaty Series, 1648–1918.* Dobbs Ferry, N.Y.: Oceana, 1969–   .

Rohn, Peter H., ed. *Treaty Profiles.* Santa Barbara, Calif.: A.B.C.-Clio Press, 1976.

————. *World Treaty Index.* 5 vols. Santa Barbara, Calif: A.B.C.-Clio Press, 1975.

Scott, James Brown, ed. *The Hague Conventions and Declarations of 1899 and 1907.* 3d ed. 5 vols. New York: Oxford University Press, 1918.

————. *Treaties for the Advancement of Peace.* New York: Oxford University Press, 1920.

United Nations, Legal Dept. *Law and Practices concerning the Conclusion of Treaties, with a Select Bibliography on the Law of Treaties.* New York: United Nations, 1953.

Vambery, Joseph T., and Vambery, Rose V., eds. *Cumulative List of Treaties and International Agreements Registered with the United Nations, December 1969–December 1974.* 2 vols. Dobbs Ferry, N.Y.: Oceana, 1977.

Wiktor, Christian L., ed. *Unperfected Treaties of the United States of America.* 5 vols. Dobbs Ferry, N.Y.: Oceana, 1976.

For additional references, including literature on individual treaties and agreements, see the following section and Plischke, *U.S. Foreign Relations: A Guide to Information Sources,* pp. 571–94.

BOOKS, MONOGRAPHS, AND PAMPHLETS

This selected compilation is limited to books, monographs, and pamphlets in the English language that are concerned primarily with the Department of State, the Foreign Service, and the administration and conduct of foreign relations. Studies dealing principally with substantive American foreign policy and diplomatic history, as well as biographies, autobiographies, and commentaries on policy, are not included. While attention is concentrated on American practice, some volumes on diplomacy in general are also listed. For article literature, see Plischke, *U.S. Foreign Relations: A Guide to Information Sources.*

Acheson, Dean G. *Power and Diplomacy.* Cambridge: Harvard University Press, 1958.

Akzin, Benjamin. *Propaganda by Diplomats.* Washington: Digest Press, 1936.

Aldridge, James. *The Diplomat.* Boston: Little, Brown, 1950.

Allan, Pierre. *Crisis Bargaining and the Arms Race: A Theoretical Model.* Cambridge: Ballinger, 1983.

Allen, Florence E. *The Treaty as an Instrument of Legislation.* New York: Macmillan, 1952.

Allison, Graham, and Szanton, Peter. *Remaking Foreign Policy: The Organizational Connection.* New York: Basic Books, 1976.

Almond, Gabriel A. *The American People and Foreign Policy.* New York: Praeger, 1960 (earlier ed., 1950).

American Assembly. *Cultural Affairs and Foreign Relations*. Englewood Cliffs, N.J.: Prentice-Hall, 1963.

———. *The Representation of the United States Abroad*. New York: American Assembly, Columbia University Press, 1956.

American Foreign Service Association. *American Diplomacy and the Foreign Service*. Washington: American Foreign Service Association, 1989.

———. *Toward a Modern Diplomacy*. Washington: American Foreign Service Association, 1968.

American Political Science Association. *International Commitments and National Administration*. Charlottesville: Bureau of Public Administration, University of Virginia, 1949.

Anderson, George L., ed. *Issues and Conflicts: Studies in Twentieth Century American Diplomacy*. Lawrence: University of Kansas Press, 1959.

Anderson, M. S. *The Rise of Modern Diplomacy, 1919–1950*. New York: 1993.

Angel, Juvenal L. *Careers in the Diplomatic Service*. 4th ed. New York: World Trade Academy Press, 1961.

Arnold, Ralph, comp. *Treaty-Making Procedure: A Comparative Study of the Methods Obtaining in Different States*. London: Oxford University Press, 1933.

Bacchus, William I. *Foreign Policy and the Bureaucratic Process: The State Department's Country Director System*. Princeton: Princeton University Press, 1974.

———. *Inside the Legislative Process: The Passage of the Foreign Service Act of 1980*. Boulder, Colo.: Westview, 1984.

Bailey, Thomas A. *The Art of Diplomacy: The American Experience*. New York: Appleton-Century-Crofts, 1968.

———. *The Man in the Street: The Impact of American Public Opinion on Foreign Policy*. New York: Macmillan, 1948.

———. *Presidential Greatness: The Image and the Man from George Washington to the Present*. New York: Appleton-Century-Crofts, 1966.

Baker, Roscoe. *The American Legion and American Foreign Policy*. New York: Bookman Associates, 1954.

Baldwin, David A. *Foreign Aid and American Foreign Policy: A Documentary Analysis*. New York: Praeger, 1966.

Barber, Hollis W. *Foreign Policies of the United States*. New York: Dryden, 1953.

Barnes, William, and Morgan, John Heath. *The Foreign Service of the United States: Origins, Development, and Functions*. Washington: Government Printing Office, 1961.

Barnett, James F. *International Agreements without the Advice and Consent of the Senate*. Grand Rapids, Mich.: N.p., 1906.

Barnett, Vincent M., Jr., ed. *The Representation of the United States Abroad*. New York: Praeger, 1965; earlier ed., 1956.

Barrett, Edward W. *Truth Is Our Weapon*. New York: Funk and Wagnalls, 1953.

Barron, Bryton. *Inside the State Department: A Candid Appraisal of the Bureaucracy*. New York: Comet Books, 1956.

———. *The Untouchable State Department*. Springfield, Va.: Crestwood, 1962.

Bartlett, Ruhl J., ed. *The Record of American Diplomacy*. 4th ed. N.Y.: Knopf, 1964.

Bartos, Otomar J. *Process and Outcome of Negotiations*. New York: Columbia University Press, 1974.

Bates, Lindell T. *Unauthorized Diplomatic Intercourse by American Citizens with For-*

eign Powers as a Criminal Offence under the Laws of the United States. New York: Author, 1915.

Baumann, Carol E. *The Diplomatic Kidnappings: A Revolutionary Tactic of Urban Terrorism*. The Hague: Nijhoff, 1973.

————. *International Terrorism*. Milwaukee, Wis.: Institute of World Affairs, 1974.

Beichman, Arnold. *The "Other" State Department: The United States Mission to the United Nations* . . . New York: Basic Books, 1967.

Beloff, Max. *Foreign Policy and the Democratic Process*. Baltimore: Johns Hopkins University Press, 1955.

Bemis, Samuel Flagg, ed. *The American Secretaries of State and Their Diplomacy*. 10 vols. New York: Knopf, 1927–1929.

Bendiner, Robert. *The Riddle of the State Department*. New York: Farrar and Rinehart, 1942.

Berdahl, Clarence A. *The War Powers of the Executive in the United States*. Urbana: University of Illinois Press, 1921.

Berding, Andrew. *Foreign Affairs and You: How American Foreign Policy Is Made and What It Means to You*. Garden City, New York: Doubleday, 1962.

Berman, Maureen R., and Johnson, Joseph E., eds. *Unofficial Diplomats*. New York: Columbia University Press, 1977.

Binkley, Wilfred E. *The Man in the White House: His Powers and Duties*. Baltimore: Johns Hopkins University Press, 1959.

————. *President and Congress*. 3d ed. New York: Random House, 1962.

Blancké, W. Wendell. *The Foreign Service of the United States*. New York: Praeger, 1969.

Blix, Hans. *Treaty-Making Power*. New York: Praeger, 1960.

Blix, Hans, and Emerson, Jirina, eds. *The Treaty Makers Handbook*. Dobbs Ferry, N.Y.: Oceana, 1973.

Bloomfield, Louis M., and Fitzgerald, Gerald F. *Crimes against Internationally Protected Persons: An Analysis of the U.N. Convention*. New York: Praeger, 1975.

Blum, Robert, ed. *Cultural Affairs and Foreign Relations*. Englewood Cliffs, N.J.: Prentice-Hall, 1963.

Bolles, Blair. *Who Makes Our Foreign Policy?* New York: Foreign Policy Association, Headline Series, No. 62, March–April 1947.

Booth, Ken, ed. *Statecraft and Security: The Cold War and Beyond*. New York: Cambridge University Press, 1998.

Borchard, Edwin M. *The Diplomatic Protection of Citizens Abroad: Or the Law of International Claims*. New York: Banks Law, 1915, 1916, 1927, 1928.

Boulding, Kenneth E. *The Organizational Revolution*. New York: Harper, 1953.

Brands, H. W. *What America Owes the World: The Struggle for the Soul of Foreign Policy*. New York: Cambridge University Press, 1998.

Briggs, Ellis O. *Anatomy of Diplomacy: The Origin and Execution of American Foreign Policy*. New York: McKay, 1968.

Briggs, Philip J. *Making Foreign Policy*. 2d ed. Lanham, Md.: Rowman and Littlefield, 1994.

Brookings Institution. *The Administration of Foreign Affairs and Overseas Operations*. Washington: Government Printing Office, 1951.

————. *Administrative Aspects of United States Foreign Assistance Programs*. Washington: Government Printing Office, 1957.

———. *Governmental Mechanism for the Conduct of United States Foreign Relations.* Washington: Brookings Institution, 1949.

Brown, Ralph S., Jr. *Loyalty and Security: Employment Tests in the United States.* New Haven, Conn.: Yale University Press, 1958.

Brown, Stuart Gerry. *Memo for Overseas Americans: The Many Meanings of American Civilization.* Syracuse, N.Y.: Syracuse University Press, 1960.

Buchanan, William, and Cantril, Hadley. *How Nations See Each Other: A Study in Public Opinion.* Urbana: University of Illinois Press, 1953.

Buck, Philip W., and Travis, Martin B., Jr., eds. *Control of Foreign Relations in Modern Nations.* New York: Norton, 1957.

Bundy, Harvey H., and Rogers, James G. *The Organization of the Government for the Conduct of Foreign Affairs.* Washington: Government Printing Office, 1949.

Burdick, Richard E. *Ozone Diplomacy: New Directions in Safeguarding the Planet.* Washington: Institute for the Study of Diplomacy, 1990.

Burke, Lee H. *Ambassador at Large: Diplomat Extraordinary.* The Hague: Nijhoff, 1972.

Busk, Sir Douglas. *The Craft of Diplomacy: How to Run a Diplomatic Service.* New York: Praeger, 1967.

Butler, Charles H. *The Treaty-Making Power of the United States.* 2 vols. New York: Banks Law, 1902.

Byrd, Elbert M., Jr. *Treaties and Executive Agreements in the United States: Their Separate Roles and Limitations.* The Hague: Nijhoff, 1960.

Calkin, Homer L. *Women in American Foreign Affairs.* Washington: Department of State, 1977.

———. *Women in the Department of State: Their Role in American Foreign Affairs.* Washington: Government Printing Office, 1978.

Callieres, Francoise de. *On the Manner of Negotiating with Princes.* London: Allen, 1979.

Camara, Jose S. *The Ratification of International Treaties.* Toronto: Ontario, 1949.

Cambon, Jules M. *The Diplomatist.* London: Allan, 1931.

Campbell, John F. *The Foreign Affairs Fudge Factory.* New York: Basic Books, 1971.

Cardozo, Michael H. *Diplomats in International Cooperation: Stepchildren of the Foreign Service.* Ithaca, N.Y.: Cornell University Press, 1962.

Carroll, Holbert N. *The House of Representatives and Foreign Affairs.* Rev. ed. Boston: Little, Brown, 1966.

Carroll, Wallace. *Persuade or Perish.* Boston: Houghton Mifflin, 1948.

Cater, Douglass. *The Fourth Branch of Government.* Boston: Houghton Mifflin, 1959.

Cerf, Jay H. *Strategy for the 60's: Summary and Analysis of Studies Prepared by Thirteen Foreign Policy Centers for the United States Senate.* Washington: Foreign Policy Clearing House, 1961.

Chamberlain, Joseph P. *Legislative Processes: National and State.* New York: Appleton-Century, 1936, Chap. 19 on "Lawmaking and Foreign Affairs."

Cheever, Daniel S., and Haviland, H. Field, Jr. *American Foreign Policy and the Separation of Powers.* Cambridge: Harvard University Press, 1952.

Childs, James Rives. *American Foreign Service.* New York: Holt, 1948.

Chittick, William O. *State Department, Press, and Pressure Groups: A Role Analysis.* New York: Wiley, 1970.

Choate, Pat. *Agents of Influence.* New York: Knopf, 1990.

Clark, Eric. *Diplomat: The World of International Diplomacy*. New York: Taplinger, 1974.

Clark, Joshua Reuben. *Right to Protect Citizens in Foreign Countries by Landing Forces*. Washington: Department of State Memorandum, 1912, 1934.

Cleveland, Harlan, and Mangone, Gerard J., eds. *The Art of Overseasmanship: Americans at Work Abroad*. Syracuse, N.Y.: Syracuse University Press, 1957.

Cleveland, Harlan, Mangone, Gerard J., and Adams, John Clarke. *The Overseas Americans*. New York: McGraw-Hill, 1960.

Clift, Arthur D. *With Presidents to the Summit*. Fairfax, Va.: George Mason University Press, 1993.

Coffey, Joseph I., and Rock, Vincent P. *The Presidential Staff*. Washington: National Planning Association, 1961.

Cohen, Bernard C. *Foreign Policy in American Government*. Boston: Little, Brown, 1965.

———. *The Influence of Non-Governmental Groups on Foreign Policy-Making*. Boston: World Peace Foundation, 1959.

———. *The Political Process and Foreign Policy: The Making of the Japanese Peace Settlement*. Princeton: Princeton University Press, 1957.

———. *The Press and Foreign Policy*. Princeton: Princeton University Press, 1963.

Cole, Taylor. *The Recognition Policy of the United States since 1901*. Baton Rouge: Louisiana State University, 1928.

Colegrove, Kenneth. *The American Senate and World Peace*. New York: Vanguard Press, 1944.

Coles, Harry L., ed. *Total War and Cold War: Problems in Civilian Control of the Military*. Columbus: Ohio State University Press, 1962.

Committee on Foreign Affairs Personnel. *Personnel for the New Diplomacy*. Washington: Carnegie Endowment, 1962 (Herter Committee Report).

Coombs, Philip H. *The Fourth Dimension in Foreign Policy: Educational and Cultural Affairs*. New York: Harper and Row, 1964.

Corbett, Percy E. *Law in Diplomacy*. Princeton: Princeton University Press, 1959.

Corwin, Edward S. *The Constitution and World Organization*. Princeton: Princeton University Press, 1944.

———. *The President, Office and Powers, 1787–1957: History and Analysis of Practice and Opinion*. 4th ed. New York: New York University Press, 1957.

———. *The President's Control of Foreign Relations*. Princeton: Princeton University Press, 1917.

———. *Total War and the Constitution*. New York: Knopf, 1947.

Cottam, Richard W. *Competitive Interference and Twentieth Century Diplomacy*. Pittsburgh: University of Pittsburgh Press, 1967.

Cottrell, Leonard S., Jr., and Eberhart, Sylvia. *American Opinion on World Affairs in the Atomic Age*. Princeton: Princeton University Press, 1948.

Council on Foreign Relations. *American Agencies Interested in International Affairs*. New York: Council on Foreign Relations, 1931.

———. *Documents on American Foreign Relations*. Various comps. Boston and later Princeton: World Peace Foundation; since 1952, New York: Harper and Brothers for Council on Foreign Relations. Annual after 1939.

Crabb, Cecil V., Jr. *American Diplomacy and the Pragmatic Tradition*. Baton Rouge: Louisiana State University Press, 1989.

————. *American Foreign Policy in the Nuclear Age*. 2d ed. New York: Harper and Row, 1965.

Craig, Gordon A. *War, Politics, and Diplomacy: Selected Essays*. New York: Praeger, 1966.

Craig, Gordon A., and George, Alexander. *Force and Statecraft: Diplomatic Problems of Our Time*. 3d ed. New York: Oxford University Press, 1995.

Craig, Gordon A., and Gilbert, Felix, eds. *The Diplomats: 1919–1939*. Princeton: Princeton University Press, 1953.

Craig, Gordon A., and Lowenstein, Francis L. *The Diplomats, 1939–1979*. New Haven, Conn.: Princeton University Press, 1994.

Crandall, Samuel B. *Treaties, Their Making and Enforcement*. 2d ed. Washington: Byrne, 1916. (Earlier ed., New York: Columbia University Studies in History, Economics, and Public Law, 1904).

Creaghe, John St. George. "Personal Qualities and Effective Diplomatic Negotiation." Ph.D. diss., University of Maryland, 1965.

Crosswell, Carol M. *Protection of International Personnel Abroad*. New York: Oceana, 1952.

Culbertson, William S. *Reciprocity: A Natural Policy for Foreign Trade*. New York: McGraw-Hill, 1937.

Dacor Bacon House Foundation. *American Diplomacy in the Information Age*. Lanham, Md.: University Press of America, 1990.

Dahl, Robert A. *Congress and Foreign Policy*. 2d ed. New York: Norton, 1964.

Dangerfield, Royden J. *In Defense of the Senate: A Study in Treaty-Making*. Norman: University of Oklahoma Press, 1933.

Dangerfield, Royden J., and Gordon, David. *The Hidden Weapon: The Story of Economic Warfare*. New York: Harper and Row, 1947.

Darby, W. Evans. *International Tribunals*. 4th ed. London, 1904.

David, Joan. *Inside the State Department: How It Works at Home and Abroad*. New York: Manhattan, 1952.

Davies, John P., Jr. *Foreign and Other Affairs*. New York: Norton, 1964.

Davis, John W. *The Treaty-Making Power in the United States*. London: Oxford University Press, 1920.

Deak, Francis. *Classification, Immunities, and Privileges of Diplomatic Agents*. Cambridge: Harvard University Press, 1927.

De Conde, Alexander. *The American Secretary of State: An Interpretation*. New York: Praeger, 1962.

Delany, Robert F. *Your Future in the Foreign Service*. New York: Richard Rosen Press, 1961.

Dembinkski, Ludwik. *The Modern Law of Diplomacy: External Missions of States and International Organizations*. Boston: Nijhoff, 1988.

Demiashkevich, Michael J. *Shackled Diplomacy*. New York: Barnes and Noble, 1934.

Dennison, Eleanor E. *The Senate Foreign Relations Committee*. Stanford, Calif. Stanford University Press, 1942.

Denza, Eileen. *Diplomatic Law: Commentary on the Vienna Convention on Diplomatic Relations*. Dobbs Ferry, N.Y.: Oceana, 1976.

Destler, I. M. *Presidents, Bureaucrats, and Foreign Policy*. Princeton: Princeton University Press, 1972.

Devlin, Robert T. *The Treaty Power under the Constitution of the United States.* San Francisco: Bancroft-Whitney, 1908.

Dizard, Wilson P. *The Strategy of Truth: The Story of the U.S. Information Service.* Washington: Public Affairs Press, 1961.

Druckman, Daniel, ed. *Negotiations: Social-Psychological Perspectives.* Beverly Hills, Calif.: Sage, 1977.

Dulles, Allen W. *The Craft of Intelligence.* New York: Harper and Row, 1963.

Dumbrell, John, with Barrett, David M. *The Making of U.S. Foreign Policy.* New York: Manchester University Press, 1997.

Dunham, Donald C. *Envoy Unextraordinary.* New York: Day, 1944.

Dunn, David H. *Diplomacy at the Highest Level: The Evolution of International Summitry.* New York: St. Martin's Press, 1996.

Dunn, Frederick S. *The Practice and Procedure of International Conferences.* Baltimore: Johns Hopkins University Press, 1929.

———. *The Protection of Nationals.* Baltimore: Johns Hopkins University Press, 1932.

Dyer, Murray. *The Weapon on the Wall: Rethinking Psychological Warfare.* Baltimore: Johns Hopkins Press, 1959.

Eagleton, Clyde. *The Responsibility of States in International Law.* New York: New York University Press, 1928.

Eayres, James G. *Diplomacy and Its Discontents.* Toronto: University of Toronto Press, 1971.

Eban, Abba S. *Diplomacy for the Next Century.* New Haven, Conn.: Yale University Press, 1998.

———. *The New Diplomacy: International Affairs in the Modern Era.* New York: Random House, 1983.

Egger, Rowland A., ed. *International Commitments and National Administration.* Charlottesville: Bureau of Public Administration, University of Virginia, 1949.

Ekvall, Robert B. *Faithful Echo: The Role of Language in Diplomacy.* New York: Twayne, 1960.

Elder, Robert E. *The Information Machine: The United States Information Agency and American Foreign Policy.* Syracuse, N.Y.: Syracuse University Press, 1967.

———. *Overseas Representation and Services for Federal Domestic Agencies.* New York: Carnegie Endowment, 1965.

———. *The Policy Machine: The Department of State and American Foreign Policy.* Syracuse, N.Y.: Syracuse University Press, 1960.

Eldon, Stewart. *From Quill Pen to Satellite: Foreign Ministries in the Information Age.* London: Royal Institute of International Affairs, 1994.

Eller, George. *Secret Diplomacy.* London: Swift, 1912.

Elliott, William Yandall, et al. *United States Foreign Policy: Its Organization and Control.* New York: Columbia University Press, 1952.

Espinosa, J. Manuel. *Inter-American Beginnings of U.S. Cultural Diplomacy, 1936–1948.* Washington: Government Printing Office, 1976.

Esterline, John H. *Inside Foreign Policy: The Department of State Political System and Its Subsystems.* Palo Alto, Calif.: Mayfield, 1975.

Estes, Thomas S., and Lightner, E. Allen, Jr. *The Department of State.* New York: Praeger, 1976.

Eubank, Keith. *The Summit Conferences, 1919–1960.* Norman: University of Oklahoma Press, 1966.

Farago, Ladislas. *War of Wits: The Anatomy of Espionage and Intelligence.* New York: Funk and Wagnals, 1954.

Farley, Philip F. *Rights of Foreign Consuls in the United States.* New York: C. B. Rogers, 1931.

Farnsworth, David N. *The Senate Committee on Foreign Relations.* Illinois Studies in the Social Sciences, Vol. 49. Urbana: University of Illinois Press, 1961.

Feis, Herbert. *The Diplomacy of the Dollar: First Era, 1919–1932.* Baltimore: Johns Hopkins University Press, 1950.

———. *Foreign Aid and Foreign Policy.* New York: St. Martin's, 1964.

———. *From Trust to Terror: The Onset of the Cold War, 1945–1950.* New York: Norton, 1970.

———. *Seen from E.A.: Three International Episodes.* New York: Knopf, 1947.

Feller, Abraham H., and Hudson, Manley O., eds. *A Collection of the Diplomatic and Consular Laws and Regulations of Various Countries.* 2 vols. Washington: Carnegie Endowment, 1933.

Feltham, R. G. *Diplomatic Handbook.* 2d ed. New York: Longman, 1977.

———. *Training for an International Career.* Washington: Institute for the Study of Diplomacy, Georgetown University, 1979.

Fenno, Richard F. *The President's Cabinet.* Cambridge: Harvard University Press, 1959.

Fischer, John. *Master Plan U.S.A.: An Informal Report on America's Foreign Policy and the Men Who Make It.* New York: Harper and Row, 1951.

Fisher, Glen H. *International Negotiation: A Cross-Cultural Perspective.* Chicago: Intercultural Press, 1980.

———. *Public Diplomacy and the Behavioral Sciences.* Bloomington: Indiana University Press, 1972.

Fleming, Denna F. *The Treaty Veto of the American Senate.* New York: Putnam, 1930.

———. *The United States and the World Court.* Garden City, N.Y.: Doubleday, Doran, 1945.

Ford, Corey, and MacBain, Alastair. *Cloak and Dagger: The Secret Story of O.S.S.* New York: Random House, 1946.

Forgac, Albert T. *New Diplomacy and the United Nations.* New York: Pageant Press, 1965.

"Forty Years of the Foreign Service, 1924–1964." *Department of State News Letter,* No. 39 (July 1964).

Foster, John W. *A Century of American Diplomacy, 1776–1876.* Boston: Houghton Mifflin, 1900.

———. *The Practice of Diplomacy as Illustrated in the Foreign Relations of the United States.* Boston: Houghton Mifflin, 1906.

Frankel, Charles. *High on Foggy Bottom: An Outsider's Inside View of the Government.* New York: Harper and Row, 1968.

Frankel, Joseph. *The Making of Foreign Policy: An Analysis of Decision-Making.* New York: Oxford University Press, 1963.

Franklin, William M. *Protection of Foreign Interests: A Study in Diplomatic and Consular Practice.* Department of State Publication 2693. Washington: Government Printing Office, n.d. [1946].

Friedrich, Carl J. *Foreign Policy in the Making.* New York: Norton, 1938.

Fuller, C. Dale. *Training of Specialists in International Relations.* New York: Carnegie Endowment, 1957.

Gaines, Helen F. *Cryptanalysis: A Study of Ciphers and Their Solution*. New York: Dover, 1956.

Galloway, L. Thomas. *Recognizing Foreign Governments: The Practice of the United States*. Washington: American Enterprise Institute, 1978.

Gamboa, Melquiades J. *Elements of Diplomatic and Consular Practice: A Glossary*. Quezon City, Philippines: Central Lawbook, 1966.

Gange, John. *American Foreign Relations: Permanent Problems and Changing Policies*. New York: Ronald Press, 1959.

————. *The Secretariat Function: A Staff Aid for Executive Management*. Chicago: Public Administration Clearing House (processed), 1953.

Garcia Mora, Manuel R. *International Law and Asylum as a Human Right*. Washington: Public Affairs, 1956.

Gaselee, Stephen. *The Language of Diplomacy*. Cambridge, Eng.: Bowes and Bowes, 1939.

Gauss, Clarence E. *A Notarial Manual for Consular Officers*. Washington: Government Printing Office, 1921.

Gelfand, Lawrence F. *The Inquiry: American Preparations for Peace, 1917–1919*. New Haven, Conn.: Yale University Press, 1963.

George, Alexander L. *Avoiding War: Problems of Crisis Management*. Boulder, Colo.: Westview, 1991.

————. *Forceful Persuasion: Coercive Diplomacy as an Alternative to War*. Washington: Institute of Peace, 1991.

Gerber, William. *The Department of State, 1930–1955: Expanding Functions and Responsibilities*. Washington: Government Printing Office, 1955.

————. *The Department of State of the United States*. Washington, D.C.: Government Printing Office, 1942.

Gibson, Hugh. *The Road to Foreign Policy*. Garden City, N.Y.: Doubleday, Doran, 1944.

Glick, Philip N. *The Administration of Technical Assistance: Growth in the Americas*. Chicago: Chicago University Press, 1957.

Goebel, Julius, Jr. *The Recognition Policy of the United States*. New York: Columbia University Press, 1915.

Goldblat, Jozef. *Arms Control: A Guide to Negotiations and Agreements*. Thousand Oaks, Calif.: Sage, 1994.

Goldwin, Robert A., and Licht, Robert A. *Foreign Policy and the Constitution*. Washington: American Enterprise Institute, 1990.

Gordon, Morton, and Vines, Kenneth N. *Theory and Practice of American Foreign Policy*. New York: Crowell, 1955, especially Chapters 3–4.

Goss, Hilton P. *The Administration and Execution of United States Foreign Policy, 1960–1975*. Santa Barbara, Calif.: General Electric, Technical Military Planning Operation, 1959.

Graebner, Norman A. *Cold War Diplomacy: America's Foreign Policy, 1945–1975*. 2d ed. New York: Van Nostrand, 1977.

————, ed. *Ideas and Diplomacy: Readings in the Intellectual Tradition of American Foreign Policy*. New York: Oxford University Press, 1964.

————. *The National Security: Its Theory and Practice, 1945–1960*. New York: Oxford University Press, 1986.

————. *An Uncertain Tradition: American Secretaries of State in the Twentieth Century*. New York: McGraw-Hill, 1961.

Graham, Malbone W. *American Diplomacy in the International Community*. Baltimore: Johns Hopkins University Press, 1948.

Graham, Robert A. *Vatican Diplomacy: A Study of Church and State on the International Plane*. Princeton: Princeton University Press, 1959.

Grassmuck, George. *Sectional Biases in Congress on Foreign Policy*. Baltimore: Johns Hopkins University Press, 1951.

Graves, William B., comp. *Reorganization of the Executive Branch of the Government of the United States: A Compilation of Basic Information and Significant Documents, 1912–1948*. Washington: Legislative Reference Service, Library of Congress, Public Affairs Bulletin No. 66, 1949.

Gregoire, Roger. *National Administration and International Organizations*. Paris: UNESCO, 1958.

Grothe, Peter. *To Win the Minds of Men*. Palo Alto, Calif.: Pacific Books, 1958.

Grundstein, Nathan D. *Presidential Delegation of Authority in Wartime*. Pittsburgh: University of Pittsburgh Press, 1961.

Hackworth, Green H., ed. *Digest of International Law*. 8 vols. Washington: Government Printing Office, 1940–44.

Hall, Edward T. *The Silent Language*. New York: Doubleday, 1959.

Halperin, Morton H. *Bureaucratic Politics and Foreign Policy*. Washington: Brookings Institution, 1974.

Hammond, Paul Y. *Foreign Policymaking: Pluralistic Politics or Unitary Analysis*. Santa Monica, Calif.: Rand, 1965.

Handy, Michael J. *Modern Diplomatic Law*. Dobbs Ferry, N.Y.: Oceana, 1968.

Hankey, Maurice P. *Diplomacy by Conference*. London: Smith, 1920; London: Benn, 1946.

Harper, Elizabeth J. *The Role of Women in International Diplomacy*. Washington: Department of State, 1972.

Harr, John E. *The Anatomy of the Foreign Service–A Statistical Profile*. New York: Carnegie Endowment, 1965.

———. *The Development of Careers in the Foreign Service*. New York: Carnegie Endowment, 1965.

———. *The Professional Diplomat*. Princeton: Princeton University Press, 1969.

Harris, Joseph P. *The Advice and Consent of the Senate: A Study of the Confirmation of Appointments by the United States Senate*. Berkeley: University of California Press, 1953.

Haviland, H. Field, Jr. *The Formulation and Administration of United States Foreign Policy*. Washington: Brookings Institution, 1960.

Hayden, Ralston. *The Senate and Treaties, 1789–1817*. New York: Macmillan, 1920.

Hayter, William. *The Diplomacy of the Great Powers*. New York: Macmillan, 1961.

Heatley, David P. *Diplomacy and the Study of International Relations*. Oxford: Clarendon Press, 1969.

Heinlein, J. C. *Presidential Staff and National Security Policy*. Cincinnati: Center for the Study of U.S. Foreign Policy, Occasional Papers, No. 2, 1963.

Heinrichs, Waldo H., Jr. *American Ambassador: Joseph C. Grew and the Development of the United States Diplomatic Corps*. Boston: Little, Brown, 1966.

Heller, Deane. *Paths of Diplomacy: America's Secretaries of State*. Philadelphia: Lippincott, 1967.

Henderson, John B., Jr. *American Diplomatic Questions*. New York: Macmillan, 1901.

Henderson, John W. *The United States Information Agency.* New York: Praeger, 1969.

Henderson, Loy W. *Foreign Policies: Their Formulation and Enforcement.* Washington: Government Printing Office, 1946.

Hendry, James McLeod. *Treaties and Federal Constitutions.* Washington: Public Affairs Press, 1955.

Henrickson, Alan K. *Negotiating World Order: The Artisanship and Architecture of Global Diplomacy.* Wilmington, Del.: Scholarly Resources, 1986.

Henshaw, Joshua S. *A Manual for United States Consuls: Embracing Their Rights, Duties, Liabilities, and Emoluments.* New York: Riker, 1849.

Herman, Michael. *Intelligence Power in Peace and War.* New York: Cambridge University Press, 1996.

Hero, Aldred O. *Americans in World Affairs.* Boston: World Peace Foundation, 1959.

Herring, E. Pendleton. *Public Administration and the Public Interest.* New York: McGraw-Hill, 1936, Chapter 5 on "The State Department and the Public."

Hershey, Amos S. *Diplomatic Agents and Immunities.* Washington: Government Printing Office, 1919.

Herz, Martin F., ed. *Diplomats and Terrorists: What Works, What Doesn't: A Symposium.* Washington: Institute for the Study of Diplomacy, 1982.

——. *Diplomacy—The Role of the Wife: A Symposium.* Washington: Institute for the Study of Diplomacy, 1981.

Hester, Donald C. "Practice and Procedure in Preparing for International Conferences—With Special Emphasis on United States Techniques." Ph.D. diss., University of Maryland, 1959.

Hill, Martin. *Immunities and Privileges of International Officials.* Washington: Carnegie Endowment, 1947.

——. *Immunities and Privileges of Officials of the League of Nations.* Washington: Carnegie Endowment, 1945.

Hill, Norman L. *Mr. Secretary of State.* New York: Random House, 1963.

——. *The Public International Conference: Its Function, Organization and Procedure.* Stanford, Calif. Stanford University Press, 1929.

Hilsman, Roger, Jr. *Strategic Intelligence and National Decisions.* Glencoe, Ill.: Free Press, 1956.

Hilsman, Roger, Jr., and Good, Robert C., eds. *Foreign Policy in the Sixties.* Baltimore: Johns Hopkins University Press, 1965.

Hilton, Ralph. *Worldwide Mission: The Story of the United States Foreign Service.* New York: World, 1970.

Hilton, Stephen. *Records of United States Participation in International Conferences, Commissions, and Expositions.* Washington: Government Printing Office, 1958; Supplement, 1965.

Hirschman, Albert O. *The Strategy of Economic Development.* New Haven, Conn.: Yale University Press, 1958.

Hobbs, Edward Henry. *Behind the President: A Study of Executive Office Agencies.* Washington: Public Affairs Press, 1954.

Hoffman, Arthur S., ed. *International Communication and the New Diplomacy.* Bloomington: Indiana University Press, 1968.

Holt, Robert T., and van de Velde, Robert W. *Strategic Psychological Operations and American Foreign Policy.* Chicago: University of Chicago Press, 1960.

Holt, W. Stull. *Treaties Defeated by the Senate*. Baltimore: Johns Hopkins University Press, 1933; Gloucester, Mass.: P. Smith, 1964.

Hoopes, Roy. *The Complete Peace Corps Guide*. New York: Dial, 1961.

Howe, Fisher. *The Computer and Foreign Affairs: Some First Thoughts*. Washington: Government Printing Office, 1964.

Huddleston, Sisley. *Popular Diplomacy and War*. Rindge, N.H.: Richard R. R. Smith, 1954.

Hudson, Manly O. *By Pacific Means*. New Haven, Conn.: Yale University Press, 1935.

————. *The Permanent Court of International Justice, 1920–1942—A Treatise*. New York: Macmillan, 1943.

————. *International Tribunals: Past and Future*. Washington: Carnegie Endowment, 1944.

————. ed. *International Legislation*. 9 vols. Washington: Carnegie Endowment, 1931.

Hulen, Bertram D. *Inside the Department of State*. New York: McGraw-Hill, 1939.

Hunt, Gaillard. *The American Passport* . . . Washington: Government Printing Office, 1898.

Ikle, Fred. C. *How Nations Negotiate*. New York: Praeger, 1964.

Ilchman, Warren F. *Professional Diplomacy in the United States, 1779–1939: A Study in Administrative History*. Chicago: University of Chicago Press, 1961.

Ilich, John. *The Art and Skill of Successful Negotiation*. Englewood Cliffs, N.J.: Prentice-Hall, 1973.

International Institute of Administrative Sciences and UNESCO. *National Administration and International Organization: A Comparative Survey of Fourteen Countries*. Brussels: UNESCO, 1951.

Jackson, Henry M., ed. *The Secretary of State and the Ambassador*. New York: Praeger, 1964.

Jenks, Clarence W. *International Immunities*. Dobbs Ferry, N.Y.: Oceana, 1961.

————. *The Prospects of International Adjudication*. Dobbs Ferry, N.Y.: Oceana, 1964.

Jessup, Philip C. *The Birth of Nations*. New York: Columbia University Press, 1974.

————. *Parliamentary Diplomacy* . . . Leyden: Sijthoff, 1956.

Jewell, Malcolm E. *Senatorial Politics and Foreign Policy*. Lexington: University of Kentucky Press, 1962.

Johnson, E. A. J., ed. *The Dimensions of Diplomacy*. Baltimore: Johns Hopkins University Press, 1964.

Johnson, Loch K. *The Making of International Agreements: Congress Confronts the Executive*. New York: New York University Press, 1984.

————. *Secret Agencies: U.S. Intelligence in a Hostile World*. New Haven, Conn.: Yale University Press, 1996.

Johnson, Richard A. *The Administration of United States Foreign Policy*. Austin: University of Texas Press, 1971.

Johnson, Richard A., Kast, Fremont E., and Rosenzweig, James E. *The Theory and Management of Systems*. 3d ed. New York: McGraw-Hill, 1973.

Johnson, Willis F. *America's Foreign Relations*. 2 vols. New York: Century, 1916.

Jones, Arthur G. *The Evolution of Personnel Systems for U.S. Foreign Affairs: A History of Reform Efforts*. New York: Carnegie Endowment, 1965.

Jones, Cecil B., Jr. "Mistreatment of Foreign Diplomats in the United States since World War II." M.A thesis, University of Maryland, 1963.

Jones, Chester L. *The Consular Service of the United States: Its History and Activities.* Philadelphia: University of Pennsylvania Press, 1906.

Jones, Dorothy V. *Splendid Encounters: The Thought and Concept of Diplomacy.* Chicago: Chicago University Press, 1984.

Jones, Howard. *The Course of American Diplomacy: From the Revolution to the Present.* 2d ed. Chicago: Dorsey, 1988.

Jones, John M. *Full Powers and Ratification: A Study in the Development of Treaty-Making Procedure.* Cambridge: Cambridge University Press, 1946.

Jusserand, Jean A. A. Jules. *The School for Ambassador and Other Essays.* New York: Putnam, 1925.

Kammen, Michael G. *A Rope of Sand: The Colonial Agents, British Politics, and the American Revolution.* Ithaca, N.Y.: Cornell University Press, 1968.

Katz, Milton. *The Relevance of International Adjudication.* Cambridge: Harvard University Press, 1968.

Kaufman, Johan. *Conference Diplomacy: An Introductory Analysis.* Dobbs Ferry, N.Y.: Oceana, 1968.

Kellor, Frances. *American Arbitration: Its History, Functions, and Achievements.* New York: Harper, 1948.

Kelly, Alfred H., et al. *American Foreign Policy and American Democracy.* Detroit: Wayne University Press, 1954.

Kelly, David V. *The Ruling Few: Or, the Human Background to Diplomacy.* London: Hollis and Carter, 1952.

Kennan, George F. *American Diplomacy, 1900–1950.* New York: New American Library, 1952.

———. *Realities of American Foreign Policy.* Princeton: Princeton University Press, 1954.

Kennedy, Charles S. *The American Consul: A History of the United States Consular Service, 1776–1914.* New York: Greenwood, 1990.

Kent, Sherman. *Strategic Intelligence for American World Policy.* Princeton: Princeton University Press, 1949.

Kertesz, Stephen D. *The Quest for Peace through Diplomacy.* Englewood Cliffs, N.J.: Prentice-Hall, 1967.

———, ed. *American Diplomacy in a New Era.* Notre Dame: University of Notre Dame Press, 1961.

Kertesz, Stephen D., and Fitzsimons, M. A. *Diplomacy in a Changing World.* Notre Dame: University of Notre Dame Press, 1959.

Kerwin, Jerome G., ed. *Civil-Military Relationships in American Life.* Chicago: University of Chicago Press, 1948.

Kim, Jung Gun. "Non-Member Participation in International Organizations." Ph.D. dis., University of Maryland, 1965.

Kissinger, Henry A. *Diplomacy.* New York: Simon and Schuster, 1994.

Kissinger, Henry A., and Brodie, Bernard. *Beaucracy, Politics, and Strategy.* Los Angeles: University of California Press, 1968.

Knappen, Marshall. *An Introduction to American Foreign Policy.* New York: Harper, 1956.

Laffin, John. *Codes and Ciphers: Secret Writing through the Ages.* New York: Abelard-Schuman, 1964.

Lall, Arthur S. *Modern International Negotiation: Principles and Practices*. New York: Columbia University Press, 1966.

Latham, John G. *Open Diplomacy*. Melbourne: Australian Institute of International Affairs, 1953.

Lauren, Paul G. *Diplomats and Bureaucrats: The First Institutional Responses to Twentieth Century Diplomacy in France and Germany*. Stanford, Calif.: Hoover Institution, 1976.

————, ed. *Diplomacy: New Approaches in History, Theory and Policy*. Riverside, N.J.: Free Press, 1979.

Lauterpacht, Hersh. *Recognition in International Law*. Cambridge, Eng.: Cambridge University Press, 1947.

Laves, Walter H. C., and Thomson, Charles A. *Cultural Relations and United States Foreign Policy*. Bloomington: Indiana University Press, 1963.

Lavine, David. *Outposts of Adventure: The Story of the Foreign Service*. Garden City, N.Y.: Doubleday, 1966.

Lay, Tracy H. *The Foreign Service of the United States*. New York: Prentice-Hall, 1925.

Leacacos, John P. *Fires in the In-Basket: The ABC's of the State Department*. Cleveland: World, 1968.

Lee, John, ed. *The Diplomatic Persuaders: New Role of the Mass Media in International Relations*. New York: Wiley, 1968.

Lee, Luke T. *Consular Law and Practice*. New York: Praeger, 1961.

Le Fever, Ernest W. *Ethics and United States Foreign Policy*. New York: Macmillan, 1957.

Leonard, L. Larry. *Elements of American Foreign Policy*. New York: McGraw-Hill, 1953.

Lerche, Charles O., Jr. *Foreign Policy of the American People*. 2d ed. Englewood Cliffs, N.J.: Prentice-Hall, 1961.

Letiche, John M. *Reciprocal Trade Agreements in the World Economy*. New York: King's Crown Press, 1948.

Levitt, Albert. *The President and the International Affairs of the United States*. Los Angeles: Parker, 1954.

Lippmann, Walter. *Public Opinion and Foreign Policy in the United States*. London: Allen and Unwin, 1952.

Liska, George. *The New Statecraft: Foreign Aid in American Foreign Policy*. Chicago: University of Chicago Press, 1960.

Lodge, Henry Cabot. *The Senate and the League of Nations*. New York: Scribners, 1925.

London, Kurt. *How Foreign Policy Is Made*. New York: Van Nostrand, 1949.

————. *The Making of Foreign Policy, East and West*. Philadelphia: Lippincott, 1965.

Lovell, John P. *Foreign Policy in Perspective: Strategy, Adaptation, Decision Making*. New York: Holt, Rinehart, and Winston, 1970.

Ludwig, Ernest. *Consular Treaty Rights and Comments on the "Most-Favored-Nation" Clause*. Akron, Ohio: New Warner, 1913.

Lyman, Theodore, Jr. *The Diplomacy of the United States, Being an Account of the Foreign Relations of the Country from the First Treaty with France in 1778 to the Present Time*. 2d ed. 2 vols. Boston: Wells and Lilly, 1928.

MacBride, Roger L. *Treaties versus the Constitution*. Caldwell, Idaho: Caxton, 1955.

————. *Administration in Foreign Affairs*. University: University of Alabama Press, 1953.

Macmahon, Arthur W. *Administration and Foreign Policy*. University of Illinois Bulletin, Vol. 54, No. 44. Urbana: Institute of Government and Public Affairs, University of Illinois, 1957.

Macomber, William B., Jr. *The Angels' Game: A Handbook of Modern Diplomacy*. New York: Stein and Day, 1975.

———. *Diplomacy for the 70's: A Program of Management Reform for the Department of State*. Washington: Government Printing Office, 1970.

Macridis, Roy C., ed. *Foreign Policy in World Politics*. 2d ed. Englewood Cliffs, N.J.: Prentice-Hall, 1962.

Markel, Lester, et al. *Public Opinion and Foreign Policy*. New York: Harper, 1949.

Marrow, Alfred J. *Making Waves in Foggy Bottom: How a New and More Scientific Approach Changed the Management at the State Department*. Washington: NTL Institute, 1974.

Martel, Gordon, ed. *The Broadview Book of Diplomatic Anecdotes*. Lewiston, N.Y.: Broadview Press, 1991.

Martin, L. John. *International Propaganda: Its Legal and Diplomatic Control*. Minneapolis: University of Minnesota Press, 1958.

Mathews, John M. *American Foreign Relations: Conduct and Policies*. Rev. ed. New York: Appleton-Century, 1938.

———. *The Conduct of American Foreign Relations*. New York: Century, 1922.

Mattingly, Garret. *Renaissance Diplomacy*. Baltimore: Penguin, 1955.

Mautner-Markhof, Frances, ed. *Processes of International Negotiations*. Boulder, Colo.: Westview, 1989.

May, Ernest R., ed. *The Ultimate Decision: The President as Commander in Chief*. New York: George Braziller, 1960.

Mayall, James, and Navari, Cornelia, eds. *The End of the Post-War Era: Documents on Great-Power Relations*. Cambridge: Cambridge University Press, 1980.

Mayer, Arno J. *Political Origins of the New Diplomacy, 1917–1918*. New Haven, Conn.: Yale University Press, 1959.

Mayer, Martin. *The Diplomats*. Garden City, N.Y.: Doubleday, 1983.

McCamy, James L. *The Administration of American Foreign Affairs*. New York: Knopf, 1950.

———. *Conduct of the New Diplomacy*. New York: Harper and Row, 1964.

McCamy, James L., with McCamy, Julia B. *Government Publications for the Citizen: A Report of the Public Library Inquiry*. New York: Columbia University Press, 1949.

McClure, Wallace M. *International Executive Agreements: Democratic Procedure under the Constitution of the United States*. New York: Columbia University Press, 1941.

McDonald, John W., Jr. *U.S.–Soviet Summitry: Roosevelt through Carter*. Washington: Foreign Service Institute, Department of State, 1987.

McDougal, Meyers S., Lasswell, Harold D., and Miller, James C. *The Interpretations of Agreements and Public Order: Principles of Content and Procedure*. New Haven, Conn.: Yale University Press, 1963.

McGhee, George C., ed. *Diplomacy for the Future*. Washington: Institute for the Study of Diplomacy, 1987.

McGlen, Nancy E., and Sarkess, Meredith S. *Women in Foreign Policy: The Insiders*. New York: Routledge, 1993.

McGovern, William M. *Strategic Intelligence and the Shape of Tomorrow.* Foundation for Foreign Affairs Series, No. 5. Chicago: Regnery, 1961.

McKenna, Joseph C. *Diplomatic Protest in Foreign Policy: Analysis and Case Studies.* Chicago: Loyola University Press, 1962.

McMahon, John L. *Recent Changes in the Recognition Policy of the United States.* Washington: Catholic University Press, 1933.

Meck, J. F., and Koenig, Louis William. *The Administration of United States Participation in International Organizations.* Washington: American Society for Public Administration, 1950.

Mee, Charles L., Jr. *Playing God: Seven Fateful Moments When Great Men Met to Change the World.* New York: Simon and Schuster, 1993.

Mendershausen, Horst. *The Diplomat as a National and Transnational Agent: A Problem of Multiple Loyalty.* Morristown, N.J. General Learning Press, 1973.

———. *The Diplomat as a National and Transnational Agent: Dilemmas and Opportunities.* Santa Monica, Calif.: Rand, 1969.

Mennis, Bernard. *American Foreign Policy Officials: Who Are They and What Are They?* Columbus: Ohio State University Press, 1971.

Merli, Frank J., and Wilson, Theodore A. *Makers of American Diplomacy.* New York: Scribner, 1974.

Merrillat, Herbert C. L., ed. *Legal Advisers and Foreign Affairs.* Dobbs Ferry, N.Y.: Oceana, 1964.

Michaels, David B. *International Privileges and Immunities: A Case for a Universal Statute.* The Hague: Nijhoff, 1971.

Millar, T. B., and Edwards, Robin, eds. *Current International Treaties.* New York: New York University Press, 1984.

Miller, Hope R. *Embassy Row: The Life and Times of Diplomatic Washington.* New York: Holt, Rinehart, and Winston, 1969.

Millis, Walter. *The Constitution and the Common Defense.* New York: Fund for the Republic, 1959.

Mitchell, Nicholas P. *State Interests in American Treaties.* Richmond, Va.: Garrett and Massie, 1936.

Moore, Dan Tyler, and Waller, Martha. *Cloak and Cipher.* Indianapolis: Bobbs-Merrill, 1962.

Moore, John Bassett. *Asylum in Legations and Consulates and in Vessels.* New York: Ginn, 1892.

———. *The Principles of American Diplomacy.* New York: Harper, 1905, 1908, 1918.

———. *A Treatise on Extradition and Interstate Rendition.* 2 vols. Boston: Boston Book, 1891.

———, ed. *A Digest of International Law.* 8 vols. Washington: Government Printing Office, 1906.

———. *History and Digest of the International Arbitrations to Which the United States Has Been a Party. . . .* 6 vols. Washington: Government Printing Office, 1898.

———. *International Adjudications, Ancient and Modern. . . .* 6 vols. New York: Oxford University Press, 1929.

Moreno, Salcedo L. *A Guide to Protocol.* Rev ed. Manila: University Book Supply, 1959.

Morse, Alexander P. *The So-Called Right of Asylum in Legations. . . .* Washington: 1892.

Mosher, Frederick, and Harr, John E. *Programming System and Foreign Policy Leadership.* New York: Oxford University Press, 1970.

Mowat, Robert B. *Diplomacy and Peace*. London: Williams and Norgate, 1935.

Mowrer, Paul S. *Our Foreign Affairs: A Study of National Interest and the New Diplomacy*. New York: Dutton, 1924.

Moynihan, Daniel P. *Secrecy: The American Experience*. New Haven, Conn.: Yale University Press, 1998.

Murphy, Thomas P., Nuechterline, Donald E., and Stupak, Ronald J., eds. *The President's Program Directors: The Assistant Secretaries—A Symposium*. Charlottesville, Va.: U.S. Civil Service Commission, Federal Executive Institute, 1976.

Murray, Eustace C. G. *Embassies and Foreign Courts: A History of Diplomacy*. New York: Routledge, 1855.

Neal, Harry E. *Your Career in the Foreign Service*. New York: Messner, 1965.

Needler, Martin C. *Dimensions of American Foreign Policy: Readings and Documents*. Princeton: Van Nostrand, 1966.

———. *Understanding Foreign Policy*. New York: Holt, Rinehart, and Winston, 1966.

Nero, Alfred G. *Americans in World Affairs: Studies in Citizen Participation in International Relations*. Boston: World Peace Foundation, 1959.

Newsom, David D. *Diplomacy and the American Democracy*. Bloomington: Indiana University Press, 1988.

———. *Private Diplomacy with the Soviet Union*. Washington: Institute for the Study of Diplomacy, 1987.

———, ed. *Diplomacy under a Foreign Flag: When Nations Break Relations*. New York: St. Martin's, 1990.

Nichols, Roy F. *Advance Agents of American Destiny*. Philadelphia: University of Pennsylvania Press, 1956.

Nicolson, Harold. *Diplomacy*. London: T. Butterworth, 1939.

———. *The Evolution of Diplomatic Method*. New York: Macmillan, 1954.

Northedge, F. S., and Donelan, M. D. *International Disputes: The Political Aspects*. New York: St. Martin's, 1971.

Nostrand, Howard Lee. *The Cultural Attaché*. Hazen Pamphlets, No. 17. New Haven, Conn.: Edward W. Hazen Foundation, n.d.

Numelin, Ragnar J. *The Beginnings of Diplomacy*. New York: Philosophical Library, 1950.

O'Davoren, William. *Post-War Reconstruction Conferences: The Technical Organisation of International Conferences*. London: King and Staples, 1943.

Odell, Talbot. *War Powers of the President: War Powers of the American Presidency, Derived from the Constitution and Statutes, and Their Historical Background*. Washington: Washington Service Bureau, 1942.

Offutt, Milton. *The Protection of Citizens Abroad by the Armed Forces of the United States*. Baltimore: Johns Hopkins University Press, 1928.

Ogdon, Montell. *Judicial Basis of Diplomatic Immunity*. Washington: Byrne, 1936.

Osgood, Robert E. *Ideals and Self-Interests in America's Foreign Relations*. Chicago: University of Chicago Press, 1953.

Ostrower, Alexander. *Language, Law and Diplomacy: A Study of Linguistic Diversity in Official International Relations and International Law*. 2 vols. Philadelphia: University of Pennsylvania Press, 1965.

Oudenijk, Willem J. *Ways and By-Ways in Diplomacy*. London: Davies, 1939.

Pan-American Union. *Standards regarding the Formulation of Reservations to Multilateral Treaties*. Washington: Organization of American States, 1959.

Parks, Wallace J. *United States Administration of Its International Economic Affairs.* Baltimore: Johns Hopkins University Press, 1951.

Pastuhov, Vladimir D. *A Guide to the Practice of International Conferences.* Washington: Carnegie Endowment, 1945.

Patterson, Richard S., and Dougall, Richardson. *The Eagle and the Shield: A History of the Great Seal of the United States.* Washington: Government Printing Office, 1976.

Paullin, Charles O. *Diplomatic Negotiations of American Naval Officers, 1778–1883.* Baltimore: Johns Hopkins University Press, 1912.

Pearson, Lester B. *Diplomacy in the Nuclear Age.* Cambridge: Harvard University Press, 1959.

Perkins, Dexter. *The American Approach to Foreign Policy.* Cambridge: Harvard University Press, 1952.

———. *The Diplomacy of the New Age: Major Issues in U.S. Foreign Policy since 1945.* Bloomington: Indiana University Press, 1967.

———. *Foreign Policy and the American Spirit.* Ithaca, N.Y.: Cornell University Press, 1957.

Pettee, George S. *The Future of American Secret Intelligence.* Washington: Infantry Journal Press, 1946.

Phleger, Herman. *United States Treaties: Recent Developments.* Department of State Publication 6376. Washington: Government Printing Office, 1956.

Piper, Don C., and Terchek, Ronald J., eds. *Interaction: Foreign Policy and Public Policy.* Dedicated in honor of Elmer Plischke. Washington: American Enterprise Institute, 1983.

Pitsvada, Bernard T. *The Senate, Treaties, and National Security.* Lanham, Md.: University Press of America, 1991.

Platt, Washington. *National Character in Action: Intelligence Factors in Foreign Relations.* New Brunswick, N.J.: Rutgers University Press, 1961.

———. *Strategic Intelligence Production: Basic Principles.* New York: Praeger, 1957.

Plischke, Elmer. *Conduct of American Diplomacy.* 3d ed. Princeton: Van Nostrand, 1967.

———. *Contemporary U.S. Foreign Policy: Documents and Commentary.* New York: Greenwood, 1980.

———. *Diplomat in Chief: The President at the Summit.* New York: Praeger, 1986.

———. *Foreign Relations: Analysis of Its Anatomy.* New York: Greenwood, 1988.

———. *Foreign Relations Decisionmaking: Options Analysis.* Beirut, Lebanon: Institute of Middle Eastern and North African Affairs, Catholic Press, 1973.

———. *International Relations: Basic Documents.* Princeton: Van Nostrand, 1953, 1962.

———. *Microstates in World Affairs: Policy Problems and Options.* Washington: American Enterprise Institute, 1977.

———. *Presidential Diplomacy: A Chronology of Summit Visits, Trips, and Meetings.* Dobbs Ferry, N.Y.: Oceana, 1986.

———. *Summit Diplomacy: Personal Diplomacy of the President of the United States.* College Park: Bureau of Governmental Research, University of Maryland, 1958.

———. *United States Diplomats and Their Missions: A Profile of American Diplomatic Emissaries since 1778.* Washington: American Enterprise Institute, 1975.

———, ed. *Modern Diplomacy: The Art and the Artisans.* Washington: American Enterprise Institute, 1979.

Ponsonby, Arthur. *Democracy and Diplomacy: A Plea for Popular Control of Foreign Policy*. London: Methuen, 1915.

Poole, DeWitt C. *The Conduct of Foreign Relations under Modern Democratic Conditions*. New Haven, Conn.: Yale University Press, 1924.

Price, Don K. *Government and Science: Their Dynamic Relation in American Democracy*. New York: New York University Press, 1954.

———. *The New Dimension of Diplomacy: The Organization of the U.S. Government for Its New Role in World Affairs*. New York: Woodrow Wilson Foundation, 1951.

———. *The Secretary of State*. Englewood Cliffs, N.J.: Prentice-Hall, 1960.

Pritt, Denis N. *The State Department and the Cold War*. New York: International, 1948.

Pruitt, Dean G. *Problem Solving in the Department of State*. Social Science Foundation and Department of International Relations, Monograph Series in World Affairs, No. 2. Denver: University of Denver, 1964–65.

Puente, Julius I. *The Foreign Counsul: His Juridical Status in the United States*. Chicago: B. J. Smith, 1926.

Putnam, Robert D. *Hanging Together: Cooperation and Conflict in the Seven-Power Summits*. Cambridge: Harvard University Press, 1987.

Qualter, Terence H. *Propaganda and Psychological Warfare*. New York: Random House, 1962.

Queller, Donald E. *The Office of the Ambassador in the Middle Ages*. Princeton: Princeton University Press, 1967.

Quester, George H. *Nuclear Diplomacy: The First Twenty-Five Years*. New York: Harvard University Press, 1970.

Radlovic, I. Monte. *Etiquette and Protocol: A Handbook of Conduct in American and International Circles*. New York: Harcourt, Brace, 1957.

Ranshofen-Wertheimer, Egon F. *The International Secretariat: A Great Experiment in International Administration*. Washington: Carnegie Endowment, 1945.

Ransom, Harry Howe. *Central Intelligence and National Security*. Cambridge: Harvard University Press, 1958.

———, ed. *An American Foreign Policy Reader*. New York: Crowell, 1965.

Rappaport, Armin. *Sources in American Diplomacy*. New York: Macmillan, 1966.

Regala, Roberto. *New Dimensions in International Affairs*. Manila: Phoenix Press, 1967.

———. *The Trends in Modern Diplomatic Practice*. Dobbs Ferry, N.Y.: Oceana, 1959.

———. *World Order and Diplomacy*. Dobbs Ferry, N.Y.: Oceana, 1969.

———. *World Peace through Diplomacy and Law*. Dobbs Ferry, N.Y.: Oceana, 1964.

Reiff, Henry. *Diplomatic and Consular Privileges, Immunities, and Practice*. Cairo, Egypt: Ettemad Press, 1954.

Reinsch, Paul S. *Secret Diplomacy: How Far Can It Be Eliminated?* New York.: Harcourt, Brace, 1922.

Richardson, James L. *Crisis Diplomacy: The Great Powers since the Mid-Nineteenth Century*. New York: Cambridge University Press, 1994.

Rivers, William L. *The Opinion Makers*. Boston: Beacon Press, 1965.

Robinson, James A. *Congress and Foreign Policy-Making: A Study in Legislative Influence and Initiative*. Homewood, IL: Dorsey Press, 1962.

———. *The Monroney Resolution: Congressional Initiative in Foreign Policy Making*. New York: Holt, 1959.

Roetter, Charles. *The Diplomatic Art: An Informal History of World Diplomacy.* Philadelphia: Macrae, Smith, 1963.

Rogers, James G. *World Policing and the Constitution: An Inquiry Into the Powers of the President and Congress, Nine Wars and a Hundred Military Operations, 1789–1945.* Boston: World Peace Foundation, 1945.

Ronning, C. Neale. *Diplomatic Asylum: Legal Norms and Political Reality in Latin American Relations.* The Hague: Nijhoff, 1965.

Rosenau, James N. *National Leadership and Foreign Policy: A Case Study in the Mobilization of Public Support.* Princeton: Princeton University Press, 1963.

———. *Public Opinion and Foreign Policy.* New York: Random House, 1961.

Rostow, Walt W. *View from the Seventh Floor.* New York: Harper and Row, 1964.

Roudybush, Franklin. *An Analysis of the Educational Background and Experience of U.S. Foreign Service Officers.* Washington: Government Printing Office, 1944.

———. *Cosmopolitan Conversation: The Language Problems of International Conferences.* New York: Columbia University Press, 1933.

———. *Diplomatic Language.* Basel, Switzerland: Satz, 1972.

———. *Foreign Service Training.* Besançon, France: Presse Comptoise, 1955.

———. *World Diplomatic List.* Washington: Government Printing Office, 1943.

Rourke, Francis E. *Bureaucracy and Foreign Policy.* Baltimore: Johns Hopkins University Press, 1972.

———. *Secrecy and Publicity: Dilemmas of Democracy.* Baltimore: Johns Hopkins University Press, 1961.

Rowe, James H., Jr., et al. *An Improved Personnel System for the Conduct of Foreign Affairs: A Report to the Secretary of State by the Secretary's Advisory Committee on Personnel.* Washington: Department of State (processed), 1950. (Rowe Committee Report.)

Salzman, Charles E. *The Reorganization of the American Foreign Service.* Washington: Government Printing Office, 1954.

Sapin, Burton M. *The Making of United States Foreign Policy.* Washington: Brookings Institution, 1966. (Also published by Praeger, 1966.)

Sapin, Burton M., and Snyder, Richard C. *The Role of the Military in American Foreign Policy.* Garden City, N.Y.: Doubleday, 1954.

Sapin, Burton M., Snyder, Richard C., and Bruck, H. W. *An Appropriate Role for the Military in American Foreign Policy-Making: A Research Note.* Princeton: Princeton University (processed), 1954.

Satow, Ernest M. *A Guide to Diplomatic Practice.* 4th ed. London: Longmans, Green, 1957.

———. *International Congresses.* London: H. M. Stationery, 1920.

Savelle, Max. *The Origins of American Diplomacy: The International History of Angloamerica, 1492–1763.* New York: Macmillan, 1967.

Savord, Ruth. *American Agencies Interested in International Affairs.* New York: Council on Foreign Relations, 1931.

Sayre, Wallace S., and Thurber, Clarence E. *Training for Specialized Mission Personnel.* Chicago: Public Administration Service, 1952.

Schneider, Johannes W. *Treaty-Making Power of International Organizations.* Geneva: Droz, 1959.

Schulzinger, Robert D. *American Diplomacy in the Twentieth Century.* New York: Oxford University Press, 1984.

——. *The Making of the Diplomatic Mind: The Training, Outlook, and Style of United States Foreign Service Officers, 1908–1931*. Middletown, Conn.: Wesleyan University Press, 1975.

Schuyler, Eugene. *American Diplomacy and the Furtherance of Commerce*. New York: Scribner, 1886.

Scott, Andrew M., and Dawson, Raymond H., eds. *Readings in the Making of American Foreign Policy*. New York: Macmillan, 1965.

Scott, James Brown. *Arbitration and Diplomatic Settlement of the United States*. Washington: Carnegie Endowment, 1914.

——. *The Development of Modern Diplomacy*. Washington: American Peace Society, 1921.

——, ed. *The Hague Conventions and Declarations of 1899 and 1907*. 3d ed. 5 vols. New York: Oxford University Press, 1918.

——. *Treaties for the Advancement of Peace*. New York: Oxford University Press, 1920.

Seabury, Paul. *Power, Freedom, and Diplomacy: Foreign Policy of the United States of America*. New York: Random House, 1963.

Seldes, George. *The People Don't Know: The American Press and the Cold War*. New York: Gaer Associates, 1949.

Sen, Biswanath. *A Diplomat's Handbook of International Law and Practice*. The Hague: Nijhoff, 1965.

——. *International Law Relating to Diplomatic Practice*. Delhi: Metropolitan, 1950.

Shaw, Carolyn H. *Modern Manners*. New York: Dutton, 1962.

Shaw, Gardiner H. *The State Department and Its Foreign Service in Wartime*. Washington: Government Printing Office, 1943.

Sheppard, Eli T. *American Consular Service*. Berkeley: University of California Press, 1901.

Simpson, Smith. *Anatomy of the State Department*. Boston: Houghton Mifflin, 1967.

——. *The Crisis in American Diplomacy: Shots across the Bow of the State Department*. North Quincy, Mass.: Christopher, 1980.

——. *Education in Diplomacy: An Instructional Guide*. Washington: Institute for the Study of Diplomacy, 1987.

——. *Perspectives on Diplomacy*. Washington: Institute for the Study of Diplomacy, 1986.

——, ed. *Instruction in Diplomacy: The Liberal Arts Approach*. Philadelphia: American Academy of Political and Social Science, Monograph 13, 1972.

Sinclair, Ian McTaggart. *The Vienna Convention on the Law of Treaties*. Dobbs Ferry, N.Y.: Oceana, 1973.

Siracusa, Joseph M. *New Left Diplomatic Histories and Historians*. Port Washington, N.Y.: Kennikat, 1973.

Smith, Gaddis. *American Diplomacy during the Second World War, 1941–1945*. New York: Wiley, 1965.

Smith, Louis. *American Democracy and Military Power: A Study of Civil Control of the Military Power in the United States*. Chicago: University of Chicago Press, 1951.

Smith, Steve, and Clarke, Michael. *Foreign Policy Implementation*. Boston: Allen and Unwin, 1985.

Snow, Freeman. *Treaties and Topics in American Diplomacy*. Boston: Boston Book, 1894.

Snyder, Richard C. *The Most-Favored-Nation Clause*. New York: King's Crown Press, 1948.

Snyder, Richard C., Bruck, H. W., and Sapin, Burton M. *Decision-Making as an Approach to the Study of International Politics*. Princeton: Princeton University Press, 1954.

——, eds. *Foreign Policy Decision Making: An Approach to the Study of International Politics*. New York: Free Press, 1962.

Snyder, Richard C., and Furniss, Edgar S., Jr. *American Foreign Policy: Formulation, Principles, and Programs*. New York: Rinehart, 1954.

Sorensen, Theodore C. *Decision-Making in the White House: The Olive Branch or the Arrows*. New York: Columbia University Press, 1963.

Spaulding, E. Wilder. *Ambassadors Ordinary and Extraordinary*. Washington: Public Affairs Press, 1961.

Spaulding, E. Wilder, and Blue, George Verne. *The Department of State of the United States*. Rev. ed. Washington: Government Printing Office, 1936.

Spector, Paul, and Preston, Harley O. *Working Effectively Overseas*. Washington: Institute for International Services, 1961.

Spencer, Jean E. "Soviet and European Satellite Treatment of Resident United States Diplomatic Personnel since the Second World War." M.A. thesis, University of Maryland, 1961.

Stanley, Timothy W., with Ransom, Harry Howe. *The National Security Council*. Cambridge: Harvard Defense Policy Seminar Serial No. 104, January 12, 1957.

Steigman, Andrew L. *The Foreign Service of the United States: First Line of Defense*. Boulder, Colo.: Westview, 1985.

Stein, Harold. *The Foreign Service Act of 1946*. Washington: Inter-University Case Program, 1949.

Stein, Janice G., ed. *Getting to the Table: The Processes of Prenegotiation*. Baltimore: Johns Hopkins University Press, 1989.

Steiner, Zara S. *Present Problems of the Foreign Service*. Princeton: Center of International Studies, Princeton University, 1961.

——. *The State Department and the Foreign Service: The Wriston Report—Four Years Later*. Princeton: Center of International Studies, Princeton University, 1958.

Stephens, Oren. *Facts to a Candid World: America's Overseas Information Program*. Stanford, Calif.: Stanford University Press, 1955.

Stewart, Irvin. *Consular Privileges and Immunities*. New York: Columbia University Press, 1926.

Stock, Leo F., ed. *Consular Relations between the United States and the Papal States: Instructions and Despatches*. Washington: American Catholic Historical Association, 1945.

Stoke, Harold Walter. *The Foreign Relations of the Federal State*. Baltimore: Johns Hopkins University Press, 1931.

Stone, Albert E. ed. *Twentieth Century Interpretations of the Ambassadors: Collection of Critical Essays*. Englewood Cliffs, N.J.: Prentice-Hall, 1969.

Stowell, Ellery C. *Le Consul: Fonctions, Immunities, Organisation, Exequatur*. Paris: Pedone, 1909.

——. *Consular Cases and Opinions*. Washington: Byrne, 1909.

——. *The Economic Adviser of the Department of State*. Washington: Digest Press, 1935.

———. *The Legal Adviser of the Department of State.* Washington: Digest Press, 1936.

Stowell, Ellery C., and Munro, Henry F. *International Cases: Arbitrations and Incidents Illustrative of International Law as Practiced by Independent States.* 2 vols. Boston: Houghton Mifflin, 1916.

Strang, William S. *The Diplomatic Career.* London: Deutsch, 1962.

Strauss, Lewis L. *Men and Decisions.* Garden City, N.Y.: Doubleday, 1962.

Stuart, Graham H. *American Diplomatic and Consular Practice,* 2d ed. New York: Appleton-Century-Crofts, 1952. (Earlier ed., Appleton-Century, 1936.)

Stupak, Ronald J. *American Foreign Policy: Assumptions, Processes, and Projections.* New York: Harper and Row, 1976.

———. *The Shaping of Foreign Policy: The Role of the Secretary of State as Seen by Dean Acheson.* New York: Odyssey, 1969.

Sulzberger, Arthur O. *The Joint Chiefs of Staff, 1941–1954.* Washington: U.S. Marine Corps Institute, 1954.

Sulzberger, Cyrus L. *What's Wrong with U.S. Foreign Policy?* New York: Harcourt, Brace, 1959.

Summers, Natalia. *List of Documents Relating to Special Agents of the Department of State, 1789–1906.* Washington: Government Printing Office, 1951.

———. *Outline of the Functioning of the Offices of the Department of State, 1789–1943.* Washington: National Archives, 1946.

Sweeny, Jerry K., and Denning, Margaret B. *A Handbook of American Diplomacy.* Boulder, Colo.: Westview, 1993.

Sylvan, Donald A., and Voss, James F. *Problem Representation in Foreign Policy Decision Making.* New York: Cambridge University Press, 1998.

Symington, James W. *The Stately Game.* New York: Macmillan, 1971.

Terchek, Ronald J. *The Making of the Test Ban Treaty.* The Hague: Nijhoff, 1970.

Terrell, John U. *The United States Department of State: A Story of Diplomats, Embassies and Foreign Policy.* New York: Duell, Sloan, and Pearce, 1964.

Thayer, Charles W. *Diplomat.* New York: Harper, 1959.

Thompson, Charles A. *Overseas Information Service of the United States Government.* Washington: Brookings Institution, 1948.

Thompson, James W. and Padover, Saul K. *Secret Diplomacy: Espionage and Cryptography, 1500–1815.* New York: Unger, 1963.

Thompson, Kenneth W. *American Diplomacy and Emergent Patterns.* New York: New York University Press, 1962.

———. *Foreign Assistance: A View from the Private Sector.* South Bend, Ind.: Notre Dame University Press, 1972.

———. *Interpreters and Critics of the Cold War.* Washington: University of America Press, 1978.

———. *Political Realism and the Crisis of World Politics: An American Approach to Foreign Policy.* Princeton: Princeton University Press, 1960.

Thompson, Margery B., ed. *As Others See Us: United States Diplomacy Viewed from Abroad.* Washington: Institute for the Study of Diplomacy, 1989.

Thorson, Stuart J., ed. *Timing the De-Escalation of International Conflicts.* Syracuse, N.Y.: Syracuse University Press, 1991.

Tobin, Harold J. *The Termination of Multipartite Treaties.* New York: Columbia University Press, 1933.

Tobin, Richard L. *Decisions of Destiny.* Cleveland: World, 1961.

Torre, M., and Glaser, W. *The Effect of Illness on Diplomatic Intercourse*. New York: Research Institute for the Study of Man, 1963.

Toscano, Mario. *The History of Treaties and International Politics*. Part 1: The Documentary and Memoir Sources. Baltimore: Johns Hopkins University Press, 1966.

Trask, David F. *A Short History of the U.S. Department of State, 1781–1981*. Washington: Government Printing Office, 1981.

———. *The United States in the Supreme War Council: American War Aims and Inter-Allied Strategy, 1917–1918*. Middletown, Conn.: Wesleyan University Press, 1961.

Trevelyan, Humphrey. *Diplomatic Channels*. Boston: Gambit, 1973.

Tuch, Hans N. *Communicating with the World: U.S. Public Diplomacy Overseas*. New York. St. Martin's, 1990.

Tully, Andrew M. *CIA: The Inside Story*. New York: Morrow, 1962.

———. *White Tie and Dagger*. New York: Morrow, 1967.

Turek, Miroslav. *Constitutional and Administrative Aspects of the Conduct of Foreign Affairs*. New York: National Committee for a Free Europe, 1953.

Udokang, Okan. *Succession of New States to International Treaties*. Dobbs Ferry, N.Y.: Oceana, 1972.

Ulmer, Sidney, et al. *Political Decision Making*. New York: Van Nostrand Rinehold, 1970.

United Nations, Legal Dept. *Laws and Practices concerning the Conclusion of Treaties, with a Select Bibliography on the Law of Treaties*. New York: United Nations, 1953.

United States, Advisory Commission on Information. *The World Audience for America's Story*. Department of State Publication 3485. Washington: Government Printing Office, 1949.

United States, Bureau of the Budget. *Organization and Coordination of Foreign Economic Activities*. Washington: Government Printing Office, 1961.

———. *A Study of Relationships between the Departments of State and Commerce*. Washington: Government Printing Office, 1948.

———. *The United States at War: Development and Administration of the War Program by the Federal Government*. Washington: Government Printing Office, n.d. [1946].

United States, Commission on Organization of the Executive Branch of the Government (Hoover Commission). *Foreign Affairs*. Washington: Government Printing Office, 1949.

———. *Task Force Report on Foreign Affairs* [Appendix H]. Washington: Government Printing Office, 1949.

———. *Task Force Report on Overseas Economic Operations*. Washington: Government Printing Office, 1955.

United States, Department of State. *The American Ambassador*. Washington: Government Printing Office, 1957.

———. *The American Consul*. Washington: Government Printing Office, 1955.

———. *The Country Team: An Illustrated Profile of American Missions Abroad*. Washington: Government Printing Office, 1967.

———. *The Department of State, 1930–1955*. Washington: Government Printing Office, 1955.

———. *Department of State—1963: A Report to the Citizen*. Washington: Government Printing Office, 1963.

———. *The Department of State Today*. Washington: Government Printing Office, 1951.

———. *The Foreign Service of the United States: Origins, Development, and Functions*. Washington: Government Printing Office, 1961.

———. *The Policy Planning Staff Papers*. 3 vols. New York: Garland, 1983.

———. *The Problem of Recognition in American Foreign Policy*. Washington: Government Printing Office, 1950.

———. *Publications of the Department of State*. Washington: Government Printing Office, periodically.

———. *The Revolutionary Diplomatic Correspondence of the United States*. 5 vols. Washington: Government Printing Office, 1899.

———. *The Secretaries of State: Portraits and Biographical Sketches*. Department of State Publication 8921. Washington: Government Printing Office, 1978.

———. Secretary's Advisory Committee on Personnel. *An Improved Personnel System for the conduct of Foreign Affairs*. Washington: Processed, 1950.

———. *Toward a Stronger Foreign Service: Report of the Secretary of State's Public Committee on Personnel, June 1954*. Department of State Publication 5458. Washington: Government Printing Office, 1954. (Wriston Committee Report.)

———. United States National Historical Publications and Records Commission. *The Emerging Nation: Foreign Relations of the United States, 1780–1789*. 3 vols. Washington, D.C.: Government Printing Office, 1996.

United States, Senate, Committee on Foreign Relations. *Additional Materials on Administration of the Department of State*. 87th Cong., 2d Sess. Washington: Government Printing Office, 1962.

———. *Administration of the Department of State*. 86th Cong., 2d Sess. Washington: Government Printing Office, 1960.

———. *Administration of the Department of State and the Foreign Service . . .* Washington: Government Printing Office, 1959.

———. *Background Information on the Committee on Foreign Relations, United States Senate*. 89th Cong., 2d Sess. Washington: Government Printing Office, 1966.

———. *Organization for Economic Cooperation and Development*. 87 Cong., 1st Sess. Washington: Government Printing Office, 1961.

———. *Recruitment and Training for the Foreign Service of the United States*. 85th Cong., 2d Sess. Washington: Government Printing Office, 1958.

———. *United States Foreign Policy: Compilation of Studies*. Senate Document No. 24, 87th Cong., 1st Sess. Washington: Government Printing Office, 1961. Series of special studies, 86th Cong., 1st and 2d Sess., 1959–60; especially *The Formulation and Administration of United States Foreign Policy*, Study No. 9, 1960.

United States, Senate, Committee on Government Operations. *Administration of National Security: The American Ambassador*. 88th Cong., 2d Sess. Washington: Government Printing Office, 1964.

———. *Administration of National Security: The Secretary of State*. 88th Cong., 2d Sess. Washington: Government Printing Office, 1964.

———. *The Ambassador and the Problem of Coordination*. Senate Document No. 36, 88th Cong., 1st Sess. Washington: Government Printing Office, 1963.

———. *Organizational History of the National Security Council*. 86th Cong., 2d Sess. Washington: Government Printing Office, 1960.

——. *Organizing for National Security*. 3 vols. Washington: Government Printing Office, 1961.

——. *The Secretary of State and the Ambassador*. New York: Praeger, 1964.

——. *The Secretary of State and the Problem of Coordination*. Washington: Government Printing Office, 1966.

United States, Senate, Special Committee to Study the Foreign Aid Program. *Foreign Aid Program: Compilation of Studies and Surveys*. Senate Document No. 52, 85th Cong., 1st Sess. Washington: Government Printing Office, 1957.

For certain purposes also consult the *United States Government Manual* (Washington: Government Printing Office, 1974–   ). For a more comprehensive listing of official U.S. Government publications on the Department of State, Foreign Service, and American Diplomacy, including journal articles, see Plischke, *U.S. Foreign Relations: A Guide to Information Sources*, Chapter 22, pp. 525–609, and for guidance to memoir and biographical literature, see Chapter 23, pp. 613–70.

Vagts, Alfred. *Defense and Diplomacy: The Soldier and the Conduct of Foreign Relations*. New York: King's Crown Press, 1956.

——. *The Military Attaché*. Princeton: Princeton University Press, 1967.

Van Dyne, Frederick. *Our Foreign Service*. Rochester, N.Y.: Lawyers Cooperative, 1909.

Villard, Henry S. *Affairs at State*. New York: Crowell, 1965.

Walther, Regis. *Orientations and Behavioral Styles of Foreign Service Officers*. New York: Carnegie Endowment, Foreign Affairs Personnel Study No. 5, 1965.

Wanamaker, Temple. *American Foreign Policy Today*. New York: Bantam, 1964.

Warden, David B. *On the Origin, Nature, Progress, and Influence of Consular Establishments*. Paris: Smith, 1813.

Wasson, Donald. *American Agencies Interested in International Affairs*. 5th ed. New York: Praeger, 1964.

Waters, Maurice. *The Ad Hoc Diplomat: A Study in Municipal and International Law*. The Hague: Nijhoff, 1963.

Webb, Keith. *International Mediation in Perspective*. London: Cassell Academic Press, 1995.

Weber, Ralph E. *United States Codes and Ciphers, 1775–1938*. Chicago: New University Press, 1978.

Webster, Charles K. *The Art and Practice of Diplomacy*. New York: Barnes and Noble, 1962.

Weihmiller, Gordon R., and Doder, Dusko. *U.S.–Soviet Summits: An Account of East–West Diplomacy at the Top, 1955–1985*. Washington: Institute for the Study of Diplomacy, 1986.

Weintal, Edward and Bartlett, Charles W. *Facing the Brink: An Intimate Study of Crisis Diplomacy*. New York: Scribner, 1967.

Wellesley, Victor. *Diplomacy in Fetters*. London: Hutchinson, 1944.

Werking, Richard H. *The Master Architects: Building the United States Foreign Service, 1890–1913*. Lexington: University of Kentucky Press, 1978.

West, Rachel. *The Department of State on the Eve of the First World War*. Athens: University of Georgia Press, 1978.

Westerfield, H. Bradford. *Foreign Policy and Party Politics: Pearl Harbor to Korea*. New Haven, Conn.: Yale University Press, 1955.

——. *The Instruments of America's Foreign Policy*. New York: Crowell, 1963.

Westphal, Albert C. F. *The House Committee on Foreign Affairs*. New York: Columbia University Press, 1942.

Wharton, Francis, ed. *Digest of the International Law of the United States*. 2d ed. 3 vols. Washington: Government Printing Office, 1887.

White, Nigel. *The Law of International Organisations*. New York: Manchester University Press, 1997.

Whiteman, Marjorie M., ed. *Damages in International Law*. 3 vols. Washington: Government Printing Office, 1937–43.

———. *Digest of International Law*. 15 vols. Washington: Government Printing Office, 1963–73.

Whittington, William V. *The Making of Treaties and International Agreements and the Work of the Treaty Division of the Department of State*. Washington: Government Printing Office, 1938.

Wicquefort, Abraham van. *The Ambassador and His Functions*. Trans. Mr. Digby. 2 vols. The Hague: Steucker, 1681; Cologne: Marteau, 1690, and others.

Wilcox, Francis O. *The Ratification of International Conventions*. London: Allen and Unwin, 1935.

Wilkenfeld, Jonathan, ed. *Conflict Behavior and Linkage Politics*. New York: McKay, 1973.

Williams, Benjamin H. *American Diplomacy: Policies and Practice*. New York: McGraw-Hill, 1936.

Williams, Philip M. *Crisis Management: Conflict, Confrontation, and Diplomacy*. New York: Wiley, 1976.

Williams, William Appleman, ed. *The Shaping of American Diplomacy: Readings and Documents in American Foreign Relations, 1750–1955*. Chicago: Rand McNally, 1956.

Willis, Davis K. *The State Department*. Boston: Christian Science Pub. Society, 1968.

Willson, Beckles. *America's Ambassadors to England (1785–1929)*. New York: Stokes, 1929.

———. *America's Ambassadors to France (1777–1927)*. New York: Stokes, 1928.

Wilson, Clifton E. *Cold War Diplomacy: The Impact of International Conflicts on Diplomatic Communications and Travel*. Tucson: University of Arizona Press, 1966.

———. *Diplomatic Privileges and Immunities*. Tucson: University of Arizona Press, 1967.

Wilson, Hugh R. *Diplomacy as a Career*. Cambridge, Mass.: Riverside, 1941.

Wilson, James Q. *Bureaucracy: What Government Agencies Do and Why They Do It*. New York: Basic Books, 1989.

Wood, John R., and Serres, Jean. *Diplomatic Ceremonial and Protocol: Principles, Procedures, and Practices*. New York: Columbia University Press, 1970.

Woodrow Wilson Foundation. *United States Foreign Policy: Its Organization and Control; Report of a Study Group for the Woodrow Wilson Foundation*. William Yandall Elliott, chairman. New York: Columbia University Press, 1952.

Wright, Quincy. *The Control of American Foreign Relations*. New York: Macmillan, 1922.

Wriston, Henry M. *Diplomacy in a Democracy*. New York: Harper, 1956.

———. *Executive Agents in American Foreign Relations*. Baltimore: Johns Hopkins University Press, 1929.

Wrixon, Fred B. *Codes and Ciphers*. New York: Prentice-Hall, 1992.

Yardley, Herbert O. *The American Black Chamber*. Indianapolis: Bobbs-Merrill, 1931.

Yost, Charles W. *The Conduct and Miscounduct of Foreign Affairs*. New York: Random House, 1972.

Young, George. *Diplomacy Old and New*. London: Swarthmore, 1921.

Young, Oran R. *The Intermediaries: Third Parties in International Crises*. Princeton: Princeton University Press, 1967.

————. *The Politics of Force: Bargaining during International Crises*. Princeton: Princeton University Press, 1968.

————. *Trends in International Peacekeeping*. Princeton: Center of International Studies, Princeton University Press, 1966.

Zartman, I. William, ed. *The Negotiation Process: Theories and Applications*. Beverly Hills, Calif.: Sage, 1978.

Zartman, I. William, and Berman, Maureen R. *The Practical Negotiator*. New Haven, Conn.: Yale University Press, 1982.

Index

Individual Presidents and Secretaries of State are listed chronologically as a group rather than alphabetically. Similarly, certain other items are grouped. Some of these are also listed chronologically, such as the Acts of Congress, individual international conferences, congresses, and meetings, and major treaties and agreements. On the other hand, several groups of items are arranged alphabetically, including lists of Department of State principal officers and offices, foreign policies of the United States, special types of diplomacy, titles and ranks of diplomats, international organizations, and U.S. independent agencies with foreign relations responsibilities (other than the Department of State).

About the Author

ELMER PLISCHKE is Professor Emeritus at the University of Maryland, College Park, and is a recognized authority on U.S. foreign relations and State Department matters.